# THE COMPLETE
# BIBLE
# HANDBOOK

## Consultant Editors

The Reverend Professor John Barton
Oriel & Laing Professor of the
Interpretation of Holy Scripture,
University of Oxford,
and Fellow of Oriel College, Oxford

•

Professor James D.G. Dunn
Lightfoot Professor of Divinity,
University of Durham

•

Rabbi Professor Jonathan Magonet
Principal, Leo Baeck College,
London

## Consultants

The Reverend Professor C.F.D. Moule
Lady Margaret's Professor emeritus in the
University of Cambridge

•

The Reverend Father Henry Wansbrough
Master of St. Benet's Hall, Oxford
Member of the Pontifical Biblical Commission

•

Dr. Claude-Bernard Costecalde
Doctor in the Science of Religions

•

Donald C. Kraus
Executive Editor, Bibles,
Oxford University Press

# THE COMPLETE
# BIBLE
# HANDBOOK

### John Bowker

DK PUBLISHING, INC.

Visit us on the World Wide Web at http://www.dk.com

# A DK PUBLISHING BOOK

Visit us on the World Wide Web at http://www.dk.com

| | | | |
|---|---|---|---|
| **Project Editors** | Peter Jones, Susannah Steel | **Senior Editor** | Luci Collings |
| **Art Editors** | Dawn Terrey, Tassy King | **Senior Art Editor** | Claire Legemah |
| **Editors** | Caroline Hunt, Julie Oughton, Nichola Thomasson | **Managing Editor** | Anna Kruger |
| **Designer** | Carla De Abreu | **Deputy Art Director** | Tina Vaughan |
| **Picture Research** | Julia Harris-Voss, Christine Rista | **Category Publisher** | Sean Moore |
| | | **US Editor** | Mary L. Sutherland |
| **DTP Designers** | Zirrinia Austin, Maite Lantaron | **Production** | Sarah Coltman, Alison Jones, David Proffit, Alex Bertram |
| | | **Index** | AD Publishing Services Ltd. |

## CONTRIBUTORS

Dr. Stephen Barton
Rev. Dr. Paul Beasley-Murray
Zoe Bennett Moore
Dr. Markus Bockmuehl
Peter Bolt
Dr. Mark Bonnington
Dr. Margaret Bowker
Rev. Jeremy Brooks
David W. Chapman

Rev. Richard Coggins
Dr. Katharine Dell
Rev. Dr. James Francis
Dr. Susan Gillingham
Sally L. Gold
Prof. D.A. Hagner
Rev. P. John Hoskin
Chris Jack
Rev. Dr. Ivor Jones
Dr. Bruce W. Longnecker

Dr. Rex A. Mason
Dr. Heather A. McKay
Dr. Andrew Mein
Mark Meynell
Rev. Dr. Walter Moberley
Edward Moll
Rabbi Rachel Montegu
Rev. Canon Rosemary A. Nixon
Rev. Dr. John Parr

David Pickering
Rev. John Proctor
Dr. Iain W. Provan
Dr. David Reimer
Dr. Deborah W. Rooke
Andrew Shead
Dr. Margaret Sidebottom
Rev. Dr. Keith Straughan
Dr. Loren T. Stuckenbruck
Rev. Dr. John Sweet

Dr. W. R. Telford
Rev. Dr. Janet E. Tolling
Rev. David Tomlinson
Rev. Dr. Ian Wallis
Dr. Stuart Weeks
Rev. Sue Woan

First American Edition, 1998

2 4 6 8 10 9 7 5 3 1

Published in the United States by DK Publishing, Inc.
95 Madison Avenue, New York, New York 10016

Copyright © 1998 Dorling Kindersley Limited, London

Text copyright © 1998 John Bowker

Published in Great Britain by Dorling Kindersley Limited.

Library of Congress Cataloging-in Publication Data

Bowker, John Westerdale
The Complete Bible Handbook: an Illustrated companion
/ by John Bowker
    p.   cm
    ISBN 0-7894-3568-3
    1. Bible--Introductions. 1. Title
    BS475.2.B69   1998
    220.6'1--dc21          98-4478
                       CIP

Color reproduction by Colourscan, Singapore

Printed and bound in Spain by AGT. TOLEDO

# CONTENTS

Introduction
6

About
this Book
12

## THE OLD TESTAMENT
## THE HEBREW BIBLE

Contents
16

The Pentateuch
20

The Historical Books
90

The Wisdom Books
168

The Prophets
194

The Apocrypha
252

## THE NEW
## TESTAMENT

Contents
272

The Life of Jesus
296

The Beginnings
of Christianity
366

The Letters
404

## REFERENCE
## SECTION

A–Z of People in the Bible
478

A–Z of Places in the Bible
496

Glossary
514

Bibliography
520

Index
530

Acknowledgments
and Picture Credits
542

# INTRODUCTION

W HY is the Bible important? The immediate answer is simple: about three-quarters of the entire population of the world today believe that the Bible is the Word of God. Or if not that exactly, then they accept that it is *a* word from God. This seems obvious in the case of Jews and Christians. But many others, including Muslims, Bahais, Hindus, and Sikhs, have no doubt that the Bible comes from God. Muslims, it's true, think that Jews and Christians have muddled human words with the Word of God, but even so, they believe that the Bible, in origin, came from God.

It's no surprise, therefore, to find the Bible at the heart of human lives in much of our history in many parts of the world: *"Your word is a lamp to my feet and a light to my path"* (Ps. 119:105). Those words have been true for countless multitudes of people. The Bible has been an encouragement in times of hope and a consolation in times of sorrow. It has inspired men and women to works of service in the world and of generosity to each other. It has been a guide in times of perplexity and a direct line to God.

The Judean Desert.

century BCE), the so-called "father of history", realized that events belong to each other and tell a continuous story: time is not just one thing after another but a story with meaning. In this way, the Bible writers invented history. They realized also that, like Adam and Eve in the Garden, there is no point trying to hide from God (Gen. 3:8–9). *"'Can anyone hide in secret places so that I cannot see him?' declares the Lord"* (Jer. 23:24). They therefore wrote the stories of even their greatest and godliest heroes with all their faults as well as their virtues. In doing this, the writers made certain that art and literature would be realistic. Stories, novels, text-books, even soap operas on television and the in-depth, scandal-seeking biographies of the modern world were born from the womb of the Bible. The same is true of music and art. The illustrations in this book alone show how deeply and for how long a period the Bible has been a challenge and an inspiration for musicians and artists around the world. Few direct illustrations of the time survive from long ago, but this has simply set free the human imagination.

## THE BIBLE IN LITERATURE AND ART

The Bible has also been a major source of language, and an inspiration for literature, music, and art. No other text has had so great an influence. Many writers in the past could assume a wide knowledge of the Bible, so that the Bible was used as a kind of common language. The result is that many books and poems of the past, even those which seem to have little to do with religion, often cannot be fully understood without a knowledge of the Bible. Even the ways of writing were affected. The writers of biblical books, long before the Greek Herodotus (c. fifth

## A DANGEROUS BOOK

Even for those who have no belief in God, the Bible remains an important book. That is why this *Handbook* is offered as a guide (*see p.542*). We need to understand the Bible because the Bible did so much to form the world we live in. Not least because the Bible is also a very dangerous book. On the basis of the Bible, some Christians have been murdering Jews for nearly two thousand years, and some Jews have killed others in pursuit of a promised land. On the basis of the Bible, witches have been burned alive, homosexuals executed, children beaten, Africans shipped to slavery, women treated in law as children, animals regarded as human property, and wars justified all in the name of the Prince of Peace. Thomas Paine (1737–1809) wrote: "Whenever we read the obscene stories, the voluptuous debaucheries, the cruel and tortuous executions, the unrelenting vindictiveness, with which more than half the Bible is filled, it would be more consistent that we called it the word of a demon than the word of God. It is a history of wickedness that has served to corrupt and brutalize mankind" (*The Age of Reason*, 1794).

It is true that every one of those ugly attitudes and actions has been condemned with equal vigor, also on the basis of the Bible and sometimes even within the Bible itself. This immediately makes the point that the Bible is a powerful book, open to different understandings and opposing uses. But in that case, what can it possibly mean to say that the Bible is the Word of God?

## THE WORD OF GOD AND THE PEOPLE OF GOD

Does it mean that God dictated the Bible in such a way that it contains no mistakes about anything? Is it, to use the technical words, infallible and inerrant? Those words cannot mean there are no mistakes of any kind in the Bible, because everybody agrees that there are factual errors in the Bible, although they may be explained differently (for examples and a discussion of these errors, *see Bibliography no.52*). Even Charles Hodge (1797–1878) a strong defender of the Bible as infallible and inerrant in all matters, including science and history, admitted that errors exist: "The errors in matters of fact which sceptics search out bear no proportion to the whole. No sane man would deny that the Parthenon was built of marble, even if here and there a speck of sandstone should be detected in its structure. Not less unreasonable is it to deny the inspiration of such a book as the Bible because one sacred writer says that on one given occasion twenty-four thousand, and another that twenty-three thousand, men were slain" (*Systematic Theology*, 1871, I, p.163).

Moses receiving the tablets of the Law.

What we cannot do here is paint over the specks of sandstone and pass them off as marble. In fact, the specks of sandstone are telling us a vital, liberating truth about the Bible – that it came into being, not despite the limitations of human knowledge at any given time, not despite the unfolding process of history, but making use of those limitations and of that process. God did not bypass history and human circumstances but used them to help a people to mature and come of age, making a name and nature known that people could understand and respond to, because they knew them to be true to themselves.

In fact, virtually all parents know exactly how the Bible came into being. As they encourage their children to grow up, they support them in ways that are appropriate for the age and understanding they have reached. They do not, if they are wise, force a child of three to write textbooks on physics or kick a ball as though his or her life depends on it. But they do start to kick balls with them, and they do (try to) answer questions like, "Why is the sky up?" or "Why do kettles boil?" and "Why do I have to be good?" As parents evoke from their children a curiosity and delight in the world, and an ethic not to do wrong and not to hurt others, so they treasure every effort, at every stage of the process, and they do not discard even the earliest attempts to write a poem or to sing a song. Home videos and tape recordings may not be the greatest art, but they are precious to parents beyond measure as a record, and parents are reluctant to erase them.

The Bible is the consequence of a process very like that. It came into being over a period of more than a thousand years, so that the Bible is not a single book. It is made up of hymns, histories, songs, law codes, prayers, and many other kinds of writings, focused on God and preserved by the people. The children of Israel, the descendants of Jacob, grew in understanding of God and of how they were meant to live, but their early attempts to write or say something about this, however much they may have been transcended in the process of growing up, were not discarded or erased. They were treasured and preserved, even though later parts of the Bible often contradict earlier parts, as the people living with God and with each other came to understand far more deeply and wisely the nature of God who cares for them as a parent. That is why the imagination of God as mother and God as father is so important in the Bible: "*Can a woman forget her nursing child, or show no compassion for the child of her womb? Even these may forget, yet I will not forget you*" (Isa. 49:15).

So the Bible is not a magic bullet, shot into the world as though time and circumstance make no difference. The Bible is the record of people called into a long relationship of learning about God and themselves – of growing up. The relationship became known as a Covenant (*see pp.60–61*), and Christians call Scripture the Old and the New Covenants – or, from the Latin, the Old and New Testaments. In the records of that long relationship, the early expressions of it were still preserved, however much the Covenant People later moved far beyond them. Like any parent, God guided them, but did not protect them from making mistakes. John Goldingay, in a difficult but excellent book (*see Bibliography no.333, p.243*), wrote of the activity of the Holy Spirit: "It does not bypass their distinctive humanity but uses it. They do not have to be perfect, nor do their words have to be models of balance, free of rawness or solecism, in order for God to work through them. The grace of God is such as to be entirely prepared to speak through skewed human agents and quite relaxed enough to trust that their eccentricities will do more good than harm"

**Madonna and child.**

## THE ORDER OF THE BIBLE

Two important points follow: first, the Bible is not a record of inevitable progress; the children of Israel and of the Covenant slip into error and mischief just as much as any children do. What is remarkable is that they recorded these lapses as carefully as their brilliant moves into vision and truth. It was a bumpy ride, and they learned from it as they went along. Second, the Bible is not put together in chronological order. The first words of the Bible to be written were not Genesis 1:1, and the earliest part of the New Testament is not the Gospel according to St. Matthew. When reading the Bible, it is always wise to understand first the general context of time and circumstance in which the books came into being. Most parts of the Bible have gone through a long process of editing as one generation after another brought to bear on the circumstances of their own day the words they received from their predecessors. What is extraordinary is that they really did this. They did not regard the words from the past as having a historical interest only, but they knew that through them God was speaking to them in the present. As early as Hosea (11:1–4; 12:2–2), Micah (6:3–5), and Jeremiah (4:23–28), Prophets went to the past to interpret the present, as did many of the Psalm writers. In the New Testament, Jesus, and those who wrote it, quote Scripture as having authority.

## INSPIRATION

Do the specks of sandstone mean that only parts of the Bible are inspired, or that some parts are more inspired than others? The answer must be "no," because all parts are equally a consequence of God "parenting" the children, and all are equally treasured. The Bible says very little about the way the words within it came to be spoken or written or preserved. In 2 Timothy 3:16, the Greek word *theopneustos*, literally, "God-breathed", is used of Scripture: "*All scripture is inspired by God and is useful for teaching, for reproof, for correction, and for training in righteousness ...*" This could equally well be translated, "*Every scripture inspired by God is also useful ...*" The

Prophets are the most obvious of those who fit that description of being breathed into by God, because they experienced a sense of being "taken over" by God and of becoming spokesmen (and occasionally spokeswomen) for God. Jeremiah spoke of the word of God as a fire burning within him and out of his control: *"If I say, 'I will not mention God, or speak any more in his name', then within me there is something like a burning fire shut up in my bones, I am weary with holding it in, and I cannot* (Jer. 20:9; cf. Ps. 39:3). This perception of prophecy being inspired (breathed in) directly by God is expressed in 2 Peter 1:21: *"no prophecy ever came by human will, but men and women moved by the Holy Spirit spoke from God"* (some texts read, *"... but moved by the Holy Spirit saints of God spoke"*).

That is the most obvious sense of Scripture being "God-breathed." The Latin word for this, *inspiro*, means "I breathe into," hence the word "inspiration." Jews and Christians believe that all Scripture, not just the books of the Prophets, is inspired by God. Jews, traditionally, have drawn distinctions, corresponding to the three divisions of the Hebrew Bible – Torah, Prophets, and Writings (*see pp.22–23*): Torah is the very Word of God, Prophecy is that Word mediated through the prophets, and the Writings come from less direct inspiration of the Holy Spirit. Christians regard the whole Bible as equally inspired. J.W. Burgon (1813–88)

**Jesus before the crowds.**

wrote: "Every Book of it, – every Chapter of it, – every verse of it, – every word of it, – every syllable of it (*where are we to stop?*), – every letter of it – is the direct utterance of the Most High" (*Seven Sermons*, 1851, p.69).

## TEXT AND TRANSMISSION

A claim like this is extremely misleading. Once again, we have to remember that the Bible is not isolated from history but immersed within it. Where the text of the Bible is concerned ("every letter of it"), we do not know what anyone *originally* spoke or wrote. That is because the written text has come down the years with many variations in it. Certainly the text is stable: when the text of Isaiah was discovered at Qumran (*see p.290*), it was remarkably similar

to the text stabilized about a thousand years later by the Masoretes (*see Glossary, pp.514–19*). Even so, there are important variants, and we cannot know what the original text was. Variations crept in, sometimes because a scribe made a mistake, sometimes because people deliberately changed the text to make it or its teaching clearer (*see Bibliography nos.268, 275, 807*). Occasionally there are major differences, as over the original text of Jeremiah (*see pp.206–07*) or over the Western text of Acts (*see p.395*). From the source of the river (what an author originally wrote) many different channels have diverged in families of texts containing many variants. If we say that every letter was the direct utterance of God, which of the variants did God utter?

Thinking of inspiration in that way becomes even more difficult when we remember that the decisions of Jews and Christians about the books to be included as Scripture were, for a long time, uncertain and did not turn on decisions about which books were inspired, but on which books should have God-derived authority in their communities (*see pp.189, 474–75*).

## THE AUTHORITY OF THE BIBLE

It is the word "authority" that gives the clue to the way in which God is related to the Bible as its author. The words "author" and "authority" come from two Latin words, *auctor* and *auctoritas*, and they are closely related. The standard Latin dictionary of Lewis and Short gives a definition of *auctor* that may seem, at first sight, obscure, but it turns out to be very helpful. An *auctor* is "he that brings about the existence of any object, or promotes the increase or prosperity of it, whether he first originates it, or by his efforts gives greater permanence or continuance to it." It is the finest definition of what the Bible, as a whole, understands by "creation."

From it comes the definition of *auctoritas*. It has to do with an *auctor*, author, bringing something into being, an invention. So it also means an opinion, or advice, or encouragement. It means weight, or importance, hence power and our sense of authority. To have the power to bring something into being involves the right to look after it, the "authoring" responsibility.

God is the *auctor*, the Author, of all things. God is the unproduced Producer of all that is, who continues to sustain every moment and every aspect of this creation in being. Without God, we would not be. In the quest for the growing of a people into maturity, not by force even when they went astray but by the nurturing of a parent (*see above*) and by the cooperations of faith, God evoked and brought into being the words that now stand as Scripture. God is the source of these words by being the source of the lives that wrote and spoke and edited and preserved them. The children of Israel took up the possibilities of story, kingship, priesthood, prophecy, even warfare, and so much more, and because of their confidence in God, tested through time, they turned everything that they touched into something astonishingly different (for examples of how this happened, *see Bibliography no. 122, pp. 31–96*).

**Reciting the Amidah, or "standing prayer."**

Through lives in communities that said "yes" to God, God was the real source, or in another word, author, of the words they wrote and preserved. And because God was in this sense their author, they have authority. They are the means through which God's authorship continues still in human lives, so that a new and different story is told through them, a story of holiness and love. The Bible is thus the Word of God because through these words, God becomes the author, or at least the joint author, of the continuing story of our lives, as individuals, and as communities that try to be God's story in the world. We read the Bible, not to find texts to enable us to burn witches, make slaves, subordinate women, condemn homosexuals, and murder Jews. All of those acts and attitudes were justified by taking single texts and applying them without reference to the greater purpose of God in the creation of holiness and love. If the Bible does not produce *that*, and if instead it leads to communal hatred and to acts of violence and destruction, the Bible is being misused. There is a better way: we read the Bible

in order to encounter the Word of God in the words of God and to be made a holy people for the worship of God and the service of the world.

## THE MEANING OF THE BIBLE

In reading the Bible in that way, it is wise to read it sharing the understanding of others, and not making it into a matter of private opinion – and this *Handbook* may be a help in doing that. Always it should be read with humility, realizing that your understanding will always be incomplete. It is important to remember that we never know, finally and completely, what the Bible means. That seems an odd statement, but what it means is this: the Bible was written in Hebrew, Aramaic, and Greek, and often there will be different ways to translate a word or a sentence, any one of which is legitimate or correct. Take Romans 5:12, a verse of huge importance in Christian history: *"Therefore, just as sin came into the world through one man, and death came through sin, and so death spread to all because all have sinned ..."* The word "because" is, in Greek, *eph ho*. It seems a simple translation and yet, in his commentary on Romans, J. A. Fitzmyer lists 11 different ways that those two Greek words can be translated, each of which makes a difference to the meaning of the verse. All translation is interpretation. There is no "meaning of the text" that we can hope to recover, not even the "true" meaning the author intended. That is so, not only because of the problems of text (*see above*) and translation, but also because the meaning of a text is *never* limited only to what an author intended. Authors, and poets, often intend one thing and achieve another. Even more often, we can see meanings beyond those the author intended.

For all these reasons, the text of the Bible lies before us as opportunity, the opportunity for God to break open a meaning of this word for us, at this moment, in this particular circumstance. We can know that some proposed meanings are definitely wrong (translating *eph ho*, above, as though it meant "in order that all may sin"), but we cannot know, finally and conclusively, what every word or sentence means.

## PRAYING THE BIBLE

We may want to read the Bible out of interest, or as a fascinating story, or just for enjoyment. But many read the Bible as the Word of God and the starting point of prayer. What difference does it make to read the Bible in that way? The Bible is a "hands-on" book. It's a bit like a cookbook: we can read recipes, but to make them up and then eat the result is entirely different. The Bible seems to be about God talking and interacting with people in the past, long ago. But the Bible is a means through which God extends that talking and interacting into the present. For a start, the Bible contains many prayers, especially the Psalms and the prayer that Jesus taught his disciples (*see p.333*), and we can make those prayers our own. Beyond that, the Bible offers itself as the place to meet God now and to be met by God in ways that will change our lives. The Bible comes to an end, but God does not. As *Verbum Dei*, a document from the Second Vatican Council, puts it, it is in the sacred books that God continues to meet us "with tender love and enters into conversation with us" (6:21).

But how do we start? Have a great desire or longing to be with God in the passage you have before you, as, of old, people had a great desire to be with God in the Temple (Ps. 84). Take a passage (for advice on how to do this *see Bibliography no.710, or the Daily Reading section*) and let that passage be the introduction that starts a conversation with God. The passage may draw out from you anger, happiness, fear, hope, trust. Allow time to listen to what it is saying to you and what it is drawing out from you. You may feel inspired by the words to sing or dance a passage, write a poem, or draw a picture. You may simply stay with the passage and let it rest in you. You may want to meet God by entering into a story through your imagination. Imagine you are in the scene, not necessarily as it was then but in your own world now. Be one of the people in the scene, not merely an observer of it. Then hear what is said to *you*. It may take time to hear what God is trying to say (it often did for people in the Bible). Go back to the text and add to your seeing and your hearing your sense of taste, touch, and smell. God is talking in your life now, as to others long ago.

Meditating on the Bible.

Not all the Bible is story. With other passages, read the passage slowly several times – perhaps aloud. As you do so, you will find that one sentence, or phrase, or word, becomes more prominent: it keeps coming to the front of your mind. Stay with that sentence or word, and repeat it often. Then respond to God in it *as you are*, in anger or in joy, or in any other mood, and try to hear what God is saying in it, or simply rest before God or long for God through it. Take the word or the verse with you into your day, and God will continue to be with you. " *Your word is a lamp to my feet and a light to my path*" (Ps. 119:105). And so it will be.

Is there any control over this? How do we know that it is God who speaks, and that we are not just talking to ourselves? There is a guarantee and a control. The guarantee is the Bible itself. Remember that if people had not found God and been found by God through these words in the first place, there could not possibly have been the honest, visionary, angry, encouraging, searching, hopeful words that make up the Bible. There are no words, as a whole, like this, gathered together in books of this kind, anywhere, in any religion, or in any literature. It is God, or at the very least this people's belief in God, that made the total difference. Share the belief, and the reality will become clear. As the Reformer Calvin (1509–64) put it, "Scripture will only be effectual to produce the saving knowledge of God when the certainty of it shall be founded on the internal persuasion of the Holy Spirit" (*Institutes* 1.8.1). The control is this: if you find that praying the Bible does not draw you deeper into a relationship of holiness and love with God and your neighbor, you need to pray it more receptively and attentively. Remember also that you are not on your own. The Bible is read and prayed in community, in liturgy, in the worship of synagogue and church. So may the words from that often strange and remote world of the Bible in the past come into our lives today and turn them into something better for tomorrow.

Hands at prayer.

**John and Margaret Bowker**
**July 1998**

# ABOUT THIS BOOK

ARRANGED on a book-by-book basis from Genesis to Revelation, *The Complete Bible Handbook* is divided into five types of double-page spread. **Book** spreads discuss the origin, authorship, and significance of each book in the Bible, summarizing the contents and key themes. **Story** spreads retell the principal stories of the Bible, and

focus on the lives of central biblical characters, with commentary on the meaning behind the stories' key events and passages. **Background** and **History** spreads look at the Bible's wider cultural and historical background, while **Theology**, or teaching, spreads outline the most important biblical teachings and give an understanding of the issues involved.

## BOOK SPREAD

*A coloured diagram indicates the relative position of each book within the Bible (see illustration opposite).*

*Tinted side panels provide a quick and concise reference guide to the contents and key themes of each book, together with its Hebrew name (in the Old Testament), details of its authorship, and the date of composition.*

## STORY SPREAD

*An accompanying commentary examines the content and the significance of the story, and looks at how it, or the lives of its central characters, have been interpreted.*

*Boxed quotations of key verses highlight the core issues of biblical teaching.*

*Tinted panels retell the biblical story.*

*Side columns highlight key events, while biblical references help locate the relevant passages.*

## THEOLOGY SPREAD

## HISTORY SPREAD

## BACKGROUND SPREAD

*An exciting variety of illustrations – devotional paintings and sculptures, religious and historical artefacts, manuscripts, and photographs – gives a flavour of the biblical world.*

*Side panels contain additional factual, historical, or contextual information and illustrations.*

*Maps show the location of key biblical sites or routes.*

*Suggestions for further reading are given at the base of each spread; the numbers refer to numbered entries in the Bibliography.*

# THE BOOKS OF THE BIBLE

The order of the books of the Bible in the *Handbook* follows that of Christian Bibles, which in turn follow the Greek translation (the Septuagint), compiled by Greek-speaking Jewish scholars during the second century BCE. In the Christian Bible, the books of the Old Testament are grouped into four sections, which are different from the Hebrew Bible, or Scriptures: the Pentateuch, the Historical

Books, Wisdom Literature, and Prophets. The *Handbook* also includes the Apocrypha, a collection of books written in Greek between the time of the Hebrew Bible and the New Testament. These books were not included in the Hebrew Bible and are only included in *some* Christian Bibles. Roman Catholic and Orthodox Bibles include some books that Protestants place in the Apocrypha.

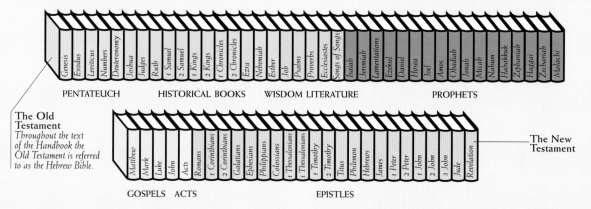

PENTATEUCH    HISTORICAL BOOKS    WISDOM LITERATURE    PROPHETS

**The Old Testament**
*Throughout the text of the Handbook the Old Testament is referred to as the Hebrew Bible.*

The New Testament

GOSPELS  ACTS    EPISTLES

## ABBREVIATIONS OF THE BOOKS OF THE BIBLE

*In alphabetical order:*

| | | | | | | | | |
|---|---|---|---|---|---|---|---|---|
| Acts | Acts of the Apostles | Ezra | – | 1 Kgs. | 1 Kings | Philem. | Philemon | Song of Thr. Prayer of Azariah and Song of the Three Young Men (Jews) |
| Amos | – | Gal. | Galatians | 2 Kgs. | 2 Kings | Phil. | Philippians | |
| Baruch | – | Gen. | Genesis | Lam. | Lamentations | Pr. of Man. | Prayer of Manasses | |
| Bel & Dr. | Bel and the Dragon | Hab. | Habakkuk | Let. Jer. | Letter of Jeremiah | Prov. | Proverbs | Sus. | Susanna |
| 1 Chr. | 1 Chronicles | Hag. | Haggai | | | Ps. | Psalms | 1 Thess. | 1 Thessalonians |
| 2 Chr. | 2 Chronicles | Heb. | Hebrews | Lev. | Leviticus | Rest of Esth. | Rest of Esther | 2 Thess. | 2 Thessalonians |
| Col. | Colossians | Hos. | Hosea | Luke | – | Rev., Apoc. | Revelation, Apocalypse | 1 Tim. | 1 Timothy |
| 1 Cor. | 1 Corinthians | Isa. | Isaiah | 1 Macc. | 1 Maccabees | | | 2 Tim. | 2 Timothy |
| 2 Cor. | 2 Corinthians | Jas. | James | 2 Macc. | 2 Maccabees | Rom. | Romans | Tit. | Titus |
| Dan. | Daniel | Jer. | Jeremiah | 3 Macc. | 3 Maccabees | Ruth | – | Tobit | – |
| Deut. | Deuteronomy | Job | – | 4 Macc. | 4 Maccabees | 1 Sam. | 1 Samuel | Sir. | (Wisdom of) Sirach, also known as Ecclesiasticus (Ecclus.) |
| Eccles. | Ecclesiastes | Joel | – | Mal. | Malachi | 2 Sam. | 2 Samuel | | |
| Eph. | Ephesians | John | – | Mark | – | S. of S. | Song of Solomon, Song of Songs also known as Canticles (Cant.) | | |
| 1 Esd. | 1 Esdras | 1 John | 1 John | Matt. | Matthew | | | Wisd. | Wisdom of Solomon |
| 2 Esd. | 2 Esdras | 2 John | 2 John | Mic. | Micah | | | Zech. | Zechariah |
| Esther | – | 3 John | 3 John | Nah. | Nahum | | | Zeph. | Zephaniah |
| Exod. | Exodus | Jonah | – | Neb. | Nehemiah | | | | |
| Ezek. | Ezekiel | Josh. | Joshua | Num. | Numbers | | | | |
| | | Jude | – | Obad. | Obadiah | S. of III Ch. | Song of the Three Children | | |
| | | Judg. | Judges | 1 Pet. | 1 Peter | | | | |
| | | Judith | – | 2 Pet. | 2 Peter | | | | |

### HEBREW BIBLE

For Christians, there are two parts of the Bible, called, traditionally, the Old Testament (Jewish Bible) and the New Testament. To make the point that there can be only one God of both Testaments, other names are becoming more usual, such as First and Second Testaments and Older and Newer Testaments. Because "Old Testament" is familiar and well known, it has been retained at the head of the page, but in the main text itself the Jewish Bible is called the Hebrew Bible.

### GENERAL ABBREVIATIONS

BCE  before the common era (= BC)
c.  *circa* (about)
CE  common era (= AD)
cf.  contrast, compare
ch. /chs.  chapter / chapters
ff.  following verses, lines, etc.
J, E, D, P  letters given to four possible sources in the Pentateuch (*see pp.*22–23)
NRSV  New Revised Standard Version
ps. / pss.  psalm / psalms
v. / vv.  verse / verses

### BIBLE REFERENCES

Chapter and verse are separated by a colon (:), and a sequence is indicated by a dash (–); book names are abbreviated when in parentheses. Thus, 1 Kings 6:14 (*1 Kgs. 6:14*) = chapter 6, verse 14 of the first book of Kings; Ruth 2:3, 15 = chapter 2, verses 3 and 15 of Ruth. Very occasionally, subdivisions of verses are indicated by letters; thus, Genesis 2:4a = the first part of verse 4 of Genesis chapter 2.

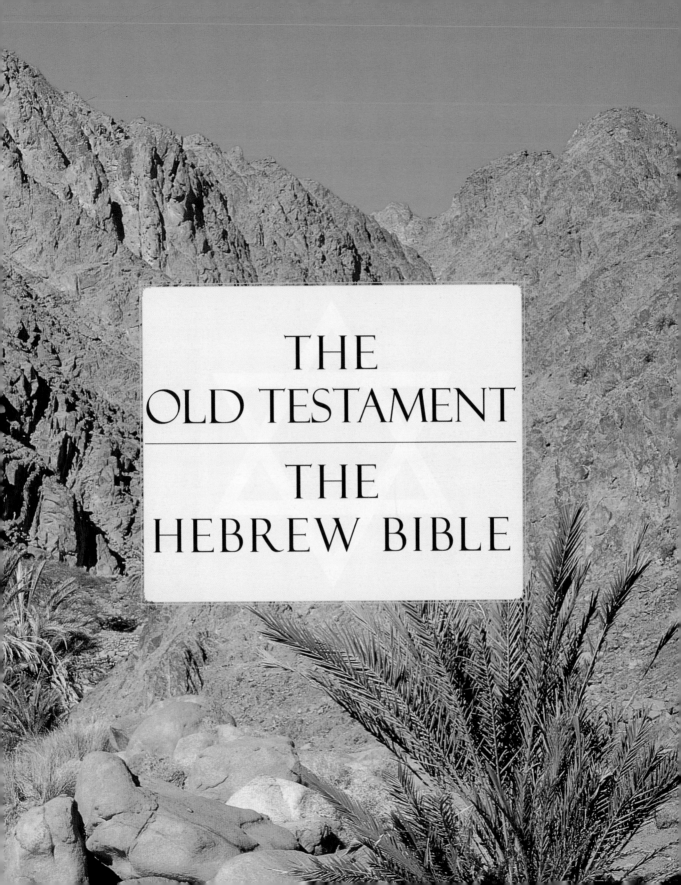

# THE
# OLD TESTAMENT

# THE
# HEBREW BIBLE

# THE OLD TESTAMENT
# THE HEBREW BIBLE

Map of the Ancient Near East    18

## BOOKS OF THE PENTATEUCH

The Composition of
  the Pentateuch    22
Torah    24
**The Book of Genesis**    26
Creation    28
The Story of Adam and Eve    30
The Story of Noah and the Flood    32
The Ancestors    34
Religion in the Period
  of the Ancestors    36
The Life of Abraham    38
The Lives of Isaac and Jacob    40
Angels in the Bible    42
The Life of Joseph    44
Everyday Life in Egypt    46
**The Book of Exodus**    48
The Story of Moses    50
Routes of the Exodus    52

The Covenant People    54
The Ten Commandments    56
The Names and Nature of God    58
The Covenant    60
**The Book of Leviticus**    62
Priests in the Bible    64
Sacrifice and Ritual    66
Fasts and Festivals    68
**The Book of Numbers**    70
The Wilderness    72
Folklore in the Bible    74
Numbers in the Bible    76
Money & Measurement    78
**The Book of Deuteronomy**    80
The Shema    82
Biblical Law in the Pentateuch    84
Crime and Punishment    86
War and Warfare    88

## THE HISTORICAL BOOKS

**The Book of Joshua**    92
Entry into the Promised Land    94
Jericho    96
Canaanites    98
Israel's Neighbors    100
The Twelve Tribes of Israel    102
**The Book of Judges**    104
Four Stories of Judges    106
Early Religion of the Israelites    108
**The Book of Ruth**    110
Women in Ancient Israel    112
**The Books of 1–2 Samuel**    114
Temples and the Tabernacle    116

The Life of Samuel — 118
The Life of Saul — 120
Kingship in the
  Ancient World — 122
The Life of King David — 124
Jerusalem — 126
**The Books of 1–2 Kings** — 128
The Times of King Solomon — 130
Solomon's Temple — 132
The Kings of Israel and Judah — 134
Empires and Kings — 136
The Stories of Elijah — 138
Gods and Goddesses
  of the Ancient Near East — 140
Assyria — 142
Josiah — 144
Exile to Babylon — 146
Babylonia — 148
**The Books of 1–2 Chronicles** — 150
Religion of the Exile — 152
Return from Exile — 154
Persia — 156
Religion after the Exile — 158
**The Book of Ezra** — 160
**The Book of Nehemiah** — 162
Education in Ancient Israel — 164
**The Book of Esther** — 166

# THE WISDOM BOOKS

Wisdom Literature — 170
**The Book of Job** — 172
Suffering — 174
**The Book of Psalms** — 176
Life after Death — 178
Music in the Bible — 180
Human Nature — 182
**The Book of Proverbs** — 184
Marriage and Family — 186

**The Book of Ecclesiastes** — 188
**The Book of The Song of Songs** — 190
Sex and Sexuality in the Bible — 192

# THE PROPHETS

The Role of the Prophets — 196
Prophetic Actions — 198
**The Book of Isaiah 1–39** — 200
**The Book of Isaiah 40–55** — 202
**The Book of Isaiah 56–66** — 204
**The Book of Jeremiah** — 206
Confessions of Jeremiah — 208
**The Book of Lamentations** — 210
**The Book of Ezekiel** — 212
Visions of Ezekiel — 214
**The Book of Daniel** — 216
**The Book of Hosea** — 218
**The Book of Joel** — 220
God's Actions in the World — 222
**The Book of Amos** — 224
Ethics and Behavior in
  the Prophets — 226
**The Book of Obadiah** — 228
**The Book of Jonah** — 230

Universalism and Particularism — 232
**The Book of Micah** — 234
Time in the Bible — 236
**The Books of Nahum
  & Habakkuk** — 238
**The Book of Zephaniah** — 240
**The Books of Haggai
  & Zechariah** — 242
**The Book of Malachi** — 244
The Greek Empire — 246
After Alexander — 248
The Maccabees — 250

# THE APOCRYPHA

Apocrypha: Fiction — 254
Apocrypha: Wisdom — 256
Apocrypha: History — 258
Apocrypha: Apocalyptic — 260

Eschatology — 262

Plants in the Bible — 264
Birds in the Bible — 266
Animals in the Bible — 268

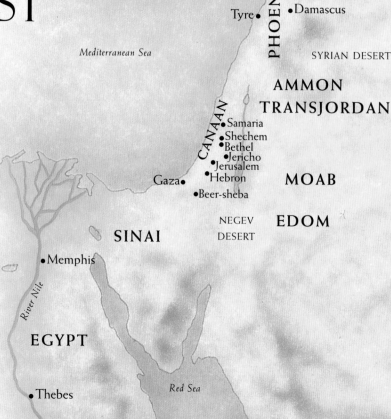

# THE ANCIENT NEAR EAST

The area stretching from the Tigris and Euphrates Rivers, through Assyria to the Mediterranean coast, and south through Palestine to the Nile Valley, has been called "the Fertile Crescent." Within this region, settled communities (as opposed to nomads) appeared, and some of the earliest civilizations were established. Major early cities, such as Mari, Haran, and Damascus, acted as a bridge for trade and the movement of armies. Powers at either end of the Crescent (Egypt, Assyria, Babylonia) tried to control Jerusalem and its surroundings, leading to their involvement in events recorded in the Bible.

CAUCASUS MOUNTAINS

*Caspian Sea*

•Nineveh

**ASSYRIA**

Asshur•

Mari•

*River Euphrates*

*River Tigris*

**PERSIA**

•Babylon

**BABYLONIA**

•Nippur

ZAGROS MOUNTAINS

ARABIAN DESERT

Susa•

Uruk•
(*Erech*)

Ur•

Eridu•

Persepolis•

**ARABIA**

*Persian Gulf*

19

# THE
# PENTATEUCH

The first five books are the same in all Bibles, both Christian and Jewish, and they follow the same order. They are Genesis, Exodus, Leviticus, Numbers, and Deuteronomy. Their Hebrew names are *Bereshith*, *Shemot*, *Vayyiqra*, *Bemidbar*, and *Debarim*. In Jewish tradition, they are known as the Torah (*see pp.24–25*). Central to the Pentateuch is the record of Moses receiving the Tablets of the Law from God (as in the illustration, left). The whole Pentateuch is thus associated with Moses. (For a discussion of authorship, *see* Composition of the Pentateuch, *pp.22–23*). Together the books form a narrative from the Creation, through the stories of the breakup and disintegration of human relationships, the Ancestors of Israel, the Exodus, the journey through the wilderness, and the giving of the Ten Commandments and other laws. The narrative draws to a close with the death of Moses on the brink of the entry into the Promised Land. A major theme in these books is the promise made by God to the Ancestors Noah, Abraham, and Jacob – a promise that takes the form of a covenant (*see pp.60–61*). This reaches its climax in the Covenant at Sinai, mediated through Moses. The Covenant establishes the people of Israel as God's people through whom God's works are performed. The Pentateuch thus contains both narratives and laws, which together constitute Torah (the guidance of God). Deuteronomy 6:20–24 shows how closely the two are related.

# THE COMPOSITION OF THE PENTATEUCH

*The word "Pentateuch," from the Greek meaning "five-volumed," denotes the first five books of the Bible – Genesis, Exodus, Leviticus, Numbers, and Deuteronomy. The origins, authorship, and composition of the Pentateuch are still a subject of much debate.*

NOWHERE in the Pentateuch is there any direct statement of authorship. It is associated with Moses, but this fact does not answer the question of how these five books came into being. The collection of the first five books (also known as Torah, *see pp.24–25*) is anonymous. The text speaks of Moses being commanded by God to record events (Exod. 17:14; Num. 33:2), laws (Exod. 24:4; 34:27), and a song (Deut. 31:22), and later tradition knew of a book of law associated with Moses (Josh. 1:7*ff.*), but nowhere does the text claim that Moses was the author of the Pentateuch. Much later, there are references to a Book of Moses (2 Chr. 25:4; Ezra 6:18; Neh. 13:1), and the New Testament associates much, if not all, of Torah with Moses (Matt. 19:7; 22:24; Mark 7:10; 12:26; John 1:17; 5:46; 7:23).

**THE STORY OF MOSES**
*This manuscript from the Pentateuch of Tours has Greek script and depicts the story of Moses.*

most scholars now see that a much longer process of composition was involved. They are not, however, agreed on what it may have been.

## THE DOCUMENTARY HYPOTHESIS

During the 19th century, the Documentary hypothesis was developed. This looked at doublets (the same story told of more than one character: as, for example, in Genesis 12:10–20; 20; 26), at the use of different names for the same place or person (Sinai/Horeb, Jacob/Israel, Midianites/Ishmaelites), at traces of two stories being woven together (e.g., the two stories of Creation in the opening chapters of Genesis), and above all at the different names for God. According to Exodus 6:3, God (*El Shaddai*) did not appear to the Ancestors of Israel with the name YHWH (conventionally Yahweh, *see pp.58–59*). This was only later revealed to Moses. Yet in other places in Genesis, God is said to have appeared with this name.

The Documentary hypothesis proposed four main sources later combined to form the Pentateuch:
• J, using the name Yahweh from the outset (in German, *Jahwe*, hence J), early in date, and speaking of God simply and directly;
• E, using *Elohim* until Exodus 6:3, possibly from the Northern Kingdom, surviving only in more fragmentary form;
• D, consisting of the book of Deuteronomy and the Deuteronomistic editing of other books, distinctive in style and attitude;

## PROBLEMS WITH MOSAIC AUTHORSHIP

But the fact that the Law and Covenant were mediated through Moses does not make him the author of the whole Pentateuch. It has long been recognized that some passages could not have been written by Moses (for example, the account of his own death, Deuteronomy 34; the mention of Dan, known by that name only much later, Genesis 14:14; the statement that Moses was the most humble man who ever lived, Numbers 12:3). However, the worth and inspiration of the Pentateuch do not turn on the question of whether the authorship of Moses must be affirmed, and

• P, the Priestly source, from the priests after the Second Temple was established and concerned mainly with ritual, emphasizing God's transcendence. The final composition combining all four sources would then be post-exilic, although earlier versions may have been unified before that date.

## TRADITION HISTORY

In recent years, the belief that all parts of the Pentateuch could be ascribed to these sources (and to a few others added later) has been questioned. Different sources were certainly used, and the Pentateuch actually names some (see Exod. 24:7; Num. 21:14). But it has been argued that the many different styles of narrative and types of composition point to a much more diverse background, and effort has been devoted to classifying the different types: each family group and tribe would have had its own stories, as would any major shrine, such as Shechem. One might then imagine a process whereby, as the tribes drew closer together (for example, during the time of David), or when together they faced a crisis, they shared their stories and traditions. These traditions may have been oral or written, but increasingly, as the stories accumulated, they would have been written down. The regulations of the Covenant, law, and ritual were added – and these held the emerging coalition together.

## RECENT THEORIES

The older theory proposed that the Pentateuch had been built up from pre-existing documents in a series of redactional stages (editing in order to join together). This theory has been modified by a proposal suggesting instead a series of stages through which the complete document was compiled from deliberate attempts to pool existing traditions. This would explain, for example, why the Priestly material, which used to be

HEBREW TEXT OF THE BOOK OF EXODUS
*The left column shows the text as it appears in the Torah scroll; the right one adds vowels and punctuation to aid reading.*

66 *Only be strong and very courageous, being careful to act in accordance with all the law that my servant Moses commanded you ... This book of the law shall not depart out of your mouth; you shall meditate on it day and night, so that you may be careful to act in accordance with all that is written in it .*99

(Joshua 1:7–8)

thought post-exilic, contains much that is early and little that is of immediate use in the post-exilic period. But much of this is bound to be speculative. We do not know what the early stages of the Pentateuch's composition were. Recently, therefore, critics have added to the quest for historical reconstruction. Of course, the historical quest remains vital, even if only to point out the undoubtedly false: we can rarely know historically what is "correct" beyond doubt, but we can know what is false or improbable (e.g., a claim that the Pentateuch was written in the second century BCE). As well as continuing historical criticism, much work is now being done in evaluating the books as they have come to us as compositions – their effect and their place in humanity's unfolding consciousness of God.

## A WORK OF GENIUS

Newer kinds of criticism, such as reader-criticism, narrative-criticism, rhetorical criticism, and ideological criticism (for these, see pp.304–5) make clear that the final form of the Pentateuch, composed as it is from such different sources and types of material, is a work of religious genius. Indeed, for that reason, some feel obliged to say that it must be, in its finished form, the work of a single author. In that sense, the author behind the author is God, since no one without the deepest sense of the presence and purpose of God in the world, in the people, and in the writer, could have written so unerringly. Not in the trivial sense of avoiding mistakes, but in the sense of consistently keeping God always in the text as the one who has brought all this into being. No matter who that author (if one there was) may have been, these books leap out from the literature of the ancient world as extraordinary in their perception of the human circumstance and its need, and of the way in which God has met that need and transformed the circumstance in the direction of holiness and love.

For further reading see bibliography numbers: 63, 94, 101, 189, 487, 590, 600, 801, 830

# TORAH

*Torah is the foundation of Israel and of the Jewish religion. Often translated as "law," it has in fact a far wider range of meanings. "Torah" is a term unique to the Hebrew Bible and later Jewish tradition.*

THE Greek translation of the Bible, the Septuagint, translated the word "Torah" as *nomos*, "law," which led to the misunderstanding that Torah implied "law" alone and thus a dry legalism, whereas, in fact, it encompasses a wide range of meanings within the Hebrew Bible. The term is expanded in later Jewish thought to include all religious interpretations and developments that take their origin in the revelation of God.

> 66 *Let your heart hold fast my words; keep my commandments, and live. Get wisdom ... do not forget nor turn away from the words of my mouth* 99
>
> (Proverbs 4:4–5)

## TORAH AS TEACHING

The word "Torah" derives from a Hebrew verb *y-r-b*. Scholars distinguish two separate roots: one meaning to "throw" and hence "shoot arrows"; the second, and more common, to "teach" or "instruct," although both contain the sense of indicating a direction. As a verb, *y-r-b* can be found referring to secular teaching in wisdom passages (Prov. 4:4, 11; Job 8:10). But the psalmists ask to be taught God's way (Pss. 27:11; 25:8; 32:8; 86:11), and the term is also used to refer to the instruction of the priests (Lev. 10:11).

In biblical stories, God may be the "teacher," guiding Moses in his negotiations with Pharaoh (Exod. 4:12) or through a "messenger," instructing the father of Samson on how to raise his child (Judg. 13:8). In the vision of Isaiah (and Micah) of the end of days, the nations will flow up to Sinai to ask to be taught God's way (Isa. 2:3; Micah 4:2). In the Pentateuch, the word "Torah" is used to describe a group of laws on a specific

READING FROM THE TORAH
*A Jewish boy who has become Bar Mitzvah reads from the Torah scroll. He uses a pointer to follow the words without touching the sacred text.*

subject, such as those concerning the Nazirites (Num. 6:21, "*this is the Torah of the Nazirite*"). However, in Deuteronomy and later books it refers to a more general collection of divine teachings, and particularly to the legal contents of the Covenant.

This is the Torah that Moses placed before the people of Israel. These are the testimonies, statutes, and judgments that Moses spoke to the people of Israel when they departed from Egypt (Deut. 4:44–45; cf. 33:4). In later books (Josh. 1:7; Ezra 3:2; 7:6; Mal. 3:22), the phrase "Torah of Moses" refers to the collection of materials that would become the Pentateuch. The king was to write out for himself a *mishneh hatorah*, "copy of the Torah" (Deut. 17:18). (This Hebrew phrase, understood as a "repeated" or "second" law, gives the book of Deuteronomy its Greek title to *deuteronomion*, "the second law.")

## THE TEACHING OF GOD

At some stage the term developed into a broader idea of the revealed teaching given by God. In Psalm 19, the center of the Psalm consists of a series of six sentences of similar construction and length whose "perfect" symmetry praises the "perfection" of the Torah: "*The law [Torah] of the LORD is perfect, restoring the soul; the decrees of the LORD are sure, making wise the simple ...*" (Ps. 19:7). These verses are placed between the opening section, which describes how the entire cosmos tells of the glory of God, and the closing section, which explores the inner "universe" of the human mind, so that the Torah is a "ladder" between these two domains. Psalm 119, on the other hand, is an extended alphabetical acrostic that is a hymn and love song to Torah, describing the joy of those who follow it.

## TORAH AND WISDOM

In wisdom literature (see pp.170–71), "Torah" is used to refer to practical wisdom to be handed down from father to son (Prov. 3:1). God creates the world with *chokhmah*, "wisdom" (Prov 3:19), and Sirach in the Apocrypha identified the Torah with this preexistent, personified wisdom, thus linking empirical knowledge (wisdom) with divine revelation (Torah). The equation of Torah and wisdom occurs in Jewish liturgy in connection with the reading of the weekly passage from the Torah in synagogue. As the scroll is returned to the ark, the congregation sings that it is *"a tree of life to all who lay hold of her"* (Prov. 3:18), the "her" being *chokhmah* in its original context.

## JEWISH TRADITION

It follows that in English the word may appear as "Torah" (particularly meaning God's foundational instruction and guidance) or as "the Torah" (particularly meaning that as guidance gathered in the Pentateuch). Jewish tradition viewed the Torah, in its limited sense of the Pentateuch, as the unmediated word of God, unchangeable and eternal. The next section of the Hebrew Bible, the *Nebi'im*, "Prophets" (the books from Joshua, Judges, Samuel, and Kings through the "Latter Prophets" Isaiah, Jeremiah, Ezekiel, and the Minor Prophets), was also "revelation," but mediated by the personal experience and abilities of the Prophets themselves

**TORAH MANTLE**
*This elaborate mantle used to cover the Torah scrolls is embroidered with a crown (the Torah being the crowning glory of Jewish life) and lions, symbols of the tribe of Judah.*

> ❝ When he has taken the throne of his kingdom, he shall have a copy of this law written for him in the presence of the levitical priests. It shall remain with him and he shall read in it all the days of his life, so that he may learn to fear the LORD his God, diligently observing all the words of this law and these statutes ❞
>
> (Deuteronomy 17:18–19)

as intermediaries. The third section, the *Kethubim*, "writings," including Psalms, Proverbs, Job, and the remaining books, were inspired by the holy spirit, so that they represent human creations, our self-revelation to God. However, this combination also becomes "Torah" in the first sense of the term.

## TWO KINDS OF TORAH

Rabbinic tradition distinguished two aspects of Torah: the "written Torah," the Pentateuch; and a commentary on it delivered to Moses on Mount Sinai at the same time, the "oral Torah." This opened the door to interpretation of the written text, enabling Torah to develop and address contemporary needs after the canon of the Bible had been closed. Thus "Torah" came to exist as a semiautonomous entity in later rabbinic thought, the total of all revelation and all subsequently derived religious teachings. In different rabbinic teachings, Torah became the blueprint God consulted in creating the world, but it was itself one of several things, like repentance, created in the twilight period between the end of the sixth day of Creation and the Sabbath. It is one of three things through which the world continues to exist, the other two being *'avodah* (Temple worship) and *gemilut hasadim* (deeds of loving kindness).

## TORAH AND OTHER PEOPLES

According to the rabbis, Torah was offered to all the nations of the world, but only Israel was willing to accept it. Nevertheless, it was given in the wilderness, not in the land of Israel, so that anyone could have access to it, and it was revealed at the same time in the 70 languages of the 70 nations of the earth.

For further reading see bibliography numbers: 416, 482, 487, 734

# THE BOOK OF
# GENESIS

*Genesis tells the story of Creation and the derivation of all life from God.
Human life begins in harmony with God, but relationships begin to break
down. God regrets the Creation but sets about the work of repair and healing.*

THE book of Genesis is a brilliant achievement of composition, drawing on different kinds of material, some of which resemble stories of neighboring civilizations (e.g., Creation, the Flood). There are connected narratives, genealogies, brief episodes (e.g., the story of Judah in ch.38), and very old poems (e.g., the blessing of Jacob, ch.49). Differences of style and theme in the material have led many scholars to conclude that Genesis was formed largely from three different earlier sources, which continue into the other books of the Pentateuch (*see pp.22–23*). Others doubt the existence of such sources and hypothesize a much larger number of stories associated with particular shrines, people, or family groups. The stories would have been gathered together later. What is certain is that the result – the book of Genesis as we now have it – is a searching and moving account of the glory and predicament of human beings and of the way in which God deals patiently with them, drawing them back into a relationship of trust and covenant.

them into a coherent narrative that still has much relevance to the human condition. The central issue in the early chapters is the quest for knowledge and power, which leads to conflict with God and conflict between humans. God is portrayed as all-powerful, but also as caring and providing for human beings as they stumble and fall. The first chapters of Genesis contain famous stories, such as those of Adam and Eve, Cain and Abel, Noah and the Flood, and the Tower of Babel. While these stories concern particular individuals, their significance is much greater, inviting readers to reflect on the relevance of these biblical figures to their own lives. From chapter 12 of the book, the focus on individuals is less symbolic and more historical.

FRONTISPIECE OF GENESIS
*This illumination from a Hebrew Bible shows some of
the many different stories in the book of Genesis.*

## THE EARLY CHAPTERS

Genesis 1–11 is a great narrative, setting human life and history in the context of God's Creation and purpose. The world is presented as an arena of opportunity, where the chances of delight and goodness are matched by the choices that take humans far from God and from one another. The book of Genesis makes use of earlier elements but weaves

## THE ORIGINS OF ISRAEL

Genesis 12–50 is ancient tribal history that also tells of origins, but this time it is the origins of Israel, a people selected by God for special blessing and special responsibility. Stories, lists and genealogies, songs and maxims, local legends and cult legends, folk history and sagas are woven together into a religious history that shaped the consciousness of the nation of Israel. The ancestral history is told in family and tribal stories about relationships and about God's promise that the people will have land and descendants. God is seen actively at work in relationship with human beings, and in the guiding of events and the bestowing of divine blessing. There are four cycles of stories in Genesis, three concerning the Ancestors, or Patriarchs, of ancient Israel: Abraham, Isaac, Jacob, and the fourth concerning Joseph.

## GENESIS AND TORAH

In Jewish tradition, Genesis forms part of Torah (*pp.24–25*). him and his descendants are set in the universal context of all Creation: these people have a specific part to play in God's purpose of repairing the breakdown in relationships recounted in the opening chapters. God's choosing of Abraham emphasizes the role of justice in human society and in the relationship of humans to God. In one rabbinic view, God created several worlds before this one, destroying each in turn and expressing satisfaction with only this last version of the Creation (*Genesis Rabbah* 3:7). In Christian tradition, the primeval history summarizes the human predicament, in relation to which Jesus is portrayed as the second Adam, who comes to reverse the sins of the first Adam and to save humanity from its sinful nature.

## CREATION IN GENESIS

It is now widely accepted that Genesis has combined two different creation stories, one running from 1:1 to 2:3 or 4a (perhaps finally composed in its present form by the Priestly editors, *see pp.22–23*), the second from 2:4b to 3:24 (coming perhaps from the J editor). The first emphasizes order and regularity under the sovereign power of God. All things that exist or come into being do so as a consequence of God's word and act. Humans are created *"in the image of God"* (Gen. 1:27), which may mean "corresponding to God" or "in the shadow of God." The second reverses the order of Creation, with Man appearing first, then plants and animals, and with Woman created later. They are the servants of a divine overlord, whereas in the first story they are raised to the dignity of God's agents in Creation. However, there are points of connection between the two stories. In both, wholeness or *shalom* is a key aspect: in the first, God rests when the work of Creation is finished (Gen. 2:2), in the second, the creation of Woman brings completion to God's work. Of special interest is the claim that humanity, male and female, black and white, old and young, believer and unbeliever, is created in God's image: *"Let us make humankind in our image, according to our likeness; and let them have dominion over the fish of the sea, and over the birds of the air ... and over all the wild animals of the earth, and over every creeping thing that creeps upon the earth,"* (Gen. 1:26–7). Long before humans fall into conflict and division, they are all equally made in the image of God. This gives humans immense worth and dignity. Human experience, however, is more familiar with the alienation, rupture, deception, striving, and pain described in Genesis 3. In one way, Genesis 1–3 speaks of what has been lost; in another, it points to the perfection yet to come. Both stories also reflect a monotheistic theology: one mediates transcendence, the other immanence. One may reflect priestly, the other prophetic, interests.

## THE BOOK

**TITLE:** Genesis

**HEBREW TITLE:** *Bereshith*
(from the first word, "in the beginning")

**DATE:** Unknown: the narratives and other material come from different periods of Israel's history, and may first have been collected in earlier sources

**AUTHORSHIP:** No author is named. The whole of Torah, including Genesis, later came to be associated with Moses. Three different source writers have been suggested, each reworking earlier oral and written material (*see pp.22–23*)

## THE CONTENTS

**CHAPTERS 1–11**
The primeval history: an account of the Creation of the world and humankind (chs.1–2), of the expulsion from Eden (chs.3–4), of near destruction in the Flood (chs. 6–9), and of the growth and increase of the human race throughout the world after the Flood (chs.10–11)

**CHAPTERS 12–25**
The Abraham cycle: stories about Abraham, the first Ancestor to whom the promise of land, blessing, and progeny is made. Stories about Abraham and his son Isaac, and about Abraham, Lot, and the destruction of Sodom

**CHAPTERS 26–36**
The Jacob cycle: the conflict between the brothers Jacob and Esau; Jacob's exile for 20 years and his quest for a wife; the conflict between Leah and Rachel; and a number of encounters between Jacob (later named Israel) and God

**CHAPTERS 37–50**
The Joseph cycle: a family history telling of the rejection of Joseph and then of his successful interpretation of dreams and rise to power at Pharaoh's palace. With the God of the Israelites on his side, Joseph saves the Egyptians from famine and is ultimately reconciled with his own family

## KEY THEMES

*Creation*

•

*The origins of Israel*

For further reading see bibliography numbers: 10, 14, 53, 105, 144, 189, 303, 324, 357, 363, 407, 427, 465, 541, 562a, 593, 628, 636, 659, 687a, 755, 763, 774, 793

# CREATION

*In the Bible, ways of thinking about Creation are not confined to the opening chapters of Genesis. Different stories and themes are drawn on, to give deeper insight into God and Creation.*

CREATION in the Bible means much more than bringing something into being. It also means sustaining and caring for that which has been created. The Bible therefore looks at Creation in many different ways. This also means that the Genesis story is not the only account of Creation in the Bible. There are several, falling into six different types:

• God creates an ordered and coherent whole (Gen. 1:1–2a; Pss. 74:12–17; 104). The last of these Psalms contains a fascinating parallel to the ordering of Creation in the Genesis account and may well be older.

• The focus of Creation is on humankind (Gen. 2:4b–25; Ezek. 28:12–19).

• Wisdom exists before the beginning of the earth, and God creates the world "in wisdom" (i.e., wisely), or "by means of wisdom" (*see also pp.170–71*). The world is an arena of learning, testing, and opportunity. This type of account is common in the wisdom literature of the Bible (e.g., Prov. 8; Job 38–41).

• God creates a people for a special divine–human relationship. There are many examples of this. Among them are the call of Abraham, the Exodus, and the interpretation of the Exile in Isaiah chapters 40–55.

• God engages in conflict with opponents (chaos, monsters, other gods), and from God's victory emerges an orderly Creation over which God rules as king. Such stories of a deity's victory over a watery chaos, often described as a sea monster, were common in the ancient Near East and are

**GOD THE CREATOR**
*This detail from part of the 16th-century Isenheim altarpiece by Mattias Grünewald depicts God the Creator.*

reflected in, for example, Psalms 74:12–17, 89:9–13, and Job 41.

• God continues to create: God will end the first Creation (Jer. 4:23–8) and after further conflict, a new Creation will emerge (Isa. 65:17–25; Ezek. 38–39; Zech. 2:1–5; 9–14; Dan. 7–12). This led to the Christian belief that the advent of Christ inaugurated the new Creation, bringing the world back to the originally intended harmony.

## WAYS OF READING CREATION

The Bible is not alone in seeing different ways of understanding the universe and the place of humans in it. There are many ways of interpreting Creation:

• As the unfolding of order in regular and reliable ways – ways that can now be described as scientific laws;

• As itself a work of art, drawing order and beauty out of unordered matter, as a potter draws a pot out of formless clay;

• As an epic poem, unfolding unceasing opportunities for new adventure and discovery;

• As a grim struggle against unyielding material in which victory is not assured. None of these ways (or the many other ways) of reading Creation is complete in itself – not even the scientific, which is always an incomplete story, correcting itself as it goes along. All of these different ways of looking at Creation and trying to understand its incredible mystery, terror, and beauty are needed. And all of these different ways are reflected in the different accounts that are given in the Bible.

## SCIENCE AND THE BIBLE

Does one of these ways, the account given in the opening chapters of Genesis, differ from the others, in the sense that it tells how the universe was brought into being – perhaps literally, perhaps figuratively, in the sense that the days of the Genesis account may stand for long periods? This has become an issue that has divided Jews as well as Christians. Some see it as an issue of truth: if the Creation did not happen as the Bible says, then the Bible is false. Among those who hold this view are Creationists. In parts of the United States they have demanded education for creation science to be taught alongside Darwinian theories of evolution.

Creationists point out that Darwin's theory of evolution has many gaps, and many things that it cannot account for. They, along with scientist and thinkers who have interpreted Darwin's work, are correct in saying that Darwin's theory, even as developed in neo-Darwinism, is incomplete. Adaption to environments through natural selection is demonstrated repeatedly in the world as we observe it now. For example, the coloration on moths changes when a city changes from a smoky to a smokeless zone; widespread use of antibiotics have led to "superbugs" resistant to them. But Darwinism is clearly far from adequate when dealing with the small-scale biochemical changes that underlie large-scale evolution. At a microscopic level, at the level of biochemistry, something more like an original design or blueprint seems inevitable. But these are arguments within science itself. They cannot be resolved by appeal to one of the several accounts of Creation in the Bible. The Bible complements the truth in any account, whether that of a poet or a scientist.

*66 Then God said, 'Let us make humankind in our image, according to our likeness; and let them have dominion over the fish of the sea, and over the birds of the air … and over all the wild animals of the earth' 99*

(Genesis 1:26)

## GOD THE AUTHOR

The major point made in the Bible is that, however Creation is interpreted, and whatever account of Creation one follows, God is the author of the story; and if there is a design, then God is the Designer. All the accounts of Creation in the Bible make this point. In this respect, the stories of the Bible differ hugely from other stories told about Creation in the religions and beliefs of the nations that surrounded Israel, such as Babylon and Assyria (*see pp.142–43, 148–49*). The biblical writers used different stories of Creation, and at least two of these accounts are shared with Israel's neighbors in the ancient Near East. But the Bible retold these stories of other nations and – from its own point of view – corrected them to make its own basic point: the true reading of Creation sees it as the consequence of One who gives it order and sustains it's being. The biblical account is coherent with many other stories, whether those of the Babylonian accounts of creation, or, much later, the theories of Darwin and his successors, and has translated them into an account that endures, even when Babylon and Darwin have faded into history. These different theories of Creation are not in competition with the Bible. The stories of Creation in the Bible give the reader the opportunity to go deeper into the understanding of the universe and of our place in it, to understand the way in which God brings all things into being and to understand how God is continually in the act of creating.

THE GALAXY
*Some have linked the biblical stories to scientific theories of the origin of the universe.*

## CREATION AND THE FUTURE

The biblical vision of Creation looks to a future that only God can create. The word *bara*, "he created," is used in the Bible only to speak of God's work. In Isaiah 65:17, it is used to describe new heavens and a new earth (*cf.* Isa. 66:22), characterized by joy, life, fruitfulness, and justice; and God will be close to the people (Isa. 65:24). The idea reappears in the New Testament (Rev. 21:2ff.), where God's compassion, combined with the absence of mourning, crying, pain, and death, are characteristics of the new Creation. For Paul, the whole of Creation groans like a woman in labor waiting for new life (Rom. 8:22). He recalls Isaiah when he writes that a person who is in Christ is a "new creation" (2 Cor. 5:17). For Paul, Christ is God's key to the completion of Creation (Col. 1:17).

For further reading see bibliography numbers: 14, 78, 105, 237, 407, 465, 564, 593, 620, 628, 792

THE STORY OF

# ADAM AND EVE

*The opening chapters of the book of Genesis tell the story of Adam and Eve, the parents of the human race, and of their sons, Cain and Abel. The story gives humans status as guardians of the earth who are morally responsible to God.*

ADAM is the first person in the Bible. There are two accounts of human creation in Genesis. In the first, *"God said, 'Let us make humankind in our image, according to our likeness ...'"* So God created humankind, male and female, in God's own image. In this first account the man and the woman are both made in the divine image and are created equal. In the second account, the man is created first, and the name Adam, which was used for all humanity in the first story, applies only to him. His name is explained: he was formed from the ground (Hebrew *adamah*), and God then put a living soul in him. Because God felt it was not good for Adam to be alone, woman was then created from one of his ribs; she was later named Eve (Hebrew *chavvah* resembles the word for living) because she is the mother of all living beings. A Jewish source suggests that Eve is more evolved than Adam because she was created from human material rather than from the earth; she is the culmination of Creation. Later legend even supposed that two different women are described in the two chapters: the first woman, Lilith, demanded complete equality in everything, so Adam asked God to replace her with someone more obliging. Eve is described as "a helper, as his partner," and the relationship between Adam and Eve becomes the pattern for all future marriages. Adam was appointed guardian of the Garden of Eden and was told that the couple might eat every fruit except that from the tree of the knowledge of good and evil. A crafty serpent in the garden asked Eve whether God had restricted what they should eat. She replied that they might neither eat nor touch the tree of the knowledge of good and evil. (A later commentary suggests that adding touch to the prohibition to Adam against eating the fruit leads to Eve's downfall: the serpent then pushed Eve against the fruit; she did not die, and so was persuaded that eating the fruit would also be harmless.) Eve ate the fruit because she was told that her eyes would be opened, to make her like God, knowing good and evil, and she gave the fruit to Adam. They saw that

Adam and Eve.

HUMANS CREATED IN GOD'S IMAGE: GEN. 1:26

THE SECOND ACCOUNT: GEN. 2:4B

ADAM MADE FROM THE EARTH: GEN. 2:7

EVE CREATED FROM ADAM'S RIB: GEN. 2:21

EVE A PARTNER: GEN. 2:18

THE SERPENT: GEN. 3:1ff.

EVE'S REPLY: GEN. 3:2

they were naked and sewed fig leaves together to make loincloths. Then they hid themselves from the sight of God. When God questioned them, Adam blamed Eve, and Eve blamed the serpent. God stated the consequences: serpents would forever slither on the ground, women would have pain in childbirth, and men would do hard work and then die. They then had to leave the Garden of Eden in case they also ate the fruit of the Tree of Life and lived forever. God made protective garments of leather for them in their new vulnerable state.

*ADAM AND EVE MAKE LOINCLOTHS: GEN. 3:7*

*GOD'S CURSE: GEN. 3:14*

## CAIN AND ABEL

When Adam and Eve's first two sons grew up, Cain became a farmer and Abel a shepherd. They both brought an offering to God: Cain of the fruits of the earth; Abel, an animal from his flock. God accepted Abel's offering but not Cain's. Cain was angry, and his face fell in disappointment – God said, *"Why are you angry, and why has your countenance fallen? If you do well, will you not be accepted? And if you do not do well, sin is lurking at the door; its desire is for you, but you must master it."* This powerful image of humanity challenged to overcome sin did not help Cain. When he and Abel were together in the fields he killed his brother. God asked Cain where his brother was, but Cain refused to accept responsibility: *"Am I my brother's keeper?"* Cain was condemned to wander as a fugitive. He was terrified, now he knew what death was, that he would be a fugitive and that someone would kill him, so God gave him a protecting sign. Then Cain went into the land of Nod, east of Eden.

*THE BROTHERS' OFFERINGS: GEN. 4:3—4*

*GOD'S ADDRESS: GEN. 4:7*

*CAIN KILLS ABEL: GEN. 4:8*

*CAIN'S FEAR: GEN. 4:14*

*THE MARK OF CAIN: GEN. 4:15*

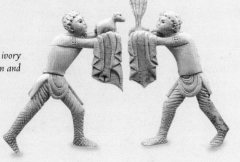

**CAIN AND ABEL**
*This 11th-century ivory carving shows Cain and Abel offering their respective sacrifices to God, who accepts only Abel's and rejects that of Cain.*

## HARMONY, CONFLICT, COVENANT

The theme that unifies all the opening stories in Genesis is their record of an original condition of harmony that is progressively broken up in contest and conflict – between humans and God and between man and woman (Adam and Eve); humans and the natural order (epitomized by the craftiness of the serpent); country-dwellers and city-dwellers (the agriculturist Cain and the herdsman Abel); the God-fearing and those who are not; and between different nations, culminating in the confusion of languages after the building of the Tower of Babel (*see p.33*). In contrast to this increasing disorder and conflict, the Bible shows God undertaking the necessary work of correction and repair. The people of Israel are to be the agents of this work, beginning with the call of Abram (Gen. 12) and continuing through successive covenants with the Patriarchs, Moses, and David. It culminates in the renewal of the Covenant after the Exile, when Ezra reads the Law to the people and they give their assent to it (*pp.160–61*). In this way the Bible sees the people of Israel as necessary for the good of all: they take upon themselves the conditions of life, summarized in Torah, which will be for the good of all people and the whole of Creation.

## THE CONCEPT OF THE FALL

Judaism does not see in the Genesis story the "Fall of Man." It may be that Adam and Eve disobeyed God, but God stayed in conversation with them. Seeking wisdom and distinguishing between good and evil become essential human attributes. Toiling for food and suffering pain in childbirth are the prices paid for knowledge. For Judaism, if there is "a fall" in Genesis, it is a fall upward into new opportunities of responsibility and achievement. Christians see a radical fault that affects all subsequent humans. The fault of the first Adam has been dealt with by Jesus, who, as the second Adam, brings redemption to the world.

## THE SYMBOLISM OF THE TREE

The Tree of Life, or the Cosmic Tree, is a symbol common in many ancient religions. In Judaism it is associated with the almond tree; the almond was used as the pattern for the cups, capitals, and flowers of the *menorah*. In the Bible it appears not only in the Adam and Eve story, but also in the New Testament. The cross is associated with the Tree of Life, mentioned again in Revelation (22:2). The Tree of Life stood at the center of the world (the Garden of Eden), and Christ's Crucifixion is said to have happened at the center of the world. The two trees of Eden (Life and Knowledge) are also reflected in ancient Babylonian religion – the Tree of Truth and the Tree of Life, which stood at the eastern entry to the Babylonian heaven.

For further reading see bibliography numbers: 39, 53, 105, 190, 582, 619, 620, 636, 659, 755

# THE STORY OF
# NOAH AND THE FLOOD

*Noah is best known as the survivor of the Flood. His righteousness and obedience to God lead to his being specially favored. God saves from annihilation Noah, his family, and a pair of every kind of bird and animal.*

GENESIS 6–9 combines two versions of the story of Noah and the Flood, closely interwoven. At the time of Noah, as the numbers of men and women began to increase, so too did evil and wrongdoing. God saw how great the wickedness had become and began to regret the creation of humans, deciding to destroy everything on the face of the earth. Noah alone found favor with God, who told him to make an ark and to take into it, not only his wife and family but a pair of each kind of bird and animal(or seven pairs of clean animals). The Flood came and lasted for 40 days. When the level of the water began to fall, Noah sent out a raven and a dove. At first, neither could find a place to land because the waters still covered everything, but at last the dove returned with an olive leaf in its beak. As soon as Noah came out of the ark, he made an altar and offered a sacrifice to God, who smelled the pleasing aroma and said, *"Never again will I curse the ground because of humankind … As long as the earth endures, seedtime and harvest, cold and heat, summer and winter, day and night, shall not cease."* Then God made a covenant with Noah, and the rainbow became the sign of this covenant. Up until this point, people had been vegetarian, but from this time on they eat meat provided

Noah's ark.

it did not still contain blood. Additional narrative about the character of Noah describes his discovery of the grapevine and the consequences of drinking wine. An inexperienced Noah is found drunk in his tent by his son Ham, who then tells Noah's other sons Shem and Japheth, who covered up Noah's nakedness. Ham is cursed for seeing his father's nakedness – the others are careful to walk into the tent backward. Ham's progeny, the Canaanites, thus became subject to the descendants of the other sons. There are two origin stories here – the origins of winemaking, and with that the change from nomadic to agricultural life; and the origin of the hierarchy of the nations as it existed in later times.

Noah is the son of Lamech, the ninth descendant of Adam through Seth. He is the first to be born after the death of Adam, when the curse on the ground, which was to last through Adam's life (Gen. 3:17), was lifted. Both the Jewish and Christian traditions consider him to be the second father of humankind (with Adam as the first), after all the other descendants had been destroyed. He died at age 950, the last of the "pre-Flood" generation who lived to extraordinary ages.

GOD DECIDES TO DESTROY THE EARTH: GEN. 6:7

THE FILLING OF THE ARK: GEN. 7:5

THE DOVE IS SENT OUT: GEN. 8:8

NOAH'S SACRIFICE: GEN. 8:20

GOD'S PROMISE: GEN. 8:21–22

THE RAINBOW: GEN. 9:12–13

NOAH BECOMES DRUNK: GEN. 9:21

THE CURSE ON CANAAN: GEN. 9:25–27

## THE NOACHIDE COVENANT

Within the structure of the Bible as a whole, the covenant with Noah is the beginning of God's work of repair and healing. Having come to regret making humans on the earth (Gen. 6:6), God now blesses Noah and his descendants and makes promises of further blessings, tied to certain conditions that they must keep. Then God gives the rainbow as a sign of the covenant that they have entered into (Gen. 9:1–17). This covenant later came to be understood as one that embraces all people,

### THE TOWER OF BABEL (GEN. 11:1–9)

*This story also has Mesopotamian connections. People discover how to make building materials and then build a tower reaching to heaven. They intend to "make themselves a name so that they may not be scattered over all the earth." God's disapproval is not explained. Many suggestions have been made – that they are storming heaven to displace God; that they are too proud; that they contradict God's command (Gen. 1:28). The story is also about language: once words and the things they denoted were the same; now they are not, so confusion arises. The direct relationship between words and reality is lost when God confuses language (babel, meaning Babylon, is taken to mean "babble"), so people no longer understand one another.*

not just the Israelites and Jews, because in chapter 10 the three sons of Noah – Shem, Ham, and Japheth – become the fathers of all the nations of the world. Noah is thus sometimes seen as the "second Adam." This all-embracing covenant came to be known in later Christian and Jewish tradition as the Noachide covenant, and it was thought to contain seven commands. These are listed differently in different texts, because they are derived not from this chapter in Genesis alone but from the appeals in the rest of Scripture to the Gentiles (non-Jews) to live justly. The usual list of seven is the command to establish a system of justice, prohibitions against idolatry, blasphemy, murder, adultery and incest (regarded as one, and often interpreted as sexual immorality in general), robbery, and eating flesh torn from a living animal. A Gentile who keeps these laws is already in the covenant with God and does not have to convert to Judaism in order to become a part of the "world to come" ('olam ha-ba). Jews have a special vocation to keep the 613 commands and prohibitions of Torah, not for themselves or for their own advantage (since "righteous Gentiles" stand on the same footing), but for the good of the whole world, in order to show what life lived under the guidance, or Torah, of God can be like. At the outset of the development of Christianity, a decision had to be made concerning how many, if any, of the laws in Torah a new convert was obliged to follow. It is possible that the decision in Acts 15:20 is an early reflection of the Noachide covenant.

# OTHER FLOOD STORIES

*Seasonal flooding occurred in both Egypt and Mesopotamia. The story of a vast deluge of water that flooded the known world is one that Israel shared with its ancient Near Eastern neighbors.*

The oldest parallel to the story of Noah discovered so far is the fragmentary Sumerian version of the flood story found at Nippur. It dates to the third millennium BCE. However, the most famous parallel to the biblical Flood story is the Mesopotamian *Epic of Gilgamesh*, discovered in 1878 written on clay tablets in the library of Ashurbanipal at Nineveh. Tablet 11 of this epic concerns a hero called Utnapishtim, who eventually discovers the secret of eternal life, and it contains a version of the story of the Flood. Utnapishtim is the parallel figure to Noah, and like him is saved from the coming deluge with his wife, family, and selected animals in an ark, while the rest of humankind is destroyed. The similarities in the circumstantial details of the stories are striking and open up the possibility of dependence of some kind. The ark is constructed in a similar way, the birds sent out from the ark are the same, and the ark lands on a high mountain. Equally striking, however, are the theological differences: the gods of the *Epic of Gilgamesh* squabble and fight; they decide to destroy humans because of the noise they are

making; and at the end of the story, when a sacrifice is made, they gather like flies in order to smell its sweet savor. The gods decide that in the future humans should be punished if they behave wickedly, but not destroyed.

### The Epic of Atrahasis

Before God sends the Flood, the Bible says that human beings "began to multiply on the face of the ground" (Gen. 6:1). A similar expression occurs in the flood story of the Akkadian *Epic of Atrahasis*, where the reason for the deluge is the gods' desire to curb human overpopulation. Atrahasis builds a boat and rides out the flood. After seven days the boat comes to rest on dry land, and he offers a sacrifice to the gods. They then decide to reinstitute rules of individual punishment rather than collective guilt.

### Gilgamesh

*The story of Gilgamesh probably dates to the third millennium BCE. It tells of the king of Uruk and his search for immortality. A series of incidents illustrates Gilgamesh's refusal to accept his mortality. The flood story that forms a part of the epic may be a later insertion.*

For further reading see bibliography numbers: 34, 35, 105, 223, 384, 476, 628, 636, 774, 793

# THE ANCESTORS

*The Ancestors of Israel are traditionally referred to as the Patriarchs and, more recently, the Matriarchs. They played a vital part in the founding of Israel before the Covenant with Moses on Mount Sinai.*

## POSSIBLE ROUTES FOR ABRAHAM'S JOURNEY

The Ancestors moved across a wide stretch of land from Mesopotamia to Egypt. Towns referred to in the biblical text include Ur, Haran, Jerusalem, Bethel, Gerar, Shechem, and Hebron. Abraham traveled from the city of Ur in southern Mesopotamia, northward to Haran, and then on to Canaan and eventually Egypt. Jacob traveled from Palestine to Haran and back, before continuing to Egypt. Both would have traveled along the many trade routes that had been established by this time.

AFTER the story of the Tower of Babel in chapter 11, the book of Genesis focuses its attention on successive generations of the Ancestors of Israel, leading to the captivity in Egypt. Abram is summoned by God to the land of Canaan, the land that is promised to the people of the great nation who are to be his descendants. Abram travels there with his nephew, Lot, and his wife, Sarai, who eventually gives birth to a son, Isaac. Isaac's own son, Jacob, then inherits the birthright and blessing of the lineage (pp.40–41). Finally, Jacob's sons become the ancestors of the individual tribes of Israel. The stories of Abram, Isaac, and Jacob are collectively known as the "Patriarchal Narratives."

God promised Abram that he would be the ancestor of a mighty nation, and that the land of Canaan would be given to his descendants (Gen. 12:2–3). This promise is affirmed in Genesis 17 in return for the circumcision of all subsequent generations, and God changes Abram's name to Abraham. Similar promises are made to Isaac (Gen. 26:3–4, 24) and to Jacob (Gen. 28:13–15). The stories clearly seek to show how Israel's existence is the fulfillment of God's will and plan.

## DATING THE NARRATIVES

The stories portray a relationship with God that precedes the Covenant at Sinai and that does not require the Patriarchs to adopt all the practices later required under the law of that Covenant. However, the narratives also include a number of stories only loosely related to this theme; some of these are very similar to one another (Gen. 12:10–20; cf. 20:1–18; 26:7–11). It seems probable that the narratives have been constructed from earlier written or oral sources (see pp.22–23 for the Composition of the Pentateuch).

**SACRED ZIGGURAT OF UR**
*In the third millennium BCE, Ur was one of the most important cities in Mesopotamia. The city center was dominated by a sacred enclosure of temple buildings, the most important of which was the three-story tower, or ziggurat, surmounted by a temple. The restored remains of the ziggurat can be seen at Tel el-Muqayyar in southern Iraq.*

**ANCIENT STATUE**
*This figurine was discovered in the excavated ruins of the city of Ur. It dates from c.2500BCE.*

The Patriarchal Narratives presuppose the existence not only of Israel but of particular relationships between the Israelites and those other nations whose ancestry can be traced back to Abraham. It is unlikely, therefore, that the basic framework of the stories can be dated before the first millennium BCE. That does not rule out the clear probability that some or all of the individual stories originated before this time and contain memories of some earlier period.

## THE NARRATIVES AND HISTORY

Many attempts have been made in the 20th century to link the Ancestors to specific times or events in the ancient Near East and to establish a "Patriarchal Age." Such attempts have generally sought to establish a particular context in which parallels to the personal names and customs of the Ancestors can be found. On the basis of such inquiries, it was widely accepted for a number of years that the Ancestors must have lived in the early or mid-second millennium BCE: the name "Jacob" was widely known at this time, and certain customs – such as a barren wife providing a maidservant as mother for her husband's children – are confirmed in texts from the Hurrian community at Nuzi, located in upper Mesopotamia in the mid-second millennium BCE. Some scholars further associated the narratives with a supposed massive influx of a nomadic people known as "Amorites" (whose language was closely related to Hebrew) into Syria and Palestine at this time.

## MODERN INTERPRETATION

Today, many scholars are inclined to be more cautious. Further examination has shown that the Patriarchal names and customs fit no single historical period: strong parallels can be cited as readily for the sixth or seventh centuries as for the 20th century BCE. The hypothesis of an Amorite invasion is no longer widely supported, and it has become clear that many of the Nuzi parallels are less precise than were once thought. It does seem apparent, however, that the individual stories in the Patriarchal Narratives are set against a broadly realistic Near Eastern background, but we have no way of assigning any

**THE DEPARTURE OF ABRAHAM**
*Abraham sets out to offer his son to God (Gen. 22:3). The artist, from the school of the Venetian painter Jacopo Bassano, puts him in a 16th-century setting.*

particular date to them. Where very specific names and events are mentioned, as in Genesis 14, it would seem that genuinely old reminiscences have been combined and reworked to tell an important story.

## THE ANCESTORS AND THE BIBLE

The final form of narratives comes probably from a time between the period of the Monarchy (tenth century BCE), and the Babylonian Exile (sixth century BCE). It is striking that the Ancestors are viewed with approval in these stories, despite not only the absence of the later covenant law but also their sometimes questionable behavior – for instance, Jacob's deceitfulness in fooling his father into giving him the blessing intended for his older brother, Esau (Gen. 27:18–29). It seems likely that the stories are supposed to represent a previous period, which has now been replaced by Israel's new covenant relationship with God in the land. The Ancestors appear in the Bible not just as "ancient history" but also as a prefiguration of the later nation of Israel.

### UR OF THE CHALDEES

The Babylonian city of Ur was home to Abraham's family before they began their journey to the Promised Land. Excavations of the site (at Tel el-Muqayyar in modern-day southern Iraq) in the early 20th century revealed many examples of beautiful craftsmanship, including gold weapons and figurines from the royal tombs (c.2500BCE). A large number of inscribed tablets have provided valuable information about the history of the city. Ur was occupied for several thousand years by a highly civilized population before being abandoned in c.300BCE.

For further reading see bibliography numbers: 6, 131, 189, 402, 490, 541, 558b, 559, 562a, 562b, 639, 763

# RELIGION IN THE PERIOD OF THE ANCESTORS

*Vivid stories are told about the Ancestors of the Israelite people, often called the "Matriarchs" and "Patriarchs". The stories are very old, even though they were written in their present form long after the Ancestors lived.*

THE Bible recognizes that the distinctive content and character of Israel's religion were associated with Moses. But the religion of the Ancestors prepares the way for this, especially in its themes of the promises of God to a particular kinship group, associated with a covenant. The character of worship at that time can be discerned from the stories of Genesis, and it is clear from comparing archaeology with details in Genesis that some stories, at least, belong to an early period. In fact, it is remarkable that the Bible records a time when the religion and worship of the Ancestors were different from the later Mosaic religion, and while it traces the way in which God moved Israel into a new acknowledgment of the truth about God, it does not erase all trace of that earlier religion. Joshua reminds the assembled people of their past and states openly: *"Thus says the LORD, the God of Israel: long ago your ancestors – Terah and his sons Abraham and Nahor – lived beyond the Euphrates and served other gods [elohim]"* (Josh. 24:2; for the meaning of YHWH and *elohim*, see pp.58–59).

**BABYLONIAN GOD**
*The Ancestor Abraham journeyed from his homeland in ancient Babylonia. This statue of the sun god Shamash comes from Ur and dates to c.1900BCE.*

what religion in the period of the Ancestors (of which many traces remain) may have been, and what later generations wrote about it. Later generations knew that YHWH was the only God, but earlier generations clearly did not worship only YHWH. The clue to this is in the explicit statement that knowledge of God's name as YHWH, which was given to Moses (Exod. 3:13–15) and was basic to Israel, was not given to the Ancestors (Exod. 6:2–3). If the Ancestors knew God differently, then it would follow that patterns of religious life and practice would differ also. Such differences are indeed to be found in the narratives of Genesis 12–50; the writers take for granted that it is the one God, YHWH, who is encountered in those differing ways. This means that there is an assumption of monotheism. Although the people encountered in the stories of the Ancestors had different names for God and different practices in worship, it is assumed that there is only one God (see the example of Abimelech, king of Gerar, in Gen. 20:3ff.).

## GENESIS

The stories of Genesis are now organized to tell how, under the leadership first of the Ancestors and later of Moses, the people moved from the worship of other gods and of El and Baal as Canaanite gods, to the worship of YHWH alone and to the worship of El as none other than YHWH (*see* Names and Nature of God, pp.58–59). But a distinction has to be made between

> **❝** *God also spoke to Moses and said to him: 'I am the LORD. I appeared to Abraham, Isaac, and Jacob as God Almighty, but by my name "The LORD" I did not make myself known to them.'* **❞**
>
> (Exodus 6:2–3)

## OTHER PEOPLES

Because of this assumption about God, the stories display no antagonism between the religious practices of the Ancestors and of the native inhabitants of Canaan. Apart from the people of Sodom and Gomorrah, there is no suggestion that the Canaanites behave in idolatrous ways. Abraham's assumption that the people of Gerar would have no fear of God (Gen. 20:11) is shown to be misplaced. Although there is a concern that Isaac and Jacob should not marry Canaanite women (Gen. 24:5–8; 34:13–17), this is never said to be because of the dangers of religious apostasy that elsewhere characterize Israel's strictures on intermarriage (e.g., the condemnation of Solomon's taking of many wives, 1 Kgs. 11:1–10).

## CANAANITE INFLUENCE

This early tolerance of the Canaanites is not surprising because it is clear that the religion of the Ancestors owed much to the genius of the Canaanites (*pp.98–99*). That is why the religious practices of the Ancestors differ from those prescribed in Mosaic Law. Trees and pillars (Gen. 12:6–7; 21:33; 28:18, 22) play a role whose precise nature is unclear but that is later prohibited in Deuteronomy 16:21–22: *"You shall not plant any tree as a sacred pole beside the altar that you make for the LORD your God; nor shall you set up a stone pillar – things that the LORD your God hates."*

There is no hint of Sabbath observance by the Ancestors and, unlike Leviticus 11, the only mention of dietary restrictions is that Egyptians do not eat with Hebrews (Gen. 43:32), not *vice versa*. Places and altars are of great importance to the Ancestors, as is the securing of blessings from God.

The Ancestors have neither prophet nor priest to mediate between themselves and God, nor do they fulfill such roles with regard to others as Moses does. The one exception is the brief appearance of King Melchizedek of Salem, who is described as "priest of God Most High" and blesses Abraham (Gen. 14:18–20).

## THE PEOPLE AND THE LAND

The lack of a priesthood and organized state religion is partly explained by the fact that the Ancestors are individuals, and Israel as a people does not yet exist. As with the Canaanites, loose federations of families in a kinship group are the nearest one gets to "a people." But while Abraham intercedes for Sodom (Gen. 18:22–33), and such intercession is one of the marks of a prophet (Gen. 20:7; cf., 1 Sam. 12:19, 23),

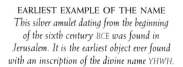

EARLIEST EXAMPLE OF THE NAME
*This silver amulet dating from the beginning of the sixth century BCE was found in Jerusalem. It is the earliest object ever found with an inscription of the divine name YHWH.*

there is no suggestion that he speaks the kind of prophetic message that Jeremiah does. That this kinship group lived easily with its neighbors in Canaan is shown by the fact that there is no suggestion that the land really belonged to them rather than to the Canaanites. They display no aggression with regard to the land. If they want land, they buy it (Gen. 23; 33:19). Abraham refers to the land he has come from as "my land" (Gen. 24:4), and the Ancestors' presence in Canaan is always depicted as "sojourning" (Gen. 17:8), or visiting, so they are temporary residents dependent on the hospitality of the Canaanite people.

## OTHER DIFFERENCES

A further difference can be seen in the fact that there is far less moral content in the religion of the Ancestors than there is in that after Sinai. Blessings are given, usually with no moral stipulation attached (most strikingly in the case of Jacob, who is told *"May God Almighty bless you and make you fruitful and numerous, that you may become a company of peoples,"* Gen. 28:3), and there are no warnings of judgment or curse if the Ancestors are disobedient. This is unlike the stipulation of Deuteronomy 28:15 that claims, *"If you will not obey the LORD your God by diligently observing all his commandments and decrees, which I am commanding you today, then all these curses shall come upon you and overtake you."*

## HOLINESS

From Moses' first encounter with God (Exod. 3:5) onward, it is clear that the notion of holiness is a basic characteristic of God and a major requirement for Israel: *"Speak to all the people of Israel and say to them: you shall be holy, for I the LORD your God am holy"* (Lev. 19:2). The notion is lacking in the stories of the Ancestors, and it draws together the previous points. The unstructured character of the religion of the Ancestors differs significantly from the structured religious organization later required for an entire people and society, the goal of which is holiness.

For further reading see bibliography numbers: 6, 490, 541, 558b, 561, 639, 649a, 763

# THE LIFE OF

# ABRAHAM

*Abraham marks the beginning of the particular story of Israel. He is the Ancestor of Israel, and his story in many ways anticipates that of the nation. His response to God is referred to as a model of how human life should be lived.*

THE story of Abram (Abraham), the father of the Jewish people, begins with God's command to him, "Go from your country": he is to leave the safety of his family home in Ur and go to a new land. He leaves with his wife, Sarai, and his nephew, Lot. His first act on arrival in Canaan is to set up an altar and to worship God. He is pitched into many adventures, losing his wife to the Egyptian Pharaoh for a while and parting from Lot after their herdsmen quarrel – only to rescue Lot in a dramatic encounter with local rulers. God then makes a covenant with Abram, promising him descendants as numerous as the stars in the sky, even though Sarai has not borne children. It is she who encourages Abram to start a family with a servant, Hagar, but this leads to conflict. God therefore confirms his covenant with Abram, changing his name to Abraham and introducing the sign of circumcision. Sarai's name is also changed, to Sarah. Three strangers visit Abraham in Mamre; he entertains them hospitably, and they confirm the promise of a son to Sarah,

*ABRAM LEAVES HIS HOME:*
*GEN. 12:1*

*ABRAM SETS UP AN ALTAR:*
*GEN. 12:7*

*ABRAM AND LOT GO SEPARATE WAYS:*
*GEN. 13:11*

*THE COVENANT:*
*GEN. 15*

*ABRAM TAKES HAGAR AS HIS CONCUBINE:*
*GEN. 16:3*

*GOD CHANGES ABRAM'S NAME TO ABRAHAM:*
*GEN. 17:5*

**Abraham prepares for God's test.**

despite the fact that she and Abraham are now advanced in years. The strangers continue on their journey to Sodom. The sin of Sodom is so great that God determines to destroy it. Informed by God, Abraham challenges God's justice – can the judge of the world destroy the innocent with the guilty? But in contrast to Abraham's hospitality, which is repeated by Lot, the people of Sodom attempt to abuse the strangers who are visiting, confirming that the city must be destroyed. Lot and his family are warned to escape and not to glance back at the scene of destruction behind them – a command disobeyed by Lot's wife, who is turned into a pillar of salt. Isaac is born to Sarah and Abraham, and the great test, the binding (*Aqedah*) of Isaac in readiness for sacrifice, is given to Abraham. When his faith does not falter, he is again promised descendants as numerous as the stars. Sarah dies, and the story moves on to Isaac and Jacob. When Abraham dies, he is buried with Sarah in the cave of Machpelah in Hebron, a site that can be visited to this day.

*ABRAHAM ASKS GOD NOT TO DESTROY SODOM:*
*GEN. 18:23–33*

*LOT'S WIFE IS TURNED TO A PILLAR OF SALT:*
*GEN. 19:26*

*ABRAHAM'S TEST:*
*GEN. 22:2*

# THE SACRIFICE OF ISAAC

The account in Genesis 22 of Abraham's near-sacrifice of Isaac – known in Jewish tradition as the *Aqedah*, the "binding" of Isaac – is one of the most memorable and influential stories in the Bible. Traditionally, Jews, Christians, and Muslims have regarded it as a supreme example of the need to place faithfulness to God above all else. The call of the one true God makes all other loyalties relative. In modern times, however, the story has often been considered a problem on the grounds that to kill a child is always wrong; therefore, the story is not admirable but horrible, showing cruelty on God's part.

In its biblical context, the story is clearly intended as an example. God's action is depicted as a "test" (v.1). Testing is a prime category in the Hebrew Bible, whereby God seeks to draw Israel into fuller obedience (*see also* Exod. 20:20). The purpose of the test is to confirm that Abraham is one who fears God (v.12): the "fear of God" summarizes the appropriate human attitude to God. Despite modern anxieties that the story might be used to sponsor immoral action by ascribing it to God, Jews and Christians have never interpreted the story in this way. Isaac is readily seen as a metaphor or symbol, representing not only whoever or whatever is dearest to a person but also that which must be relinquished to God if God requires it.

**The Sacrifice**
*This sixth-century floor mosaic depicts Abraham preparing to sacrifice his son, Isaac.*

## GOD'S COVENANT WITH ABRAHAM

Although the stories about Abraham are diverse, presumably coming from different sources, they have been worked together into a dramatic narrative. They display human problems that are familiar to many people – childlessness, family disputes, jealousy, cruelty, cowardice, and deception. But they combine them with a portrayal of a better way – obedience to God, generosity, courage, faith, and sacrifice.

The story of Abraham is framed by two divine commands (in identical Hebrew idiom): "Go" (Gen. 12:1; 22:2). On the first occasion, Abram (as he is called until his name is changed) has to forsake his family and country (his past), while on the second occasion, he has to relinquish his long-awaited and beloved son (his future). The trusting obedience shown on these two occasions has been central to the significance that Abraham has had for his descendants, whatever his actions at other times.

The main narrative thread is provided by a divine promise and Abram's responses. God promises to make of Abram a great nation, even though his wife, Sarai (later Sarah), is childless. This promise could be fulfilled through Sarai or through Abram's nephew, Lot. However, Abram lets Sarai be taken into the Pharaoh's harem (Gen. 12:10–20), and Lot leaves Abram and settles in Sodom (Gen. 13:5–12). The promise could also be fulfilled through a slave born in Abram's house or through Hagar, the servant whom Abram takes as his concubine. Their son Ishmael, though the father of many, will be "a wild ass of a man" in perpetual conflict (*see* Gen. 16, esp. 16:10–12). The promise seems impossible, but by the gift of God, it will be fulfilled through Isaac, the son of Abraham and Sarah in their old age. Yet Abraham again appears to jeopardize the possibility of their having a son by allowing Sarah to be taken into another man's harem (Gen. 20). Even when Isaac is born to Abraham and Sarah, the story is not finished. There is conflict with Ishmael; then God tells Abraham to offer up Isaac as a sacrifice. Only after Abraham has been willing to do this does the focus move to a wife for Isaac and the future of the family.

## JEWS, CHRISTIANS, AND MUSLIMS

A common reverence for Abraham as a model of true human response to God and as ancestor of subsequent believers is one of the prime links between Jews, Christians, and Muslims.

Abraham's responsiveness to God is summed up in his epithet as "the friend of God." This title is first given in Hebrew scripture (Isa. 41:8; 2 Chr. 20:7); it is taken up in the New Testament (Jas. 2:23); and in Islam, Abraham (*Ibrahim*) is known simply as "the friend" (*Al Khalil*).

Each religion gives content to Abraham's friendship with God in terms of its own characteristic emphases, on the supposition that Abraham is best understood in terms of that to which he helped give rise. Thus for Jews (appealing to Gen. 26:5 as well as to more general considerations), Abraham is an example of one who was obedient to God's commandments, or Torah, even before Torah was given to Israel at Sinai. For Christians, following Paul's exposition (Rom. 4), Abraham is a model of one who has faith (*pistis*) in God. For Muslims, Abraham demonstrates *islam*, unconditional submission to the will of God, as in his willingness to sacrifice his son. Though Jews, Christians, and Muslims differ about the true human response to God as exemplified by Abraham, they agree that he provides a model of how human life should be lived.

For further reading see bibliography numbers: 427, 541, 558b, 559, 763

## THE LIVES OF

# ISAAC AND JACOB

*The stories of Isaac and his sons, Jacob and Esau, are told in Genesis 24–36.*
*While all three are important representatives of Israel, the Bible nevertheless*
*portrays them as human characters with very real faults and virtues.*

THE story of Isaac's search for a wife is told in great detail. As his father, Abraham, grew old, he was anxious that his son should take a wife from his own people and not from the Canaanites among whom they lived. Concerned not to let Isaac return to his homeland – thus breaking the agreement with God – Abraham sent out his servant in search of a wife for his son. The servant traveled to the city of Nahor and waited by the city well for the women to come and draw water. He prayed to God, asking that the girl who offered to water his camels should be Isaac's wife. Rebekah appeared and, drawing water from the well, offered him some for his animals. When she revealed her parentage to the servant, he negotiated with her family for her hand. Rebekah consented to return with him and later married Isaac.

The first children born to Isaac and Rebekah were the twins Esau and Jacob. The primary theme of the story of Jacob is his rivalry with Esau – a rivalry that began in their mother's womb and in Esau selling his birthright (Gen. 25:29–34). As time went on, Isaac grew old and his eyesight failed.

SERVANT TRAVELS TO NAHOR: GEN. 24:10

SERVANT PRAYS TO GOD: GEN. 24:14

REBEKAH REVEALS PARENTAGE: GEN. 24:47

ISAAC AND REBEKAH MARRY: GEN. 24:67

TWINS BORN: GEN. 25:24–26

William Blake's depiction of Jacob's ladder.

His favorite was his elder son, Esau, and he asked Esau to bring him some food. But the conversation was overheard by Rebekah. Taking the part of Jacob, her younger son, she made a dish, which she then made him take to his father. By covering Jacob's smooth flesh with hairy animal skins, Rebekah fooled Isaac into thinking that it was his more hairy-skinned son Esau who gave him the food. As a result, Jacob, rather than Esau, received his father's blessing. Thus by a trick, Jacob pretended to be Esau and received the blessing intended for his brother. The blessing was more than it appeared, effectively a promise of material success that should go to the first-born. The cheated brother Esau received another blessing, but he responded to Jacob's deceitfulness with heartrending anguish. This later turned to murderous resentment toward his brother, and Jacob fled, fearing for his life. Before he left, Isaac blessed him with the words used by Abraham. This time Isaac knew which son he was blessing. Rebekah advised Jacob to flee to her brother, Laban, who lived in Haran. Such refuges for those who had committed crimes were common in ancient times.

ISAAC ASKS ESAU TO BRING FOOD: GEN. 27:4

JACOB DECEIVES ISAAC: GEN. 27:19

ISAAC'S BLESSING: GEN. 27:4

JACOB FLEES: GEN. 27:41–45

## JACOB'S LADDER

On his way to his uncle, Jacob dreamed of a ladder between earth and sky, with angels passing up and down. He received a blessing from God, who promised Jacob and his descendants land and support: *"Know that I am with you and will keep you wherever you go, and will bring you back to this land; for I will not leave you."* Jacob set up an altar at the place and called it Bethel. Jacob then traveled on to the land of his uncle Laban for whom he worked. He married Leah and Rachel, who bore his children, the ancestors of the tribes of Israel. Years later, Jacob returned home to restore his relationship with Esau. On the way, he wrestled with a mysterious figure. He would not let the figure go, and asked for a blessing. God was acting through this encounter, and Jacob's name was changed to Israel: one who struggles with, or for, God. The promises granted to Abraham and Isaac were reconfirmed.

Isaac's blessing.

## RECONCILIATION

When told that Esau was coming toward him with enough men for a small army, Jacob interpreted this as a threat and, in his terror, prayed to God for help. But despite Jacob's fears, when Jacob and Esau met, Esau took no vengeance but welcomed his brother warmly, and the brothers were reconciled. Jacob offered him the vast numbers of flocks and herds that he had sent ahead, which Esau finally accepted. Jacob referred to these several times as "my gifts," but later as "my blessing," thus showing that, in the end, he restored the blessing of material property that he had stolen from his brother. Altars were built wherever the two brothers went. Isaac and Rebekah died, and the story moves on to the episodes with Joseph (*see pp.44–45*) before Jacob gave a final blessing to his sons, the Twelve Tribes of Israel.

JACOB MARRIES: GEN. 29:23–30

JACOB WRESTLES WITH ANGEL: GEN. 32:24

JACOB AND ESAU MEET: GEN. 33

JACOB'S GIFTS: GEN. 33:10

ISAAC DIES: GEN. 35:29

## THE IMPORTANCE OF ISAAC AND JACOB

Isaac is the most passive of the Patriarchs. In Genesis 22 he is silently bound by Abraham (though much subsequent Jewish tradition ascribes to him a more active participation). Isaac plays no active role while Abraham's servant acquires a wife for him. A blind and bedridden Isaac is deceived by his wife and younger son. Only in Genesis 26 does Isaac act in his own right – and here, all the stories are reminiscent of earlier episodes in Abraham's story. Perhaps one implication of Isaac's story is that God's purposes do not necessarily need strong, active, and distinctive people for their continuation and fulfillment.

Jacob is different. His name becomes that of the nation Israel, and his 12 sons become the ancestors of the Twelve Tribes of Israel. In telling of its eponymous ancestor, one might expect the Israelites to tell of a courageous, faithful, God-fearing hero. But Jacob's faults are shown along with his virtues. In his youth, he connives in deception and is a liar as well. When, later in life, he is transformed by a mysterious encounter with God and his name is correspondingly changed, he is still no model. He is a poor parent, showing favoritism among his children and provoking deadly sibling rivalry. The Bible's portrayal of this man as Israel's ancestor is remarkable. It is a reminder that God can use even the weak to do good things. It is a story acting as a reminder that there are many baffling paradoxes in the encounter between God and humanity.

In these narratives, it is made clear from the outset that Jacob and Esau represent the two peoples of Israel and Edom (Gen. 25:23, 30; 27:29a; *see also pp.100–1*). However much the stories embody the historic rivalries of these two peoples, the chief figures are important in their own right. Their difference is most obvious when Esau forgives Jacob, for in Israel's history – and especially in Obadiah (*pp.228–29*) – Edom is particularly remembered for its ruthless exploitation of Jerusalem when the latter was overthrown by the Babylonians.

## FAMILY TREE

*The chart shows the first three generations of the Ancestors of Israel. The 12 sons of Jacob then form the Twelve Tribes of the nation.*

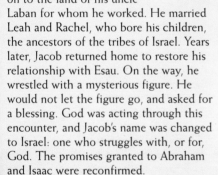

SARAH ⫟ ABRAHAM + HAGAR

LABAN    REBEKAH ⫟ ISAAC    ISHMAEL

LEAH    RACHEL    JACOB    ESAU

**For further reading see bibliography numbers:** 427, 687a

# ANGELS
## IN THE BIBLE

*Angels are heavenly beings who carry God's messages between heaven and earth.
They are agents and assistants of God and appear throughout the Bible,
especially at the strategic moments in the history of God's people.*

THE most common words in the Bible to denote an angel are the Hebrew *mal'akh* and Greek *angelos*. Both terms are used to describe messengers, whether human or from the realm of God. In the latter case, angels are not only the messengers of God but also the agents of, and assistants to, God, although they are always regarded as far inferior to God. As God's messengers, angels appear to the Patriarchs, they commission and announce leaders, and they deliver God's word to the people. As agents of God, angels deliver judgments, punishments, and guidance, and they help to bring about important victories. Their presence often evokes reverence and worship of God.

## THE ANGEL OF THE LORD

This particular angel is portrayed as one whose coming seems to mediate the very presence of God, and at times it is hard to tell whether it is God or a separate figure who is being spoken of. It is likely that stories concerning the Angel of the LORD were originally told about the presence of God, but that the sense of God's holiness and transcendence led to these stories being transferred to a separate figure. When the Angel of the LORD spoke to Hagar in the wilderness, she *"named the LORD who spoke to her, 'You are El-roi'"* (Gen. 16:13; cf. Exod. 3:2–4; Judg. 6:11–23).

**THE ARCHANGEL MICHAEL**
*This image of the archangel Michael shows him with his emblem, the sword. Jewish and Christian sources identify seven archangels, and these are believed to be the angels who stand before God in Revelation.*

## ANGELS AS HEAVENLY BEINGS

Other terms used to describe angels and to denote their heavenly character include "sons of God" and "holy ones." "Seraphs" and "cherubs" are supernatural beings but not angels. Angels are mentioned among the divine council of God as members of a heavenly chorus: *"when the morning stars sang together and all the heavenly beings shouted for joy"* (Job 38:7); they are also associated with descriptions of God's chariot or throne. The Bible does not make explicit reference to each of these beings as "angels," and while depictions of Heaven are usually found in poetic or apocalyptic passages, the reality of Heaven and of spiritual beings is not in doubt. Angels are powerful heavenly beings, whose agency is not only an assurance of God's activity in the world but also a guarantee of the eventual vindication of the faithful people.

**THE THREE ARCHANGELS AND TOBIAS**
*This 15th-century painting by Francesco Botticini depicts Tobias and Raphael's journey to Media, as described in Tobit 5–6. The artist has added the archangels Michael (in armor) and Gabriel (with Mary's emblem, the lily) to the scene, even though they are not mentioned in the story.*

## MESSENGERS OF GOD

In the early parts of the Hebrew Bible, God was often described as appearing on earth: *"God [was] walking in the garden at the time of the evening breeze"* (Gen. 3:8). Later, the impossibility of God, the Creator of all things, appearing in Creation led people to wonder how God could communicate with those on earth. Prayer and sacrifice, and priests and prophets, have major parts to play in this, but increasingly so does the belief that God sends messengers to earth. Jacob's vision of *"a ladder set up on the earth, the top of it reaching to heaven; … the angels of God were ascending and*

## AGENTS OF GOD

*Angels are often regarded as a graphic way of asserting that God is not far distant, and cares greatly for the smallest details of life. This detail is taken from a 15th-century Italian manuscript entitled "Life of Monks."*

## JACOB'S LADDER

*This detail from a 16th-century stained-glass window depicts Jacob resting at Bethel on his journey to Haran. He dreamed of a heavenly ladder on which angels ascended and descended.*

## ANGEL TRAVELER

*Depictions of angels have changed dramatically with time. This elaborate portrait was painted by the French artist Gustave Moreau (1826–98).*

*descending on it"* (Gen. 28:12) is both immediate and graphic. Angels in the earlier parts of the Bible have human form and are, at times, referred to as "men" (Gen. 18:2; Josh. 5:13). Only much later do they get the wings of seraphs: *"Seraphs were in attendance above him; each had six wings: with two they covered their faces, and with two they covered their feet, and with two they flew"* (Isa. 6:2). The idea of good and bad angels in conflict may have been introduced at the time of the Babylonian Exile.

## THE NATURE OF ANGELS

Biblical data on the form and nature of angels is scarce. It seems clear, in general, that angels are created, spiritual beings, who may or may not have physical form. Their appearance is rarely described and is best understood as being able to adapt to the task at hand. While some are human in appearance, others are more fantastic to behold. Few clues are given as to the name, rank, or individuality of these creatures. Not until Daniel, late in the biblical period, are two angels, Michael and Gabriel, named. Raphael and Uriel are also named in the books of the Apocrypha. The later view that angels do not marry

(Mark 12:25) implies that they do not share the male and female nature of humanity; much earlier, however, they are described as sexual beings (Gen. 6:4; Zech. 5:9). While angels do not act of their own accord, they are capable of waywardness and rebellion (Gen. 6:1–4). The existence of "fallen" angels also suggests a capacity for moral judgment (in both 1 Corinthians 6:3 and Jude 1:6, angels are in need of supervision).

## THE PORTRAYAL OF ANGELS

Both Jewish and Christian literature elaborated greatly on the names and nature of angels. Vivid apocalypses fed a heightened interest in the participation of heavenly realities in earthly events. More detail on the names, nature, and organization of angels is given in these literary texts than in the Bible. The New Testament continues the biblical tradition. Heavenly messengers are in evidence at the key stages of the birth and Resurrection of Christ, and are also associated with Heaven and the return of Christ. Their appearance is described as white or shining, consistent with later Jewish depictions of angels in terms of fire, shining metals, and precious stones. Angels remain an important part of both Jewish and Christian belief. As with all biblical language, it is important not to confuse the words that are used to describe angels with the truths that angels themselves represent. The real purpose of God is brought to bear in ways that are more easily represented in pictorial form. Both Jewish and Christian traditions elaborated those pictures in great detail in postbiblical times.

For further reading see bibliography numbers: 47, 330, 597, 649a, 669, 778

# THE LIFE OF

# JOSEPH

*The story of the Ancestor Joseph, as told in Genesis 37 and 39–50, is a self-contained narrative structured around symbolic dreams. It provides a transition from the period of the Ancestors to the Exodus, but its style sets it apart from both.*

JOSEPH, whose name means "may God give increase," is the son of Jacob and Rachel. He becomes his father's favorite and is given a splendid "coat of many colors" (some modern versions translate this as "long-sleeved coat").

*JOSEPH'S COAT: GEN. 37:3*

This arouses the resentment of his brothers, and the situation is exacerbated when he relates his two dreams that foretell his own power over the rest of the family. His

*JOSEPH'S DREAMS: GEN. 37:5–9*

angry brothers abduct him and sell him to foreign merchants and into slavery, telling Jacob, their father, that Joseph has been killed by an animal. They produce Joseph's blood-stained "coat of

*JOSEPH SOLD INTO SLAVERY: GEN. 37:28*

Joseph being thrown into the well.

many colors" as proof. Taken to Egypt, Joseph rises to a senior position in the household of Potiphar, head of the royal guard. Joseph rebuffs the advances of Potiphar's wife, who retaliates by falsely accusing him of rape. Thrown into prison, Joseph encounters the king's butler and baker and interprets a dream for each of them. Events unfold as Joseph has predicted: the baker is executed, but the butler is released. Two years later, the Pharaoh has a dream in which seven fat cows come out of the Nile followed by seven thin cows, which then eat the seven fat cows. A second dream

*JOSEPH FALSELY ACCUSED: GEN. 39:17*

*JOSEPH INTERPRETS PRISONERS' DREAMS: GEN. 40:9–15*

follows in which seven plump ears of corn are swallowed up by seven thin ears of corn. When all attempts to interpret the Pharaoh's dreams fail, the butler remembers Joseph. The Pharaoh sends for Joseph, who announces that the dreams predict seven prosperous years, followed by seven years of famine. Joseph is put in charge of preparations and raised to a position of influence. When ten of his 11 brothers come to Egypt in search of food, they do not recognize him. Joseph gives them food and tells them to return later for more. He demands

*PHARAOH'S DREAMS: GEN. 41:1–7*

*JOSEPH INTERPRETS PHARAOH'S DREAMS: GEN. 41:25–36*

*THE FAMINE SPREADS: GEN. 41:54*

*JOSEPH PUTS HIS BROTHERS TO THE TEST: GEN. 42:25*

that one of them remain as a hostage and that they bring the youngest brother, Benjamin, with them on their return. When Benjamin returns with his brothers, Joseph plants a silver cup in his sack. After the brothers have left, Joseph orders that they be followed and Benjamin is accused of the theft of the cup. The brothers return to Egypt and beg for Benjamin to be spared, at which point Joseph reveals his true identity to his brothers, and announces that his own story has been part of a divine plan to save the family. The father, Jacob, settles in Egypt with his household. After his death, his body is returned to Canaan.

*BROTHERS RETURN TO EGYPT: GEN. 43:15*

*JOSEPH REVEALS HIMSELF TO HIS BROTHERS: GEN. 45:3*

## AN INDEPENDENT STORY

There are some inconsistencies in the later chapters of Genesis that point to more than one source for the biblical account of Joseph: in Genesis 37:25–28, for instance, the Ishmaelite merchants suddenly become Midianites, and in Genesis 37:26 the "good" brother who seems to save Joseph's life is Judah, while in Genesis 37:22, 29, it is Reuben. Against this, though, there is a strong structural unity in the narrative, based on the dreams, which both predict and provoke developments in the plot. The story of Joseph was probably created independently in more or less its present form, and then was subjected to further minor editing. When it was linked to the other material in Genesis, some sections were added – most notably, the tale in Genesis 38 and the poem in Genesis 49. The narrative of Joseph is different from other stories in the Patriarchal tradition, not least because its portrayal of divine action is more subtle and indirect than that in the surrounding stories of Genesis. The picture of God is different from that revealed in the Abraham stories. This distinctiveness is underlined by the confusion in the historical traditions about the tribe of Joseph. The tribe is sometimes mentioned as a distinct entity (e.g., Josh. 18:11), in keeping with the idea that the tribes are named after the sons of Jacob, but it is also often replaced by the tribes of Ephraim and Manasseh, which were named after two of Joseph's sons. The Joseph narrative is then commonly considered to be a separate composition and set apart from the main Patriarchal tradition, which surrounds it in the book of Genesis.

## THE DATE OF THE STORY

The date of the story's composition is unknown. Although it does reflect some general knowledge of Egypt, this is too vague to tie the story to a particular period. At best, we can say that it is earlier than the books of Daniel and Esther, which it has influenced, and that, if it is later than the Exodus account, it must have replaced some other explanation of the Israelites' presence in Egypt – perhaps an earlier version of the story. Some attempts have been made to view it as a "wisdom story," illustrating the kinds of themes found in Proverbs, but these are difficult to sustain; it is probably designed to be morally elevating entertainment. Egyptian sources neither confirm nor deny the story's historical details, but some elements of the story, especially the tale of Potiphar's wife, are common folk-tale motifs.

# OTHER JOSEPH STORIES

*Joseph became the hero of several much later works. The first of these belong in the early Jewish tradition. However, Joseph also appears in Islamic works, and the Qu'ran includes an entire chapter dedicated to his story.*

The figure of Joseph appears in many works, used for both religious and secular purposes, and the character seems to have been well known outside its biblical context. The most notable of the early Jewish works is the romance *Joseph and Aseneth*, which was probably composed in the first century BCE or CE. After rejecting many suitors, the Egyptian king's daughter is overcome by Joseph's beauty, falls desperately in love with him, and then converts to Judaism so that the two can marry; the couple later survives a plot against them by a group composed of some of Joseph's brothers and brothers-in-law. The apocalyptic *Prayer of Joseph* is probably of about a similar date, and we also have the *Testament of Joseph* and the *History of Joseph* (which is very fragmentary). These early Jewish works show a general trend to emphasize Joseph's piety and perfection. In later tradition, Joseph is regarded as the model of a righteous man (*tzaddik*), who was protected from harm by the Divine Spirit and whose descendants, the tribe of Joseph, are protected against the evil eye. In the New Testament, Hebrews 11:22 lists Joseph as a hero of faith, and his career is summarized by Stephen in Acts 7:13–17.

### Joseph in modern works

The supreme achievement in building on the story of Joseph was that of Thomas Mann, perhaps from a remark in Goethe's autobiography that the story of Joseph is "fascinating, but thin." Mann "filled out" the story in four volumes of more than 2,000 pages. They were published from 1933 to 1944 as *Joseph and His Brothers*, *Young Joseph*, *Joseph in Egypt*, and *Joseph the Provider*. Mann's own experience as an exile from Germany in the United States is evident in the later volumes (Joseph's agrarian reforms, his rationing and taxation, and his regulation of business reflect Roosevelt's New Deal in 1930s America), but overall the journey from Canaan into Egypt is the movement of humanity from the primitive and community-bound to the cultured and individual. Others before Mann had retold the story on the stage. From the 17th century come Robert Aylet's *Pharaoh's Favorite* (1623) and Francis Hubert's *Egypt's Favorite* (1631), in which Potiphar, with his capricious judgments, is called "rashly heady" and is likened to a field of grain that bends whichever way the wind blows. Perhaps the most famous stage interpretation of the story, however, is Tim Rice and Andrew Lloyd Webber's modern rock musical, *Joseph and the Amazing Technicolor Dreamcoat*.

**Interpreting Pharaoh's dreams**
*This 18th-century Islamic watercolor comes from a Persian manuscript.*

**For further reading see bibliography numbers:** 11, 303, 422, 427, 516, 637, 687a

EVERYDAY LIFE IN
# EGYPT

*Ancestors of Israel settled in Egypt, and some were conscripted for hard labor. The memory of this time produced the stories of Joseph (pp.44–45) and of the dramatic escape in Exodus (pp.48–49).*

FROM its origins as a separate state in about 3100BCE, through to Roman times, Egypt remained one of the most important and distinctive ancient cultures. It is frequently mentioned in the Bible, not least because it often sought to extend its empire northward and threatened Israel and Judah. Our knowledge of Egyptian life is derived mainly from records and monuments left by the small ruling class, so much detail about everyday existence remains obscure or poorly understood. Most people lived in small mud-brick houses, and all record of them has been washed away.

## THE RIVER ECONOMY

Egyptian agriculture was not directly dependent on rainfall, but on the annual flooding of the Nile, fed by the summer rains in Ethiopia. Between May and September, the river usually rose about 20 feet (8 meters), covering the surrounding fields with a layer of fertile silt and enabling the cultivation of crops between November and June. The delta area provided pasture for sheep and cattle, as well as land suitable for viticulture.

### PAPYRUS GRASS

*Papyrus reeds grew in the marshy ground of the Nile delta (see map, above), providing thick fibers for rope and a soft pulp from which writing sheets were made.*

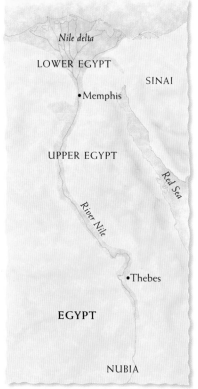

*Nile delta*

LOWER EGYPT

SINAI

•Memphis

UPPER EGYPT

Red Sea

River Nile

•Thebes

EGYPT

NUBIA

### THE FLOODED NILE
*Where the Nile flooded, it made the land fertile, shown above in green. A water supply independent of weather supported farming when other lands suffered drought, and hungry refugees often sought food in Egypt.*

### FISHING ON THE NILE
*The Nile provided fish, as well as an easy method of travel. The first boats were made of papyrus stalks bound together with twine; they were later replaced by wooden vessels.*

### BURIAL GOODS
*Egyptian tombs often held model boats for the owner's use in the afterlife. At the right, a figure holds a plumb line to measure the depth of the water.*

## WORK AND HOUSEHOLD

Egyptian women enjoyed a degree of independence and legal equality with men that was unusual in the ancient world, and some played an important role in society and its religious institutions; most, though, were probably occupied in household tasks and child rearing. Men were liable to conscription for military service or building projects, especially during the period when the fields were flooded and farming was impossible, while poorer Egyptians were under an obligation to the estate on which they worked. Slaves were relatively

**HARVESTING THE GRAIN**
*Grain was harvested with a sickle and, when gathered together, it was thrown into the air with wooden fans (see left). The chaff would be carried off by the breeze, and the grain would fall to the floor.*

uncommon, even in rich households, although many servants were often employed. Pets, especially monkeys and dogs, were kept by many homes in ancient Egypt; dogs also had a practical role to play in the suppression of vermin and in hunting, which was a favorite pastime of the Egyptian upper classes.

## LUXURY GOODS

Wealthy Egyptians used a variety of luxury goods. For formal meals and special occasions, they wore jewelry and wigs made of human hair, perhaps topped by a cone of perfumed fat that slowly melted and released scent (*see right, above*). Cosmetics, including eye-paint, were used by both sexes; many cosmetic jars have been found. Such luxuries reflect not only Egypt's thriving trade, but also the activities of many specialists in its society.

**GRAPE PICKING**
*Produced in the western delta, wine was a luxury product.*

## ISRAEL IN EGYPT

Chapter 46 of the book of Genesis reports that the family of Jacob came to settle in Goshen, probably in the eastern delta, where they worked as herdsmen; this is an area in which other foreigners seem to have settled. How much they took part in normal Egyptian life is unclear, but Exodus 1 suggests that they were conscripted for construction projects at "Raamses" (probably Per Ramses, modern Qantir) and "Pithom" (the location of which is uncertain); native Egyptians were probably themselves liable to such conscription.

**Women wearing perfumed wigs.**

# RAMESSES II

*This Nineteenth-Dynasty Pharaoh ruled Egypt from 1279 until 1213 or 1212BCE. He may have been the Pharaoh of the Exodus. His name is also spelled Ramses and Rameses.*

There is no Egyptian record of the Exodus. The Egyptian army could not have been annihilated without there being a record, but conflicts with nomadic and other foreign groups were common. As a result, the departure of the group that became Israel might have attracted little attention.

The Bible does not mention Ramesses by name, but there is some archaeological evidence to fill out the story of his reign. He came to power at a time when Egypt was a prosperous empire with control over Palestine and southern Syria. Ramesses' establishment of a residence in the eastern delta reflects the shift of Egyptian interest toward that region. This empire, though, brought the Egyptians into conflict with the Hittites, whose own influence stretched far beyond their native Anatolia into northern Syria. Despite extensive preparations for war, Ramesses only narrowly escaped absolute defeat, when his army was surprised and routed at Qadesh, but the battle was followed by stalemate and eventually by a formal treaty.

The remainder of Ramesses' long reign was peaceful. He undertook a vast number of building projects, leaving more buildings than any other Pharaoh. He also fathered over 80 children, which may have contributed to later problems over the Egyptian succession. After Ramesses' reign, Egypt suffered a number of serious setbacks: his son Merneptah claims to have campaigned against various peoples in Palestine, including Israel.

**Ramesses II.**

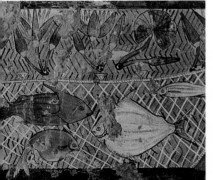

**For further reading see bibliography numbers:** 37, 170, 171, 277, 565, 569, 573, 633, 634, 719, 803

# THE BOOK OF
# EXODUS

*The second book of the Bible records the power of God in choosing Moses to lead the people of Israel out of Egypt and into the Promised Land. In the wilderness, God establishes a covenant with the people at Sinai.*

THE book of Exodus marks the transition from the individual narratives about the Ancestors to the beginnings of the "children of Israel" as a coalition of tribes and ultimately a people in their own land. At the beginning of the book, the Israelites are enslaved in Egypt and demoralized. Under God's guidance, Moses, who had grown up in the palace of the Pharaoh, had given to him the leadership qualities to rescue them. On escaping from Egypt, the new covenant made with God at Mount Sinai became the constitution for the nation, defining their responsibilities toward one another and toward God. The book dramatically contrasts the heights of religious awareness, marked by the theophany of God at Sinai, with the depths reached by the worship of the Golden Calf. The need to create a tangible focus for communicating with God is met by the establishment of the Tabernacle with its accompanying rituals.

**JOURNEY OF THE EXODUS**
*One of the central events of the Exodus narrative is the crossing of the Red/Reed Sea, shown here in a painting by the modern artist Tamas Galambos.*

## THE LAWS OF THE COVENANT

The Covenant becomes extremely important in Exodus. There are memories of earlier covenants with the Ancestors in Genesis, but now in Exodus 19–24 the story is told of a covenant made on Mount Sinai that becomes the foundation of the people, Israel. While attention is understandably focused on the Ten Commandments (20:1–21; *see pp. 56–57*), the subsequent chapters are a practical application of the principles in the Commandments. This section has sometimes been regarded as a separate unit, later incorporated in the book of Exodus. It has been called the Book, or the Code, of the Covenant. The laws begin by

setting limits on slavery within Israelite society, in deliberate contrast to Egypt. At the heart lies the command, *"You shall not wrong or oppress a resident alien, for you were aliens in the land of Egypt"* (22:21). The subsequent laws explore the limits of freedom, by examining situations in which the Israelite or his possessions impinge on the freedom of another by causing damage to others or their possessions. Some laws apply to those who come under God's special protection, where God's honor may also be damaged. These "negative" situations point the way to a society where mutual respect and support are the norm.

## THE DIVINE QUALITIES

After the episode with the Golden Calf, when Moses tries to reconcile God to the children of Israel, God describes a series of divine qualities of patience, love, and mercy (34:6–7) that are repeated with variations throughout the Hebrew Bible. They are also central to the liturgy of the Jewish Day of Atonement, when Israel depends on God's mercy for forgiveness. The concluding part, that God visits the sins of the parents on the children down to the third and fourth generation, is often misunderstood as a punishment passing through time. But in the Hebrew Bible, an individual might expect to be alive at the birth of his great-grandchildren, the fourth generation. So the warning means that all those of his family who are currently alive may suffer for his wrongdoing.

Few biblical themes have had such an impact as that of the Exodus from Egypt. It has become the model for innumerable struggles against tyranny throughout history. It was evoked in the American Revolution, and in recent times "Let my people go!" became the slogan for helping Jews leave the Soviet Union. The Exodus became a central concept in South American liberation theology. The *Haggadah*, the order of service for the Jewish domestic service of the Passover, explores the themes of both physical and spiritual slavery.

## THEMES IN THE BOOK OF EXODUS

Those who discern different sources underlying the final composition of Exodus see different strands of emphasis in the book (*see pp.22–23*). In one (attributed by some to J), the covenant history is continued from Genesis, with people showing need of God's help but often acting against God. The Golden Calf (ch.32) exemplifies the way in which a whole generation can reject God, but God does not abandon them. In another strand of emphasis in the book (attributed to P; *see pp.22–23*), the focus is on the Sinai Covenant and the instructions for the proper performance of worship. The Exodus points to the Temple as the completion of what God has begun on Sinai. Thus the genealogy of Moses and Aaron (6:20) is extended a further generation to Phinehas (6:25), to whom God eventually gives "the covenant of perpetual priesthood" (Num. 25:6–13). These themes, however, have been combined in the book of Exodus in a dramatic vision of overwhelming power. The escape from Egypt, God's defeat of armies and magicians and all obstacles, the Passover enacting the drama into every subsequent Jewish life, and the providence of God making God's name and purpose known, make the book an outstanding witness to God's encouragement of faith and trust.

## THE TEN PLAGUES

The ten plagues described in the book of Exodus (7:14–12:32) have two purposes: to enable the Israelites to go free and to teach the Egyptians the power of God. They are referred to elsewhere in the Bible as the summary of God's authority over creation and over humans, including the strongest nations (*see* Pss. 78:43–51; 105:28–36). In Exodus they are organized in three sets of three plagues, in each of which they grow in severity through the set, and each set is more severe than the previous one. The first two in each set come with a prior warning, the third without.

| PRELUDE | FIRST SET | SECOND SET | THIRD SET |
|---|---|---|---|
| Warning | 1 Blood | 4 Swarm of Flies | 7 Hail |
| Warning | 2 Frogs | 5 Pestilence | 8 Locusts |
| No Warning | 3 Gnats | 6 Boils | 9 Darkness |

The tenth plague is the death of the firstborn.

## THE BOOK

TITLE: Exodus ("Departure [from Egypt]") – the word is derived from the Greek title in the Septuagint

HEBREW TITLE: [*v'aleh*] *shemot* "[and these are] the names," the opening words of the book

DATE and AUTHORSHIP: For the Composition of the Pentateuch, *see pp.22–23*

## THE CONTENTS

1 Egyptian oppression

2–4 Moses' birth, exile, call, and return

5–12:32 The struggle with Pharaoh and the ten plagues

12:33–15:21 The Exodus and the crossing of the Red/Reed Sea

15:22–17:7 The need for water and food

17:8–16 The battle with the Amalekites

18 The visit of Jethro, Moses' father-in-law

19 The theophany at Sinai

20 The Ten Commandments

21–23 The laws of the Covenant

24 The sealing of the Covenant

25–31 Instructions for building the Tabernacle and its service

32 The Golden Calf

33 Moses' struggle to retain God's presence

34 The divine qualities are revealed and the Covenant is renewed

35–40 The Tabernacle is built

## KEY THEMES

*The Exodus from Egypt*

•

*Sinai and the Covenant*

•

*Moses as a sign of God's authority*

**For further reading see bibliography numbers:** 113a, 150, 168, 174, 220, 248, 456, 588, 599, 685, 686, 687, 765, 775

# THE STORY OF
# MOSES

*Moses lies at the foundation of the faith and life of Israel. The story of his life and works, and of all that God did through him, are told in the books of Exodus, Leviticus, Numbers, and Deuteronomy.*

*ISRAELITE CHILDREN TO BE KILLED: EXOD. 1:16*

*THE PHARAOH'S DAUGHTER: EXOD. 2:5*

THE story of Moses begins in Egypt. He was born there at a time when the Pharaoh had ordered that the male children of the Israelites should be killed. His parents hid him among the bullrushes, where he was rescued by the Pharaoh's daughter. His name means "one who draws" because he was drawn out of the river (although the Egyptian *mesu* simply means "a son"). Brought up by the Pharaoh's daughter, Moses stumbled upon an Israelite being beaten by an Egyptian, whom he killed. He was then forced to flee to Midian, where he married. God appeared to Moses in a burning bush, which burned without being consumed by the fire. God told Moses that he, with his brother Aaron, must lead the people of Israel out of Egypt and into a land of milk and honey. The name of God was then revealed to Moses: *"I AM WHO I AM."* Moses appealed to the Pharaoh to "let my people go," but the Pharaoh increased the workload of the Israelites. Aaron then performed various miracles to convince the Pharaoh to free the Israelites

*NAME OF GOD REVEALED IN THE THE BURNING BUSH: EXOD. 3:13ff.*

*PLEA TO LEAVE EGYPT: EXOD. 5:1*

*AARON'S MIRACLES: EXOD. 7:8–13*

Moses receiving the tablets of the Law from God on Mount Sinai.

but was still refused. Moses and Aaron brought plagues from God to secure the escape of their people from Egypt – they were safe because God passed over the Israelites. Finally, at the tenth plague, the Israelites were allowed to leave. Passing through the Red, or Reed, Sea, Moses led the Israelites into the wilderness, where the people complained about their hardships. Moses found drinking water, quail, and manna from God and brought the people to Mount Sinai. Here, Moses received the tablets of Law from God, with the Ten Commandments written on them. But when he came down from the mountain he had to contend with the people's idolatrous worship of a Golden Calf. God also gave Moses elaborate instructions for the furnishings of the Tabernacle, where the Israelites would worship while in the desert. After more wandering, Moses brought the people to the border of the Promised Land but died before he himself could enter, and different reasons are given why this was so. The story then moves on to the entry into the Promised Land.

*PLAGUES IN EGYPT: EXOD. 7:14–12:32*

*MOSES PARTS THE RED SEA: EXOD. 14:21*

*THE TEN COMMANDMENTS: EXOD. 20:1–17*

*TABERNACLE: EXOD. 25, 26, 27*

*REASONS GIVEN: NUM. 20:10–13; 27:12–14; DEUT. 32:48–52; 1:37ff; 3:18–28*

## MOSES' RELATIONSHIP WITH GOD

God spoke to Moses *as one speaks to a friend* (Exod. 33:11). And the Bible emphasizes Moses' unique access to God: *"[Moses] is entrusted with all my house. With him I speak face to face, clearly, not in riddles; and he beholds the form of the LORD."* It was because of this that Moses could be the agent of God's deliverance of Israel from Egypt, of God's guidance of Israel in the desert, and of God's laws for Israel at Sinai and on the plains of Moab. Moses first encountered God at Sinai in the burning bush. God was going to deliver Israel from Egypt, and Moses was to be the human agent who spoke and acted on God's behalf to bring this about. Moses expressed great reluctance, and his four difficulties were all taken seriously by God; only when Moses refused to go did God get angry and conclude matters. Thereafter, although many difficulties followed, Moses consistently acted in obedience to God's wishes – with one notable, though obscure, exception (Num. 20:2–13).

*MOSES UNIQUE ACCESS TO GOD: NUM. 12:7–8; DEUT. 34:10*

*THE BURNING BUSH: EXOD. 3*

*GOD'S ANGER: EXOD. 3:11–4:17*

## AN ELUSIVE FIGURE

For the modern historian, Moses is an elusive figure. The details seem clear but present difficulties. For example, Moses is born in Egypt and has an Egyptian name (Exod. 22:1–10), but the name is based on a play on *Hebrew* words made by an *Egyptian* princess. The story of heroes abandoned as infants and rescued is a common theme in folklore (Hercules, Oedipus, Cyrus, and the Babylonian Sargon). But this must not be misunderstood. To say that a story exhibits the characteristics of folklore is only to say that a story is so important for a group of people that the group preserved it. In itself, it says nothing about the origins of the story, whether they lie in fact or fiction, both are equally capable of telling truth (for folklore, *see pp. 74–75*). Thus the Bible conveys the truth of Moses for Israel in ways that emphasize his real humanity. He is the key intermediary between God and humans, who teaches Torah and is the instrument of its revelation. The Song of Moses (Deut. 32) summarizes the vocation of Israel, as *"the LORD's own portion"* (v.9), the Rock on whom they are founded. And yet, although Moses saw more of God's self-revealed glory than anyone else in the Hebrew Bible (Exod. 33:17–24; 34:29–35), the Bible makes it clear that he is a human figure with human weaknesses. He was reluctant to be God's messenger (Exod. 3:11); he lost his temper (Num. 20:9–11; 31:14); and in the end he died and was buried (Deut. 34), unlike Enoch and Elijah who were exempted from death.

## MOSES AND THE KENITES

Some features in the account of Moses point to important historical foundations, even though the details are elusive. For example, Moses is connected through Jethro with the Kenites. Exodus 3:1–15 tells of Moses first encountering YHWH while in the service of Jethro: *"Moses was keeping the flock of his father-in-law Jethro, the priest of Midian; he led his flock beyond the wilderness, and came to Horeb"* (Exod. 3:1). Jethro is described as a Kenite (Judg. 1:16; 4:11). The Kenites are portrayed in the Bible as strong supporters of Israel and of the worship of YHWH, although they were never incorporated into the tribal system (*see e.g.*, 1 Sam. 15:6). Historically, therefore, there is support for the view that God known as YHWH was indeed brought to Israel by Moses from the Kenites (this view is known as "the Kenite hypothesis"). The historical foundations of the life of Moses are clear. Through the figure of Moses the truth is constantly reiterated that God becomes known through the lives of ordinary people – in them the stories of life become the stories of God.

For further reading see bibliography numbers: 23, 150, 192, 343, 402, 559, 599, 687, 765

# ROUTES OF THE EXODUS

*The Exodus is the dramatic story of the people of Israel's escape from slavery in Egypt. It has remained the inspiration not only of Jews but of all those seeking liberation.*

## THE "RED SEA"

Versions of the Bible that tell of the crossing of the Red Sea probably mistranslate the Hebrew *yam suf*. More accurate is "sea of reeds," and its exact location is unknown.

THE Exodus is celebrated in the Bible as the demonstration of God's power and commitment to the Chosen People. The event is referred to in Exodus (esp. Exod. 15), in the Psalms (e.g., Ps. 114), in Isaiah 40–55, and also in the New Testament (Matt. 2:15; Luke 9:31). The date and route of the Exodus, and the site of Mount Sinai, are all much debated. None of the Pharaohs with whom Joseph, Moses, and Aaron had dealings is named in the Exodus account; nor do the Egyptian records mention these events. A period of 480 years from the Exodus to the dedication of the Temple is given at 1 Kings 6:1. On that rough basis some scholars have linked the Exodus to the expulsion of the Hyksos kings from Egypt, c.1550BCE. More likely is a date during the reign of Ramesses II (*cf.* Exod. 1:11), during the 13th century BCE.

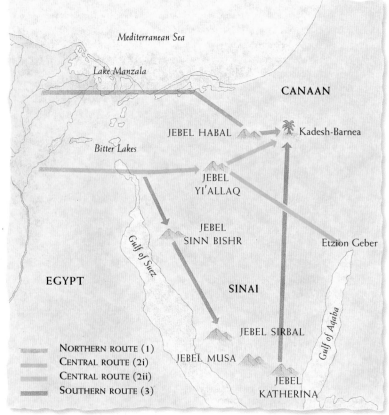

POSSIBLE SITES OF MOUNT SINAI AND THE POSSIBLE ROUTES OF THE EXODUS
*(1) The Northern Route. From Egypt along the Mediterranean coast, across Lake Manzala or one of the lagoons, then southeast through the Sinai peninsula to Mount Sinai and on to the oasis at Kadesh-Barnea. (2) The Central Route. From Goshen in Egypt, east across one of the Bitter Lakes to Mount Sinai, then either (i) northeast to Kadesh-Barnea or (ii) southeast to Etzion Geber. (3) The Southern Route. Across the northern tip of the Gulf of Suez, then south through the Sinai peninsula to Mount Sinai.*

SINAI DESERT
*Measuring approximately 130 miles (209km) east to west and 240 miles (386km) from north to south, the Sinai Desert is still inhabited by bedouin, as it was at the time of the Exodus.*

## THE ROUTE TO MOUNT SINAI

The immediate aims of the Exodus were to redeem the Israelites from slavery and to lead them into the land of Canaan (Exod. 6:1–8). The most direct route between Egypt and Canaan would have been along the Mediterranean coast, "the way of the Philistines" (Exod. 13:17), but this route was deliberately not taken. Instead, God took the Israelites

**THE MONASTERY OF ST. CATHERINE**
*This Greek Orthodox monastery, founded by Justinian in the fourth century CE, lies on the northern slopes of Jebel Musa ("the mountain of Moses") in the south of the Sinai peninsula. It claims to be the oldest monastery in existence.*

events that took place on Mount Sinai resist precise definition. Some have even argued that traditions about the Exodus, about the Wilderness Period, and about the revelation of God on Mount Sinai came originally from different parts of the kinship group and were put together at a later date only when the tribes were seeking to achieve a greater unity and were pooling their stories and traditions. At the very least, it is clear that a family or kinship group of escaping slaves found a faith and an identity under God, which they took with them into a new land and life. This event became the foundation of a people who have endured

**THE TABERNACLE**
The center of religious life in the desert was the Tabernacle or the "tent of meeting." The tent stood outside the main encampment. Moses would go into the tent and the pillar of cloud would come down and hover outside, showing the divine presence, while God spoke with Moses. The Tabernacle was a sanctuary that the Israelites carried with them across the desert. It held the Ark of the Covenant, containing the tablets with the Ten Commandments inscribed upon them, which Moses had brought down from Mount Sinai.

"through the way of the wilderness" (Exod. 13:18), a journey that led first to Mount Sinai, then to the oasis of Kadesh-Barnea, and ultimately, after a whole generation in the wilderness, to Canaan. The Bible records many place names along the route, but few can now be identified with any certainty. Of the possible routes from Egypt to Mount Sinai, there are three main theories (*see map, opposite*).

through continuing persecution, and who, at Passover each year, keep faith with their origins: "In each generation, every one must think of himself as though he personally had gone forth from Egypt" (*Mishnah Pesachim* 10:5).

## THE SITE OF MOUNT SINAI

The Bible also refers to Mount Sinai as "the mountain of God," "the mountain at Horeb," and simply "the mountain," but its exact location is never identified. Several have been proposed, consistent with the theoretically possible routes of the Exodus (*see map, opposite*). The biblical accounts of events at Mount Sinai mention fire, smoke, and earthquakes. Such volcanic imagery does not fit with mountains in the Sinai peninsula but could fit a location in the Arabian peninsula. It may be that the Bible is using imagery to suggest a theophany, a dramatic manifestation of God, rather than recording actual eruptions.

Given the scarcity of hard evidence, it is unlikely that theories regarding the route of the Exodus or the site of Mount Sinai can ever amount to more than a balance of probabilities. Despite their effects on later history, the

**OASIS IN THE SINAI DESERT**
*There are indications of a tradition that Kadesh-Barnea, an oasis (see map, opposite), was the central place in the movement to Canaan and the site of the giving of the Law. The tradition would have represented the experiences of one of the groups that made up the later nation of Israel.*

**For further reading see bibliography numbers:** 131, 193, 230, 283, 374, 402, 559, 588, 639, 757

# THE COVENANT PEOPLE

*In the long work of repairing the broken and divided human condition described in Genesis, the Bible shows God calling a particular people to play a special part. The idea of a chosen people is not one of privilege but of service and obligation on behalf of others.*

GOD'S choice, or "election," of a people to live as the Covenant People is one of the most fundamental and persistent themes of the Hebrew Bible. God commands Moses to speak to the people of Israel, telling them, *"For you are a people holy to the LORD your God; the LORD your God has chosen you out of all the peoples on earth to be his people, his treasured possession"* (Deut. 7:6). These words link *"chosen"* with *"holy,"* and, with *"his treasured possession,"* emphasize the special relationship between God and Israel. The gracious initiative and faithfulness of God is the sole reason given for God's action rather than any intrinsic quality of the people: *"It was not because you were more numerous than any other people that the LORD set his heart on you and chose you – for you were the fewest of all peoples. It was because the LORD loved you and kept the oath that he swore to your ancestors …"* (Deut. 7:7–8).

> " … the LORD has brought you out with a mighty hand, and redeemed you from the house of slavery, from the hand of Pharaoh king of Egypt. Know therefore that the LORD your God is God, the faithful God … "
>
> (Deuteronomy 7:8–9)

## UNDERSTANDING GOD'S CHOICE

The meaning of God's choice is further illuminated by regular poetic parallelism between *"my chosen"* and *"my servant"* in Isaiah 40–55. God's choice is a vocation to service: *"But you, Israel, my servant, Jacob, whom I have chosen"* (Isa. 41:8); *"Here is my servant, whom I uphold, my chosen, in whom my soul delights"* (Isa. 42:1); *"But now hear, O Jacob my servant"* (Isa. 44:1). The Prophets make it clear that if the people of Israel are faithless in their vocation, there will be no special favors; they will instead incur God's judgment. As Amos declares: *"You only have I known of all the families of the earth; therefore I will punish you for all your iniquities"* (Amos 3:2). None of this means that God has a concern for Israel alone (*see box, opposite*). In fact, the Bible makes it clear that God has command of all nations and uses them

**THE SETTLED PEOPLE OF ISRAEL**
*Following the Exodus, the Israelites became a settled people who depended on farming for survival. Staple crops grown included wheat, barley, and flax. Fields were cultivated by wooden plows drawn by oxen, and seed was sown by hand.*

# CHOSEN PEOPLE IN THE GENESIS STORIES

*Does God's choice of Israel imply a lack of concern for other peoples? Some Israelites clearly thought so, and the book of Jonah responds with a devastating critique of chauvinism and bigotry (esp. Jonah 4:1–11). The issues are also examined in the Genesis stories of Israel's ancestors, Cain and Abel, and Jacob and Esau.*

In the story of Cain and Abel, God accepts Abel's offering of the fat portions from the firstborn of his flock, but rejects the fruits of the soil offered by Cain (Gen. 4:4–5). No reason is given for this rejection, which points to the fact that God's decision here is dependent upon God alone and not upon a virtue or vice in the one chosen or not chosen. Similarly, God has decided in favor of Jacob before Jacob and Esau are even born: *"one shall be stronger than the other, the elder shall serve the younger"* (Gen. 25:23). Virtue is certainly not Jacob's strong point as he deceives his father, cheats his brother, and is forced to flee for his life (Gen 27:1–45; *see also pp.40–41* for the story of Jacob and Esau).

### The response to choice

The stories explore how people respond to the situation of being rejected in favor of another: not to be chosen can naturally provoke feelings of resentment. God pictures this resentment as a wild animal crouching, about to jump up and devour Cain. Cain has a choice that makes it possible for him to master this resentment:

*"If you do well, will you not be accepted? And if you do not do well, sin is lurking at the door; its desire is for you, but you must master it"* (Gen. 4:7). In reality, however, Cain fails to master his resentment and he kills Abel.

### Jacob's encounter with God

The same issue can be seen in the relation between Jacob and Esau. Jacob flees for his life from his brother, whose resentment is great enough to lead him, too, to murder (Gen. 27:41–45). Years later, Jacob returns home with wives, children, and great wealth, yet is terrified of what Esau may do to him. When initially he hears that Esau is coming to meet him with enough men for a small army, he fears the worst (Gen. 32:3–8). At this moment of truth, Jacob mysteriously wrestles with God in the form of another man (Gen. 32:22–32), and when Jacob finally encounters Esau, Esau welcomes him in a way that becomes a model for Jesus' story of the father welcoming his wasteful, prodigal son (Gen. 33:4; Luke 15:20). Esau has mastered the beast that Cain failed to master.

to bring the divine purposes into effect. God instructs Amos to ask the people of Israel, *"Are you not like the Ethiopians to me, O people of Israel? Did I not bring Israel up from the land of Egypt, and the Philistines from Caphtor and the Arameans from Kir?"* (Amos 9:7). Isaiah imagines God as a beekeeper who summons his bees to do his work. In God's case, the summons is to Assyria to be an instrument of punishment (Isa. 7:18; cf. Hab. *pp.238–39* for the question of God using a violent nation to do the divine work).

## THE ELECTION OF ISRAEL

The Prophets make it clear that many understood the election of Israel as a matter of exclusive privilege. Gradually, that attitude changed. In Exodus 19:5–6, a passage of central importance, God tells Moses, *"if you obey my voice and keep my covenant, you shall be my treasured possession out of all the peoples. Indeed, the whole earth is mine, but you shall be for me a priestly kingdom and a holy nation."* This passage might be understood as exclusivity, but it could mean that Israel was to be a mediator or bridge between nations and God, just as a priest acts as a mediator

between people and God. In the Hebrew Bible, holiness means being set apart from all that might damage or corrupt in the world in order to be close to God. Thus, Israel is to keep faith with God, not for itself alone but so that one day the whole world will know God for itself. This is the day when *"the earth will be filled with the knowledge of the glory of the LORD, as the waters cover the sea"* (Hab. 2:14; cf. Isa. 11:9). Zechariah 8:23 describes this as the day when *"ten men from nations of every language shall take hold of a Jew, grasping his garment and saying, 'Let us go with you, for we have heard that God is with you.'"*

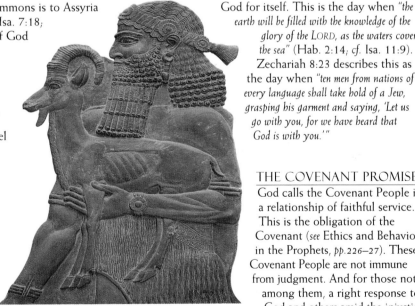

ANIMAL SACRIFICE
*At the covenant with Abraham, a heifer, a goat, a ram, a turtledove, and a pigeon are offered for sacrifice (Gen. 15:17–21).*

## THE COVENANT PROMISE

God calls the Covenant People into a relationship of faithful service. This is the obligation of the Covenant (*see* Ethics and Behavior in the Prophets, *pp.226–27*). These Covenant People are not immune from judgment. And for those not among them, a right response to God and others amid the injustices of life remains a real possibility (*see* Noachide Covenant, *p.33*).

For further reading see bibliography numbers: 270, 306a, 482, 830

# THE TEN COMMANDMENTS

*The Ten Commandments, or in Hebrew "the Ten Words" (Exod. 20:1–17; Deut. 5:6–21), are one of the most famous, and historically most influential, passages in the Bible. They have often been taken as a summary expression of morality and of God's will for humanity.*

THE importance of the Ten Commandments is clear from their biblical context. They are the first of the laws given to Israel at Sinai (Exod. 20:1–17); they are repeated in full (with some differences) at the beginning of Moses' exposition of the Covenant between God and Israel (Deut. 5:6–21); and they are the sole laws spoken by God directly without the mediation of Moses (Exod. 20:18–20; Deut. 5:22–31) and written by God on tablets of stone.

The Commandments are spoken by God and written on stone, but, if these are the words of God, why does the wording in Deuteronomy differ from that in Exodus? Some human involvement is clearly implied, and Deuteronomy itself suggests this with a reference to the involvement of Moses, which is a little awkward in the context of God's

direct address to Israel (Moses stands between God and the people, *see* Deut. 5:5). The difficulty suggests that God's speaking and writing has a symbolic significance that is not identical with a "literal" interpretation.

## THE NUMBERING OF THE COMMANDMENTS

The precise numbering of the Commandments has often been disputed, depending on how Exodus 20:2–6 is divided into the first two Commandments. The form of the Commandments is varied: two long ones (2, 4), five short ones (1, 6, 7, 8, 9), three of intermediate length (3, 5, 10); eight in negative form as prohibitions; two as positive commands (4, 5); two are spoken by God in the first person (1, 2), the others refer to

**THE TEN COMMANDMENTS BY LUCAS CRANACH THE ELDER**
*(Top row, l to r): there is one God and the prohibition against graven images (1&2), respect for God's name (3), the holy Sabbath (4), the commandment to respect one's parents (5); prohibition of murder (6), (bottom row): stealing (8), adultery (7), false testimony (9), coveting neighbor's wife (10), coveting neighbor's goods (10).*

God in the third person. These variations have led commentators to suggest a possible earlier, more consistent form of the material; but there is a lack of evidence to fully substantiate this view. Among Jews, the Commandments are divided into five positive and five negative commands. An early commentary observes that the first five are "between humans and God," the second five between humans themselves. To "honor your father and your mother" is thus a religious rather than an ethical command, because there are three partners in the creation of a child, the parents and God. To honor parents is to honor God, the Creator of life.

## CONTENT AND MEANING

The content of the Commandments relates initially to Israel's relationship with God (1–4) and then addresses conduct with other people (5–10).

• The first Commandment (Exod. 20:2–3) requires exclusive allegiance to God alone.

• The second Commandment (20:4–6) prohibits idolatry, as incompatible with exclusive allegiance to God. This has come to mean a purity of relationship, in which idolatry is a metaphor for any person or thing that takes the place of God.

• The third Commandment (20:7) is probably concerned not just with obvious profanity of speech but with any attempt to manipulate the name of God to further human schemes.

• The Sabbath, or fourth, Commandment (20:8–11) gives symbolic structure to ordinary, mundane time and prescribes a weekly holiday (holy day) as a pattern of life that conforms to the nature of God.

• The command to honor parents (20:12) probably intended adults to care for their elderly parents (for all the other Commandments envisage male adults as the primary audience).

• The reference of the sixth Commandment (20:13) is unclear. It is likely that "you shall not murder" is closer to the sense of the Hebrew than "you shall not kill," for, in appropriate legal and military contexts, the Bible accepts the taking of life.

## THE COMMANDMENTS

**1** *I am the* LORD *your God ... you shall have no other gods before me*

**2** *You shall not make for yourself an idol, whether in the form of anything that is in heaven above, or that is on the earth beneath, or that is in the water under the earth. You shall not bow down to them or worship them; for I the* LORD *your God am a jealous God*

**3** *You shall not make wrongful use of the name of the* LORD *your God*

**4** *Remember the Sabbath day, and keep it holy*

**5** *Honor your father and your mother*

**6** *You shall not murder*

**7** *You shall not commit adultery*

**8** *You shall not steal*

**9** *You shall not bear false witness against your neighbor*

**10** *You shall not covet your neighbor's house; you shall not covet your neighbor's wife*

Exodus 20:1–17

• The prohibition of adultery (20:14) seeks to preserve marriage from being undermined by infidelity. In the Bible, it was more restrictive on the woman than the man: a married man could have sex with an unmarried woman without constituting adultery because a married woman was considered the property of her husband.

• The eighth and tenth Commandments (20:15, 17) are closely related; one prohibits all acts of misappropriation, the other deals with the underlying motive. Their concern is to protect communal life from practices that undercut it.

• The prohibition of false witness (20:16) envisages a legal context, which protects the neighbor's well-being.

## JEWISH TRADITION

According to the Babylonian Talmud (the major collection of rabbinic interpretations of Torah), the priests would recite the Ten Commandments as part of the liturgy, and people in general also wanted to do so. "But they were stopped on account of the insinuations of the *minim* [heretics; possibly Christians]." This suggests Christians were making the Ten Commandments into a summary of the essential meaning of Torah arguing that the rest of the laws were unnecessary. As a result, the Ten Commandments are not prominent in Jewish worship or liturgy, although they are read. The revered teacher Maimonides (1135–1204) said that no one should pay special reverence to them. For the rabbis, the Ten Commandments were brought into being before the Creation, so they are universal in their application: they precede a specific time and place. They were offered to the peoples of Edom and Moab, and the Ishmaelites, but they all refused them.

Recent scholarship has drawn attention to the question of who is being addressed by the Ten Commandments. In the context of the Torah, the people spoken to directly are adult Israelite males. If the Ten Commandments are addressed to men, and only indirectly to women in their role as wives, then this sets limits on using them as a basis for a general and nonspecific morality.

For further reading see bibliography numbers: 63, 687, 723, 830

# THE NAMES AND NATURE OF GOD

*God is known by many names in the Bible, perhaps from a time when people believed in different gods. But these different names were recognized in Israel as manifestations of the one God, the only God there is or has ever been.*

NAMES in the Bible can often be full of meaning, in that they may express something of the character of the one who bears the name. After his encounter with God (Gen. 32:28), Jacob is called Israel, while Naomi ("Pleasant") wishes to be called Mara ("Bitter") after her bitter experiences in Moab (Ruth 1:20–21). Similarly, the names of God in the Bible are closely connected with the nature of God.

As in Canaanite religion (*pp.98–99*), so also in the Bible God is El, supreme over the Earth and all other heavenly beings. El was brought into contact with the Earth by association with particular places (El Bethel, Gen. 35:7) or functions, as El Roi (God who sees, Gen. 16:7–14), El Berith (God of the Covenant, Judg. 9:46), or attributes, as El Olam (God who endures, Gen. 21:33). God in supreme majesty was also called Elohim. Elohim is, strictly speaking, the Hebrew plural, "gods," and it is sometimes used in the Bible in a plural sense (the images are called *elohim* in Gen. 31:30; *cf.* Judg. 17:5; Dan. 11:8). But usually Elohim means *the God*, the one above all others that are claimed to be God. That is why we get the otherwise strange phrase in Genesis 33:20: *El Elohe Israel*, meaning "El is the Elohim of Israel".

> *❝ So Moses … went up on Mount Sinai … The LORD descended in the cloud and stood with him there and proclaimed the name, 'The LORD.'❞*
>
> (Exodus 34:4–5)

## A NEW NAME IS GIVEN

All this a Canaanite would recognize. But Israel voyaged into a new world of faith and understanding when an entirely different name of God was entrusted to the people – a name that we no longer know how to pronounce. Because of its holiness, Orthodox Jews would not even wish to pronounce it, and they refer to it in Hebrew as *haShem*, literally "the Name." This rests on three key passages: Exodus 3 (esp. 3:13–15), Exodus 6 (esp. 6:2–3), and Exodus 33–34 (esp. 33:19; 34:6–7). What is said here about the name of God is set on God's own lips and is spoken to Moses alone. No matter how we may now think these passages came to be written, they remain the foundation of Israel's faith and new direction in life. But what is the name, and what is its significance?

## THE NAME

Hebrew was initially written with consonants only. Vowels were pronounced when the text was read aloud, but they were not written down until the work of the Masoretes in the latter part of the first millennium CE. In the Hebrew text of Exodus 3:15 and elsewhere, the consonants of the divine name are given as *y h w h*. For reverential reasons, Jews did not pronounce the name of

**MOSES AND THE PILLAR OF SMOKE**
*During the Exodus, Moses parts the sea and the people are guided through the wilderness by God in the form of a pillar of smoke and a pillar of fire.*

God and used substitute words and alternatives such as Adonai ("LORD" in traditional English translation, the capitalized form indicating that it is the name of God). The Masoretes put the vowels of Adonai into the Hebrew y h w h, to make sure that no one said the name, but said Adonai instead. When the vowels of AdOnAi were added to *y h w h* in English translations, this produced the form Yahowah, or Jehovah. In fact, the vowels originally belonging to *y h w h* have long been forgotten.

## THE UNIQUE GOD

There is a consensus among modern scholars that the most likely original form of the name is "Yahweh." This is not beyond dispute, and many prefer a reverential capitalizing of the name without vowels, so YHWH. The origin of the name Yahweh is said in the Bible to connect with the Hebrew verb "to be" (*bayab*) as is shown in the form "I AM WHO I AM" or "I WILL BE WHAT I WILL BE" (Exod. 3:14). This can be understood in more than one way. For example, it could indicate divine freedom ("I am who I want to be"), divine faithfulness ("I always am who I really am"), or divine uniqueness ("I only am the one who I am").

The immediate narrative context, the burning bush where a fire burns that does not consume (Exod. 3:2), may suggest the uniqueness of a God who transcends familiar human categories. A classic Jewish and Christian understanding of this concept is the belief that the more you know about God, the more you know you don't know. In Exodus 34:6–7 comes the fullest statement about the nature of God in the Hebrew Bible. The context, remarkably, is that of Israel's unfaithfulness. While still at Sinai the idolatrous Israelites fashion a Golden Calf (Exod. 32:1–6). Although God almost destroys Israel, Moses' prayer elicits a divine promise of mercy in a way that definitively links this mercy to God's name as YHWH ("*I will make all my goodness pass before you, and will proclaim before you the name, 'The LORD'; and I will be gracious to whom I will be gracious, and will show mercy on whom I will show mercy,*" Exod. 33:19). Only after the text emphasizes that this is still a limited vision of God ("*and you shall see my back; but my face shall not be seen,*" Exod. 33:23) does God's proclamation of the divine name to Moses take place (Exod. 34:1–9). The text strongly emphasizes that grace and love characterize YHWH, while making clear that this mercy cannot be taken for granted by Israel. On this basis YHWH's Covenant with Israel, imperiled by Israel's unfaithfulness, is renewed (34:8–10). Throughout the Bible, we can see how YHWH gradually invades the territory of El, first taking over the functions of El (much as Baal-Hadad does in the Ugaritic texts, *see p.99*), and then becoming the one who El is. Thus, YHWH becomes what God is and is recognized as the only God. This extraordinary exploration and discovery of faith, led on by God as the one who invites and encourages the people into this deeper understanding, is the supreme achievement that creates the phenomenon of Israel: it is also the supreme achievement of the Bible itself.

**A BRIGHT LIGHT**
*God is described as being like various natural phenomena and objects – a shield, a fortress, and a bright light shining through the darkness.*

> 66 *Who is like you,*
> *O LORD,*
> *among the gods?*
> *Who is like you,*
> *majestic in holiness,*
> *awesome in splendor,*
> *doing wonders?* 99
>
> (Exodus 15:11)

## JEWISH TRADITION

Jewish tradition recognized several names used of God in the Hebrew Bible and interpreted them as different divine aspects or attributes. For instance, in *Midrash Haggodol*, God said: "You want to know My name? I am named after my acts. As the judge of people I am called *elohim* ["God"]; as the one who battles the wicked I am called *tzevaot* ["military hosts"]; as the delayer of punishment, *shaddai* ["almighty"]; as the compassionate ruler, *rachum* ["compassionate"]; and similarly *kano* ["jealous"]; *nokem* ["the one who brings appropriate punishment"]; *morish uma'asheer* ["the one who makes poor and makes rich"]; *dayyan* ["judge"]; *tzaddiq* ["the righteous"]; *chasid* ["the faithful"]; *qadosh* ["the holy"]; *ne'eman* ["the trustworthy"]; *chazaq* ["the powerful"]; *gadol* ["great"]; *gibbor* ["mighty"]; *nora* ["awesome"]" (*Midrash Haggadol* on Exodus 3:14).

For further reading see bibliography numbers: 122, 549, 563, 649a, 711

# THE COVENANT

*The Covenant is an agreement between God and the people of Israel. It requires that the
people will remain faithful and put their trust in God; in return God will protect Israel
from its enemies and will exalt Israel.*

THE making of covenants, in the sense of treaties or
pacts, was a common feature in the world of ancient
Israel, well attested to in the Hebrew Bible and in
texts from adjacent Hittite and Assyrian cultures. Like many
everyday terms, "covenant" was taken
up as a model for God's relationship
with Israel, and it became the central
category for depicting that relationship.

The idea of a covenant is that of two
people or two parties entering into a
formal agreement. In biblical times,
a covenant would often be made with
solemn actions, such as blood sacrifice
or a sacred meal. Archaeologists have
found evidence of a number of covenants
from the ancient world, and it may be
that the importance of the covenant
form in Israel is derived from a
knowledge of these other covenants.
The major difference between those documents and the
covenants of the Hebrew Bible is that in the latter God,
not the king or ruler, is the senior partner. So important is
the idea of covenant in the Bible that the two parts of the

Christian Bible came to be called by Christians the Old
and the New Testaments (*testamentum* being a Latin word for
covenant). Many covenants are mentioned in the Bible,
but perhaps the most binding and solemn was that made
between God and Israel at Sinai.

> **❝ *I hereby make a covenant.
> Before all your people I will
> perform marvels, such as have
> not been performed in all the
> earth or in any nation; and
> all the people among whom
> you live shall see the
> work of the LORD.* ❞**
>
> (Exodus 34:10)

## THE NATURE OF COVENANT

The nature and meaning of the Mosaic
Covenant between God and the Israelites
is explored in certain foundational texts,
especially Exodus 19–24, 32–34 and
Deuteronomy 4–11, 26–30. These texts
describe several fundamental characteristics of the Covenant:

• God is the stronger party in a
relationship of unequals and takes
the initiative in making the Covenant
(shown also in delivering Israel from
Egypt, Exod. 19:4; 20:2) and on God's terms (summarized
in the Ten Commandments, *cf.* Deut. 4:13; *see also pp. 80–81*).
• Israel willingly enters the Covenant (Exod. 19:8; 24:3–8)
and is taught to regard its covenantal status as its key

**THE RETURN OF THE ARK OF THE COVENANT**
*This representation of the return of the Ark takes its subject from 1 Samuel 6. In the foreground the Ark of the Covenant
has stopped by the great stone of Abel on its way to Jerusalem. The Philistines are shown crossing the bridge behind.*

distinguishing feature (Deut. 4:5–8; 32–40).

• Like a marriage, the Covenant requires the exclusive loyalty of Israel to Israel's God, YHWH, corresponding to YHWH's unique commitment to, and activity on behalf of, Israel (Exod. 34:11–16; Deut. 4:9–24). This is a theme taken up by some of the Prophets, in particular Hosea and Ezekiel.

• The Covenant should lead to the glory and exaltation of Israel as a holy people (Deut. 26:16–19).

• While blessings are promised when Israel is faithful, warnings of dire curses – famine, distress, exile – result from Israel's unfaithfulness (Deut. 28:1–68; 29:16–28).

• Although, if unfaithful, Israel is urged to turn again to God so that it may be restored (Deut. 30:1–10), and although Israel's responsiveness to God always matters, the continuation of the Covenant depends ultimately on the mercy and faithfulness of God, which is greater than the faithlessness of Israel (Exod. 33:11–34:10; Deut. 32).

• Moses is the mediator of the Covenant, the archetype of subsequent prophets and priests who continue this role (Exod. 24; 33:11–34:35; Deut. 18:15–20).

• The Covenant is an enduring reality for Israel in every generation (Deut. 5:3; 29:14–15).

**THE RITE OF CIRCUMCISION**
*Circumcision is one of the rites by which the Israelites showed their loyalty to God's Covenant. It is still performed on all male Jews today.*

covenant with Abraham, Isaac, and Jacob" (Exod. 2:23–24; cf. Deut. 7:8). These two covenants with Abraham and David thus have a different dynamic from the Sinai Covenant, where far greater emphasis is laid on the responsibilities of the recipient. Prophets rarely quote the Covenant but show awareness of it (see pp.219, 227, 235).

## THE ARK OF THE COVENANT

The Ark of the Covenant is one of the most important objects in the Hebrew Bible. It was a small wooden chest that symbolically represented the presence of God with Israel (for its description, see Exod. 25:10–22). Its construction is associated with the making of the Covenant between God and Israel at Sinai (Exod. 24:15–25:22; Deut. 10:1–5). Appropriately, acacia, the wood of the Ark (Exod. 25:10), is found growing in the Sinai peninsula. As a sacred object, the Ark was usually kept in a shrine (in the Tabernacle or the temples at Shiloh and Jerusalem), but it could be brought out on special occasions. The most illuminating story about the Ark and divine presence is told in 1 Samuel 4–6. Here, the Israelites presumptuously suppose that the Ark will guarantee them victory in battle, which it does not. The Philistines suppose they can keep it as a trophy in the temple of Dagon, which they cannot. To emphasize that the Ark cannot be regarded as a kind of magic "fix" or talisman against Israel's enemies, the designation changes in these chapters: when the Ark is effective, it is called "the Ark of YHWH" (Israel's God, the LORD); when it is ineffective, it is called "the Ark of God" (Elohim). King David installed the Ark in Jerusalem to help consolidate his new capital (2 Sam. 6; see also pp.124–25), and it was as a shrine for the Ark that the Jerusalem Temple was built (2 Sam. 7; 1 Kgs. 8:1–11; see pp.132–33).

The ultimate fate of the Ark is unknown. It is generally supposed to have been destroyed when the Jerusalem Temple was destroyed by the Babylonians in 587BCE. Later tradition told of the Prophet Jeremiah hiding the Ark in a cave (2 Macc. 2:4–8), which has sometimes encouraged people to suppose – unwisely – that the Ark might yet be rediscovered.

## OTHER BIBLICAL COVENANTS

The Mosaic Covenant with Israel at Sinai, confirmed in Joshua 24, is not the sole divine covenant in the Hebrew Bible. God also makes covenants with Noah (see p.33), Abraham (Gen. 15, 17), and David (2 Sam. 7:1–29; 23:5; Ps. 89). In these covenants, much emphasis is placed upon the covenant as a divine initiative and gift. In Psalm 89:3 the parallel between *"I have made a covenant with my chosen one"* and *"I have sworn to my servant David"* shows that the covenant with David is essentially an oath, a solemn promise on God's part. Solemn promises are also the content of Genesis 15 and 2 Samuel 7. At some points in the Bible, the making of the Covenant with Israel as a nation is depicted as a fulfillment of God's promise to Abraham: *"The Israelites groaned under their slavery and cried out ... God heard their groaning, and God remembered his*

> ❝ *In your distress, when all things have happened to you in time to come; you will return to the LORD your God ... Because the LORD your God is a merciful God, he will neither abandon you nor destroy you.* ❞
>
> (Deuteronomy 4:30–31)

For further reading see bibliography numbers: 43, 89, 183, 270, 492, 559, 588, 589, 787

# THE BOOK OF
# LEVITICUS

*"The priestly book," Leviticus consists mainly of legislation. Nearly half the 613 commandments in the Torah are in this book, which deals with the priesthood, rituals, feasts, fasts, purity, and holiness.*

LEVITICUS is set in the Wilderness Period, when the Israelite nation was still encamped at Mount Sinai. This encampment, which had at its center the sanctuary, was considered part of God's domain, so while there, the Israelites had to keep themselves in a state of purity. The world of Leviticus, with its detailed accounts of ritual and blood sacrifice, seems remote from our own world. Ritual and cultic laws cannot be transferred directly into modern life. But the question remains: how do we draw a distinction in our lives and behavior between what is corrupt and what is clean and holy? Fundamental to the book is the command, *"You shall be holy, for I the LORD your God am holy"* (19:2; cf. 11; 45; 20:7, 26). All of Leviticus' regulations concerning the encampment and its sanctuary were meant to prevent what was impure from coming into contact with what was holy.

## THE REGULATIONS OF LEVITICUS

On entering the sanctuary, the priests had to be sure that they were in no way contaminated, either in their physical condition or through contact with "impurity" (such as a dead body). The regulations also had a medical function: the book describes physiological and pathological conditions that were considered impure. The priest distinguished between illnesses, particularly those involving bodily discharges that required quarantining due to the risk of spreading infection, and physiological states, such as

menstruation, postpartum discharges, and discharges of semen. In the case of illness, a certain amount of time had to elapse after the symptoms had cleared before the individual could be readmitted to the Temple. For other states, a fixed period of time had to elapse and the individual would have to undergo simple ritual washing. Certain ritual sacrifices were then offered, signifying that he or she was again "pure" and able to reenter the community. The sacrificial system was the means for regulating the relationship between God and the community. If the priests did not follow the strict code of behavior in the sanctuary, there would be devastating consequences (Lev. 10:1–2), such as an outbreak of plague in the encampment (Num. 1:53; 8:19; 17:11). Similar, but less stringent, requirements affected the Levites who served the priests. Since the entire Israelite encampment was part of the divine domain, the ordinary people also had to keep themselves in a state of purity, which included being selective in the food they ate. Leviticus gives a series of rules as to which animals can be eaten and which are considered unclean. Many of these food laws are still observed by Orthodox Jews today. Chapter 19 stands at the heart of Leviticus, and, as a whole, it defines holy behavior – the behavior demanded of everyone. Perhaps the overriding command is the well-known verse *"you shall love your neighbor as yourself."* It was not only one's physical state that affected one's presence in the sanctuary. Israel itself was to be a nation of priests (Exod. 19:6).

**NADAB AND ABIHU OFFER UNHOLY FIRE**
*Aaron's two sons put incense in their censers and offered fire to God, when it had not been commanded. Fire came down from God and they were killed (Lev. 10:1–2).*

## A HOLISTIC VIEW

In reading Leviticus it should be remembered that the special Covenant between God and the people is actually made with the adult Israelite male, whose family, property, and possessions are considered as extensions of himself. Central to this Covenant are two principles made clear in Leviticus 25: Israelites are the property of God alone (25:42, 55), so no one can own – that is enslave – a fellow Israelite. The other is that the land of Israel itself belongs to God and those who live there are merely tenants (25:23), so the land should be redistributed every Jubilee (50th) year when all debts are canceled. Both of these principles represent ideals that were often forgotten in the record of the biblical period.

Nevertheless, they are a reminder that Leviticus takes a holistic view of the human being: body and spirit, ritual life and ethical life, individual and collective, are intimately bound up each with the other. The early rabbis called the book of Leviticus *Torat Kohanim*, "Guidance for Priests." According to *Leviticus Rabbah* (7, 3) God has said, "If you study the sacrifices, I will reckon it to you as though you have offered them up." So study was seen as being as worth-while as the sacrifice. Traditionally, it is the first book taught to children: "Young children are pure and the sacrifices are pure, so let the pure come to study the pure."

## HOLINESS

In the Bible, the word "holy" has a very specific meaning. Since God is the Holy One, holiness involves being close to God, belonging or being consecrated to God. That at once means being separated from what is unclean or contaminating. In fact, the Hebrew words *qadosh* (holy one) and *qodesh* (holy things/holiness) come from a root meaning "to cut off" or "separate." There are many examples of this "being separate in order to be close." As Moses approaches the burning bush, he hears God saying *"Come no closer! Remove the sandals from your feet, for the place on which you are standing is holy ground"* (Exod. 3:5). When Israel is called to be a holy nation (Exod. 19:5–6; Deut. 26:19; 28:9; Jer. 2:3), it too must separate itself from what is unclean if it is to draw close to God.

But holiness also embodies the power of God to destroy what is unworthy of God, and thus may be considered a danger to those who treat it lightly or carelessly. This is evident in the story of Nadab and Abihu (Lev. 10:1–2). On another occasion, when the Ark of the Covenant was being moved, a man called Uzzah put his hand on the Ark to steady it, and he immediately fell down dead (2 Sam. 6:1–8). The word "holiness" is used in a similar sense in the New Testament, where it can be defined as meaning "closeness to God, by separation from all that is unworthy of God": *"present your bodies as a living sacrifice, holy and acceptable to God"* (Rom. 12:1; cf. 1 Cor. 6:19ff.; Eph. 2:21ff.; Heb. 12:10).

## THE BOOK

**TITLE**: Leviticus. From the Latin title meaning "having to do with priest and priestly matters"

**HEBREW TITLE**: *Vayyiqra* ("and he summoned")

**DATE**: Unknown, but set in the Wilderness Period (*see pp. 62–63*)

**AUTHORSHIP**: The book describes itself as a series of instructions given by God to Moses. It is a collection of laws thought by some to have been gathered as a rule book for rituals of the Second Temple (after the Babylonian Exile, post 538BCE) drawing on earlier material; but much of that earlier material has little relevance in the Second Temple, so the book may be earlier

## THE CONTENTS

**CHAPTERS 1–7**
Laws on sacrifices and offerings

**CHAPTERS 8–9**
Aaron and sons appointed priests

**CHAPTER 10**
Two of Aaron's sons, Nadab and Abihu, offer unholy fire and perish

**CHAPTERS 11–15**
Laws concerning purity, and the distinction between clean and unclean

**CHAPTER 16**
The Day of Atonement

**CHAPTERS 17–26**
Regulations for the life of Israel (these chapters have been called "The Holiness Code")

## KEY THEMES

*Sacrifice and ritual*

•

*Holiness*

•

*The difference between what is clean and unclean*

**For further reading see bibliography numbers:** 198, 247, 601, 693, 789

# PRIESTS
## IN THE BIBLE

*The priest was an important figure in Israelite religion, a member of a specific family.
The mediator between the people and God, he served in the sanctuary and acted as
a buffer between the profane world of everyday life and the holiness of God.*

PRIESTHOOD was hereditary, running in families, several of which are mentioned in the Hebrew Bible. Eli and his two sons, Hophni and Phinehas, were priests at the sanctuary of Shiloh (1 Sam. 1:3, 9). Ahimelech was priest at Nob, where his family was established in the priesthood (1 Sam. 22:11). The Prophet Jeremiah is described as one of the priests who were in Anathoth in the land of Benjamin (Jer. 1:1). There seem never to have been female priests. Such a concept was probably thought to be far too dangerous in a context where fertility cults and their associated sexual rites – including cultic prostitution – were a constant threat to the purity of the Israelite religion (*see* Hos. 4:11–14).

## WHAT DID PRIESTS DO?

The priest's duties developed over time. He was involved in making sacrifices; indeed, his livelihood largely depended on the sacrifices, because he was entitled to specified portions of all the offerings that were brought to the sanctuary. Priests had no inheritance of land, but they did receive tithes from the people. There were other duties too. In early times, a priest was keeper of the divine lots, the Urim and Thummim, which he would use to consult God for an oracle of guidance.

The lots were probably sticks or stones that could be drawn out of, or cast from, a container, and the outcome would be interpreted by the priest to give a yes/no answer or to make a choice between two alternatives (*cf.* 1 Sam. 14:41–42). Later, the lots were replaced by prophecy as the way of asking God for guidance.

Priests were also responsible for giving Torah or judgments, teaching the Law to the people, and deciding on matters of ritual purity (Hag. 2:11–13). A fourth area of priestly responsibility was burning incense in the sanctuary (*see opposite*).

## WHO COULD BE A PRIEST?

In the books of Exodus, Leviticus, and Numbers only the sons of Aaron, brother of Moses and descendant of Levi, are allowed to be priests. In Deuteronomy, however, not just the sons of Aaron but all descendants of Levi can be priests. A third group claiming priestly rights were the descendants of Zadok, David's priest in Jerusalem (2 Sam. 8:17). The Zadokites came to dominate the priesthood at the Jerusalem Temple and eventually

**PRIESTS IN THE TEMPLE**
*Different parts of the priesthood were responsible for the upkeep of different parts of the Temple. Even the carrying of the Ark was specifically entrusted to priests due to its extreme importance, especially during the entry into the Promised Land. But priests also carried out sacrifice and other sacred rites. The illustration above from a 13th-century French manuscript shows the High Priest pouring oil into the seven-branched golden lampstand or menorah. The Bible describes the menorah at Exodus 37:17–24.*

**BLESSING AT THE WESTERN WALL**
*Priests (kohanim) wearing white prayer shawls bless people at the Western Wall in Jerusalem, as the priests of the Temple did in the period of the Hebrew Bible.*

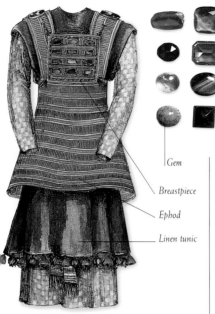

*Gem*

*Breastpiece*

*Ephod*

*Linen tunic*

### PRIEST'S CEREMONIAL COSTUME

*Priests wore a linen sleeved tunic and a garment called an ephod. This reached from the chest down to the hips, and was held in place by two shoulder bands and tied around the waist. The Urim and Thummim, the divine lots used to consult God, may have been held in the ephod. The ephod of the High Priest held a breastpiece with 12 gems on it engraved with the names of the Twelve Tribes of Israel. The breastpiece symbolized the priest as the announcer of God's will to humankind. Priests were not allowed to wear woolen clothes and were forbidden from wearing sandals in the Temple.*

became the accepted family line from which the High Priest had to come. Before the Monarchy, priests were not as restricted, but members of the tribe of Levi were always preferred for the priesthood (*see* Judg. 17:5, 13). After the Exile (587/6–38/7BCE), when the Jerusalem Temple had become the country's only legitimate site of worship, the claims of the different priestly groups were brought together, so that the Zadokites were regarded as a subgroup of the Aaronides, who were in turn a subgroup of the Levites (1 Chr. 6:1–30). This meant that all those who served in the Temple were regarded as being of Levitical descent. However, under this arrangement, those who were simply descendants of Levi and not linked to Aaron or Zadok were no longer entitled to be full priests. They served as musicians, gatekeepers, and officials and laborers concerned with

the upkeep of the Tabernacle, but then were not allowed to approach the altar and perform sacrificial duties. Responsibility for those duties was reserved for the Aaronides, who were the full priests. The significance of the priesthood was greatly diminished with the destruction of the Temple in 70CE. Today, rigorous proof of descent from the line of Aaron is no longer possible, and the authority of modern-day *kohanim* (priests) usually rests on family tradition.

#### INCENSE BURNER

*Burning incense was a common feature of priestly ritual. It was burned in the Temple's inner sanctum as an acknowledgment of God. Frankincense, a type of aromatic tree resin, was normally used. This incense burner, from Beth Shean in modern Israel, dates from the tenth/ninth centuries BCE.*

# AARON

*The brother of Moses, Aaron became the High Priest of the Israelites. The later priesthood was believed to be descended from him.*

Aaron appears in several different capacities in the wilderness narratives. Introduced as Moses' brother, he is also his spokesman before Pharaoh (Exod. 4:14–16). Aaron appears with the elders of Israel as one of the leaders of the people (Exod. 18:12; 24:1, 9–11, 14) and is also portrayed as responsible for leading the Israelites into idolatry during Moses' absence on Mount Sinai (Exod. 32:1–6). However, his most significant and enduring role is that of High Priest (Exod. 28:1). This role belongs to a religious worldview whereby the right to approach God depends on each individual's degree of holiness. In this system, the High Priest was the most holy person, a status expressed in his elaborate costume (*see above, left*) and the rules for his conduct (Lev. 21:10–15). He was the only one allowed to come into God's presence, the innermost part of the sanctuary (*see* Lev. 16:1–4). Aaron is shown as the founding father of the only legitimate priesthood; his sons alone are summoned by God to serve as priests and enter the sanctuary (Exod. 28:1). That this was a controversial claim is implied by the story of opposition to Aaron from others who also claimed the right to be priests, and the subsequent tale of Aaron's rod that sprouted, proving that God had chosen him (Num. 16; 17:8–9).

For further reading see bibliography numbers: 148, 194, 314, 470, 551, 561, 649a, 720, 766, 767

# SACRIFICE AND RITUAL

## IN THE BIBLE

*Sacrifice and ritual are important for religions. They often mark the boundaries of sacred time and space, and so are a way of interacting with the spiritual world. This was certainly true of their use in the religion of ancient Israel.*

FROM the beginning of the biblical narrative, sacrifice is taken for granted as part of Israel's religious observance. It first appears in the story of Cain and Abel (Gen. 4:3–8), and thereafter it appears regularly throughout the Hebrew Bible. The Book of the Covenant (Exod. 20–23), probably the oldest legislative code in the Bible, also mentions sacrifice with a familiarity that shows that, even at this early stage, the practice was well established in Israel (Exod. 20:24; 23:18). The most detailed instructions about sacrifice come in the book of Leviticus (*pp.62–63*). Three basic types of animal sacrifice are described: the burnt offering (whole offering, holocaust), in which the entire animal was burned on the altar; the peace offering, where only the fat and some internal organs were burned on the altar, and the rest was eaten by the worshipers; and the purification, or sin, offering, where the animal's blood was sprinkled or daubed on various parts of the sanctuary, the fat parts were burned on the altar, and the rest of the animal was either burned or eaten by the priests. There are also regulations for cereal offerings, some of which were brought if people could not afford animals, and some of which were brought along with the animal sacrifices. To the people offering these sacrifices, there were many possible meanings. It could be a way of "feeding" or sharing a meal with a deity, or it could be an expression of devotion or thanksgiving, an attempt to influence the deity in the worshiper's favor, or a means of expiation or purification.

**EARLY SANCTUARIES**
*The altar for the burnt offerings in the Holy of Holies at the temple of Arad. The inset shows a horned altar from the sanctuary at Megiddo in central Israel. Both date from the ninth century BCE.*

**RITUAL TODAY**
*Ritual is a major part of the traditions of both modern Judaism and Christianity. In the photograph on the left, Orthodox Jews are seen burning* chometz, *leftover leavened bread, before the beginning of the Seder on the first night of Passover. The custom follows the words laid down in* Exodus 12:15.

However, all sacrifices outlined in the Bible were probably thought to be effective on several levels at once. Thus it may not be possible to isolate a single meaning for each sacrificial type.

## BLOOD SACRIFICE

One distinctive characteristic of the Israelite understanding of sacrifice is its attitude toward blood. Both Leviticus and Deuteronomy forbid the eating of blood because it is seen as the seat of life (Lev. 17:10–14; 19:26; Deut. 12:16; 23–24) and therefore as

**SACRIFICE IN OTHER CULTURES**
*Sacrifice was a part of all cultures of the ancient Near East. It is clear in Solomon's prayer at the dedication of the Temple (1 Kgs. 8:41–43) that Gentiles as well as Jews brought sacrifices to the Temple. Similarly, in Isaiah 56:6–7, the Temple is seen as a house of prayer for all peoples. The image above, a wall painting from the grave of an Egyptian high official, shows the sacrifice of a bull. It was painted toward the end of the third millennium BCE.*

belonging to God, who is by nature everliving and the giver of life. The proper place for the blood is at the altar (Deut. 12:27), since it has been given for atonement purposes (Lev. 17:11). Blood is also used in some of the ceremonies outlined in the Hebrew Bible to purify the sanctuary from the desecrating effects of the people's sin, and from other ritual impurity (cf. Lev. 16:11–19). Other ritual requirements

were just as important as sacrifice and range from rules about diet and dress to festival observances. Although these strictures may appear arbitrary, they can be understood as marking out what is holy, what is profane (i.e., clean but not holy), and what is unclean. Thus, when lepers are cleansed from the unclean leprous state, there is ritual and sacrifice to show that they are no longer unclean but clean (Lev. 13). Ritual requirements such as dietary laws (Lev. 11:1–46) and dress codes (Lev. 19:19; Deut. 22:5) help to align Israel with the divinely ordained distinctiveness of different parts of the Creation. Festivals, ritual, and sacrifice mark out the periods of holy time (e.g., Exod. 12:14–20). Hence, both sacrifice and ritual appear as part of a carefully ordered system of holiness.

## LATER TRADITIONS
Sacrifice and ritual were intended to be a way of expressing true devotion and not a substitute for it. Indeed, there is harsh criticism in the Prophets for those who thought that sacrifice without devotion was all that was necessary (Amos 5:21–24; Mic. 6:6–8). Although sacrifice ceased when the Temple was destroyed in 70CE, the ritual requirements have remained important for many Jews to the present day. The symbolism of the priesthood has been preserved in Judaism through the tradition that all Jews still belong to one of the three biblical divisions: priest, Levite, or Israelite – hence, characteristic names, such as Cohen (priest) or Katz (an abbreviation of *cohen tzedek*, "righteous priest"). Prayers

for the restoration of the Temple and its sacrificial system continue in traditional Jewish liturgy, although these forms have been largely dropped in non-Orthodox forms of Judaism. In Christianity, much sacrificial imagery became associated with the death of Jesus, and in the Letter to the Hebrews (*pp.450–51*) the sacrifice of Jesus supplants the sacrifices of the Hebrew Bible. But the symbolism of sacrifice has been continued in the Catholic Eucharist and in the role of the priest as understood in some Christian traditions.

**SAMARITANS**
*The Samaritan religion shares affinities with Judaism and a belief in the five books of the Pentateuch as the word of God revealed to Moses. Samaritan sacrifice involves the burning of the entire animal carcass, according to the ritual prescriptions outlined in the book of Leviticus.*

**HOLY COMMUNION**
*Christians participate in the sharing of bread and wine in remembrance of Christ. This practice is known as Communion or the Eucharist.*

**For further reading see bibliography numbers:** 13, 116, 148, 194, 317, 470, 479, 561, 649a, 661, 767

# FASTS AND
# FESTIVALS

*Festivals draw people together in celebration: they are enjoyable and worth a journey or,
in religious terms, a pilgrimage. But people also need to express sorrow together
when things go wrong, so fasts are a public expression of regret and grief.*

B Y the end of the biblical period,
festivals and fasts had been organized so that in each year there
were a mix of agricultural observances,
and those that commemorated the history of God's dealings with Israel (for
the calendar *see pp.236–37*). At least
three pilgrimage festivals were celebrated before the Exile to Babylon
in the sixth century BCE. These were
Passover, in early spring, Weeks (or
Pentecost), so called because it took
place seven weeks after Passover, and
Tabernacles (Booths, or Sukkot) in
early autumn. Four other feasts or holy
days developed, probably after the
Exile. At the end of summer, the Feast
of Trumpets called the people to a fast

**THE FESTIVAL OF PASSOVER**
*Passover became linked to the story of the
escape from slavery in Egypt, when God
killed the firstborn of the Egyptians, but
"passed over" the Israelites and granted
their release. The account of this event
in Exodus 12–14 shows the close
relationship between the escape from
Egypt and the celebration of Passover
and Unleavened Bread.*

Matzo (bread
made without
yeast)

Cup of
wine

Passover
prayer book
(Haggadah)

Egg
symbolizes
sacrifice

Lamb recalls
first Passover

Nut and
fruit paste

The "bitter
herbs" of slavery

Pesach meaning
"Passover"

**Passover meal.**

before the beginning of the New Year
(Rosh Hashanah). This ended with the
Day of Atonement (Yom Kippur), when
repentance and forgiveness took place.
At the beginning of winter, a post-
biblical festival, Hanukkah, ("dedication")
commemorates the rededication of
the Temple after the victory of the
Maccabees. At the end of winter,
Purim celebrates deliverance from
the murderous plans of Haman in
the book of Esther (*see pp.166–67*).

An additional weekly feast was
the Sabbath. Beginning at sundown
with a family meal, it marked the
division between rest and work, and
highlighted the people's dependence
upon God alone.

**PREPARATIONS FOR THE FESTIVAL**
*A street stall in Israel laden with decorations
during the festival of Purim. Purim means "lots,"
a reference to Haman's cruelty in drawing
lots to see when the Jews would die.*

## SUKKOT

*The Festival of Tabernacles, or Sukkot, became linked to the time after the escape from Egypt. During this period, the Israelites lived nearly 40 years in the wilderness in shelters or "tabernacles," commemorated today in the building of shelters (see left). As the feast of Weeks followed Passover, it became attached to the story of the giving of the Law to Moses at Sinai, which took place seven weeks after the escape from Egypt (Exod. 19:1ff.).*

## THE AGRICULTURAL YEAR

The connection of the main festivals with the rhythm of the seasons suggests an agricultural setting for the three main festivals. The earliest calendars in Exodus 23:14–17 and Exodus 34:18–24 confirm this. The Feast of Unleavened Bread, which later became part of Passover, is described as a thank-offering at the beginning of the grain harvest. The Festival of Weeks, 50 days later, was held to celebrate the end of the grain harvest. Tabernacles was an autumn thanksgiving for the wine harvest. Such agricultural associations pre-suppose a time after the settlement, when a people tilled the land and survived on the crops. However, it is likely that some earlier pastoral rites lie behind at least two festivals. Being common practices among nomadic peoples, these festivals would have originated in presettlement times. Thus the offering to God of the firstborn spring lamb at Passover would have been in order to gain protection for the rest of the flock during the search for pasture in the dry summer months. It is possible that the sending away of the Scapegoat, on the Day of Atonement, laden with the sins of the people, may have had its origins in an earlier custom of sending a goat into the wilderness to placate the desert demons, and thus guaranteed the protection of the herd.

## THE NATION AND MORALITY

These local harvest festivals gradually took on a historical significance; they became pilgrimage occasions when the people heard their early history narrated at a central shrine. This created a sense of national bonding. The story in 2 Kings 23 concerning King Josiah's reinstatement of the Passover festival at Jerusalem is one example of this, as also are the laws about keeping the Passover in Deuteronomy 16:1–17. Although some festivals and feasts did not originally have historical associations, all were eventually given them: indeed one of the distinguishing aspects of Israelite religion is the setting of its religious observances within the history of the people and their God. In addition, this history brought particular obligations: the moral element is another distinctive characteristic of Israelite religion. In Deuteronomy, feasts are also an occasion for sharing food with the poor (ch.16).

## FASTING

This is a discipline where people abstain from food, drink, and physical pleasures, in penitence for sin, in commemoration of national tragedies, or as an offering to God. The most important fast is the Day of Atonement (Yom Kippur). Four disasters, later commemorated by fasts, are mentioned in the Bible: 10 Tevet, the beginning of the siege of Jerusalem (2 Kgs. 25:1), which led to the destruction of the first Temple; 17 Tammuz (commemorating the breach in the Wall); 9 Av (the destruction of the First and Second Temples; and 3 Tishri (the fast of Gedeliah, Jer. 40–43). The fast of petition can be seen in Esther 4:16–17.

## HANUKKAH

*The Temple was rededicated after being desecrated by the Seleucid powers in the late second century BCE (1 Macc. 4:52–59; see pp.258–59); the importance of light arises because when only a one-day supply of oil remained, it kept burning miraculously throughout an eight-day period.*

### NEW YEAR FOR TREES
*In the image above, a young girl is seen planting a tree to celebrate the festival of the "New Year for Trees" (Hebrew Tu bishvat). This minor Jewish festival falls on the 15th day of the month of Shvat in the early spring.*

For further reading see bibliography numbers: 470, 767, 777

# THE BOOK OF
# NUMBERS

*Numbers relates events during Israel's journey through the desert from Mount Sinai to the borders of Canaan, the "Promised Land." The book tells of Israel's "wilderness experience," a journey that was both geographical and spiritual.*

THE major theme of the book of Numbers is the journey of the people of Israel from a lack of faith in God and in their leaders, including rebellion against them, through the consequences of punishment and suffering, leading to acceptance of their destiny as God's people and preparation for a new life. The first ten chapters represent the ideal structure of the encampment, the Tabernacle, and the march. The next chapters show how the realities of life intrude upon this ideal scene. The book contains many different types of writing: narratives, poetry, songs, prayers, prophecy, blessings, laws, and lists. While this can seem confusing at first, the book's major theme of the people's journey is carried forward with great vigor.

## LISTS AND LEGISLATION

The narrative of the people's journey through the wilderness is interspersed with dense genealogical, geographical, and legal material, much of it in the form of lists: peoples, laws, and places are "numbered" throughout the book. The book begins with a census of the adult males, listing tribes, leaders, offspring, and their appointed ranks. It records the specific arrangements for encampment around the sanctuary and the sacrifices offered at its dedication. A second census takes place, and the precise boundaries of the Promised Land are defined. The purpose of such details seems to be to establish continuity with the past – with the figures of the earlier period of the Ancestors – and with the future. They provide a historical basis for the division of the land and the tribal confederation into which Israel is organized in the later period of the Judges; they also legitimize later institutions and rituals. Much of the later material is continuous with that found elsewhere in the Pentateuch. In Numbers, however, it is not presented in a systematic way, as the Holiness Code is in Leviticus (*pp. 62–63*), but it is more integral with the narrative of the people's journey through the wilderness and is often determined by the events of the narrative. For example, elaborate laws governing the duties and rights of the priests and Levites arise in the aftermath of the rebellion led by Korah; the law of female inheritance is told through the story of Zelophehad's daughters; laws relating to open and deliberate violation of a commandment, acting "with a high hand," is illustrated by the case of the man caught gathering wood on the Sabbath ("*But whoever acts high-handedly, whether a native or an alien, affronts the* LORD, *and shall be cut off from among the people*," 15:30). These and other miscellaneous laws, such as those relating to daily and festival sacrifices, cities of refuge, and the making of vows, reflect a settled society and tell us much about its structure and values.

THE WILDERNESS
*Various physical features of the Sinai peninsula may be reflected in the biblical account of the journey through the wilderness: mudflats in the desert do occasionally collapse (cf. Num. 16:31–32), and the porous limestone of the area can even hold water (cf. Num. 20: 2–13).*

## DISSATISFACTION AND REBELLION

The themes of challenge to the leadership of Moses and of rebellion punctuate the book. The people's dissatisfaction begins to surface early on. Aaron and Miriam, the brother and sister of Moses, openly express disapproval of him, and the spies who return with reports from Canaan foment unrest and "murmuring" (14:2).

As punishment for their lack of faith, the generation who experienced the Exodus are condemned to wander in the wilderness until all have died. Korah, Dathan, and Abiram attempt a serious rebellion, and, in the divine punishment that follows, many lose their lives ("*The earth opened its mouth and swallowed them up, along with their households — everyone who belonged to Korah and all their goods. So they with all that belonged to them went down alive into Sheol; the earth closed over them, and they perished from the midst of the assembly ... And fire came out from the LORD and consumed the two hundred and fifty men offering incense,*" 16:32–35). The final revolt is the betrayal of YHWH for a Moabite god. The ensuing plague destroys 24,000 people (25:9). As a result, a new census is required, and this proves to be a turning point: it numbers the new generation, and it introduces a people more directed in their preparations to enter the Promised Land under their new leader, Joshua.

## DIFFICULTIES AND CONTRIBUTIONS

Numbers is considered a difficult book for several reasons: the diverse nature of its material, the apparent lack of structure or an obvious unifying theology, and the statistical listings and legislative information that interrupt the smooth flow of the narrative. In a different way, questions are raised by the acceptance of violence as a means to God's end and purpose (*cf.* the issue of cities given over to destruction, *pp.88–89, 93*). The context in Numbers makes it clear that God's justice cannot live with rebellion and apostasy, yet even so, God leads the people on. Thus, the theme of spiritual development through trial may be the key to understanding this book.

## NUMBERS AND JEWISH RITUAL

Numbers has contributed two essential elements of Jewish liturgy and practice. The passage (15:37–41) in which God commands the wearing of "tzitzit," or fringes, as a daily reminder to observe the commandments, "so that you shall be holy," is part of the central prayer, the Shema (*pp.82–83*). The blessing that Aaron and his sons are commanded to recite over Israel ("*The LORD bless you and keep you; the LORD make his face to shine upon you, and be gracious to you; the LORD lift up his countenance upon you, and give you peace,*" 6:24–26) has become part of synagogue and home ritual: one who so mediates the divine blessings to others must do so with love.

# THE BOOK

TITLE: Numbers (from the Latin title)

HEBREW TITLE: Known as *BeMidbar*, "in the wilderness"; it is also referred to as *Homesh Happiqqudim*, "that part of the Pentateuch dealing with the numbering of the Israelites"

DATE AND AUTHORSHIP: *See* Composition of the Pentateuch, *pp.22–23*

# THE CONTENTS

**CHAPTERS 1–6**
The census of Israel (ch.1); the arrangement of the camp (ch.2); the numbering of the Levites and the census of the clans (chs.3–4); various laws (cleanliness, wives, Nazirites); the priestly blessing (chs.5–6)

**CHAPTERS 7–12**
Consecration of the Tabernacle and of the Levites (chs.7–8); Passover, the cloud of God's presence; the silver trumpets (chs.9–10:10); Israel leaves Sinai and is fed on quail (chs.10:11–11); Aaron and Miriam complain against Moses (ch.12)

**CHAPTERS 13–17**
Spies in Canaan; the rebellion of the people (chs.13–14); various laws (offerings, sin, dress) (ch.15); rebellion of Korah, Dathan, and Abiram; Aaron's staff (chs.16–17)

**CHAPTERS 18–25**
Priestly duties (chs.18–19); death of Miriam; water from the rock; Edom refuses entry; death of Aaron; defeat of Arad; the bronze snake (20–21:19); the Moabites and Balaam (21:20–25:18)

**CHAPTERS 26–30**
A census; Zelophehad's daughters; Joshua as Moses' successor (chs.26–27); laws on sacrifices and offerings (chs.28–30)

**CHAPTERS 31–36**
Defeat of Midian; summary of the journey; plans to conquer Canaan (31–35:5); cities of refuge (35:6–34); inheritance of daughters (ch.36)

# KEY THEMES

*The Promised Land and the journey toward it*

•

*The faithfulness of God*

•

*Rebellion, complaints, and human weakness*

For further reading see bibliography numbers: 94, 150, 193, 230, 494, 602, 605

# THE WILDERNESS

*After the Exodus from Egypt, the people of Israel spent 40 years in the wilderness of the Sinai peninsula before arriving in Canaan, the Promised Land. They are prepared for life in a new covenant with God.*

### MANNA
The inhospitable nature of the Sinai is clear from its arid aspect. During their sojourn in the desert, the Israelites lived on quails, small birds, and manna, a flaky breadlike food that they found each morning lying on the ground like dew. On the sixth day they gathered twice the usual amount, providing them with food for the Sabbath.

THE material relevant to the Wilderness Period is not found in a continuous narrative but is spread throughout the books of Exodus, Leviticus, and Numbers. Far from a period of aimless wandering, the accounts describe a physical and spiritual journey and events that were crucial to the development of Israel as a nation and to its understanding of its relationship with God. The story as it now stands in these books has been assembled from different sources, and it is no longer possible to reconstruct the history of the period as a whole. Indeed, some think that the major elements did not originally belong together, and that not only the collection of laws but also the events came from different parts of the kinship (family) group. Thus some believe that

the Sinai revelation may not originally have belonged with the rest of the wilderness stories. However, for Israel and its faith, the story is now inextricably bonded into a single whole. As a motif, the wilderness expresses hardship and testing in inhospitable, often dangerous, surroundings, but it is also a neutral space, where the old can be discarded and the new can be instituted and practiced.

## A PERIOD OF TRANSITION
Jewish tradition understands the Israelites' experience in the wilderness as a necessary period of transition. The Exodus from Egypt catapulted into freedom people who had been born into slavery; their psychological adjustment, however, took longer. It required time for them to relinquish the old and familiar ways, to understand and accept the demands of their new life under God's direction, and to grow into the responsibilities of their freedom. The slaves whom Moses led out of Egypt become, by the end of their journey through the wilderness, the committed nation that stands ready to cross the Jordan River.

However, the journey from one state of mind to the other is not an easy one, and there are many crises along the way. Early anxieties concern pressing physical needs; these are resolved by the divine provision of food, in the form of quails and manna (a breadlike substance), and fresh water to drink. There is a simmering lack of trust in Moses' leadership that boils over into rebellion. Nostalgia for old gods, for the lost security of the familiar, culminates in a determined episode of idolatry with a Golden Calf when Moses' back is

### BEDOUIN
*The nomadic tribes of the Middle East are mainly animal herders who move into the desert during the rainy season and return to cultivated land in the dry summer months. Religion is an important part of bedouin life, as it was for the Israelites; elements of bedouin custom are traceable in early Israelite life.*

**THE ENCAMPMENT AT THE WELL (NUM. 21:16)**
*The mosaic above comes from Dura-Europos, an ancient synagogue in Iraq, dating from c.245BCE.*

turned, and later a flirtation with a Canaanite god. The divine response to these episodes is severe: many people are executed or die in plagues, fires, and earthquakes. Yet throughout their journey the people are accompanied by a pillar of smoke by day and a pillar of fire at night, assurances of God's continuing presence, protection, and guidance.

## A PERIOD OF COMMITMENT

While the Israelite people were shaking off the past, they were also taking on a new identity. The central event of the Wilderness Period is God's revelation of Torah, the teaching of the law, at Mount Sinai. God's giving of Torah and the people's acceptance of its requirements – *"Everything that the LORD has spoken we will do"* (Exod. 19:8) – constitute a covenant between them and a defining moment in Israel's relationship with God. The people's positive acceptance of their role is the backdrop against which the episodes of backsliding, revolt, and uncertainty should be seen, for they are the birthpangs of this new relationship. In the wilderness, just as through their subsequent history, the people of Israel accept their destiny while struggling with its reality. On the whole, Jewish tradition views the Wilderness Period favorably. With the giving of the Torah at its heart, and with many treasured institutions such as the priesthood, the Levites, the Tabernacle, and the festivals of Sukkot and Shavu'ot all tracing their ostensible origins to this period, it has been regarded as a time of many blessings.

# THE FESTIVAL OF SUKKOT

*This festival falls in early autumn, in the Jewish month of Tishri, and lasts for seven days. Its background lies in a harvest festival, but later tradition associates it with the period of wandering in the wilderness.*

Sukkot is traditionally the time when the community of Israel could thank God for the bounty of the land and rejoice in the harvest safely gathered. Four items were used in the Temple ritual: palm, willow, citron, and myrtle. The ritual was connected to the Wilderness Period, when the Israelites lived in temporary dwellings. In commemoration of this, the central act of the festival became the building of, and living in, temporary shelters or huts (*sukkot*). Seventy bullocks were sacrificed, 13 on the first day, down to seven on the last day (Num. 29:12–35). Since 70 is the number of nations descended from Noah (Gen. 10), the number of animals was seen as being offered on behalf of all people, giving the festival a universal dimension.

In today's festival, the main symbols remain. It falls immediately after the Day of Atonement (Yom Kippur), and its characteristic flavor of celebration is welcome after the seriousness and introspection of that period. Many families build their own makeshift structure (*sukkah*), sufficient to

withstand rain and wind but through which the stars can be seen at night. For the seven days of the festival, it is used as a place to eat and even sleep. Some congregations build a communal *sukkah* where community meals can be held. The festival is also called Tabernacles (from the Latin).

**Inside the** *sukkah*
*The interior of the* sukkah, *where the family eats and even sleeps, is often hung with pictures and decorations.*

### FOUR SPECIES

During Sukkot, psalms of praise and thanksgiving are sung in the synagogue. The symbols of the Temple ritual, the four "species," are held aloft: an etrog (a sweet citrus fruit) and branches of palm, willow, and myrtle. Representing the presence of God in the four corners of the world, they are waved in six directions, to the four points of the compass and then above and below, toward Heaven and earth.

There is a custom to say a prayer over the four species before each meal in the *sukkah*.

For further reading see bibliography numbers: 6, 89, 131, 193, 230, 374, 402, 456, 559, 561, 588, 602, 775, 777

# FOLKLORE

## IN THE BIBLE

*The Bible is full of stories. Many of them originated as popular stories much loved by ordinary people and then were used to pass on information from generation to generation. Some of them have been identified as "folklore."*

THE word "folklore" means "folk-learning," and it applies to traditions and wisdom passed on by word of mouth from one generation to another. It thus involves traditional practices (including medicine and healing), but frequently it refers to stories, legends, myths, and proverbs. Often told for entertainment, these tales were also important for the education of the next generation in the ways and customs of the family or group. The relation of folklore to the Bible has been a controversial topic for more than a century. Some have used it as a term of abuse, and those who have wished to denigrate parts of the Hebrew Bible have referred to many of its stories as "no more than folklore," implying that "folklore" automatically suggested a primitive viewpoint, unconcerned with historical truth. The classic example of this approach was Sir James

Frazer's *The Golden Bough* (1890–1915), which brought together examples of such "primitivism" from all over the world; he applied this more specifically to the Hebrew Bible in his *Folklore in the Old Testament*. Much of Frazer's work consists of the uncritical comparison of popular customs as if to illustrate a primitive past that modern societies have left behind.

## THE ACCEPTANCE OF FOLKLORE

More recent studies of folklore have rejected this approach. The idea of a steady progress in human history, which has left the primitive behind, has been profoundly contradicted in the 20th century, with supposedly advanced societies engaging in horrific acts of genocide, and so-called primitive societies often demonstrating how well they are adapted to life in their local environments. This revaluing of the style of early forms of society has been reinforced by work in the sociology and the anthropology of religion. Studies have shown that folklore is a powerful way of conveying extremely profound beliefs about the nature of the world that we inhabit. Thus, to say that an item in the Bible comes from a background of folklore should no longer be regarded with suspicion. Folklore may be of great

## BALAAM'S DONKEY

The story of Balaam, a non-Israelite prophet, and his talking donkey is told in Numbers 22:1–24:25 (a prophecy of Balaam survives outside the Bible). Folklore records Balaam as a prophet who sold his prophecies to the highest bidder but could not see as much as his talking donkey (Num. 22). However, Balaam is also the prophet who foresees a Messiah (Num. 23–24).

value in preserving truths and insights about people's knowledge of God and of the world around them.

In light of this perception, there should be no embarrassment in describing, for example, Jacob's wrestling with the angel (Gen. 32:24ff.) or the story of Job based on, or reminiscent of, folklore. This reevaluation has been accompanied

JONAH AND THE WHALE
*Individuals being swallowed by sea monsters and surviving is a common theme in folklore. Such tales lead us to question the reasons why these people survived.*

by increased interest in the literary forms of folklore. Studies had already developed independently of biblical scholarship, but they were applied to the Bible – particularly through the work of the German scholar H. Gunkel. He made the distinction between "legends" and history writing, and he viewed such books as Genesis as primarily a collection of legends, many of them embodying popular folklore. This is a useful category for much of the material in the Hebrew Bible, such as the exploits of Samson (Judg. 13–16) or Jonah and the whale; it is less likely to be useful in the New Testament, which was compiled and composed over a shorter timespan.

## THE NEW TESTAMENT

In the New Testament, a few stories have been classified as legends, but it is difficult to see anything that came from a long tradition of folklore. However, such stories as that of the demon-possessed man and the herd of pigs (Mark 5:1–13) have certain folkloric elements.

It is helpful, therefore, when considering the relationship between the Bible and folklore to have two approaches in mind. One will concern particular themes and motifs: traditional stories, often involving supernatural beings or humans endowed with more than human qualities. The other is a more formal literary study, concerned with the proper classification and understanding of the biblical material.

JOB AND HIS BOILS
*The book of Job is a mixture of dramatic dialogue between God and Job, and folkloristic elements such as Job's affliction with boils.*

## MODERN STUDIES

Finally, it should be noted that much folklore study has concentrated on identifying basic motifs common to popular tales from many different cultures. A classic reference is Propp's *The Morphology of the Folktale* (1968), which is not directly concerned with the Bible, but has been used by many biblical scholars. The interest of folklore for biblical studies ranges widely. For some, it is still regarded with suspicion, as liable to weaken what they regard as the essential historicity of the Bible. Folklore may in fact transmit historical events, but its focus and interest are the story and the message it conveys.

### THE TOWER OF BABEL
*Many commentators have claimed that the form of the Tower of Babel was based on the ziggurats of ancient Mesopotamia (see pp.34–35). Like many stories in the early part of the Hebrew Bible, this tale is used to explain origins, in this case the origins of language.*

**For further reading see bibliography numbers:** 72, 79, 120, 255, 324, 353, 357, 461

# NUMBERS
## IN THE BIBLE

*Many numbers in the ancient Near East were given a significance that went far beyond a representation of quantity. Numbers were full of symbolic meaning and could also be used for a variety of theological purposes.*

FROM about the fourth millennium BCE, separate mathematical traditions evolved in Egypt and Mesopotamia that, at first, fulfilled a purely practical need in the societies of each region. The two systems were very different in a number of key respects: Egypt used a decimal system that, in its day-to-day form, employed separate signs for each of the units (1–9), tens (10–90), hundreds (100–900), and thousands (1,000–9,000); no zero was used. In Mesopotamia, the system was essentially sexagesimal – that is, based around units of 60 instead of ten; our system of hours, minutes, and seconds originates from this period. By the second millennium BCE, a system that used signs for one, ten, and (later) zero was in place.

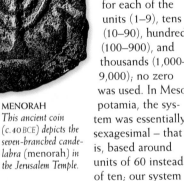

**MENORAH**
*This ancient coin (c. 40 BCE) depicts the seven-branched candelabra (menorah) in the Jerusalem Temple.*

## COMPLEX SYSTEMS

Both Egypt and Mesopotamia developed quite sophisticated techniques of arithmetic and geometry, along with an interest in mathematics that went beyond the purely functional. Together with that of Greece, these systems exerted a long-lasting influence on the Near East and, ultimately, the rest of the world. Israel was not alone in this respect: Egyptian numerals are found in early Israelite documents, while the many multiples of 60 found in the Bible and Apocrypha (2 Sam. 2:31; cf. Neh. 7:66) suggest the influence of Mesopotamia's sexagesimal system. There is little direct evidence of Israelite mathematics, although 1 Kings 7:23 indicates knowledge of the approximate relationship between the diameter and circumference of a circle.

## SIGNIFICANT NUMBERS

Many numbers have symbolic or theological significance. The number three is often associated with the Trinity: Jesus tells his disciples to *"make disciples of all nations, baptizing them in the name of the Father and of the Son and of the Holy Spirit"* (Matt. 28:19). Three is also associated with God's actions.

**THREE INTO ONE**
*Three fish together represent the Trinity: the Father, the Son, and the Holy Spirit. The fish is also a symbol of Jesus and, later, of Christians.*

**RULE OF THREE**
*The dimensions of Solomon's Temple were elaborated in later tradition and symbolic meanings were assigned to them.*

For instance, it was on the third day that God came down upon Mount Sinai to deliver the Ten Commandments (Exod. 13:11); Hosea told the people that God would raise them *"on the third day"* (Hos. 6:2). Mathematics may possibly explain the strong interest shown by Jewish and Mesopotamian writers in the number seven – the first

**FORTY DAYS IN THE WILDERNESS**
*The number 40 is associated with many acts of salvation. Jesus fasted in the wilderness for 40 days and 40 nights prior to his temptation (Matt. 4:2).*

of the Babylonian "prime" numbers – which is indivisible by two, three, or five. It will hardly explain, though, the use of the number seven to suggest a figure "beyond counting." When Peter asks Jesus how many times he should forgive a sinner, Jesus replies, *"Not seven times, but, I tell you, seventy-seven times"* (Matt. 18:22; cf. Sir. 20:12). The derivation of some significant numbers is obvious. For example, Enoch lived for as many years as there are days in a year (Gen. 5:23). More often, we can only observe the use of, and relationship between, such numbers without being able to pinpoint the origin of their significance. We may note, for instance, that 40 is often used as a measure of significant time: the Flood lasted for 40 days, and Moses was on Mount Sinai for 40 days. Similarly, 40 years apparently represented a generation – the length of time spent by Israel in the wilderness, the conventional period of Israel's rests and captivity in Judges, and of David and Solomon's reigns.

Twelve Tribes of Israel, but the names of the disciples (and of the tribes) may vary between lists. Chronology in the Hebrew Bible may have been adapted to represent "significant" periods, so that, for example, the founding of the Temple is set 480 years (40 x 12 years) after the Exodus. Apocalyptic literature shows a strong interest in the division of history into such periods.

**THE FLOOD**
*"… the windows of the heavens were opened. The rain fell on the earth for forty days and forty nights"* (Gen. 7:11–12).

## SIGNIFICANT PERIODS

Numbers were also used to relate events to each other; for instance, Jesus' 40 days in the wilderness reflected Israel's time of testing in the wilderness. In such cases, the number sometimes seemed more important than the people or places counted. For instance, there were clearly 12 disciples, reflecting the

## BIBLE "CODES"

Through the assignment of numbers to gods and particular words, Mesopotamian scribes were able to connect numbers and words, and to manipulate the words mathematically and cryptographically. In this way, King Sargon II could proclaim that the dimensions of a city were "the number of his name." Similar techniques became possible in Judaism after the second century BCE, when special numerals were replaced by letters. Thereafter, like the Greeks, the Jewish people used letters as numbers in the order of the alphabet, so that *Aleph* = 1, *Beth* = 2, and so on. By reading letters as

numbers, and adding or manipulating the values of each, words could be said to have a particular numerical value. This allowed the encoding of words. Thus the number 666 in Revelation 13:18 is believed to encode in Hebrew letters the name of the persecutor Nero. At the same time, the use of letters as numbers allowed early Jewish and Kabbalistic interpreters to seek quasi-mathematical relationships between words and to draw out meanings supposedly hidden in the text. "Code-breaking" remains popular among some readers of the Bible, who often ignore its complicated textual history to seek messages by, for example, taking every *n*th letter. Although the biblical writers often did use numbers in a very symbolic way, it is certain that they did not put hidden codes into the text.

**THE DEVIL**
*In Revelation, the horned beast caused people to be marked on their right hand or forehead with the number 666.*

For further reading see bibliography numbers: 232a, 311, 558a

# MONEY & MEASUREMENT
## IN THE BIBLE

*Coins did not become a recognized medium of exchange in the ancient Near East
until the seventh century BCE. Systems of weights and measures varied between
districts, and different systems may also have been merged over time.*

UNTIL the seventh century BCE, most trade was based on barter. Various goods were used in commercial transactions, including staple commodities such as wheat, barley, wine, metal, and timber. Livestock and precious metals – gold, silver, iron, and bronze – were often used to assess wealth. In New Testament times, official Roman money, provincial coins, and local Jewish coins were all in circulation in Palestine (*see p.371*).

JEWELER'S SCALES
*This painting from the tomb of the Egyptian king, Amenhotep III (1417–1379 BCE)
in Thebes, depicts a jeweler in his workshop, weighing a piece of jewelry.*

## UNITS OF WEIGHT

In the Hebrew Bible, the basic unit of weight was the *shekel*, for which surviving stone weights – carved into shapes that made them easily recognizable – indicate a value of about $2/5$ ounce (11.4 grams). Half a shekel was called a *beka*, while one-twentieth was a *gerah*; the *pym* weight mentioned in 1 Samuel 13:21 may have been two-thirds of a shekel. For larger quantities, the *talent*, equivalent to 3,000 shekels, was also used, as, occasionally, was the *mina*, equivalent to 50 shekels. A number of weights were inscribed with the term *netseph*, a unit of 0.32–$1/3$ ounces (9–10 grams), which was slightly less than the shekel.

ANCIENT WEIGHTS
*A shekel was the principal unit of weight
in ancient biblical times. These silver
shekels, and the oil lamp with which
they were found, date from 66–70CE.*

In New Testament times, Roman measures were associated with older units of weight. The Roman pound weighed approximately $11\frac{1}{2}$ ounces (326 grams). It was equivalent to 84 *denarii* at the time of Augustus but increased to 96 denarii during the reign of Nero. In Palestine, two denarii became equal to one shekel. A mina of 50 shekels weighed approximately 12 ounces (340 grams), while a talent of 3,000 shekels weighed about 45lbs (20.4 kilograms).

These equivalences did not prevail everywhere, and, at times, the shekel seems to have been identified with the Tyrian *tetradrachma*, which weighed approximately $1/2$ ounce (14.2 grams).

## MEASURES OF VOLUME

In ancient times, liquids were most probably measured using a system whereby one *bath* of $5\frac{1}{3}$–8 gallons (20–30 liters) was equal to four *hin* or 48 *log*. However, the hin came to be identified with the *ephah*, and both the hin and the log may have been redefined. In the New Testament, the *quart* (Rev. 6:6) is probably about 2 pints (1 liter), and the bushel (Matt. 5:15) equivalent to approximately 17 pints (8 liters).

## UNITS OF AREA AND CAPACITY

Land was generally measured in terms of the area plowed or seeded per day (a yoke). We do not know the precise area of a yoke in Israel, but the Romans estimated it to be approximately three-fifths of an acre. A *seah* of seed would probably have been required to cover 2,500 square cubits of land (*see box, right*). In Isaiah's song about the unfruitful vineyard, *"ten acres of vineyard shall yield but one bath, and a homer of seed shall yield a mere ephah"* (Isa. 5:10).

Many units of capacity are mentioned in the Hebrew Bible, although some of their values are unclear. For instance, the *homer* – in theory, an ass-load – must have been equivalent to about three to six bushels; the ephah was one-tenth of a homer, and the *omer* or *issaron* was one-hundredth of a homer. Other measures included the *lethech*, approximately half a homer, the *kor*, which came to be identified with the homer, the seah, probably one-thirtieth of a kor, and the *kab*, one-sixth of a seah.

**EARLY COINS**
*This is one of the first Jewish coins, struck in the land of Israel c.333BCE. It bears the Hebrew inscription yehud – the Aramaic name of the Persian governor of Judea at that time.*

# LINEAR MEASURES

The principle unit of length in the Hebrew Bible was the cubit – approximately the length of an arm from the elbow to the fingertips. The precise value of the Israelite cubit is uncertain, but it varied from 17–21 inches (44–53cm). A span – the width of a hand from the tip of the thumb to the tip of the little finger – was taken to be half a cubit, while the handbreadth was equivalent to the width of the four fingers at the point where they join the palm. The New Testament refers to the fathom (Acts 27:28), which was equal to four cubits, and the *stadion* or furlong, probably equal to 360 cubits. Reference is also made to the Roman mile (Matt. 5:41), which was approximately 4,855 feet (1,480m) in length.

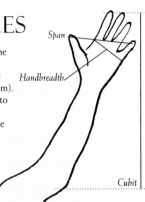

# MONETARY UNITS

Although most trade in ancient times was based on barter, silver and other metals could also be used as a convenient medium of exchange. Monetary units were not units of currency in the modern sense but were, effectively, units of weight. Coins first appeared in Palestine during the fifth century BCE and were introduced as a way to guarantee the purity and weight of metal. Coins issued by many different authorities were used side by side, which makes it difficult to identify some of the coins mentioned. This seems rarely to have been a problem for the ancient Jews, except when they paid their annual Temple tax in Tyrian silver *didrachmas*, obtained from the money-changers in the Temple (Matt. 21:12).

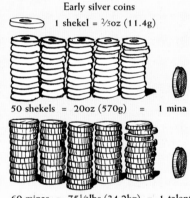

Early silver coins

1 shekel = ²⁄₅oz (11.4g)

50 shekels = 20oz (570g) = 1 mina

60 minas = 75½lbs (34.2kg) = 1 talent

# WEIGHTS AND MEASURES

Only basic, standardized weights and measures were used in the ancient Near East. Stone weights were often carved into characteristic shapes such as animals or birds. Larger weights were used by merchants to weigh commodities including gold, silver, and bronze. These weights did not constitute an integrated system and can be given only approximate values in modern terms.

10 gerahs ⟶ 1 bekah (or 1 denarius)

¹⁄₅oz (5.7g)

2 denarii ⟶ 1 shekel

²⁄₅oz (11.4g)

50 shekels ⟶ 1 mina

20oz (570g)

3,000 shekels ⟶ 1 talent

75½lbs (34.2kg)

**METAL WEIGHTS**
*Before coins were invented, a currency of established weight and value, such as these ingots, was used.*

For further reading see bibliography numbers: 87, 625

# THE BOOK OF
# DEUTERONOMY

*Deuteronomy continues the wilderness story from Sinai to the death of Moses.*
*As well as laws, it contains a vision of history and of the relationship between*
*God and the people, which has influenced many other parts of the Bible.*

D EUTERONOMY is essentially a book of speeches and laws, brought together under the watchword "covenant" (Hebrew *berith*). A covenant was part of a treaty-form often used in ancient times, whereby the Suzerain or Overlord (here, YHWH) promised to protect his vassals (here, Israel) on condition that they give him their full allegiance. The treaty-form is set out as 1) preliminary address (4–11); 2) laws and obligations (12–26); and 3) blessings and curses in relation to breaking the Covenant (27–28). The section 4:44–28:68, thus makes up the core of the book.

## LINKS WITH
## HISTORICAL BOOKS

The three speeches in the book (chs.1–3; 7–10; 29–30) resemble the rhetoric and theology of other speeches, such as that in Joshua 1 (Moses), Joshua 24 (Joshua), 1 Samuel 12 (Samuel), 2 Samuel 7 (Nathan), and 1 Kings 8 (Solomon). Such associations with the narrative Joshua–2 Kings suggest some literary and thematic unity between Deuteronomy and these books, which are sometimes called the "Deuteronomistic history." If Joshua–2 Kings is seen as "preached history," then Deuteronomy is "preached law." The law sets the ideal; the Historical books show the consequences of failing to meet that ideal in reality: thus, these two sections of the Hebrew Bible belong together. The first of the legal collections (chs.4–6; 12–26) centers on the Decalogue or Ten Commandments (*see pp.56–57*), in Deuteronomy 5. This has a parallel form in Exodus 20; parts of Deuteronomy are a

**MOSES HOLDING THE TABLETS OF STONE**
*Rembrandt's portrait of Moses shows him holding up the tablets of stone with the Ten Commandments.*

later expansion, although the structure and form are the same. The second legal collection in chapters 12–26 has many correlations with an early law code in Exodus 20:22–23:19, known as the "Book of the Covenant," and it seems likely that the Deuteronomistic Code is again a later adaptation; it explains ancient law and applies it to later life, being close to the Prophets in their social and humanitarian concerns.

## MISCELLANEOUS
## MATERIAL

The miscellaneous material (chs.11, 27, 28, 31, 32, 33, 34) develops the covenant theme further, part prose and part ancient poetry (chs.27, 28, 32, 33). These passages provide good examples of the composite growth of this book. Chapter 31, which speaks of the reading of this "second law" every seven years at the Covenant Renewal Festival, illustrates how the traditions might have been preserved in the liturgical life of the people. The book served many purposes: with its prophetic, liturgical, and didactic concerns, it embraces both public and private interests and appears to have been preserved for teaching purposes in family and court circles alike. These dual interests are especially evident in the two legal collections. By contrast, the speeches are crafted to address the whole "community," whether family or nation, in more general terms. For example, chapters 4–6 emphasize the importance of keeping the Covenant in family life. The last six of the Ten Commandments (Deut. 5:12–21), on respect for one's neighbor, make clear that the well-being of society is achieved by means of a secure family life – the honoring of parents, marriage, property, and resting from work. Similarly, the Shema (*see pp. 82–83*) has the same family interests: teaching takes place within the family (Deut. 6:4–9). So too does the creed in 6:20–25. The importance of the family is also stressed in many of the laws in chapters 12–26, particularly those in the latter part of the Code. One key vision is of a people bound together under the covenant of family bonds: and may well account for the survival of the book after the end of the nation under their king in 587/6BCE.

## THE CONCERNS OF THE NATION

Nevertheless, national and institutional concerns are also evident. The Law Code in 12–26 begins and ends with the law about making pilgrimage to one central sanctuary (later seen as Jerusalem), and was probably designed to correct heterodox worship in local sanctuaries (*"You must demolish completely all the places where the nations whom you are about to dispossess served their gods, on the mountain heights, on the hills, and under every leafy tree,"* 12:2). The instructions about the accountability of prophets, judges, priests, military leaders, and especially the king to the laws of God reveal a more public moral concern. These parts of Deuteronomy see a people bound together under their leader in the worship of one God. In this way Deuteronomy safeguarded the people's loyalty to their God by appealing to them both in the public and private domain.

## COMPOSITION AND TRADITION

The book of Deuteronomy was perhaps first compiled at sanctuaries, such as Shechem and Shiloh in the north; after the fall of the Northern Kingdom in 722BCE, it would have been taken down to Judah. From the accounts in 2 Kings 22–23, the book seems to have been popularized after 621BCE during the reign of King Josiah. It is possible that all or part of Deuteronomy was the law book discovered during the restoration of the Temple during the reign of Josiah (2 Kgs. 22:8–10). Although some laws became difficult to obey, they were still carefully preserved. For example, once the Temple had been destroyed, it became impossible to make any pilgrimage to the Jerusalem sanctuary (Deut. 12); once the Monarchy had ceased, the laws about the king (Deut. 17) were anachronistic; and when the political situation changed dramatically under the Persians, the laws on the total destruction of the enemy in war (Deut. 20) could no longer be applied. But the essence of the book of Deuteronomy has endured – the worship of one God (monotheism), and a humanitarian concern for the well-being of the community – the hallmark of both Jewish and Christian religions.

## THE BOOK

**TITLE**: Deuteronomy. From the Greek title *to deuteronomion* meaning "the second law," probably a reference to Deuteronomy 17:18, which refers to the need to make "a copy of this law"

**HEBREW TITLE**: *Debarim* (from the first line, "These are the words [*debarim*] that Moses spoke")

**DATE**: Set at the same time as *Leviticus* and *Numbers*, in the Wilderness Period

**AUTHORSHIP**: The book is presented as the last will and testament of Moses, addressing the people on the plains of Moab just before his death and before their promised entry into the land over the Jordan River (1:1; 3:1). The contents of the sermons and the laws throughout the book reflect the concerns of a settled people. The book is most probably *composite*, that is, the work of several authors

## THE CONTENTS

**CHAPTERS 1–11**
1–3 Moses first speech
4–6 Introduction to the Decalogue and the Covenant commands; 7 Instructions for the conquest of Canaan
8 Reminder to obey God
9 Reminder of Israel's disobedience;
10–11 The Ten Commandments on stone and obedience

**CHAPTERS 12–26**
12 Centralization of worship
13 Other gods and false prophets; 14–18 Laws on worship, kings, and priests
19–25 Laws on community life; 26 Two rituals and a covenant warning

**CHAPTERS 27–34**
27–28 Blessing and curses of the Covenant; 29–30 Moses' third speech: "the Moabite Covenant"; 31 Succession of Joshua; the seven-year reading of the Law; 32 The Song of Moses; 33 The Blessing of Moses; 34 The Death of Moses

## KEY THEMES

*God's willingness to enter into a covenant*

•

*The need to keep and renew the Covenant*

•

*The Promised Land*

For further reading see bibliography numbers: 182, 309, 532, 587, 598, 618, 621, 622, 635, 687, 787

# THE SHEMA

*The words of Deuteronomy 6:4–9 are called the Shema, a foundational biblical text within Judaism. It is so called because of its opening word in Hebrew, shema, meaning "hear." Christians have also regarded the words as a summary of the heart of their faith.*

THE book of Deuteronomy (pp. 80–81) is central to the understanding of God and God's dealings with Israel, and the Shema lies at the heart of Deuteronomy. It is the beginning of Moses' exposition of the Covenant between God and Israel. It follows the Ten Commandments after Moses has been appointed as spokesman (i.e., a "prophet") for God (Deut. 5:22–33). Observant Jews recite these words in their morning and evening prayers (in line with Deut. 6:7, *"talk about them … when you lie down and when you rise"*). They have often made these words their last at the moment of death. When asked which was the most important commandment, Jesus replied with the words of the Shema (*see* Mark 12:28–34). The claim of these words – that a total, undivided, and unreserved response to God is the only appropriate response – is, in one way or another, the foundation of Judaism, Christianity, and Islam. Because the verb "to be" is usually understood in Hebrew, the opening words of the Shema can be translated with slight variations; thus: "YHWH [i.e., the LORD] is our God, YHWH alone" or "is one." The translation of the Jewish Publication Society has: "The LORD is our God, the LORD alone."

> **❝ Hear, O Israel:**
> **The LORD is our God**
> **the LORD alone. You shall**
> **love the LORD your God**
> **with all your heart,**
> **and with all your soul,**
> **and with all your might. ❞**
>
> (Deuteronomy 6:4–5)

**OSTRACA**

*This pottery fragment, or ostraca, from the second century BCE is inscribed with the first Hebrew words of the Shema, "Hear O Israel!" This is the essence of the Jewish belief in one God, the essence of monotheism. The words of the Shema were often inscribed on amulets and written on the doorposts of Jewish buildings.*

## WHAT DOES THE SHEMA MEAN?

There have been numerous debates about the understanding and obeying of the Shema. First, what does it mean that the LORD is "the only one"? The most illuminating biblical parallel is Song of Songs 6:9, where the lover says of his beloved that she is "one." Although there are other queens, concubines, and maidens, this woman is unique as the object of love and praise. Similarly, the Shema summarizes the sense of the first two of the Ten Commandments, that the LORD is unique and so is to be the sole recipient of Israel's loyalty; beside the LORD, all other claimants for ultimate human loyalty are idols, false gods. Second, within Deuteronomy 6:5 the words are easily misunderstood. "Love" is not a matter of feeling but of doing (cf. Deut. 5:10, where "love" is linked with "keeping commandments"). In Hebrew thought, "heart" means the place of thinking (cf. Ps. 14:1), "soul" means the life and vitality of a person (Ps. 146:1–2). The only other use of the word "might" is in 2 Kings 23–25 where Josiah is presented as a model of fulfilling the Shema. In the context of Josiah's reform (2 Kgs. 22–23), "might" means something like "resources"; traditional rabbinic interpretation shrewdly understood "might" to be "money." Another question raised by the Shema is who is meant by Israel. It is clear who is meant in the time of Moses, but who is addressed now? Does Jew exhort fellow Jew to hear the word of God? One interpretation of the Midrash (the Jewish commentary) is to suggest that Israel is the ancestor Jacob and that in reciting the Shema the modern Jew reaffirms devotion to Jacob's teachings.

## HOW LITERAL IS THE SHEMA?

The instructions to attend constantly to the Shema (Deut. 6:6–9) have given rise to recurrent debates about how literally the instructions are to be taken, not least because other passages in the Hebrew Bible (e.g., Prov. 6:20–21) refer to "binding" commandments upon oneself in a figurative way. Whichever view is taken, it seems clear that what is envisaged is a range of symbolically significant actions demonstrating Israel's allegiance to the LORD. In original context, verse 8 – "*Bind them [the words of the Shema] as a sign on your hand, fix them as an emblem on your forehead*" – probably envisaged armbands and headbands, and verse 9 "*write them on the doorposts of your house and on your gates inscriptions*" on domestic doorposts and city gates. Early Jewish tradition interpreted the instructions in terms of phylacteries (cubical boxes containing the text of Deuteronomy 6:4–9 and other related texts, bound on the left arm and forehead at times of prayer) and *mezuzot* (containers with two of the same texts affixed to the doorpost).

In rabbinic tradition recitation of the Shema represents "accepting the yoke of the kingdom of heaven," a yoke that is not a burden but a privilege.

Wooden ark contains and protects scroll

Sacred Torah scroll

Prayer shawl

PRAYERS AT THE WESTERN WALL
*In the image right, Jews are shown praying at the Western Wall in Jerusalem. They hold aloft the Torah scroll, which may not be touched and is covered by a mantle or, as with these oriental Jews, by a wooden case.*

# THE BIBLICAL ATTITUDE TO TORAH

*In Judaism, Torah refers to the first five books of the Bible and is traditionally translated as "law." But this is misleading, especially if it is then used to make the claim that "Judaism is a legalistic religion."*

The word "Torah" comes from a Hebrew root meaning "to shoot at a target." Thus it means "to indicate a direction," and "teaching," "guidance" – and so may include specific laws (*torot*). The word can be used to denote a particular law or ritual; for example, the Torah of the burnt offering at Leviticus 6:8–9 (Heb. 6:2). But because Torah also refers to the Pentateuch, clearly much more than law is involved in the guidance of Israel.

In the Hebrew Bible the word "Torah" can be used for any instruction ascribed to God (e.g., Isa. 8:16; Jer. 18:18), but more specifically it refers to the "legislation" of Moses (Deut. 1:5; 4:8). The Bible claims that the content of this Torah is so rich that it should be constantly pondered and will be an unfailing source of wisdom (Josh. 1:7–8; Ps. 1:1–3) to those who study it. This belief in Torah as a unique source of inspiration and goodness is taken up elsewhere and becomes a distinctive note

of Hebrew spirituality in Psalms 19 and 119. In Psalm 119, the word "Torah" or a synonym is used in 173 of the 176 verses: the psalm is a love song of the delights and riches of Torah. It may not be accidental that the second main division of the canon, the books of the Prophets, begins with the injunction to Joshua to live by Torah (Josh. 1:2–9), while the third division, the Writings, begins with the psalmist's picture of the blessedness of the one who lives by Torah (Ps. 1:1–3). Although Torah is to be studied, it is not to be worshiped – this would be idolatry. As the Shema makes clear, there is only one God to worship. However, the Hebrew canon as a whole puts Torah at its heart (*see further pp. 24–25*).

### Morning prayer
*This devout Jewish man is shown in the act of praying. He wears a prayer shawl and strapped to his forehead is a phylactery, a cubical box containing the text of the Shema.*

For further reading see bibliography number: 113a

# BIBLICAL LAW
## IN THE PENTATEUCH

*"Law" usually translates as Torah but misleadingly so, because Torah is more literally the "instruction" or guidance given by God to Israel. More than simple sets of regulations, the laws demonstrate the justice of God and draw on a long tradition of law codes in the Near East.*

THE key sources for biblical law are Exodus 20–34, Leviticus, and Deuteronomy. The content ranges widely, but, broadly speaking, Leviticus focuses upon issues of purity and cult, as does Exodus 24–30. Deuteronomy and Exodus 20–23 include laws relating to religious practice but are also concerned with social and criminal matters. In each case, series of laws are presented as regulations given directly to Moses by God. More recently, though, the texts we now have are thought to date from no earlier than the Monarchic period (tenth century BCE), incorporating or adapting existing materials. These probably included earlier sets of laws, such as the Ten Commandments, or Decalogue (*see pp.56–57*), or the Holiness Code (Lev. 17–26), so it is not easy to identify the dates or interrelationship of the materials. Some codes may not have been generally known even after their composition. In 2 Kings 22, it is suggested that a law book had lain forgotten in the Temple until it was found during repairs.

READING THE LAW IN THE SYNAGOGUE
*The books of the Pentateuch, or Torah, are particularly sacred to Jews. Written on long scrolls of parchment, they are kept in a special container sometimes called an "ark."*

## FORM AND CONTENT

The laws of the Bible are expressed in two main ways: as conditional sentences, starting with "if" or "when" (*"When a man sells his daughter as a slave, she shall not go out as the male slaves do,"* Exod. 21:7), and as direct, general commands (*"You shall not steal,"* Exod. 20:15). The former identify the proper action to be taken in specific cases and are sometimes called "casuistic"; they resemble other Near Eastern law codes. The latter prescribe or prohibit particular actions and are sometimes called "apodeictic." Such laws are often formally indistinguishable from the advice given in wisdom literature (*see pp.170–71*). Religious regulation is not specifically separated from secular law, and both are combined with narrative or other material in the books of Exodus and Deuteronomy.

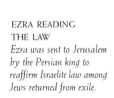

EZRA READING THE LAW
*Ezra was sent to Jerusalem by the Persian king to reaffirm Israelite law among Jews returned from exile.*

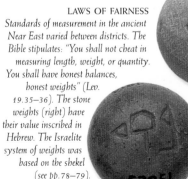

LAWS OF FAIRNESS
*Standards of measurement in the ancient Near East varied between districts. The Bible stipulates: "You shall not cheat in measuring length, weight, or quantity. You shall have honest balances, honest weights" (Lev. 19.35–36). The stone weights (right) have their value inscribed in Hebrew. The Israelite system of weights was based on the shekel (see pp.78–79).*

**LAWS OF OTHER NATIONS**
*The Bible shows many aspects of life that were regulated in the ancient Near East. This Babylonian tablet is inscribed with a charter for a grant of land.*

## NATURE AND SIGNIFICANCE

The biblical laws are not an all-embracing system of civil legislation, and many would have been difficult or impossible to enforce. They are presented as the agreed terms of a covenant between God and Israel. Furthermore, Deuteronomy 4:6–8 suggests that they are a model of wisdom, understanding, and righteousness, to be admired by the peoples of other nations. Considered in the light of law codes and attitudes to law found elsewhere in the ancient world, it seems likely that the social and criminal laws, at least, were

also intended to have a symbolic significance that went beyond their actual content. Where foreign kings promulgated law codes that advertised their justice and good stewardship to the people and the gods, Israel's laws shifted the basis of legal authority away from the king and demonstrated these same qualities in God. However, the various texts also reflect individual emphases upon what constitutes justice and right order, so that there are differences in, for example, the explan-ation for the Sabbath or the prescriptions for Passover (*cf.* Exod. 12:3–11 and 20:10 with Deut. 16:1–7 and 5:15), which embody more general differences in outlook. The laws are not, then, merely requirements to be met but are vehicles for religious thought and symbols of divine justice.

**SHOPPING FOR SABBATH**
*The importance of the Sabbath is clear from the Creation story in Genesis 2:2–3, and the law to keep the Sabbath holy is one of the Ten Command-ments. Among Orthodox Jews, cooking is forbidden on the Sabbath, and so the food is prepared and cooked beforehand and kept hot until needed.*

# NEAR EASTERN LAW CODES

*Israelite law had much in common with the laws of its neighbors; it shows these resemblances both in form and subject matter.*

As well as some Hittite collections, there are more than a dozen codes from Mesopo-tamia, dating from about the end of the third millennium BCE through the middle of the first millennium. The best known, the law code of Hammurabi, is broadly typical of the genre and was set out by King Hammurabi of Babylonia in the 18th century BCE.

The code's 282 laws (a number of which are no longer legible) are phrased in the "if/then" style, deal with very specific situations and are arranged by topic. The topics are limited in scope, and the coverage of each is far from comprehensive. Moreover, no reference is ever made to this code in any of the legal documents that survive from the time; indeed, none of the codes seems to have functioned as an authoritative guide for use in the courts. Each probably served to demonstrate that the king was performing his role properly. The prologue to Hammurabi's code lists his conquests, illustrating his competence in the military aspect of kingship, while he stresses that he has been a good and just shepherd to his people, protecting the weak and oppressed.

In that sense, such law codes are essentially royal propaganda, but they also have an instructional aspect, with the laws held up as models for future rulers to imitate. It is this element that gave them a more permanent value, and the code of Hammurabi was itself copied, read, and used as a model for more than 1,000 years.

For further reading see bibliography numbers: 43, 90, 104, 110, 115, 161, 276, 286, 297, 600, 611, 617, 723

# CRIME AND PUNISHMENT

## IN THE BIBLE

*In Israel's law, religious considerations are prominent: there may be offenses or "crimes" against God. But equally the Covenant requires appropriate behavior between humans, so that there are also crimes against human beings. It follows that there is little or no distinction between religious and secular offenses.*

LAW is embedded in Torah (pp.24–25), and Torah establishes the covenant relation between God and Israel. The people of Israel are called to observe the commandments given them by God, so that God is the source of all law and punishment. A whole category of punishment (*karet*, "cutting off" from the people) is believed to be exercised by God, by such means as early death or childlessness.

## CRIMES AGAINST OTHERS

Seen in this perspective, crimes against God, such as idolatry (the worship of other gods) and blasphemy, are particularly serious, since they are seen to pollute the land and people, thereby threatening the security of society as a

whole. However, the bulk of criminal law is taken up with offenses against individuals such as murder, personal injury and rape, kidnapping, theft, and damage to property. The discussion is often complex, dealing with a number of possible cases. To take the example of murder, the sixth Commandment, "you shall not kill," seems like a general principle, but the laws nevertheless

**STONING**
*The most common form of punishment was stoning, where the whole community took part in the punishment of the criminal. Such punishment was seen to have a deterrent effect: "the rest shall hear and be afraid, and a crime such as this shall never again be committed among you" (Deut. 19:20).*

make such distinctions as those between premeditated murder and accidental homicide. Thus in the case of those who have killed a person without intent, provision is made for six *"cities of refuge,"* to which they might flee from vengeful relatives (Num. 35:9–15; Deut. 19:1–6).

It is clear the legislators counted some actions as criminal that others might consider matters of civil law or private morality. Adultery (*see p.187*) is seen as a serious crime for which both the man and woman must be stoned to death, and the same penalty is deemed

**THE SCAPEGOAT**
*Mention is made in Leviticus 16:7–10 of the goat that was expelled from the community into the wilderness, taking the sins of the people with it. The sin-laden goat was sent to Azazel, a demonic figure whose name may mean "angry god."*

**THE SUPREME GOD**
*The idea of a divine being as the supreme judge was common in the ancient Near East. In Egypt, this belief was linked to the idea of life after death. Here the Egyptian Pharaoh holds Nubian, Syrian, and Libyan prisoners by the hair.*

appropriate for a persistently obstinate teacher who refuses to submit to the opinion of the highest judge of the time – because such alternative teaching destroys Israel (see Deut. 17:8–13). However, the law codes that we find in these first books of the Bible may represent an ideal rather than actual practice, and when we read of such cases elsewhere in the Hebrew Bible, we often find that such penalties were not rigorously applied.

## TYPES OF PUNISHMENT

In contrast to modern systems of justice, imprisonment was not used as a standard penalty in ancient Israel, although an offender might be kept in custody until the court decided the punishment (Num. 15:34). For the most serious crimes, such as murder, adultery, and idolatry, the death penalty was prescribed. Other punishments (in addition to *karet*, *see opposite*) were stoning (*see opposite*); exclusion from the community (*herem*, "the ban"); and corporal punishment, limited in Deuteronomy 25:3 to 40 lashes: *"Forty lashes may be given but not more; if more lashes than these are given, your neighbor will be degraded in your sight."* Fines and financial compensation were also used, as in Deuteronomy 22:13–19, where the man who falsely accuses his wife of adultery is fined by the elders, and verse 28, where a man who rapes a virgin pays her father compensation. Other penalties include the confiscation of property (Ezra 10:8), and the *lex talionis*, the law of retaliation: *"Show no pity: life for life, eye for eye, tooth for tooth, hand for hand, foot for foot"* (Deut 19:21; cf. Exod. 21:3–25; Lev. 24:20). This may sound severe, but it was originally intended to set a limit on the revenge taken by injured parties. It was often taken to mean financial compensation (as above), and in any case, in contrast to the code of Hammurabi, Deuteronomy 24:16 states that retaliation cannot be exacted from relatives, but only from the offender.

**THE STONING OF ACHAN**
*During the entry into the Promised Land, Achan "took some of the devoted things." As a result, the Israelite attack on Ai failed, and Achan and his family were stoned to death and burned (Josh. 7).*

of retribution against those who have offended. The role of the courts is to arbitrate retribution between the accused and the injured parties, establishing the facts of the case and making sure revenge is kept within strict limits. By contrast with other Near Eastern law codes, the law of the Bible often seems to display a more humanitarian or egalitarian concern for the individual, as, for example, in Exodus 21:26–27: *"When a slaveowner strikes the eye of a male or female slave, destroying it, the owner shall let the slave go, a free person, to compensate for the eye. If the owner knocks out a tooth of a male or female slave, the slave shall be let go, a free person, to compensate for the tooth."*

## OTHER NATIONS

The biblical law codes have connections with legal traditions in the ancient Near East but change them in the light of their own understanding of God and of God's justice (see pp.84–85). Criminal acts are breaches of an established moral code set down in law, and victims have the right

**COMPENSATION**
*The Bible requires that those guilty of certain crimes compensate their victims, often with goods four or five times the value of those stolen (see Exod. 22:1).*

**For further reading see bibliography numbers:** 110, 315, 558, 611, 617, 791

# WAR AND WARFARE
## IN ANCIENT ISRAEL

*In the Hebrew Bible, God is characterized as king of Israel and, therefore, like kings in the ancient Near East, as a warrior. The Bible interprets the wars of these kings as acts of rescue and of judgment.*

THE God who is Israel's king is a God who fights – one whose principal epithet, in fact, is "the LORD of hosts," the LORD of armies (1 Sam. 17:45; Isa. 1:24; Amos 5.27; Ps. 24:7–10). This theme of "God the Warrior" is prominent in the Exodus and conquest of Canaan, where cities and people are "de-voted" (Hebrew. *herem*) to God and thus to total destruction (*see p.93*).

## GOD'S WRATH

In this destruction, Israel is an instrument of God's wrath, a theme picked up in the Prophets (e.g., Amos 2:9) and the Psalms (e.g., Ps. 78:53–55). God conquers the land of Canaan and gives it to Israel – Israel's battle is God's battle. Later stories adopt the same attitude. When Israel acts as it should, it fights God's battles, not its own. The Israelites are merely the executors of God's battle plans. It is significant, then, that when 1 Samuel 8 repre-sents Israel's request for a human king as a rejection of divine kingship, so much of the emphasis should fall on the creation of a standing army for Israel's own use, rather than for God's.

### METAL WEAPON
*This vast sword dates from the time of the Ancestors (see pp.34–35). It comes from Beit Dagin, near Tel Aviv in modern Israel.*

## WAR AS JUSTICE

Divine kingship had a judicial nature: the ancient Near Eastern king was judge as well as warrior (e.g., 1 Kgs. 3:16–18). So too is the divine king of the Hebrew Bible a judge, regarded by worshipers as having ultimate jurisdiction over the whole world (e.g., Pss. 24; 82:1–4). When the Hebrew Bible speaks of war, therefore, talk of justice is never far away. An example is Judges 11, with its long preamble to the battle in verses 12–28, concerning the justice of the case; another is 2 Chronicles 20, where Jehoshaphat likewise prays in verses 6–12 for God's judgment. There is no "might is right" view of God in the Hebrew Bible: war is a judicial business (*cf. also* Joel 3:2; 9–21; Amos 1). Several implications follow. First, Israel's God could fight against Israel as well as on its side (e.g., 1 Sam. 4; Isa. 10:5–6; Jer. 25:9–11). Indeed, God never fought on Israel's side at all.

### BRONZE WARRIOR
*This bronze or copper figure holds a spear and a sickle sword, a weapon known throughout the ancient Near East. The warrior, naked except for his belt, probably comes from Syria and dates from about 2000–1750BCE.*

The question was always whether Israel was about to fight on God's side, the side of justice. If not, God could as easily use other nations to bring divine judgment against the wicked – who might include Israel. Second, the Hebrew Bible outlines rules of war. This is made explicit in Deuteronomy 20; 21:10–14, where laws forbid undue brutality against a besieged city, urge ecological awareness while a siege is

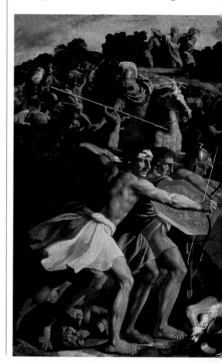

taking place, and put certain limits on the treatment of prisoners. If such specific rules did not apply when Israel dispossessed the Canaanites at the point of entry into the land (Deut. 20:16–18), it is nevertheless important to realize that this war too is presented as part of a judicial process.

Success in war was therefore dependent on God's favor. God was consulted before going to war, sacrifice was offered, and a degree of personal purification was required. This is shown in David's conversation with the priest Ahimelech (1 Sam. 21:4ff.). But war was to be valued less than building the society, so those who had begun essential domestic matters and not completed them (building a house, planting a vineyard, marrying) were exempt.

## THE AIM OF PEACE

If the reason for war is justice, then its aim is peace – the real peace that arrives in the aftermath of justice, and not at its expense. Peace is envisaged at various points in Israel's story (e.g., in the idyllic picture in 1 Sam. 7, where peace and justice both feature, or in the so-called Messianic oracles), but it came eventually to be expected only in the future, and not until after "the Day of the LORD" (p.241) when the kingdom of God finally arrives in all its fullness.

**SYRIAN SLINGER**
*This Syrian warrior is shown using a sling, perhaps similar to that used by David against Goliath. The relief comes from the royal palace at Tel Halaf and dates from the ninth century BCE.*

**JOSHUA'S VICTORY OVER THE AMALEKITES**
*God makes war on Israel's neighbors, bringing judgment on them for their sins. Although the Israelites are actively involved, as in Joshua's battle (left), they are simply the vehicles of divine wrath.*

**RAMESSES THE CHARIOTEER**
*God made war on the Egyptians to rescue the Israelites from oppression (e.g., Exod. 15:1–6). The Egyptians used light, swift chariots made of wood and leather. They were driven by esteemed individuals such as the Pharaoh Ramesses II.*

**ARROWHEADS**
*Bows, arrows, and battering rams were often used in siege warfare. Bronze arrowheads such as those at right were used after about 2000BCE in the Near East. Iron arrowheads (bottom) appeared after about 1100BCE.*

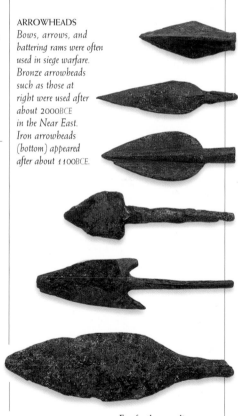

For further reading see bibliography numbers: 355, 410, 594, 672a, 835

# THE HISTORICAL BOOKS

The Historical books tell the story of the Covenant People, from the entry into the Promised Land to the return from exile, and the Maccabean revolt (*see pp.250–51*). In the Hebrew Bible, six of these books – Joshua, Judges, 1 and 2 Samuel, and 1 and 2 Kings – are gathered in the section known as *Nebi'im* (Prophets) and are known as the Early, or Former, Prophets. This draws attention to their character of making God's purpose and action in history known. Ruth, Esther, Ezra, Nehemiah, and 1 and 2 Chronicles are in the section known as the *Kethubim* (Writings). In Christian Bibles, the Historical books are not given a separate name but are distinguished from the books of the Prophets (the Wisdom books come between the two). There are also differences in Christian Bibles about the books to be included, because Roman Catholic and Orthodox Bibles include books that others place in the Apocrypha (*see pp.252–53*). The two major lists, in the order in which the books will be found, are as follows:

| | |
|---|---|
| Joshua | Joshua |
| Judges | Judges |
| Ruth | Ruth |
| 1 and 2 Samuel | 1 and 2 Samuel |
| 1 and 2 Kings | 1 and 2 Kings |
| 1 and 2 Chronicles | 1 and 2 Chronicles |
| Ezra | Ezra |
| Nehemiah | Nehemiah |
| Esther | Tobit |
| | Judith |
| | Esther |
| | 1 and 2 Maccabees |

# THE BOOK OF
# JOSHUA

*The book of Joshua relates the conquest of the Promised Land in fulfillment of God's promise to Abraham to give Canaan to the obedient people of Israel.*

THE book of Joshua opens with the people of Israel on the plains of Moab, the charges of Deuteronomy (*see pp.80–81*) still ringing in their ears. As the narrative unfolds, victory and success accompany obedience to God's commands, while unfaithfulness and sin meet with failure and judgment. The book bears witness to the work of God in driving out the inhabitants of the land and in giving the land to Israel, thus keeping the divine promise.

## A CHRONICLE OF FAITHFULNESS

In the Hebrew Bible, the book of Joshua stands at the head of the Former Prophets (the books of Joshua, Judges, 1–2 Samuel, 1–2 Kings). The book does not deal with "history" in any modern sense; in the books of the Former Prophets, Joshua is not an exhaustive military history of the conquest. It is instead a prophetic interpretation of God's dealings with the Covenant People, Israel: a chronicle of the people's faithfulness and obedience to God and of God's faithfulness to the covenant promises. It is not possible to reconstruct a connected history of events from this book, which draws on diverse materials to tell its own story. The book's account of the conquest gives the impression of a single unified onslaught, which was brought to completion. In fact, much remained to be done, some of it in the piecemeal approach described in

Judges 1. While the exact course of events was clearly more complex, and cannot now be recovered with certainty (*see pp.94–95*), Joshua's account focuses on the spiritual themes of the conquest, praise, and fulfillment. The book pays scant regard to the original inhabitants of the land, who experienced the effects of the conquest on themselves.

"I WILL GIVE TO YOU ... ALL THE LAND OF CANAAN" (GEN. 17:8)
*The book of Joshua gathers together different stories of the conquest of the land.*

## JOSHUA THE MAN

Joshua succeeded Moses as leader of Israel, and throughout his leadership Israel remained faithful to the Covenant (Josh. 24:31). He was well qualified for the role (Josh. 1:5). Of the spies sent by Moses, only he and Caleb had reported favorably on the land and, of the Exodus generation, only they entered the land.

The preparation and entry into the Promised Land (Josh. 2–5) are in contrast to the attempt made under Moses some 40 years earlier. Spies are again sent out, but this time report favorably: *"Truly the LORD has given all the land into our hands"* (Josh. 2:24). Through God's miraculous intervention, Israel crossed the Jordan River, which was in flood at that time of year. They were then in dangerous enemy territory, but Joshua's first action in the land – to circumcise all males so that they might keep the Passover – shows that obedience to God is more important than military caution. Their obedience is rewarded: no longer dependent on manna, they eat food from the land they have entered.

Three features in the narrative of the conquest illustrate the main themes of divine action and human obedience:

• The miraculous fall of Jericho (Josh. 6, *see pp.96–97*) reveals God's hand in the conquest: the land is "given" in fulfillment of promises made to Abraham (e.g., Gen. 17:8).

• Success in battle is dependent on obedience to God: Israel's failure to capture Ai is caused by Achan's sin, which affects the whole people (Josh. 7).

• Success returns only when Achan's sin is discovered and blotted out. Ai was eventually taken by deception and ambush (Josh. 8); even cities "given" to Israel are hard-won.

The division of the land for the Twelve Tribes of Israel (Josh. 13–22) was a program of allocations to be made once the territory had been captured. The land was not fully conquered in Joshua's time (Josh. 13:1–6), or afterward (Judg. 1–2). The so-called trans-Jordanian tribes (Reuben, Gad, and the half-tribe of Manasseh) had been allocated land on the east side of the Jordan. It seems that the physical barrier caused misunderstandings (*see* Josh. 22).

## MODERN QUESTIONS

The moral issues raised by the book are complicated for the modern reader, not least the practice of "devoting" (Hebrew, *herem*) cities to total destruction at God's specific command. The later importance of preserving the Covenant, and the threat to monotheism presented by the local religion and by intermarriage with Canaanites, may explain why extermination was seen as the only safeguard against idolatry (for the earlier relationship, *see pp.36–37*).

With this book it is important to recognize the dangers of taking the Bible so literally that the time and context of its production are forgotten. The conquest chapters (5:13–12:24), followed by those dividing up the land, show God as a ruthless predator who destroys those who stand in the way of the faithful and obedient. Applied as a timeless portrayal of God and of "what God wants," these chapters may lead not only to obedience, but also to acts of imitative ruthlessness. However, understood as a stage in the process toward a deeper understanding of the nature of God and of the character of obedience, the chapters stand more as a warning than as an encouragement.

**THE FALL OF JERICHO**
*This 16th-century painting is a European depiction of the event.*

# THE BOOK

TITLE: Joshua

HEBREW TITLE: *yehoshua*. The name means "YHWH is salvation." The Greek form of the name (*Iesous*) is known to us as Jesus (*see* Matt. 1:21)

DATE: Joshua opens on the eve of the conquest but was written after the settlement

AUTHORSHIP: The author or compiler of Joshua is not identified. In several places references are made to objects still standing "to this day," which may suggest that little more than a generation had elapsed since the events narrated took place. On the other hand, the way Joshua expounds the link between faith and the occupation of Canaan may reflect the concerns of a people coming to terms with their expulsion from the land (in 587BCE). Scholars remain divided on the final date

# THE CONTENTS

**CHAPTER 1**
Joshua charged by God to finish Moses' task

**CHAPTERS 2–5**
Preparation and entry into the Promised Land. The miraculous crossing of the Jordan River

**CHAPTERS 6–12**
Conquest of the land. Success in battle is linked with obedience to God

**CHAPTERS 13–22**
As Joshua grows old, God tells him to divide the land among the Twelve Tribes. The allocation of land and the inheritances of Caleb and the Levites

**CHAPTERS 23–24**
Continuing obedience in the land necessary for God's blessing. Joshua's sermon and death

# KEY THEME

The covenant promises are fulfilled in the conquest of Canaan

For further reading see bibliography numbers: 24, 343, 355, 530, 532, 639

# ENTRY INTO THE PROMISED LAND

*Israel's entry into the land of Canaan was seen as a fulfillment of God's Covenant with the people. That Israel occupied the land is beyond doubt; the details of how it came into the Israelites possession are more complex.*

### HEBREWS

Early Israelites are sometimes called Hebrews,
usually to distinguish
them from foreigners
(Exod. 1:19). Are they the
same as the Habiru (of
Sumerian texts), or the
Hapiru (of the 14th
century BCE diplomatic
correspondence)? The
letters refer to "Hapiru"
people who are causing
disruption in Palestine.
They are a people with no
assured place in society –
slaves, mercenaries,
bandits. The issue is
disputed, but if these are
the Hebrews, it points to
the conquest of Canaan
being more of a takeover
from within the area
than an invasion.

ACCORDING to the biblical account, related chiefly in Joshua, the conquest of the Promised Land was achieved by united military forces that entered the land from the west. They crossed the Jordan River at Gilgal, and the destruction of the cities of Jericho and Ai followed in quick succession. Following campaigns in the south and the north, the united armies were disbanded and

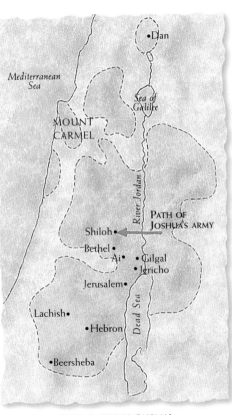

SETTLEMENT IN CANAAN
*The shaded area of the map shows the regions of Palestine that were settled by the Israelites under Joshua.*

dispersed. Yet in many areas the indigenous peoples remained and were never completely driven from the land. Judges 1–2 suggest that this was as a punishment for Israel's unfaithfulness.

The archaeology of Palestine is extensive, but surprisingly no documents exist that reliably refer to the history of the Israelites before the Monarchy (tenth century BCE).

JOURNEY TO THE PROMISED LAND
*This painting by Michael Rothenstein depicts the Israelites as they journey to claim the land that God had promised to the Ancestors.*

Such evidence as there is of the Middle to Late Bronze Age – mainly pottery, house construction, cistern design, and signs of fire in cities – suggests a different picture of Israel's origins in Canaan. More recently, sociological insights based on assumptions about the behavior of different nomadic groups have been applied to the archaeological data, and they provide additional models to explain Israel's occupation of the Promised Land.

## THEORIES OF OCCUPATION

One view of the occupation suggests that the Hebrews made a long-term, and mainly peaceful, infiltration into the hill country. Seminomadic clans grew in strength and eventually gained dominance over the other peoples of Canaan. A second view holds that some form of peasant revolt took place. In the face of increasingly oppressive taxation, the peasants fled from the plains and gathered in bands in the hill country. An eventual revolt saw the overthrow of Egyptian rule and the resettlement of the peasants in the plains. A final theory proposes that a dramatic shift in living patterns among the seminomadic Canaanites was responsible for the changed population. Forced to abandon the plains by drought, these groups then formed settlements in the hills, constituting themselves a people. This final theory requires no influx of outsiders to account for the evidence.

## UNANSWERED QUESTIONS

These models are not mutually exclusive and, whether based on biblical, archaeological, or sociological information, they leave some questions unanswered. The accounts of the Hebrew Bible are best understood as a "prophetic history," providing a theological commentary on Israel's origins. This, however, does not eliminate their historical reliability at particular points. What seems clear is that there was a long and complex sequence of events: some of the tribes never went to Egypt, but remained all the time in Canaan; some entered from the south, others from the east. The Bible unifies the different experiences and traditions, and Joshua 24 may reflect a deliberate attempt to draw the elements of the kinship group together.

## REST FROM THE ENEMY

The uncertainty surrounding both the date of the Israelites entry into Canaan and the specific details of the conquest, does not affect the way in which the occupation and settlement became foundational in Israel's self-understanding and faith in God. Israel's presence in Canaan demonstrated that God's promises come true (Josh. 21:45). For centuries, Israel's military fortunes became a barometer of its spiritual faithfulness to the Covenant. At high points in Israel's national life there was "rest" from its enemies. At other times, when Israel faced defeat, the Prophets called on the people to forsake alliances and return their trust to God, who gave them the land. Persistent rebellion against God eventually led to Israel's expulsion from the land (see pp. 146–47).

The New Testament continues the theme of the "rest." Occupation of the land was never actually completed, as Israel continued to share Canaan with indigenous peoples. According to the Letter to the Hebrews, this incomplete conquest points to a greater reality, yet to be consummated, when Jesus (believed by Christians to be greater than both Moses and Joshua) will lead his people to the perfect rest of Heaven (Heb. 3–4).

JEBUSITE CITY
The date of Israel's entry into the Promised Land is as difficult to ascertain as the date of the Exodus (pp. 52–53). Evidence of fire and destruction in several Canaanite cities in the same period is not sufficiently conclusive. If the final conquest of the Promised Land started 40 years after the Exodus, the entry probably began in either c.1400BCE or c.1240BCE (see also Jericho pp. 96–97). During this period, the city of Jerusalem, situated high in the Judean hills, remained in the hands of the Jebusites. It was not conquered until the reign of David.

# FROM SINAI TO CANAAN

*Before their entry into the land of Canaan, the Israelites lived in seasonal encampments in the desert and led a nomadic lifestyle.*

The Bible indicates that approximately two million Israelites wandered "in the wilderness of Sinai" (Num. 1:1) during the 40 years of the Exodus. The actual numbers were smaller, but even so, the barren landscape and scarce resources of the desert could not support a fraction of this population so God provided "bread from heaven" (Exod. 16:4) and water (Exod. 17:6). The Israelites lived in tribal groups throughout the Sinai region, where they tended herds and traveled in search of new pastureland.

Sinai desert.

The contrast with Canaan, "a land of wheat and barley, of vines and fig trees and pomegranates, a land of olive trees and honey" (Deut. 8:8), was vast. After Joshua had led the Israelites into the Promised Land, they became a settled agricultural community.

For further reading see bibliography numbers: 6, 131, 231, 343, 355, 410, 490, 530, 532, 559, 639, 672a, 788, 799

# JERICHO

*Jericho is mentioned in the Bible as the first city conquered by the Israelites under Joshua. But the city itself had already enjoyed a long history, and today it claims to be the oldest continually inhabited oasis in the world.*

## THE SITES OF JERICHO

Jericho is strategically placed on the eastern border of Canaan in what is now the West Bank. Several different sites were developed in the area. Er-Riha (modern Jericho) is about 17 miles (27km) east-northeast of the capital, Jerusalem, while the ancient city is thought to lie 1 mile (2km) northwest of Er-Riha at Tell es-Sultan. Roman Jericho is to the west of Er-Riha.

•Jericho

D UE to its abundant spring, the site of Jericho has been settled without break for thousands of years. The remnants of successive civilizations, layered one upon the other, contain a multitude of artifacts and human remains. As a result, Jericho has been the subject of extensive excavations. Findings from these have raised questions in relation to understanding biblical accounts.

## ANCIENT JERICHO

Ancient Jericho is of enormous archaeological importance and a primary source of information on the earliest settled life in Palestine (until 1200BCE). From archaeological evidence, it is clear that the first settlements were founded around 8000BCE. Over the following millennia, the site was periodically destroyed and resettled. During the Patriarchal Period (Middle Bronze Age, 1900–1600BCE) Jericho was an important city. After being violently destroyed in about 1550BCE, the site seems to have been left without major occupation for several hundred years.

## JOSHUA'S CONQUEST

Jericho is described in the Bible as the first town captured by the nation of Israel under Joshua's leadership. The collapse of Jericho's walls at the mere shout of Israel (Josh. 6) was symbolic, demonstrating that God was indeed on Israel's side. The basis of this account has been

questioned, not least in the light of archaeological evidence. K. M. Kenyon, who carried out major archaeological excavations at the site in the 1950s, put the latest date for the walled city's complete destruction at c.1550BCE – significantly before the earliest likely date (1400BCE) for the Israelite conquest of Canaan and the date of the Exodus (*see pp.94–95, 52–53*). It is more likely that the 18th Dynasty of Egypt was the aggressor in Jericho at this time. It is still possible that what Joshua encountered was a small town, built on the ruins of ancient Jericho.

According to the biblical narrative, everyone in the city was killed, and the site placed under a powerful curse:

> *Cursed before the LORD be anyone who tries to build this city – this Jericho!*
>
> *At the cost of his firstborn he shall lay its foundation,*
>
> *and at the cost of his youngest he shall set up its gates!*
>
> (Joshua 6:26–27)

Before the Late Monarchy (tenth century) Jericho is referred to sparingly, suggesting that there was only light occupation, perhaps in awe of Joshua's curse. When in the ninth century BCE, Hiel of Bethel rebuilt the foundations, he suffered the loss of his eldest and youngest sons, as the curse of Joshua predicted (1 Kgs. 16:34). Jericho continued to be settled, though, and was home to Elijah and Elisha's school of prophets (2 Kgs. 2). The town probably remained occupied after the deportation of the Israelites into exile in 598/7BCE. Three hundred and forty-five "sons of Jericho" returned to Judah from Babylon after the Exile (post 538BCE), to what by then was probably a modest settlement.

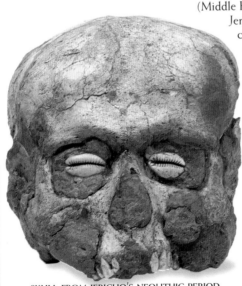

**SKULL FROM JERICHO'S NEOLITHIC PERIOD**
*Skulls dating from the Neolithic period and decorated with shells, clay, and human hair have been found at Jericho. They may have been connected with some form of ancestor worship.*

## ROMAN JERICHO

The city of Jericho is mentioned in the Apocrypha as the site of Bacchides' fortress (1 Macc. 9:50), and of the slaughter in 143BCE of Simon and his sons (1 Macc. 16:11–17).

During the Roman period (from the second century BCE onward), the Hasmonean rulers (see pp.250–51) built and added to a winter palace to the south of the old city. Proximity to Jerusalem and to a warmer climate made this an ideal location. Herod the Great

(37–4BCE) continued the building at Jericho, and added his own winter palace with a fine classical frontage. The palace stood near fertile palm and balsam groves and had its own ornamental gardens. It is thought to have been the site of Herod's death in 4BCE.

### HEROD'S WINTER PALACE
*Only part of Herod's lavish palace has been excavated; much still lies buried beneath the sands.*

## JERICHO IN THE NEW TESTAMENT

The city of Jericho is also the site of several episodes in the New Testament. Jesus traveled in the region of Jericho, where he encountered and healed the blind men, including Bartimaeus. Zacchaeus, a wealthy tax-collector, encountered Jesus as he was passing through the city. Finally, in the parable of the Good Samaritan, the Samaritan is said to be traveling on the road from Jerusalem to Jericho, which was notorious in New Testament times as a place for bandits. The Samaritan is said to be going "down" from Jerusalem because Jericho is so much lower in altitude.

### OASIS
Jericho was a natural site for settlement because of its abundant freshwater spring, which has supported an oasis at the site for several thousand years. At about 700ft (213m) below sea level, the oasis is often claimed to be the lowest in the world. The Bible sometimes refers to the city as the City of Palms. Wisdom is said to grow *"like the rosebushes in Jericho"* (Sir. 24:14), perhaps an allusion to the fertility of the oasis.

# THE MOUND OF JERICHO

*A crosssection through the hill of Jericho shows a multitude of layers, providing evidence of many different stages of human occupation and long periods when it was largely abandoned.*

Apart from its biblical importance, Jericho provides one of the first examples of a continuously inhabited site. Although there is evidence of earlier human remains, the first development was a Neolithic settlement from about 8000BCE of mud-brick houses, a stone-built surrounding wall, and, remarkably for this period, a large central tower (see below). The inhabitants practiced hunting, herding, and primitive agriculture and seem to have taken particular care to preserve the skulls of the dead (see opposite), which were mostly buried beneath the floors of the houses. From the third and fourth millennia BCE, the town was defended by mud walls; 17 different phases have been traced by archaeologists. Other inhabitants of the site include the Canaanites (see pp.98–99), who probably lived at Jericho from c.1900BCE.

Tower

Spring

### The tower
*Containing a flight of internal steps, the tower dates from the Neolithic period (c.8000BCE).*

Wall

**Aerial view of the mound.**

### SOME REFERENCES TO JERICHO
Collapse of the walls of Jericho (Josh. 6)

•

Rebuilding of city by Hiel of Bethel (1 Kgs. 16:34)

•

Elijah and Elisha's school of prophets (2 Kgs. 2)

•

Christ healing the blind (Matt. 20:29–34; Mark 10:46–52;

•

Zacchaeus (Luke 19:1–10)

•

The Good Samaritan (Luke 10:29–37; see also p.339)

**For further reading see bibliography numbers: 93, 322, 454, 757**

# CANAANITES
## CULTURE AND RELIGION

*Canaanite culture dominated Syria and Palestine in the second millennium BCE, and some Canaanite peoples, especially the Phoenicians, were still influential many centuries later. Despite conflict and contest, Israel inherited much from this culture.*

DESPITE the frequency of its use in the Bible and elsewhere, the meaning and reference of the name "Canaan" remain rather unclear. As a geographical term, it seems to have been used to describe the whole area of Syria and Palestine, or at least some large part of it. When applied to people, though, it does not usually describe the whole population of that area, but only a group within it. The nature and extent of that group varies: in Exodus 3:8, for example, the Canaanites are distinguished from Hittites and Hivites, yet in Genesis 36:2 the Canaanite wives taken by Esau include a Hittite and a Hivite (*cf.* Num. 13:29; Judg. 1:9).

In Genesis 9:18–27, Canaan is the son of Ham, who was cursed by Noah, and in the Table of Nations he is the father of many peoples in the land later occupied by Israel (Gen. 10:6, 15–20). The name "Canaanite" came to denote peoples in general who would also have used more specific terms to describe themselves. The word may be connected with a word expressing descent or lowliness – perhaps a reference to the sun's descent, indicating that the Canaanites were "westerners." Modern scholarship usually employs the term in a similarly general way, to describe the section of the Syrian–Palestinian

CANAANITE CRAFTSMANSHIP
*Canaanite artifacts reflect both indigenous styles and influences from other nations. In the Fosse Temple, a sanctuary at Lachish, a number of gold pendants were found (left). They probably formed part of an offering to the deity. The decoration was made by an impression formed when gold was beaten over a patterned object. The Egyptian-style seal (right) was made by Canaanites and was used to denote ownership.*

population that spoke variants of a particular Semitic language: the "Canaanite" dialects, which include Hebrew (*see* Isa. 19:18) and Phoenician, and are distinct from Aramaic, Akkadian, Arabic, and the other Semitic tongues. It seems unlikely that any strong differentiation can be made between these Canaanites and the "Amorites," except, perhaps, on geographical grounds: the term "Amorite" is often used of peoples found farther east.

## CANAANITE SOCIETY
Archaeological evidence for the Middle and Late Bronze Ages in Palestine suggests that the region was fairly uniform in culture during the centuries before Israel's emergence and was not divided into radically different societies. There may never have been any single

Canaanite nation. Rather, the Canaanites were organized into city-states, with each city ruled by its own king and patrician class, exercizing authority over the surrounding countryside. For much of the second millennium BCE, these city-states were subject to Egypt, and 14th-century letters to the Egyptian king, found at Amarna, give many insights into their political methods and problems. Their economies were essentially agricultural, but the Canaanites were

Connection between

---

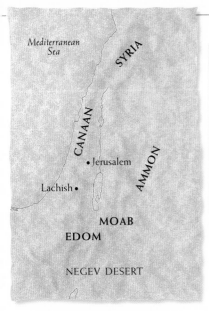

THE LAND OF CANAAN
*The ancient boundaries of the land of Canaan are described in the book of Genesis 10:19.*

**CANAANITE SARCOPHAGI**
*Over 50 pottery sarcophagi, some showing Egyptian influences, were found at Deir el-Balah, south of Gaza city. The embalmed body of the deceased was laid in the sarcophagus, together with jewelry and funeral gifts. The sarcophagi date to the 14th/13th centuries BCE.*

also famous for their trading (*see* Isa. 23:8). Their art seems to have drawn on traditions from many areas, but it also developed its own distinctive character; some of the surviving pieces are exquisite. Although little remains, it seems that the Canaanite people also had a strong tradition of literature and were an essential link in developing the alphabet (*p.165*), without which the writing of the works that became Scripture would have been impossible.

## CANAAN AND ISRAEL

The historical relationship between Israel and Canaan is not yet wholly understood, although it seems clear the two were more closely connected than the biblical text suggests. While there was clearly contest and conflict over the nature and demands of God, it is also clear that Israel derived much from the culture of the Canaanites.

IVORY HEAD
*This portrait of a Canaanite comes from Lachish.*

Connection between the two is clear in archaeological evidence from towns and cemeteries of Syria and Palestine. Not only did the ancient Israelites speak a Canaanite language, but their culture seems to have drawn on Canaanite poetic traditions, religious ideas, and myths (for additional parallels with other neighboring religions, *see pp.140–41*). Examples of these traditions were uncovered among the remains of Ugarit (*see box, below*). Such parallels are reflected at various levels, from the adoption by the Israelites of the mythical Canaanite beast Leviathan – whom God is described as defeating in Psalm 74 – to the eventual identification of the Israelite God with the chief Canaanite deity, El. The later religion of the Israelites wrote or edited the texts to give the impression of constant conflict and differences between the two cultures.

## CANAANITE RELIGION

*The Canaanites were not a single nation, so it is likely that their religious ideas varied to some extent across the region.*

A general picture of Canaanite beliefs emerges from biblical and classical sources, especially in the texts discovered (from 1928 onward) at Ras Shamra, in modern northern Syria, the site of ancient Ugarit – called the Ugaritic texts. They date from the late second millennium BCE and include a number of poems on legendary or mythological themes. They also give important insights into Ugaritic religion, which was probably similar to the religion of most Canaanite city-states.

El, father of the gods, stands at the head of the pantheon with his consort Athirath, the biblical Asherah. He is portrayed in terms of a king but plays little direct part in the poems. His court is composed of other deities, who often fight among themselves. Yam, the god of the sea, and Mot, the god of death and the underworld, are powerful, but it is the storm-god, Hadad, usually called Baal, "Lord," who dominates many of the stories; he is sometimes helped by his bloodthirsty sister, Anat.

These myths may have been connected with rituals based on the cycle of seasons. From administrative texts and archaeological evidence, we know that Ugarit had a hereditary priesthood and at least two temples, one for Baal, the other for the god Dagon. In addition, platforms, or the "high places" often mentioned in the Bible, have been found in Palestine.

Temple offering.

For further reading see bibliography numbers: 95, 98, 210, 221, 231, 235, 251, 327, 346, 351, 372, 413, 572, 585, 628, 651, 688, 694, 799, 820

# ISRAEL'S NEIGHBORS
## IN THE ANCIENT NEAR EAST

*Until recently, little was known about ancient Israel's smaller neighbors, and the Bible was the principal source of information. Recent archaeological work has provided a better understanding of these ancient nations and of their historical relationship to Israel.*

SURROUNDED by impressive empires, such as Egypt and Assyria (*see pp.46–47, 142–143*), and seafaring traders such as the Phoenician and Philistine nations, Israel also had a number of smaller neighbors. They are sometimes described as the illegitimate children of Israel's ancestors (Gen. 19:30–8). However, despite the emphasis the Bible lays on their differences, it is clear that Israel also gained much from them.

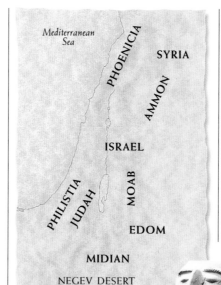

BIBLE LANDS
*In the ancient Near East, the exact boundaries of other nations were indistinct, and people would have moved back and forth across the land.*

NOMAD
*Because of the nomadic lifestyle among some of the peoples neighboring Israel and Judah and the lack of fixed settlements, remains are relatively scarce.*

## AMMON

Ammon was located across the Jordan from Israel, in the area of the modern Jordanian capital of Amman. Its inhabitants are mentioned frequently in the Bible, where they are identified as the descendants of Ben-ammi. According to Genesis 19, Ben-ammi was the cousin and

FERTILITY GODDESS
*This pottery figurine of Ashtar, a fertility goddess, dates from about the 13th century BCE. Its form is similar to that of some early Mesopotamian figures.*

half-brother of Moab, the two having been born out of incestuous relationships between Lot and his daughters. The story acknowledges a close link between Israel, Ammon, and Moab, but is further intended, of course, to show the origins of these neighbors in a poor light. The Ammonites are also said to have been given land by God, who enabled them to conquer the legendary Rephaim. For this reason, the Israelites are forbidden

CULT STAND
*This anthropomorphic cult stand was found in an Edomite shrine in Hurbat Quitmit in the eastern Negev Desert. It dates from the seventh/sixth centuries BCE. It would have been used to contain incense and may resemble the people who made it.*

to fight with them as they approach their own Promised Land (Deut. 19–21). Archaeological evidence seems to suggest strong cultural, perhaps even ethnic, continuity between the Ammonites and the earlier inhabitants of the region, but it is more than likely that Ammon came into being as a result of the same unknown historical forces and changes that led to Israel's emergence in Canaan. In any case, the Ammonites and Israelites are depicted as antagonists from an early period (Judg. 3:13), with the Israelites increasingly having the upper hand. Both, however, became subject to the powerful empires of Assyria and Babylon. We know little about the culture and religion of Ammon, although a number of short inscriptions have been found. These confirm that the Ammonites spoke a language closely related to Hebrew, and that their national god was Milkom.

## MOAB

The Moabites, who inhabited the more desolate region east of the Dead Sea and Arabah, are closely linked in the biblical sources with their Ammonite neighbors to the north, and their history is similarly intertwined with that of Israel. The nation's origins are not entirely clear, but archaeological evidence tends to suggest that Moab also developed, in part at least, out of the indigenous culture of the area. Important knowledge about Moab comes from an inscription composed by King Mesha of Moab in the ninth century BCE. This inscription describes his successful attempt to throw off Israelite control, with the assistance of the national god, Kemosh; a different version of these events is given in the Bible in 2 Kings 3. The inscription is in Moabite, a language very similar to Hebrew, and portrays Kemosh's actions on behalf of his nation in terms reminiscent of those used by the Bible about the Israelite God. References to Moab cease after its conquest by Babylon, suggesting that the nation then no longer had an independent existence.

*SYRIAN*
*This splendidly preserved faience tile comes from a tomb in the mortuary temple of the Egyptian Pharaoh Ramesses III. It shows a Syrian prisoner from the area north of Israel dressed in a highly decorated robe.*

## EDOM

The land of Edom lay to the south of Moab, on a high rocky plateau, and its inhabitants, of whose origins we know little, inspired mixed reactions among the biblical sources. On the one hand, the Edomites are portrayed positively in the Hebrew Bible as descendants of Esau, and so were close relatives of the Israelites, who had similarly been granted their land by God (Deut. 2:22); indeed, Israel claimed brotherhood with them (Num. 20:14; Deut. 23:8). This friendly attitude might be linked with a tradition that God actually came from Edom (Hab. 3:3; Judg. 5:4), with the unusual lack of biblical attacks upon Edom's religion, and with the permission given in Deuteronomy 23:8 for those of Edomite descent to enter the assembly. On the other hand, though, there is a strong prophetic condemnation of Edom in other parts of the Hebrew Bible (e.g., Ezek. 25:12–14). This may

*EDOMITE GODDESS*
*This horned goddess from an Edomite shrine in the eastern Negev dates from the seventh/sixth centuries BCE.*

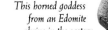

*MIDIANITE POT*
*This late Bronze Age pot was found in Timnah in the southern Negev Desert.*

have been provoked by an Edomite seizure of Judahite land after the destruction of Jerusalem – the last, perhaps, in a series of such annexations. Edom itself suffered similar destruction by the Babylonians a few years later, although its territory then became known as Idumea, the homeland of Herod the Great (*see pp.276, 278*). There are various references to the land of Edom in a list of tributes from subject nations, and some information has been preserved in Assyrian records of the eighth century BCE. The national god of the Edomites was apparently called Qos, or Qaus, a form that appears in personal names from the region. There is also evidence of other gods and goddesses. Otherwise, we know very little about the nation's religious beliefs or culture, although there have been some archaeological finds of ostraca and seals.

**For further reading see bibliography numbers:** 210, 231, 372, 413, 572, 573, 628, 651, 820

## THE SONS OF JACOB

Jacob is considered to be the father of the Covenant People. His sons later became the ancestral heads of the Twelve Tribes of Israel.

*Their names were:*

| | |
|---|---|
| REUBEN | SIMEON |
| LEVI | JUDAH |
| ISSACHAR | ZEBULUN |
| JOSEPH | BENJAMIN |
| DAN | NAPHTALI |
| GAD | ASHER |

# THE TWELVE TRIBES OF ISRAEL

*In biblical times, Israel was composed of twelve tribes, who made up a single kinship group. They were named after the sons of Jacob. It is not easy to trace their early history, but they later became essential to the nation's identity.*

THE Hebrew Bible, in its finished form, assumes that the people of Israel are descendants of the 12 sons of Jacob (subsequently called Israel). It is no longer possible to reconstruct the history of individual tribes in the kinship group, but the stories reflect their varied early histories. Levi is particularly difficult – it is described in Genesis as being similar to the other tribes, but it had no land. The Levites in the cities were supported by other tribes, on whose behalf they ministered before God. The tribe of Joseph received a double inheritance (rightly due to Reuben as the firstborn son), known by the names of his two sons, Ephraim and Manasseh. In lists related to land, these names replace Levi and Joseph.

The division of land was seen as follows: the tribes of Gad, Reuben, and one half of Manasseh were granted land to the east of the Jordan (*see left*). Their geographical isolation from the rest of Israel led to a mutual suspicion on more than one occasion (Josh. 22). The tribes of Asher, Naphtali, Zebulun, Issachar, Ephraim, and the second half of Manasseh occupied the heart of the Northern Kingdom. To the south, initially separated by unconquered cities, lay the southern tribes of Dan, Judah, Simeon, and Benjamin. Dan initially settled in the south but migrated to the northernmost tip of Israel as a result of relentless Philistine pressure (Judg. 18:21–28).

## KINSHIP GROUPS

In Exodus 1:1, the Twelve Tribes are known as *Bene Ya'aqob*, or *Bene Yisrael* (*Bene* meaning "sons of"). The birth of Jacob's sons is recorded in Genesis 29–35. At this point, they are grouped according to their mothers: Reuben, Simeon, Levi, Judah, Issachar, and Zebulun were the sons of Leah; Joseph and Benjamin were the sons of Rachel; Dan and Naphtali were the sons of Bilhah; and Gad and Asher were the sons of Zilpah. The Bible makes it clear that this is not a definitive list, and that different names are sometimes used. For instance, in Genesis 48:8–20, Ephraim and Manasseh appear as separate tribes. Elsewhere, Simeon and Levi are omitted (Genesis 34 records a story that explains why they fell out of favor with Jacob).

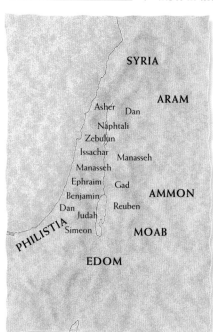

## ISRAEL'S TRIBAL TERRITORY

Whatever their early history, the Twelve Tribes of Israel became the mark of the Covenant People. This map shows the division of the kingdom after the Exile, when the tribal boundaries were established (Josh. 13–19).

**THE TWELVE TRIBES**
*This 14th-century illustration from a French manuscript depicts the ancestors of the Twelve Tribes of Israel.*

The Song of Deborah (Judg. 5) suggests that there are only ten tribes – neither Judah nor Gad is mentioned. In Joshua 17:1, Machir is substituted for Manasseh.

From this information, it is clear that the lists reflect the changing histories of these family groups, but that there was an overriding and continuing sense of a kinship group. Even though some members were replaced by others, the sense of belonging to a kinship group prevailed. That it was made up of disparate units is evident from the way that the sons were grouped by their mothers (*see opposite*), who were differently related to Jacob – Leah and Rachel were wives, Bilhah and Zilpah were concubines. Thus it was possible to be brought into a relationship with the kinship group in different ways and at different times. This helps to explain the importance of genealogies throughout the Hebrew Bible – of knowing who is descended from whom, and the ways in which people are related.

## ORGANIZATION OF TRIBES

The "tribes" are known by three main names in the Hebrew Bible: *bet ab*, which means the immediate "family"; *mishpachah*, which refers to the wider family and is often translated as "clan"; and *shebet*, which points to a larger unit of organization, such as a tribe that unifies several families. Each of these terms relies on the importance of lineage – of knowing who is related to whom – and that is why the larger unit of organization is best known as a kinship group. Although the kinship may not have been actual, it was affirmed for all members of the group and allowed stories to be told of how each of the members came to belong.

The members of the kinship group known as *Bene Yisrael* followed very different and often independent histories. This can be seen in the stories gathered in Judges, especially in the Song of Deborah (ch.5), where the lack of unity is deplored and derided. In other kinship groups of this kind, such as those among Arab tribes of the seventh century CE, it was usual for members to insist on their independence. If there was a crisis for one or more members of the group, other members were obliged to assist until the crisis had passed. It was also usual for members to have

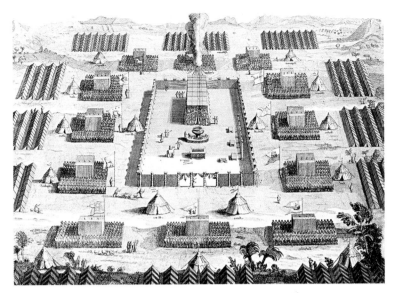

TRIBAL ENCAMPMENT AROUND THE TABERNACLE
*Pivotal to Israel's early religious life, the Tabernacle stood at the center of the encampment. It was surrounded by the tents of the Twelve Tribes of Israel – three tribes on each side.*

their own leaders, unless, in a crisis, a gifted leader emerged to deal with it, such as Saul, who encouraged other members of the group to respond to the crisis of the Philistines and the Ammonites (1 Sam. 11).

## ISRAEL IN CONFLICT

David kept the kinship group unified beyond the moment of immediate crisis. This unity continued under his son and successor, Solomon, but when he died, the northern members of the kinship group asked, *"What share do we have in David? We have no inheritance in the son of Jesse. To your tents, O Israel! Look now to your own house, O David"* (1 Kgs. 12:16). On Solomon's death, Jeroboam's Northern Kingdom – known as Israel or Ephraim – split from Rehoboam's Southern Kingdom of Judah. Northern Israel was raided by the Assyrian king, Tiglath-Pileser III, in 733BCE, and was finally crushed when Samaria fell (722BCE). The inhabitants of Samaria were deported, and nothing more is heard of these "lost" tribes. The Southern Kingdom survived until the fall of Jerusalem in 587BCE (*pp.146–47*). The tribes of Judah, Benjamin, and Levi seem to have continued (Ezra 1:5), and to have responded to Cyrus' edict that allowed them to return to their lands (*pp.154–55*).

VILLAGE OF CARMEL
The city of Hebron and its surrounding territory were conquered by Caleb, son of Jephunneh of the tribe of Judah (Josh. 14:6–15). The village of Carmel (meaning "garden") is in the south of the region. It was here that the wealthy landowner Nabal (meaning "foolish") refused hospitality to David's men (1 Sam. 25:5). Abraham and Jacob were later buried at the cave of Machpelah, near Hebron.

**For further reading see bibliography numbers:** 6, 131, 210, 326, 343, 345, 402, 490, 659, 821

# THE BOOK OF
# JUDGES

*The book of Judges tells vivid and dramatic stories of Israel in search of its identity during the settlement. The tribes had scattered over a wide area, but they still might help one another in times of crisis.*

IN the Hebrew Bible, Judges is the second book of the Former Prophets, coming after Joshua. It describes the exploits of various tribal leaders and heroes during the period of the settlement in Canaan – between the entry into the Promised Land and the rise of the Monarchy under the Prophet Samuel. Judges' account of the settlement shows that it took far longer, and involved more episodes, than the book of Joshua suggests.

## HOSTILE THREATS

The biblical account of the settlement of the Israelite tribes in the Promised Land, begun in the book of Joshua, continues throughout the book of Judges. It describes how the tribe of Dan attempted to find a place of settlement in the north, and how various Canaanite factions exerted hostile pressures on the tribes that attempted to settle in central Palestine. Gradually the tribes extended and strengthened this area of settlement.

Strong pressure was later felt from the Philistines in the south-west, as they attempted to extend their territory into the central area (the main theme of the Samson stories). Gradually the Israelites realized that a loose confederation of tribes under a charismatic leader, or "judge" (who was recognized only as long as a crisis lasted), was no match for the Philistine enemy, and the demand for a monarch became stronger.

**SAMSON DESTROYS THE PHILISTINE TEMPLE**
*This illustration from a 19th-century Jewish manuscript depicts Samson destroying the Philistine temple after regaining his strength.*

## JUDGES AS LEADERS

There were twelve "judges," probably corresponding to the Twelve Tribes of Israel. Five of these – Tola, Jair, Ibzan, Elon, and Abdon – are said to have been judges of all Israel and were also known as the "minor judges" (10:1–5; cf. 12:8–15). The remaining seven judges seem to have been tribal leaders who fought against specific Canaanite tribes: Othniel versus nomads; Ehud versus Moabites; Shamgar versus Philistines; Deborah versus Canaanites; Gideon versus Midianites; Jephthah versus Ammonites; Samson versus Philistines. These judges did not have similar backgrounds or patterns of behavior, but they were leaders of tribes that sometimes rallied other tribes to fight with them. For instance, Deborah called on Naphtali and Zebulun (4:6) and on Benjamin and Issachar (5:1–15). The leaders were raised up as deliverers (3:9); the Spirit of God came upon them; they judged Israel; they went out to war at the head of the army (3:10) (or in Deborah's case deputized someone to do that for her, 4:6); they took tribute on behalf of Israel (3:15); and they delivered judgments (4:5). Deborah was a prophetess (4:4); Gideon and Jephthah made sacrifices (6:24; 11:31); Jephthah was a mighty warrior but also a bandit (11:1–3); Samson was a Nazirite dedicated to God (13:5). However, the authors of Judges make it clear that they were all charismatic leaders, through whom God worked to deliver Israel from its enemies.

## THE DEUTERONOMISTIC VIEW OF HISTORY

The books from Joshua–2 Kings tell the story, or stories, from the viewpoint of the vision in Deuteronomy (pp.80–81) of God's dealings with the people; thus they are known as "the Deuteronomistic history." Judges is the second book in the Deuteronomistic history. Deuteronomistic history is a theological history, influenced by the teaching of the great Prophets of the eighth and seventh centuries BCE. The Deuteronomists wanted to show that peace in the Promised Land was constantly threatened by the disobedience of the people. This threat could be removed only when the people repented and returned to worshiping YHWH, their God.

The Deuteronomistic view of history is summarized most clearly in Judges 2:6–3:6. Israel commits *"evil in the sight of the LORD"* by worshiping Canaanite gods (2:11); God's anger is kindled, and the Israelites are overpowered by their enemies and lose their struggle for Canaanite territory (2:14). Overcome by disaster, the Israelites repent and cry to God for help. God is *"moved to pity"* (2:18) and raises a judge to help them. The judge is victorious in battle over the current enemy, but as soon as the disaster has ended, Israel rebels again and returns to its apostasy. This interpretation of history is used to explain why Israel had such a struggle in the Promised Land after the death of Joshua (2:21–23).

# ROLES OF THE JUDGES

The Hebrew word that we translate as "judge" – *shophet* – is a participle of the Hebrew verb *shaphat*. In the Hebrew Bible, *shaphat* is used to describe roles that include a giver of the law, a judge, or a governor. These people would be responsible for making decisions in controversial situations, executing judgment, discriminating, condemning, punishing, and vindicating. There are only two instances in the book of Judges where the word is used in its legal sense – first, when the Israelites came to Deborah *"for judgment"* (4:5), and second, when Jephthah warns the king of the Ammonites to *"Let the LORD, who is judge, decide today for the Israelites or for the Ammonites"* (11:27). The minor judges – Tola, Jair, Ibzan, Elon, and Abdon – are described as "judging," or administrating justice, rather than acting as military leaders.

In the Mari texts from the upper Euphrates (c.1800BCE), an official, or "judge," was a type of local governor whose functions included the administration of justice and the mustering of troops (in a similar way that some of the "major" judges acted). Jephthah, in particular, was clearly both a governor and a military leader. The use of the word *shophet* for tribal heroes is found only in the book of Judges. With the rise of the Monarchy, judicial authority became invested in the institution of the king.

## THE BOOK

**TITLE:** Judges

**HEBREW TITLE:** *Shophetim*, meaning "judges"

**DATE:** The book is set during the period of the settlement of Canaan. It was based on old stories, gathered and edited at a later date

**AUTHORSHIP:** Unknown. Chapters 1–8 and 10–16 may have been compiled by the Deuteronomists from old traditions, perhaps mainly from northern tribes. Chapters 9 and 17–20 may have been added by a post-exilic editor

## THE CONTENTS

**CHAPTERS 1–5**
Introduction to bridge the gap between Joshua and Judges. The people of Israel are unfaithful to God (chs.1–3:6). Othniel, Ehud, and Shamgar save the Israelites from their oppressors (chs. 3:7–31). Deborah defeats the Canaanites (ch.4), and sings her song of victory (ch.5)

**CHAPTERS 6–12**
Gideon destroys the altar of Baal (ch.6), and leads the people to victory over the Midianites (chs.6–8). Abimelech, son of Gideon, kills his brothers to become king (ch.9). Tola and Jair are judges (ch.10). Jephthah defeats the Ammonites (chs.10–12:7). Ibzan, Elon, and Abdon judge Israel (chs.12:8–15)

**CHAPTERS 13–21**
Samson defeats the Philistines and destroys their temple after they cut his hair and blind him (chs.13–16). Epilogue (chs.17–21)

## KEY THEMES

*The importance of obedience to God*
•
*Abandoning God leads to punishment*
•
*God's mercy upon repentance*

For further reading see bibliography numbers: 15, 24, 39, 40, 249, 312, 326, 369, 402, 530, 531,532, 559, 598, 715, 756, 782

# FOUR STORIES OF

# JUDGES

*The stories of the book of Judges reflect aspects of life during the settlement of Canaan. They show how God raised up leaders ("judges") in times of threat and crisis.*

THE story of Deborah is found in the parallel accounts of Judges 4 and 5. Chapter 4 is a narrative from the Deuteronomists (*see p.105*); chapter 5 covers the same events and is known as the "Song of Deborah" – an ancient poem, full of wonderful imagery and drama generally agreed to be a first-hand historical account dating from c.1125BCE. The main event in Deborah's story is the Battle of Megiddo. Although the battle was fought against Jabin, king of Hazor, a more important figure in the story is the Canaanite commander, Sisera. The battle began on Mount Tabor, on the northeast edge of the plain of Jezreel, situated on one of the main commercial routes from Egypt to Mesopotamia. Sisera's troops were encamped in the valley, along the bed of the Kishon River, which was dry in the summer months. According to the Song of Deborah, it was flooded by a sudden rainstorm that caused the heavy Canaanite chariots to become stuck in the clay. Barak, Deborah's commander, slaughtered the beleaguered Canaanites, while Sisera sought refuge with Jael, a woman from the Kenite tribe,

THE TRIBES ASSEMBLE AT MOUNT TABOR: JUDG. 4:6

SISERA'S TROOPS: JUDG. 4:13

THE STORM: JUDG. 5:21

THE FALL OF SISERA'S ARMY: JUDG. 4:15–16

whom he considered to be an ally. However, the Kenites had close links with the worship of YHWH, and Jael acted for Deborah. When Sisera was asleep, Jael drove a tent-peg through his head and then displayed the corpse to Deborah.

SISERA FLEES: JUDG. 4:17

SISERA'S DEATH: JUDG. 4:21

Jephthah's daughter goes out to meet her father.

## GIDEON AND THE MIDIANITES

The story of Gideon (Judg. 6–8) begins when Midianite raids threatened central Canaan. Gideon's troops were selected according to the way in which they drank water: only those who did not kneel, but lapped water from their hands (thus leaving them more alert for signs of the enemy), were chosen – 300 men out of 10,000. Before the battle, Gideon heard a man telling of his dream in which a barley loaf fell into the Midianite camp and flattened it. The dream was fulfilled that night when Gideon's troops defeated the Midianites by blowing trumpets (animal horns) and breaking pottery jars. Their famous cry, *"A sword for the LORD and for Gideon!"* thus convinced the Midianites that they were about to be overwhelmed by superior numbers, and they fled in

THE MIDIANITE THREAT: JUDG. 6:2–6

GIDEON SELECTS HIS TROOPS: JUDG. 7:4–8

THE DREAM: JUDG. 7:13

THE MIDIANITE ARMY FLEES: JUDG. 7:22

confusion. Gideon was offered a crown and the chance to found a ruling dynasty, but he refused for himself and for his family. Later, however, his son Abimelech proclaimed himself king with Shechem as his capital, but his reign lasted only three years.

*ABIMELECH BECOMES KING: JUDG. 9:6*

## JEPHTHAH'S VOW

Jephthah was one of the principal judges of Israel. He was an illegitimate child and was forced to flee from his family after being disinherited. He became a bandit, which later made him the ideal choice to lead an army against the Ammonites. Jephthah made a vow that on his return from defeating the Ammonites, he would sacrifice the first person who came to meet him; unfortunately, this was his (unnamed) daughter. She did not argue or rebel against her father, and asked only for two months to mourn her virginity on the mountains of Israel before accepting her fate. Jephthah is also remembered for the use of a password – *shibboleth* – in a civil war between the Gileadites and the Ephraimites. It was a password that enemies of the Gileadites could not pronounce.

*JEPHTHAH BECOMES AN OUTLAW: JUDG. 11:3*

*JEPHTHAH'S VOW: JUDG. 11:31*

*JEPHTHAH'S PASSWORD: JUDG. 12:6*

## SAMSON AND DELILAH

The story of Samson begins with the divine announcement of his birth, in which he is dedicated to be a Nazirite. Samson is very different from the other judges; he did not lead tribes against the enemy, but fought personal battles against the Philistines. He also had a weakness for Philistine women, including Delilah. Most of all, Samson was famous for his great strength – he killed a lion with his bare hands and slew a thousand Philistines with the jawbone of an ass. As a Nazirite, he did not cut his hair and claimed that this was the secret of his strength. Delilah betrayed his secret to the Philistines; they cut his hair while he was sleeping, and *"his strength left him."* After his hair had regrown in prison, Samson destroyed the Philistine temple in Gaza by pushing out the two central pillars, thus killing both the worshipers and himself.

*SAMSON IS DEDICATED TO BE A NAZIRITE: JUDG. 13:5*

*SAMSON'S STRENGTH: JUDG. 14:6–8*

*DELILAH BETRAYS SAMSON'S SECRET: JUDG. 16:18*

*SAMSON'S DEATH: JUDG. 16:30*

## WOMEN IN THE JUDGES STORIES

In the Judges stories, women are at the disposal of men (e.g., Achsah offered as a prize, 1:11–15) and are victims of violence. But they also have control in life, a fact less evident in Israel's later history. Thus Deborah is described as both a "prophetess" and a judge – this term may be an anachronism, but it seems certain that she was a charismatic leader who revealed YHWH's word and will. As a woman, Deborah could not lead the Israelite army, so she appointed Barak as her commander, and he acted on her orders.

The story of Jephthah (Judg. 11–12:7) is also notable for its portrayal of a strong female protagonist, although Jephthah's unnamed daughter is quite different from both Deborah and Jael. This tragic story explains the local custom that arose in Israel, whereby *"for four days every year the daughters of Israel would go out to lament the daughter of Jephthah the Gileadite"* (Judg. 11:40). Human sacrifice was forbidden (Lev. 18:21; cf. 20:2), but this story may represent a time when the practice still occurred out of desperation, such as when God's special aid was needed (2 Kgs. 3:27).

## HEROIC FIGURES

The call of Gideon has two notable signs of God. First, both a kid and unleavened bread are consumed by fire (Judg. 6:19–21), and second, the sign of dew on the fleece that was left out all night when the surrounding floor was dry, followed by the next trial with dew on the floor but not on the fleece (Judg. 6:36–40). Gideon's reluctance to accept his commission echoes the call and commission of Moses (Exod. 3), thus emphasizing the important role that Gideon was to play in rescuing God's people. When they were victorious over a vastly superior enemy, which *"lay along the valley as thick as locusts"* (Judg. 7:12), the rightness of God's cause was demonstrated.

The stories of Samson are likely to have been transmitted as folklore (*pp.74–75*) before being written down and set in a Deuteronomistic framework. They have typical folklore motifs, including the barren wife being promised a special son, and a hero with a secret strength but a fatal weakness. These stories also typically contain riddles and heroic deeds, and explain the causes of things. Samson became a major inspiration for art, music, and literature, showing the power of folklore to persist, especially when it has been embodied in the Bible. Through his struggles with the lion and his suffering under the Philistines, he became a Christlike figure. Representations of Samson are found in medieval churches, and many famous artists were inspired to paint him, including Doré, Ghiberti, Dürer, Rubens, Mantegna, and Rembrandt. John Milton transformed him into a tragic hero in his poem *Samson Agonistes*, and this, in turn, provided the inspiration for Handel's oratorio *Samson*.

For further reading see bibliography numbers: 39, 40, 217, 369, 715, 756

# EARLY RELIGION

## OF THE ISRAELITES

*Our understanding of early Israelite religion rests very heavily on later sources, which portray it in terms of their own ideas and concerns. There is evidence to suggest that early religion differed from later belief and practice in certain key respects.*

NO biblical text sets out comprehensively to describe religious practice in Israel before the Monarchy (tenth century BCE), but frequent references are found to this practice in the books of Joshua through to 1 Samuel. These are part of the so-called "Deuteronomistic History" (p.105), which explains Israel's later troubles in terms of its failure to obey the laws set out in Deuteronomy.

## THE LAWS OF DEUTERONOMY

According to the account in Deuteron-omy, Israelite religion was intended to be centered on one location, chosen by God (cf. Deut. 12:13–14). From the time of Solomon, this was the Temple in Jerusalem; previous to this, it had been whatever place held the Ark of the Covenant. The Ark moved around: in Judges 20:27 it is at Bethel, while in 1 Samuel 3:3 it is at Shiloh (*see below*). It was finally brought to Jerusalem by King David (2 Sam. 6). The texts also stress that the laws and practices of the religion were set out from the beginning in the Covenant with God to which the Israelites had assented. So the practice was the same at the time of the Judges as it was in the late monarchic period. Any religious belief or practice that was at variance with the account in Deuteronomy was an offense or a rebellion against God, to be

> **❝** *Take care that you do not offer your burnt offerings at any place you happen to see. But only at the place that the* LORD *will choose.* **❞**
>
> (Deuteronomy 12:13–14)

excised from Israel. But reality was more diverse than this, and attempts to describe early Israelite religion can only catch glimpses of it through the later interpretations. The mobility of the Ark, for instance, is used to explain the previous legitimacy of sacrifice outside Jerusalem; many scholars now doubt whether there was only one fixed covenant in the early period. The biblical account, then, is measuring early practices against its own, later, standards, and what it deems to be unacceptable may well have been ordinary practice at an earlier date.

## SANCTUARIES AND SHRINES

Families were central in religion, and when they moved they took their worship with them, building altars (Gen. 13:18; 33:20) or pillars (Gen. 28:18; 31:45) where they settled. So there were many sacred places. Of note were Shechem (Gen. 12:6; 33:18–20; Josh. 24; 1 Kgs. 12:1) and Shiloh (Josh. 18:1; 1 Sam. 1–4), but many other sacred places are mentioned – for example, Gilgal (Josh. 4:20), Bethel (Gen. 28:10–22), Mizpah (1 Sam. 7:5ff.), Gibeon (1 Kgs. 3:4), and Ophrah (Judg. 6:11–24). It now seems clear that there was much con-tinuity between Canaanite and Israelite culture and religion, despite the later sense of conflict between them. God was often called by the name El, the name of the Canaanites' chief deity, and shares many of the characteristics of that deity; certain myths and stories may also have a Canaanite

**SHILOH**
*It was at Shiloh that the tent of meeting was set up in the first days after the conquest, and it was the main sanctuary at the time of the Judges. The image (right) shows the remains of the sanctuary.*

# THE ORAL TRADITION

*When considering the early religion of the Israelites, it is important to remember that the material of this religion would have been passed on from generation to generation by word of mouth, and that this transmission took particular forms.*

In the days before the invention of printing and books, information had to be memorized and passed from person to person and from generation to generation by word of mouth. Information about everything: how to do things like fighting a war or making a boat; the history of one's family and people; the origin of the world and of all that happens in it (accounts of why or how things have come into being are known as "etiological," from Greek *aitia*, "a cause"); how to behave and what to do in times of birth, marriage, illness, and death. Most of this is so important for the survival and well-being of the people in question that the information was told in forms that could easily be remembered – such as myths, sagas, folk tales, legends, riddles,

**Jewish children receiving oral instruction.**

songs, and proverbs. That is why oral traditions change very little over time, as we can still see today in areas like parts of Africa and India. Even in countries where books are plentiful, children at play recite rhymes that have varied little from generation to generation. Before the arrival of paper and books, memory and learning played a vital part, which is why oral tradition is remarkably stable. This is important when considering such things as the composition of the Pentateuch (*pp.22–23*) and the transmission of the words of Jesus before the Gospels were written down. In Judaism the Written Torah of the Pentateuch is augmented by the Oral Torah (*Torah sheb'al peh*, "Torah according to mouth"), culminating in collections known as the Mishnah and the Talmud.

background. It seems very likely, therefore, that Canaanite religion was not simply in contest with Israel, but that it contributed to the later character of religious belief and practice. Even practices often regarded as distinctively Israelite, such as circumcision or the rejection of images, are to be found elsewhere among the cultures of Syria–Palestine, emphasizing the degree to which Israelite tradition developed within this context, not simply in opposition to it.

## GENERAL OUTLINE

It is as hard to reconstruct early Israelite religion as it is to reconstruct early Israel. There was a sense of certain families belonging to a kinship group, but the components of the kinship group changed and followed different histories, although they could call on one another in times of crisis. The belief that they were organized into a formal bond like the Greek city-states (*amphictyonies*) now seems improbable. Worship was focused on local sanctuaries or shrines, each with its own practices and stories, often associated with a specific God or name of God. Thus El is often qualified by being called El Bethel, El Berith, El Shaddai, El Olam, El Roi, El Elyon, or even El Elohe Yisrael, El of the God (or "god") of Israel (Gen. 33:20: *"There be erected an altar and called*

*it El-Elohe-Yisrael"*). Many stories in the Bible, especially in Genesis, Joshua, and Judges, are likely to have come from these early sanctuaries. The early religion allowed that El, the supreme God, had heavenly agents or deputies, especially in the form of angels or messengers (Greek, *angelos*, Hebrew *mal'ak*, "messenger") (*see pp.42–43*).

> ❝ I am the LORD your God, who brought you out of the land of Egypt, out of the house of slavery; you shall have no other gods before me. ❞
>
> (Deuteronomy 5:6–7)

## YHWH, THE ONE GOD

Since there was not yet a nation of Israel, as such, we cannot state that YHWH was strictly a national god, but common worship of YHWH became a key factor in the growth of Israelite self-identity. Gradually, YHWH took over the domain and functions of the Canaanite god El, until the claim could be made that YHWH *was* El, creator of the world and ruler of the heavens. This fact is reflected, for instance, in the book of Deuteronomy 32:8. The earliest text of this (Qumran and LXX, the Septuagint, the Greek translation) read: *"When Elyon [the Most High] apportioned the nations, when he divided humankind, he fixed the boundaries of the peoples according to the number of the gods; the LORD's own portion was his people."* This translation of the text was later revised to read *"... according to the number of the sons of Israel,"* because YHWH was no longer distinct from El.

For further reading see bibliography numbers: 6, 95, 237, 470, 490, 532, 561, 711

# THE BOOK OF
# RUTH

*This short book tells the story of a widow whose devotion to her mother-in-law, faith in God, and integrity in the face of hostile circumstances are recognized and rewarded by God.*

THE book of Ruth is a moving story set in the time of the judges (*see pp.104–5*). It tells the story of a widow from Moab. By her good works and faith she attracts the attention of a wealthy Israelite who marries her and by whom she has a son. Through her son, the story establishes Ruth as an ancestor of King David. Ruth is regarded as the great example of a Gentile becoming a Jew, in other words, a righteous convert to Judaism. One main purpose of the book is to show how God's goodness extends beyond the Covenant People of Israel to a foreigner. In the Christian Bible, the book of Ruth is placed between the books of Judges and 1 Samuel, while in the Hebrew Bible it is the first of the five *Megillot* (Festival Scrolls), usually found after Proverbs. In Jewish tradition, the book is read at the Festival of Weeks (Shavu'ot, or Pentecost), the festival of harvest, because the story of Ruth is set at the time of the barley harvest.

**RUTH AND NAOMI**
*This 19th-century English painting shows the devoted Moabitess Ruth with her mother-in-law, Naomi.*

## JEWISH INTERPRETATIONS

The *Great Midrash* (*Midrash Rabba*), one of the ancient Jewish commentaries, says of Ruth 2:12: "Come and consider how great is the power of the righteous, and how great is the power of righteousness [or *tsedeqah*, "charity"], and how great the power of those who do good deeds, for they shelter neither in the shadow of the morning, nor in the shadow of the wings of the earth, nor in the shadow of the sun, but under the shadow of God at whose word the world was created" (5:4). The Jewish commentator Rabbi Zeira said of the book of Ruth: "This scroll, there is nothing in it about impurity and purity, about things permitted, or not permitted – so why was it written? To teach you how great is the reward for performing deeds of faithful love" (*Ruth Rabba* 2:15). Ruth is rewarded for her attention to her mother-in-law, Naomi.

## REDEEMERS AND REDEMPTION

Although it is a short, moral tale of faith and devotion, the book of Ruth is also an account of the harsh realities of life as a widow on the margins of Israelite society. Not only does Ruth encounter hostility as a Moabitess (Ruth 2:9, 15, 16), but she and Naomi are impoverished, unprotected, and at risk. Structures existed to make sure such people were cared for. The responsibility traditionally fell on a husband's relative, a "kinsman," who redeemed the dead man's land and cared for his widow. Naomi's kinsman Boaz replaces her husband Elimelech's closest "redeemer" relative, who might otherwise obtain the land belonging to Naomi and claim it for himself. On marrying Ruth, Boaz also promises to preserve the family property and name.

## THE LAW OF REDEMPTION

This law, based on Leviticus 25, instructs a redeemer to buy back land forcibly sold by someone in debt, or buy him out of slavery. The law underlies Ruth 4:1–12. The marriage of Ruth and Boaz has a loose connection with levirate law, the ancient Jewish code that ensures succession, and which is contained in Deuteronomy 25:5–10, deals with the case of a man who dies childless. The brother of the dead man *either* must marry the widow and father a son, who takes the name of the dead man and inherits his portion in the Promised Land, *or* must release her to marry another man through the rite of *Halitzah*, or "taking off the shoe" (Deut. 25:7–10).

## THE PROVIDENCE OF GOD

The engaging storyline and vivid language of this book give the impression of a deceptively simple folktale. However, the book of Ruth also displays the providence of God, the hidden way in which God works out a purpose, even through the hardest and most bewildering circumstances (*see also* The Life of Joseph, *pp.44–45*, and the "Succession Narrative," 2 Sam. 9–20). Boaz says to Ruth: *"May the LORD reward your deeds. May you have a full recompense from the LORD, the God of Israel, under whose wings you have sought refuge,"* but only at the beginning and the end of the book (1:6 and 4:13) is God described as acting directly. The book of Ruth gives a high status to non-Jews, so some think that it was written to reject the policy of Ezra (*pp.160–61*) on mixed marriages, but the book is not direct enough for that to be likely. Certainly it shows that the Gentiles can be welcomed into the Covenant People with important roles. Ruth becomes the ancestor of David, to whom the Messianic promises are later made. In his genealogy of Jesus, Matthew includes Ruth and four other women with unusual marriage relations who played a part in God's purpose (1:2–16).

---

## THE LAMENT OF RUTH

The character of Ruth is often taken as a prime example of forbearance in the face of difficult circumstances. But because of her situation, Ruth is also often depicted as expressing the sadness of exile. This is the interpretation put on the story by the English Romantic poet John Keats (1795–1821), who wrote of the song of Ruth in his poem *Ode to a Nightingale*:

> **❝**The voice I hear this passing night was heard
> In ancient times by emperor and clown;
> Perhaps the self-same song that found a path
> Through the sad heart of Ruth, when sick for home,
> She stood in tears amid the alien corn**❞**

---

# THE BOOK

**TITLE**: Ruth

**HEBREW TITLE**: *Rut*

**DATE**: The setting of the book is the time of the judges (c.1100–1000BCE), but the writing belongs to a later date. This is indicated when the author explains former customs (Ruth 4:1–12). It is thought by some to be a post-exilic work, i.e., after 538BCE

**AUTHORSHIP**: Unknown; tradition attributes it to Samuel

# THE CONTENTS

## CHAPTER 1

Ruth had married Mahlon, the elder son of Elimelech and Naomi. After the deaths of Elimelech, Mahlon, and another son in Moab, Naomi is left without heirs in a foreign land. She decides to return home after the end of a famine there. This upsets her daughter-in-law Ruth, herself a Moabitess, who offers to accompany Naomi. Naomi and her daughters-in-law, Ruth and Orpah, leave Moab to travel to Bethlehem in Judah. Naomi and Ruth continue alone

## CHAPTERS 2–3

Ruth supports Naomi by gleaning in the fields of Boaz, a wealthy "kinsman." He shows his kindness to Ruth by allowing her special privileges. Ruth goes to Boaz at night, and he offers to support her if another kinsman will not redeem Naomi's land

## CHAPTER 4

Boaz redeems Ruth and marries her. Ruth gives birth to a son, Obed, the grandfather of David. Outline of the genealogy of David

# KEY THEMES

*God's goodness extends beyond the Covenant People of Israel*

•

*Redemption*

•

*The harsh realities of life as a widow*

For further reading see bibliography numbers: 24, 39, 76, 128, 296, 475, 482a, 690

# WOMEN
## IN ANCIENT ISRAEL

*Ancient Israel was a patriarchal society where family lines were male-based and polygamy was accepted. Women had few legal rights and were excluded from the ranks of religious officialdom. Yet this is far from a complete picture of the position of women in ancient Israel.*

LIVING in a male-dominated society, women had few social and legal rights, and were highly vulnerable without the protection of a male relative. Yet the Bible shows us that many women still exerted their influence on family and society. As matriarchs, prophets, rulers, and wives, women in the Bible enjoyed a role far superior to that which these broad descriptions of their circumstances might suggest (*see also p.107*).

## MATRIARCHS

Genesis tells the story of the Ancestors of Israel (the Patriarchs) from a male point of view, but it recognizes the prominent part played by the "mothers" (*immahot*) in establishing Israel. All four, Sarah, Rebekah, Rachel, and Leah, were chosen as the wives of the Patriarchs, rather than simply being found, and, with the exception of Sarah, the Bible recounts in

detail how they were chosen. Jews call them "Our mother ..." and they are increasingly entering Jewish liturgy outside Orthodox circles.

## PROPHETESSES

Although women could not be priests, there are a number of biblical women who are called prophetess. Later Jewish tradition named seven such women – Sarah, Miriam, Deborah, Hannah, Abigail, Huldah, and Esther – but only three of these seven actually have the title of prophetess in the Hebrew Bible. The first is Miriam, the sister of Aaron and Moses, who led the women of Israel in a celebratory dance and sang a song of praise to God after the Israelites

had crossed the Red (Reed) Sea (Exod. 15:20–21). Tradition remembers not only the site of her death and burial (Num. 20:1) but also her leading role in the Exodus (Mic. 6:4) and her punishment with leprosy for challenging Moses (Deut. 24:9; cf. Num. 12:1–16). Deborah, too, is called a prophetess (Judg. 5:2–31). The Song of Deborah, one of the oldest passages in the Bible,

**SONG OF THE SEA**
*Miriam headed the festivities of song and dance among the Israelite women as they celebrated victory over the Pharaoh's army and gave thanks to God. The sister of Aaron and Moses, Miriam is one of the women in the Bible cited as a prophetess.*

**A WIFE FOR ISAAC**
*Abraham sent his servant Eliezer to find a wife for his son Isaac. This 17th-century painting, by the Spanish artist Murillo, shows Rebekah offering Eliezer water while at the well with a group of other women. The servant identifies her as God's choice, and Rebekah returns with him to become Isaac's bride.*

**For further reading see bibliography numbers:** 29, 39, 90, 129, 150, 274, 286, 313, 427, 475, 555, 563, 582, 619, 665, 670, 756, 786, 871

**THE GOOD WIFE**
*"She rises while it is still night and provides food for her household and tasks for her servant-girls" (Prov. 31:15).*

calls her a "mother in Israel" (Judg. 5:7) and praises her leadership, which united the tribes of Israel. Finally, Huldah was a prophetess in the days of King Josiah of Judah (pp.144–45). After the Book of the Law had been found in the Temple, she received a delegation from Josiah in order to validate its authenticity and sent the king a message of consolation because of his piety (2 Kgs. 22:14–20).

## RULERS

Women are shown as powerful rulers, both good and bad. Deborah, the judge and prophetess, was good, but Jezebel, the wife of King Ahab of Israel (1 Kgs. 16:31),

persecuted God's prophets in the ninth century BCE (1 Kgs. 18:13; 19:1–3) and had Naboth killed in order to confiscate his land (1 Kgs. 21:1–16). Similarly, Athaliah seized power in Judah by killing all the royal family, and reigned for six years until she herself was deposed by a coup (2 Kgs. 11:1–20). Athaliah's coup can be understood in the light of the fact that she was the queen mother, and "queen mother" was an official position of great importance and influence (cf. 1 Kgs. 2:19; 15:9–10, 13).

## WIVES AND MOTHERS

Women were primarily wives, mothers, and household managers (see also pp.186–87), and the picture of the good wife in Proverbs 31:10–31 gives an idea of the skill and responsibility a woman could exercise in the domestic sphere. Hence, it is not surprising that many women are shown exerting a strong influence in this context. Rebekah's plans enable her son Jacob to steal his brother's blessing from their father Isaac (Gen. 27:1–40); the widows Ruth and Naomi use the kinship laws to their advantage in order to procure a husband for Ruth (Ruth 2–4); and Hannah takes the initiative and prays for a son (Samuel) despite her husband's acceptance of her barrenness (1 Sam. 1:1–28). Hannah's song of praise to God (1 Sam. 2:1–10) is echoed in Mary's Magnificat (Luke 1:46–55), and has a prophetic flavor. On a less maternal level, Abigail's diplomacy placates David after

**INSIDE AND OUTSIDE THE HOME**
*Aside from their roles as wives and mothers, the Bible also shows us how women worked outside the home. Royal establishments employed women as cooks and bakers (1 Sam. 8:13) and also as singers (2 Sam. 19:35). The terra-cotta figurine on the right shows a woman kneading dough, and the clay figurine on the left depicts a woman bathing. Both date from about the 12th century BCE.*

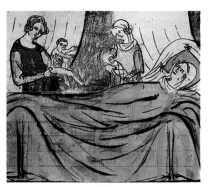

**THE MIDWIFE**
*Another possible role for women outside the home was that of midwife. This 14th-century manuscript depicts the midwives at Rebekah's bedside after she has given birth to her twin sons, Esau and Jacob.*

her husband Nabal has antagonized him, and she thereby not only preserves her own household but prevents David from taking unlawful revenge and incurring blood guilt (1 Sam. 25:2–35). Women are also shown as midwives (Exod. 1:15–21; 1 Sam. 4:20), mediums (1 Sam. 28), herders (Gen. 29:9), harvesters (Ruth 2:8–9), perfumers, cooks and bakers (1 Sam. 8:13), and, inevitably, prostitutes, both cultic and profane (Deut. 23:17–18; 1 Kgs. 3–16). All these examples go to show that, despite their limited public role and inferior status in the law, the presence and influence of women in Israelite society was considerable.

### NURTURING AND EDUCATING

*Mothers were expected to provide the primary care for their young, until they were weaned at the age of three. From the instructions in Proverbs 6:20, "do not forsake your mother's teaching," we may also presume that mothers played an important role in the moral and religious education of their young children. This Phoenician fertility goddess was probably used to protect the pregnant woman while she was at home.*

# THE BOOKS OF
# 1-2 SAMUEL

*The two books of Samuel tell the history of Israel from the time of the judges, through the establishment of the Monarchy and David's reign. The narrative with which Samuel ends is picked up at the beginning of First Kings.*

THE two books of Samuel are in reality one book, split at the time of the Greek translation, the Septuagint. In Hebrew tradition, they are considered one book. Many different kinds of writing are brought together in Samuel, and the book has been composed from different sources. One source is cited, though it has not survived: David's lament (2 Sam. 1:18–27), which comes from the *Book of Jashar* (*cf.* Josh. 10:13*ff.*). But Samuel was clearly considered as a whole, sustaining, as it does, a number of recurring themes (the fate of the Ark, the contested move from the rule of judges to the innovation of monarchy, the emergence and independence of prophets). Some episodes are out of sequence, but the overall narrative is driven forward with skill. The focus is the transition of a loosely related kinship (family) group, intermittently ruled by judges, to an embryonic nation ruled by a monarch. In this way, Israel resembled the nations that surrounded it: the nation comes of age. How realistic this picture actually is in relation to the history of the surrounding nations is now difficult to know, since so little evidence has survived apart from the biblical record, but what the picture conveys is powerful indeed. Impressive, too, is the way in which the picture is not wholly idealistic. It includes the problems: there was a false start in Saul, and David was by no means the perfect man or king.

**SAMUEL ANOINTS DAVID**
*The Prophet Samuel anointing King David: "Then Samuel took his horn of oil and anointed him in the midst of his brethren" (1 Sam. 16:13).*

## TO HAVE OR NOT TO HAVE A KING

A refrain in the book of Judges had been, *"In those days there was no king in Israel; all the people did what was right in their own eyes"* (Judg. 21:25): having a king was perceived by some to be the solution to Israel's problems. Yet when Samuel was asked by the elders to give them a king (1 Sam. 8:6–9), he saw it as a rejection both of himself as a judge and of God. He alluded to the warnings of Deuteronomy 17 about the dangers of having a king (1 Sam. 8:11–18). Nevertheless, the people still demanded a king *"so that we also may be like other nations"* (1 Sam. 8:20), and Samuel reluctantly acquiesced. This reluctance reflected the continuing conflict about the innovation. David's reign seemed to offer the national unity and stability that was lacking in the period of the Judges, but the tensions – between centralized power and the traditional independence of members of the kinship group – remained, as 1 and 2 Kings make clear.

## THE LORD'S ANOINTED

The word *mashiach*, transliterated as "Messiah," means "anointed." Someone anointed is set apart for God's work, and the Bible tells of other anointed figures. It was appropriate for kings who received their commission from both priests and prophets (Zadok the priest and Nathan the prophet anointed Solomon king), and that is why Samuel uses the word as a description of the king. After Saul had tried to have David killed (e.g., 1 Sam. 19), David refused to harm him, as he was the LORD's anointed – even though he had opportunities to do so (*"the LORD gave you into my hand in the cave; and some urged me to kill you, but I spared you. I said, 'I will not raise my hand against my lord; for he is the LORD's anointed,'"* 1 Sam. 24:10).

However, being "the LORD's anointed" meant that the king was bound to act as God required: he could not consider himself above the law of God, although many of the kings of Israel and Judah clearly acted as if they thought they could. God monitors David through the prophet Nathan (2 Sam. 12:1), who rebukes him for adultery and murder by telling a parable in which the king is meant to recognize himself (*"You are the man!"*). David is warned that his descendants will be accountable to God like others within the covenant community (*"I will be a father to him, and he shall be a son to me. When he commits iniquity, I will punish him with a rod such as mortals use, with blows inflicted by human beings,"* 2 Sam. 7:14). Kings have great authority, but always authority under God, as 1–2 Kings show.

## DAVID'S HOUSE AND GOD'S HOUSE

When David conquered Jerusalem, it brought a degree of stability (*"the king was settled in his house, and the LORD had given him rest from all his enemies around him,"* 2 Sam. 7:1). In particular, it offered to the members of the kinship group a neutral place to serve as capital – Jerusalem had not belonged to any one of them. This was reinforced by moving the Ark to Jerusalem, thus beginning the process of concentrating the worship of Israel's God in Jerusalem.

The process culminated in the next generation with Solomon's building of the Temple (also contested, because it contradicted the traditional independence of the tribes). It seems likely that David also took over some of the ritual and ideology of the original inhabitants (the Jebusites; cf. Gen. 14:18–20). This resulted in a high estimate of kings, who acquired a prominent role in the cult. The later concept of the Messiah is modeled on the kings of David's line. God thus offers to build a house, or dynasty, for David that will last forever (*"Your house and your kingdom shall be made sure forever before me; your throne shall be established forever,"* 2 Sam. 7:16).

The extravagant hopes that were invested in the royal descendants of David (*see,* for example, Pss. 2, 45, 72, 110; Isa. 7:10–16; 9:2–7; 11:1–5; Mic. 5:1–7) were repeatedly contradicted by their behavior, which was often immoral and in direct contradiction of the word of God. As a result, the Exile could eventually be seen as a just punishment. Even so, the hopes invested in the Messiah of God did not disappear with the last of the kings of Judah. The hopes were transferred to a future figure yet to come, and thus began the Messianic hope in a new and future sense.

## THE BOOK

**TITLE**: 1–2 Samuel

**HEBREW TITLE**: Originally one book named after Samuel. The Septuagint divided it into two parts

**DATE**: The text gives no clues, but it is now part of the Deuteronomistic History (completed, at the latest, during the Exile)

**AUTHORSHIP**: No author is named. The Talmud attributes it to Samuel, and after his death to Gad and Nathan

## THE CONTENTS

**1 SAMUEL 1–12**
**THE LAST OF THE JUDGES, SAMUEL**
1 God answers Hannah's prayer: Samuel is born
2:1–10 Hannah's song of thanksgiving
2:11–36 The end of the line of Eli as priests
3 The call of Samuel
4–6 The Philistines and the Ark
7 Samuel as judge
8–12 Saul becomes Israel's first king

**1 SAMUEL 13–31 THE FIRST KING, SAUL**
13–15 Saul's disobedience and rejection
16–31 Saul and David; death of Saul and Jonathan

**2 SAMUEL 1–20**
**DAVID – THE FIRST IN A NEW DYNASTY**
1 David's lament
2–4 Abner's revolt and the murder of Ishbaal
5–7 David establishes his throne and moves his capital and the Ark to Jerusalem
8–10 David's conquests
11–12 David and Bathsheba, and Nathan's rebuke
13–20 The revolt of Absalom and Sheba

**2 SAMUEL 21–24**
Epilogue; David's Song of Victory; his last words; the census and the plague

## KEY THEMES

*Kingship and its relation to the Covenant*

•

*Obedience and disobedience*

For further reading see bibliography numbers: 41, 131, 302, 342, 358, 359, 404, 548a, 622

# TEMPLES

## AND THE TABERNACLE

*The Jerusalem Temple became the center of pilgrimage and worship — indeed, it came to be
regarded as the center of the world. But it was not always so. The First Temple in Jerusalem
was built in the reign of Solomon, and the Bible mentions other earlier temples or shrines.*

A TEMPLE in the ancient world
was regarded as the dwelling
place of a god, and this concept
was reflected in both its structure and
its furniture. Temples are common in
virtually all religions. The strongly
exclusive character of the religion of
YHWH may be one reason why the
building of the Temple by Solomon
was bitterly opposed by those who
looked back to the wilderness days,
when God did not need a house to
dwell in. In general, a temple was a
roofed building, as a house would be,
and it was furnished with items that
symbolized the divine presence in
the building, such as a lampstand, a
table for ceremonial bread ("shew-
bread"), a seat or throne of some
kind, and occasionally a statue.

## THE TABERNACLE

Exodus 33:7–11 records the tradition
of a "tent of meeting" outside the
camp, where Moses and others
would go. The basic tent concept is
expanded into a splendid "Tabernacle"
(Exod. 25–27; cf. 1 Kgs. 6–7). The
Tabernacle had all the equipment of a
permanent temple (Exod. 25; 26; 40):
an inner sanctum where God could be
consulted, symbolized by the mercy
seat above the Ark; a courtyard with
an altar upon which sacrifice was
offered; and a family of priests to serve
there. The picture of the Tabernacle
expresses God's constant presence
in the midst of a wandering people.
Whatever the actual form of the tent
shrine, though, once Israel settled in
the land, it was superseded by
permanent temples.

CONSECRATION OF THE TABERNACLE
*The place where God could be consulted during the
wilderness years was the "tent of meeting." This
wall painting shows the consecration of the Tabernacle.*

## THE HOUSE OF GOD

Because a temple was dedicated to God, it was a place where God might be revealed to worshipers (1 Sam. 3:2–10; cf. Isa. 6:1–5), and where people could go to ask for divine guidance (1 Sam. 22:11–15). Every temple had an altar associated with it, where offerings could be brought, and this stood outside in the temple courtyard. Temples would be served by resident families of priests (1 Sam. 1:3; 2:11). Great feelings of awe and holiness are associated with temples. Holiness (see p.63) is a dynamic and powerful sense that God cannot stand anything that defiles or corrupts. As in a nuclear reactor, the core is the source of energy, but if mishandled, it can be destructive. Only the highly trained and pure can work near the holy, hence the development of priests (not at random, but in families) to undertake this. Others cannot draw near. To infringe upon this is to invite destruction of oneself (see 2 Sam. 6:1ff.), or of a larger group through plague.

## EARLY TEMPLES AND SHRINES

The most famous of the early temples is the one at Shiloh, where the boy Samuel served alongside Eli the priest (1 Sam. 1:9; 2:18). It gained its reputation from being the place where the Ark of God, the ultimate symbol of the divine presence, was installed after the conquest of Israel (1 Sam. 3:3). But once the Ark had been moved elsewhere, the temple at Shiloh declined in importance. However, there were two other early shrines that kept their importance well into the Monarchy (tenth century BCE): those at Bethel, just to the north of Jerusalem, and Dan in northern Israel. An image was set up at Dan

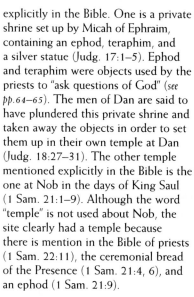

**CANAANITE SHRINE**
*This clay model of a shrine with idols dates from the eighth century BCE. They are identifiable as Canaanite fertility figures, while the two pillars at the entrance to the shrine recall the two pillars that stood at the entrance to Solomon's Temple (see pp.132–33). Such archaeological finds suggest that Canaanite religious practice coexisted with, and influenced, Israelite religion.*

(Judg. 18:27–31), and glimpses of the temple at Bethel are found in Genesis 28:10–22, Judges 20:18–28, Amos 7:12–13, and 2 Kings 23:15–20.

Later on, in the days of the Monarchy (tenth century BCE), Jeroboam, the first king of Israel, capitalized on the religious significance of the two sites by setting up cultic statues at both of them (1 Kgs. 12: 26–30). By the second half of the eighth century BCE, the site of Bethel was referred to as a royal temple (Amos 7:13), and it was still an important religious site in the days of Josiah at the end of the seventh century BCE (cf. 2 Kgs. 23:15–16). Although several other temples probably existed, only two more are mentioned

**CANAANITE ALTAR, MEGIDDO**
*Megiddo is where it is said the final battle between good and evil will take place.*

**EARLY ISRAELITE BUILDINGS**
*Relatively few structures survive from the Israelite period, and our knowledge of their style is limited. Such buildings were probably simple, as suggested by this storehouse from Tel Hatzor in Galilee. It dates from about the eighth century BCE.*

explicitly in the Bible. One is a private shrine set up by Micah of Ephraim, containing an ephod, teraphim, and a silver statue (Judg. 17:1–5). Ephod and teraphim were objects used by the priests to "ask questions of God" (see pp.64–65). The men of Dan are said to have plundered this private shrine and taken away the objects in order to set them up in their own temple at Dan (Judg. 18:27–31). The other temple mentioned explicitly in the Bible is the one at Nob in the days of King Saul (1 Sam. 21:1–9). Although the word "temple" is not used about Nob, the site clearly had a temple because there is mention in the Bible of priests (1 Sam. 22:11), the ceremonial bread of the Presence (1 Sam. 21:4, 6), and an ephod (1 Sam. 21:9).

For further reading see bibliography numbers: 49, 95, 183, 371, 381, 456, 470, 506, 607

# SAMUEL

*Samuel is portrayed as a man of power and influence. Dedicated to God before he was born, Samuel heard the prophetic call at an early age and went on to become a figurehead for the people of Israel.*

SAMUEL was the son of Elkanah and Hannah, and a descendant of Levi. He was not of the line of Aaron, but was able to act as a priest because the later rules reserving this privilege for the sons of Aaron had not yet been put into effect.

HANNAH IS UNABLE TO BEAR CHILDREN: 1 SAM. 1:5

Because she was barren, Hannah went to the sanctuary at Shiloh where Eli and his sons were priests. There, she and her husband made offerings and prayed for a son. Hannah promised to dedicate to God any son who was born, and, in due course, she gave birth to Samuel. After he had been weaned, Hannah dedicated him to God as she had promised, and spoke the famous prayer that (like the Magnificat of Mary, *p.317*) celebrates the power of God to reverse the ordinary expectations of life.

HANNAH PRAYS FOR A SON: 1 SAM. 1:11

HANNAH'S PRAYER: 1 SAM. 2:1–10

At an early age, Samuel began to serve God in the sanctuary at Shiloh, where Eli's sons were becoming notorious for their corrupt behavior – so much so that a *"man of God"* prophesied that God would overthrow them. Samuel, however, kept faith and was called by God

SAMUEL ENTERS THE HOUSE OF ELI: 1 SAM. 2:11

PROPHECY AGAINST ELI'S HOUSEHOLD: 1 SAM. 2:27–36

Samuel relates God's message to Eli.

during the night to hear the same message of threat against the house of Eli. As Samuel grew up, he kept the word of God carefully and was recognized by the people as a *"trustworthy prophet of the LORD."* The meaning of this soon became apparent. The threat against the house of Eli was brought to pass when the Philistines captured the Ark: Eli's two sons were killed, and Eli, too, died when he heard the news.

SAMUEL KEEPS THE WORD OF GOD: 1 SAM. 3:19–21

THE DEATH OF ELI: 1 SAM. 4:18

Samuel appeared as a new leader who defeated the Philistines. In the role of priest, he *"cried out to the LORD for Israel,"* yet is later described as one who *"judged Israel all the days of his life"* (7:15). Some people among the tribes, or family groups, decided that it was time for a more permanent form of leadership, and they asked Samuel to appoint a king. Samuel warned them against this request, but the people of Israel refused to listen. God then told Samuel that Saul would become king: *"I will send to you a man from the land of Benjamin, and you shall anoint him to be ruler over my people Israel."* Saul was searching for his lost

SAMUEL MAKES AN OFFERING TO GOD: 1 SAM. 7:9

THE PEOPLE ASK SAMUEL TO APPOINT A KING: 1 SAM. 8:5

GOD CHOOSES SAUL TO BECOME KING: 1 SAM. 9:16

donkeys and was looking for a seer ("seers" were later called "prophets," 1 Sam. 9:9). Samuel not only acted as a seer in the matter of the donkeys but also anointed Saul as king. Saul immediately began the task of unifying the tribes into a common enterprise against the Ammonites, and thus began the task of creating a nation, or a people, as opposed to a coalition of family groups.

*SAMUEL ANOINTS SAUL AS KING: 1 SAM. 10:1*

## SAMUEL'S WARNING TO SAUL

By now, Samuel was *"old and gray."* The argument about Saul's appointment as king continued, and Samuel could only advise the people of Israel that, provided they keep faith with God, all would be well; otherwise they and their king would be swept away (this is the understanding of history expressed in the book of Deuteronomy, used to give thematic order to the books of history in the Bible). As if to illustrate this point, Saul panicked at the threat of the Philistines and failed to trust God and Samuel. As a result, Samuel foretold the fall of Saul's house and kingdom. Saul's disobedience became even more flagrant when he refused to destroy completely the Amalekites, killing the people but keeping *"all that was valuable,"* including their best sheep and cattle for sacrifice. Samuel replied with words that became characteristic of later prophets: *"Has the LORD as great delight in burnt offerings and sacrifices, as in obedience to the voice of the LORD? Surely, to obey is better than sacrifice, and to heed than the fat of rams"* (15:22).

*SAMUEL'S FAREWELL ADDRESS: 1 SAM. 12:2–18*

*SAMUEL WARNS THE PEOPLE TO KEEP FAITH IN GOD: 1 SAM. 12:24–25*

*SAUL FAILS TO TRUST IN GOD: 1 SAM. 13:8–14*

*SAUL SPARES THE AMALEKITE KING: 1 SAM. 15:8*

Samuel then broke with Saul and anointed David as king. From this point on, Samuel withdrew to Ramah, and eventually he died there. Even so, he had a final word to say to Saul, when, in desperation at the threat of the Philistines, Saul went to a woman who could summon Samuel's shadow from the dead (the dead at that time were believed to be a weak shadow cast into the grave, so Samuel could be recognized only by his prophet's mantle). But Samuel could only repeat his words of doom as a consequence of Saul's earlier disobedience.

*SAMUEL ANOINTS DAVID AS KING: 1 SAM. 16:1–13*

*SAUL CONSULTS A MEDIUM: 1 SAM. 28:8–25*

## THE ROLES OF SAMUEL

Samuel lived in a time of unrest and transition as Israel moved from local leadership to a system of national unity. At the time of the Philistine threat and in the absence of another figurehead, the Israelites looked to Samuel for leadership. He was a man of power and influence and is depicted in many roles, including prophet, judge, priest, and leader of the nation (although some of these roles, particularly in the judicial sense, may have been combined). Samuel appointed Saul and David as the first two kings of Israel. The policy of introducing kings was contested until long after the time of Samuel, but under David this system became widely accepted, not least for the advantages it gave in strengthening the otherwise divided family groups for defense and eventually attack.

## THE TRANSITION FROM JUDGES TO KINGS

The story of Samuel has been told in a way that makes it clear how Israel moved from one system of authority and government to another. Samuel is the bridge from the old system of judges *(pp. 104–5)* to a new system of kings: the long speech in 1 Samuel 12 summarizes the transition from judges to kings, connecting it with the continuing story of God and the people. Under the old system, the families had their own authorities and elders, but in a time of crisis, the best person for the task at hand was appointed the overall leader. When the crisis was over, the family groups reverted to their ordinary practice of looking after themselves. Samuel is portrayed as a God-chosen leader of the charismatic kind, but he looks beyond himself to a hereditary type of kingship. The unnamed *"man of God"* who prophesied that God would overthrow the house of Eli (1 Sam. 2:27–36) is a reminder that events are shaped by God. Death, panic, and disaster result from both the wickedness of leaders and the unfaithfulness of the people. This theme continues throughout the book of Samuel.

In the New Testament, Samuel was regarded as the last of the judges (Acts 13:20), the first of the Prophets (Acts 3:24), and one of the great heroes of faith (Heb. 11:32). The dispute about the intrinsic rights and wrongs of kingship became of great importance in the debates of the 17th century, leading up to the French Revolution and the establishment of the United States as a republic. The debate centered on whether God approves of kings, irrespective of their personal behavior (the divine right of kings to rule), or whether God's approval is dependent on their obedience to divine moral law. If kings disobey the word of God, as Saul did, then the overthrow, not just of a house but of kingship itself, is not against the will of God.

For further reading see bibliography numbers: 42, 267, 312, 559, 622, 640

THE LIFE OF

# SAUL

*Saul was the first king of Israel. Despite victory over the Ammonites in the early days of his reign, he later disobeyed the command of God on three occasions, and his kingship was eventually passed to David.*

THE story of Saul is told in 1 Samuel 9–31. He is introduced as a handsome young man, standing *"head and shoulders above everyone else."* He was the son of Kish, a man of wealth, but evidently not so wealthy that he could afford to overlook the loss of three donkeys. Saul and a servant were sent to search for the donkeys but without success. The servant urged Saul to go to a man of God, a seer (later to be called a prophet), to see if he could find the lost animals. The seer, Samuel, had been alerted by God that he would meet a man whom he was to anoint as the first king of Israel. Samuel told Saul that the donkeys had been found, and he should meet Samuel at a place of religious celebration – a "shrine" – where he should prepare for other things. Even though Saul demurred on the grounds that he came from a humble family, Samuel anointed him the next morning to be leader over God's inheritance: *"The LORD has anointed you ruler over his people Israel. You shall reign over the people of the LORD and you will save them from the hand of their enemies all around."* Samuel told Saul that

mysterious signs would be offered, including an encounter with a band of prophets coming down from the shrine. A graphic description of the way in which the earliest prophets used music to induce ecstatic states is offered in verses 5–7. Samuel told Saul that as the prophets played their music, *"the spirit of the LORD will possess you"* and he too would prophesy, leading the people to question: *"Is Saul also among the prophets?"*

Saul returned home, and in a second story of selection, Samuel again designated Saul as the one whom God had chosen to be king. Saul set about the task of unifying the tribes: Nahash, king of the Ammonites, besieged Jabesh-gilead, a town to the east of the Jordan, and only agreed to peace provided he could gouge out the right eye of each of the tribespeople *"and thus put disgrace upon all Israel."* When the people of Jabesh were given seven days' respite, Saul heard of their plight and was greatly angered. He sent the cut-up parts of two oxen to each of the Twelve Tribes, with the message that if the tribes did not rally, their own oxen would

**Saul and David, the first kings of Israel.**

*DESCRIPTION OF SAUL: 1 SAM. 9:2*

*SAUL SEARCHES FOR THE LOST DONKEYS: 1 SAM. 9:3*

*GOD TELLS SAMUEL THAT SAUL WILL BE KING: 1 SAM. 9:16*

*SAMUEL ANOINTS SAUL: 1 SAM. 10:1*

*SAMUEL INSTRUCTS SAUL: 1 SAM. 10:5*

*SAUL PROPHESIES: 1 SAM. 10:10*

*SAUL IS PROCLAIMED KING: 1 SAM. 10:20–24*

*AMMONITE THREATS: 1 SAM. 11:2*

*SAUL SEEKS SUPPORT FROM THE TWELVE TRIBES: 1 SAM. 11:7*

be treated in the same way: *"Whoever does not come out after Saul and Samuel, so shall it be done to his oxen."* The tribes came to Saul, who then led them in the defeat and destruction of the Ammonites. In this way, the first steps were taken toward a kingdom in which the interests of the parts were given up for the good of the whole.

After the defeat of the Ammonites, Saul was confirmed as king and, soon after, set about defeating the Philistines. Despite the signs and proofs that had accompanied his rise to power, he failed at his first test: having been told to wait for Samuel's arrival, Saul panicked and was rebuked for his disobedience. Even so, he defeated the Philistines and embarked on raids and campaigns in the surrounding territories.

## SAUL LOSES HIS KINGSHIP

Saul was entrusted with a command from God to destroy the Amalekites and to do so completely: *"utterly destroy all that they have; do not spare them, but kill both man and woman, child and infant, ox and sheep, camel and donkey."* Once again, he compromised, sparing the life of Agag, the king, and keeping back the best of the Amalekite possessions, ostensibly for a sacrifice. Samuel ferociously denounced any reliance on sacrifice rather than on obedience and told Saul that he had been rejected as king. As Samuel turned to go, Saul caught hold of his mantle to stop him. As the mantle tore, Samuel told him that the kingdom had been given *"to a neighbor of yours, who is better than you."*

This episode is followed by Samuel anointing David, a source of trouble for Saul. David entered Saul's service and gained renown through his killing, as Israel's champion, of Goliath. Saul became increasingly jealous of David and of his fame among the people, and made several attempts to kill him. Driven to increasing desperation by the threat of the Philistines, Saul visited a medium to consult the spirit of Samuel, only to hear that the judgment of God against him for his disobedience was irrevocable. In a last battle against his old enemies on Mount Gilboa, before the Philistines could capture him, Saul *"took his own sword and fell upon it."*

*SAUL DEFEATS THE AMMONITES:*
*1 SAM. 11:11*

*SAUL IS CONFIRMED AS KING: 1 SAM. 11:15*

*SAUL'S FIRST TEST: 1 SAM. 13:13–14*

*SAUL FAILS TO DESTROY THE AMALEKITES: 1 SAM. 15:9*

*SAUL IS REJECTED AS KING: 1 SAM. 15:23*

*DAVID IS ANOINTED AS KING: 1 SAM. 16:13*

*SAUL'S ATTEMPTS TO KILL DAVID: 1 SAM. 18:11*

*SAUL TAKES HIS OWN LIFE: 1 SAM. 31:4*

## THE INTRODUCTION OF KINGSHIP

Saul is an enigmatic figure, standing halfway between the charismatic "judges" (leaders without successors, who took charge in a particular crisis) and the kings, who expected their sons to succeed. Saul attempted to draw the tribes of Israel together and to found a dynasty, but it was left to David to achieve this. Much care is taken in the stories to show that Saul had received authority from God: not only was he anointed, but he received the direct inspiration of an authentic prophet, even though he had not been brought up or trained in a prophetic group. The Deuteronomistic understanding of history (used to give thematic order to the Historical books of the Bible; see p.105) found a ready explanation for the failure of Saul: he disobeyed the commands of God and brought upon himself the punishment that opened the way for David. It may be that the experiment of kingship was still too unfamiliar and contested during the time of Saul (see pp.118–19). What made Saul different from the judges, and the experiment in kingship necessary, was the *constant* threat of Philistine attack.

In the past, judges had come to the fore in order to deal with a particular crisis. When the crisis was over, family and tribal groups returned to their everyday forms of organization and authority. During the time of Saul, the Philistines attempted to move inland from the coastal plain, and they were successful in many of their campaigns. Saul fulfilled the people's need for a permanent kind of leadership, but it was left to David to find the ideology to transform it into kingship. This he did when he captured Jerusalem and adapted the forms of kingship and ritual of the Jebusites.

## LATER INTERPRETATION

The Bible does not conceal weaknesses in Saul's character, but Jewish tradition is able to treat him sympathetically. In a ninth-century CE collection of sermons (*Pesiqta Rabbati*), careful attention to the text in 1 Samuel shows that Saul was humble (10:22), that he kept the Levitical rules of purity even when eating common food (9:24), that he spent his own money to save Israel (11:7), and that he deemed his servant equal in worth to himself (9:5). Christian interpretation has been more inclined to stress his disobedience and suicide, but the tragedy in his history has proved fascinating to artists, writers, and composers. Browning, in his long poem *Saul*, looks at the story through the eyes of David, who, in a memorable passage, prophesies Saul's redemption. Rilke (*David Sings Before Saul*) stayed closer to the tragic earth than to the dream: "Come down from your throne and break in pieces / This my harp you are exhausting so."

**For further reading see bibliography numbers:** 97, 102, 131, 266, 267, 358, 402

# KINGSHIP
## IN THE ANCIENT WORLD

*In the ancient world, kings played a key role in linking Heaven and earth. Kings were sacred, and in some countries they were regarded as divine. How far did the idea of sacral kingship influence the ideas of kingship in Judah and Israel, and of the coming Messiah?*

ACROSS the ancient Near East, different cultures held different views of kingship that linked the king in some way with God or the gods. Vast, monumental buildings, palace and temple complexes, royal tombs, city walls, gateways, fortifications, storerooms, archive collections, and other buildings are testimony to the impact of the ideology of royalty on ancient civilization.

Early civilizations were characterized by centralized state or city-state administrations. In the unified state of Egypt, power was concentrated in the hands of the king. By contrast, Mesopotamian cities were originally independent, and the land was divided among city-states and independent rulers engaged in a constant struggle for hegemony. The ideas of kingship reflect these differences.

**SYMBOLS OF KINGSHIP**
*The construction of the pyramids in ancient Egypt required massive investment of state resources, both raw materials and human labor. They boldly articulate the awesome sense of security, authority, and power in which kingship was grounded.*

## EGYPT

In Egypt the king was regarded as a deity. A god from birth, on his death he was worshiped in temples of the dead. His divinity did not depend upon his political power, nor did political decline mean the demise of his divinity. During his life he was priest to other gods; his word was law. Evidence suggests that in later Egypt the king moved farther down in the hierarchy of gods.

## MESOPOTAMIA

The peoples of Mesopotamia held various views of kingship. To the Sumerians, the king was a "great man," the agent of the gods, while the Semitic kings of Akkad were identified with the god of the city-state over which they ruled. The Babylonians and Assyrians believed that the office of king was divinely ordained, although the kings themselves were not divine.

The rule of the Babylonian kings mirrored the rule of their god. The well-known Babylonian text *Enuma Elish* (a copy of which was excavated from the library of King Ashurbanipal in Nineveh c.650BCE) provides a religious justification for kingship in Babylonian society: the god Marduk had created order from chaos, and the role of the king was to do the same.

**THE HANGING GARDENS OF BABYLON**
*The hanging gardens were one of Babylon's most lavish features. The king provided a temple for the god of the state, a symbolic representation of the center of the cosmos and of the king's relationship with the state deity.*

## ASIA MINOR

In the Hittite culture, which dominated much of the area of modern Turkey and Iran, the kings were high priests, chiefly responsible for the religious well-being of the people. They adopted the title "My Sun," a form borrowed from Egypt, where it was used to address the Pharaoh, but they were not thought to be gods during their lifetime. It was believed that when the king of the Hittites died, he became a god.

**SEAL OF JEROBOAM**
*The cast of this seal, inscribed "Shema, servant of Jeroboam," was found at Megiddo and may refer to Jeroboam II, king of Israel in the ninth century BCE.*

## DIVINE RULE

The rule of the king of Babylon mirrors the rule of Marduk. The king served the deity as a priest, and by maintaining the cosmic concept of justice – *mesarum* in Mesopotamia and *ma'at* in Egypt – prevented the triumph of the powers of chaos that constantly threatened to overwhelm the cosmic order. The great law codes of Lipit-Ishtar (c.1830–1550BCE) from Sumer and King Hammurabi of Babylon (1792–50BCE) articulate axioms of the cosmic concept of justice. Its origins were believed to be divine.

## THE KING'S ROLE

The role of the king as judge in the maintenance of justice, as warrior in the protection of society, and as priest in the ordering of worship is fundamental to the well-being of society. Following the demise of Egyptian power in Syria–Palestine around 1000BCE, comparatively small city-states in Philistia, Phoenicia, Damascus, Aram, Moab, and Ammon emerge alongside Israel. Each struggled for hegemony, but the region was dominated in turn by the rulers of Assyria, Babylon, Persia, Greece, and finally Rome. Not surprisingly, ideas about kingship reflect those of the dominant powers in the area.

## KINGSHIP IN THE BIBLE

In the Bible, kingship becomes important (though contested) from the time of Saul, David, and Solomon onward. When David captured Jerusalem from the Jebusites, he seems to have taken over a royal ideology "after the order of Melchizedek," the king of Jerusalem (Gen. 14:17–24; Ps. 110). But we know nothing of that earlier ideology of kingship, and can only infer what David and his successors made of it from the Psalms and from oracles concerning kings in the Prophets. In the Psalms, the kings are closely associated with God and God's work (in Psalm 45:6, the king is actually addressed as God, Elohim, even though English translations may obscure this).

## THE MESSIAH

God mediates blessings through the king, so that the great oracles celebrating the birth of a new royal child are rightly called Messianic (dealing with the LORD's anointed one), although they are not referring to a distant future figure (e.g., Isa. 9:1–7). The king is closely associated with God (2 Sam. 14:17; Ps. 2:7ff.; 89:27). Did he play the part of God in rituals and liturgies, as kings did elsewhere? This is unlikely, as no such ritual has been described; thus it has to be inferred from the Psalms. At the least, it is clear that the king represented the people before God and that the Messianic hope, in its futuristic sense, is derived from these early hopes invested in the king.

**SOLOMON**
*Most resplendent of the kings of Israel, Solomon's wealth and wisdom were legendary. He is shown here receiving the attentions of the Queen of Sheba and her retinue.*

**For further reading see bibliography numbers:** 4, 97, 186, 242, 264, 307, 374, 383, 548a, 550, 650

# THE LIFE OF
# KING DAVID

*In the history of Israel, David is the king who dramatically transformed the tribes into a nation. He is also credited with authorship of the Psalms. But the story of David is told in realistic detail, and his faults are not concealed.*

*DAVID THE SHEPHERD: 1 SAM. 17:37*

*DAVID DEFEATS GOLIATH: 1 SAM. 17*

*DAVID AND JONATHAN LOVE EACH OTHER: 1 SAM. 18:1–4*

D AVID was the youngest of the eight sons of Jesse. His story is told in 1 Samuel 16–1 Kings 2:12. In his youth, he cared for the family flocks and became a good musician. He was selected by Samuel to be the king that Saul had failed to be, and was soon involved in the conflicts with the Philistines. When he defeated their champion, Goliath, a rout of the Philistines followed. But the success of David made Saul jealous. When David and Jonathan, Saul's son, became devoted to each other, the women greeted David as greater than Saul: "Saul has slain his thou-sands, but David has slain his tens of thou-sands." Saul began to plot against David, hoping to use his daughters Merab, and then Michal, to ensnare him. Saul deter-mined to kill David, but Jonathan told David about the plot and Michal helped him to escape. David and Jonathan had a common cause, but those who supported David, like the priests of Nob, were killed. Abiathar, the son of Ahimelech, one of the priests, escaped and warned David so that he had to flee even farther and take refuge in the cave of Adullam.

*MICHAL HELPS DAVID ESCAPE: 1 SAM. 19*

David slaying Goliath.

## DAVID AS AN OUTLAW

There then followed a period when David was the head of an outlaw band. During this time, he married Abigail. He could have killed Saul but spared him twice, even though he was being driven to desperate straits. At one point, David had to take refuge in Philistine territory because he was sure that Saul would not look for him there, and thus came close to fighting on the Philistine side. It was only because the Philistines did not trust a former enemy that he took to raiding the Amalekites instead. Meanwhile, the Philistines won a great victory against Saul at Mount Gilboa, during which they killed Saul's sons, including Jonathan. The distraught Saul told his armor bearer to kill him also, and when the armor bearer refused, Saul fell on his sword and committed suicide. When David heard of the deaths of Saul and Jonathan he uttered his famous lament, recorded in the Book of Jashar (2 Sam. 1): *"How the mighty are fallen in the midst of battle! Jonathan lies slain upon your high places. I am distressed for you, my brother Jonathan; greatly beloved were you to me; your love to me was wonderful, passing the love of women."*

## DAVID'S LATER YEARS

The subsequent story of David shows great success, above all in the capture of Jerusalem, but also continuing trouble and conflict (*see right*). As his days drew to a close, his association with the Psalms (many of which are hymns for royal occasions) is marked by his reciting Psalm 18:1–50 and his last words. Even so, his troubles were not at an end. God, in anger against the people, provoked David into taking a census of Israel and Judah, thus indicating an inappropriate pride. The plague that was sent as a punishment stopped only when David showed his penitence and built an altar. He was now so old and feeble that a young virgin, Abishag the Shunamite, was sent to warm him, and in these circumstances, Adonijah made a bid for power and declared himself king. David's last act was to ensure the succession for Solomon and to give him his final instructions, *"Then David slept with his ancestors, and was buried in the city of David."*

*DAVID MARRIES ABIGAIL: 1 SAM. 25:42; AND SPARES SAUL: 1 SAM. 24, 26*

*CAPTURE OF JERUSALEM: 2 SAM. 5:6–17*

*SAUL'S SUICIDE: 1 SAM. 31*

*DAVID'S LAMENT: 2 SAM. 1*

*DAVID'S THANKSGIVING: 2 SAM. 22*

*DAVID'S LAST WORDS: 2 SAM. 23*

*BUILDING OF THE ALTAR: 2 SAM. 24*

*FINAL INSTRUCTIONS: 1 KGS. 1:28–2:12*

## THE IMPORTANCE OF KING DAVID

The later memory of David is of one who *"wiped out his enemies on every side,"* and was given *"a covenant of kingship and a glorious throne in Israel"* (Sir. 47:7, 11). With him is begun the royal line, from which the Messiah (*see pp.123, 201*) will come. But his story is told in the Bible with such honesty that his sins and struggles are completely revealed. This combining of tragedy and triumph can be seen in repeated civil war. When Saul died, the tribes looked for a new leader in different ways: the northern tribes went for a descendant of Saul, Ish-bosheth, but the tribe of Judah supported David as the best leader for the times. Gradually David prevailed, and Ish-bosheth was murdered. An alliance was made, and David immediately set out to conquer the Jebusites and capture their capital city, Jerusalem (2. Sam. 5:6–17). In a shrewd move, David made it his new capital, because none of the rival tribes had ever possessed it, so that it was neutral territory. It had a long history of sacred rituals associated with the kings, and David adapted these to the new institution of kingship, determining also to build a Temple (2 Sam. 7). He defeated the Philistines and recaptured the Ark, bringing it into Jerusalem with great triumph.

David set out on further conquests (2 Sam. 8, 10), and, for Jonathan's sake, tried to reconcile the descendants of Saul. But his success was marred by his lust for Bathsheba and his cruel plot to secure her for himself (2 Sam. 11). When her husband Uriah was killed, David married her. This evoked the fearless rebuke of the prophet Nathan (2 Sam. 12:7). David was punished by the death of his child, but then another son, Solomon by name, was born, who became David's successor.

## DAVID IN CONFLICT

Even to the end, David's story is honestly told. A disastrous family conflict followed the rape by one of David's sons Amnon of his sister Tamar. Another son Absalom took revenge by killing Amnon but then had to take refuge, eventually leading to a conspiracy against David who was forced out of the city (2 Sam. 14, 15). At the end of the civil war, Absalom was trapped in a tree and killed by Joab, but the grief of David was great (2 Sam. 18, 19). Even then, his troubles were not over: the old rivalry between the northern tribes and Judah broke out again because of the possessiveness of the men of Judah (2 Sam. 19:40–43). A revolt against David began under the leadership of Sheba, a Benjaminite, and under the slogan *"We have no portion in David, no share in the son of Jesse! Everyone to your tents, O Israel!"* (2 Sam. 20:1). When that revolt was put down (2 Sam. 20), David reburied the bones of Saul and Jonathan and pursued his final battles against the Philistines.

For further reading see bibliography number: 6, 97, 131, 160, 299, 359, 402, 559, 803

# JERUSALEM

*Standing on a small spur of hill, Jerusalem was not originally
of importance, but it became a powerful symbol of belief,
identity, and aspiration.*

### ZION

Jerusalem is often called Zion.
The name may mean "citadel"
or "fortress." It seems initially
to have referred to the ridge
on which the Jebusite fortress
was placed. From this it was
transferred to the Temple
Mount, hence the references
to Zion as God's holy hill
(Ps. 2:6). Thus Zion is often
the holy center of Jerusalem,
not Jerusalem itself.

JERUSALEM was probably first settled and
built in the early second millennium BCE.
*Urushalim,* its Canaanite name, means
"foundation of the God Salem." It may
have been a holy city: Genesis 14:18–24 and
Psalm 110:4 point back to an earlier priesthood, taken up by David. When David
attacked Jerusalem, the inhabitants (the
Jebusites) regarded it as impregnable. But
David did capture it (2 Sam. 5:6–10; cf. Judg.
19:10–12) and made it the capital of his
newly established kingdom. The natural
resources of the site (valleys on three sides

and a water supply) together with its
strategic location (between David's home
in the territory of Judah and the northern
Israelite tribes) no doubt influenced David's
choice. In his endeavor to draw the scattered
parts of the kinship or family group together,
it was important to have a neutral site as
capital, one that had not been inhabited by
any of the tribes before that time. Under
David and Solomon, Jerusalem was the
center of a united kingdom with the newly
built Temple as the home of the Ark of the
Covenant (see pp.60–61; cf. Ps. 132). After this
period, until its capture and destruction by
the Babylonians in 587/6BCE, Jerusalem was
the capital of the small and often embattled
kingdom of Judah. As Jews began to return
from exile in Babylon, the Temple was
rebuilt, probably in about 520BCE.

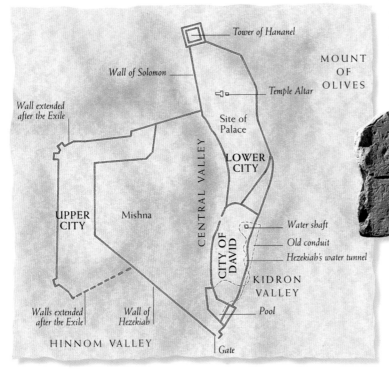

### JERUSALEM AFTER THE EXILE (SIXTH CENTURY BCE)

*The original city of Jebus (later the city of David) was bounded on three sides by valleys. It was a
natural stronghold and was not conquered before the time of David. Solomon extended the city north
(lower city), and additional building took place to the west during Hezekiah's reign and after the Exile.*

### TUNNEL INSCRIPTION

*This early Hebrew inscription was found in Hezekiah's
tunnel (see left) and describes the digging of the tunnel.*

## RELIGIOUS SIGNIFICANCE

The religious and symbolic significance of
Jerusalem has always outweighed its political
or economic significance. Its importance is
most eloquently attested by literature written,
or compiled, in Jerusalem. In general terms,
this literature means the Hebrew Bible as a
whole and specifically the Psalms (e.g., 102,

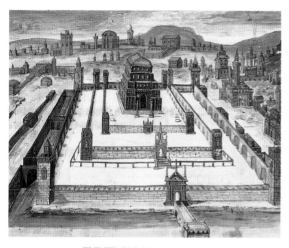

**THE TEMPLE IN JERUSALEM**
*This 18th-century book illustration shows the Temple in the center of Jerusalem. The city became not only a capital, but the center of Israelite faith.*

116, 122, 126, 137, 147) and the book of Isaiah. Here, there is a strong sense that Jerusalem – or Zion – is chosen by God as a place where God is present with the Covenant People, a presence focused in the Temple where the Ark is located (Pss. 78:67–69; 132:13–18). God's presence gives an assurance of blessing and protection against enemies (Pss. 46, 48, 76; Isa. 29:5–8; 31:4–5), an assurance given remarkable content in the account of Jerusalem's deliverance from the Assyrians in the time of Hezekiah (Isa. 36–37; 2 Kgs. 18–19).

## GOD'S JUDGMENT

The Prophet Jeremiah warned that the inhabitants of Jerusalem could not rely upon God's protection if they did not live faithfully and uprightly (Jer. 7:1–15). The fall of Jerusalem to the Babylonians in 587/6BCE was understood as a judgment upon the people's failure to turn genuinely to God in trust (Jer. 25:1–14). The impact of the fall of Jerusalem, the destruction of the Temple, and the sense of loss that this caused is movingly expressed in Lamentations (*pp.210–11*). The Psalms had celebrated the beauty of Zion as *"the joy of all the earth"* (Ps. 48:2), but these very words then became used as a mocking taunt by passersby: *"Is this the city that was called the perfection of beauty, the joy of all the earth?"*

(Lam. 2:15). Yet the anguish of desolation resulted in a renewed conviction of God's good purposes for Jerusalem. The city's restoration is lyrically proclaimed in chapters 60–62 of the book of Isaiah, and in Ezekiel 40–48 comes a vision of the rebuilt Temple.

## THE LATER TEMPLE

The Temple was probably rebuilt in 520BCE. This "Second Temple" was enlarged and embellished by Herod the Great in an extended building project around the turn of the era (reported as taking 46 years in John 2:20). It was destroyed by the Romans in 70CE and, despite occasional abortive attempts, was never rebuilt. The sole physical remains of the Temple are parts of the retaining wall around the Temple enclosure, most famously the Western Wall, known as the Wailing Wall, where Jews would lament what they had lost. Otherwise, there are various archaeological remains from almost every period of Jerusalem's long and turbulent history in both the biblical and postbiblical periods. The symbolism of Jerusalem as the holy city remained potent, not only for Jews but for Christians and Muslims as well.

### BEFORE THE EXILE

**Second millennium BCE**
Origins of the city

**Time of the conquest**
Jerusalem ruled by Jebusites, an indigenous Semitic tribe

**Reign of David**
Capital moved to Jerusalem, becomes center of Twelve Tribes. Ark installed

**Reign of Solomon**
Temple built

**Reign of Rehoboam**
Royal palace plundered by Egyptian troops. Jerusalem capital of Judah alone

**Reign of Hezekiah**
Water conduit built. City fortified

**597BCE**
Capture of city by Babylonians

**587/6BCE**
Destruction of much of the city by Babylonians

**EARLY MORNING OVER JERUSALEM**
*This view of the city of Jerusalem today shows the old city bounded by its medieval walls in the center of the image. In the foreground are the lower slopes of the Mount of Olives.*

**For further reading see bibliography numbers: 21, 28, 454, 458, 632, 836**

# THE BOOKS OF
# 1-2 KINGS

*These two books trace the history of Israel and Judah from the time of Solomon until their destruction by the empires of Assyria and Babylon. They present this destruction as the inevitable outcome of the people's disloyalty to God.*

THE overriding vision of history and its meaning, found in the books of Joshua, Judges, Samuel, and Kings, is established in the book of Deuteronomy. It is therefore known as the Deuteronomistic history (*see pp.80–81, 105*). It explains why failure and decline occur in that history, and it is a theological analysis of the past, rather than a simple catalog of events. This history is explicitly selective, often referring readers to other sources for more information. Occasional comments on events serve to drive home the message that Israel and Judah were destroyed because of their own faults, not through divine malevolence or weakness (e.g., 2 Kgs. 17:7–23). The narrative also emphasizes the role of prophecy, both through demonstrations that events had previously been prophesied (e.g., 1 Kgs. 11:31–36), and through stories of prophetic activity or intervention (e.g., 2 Kgs. 19–20).

and coups led to the eventual defeat of the Northern Kingdom at the hands of the Assyrians. The kings of Judah, the continuing dynasty of King David, suffered less, the book suggests, because of God's promise to their ancestor David. Prophets are important in Kings, bringing God's judgments to bear. This is most obvious in the case of Elijah and Elisha, both of whom interact with other prophets, but revealing stories are recorded of Nathan (1 Kgs. 1), a man of God and an old prophet of Bethel (ch.13), Ahijah (14:1–8), Jehu (16:1–14), Obadiah and the hundred prophets (ch.18), one of the sons of the prophets (20:35–43), the 400 prophets and Micaiah ben Imlah (ch.22), Isaiah (2 Kgs. 19–21), and other unnamed prophets.

**FOUNDER OF THE DYNASTY**
*On his deathbed, David gave Solomon a solemn charge. This establishes his dynasty (1 Kgs. 2), which survived in the kings of Judah.*

## A THEOLOGICAL VIEW OF HISTORY

In 1–2 Kings the unifying vision of the Deuteronomistic history also lays emphasis upon the responsibility of individual monarchs, classifying each as good or bad in terms of religious fidelity and adherence to the Law and the requirements of the Covenant. It would be a mistake to assume that these books are unimaginative accounts of the past; they represent, rather, a sophisticated theological explanation for the destruction of the two kingdoms. Scholars are divided over the work's expectations for the future, some seeing its message as unalloyed gloom, others taking the final account of Jehoiachin's release (2 Kgs. 25:27–30) as an indication of hope that God has not forgotten the promise

## THE EVENTS OF KINGS

The books of Kings open with the old age of David and go on to describe the accession of his son Solomon, the successes of his reign, including the building of the Temple, and his failures caused by reliance on foreign alliances. The books then describe the division of the kingdom on Solomon's death into the Northern Kingdom of Israel under Jeroboam, and the smaller Southern Kingdom of Judah under Rehoboam. Israel succumbed to pagan influence, and a succession of rebellions

made to David in 2 Samuel 7:15: *"I will not take my steadfast love
from him, as I took it from Saul, whom I put away from before you.
Your house and your kingdom shall be made sure for ever before me;
your throne shall be established for ever."*

## THE SOURCES OF KINGS

The reigns of the kings are dealt with unevenly, and this may
reflect the availability of sources, such as the Acts of Solomon
(1 Kgs. 11:41), the Annals of the Kings of Israel (1 Kgs. 14:19),
and of Judah (1 Kgs. 14:29). Equally, it is not always easy
to reconcile figures given for the length of each reign with
the dates given for particular events or the synchronization
of northern and southern kings. For example, 1 Kings 16:23
states, *"In the thirty-first year of King Asa of Judah, Omri began to reign
over Israel; he reigned for twelve years,"* while 1 Kings 16:29 states,
*"In the thirty-eighth year of King Asa of Judah, Ahab son of Omri began
to reign over Israel."* This may reflect both a tendency to arrange
history into periods of symbolic length and a reluctance to
allow chronology to obscure the message of the work. The
analysis presented in the Deuteronomistic history has much
in common with the early Prophetic books. It was to prove
immensely influential, and undoubtedly contributed to many
key aspects of later Judaism – especially the religious focus
on the Covenant. More immediately, most scholars believe
that 1–2 Kings provided much of the material for 1–2
Chronicles and that they were probably the source
for Isaiah 36–39.

## THE DIVISION OF THE KINGDOM

The opening chapters of 1 Kings (1–8) describe the building
of the Temple, but for all its splendor it did not reconcile
all the tribes to the house of David and Solomon. Did all
the tribes really owe allegiance to the house of David,
centered on the Temple and the association of the king
with it? When Rehoboam succeeded Solomon, his father,
the northern tribes refused to continue their allegiance;
and they reverted to their own tribal leaders: *"When all Israel
saw that the king would not listen to them, the people answered the king
'What share do we have in David? We have no inheritance in the son of
Jesse. To your tents, O Israel! Look now to your house, O David'"* (1
Kgs. 12:16). So began the schism between North and South
that prevails in the period covered by 1–2 Kings. Beyond
that, there were some "tradition-fundamentalists" who tried
to keep the religion as it had been in the wilderness days.
The followers of Jehonadab ben Rechab (the Rechabites)
protested against anything that took people away from
the wilderness tradition: strongly in favor of Israel's God
(2 Kgs. 10:15), they protested the planting of grapevines
and also, therefore, the drinking of wine, because such
things would have been impossible while Israel was
traveling through the wilderness (Jer. 35:6ff.).

# THE BOOK

**TITLE**: 1–2 Kings. The title of these books reflects their content.
In the Greek Septuagint version, they are grouped with the
books of Samuel to form "1–4 Kingdoms." The division into
two parts was probably made necessary by the limited size of
ancient scrolls. In the Hebrew Bible these books are among
the "Former Prophets"

**HEBREW TITLE**: *Melakhim* (Kings)

**DATE**: The latest events described in Kings occurred in about
561BCE, but many scholars believe that there was an earlier pre-
exilic edition, perhaps written in the late seventh century BCE.
The books may have incorporated some stories and texts that
were already in existence

**AUTHORSHIP**: Not known. In Jewish tradition, the author was
Jeremiah. Most modern scholars believe that 1–2 Kings are the
final part of a Deuteronomistic history (*see pp.80–81, 105*), since the
content of books illustrates principles set out in Deuteronomy

# THE CONTENTS

**1 KINGS 1–11**
The accession and reign of Solomon

**1 KINGS 12–16**
The divisions of the kingdom

**1 KINGS 17–2 KINGS 13**
Elijah and Elisha

**2 KINGS 14–17**
The history of Judah and Israel until the exile
of Israel

**2 KINGS 18–25**
The history of Judah until the exile of Judah

# KEY THEMES

*The importance of being faithful to the Covenant*

•

*The building of the Temple*

•

*The role of prophets in general and of Elijah and Elisha in particular*

**For further reading see bibliography numbers:** 347, 438, 559, 631, 764

# THE TIMES OF

# KING SOLOMON

*The builder of the First Temple and the successor to King David, Solomon is a key figure in the development of Israel. His wisdom was legendary and "surpassed the wisdom of all the people of the east, and all the wisdom of Egypt" (1 Kgs. 4:30).*

THE accounts of Solomon in 1 Kings 1–11 and 2 Chronicles 1–10 give many details of his life, but despite the account of vast international dealings, no trace of him appears in other records. He has attracted stories of a symbolic and exemplary kind, so that interpretation is now part of the biography. According to the narrative between 2 Samuel 9 and 1 Kings 2, Solomon was the son of David and Bathsheba, and was also known as Jedidiah. He was not the natural heir but attained the throne after a series of intrigues and the defeat of his brothers Absalom and Adonijah. Once established, he married the daughter of an Egyptian king,

the first of many marriage alliances. Early in Solomon's reign, God asked him to name a gift, and Solomon asked for wisdom. The gift is shown in the story of the two women. Using wood and builders supplied by King Hiram of Tyre – with whom he had an important trading alliance – Solomon constructed and furnished the Temple as well as many other buildings. He also established trading links and a powerful army and fleet, becoming the richest and wisest king in the world. However, the foreign women among his 700 wives and 300 concubines led him to follow foreign gods. As retribution for his disobedience, God decided to tear the kingdom from Solomon, a punishment moderated so that Solomon's descendants could inherit part of the land. This resulted in the division of the kingdom after Solomon's death.

*DEFEAT AND DEATH OF ADONIJAH: 1 KGS. 2:25*

*THE TWO HARLOTS: 1 KGS. 3:16–28*

*DEALINGS WITH KING HIRAM OF TYRE: 1 KGS. 5*

*SOLOMON RICHEST AND WISEST KING IN THE WORLD: 1 KGS. 10:23*

*SOLOMON'S PUNISHMENT: 1 KGS. 11:31*

*SOLOMON'S DEATH: 1 KGS. 11:40*

Solomon dictating wise judgment.

## READING THE STORIES OF SOLOMON

The stories of Solomon's wealth, of the prodigious number of his consorts, and of the extent of his influence have almost certainly been told with a view toward glorifying Israel's heyday. No mention of Solomon is found in foreign sources, and the Bible gives no adequate explanation for the staggering riches that would have been needed for even a fraction of the projects described: his annual income is simply described as 666 talents of gold (about 25 tons). In fact, strong theological elements dominate the account, from the symbolic 480 years between Exodus and Temple through the explanations for the collapse of the kingdom, embracing also the lengthy prayer of 1 Kings 8:12–61 that begins *"Blessed be the* LORD, *the God of Israel, who with his hand has fulfilled what he promised from his mouth to my father David …"*

There is also a series of stories that are associated with Solomon's wisdom, including the visit of the Queen of Sheba (*see right*) and the story of the two women in 1 Kings 3:16–28. (Confronted by two harlots, who each claimed to be the mother of a child, Solomon ordered that the child be cut in half; the real mother then revealed herself by abandoning her claim.) The biblical materials do not give a detailed reconstruction of his reign: the stories exhibit the transition of Israel from tribes to nation-state and show how God is the guide and monitor of all that happens.

## SYMBOL OF THE NATION

Through the influence of his mother, Bathsheba, Solomon became second in the line of the dynasty of David and the third king of Israel. But his significance is far greater than as a royal figurehead: he is also a symbol of nationhood, associated with a golden age of the distant past, and the founder of the First Temple. Therefore, he was a figurehead, not only of nationhood but also of a religion. His relationship with gods other than YHWH foreshadowed that of the nation, fulfilling warnings about foreign influence and the worship of foreign gods that was to lead to the calamity of exile.

Solomon was famous for his wisdom and became the patron of wisdom literature, with later books attributed to him including the Proverbs, the Song of Songs, Ecclesiastes, and the Wisdom of Solomon in the Apocrypha. The attribution of these books to Solomon may have occurred long after the historical figure lived and perhaps resulted from the many legendary elements that surrounded him. Linked to both wisdom and wisdom literature is a certain emphasis on sexuality, reflected in the later attribution to Solomon of the Song of Songs (*pp.190–91*): he is a lover of many exotic women, and they bring about his downfall.

A number of stories later arose in Jewish and Islamic traditions (for the latter, *see* Qur'an 21:82; 27:16–45) concerning Solomon's relationship with the Queen of Sheba, and there are several apocryphal stories associated with him.

## THE QUEEN OF SHEBA

Impressed by stories of Solomon's great wisdom, the Queen of Sheba journeyed from her homeland in southwest Arabia with great pomp and ceremony. The biblical account (1 Kgs. 10) tells how Solomon's wisdom surpassed her expectations, and she was overcome by the splendor of his court. She sought his favor with gifts of spices, gold, and precious stones – luxury goods typical of the trade routes that crossed Arabia and East Africa. The Bible relates that Solomon *"gave to the Queen of Sheba every desire that she expressed,"* after which the Queen returned home laden with the gifts of Solomon.

**Woman from Sheba**
*This stone head of a woman from Saba (Sheba) in south Arabia dates from the first millennium* BCE. *Her name is written on her brow in the Sabean script. In Ethiopian legend, the Queen of Sheba was famous as the queen of Ethiopia who bore Solomon's son, the first king of Ethiopia.*

## SOLOMON'S WISDOM AND FOLLY

*Solomon displays wisdom in the way that he rules Israel, but he is also the archetype of the foolish man led astray by a foreign woman.*

The wisdom granted to Solomon in 1 Kings 3 is very specific: it is the understanding of how to rule and judge the nation, and it is probably the wisdom for which Solomon was at first remembered. The later rise of "wisdom literature" associated the term with certain types of literature and probably provoked a shift in the understanding of Solomon's famed wisdom. This dovetailed neatly with an earlier tendency for one type of wisdom literature, the "instruction," to be presented as a speech by some famous individual, who lent it authority. One instance of this is especially interesting: the instruction in Proverbs 1–9 is apparently attributed to Solomon and makes extensive use of a contrast between wisdom and the "foreign woman," also called "folly," who leads the unwary to destruction. There may be a reference here to the turning from God for which Solomon was also remembered (Neh. 13:26). From the warnings of Deuteronomy (e.g., 7:3–4) through the divorces forced upon those returning from exile (*see p.160*), foreign women were viewed as dangerous and subversive, liable to lead the Israelites into the worship of other gods. If Jezebel is arguably the prime example of such a woman, then Solomon is certainly held up as the most notable victim – a man famous for his wisdom, who could yet be seduced into folly.

For further reading see bibliography numbers: 131, 180, 312, 383, 402, 539, 551, 559, 629

# SOLOMON'S TEMPLE

*From the tenth to the sixth centuries BCE, the Temple of Solomon was the heart of religion in Judah; its dedication to God is described in 1 Kings 6–8. It provided a permanent dwelling place for the Ark.*

## THE TABERNACLE

During the journey through the wilderness, the Tabernacle was a movable shrine, a gathering point for the Israelites. The instructions for its construction are given in Exodus 25–31 and 35–40. The elaborate details may anticipate the Temple itself.

Once King David had established the centralization of power in Israel, the persistence of the Tabernacle seemed incongruous, and the building of the Temple was left to his son Solomon.

## CEDAR WOOD

This relief from the palace of King Sargon II in Khorsabad shows boats with horse-headed prows transporting logs. King Solomon brought cedar wood for building the Temple from Lebanon: *"My servants shall bring it down to the sea from the Lebanon; I will make it into rafts to go by sea"* (1 Kgs. 5:9). He appealed to King Hiram of Tyre, who supplied the wood and was paid in wheat and oil.

SOLOMON'S Temple was built next to his palace, in a compound on what is now called the Temple Mount. Its construction is described in the Bible in 1 Kings 6, where it is said to have been a rectangular stone building divided into three sections: the portico, the main sanctuary, and the inner sanctuary. The building is described as being 60 cubits long, 20 cubits wide, and 30 cubits high; the precise length of the cubit at this time is not known (*see pp. 78–79*), but the building was probably about 98 feet (30 meters) long, 33 feet (10 meters) wide, and 49 feet (15 meters) high. The total lengths for each section add up to 70 cubits, though, and the portico may have lain outside. Rooms were also built around the side and rear walls, probably for the use of priests. Most religious activities were carried out in the main sanctuary, while the inner sanctuary, the "Holy of Holies," contained the Ark beneath two wooden cherubim. This overall structure is broadly similar to that of many other temples in the region. Contemporary architectural techniques imposed considerable limits upon the size of such buildings, and Solomon's Temple was large for its time. By modern standards, though, it was very small and could have contained relatively few people.

## FURNISHINGS

The Temple is said to have been richly decorated, with a carved cedar-wood lining on the inside walls and floor, overlaid with gold, and with decorative carvings on the doors and doorposts. The many objects placed in and around the building were similarly magnificent, although their function often eludes us. Two

features are of particular interest: the pillars in the vestibule and the "molten sea," both of which are described in 1 Kings 7:23. The pillars, called Jachin and Boaz, are not structural supports but freestanding columns set on either side of the entrance, like the gold and emerald pillars at the Phoenician temple of Melqart at Tyre. Their names may mean "he will establish" and "in strength," and their basic purpose was probably to provide an impressive entrance. The "molten sea" is more mysterious. It seems to have been a giant basin, possibly used for purification, but it may also have had some symbolic links with mytho-logical ideas.

*Jachin*

*Sacrificial fire*

*Porch area*

*Boaz*

## THE HISTORY OF THE BUILDING

In 2 Samuel 7 God refuses David permission to build a temple but promises that his son will do so, linking this to a promise that his dynasty will be established forever. Solomon duly began to build the Temple in the fourth year of his reign, 480 years after the Exodus. The task took seven years. Both numbers are probably symbolic figures, and may give no reliable date for the construction. As with the institution of monarchy, not all people agreed: why should God, who had protected them safely through the wilderness and after, be shut up in a house? (for this devotion to wilderness tradition, *see p.129*). The subsequent history is mentioned from time to time in the biblical histories.

**LATER INTERPRETATIONS**
*Representations of the building have been influenced by later architecture. This classical version is shown on the walls of an early synagogue and dates to the third century* BCE.

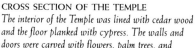

*Inner sanctuary (Holy of Holies)*

*Large chamber*

**CROSS SECTION OF THE TEMPLE**
*The interior of the Temple was lined with cedar wood and the floor planked with cypress. The walls and doors were carved with flowers, palm trees, and cherubim, and overlaid in gold, a feature common in ancient temples. No stonework was visible.*

At various times the Temple is said to have been stripped of some or all of its furnishings, when money was needed to provide gifts or tribute to foreign rulers. But new vessels and furnishings were probably often created or received as gifts: a good description of such periodic refurbishment is given in 2 Kings 12, when King Jehoash instituted repairs. Various alterations and additions were made by the reforming kings Hezekiah and Josiah and also by Ahaz and Manasseh, who are said to have introduced certain foreign elements. However, our knowledge of these events depends on sources that were eager to illustrate their opinion of particular rulers, and so must be used with caution. The Temple was finally destroyed by the Babylonians, who ransacked it after Jehoiachim's rebellion (598BCE), and burned it down after that of Zedekiah (587BCE). In its time, Solomon's Temple was the center of the national religion of the Judeans, although it was not, perhaps, the only temple to YHWH. Its presence in the capital, Jerusalem, signified the actual presence of God among the people, and it became for them a powerful symbol. It also gave rise to a complicated priestly system, with its associated ideology of holiness and purity (see pp.64–65); this system was to be highly influential upon the later development of Judaism.

### WALL HANGING
Many features of the Temple, and decorations associated with it, are reflected in the furnishings of later Judaism.

The ornate curtain or parochet (Exod. 26:31–33) below was made in the 18th century and hung from the wall, serving to cover the scrolls containing the Torah in a synagogue. The two pillars represent the pillars, Jachin and Boaz, that stood at the entrance of Solomon's Temple. The cover is made of gold-embroidered velvet and comes from Germany.

Torah curtain.

For further reading see bibliography numbers: 49, 183, 371, 381, 470, 506, 607, 767

# THE KINGS OF ISRAEL AND JUDAH

*The kings of Israel and Judah are known, almost entirely, from the account that is given of them in the books of Kings and Chronicles. Few references to them have survived in the records of other nations.*

## THE DIVIDED KINGDOM

Solomon's son Rehoboam was challenged by Jeroboam, who saw no need to continue allegiance to the the house of David. This led to the secession of the Northern Kingdom (*see p.129*). The Davidic dynasty ruled in Judah for nearly 350 years, while the northern state of Israel fell in 722BCE following a series of attacks.

THE reigns of the kings of Israel and Judah are described in 1 Kings 12 to 2 Kings 25 and in 2 Chronicles 10–36. Chronicles depends to a great extent on the prior account in Kings, although it deals mainly with Judean kings only (for differences, *see p.151*).

After the death of Solomon, the empire that he ruled is described by the biblical sources as fracturing into two separate kingdoms. Jeroboam, son of Nebat, ruled the north (Israel) and Solomon's son Rehoboam ruled the south (Judah). The history of both kingdoms is described by the biblical authors as one largely characterized by the abandonment of the true religion. The Northern Kingdom was immediately taken over by other gods and never again succeeded in breaking free of their influence (1 Kgs. 12:25ff.; 16:29ff.). Prophets – most notably Elijah and Elisha – opposed the apostate

kings, whose dynasties come and go as the judgment of God falls upon them. Final judgment is slow in coming because of God's promises and compassion for the people (2 Kgs. 10:30; 13:23). Eventually, however, judgment arrives, and northern Israel goes into exile in Assyria for its sins (2 Kgs. 17).

## SINS OF THE KINGS

According to Kings, the religious situation in Judah was initially no better than that in Israel (1 Kgs. 14:22–24; 15:3–5; *cf.* 2 Chr. 10–13). However, Judah's story is not thereafter one of continuous apostasy. Kings who keep faith with the commands of God, such as Asa (1 Kgs. 15:9–24; 2 Chr. 14–16), do rule in the gaps between the wicked kings; and toward the end of the story we meet two of the most devout kings, Hezekiah and Josiah, who reform Israelite worship, and obey and trust in God. Nevertheless, sin gradually accumulates. Although it appears at first that God will treat Judah with less severity than Israel because of his commitment to David, in the end the commitment only delays the judgment. For the authors of Kings, the sins of Manasseh in particular (2 Kgs. 21) are too much for God to bear. Judah duly suffers the same fate as Israel (2 Kgs. 23:26–27; 24:1–4).

## ROYAL SIGN

This jar handle is stamped with a winged scarab, the sign of the Judean royal family. Over a thousand such seals have been found, all of them dating to the reign of King Hezekiah in the eighth century BCE. They may relate to stockpiling carried out to withstand Assyrian attack.

### THE KIDRON VALLEY

*This valley, to the north of Jerusalem, was an important place of burial and contains many rock-cut tombs. The reforming kings, such as Asa, Hezekiah, and Josiah, used the valley as a place of destruction where heathen idols and altars were burned or ground to powder.*

**THE BLACK OBELISK**
*"Ia-u-a" or "Ia-a-u," "son of Omri," is shown paying tribute to the Assyrian ruler Shalmaneser III (858–824BCE). This is possibly Jehoram, but more likely Jehu.*

## A CRAFTED ACCOUNT

Like all historians, the biblical writers selected and arranged their material in order to tell a certain story. Not everything narrated is given equal importance. A striking feature of Kings, for example, is that fairly long periods of time are passed over relatively briefly, while periods of a year or less are described at great length (e.g., the account of Manasseh's reign of 55 years occupies only 18 verses [2 Kgs. 21:1–18], but the account of religious reform in Josiah's 18th year [2 Kgs. 22:3–23:23] takes up 41 verses).

## A MORAL VIEW

The telling of the biblical story is dominated by the religious convictions of its authors. From this point of view, what is most important about the kings of Israel and Judah is that they failed corporately to lead Israel in the ways of God, and specifically in accordance with the law of Deuteronomy (for the Deuteronomistic history, *see pp.80–81, 105*).

At the heart of the material in the book of Kings and in the midst of factual information concerning, for example, the length of a king's reign and the name of his capital city, is an evaluation of the king in terms of his religious policy (*see* 1 Kgs. 22:41–43, 45, 50). All the kings of Israel and Judah are here weighed in relation to the Mosaic Covenant, and almost all are found wanting (e.g., Jeroboam in 1 Kgs. 12:25–33; 14:1–16; Ahaz in 2 Kgs. 16:1–4). It is this lack of obedience to God that eventually brings the Monarchy to an end, in defeat at the hands of the Assyrian and Babylonian invaders.

### FOREIGN GODS

Many of the kings of Israel and Judah were tempted to worship foreign gods, The figure above represents one such god, probably either Reshef or Baal.

# THE KINGS OF ISRAEL AND JUDAH

*Before the division into the kingdoms of Israel and Judah (see The Divided Kingdom opposite), the land was governed by a united monarchy. The first of the kings, **Saul** (c.1050–10BCE), was elected by the people. His successor **David** (c.1010–970BCE) expanded the territory of the Israelites and formed the dynasty that lasted 400 years. David was succeeded by his son **Solomon** (c.970–30BCE), who built the Temple in Jerusalem. Few dates, however, can be given with certainty. Those given here should be regarded as approximate only.*

### JUDAH

| Rehoboam (924–07) | Asa (905–874) | Jehoram (850–43) | Athaliah (843–37) | Amaziah (800–791) | Jotham (?–742) | Hezekiah (727–698) | Amon (642–40) | Jehoahaz II (609) | Jehoiachin (598–97) |
|---|---|---|---|---|---|---|---|---|---|
| 950BCE | 900BCE | 850BCE | 800BCE | 750BCE | 700BCE | 650BCE | 600BCE | | 550BCE |
| Abijam (907–06) | Jehoshaphat (874–50) | Ahaziah (843) | Joash (837–800) | Uzziah (?–?) | Ahaz (742–27) | Manasseh (697–42) | Josiah (639–09) | Jehoiachim (608–598) | Zedekiah (597–87/6) |

### ISRAEL

| Jeroboam I (924–03) | Baasha (902–886) | Omri (885–73) | Ahaziah (851–49) | Jehu (843–16) | Joash (800–785) | Zechariah (745) | Menahem (745–36) | Pekah (735–32) |
|---|---|---|---|---|---|---|---|---|
| 950BCE | 900BCE | 850BCE | 800BCE | 750BCE | | 700BCE | | |
| Nadab (903–02) | Elah (886–85) | Ahab (873–51) | Jehoram (849–43) | Jehoahaz (816–800) | Jeroboam II (785–45) | Shallum (745) | Pekahiah (736–35) | Hoshea (732–23) |

For further reading see bibliography numbers: 4, 6, 25, 97, 131, 312, 383, 402, 424, 548a, 550, 559

# EMPIRES AND KINGS

*The chart below shows the major empires of the Near East during the period of the Hebrew Bible. The period begins with the earliest civilization in the Sumerian city-states and draws to a close with the eclipse of Greece and the rise of Rome.*

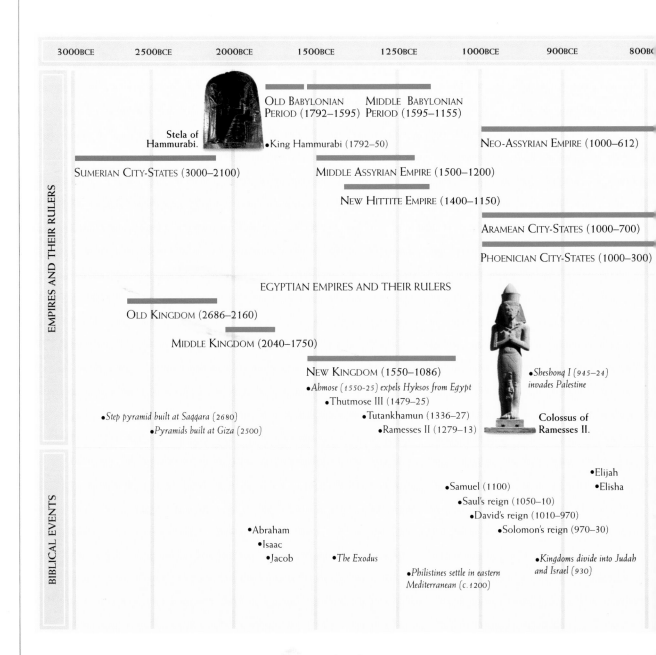

| 3000BCE | 2500BCE | 2000BCE | 1500BCE | 1250BCE | 1000BCE | 900BCE | 800BC |

**EMPIRES AND THEIR RULERS**

OLD BABYLONIAN PERIOD (1792–1595)   MIDDLE BABYLONIAN PERIOD (1595–1155)

**Stela of Hammurabi.**

•King Hammurabi (1792–50)

NEO-ASSYRIAN EMPIRE (1000–612)

SUMERIAN CITY-STATES (3000–2100)

MIDDLE ASSYRIAN EMPIRE (1500–1200)

NEW HITTITE EMPIRE (1400–1150)

ARAMEAN CITY-STATES (1000–700)

PHOENICIAN CITY-STATES (1000–300)

EGYPTIAN EMPIRES AND THEIR RULERS

OLD KINGDOM (2686–2160)

MIDDLE KINGDOM (2040–1750)

NEW KINGDOM (1550–1086)

•Ahmose (1550–25) expels Hyksos from Egypt
•Thutmose III (1479–25)
•Tutankhamun (1336–27)
•Ramesses II (1279–13)

•Sheshonq I (945–24) invades Palestine

**Colossus of Ramesses II.**

•Step pyramid built at Saqqara (2680)
•Pyramids built at Giza (2500)

**BIBLICAL EVENTS**

•Elijah
•Elisha

•Samuel (1100)
•Saul's reign (1050–10)
•David's reign (1010–970)
•Solomon's reign (970–30)

•Abraham
•Isaac
•Jacob

•The Exodus

•Kingdoms divide into Judah and Israel (930)

•Philistines settle in eastern Mediterranean (c.1200)

URING the biblical period, many different states and empires rose and fell. Situated near the mid-point of the Fertile Crescent (pp.18–19), Palestine and Jerusalem became increasingly involved in the attempts of major powers to gain control of the area. Generally speaking, dates from this period are approximate. The Bible does not offer a full chronology of events. Although many of the books of the Bible contain genealogies and chronologies of ancient Israel, the dating of many biblical events (such as the Exodus, *see pp.52–53*) remains in doubt. The accounts of the two divided kingdoms of Israel and Judah dated biblical events according to the reigns of different kings, as did many other nations of the ancient Near East, and this has created confusion and conflicting dates. Many of the dates given on this chart are therefore approximate. Historians have also subdivided the dynasties even further than shown on the chart here. For additional details on Egypt, *see pp.46–47*, for the kings of Israel and Judah *see pp.134–35*, for Assyria *see pp.142–43*, for Babylonia *see pp.148–49*.

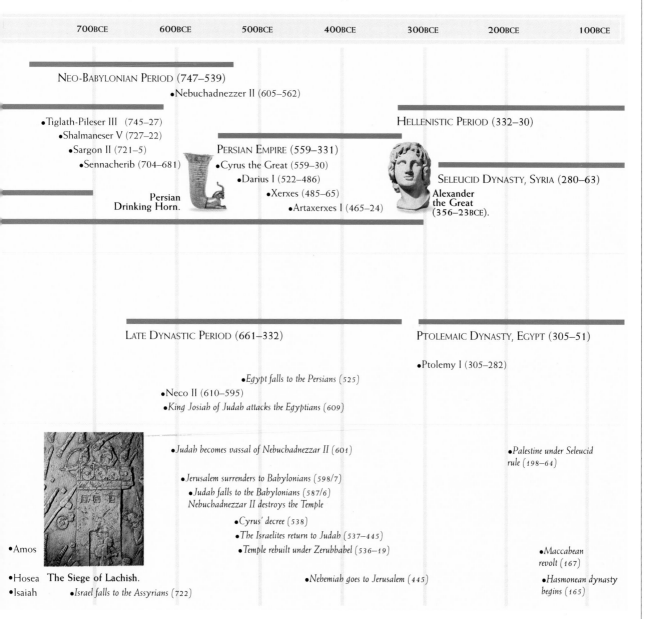

| 700BCE | 600BCE | 500BCE | 400BCE | 300BCE | 200BCE | 100BCE |
|---|---|---|---|---|---|---|

NEO-BABYLONIAN PERIOD (747–539)

•Nebuchadnezzer II (605–562)

HELLENISTIC PERIOD (332–30)

•Tiglath-Pileser III (745–27)
•Shalmaneser V (727–22)
•Sargon II (721–5)
•Sennacherib (704–681)

PERSIAN EMPIRE (559–331)
•Cyrus the Great (559–30)
•Darius I (522–486)
•Xerxes (485–65)
•Artaxerxes I (465–24)

**Persian Drinking Horn.**

SELEUCID DYNASTY, SYRIA (280–63)

**Alexander the Great (356–23BCE).**

LATE DYNASTIC PERIOD (661–332)

PTOLEMAIC DYNASTY, EGYPT (305–51)

•*Ptolemy I (305–282)*

•*Egypt falls to the Persians (525)*
•*Neco II (610–595)*
•*King Josiah of Judah attacks the Egyptians (609)*

•*Judah becomes vassal of Nebuchadnezzar II (601)*

•*Palestine under Seleucid rule (198–64)*

•*Jerusalem surrenders to Babylonians (598/7)*
•*Judah falls to the Babylonians (587/6)*
*Nebuchadnezzar II destroys the Temple*
•*Cyrus' decree (538)*
•*The Israelites return to Judah (537–445)*
•*Temple rebuilt under Zerubbabel (536–19)*

•Amos

•*Maccabean revolt (167)*

•Hosea  **The Siege of Lachish.**
•Isaiah  •*Israel falls to the Assyrians (722)*

•*Nehemiah goes to Jerusalem (445)*

•*Hasmonean dynasty begins (165)*

# THE STORIES OF

# ELIJAH

*During the reign of the ninth-century king Ahab, idolatry was widespread in Israel.*
*Elijah's message was total commitment to God and the Commandments, and he*
*dedicated his life to opposing the worship of other deities, particularly Baal.*

ELIJAH was a prophet whose life demonstrated the tensions that could exist between prophet and king, particularly if that king was not committed to Israel's God. His name means "My God is YHWH," the Lord of Israel. The most significant events of Elijah's life were his contest with the pagan prophets of Baal on Mount Carmel, his vision of God as a still small voice, and his being swept up to heaven in a whirlwind by a chariot of fire. Elijah's story is told among the accounts of the kings of Israel and Judah, from 1 Kings 17 to 2 Kings 2.

CONTEST WITH THE PROPHETS OF BAAL: 1 KGS. 18:20–40

THE VOICE OF GOD: 1 KGS. 19:11–18

ELIJAH'S ASCENT: 2 KGS. 2:1–12

## ELIJAH'S EARLY LIFE

Elijah appears in the Bible warning King Ahab that God would end a drought only by God's word spoken through Elijah. God then instructed Elijah to hide in the desert: *"You shall drink from the wadi [valley], and I have commanded the ravens to feed you there"* (1 Kgs. 17:4). When the brook dried up, Elijah lodged with a widow whose only supplies were a handful of flour and a small amount of oil. Elijah assured her that she would be able to feed her household for

ELIJAH'S WARNING: 1 KGS. 17:1

ELIJAH AND THE WIDOW: 1 KGS. 17:9FF.

**Elijah ascends in his fiery chariot.**

many days, and the supplies would not diminish *"until the day that the LORD sends rain on the earth"* (1 Kgs. 17:14). However, the widow truly acknowledged that Elijah was a "man of God" when he revived her dead child: *"Now I know that you are a man of God"* (1 Kgs. 17:24).

## THE PROPHETS OF BAAL

After three years of drought, Ahab accused Elijah of troubling Israel. Elijah responded by telling Ahab to summon the prophets of Baal to Mount Carmel, where he issued a challenge. Elijah proposed that both he and the prophets of Baal set up an altar and prepare a sacrifice. The people would then recognize as God the one whose altar caught fire. Baal's prophets called on Baal all day, danced around the altar, and mutilated themselves, but there was no reply. Elijah built his altar with twelve stones, to represent the unity of the Twelve Tribes of Israel. He then called to God, and the altar was immediately consumed by fire. The rains came later that day, proving to Ahab that God, unlike Baal, could end the drought at will.

AHAB ACCUSES ELIJAH: 1 KGS. 18:17

AHAB SUMMONS THE PROPHETS OF BAAL: 1 KGS. 18:19

THE CONTEST IS PREPARED: 1 KGS. 18:24

NO REPLY FROM BAAL: 1 KGS. 18:29

THE RAINS: 1 KGS. 18:45

## ELIJAH'S VISION

After Ahab's wife, Jezebel, threatened to kill Elijah, he fled to the wilderness and prayed to die: *"It is enough, now, O LORD, take away my life, for I am no better than my ancestors"* (1 Kgs. 19:4). An angel fed him, and he traveled to Horeb where Moses and the children of Israel had received the Ten Commandments in a dramatic revelation with thunder and lightning. Elijah's experience was very different: he complained that to be a fugitive fearing for his life was poor reward for his zeal in defending God. A wind, an earthquake, and fire all passed by the cave in which Elijah waited. God was not there, but God spoke to Elijah in a still small voice, *"a sound of sheer silence"* (1 Kgs. 19:12).

**Flour & oil**
*During the famine, Elijah assured the widow that her supplies of flour and oil for making bread would last until the rain came.*

## NABOTH'S VINEYARD

King Ahab coveted a vineyard owned by a man called Naboth, but Naboth refused to sell. Ahab's wife, Jezebel, had Naboth accused of blasphemy and he was killed. In a dramatic confrontation, Elijah prophesied that for this abuse of royal power, Ahab and Jezebel would die disgracefully: *"Because you have sold yourself to do what is evil in the sight of the LORD, I will bring disaster on you"* (1 Kgs. 21:20–21). Ahab's subsequent repentance lessened his punishment.

NABOTH IS KILLED:
1 KGS. 21:13

## ELIJAH'S ASCENT TO HEAVEN

Elijah passed his ministry on to another prophet, Elisha, by casting his mantle over Elisha while Elisha was plowing. Later, on the day of Elijah's ascension, Elisha refused to leave his master three times: *"As the LORD lives, and as you yourself live, I will not leave you"* (2 Kgs. 2:2). Finally, a fiery chariot and horses separated them, and Elijah ascended to heaven in a whirlwind. Elisha then picked up Elijah's fallen mantle and assumed his role. When they saw Elisha coming, the prophets at Jericho declared: *"The spirit of Elijah rests on Elisha"* (2 Kgs. 2:15).

ELISHA TAKES OVER
ELIJAH'S MINISTRY:
1 KGS. 19:19

ELIJAH ASCENDS
TO HEAVEN:
2 KGS. 2:11

## THE CONTEXT OF THE ELIJAH STORIES

Elijah's background is known only from his description as *"Elijah the Tishbite, of Tishbe in Gilead"* (1 Kgs. 17:1). He first appears to warn Ahab of the impending drought. The contest with the prophets of Baal on Mount Carmel takes place approximately three years later, marking the end of the drought. Baal means "owner" or "lord" and is the name of the Canaanite god of storms and weather. Because he was "owner of the land," the inclination to worship Baal was strong.

The incident at Naboth's vineyard demonstrates the principle that land owned by an Israelite family was regarded as a gift from God, and that the right of the individual or family to retain ownership should be respected. Throughout the story, Elijah displays the strong ethical qualities of his faith, which were not regarded as an important part of Baal's faith.

When God spoke to Elijah in the cave, the divine voice came out of the *"sound of sheer silence"* (1 Kgs. 19:12). This manifestation of God is particularly appropriate for Elijah, who so fiercely and dramatically proved God's power to others. Elijah considered his work to be finished, but God restored his sense of worth and granted him a companion and successor. Following Elijah's ascent to heaven, Elisha assumed responsibility for continuing Elijah's work, ensuring that prophecy and faith in God would continue.

## ELIJAH IN TRADITION

In Malachi 4:5, God says: *"I will send you the prophet Elijah before the great and terrible day of the LORD comes"* to reunite families in disagreement. Since Elijah did not die, it is assumed that he can return to this world at will, and he often appears in legends as a messenger between Heaven and earth.

Jews believe Elijah will come at the end of days to decide all those questions of Jewish law upon which the rabbis were unable to reach consensus; they also believe he will announce the coming of the Messiah. His presence is hoped for at the Passover Seder, the ritual for the first night or the first two nights of Passover. It is hoped that he will appear in both roles – to decide whether a fifth cup of wine should be drunk, and to proclaim the Messiah's imminent arrival. Many of the stories about Elijah in Jewish legend describe his help with the poor and those in danger. A chair is dedicated to him at circumcision ceremonies, which he has to attend as each child might be the future Messiah.

In early Christianity, the return of Elijah was applied to John the Baptist: *"Elijah is indeed coming first to restore all things"* (Mark 9:12; cf. Matt. 11:14; 17:10–13). In the New Testament, Elijah was also associated with Jesus at the Transfiguration: *"Suddenly there appeared to them Moses and Elijah"* (Matt. 17:3; cf. Mark 9:2–10; Luke 9:28–36).

For further reading see bibliography numbers: 209, 347, 804

# GODS AND GODDESSES

## OF THE ANCIENT NEAR EAST

*Many different religions were practised in the ancient Near East. We know something of those
in the more powerful or influential areas, but others remain obscure. Popular religious beliefs
were probably different from the "official" faiths in many important ways.*

THE biblical estimation of other
religions is usually hostile. But
it is made obvious throughout
their history that the people of Israel
were involved in the practices of those
religions, and that the religion of Israel
gained and assimilated much in this way.

## MESOPOTAMIAN RELIGION

Most Mesopotamian religion was based
on the polytheistic Sumerian religious
system, which elevated three gods – An,
Enlil, and Enki – above the others. The
most senior god was An, but his power
was vested in his son, Enlil, the king of
the gods, who was advised by Enki.
Babylonians and Assyrians called An
"Anu" and Enki "Ea." Other, less senior
deities met in an assembly chaired by
An or Enlil, and the decisions made by
the gods were said to be written down
on a Tablet of Destinies. Initially, deities

**ANUBIS, LORD OF THE UNDERWORLD**
*The status of certain Egyptian gods varied over time,
partly through changing political circumstances:
from being the god of death for only the Pharaoh,
Anubis became the god of death for all.*

were associated with, and responsible
for, natural or cosmological phenomena.
For example, the pantheon includes
a moon god (Sumerian Nanna=
Babylonian/Assyrian Sin) and a sun
god (Utu=Shamash), as well as gods
of crops, husbandry, and even
fermentation. The underworld
was an independent dominion,
ruled over by its own king and
queen, Nergal and Eresh-kigal.
The religious system was
altered and adapted considerably
over time by different cities or
regions. In particular, the growing influence of Semitic peoples
led to the inclusion of new
deities or to the merger of
Sumerian with Semitic gods.
Such mergers (known as
syncretism) occurred anyway,
as prominent gods absorbed

characteristics of others: most notably,
Ishtar came to be *the* Goddess, embodying the natures of other goddesses.
Political considerations also altered the
balance of divine power, so that Babylon
promoted its city-god Marduk to chief
god, as did the Assyrians for Ashur.

## EGYPTIAN RELIGION

Although paintings often show Egypt's
gods as animals or with animal features,
they were generally thought to have
human forms. Their numbers could
likewise be increased
or decreased

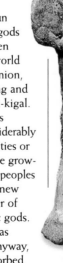

**MESOPOTAMIAN WATER GODDESS**
*Many gods and goddesses were linked to the fertility of crops
and the provision of land. Here, a water goddess is
being worshiped by other gods.*

**IDOL WORSHIP**
*The worship of a calf was common throughout the ancient Near East and appears in the biblical story of Moses (see pp. 50–51). The bronze calf covered in silver and the clay shrine in which it was found (above left) were excavated at the sanctuary of Ashkelon.*

through the import of new deities or through syncretism. Egyptian gods could also be linked together to express possession of one another's attributes: the Theban god Amun, for instance, could be linked with the sun god Re to become Amun-Re. The status of particular gods varied over time, partly through changing political circumstances, but the sun god remained the principal focus of belief for Egyptians. For a brief period in the 14th century BCE, the Aten, the visible disk of the sun, was made the sole object of worship by King Akhenaten.

From early times, the Egyptian king was strongly associated with the god Horus, who, assisted by his mother, Isis, struggled against his uncle, Seth. Seth had killed Horus' father, Osiris, whose resurrection to become god of the dead played a key role in ideas of the afterlife. The Egyptian gods were responsible for the preservation of Maat at the cosmic level: Maat, sometimes depicted as a goddess, is the order and truth that maintains the integrity of the world, and that is under constant threat from the forces of chaos.

## OTHER RELIGIONS

Much of Syria and Palestine was dominated by the polytheistic Canaanite religion (see pp. 98–99), which probably served as a framework for numerous local cults; this religion seems also to have been adopted by the Philistines. Across the Jordan River, Ammon, Moab, and Edom (pp. 100–1) all had national gods, but we know little about them. Farther south, the Arabian kingdoms worshiped many local deities, but all appear to have venerated (under different names) gods of the moon and of the morning star, and a goddess of the sun. From the time of the Persian empire, Persian religion may have had some influence in the region, although the Persians seem to have encouraged local beliefs instead of imposing their own. Early Persian religion has links with Indian religion, but, probably between the tenth and sixth centuries BCE, Zoroas-

**CANAANITE GODDESS**
*This representation of Astarte, the goddess of fertility, shows how sexuality was important in many religions.*

trianism led to a focus upon the god Ahura Mazda (see p. 157) and a tendency to move away from polytheism toward a form of dualism.

In the Bible, the classic picture of conflict between YHWH and other gods is that of Elijah and the prophets of Baal (see pp. 138–39). The basic acknowledgment of a diverse loyalty is that of the early statement in Joshua 24:2, "Thus says the LORD, the God of Israel: Long ago your ancestors — Terah and his sons Abraham and Nahor — lived beyond the Euphrates [River] and served other gods" (Elohim in the plural). The Bible story emerges from the conflict to assert YHWH as the only Elohim.

**MESOPOTAMIAN FIGURES**
*These figurines from northern Syria date from the third millennium BCE. They may have functioned as votive offerings, representing the worshiper who dedicated them, or they may have served as protective house gods. Many figurines have been found near the Euphrates.*

**METAL WAR GOD**
*This figure of the war god Reshef comes from Megiddo in Israel. Reshef was connected with Phoenician and Canaanite religion, where he was also the god of the "West."*

For further reading see bibliography numbers: 115, 170, 233, 277, 513, 565, 569, 572, 628, 633, 651, 873a

# ASSYRIA

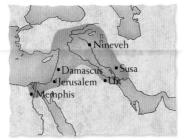

*From their heartland in northern Mesopotamia – modern Iraq – the Assyrians built one of the most powerful ancient empires. They played a crucial role in Israelite history, destroying Israel and invading Judah.*

## THE EMPIRE

Originating in the fertile land of the Tigris and Euphrates Rivers, the nation of Assyria soon expanded. At its greatest extent, in the seventh century BCE, the empire stretched from modern Iran to Egypt. Although the small Southern Kingdom of Judah was invaded by the Assyrians, it managed to escape occupation.

ALTHOUGH the principal cities of the region, including Asshur and Nineveh, had long histories of their own, Assyria did not emerge as a distinct nation until the second millennium BCE. The Assyrian people originally spoke a dialect of Akkadian (a form of the Babylonian language) that was written on clay tablets using cuneiform script. But during the first millennium BCE a growing Aramaean presence led to the widespread adoption of Aramaic. From the 13th century BCE, the Assyrians began a series of conquests in the surrounding region, including territory that had belonged to the crumbling Mitannian empire. With some significant setbacks, these conquests continued for about two centuries, during which period the Assyrians established a reputation for cruelty and ruthlessness, useful to themselves. A partial collapse of their empire during the 11th century was followed by a revival in the late tenth century. This was to continue until the early eighth century BCE, when central power collapsed and much of the territory was lost to the rival empire of Urartu (covering parts of modern Iran, Turkey, and Armenia).

## ASSYRIA IN PALESTINE

Territory lost to Urartu was swiftly regained by the Assyrian Tiglath-Pileser III (745–27BCE), known in some Bibles as Pul (*see* 2 Kgs. 15:19; 16:10; 2 Chr. 28:20–21). He extracted tribute from states in Syria and Palestine and, in 734BCE, captured Gaza in southern Palestine. Shortly after this, a series of revolts was put down by Tiglath-Pileser and his successors, Shalmaneser V (726–22BCE) and the usurper Sargon II (721–5BCE). Among the rebels was the Northern Kingdom of Israel. Its capital, Samaria, was sacked, probably by Shalmaneser, in 722BCE, and much of the population deported. Deportation had been normal practice for some time: the movement of people around the empire removed

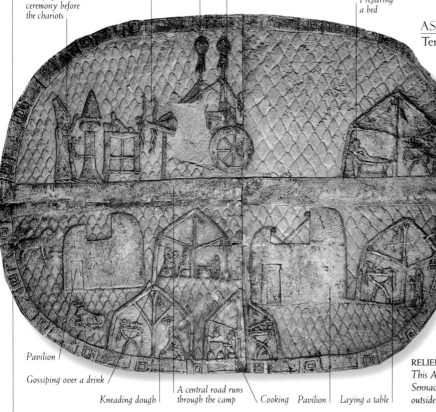

*Two priests in tall hats perform a ceremony before the chariots*

*Incense burner*

*Standard of Sennacherib*

*A chariot of the gods, which would have been driven into battle*

*Preparing a bed*

*Pavilion*

*Gossiping over a drink*

*Kneading dough*

*A central road runs through the camp*

*Cooking*

*Pavilion*

*Laying a table*

### RELIEF OF THE ENCAMPMENT
*This Assyrian relief from the walls of a central room in Sennacherib's palace depicts the encampment of the king's army outside Lachish. Assyrians are shown at a variety of activities.*

# THE SIEGE OF LACHISH

*When the Assyrians invaded Judah, they captured many fortified cities, among them the ancient stronghold of Lachish. A record of the capture exists on large Assyrian reliefs.*

**The ruins of Lachish**
*Ruins at the fortified city of Lachish, settled in 2500BCE, show evidence of both Canaanite and Israelite religions.*

In 701BCE, after King Hezekiah withheld tribute, the Assyrian king Sennacherib invaded Judah, forcing Hezekiah's surrender (2 Kgs. 18:13–15). Sennacherib received the Judahite messengers at Lachish. His conquest is depicted on large stone reliefs that once covered the walls of a central room in Sennacherib's palace. From these, and from other archaeological evidence, it is clear that Lachish resisted the Assyrian attack and was besieged for some time (*see opposite, below*). Although the reliefs conform to Assyrian artistic conventions, they do appear to reflect details of the actual siege, showing captives and plunder being taken from the defeated city. A mass burial has been found with the remains of around 1,500 bodies, probably citizens killed during or after the siege. Lachish never fully recovered; its defenses were repaired in the late seventh century, but the city was destroyed again during the Babylonian conquest in the 580's BCE.

ASSYRIAN RELIGION
Often derived from the Babylonian religion, many Assyrian gods were associated with particular cities. The national god Ashur was worshiped at the city of Asshur. The Assyrian king acted as the representative of Ashur. As a result, military campaigns were often viewed as holy wars. The small household god, above, was one of several figures found under the floor of the royal palace at Nineveh.

potential troublemakers, and created communities dependent on Assyrian good-will and protection. Slightly later Assyrian sources mention Israelite troops conscripted into the Assyrian army. Judah did not join the rebellion, and may have received Assyrian assistance against Israel and Damascus (2 Kgs. 16:5–18). When the Israelite king Hezekiah withheld tribute in the late eighth century BCE, Sargon II's successor, Sennacherib (704–681BCE), invaded. The biblical account of the invasion (2 Kgs. 18–19) depicts an Israelite surrender that agrees closely with Assyrian sources. These sources do not mention God's destruction of the Assyrian army's second attack, described at 2 Kings 19:37. Some scholars speculate that the Assyrians invaded a second time, but there is no evidence for this.

## THE FALL OF THE EMPIRE
Assyria's dominance over the powerful city of Babylon was challenged by a series of rebellions; in 652BCE this turned into open civil war. Although the Assyrians won, they were unable to repress Babylonian resistance completely. In 626BCE, the Babylonians repelled an Assyrian attack on Babylon and turned the tables, beginning an assault on Assyria itself.

The important city of Asshur was captured in 614, and two years later, the capital Nineveh fell. By this time, Assyria had allied itself with Egypt, but their combined forces were driven out to Syria, and finally defeated by the Babylonian king Nebuchadnezzar II at Carchemish, in 605BCE. Almost as a footnote to this great campaign and the defeat of Assyria, in 609BCE the Judahite king Josiah was killed by an Egyptian army at Megiddo, in northern Palestine: Egypt and Judah were probably each attempting to fill the regional power vacuum left by Assyria's collapse.

# ASSYRIA IN THE BIBLE

The rise and fall of the Assyrian empire left a profound mark on biblical writings. The Assyrian campaigns are described in the books of Kings and Chronicles, but there are also frequent references in the Prophets. The historians' accounts of the Assyrian invasion are found in 2 Kings 15–19 (and the parallel passages in 2 Chronicles 22–29) and Isaiah 36–39. Much of this history is also found in Assyrian reliefs. The reactions of the Prophets are more scattered and take a number of forms, from the period of Assyria's threat to the fall of Nineveh come Isaiah 1–12 (note chs.9 and 10); 14:24–16:14; 20:1–6; 21:11–23:18; 29:1–30:17; 30:27–32:14; Micah 1–3:10; Amos and Hosea; Zephaniah, and Nahum. Nahum is a particularly fierce denunciation of Nineveh. Assyria is often seen in the Bible as the scourge of Israel and Judah, and its invasions of both are reported as divinely permitted – God's punishment for their disobedience. But Assyria was destroyed for its godlessness.

For further reading see bibliography numbers: 176, 204, 348, 413, 572, 651, 663, 674, 675, 820

# JOSIAH

*Josiah was king of Judah shortly before the Exile, ruling from 639 to 609BCE.*
*He made an attempt to reform religion in the land, influenced by the discovery*
*of an old law book during repairs to the Temple.*

IN the Bible, Josiah is regarded as one of
Israel's most important kings due to his
religious policy. His story is told in 2 Kings
22–23 and 2 Chronicles 34–35. Josiah
succeeded to the throne at the age of eight
during a time when the power and threat of
Assyria was declining. He ruled for 30 years
(c.639–9 BCE), and during that time, *"walked
in all the way of his father David"* (2 Kgs. 22:2). In
the 18th year of his reign (according

to 2 Kings, the eighth according to 2 Chronicles), Josiah started the restoration of the Temple, and so began his great reform of religion.
In c.622BCE, "the book of the law" was found
during the repair work. Although not identified, it seems likely that the scroll contained
at least a part of the book of Deuteronomy, as
there are connections between Josiah's reforms
and the demands of the book. Following the
discovery of the scroll, the words of the

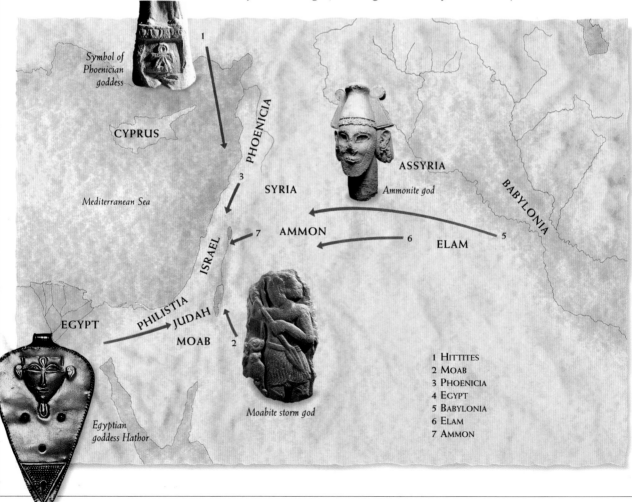

*Symbol of
Phoenician
goddess*

CYPRUS

*Mediterranean Sea*

PHOENICIA

SYRIA

ASSYRIA

*Ammonite god*

BABYLONIA

AMMON

ELAM

ISRAEL

PHILISTIA

EGYPT

JUDAH

MOAB

*Egyptian
goddess Hathor*

*Moabite storm god*

1 HITTITES
2 MOAB
3 PHOENICIA
4 EGYPT
5 BABYLONIA
6 ELAM
7 AMMON

Covenant were read aloud to the people, and the Covenant was renewed. There followed a purge of religious beliefs and practices throughout the land, and Josiah ordered the Passover to be kept *"as prescribed in this book of the covenant"* (2 Kgs. 23:21–23).

## JOSIAH'S REFORMS

In 2 Chronicles, there is more emphasis on Josiah's connection with David, and the way in which he fulfilled the role of the anointed one of God. Like David, Josiah also restored the Ark and the singers to the Temple. According to the book of Chronicles, these reforms began ten years earlier, so the finding of the "book of the law" did not initiate these reforms but was discovered during the course of them. Both 2 Kings and 2 Chronicles record the fatal wounding of Josiah at the Battle of Megiddo in 609BCE, where Josiah intervened to stop the Egyptians from proceeding north to fight the Babylonians. Chronicles, however, attempts to explain why a king as good as Josiah should have come to such an untimely end (2 Chr. 35:20*ff*). Both books agree in portraying Josiah as one who pursued what was, from their point of view, a pure form of devotion to YHWH, in line with the covenant law of Moses. Josiah introduced the reforms to Judah and extended them to territory that had belonged to the Northern Kingdom of Israel.

## THE POWER OF BABYLON

In 627BCE, political circumstances changed and an opportunity for action in the north occurred. The death of the Assyrian king Ashurbanipal (c.668–27BCE) plunged the empire into a civil war from which Babylon eventually emerged as the new imperial power in the east. From this time on, Assyria could no longer control Palestine. Egypt increasingly became the major threat to Syria–Palestine and secured control of the "Way of the Sea" (the main route that passed from Egypt along the western coast of Palestine and then northeast via Megiddo and Damascus). It was only

FOREIGN INFLUENCE
*The history of Israel from the conquest to the Exile is portrayed as a period of struggle against the influence of foreign nations and gods. The map (opposite) shows the major nations.*

at the end of Josiah's reign, when he moved to confront Egypt directly and interfered with movement along the "Way of the Sea," that direct Egyptian interest in the Judean king arose. During the battle at Megiddo in 609BCE, Josiah was killed, perhaps in the attempt to establish his independence from Egypt early in the reign of the new Pharaoh, Necho II. Any limited independence that Judah might have gained during the period of Assyrian decline had now been entirely lost.

## THE FALL OF JERUSALEM

King Jehoahaz of Judah was immediately removed from power and replaced by his brother Eliakim, who subsequently changed his name to Jehoiachim. Syria–Palestine was described as a territory that *"belonged to the king of Egypt"* (2 Kgs. 24:7), but this situation did not last for long. After the Babylonians won crushing victories at Carchemish (northern Syria) in 605BCE, and then farther south at Hamath, Jehoiachim switched his allegiance to the Babylonian king, Nebuchadnezzar II.

Only a few years later, however, he rebelled, perhaps in the context of Nebuchadnezzar II's failed attempt to invade Egypt in 601BCE. At the end of 598BCE, the Babylonian army arrived at the gates of Jerusalem, and there were no Egyptian forces on hand to help. The city surrendered to the Babylonians in March 597BCE, and the new king of Judah, Jehoiachin, was deported to Babylon along with many other leading citizens. Mattaniah, uncle of Jehoiachin, then succeeded to the throne and was given the name Zedekiah.

Another rebellion followed, in connection with the resurgent power of Egypt under Psammetichus II. Jerusalem was besieged for two years and finally fell in 587/6BCE when supplies of food had been exhausted. Zedekiah managed to escape when defeat was imminent and fled in the direction of the Jordan, only to be overtaken by the Babylonians near Jericho. His sons were executed, and he himself was blinded and then deported to Babylon. A few weeks later, the walls of Jerusalem were dismantled, and the city was razed to the ground. The period of the Exile had begun.

JORDAN VALLEY
The Jordan River provided a natural barrier to foreign influence. "Evil" spirits were often thought to inhabit the desert that lay beyond it.

EVENTS
LEADING UP
TO THE EXILE

Restoration of the Temple 622BCE

Josiah killed at Megiddo 609BCE

Jehoahaz king of Judah 609–8BCE

Jehoiachim king of Judah 608–598BCE

Babylonian victory at Carchemish 605BCE

Nebuchadnezzar II's attempts to invade Egypt 601BCE

Jehoiachin king of Judah 597BCE

Surrender of Jerusalem to Babylonian army 597BCE

Zedekiah king of Judah 596–86BCE

Fall of Jerusalem 587/6BCE

For further reading see bibliography numbers: 131, 402, 473, 550, 559,

ROUTE OF THE EXILES

# EXILE TO BABYLON

*The early sixth century BCE was a time of almost unparalleled crisis for the Jewish people. Their leaders were removed, and many of them were forced to rebuild their lives and communities in a foreign land.*

## ROUTE TO BABYLON
Following the surrender of Jerusalem in 597BCE, the exiles traveled north through Bethel, Riblah, and the Sea of Galilee, and onward to the Euphrates. They then followed the path of the river southward into Babylon.

THE threat of exile would have been familiar to the people of Judah from the time of Assyrian domination in the eighth century BCE (*see pp.142–43*). It was only with the arrival of the Babylonian king Nebuchadnezzar II that the threat became a reality for many of Judah's citizens.

At the beginning of the sixth century BCE, the kings of Judah rebelled against their Babylonian overlord, King Nebuchadnezzar II. His response was swift and decisive – in 597BCE he accepted the surrender of Jerusalem and took many of the city's leading citizens into exile in Babylonia. King Jehoiachin of Judah and his family were deported, together with many of Judah's chief officials of state, military leaders, craftsmen, and smiths (2 Kgs. 24:14–16). Further deportations followed in the wake of the city's final destruction in 587/6BCE, when *"Nebuzaradan the captain of the guard carried into exile the rest of the people who were left in the city and the deserters who had defected to the king of Babylon"* (2 Kgs. 25:11; cf. Jer. 52:15–16). It is difficult to gauge the exact number of people who were deported to Babylon – Jeremiah 52:30 gives a figure

## THE PROPHETS OF THE EXILE
The Prophets brought messages of both warning and hope. Jeremiah foretold the disaster of the Exile and warned the people that God's judgment for their disobedience was inevitable. During the Exile, the Prophets spoke of hope for the future in a new covenant that God would establish with the people to *"forgive their iniquity, and remember their sin no more"* (Jer. 31:34).

EARLIER EXILES
*The exile of the people of Judah echoed that of the people of Israel by the Assyrians. This relief dates from the eighth century BCE and depicts Israelite captives leaving Lachish after the city was besieged.*

of *"four thousand six hundred"* – it would certainly have been in the region of several thousand men, women, and children. The biblical record claims that all were taken except *"some of the poorest people of the land,"* who were left to become *"vinedressers and tillers of the soil"* (2 Kgs. 25:12). It is worth remembering, however, that in an ancient agricultural society like Judah, such people probably constituted the majority of the population.

## THE AIMS OF DEPORTATION

Mass deportations formed a fundamental part of Assyrian and Babylonian foreign policy. The resettlement of whole communities far away from their original homes was a powerful method of demonstrating the empire's might to its subjects. There were also other practical benefits: rebellious community leaders could be moved from their former positions of influence to a safe distance, where it was hoped the presence of their families would encourage them to remain. These "dangerous elements" of the conquered population could then be usefully redeployed as soldiers, construction workers, or farmers in the service of the empire. Areas of the kingdom that had been depopulated through war or natural disaster often received communities of deportees to help with such tasks as agricultural and civic reconstruction.

## LIFE IN EXILE

Little is known about the immediate fate of the exiles. King Jehoiachin was imprisoned in Babylon with a small retinue, but he was still alive in 562BCE when he was granted special privileges by Nebuchadnezzar's successor Amel-Marduk, who *"spoke kindly to him, and gave him a seat above the other seats of the kings who were with him in Babylon"* (2 Kgs. 25:28). Craftsmen and smiths may have continued their trades, but the majority of exiles would probably have been settled into farming communities, and put to work on both the land and the canals that watered the grain fields of Mesopotamia. As they faced the task of rebuilding their lives and communities, the Babylonian policy of keeping deportees together allowed them to retain their national groups. It also permitted them limited

**MODERN-DAY EXILES**
*For some people, the threat of exile continues to the present day. These Kurdish refugees seek shelter and protection in a foreign land due to conflict at home.*

control over their own social and religious affairs. The prophecies of Ezekiel (*pp.212–13*), Isaiah 40–55 (*pp.202–3*), and Jeremiah (*pp.206–7*) interpreted the Exile to the people as they learned to worship God without a Temple or sacrificial offerings.

There is evidence that many people were sent to the region of Nippur in southern Mesopotamia, where the Prophet Ezekiel lived and worked. The cuneiform records of the Murashu banking firm suggest that the area still held a sizable Jewish population in the late fifth century BCE. Such communities followed the advice of Jeremiah, who wrote in a letter to one group of exiles: *"Build houses and live in them; plant gardens and eat what they produce. Take wives and have sons and daughters; take wives for your sons, and give your daughters in marriage, that they may bear sons and daughters; multiply there, and do not decrease. But seek the welfare of the city where I have sent you into exile, and pray to the LORD on its behalf, for in its welfare you will find your welfare"* (Jer. 29:5–7). Many Jews did indeed find their welfare in Babylonia; some continued to farm, and others became successful in business and in the royal administration. When the Jews were finally allowed to return to Judah, large numbers remained in Babylonia. It continued to be one of the most important centers of Jewish culture and learning into the Middle Ages.

MOROCCAN JEW
The Exile began the process known as the Diaspora – the settlement of Jews in countries around the world. These included, early on, Egypt (*see* Elephantine Island, *pp.159, 247*) and Syria. Communities were also established in regions as diverse as North Africa, Persia, and Asia Minor.

For further reading see bibliography numbers: 2, 3, 92, 131, 144, 206, 402, 464, 559, 586, 707, 751

# BABYLONIA

*The Babylonians exerted a lasting influence on Israelite culture and history. Heirs to, and propagators of, the ancient Sumerian and Akkadian cultures, they enjoyed increasing political power. It was they who conquered Judah and took many into exile.*

## THE EMPIRE

The map above shows the extent of the Babylonian empire at the time of Nabopolassar (625–5BCE), who conquered the Assyrian empire and took over the lands that the Assyrians controlled. These included Judah; in 597BCE Nabopolassar's son, Nebuchadnezzar II, raided Jerusalem, destroying the city ten years later.

THE name "Babylonians" was used by the Greeks to describe the people of the area at the southern end of the Tigris and Euphrates plain. It was not a word used by the people there themselves. Babylon was the city and capital; the area was Sumer and Akkad (from the main language) or Akkad alone. The founding of a great empire was largely due to Hammurabi (c.1792–50BCE). He took advantage of the delicate balance of power between Amorite city-states and strengthened Babylon's political and defensive position. By 1759BCE the whole of southern Mesopotamia was for the first time united into a single empire, with a magnificent capital, Babylon, and a common language in Akkadian. Only later did a group of incoming tribes called Chaldeans so mix with the indigenous people that Babylonians and Chaldeans become virtually synonymous.

## BABYLONIAN CULTURE

Hammurabi's Babylonia propagated the cultural treasures inherited from Akkadian-Sumerian cultures of the third millennium BCE. Chief among these was cuneiform writing. Learning had flourished, producing word lists, dictionaries, grammars, mathematical treatises, and astronomical data. So too did the recording of magic spells and texts, a tradition that led to the Chaldeans being especially associated with magic (*see* Dan. 2:2).

Most important was the transmission of Sumerian epics such as the *Enuma Elish* (a tale of cosmic conflict in creation), the *Gilgamesh Epic* (which includes a tale of a flood, *see p.33*), and wisdom literature (such as *I Will Praise the Lord of Wisdom*). This literature paints part of the intellectual background against which the worldview of the Hebrew Bible developed, especially the themes of creation, flood, and suffering (*pp.174–75*). The code of Hammurabi (*see opposite, above*) bears witness to the existence of legal codes in the previous millennium. Whether this had direct influence on the Pentateuch is doubtful, although there are some parallels of a general kind (*see pp.84–85*).

### THE ISHTAR GATE

*This splendid archway is a reconstruction of the Ishtar Gate, which opened onto the Processional Way leading to the main temple in Babylon. Built by Nebuchadnezzar II in about 580BCE, it was part of the reconstruction of the city. The gate is decorated with figures of a bull and the dragon of Marduk.*

**THE LAWS OF HAMMURABI**
*This detail from the Stela of King Hammurabi shows the Babylonian king standing before the sun-god Shamash. Hammurabi was responsible for unifying Mesopotamia in the 18th century BCE. Some of the laws of Hammurabi may show similarities with the laws of Exodus and Deuteronomy.*

## LATER BABYLONIA

After Hammurabi's death, the empire weakened greatly, but, from the surviving texts, it seems the tradition of learning was maintained. For a brief while, Nebuchadnezzar I (1125–4BCE) made gains and raised Babylon's profile and morale, but this was short-lived. To the south, the Chaldeans presented a growing threat, and from 911BCE onward vied with Assyria (to the north) for control of Babylon.

## THE NEO-BABYLONIAN EMPIRE

The city of Babylon changed hands several times, but after the fall of Assyria in the seventh century BCE, the Medes Nabopolassar and his son, Nebuchadnezzar II, seized their chance and revitalized the empire. This period of the second (Neo-Babylonian) empire lasted only from 625–539BCE, but it was a marvel of splendor and magnificence. Within two decades, Nabopolassar had gained control of central Mesopotamia and Syria.

The political fate of Judah was decided by changes in the hostile international environment. The fall of Assyria had been predicted by the Prophets, but the threat of neither Egypt on one side, nor Babylon on the other, gave cause for any comfort.

Nebuchadnezzar II of Babylon defeated Egypt and demanded tribute from Judah and its neighbors. A first rebellion against him by Jehoiachin was put down in 597BCE with the deportation of Judah's royal family. A second rebellion, by Zedekiah, resulted in the catastrophe of 587/6BCE, when Jerusalem was razed, and many Jews were either killed or deported to Babylon.

## THE END OF THE EMPIRE

Three weak rulers followed Nebuchadnezzar II in quick succession and were unable to hold onto his gains. They gave way to the usurper Nabonidus (555–39BCE), whose campaigns enlarged the empire but failed to command the complete loyalty of the Babylonians. His worship of the moon-god Sin and his failure to attend the all-important New Year festival in Babylon only added to the ease with which the Persian Cyrus took Babylon from Nabonidus and his son and regent Belshazzar in 539BCE.

## INFLUENCE ON ISRAEL

By the time the Jews were taken as captives to Babylon, Israel's cultural and religious identity had been established, and it was by no means lost during the Exile. However, Israel's religion was affected: the Israelites took over, but severely adapted, opportunities they found in the surrounding culture. Thus Jews did not join in the worship of Marduk and the Babylonian pantheon, and they refused the practices of astrology and divination, as the book of Deuteronomy makes clear (*"No one shall be found among you who makes a son or a daughter pass through fire, or who practices divination, or is a soothsayer, or an augur, or a sorcerer, or one who casts spells, or who consults ghosts or spirits, or who seeks oracles from the dead,"* Deut. 18:10–11; cf. 13). But they developed further their beliefs in angels and in the powers of evil. The Babylonian Exile forced a reassessment of Israel's relationship with YHWH, issuing with renewed and assured hope of Israel's restoration and release from exile (*see* especially Isaiah 40–55, *pp.*202–3). Much later, "Babylon" becomes a symbol for powers opposed to God's rule, from which believers pray for rescue.

see especially Isaiah 40–55, pp.202–3

---

**THE NEO-BABYLONIAN KINGS**

Nabopolassar
625–5BCE

Nebuchadnezzar II
604–562BCE

Amel-Marduk
561–60BCE

Nergal Sarussur
559–56BCE

Nabonidus 555–39BCE

**BABYLONIAN RELIGION**
Of the Babylonians' religion, only the main cult is well known. There were temples to different deities, often personifying or manifesting aspects of nature. There were also ziggurats (stepped towers), whose function is not clear; perhaps they were the model for the Tower of Babel. Babylon adopted the Sumerian pantheon with Marduk as the head of the gods. He was known as Bel (i.e., Lord, cf. the Hebrew word *Baal*, which also means "Lord"). There were seasonal festivals in which the king took an important part, especially in a New Year festival; some see reflections of this in some of the Psalms.

---

For further reading see bibliography numbers: 115, 204, 349, 413, 572, 663, 674, 820

# THE BOOKS OF
# 1-2 CHRONICLES

*Based mainly on the books of Samuel and Kings, the books of 1–2 Chronicles
tell the story of the covenant people. The books place emphasis on the covenant
with David, the Temple and its priests, and the responsibilities of the people of God.*

TO a large extent, the content of the books of Chronicles is paralleled elsewhere in the Hebrew Bible. Many (though by no means all) of those mentioned in the genealogies of 1 Chronicles 1–9 are also in the books of Genesis, Exodus, or Numbers. The account from David to the Exile mostly describes the same events as Samuel–Kings, often in identical or very similar words. Hence the Greek title of *Paraleipomena*, "The Things Omitted," and also the relative neglect into which Chronicles was consigned until quite recently. This neglect is also due to the long lists of names characteristic of Chronicles. Less interesting for us, they were important for the original readers in helping to establish their identity within the community.

## SOURCES

As regards history, Samuel–Kings has usually been regarded as the primary, more reliable source, and Chronicles has been neglected, despised – because, for example, it turned the figure of David into a meddling ecclesiastic – or subjected to desperate interpretation by those anxious to present it as historically reliable. In recent years, however, a better understanding of Chronicles has emerged. Together with Ezra–Nehemiah, the book offers a picture of the past with somewhat different emphasis from that of the Genesis to Kings narrative. The last verses of 2 Chronicles are found again in Ezra 1, so it is either a continuous history from the same source (the majority view until recently) or distinct pieces worked together into one overall structure (the usual view now). Chronicles was compiled when the Jews were essentially a

religious congregation gathered around the Jerusalem Temple, so the genealogies focus especially on Judah (1 Chr. 2–3), the main group in that area, and on Levi (1 Chr. 6), the priestly tribe. Here, attention is devoted to the Levites, responsible for most of the secondary aspects of Temple worship. The Second Book of Chronicles contains several sermons attributed to Levites, setting out how God will reward the community if they remain faithful. The proper conduct of worship is important: even kings could not take matters into their own hands (e.g., Uzziah's punishment in 2 Chr. 26).

## THE CHRONICLER

Much recent attention has focused on the way the Chronicler has interpreted and reshaped older traditions (*see opposite*). Thus differences in Samuel as to who killed the Philistine giant Goliath (David in 1 Sam. 17; or Elhanan in 2 Sam. 21:19) are resolved by making Elhanan's victim Goliath's brother. King Manasseh is condemned in 2 Kings 21, but he reigned for 55 years, implying divine favor, so 2 Chronicles 33:12–13 describes Manasseh's otherwise unattested repentance. Chronicles gives a brilliant theological interpretation of history for the needs of the post-exilic community: from the earliest days (Adam, 1 Chr. 1:1) to the present, this people, so recently defeated and still subject, is the center of God's purpose and providence. One of the most attractive and often over-looked stories in Chronicles is that of the prophet Oded, whose concern for captives from Judah may have provided the model for Jesus' parable of the Good Samaritan (2 Chr. 28:8–15).

**THE ARK OF THE COVENANT**
*At the center of the Chronicler's belief is adherence to
the Covenant and the promises God made to David.*

# DIFFERENCES BETWEEN CHRONICLES & KINGS

Most of Chronicles (1 Chr. 10:1 to 2 Chr. 36:19) describes events also found in Samuel and Kings. Both the similarities and the differences raise questions. The similarities raise the question: why were the same people and events described twice? The differences raise the question: why were omissions and changes introduced? Most probably, Chronicles used Samuel–Kings as a source, so that differences came from the editorial policy and vision of the Chronicler. Some have held that Samuel–Kings and Chronicles used a common source, but that would require a very late dating for Samuel–Kings.

For the sections in common, Chronicles is shorter than Samuel–Kings, mainly because Chronicles gives no independent treatment of Israel, the Northern Kingdom. By the time Chronicles was written (c.350BCE), that kingdom had long since fallen, and those who lived in its territory were not regarded as true Israelites.

### Alterations to Samuel–Kings

There were other changes, smaller but significant. The picture of David is very different. In 2 Samuel/1 Kings he is shown with faults – as an adulterer who organizes the murder of the husband of his pregnant mistress and who cannot control his own family; one who is reduced to senility. None of this is in Chronicles, where David is devoted to making everything ready for the Temple to be built by his son Solomon. This may be censorship, but more probably it reflects Jerusalem and its Temple as now the center of the people's concern.

Other differences reflect a later religious understanding. David's census brought disaster (2 Sam. 24), so the Chronicler introduces "Satan" instead of God as its instigator (1 Chr. 21:1) – the first time that Satan is found in the Hebrew Bible as a direct agent of evil. King Uzziah suffered from an infectious skin disease (2 Kgs. 15:5); 2 Chronicles 26 explains this as a result of his interference in religious matters. In 2 Kings 21–23 Manasseh is condemned and Josiah praised, yet one lived a long life, while the other was cut off in his prime. 2 Chronicles 33 and 35 explain that Manasseh repented, while Josiah ignored a prophetic word.

### A different understanding of history

Overall, therefore, Chronicles gives a different assessment of the kings of Judah. In 1 Kings 15:3, Abijam *"committed all the sins that his father did before him,"* but in 2 Chronicles 13:1–22 Abijah [sic] is a loyal defender of YHWH's cause. In 2 Kings 21:1–17, Manasseh is among the worst kings, but in 2 Chronicles 33:1–20, he repents of his evil and symbolizes God restoring the people. "Seeking God" is, for Chronicles, a key to prosperity or disaster, just as "humbling oneself," or failing to do so, leads to the appropriate response on the part of God. To a people asking, in the light of the Exile, whether God has abandoned the Covenant with them, Chronicles answers emphatically that God has not done so, and that history shows what kinds of behavior will restore the people to God.

## THE BOOK

**TITLE:** 1 and 2 Chronicles – the usual name since the time of the scholar Jerome (fifth century CE)

**HEBREW TITLE:** *Dibre hayyamim* (literally "accounts of the days"); the books in the Hebrew Bible are not divided into two parts and are the last of The Writings; that is, they are the last books in the Hebrew Bible

**GREEK TITLE:** *Paraleipomena* (literally "things omitted," that is omitted from the books of Kings)

**DATE:** Certainly later than 540BCE (the last event recorded); otherwise not known

**AUTHORSHIP:** Perhaps a Levite in the service of the Second Jerusalem Temple

## THE CONTENTS

### 1 CHRONICLES 1–9
The period from Creation to the rise of David is traced almost exclusively by means of genealogies

### 1 CHRONICLES 10–29
The reign of David, with special emphasis on his preparation of a site and materials for the Temple

### 2 CHRONICLES 1–9
The reign of Solomon. The Temple is built and dedicated to God's service

### 2 CHRONICLES 10–36
The reigns of the kings of Judah are described from Solomon to the Exile. A brief appendix heralds the end of exile with the reign of Cyrus of Persia

## KEY THEMES

*The Covenant*

•

*Temples, priests, and worship*

•

*The reasons for success and failure in history*

For further reading see bibliography numbers: 195, 436, 437, 583, 812, 813

# RELIGION OF THE EXILE

*In the sixth century BCE, Jerusalem fell to the Babylonian armies. Many important religious developments took place among the exiles in Babylon, as they questioned whether God had abandoned the people or was strong enough to defend them.*

THE Exile raised many questions that were tremendously important for the future of Israel's faith. The people wanted to know if God's promises were false (Ps. 77:7–9; cf. 89:49–51), and whether God now lacked strength (Isa. 50:2). Not all Israelites were taken into exile, and the land of Judah was not left completely uninhabited. However, those left behind were in a wretched condition (*see* Lamentations, *pp.210–11*), with constant raids from outsiders. Others fled to Egypt, where important letters from a community settled at Elephantine have survived (*see pp.159, 247*). In accordance with Babylonian policy, those taken to Babylon established their own areas of settlement. The question now arose of whether they should worship the gods of Babylon, who had proved stronger. The Prophets of the Exile warned the people to remain faithful to their God.

> **❝** *Those who trust in the LORD are like Mount Zion, which cannot be moved, but abides forever.* **❞**
>
> (Psalm 125:1)

## TRADITIONAL VALUES

The exiles were helped by the reconstruction of worship. It had only been during the reign of King Josiah that an attempt had been made to centralize all worship in the Temple in Jerusalem (*pp.144–45*). The more common practice of worshiping God wherever the people were living now proved its worth. Provision for this circumstance is included in Solomon's prayer of dedication to the Temple (1 Kgs. 8:46–51). In priestly thought and in the Deuteronomistic History (*see pp.80, 105*) family observances are stressed: circumcision, observance of the Passover, the keeping of the Sabbath (Exod. 31:13), and laws of diet and purity are signs of faithful observance and became an important part of the people's common life. Throughout this period, however, the memory of what had been lost remained dominant (Ps. 137).

**A PORTRAIT OF SUFFERING**
*This 19th-century etching by Goya, entitled "There is no one to help him," depicts a dying man, overcome by grief at the plight of his family. During the Exile, the Prophets reassured people that faith in God would bring renewed hope for the future.*

# THE LACHISH LETTERS

*The Lachish Letters were discovered during excavations at the Judean city of Lachish in 1935–38. They can be precisely dated and thus throw vivid light on the Babylonian attack of the city.*

Lachish was one of the major fortified cities of Judah, located to the southwest of Jerusalem (*see p.143*). The Lachish Letters, inscribed on broken pieces of pottery known as potsherds or *ostraca*, were written between an officer at an outpost and his commanding officer in Lachish and can be dated to the final months before the kingdom of Judah fell to the Babylonians. One of the letters (no.4) records the very moment that the Babylonian army swept over Azekah on its way to Jerusalem. It states that the signal fires of Lachish could still be seen, but that those of Azekah had disappeared. This letter must have been inscribed on the sherd just after Jeremiah

**Lachish potsherd.**

34:7 was written. It refers to a time *"when the army of the king of Babylon was fighting against Jerusalem and against all the cities of Judah that were left, Lachish and Azekah; for these were the only fortified cities of Judah that remained."*

Other letters are of great importance, showing, for example, that the name of YHWH was paramount. The officer at the outpost began each letter to his commanding officer with the greeting, *"May YHWH cause my lord to hear tidings of peace this day."* This suggests that the reforms of Josiah (*see pp.144–45*) had been effective. Several letters also refer to "the prophet"; no name has survived in the text, but possible identities include Jeremiah and Uriah (Jer. 26:20–21).

## THE IMPORTANCE OF FAITH

Among the exiles, some began to remember also the consistency and faithfulness of God in their history – in the promises to the Ancestors, during the Exodus, throughout the settlement of the Land, and in the Covenant with the house of David (2 Sam. 7). These memories became the underlying themes of Isaiah 40–55 (*see pp.202–3*), and led to the leap of faith that Cyrus, king of Persia, was God's new Messiah. When Cyrus began to move against Babylon, the Prophet saw that his campaign route followed the route of Abraham when he, in obedience to God, set out from Ur to go where God had commanded. Cyrus was the instrument of God in bringing about the return of the Jews to their land: he is described as *"my shepherd"* (Isa. 44:28), and as God's Messiah in Isaiah 45:1.

This profound faith that God had not been defeated in the defeat of Israel did not, however, answer the all-important question of why the disaster had happened. The simple and traditional answer assumed that it was the fault of those who had lived before the Exile – they had clearly sinned greatly, and their descendants were paying the price: *"The parents have eaten sour grapes, and the children's teeth are set on edge"* (Jer. 31:29). Both Jeremiah and Ezekiel contested this view. Although they agreed that there had been grievous fault in the past, they emphasized that people in the present must recognize their own responsibility (Ezek. 18:1–4). In the same spirit, work began on editing the traditions and existing records to tell a continuous story of faith and betrayal, of reward and punishment. Telling the story from the point of view now

> **❝ As I live, says the Lord GOD ... Know that all lives are mine ... it is only the person who sins that shall die. ❞**
>
> (Ezekiel 18:3–4)

found in the book of Deuteronomy was a long process, but its unmistakable mark was left on the Historical books as we now have them. On the basis of this acceptance of responsibility, Isaiah 40–55 could put forward the view that those in Exile should prepare the way for a renewal of Israel. Similarly, Ezekiel 40–48 could look forward to a rebuilt Temple. In even more visionary style, the commentary of prophets gave way to visions of the future that issued in works now known as "Apocalyptic" (*see pp.260–61*).

## A NEW IDENTITY

During the Exile, a new sense of what it meant to belong to the people of Israel began to emerge – a move from an identity fixed by geographical location and national institutions to one based on commitment to a religious and cultural tradition. For the first time, it became possible to think of "Judaism." Of course, the religion of the exilic period was not monolithic – not all people had been deported by Nebuchadnezzar: some remained in Israel, and others fled to the nearby countries of Egypt and Syria. However, many of the most significant religious developments took place among the exiles in Babylon. After the return from exile, it was their descendants who took control in Jerusalem and who largely molded the official religion of the Restoration Period (*see pp.160–63*). The new shape of religious life that began with the Babylonian Exile continued to sustain Jewish communities in Judah and throughout the Diaspora. It also provided an important model for the rabbinic Judaism that emerged after the destruction of the Second Temple in 70CE.

**For further reading see bibliography numbers:** 2, 3, 6, 92, 144, 301, 464, 586, 707

# RETURN FROM EXILE

*The return of the Jews from exile in Babylon proved to be a bitter disappointment.
Hopes of a restored nation and monarchy were not fulfilled. Economic hardship,
aggressive neighbors, and reduced population impeded the revival of Judah's fortunes.*

### ROUTE OF RETURN
The Jews returned from
Babylon in stages and may
have taken different routes
to come back to Israel. The
journey was a dangerous
one, and many remained in
Babylon. The Medo-Persian
empire included all the
area on this map.

IN 539 BCE, Cyrus, king of Persia, finally
entered Babylon and deposed Nabonidus
as ruler. His decree in the following year,
that the Temple of the Jews be rebuilt and
that stolen items be returned to it, was in
keeping with his – for the time – remarkably
tolerant and generous policy toward his
subjects. In the years after the decree, some
Jews trickled back to the land, but many
more stayed behind. The uncertainty of the
whole venture, the prosperity of the Jews in
Babylon, and fading memories of the land
itself may explain why only relatively few
took the opportunity to return. A first group
probably returned in about 538/7BCE, under
Sheshbazzar, a prince of Judah. The land
was sparsely inhabited, hard to farm, and
subject to poor climate and seasonal crop
failure. In addition, the non-Israelite occupants
of the land, unwilling to relinquish their
possession, opposed the efforts at resettling
and rebuilding. The rebuilding of the Temple –
so central to Judah's identity – ceased very
soon after the initial foundations were laid.

It seems that a second wave of exiled
Jews returned shortly before 520BCE, under
Sheshbazzar's nephew Zerubbabel, by now
the heir apparent of Judah.

### CYRUS THE GREAT
This head of a Persian king
is believed to be that of
Cyrus the Great, who was
famed for his leniency in his
treatment of subject peoples,
including toleration of non-
Persian religions and gods.

**TOMB OF CYRUS THE GREAT (559–29BCE)**
*The final resting place of Cyrus the Great lies several hundred feet west of the royal palace at Pasargadae in modern
Iran. Cyrus built the palace and its city shortly after his conquest of the wealthy state of Lydia in Asia Minor.*

THE CYRUS CYLINDER

*The cuneiform script on this clay cylinder tells how King Cyrus allowed people captive in Babylon to return to their homelands. Among them would have been the Jews, who are not mentioned here by name.*

## MESSIANIC HOPE

Following the accession of the Persian Darius I in 522BCE, political upheaval in the wider Near East may have rekindled a hope that a Davidic ruler might be enthroned, one who would restore a strong national independence. God's covenant with David (2 Sam. 7:16) had been remembered during the Exile (Jer. 23:5–6), and its renewal was still anticipated after the return of the Jews (Zech. 6:9–14). The Prophets Haggai and Zechariah (*pp.242–43*) challenged the complacency of the people, and looked for work on the Temple to restart. The Second Temple (as it became known) was completed four years later, and consecrated in 515BCE.

## PROPHETS OF THE EXILE

Ezra and Nehemiah continued to rebuild and reorganize Jerusalem. The books bearing their names are the main sources of information for this period. Accounts are conflated in places, and exact dates are hard to assign. According to the books' datings, from about 458BCE Ezra established the place of Torah and of the Law as the constitution of the community, and Nehemiah's work on the city wall proceeded during 445–33BCE. Whatever the exact date, both men were active a considerable time after the first return of 538/7BCE. Prophets of the Exile (especially Ezekiel, Jeremiah, and Isaiah 40–55) had written and spoken of the day in which God would redeem the people and restore Israel to unity and supremacy. The so-called post-exilic Prophets (especially

Haggai, Zechariah, Isaiah 56–66, and Malachi) still looked for these hopes to be realized – but in the sixth and fifth centuries BCE these hopes were in vain. Not until the Hasmoneans (*see pp.250–51*) did Israel regain national independence and move tentatively to restoration of a monarchy. By then the High Priest (also an anointed figure, i.e., "Messiah") was more important in practice, and the Messianic hope focused on the line of David was increasingly looked for elsewhere.

## REBUILDING THE TEMPLE

*Backed by Ezekiel's vision of a spendidly restored Temple, the priests pressed for a rebuilt Temple as the center of their own authority.*

Ezra 1–6 gives the impression that the return from exile moved with purpose to the rebuilding of the Temple. But Ezra was written later, and writings closer to the time make it clear that a bold start had been followed by apathy – or by remembering that Jeremiah had warned against trust in the Temple (Jer. 7:1–9). Haggai and Zechariah (*pp.242–43*) were vital in motivating people and thought in terms of a glorious restoration of Israel as it had once been, with even the Davidic line restored in Zerubbabel. Zechariah may have envisaged a "diarchy" (joint rule by two leaders), with Zerubbabel and Joshua the High Priest sharing the throne (Zech. 6:9–14).

The Temple was rebuilt on the ruins of the old one, divided into three areas of differing degrees of holiness: the Holy of Holies (now empty after the loss of the Ark, and entered only once a year on the Day of Atonement by the High Priest); the main holy area (*hekal*, a word sometimes used for the Temple as a whole); and the entrance area. Introduced were an incense altar and a seven-branched candlestick, the *menorah*, later to become a symbol of Israel. Also built was the altar of burnt offering, approached by a ramp on the south side, to which private offerings could be brought, so that Ezekiel's vision (Ezek. 40–48) of excluding laypeople from all holy areas was not put into effect.

For further reading see bibliography numbers: 2, 3, 6, 131, 344, 370, 402, 559, 702

# PERSIA

*The Persians succeeded the Babylonians as masters of Mesopotamia and of the known world. Their huge empire was conquered by Alexander the Great in 331BCE. During the Persian period, the Jews returned to Jerusalem.*

## THE ACHAEMENID EMPIRE

At its maximum extent, during the reign of Darius I (522–486BCE), the Achaemenid empire stretched from the land of the Pharaohs in the west to the Indus River in the east. The area was divided into large regions ruled over by satraps, or governors, chosen from Persian and Median nobles but with native officers of the region under them. Under Darius I there were about 20 satraps in all.

THE Persian period saw stability and prosperity for many, and brought standardization across many nations. During this time, some Jews returned to Jerusalem and were able, under Ezra and Nehemiah, to rebuild the city and the Temple. The exact extent of Persian influence on Israel's religion is harder to gauge.

## PERSIAN ORIGINS

Medes and Persians both entered the Iranian plateau in the second millennium BCE. Both are mentioned in texts of the ninth century BCE, from which time they seem to have existed as independent kingdoms. Two centuries later, a united Median state was formed and, together with the Chaldeans, achieved the overthrow of Assyria and Babylon (*see pp.142–43, 148–49*).

The Chaldeans entered Babylon from the south; Cyaxares the Mede (625–585 BCE) besieged and took the cities of Asshur (614BCE) and Nineveh (612BCE) and with them control of Assyria. The rise of the Persian empire began with Cyrus the Great (559–29BCE), who in 550BCE defeated the Medes, adding to their empire that of Lydia (546BCE) and eventually Babylon (539BCE). His surprisingly easy entry into Babylon is attested by both Babylonian and Median sources: the subjects of the Babylonian kings were ready for change.

Cyrus' policy toward subject peoples was extremely tolerant for the time: he encouraged them to worship their own gods and perpetuate their own culture. Having restored to the Babylonians their local gods, Cyrus himself participated in the worship of Marduk, head of the Babylonian pantheon. There were no

**STAIRCASE TO THE AUDIENCE HALL AT THE PALACE OF DARIUS, PERSEPOLIS**
*The ceremonial city of Persepolis was founded in 520BCE and took 60 years to complete. The city's architecture shows influences from Egypt, Babylonia, Assyria, and eastern Greece, all of which were captured by the Persians.*

**ZOROASTRIAN**
*A gold votive plaque from the Oxus treasure showing a male figure holding a bundle of rods used in Zoroastrian ritual.*

"local gods" to return to the Jews, who were instead allowed to return to Jerusalem to rebuild the Temple and restore the cult. Cyrus issued this decree, which is mentioned in Ezra 6:3ff. Cyrus retained a firm grip on his

empire through a complex bureaucracy staffed by Medes and Persians. The Persian empire continued to grow under his successors: Cambyses II (528–23BCE) conquered Egypt; Darius I (522–486BCE) attempted to conquer Greece, the last area to elude Persian power but was turned back at Marathon (490BCE). Darius standardized weights and measures and established a wide network of roads to cover the 20 satrapies or provinces. Xerxes I (485–65BCE, called Ahasuerus by Esther and Ezra) did invade Greece but was repelled in 479BCE. Egypt finally managed to extricate itself from Persian rule (401BCE) under Artaxerxes II (404–359BCE) but was brutally retaken by Artaxerxes III (358–38BCE). Meanwhile, Philip II of Macedon (359–36BCE) was uniting the Hellenic states. His son Alexander tore apart the Persian army in 333BCE and finally overthrew Darius III (335–31BCE) at Gaugamela.

## RELIGION OF THE PERSIANS

The early Persians revered gods of nature, fertility, and the heavens. Sometime around 1200BCE, Zoroaster founded a religion that taught ethical dualism: the choice was between Righteousness and the Lie. This was no unqualified monotheism, but one in which uncreated good and evil spirits (Ahura Mazda and Angra Mainyu) battled against each other. It is uncertain to what extent the kings were Zoroastrian in their own religion. Darius I recognized the god Ahura Mazda, along with a host of others. Some biblical concepts (dualism, Satan, angels, and resurrection, for example) may parallel aspects of Iranian thought, but it may not directly relate to any Persian influence. Israelite thought was quite fertile in this period, as in others, and did not depend on Persian influence for its vitality.

**ZOROASTRIAN CEREMONY**
Zoroastrian teaching is mainly preserved in 17 hymns, known as Gathas, which are in the Yasna, part of the sacred Avesta scripture. The image above shows the coming of age, or Navjote, ceremony.

**SILVER RAM**
Persian art drew on different parts of the empire for inspiration. The ram pictured above originates from Persepolis, and dates from the fifth century BCE.

# THE ACHAEMENID KINGS OF PERSIA

| | Cambyses II (528–23) | | Xerxes (485–65) | | | Darius II (423–05) | | Artaxerxes III (358–38) | | Darius III (335–31) | |
|---|---|---|---|---|---|---|---|---|---|---|---|
| 560BCE | 530BCE | 500BCE | 470BCE | 440BCE | 410BCE | 380BCE | 350BCE | 320BCE | | | |
| Cyrus the Great (559–29) | | Darius I (522–486) | | | Artaxerxes I (464–24) | | | Artaxerxes II (404–359) | | Arses (Xerxes II) (338–35) | |

For further reading see bibliography numbers: 2, 3, 125, 207, 344, 413, 513, 651

# RELIGION AFTER THE EXILE

*The disaster of the Exile resulted in change for many people. Israel's kings and Temple had been swept away, and, for some, the rebuilding of faith meant a reconstruction of what they had lost. For others, it involved the acceptance of loss and the possibility of striking out in new directions.*

BEFORE the Exile, Israel's religion was characterized by the sense of security felt by the people, who were certain of God's presence and protection while living in God's land. That security was shattered by the crisis of the Exile (598/7–538/7BCE), when it seemed that God had abandoned the people to the Babylonian conquerors. Following this period, the religion that had existed before the Exile had to be fundamentally redefined. The religion that developed during this period is the predecessor of what the Jewish people, in the first century CE, began to call "Judaism."

Before the Exile, the people of Israel and Judah were independent nations whose monarchs were regarded as the channels of divine favor and blessing for the people. After the Exile, the Jews of Judah had no king of their own, and their religion (which had recognized the people's king as its most significant official) had to be reassessed. Even though the Jews made several attempts to restore the Monarchy (*see* Haggai and Zechariah, *pp.242–43*), the importance of the priests of the Temple increased, and the High Priest assumed the role of chief mediator between the people and God, a

**HISTORIC CENTER OF WORSHIP**
*After the Exile, the Temple played an important role in reestablishing the presence of God by providing a focal point for worship and sacrifice. Here, Jews gather at the Western Wall in Jerusalem to mark the destruction of both the First and Second Temples.*

role that had been filled previously by the monarch. Once the Temple had been rebuilt, the priests who officiated there took on a major role in interpreting the will of God, a role that had once belonged mainly to the prophets. Prophets became far less important, and the end of their visions gave way to Apocalyptic (*see pp.260–61*), predicting that there would be a universal judgment of the nations.

> *"… this is the place of my throne and the place for the soles of my feet, where I will reside among the people of Israel forever. The house of Israel shall no more defile my holy name, neither they nor their kings "*
>
> (Ezekiel 43:7)

## TEMPLE WORSHIP

The second important feature of the newly formed religion was the uniqueness of the Temple. Despite the ruling in the book of Deuteronomy that there should be only one place of worship – *"But you shall seek the place that the LORD your God will choose …"* (Deut. 12:5–6; cf. 12:13–14) – worship and sacrifice had taken place before the Exile at a number of shrines. The Exile was partly interpreted as God's punishment for worshiping at these other, illegitimate shrines – even more reason for the centralization of worship in Jerusalem. Ezekiel's dream had been of a restored Temple (*see pp.214–15*). After the Exile, therefore, the rebuilt Temple became a focal point for devotion and a symbol of God's presence in a far greater way than it had before the Babylonian Exile (Ezek. 43:1–7).

**ELEPHANTINE ISLAND**
*Located at Aswan on the Nile, this island was home to a colony of Jews who were exiled following the destruction of Jerusalem in 587BCE.*

remained loyal to Jerusalem and the Temple, and maintained their Jewish identity by studying and observing their own tradition, especially Torah. Later, Diaspora communities became important for Jewish scholarship. Jews based in Egypt translated the Hebrew Bible into Greek, and Babylonian Jews developed Jewish teaching through the interpretation of Torah, first through oral transmission, then in the codification of the Mishnah and, eventually, the Talmud. The growing importance of the written tradition, above all of Torah, was a distinctive feature of the renewed religion. Prophecy declined, but the words of the Prophets were carefully preserved. Both during and after the Exile many writings were produced, both to preserve national traditions and identity and to give theological explanations of the Exile to enable faith to continue.

## COMMITMENT TO TORAH

In the view of many scholars, it was during this period that the the Pentateuch (the five books of the Hebrew Bible from Genesis to Deuteronomy) received its final editing. Whether that is so or not, there was certainly a renewed commitment to the Law: note especially Nehemiah 8:1–6. The five books came to be known as Torah, a term indicating "teaching" or "direction" (not just "Law," it includes narrative as well as legal elements, *see pp.24–25*). Torah was an important expression of faith and identity for those in exile. Its importance for the whole Jewish community was established in the fifth century BCE, when Ezra brought an official edition of Torah to Judah and made it the law of the land.

Along with this new focus on the written word came synagogues, where the faithful gathered to pray and study Torah, and scribes, who were legal experts. The importance of the written word meant that the Jews truly became a people of the Book.

## THE SIGNIFICANCE OF THE DIASPORA

A third feature of the redefined religion was the increased significance of the Diaspora – Jewish communities outside the land of Israel. One of the largest and most important of these was located in Babylon. The Exile had proved that God could be worshiped both in Babylon and without the Temple (Ezek. 1:1–3; cf. Jer. 29:1–7). Many people born and raised in Babylon during the decades of exile chose to stay there. However, they

> *" Thus says the LORD of hosts, the God of Israel, to all the exiles whom I have sent into exile from Jerusalem to Babylon … pray to the LORD on its behalf, for in its welfare you will find your welfare "*
>
> (Jeremiah 29:4–7)

**For further reading see bibliography numbers:** 2, 3, 6, 65, 206, 344, 370, 624, 668, 702

# THE BOOK OF
# EZRA

*After the Exile, people asked how they were to pick up their lives again.
The book of Ezra shows how this was done – partly through the
rebuilding of the Temple and then through the leadership of Ezra himself.*

THE first six chapters of the book of Ezra are concerned directly and indirectly with the rebuilding of the Temple in Jerusalem. They begin with Cyrus' decree, then list the returnees (ch.2) and the beginnings of sacrifices (ch.3). Chapters 4 and 5 record opposition to this, but in chapter 6 the right to rebuild the Temple is confirmed and the work is completed. Chapter 7 introduces Ezra, and although he is described as a "scribe," a senior official responsible for Jewish affairs, the main emphasis is on his descent from Aaron, the first High Priest, and Zadok, the line of High Priests from the time of King David. Chapter 8 lists those going with Ezra, then concentrates on the preparations for going up to the Temple and for sacrifices. Chapters 9 and 10 deal with Ezra's concern about the "pollution" brought about by marriage with foreign wives.

## THE COMPOSITION OF
## EZRA AND NEHEMIAH

The books of Ezra and Nehemiah were originally a single volume. They were first separated by Origen in the third century CE. The division into two books appears in Hebrew Bibles only after the 15th century, and the Jewish scribal (Masoretic) tradition treats the two of them together. The language is Hebrew with occasional Aramaic portions (Ezra 4:8–6:18; 7:12–26). In addition to the canonical Ezra, there exist other books with the name Esdras, Greek for Ezra, notably 1 Esdras, a Greek translation of 2 Chronicles 35–36; Ezra 1–10 and Nehemiah 8:1–13 plus a major addition not present in the Hebrew (it appears as an appendix to the Vulgate as 3 Esdras); and 2 Esdras (known also as 4 Ezra),

an apocalyptic work in the Apocrypha (*pp.260–61*). A number of different sources or documents are included in the books; in the case of Ezra, there is the so-called Ezra memoir, written in the first person, but with some parts in the third person. Although the view is contested, some scholars believe that the Chronicler (i.e., whoever was responsible for producing the books of Chronicles) was also responsible for the form of the books of Ezra and Nehemiah as we now have them. Those books (Ezra and Nehemiah) discuss the same period of time and events, but they discuss them from the two different perspectives of the two named figures.

**EZRA THE SCRIBE**
*This eighth-century Bible illustration shows Ezra copying
out the books of the Law on his return to Jerusalem.*

## FOREIGN MARRIAGES

The story of Ezra himself is told in Ezra 7–10 and Nehemiah 8–9, but virtually no information is provided about Ezra's life and background. He is not even mentioned in the list of "famous men" to be praised in Sirach (*pp.256–57*). What is clear is that he emphatically opposed marriages to non-Jews (Ezra 9–10), demanding that foreign wives should be divorced. Nehemiah also opposed such marriages (Neh. 13:23– 27), regarding the marriages of Solomon to non-Jews as having led him into great sin. But Nehemiah simply prohibited such marriages. Unlike Ezra, he did not demand divorce. This seems strange if Nehemiah was working with, or soon after, Ezra, and so some regard these differing views as an argument for reversing the order of the two – with Nehemiah coming first and Ezra, working at the time of Artaxerxes II (404–359BCE), making Nehemiah's earlier prohibition even more severe. But this is only a matter of speculation.

## BACKGROUND TO THE BOOK

The books of Ezra and Nehemiah refer to five Persian kings: Cyrus (Ezra 4:5), Ahasuerus or Xerxes (Ezra 4:6), two by the name of Artaxerxes (Ezra 4:7; Neh. 2:1; 5:14; 13:6), and Darius (Ezra 4:5). However, the order in which they are mentioned does not follow a clear historical sequence, and scholarly opinion differs as to the exact period referred to in the books and as to which kings bearing the same name are intended. Given also that different sources have been used, the reconstruction of this period from these books is uncertain.

One possible chronology is as follows: under Cyrus of Persia the first attempts were made to rebuild the Temple (537BCE). Cyrus was succeeded by Cambyses, but it was under his successor Darius I that the Temple was actually rebuilt (520–16BCE). Darius was, in turn, succeeded by Xerxes, and it was his successor, Artaxerxes I, who sent the scribe Ezra to Jerusalem (458BCE), presumably to look after the religious needs of the community in line with the liberal policies of the Persian kings of supporting local traditions in exchange for loyalty. Thirteen years later, Nehemiah was sent to become the governor of Judah and returned again for a second period at a later date. However, if the king mentioned in Ezra 7:7 is Artaxerxes II, then the date of Ezra's arrival would be 398BCE, and his work would come after that of Nehemiah.

## THE THEME OF EZRA

Throughout the book, the focus is on priestly concerns when it comes to restoring the religious basis of the community and rebuilding its relationship with God. This is in contrast with the more political focus of Nehemiah as a layman and governor of the community (*see pp.162–63*). The importance of the Law for Ezra is made clear (7:6ff.), although otherwise the Law is not stressed. Great emphasis is placed on the work of God in history and on the control that God has over all the nations of the earth: Ezra in his prayer accepts that God is able to move the decision of the Persian king (Ezra 9:8ff.).

## EZRA IN JEWISH TRADITION

The book of Ezra describes Ezra himself as *"skilled in the law [Torah] of Moses"* (7:6) and as a *"scribe of the law [Aramaic dat] of the God of heaven"* (7:12, 21), but it is unclear as to which part of Torah (the entire Pentateuch, parts of it, or possibly the book of Deuteronomy) this refers. In Jewish tradition, the scribe Ezra is considered as having reestablished the Torah in the lives of the Jewish people and as being almost equal in stature to Moses. He introduced public readings of Torah and had the scrolls written in "Assyrian" characters – the square script still in use today. He was also responsible for introducing schools in which to study and debate the Torah.

## THE BOOK

**TITLE:** Ezra

**HEBREW TITLE:** In Hebrew *ezra* means "[God] helps"

**DATE:** The book records incidents that occurred in the sixth, fifth, and possibly fourth centuries BCE, and was probably composed in the fourth century BCE

**AUTHORSHIP:** The book incorporates a variety of sources and is part of a joint volume "Ezra–Nehemiah." This was probably composed as a supplement to 1 and 2 Chronicles and comes from the same author or authors

## THE CONTENTS

**CHAPTERS 1–6 RETURN AND REBUILDING**
The beginning of the return from Babylon and the rebuilding of the Temple. The decree of Cyrus to rebuild the Temple and the response of those in exile. 2:1–70 The list of those who returned with Zerubbabel. 3:1–13 The restoration of worship and the laying of the foundations of the Temple. 4:1–24 Opposition to the building from the local Samaritan population. 5:1–6:22 Permission is granted, and the work on the Temple is completed

**CHAPTERS 7–10 THE WORK OF EZRA**
7:1–28 Ezra journeys to Jerusalem with authorization from King Artaxerxes. 8:1–14 List of the exiles who returned with Ezra, the preparations, and the journey. 9:1–10:44 The sin of the community – marriage with foreign wives

## KEY THEMES

*The Temple and its rebuilding*
•
*Religious reforms to establish the distinctiveness of Israel*
•
*National repentance*

**For further reading see bibliography numbers:** 99a, 188a, 278, 288a, 402, 424a, 436, 462, 559, 810, 811

# THE BOOK OF
# NEHEMIAH

*The book of Nehemiah was originally joined to the book of Ezra. It is written in the first person and reveals Nehemiah, the governor of Judah, as a man of purpose, dedication, and commitment to duty.*

NEHEMIAH, son of Hacaliah, held an honored position as cupbearer to the Persian king Artaxerxes I, in Susa. When Nehemiah learned of the difficulties faced by Jewish settlers who had returned to Judea, and that the wall and gates of Jerusalem had been damaged by fire, he obtained permission from the king to reconstruct them. On arrival in Jerusalem, he carried out a secret inspection of the ruins and organized a rebuilding plan using the voluntary services of the exiles who, led by Zerubbabel, had returned from Babylon. This work was opposed by Sanballat the Horonite and Tobiah the Ammonite, leaders of the local population, first by ridicule and later by the threat of force. To prevent further direct threats to the rebuilding work, Nehemiah armed and defended the builders. Despite several plots against him, the walls of Jerusalem were rebuilt in 52 days. Nehemiah then set about repopulating the city, taking one in ten people from the surrounding areas. After 12 years, Nehemiah returned to Babylon. In his absence, certain problems arose, which he dealt with on his subsequent return.

**THE ISRAELITE TOWER**
*This tower, forming part of the wall that surrounded Jerusalem, was partly destroyed in 586BCE during the Babylonian conquest.*

Throughout the book, Nehemiah's concerns are both political and practical, although the account is interspersed with prayers to God. This practical emphasis is in marked contrast to the "priestly" interests in the book of Ezra (*pp.160–61*), which center on sacrifice, purity, and the Temple.

In both books there is a major preoccupation with marriage to "foreign," or non-Jewish, women. In Ezra 9–10, those who had married non-Jewish women were compelled to separate from them. In Nehemiah 13:23–27, the people were prohibited from entering into such marriages.

## THE PERSONALITY OF NEHEMIAH

Because the book is based on a personal memoir, Nehemiah's personality stands out more than that of almost any other figure in the Hebrew Bible. He was forceful and highly practical – both in his organization of the rebuilding plan and in his ability to mobilize support. However, he had strong opinions that were often violently expressed, and he employed shrewd defensive tactics against local opponents from the non-Judean population. Nehemiah possessed personal courage and refused to go into hiding when his life was in danger (6:11).

He was a religious man, as demonstrated by his frequent appeals to God and his commitment to religious traditions, such as the Sabbath: *"We also lay on ourselves the obligation to charge ourselves yearly one-third of a shekel for the service of the house of our God"* (10:32; cf. 13:15–22) and the provision of offerings (10:33–39). Nehemiah's memoir might be seen as an arrogant exercise, even though it was probably composed in response to criticism from his opponents. In contrast to the behavior of his predecessors (5:15), Nehemiah was proud of the fact that he did not receive payment for his work, or *"demand the food allowance of the governor, because of the heavy burden of labor on the people"* (5:18). He was a man whose dedication, single-mindedness, and spiritual strength enabled him to carry out his purpose.

## THE TORAH AND COVENANT

In both Ezra and Nehemiah, reference is made to the "Torah of Moses." However, in Ezra it is mentioned only in relation to restoring elements of the Temple tradition, but in Nehemiah it plays a central role once the walls have been restored. In a major ceremony lasting seven days, the words of Torah were read in public and explained before "the whole people" (ch.8). From this, the people found that they were to celebrate Sukkot, the Festival of Booths, and also that they should separate themselves from their foreign wives. Associated with this event was a confession that summarized the history of Israel's relationship with God, which became a prelude to a solemn recommitment to the Covenant with God. Thus, the book placed great importance on the centrality of Torah and its availability to the people, in contrast to the emphasis on the Temple in the book of Ezra. This proved to be an early stage in the process that led to those forms of Jewish spirituality that depended less on the priesthood and fostered a more democratic approach to learning and interpretation – a key element in the later emergence of rabbinic Judaism.

## NEHEMIAH IN TRADITION

Nehemiah is praised in Sirach (49:12b–13) and also in 2 Maccabees (1:18, 20–36). The Jewish historian Josephus (c.37–100CE) wrote at length about Nehemiah's achievements (*Antiquities* 11:159–74). The rabbis, however, unhappy with his apparent arrogance, called the book Ezra (b. *Sanhedrin* 93b). Nehemiah's rebuilding of the walls of Jerusalem led to his being celebrated in post-Reformation Protestant writings as a "restorer of the Church." In *Magnalia Christi Americana*, Cotton Mather (1663–1728), the American clergyman, hailed John Winthrop (1639–1707), governor of Connecticut, as "Nehemias Americanus" – the builder of Christian civilization in the New World. Writer T. S. Eliot (1888–1965) made Nehemiah a central figure in the chorus of his play *The Rock*.

# THE BOOK

**TITLE:** Nehemiah

**HEBREW TITLE:** *n'hemyah*
(meaning, "YHWH has comforted")

**DATE:** The book records incidents that occurred in the fifth century BCE and was probably composed in the fourth

**AUTHORSHIP:** The book, which incorporates materials from a variety of sources, including a "memoir" by Nehemiah himself, is part of a joint volume "Ezra–Nehemiah." It may have been composed as a supplement to 1 and 2 Chronicles

# THE CONTENTS

**CHAPTERS 1–4**
Concerned about the people, Nehemiah prays to God (ch.1). He visits Jerusalem, resolves to rebuild the walls of the city (ch.2), and organizes the restoration work (chs.3–4)

**CHAPTERS 5–10**
Despite community problems and hostile plots, the walls are completed (chs.5–6). Exiles who returned for the rebuilding are listed (ch.7), there is a public reading of the Torah and worship services (chs.8–9), and the people enter a formal covenant (ch.10)

**CHAPTERS 11–13**
People are resettled in Jerusalem (ch.11). A list of priests and Levites who helped with the rebuilding is followed by the dedication of the wall of Jerusalem (ch.12). During his second period as governor, Nehemiah undertakes a number of reforms (ch.13)

# KEY THEMES

*The Temple and the security of Jerusalem*
•
*The importance of holiness*
•
*Centrality of Torah and its availability to the people*

For further reading see bibliography numbers: 99a, 188a, 278, 288a, 402, 424a, 436, 462, 559, 811

# EDUCATION
## IN ANCIENT ISRAEL

*Boys and girls were well educated or instructed to understand themselves and their roles in society. Education took place largely in the home. Little information about how this was done has survived.*

IN the early biblical period, there is little trace of formal education. The name of a town, Kiriath-sepher (Josh. 15:15ff.; Judg. 1:11ff.), which means "Town of the Book," is hardly enough to warrant the suggestion of a school. Basic education rested in the home, where the role of mothers was paramount. The Bible, however, is written from the perspective of men and places emphasis on the male transmission of skills: in ritual (1 Sam. 3:1), farming (1 Sam. 16:11), or warfare (2 Sam. 22:35; cf. Judg. 8:20). Thus, with the exception of Proverbs 31:10–31, the importance of mothers in this respect has virtually been ignored. Other passages in Proverbs reflect the importance of the home in education (see 4:1–9; 6:20). The Bible also developed an awareness of the child as a metaphor for faith in characteristics of trust and teachability:*"But I have calmed and quieted my soul, like a weaned child with its mother"* (Ps. 131:2).

## DIFFERENT ROLES

While education in the Hebrew Bible is informed by the overarching dimension of faith in God, learning and instruction find expression in a number of different ways. These include learning related to general abilities, training relevant to particular trades and occupations, and skills needed by specific individuals relevant to government and diplomacy or the interpretation of the law. In a patriarchal society, children's education was influenced by the roles they were expected to play, so that farming and herding or military skills were expected for boys, while girls learned domestic crafts.

## AIMS AND METHODS

The learning of particular roles was supplemented by the learning of the traditions of the people and of God's dealings with them. This meant that the family played a central role in the nurturing and transmission of faith. The family held the narrative and

DEVELOPMENTS IN THE ALPHABET
*By the third century BCE, cuneiform scripts had begun to be replaced by the new alphabetic scripts of Aramaic and Greek. This clay tablet comes from Iraq and is inscribed with Greek letters; the language, however, is unknown.*

passed it on, as in the celebration of Passover (*p.68*), and this narrative gave the individual an identity within the family and the nation. Allusions to events of the past in the Psalms or in the prophetic writings confirm the broad educative significance of history for an awareness of ethnic and religious identity. The connection between the home and religious festivals (Deut. 16:1–12; 1 Sam. 20:5–6) further strengthened the family as the primary educational context.

It was regarded as the duty of the head of the household to teach his children (Exod. 13:8; Deut. 4:9; 6:6–9; 6:20; Josh. 4:21–22), if necessary with discipline (Prov. 22:15; cf. 3:11–12; Sir. 30:1–13). The Law itself required children to honor their parents (Exod. 20:12; Deut. 5:16), and this would have reinforced the child's respect for elders,

EDUCATION IN THE HOME
*The family plays a central role in education of the young in the Hebrew Bible: "Remember the days of old, consider the years long past: ask your father, and he will inform you; your elders, and they will tell you" (Deut. 32:7).*

Recommends Torah, marriage, and good deeds | Marriage ceremony | The Torah

**CIRCUMCISION CLOTH**
*This cloth shows various aspects of Jewish life and education. It is made for a baby boy at the time of his circumcision, which takes place eight days after the child's birth. Such decorated cloths may later be presented to the synagogue and used as "binders" to fasten the Torah scroll beneath it's mantle.*

itself important in education of this kind. Consequently, a disobedient child is a source of shame to parents (Deut. 21:18–21; Prov. 10:1). The natural inquisitiveness of the child was encouraged as a means of initiating teaching, and learning was predominantly achieved orally and by repetition. Education would have included such aspects of numeracy and literacy as were relevant to wider domestic life (Isa. 10:19), although it was not until much later that education relevant to different stages in life was identified.

Particular importance was attached to the education of royalty relevant to military prowess (1 Sam. 20:19–20, 35ff.), government and diplomacy (2 Kgs. 15:5), and patronage of the Temple (1 Kgs. 8:63). A prince would receive formal instruction and advice from court prophets, and his rule was judged by the values of the Law.

**WRITING TOOLS**
*This Egyptian writing equipment includes reed pens, an inkwell, and a knife to sharpen the pens. Egyptians were among the first to develop papyrus as a writing material (see pp.46–47).*

(2 Kgs. 20:9–11), medicine, rulings on diseases (2 Chr. 16:12), and the copying of the Torah and other texts (Deut. 17:18–19). The prophetic tradition also provided instruction (Isa. 8:16), often obtained through attending to the needs of a master, although a prophet's own education might also be acquired through a court or a priestly school; the first reference to a school appears in Sirach 51:23. Some training in oration and music may have been part of that learning (Ezek. 33:30–33). Unlike the priesthood, no qualifications of birth or gender were necessary for the prophetic order, which included women, some of considerable repute (Miriam, Deborah, and Huldah).

**JEWISH SCRIBE**
*The importance of education increased when the Jews went into exile, and the study of Torah came to the center of religious life. The care taken by the scribe reflects the value of each letter of the Torah.*

## THE EDUCATION OF OFFICIALS

The royal patronage of the arts (music and wisdom) also had important consequences for education (1 Kgs. 5:7–14; Prov. 25:1; Amos 6:5). The education of scribes and priests, who served the administrative needs of government and Temple, provided another important structured pattern of learning. This was no doubt aided by the introduction of alphabet writing (cf. Isa. 28:9–13), which would have been required for calendrical and census calculations, engineering

## THE ALPHABET

Among the prototypes for the early alphabet, which emerged in the land bordering the eastern shores of the Mediterranean between 1700–1500BCE, were the cuneiform and hieroglyphic scripts of Mesopotamia and Egypt. The Canaanites developed a simplified form of writing that underlies our own alphabet, whereby symbols or characters were used to represent the individual sounds (vowels and consonants) of the language rather than objects or ideas. Known as the North Semitic alphabet, this precursor of the modern Hebrew alphabet remained unchanged for centuries. The geographical location of Israel was significant in its development of a sophisticated literary tradition.

For further reading see bibliography numbers: 48, 313, 489, 517, 585, 688, 737, 766, 767, 783, 785, 892

# THE BOOK OF
# ESTHER

*Set at the Persian court, Esther is the dramatic story of the Jewish people in danger and how they are rescued. It inspired the Jewish festival of Purim.*

THE book of Esther is a story of court intrigue, relating the triumph of the Jews over those seeking to harm them. Esther, the queen of Persia, intercedes with the king to save the Jews from a cruel fate devised by the king's chief adviser, Haman. Haman has a personal vendetta against Mordecai, Esther's guardian and himself a Jew. The tale is retold every year at the Jewish festival of Purim, when the deliverance of the Jews is celebrated and gifts are exchanged. The book is unusual in that God is not directly mentioned – although the providence of God is in the background – and there is no religious observance except fasting and the ethic of self-defense. The story may contain a historical core, but its purpose seems to be mainly an explanation of how the festival of Purim came into being. Esther also has a strong theological message about the liberation of the oppressed.

**ESTHER WITH TWO MAIDS**
*Esther is shown kneeling before the king, begging for the safe deliverance of the Jews.*

## FORM AND MEANING

An understanding of Esther's literary qualities has served to increase appreciation of the book, in particular the noting of the many ironies in the story and its colorful characters and setting. The book utilizes the conventions of wisdom literature *(see pp.170–71)* to describe ways of behaving in the royal court. Even more than other Wisdom books, the book avoids making explicit reference to the action of God, but does see God acting behind events. It can be read as a straight struggle between two outsiders (Mordecai and Haman) to gain influence with the king. But at a deeper level, it reflects the biblical view that God has the greater struggle with the powers of evil, characterized by the "Amalekites" (Exod. 17:14–16; Deut. 25:17–19): Haman is a descendant of Agag (3:1), the Amalekite king whom Saul failed to kill (1 Sam. 15:9); Mordecai is a descendant of Kish, the father of Saul, so that in this "replay," evil is defeated.

## ESTHER IN THE CANON

There may have been uncertainties about including the book in the canon – perhaps, in part, because it does not mention the name of God (an omission put right in the Greek additions; *see below*). No part of Esther has been found among the Dead Sea Scrolls *(see pp.290–91)*, although some scholars have claimed the manuscript 4Q550 as a prototype of Esther.

In the Hebrew Bible, the book of Esther is one of the Five Scrolls (*Megilloth*), and is thus in the third section of the Bible, the Writings (*Kethubim*). In the Christian Bible, the book is placed among the Historical books. It exists in three versions: (1) the (shorter) Hebrew Masoretic text; (2) the Septuagint (Greek translation), which contains six additions; when making the Latin (Vulgate) translation, Jerome recognized the additions and added them to the end of the book as chapters 11–16; (3) a longer and independent Greek translation, perhaps of a different Hebrew original. During the Reformation, the Reformers reverted to the original Hebrew canon of Scripture, and the Additions to Esther were put into the Apocrypha.

## LATER INTERPRETATIONS

The book has remained extremely popular among Jews partly due to its important place in the liturgical year and the opportunity it affords to celebrate. The Jewish philosopher Maimonides (1135–1204) regarded the book as second only to the Torah in importance. Rabbinic tradition is very positive about Esther's character, and she is one of the seven female prophets of Israel. Christian tradition has also praised Esther's virtuous and courageous action, even seeing her as prefiguring the Virgin Mary, in her chastity, beauty, and ability to intercede for others. Some have seen renewed significance after the Holocaust as an exploration of the dangers of life in exile: the absence of God's name has been linked to questions about the apparent "silence" of God in that period.

## PURIM

*Purim is an annual Jewish festival celebrated on the 14th and 15th days of Adar (in February/March).*

The name Purim probably derives from the Hebrew *pur* meaning "lot," since the wicked Haman cast lots as to the day on which he should destroy the Jews. In the end, it was the Jews who were able to destroy their enemies. The Jews are enjoined at the end of the book (9:28) never to forget this deliverance and to keep these days of Purim in perpetuity from generation to generation. It is thought that the festival was first celebrated in the Diaspora and was accepted in Judah later.

During Purim, the Esther scroll is read aloud in synagogues. There are often pageants and masquerades and also plays based on the book, a practice influenced by the injection of elements of the Italian carnival in later centuries. A festival meal takes place that lasts late into the night, and mourning is forbidden. The Talmud instructs "Drink wine until you can no longer distinguish between 'Blessed be Mordecai' and 'Cursed be Haman'" (Meg. 7b).

**In the synagogue Esther is read during Purim.**

## THE BOOK

**TITLE:** Esther

**HEBREW TITLE:** *Ester*

**DATE:** Post-exilic, probably written during the Persian period

**AUTHORSHIP:** Unknown

## THE CONTENTS

### CHAPTERS 1–2

Background to the plot to destroy the Jews. Queen Vashti of Persia refuses to appear at a feast and is deposed. The king holds a contest to find another queen, and Esther (who, unknown to him, is Jewish) is chosen. Mordecai, her guardian, uncovers a plot to assassinate the king. Esther makes the plot known, and the culprits are hanged

### CHAPTERS 3–7

The threat to the Jews. Haman's plot. Mordecai persuades Esther to help. Esther's banquet. Haman builds a gallows for Mordecai. The king honors Mordecai. Esther intercedes for the Jews. Haman is hanged

### CHAPTERS 8–10

The reward for the Jews and the institution of the feast of Purim. The king's edict on behalf of the Jews. The triumph of the Jews and the celebration of Purim. Praise for Mordecai

## KEY THEMES

*The providence of God*

•

*The origins of the feast of Purim*

•

*Threats against the Jews*

•

*A woman as the protagonist*

For further reading see bibliography numbers: 80, 91, 188, 188a, 284, 304, 475, 482a, 567, 814

quedam de argento ductilis et tube
cornee de quibus dicitur psalmo nonage
simo septimo ubi dicitur in tubis ducti
libus et voce tube cornee. Erat autem
tuba cornea istius
figure et forme

Tuba v[illegible]
diuersis sicut forma [illegible]
debat. Laudate enim in psalterio et
cithara. Sed descriptiones doctorum
non multis euidenter assint in instru
mentis modernis. forma psalterii
quorum differentiam expositores as
signant quod cithara reddit sonum ab
inferiori et psalterium a superiori.
Si quidem quod ymaginemur ali
quem stantem cum psalterio mo
derne forme ita quod pes longior ia
ceat super brachium et pes [illegible]
brachia pendeat sonus quidem
canorum reddetur a superiori [illegible]
[illegible] ab inferiori
[illegible] in hac fo[rma]

Sed et ci
thara pendens
ab inferiori
et contra acu
tiorem sonum
a superiori red
dit et grauio
rem ab infer
iori ut patet
in hac forma.

Sed quia
psalterium ethi
mologice [illegible]
tio dicat quod psal
terium sit fig
ure concaui
[illegible] reddentis sonum in parte supe
riori et quod eius forma est sim [illegible]
[illegible]

cordis signum concauum. ubi sonus
redditur sunt superius applicationem ad
similitudinem [illegible] cum corde [illegible]
[illegible] virgule [illegible]
modulatio illius soni fit [illegible]
tangendo cordis digitis [illegible]
[illegible] ut acuimus uel [illegible]
sonent. Conuenit quod psalterium [illegible]
cum viella [illegible]
diuisis una quod habent figuram
concauum [illegible] reddentem sonus supe
rius quod modulatio eius fiat [illegible]
in digitorum [illegible] in [illegible]
differentia in figura [illegible] forma [illegible]
[illegible] ad modum
[illegible] que [illegible]
[illegible] forme. [illegible] instru
menta moderna [illegible]
[illegible] uel [illegible]
differentia est in [illegible] cordarum [illegible]
[illegible] moderne
[illegible]
[illegible] psalterium uel [illegible]
uel [illegible] differentia [illegible]
[illegible] moderne
[illegible]
Cithara autem [illegible] psalterio
signum concaui [illegible] inferiori [illegible]
ad modum [illegible] red
dat sonum [illegible] descriptio [illegible]
conuenit cum forma cithare mo
derni temporis. [illegible]
[illegible] et [illegible]

Timpanum [illegible]
[illegible] est
est pellis uel
corii signo [illegible]
[illegible] est [illegible]
[illegible] est [illegible]
media [illegible]
[illegible]
[illegible] et [illegible]

# THE WISDOM BOOKS

The Wisdom books are extremely varied. Some are concerned with questions about the meaning of human experience, such as desire and love (The Song of Songs) or the inequalities of life and suffering (Job, Ecclesiastes), others with the wise ordering of daily life (Proverbs), or with praise and prayer to God (Psalms). The title "Wisdom books" is thus misleading if it gives the impression that these books come from one style of writing or from a single school of writers. In the Hebrew Bible, these books are not distinguished as a separate group, but are gathered into the *Kethubim* (the Writings, the third and last section of the Hebrew Bible), along with Ruth, Lamentations, Esther, Daniel, Ezra, Nehemiah, and 1 and 2 Chronicles. In Christian Bibles, the Wisdom books come between the Historical books and the Prophets. The books included vary, because Roman Catholic and Orthodox Bibles include works that are not in the Hebrew Bible and that others place in the Apocrypha. The two main lists are as follows, in the order in which they are found:

| | |
|---|---|
| Job | Job |
| Psalms | Psalms |
| Proverbs | Proverbs |
| Ecclesiastes | Ecclesiastes |
| The Song of Songs | The Song of Songs |
| | Book of Wisdom |
| | Sirach |

# WISDOM LITERATURE
## IN THE BIBLE

*Wisdom literature is the term generally used to describe the books of Proverbs, Job, and Ecclesiastes.*
*It is also applied to certain Psalms and to some of the books in the Apocrypha, especially Sirach*
*and the Wisdom of Solomon. Wisdom literature is recognized by its content rather than its style.*

IN the Bible, *"The fear of the LORD is the beginning of wisdom"* (Prov. 9:10; Ps. 111:10). Wisdom is to be applied to the living of life day by day. Deep questions are raised in wisdom literature, and practical advice is offered in writings that are carefully crafted and often profoundly beautiful. Some scholars include other parts of the Hebrew Bible in this category (e.g., the story of Joseph, *pp. 44–45;* Pss. 1, 37, 49, 73, 112), but this remains questionable. Wisdom literature is marked by an emphasis on the fate and behavior of the individual, in contrast to the emphasis on nation and history found in the Historical and Prophetic books, but there is no good reason to believe that it was composed in different circles, or that it was produced by a consciously distinct group.

**"DAVID THE PSALMIST"**
*Over 70 of the Psalms are attributed to King David (see pp. 176–77), some are of a wisdom type. The royal court may have been a center for the transmission of learning, as it was in Egypt, where wisdom literature was used in the training of the Pharaohs and their courtiers.*

## WISDOM

"Wisdom" is the word used in the Hebrew Bible to describe a wide range of human skills, from embroidery to divination, and it means something like "know-how." In the wisdom literature, its sense is very general, and it is used alongside terms like "knowledge" and "understanding" to describe the ability to discern what is the proper course of action. In Proverbs 1–9, wisdom is poetically personified as a woman (the Hebrew word *chokmah* is feminine), and is contrasted with the situation of the "foreign woman" who leads the unwary individual off the right path and to death. Wisdom acts as a guide, enabling those who follow her to stay on the proper path through life, a path on which they will enjoy divine favor and protection. The language strongly suggests that

**MESOPOTAMIAN WISDOM**
*In Mesopotamia, wisdom was used in an attempt to secure help from the gods, and thus ensure prosperity. The tablet above comes from the city of Babylon and dates from the eighth-seventh centuries BCE. It lists some of the names of the gods worshiped by the Babylonians*

this path is identified with obedience to the Torah, and wisdom is portrayed as open and accessible – she invites humans to join her and promises life. This portrayal exerted a deep influence on later literature, especially the book of Sirach in the Apocrypha, but the idea of accessible wisdom is questioned by Job and the author of Ecclesiastes.

**THE WISDOM OF AMENEMOPE**
*This Egyptian work was influential throughout the ancient Near East, and
it shares similarities with certain passages in Proverbs (see box, below).*

of Wisdom are paired with contrary speeches by other characters. The book of Job takes this even farther, exploring its themes through a dialogue between Job and his friends. There is also a strong concern with language, reflected in the wisdom writers' extensive use of poetic imagery, form, and vocabulary. The theme of true wisdom being derived from God is continued in the New Testament, where Jesus not only is a wisdom teacher greater than Solomon (Luke 1:31), but is the embodiment of wisdom: *"... but to those who are called, both Jews and Greeks, Christ [is] the power of God and the wisdom of God"* (1 Cor. 1:24; cf. Col. 1:15–20).

**PAPYRUS SHEETS**
*Before the development of paper, works of literature, such as that above left, were written on overlapping sheets made from the beaten pulp of stems from the papyrus plant.*

In both those books, the writers suggest that humans cannot fully understand the world or the ways of God, and both advocate an acceptance of one's circumstances. It is only God who can understand everything in the world, and the advice of these complex Wisdom books is for humans to put their complete faith in God's wisdom.

## LITERARY CHARACTER

Wisdom literature is recognized by its subject matter rather than its form, but certain styles of composition are particularly associated with the topic of proper behavior. The most obvious of these is often called "sentence-literature," and consists of short sayings or aphorisms arranged in series, often linked by catchwords (*see* Prov. 10:1–22:16, although these are not always obvious in translations). Such series can play a part in another

**SCRIBES**
*The skill of scribes was sometimes associated with wisdom. In the Bible, Psalm 45:1 compares a tongue speaking praise to the pen of a "ready scribe."*

genre, the "instruction," which presents itself as a father's words to his son or children, passing on to them his own experience of life (*see* Prov. 1–9). This teaching is often given added weight by the identification of the father with some famous figure of the past, such as Solomon. Speech is an important element in much wisdom literature: instructions, after all, are supposed to be reports of the father's speech. In Ecclesiastes, the content is a speech by the Qoheleth or Teacher, while in Proverbs 1–9 speeches by the figure

# EGYPTIAN INFLUENCE

*Instructions and sentence literature are among the earliest literary compositions found in Egypt and Mesopotamia and may have influenced biblical writing.*

A number of dialogues about justice or suffering were written outside Israel. Foreign wisdom literature was widely popular, and biblical writers were probably aware of such works and tried to imitate their conventions; Proverbs 30:1–9 may, indeed, be a foreign composition.

Such borrowing, though, is usually very general: it is unlikely that many foreign writings were available or accessible to Israelite authors. However, one Egyptian work, the *Instruction of Amenemope* (c.11th century BCE), was almost certainly known and read, perhaps in translation: Proverbs 1–9 imitates certain features otherwise found only in this text, and close parallels

to its content are concentrated in Proverbs 22:17–23:10. This does not imply active collaboration between "wisdom" authors or groups in different countries but reflects the wide popularity of wisdom literature in the ancient world. It is sometimes thought that wisdom literature entered Israel as an imitation of the Egyptian educational system, but there is little evidence for this. Egyptian writers seem to have been strongly influenced themselves, in the last few centuries BCE, by a text called *The Sayings of Ahiqar*, probably composed in eighth-century Syria. There may well have been a thriving local tradition of composition in Syria-Palestine during the biblical period.

**For further reading see bibliography numbers:** 103, 104, 124, 180, 215, 336, 480, 539, 638, 785, 809

# THE BOOK OF
# JOB

*The book of Job is largely concerned with an entirely just and righteous man
and his relationship with God. It raises important questions about divine
justice and the nature of suffering (see pp.174–75).*

To solve a dispute between God and Satan, suffering is inflicted upon a totally righteous man, who protests his innocence to disbelieving friends. When he appeals to God for an explanation, God allows that the conventional explanations of Job's friends are inadequate but shows that the divine ways are beyond human understanding. In the end, Job's fortunes are restored.

## MEANING AND INTENTION

The book of Job focuses on the issue of the suffering of innocent people (*see pp.174–75*). The main part of Job is made up of cycles of speeches between Job and his three friends, Eliphaz, Bildad, and Zophar. In a prologue he is defined as completely innocent, but his friends urge that suffering only follows sin. Job rejects their argument and appeals to God, who eventually responds in a majestic appeal to the greater power and wisdom displayed in Creation. By defining Job as a completely innocent man, the author is able to call into question the conventional wisdom of the time, which insisted that suffering is always the result of some wrongdoing. In fact, the friends could be right, because Job is the *only* wholly righteous person (defined as such for the book). It is also difficult to take the portrayal of Job as a

**THE SUFFERING OF JOB**
*This illustration shows Job afflicted by boils and seated on a dung heap.
He argues with the misguided attempts of friends to comfort him.*

model of patience in adversity, since Job becomes increasingly frustrated and angry. He does not curse God, as his wife suggests, but does want to confront God. In the end, it seems that the author is not concerned as much with explaining as with exploring: raising awkward questions about conventional ideas and implicitly affirming the human right to ask such questions, even though it is shown that the answers, in the context of God's amazing Creation, lie far beyond human comprehension. Some writers have seen a parallel to this in the style of composition, since some of the poetry in the book of Job seems to parody conventional forms.

## CHANGES TO THE TEXT

The text of Job is extremely difficult, and the book has almost certainly been disturbed and supplemented at points. Most notably, Elihu's speech criticizing Job has been inserted so that it falls between Job's challenge to God and God's response. It looks as though a later writer thought that the answers offered by Job's friends were too weak and has offered some further considerations. The pattern of speeches in chapters 3–31 is also broken after two cycles. In addition, the prose narrative at the beginning and end of the book does not seem to be coherent with the poetry. In the poetry, Job argues that the innocent can and do suffer, so that to prosper is not necessarily a mark of piety. But the narrative shows Job being rewarded for his piety, and that link is a basic assumption in the dispute between God and Satan. It appears as though the narrative did not originally belong with the dialogues. The lack of coherence even within each section means that the author deliberately employed contradiction and paradox to question the superficialities of the story.

**JOB AND HIS WIFE**
*Job's wife encourages him to "curse God and die," but he rejects her advice.*

## DOES JOB APPEAL TO LIFE AFTER DEATH?

Job 19:25–27 seems to be Job's great cry of faith that even if in this life he suffers unaccountably, at least after his death he will be raised up from the dead to see God:

> *I know that my Redeemer lives,*
> *and that at the last he will stand upon the earth;*
> *and after my skin has been thus destroyed,*
> *then in my flesh I shall see God.*

Christians have often understood these words, as translated here in the Authorized Version, to be alluding to Jesus' Resurrection. The composer George Frideric Handel (1685–1759) used the words from Job for the text of one of the most famous arias in the *Messiah* (1742).

In fact, the Hebrew text here is extremely uncertain. Job uses the common biblical theme of a law court, insisting that he is innocent and that God will come as his defending counsel to prove it. A likely translation is: "I know that the one who takes my side is active, and that one will stand up as the final speaker in court. I will see my witness standing beside me, and see my defending counsel to be God."

## JOB'S PLACE IN LITERATURE AND THOUGHT

The themes of justice and suffering that are discussed in this book also occur in dialogues in the ancient world, and the book of Job may have been written in this tradition. There are obvious similarities between the book and several Mesopotamian works; in addition, there are links with other biblical literature, especially the book of Ecclesiastes and the Psalms of Lament (p.209). Subsequently, the story was sometimes interpreted as a recommendation for patience, as in James 5:11 and the apocryphal *Testament of Job* from the first century BCE. However, the rabbis were more critical in their opinions of the character, some portraying Job as a rebel or chatterer, and most justifying God at Job's expense.

# THE BOOK

**TITLE**: In both Hebrew and Christian Bibles, the book is named after its protagonist, Job

**HEBREW TITLE**: *Iyyob*

**DATE**: The story is set in the distant past, but the work was probably composed in about the fifth or fourth century BCE

**AUTHORSHIP**: No information is given about the original author, and the story includes matters of which Job himself is explicitly ignorant. Some significant parts of the book may have been added after its initial composition

# THE CONTENTS

**CHAPTERS 1–2**
A prologue describes Job, a wealthy and righteous man. The dispute between God and Satan. Satan is allowed to test Job. Job loses his sons and daughters, and his flocks are driven away by enemies

**CHAPTERS 3–31**
Dispute between Job and his three friends Eliphaz, Bildad, and Zophar. Job complains against God that God does not hear him, God is punishing, and God allows the wicked to prosper

**CHAPTERS 32–37**
Elihu's speech criticizes Job and outlines the nature of God's justice

**CHAPTERS 38–41**
God's response to Job, revealing God's will. Job accepts that God is capable of matters he cannot understand

**CHAPTER 42**
Job's repentance, vindication, and restoration

# KEY THEMES

*If God is just and all-powerful, why do the righteous suffer?*

•

*Human suffering*

•

*The justice and nature of God*

For further reading see bibliography numbers: 53, 190, 237, 239, 263, 339, 363, 364, 683, 768

# SUFFERING

*Why do the innocent suffer? Various books of the Bible raise the question why some people suffer more than others. Often the innocent seem to suffer more than the wicked, who appear to "flourish like a bay tree" (Ps. 37:36).*

IN a just world, it seems that the innocent should prosper and the wicked suffer – a view affirmed in some texts of the Bible, such as Psalms 37:11–13: *"But the meek shall inherit the land, and delight in abundant prosperity. The wicked plot against the righteous, and gnash their teeth at them; but the LORD laughs at the wicked, for he sees that their day is coming."*
Yet in life the reverse often seems true: the innocent seem to suffer more, and, in the Bible, they protest. The common answer, especially in Psalms, is that sin leads to suffering. Several writers, in Ecclesiastes, Job, and Habakkuk, question this. This is also the theme of a number of Psalms – the so-called "Psalms of Lament" (*p.209*) – that appeal directly to God, sometimes complaining that God seems to be absent, or even asleep: *"Why do you hide your face? Why do you forget our affliction and oppression?"* (Ps. 44:24). Such Psalms often end with reconciliation and thanksgiving, which relieve but do not explain the suffering, or they make a plea to God for redemption (*"Redeem us for the sake of your steadfast love,"* 44:26).

> **❝** Will you even put me in the wrong? Will you condemn me that you may be justified? Have you an arm like God, and can you thunder with a voice like his? **❞**
>
> (Job 40:8–9)

## CHALLENGING GOD

The note of challenge to God in the Psalms is picked up again in the "Confessions" of Jeremiah (*see pp.208–9*), which have a similar style but a more concrete context: Jeremiah 15:18, for instance, asks whether God will prove to be like an untrustworthy stream, drying up when it is needed – *"Truly, you are to me like a deceitful brook, like waters that fail."* Such direct questioning of God is the key motif in the book of Job. Convinced of his own innocence, and unaware of the heavenly debate that has led to his problems, Job demands a confrontation and explanation; God does answer him, but denies Job's right to any such explanation. However, God is not always portrayed as so far beyond human challenge on such issues. For example, Abraham asks, *"Shall not the Judge of all the earth do what is just?"* (Gen. 18:25) and is able to extract a promise that Sodom should not be destroyed if ten righteous people are to be found there, persuading God to show justice on an individual, rather than a collective, basis (Gen. 18:23–33).

**THE DAMNED ON THE DAY OF JUDGMENT**
*Theology that came after the Hebrew Bible developed a whole system of belief based around the figure of Satan. This mosaic from the Baptistery in Florence, Italy, shows the Devil at the center of the damned on the Day of Judgment.*

# SATAN

*In modern culture Satan is a ruthless instrument of evil, but the portrayal of this figure in the Hebrew Bible is different. This earlier figure is far more closely linked to God and the concept of divine judgment.*

The basic sense of the Hebrew term *satan* is something like "accuser" or "adversary." It is used a number of times in the Hebrew Bible to describe humans who are in this position: e.g., 2 Samuel 19:22 – *"What have I to do with you, you sons of Zeruiah, that you should today become an adversary to me?"* In Numbers 22:22 it is a role undertaken by an angel: *"God's anger was kindled because he was going, and the angel of the LORD took his stand in the road as his adversary."* A heavenly Satan appears only in the relatively late books of Job (chs.1–2), where God allows Satan to test Job; Zechariah (3:1–2), where Satan accuses Joshua and is rebuked by God; and 1 Chronicles (21:1), where Satan is responsible for the census of the people – *"Satan stood up against Israel, and incited David to count the people of Israel."* In the first two the term is a title, rather than a name – he is "the Satan" – and Job suggests that he is one of the "sons of God" who constitutes the divine council. This Satan is an awkward and antagonistic character, whose role seems to be one of questioning and testing

**Satan and the Archangel.**

piety: that makes him dangerous to humans, of course, but he is not portrayed as an opponent of God. In the Greek translations, the title is translated as *diabolos*, or "devil," but at the time this word meant simply an "enemy."

### Later versions of Satan

During the intertestamental period, Jewish literature shows interest in demons and in organized powers of evil opposed to God. These ideas influenced the New Testament portrayal of Satan; even so, Satan retains much of his old character in the Temptations (*pp.326–27*). In Revelation, Satan develops into God's absolute enemy. The Christian idea of a Satan who is "prince of evil," a powerful enemy of God who rules the region of hell and a host of demons, is really a post-biblical synthesis of characters and concepts. Rabbinic Judaism connected Satan principally with the human temptation to sin, identifying him with the "crafty" serpent of Genesis 3. In Revelation 20:1–10 Satan is the serpent, but a more malevolent figure.

## SOCIETY AND NATION

National gods were generally expected to defend their people, although on occasion they might decide to punish them, or might prove unable to resist attack from a more powerful god. So the fall of first Israel and then Judah provoked various attempts to justify God's treatment of the Israelites. In the Historical and Prophetic books, individual suffering of the innocent is widely treated as one symptom of collective corruption and guilt, and is the responsibility of society, rather than of God: the nation is punished, in part, for allowing such injustice (e.g., Amos 5:1–15). For some of these writers or their audiences, though, the collective punishment of the nation seemed excessive. Isaiah 40:2 (*"Jerusalem ... has received from the LORD's hand double for all her sins,"*) suggests that the exiles have received a double punishment, perhaps because they have suffered on behalf of others – as is possibly meant in 53:4–5. In Ezekiel 18, on the other hand, the exiles complain that they are paying for the sins of a previous generation, to which the Prophet responds that they

are being punished by a just God for their own sins: *"Yet you say, 'The way of the LORD is unfair.' Hear now, O house of Israel: Is my way unfair? Is it not your ways that are unfair? When the righteous turn away from their righteousness and commit iniquity, they shall die for it; for the iniquity they have committed they shall die"* (Ezek. 18:25–26).

> ❝ *God will judge the righteous and the wicked, for he has appointed a time for every matter, and for every work. I said in my heart with regard to human beings that God is testing them to show that they are but animals.* ❞
>
> (Ecclesiastes 3:17–18)

## JUDGMENT

The perception that, too often, the innocent suffer and the wicked prosper was only strengthened by the failure of post-exilic aspirations and the events of the Maccabean revolt (see pp.250–51). Rather than concede that national martyrs might have been punished for some wickedness, or that God might be unjust, certain groups within Judaism adopted the view that there would be an ultimate judgment after death. This was a new development, although it may have had some earlier basis (see Sir. 3:17), but it was to become accepted within both Christianity and rabbinic Judaism. Restricted to *this* life, the inequalities mean that humans cannot comprehend God's ways.

**For further reading see bibliography numbers:** 121, 218, 283, 284, 363, 768

# THE BOOK OF
# PSALMS

*Also known as the Psalter, the book of Psalms contains hymns and laments of ancient Israel. Many commentators now believe that many of these formed part of the ritual of worship in the Temple and would have been set to music.*

THE Psalms have been inspired by the heights and depths of human experience: they express great faith, great doubt, and timeless prayer. In origin, it is clear that the Psalms played a crucial part in the ritual and sacrificial life of the people. Psalms offer a contrast to the world of Leviticus (*pp. 62–63*), where the actions of sacrifice are described but there is little or nothing of what was spoken during the ritual. In the book of Psalms, all we know is what is spoken, for the rubrics (the introductory passages that describe the liturgical action) are missing. We hear in passing of processions, of sacrifices, of festival days, and of music. Yet it is equally clear that a few psalmists considered the life of prayer to be more important to God than outward forms of worship.

**MANUSCRIPT ILLUSTRATION**
*The Psalms have been a source of inspiration for many different artists. This attractive illustration comes from a tenth-century Anglo-Saxon Psalter.*

in times of defeat. After the Exile, when the Temple and the priesthood were paramount, and personal piety was also more significant, psalms would have been composed for both corporate and individual concerns. They served both a liturgical and an ideological purpose, in that they established the people's faith in YHWH, the LORD, as their God and in themselves as God's people. The fact that the Psalms were not tied to one particular occasion, either a festival or a national event, means that they have been able to be used as hymns and prayers in both Jewish and Christian traditions. They can still be understood and used today, despite the loss of the king, the land, the Temple, and the priesthood for which they were originally composed. This longevity of the Psalms illustrates not only the appeal of the poetry of the Psalms, but also the breadth and depth of their spirituality.

## THE HISTORY OF THE PSALMS

Many commentators have emphasized the importance of one annual festival for which, they claim, many of the Psalms were composed. There is evidence of such a festival in the spring in Babylon and in the fall in Canaan. But there is virtually no evidence for such a festival in the Bible, since the cultic calendars prescribe three (Passover, Weeks, and Tabernacles). Psalms would probably have been used at each of these. Before the Exile, the king and the Temple played a vital role in worship. This is illustrated not only in the Psalms but also in the books of Samuel and Kings. Sacred songs or psalms would have been composed to celebrate the anniversary of the king's accession, to commemorate times of victory over enemy nations, and to lament loss

## THE IDEA OF GOD IN THE PSALMS

Because the Psalms were written over such a long period of time, they display many facets of the character of God. Some psalms, written for the king and the Temple, speak of the God of one particular people and place; others, written in praise of God's might and majesty in Creation, speak of a God of all peoples and of the whole universe. In one psalm we may hear of God's anger and judgment; in another, of God's mercy and salvation. In this sense, in its paradoxical voices, the Psalter contains in miniature the many different ideas about God found in the Hebrew Bible as a whole.

## THE FORMS OF THE PSALMS

Hymns and laments (p.209) are the most common forms in the Psalter. These two forms were also used in Babylonian and Egyptian liturgies. This suggests that some of the Psalms have been written in a common form for use in liturgy. Many other psalms are better classified according to content rather than form. For example, the psalms that refer to the king ("royal Psalms," Pss. 2, 18, 20, 21, 45, 72, 89, 101, 110, 132) have no one form in common. There is similarly no shared form in psalms that are didactic in tone ("wisdom Psalms," Pss. 1, 19, 37, 49, 73, 112, 119, 127, 128, 139) or in those psalms that have a prophetic emphasis (prophetic exhortations, Pss. 14, 50, 52, 53, 58, 75, 81, 95). Many other psalms use a combination of forms ("mixed Psalms"). Understanding the two basic forms of hymn and lament in the Psalms, however, can be an important tool in understanding the meaning of each individual psalm.

The Psalms are not poems with a regular meter and distinctive line forms: some rhythm is evident and line forms are often intended, but the essence of Hebrew poetry lies in its sense rather than in its metrical form. Thus the Psalms retain their poetic quality even in translation. Their key poetic feature is "parallelism." For example, ideas expressed in one line are echoed in another, or ideas expressed in one line are set alongside a contrasting idea in another. Hebrew poetry defies hard-and-fast rules, but as with poetic form, there is also some adherence to convention in the meaning of the poetry itself.

## LATER UNDERSTANDING

The Psalms have been viewed in at least five different ways over the past 200 years. An early view was to attribute them to a very late era and then to see them as personal outpourings of the human spirit. This was modified by commentators who understood them to be late, but written for corporate use by gifted representatives of the community. By the turn of the 20th century, this view had changed so that the "representative" was seen as a cultic official writing liturgies for special annual festivals. Because the king was seen to play a vital role in such ceremonies, many of the Psalms were accepted as belonging to the pre-exilic period (the period of kingship). This view was subsequently altered by those who agreed that the key influence on the Psalms was the cult (the Temple ritual); but this was also bound up with private ceremonies (dealing with those suffering, recovering from illness, sorcery, or persecution, and those who are dying). Most recently, some writers have proposed that the original historical contexts of the Psalms will always be a puzzle, and hence it is best to see them more generally as written "from life's experiences and for life's experiences." It is their common humanity that binds together the earliest composers with those who have used the Psalms through the centuries.

# THE BOOK

**TITLE:** Psalms. A translation of the Greek *psalmoi*, itself a rendering of the Hebrew *mizmorim*, meaning "hymns." Psalter is from the Greek *psalterion*, probably taken from the Hebrew word *nebel*, meaning "stringed instrument"

**HEBREW TITLE:** *Sepher tehillim*, meaning "book of praises," and *sepher tephillot*, meaning "book of prayers"

**DATE:** The 150 Psalms were composed over a long period but are not arranged chronologically. Some date from the monarchic period (tenth century BCE onward); others are as late as the Greek period (up to the third century BCE). Not all can be dated

**AUTHORSHIP:** The heading "a Psalm of David" in about 73 psalms need not denote authorship; the preposition *le*, here translated "of," can mean "for" or "belonging to." There were probably many psalmists – some serving as court poets, some as cultic prophets, priests, and scribes

# THE CONTENTS

The Psalter consists of ten major collections formed over time into five "books," echoing each of the five books of the "The Laws of Moses":
Book I, Pss. 1–41
Book II, Pss. 42–72
Book III, Pss. 73–89
Book IV, Pss. 90–106
Book V, Pss. 107–150
Three of the ten collections have the heading "To [for] David" (Pss. 3–41; 51–72; 138–145). Another three have headings linking the psalms with guilds of singers – Asaph (Pss. 73–83), and Korah (Pss. 42–49), and a mixed collection (Pss. 84–89). Two others are termed Hallel collections (Pss. 112–118; 146–150) because of their shared themes of praise to God (in Hebrew *halal* means "praise"). Psalms placed alongside each other share catchwords, similar contents, and common superscriptions, and there is a careful choice of appropriate psalms at the beginning and end of collections and "books"

# KEY THEMES

*God who rules over Creation*

•

*Prayer, petition, and lament*

•

*Hymns for liturgy, especially involving kings*

For further reading see bibliography numbers: 12, 146, 219, 237, 238, 264, 265, 295, 328, 471, 51

# LIFE AFTER DEATH

*In the Hebrew Bible, the idea of life after death is open to two different interpretations.*
*Each is a development of the belief that God is able to "deliver" the soul from death,*
*from the pit, from destruction, from what is called Sheol.*

THE Hebrew Bible holds that human beings are made up of ordinary material into which God breathes life as breath. Blood is the key to life, not an immaterial substance like a soul (for this, *see* Human Nature, *pp.182–83*). Certainly, until the later stages of the Hebrew Bible, there is nothing that can escape from the body and its subsequent death and go to live with God after death. On the other hand, there is survival of a kind: the dead were remembered and were seen in dreams, so that clearly a trace of them continues. This shadowy and weak existence, cut off from humans and from God, goes on in Sheol – the depths of the earth, the grave. Equally, it was recognized that offspring often resembled parents and grandparents, so that there was survival through the family or nation: hence the importance of remembering ancestors and of such institutions as the levirate marriage (*see p.111*).

## DELIVERANCE

But those views of "life after death" are scarcely vigorous, and that is why the Hebrew Bible is concerned mostly with avoiding or postponing death, relying instead on the power of God to deliver the living from falling into the pit, or grave. God certainly has the power to rescue and deliver, but in what sense? One sense, used especially in the Psalms, concerns a deliverance from a close-to-death experience. This has nothing to do with life beyond the grave, but rather it is about prolonging life here and now. Similarly, expressions about God giving "life for evermore" refer to God continuing life in this world, intensified by a sense of release from a

**THE BURIAL OF THE DEAD**
*Wrapped in linen cloth, bodies were buried in tombs cut from the rock. After the flesh had rotted away, the bones were gathered by the relatives of the deceased and placed in a box called an ossuary (see also pp.362–63).*

premature death. This view of "life before death" is clear in two psalms found in Isaiah 38 and Jonah 2: the suppliants speak of being released from death, and the narrative context clearly reveals that they are referring to their corporeal existence.

Does God deliver in a second sense, from Sheol after death, so that life with God continues? This was a late belief, and there are only a few examples of it in the Hebrew Bible. Two passages (both possibly written after the Exile) are concerned with the fate of the righteous and God's ultimate reward for innocent suffering. In Psalm 49, the suppliant is surrounded by people of iniquity, who nevertheless enjoy success (vv.5–6). Yet, the psalmist reflects, they must die, as all must die: *"Truly, no ransom avails for one's life, there is no price one can give to God for it. For the ransom of life is costly, and can never suffice, that one should live on for ever and never see the grave … Like sheep they are appointed for Sheol … Sheol shall be their home"* (vv.7–14). What then of the fate of the righteous? Not having enjoyed the success that wrongdoers have experienced in this life, are they even worse off than the wicked? To this the psalmist declares, in faith, *"but God will ransom my soul from the power of Sheol, for he will receive me"* (v.15). The psalmist sees his salvation and that of the righteous taking place in a future life. In Daniel 12:1–3, the same belief is expressed. The last few chapters of the book of Daniel reveal how the faithful are suffering innocently, while the wicked escape without injury. Vindication must take place, but this can happen only beyond death: *"at that time your people shall be delivered … those who are wise shall shine like the brightness of the sky … like the stars for ever and ever"* (vv.1–2).

## THE BOOK OF LIFE

The registering of the names of the righteous in a book of remembrance illustrates the two views of what "life after death" may mean. More often than not, in the Book of Life, "life" is about the here and now; Exodus 32:32 and Malachi 3:16 fit into this category, as do Psalms 56:9 and 69:28. In Psalm 59 – *are they [my tears] not in your book?"* – there is a prayer for release from premature death. In Psalm 69:28, the prayer is for the suppliant's enemies' names to be removed from the book of the living, so that they will suddenly die. But occasionally it may mean the ultimate vindication of the righteous by being given life with God beyond the grave. Daniel 12:1, in the context of verse 2, is open to this interpretation: *"your people shall be delivered, everyone who is found written in the book."* Psalm 139:16 speaks of the suppliant being known by God even before birth; his (as yet unformed) days and deeds were written "in the book." Later texts, including a collection of writings attributed to Enoch (47:3; 108:3), could also be read in this way.

## AN ASCENT TO HEAVEN?

Psalm 49:15 speaks of God "receiving" the psalmist after ransoming him from Sheol. This word, *laqach*, is used in another Psalm, 73:24, referring to the grave. It is used of two exceptional individuals who were "taken" to heaven, (i.e., exempted from Sheol): Enoch (Gen. 5:24) and Elijah (2 Kgs. 2:3ff.). So the exceptionally righteous, following these examples, may be exempted from Sheol, as we find in later texts of Abraham, Moses, and Isaiah – and, in the New Testament, of Jesus.

How might the "exemption from death" happen? No one knew, but they speculated that it might be by resurrection of the body, or – as the Greeks supposed – by immortality of the soul. The Bible does not say, and early Christians simply put the two ideas together. More important is the trust in God that the One who creates in the first place will continue to do

> 66 *Many of those who sleep in the dust of the earth shall awake, some to everlasting life, and some to shame and everlasting contempt. Those who are wise shall shine like the brightness of the sky.* 99
>
> (Daniel 12:2–3)

**TOMB OF ZECHARIAH**
*This rock-hewn structure in the Kidron Valley near Jerusalem, east of the Temple Mount, was built in the first century BCE and is traditionally regarded as the tomb of Zechariah.*

> 66 *Your dead shall live, their corpses shall rise. O dwellers in the dust, awake and sing for joy! For your dew is a radiant dew, and the earth will give birth to those long dead.* 99
>
> (Isaiah 26:19)

so in the future. Passages that have been used as "proof texts" to illustrate a belief in the resurrection of the dead are largely to be found in the Prophets. Hosea 6:2 is one: *"After two days he will revive us; on the third day he will raise us up,"* and Hosea 13:14: *"Shall I ransom them from the power of Sheol?"* is another. Ezekiel 37, concerning the bringing to life of a valley of dry bones, and Isaiah 53, which describes a figure who suffers and dies for the people and who is then brought back to life, are two other examples. Yet all of these, in their context, are probably graphic metaphors describing the future restoration of the whole people, after a time of national calamity. The most important thing to a people under oppression was that God's justice had to be seen to be done – in this life.

## A LATE BELIEF

The belief in life beyond death did not flourish until very late in the period of the Hebrew Bible, during times of intense persecution when the need arose to see God vindicating faith – if not in this life, at least in a world beyond. The biblical texts that give the clearest examples of any belief in life after death are Daniel 12:1–3, Psalms 49:15 and 73:24–26, and Isaiah 26:19. Among the books in the Apocrypha, the belief in life after death is expressed strongly in Wisdom 2:1, 5:15, 6:18–19. It appears in post-biblical works, such as Jubilees 23:31.

This is one of the most extraordinary facts of the Bible. Virtually the whole of the Hebrew Bible came into being without any belief that faith would be rewarded after death. The Psalms, the prayers, the stories, the Covenant and the keeping of its conditions – all this came into being because of the existence of God, not because there was any hope of earning a passage through death as a reward. It makes the Hebrew Bible a truly extraordinary achievement, not for the sake of reward but for the sake of keeping faith with God.

**For further reading see bibliography numbers:** 118, 236, 238, 521, 646, 698, 721

# MUSIC
## IN THE BIBLE

*Psalm 150 declares that music and praise belong together. The Hebrew Bible refers to many occasions to which music contributed an important part – in times of rejoicing, during religious worship, and to celebrate victory in battle.*

MUSIC has played a part in almost every culture. Although the archaeological evidence about music in biblical times is very limited, both the Bible and other ancient literature provide a vivid picture of music making at the time. References to music are made in the earlier chapters of Genesis and continue through the period of the Exodus to the Restoration. The Bible makes many references to skilled musicians, such as Jubal as *"the ancestor of all those who play the lyre and pipe"* (Gen. 4:21). Music is played at

**MUSICAL ENSEMBLE**
*In early biblical times, music was composed and played on solo instruments; ensemble playing did not develop until later on. The instruments in this group include the drum, horn, triangle, and lute.*

weddings (1 Macc. 9:37–39) and during pilgrimages (2 Sam. 6:5). References to singing are made at the making of wells (Num. 21:17–18), in matchmaking (S. of S. 2:12), and at victory celebrations (Exod. 15:1–18; cf. Judg. 11:33–34); reference is also made to songs of mourning at funerals (2 Sam. 3:33–34; cf. Judg. 11:40). Music was also played at coronations (2 Sam. 15:10), to deflect evil powers (Exod. 39:24–26), and during military maneuvers (Judg. 3:27). When Jericho was destroyed, God told Joshua that seven priests should carry *"seven trumpets of rams' horns"* in front of the ark (Josh. 6:4). The ram's horn is called the shofar (see left).

## MUSIC AND PROPHECY

Accounts of Israelite prophecy describe musical features also found in other cultures. The group of players and singers accompanying the prophets in 1 Samuel 10:5 resemble the Canaanite bands, of which evidence has been found on a pottery incense burner from Ashdod. Music enabled prophets to enter a trance and receive divine oracles (2 Kgs. 3:15). There are also prophetic song parodies (Isa. 5:1–7), and prophetic attacks on the use of music in worship (Amos 6:5–6) and on music and drinking: *"you who rise early in the morning … whose feasts consists of lyre and harp, tambourine and flute and wine, but who do not regard the deeds of the LORD"* (Isa. 5:11–12).

**SOUNDING THE SHOFAR**
*"Shofar" (Hebrew shophar) is the traditional name for the ram's horn that is blown on special occasions during the Jewish year, particularly on New Year's Day and on the Day of Atonement.*

## MUSIC DURING WORSHIP

The worship in the Temple, like that at the shrines of other cultures, undoubtedly involved various kinds of music. References to singing and playing during religious worship are frequent, but the translations of musical terms can rarely be certain. From the description given, we can reconstruct the

**CEREMONIAL MUSICIANS**
*These musicians, playing reed pipes and a lute, appear in a 14th-century fresco entitled "The Investiture of St. Martin of Tours to a Knight," by the Italian painter Simone Martini.*

# MUSICAL INSTRUMENTS

*Percussion, wind, and stringed instruments are all mentioned in the Bible, although information about their structure and composition is limited.*

Percussion instruments mentioned in the Bible include shakers or castanets – handheld pottery shapes containing rattling pellets – (2 Sam. 6:5), small, twin cymbals (2 Chr. 5:12), the Egyptian sistrum, or triangle, and the frame drum – also called the tambourine (Gen. 31:27), or timbrel (Judg. 11:34). Wind instruments included pipes, or flutes (Jer. 48:36), and various horns or trumpets (1 Kgs. 1:34). Among stringed instruments mentioned are the lyre (Job 21:12), the lute, and the harp, which was associated with contentment and joy.

**Copper or bronze cymbals, c.2100BCE.**

character of the chanting and of the different kinds of cymbals, drums, pipe-horns, and trumpets used during Temple worship. The most famous of the Temple instruments is the long silver trumpet, which was particularly employed to signal the daily watches. In Hellenistic times (*see pp.246–47*), major musical developments took place. Evidence of changing attitudes to music in Hellenistic society began to appear in biblical material, and music became a more integral part of social life, featuring especially at banquets. The pagan band described in Daniel 3:5 as *"the sound of the horn, pipe, lyre, trigon, harp, drum, and entire musical ensemble"* illustrates how wind, stringed, and percussion instruments were now grouped into an ensemble and played simultaneously.

**MUSIC AND DANCING**
*Music and dance were often performed at times of celebration. This 19th-century painting by Edward A. Armitage depicts the scene at King Herod's birthday feast (Mark 6:21).*

## MUSIC IN THE NEW TESTAMENT

Several of the cultural uses of music reappear in the New Testament: the dancing at King Herod's birthday (Mark 6:22), music and dancing to celebrate a homecoming (Luke 15:25), and the playing of the flute at a time of mourning (Matt. 11:16–17). One significant reference is the addition of a song to the Last Supper (Matt. 26:30), a tradition that was extended into the life of the early Church and continues today. References to music in the writings of Paul include songs and singing (Col. 3:16), the final sounding of the trumpet (1 Cor. 15:52), a reference to the call to battle (1 Cor. 14:8), and possibly to the Temple cymbals (1 Cor. 13:1).

**TAMBOURINE PLAYER**
*This figurine of a female tambourine player dates from the eighth/ninth centuries BCE.*

For further reading see bibliography numbers: 265, 440, 542a, 699b

# HUMAN NATURE

*"What are human beings that you are mindful of them, mortals that you care for them? You have made them a little lower than God, and crowned them with glory and honor"* (Ps. 8:4–5).

THE question, "What is a human being?" is answered in the book of Genesis: *"the LORD God formed man [Adam] from the dust of the ground, and breathed into his nostrils the breath of life"* (2:7). In one account (2:21), Eve was then derived from the man in order to form a complementary bond; in the other account (1:27) they are created in equal balance. Thus humans depend on God and require one another. They are alive but not simply in the way that birds and animals are alive. They are alive in a spirited way, and several words in the Hebrew Bible draw attention to the emotional and reflective capacity of humans – such Hebrew words as *nephesh, neshemah,* and *ruach.* Sometimes these words are translated as "spirit" or "soul," but they do not imply a soul that leaves the body at death and goes on to eternal life.

## LIFE AND DEATH

When humans die, the body returns to dust and the breath to air. Body and spirit form an essential unity (Ps. 63:2), and nothing can survive death. That is why some citations of "the son of man" (in Hebrew, "son of Adam") are in contexts where the weakness of humans and their mortality is clear (*see* Pss. 144:3*ff.*; 146:3*ff.*; Job 16:21*ff.*; 25:6; Isa. 51:12). In Psalm 8:4 (*see above*) "mortals" are literally "sons of man" or "sons of Adam." A son of man is a son of Adam who is subject to the eventual fate of death (Gen. 3:19). Death breaks up the body, and nothing but a slight memory of a person continues in Sheol (the shadowy underworld, equivalent to the grave) and in the memory of descendants. Only at the very end of the period of the Hebrew Bible does the belief begin to grow that God as creator will be able to continue a

> **❝** O LORD, what are human beings that you regard them, or mortals that you think of them? They are like a breath; their days are like a passing shadow. **❞**
>
> (Psalm 144:3–4)

**ADAM AND EVE**
*The first humans are often portrayed as a perfect balance of each other.*

faithful love for humans even beyond death. The Hebrew Bible's realistic account of human nature attaches great importance to the present life since there is no afterlife (a point well grasped by the author of Ecclesiastes).

## WHAT IS A HUMAN BEING?

The body and spirit together constitute a human being. The Bible does not give the brain, and the relation of thoughts and feelings to the brain, the isolated significance given to them today. Different words indicate the different parts of the person, but it is the whole person that is important. Thus "heart" (*leb/lebab*) is the seat of feelings and mind alike and the governing center that makes people who they are (Ps. 51:10); "soul" (*nephesh*) is the seat and action of spiritual experiences and emotions (S. of S. 1:7); "flesh" or "body" (*basar*) indicates vulnerable, bodily existence within a social group (also translated at Isa. 58:7 by "kin"); "spirit" (*neshemah*) relates the life-giving power that comes from God with the one who is thus empowered (Job 34:14). These terms relate, then, not to a medical or psychological analysis, but to the way that people live. Thus *leb* sums up humans as they feel emotions, *nephesh* as they are in precarious need, *basar* as they are vulnerable, and *ruach* as they are empowered. The other important feature of human nature in the Hebrew Bible is that the importance of the individual is often bound up with the identity of the group or nation as a whole. In Joshua 7:1, for example, *"the anger of the LORD burned against the Israelites"* as the sin of one person is visited on the whole group. In the Psalms, the pronoun "I" may express the worship of the individual or the worship of all.

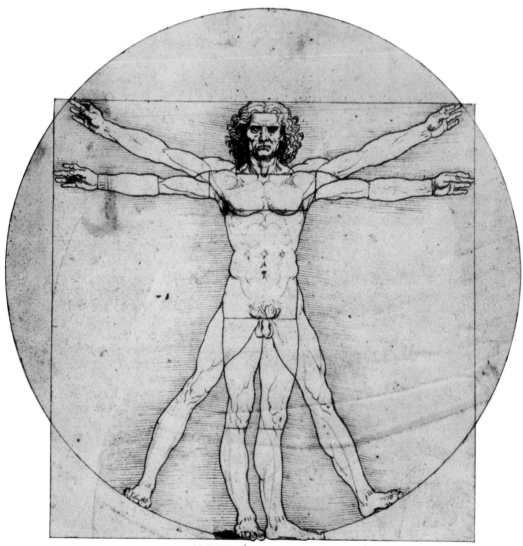

LEONARDO'S VITRUVIAN MAN
*The book of Genesis describes how God creates a world of balance in perfect harmony: "God saw everything ... and indeed,
it was very good" (1:31). Ideas of harmony and balance were central to much of Renaissance thought, a fact reflected in
Leonardo da Vinci's Vitruvian Man, where an idealized human body is shown in perfect proportion.*

## GOOD AND EVIL

The Hebrew Bible does not dwell on motives, leaving it to the reader to try to understand what makes human beings act as they do – although the stories may be told in a way that offers a kind of value judgment. However, in some of the Psalms, and some prophetic and wisdom passages, a kind of introspection does appear, often in symbolic language – the journey into the underworld, or the experience of drowning (Pss. 69:1–2; 14–15), or the description of forces within the speaker as "enemies" that surround him. The Bible acknowledges that humans "go wrong." From Genesis 2:9 (know-ledge of good and evil), and from the verb *yazar* ("formed") in 2:7, later interpreters thought that God had created humankind with two inclinations (*yezer*): one to good, the other to evil. The "fall" of Adam and Eve is thus a fall upward into new opportunities, including the opportunity to sin. There is no *original* sin – i.e., fault derived from the first Adam – as Christianity later came to believe. But sins there certainly are – enough at one stage to make God regret having created (see pp. 28–29). At the same time, there are provisions in the Bible, especially in Torah, that deal with the consequences of sins.

For further reading see bibliography numbers: 53, 373, 407, 433, 472, 826

# THE BOOK OF
# PROVERBS

*The book of Proverbs is a handbook of sound advice, containing proverbs and instructions on many themes. Its purpose is to persuade the reader to acquire wisdom, and it believes "the fear of the LORD is the beginning of knowledge" (1:7).*

THE book of Proverbs answers the question: how is life to be lived day by day? Proverbs gathers together advice and wisdom. Sayings from this book have gone deep into our language; many are still used in everyday life, long after the book was written. The purpose of Proverbs is to establish what constitutes wise and foolish behavior. The book contains the concept of life as a path along which one walks, making choices along the way, and there is much confidence that, through experience, the wise person can learn what kinds of behavior will lead to success and happiness.

## USES AND DATE

The various sections of the book are hard to date, but Proverbs 10:1–22:16 represents the earliest collection. Probably the context of this material is educational. Much of it may have originated in the family or tribe from early times, passing down through generations. Some proverbs concern the king and may represent a courtly background, although these are not extensive.

It is likely that the Proverbs were used for schooling, although their character suggests they were not simply used to educate an elite, administrative group at court, as some have argued. There may have been groups of "the wise" who propagated moral advice such as we have in the Proverbs, or they may have simply gathered the material together in its final stages. The attribution to Solomon (1:1) is generally thought to be secondary, based on his important reputation for wisdom (*see* 1 Kgs. 4:33).

## THE HUMAN ANGLE

A striking aspect of the book of Proverbs is that, like the rest of the wisdom literature in the Bible (*see pp.170–71*), it contains no reference to the salvation history of Israel. Instead, God is shown as creator rather than redeemer, and the world is looked at very much from the angle of human experience. Much of the material shows a very broad understanding of human life, its problems and contradictions. Scholars have debated whether the different sections of Proverbs show a development from a less theological world view to one that is more overtly so. Proverbs 1–9 seems to have a more theological character and may represent the fruits of more mature reflection upon the experience expressed elsewhere.

However, God is never absent – at times God is on the edge of an essentially human quest; at other times God is more centrally placed and is the means through which knowledge is attained. This is especially true when the experience is mediated through the figure of Wisdom, who provides a link between God and humankind. Wisdom is made so clearly a personal agent of God in 8:22 (*see also* 1:20–33 and chs.8–9) that some have thought that an original goddess of wisdom has been absorbed here into the representation of Israel itself, often referred to as a female (the God at Elephantine [*see pp.159, 247*] is referred to as having consorts). As Israel is the chosen consort of God, so Wisdom too is God's natural companion.

**PROVERBS IN PAINTING**
*The lazy man is a common feature of allegorical art. Breughel's painting illustrates the proverb "Go to the ant, you lazybones; consider its ways, and be wise" (Prov. 6:6).*

## PROVERBS IN LATER TRADITION

In later tradition, personified Wisdom became Dame Wisdom, and her opposite became Dame Folly, who is often depicted as a whore luring men to hell. The Christian moral philosopher Boethius developed this antithesis in his book, *De Consolatione Philosophiae* (523CE), depicting Dame Wisdom as Lady Philosophy who woos her student, Boethius, away from "strumpet muses": they personify fleeting, temporal prosperity, here depicted as Lady Fortune. In Jewish tradition, much was made of the association of Proverbs with Solomon, and he was thought to have written it at the peak of his maturity, in middle age. In the later Wisdom books, wisdom and Torah are identified, and this is taken up by the rabbis who increasingly saw Proverbs as "Torah commentary." Wisdom remained a popular theme in literature up to the period of the Enlightenment.

# ANCIENT NEAR EASTERN WISDOM

The literature of the ancient Near East had a tradition of writings containing wise sayings and proverbs. These writings of the wisdom of the past, and the wisdom literature of Egypt and Mesopotamia in particular, provide many close cultural parallels with that of Israel. The tradition in these countries is older than the tradition in Israel, some of the Egyptian Instructions dating from the third millennium BCE. Such comparisons are often used to illuminate the possible context of Israelite wisdom.

For example, on the basis of a close parallel with the Egyptian *Instruction of Amenemope*, a school textbook, it is argued that Proverbs 22:14–24:22 was probably used as a handbook for training administrators in a school context, paralleling the Egyptian one. Such a context may have been in "wisdom schools" at the court of King Solomon during a period of Solomonic Enlightenment, when a class of administrators may have needed to service a growing monarchic state.

The wisdom literature of other cultures also provides interesting theological parallels. The Egyptian conception of Ma'at has much in common with the Israelite figure of personified wisdom. Ma'at is described as having a role alongside God in Creation and in the ordering of the world, which closely parallels the description in Proverbs 8.

We also find ancient Near Eastern wisdom of a more questioning kind that parallels sentiments in the later Israelite wisdom books of Job and Ecclesiastes regarding the justice of God, the meaning of human life, and the difficulties involved in the relationship between humans and God. The Babylonian Theodicy, Babylonian *I Will Praise the Lord of Wisdom*, and the Egyptian *Dialogue Between the World Weary and His Soul* are comparable.

## THE BOOK

**TITLE**: Proverbs

**HEBREW TITLE**: *Mishle Shelomoh* (The Proverbs of Solomon)

**DATE**: A mixture of material from many different periods of Israel's life

**AUTHORSHIP**: Unknown. They are attributed to Solomon but include collections from other wise men, including foreigners. Probably they were collected by groups associated with the teaching of wisdom

## THE CONTENTS

**CHAPTERS 1–9**
Instructions, warnings, and hymns to wisdom, less proverbial and more theological in character

**CHAPTERS 10:1–22:16**
A very varied section of proverbs covering many topics such as wealth and poverty, wise and foolish behavior, etc.

**CHAPTERS 22:17–24:22**
A section resembling an Egyptian school text, *The Instruction of Amenemope*

**CHAPTER 24:23–34**
Wise sayings and an example story

**CHAPTERS 25–29**
More "proverbs of Solomon" transcribed by the "men of Hezekiah"

**CHAPTERS 30–31**
Appendices containing small collections

## KEY THEMES

*The way to attain wisdom and self-discipline*

•

*Wisdom revealed in God's creation*

•

*The deceptive ways of folly*

**For further reading see bibliography numbers:** 124, 157, 215, 240, 336, 455, 480, 520a, 540, 801a, 809

# MARRIAGE AND FAMILY

## IN ANCIENT ISRAEL

*Through its stories and laws, the Hebrew Bible portrays a carefully regulated system of households and clans that offers protection to their members, and also functions to retain the proper inheritance and possession of ancestral land.*

BELONGING to a family and thereby securing inheritance and descent were important issues in ancient Israel, perhaps especially after the destruction of the Monarchy and the national political systems. Marriage played a key part in this system.

## HOUSEHOLD AND CLAN

The immediate family of every Israelite was known as the "household" or "the father's household." Each family constituted one branch of an extended family, or "clan," or "kinship group," whose members considered themselves to be the descendants of a single ancestor, protecting one another. Upon marrying, women left their own household to join that of their husband, and their property became his. If this property included land, they were obliged to marry within their own clan to prevent its loss (Num. 36:1–12). Similarly, if a man was forced to sell some of his property, it was a family duty to buy and keep it until he could afford to buy it back (Lev. 25:25–28). Such rules applied only to agricultural land, and not to city property: the family and clan system was geared to country life, and stood apart from city and

**ABRAHAM, HAGAR, AND ISHMAEL**
*Abraham's wife, Sarah, gave him Hagar as a concubine and she bore him a son, Ishmael. When Sarah bore Isaac, Hagar and her son were expelled.*

governmental institutions. After the Exile, a new unit of several families, "the household of the fathers," emerged among the exiled families of the ruling classes. They had a strong interest in regaining family status and property.

The Hebrew Bible gives us no clear picture of marriage customs. Polygamy was apparently accepted as normal, with the wealthy having many wives and concubines, which poorer men could not afford. Women were permitted only one husband at a time. It is likely that marriages were arranged within the clan, with both parties marrying very young, but love matches are reported, and the couple could force the issue themselves (Deut.

**THE JEWISH BRIDE**
*This 17th-century oil painting by Rembrandt shows Isaac with his wife, Rebekah. Abraham was determined that Isaac should marry a Jewish woman, and he sent a trusted servant to search for a wife for Isaac.*

# OLD AGE

Israelites believed 70 years to be the normal human life span (Ps. 90:10), and 120 years to be the absolute maximum (Gen. 6:3), although few reached those ages. Ecclesiastes 12:1–7 depicts old age as a time of frailty and failing senses. Nevertheless, to reach old age was recognized as an achievement worthy of respect, which indicated divine blessing. Long life spans are attributed to many great men in the Bible.

**MARRIAGE CONTRACT**
*This Jewish marriage contract, or ketubah, dates from the 19th century and comes from Turkey.*

22:28–29). Marriages ended either through divorce, which left both partners able to remarry (although not to each other), or through the death of one partner. If this partner was the husband, and he left no children, then it was a family duty, although not an absolute obligation, for one of his brothers to marry the widow. Widowed partners were otherwise free to remarry. Since property normally passed to male heirs, marriage offered financial protection to women, and the vulnerability of widows is a common theme (e.g., Deut. 27:19; see Ruth, *pp.110–11*). Marriage was a valued institution (Ps. 128; Prov. 31:10–31), and it was a key to understanding God's relation to Israel. Monogamy (as the increasingly practiced ideal) represents God's choice of Israel out of all nations and God's faithfulness; in Hosea 1–3 and subsequent Prophets (e.g., Jer. 3:1–5; Isa. 54:5–8) the covenant relationship between them is likened to a marriage bond. Whereas other gods and goddesses can marry each other, God has no divine spouse and is "married" to Israel.

Wedding ring.

### WEDDING CEREMONIES
*In ancient Israel, marriages seem to have been celebrated as a special event; both parties were richly dressed (Isa. 61:10), and the groom apparently paid a sort of dowry to the bride's father. During the Middle Ages a ring was given to the bride at the betrothal (kiddushin), which took place in the bride's house. The marriage itself, including the signing of the contract (see left), takes place under the huppah, or wedding canopy (see below), which represents the entry of the bride into the groom's house.*

A modern Jewish wedding ceremony

# ADULTERY

*In the Hebrew Bible, adultery is sex between a man and a woman who is married to someone else. It does not include relationships between married men and unmarried women.*

Adultery is not a simple issue of fidelity between partners in marriage but rather addresses the need to make sure that heirs are legitimate. At times, it is portrayed as a crime committed by one man against another (e.g., Gen. 39:8–9). It is the sexual relations of a man (married or not) with another married woman, but not with a single, divorced, or widowed woman. Adultery is punishable by death (Lev. 20:10; Deut. 22:22), although perhaps the woman's husband may have had some discretion in the matter. The adulteress herself was possibly stripped in public before execution (Hos. 2:3), and it is likely that both parties would have been stoned to death, although the method of killing is not specified in the laws. Adultery was one of the most serious crimes, perhaps because it is linked to Israel's betrayal of God. Israel's pursuit of other gods is compared to lust leading to adultery (e.g., Ezek. 16; Jer. 2:32; 3:6–10). In the wisdom literature adultery is associated with folly (e.g., Prov. 6:20–35).

**David and Bathsheba**
*David seduced Bathsheba while she was married to Uriah the Hittite. He later had her husband killed by sending him first into battle.*

For further reading see bibliography numbers: 29, 66, 129, 368, 489, 744

# THE BOOK OF
# ECCLESIASTES

*The writer of Ecclesiastes looks at existence without a belief in a life after death and, with great honesty, considers the implications. The book affirms the goodness of what God has created.*

THE book of Ecclesiastes begins with the words, *"Vanity of vanities ... vanity of vanities! All is vanity."* The English word "vanity" suggests the emptiness and futility of everything, with the result that the rest of the book is then read as a long rendering of this basic observation. But the Hebrew word here translated as vanity (*hebel*) means something more like the steam that rises in a bathroom, the mist that evaporates at sunrise. Understood in this sense, the book begins with a plain statement of fact, that a human life is nothing more than a breath (*cf.* Gen. 2:7). The book of Ecclesiastes looks at life on the terms that life offers: that is, a brief interval full of possible delight and pleasure, but one in which most human pretensions to worth, grandeur, and importance are *hebel*, a fleeting mist that passes with the dawn. As with the book of Job (*pp.172–73*), the writer refuses to take refuge in a belief that this brief life will lead to something better or more enduring after death.

endurance of God and of the created order, and invites its reader to affirm the value of life as it is, not to hunt around for spurious consolations: *"a living dog is better than a dead lion"* (9:4), and what could be better than the following advice? *"Enjoy life with the wife whom you love, all the days of your vain life that are given you under the sun, because that is your portion in life"* (9:9).

**ALLEGORY OF THE VANITIES OF HUMAN LIFE**
*Steenwyck's still life, based on the text of Ecclesiastes, is rich in symbolism. The expiring lamp represents the transience of human life, the skull, death.*

## REALISM AND FAITH

Some have read the book of Ecclesiastes as an expression of skepticism and lack of faith, and have wondered how the book came to be included in the canon. It was indeed a book that was disputed. But on its own terms, it is one of the most devout books in the Hebrew Bible. It accepts the

## AUTHORSHIP

The author of Ecclesiastes is identified only as "Qohelet," which is thought to mean "the one who gathers," an idea reflected in the Greek translation Ecclesiastes (the Greek word *ekklesia* means "a gathering"). Qohelet may have gathered proverbs and sayings (12:9), but it is more likely that it was people he gathered, as seen in English translations that render Qohelet as "the Teacher" or "the Preacher." Long-standing tradition identified Solomon as the author of this book, based on references in 1:1–2:26 to the author's royal status and great wealth, and on Solomon's famed wisdom. However, it is now acknowledged that the text neither demands nor supports this. Ecclesiastes belongs to the wisdom tradition of Israel (*see pp.170–71*). It makes use of wisdom forms – such as short, pithy sayings – and covers the major topics of wisdom interest: life and death, work and profit, folly and wisdom. In common with other literature of its type, there are no precise historical references (the reference to the building of a city at 9:14*ff.*

is not specific), and the general nature of the observations makes it hard to assign a date or place of composition with confidence. A date in the third century BCE is most consistent with the book's language and its subsequent use by other writers, a date agreed on by most scholars. This makes the book a conservative work, refusing to endorse the increasing speculations about life after death (as the Sadducees were still doing at the time of Jesus).

The book of Ecclesiastes goes even further and questions whether retribution (the idea that wise and foolish actions bring appropriate rewards) actually operates in this life. The author's observations lead him to conclude that the wise and the foolish, the wicked and the righteous are not rewarded according to their actions: death takes no account of wisdom and folly, and injustice and oppression continue. All the more reason, then, to enjoy one's work, food, and family. Nevertheless its concern with the transience of life fits well with the autumnal mood of the Jewish festival of Sukkot (*see pp.68–69, 73*).

# THE EMERGENCE OF THE CANON

The process of deciding which books should be accepted into the canon was a long one. In the case of the Hebrew Bible, a 15th-century Jewish scholar, Elias Levita, suggested that Ezra had decided the matter, but that guess, based on 2 Esdras 14:44–48, is clearly wrong. The Greek Bible of Alexandria (the Septuagint) contained more books (*see Apocrypha, p.253*). Mishnah *Yadaim* 3:5 states that the assembly of rabbis at Jamnia/Yavneh after the fall of Jerusalem in 70CE debated the status of Ecclesiastes and the Song of Songs, leading to the belief that the canon was settled there. It now seems unlikely that there was a formal "Council of Jamnia," and more apparent that the process was gradual.

Some have argued that the first two parts of the Hebrew Bible (Torah and *Nebi'im* [Prophets]) were decided much earlier than the *Kethubim* (Writings), so that the former were already an acknowledged authority by New Testament times. In 2 Maccabees 2:14 it is recorded how after the loss of books in the Maccabean revolt, Judas Maccabeus collected them again. While this illustrates the importance of preserving the books, it does not say which they were at that time.

It took a long time to establish which books had authority in Jewish life. Some books – among them the Torah – had very ancient authority, while that of others was not so clear. They may have become "canonical" relatively late (from the second century CE onward), even though they were regarded as the word of God long before. In addition to uncertainties about Ecclesiastes and Song of Songs, doubts were also raised in the rabbinic period about Esther and Ezekiel, the latter because some of its laws seemed to conflict with those of Torah.

# THE BOOK

**TITLE:** Ecclesiastes

**HEBREW TITLE:** *Qohelet* (*see below*)

**DATE:** c.250–25BCE

**AUTHORSHIP:** The book is attributed to "Qohelet, the son of David" (i.e., Solomon), but the identity of the author is not known

# THE CONTENTS

**CHAPTERS 1–2**
Superscription. The endurance of the earth while human life comes and goes. The pursuit of wisdom does not alter this, nor does the pursuit of pleasure. Death comes equally to all

**CHAPTERS 3–6**
Everything has its time in God's world. Wretchedness of life on its own

**CHAPTERS 7–9**
The place of wisdom. The place of government. The wise way to live. Idea of living under sentence of death is developed

**CHAPTER 10**
Folly

**CHAPTERS 11–12**
Life is uncertain, so enjoy youth before old age comes and remember God. Conclusion

# KEY THEMES

*Life is fleeting and transient*

•

*The just and the unjust suffer equally*

•

*Life without God is meaningless*

•

*Enjoy the good gifts of God*

For further reading see bibliography numbers: 213, 215, 305, 340, 394, 785

# THE BOOK OF THE
# SONG OF SONGS

*Solomon's "Song of Songs" is a celebration of love, of which Rabbi Akiba
(c.50–135CE) said: "All the ages are not worth the day on which the
Song of Songs was given to Israel, for all the Writings are holy, but the
Song of Songs is the Holy of Holies."*

JUST as "the Holy of Holies" means the holiest of
places, so "the Song of Songs" means the greatest
of songs. This is no idle boast, for the book is full
of exquisite poems that use almost every device
available to the Hebrew poet. It is a rhapsody of the
thoughts and feelings of a young woman and her beloved
as they journey toward the consummation of their love.
Rarely has a book been interpreted so diversely over the
millennia. Until the 19th century, the Song of Songs
was mostly read as an
allegory whose real
meaning was spiritual,
concerning God's
dealings with Israel,
or Christ's love for the
Church. Then more
literal readings began
to prevail, so that some
saw it as a cycle of love
songs to be sung at a
wedding, others dis-
cerned a fertility cult
ritual, and others sim-
ply an anthology of
unconnected poems.

as such – this is not a play, but a song cycle united by
common themes, catchphrases, and refrains. Between
outpourings of mutual praise, intimate longings, fears
of loss, tensions of separation, and happiness in love,
the following refrain is repeated three times: *"I adjure you,
O daughters of Jerusalem … do not stir up or awaken love until it
is ready!"* (2:7; 3:5; 8:4). This repetition provides a sense
of movement, and suggests a relationship progressing
steadily toward consummation.

HOMECOMING OF THE BRIDE AND GROOM
*"Set me as a seal upon your heart, as a seal upon your arm;
for love is strong as death, passion fierce as the grave."*

## THE MEANINGS
## OF THE BOOK

There are many ways to
hold the poems together
in our imagination; the
contents in the panel
opposite provide one
possibility. Chapters 3–6
describe a dream sequence
(3:1; 5:2; 6:12), where the
bride-to-be has dreams (and
nightmares) about her
wedding and of what will
follow. In the wedding
passage (3:6–11), she
imagines the day as a royal
occasion, and her lover as
Solomon. In 8:5 the first
line of this wedding dream is repeated, as the dream gives
way to reality. The last part of the Song (8:5–14) resembles
a curtain call, with every character making a final appearance.

## CHARACTERS
## IN THE BOOK

The two leading characters in the book are a young
country girl and her lover (1:5–7). Minor characters
include the mothers of the bride and groom, brothers,
watchmen, and the women of Jerusalem. Solomon is
mentioned seven times, and some consider that he plays
the third main character, who tries to win the girl but
ultimately fails. However, it is more probable that the
girl is speaking metaphorically when she describes her
lover as a "Solomon" of splendor. The book has no plot

In the Christian Bible, the Song comes after Proverbs
and Ecclesiastes – the other books associated with Solomon.
In one rabbinic view, Solomon wrote these poems when
he was young and passionate, the book of Proverbs when
middle-aged, and the book of Ecclesiastes when he was old
and weary of life. However, another view reverses the order,

and believes that Ecclesiastes was written when Solomon was young and expressed the cynicism of a youth, Proverbs in middle age, and the Song of Songs in old age (all theories are combined in *The Book of Wisdom* by the American poet Robert Lowell). Some editions of the Hebrew Bible place the Song of Songs second in the collection of Festival Scrolls (known as *Megilloth*). In other editions, particularly those in common Jewish use, it appears first, following the order of the scrolls as they are read during the Jewish festivals throughout the year, beginning with the Passover. The pastoral atmosphere, and the links to the flowers and animals of the land, made it a source for popular songs by those who founded the State of Israel.

## LATER UNDERSTANDINGS

There was much debate among the rabbis about whether this book should be included in the canon (*see p.189*). It does not mention God, and it seems to be about an entirely human concern. Rabbi Akiba and others after him took the Song to be a celebration of God's love for Israel. Even the title in verse 1, "Song of Songs of Solomon [*shelomo*]", was understood as "Song of Songs about the One to whom peace [*shalom*] belongs," that is, God. Then the verses are understood as particular examples of that love. For example, on 3:6, "perfumed with myrrh," the Great Commentary on Song of Songs (*Midrash Hazitah*) says: "this refers to our father Abraham. As myrrh is the first of all spices, so our father Abraham was the first of all the righteous."

## ALLEGORICAL INTERPRETATIONS

Christians have also made allegorical interpretations from at least the time of Origen (c.185–c.254CE) onward, seeing the book as a description of the coming of Christ in his incarnation as the supreme lover of the soul, and as a description of the soul's response in yearning for God. Ambrose (c.339–97CE), for example, saw in the text four stages of the soul's progression to God (*On Isaac* 6:50). It has been read as an allegory of the love between God (Christ) and the Church or the soul, or the Virgin Mary. But the finest example of this use of the text is St. John of the Cross, who had the book read to him on his deathbed. The song became a foundation for his own spiritual poetry, as in *The Living Flame*:

> Ah gentle and so loving
> you wake within me proving
> that you are there in secret and alone,
> your fragrant breathing stills me,
> your grace, your glory fills me
> so tenderly your love becomes my own.
>
> [*The Living Flame*, trans. M. Flower]

## THE BOOK

**TITLE:** Song of Songs

**HEBREW TITLE:** *Shir haShirim*

**DATE:** Uncertain. Estimates range between the tenth and fifth centuries BCE

**AUTHORSHIP:** Uncertain. The book is linked with Solomon through the title *"The Song of Songs of Solomon,"* but *"of"* can also be translated *"about."* The poems do not claim unambiguously to be written by Solomon

## THE CONTENTS

**CHAPTERS 1–2**
Title (1:1). Mutual praise and longing between the lover and the beloved

**CHAPTERS 3–6:3**
The bride's dream (3:1–5). The groom and his party approach (3:6–11). Praise for the beauty of the bride (4:1–5:1). Description of the bride's dream (5:2–8). The bride and her friends discuss the groom (5:9–6:3)

**CHAPTER 6:4–8:14**
The groom extols the beauty of his bride (6:4–13). Expressions of praise and longing between the bride and groom (7:1–8:4) The dream gives way to reality (8:5) Concluding passage (8:6–14)

## KEY THEMES

*The celebration of mutual love between a woman and a man*

•

*The analogies of love and beauty in nature*

For further reading see bibliography numbers: 39, 285, 300, 329, 477, 486, 527, 528, 578, 623

# SEX AND SEXUALITY
## IN THE BIBLE

*Sexual imagery is used widely in the Hebrew Bible: in the laws of Leviticus, the erotic love poetry of the Song of Songs, and the proscriptions of the prophets' warnings. But sex itself is not a major preoccupation. It is rarely treated as a straightforwardly moral issue.*

WHEN reading the Bible, it is important to realize that the biblical writers' understanding of sex and procreation differed from our own. The biblical writers understood that pregnancy depends upon a woman receiving a man's "seed." They seemed unaware that semen was a vehicle for sperm, and that a man who could produce it might still be infertile. Equally, they showed no knowledge of the ovum, and, although inherited characteristics must have suggested that the woman was more than just a receptacle, formation of the fetus remained a mystery (Jer. 1:5). They were aware, though, of menopause (Gen. 17:17), and perhaps also of the link between fertility and the menstrual cycle (Lev. 15:19; cf. 2 Sam. 11:4). Although Onan is condemned for deliberately failing to impregnate Tamar when obliged by custom to do so (Gen. 38:9–10), there is no indication that procreation

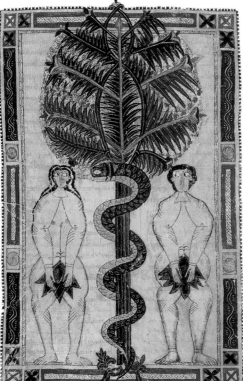

ADAM AND EVE
*With the disobedience of Adam and Eve comes the discovery of the couple's nakedness, shown here in this Spanish manuscript.*

ASTARTE
*Before and even after the arrival of the Israelites, the worship of fertility deities such as Astarte was common in the land of Canaan.*

was considered the sole purpose of sex. The sexual urge is explained in Genesis 2:23–24 as an urge to reunite as one, woman having been created from man's body. In Genesis 3:16, woman's love for man drives her to have sex despite the prospect of childbirth, which was very dangerous in the ancient world. Erotic love is most obviously celebrated in the Song of Songs. No

clear reference, incidentally, is made anywhere in the Hebrew Bible to nonpenetrative sex, which may not actually have been seen as coming under the laws on sexual relationships. Contraception is not mentioned, although the story of Onan reflects a knowledge of coitus interruptus, and long periods of breast-feeding (three years in 2 Macc. 7:27) would have regulated female fertility.

## INCEST AND EXTRAMARITAL SEX
The idea that sexual partners become united as one may underlie Leviticus' curious identification of partners with each other's genitals (e.g., Lev. 18:7), which is used to explain some of the many regulations about incest. These regulations, and the penalties they prescribe, follow no obvious order or pattern. They probably reflect the customary practices and taboos of a sort found in many societies, which encourage intermarriage between separate family groups. The clarification and regulation of such matters may have become especially important for the relatively small groups who went into the Babylonian Exile or those who subsequently returned to Jerusalem. The regulation of other extramarital sex is motivated by additional concerns: for the proper distribution of family property, it was important to know the paternity of any offspring; furthermore, the adult Israelite male was regarded as having

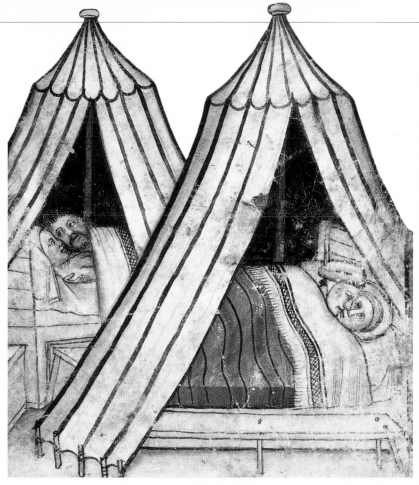

**AN IDEAL STATE**

*This illustration from the 15th-century "Bible History of the Jews" shows couples in bed in their tents in the desert. Monogamy and polygamy existed side by side.*

The choice of sexual partner was regulated even outside the immediate family circle: Israelites, after the Exile, were prohibited from marrying foreigners (*p.160*). In earlier times many apparently did so, suggesting that laws such as Deuteronomy 7:3 were not always known or applied.

## HOMOSEXUALITY

The grouping of such regulations often suggests a rationale that is obscure or incomprehensible to us: in Leviticus 18:23, for example, bestiality is linked with impurity and defilement, and it is grouped alongside sex with a menstruating woman, adultery, and male homosexuality. The last of these is also condemned: *"If a man lies with a male as with a woman, both of them have committed an abomination; they shall be put to death; their blood is upon them"* (Lev. 20:13). The verse probably refers to penetrative homosexual sex: lesbianism is never mentioned in the Hebrew Bible.

Apart from these prohibitions, little interest is shown in homosexuality. The stories in Genesis 19, relating to the men of Sodom, and Judges 19:22–30, where a guest is abused, are concerned with homosexual rape by heterosexuals: this was well known in the ancient world as a humiliating form of assault.

extended rights, in the sense that his wife, children, servants, animals, and land were believed to be extensions of himself. As a result, adultery was thought of as a form of assault and theft. For these reasons, adultery attracts particular condemnation throughout the Hebrew Bible and becomes the model of Israel's offense in running after other gods (*see also* Marriage and Family, *pp.186–87*).

According to Deuteronomy 22:20ff., a woman was expected to be a virgin when she married and could be killed if unable to prove this when challenged. If a man had sex with a virgin, he was obliged to marry her (e.g., Exod. 22:16) and to pay compensation to her father. Equally, though, a man might choose to marry a prostitute (if he was not a priest), while a father might refuse to allow his daughter to marry her lover. Male chastity is not strictly regulated in the Hebrew Bible, and the widowed Judah fears no more than ridicule for sleeping with a prostitute (Gen. 38). But there are warnings against the potentially corrupting influence of female sexuality (e.g., Prov. 7).

**DAVID WATCHES BATHSHEBA**

*This 16th-century painting by Wolfgang Krodel depicts David as he caught sight of Bathsheba, wife of Uriah the Hittite, from his rooftop while she was bathing. His sleeping with her and his murder of her husband were condemned (2 Sam. 11–12).*

For further reading see bibliography numbers: 211, 483, 619, 755

# THE
# PROPHETS

In the Hebrew Bible, the second major division begins after Deuteronomy. It is called the Prophets. At this point, major differences occur in the classification and order of books. In the Jewish Bible, the section "Prophets" includes some of the Historical books, but not Ruth, Esther, Ezra, Nehemiah, or 1 and 2 Chronicles; nor does it include Lamentations or Daniel. All these are in the third section, *Kethubim*, the Writings. Prophets are divided into Former Prophets (the narrative works) and Latter Prophets (the Prophetic books). Among Christians, the Historical books are kept separate, and Roman Catholics include Baruch as part of the canon.

| JEWISH | CHRISTIAN |
|---|---|
| *Former Prophets:* | Isaiah |
| Joshua | Jeremiah |
| Judges | Lamentations |
| 1 and 2 Samuel | [Baruch] |
| 1 and 2 Kings | Ezekiel |
| *Latter Prophets:* | Daniel |
| Isaiah | Hosea |
| Jeremiah | Joel |
| Ezekiel | Amos |
| Hosea | Obadiah |
| Joel | Jonah |
| Amos | Micah |
| Obadiah | Nahum |
| Jonah | Habakkuk |
| Micah | Zephaniah |
| Nahum | Haggai |
| Habakkuk | Zechariah |
| Zephaniah | Malachi |
| Haggai | |
| Zechariah | |
| Malachi | |

# THE ROLE OF THE PROPHETS

*Prophets existed in Israel from at least the tenth century BCE. They became increasingly individual figures. From the early fifth century BCE, their function of communicating the will of God was increasingly taken over by priests and Torah.*

PROPHETS functioned as channels of communication from God to humans, and from humans to God. Typically their oracles begin, "Thus says the LORD …" As agents of God to the people, Israelite prophets brought the people messages from God – either about everyday matters, such as the location of lost animals (1 Sam. 10:2), or about matters of state and the whole future of the nation (Amos 1–2). As the people's representatives to God, prophets had a duty to intercede. Their intercession might be for domestic concerns (Elijah prayed for a dead boy who returned to life, 1 Kgs. 17:17–24) or for deliverance from national emergencies (Isa. 37:21–35). Prophets were originally called "those who see," but the "seers" (Heb. *roeh, chozeh*) were later called "prophets" (*nabi/nebi'im*).

## BACKGROUND

Figures who resembled Israelite prophets existed in other parts of the ancient Near East. Tablets discovered at Mari, a Mesopotamian city, tell of figures known as "answerers" or "ecstatics" who gave the kings communications from the deity. Some Assyrian texts from the seventh century BCE are oracles from "shouters," "revealers," and "ecstatics," and texts from Mari and Emar in Syria use a word close to the Hebrew *nabi*. It is clear that prophets were commonly associated with the cult, working alongside priests, supplying oracles and answers to questions for the worshipers. There are traces of cultic prophets in the Bible, including bands of professional ecstatic prophets (1 Sam. 10:5–8). It may be that some of the Psalms originated as oracles of cultic prophets.

**THE PROPHET EZEKIEL**
*Perhaps most visionary of the canonical Prophets, Ezekiel was probably one of the deportees taken to Babylon in the sixth century BCE.*

## CANONICAL PROPHETS

If the canonical Prophets (whose oracles are now collected in the books of the Bible) emerged from a cultic background, how did they come to be so separated from the cult that many of them uttered fierce oracles against reliance on the cult as a substitute for the true service of God (e.g., Isa. 1:10–17; 66:1–6; Jer. 6:20; 7:1–15; Hos. 6:6; Amos 5:21–4; Mic. 6:6–8)? What distinguished particular individuals from the common run of prophets so that their words or oracles came to be collected in Prophetic books? And what so distinguished them from the world of cultic prophets that eventually the Prophets whose oracles were collected could look at the cultic prophets from a distance and call them false?

## TRUE AND FALSE PROPHETS

The initial distinction between a true and a false prophet was simple. Did the word that the prophet had spoken come true or not? That was the issue in the story of Micaiah ben Imlah (1 Kgs. 22). But if people had to wait to find out whether the words came true in the event, then they could not know the difference between a true and a false prophet until it was too late (i.e., after the event). Deuteronomy 18:15–22 gives exactly that test. In Deuteronomy 13:1–5, however, an all-important change takes place. It says that even if the words of a prophet come to pass, but the prophet has not spoken according to God's voice and commandments, then that prophet is false. A shift has been made from the outward form of a prophecy (for example, going into an ecstatic trance, as with Saul, or speaking in tongues, as recorded in Isaiah 28:10, where the words are gibberish and cannot be translated) to the content of what is spoken. Anyone can say *koh amar Adonai*, "thus says the LORD," but if the claimed word is not coherent with the accumulating knowledge of the word and the will of God, that prophet is false. Although the particulars of the Prophets' message are diverse (as applied to specific people or situations), the whole is remarkably consistent. They are confident what the word and the judgment of God are. In this way, although they do not refer much to the great and still-forming tradition of law and narrative in Torah, these messages certainly speak in the same moral and ethical tradition. In particular, see the message in Deuteronomy, where the well-being of the people depended directly on their behavior.

## ETHICS

The ethical focus of the Prophets is apparent even outside the Prophetic books (*see* Nathan in 2 Sam. 12; Ahijah in 1 Kgs. 11:29*ff.*; Elijah in 1 Kgs. 21), and it explains why there is so often a dramatic statement of the issues of judgment, combined with an appeal that the people addressed will change their ways and avoid the catastrophe before them. The Prophets not only address a crisis (sometimes addressing particular kings) but may actually create a crisis by bringing the judgment of God to bear. The Prophets consistently point to the absolute sovereignty of Israel's God – so much the One who *is* God that the gods of other nations are nothing and not to be followed. Indeed, since there is none other that can count as God, it must be Israel's God who controls the fate of all nations and uses them for the divine purpose (*see pp. 88–89*).

> **"** If a prophet speaks in the name of the LORD but the thing does not take place or prove true, it is a word that the LORD has not spoken. The prophet has spoken presumptuously; do not be frightened by it. **"**
>
> (Deuteronomy 18:22)

**THE ROLE OF SACRIFICE**
*Despite the role of cultic prophets in the Temple, and thus their association with sacrifice, several of the major Prophets make it clear that sacrifice alone, without obedience to God's will, is not enough.*

> **"** If prophets ... appear among you and promise you omens or portents, and the omens or the portents declared by them take place, and they say 'Let us follow other gods ... and let us serve them,' you must not heed the words of those prophets. **"**
>
> (Deuteronomy 13:1–3)

## THE PROPHETS AND SACRIFICE

But this does not give God's people a privileged place of favor. On the contrary, it focuses on them the demand for justice and righteousness (*see* the recital in Amos 1:3–2:8). The Prophets were equally clear that the word and the will of God take total precedence over the performance of ritual actions. God is not persuaded by any number of sacrifices. Samuel had already made the point to Saul that obedience is more important than sacrifice (*see p. 119*), and the Prophets repeat it in no uncertain terms (*see* Isa. 1:11–17; Amos 5:21–27; Hos. 6:4–6; Mic. 6:6–8). So strong is the contrast that Jeremiah seems to claim that God never commanded the rituals and sacrifices in the first place (Jer. 7:21–29).

## PROPHECY AS PREDICTION

Because of the original connection of the Prophets with the cultic functionaries who were there to provide guidance for a king or to find lost property, the Prophets continued to point to the future. The importance of the predictive element of prophecy was heightened when the first Christians took texts from the Prophets that in their view pointed to Jesus as the fulfillment of that prophecy.

The Prophets did indeed lay out the consequences of behavior in a general way, for good and for ill, but there are few specific prophecies in a "foretelling" sense (i.e., that actually foretell specific events in the future). The purpose of the Prophets was to bring the people of their day back to their proper obedience to God. Thus in general they were offering not foresight but insight. They do point to consequences of behavior in the judgment of God, but this is not offered as a map of the future.

For further reading see bibliography numbers: 65, 99, 103, 130, 216, 276, 345, 382, 501, 539, 692, 771

# PROPHETIC ACTIONS

*Biblical Prophets communicated their message in different ways: in songs
and oracles, in prose and poetry. But the Prophets also put their urgent message
into actions, which could initiate the events they portrayed.*

**W**HAT happens when words fail?
Prophets put their message into
an acted form. The action
brings into being the message that it
carries: when the Prophet Jeremiah wore a
yoke (*see opposite*), it meant that the yoke of
exile, already threatened in his words, had
come into being. Prophetic actions were
much more than visual aids. Actions
are found throughout the
period of prophecy, from the
Monarchy until after the Exile.

## THE TRUE PROPHET

The outcome of battle
concerned kings and prophets.
When the prophet Zedekiah
used iron horns to enact the
overthrow of the Syrians by
the kings of Israel and Judah
(1 Kgs. 22:11), he shared a
prophetic tradition common
in the ancient Near East. At
Mari, for example, an ecstatic
prophet devoured a raw lamb
as a symbol of coming trouble.
In the early period of prophecy,
the test of a true prophet
was whether the prophecy
(enacted or spoken) came true
in the future. Elisha's acted
prophecy of Syrian defeat in
the next century showed him
to be a true prophet, but rather
too late to be of interest.
However, gradually Israel's
prophets came to realize that
the only test was whether a
prophet had spoken truly
according to God's word
(*see pp.196–97*).

> **"** *... the spirit of the LORD
> will possess you, and you will
> be in a prophetic frenzy ...
> and be turned into a
> different person* **"**
>
> (1 Samuel 10:6)

**ELIJAH FED BY RAVENS**
*The Prophet Elijah took on King Ahab and his queen, Jezebel, but he was
protected by God and hid by the brook Cherith, where he was fed by ravens.*

## THE MEANING OF NAMES

The Prophets' actions were also symbolic
of Israel's unfaithfulness to God. Hosea
married a harlot, Gomer, reflecting Israel's
idolatrous prostitution to the fertility
cult of Baal (*see pp.218–19*). The names of
the Prophet's children, Jezreel (a place
of defeat for Israel), Lo-Ruhamah ("Not-
Pitied" or "Not Loved"), and Lo-Ammi
("Not My People"), further symbolize
the deteriorating relationship
between Israel and God (Hos.
2:13; *see also* 1–3). Symbolic
names are used frequently.
Thus Isaiah spoke to beleaguered Judah through the
naming of three children:
Shear-Jashub (which means "a
remnant shall return," Isa. 7:3),
Maher-shalal-hash-baz ("The
spoil speeds, the prey hastens"
Isa. 8:1–4: an indication of
defeat), and Immanuel ("God
with us," Isa. 7:14).

## WARNINGS OF EXILE

But Hosea and his contemporaries were unable to shake
Israel and Judah's complacency.
Prophetic actions reinforced
the ineffective oracles to warn
of the unprecedented and the
unthinkable: exile from the
land. Isaiah, Jeremiah, and
Ezekiel were commanded to
break social taboos and so
embody the shame of coming
exile. Isaiah, for example,
walked barefoot and naked for
three years ("The LORD said, 'Just
as my servant Isaiah has walked

naked and barefoot for three years as a sign and a portent against Egypt and Ethiopia, so shall the king of Assyria lead away the Egyptians as captives and the Ethiopians as exiles, both the young and the old, naked and barefoot, with buttocks uncovered, to the shame of Egypt,'" Isa. 20:3–4). The reality of deportation was acted out as Ezekiel packed his bags and left home, breaking through a wall of his house: *"you shall cover your face, so that you may not see the land; for I have made you a sign for the house of Israel"* (Ezek. 12:6ff.). He had already enacted the siege of Jerusalem with clay tablets, bonds, a starvation diet, and the shaving of his hair (Ezek. 4–5). The Prophet Jeremiah smashed a clay jar to show how God would smash the nation and the city (Jer. 19). As he spoiled a loincloth by burying it, so God would spoil Judah (Jer. 13).

## JEREMIAH'S YOKE

The prophet Jeremiah made and wore a yoke to illustrate the captivity that would come upon the kingdoms of Israel and Judah (Jer. 27). The yoke was a sign of servitude to Babylon: *"But if any nation or kingdom will not serve this king, Nebuchad-nezzar of Babylon, and put its neck under the yoke of the king of Babylon, then I will punish that nation with the sword, with famine, and with pestilence, says the LORD, until I have completed its destruction by his hand"* (Jer. 27:8). This example is instructive, because another prophet, Hananiah, knowing that he could not contradict an enacted sign, took Jeremiah's yoke and broke it, thereby extending the sign to say that the captivity would last only two years. The word of God then came to Jeremiah, telling him to get an unbreakable iron yoke: the next stage will be a more severe defeat (Jer. 28:14).

Jeremiah challenged Hananiah, the false prophet, *"I am going to send you off the face of the earth. Within this year you will be dead, because you have spoken rebellion against the LORD"* (Jer. 28:16). By contradicting the word of God spoken through Jeremiah, Hananiah gave false prophecy and soon paid the price with his life: *"In that same year, in the seventh month, the prophet Hananiah died"* (Jer. 28:17).

> **"** Mortal, prophesy against the prophets of Israel who are prophesying; say to those who prophesy out of their own imagination: 'Hear the word of the LORD!' **"**
>
> (Ezekiel 13:2)

**FALSE GODS AND PROPHETS**
*Many of the actions of the Prophets are directed against the worship of gods other than YHWH, such as Baal (above). Elijah took on the 450 prophets of Baal and, supported by God, proved the falseness of their worship (see pp.138–39).*

> **"** ... you shall go to all to whom I send you, and you shall speak whatever I command you. Do not be afraid of them, for I am with you to deliver you, says the LORD. **"**
>
> (Jeremiah 1:7–8)

## HOPE AND RESTORATION

Not all the enacted signs brought about destruction and defeat. Some offered hope. Jeremiah bought a field at Anathoth to show that an invasion would not be permanent (Jer. 32). Later, the exiles were assured that Babylon would one day sink like a scroll weighted with a stone. Ezekiel joined two sticks together to symbolize the restoration of God's covenant blessings and the reunification of Israel and Judah: *"Thus says the Lord GOD: I will take the people of Israel from the nations among which they have gone, and will gather them from every quarter, and bring them to their own land. I will make them one nation in the land, on the mountains of Israel; and one king shall be king over all of them"* (Ezek. 37:21–22ff.). A crown of gold and silver was crafted by Zechariah after the return of the exiles to show that God's promises to David would be fulfilled (Zech. 6:9–15).

The Prophets spoke directly for God, perhaps even bringing the word of God from the divine Council (1 Kgs. 22:19–20; Jer. 23:18–22). In extreme circumstances, the Prophets translated the word of God into actions that brought into being and made inevitable the future they foretold.

## THE ACTIONS OF JESUS

By New Testament times, prophets had been virtually eliminated from official, Temple-based religion, but they continued their role in popular religion, and actions of this type were still performed when the urgency of the message was great (see Acts 21:10ff.; cf. 11:27ff.). It is possible that this underlies Jesus' action at the Last Supper (pp.350–51), when he said of bread *"This is my body"* and of wine *"This is my blood"*. These actions bring into being his promise that, although he has to die, he will be with his followers to the end of the age (Matt. 28:20). The only difference would be that in the Hebrew Bible there is but one event to be appropriated in the future, yet Paul states in the earliest account of the Last Supper that this action is to be appropriated again and again (1 Cor. 11:25ff.). The entry of Jesus into Jerusalem and the clearing of the Temple have also been interpreted this way.

For further reading see bibliography numbers: 65, 99, 103, 130, 216, 276, 345, 382, 501, 539, 692, 771

# THE BOOK OF
# ISAIAH 1-39

*Like other prophetic writings, the first section of the book of Isaiah contains prophecies against foreign nations and condemnation of Israel's waywardness. It also includes Isaiah's dramatic vision of God and his call to prophecy.*

ALL 66 chapters of the book of Isaiah appear in the Bible as a single work made up of oracles and visions of the prophet Isaiah. In the 12th century CE, Abraham Ibn Ezra suggested that parts of the section beginning with chapter 40 were written by a later author or compiler, and since then, many scholars have concluded that 1–39 (First or Proto-Isaiah), 40–55 (Second or Deutero-Isaiah), and 56–66 (Third or Trito-Isaiah) are from different periods. The three main reasons are: Isaiah is not mentioned by name after chapter 39; Isaiah 40–55 deals with the period of the Exile (Cyrus is mentioned by name, 44:28; 45:1); and Isaiah 56–66 deals with the post-exilic period. Those who defend the single authorship of Isaiah point to the traditional acceptance of the book as a single whole and to its many recurrent themes. For instance, throughout the book, God is called "the Holy One of Israel."

## ISAIAH AS PROPHET

The prophet Isaiah, son of Amoz, lived in Jerusalem at the end of the eighth and the beginning of the seventh centuries BCE, the period during which the Northern Kingdom was conquered by the Assyrian empire and the Southern Kingdom, Judah, survived by paying tribute. Isaiah seems to have been from a priestly family. He had access to the king and knew intimately the ruling classes of his society, whose

**THE PROPHET ISAIAH**
*Four kings reigned over the Southern Kingdom of Judah during the period of Isaiah's life: Uzziah, Jotham, Ahaz, and Hezekiah.*

corruption he condemned. He brought to his critique a range of poetic gifts, composing songs (5:1–7), satirical sketches (3:6–7; 28:7–8), and rhythmic images (5:27–29); these are often dependent on word plays that have been lost in translation.

Isaiah's work began in a dramatic vision in the Temple, described in Isaiah 6. Other Prophets had had visions of God in cultic settings (e.g., Amos 9:1), but none had the same lasting impact. The difference between holiness and uncleanness, so important in the book of Leviticus (11:44–5; 19:2; 20:7), was made so clear to Isaiah that he called God repeatedly "the Holy One of Israel." Outside Isaiah the phrase is found only six times in the Bible. According to later tradition, Isaiah ended his life by being martyred: he was sawn in half during the reign of Manasseh (*cf.* Heb. 11:37).

## THE VISIONS OF ISAIAH

Isaiah's first vision (2:1–4) is also present in the book of Micah (Mic. 4:1–4). It concerns the end of days when the nations will flow toward the Jerusalem Temple to learn Torah from God, so that they will *"beat their swords into plowshares"* (Isa. 2:4; *cf.* Mic. 4:3). The second, which contains a profound religious paradox, comes from his vision of God seated on a throne while the fiery seraphim chant: *"Holy, holy, holy is the LORD of hosts; the whole earth is full of his glory"* (Isa. 6:3). The word "Holy" means that God is "other," set apart and separate from this world. But at the same time, God's "glory" and "presence" fill the world, so that God can be encountered, and is "among us." In an oracle concerning the king as God's Messiah (*see p.123*), Isaiah speaks of Immanuel, "God is with us" (*see* Isa. 7:14), which is later applied to Jesus (Matt. 1:23).

In chapter 6, Isaiah "sees" God seated on the divine throne. He experiences himself as having unclean lips, the terms used of a leper, but a seraph, a fiery creature, touches his lips with a coal and purifies them. Isaiah volunteers his services as a messenger to the people but is given the paradoxical task of making them even less able to hear and understand the word of God. This dramatic scene connects the divine and the earthly, and imagines the Temple as the intermediate place where the Prophet and heavenly being meet. The Prophet, having entered the divine counsel, now finds himself estranged from his own world. The passage points to the paradox at the heart of prophecy: to be party to the word of God may lead to an inability to communicate effectively with society, an experience echoed in the lives of the great biblical Prophets.

## ISAIAH'S MESSAGE

Isaiah addressed the injustice of his time, particularly the exploitation of the poor by the wealthy (1:15–17; 5:8–10) but also the corruption of the priests and prophets (5:11–17; 28:7–8), politicians (5:18–21; 28:14–15), and military (5:22; 22:8–14). His second target was the foreign policy that sought alliances with Assyria or Egypt instead of seeking security in the Covenant with God. But God's holiness also meant that faith would be kept with the people, no matter how wayward they had become. There will be a destruction so devastating that only a remnant will remain – nothing more than the stump of a felled tree (6:13). But the idea of this remnant also meant that at least a part would remain: from the shattered tree a new shoot *will* sprout (10:20–23). The names of Isaiah's two sons express the two sides of the remnant of belief (7:3; 8:1–3; *cf.* Hos. 2:1–9): one means "A remnant shall return"; the other means "The spoil speeds, the prey hastens."

## THE HOPE FOR THE MESSIAH

Isaiah shared the hope that the successive kings of the house of David would represent the people before God and would be the means through which the blessings of God would pour upon the people. The birth of a new successor in the palace gives rise to the hope that this Messiah (or anointed king) will bring all this to pass: *"For a child has been born for us, a son given to us; authority rests upon his shoulders ..."* (9:6–7; *see also* 7:10–16; 11). But the realization of hope requires living as God demands. There is no substitute for this, and Isaiah, in common with other Prophets, insisted that ritual and sacrifice were not enough on their own to please God (1:11–17).

# THE BOOK

**TITLE:** Isaiah. This section (chapters 1–39 of the book of Isaiah) is also referred to as "First Isaiah" or "Proto-Isaiah"

**HEBREW TITLE:** *Yesa'yahu* or "YHWH [the LORD] is helper [or savior]," taken from Isaiah 1:1

**DATE:** Set in the eighth century BCE

**AUTHORSHIP:** Oracles of Isaiah or the school of Isaiah (Isa. 8:16); chapters 36–39 reappear in 2 Kings 18:13–20:19 with minor variations

# THE CONTENTS

## CHAPTERS 1–11

1:1–31 Prologue to chapters. 2–12: Judah and Jerusalem will be destroyed because of their lack of justice

2:1–5:30 Future visions contrasted with present corruption:

   a) Zion at the center of a world of peace (2:1–4)

   b) Corrupt leadership to be destroyed (2:5–4:1)

   a) Zion destroyed for a "holy" remnant (4:2–6)

   b) Song of the Vineyard. Corrupt leadership to be destroyed (5:1–30)

6:1–13 Isaiah's inaugural vision. 7:1–9:1 The Syro-Ephraimite war; Political alliances or trust in God.

9:2–7; 11:1–16 The promise of a royal savior

9:8–10:34 The destruction of Assyria

## CHAPTERS 12–27

12:1–6 Hymn in praise of God

13–23 Prophecies against foreign nations

24–27 The "Apocalypse" of Isaiah – God's future judgment and final victory

## CHAPTERS 28–39

28–33 Prophecies concerning Judah, in particular its political ties with Egypt. 34–35 The coming judgment and the restoration of Jerusalem

36–39 The Isaiah narratives

# KEY THEMES

*The sovereignty of God and God's judgment*

•

*God's faithfulness to the people and to Jerusalem*

•

*Hopes centered on God's anointed (Messiah)*

For further reading see bibliography numbers: 64, 176, 177, 184, 415, 444, 445, 691, 780, 794, 805

# THE BOOK OF
# ISAIAH 40-55

*Chapters 40–55 of Isaiah deal with the period of exile in Babylon. In place of despair, they look to the future and offer hope; in place of defeat and the humiliation of exile, they offer God.*

THE message of Isaiah 40–55 clearly fits the period of the Exile. There are no references to Judean kings, or to Temple worship, or to international alliances with other nations; instead, the central concern is the longing for a return to Judah. Jerusalem (or Zion) and its Temple need to be rebuilt; the Babylonians (or Chaldeans) have brought about this destruction, and their idols are a threat to the people's faith in YHWH. Most important, the figure of Cyrus of Persia (who had conquered Babylon by 538/7BCE; *see pp.156–57*) is both implicitly and explicitly a sign of hope: through him God will bring about a "new thing." Either God inspired Isaiah to give this message two hundred years before the Exile, or these oracles, which do not mention Isaiah by name, bring the message of Isaiah to bear on these later events, perhaps through his school of disciples (8:16–18; 50:4). For example, Isaiah 35 pictures restoration through images of the wilderness (vv.1–2, 6–7) and Zion (v.10) – images that are also used in chapters 40–55. Similarly, Isaiah 12 is a collection of thanksgiving songs anticipating future restoration, in style and content like Isaiah 42:10; 44:23; and 45:8. And the attacks on Babylon in chapters 13–20 are very like the attacks on Babylon in 47:1–7. Chapters 40–55 of the book of Isaiah use several forms only rarely used in Isaiah chapters 1–39. The most obvious are the calls of praise to YHWH for what he is about to do; the long oracles that predict salvation; and the attacks against the other nations and their deities in the form

**MAKING THE DESERT BLOOM**
*"For I will pour water on the thirsty land, and streams on the dry ground" (Isa. 44:3).*

of a legal prosecution. We may note here the influence of the arrangement and singing of the Psalms; the Prophet has clearly been influenced by liturgical forms, and these have been adapted to suit the message of salvation. In any view, chapters 40–55 of the book concern a dispersed people, laboring under the hand of Babylon, in need of promises of restoration.

## COMMON THEMES AND MOTIFS

One motif that in Isaiah 1–39 is used as a message of judgment, and in Isaiah 40–55 of salvation, is of God the "Holy One [of Israel]." A second motif used in the same way is of God as King: God is sovereign and so can work throughout all the nations for good or ill. An additional motif is of the people being "blind and deaf": in Isaiah 1–39, this concerns their attitude to the message of judgment (6:9–10), and in chapters 40–55 to the message of salvation (42:16, 18–19; 43:8; 44:18). One very important theme in both books is that of God's purpose of peace for Jerusalem, or Zion (Isa. 2:2–4; 4:2–6; 29:5–8; in Isaiah 40–55, 40:9–11; 44:26–27; 48:1–2; 49:14– 23; 51:3, 11, 16–20; 52:1–2, 7–10; 54:11–14). From these similar motifs, we can deduce a theology shared by both Prophets with the following characteristics: God is holy, sovereign, transcendent, and hence capable of reversing the people's fate both before and after the Exile; what is required of the people is that they respond to God in trust.

## THE SERVANT

Of major importance in chapters 40–55 are the passages describing the work and vocation of the Servant of God. Four passages (42:1–4; 49:1–6; 50:4–9; 52:13–53:12) are sometimes called "The Servant Songs," although it is not agreed whether they are separate songs, whether they belong together, or whether they have the same subject in mind. The Servant is unmistakably Israel in 49:3, but some have thought that the songs may originally have been concerned with, or arisen from, the experience of a particular historical figure – such as, Hezekiah or Jeremiah. The Suffering Servant, who later became so associated with Jesus, would then have been applied to the experience of Israel in exile: like the remnant of Isaiah 1–39, the disheartened people in exile are urged to keep faith and to see the sufferings they are bearing as the means through which God, having justly punished them for the offenses that led to the Exile, will restore the people to their land. *"He was oppressed, and he was afflicted, yet he did not open his mouth; like a lamb that is led to the slaughter, and like a sheep that before its shearers is silent, so he did not open his mouth. By a perversion of justice he was taken away. Who could have imagined his future? For he was cut off from the land of the living, stricken for the transgression of my people. They made his grave with the wicked and his tomb with the rich, although he had done no violence, and there was no deceit in his mouth"* (Isa. 53:7–9).

## THE MESSAGE OF HOPE IN ISAIAH 40–55

Other theological themes are developed in a new way in Isaiah 40–55. One is the repeated emphasis on God as the "Redeemer" of the people (*"Do not fear, for I have redeemed you; I have called you by name, you are mine,"* Isa. 43:1). The word is connected with the language used about the redemption of a slave from bondage and recalls the time when the Israelites escaped from Egypt. Hence the new use of the Exodus tradition (*"Awake, as in days of old, the generations of long ago,"* 51:9): the time in Egypt and the time in Babylon have correspondences, because in both the people need redemption. The title of God is given as "I am" (this is one interpretation of YHWH: *"I AM WHO I AM,"* see p.59); this was the name God gave to Moses during the Exodus (see Isa. 43:11: *"I am the LORD, and besides me there is no savior"*) and it further expands the Exodus theme. To this is added the belief in God as Creator, using not only the traditions of God's creation of the cosmos (see Isa. 40:12, 22; 44:24; 45:18) but also the traditions of the Garden of Eden (see Isa. 51:3: *"[God] will make her wilderness like Eden"*). This combining of the idea of God as both Creator and Redeemer is a distinctive quality of the book. It is an important means of announcing God's salvation, for it shows to those in exile the redeeming compassion and the transcendent power of their God, YHWH.

# THE BOOK

**TITLE**: Isaiah. This section (chapters 40–55 of the book of Isaiah) is also referred to as "Second Isaiah" or "Deutero-Isaiah"

**DATE**: These chapters deal with the period of the Exile

**AUTHORSHIP**: (For discussion of date and authorship, *see* text)

# THE CONTENTS

**CHAPTER 40:1–8**
Prologue: Salvation announced; God's words stand forever

**CHAPTERS 40:9–48:22**
The historical process of salvation in form abcba:
a) Salvation for Jacob/Israel (40:9–44:8)
b) Diatribes against Babylon and its idols (44:9–20)
c) Salvation for Jerusalem through Cyrus (44:21–45:25)
b) Diatribes against Babylon and its idols (46:1–47:15)
a) Salvation for Jacob/Israel (48:1–22)

**CHAPTER 49:1–7**
The Servant's mission: salvation now, salvation later

**CHAPTERS 49:8–55:13**
The supra-historical process of salvation, in the form aba:
a) Salvation for Zion (49:8–52:12)
b) The Suffering Servant (52:13–53:12)
a) Salvation for Zion (54:1–55:5)

**CHAPTER 55:6–13**
Epilogue: Salvation; God's word stands forever

# KEY THEMES

*God remains sovereign despite the military strength of Babylon*

•

*Salvation is certain*

•

*The work and suffering of the Servant*

•

*The impotence of Babylonian idols*

For further reading see bibliography numbers: 2, 144, 181, 187, 597a, 781, 795, 800, 802

# THE BOOK OF
# ISAIAH 56-66

*The third part of the book of Isaiah (chs. 56–66) continues the themes of
the earlier parts but puts them in the context of the return from exile. The
emphasis is on the importance of keeping the laws and on the triumph of God.*

**W**HILE chapters 40–55 of the book of Isaiah
(*see pp.202–3*) deal with the Exile in Babylon
and imply that the Temple has been
destroyed, the later chapters of the book
(56–66) assume that the Temple has been rebuilt (*"these
I will bring to my holy mountain, and make them joyful in my house
of prayer,"* 56:7) and the focus is on Jerusalem. Despite
the miscellaneous character of
the various passages, they seem
to be addressed to those who
have returned from exile and
are facing the problems of
reconstructing their lives, even
though they are also repeating
previous mistakes, such as
idolatry and acts of injustice.

the ruins of their former society. There were also disagreements about priorities among the returning exiles,
particularly with regard to the rebuilding of the Temple.
These prophecies both criticize what is seen to be wrong
and offer reassurance for the future.

## THE HISTORICAL CONTEXT

Our knowledge of the period
when the exiles returned to
Israel (after 538BCE) is limited
and must be constructed from
contemporary biblical texts.
The returning exiles faced a
variety of problems. One was
their relationship with those
who had remained in the land,
as well as with foreigners who
had been "imported." Among
these people, certain religious
practices, condemned in the
past, were still retained. They
also had to cope with the gap
between the glorious promises
of restoration from Isaiah 40–55
and others, and the practical
difficulties of starting again in

**CARE FOR THE DEFENSELESS**
*In Isaiah, religious observances mean little if they are not accompanied
by compassion and care for the weak and needy.*

## IMPORTANT THEMES

The oracles gathered in these
chapters show marked contrast
between threat and promise (*see
p.219*). Chapters 56–59 contain
accusations and laments.
They are followed in chapters
60–62 by promises of imminent
salvation – indeed, for those with
eyes to see, it is already at hand:
*"Arise, shine; for your light has come,
and the glory of the LORD has risen
upon you"* (60:1). Central is the
word *tzedaqah*, "righteousness":
it features in the accusations and
laments as the quality that is
now lacking in the behavior
of the people (57:1; 58:2; 59:4,
9, 14). But at the same time, it
is the clear and consistent
attribute that enables God
to bring rescue and salvation
(59:16ff.; 60:17; 62:1ff.; 63:1).
The theme of new creation,
especially through the word *bara*
(*p.29*), is continued from Isaiah
40–55 (41:20; 48:7; 65:17), and
other themes and words from
Isaiah 1–39 appear. For example,
Isaiah 57:15 uses the phrase
"high and lofty" (*"For thus says
the high and lofty one who inhabits*

eternity, whose name is Holy: I dwell in the high and holy place"); this is also used to describe God's appearance seated on the throne "high and lofty" in Isaiah 6:1 ("I saw the LORD sitting on a throne, high and lofty; and the hem of his robe filled the temple"). God is described as "holy," yet present with those of a "crushed and humble spirit." This appears to be an interpretation of 6:3, which describes God as "Holy, holy, holy" – meaning transcendent and beyond humans, yet filling the earth with the divine presence ("the whole earth is full of his glory").

Similarly, Isaiah 65:25 ("The wolf and the lamb shall feed together, the lion shall eat straw like the ox") links with 11:7 ("The cow and the bear shall graze, their young shall lie down together; and the lion shall eat straw like the ox") in suggesting changes to the natural order in the Messianic age to come, when animals that are enemies will be at peace with one another. In Jewish tradition the predatory animals that will live in peace with their natural victims are understood to refer to the aggressive nations that, one day, will be at peace with one another.

## THE LANGUAGE OF ISAIAH 56–66

Isaiah 56–66 shares with Isaiah 1–39 a fascination with wordplay that underpins the contents of its message. In a passionate address on a fast day, the Prophet berates the wealthy for taking on the outer trappings of fasting without any real inner commitment or change ("Look, you serve your own interest on your fast day, and oppress all your workers. Such fasting as you do today will not make your voice heard on high," Isa. 58:3–4). The Hebrew word for "fast" is tzom. Isaiah challenges them: "on the day of your tzom, you find [timtz'u] business … For strife and 'contention' [matzah] you fast." Their fasting is literally backward: sacrificing or fasting for their own gain but not for the sake of God or so that others may benefit.

## ISAIAH 56–66 IN LATER TRADITION

Isaiah 58 is the prophetic reading for the morning of Yom Kippur, the Jewish Day of Atonement. The phrase "humble our souls" (translated in the NRSV as "humble ourselves," 58:3) is a direct echo of Leviticus 23:27 "it shall be a holy convocation for you: you shall deny yourselves …" which calls for such a practice on the Day of Atonement. Jewish tradition understands this to refer to "fasting." By introducing such a reading on this most important of fast days, the rabbis effectively continued the message of Isaiah 56–66 that fasting without a change of behavior is of little consequence.

The passage in 61:1–4 ("The spirit of the Lord GOD is upon me, because the LORD has anointed me; he has sent me to bring good news to the oppressed, to bind up the brokenhearted, to proclaim liberty to the captives … to proclaim the year of the LORD's favor, and the day of vengeance of our God; to comfort all who mourn") was read by Jesus in the synagogue in Nazareth and applied to himself (Luke 4:16–21).

## THE BOOK

**TITLE:** Isaiah. This section (chapters 56–66) is also referred to as "Third Isaiah" or "Trito-Isaiah"

**HEBREW TITLE:** see the book of Isaiah 1–39 (pp.200–1)

**DATE:** The period following the return from Babylon, between 530 and 510BCE

**AUTHORSHIP:** see the book of Isaiah 1–39 (pp.200–1)

## THE CONTENTS

**CHAPTERS 56–60**

56 Welcoming foreigners into the Covenant with Israel's God. Corrupt leaders condemned
57 Against idolatry. A poem of consolation (similar to passages in Isaiah 40–55)
58 God does not desire fasting but justice
59–60 Corruptions and injustice in the restored community. The glorious restoration of Jerusalem

**CHAPTERS 61–66**

61 The Prophet's mission to restore the people
62 The glory of the people is restored in Zion
63–64 God's punishment of Israel's enemies. Prayer for God's intervention to deliver Israel
65:1–16 God was willing to respond, but the people were silent
65:17–66:24 A new Heaven and earth. Israel rejoicing again on their land; nature in harmony. Concluding oracles: on the Temple; the miraculous "rebirth" of Jerusalem; the return of Israel and the fate of the wicked

## KEY THEMES

*Judgment and calls to repentance*

•

*Promises and visions of salvation*

For further reading see bibliography numbers: 2, 144, 272, 781, 795, 800

# THE BOOK OF
# JEREMIAH

*Jeremiah was a Prophet during the period that led into the Babylonian Exile. He warned of the consequences of forsaking God, but he also pointed to new life and restoration.*

JEREMIAH is the longest of the Prophetic books, and tells us much about the Prophet himself. He was born in Anathoth, about three miles (5 kilometers) north of Jerusalem, and began preaching around 627BCE, during the reign of King Josiah of Judah. Josiah's grandfather, who reigned for 40 years, had led the people away from monotheism and into idolatrous worship on the "high places." Josiah restored monotheism and once again centralized worship in the Temple. Jeremiah witnessed the fall of the Assyrian empire to Babylon in 606BCE, the death of Josiah in 605BCE, the destruction of the Jewish state by the Babylonians in 586BCE, and the removal of the people into captivity in Babylon. Jeremiah himself was taken to Egypt by fugitive Judeans. There he died, according to the legend, a martyr's death.

## THE BOOK'S COMPOSITION

The book of Jeremiah contains individual sayings, short sermons, and episodes from his life, and oracles, few of which are dated. The book is not arranged in chronological order. It may be that the scribe Baruch (ch.36) put a collection together, or it may have been later editors. The Greek version (the Septuagint) is arranged in a different order and is about 2,700 words shorter than the Hebrew version. Some fragments from the Dead Sea Scrolls (*see pp.290–91*) follow the Hebrew, but one (in Hebrew) follows the Greek, so it is not certain which version of the text is the original.

**JEREMIAH**
*In a time of political threat, Jeremiah's continuing message to the people of Judah was the coming of God's judgment.*

## THE MESSAGE OF JEREMIAH

The impassioned outbursts known as Jeremiah's "Confessions" (*pp.208–9*) bring him personally close to the modern reader. He portrays God as one who offers loyalty to those who are loyal in return, and who has been hurt through the people's infidelity. The marriage metaphor (chs.2–3) makes clear the outrage that God feels at Judah's unfaithfulness: *"If a man divorces his wife and she goes from him and becomes another man's wife, will he return to her? Would not such a land be greatly polluted? You have played the whore with many lovers; and would you return to me? says the LORD"* (3:1). Just as YHWH has been rejected by the people – principally for idols or the "queen of heaven" – so now he rejects them, at times with a terrifying finality. The Prophet is commissioned to communicate this rejection in 1:10: *"to pluck up and to pull down, to destroy and to overthrow, to build and to plant."* Jeremiah employs the menacing image of the *"foe from the north"* for the agent of doom that came to be associated with the mighty empire of Babylon.

Inevitably, such a message brought the Prophet into conflict with the authorities. Both in the oracles (21:1–23:6) and in the narratives (e.g., chs.37–38), Prophet and king are found in conflict, which in turn involves wider circles of officials, especially the religious professionals. Note the conflict between Jeremiah and the prophet Hananiah (ch.28). Even the Temple itself is threatened, in a chilling oracle of doom. Jeremiah insists on a future for God's people in their own land, but it requires submission to the Babylonians: *"For thus says the LORD of* hosts, the God of Israel; I have put an iron yoke on the neck of all these nations so that they may serve King Nebuchadnezzar of Babylon, and they shall indeed serve him," (28:14) and acceptance of the life there: "Take wives and have sons and daughters ... multiply there, and do not decrease. But seek the welfare of the city where I have sent you into exile, and pray to the LORD on its behalf, for in its welfare you will find your welfare" (29:6–7). He commends the exiles living in Babylon rather than those who remain in the land. Beyond this, Jeremiah's ministry is not only to Judah but also to the other nations; all nations come under God's judgment (25:15–31). Most clearly this is seen in the foreign nation oracles, where the Prophet denounces nine nations, including Babylon, to which they must submit. This apparent contradiction arises from the notion of fidelity to a God who longs to be faithful, and that might mean submission to his enemies. But YHWH must still be revered as the supreme God, and those who do not do so remain under divine judgment.

## A HOPEFUL FUTURE?

God's fidelity is not contradicted by God's judgment. After the "plucking up" and "breaking down" come the building and planting (1:10). Hope for a new future comes only after the past has been dealt with and a reorientation embraced. Chapters 30–33 are sometimes called "the Book of Consolation," but, in fact, they are made up of material of diverse origin; some (e.g., 31:1–6) is reminiscent of Hosea. The "new covenant" passage of 31:31–34 is well known, but it is only one among others in the book: "The days are surely coming, says the LORD, when I will make a new covenant with the house of Israel and the house of Judah. It will not be like the covenant that I made with their ancestors when I took them by the hand to bring them out of the land of Egypt – a covenant that they broke, though I was their husband, says the LORD." Even there the new situation is rooted in the Law, and it remains one of faithful relationship: no longer is this relationship to be maintained by external constraint, for it flourishes out of intimate knowledge.

## JEREMIAH'S INFLUENCE

The figure of Jeremiah the suffering Prophet has been influential in both the Jewish and Christian traditions. Such a model lies behind the presentations of both Jesus and his near-contemporary, the Jewish historian Josephus (37–100CE). In the collection of rabbinic sermons known as *Pesiqta Rabbati*, Jeremiah's role in the fall of Jerusalem is considered: there the Prophet's righteousness protects the holy city of Jerusalem, and when he is absent the city is destroyed. Jeremiah's life both condemns the faithless and promises hope to the faithful. In Jewish tradition, Jeremiah is the author of the book of Lamentations (*pp. 210–11*) and of the books of Kings (*pp. 128–29*). The word "jeremiad," meaning any type of declamation that promises nothing but doom unless one amends one's life, comes from his name, and this became a form of rhetoric in colonial America.

# THE BOOK

**TITLE:** Jeremiah

**HEBREW TITLE:** *Yirmeyahu*

**DATE:** The oracles cover a period mainly from the 13th year of Josiah as king (627BCE) to the beginning of the Exile (587/6BCE). Verses 43:8–44:30 come from Egypt and date to the period after 586BCE

**AUTHORSHIP:** The book is a collection of Jeremiah's oracles. The scribe Baruch had a part to play in their preservation. The final ordering of the book may have come from editors associated with the views of Deuteronomy (*pp. 80–81*)

# THE CONTENTS

**CHAPTERS 1–36**
Jeremiah's call, oracles of judgment and repentance
1:1–19 The call of Jeremiah
2:1–4:4 Judah called to repentance
4:5–8:3 Anger of God and the charge of false worship
8:4–10:25 Grief over the sinful people, and the true worship of God as Creator
11–15 Judah's rebellion and the coming judgment
16–20 Jeremiah's life gives God's message: he laments his fate

21–29 Zedekiah rejected; the Exile foretold
30–33 Prophecies of restoration
34–36 Jeremiah resisted

**CHAPTERS 37–45**
The fall of Jerusalem and Jeremiah's fate

**CHAPTERS 46–51**
Oracles against various nations

**CHAPTER 52**
Another record of the fall of Jerusalem

# KEY THEMES

*Lack of trust in God will lead to disaster*

•

*The honesty and integrity of Jeremiah before God*

•

*Judgment is certain but so too is new life beyond it*

For further reading see bibliography numbers: 162, 163, 164, 185, 457, 537, 704

# CONFESSIONS OF JEREMIAH

*The book of Jeremiah contains passages expressing Jeremiah's anguish and anger at the conflict both within and in his surroundings. These six vividly portrayed passages are known as his "Confessions."*

WHAT emotions are people allowed to express in their prayer to God? The Confessions of Jeremiah show a Prophet cursing, lamenting, and expressing anger – emotions that are embedded in the Bible. Sometimes these emotions are directed against enemies, but, in moving honesty, they are sometimes expressed against God: both Abraham and Job struggle with God (*see box, right*), and psalms of lament make up a large part of the book of Psalms (*see opposite*). Such laments have a number of common features: usually addressed to God, they complain about an enemy, they assert the individual's innocence, they demand action from God, and they express confidence in the outcome. Around the time of the Exile, the lament tradition took on a strongly accusatory tone against God: *"But now you have spurned and rejected him; you are full of wrath against your anointed. You have renounced the covenant with your servant; you have defiled his crown in the dust"* (Ps. 89:38–39). The six laments voiced by the Prophet Jeremiah arose out of a profound paradox: how could one approach a God thought to be a friend, but experienced as a foe?

One of the most potent elements of the Bible's lament tradition is that of protest. The person crying out to God has experienced a gap of such decisive proportions between experience and expectation that the only course open is to protest to the God who seems to be both the origin and the goal of human suffering. Such protests sound clearly throughout this series of "Confessions" by Jeremiah, as the Prophet who was compelled to utter God's words, suffers God's pain.

## THE PLIGHT OF JEREMIAH

Laments typically involve three parties: the sufferer who cries out, the God to whom the lament is addressed, and the enemies of the sufferer. In Jeremiah's laments, the "enemies" are at first seen to be "the men of Anathoth," the Prophet's hometown. So deep was the offense, and so distressing the message, that Jeremiah was threatened with death if he persisted in speaking (Jer. 11:21). Because of the words he uttered on God's behalf, Jeremiah was isolated from human society (Jer. 15:16–17) and faced persistent hostility (Jer. 18:18–20). The Prophet also faced the perennial dilemma: why is it that those who oppose God prospered, while he – who proclaimed the word of God – experiences deprivation of every kind (Jer. 12:1)? Jeremiah later protested, *"Is evil a recompense for good?"* (Jer. 18:20). He reasoned that if natural justice prevailed, the wicked would be punished, and those in the right would be rewarded. But this seemed not to be so.

**JEREMIAH'S LAMENT**
*This 19th-century German painting depicts the Prophet Jeremiah with "eyes a fountain of tears … for the slain of my poor people!" (Jer. 9:1).*

## A DEEPER ENEMY

In desperation, this dilemma led the Prophet to question the identity of the real enemy. Clearly there was human opposition, but there was also a deeper enemy. God sent the Prophet Jeremiah, and could also save him (Jer. 17:14, 17), but God was a source of suffering too: *"Why is my pain unceasing, my wound incurable, refusing to be healed? Truly, you are to me like a deceitful brook, like waters that fail"* (Jer. 15:18). Jeremiah was God's own Prophet, but God evidently opposes him and acts on behalf of the wicked (Jer. 12:2). Jeremiah also forcefully accuses God: *"O LORD, you have enticed me, and I was enticed; you have overpowered me, and you have prevailed"* (Jer. 20:7). He is tired of bringing "terror on every side," yet is unable to give up the divine word: *"If I say, 'I will not mention him, or speak any more in his name,' then within me there is something like a burning fire shut up in my bones; I am weary with holding it in, and I cannot"* (Jer. 20:9).

**DESERT WADI**
*This dried-up riverbed resembles Jeremiah's description of God: "a deceitful brook, like waters that fail" (Jer. 15:18).*

## THE CURSES OF JEREMIAH

Curses figure prominently in ancient laments. In his Confessions, Jeremiah curses the enemy: *"Let my persecutors be shamed, but do not let me be shamed; let them be dismayed, but do not let me be dismayed; bring on them the day of disaster; destroy them with double destruction!"* (Jer. 17:18; cf. 18:21–23). He calls on God's punishment to fall on those who oppose God. Such is the depth of Jeremiah's pain that he curses himself, as does Job, ruing the day of his birth: *"Cursed be the day on which I was born!"* (Jer. 20:14–15; cf. Job 3) (see box, below). The assurances that Jeremiah received fail to be realized, and the book ends with him being taken – against his will and the word of God – to Egypt. It is assumed that he died a hostage there among his own people.

---

### CONFESSIONS OF JEREMIAH

*The Confessions of Jeremiah are one part of the book of Jeremiah and consist of the following sections:*

11:18–23 *Human opposition*

12:1–6 *Why do the wicked prosper?*

15:10–21 *Pain in devoted service*

17:14–18 *Has prophecy failed?*

18:18–23 *Receiving evil for good*

20:7–18 *Divine deception and prophetic compulsion*

---

## CONFESSIONS IN CONTEXT

The Confessions of Jeremiah eloquently portray the breakdown of a prophet in despair over the conflict both within and around him. And yet, embedded as they are among the oracles of Jeremiah, his Confessions serve to vindicate his message. While Jeremiah resisted the words he knows he must speak – *"But I have not run away from being a shepherd in your service, nor have I desired the fatal day. You know what came from my lips; it was before your face"* (Jer. 17:16) – he was eventually proved to be right, but beyond the horizon of his own life. There is another sense, too, in which Jeremiah's Confessions transcend his own experience. These laments are spoken in Jeremiah's voice, but interpreters have long noted how much the voice of this individual resonates with the voice of God's faithful people. There is a close connection with many Psalms. In bad situations, people cry out honestly to God (see Pss. 4, 6, 12, 13, 22, 35, 38–44, 55, 60, 69, 74, 77, 79, 83, 88, 102, 109, 137, 140–143).

In these heartfelt prayers, the sufferer feels abandoned by God, yet the only course of action open is to cry out to the absent God. The expression of this feeling is essential if prayer and public worship are to approach God with integrity.

---

# PUTTING GOD ON TRIAL

*Other key biblical figures such as Abraham and Job also experienced periods of conflict with God, particularly in relation to suffering and justice.*

Abraham and Job both struggled with God (see pp.38–39, 172–73). When God disclosed to Abraham an intention to destroy Sodom and Gomorrah (Gen. 18:17–19), the Patriarch attempted to save the righteous. He asked for assurance that God would not destroy the citizens of Sodom and Gomorrah if even ten righteous people were to be found within the city walls. While God had confidence in Abraham to *"keep the way of the LORD by doing righteousness and justice"* (Gen. 18:19), it is precisely at this point that Abraham has doubts: *"Far be it from you to do such a thing, to slay the righteous with the wicked … Shall not the Judge of all the earth do what is just?"* (Gen. 18:25). The incident shows how Abraham both trusts in God and questions what he thinks God will do.

Job's oppressive experience of God's presence provoked even further accusations against God. Like Jeremiah, Job rues his own birth (Job 3), and soon blames God for his misery: *"If I sin, what do I do to you, you watcher of humanity? Why have you made me your target?"* (Job 7:20). Job despairs of having his integrity recognized (Job 9:20), for *"he crushes me with a tempest"* (Job 9:17a; cf. Job 38:1), *"and multiplies my wounds without cause"* (Job 9:17b; cf. Job 2:3). Still Job persists in his railing against God, convinced both of his own innocence and of God's injustice (Job 27:5–6). As lament seeks confrontation rather than explanation, Job's questions are never answered. God responds to Job (Job 38–41), and Job realizes that although the mystery of suffering remains, the struggle with God was the right path to take (Job 42:7).

---

For further reading see bibliography numbers: 62, 100, 219, 227, 240, 603, 700, 704, 712, 797

# THE BOOK OF
# LAMENTATIONS

*This collection of five poems is an outpouring of grief at the destruction of Jerusalem.
It does not attempt to explain the disaster or draw lessons from it. Rather, it gives
vent to deep emotion and attempts to restore life and a stable relationship with God.*

AS in other biblical laments, the embittered voices of Lamentations seek confrontation with a God who seems to have turned from friend to foe. Lamentations is a highly crafted piece of poetry that conveys deep and spontaneous emotion. Its five intense poems contain themes of dismay, mourning, betrayal, and outrage intertwined with a pervasive sense of guilt and shame. Sometimes these words are spoken within the hurting community, sometimes they are directed at God, and sometimes they are spoken into the air – undirected and forlorn. For all that, much of the book's language comes from the traditional forms of mourning and liturgy long used in the ancient world. A wide array of reactions answers questions about what happened, what the consequences are, who did it, and what is going to happen next.

**MOURNING WOMEN**
*These clay figures of women grieving – probably used as burial goods – were found at Azor in modern Israel. They date from the seventh century BCE.*

## AUTHORSHIP

All the five poems of Lamentations follow an "alphabetic acrostic" pattern, each stanza beginning with a successive letter of the Hebrew alphabet (the fifth poem retains the 22-verse structure without the acrostic). The Prophet Jeremiah has traditionally been assumed to be the author, and there are language links between this and the book that bears his name. The pre-Christian Greek translation of the book begins with this explicit identification ("And it came to pass after Israel was taken captive, and Jerusalem made desolate, that Jeremias sat weeping and lamented with his lamentation over Jerusalem and said …"). Its notice of Jeremiah "weeping" draws attention to the evocative shared language between the two books (Jer. 9:1; 14:17; cf. Lam. 2:18; 3:48). Recently, recognition of the traditional phrases and composite nature of the work (chs. 3 and 5 standing apart) has led to a consensus that authorship remains anonymous.

## DESTRUCTION

Reflections on the disaster relate first of all to the destruction of the holy city of Jerusalem. The empty isolation of the city is immediately evident; it lies alone, without comforter. In 2:5–9 the poet embarks on a tour of the devastation. While the physical destruction of the holy city never quite fades from view, the focus of the book of Lamentations shifts to the violation of the inhabitants of Jerusalem themselves. Gut-wrenching grief is confused with pangs of hunger, while the famine that the people suffer reaches grotesque proportions. The carnage finally arrives at a grisly climax where the mothers of the city prepare their own children as food (4:4–10). It is sobering, then, to realize that the only agent of destruction that can be directly identified in all of this calamity is God: *"The LORD has become like an enemy; he has destroyed Israel … The LORD has done what he purposed"* (2:5–17).

## A FORSAKEN PEOPLE

Elsewhere the poet rails against enemies, but these seem to be those who have betrayed Israel and gloated over the destruction, rather than the destroyers themselves. Only in the third poem, which is distinct from the others, is hope held out. Triple the length of the other poems, and mostly spoken in an individual male voice, this psalm claims that *"although he causes grief, he will have compassion"* (3:32), a hope expressed nowhere else in the book. One question hangs unasked until the very end but is implied everywhere: *"Why have you forgotten us completely? Why have you forsaken us these many days?"* (5:20). Why has this happened? God has acted on plans made long ago, but this response comes as punishment on a guilty people: *"Jerusalem sinned grievously"* (1:8), but through the disaster *"the punishment of your iniquity, O daughter Zion, is accomplished"* (4:22).

## GRIEF OBSERVED

The book of Lamentations expresses grief seeking God. Its language is not logical, but neither is it inexplicable. Elisabeth Kübler-Ross' book *On Death and Dying* identifies five stages connected with the experiences of both grieving and death. These stages of loss and grieving can be identified in the book of Lamentations. They help explain the outcries of Lamentations.

The five poems share various themes, but each poem also has a distinctive orientation usually expressed in the first line. The first chapter surveys the "lonely city" that is left without comforter (stage one: isolation). In the second, the destruction by an angry God provokes shock from other observers (2:15–16) and an embittered response (2:18–20; stage two: anger). The third poem attempts to provide hope for the destitute and get God back on their side: since *"the LORD is good to those who wait for him,"* then *"let us test and examine our ways, and return to the LORD"* (3:25, 40; stage three: bargaining). The fourth poem sinks back into despair, comparing how good things were with how horrible they have become. It is the only poem in the book that lacks prayer (stage four: depression). Then the book breaks with Ross' pattern (her fifth stage is acceptance). In the fifth chapter, the poet reaches a final crescendo of complaint, urging God to restore the relationship and life itself (5:1, 21). There is not acceptance here, only the desolation of a people abandoned by God.

The destruction of Jerusalem played a significant role in the formation of Jewish consciousness. The importance of the book of Lamentations in this process is seen in the rabbinic commentary *Lamentations Rabbah* – one of the oldest works of its kind. These sad words continue to play a role in the life of the Jewish community, being recited on the fast day of the ninth of the month of Av (*see pp.236–37*), the commemoration of the destruction of Jerusalem by both the Babylonians (587/6BCE) and the Romans (70CE).

## THE BOOK

TITLE: Lamentations

HEBREW TITLE: *'Eykah* ("how", 1:1)

DATE: Exilic period (598/7–38/7BCE).

AUTHORSHIP: While the book itself remains anonymous, it has traditionally been ascribed to the Prophet Jeremiah. In the Hebrew Bible, it does not follow the book of Jeremiah it is one of the Five Scrolls in the Writings

## THE CONTENTS

CHAPTER 1
*"How lonely sits the city ..."* Mourning the desolation of the bereft city

CHAPTER 2
*"How the LORD in his anger ..."* Catalog of destruction and angry response

CHAPTER 3
*"I am the one who has seen affliction ..."* A sufferer turns to God to find respite

CHAPTER 4
*"How the gold has grown dim ..."* Traumatized survey of the reversals brought by destruction

CHAPTER 5
*"Remember O LORD ... Restore us ..."* Final plea for restoration

## KEY THEMES

*The destruction of Jerusalem*

•

*God's rejection of the people*

For further reading see bibliography numbers: 8, 198, 408, 630, 676, 796

# THE BOOK OF
# EZEKIEL

*Ezekiel was one of the exiles taken to Babylonia by Nebuchadnezzar II in 597BCE. There he received his first call to be a prophet. The book contains oracles concerning Jerusalem and the exiles, and provides a vision of the rebuilt Temple.*

THE book of Ezekiel contains the oracles and visions of the Prophet Ezekiel, a younger contemporary of Jeremiah. His prophecy concerns itself with the religion of the exiles, first warning of further disasters for the people of Israel and the city of Jerusalem, then turning to console God's people and to promise an end to their suffering, and finally recording a great vision of the restored Temple after the Exile is over.

## THE PROPHET

The Prophet Ezekiel came from a priestly family, and in sharp contrast to Prophets such as Amos, Micah, and Isaiah, he placed a high value on the Temple and its worship. The holiness of God is the theological center of the book, and Israel's security depends upon God's presence in the Temple. Ezekiel used the ritual language of purity and defilement to describe sin and virtue, and his arguments often adopt the style of priestly case law.

Yet Ezekiel was also a Prophet of the most ecstatic and visionary kind: the book describes in detail the visions of God that punctuated his ministry (*see Visions of Ezekiel, pp.214–15*), the first of which left him greatly affected (*"And I sat there among them, stunned, for seven days,"* 3:15). He performed many symbolic actions (*pp.198–99*), and was afflicted with periods of muteness (3:24–27; 24:25–27; 33:21–22). People were impressed but

**THE PROPHET EZEKIEL**
*This lively representation of the Prophet comes from a Greek monastery.*

resistant to the message. The oracles of Ezekiel are all unified by a heavy stress on the sovereignty and freedom of God, who both punishes and restores, *"then you shall know that I am the LORD"* (6:7, 10, and about 60 additional times elsewhere in the book).

## ORACLES OF DOOM

The Prophet's early oracles focus on sin and punishment (Ezek. 3–24). The sins of Judah and Jerusalem have reached such epic proportions that God has no remedy other than destruction and exile. God's people have shown themselves to be faithless and disobedient in rampant idolatry, which has penetrated God's own Temple: *"Your altars shall become desolate, and your incense-stands shall be broken; and I will throw down your slain in front of your idols. I will lay the corpses of the people of Israel in front of their idols; and I will scatter your bones around your altars"* (6:4–5). They have broken God's Covenant in the alliances that they have made with foreign powers; as a result, lawlessness and violence are rife everywhere.

Ezekiel vehemently rejected the people's plea that they are being punished only for sins committed by their predecessors. Like Jeremiah (*pp.206–7*), he repudiated their glib proverb, *"What do you mean by repeating this* proverb concerning the land of Israel, 'The parents have eaten sour grapes, and the children's teeth are set on edge'? As I live, says the Lord GOD, this proverb shall no more be used by you in Israel" (Ezek. 18:2–3; cf. Jer. 31:29). Ezekiel pulled no punches as he attempted to convince the people that they are indeed a rebellious house that deserves punishment: "I will not refrain, I will not spare, I will not relent. According to your ways and your doings I will judge you, says the Lord GOD" (24:14).

## JERUSALEM, THE UNFAITHFUL WIFE

Perhaps most startling of the language in the book of Ezekiel are the two allegories in chapters 16 and 23 where Jerusalem is portrayed as an adulterous and promiscuous wife: "How sick is your heart, says the Lord GOD, that you did all these things, the deeds of a brazen whore; building your platform at the head of every street, and making your lofty place in every square!" (Ezek. 16:30–31; cf. Hosea). The city's sins and ultimate punishment are described in graphic detail: "... she increased her whorings, remembering the days of her youth, when she played the whore in the land of Egypt and lusted after her paramours there, whose members were like those of donkeys, and whose emission was like that of stallions. Thus you longed for the lewdness of your youth, when the Egyptians fondled your bosom and caressed your young breasts" (Ezek. 23:19–21).

## THE PROMISE OF RESTORATION

A dramatic shift came after Ezekiel learned of the fall of Jerusalem in 587/6BCE (33:25). He turned from judgment to consolation, and promised a return from exile, the rebuilding of national institutions, and renewed prosperity and security for the people (chs.33–48, see also Visions of Ezekiel, pp.214–15). God will give the people strength to obey the commandments where they had so conspicuously failed in the past: "A new heart I will give you, and a new spirit I will put within you; and I will remove from your body the heart of stone and give you a heart of flesh. I will put my spirit within you, and make you follow my statutes and be careful to observe my ordinances. Then you shall live in the land that I gave to your ancestors; and you shall be my people, and I will be your God" (36:26–28).

Given the apparent contradiction between Ezekiel's messages of judgment and restoration, we might ask if Israel does anything to deserve the better treatment it receives. The answer is no. Restoration comes about not through human effort but solely as the result of divine grace. God's prime concern even in restoration is not the people's well-being but God's own holiness: "It is not for your sake, O house of Israel, that I am about to act, but for the sake of my holy name, which you have profaned among the nations to which you came" (36:22). The central focus here, as throughout the book of Ezekiel, is the power and glory of God.

# THE BOOK

TITLE: Ezekiel

HEBREW TITLE: Yehezkel

DATE: An exilic work: the earliest oracle is dated 593BCE, the latest one 571BCE

AUTHORSHIP: Most of the book goes back to the Prophet Ezekiel himself, but his oracles may have been arranged and supplemented by later editors

# THE CONTENTS

CHAPTERS 1–24
Oracles and visions concerning the sins and impending punishment of Jerusalem

CHAPTERS 25–32
Oracles against the nations of Ammon, Moab, Edom, Philistia, Tyre, Sidon, and Egypt

CHAPTERS 33–39
Oracles and visions of comfort and reassurance, mostly about the restoration of Israel

CHAPTERS 40–48
A vision of the restored city and Temple

# KEY THEMES

Sin and its punishment
•
God is not confined to Jerusalem, but reigns everywhere
•
The restoration of the Temple and Jerusalem

For further reading see bibliography numbers: 2, 99, 100, 144, 145, 269, 354, 375, 463, 542, 743

# VISIONS OF EZEKIEL

*A number of the Prophets saw visions, not least in the Temple or by an altar, but the visions of Ezekiel – his visions of God, of Jerusalem, and of the valley of bones – are particularly dramatic and form a bridge to apocalyptic writings.*

THE Prophets had a strong sense of speaking the word of God: many oracles begin: *Koh amar Adonai,* "Thus says the LORD …" This was powerfully reinforced for those who had a vision of God (*see* 1 Kgs. 22–19; Isa. 6:1; Amos 9:1). In the case of Ezekiel, these visions were so rich that later, when prophecy ceased in mainstream Jewish religion, they led the way into Apocalyptic (*pp.260– 61*), which frequently recounts visions as a vehicle for its message. Not surprisingly, Ezekiel was remembered in later Jewish tradition as one *"who saw the vision of glory, which God showed him"* (Sir. 49:8). Even later than that, Ezekiel's visions of the *merkabah,* or chariot, became a focus of meditation, so that the vision was reproduced for the meditator.

## THE VISION OF GOD

Among the best known parts of the book, Ezekiel's visions appear at the beginning of his prophetic ministry and at key points in his proclamation of Israel's future. The book of Ezekiel opens with a divine vision, which he saw while among the exiles in Babylonia (1:1–28). The Prophet describes four bizarre living creatures, each with four faces and four wings, accompanied by gleaming wheels within wheels. Upon a throne above the creatures sat *"something that seemed like a human form,"* whose gleaming brightness was surrounded by splendor like a rainbow's.

Ezekiel's hesitation to state that he has seen God is evident as he writes *"This was the appearance of the likeness of the glory of the LORD"* (1:28). But this is perhaps the closest anyone comes in the Hebrew Bible to offering a description of God.

**THE VALLEY OF DRY BONES**
*"He brought me out by the spirit of the LORD and set me down in the middle of a valley; it was full of bones" (37:1). Drought and famine were a constant threat to Israel.*

> **"**… as the glory of the LORD rose from its place, I heard behind me the sound of loud rumbling; it was the sound of the wings of the living creatures brushing against one another and the sound of the wheels beside them.**"**
>
> (Ezekiel 3:1–3)

## THE VISION OF JERUSALEM

What did it mean for God to appear to Ezekiel in Babylonia? It might have been a positive sign: God could still be present with the exiles even in a foreign land. But it could also threaten the possibility that God had abandoned Jerusalem to destruction, and Ezekiel's initial call is to proclaim *"words of lamentation and mourning and woe"* (2:10). This threatening aspect is evident as God's glory reappears in Ezekiel's first Temple vision (chs.8–11). Here the Prophet is carried into Jerusalem, where he is shown all the abominable practices that pollute the Temple. Instructions are given to six angelic executioners to begin Jerusalem's punishment, starting from the polluted sanctuary. The most ominous sign of all is that the glory of God rises up from its place in the Temple and moves outside the city, leaving the city to its fate.

## THE VALLEY OF BONES

In this, perhaps the best known of Ezekiel's visions, the Prophet is shown a valley full of dry bones. He is commanded to prophesy to them that they will live again, and as he prophesies, he sees the bones join together and become covered with sinews, flesh, and skin. Finally breath comes into them, at which point they live and stand on their feet, "a vast multitude." The vision clearly relies on the account of human nature and its composition in the book of Genesis (*see pp.182–83*). Eventually, Ezekiel's vision became the basis for a belief in life after death: if God can create in the first place, God can surely do so again, especially for the faithful of Israel who may have fallen in battle defending God (as many did during the Maccabean revolt, *pp.250–51*). But in Ezekiel the vision is not a prediction of wholesale resurrection for individuals. It is used to speak of the state of the people of Israel. It is the hopeful answer to the exiles' complaint, *"Our bones are dried up, and our hope is lost; we are cut off completely"* (37:11). God promises the people that they will be created anew in the land of Israel: *"I will put my spirit within you, and you shall live, and I will place you on your own soil"* (37:14).

## THE NEW TEMPLE

In Ezekiel's last and most extended vision (chs.40–48), the catastrophe of the First Temple vision is finally undone. Again he is carried to the land of Israel and shown around the new Temple by a man *"whose appearance shone like bronze, with a linen cord and a measuring reed in his hand"* (40:3). There follows a very detailed physical description for the new Temple and city that God will provide for the people. Ezekiel is shown the return of the divine glory to its place in the Temple, *"the glory of the God of Israel was coming from the east; the sound was like the sound of mighty waters; and the earth shone with his glory"* (43:2). He hears a voice say: *"... this is the place of my throne and the place for the soles of my feet, where I will reside among the people of Israel forever"* (43:7).

God's permanent presence is secured by new regulations for sacrifice and worship, and the land is redistributed among the tribes of Israel. Institutions that have failed God and the people before are reduced in significance. There is no king as God's anointed one, or Messiah; the king is virtually reduced to a temple official as *nasi*. The new Temple lies at the geographical and theological center of the new Israel, and a great

> **❝** As for you, mortal, describe the temple to the house of Israel, and let them measure the pattern; and let them be ashamed of their iniquities ... make known to them the plan of the temple. **❞**
>
> (Ezekiel 43:10–11)

river flows out from it to the Dead Sea to make the desert of Judah fertile and prosperous: *"This water flows toward the eastern region ... and when it enters the sea, the sea of stagnant waters, the water will become fresh ... and everything will live where the river goes"* (47:8–9). The final verse of the book well expresses Ezekiel's theology of the divine presence as the city is renamed: *"And the name of the city from that time on shall be, The LORD is There"* (48:35).

## FURTHER USES OF THE VISIONS

The extraordinary description given by the Prophet Ezekiel in his vision of the New Temple (Ezek. 40–48), with its scrupulous dimensions and attention to detail, makes a reconstruction of the building itself quite easy. In the first millennium CE, the Prophet's vision of God became the basis for the *merkabah*, or chariot, form of Jewish mysticism (for possible connections with Paul, *see p.391*). Mystics who follow this form of belief are known as the *yoredey merkabah*, or "Riders of the Chariot." According to this belief, by following various ascetic practices the soul of the believer can ascend to a heavenly realm; looking within his heart, the believer will eventually be able to gaze at the heavenly chariot and the seven halls of the angels. The belief continued in the form of mysticism known as the Kabbalah.

Floor plan of sanctuary

Sanctuary

Temple

Altar

Gateway

Outbuildings

Pavement

Eastern gate

Outer court

**EZEKIEL'S TEMPLE**
*The temple of Ezekiel's vision is not dissimilar from the Temple of Solomon (see pp.132–33). The Temple building, with its outer sanctuary and inner Holy of Holies, was surrounded by an outer court. To either side of the sanctuary were priests' quarters. Around the outer court were various buildings; kitchens stood in each of the four corners, and the whole complex was surrounded by an outer wall. The entrance to the Temple faced east, and it was at the east gate that Ezekiel saw his vision of God.*

For further reading see bibliography numbers: 99, 144, 354, 463, 501, 664, 696

# THE BOOK OF
# DANIEL

*The book of Daniel contains lively stories and far-reaching visions. Set in the sixth century BCE, it deals with the challenges and problems in the second century BCE.*

DANIEL is an unusual book on many counts. It divides into two parts, narratives and visions, but it is also divided in terms of the language in which it is composed. It opens in Hebrew (1–2:4a), continues in Aramaic (possibly the original language of the entire book) to the end of chapter 7, and from here reverts to Hebrew until the end. Descriptions of the visions of future events and the end of days put it into the category of Apocalyptic (Greek, meaning "revelation"; *see pp.260–61*); it is the most developed example of this in the Hebrew Bible. Questions about the nature of the book have influenced its location in different versions of the Bible. In the Hebrew Bible it is in the Writings, possibly because of the different material in it, or because it was composed later than the Prophets. However, in the Greek translation of the Bible, and thus in Christian Bibles, it is located among the Prophetic books.

DANIEL IN THE LIONS' DEN
*"My God sent his angel and shut the lions' mouths so that they would not hurt me, because I was found blameless before him; and also before you, O king, I have done no wrong" (Dan. 6:22).*

to be a court name for Cyrus). The vision of the sequence of four kingdoms was a common Near Eastern concept relating to Babylon, Media, Persia, and Greece. Daniel 11 appears to describe in great detail the wars between the Seleucids and the Ptolemies. Thus, many assume that the book was composed at the time of the persecution of the Jews by Antiochus IV Epiphanes (168–64BCE). Others regard the book as a visionary foretelling. Either way, it shows faithful Jews, loyal to their God, surviving in an alien environment with the promise of a triumphant and peaceful future.

## THE INFLUENCE OF DANIEL

The combination of precise descriptions of times and events to come, of the rise and fall of kingdoms, and of the certainty of God's hand in events, together with an imagery that is open to many interpretations, have made this book one of the most studied and influential in the Bible. Daniel's influence can be seen in the Gospels, the Letters of Paul, and the Apocalypse of John. The phrase "the son of man" (*see* Dan. 7:13; *cf.* 9:22) was used by Jesus of himself, and since he said *"the* Son of Man" (i.e., the one you know about), Jesus was drawing on Daniel and other biblical passages to convey his own understanding of his own work and person (*see p.348*). The rule of God promised by Daniel was then seen as being fulfilled in the coming of Jesus. The book lends itself to religious polemic, with Daniel's image of the terrible fourth

## THE HISTORICAL PROBLEM

The dates given in the book cover the period of the Babylonian Exile – opening with the arrival of Nebuchadnezzar II in Syria–Palestine and ending with the third year of King Cyrus, just after the first exiles had returned to Judah. The name Danel ("Daniel" in some translations) occurs twice in the book of Ezekiel (Ezek. 14:14; 28:3), but this may be a different person. Reference is made to Darius the Mede – who is not otherwise known – conquering Babylon (some assume Darius

beast (Dan. 7:19–27), the last evil kingdom, representing opponents. There have been interpretations of this beast as varied as the "Wicked Priest" of the Qumran community to Luther's attacks on the papacy. While Jewish commentary in the Middle Ages was cautious about identifying the exact timing of "the end," the book had a great influence on millennarian movements in Christian Europe, and has been the source of visions of the end that have influenced individuals and movements until today. The fact that all the proclaimed "end of days" have come and gone without effect has not deterred people in the past or present from using the book to prove that the "end" is imminent.

The major purpose of Daniel was to offer hope and encouragement to Jews being persecuted, particularly under Antiochus Epiphanes. It does not support armed resistance, as of the Maccabees (pp.250–51), but rather advocates acceptance and trust, even if it means martyrdom. Daniel is the most explicit of all the books in the Hebrew Bible in affirming resurrection.

## LATER INTERPRETATIONS

Two episodes from the book of Daniel have had a major impact on the popular imagination: the refusal of Daniel's companions to bow to an idol and their subsequent survival in the "fiery furnace" (3:19–30), and Daniel's survival in the "lions' den" (ch.6). A rabbinic comment links these two "supernatural" events along with the fish that swallowed the Prophet Jonah and Balaam's talking donkey (Num. 22:22–40) as being created in the twilight period between the end of the sixth day of Creation and the onset of the first Sabbath day: even the unlikeliest events do not take God by surprise. Daniel was punished because he continued to pray to God three times a day (ch.6). Early illustrations of this in Jewish and Christian sources show Daniel, often flanked by the lions, with his arms extended in prayer. He was seen as someone so devoted to prayer that he was willing to risk martyrdom.

## BELSHAZZAR'S FEAST

In Daniel 5, Belshazzar holds a great feast and in his arrogance has the gold and silver vessels of the Jerusalem Temple, captured by his father, Nebuchadnezzar, brought in and used for the banquet. At once the fingers of a hand appear and write on the wall the words *Mene mene tekel upharshin*, which Daniel interprets to mean *"your days are measured* [mene]*, you have been weighed* [tekel] *(and found wanting), and your kingdom will be given over to the Medes and the Persians* [pharshin]*."* This event inspired writings by Chaucer, Claderon, Goethe, Lord Byron, and Heine, whose poem was set to music by Schumann. The words of this proverbial "writing on the wall" are often quoted in political struggles against authoritarian regimes.

# THE BOOK

**TITLE:** Daniel

**HEBREW TITLE:** *dani'el*, which may mean "my God is judge" or "judge of God"

**DATE:** Though the book is set in the sixth century BCE in the period of the Babylonian Exile, many now believe that it was written in the second century BCE

**AUTHORSHIP:** Not stated in the book, but from Daniel's being told (12:4) to seal up the book, he has traditionally been identified as its author

# THE CONTENTS

### CHAPTERS 1–6: NARRATIVES

1:1–21 Four young exiles show wisdom and piety in the Babylonian court. 2:1–49 God reveals Nebuchadnezzar's dream of the four kingdoms to Daniel. 3:1–30 Daniel's three companions refuse to bow to Nebuchadnezzar's idol and survive the fiery furnace. 4:1–37 Nebuchadnezzar's dream and madness interpreted by Daniel. 5:1–30 Belshazzar is judged by God and is slain. 6:1–28 Darius the Mede sees Daniel survive in the lions' den

### CHAPTERS 7–12: VISIONS

7:1–28 Daniel's vision of the four kingdoms and God's kingdom. 8:1–27 Gabriel explains Daniel's vision of the fall of the Greek empire. 9:1–27 Daniel's prayer for the end of exile and the vision of the 70 "weeks." 10:1–12:13 A heavenly messenger reveals what will happen to Daniel's people at the end of time

For the additions to Daniel, *see pp.254–55*

# KEY THEMES

*Maintaining faith under persecution*

•

*Knowledge and power lie with God alone*

•

*Stories of Daniel*

**For further reading see bibliography numbers: 201, 332, 375, 394, 474**

# THE BOOK OF
# HOSEA

*Hosea has much to say about unfaithfulness, using adultery
as the basic example. While this will be punished, Hosea
speaks also of God's enduring love and faithfulness.*

THE book of Hosea is the longest of the so-called Minor Prophets and is vivid in the emotional intensity of its prophecies. Hosea rebukes Israel for its infidelity to the Covenant with God: the tragedy of its situation is mirrored in the provocative parallel of Hosea's relationship to his unfaithful wife, Gomer. It was a situation that God could not leave unchecked. Yet in spite of God's inevitable judgment, the people of Israel are still loved (3:4–5), and God longs for them to return, just as Gomer returned to Hosea.

## HISTORICAL BACKGROUND

The Northern Kingdom had enjoyed a period of great stability and peace under King Jeroboam II. However, when he died in about 750BCE, there followed a series of coups and six kings in quick succession, causing and reflecting deep political unrest and national vulnerability. The kingdom was easy prey for the emerging empires to the east – Assyria was gaining in power under the ambitious Tiglath-Pileser III (c.745–27BCE). Israel alternated between submission and rebellion but could never escape its powerful neighbor. Assyria eventually destroyed Samaria and carried its people off into exile in about 722BCE (2 Kgs. 17, especially vv.3–6). According to Hosea, this disaster was a consequence of the people's rejection of God. There is evidence to suggest that the Prophet himself came from the Northern Kingdom. Much of Hosea's message about faithfulness and infidelity is

concentrated in the account of his marriage to Gomer, a prostitute, which Hosea presents as the result of a command by God. How could God issue such a command, even as a prophetic action (*see pp.198–99*)? Some take it as an allegory (noting the names of the children, *see p.198*), but it reads like an account of an event. Perhaps Gomer was a sanctuary (cultic) prostitute, involved in fertility rites for the Phoenician god Baal. In that case, her marriage is redemptive (ch.3), for Israel could also be redeemed from Baal worship. According to Leviticus (21:7, 14), only priests were forbidden to marry prostitutes.

HOSEA PREACHING
*This 14th-century illustration from a French manuscript depicts the Prophet Hosea preaching.*

## ISRAEL'S DIVORCE FROM YHWH

A marriage breakdown was a stark illustration for what had gone wrong in Israel – it powerfully conveys God's pain at being rejected by the people of Israel: *"For a spirit of whoredom has led them astray, and they have played the whore, forsaking their God"* (4:12). Their alliances with pagan nations demonstrated this (7:11), as did their pagan practices: sacrifices that God had forbidden (4:13) and idolatry (10:4–5). The leaders (the priests, king, and Prophets) did nothing to prevent this decline, for they were deeply embroiled in it (5:1; 7:3; 4:5). The covenant blessings of the good life in the land, which had been promised in Deuteronomy, are now abused and contaminated. In effect, a generation had grown up not knowing their God (4:4; 8:14).

## JUDGMENT AND HOPE

God had to judge this, and punishment would follow. Hosea holds nothing back in his description of what it will be like (e.g., 12–13:14); the seriousness of the situation called for the strongest language possible. The Blessings of Deuteronomy will give way to the Curses (4:10–11a; cf. Deut. 28:17–18; 32:24–28). The people of Israel had adopted the pagan lifestyle of their Canaanite neighbors, worshiping the local gods to ensure the fertility of crops and financial prosperity. Hosea directed his invective most especially at the rulers, priests, and merchants, who he felt had led this corruption. They would become the captives of the pagan nations they had tried to placate, and it would be like their former slavery in Egypt (11:5).

In spite of Israel's betrayal, the book also gives a moving portrayal of God's love for Israel. Hosea gives a remarkable insight into God's inner turmoil over what to do: *"How can I give you up, Ephraim? How can I hand you over, O Israel? How can I make you like Adhmah? How can I treat you like Zeboiim? My heart recoils within me; my compassion grows warm and tender"* (11:8). The imagery of God as a caring and devoted parent torn between anger and love is strong. After the Exile, there will be a time when the people will return – and a second Exodus will take place (2:14–15). Hosea was clearly no mere herald of God's judgment; he was deeply concerned for God's love for the people of Israel, bound together as they were, with the divine name YHWH as pledge and token of God's love (12:9).

## THREAT AND PROMISE

Some scholars have argued that promises of hope are incongruous in a book containing severe notes of judgment. They find that the book is dated (inaccurately) by a list of kings of *Judah* (although Hosea is a Prophet to *Israel* in the north,) and that some of the promises of hope are addressed to Judah (but so are some of the condemnations). The scholars suggest that the book was edited, and that promises of hope for Judah were added when the book was included among the Prophets in the south. But there is no reason why threat and promise cannot be found in the same Prophet. In fact, the two occur together in many of the Prophetic books. The truth is that, in the context of the Covenant, threat and promise belong inevitably and necessarily together, because the Covenant contains promises of reward if its conditions are kept, and punishment if they are not. In the book of Hosea in particular, the blessings and curses of the Covenant, especially as formulated in Deuteronomy, form the background to the message. The Prophet explicitly mentions the Exodus and interprets its message for his own time (ch.11). There is also direct reference to God's Covenant with Israel (ch.13). Thus Hosea is seen dealing directly with the concerns of the Pentateuch.

## THE BOOK

**TITLE:** Hosea

**HEBREW TITLE:** *Hosea'* meaning "help" or "salvation," perhaps shortened from *Yehoshua'*, "YHWH is salvation"

**DATE:** Written between 750BCE and 720BCE (culminating in the fall of Israel to Assyria)

**AUTHORSHIP:** A prophet of the Northern Kingdom of Israel. Very little is known apart from his date and his troubled marriage to Gomer, supposing that that was an actual event, rather than an allegory. Parts of the book may have been added later by editors in the Southern Kingdom

## THE CONTENTS

**CHAPTERS 1–2**
Superscription. Hosea's marriage. Israel's adultery and idolatry. God's promise of mercy

**CHAPTERS 3–5**
Hosea is reconciled with Gomer. The sins of Israel. Judgment on Israel and Judah

**CHAPTERS 6–10**
Israel's lack of trust. Israel's rebellion. False worship and idolatry. Punishment in exile threatened

**CHAPTERS 11–14**
God's love for Israel endures. Both Israel and Judah have failed God. God's anger. Repentance will lead to forgiveness

## KEY THEMES

*Hosea's marriage as a sign of God's relationship with Israel*

•

*The love and compassion of God for Israel*

•

*The consequences of unfaithfulness and of repentance*

For further reading see bibliography numbers: 17, 131, 147, 226, 228, 229a, 271, 341, 701, 739

# GOD'S ACTIONS IN THE WORLD

*An "act of God" has come to mean something so unlikely or unpredictable that no one really could have expected it. But in the Bible, acts of God are real and predictable, and make a great difference, not just to Israel but to the whole world.*

BASIC to the Bible is a belief that God is active in the world: God is the creator and sustainer of the world, and a general guidance of the world (known later as "providence") is combined with specific actions and self-disclosures to particular people in particular times and particular places. This has become problematic in modern times, when it has regularly been supposed that such belief can be meaningful only if God can be identified and analyzed as a cause of events like other agents (physical, biological, chemical, economic, political, etc.). Since this cannot be done, God has disappeared from scientific and social-scientific discourse, and belief in God's activity has, generally, been relegated to the realm of private fancy. Yet in terms of classic theology it is a mistake ("idolatry") to treat anything in Creation as though it alone were the creator, and the discernment of God's action is always a moral and spiritual task.

## THE CAUSES OF AN EVENT

In recent years, the understanding of the very difficult notion of "cause" has been much developed. It is now recognized that all events are brought into being by an immense network or coalition of causes, and that we talk about only the most immediate, or proximate, causes in the case of any event – we do not have enough time to do otherwise. Drop a piece of paper to the floor: what caused it to fall? We might say, "You caused it to fall: you picked it up and let it drop." But there are many more causes than

**VICTIMS OF VIOLENCE**
*Human disasters often lead people to question how a just God can let this happen. The Bible reveals that God's purposes and ways of acting embrace and redeem disasters.*

that which is immediately apparent, like gravity and the laws of motion. In a sense, gravity caused the paper to fall. But usually we do not have time to mention all the causes of the event, and people would think us very strange if we did. This means that generally we specify only the causes of an event that happen to interest us.

## THE CAUSE OF ALL THINGS

God *as creator* is the cause of all causes, the reason why things exist at all, and why things happen with any regularity: fires burn and paper falls with any regularity in appropriate circumstances. We do not need to specify God among the causes of particular events, because it adds no further relevant information. But because God is the "cause of all causes," it means that God can come into particular events as a more focused cause, in response, for example, to prayer or to faith.

While science or poetry or art do not need to specify God as involved in the network or coalition of causes, sometimes they must: truth demands it. To rely on scientific positivism to give the whole truth may be foolish. Science yields truth but not the whole truth about us or about the world.

At first, the Bible may seem strange by going to the opposite extreme and by specifying God as the cause, while ignoring other causes that are of interest to us now. But that is because, in biblical times and in the Bible itself, God was the main interest. Actions of many different kinds are attributed to God, and these are often expressed in direct and pictorial terms, as though God is a superperson who dashes in and out of the world, smiting enemies and causing amazing – even impossible – things to happen. It is essential, when reading the Bible – or any ancient text – not to confuse the elementary and pictorial language that is used with what it is trying to explain or narrate. The reader must always ask, "What made them speak or write in this way?" The issue raised by God's actions in the Bible is never whether God could have really made the sun stop or an axhead float. The issue is *why* these people thought of God as one who might act in these ways and *what* they are trying to say. They may be describing things as they happened, or they may be using popular stories, but what matters is what they are saying through these narratives: God as cause is one who never abandons the world or the people in it who are being led to a new life.

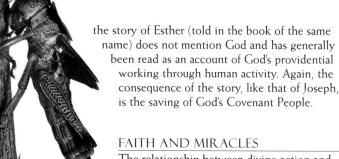

**LOCUST**
*The Bible often interprets the destruction wrought by plagues of locusts as God's punishment.*

the story of Esther (told in the book of the same name) does not mention God and has generally been read as an account of God's providential working through human activity. Again, the consequence of the story, like that of Joseph, is the saving of God's Covenant People.

## FAITH AND MIRACLES

The relationship between divine action and human ability to perceive this action is a recurrent theme in the Hebrew Bible. An example is the story in 2 Kings 2:1–18. Elisha asks to be Elijah's authentic successor as prophet (2:9; the "double portion" marks the inheritance of a first-born son, Deut. 21:17). Elijah sets as a condition for this that Elisha must be able to see Elijah being taken from him (2:10) – a true prophet must be someone who can discern God's actions. When God subsequently takes Elijah, Elisha sees it (2:11–12) – unlike the sons of the prophets at Jericho, who note that Elijah has gone but think they should send out search parties for him (2:15–18).

There is a regular tension between "miracle" and "faith." In the Bible, divine action can sometimes create an appropriate human response – perhaps most famously in the contest on Mount Carmel between Elijah and the prophets of Baal (1 Kgs. 18), although here the impact on the people is short lived. Similarly, the most dense sequence of "miracles," in the plagues on Egypt and the crossing of the Red, or Reed, Sea (Exod. 7–15), prefaces stories of Israel's grumbling and disobedience (Exod. 16–17); seeing is not believing. What is important for the Hebrew Bible is not the occasional intrusion of supernatural events into daily life, but the regular acknowledgment of God's engagement with, and concern for, the world. This is summarized in the call to Israel to act as witnesses (*edim*) to God's actions in the world (Isa. 43:10; 44:8).

## GOD WORKING THROUGH OTHERS

Unusual or spectacular actions of God – what we commonly speak of as "miracles" – do not occur evenly throughout the Bible but cluster around particular figures, such as Moses, Elijah, Elisha, and eventually Jesus. These "miracles" occur in contexts where the response to God – for whom these people speak and act – is acutely problematic. More common than "miracles" is a sense of God working in and through familiar, everyday actions. On one level, the story of Joseph in Egypt (Gen. 37–45; see pp.44–45) is a story of resentment, malice, and deception on the part of Joseph's brothers, and of vanity, suffering, endurance, and success on Joseph's part; yet it is also depicted as part of God's providential guidance and preservation of the people (Gen. 45:4–8; 50:20). Likewise,

# PLAGUES AND PESTILENCES

*Among the "acts of God" are plagues and pestilences that are sent by God for various different reasons and appear in different contexts.*

In the Bible, plagues and pestilences are sent by God to serve the divine purposes, often that of judgment. In Joel 1–2 the plague of locusts may be literal, or it may be a metaphor for an invading army, but in either case it is linked to the Day of the LORD (p.241) and to judgment. Best known are the plagues sent against the Egyptians (see pp.48–49). In Exodus 7:3 and 13, the ten plagues are called signs and wonders, and much later they were understood by Paul to have served God's purpose that God's *"name might be declared throughout all the earth"* (Rom. 9:17). The plagues are celebrated in two Psalms (78 and 105), but not all ten are mentioned. Pestilence was equally understood to be sent by God in Exodus 9:15, Jeremiah

15:2, Habakkuk 3:5, and Amos 4:10. It was sent as a punishment for unbelief (Num. 14:12) and for failure to keep the terms of the Covenant (Deut. 24:24; 28:21), but also to evoke to repentance (*"I sent among you a pestilence after the manner of Egypt; I killed your young men with the sword; I carried away your horses; and I made the stench of your camp go up into your nostrils; yet you did not return to me, says the LORD,"* Amos 4:10). The pestilence might be sent by means of a destroying angel (2 Sam. 24:16; 1 Chr. 21:15). This scourge might be averted by prayer (see 1 Kgs. 8:37, Solomon's prayer), but fasting and sacrifice alone were insufficient to avert it if they were not accompanied by repentance.

**For further reading see bibliography numbers:** 7, 117a, 283, 306a, 660

# THE BOOK OF
# AMOS

*Amos was a businessman and farmer who was called to be a prophet.
He spoke out strongly for justice and against the religious officials of
his day, for which he was expelled from the royal sanctuary at Bethel.*

AT the heart of Amos' message lies an impassioned plea for social justice: *"Let justice roll down like waters, and righteousness like an ever-flowing stream"* (5:24; see also 5:7; 6:12). Here, people have forgotten the most basic demand of their law: respect for their neighbors. Amos repeatedly refers to ways in which the people have failed the Law, referring to a collection called the Covenant Code (Exod. 20:22–23:33). They abuse the poor (Amos 5:11; *cf.* Exod. 22:25); take advantage of those in debt (Amos 2:8; *cf.* Exod. 22:26–27); pervert the course of justice (Amos 5:10, 12; *cf.* Exod. 23:6–8); and deal deceitfully, even on the Sabbath (Amos 8:4–6; *cf.* Exod. 23:12). In addition to specific legal offenses, they have lost all sense of right and wrong: they applaud the forthcoming judgment on their enemies because of their appalling war crimes (1:3–2:5), but they are guilty of inflicting even greater atrocities on their own people (2:6–16). Worst of all, their sin has religious roots: believing their prosperity to be a sign of God's pleasure, they think they can placate God with sacrifices without seeing any integral relationship between justice and worship. Self-destruction is inevitable: thus Amos uses shock tactics to shake the people from their complacency.

**THE PROPHET AMOS**
*Amos' work as a farmer led him to employ many agricultural images.*

## IS THERE ANY HOPE IN AMOS?

Initially, Amos may have held out hope for some repentance: at the heart of the book, chapter 7 describes two visions where Amos intercedes but with little effect. The second pair of visions in chapters 7 and 8 could not be more clear: *"The end has come upon my people Israel; I will never again pass them by"* (8:2). Such a message sounded like treason, for Amos held

King Jeroboam as accountable as any (7:1–17). Once God's Prophet had been expelled from the Northern Kingdom, the people were left to their own fate. So in this sense the people bring the judgment upon themselves, and there is no hope for them. Yet the book ends with oracles of hope. This is probably the usual combination of threat and promise (*see p.219*), but it may also be that, after the defeat of Judah by the Babylonians in 587/6BCE, Amos explained why the disaster had happened. But in the disaster, words of hope (*cf.* Second Isaiah, pp.202–3) could be added: the Day of the LORD regains its redemptive meaning, for Amos 9:11, 12, 13–15 speaks of the Monarchy being restored, enemies being defeated, and the people repossessing the land. So while the message of the Prophet Amos moves from hope to judgment, the overall schema of the book moves from judgment to hope.

## RHETORICAL FORMS

Amos used many different ways of speaking (rhetorical devices), turning forms that had affirmed Israel as God's people into a message of judgment. Thus such liturgical forms as calls to worship (4:4–5; 5:4–5), the blessing after sacrifice (5:21–24), and hymns to God as Creator (4:13; 5:8–9; 9:5–6) are all used instead to show God's displeasure with the people. Or again, wisdom teaching, such as rhetorical questions drawing out inferences about right behavior (3:3–6, 8; 5:25; 6:12; 9:7–8), are turned into accusations against the people. He was the first of the biblical Prophets to take the popular Day of the LORD (p.241), when people believed God would give them great harvests and victory over their enemies, and view it as *"darkness, not light"* (5:18). Amos described it as a series of natural disasters (4:6–13) and as Israel's defeat by an enemy nation (probably Assyria, 3:9–11; 6:11–14). Another example is the tradition of the Exodus (*pp.48–49*): in Amos it is a sign, not of liberation but of judgment: *"You only have I known of all the families of the earth; therefore I will punish you for all your iniquities"* (3:2; see also 2:9ff.; 5:25; 7:8; 8:2; 9:7).

## WHAT IS THE SIGNIFICANCE OF AMOS?

Amos' significance might be neatly summarized in the fact that he was the first Prophet whose oracles were compiled as a book. But his importance is more complex than this. Over the last two centuries, Amos has been interpreted in at least four different ways. At the beginning of the 19th century, commentators saw the Prophet as a great spiritual innovator, with a unique experience of God, preaching for conversion. Toward the end of the same century, Amos' teaching, as much as his experience, was emphasized: he initiated the reasonable and coherent case for "ethical monotheism" – the worship of one God, accompanied by a strict moral code of behavior. For the first half of the 20th century, Amos was primarily understood as a great ritualist. He was a cultic prophet, seeking to reform the worship at the sanctuaries by attempting to reform the people who corrupted them. More recently, Amos has been seen more as a social reformer than a liturgical one; he is portrayed as a political radical, reminding the people of the social implications of their ancient traditions. An isolated figure who spoke out against society only to reform it, he opposed all the bastions of power – the king, the institutions, the leaders – in support of the oppressed and the poor.

## AMOS AS A PROPHET

In 7:10–15, Amaziah, the priest in the royal sanctuary, tries to expel Amos for prophesying against the king, and because, as a Southerner, he has no place as a prophet in the sanctuary. The verb "to be" is understood in Hebrew, so Amos replies, "I not a prophet and I not a son of a prophet." We can add the verb "to be" in two different ways; to mean "I *am* not a prophet or a son of a prophet" ("son of a prophet" means "member of a prophetic guild"), or "I *will* not *be* a prophet …"; in that case, Amos is stating strongly that he is not a prophet of a cultic kind (v.14). It could mean "I *was* not a prophet … [but I am now]." However, biblical Hebrew has no punctuation, so it may be a question: "I not a prophet? I not the son of a prophet? … [I most certainly am, because God called me directly]." In other words, what looks like a strong negative in translation may be a question turning the sentence into a strong affirmative (cf. Jer. 4:27b).

## THE BOOK

**TITLE:** Amos, referring to the eighth-century Prophet who, according to 1:1, worked as a shepherd in Tekoa in the Southern Kingdom, yet was called to prophesy in the Northern Kingdom

**DATE:** 1:1 sets Amos in the reigns of Uzziah, king of Judah (783–42BCE), and Jeroboam II, king of Israel (786–46BCE). The later oracles refer to a time of peace, prosperity, and national expansion; this, together with the biblical and archaeological evidence for the earthquake referred to in 1:1, would suggest the latter part of Jeroboam's reign, between 760 and 750BCE. Other biblical material on this period is found in 2 Kings 14–15

**AUTHORSHIP:** Amos, whose oracles have been redacted for the final form of the book

## THE CONTENTS

**CHAPTERS 1–2: ORACLES AGAINST THE NATIONS**
1:1–2 Title and announcement of judgment
1:3–2:5 Oracles against Damascus, Philistia, Tyre, Edom, Ammon, Moab, and Judah
2:6–16 Oracle also against Israel

**CHAPTERS 3–6: JUDGMENT AGAINST ISRAEL**
3:1–15 Israel as God's Covenant People
4:1–13 Israel fails to repent

5:1–17 Injustice in Israel
5:18–6:14 The Day of the LORD and the certainty of judgment

**CHAPTERS 7–9**
7:1–9 Three visions
7:10–17 Judgment against Amaziah
8:1–3 Vision of ripe fruit
8:4–10 Condemnation and punishment
9:1–6 Vision of God beside the altar
9:7–15 Promises to a righteous remnant of restoration and prosperity

## KEY THEMES

*God's concern with social justice*

•

*God as judge of all nations*

•

*Visions revealing God's purpose*

For further reading see bibliography numbers: 16, 62, 208, 245a, 378, 446, 466, 533, 716, 827

# ETHICS AND BEHAVIOR IN THE PROPHETS

*"He has told you, O mortal, what is good; and what does the LORD require of you but to do justice, and to love kindness, and to walk humbly with your God?" (Mic. 6:8). What God requires is clear from the prophetic message: each individual has obligations to both God and community.*

PROPHETS attached to the cult (to shrines or to the Temple, *see p.196*) gave oracles of advice or warning to individuals or to the ruler. The Prophets whose oracles are now in the biblical books of the Prophets had connections with that background, but increasingly their truth as prophets came to depend on the content of the message, not on the crude test of whether their prophecies had come true. They spoke words that they often said had come directly from God: Isaiah related not only the vision that he saw, but also the word that he saw (Isa. 1:1; 2:1), the word that God spoke to him (Isa. 8:1, 5, 11). They spoke in the name of God, saying "Thus says the LORD."

> ❝The LORD does nothing without revealing his secret to his servants the prophets. The lion has roared; who will not fear? The LORD has spoken, who can but prophesy?❞
>
> (Amos 3:7–8)

## THE FATE OF THE NATION

Increasingly, that word was addressed, not just to individuals or to kings, but to the whole people. Prophets were set as watchmen on the lookout for God's word (Ezek. 3:17; Hab. 2:1). Prophets such as Nathan, Ahijah, and Elijah, whose stories are told in the Historical books of the Bible, confronted individual kings whose evil ways did indeed pose a threat, endangering the whole nation. But in the Prophetic books, it is far more often the nation itself that is confronted; it is the evil ways of the whole people that threaten to bring punishment.

**PROTEST AGAINST OPPRESSION**
*The Prophets demand that more vulnerable and powerless members of society be protected and treated fairly. Justice should prevail, even in difficult situations.*

## THE PROPHETS AND TRADITION

Not unlike the book of Deuteronomy and the Deuteronomistic understanding of history (*pp.80–81, 105*), the Prophets saw the future depending on ethical choices to be made in the present – "justice," "righteousness," and "holiness" are linked together (see Isa. 5:16; cf. Amos 5:24). It seems natural that, in the context of the Covenant, keeping its terms will lead to reward, and disobedience to punishment. Yet the Prophets barely ever mentioned the Covenant, nor did they make an appeal to the past traditions of Israel in order to demonstrate God's purpose and character. Far from reminding people of the laws, the Prophets usually spoke in more general terms and often set themselves against reliance on the sacrifices so important in Torah (*pp.66–67*).

## PROPHETS AND TORAH

Some biblical scholars used to contrast the legalistic religion of Torah with the ethical religion of the Prophets. This is a disastrous misreading of the Bible. Torah includes much more than law, and the Prophets do appeal to the tradition of Israel's history, usually in ways that assume the people know the context. Thus Hosea 12:2–6 can be understood only by those who know the original story; in Micah 6:3–5, the historical recital breaks off mid-sentence as though the people know the story well enough; and Jeremiah 4:23–28 is an exegesis of Genesis 1:1–2.

## COVENANT LAW REQUIREMENTS

The more important truth is that while the Prophets are aware of the Covenant (e.g., Hos. 6:7; 8:1; Jer. 31:31–4; 33:19–23), they deal with the actual behaviors before them, not in theoretical conditions. For that reason, the Prophets preferred to set the demands and judgments of God in the context of a court of law (see p.235), where God brings a charge against the people: *"Hear the word of the LORD, O house of Jacob, and all the families of the house of Israel"* (Jer. 2:4); *"Hear what the LORD says: Rise, plead your case before the mountains, and let the hills hear your voice"* (Mic. 6:1–8; cf. Isa. 1:1–2). The Prophets, therefore, insist on exactly the kind of behavior that is demanded in the Covenant. They are often relying on specific laws in the Covenant as the basis of the charge (see pp.224–25). Zechariah 7:8–10 provides an excellent summary of the covenant law requirements.

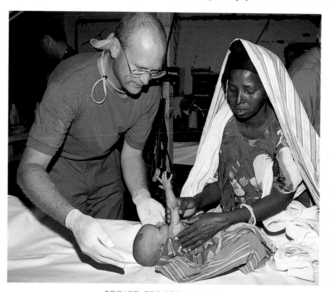

**REGARD FOR HUMANKIND**
*The Prophets believed the bonds of society could be maintained through consideration for God and for fellow humans. Here, an army doctor treats patients in a Somalian village.*

## RELATIONSHIPS AND THE PROPHETS

Both Prophets and the Covenant address the breakdowns in relationship between humans and God (the "vertical" plane) and between humans and humans (the "horizontal" plane). A rupture in the horizontal plane affects the vertical plane, and vice versa. This is the central point of covenant regulations, from the release of slaves to the proper assessment of damages, and from the correct treatment of widows, orphans, and strangers to making sure that weights and measures are true. Ethics cannot, in the Hebrew Bible, be distinguished from their context in the Covenant. The essence of prophetic and covenantal ethics is to maintain the bonds of society through a proper regard for God and for fellow humans.

This dynamic is seen as clearly in the denunciations of the worship of false gods in Torah as it is in the Prophets' denunciation of worship fouled by unacceptable behavior: *"I hate, I despise your festivals ... Take away from me the noise of your songs ... But let justice roll down like waters"* (Amos 5:21–24).

> **❝ *Render true judgments, show kindness and mercy to one another ... do not devise evil in your hearts against one another.* ❞**
>
> (Zechariah 7:9–10)

These words echo through the Prophets (Isa. 1:12–17; cf. Hos. 6:6; Mic. 6:6–8) so much so that at least two Prophets question whether God commanded this kind of worship in the wilderness at all: *"Did you bring to me sacrifices and offerings the forty years in the wilderness, O house of Israel?"* (Amos 5:25). But that may simply refer to the elaboration of sacrificial practices, in which case Amos is disapproving of outside influences on traditional ceremonies. Even the late prophetic text on fasting (Isa. 58) leaves the impression that God responds to acts of kindness rather than to prescribed religious observance (Isa. 58:6–9).

## RIGHTEOUS BEHAVIOR

The demand for "justice" or "righteous" behavior is vague. Some oracles in the Prophets identify precisely forms of abuse and their remedies – these are known as the "woe" oracles (Isa. 10:1–4; 5:8–23; cf. Hab. 2:6–20). By far the most common indictment involves abuse of power through the accumulation of wealth. The more power one holds, the greater the opportunity for abuse. Thus Jeremiah railed against the kings of Judah who thought their greatness lay in the wealth they could gain at the expense of their subjects, rather than in their care of the poor and needy: *"But your eyes and heart are only on your dishonest gain, for shedding innocent blood, and for practicing oppression and violence"* (Jer. 22:17). Although kings had unique opportunities for this kind of action (2 Kgs. 21), others clearly succumbed to the same temptation: *"Alas for those who devise wickedness and evil deeds ... they covet fields, and seize them; houses, and take them away"* (Mic. 2:1–2; cf. Isa. 5:8–10). The God of the Prophets is the same God of the Covenant who demands that those members of society who are weak and powerless be protected and treated fairly. The vulnerable in that community are those without personal power or patron – the destitute, widows, orphans, and aliens (Isa. 1:17; cf. Jer. 7:5–10). One day, the ideal human ruler will put this into effect (Isa. 11:3–4; 41:17).

For further reading see bibliography numbers: 63, 96, 161, 229, 276, 404a, 585b, 560, 750, 773, 830

# THE BOOK OF

# OBADIAH

*This, the shortest book in the Hebrew Bible, consists of an oracle of judgment against Edom and a promise of God's purpose ultimately to deliver the people and rule over the world from Jerusalem.*

THE book of Obadiah consists of one chapter of 21 verses. The first 16 verses are an oracle against the people of Edom, one of Israel's neighbors; the later verses promise the victory of Israel over Edom. Such "Oracles Against the Nations" (*see box, opposite*), as they are known, occur in all the major Prophetic books, but this is the only example of a detached one.

## THE EDOMITES

This nation (*pp. 100–1*) occupied territory to the southeast of Judah, on the other side of the Dead Sea. The Hebrew Bible records long and continuing enmity between Edom and Judah, so Obadiah could refer to a number of occasions when hostilities broke out between the two nations. However, it is clear that the part played by the Edomites in the Babylonians' invasion of Judah in the early sixth century BCE left a special mark on the exilic and post-exilic literature (e.g., Ps. 137).

The invasion culminated in the destruction of the Temple and the fall of Jerusalem in 587/6BCE, so clearly it would have had a profound effect upon the Hebrew religion of this period. Such passages reveal that the Edomites were thought to have shown a combination of indifference and active participation in that period of life-and-death crisis for Judah. Since this is exactly the note of Obadiah, most scholars date the book

**THE PROPHET OBADIAH**
*This illustration of the Prophet Obadiah comes from a 13th-century French manuscript.*

to around that time. In the tradition, Edom is identified with Esau, Jacob's brother, testifying to a sense of kinship between the two peoples (vv.6, 8, 19, *cf.* Gen. 25:19–34). Family squabbles are sometimes the worst, however, and perhaps the very closeness of the two nations added a special tinge of bitterness. Indeed, Edom's lack of help may have led to a sharp sense of betrayal and the vehemence of the Prophet's words.

In the Hebrew Bible, Obadiah follows the book of Amos, perhaps because it was seen to be related to the passage at Amos 9:11–12: *"I will raise up the booth of David that is fallen, and repair its breaches, and raise up its ruins, and rebuild it as in the days of old; in order that they may possess the remnant of Edom and all the nations who are called by my name, says the LORD."* Obadiah is followed by the book of Jonah, which stresses a more universal aspect to the love of God, partly, perhaps, to counteract the impression of xenophobia in Obadiah.

## PARALLELS WITH OTHER BOOKS

There are some striking parallels between Obadiah and other Prophetic books in the Hebrew Bible. The most obvious is between verses 1–5 of Obadiah and Jeremiah 49:14–16, but see also Obadiah 1:17 and Joel 2:32. Ezekiel 35, especially verse 5, is also close to the thought of Obadiah verses 10–14. Most scholars now doubt whether this is a case of one individual prophet borrowing from another. It is perhaps more likely that there could have been a "stock" of prophetic material used in the Temple worship that, rather like liturgical material today, could be used differently according to context and purposes. If that were so, it illustrates the way in which the Prophets remained close to the cult, even though they increasingly distanced themselves from cultic prophets (*see p.226*).

## THE BOOK'S VALUE

The book of Obadiah has often been condemned as an unworthy outburst of vengeful hatred. However, in the course of time, nations once hostile (such as Babylon and Edom) could come to symbolize "all that is opposed to God's will for his world" (*cf.* the use of "Babylon" in Revelation 14:8). Edom later came to symbolize Rome and its empire. Note that Edom is attacked for widespread evils such as its "pride" and "arrogance" (v.3), its betrayal of treaty and kinship ties (vv.10–14), and inhuman cruelty (vv.15–16). Thus the words of this early Prophet have seemed all too applicable throughout the centuries.

Ultimately the book of Obadiah moves beyond narrow nationalism to envisage the salvation of all who turn to God. All nations will be judged on the Day of the LORD. The promise of this book, like that of the other Prophetic books, is that all such evil, whomever it is committed by, will be rooted out by God, who will ultimately rule as universal king, establishing freedom and justice for all the oppressed (v.21). Its message is ultimately one of hope rather than condemnation.

## ORACLES AGAINST THE NATIONS

Oracles against other nations in the world are not uncommon in the Prophetic books. A whole section of the book of Isaiah (chs.13–23) gathers oracles of this kind. While their language may be as vigorous as that of Obadiah, none of them is a matter of simple malice and hatred. They are a way of expressing important truths about Israel's God, who is sovereign over *all* the nations, not just over Israel and Judah. The moral life that is demanded by God is universal (it does not apply only to Judah and Israel); God can use the nations to accomplish the divine purpose, but also they will be punished if they continue in their wicked ways.

These themes are drawn together in the book of Jeremiah (ch.25). In a world where each nation had its own gods and its own morality, these recognitions – that if God is God at all, then there can be only one God – became an extraordinary breakthrough. Only on the basis that there is one God whose world this is could the oracles against the nations be spoken with such confidence as we read in the book of the Prophet Obadiah.

## THE BOOK

**TITLE**: Obadiah. The title signifies either the name of the Prophet or a description of his role. In Hebrew it means "Servant of YHWH"

**DATE**: Probably in the time of the Babylonian Exile, or soon after

**AUTHOR**: The name Obadiah occurs several times in the Hebrew Bible, but the lack of any biographical details means we cannot identify this particular individual

## THE CONTENTS

**VERSES 1–4**
Predictions of the disaster coming to Edom

**VERSES 5–7**
The destruction of Edom will be total

**VERSES 8–9**
The wise and the warriors will be destroyed

**VERSES 10–14**
Edom's disgraceful treatment of Judah

**VERSES 15–21**
The coming Day of the LORD

## KEY THEMES

*God's judgment includes other nations*

•

*The sovereignty of God is universal and prevails*

•

*The Day of the LORD*

For further reading see bibliography numbers: 9, 197, 510, 524, 739, 779, 839

# THE BOOK OF
# JONAH

*Reading through the Prophets of the Hebrew Bible, Jonah comes as a surprise.
It is not a collection of oracles, but a vivid story. After the violent denunciations
of Obadiah, here is a story that tells of God's mercy — even for hated enemies.*

THE book of Jonah is a colorful story about the relationship between God and humans, about forgiveness and repentance, about obedience and punishment for disobedience, and about God's boundless compassion and mercy. The story concerns an unwilling Prophet who runs from God and the miraculous repentance of a whole city of foreigners. Elements of folklore (for example, Jonah, the unwilling Prophet, being cast into the sea and swallowed by a great fish) show how treasured the story was (*see pp.74–75*). Jonah the Prophet is mentioned in 2 Kings 14:23–29.

## THE STORY OF JONAH

Jonah is told by God to prophesy against Nineveh, and he flees to Tarshish on a ship. While Jonah sleeps, a storm rages; the pagan sailors are afraid and pray unsuccessfully to their gods. The captain wakes Jonah and asks him to call upon his God to save them. The sailors cast lots to discover the cause of the evil, and the lot falls on Jonah, who admits his responsibility for the storm. Jonah suggests they throw him overboard; when they do, the sea is calmed and they are converted to Jonah's God. God sends a fish to save Jonah by swallowing him whole, and he delivers to God a psalm of thanksgiving from the belly of the fish. At God's word, the fish spews Jonah out onto dry land. God again instructs Jonah to proclaim the message to Nineveh, and he obeys. The people respond with a fast, which the king of Nineveh reinforces, calling on everyone to renounce evil and violence. When they do so, God withdraws the threat. Jonah argues with God that his journey was a waste

of time. He asks to die, and God questions his anger. Jonah leaves the city and sits down. God makes a bush grow up and shade Jonah's head, and Jonah is glad. The next day a worm appears and attacks the plant. God sends a sultry east wind, and Jonah asks to die once more. He is angry that the bush died. God points out that if Jonah is sorry about the death of the plant, much more should he pity Nineveh. The astonishing final words show God's encompassing concern for animals as well.

JONAH AND THE WHALE
*The Bible speaks only of "a large fish" (Jonah 1:17),
but popularly it has been called a whale.*

## THE PROPHET JONAH

Jonah is one of the Minor Prophets, found in the Book of the Twelve Prophets. Unlike other Prophetic books, it consists of mainly narrative rather than prophecies. It is thought to have been written to expose the narrow nationalism of some Israelites and to state that God acts to redeem nations other than Israel, even the much-hated Nineveh (*see Nahum, pp.238–39*). It is thus often related to the book of Ruth (*pp.110–11*), a book that shows that David had non-Jews in his immediate ancestry. As a beautifully constructed story, it achieves its effect through its ironic style, which inverts the usual convention of the "righteous prophet" and the "evil people." In the Jewish liturgical calendar, the book of Jonah is traditionally read on the Day of Atonement (*see pp.68–69*), when its themes of repentance and universalism are particularly appropriate.

The description of the Prophet Jonah contains similarities with those of other figures from the Hebrew Bible, such as the Prophet Elijah, who also sat under a broom tree and wished for death (1 Kgs. 19:4), and who also fled from God.

The book contains words and phrases that echo passages from other books of the Hebrew Bible, the most famous of which is the description of God as *"merciful, slow to anger, and abounding in steadfast love, and ready to relent from punishing"* (Jonah 4:2), found in the books of Exodus, Joel, Nahum, Nehemiah, and some Psalms. Rabbinic tradition elaborated these parallels, linking Jonah with Moses. The action of Jonah descending into the sea was seen as paralleling Moses descending from Mount Sinai. Jonah was also linked with Adam, another figure who hid from God's presence.

## CHRISTIAN READINGS

The figure of the Prophet Jonah had a prominent place in Christian tradition. Jesus used the sign of Jonah and the repentance of the Ninevites to warn nonbelievers (Matt. 12:38–45; 16:1–4; Luke 11:29–32). Because of his "three days and three nights" in the belly ("darkness") of the great fish, Jonah was regarded as a type or an emblem of the crucifixion leading to resurrection. This image can be seen as early as those in the Roman Catacombs. The early Church fathers drew out themes of repentance and the mercy of God; of God's mission being extended to the Gentiles; and of the link with the Holy Spirit, since the name Jonah means "dove." Following the New Testament, they compared Jonah's time in the belly of the fish to the period that Jesus spent in hell before his Resurrection. The Reformers saw Jonah as a fallible human saved by grace. The story of Jonah has also been seen as a moral tale demonstrating the power of prayer, the efficacy of fasting, and the merit of good deeds.

## LATER INTERPRETATIONS OF THE STORY

Artistic representations of Jonah on his exit from the fish often depict him naked and bald. In literary interpretations (Milton, Defoe, Emily Brontë, Byron, Kipling) he has often been portrayed as one who brings trouble on his companions, and a transient good is referred to as a "Jonah's gourd" (Tennyson, Hardy). Jonah's tale has been retold in many different ways and styles. The fish caused imaginations to wander with thoughts of what the inside of the belly might have looked like (a line of thinking followed in poems by Aldous Huxley and A. M. Klein), and the grotesque image of Jonah using the whale's eyes as windows.

In Robert Frost's poem *A Masque of Mercy* (1947), Jonah and Paul (and others) debate a universe that may be God-directed, but, to Frost at least, is largely inscrutable. In order to find a place to stand in the world, the major quality needed is courage, but what does that say of the nature of the world? "The saddest thing in life/Is that the best thing in it should be courage." Jonah's fault is that he lacks courage to do the disagreeable thing.

# THE BOOK

**TITLE:** Jonah

**HEBREW TITLE:** *Jona*

**DATE:** Probably after the Exile (sixth century BCE)

**AUTHORSHIP:** Unknown

# THE CONTENTS

**CHAPTER 1**
Jonah is commissioned by God to prophesy against Nineveh, but he flees. In the great storm that God sends, Jonah is thrown overboard, and is swallowed by a great fish

**CHAPTER 2**
Jonah's prayer; he is vomited onto dry land

**CHAPTER 3**
God again instructs Jonah to proclaim his message to Nineveh, and he obeys. The people repent and fast, and God does not destroy them

**CHAPTER 4**
Jonah is angry that Nineveh has not been destroyed, but God teaches him the lesson of compassion and mercy

# KEY THEMES

*The sovereignty of God over all nations*

•

*The universal mercy of God*

•

*The power of repentance*

For further reading see bibliography numbers: 9, 123, 337, 509, 510, 676, 689, 739, 768, 779, 829

# UNIVERSALISM AND PARTICULARISM

*"Particularism" is a belief in God's salvation of one people (pp. 52–53). "Universalism"*
*is the belief in God's salvation of all people, regardless of race or creed. In Israelite religion,*
*the purpose of being the Covenant People of God is to bring the knowledge of God to all.*

IN the Bible, God deals with one particular people and nation in order to make the knowledge of God universal – *"the earth will be filled with the knowledge of the glory of the LORD, as the waters cover the sea"* (Hab. 2:14). But the two viewpoints of universalism and particularism are not always held together. The most important traditions of particularism are those concerning the Exodus (pp. 48–49) and Zion (pp. 126–27). By contrast, universalism rests mainly on creation traditions, holding that God as Creator of all humankind is the sovereign LORD of all peoples.

## ELECTION TRADITIONS
The Exodus traditions are found in Exodus and Deuteronomy; they are used and adapted in some of the Prophets and in a few Psalms. The core belief is that Israel's God rescued the Hebrew people from slavery, under the leadership of Moses, in order to bring them to Canaan, a land promised long ago to the Patriarch Abraham. Those who oppose God's purpose are therefore the enemies of Israel and, to that extent, the enemies of God. However, God's much larger purposes must also include other peoples. For example, the Egyptians opposed the Exodus and suffered plagues in Egypt

> **❝** *Are you not like the Ethiopians to me, O people of Israel? says the LORD. Did I not bring Israel up from the land of Egypt, and the Philistines from Caphtor?* **❞**
>
> (Amos 9:7)

**UNIVERSALISM**
*The fundamental belief of universalism is that God cares for all peoples and is sovereign over them.*

and defeat at the Red or Reed Sea, but the larger purpose was *"The Egyptians shall know that I am the LORD"* (Exod. 7:5; 8:6, 18; 9:14, 29; 11:7; 14:4, 18). Even so, with mention of some nations, especially the Canaanites, Ammonites, Moabites, and Edomites, the emphasis is on particularism, and the command to destroy their gods and culture is unrelieved. Traditions relating success in war (pp. 84–85) reinforced the belief that Israel's God is the only one able to defeat all non-Hebrew peoples – an act that makes God victorious over their gods as well. At the heart of these traditions, developed at length in Deuteronomy, is the belief that God has made a "covenant" with the people, through Moses (see pp. 60–61).

## ZION TRADITIONS
The Zion traditions lie in the books of Samuel and Kings and are affirmed in many of the royal Psalms and Zion hymns, in earlier Prophets such as Isaiah, and in later Prophets such as Zechariah. The core belief is that, following the promises made of the land, God has provided the people with a city – Zion, or Jerusalem. The divine presence will dwell in the holy Temple, protecting the people of Israel forever. The enemies are now all those

who threaten Zion – Assyrians, Syrians, Egyptians, Babylonians. The covenantal figure is now David, not Moses – although the conditions of the Covenant are less defined, the same nature of an agreement binding on both sides is still evident (*see 2 Sam. 23:5; Ps. 89:29–37*).

## CREATION TRADITIONS

While the election traditions may be traced back to the pre-exilic period, the creation traditions are found mostly in literature from the exilic and post-exilic periods in the Priestly account of the creation of the world in Genesis; in parts of the wisdom literature (for example, in Proverbs and Job); in some hymns in the Psalter that extol God as Creator of the cosmos; and in Isaiah 40–55 (*see below*). The examples from the Priestly and Wisdom writings and from the Psalms are less antagonistic to other nations. Usually, God's relationship with Israel's enemies is neither affirmed nor denied; the major theme is of God's kingly rule over all the created order – the heavens and the earth, the land and the sea, the animals, birds and fish, and all of humankind. If God is both Creator and King, divine rule is universal and all nations owe God homage. The creation traditions focus entirely on God, not on the Covenant, and the obligation to keep faith rests not only on Israel alone but on all the known nations of the world (*see, for example, Ps. 100:1–3*).

## ISAIAH 40–55

Isaiah 40–55 (*see pp.202–3*), a work dealing with the exilic period, combines the election traditions (those of both Moses and David) with a creation theology (again affirming God not only as Creator but also as King). This creates a "conditional" universalism. On the one hand (appealing to the election traditions), other peoples and nations are depicted as enemies, cringing before Israel who is to be the ultimate victor (*see Isa. 45:14; 49:22–23*). On the other hand (using the creation traditions), other

nations are called upon to "be saved" (Isa. 45:22) because the God of Israel, YHWH, the great transcendent King of the Universe, is concerned for the welfare of all peoples. This is not a pluralistic universalism, which would mean that all people, regardless of creed and race, can worship the Creator God in whatever way they wish. It is a "conditional universalism": provided that all people recognize the Creator God as YHWH, the God of Moses and the God of Zion, and hence worship and obey God through an Israelite (Jewish) expression of faith, they can be saved. Taken together, Isaiah 40–55 expresses this view. The same idea is developed more in other post-exilic books, for example, in Ruth and in Zechariah 8:20–23, which speaks of the pilgrimage of all nations to Jerusalem: *"Thus says the LORD of hosts: Peoples shall yet come, the inhabitants of many cities; the inhabitants of one city shall go to another, saying, 'Come, let us go to entreat the favour of the LORD, and to seek the LORD of hosts; I myself am going.' Many peoples and strong nations shall come to seek the LORD of hosts in Jerusalem and to entreat the favour of the LORD. Thus says the LORD of hosts: In those days ten men from nations of every language shall take hold of a Jew, grasping his garment and saying, 'Let us go with you, for we have heard that God is with you.'"*

**DIVINE LOVE FOR ALL NATIONS**
*This stained-glass window depicts a scene from the book of Ruth (see pp.110–11). The story demonstrates that God cares for all who turn to him, irrespective of their nationality.*

> 66 *Make a joyful noise to the LORD, all the earth. Worship the LORD with gladness; come into his presence with singing.* 99
>
> (Psalms 100:1–3)

## JONAH

A pluralistic universalism is perhaps glimpsed in the book of Jonah (*pp.230–31*). The surprising element in Jonah is that the Ninevites (i.e., the Assyrians) hear God's word and repent, but do not then adopt or assimilate Israelite beliefs and practices. No conditions for their conversion are imposed (*"When God saw what they did, how they turned from their evil ways, God changed his mind about the calamity that he had said he would bring upon them; and he did not do it,"* Jonah 3:10). It seems likely that the book of Jonah was written, at least in part, to challenge that excessive nationalism whereby even the traditions about God's care of all Creation were being turned inward to serve Israel alone.

For further reading see bibliography numbers: 522, 676, 802

# THE BOOK OF
# MICAH

*The Prophet Micah spoke strongly against injustice and corruption, and
saw God bringing an accusation against the people. But he also saw great
hope in a future salvation, both for Jerusalem and for the people.*

THE whole period of the late eighth century BCE was a
time of great political uncertainty, when both Israel
in the north and Judah in the south lived under the
lengthening shadow of Assyria (*pp.142–43*). In
721BCE, Israel fell to Assyria: an early oracle predicts this
(1:6–7); a later oracle is directed toward Judah as well (1:15).
In 701BCE, Jerusalem almost shared the same fate,
but Hezekiah bought off the Assyrian king,
Sennacherib, with a large indemnity. Micah
was the contemporary of Isaiah and
Hosea. He saw that the community was
in danger because of the moral rot
eating away at its institutions. The
rich oppressed the poor, and the
leaders corrupted justice. The
priest conspired in the corruption
of it all, and the prophets (i.e.,
the state-employed prophets, *see
p.196*) proved to be paper tigers
as they turned a blind eye to the
sins of their paymasters. No
wonder, then, that the Prophet
who threatened the rulers and
their supporters so fiercely and
who predicted the overthrow of the
whole "establishment" should be so
unpopular. Indeed, 2:6–11 is best
understood as the record of a dispute
between Micah and his opponents.

## MICAH'S USE OF
## PROPHETIC CONVENTIONS

Micah announced that God's judgment
against the kingdom was imminent. He
used a number of different prophetic forms for this, which
are familiar from other books of the Bible. In addition to
direct threats of judgment (e.g., 1:2–9), he used the form of
the lament that is introduced by the cry "Woe," and suggested

that the funeral of the kingdom was near (2:1–5). The form of
the "legal controversy" was also used as though God were
bringing the people to court (*see* The Lawsuit of God, *opposite*).
In Micah 7:17, the Prophet employed the form of the "psalm
of lament," so familiar from the Psalter (*see p.209*).

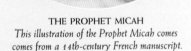

**THE PROPHET MICAH**
*This illustration of the Prophet Micah
comes from a 14th-century French manuscript.*

## VISION OF THE FUTURE

As with all the Prophetic books, the book
of Micah does not predict that sin and
judgment will finally defeat God's
purpose of love and justice for the
people. Promise and threat are
combined because that was the
structure of the covenant
relationship (*p.219*). This structure would have been very
familiar; in 6:1–6 Micah began
the historical recital that
preceded the statement of the
covenant terms, but he broke
off in midsentence, as though
this history was known well
enough. Then he gave the basic
statement of the covenant
obligation (6:6–8), reviewed the
ways in which the people had failed,
and reminded them of what their
reward would be should they turn back
to God and keep the conditions of the
Covenant. To suggest splitting off the
promises of hope at the end as though
they might be a later addition, as some
commentators have done, would be a
serious mistake. In fact, throughout the
book there are many oracles of hope for the emergence of
a new community, although it was to emerge only after the
overthrow of the present regime (3:12). Even the promise of a
new ruler to come from Bethlehem (5:2–4) presupposes the

fall of the existing line of David. A new community will emerge of those who have learned the Prophet's lesson that God requires obedience in heart and life rather than mere an outward show of religion (6:6–8). Their hope is that, ultimately, God is a "pardoning God" (7:18–20).

## KEY PASSAGES IN MICAH

The book of Micah contains some of the most familiar words of the Hebrew Bible. The basic summary of covenant conditions (6:6–8), the foundations of ethics in the Prophets (*pp.226–27*), ends with the words:

> He has told you, O mortal, what is good;
> and what does the LORD require of you
> but to do justice, and to love kindness,
> and to walk humbly with your God?

This has been regarded as one of the quintessential summaries of the 613 commandments given to Israel in the Torah: "David came and reduced the 613 commandments to eleven [Ps. 15:2–5], Isaiah came and reduced them to six [Isa. 33:15], Micah came and reduced them to three, Isaiah came again and reduced them to two [Isa. 56:1], Amos came and reduced them to one: *'For thus says the LORD to the house of Israel: Seek me and live'* [Amos 5:4]" (*B. Makkot 24a*).

There is also the promise of a future ruler who will deliver his people (5:2), a promise familiar in Christian Christmas liturgies. It shares with Isaiah the noble vision of future universal peace in 4:3, reaching a climax in the words, *"nation shall not lift up sword against nation, neither shall they learn war any more."*

## THE LAWSUIT OF GOD

As in several other books in the Bible – an example is Deuteronomy 32 – Micah used language that suggests that there is a heavenly court in which Israel is charged before (or even by) God. The charge is known as the *rib*, and prophets are present at the trial as reporters. The passages are based on the following pattern: the scene being set, the speech of the plaintiff, the appointment of Heaven and earth as judges, the charge against the defendant, the refutation of defense arguments, specific indictment, and sentence. The influence of the *rib* can be seen outside the Prophets; for example, in Job (*see pp.172–73*). It has also been argued that the lawsuit form is related to the widespread covenant forms of the ancient Near East (although how far these can be applied to the biblical material has been disputed). Among the covenant forms is one in which there is a call to witnesses to attend: the case at issue is stated (e.g., Deut. 32:4–6; Isa. 1:2*ff.*; Mic. 6:3–5; Jer. 2:5–7); the indictment is made (Deut. 32:15–18; Mic. 6:9–15); the sentence is pronounced (Deut. 32:19–27; Mic. 6:16); and the benefits of keeping the terms of the Covenant are recited (Deut. 32:28–43; Mic. 7:7*ff.*).

# THE BOOK

**TITLE**: Micah

**HEBREW TITLE**: Micah (meaning "Who is like Yah?" [YHWH], a name given to several individuals in the Hebrew Bible)

**DATE**: Eighth century BCE. The editorial superscription places Micah's ministry within a long period spanning the reigns of three Judean kings, Jotham, Ahaz, and Hezekiah, roughly 742–687BCE

**AUTHORSHIP**: Attributed to Micah. He is the only Prophet whose words are attributed to him in another Prophetic book (*see* Jer. 26:18)

# THE CONTENTS

**CHAPTERS 1–3**
Mainly oracles of judgment against Samaria and Judah but including a vision of a new Israel

**CHAPTERS 4–5**
Oracles of salvation

**CHAPTER 6:1–8**
God's lawsuit against Israel

**CHAPTERS 6:9–7:7**
God's judgments

**CHAPTER 7:8–20**
More oracles of judgment and hope

# KEY THEMES

*Warnings of condemnation and punishment*

•

*Forgiveness and restoration are promised*

•

*God's lawsuit against Israel*

For further reading see bibliography numbers: 9, 409, 524, 534, 828

# TIME IN THE BIBLE

*Different cultures have different attitudes to time. Some see history as cyclic, others as meaningless, still others as a process of human evolution from lower to higher. In the Hebrew Bible, time is seen in relation to its Creator. The biblical vision finds meaning in the turmoil of history by relating it to God and God's purposes.*

THE many puzzles of time continue to challenge both scientists and philosophers. To biblical writers, God, God's law, and God's purposes provide a unifying pattern that enabled them to find meaning in the passing of time. For them, the past may have been very much alive in the present, in the reading of a text, or in the celebration of festivals and rituals. The present may be more real in the future – in the fulfillment of prophecies and in judgment. The future may already be contained in the past – in the unfolding of the purposes of God, especially in the promises and threats made of old. Like us, the biblical writers had a sense of the past, present, and future, but expressed their relationship in spatial terms. The past is what can be seen and known, and is therefore what lies before us, ahead of us (Hebrew *qedem*); the future is unknown and therefore lies behind our backs (Hebrew *achor, acharon*). Only God can see the future of a person or a nation; and only God is able to see the future as others see the past. The whole of time and history is "in front of God's face."

God endures when all else passes away, giving meaning and perspective to time. A series of events becomes not simply one thing after another, but the unfolding of God's purpose. Considerable effort was made to include the genealogies of the tribes of Israel and the chronologies of the kings of Israel and Judah in the biblical narrative. Biblical time is a map of these vital events, moments, and encounters.

**SUNRISE OVER THE SEA OF GALILEE**
*In biblical times, a day was considered to be the length of time between sunrise and sunrise. Later it became known as the period between sunset and sunset.*

> **"** *God called the light Day, and the darkness he called Night. And there was evening and there was morning, the first day.* **"**
>
> (Genesis 1:5)

## PROPHETS AND APOCALYPTIC

The Prophets in particular unfolded the meaning of God's purpose in time, but when prophecy ceased in Israel, Apocalyptic (*pp.260–61*) took over this role. Drawing past, present, and future into a dynamic connection with one another, Apocalyptic promises huge changes in the world and in human existence, caused by the often violent action of God in the physical world. The Day of the LORD in the Prophets (*p.241*) is examined in detail. Increasingly, it is asserted that in "a little while" God will overthrow the wicked (*see* Ps. 37:10). This "little while" is not an exact measure of time, i.e., something good may happen soon, but the exact time is not specified.

## TIME IN THE NEW TESTAMENT

For the New Testament writers, time is gathered into the person of Jesus – as the promised Christ, or Messiah, the meaning of past and future are gathered into him: *"The time is fulfilled, and the kingdom of God has come near; repent, and believe in the good news"* (Mark 1:15; cf. 2 Cor. 6:2). The end has already begun, and although Jesus warned his followers not to attempt to calculate when the completion of the already inaugurated kingdom might be, many of the early Christians clearly thought that the cataclysmic event was close upon them (*see pp.470–71*). But in the biblical understanding of time that Jesus shared, past, present, and future are united in one moment. The important thing is to live the present moment for God and according to God's wishes.

## WORDS FOR TIME

In the New Testament, three words are used to describe time: *chronos* refers to time as a quantity: *"I will be with you a little while longer"* (John 7:33), while *kairos* describes time as an opportunity: *"I am not going to this festival, for my time has not yet fully come"* (John 7:8; *cf.* Mark 1:15). These distinctions are by no means absolute. The third word used to describe time is *aion* (English, eon), which refers to a long sequence of time – an age or a period – especially one in which God acts: *"whoever speaks against the Holy Spirit will not be forgiven, either in this age or in the age to come"* (Matt. 12:32; *cf.* Rom. 12:2 for "the present age"; see also Mark 10:30; *cf.* Eph. 2:7 for "the coming age"). The plural "eons" (Matt. 21:19; *cf.* John 12:34), often translated as "forever," may not mean "eternal," but rather "an unimaginably long time."

**THE HEBREW CALENDAR**
*The year of the ancient Israelite was dominated by the agricultural seasons and punctuated by festivals. The calendar follows the Western Semitic calendar with a year of 12 lunar months, beginning in the autumnal month of Tishri.*

seven-day week (the Sabbath being the only day named, as opposed to being simply numbered), and there were 12 months (the words for "month," *yerach* and *chodesh*, are both related to the words for "moon" and "new"). The names for the months changed as Israel moved from Canaanite to Babylonian influence. Not all of the surviving names for the months occur in the Bible (see chart, left), but they are known from other texts.

## MEASURES OF TIME

There was no system of continuous chronology in ancient Israel, as there is in the Muslim system of dating years "after the Hijrah" (AH) or the Christian BC or AD ("before Christ" or *"Anno Domini"*). Most chronological systems in the Bible were related to kings or rulers, or to events: *"In the four hundred and eightieth year after the Israelites came out of the land of Egypt, in the fourth year of Solomon's reign over Israel, in the month of Ziv"* (1 Kgs. 6:1). Figures from different sources, however, are often inconsistent, and the two kingdoms of Israel and Judah often dated events differently. Clearly some events had greater importance for the ancient Israelites than others. The cycle of the year was punctuated by weekly, monthly, and annual holy days (see pp.68–69). Like many other ancient civilizations, the Hebrews identified some parts of time as holy, separate, and as belonging to God. Certain days, such as the Sabbath and those of the festivals, were set apart from other times with rituals to mark their beginning and end, and with activities that were either forbidden or commanded.

## THE DIVISION OF TIME

Until the Roman system of 12 hours to the day was adopted, the day was not divided into equal units (minutes and hours). Thus, an hour was a small but undefined length of time. A day might also be a designation of significance, for example, the Day of the LORD (p.241), but in more general terms, it came to be known as the period of time between sunset on one day and sunset on the next (Gen. 1:5). In earlier times, the day may have been calculated from sunrise to sunrise (Lev. 7:15–17; *cf.* Judg. 19:4–19). The year was based on the cycle of the moon, perhaps with an additional month inserted to bring it into line with the year calculated from the sun. There was thus a

**NATURE'S TIMEPIECE**
*The sun has long been used to indicate the time of day. In the Bible it is an emblem of constancy, and God is referred to as the source of spiritual light.*

For further reading see bibliography numbers: 51, 772

# THE BOOKS OF
# NAHUM &
# HABAKKUK

*Nahum and Habakkuk are contrasting Prophets, but together they raise issues about God's use of foreign nations to achieve the divine purpose. The great powers of the world are destined to pass away, but God's love will endure.*

THE Prophet Nahum appears to breathe hatred and vengeance against a foreign oppressor, Nineveh and the Assyrians, while promising comfort for the people of God. As such, he has often been criticized and compared unfavorably with some of the other Prophets, such as Amos, Hosea, and Isaiah, who challenged their own people with God's judgment for their unethical behavior. Yet all the major prophetic collections contain "oracles against the nations" (Isa. 13–23; Jer. 44–51; see p.229). Even Isaiah 40–55 (pp.202–3), concerned with Israel's response to exile, contains threats of judgment against an oppressor (Babylon) while promising salvation for the people of God. "Comfort" in Isaiah 40:1 is Hebrew *nahamu*, as in the name Nahum. A further link between Nahum and those chapters of Isaiah can be found in the words common to both (Nah. 1:15; cf. Isa. 52:7). Perhaps the function of such oracles was to secure victory for God's people by invoking divine help against the mighty powers before which they themselves were helpless. Whether he was predicting the future or recounting the past, the events Nahum describes did happen: Assyria, under whose shadow Israel and Judah had lived for a century, collapsed before a coalition of Medes and Babylonians in 612BCE.

THE FALL OF NINEVEH
*This detail from a 19th-century painting by John Martin depicts the capture of Nineveh, the last capital of Assyria, in 612BCE.*
*The city was plundered by a combined force of Medes and Babylonians, and was subsequently left to fall into desolate ruin.*

## THE SIGNIFICANCE OF NAHUM'S PROPHECY

There are indications in the book that Nahum's prophecy is more than a piece of xenophobic nationalism. The defeat of Nineveh is set on a "cosmic" stage. The opening poem (1:2–8) depicts YHWH as the Creator God, who brought the earth from chaos and who could return it to chaos again (vv.5–6). This suggests the sole, sovereign power of YHWH over all Creation. Typical prophetic themes are used in condemnation of Nineveh: its arrogant defiance of God (1:9), its idolatry (1:4), its cruel oppression (2:11–12); the *"City of bloodshed"* (3:1) with no name is symbolic of all oppressive regimes. Nineveh therefore seems to have become representative of all that is opposed to God's just will for the world: evil that will be rooted out wherever it is found. God's great "covenant" promise to the people (Exod. 34:6–7) is recalled at 1:3, and this promise is not made lightly. Both God's supreme power and enduring purpose are the themes of this book.

## HABAKKUK QUESTIONS GOD

Most of the Prophets in the Hebrew Bible presented God's word with an assured "Thus says the LORD." This did not stop them from raising questions and even arguing with God (*see* Jeremiah, *pp.206–7*). Just as Abraham is recorded as disputing with God about divine justice (Gen. 18:22–33), so Habakkuk also complained to God about the injustice in the Judean society of his day (1:2–4). God replied that the terrible might of the Babylonians would be brought down upon the people in judgment (1:5–11). The Prophet is troubled and questions how God can use such an evil power against the just as well as the wicked (1:12–17). This echoes the exact nature of Abraham's questions to God. God answers with a second oracle (2:1–5), in which Habakkuk is assured that the righteous will live because of their faith, or faithfulness (2:4), while the evil will be judged (2:5).

## HABAKKUK, THE WATCHFUL PROPHET

In threatening times, Habakkuk is called to act as a "watchman" looking for the first signs of God's action (2:1). He is, therefore, the first to hear the good news of God's promised deliverance (2:2–5). There are descriptions of similar roles for Prophets in Isaiah 21:6–12 and Ezekiel 3:17–21. This oracle is followed by the "Woes" (a form of prophetic oracle) in 2:6–19. They culminate in the assurance of God's presence among the people as God watches over the world (v.20). The mythological language of the psalm in 3:1–19 recalls God's great actions in Creation and in the history of the people. It concludes with the assurance that God will be the joy (v.18) and the strength (v.19) of the people in every historical situation. The psalm thus "universalizes" the message of the book for people of faith in all times.

---

## THE BOOK

**TITLE**: Nahum

**HEBREW TITLE**: *nahum* (meaning "comfort")

**DATE**: Seventh century BCE. Two historical events are mentioned in the book: the capture of Thebes by Assyria (3:8) in 661 BCE, and the fall of Nineveh, the capital of Assyria (2:8), in 612 BCE

**AUTHORSHIP**: Nothing is known about a prophet of this name. Elkosh, his town of origin, is unidentified

## THE CONTENTS

1:2–8 A poem announcing the coming of YHWH

1:9–2:2 Threats against YHWH's enemies, and a promise of deliverance for the people

2:3–13 The defeat of Nineveh

3:1–4 A lament over the fall of the *"City of bloodshed"*

3:5–19 An oracle addressed to Nineveh

## KEY THEME

*God's sovereignty over all, including the Assyrians*

---

## THE BOOK

**TITLE**: Habakkuk

**HEBREW TITLE**: *habaqquq* ("embraced")

**DATE**: Probably late seventh century BCE. The reference to *"the Chaldeans"* (1:6) suggests a time somewhere between 612–586 BCE

**AUTHORSHIP**: Unknown – the book gives no details

## THE CONTENTS

1:2–4 Habakkuk asks God how long the oppression will last,

1:5–11 An answering oracle from God

1:12–17 A second lament by the Prophet

2:1–5 God assures Habakkuk that the righteous will live by faith and the evil will be judged

2:6–20 A series of "Woes" threatening God's judgment

## KEY THEME

*Sin and punishment*

---

For further reading see bibliography numbers: 197, 524, 525, 652, 653, 779, 814

# THE BOOK OF
# ZEPHANIAH

*Zephaniah, a short book, consists of a fiery oracle of judgment against
Judah and a promise of God's purpose ultimately to deliver the righteous
and rule over the world from Jerusalem.*

THE three chapters of the book of Zephaniah
outline what has gone wrong among God's people,
what God's retribution will be, and the judgment
of good and evil. Zephaniah describes how priests
and the people indulge in idolatrous worship. This is itself
an indication of widespread religious apathy. Civil and
religious leaders break God's law, and such disregard for the
duties of religion make the rich and powerful feel free to
oppress the weak and the poor. These wrongs are symptom-
atic of a universal corruption. Zephaniah speaks of God's
intention to undo the work of Creation by cutting off "Adam"
(also translated as "humanity" at 1:3 and "people" at 1:17)
and sweeping away everything of the Creation recorded in
Genesis 1. There follow "oracles against the nations" that,
while specifying certain nations, accuse them of sins similar
to those of Judah: arrogance, pride, and an almost blasphemous self-confidence. God has a "Day" (*see right*),
when both the proud and mighty of the people of God
will be judged together with those of other nations.

## THE SALVATION OF THE HUMBLE

As with most of the other Prophets of the Hebrew Bible,
Zephaniah does not see human sin and its judgment as
God's last word (*see* Threat and Promise, *p.219*). The humble
and the poor who have been on the receiving end of the
oppression by the powerful will be delivered. Indeed, both
the oppressive nations and the rich and strong in Judah itself

### THE DAY OF THE LORD

"… A day of wrath, a day of distress and anguish, a day of ruin and devastation, a day of darkness and gloom, a day of clouds and
thick darkness, a day of trumpet blast and battle cry against the fortified cities and against the lofty battlements" (Zeph. 1:15–16).

are all lumped together as the enemies whom God will defeat when the people of God are rescued. Neither human power nor wealth will enable the mighty to escape God's action. God will purify the humble so that they reflect the divine righteousness, and then all Creation will reflect the character of God, who will reign over the whole world from Jerusalem. The prophecy of Zephaniah is thus a politically, as well as religiously, radical book. The link between God's judgment and salvation is found in the call to the humble to put their trust wholly in God as they await divine action.

## THE DAY OF THE LORD

The first to mention "the Day of the LORD" in the Hebrew Bible is Amos (5:18–20). He depicts his hearers as looking forward to it, so presumably this was a concept already familiar to them. It was clearly seen as an occasion when the enemies of God would be judged, and the people of God would be delivered. Scholars disagree about whether this was an idea that originated in a war context, when God's help was summoned to defeat the enemies of Israel, or in some great occasion in Israel's religious calendar when, in the Temple, they celebrated God's "coming" to them in blessing and renewal (e.g., Ps. 50:1–3). Amos turns the concept against the Israelites. It will be a day when God comes to judge those who, by their corrupt conduct, have made themselves the enemies of God. For them it will therefore be a day, not of light but of darkness.

Amos' ideas clearly influenced Zephaniah, who had also been influenced by Isaiah. Isaiah stressed that the Day of the LORD would turn all human values upside down, when the "proud and lofty" would be brought low (Isa. 2:11–17). There was a tendency to see this prediction of the pre-exilic prophets as being fulfilled by the destruction of Jerusalem and the Exile to Babylon (e.g., Lam. 1:21). In later, more eschatological prophecy (e.g., Joel 3:1–3; Heb. 4:1–3; *see pp.262–63*), the Day of the LORD again came to be seen as a time when God would ultimately defeat the nations that had oppressed Israel. But, as in Zephaniah, even threats against specific nations are often broadened to include threats against the kind of evils they have committed. So these predictions, rather than being merely the expression of a crude nationalism, offer assurances to the faithful everywhere that God will eventually root out all evil from creation.

In the New Testament period, many speculated about the imminence of the Day of the LORD, or of Judgment (Mark 13:6), but were warned that God's plans are secret (Mark 13:32). The Day came to be identified with the Day of the Son of Man (Matt. 24:42–44; Luke 17:24, 30; Acts 17:31; Rom. 2:16), when the ascended Jesus would act as judge, and the 12 Apostles would share the throne of judgment (Luke 22:30). There were some, however, who believed that the last days had already begun in the life and ministry of Jesus on earth (*see* John 12:31; 16:8–11; Acts 2:16–21; Heb. 1:2).

## THE BOOK

**TITLE**: Zephaniah. Four people of this name are mentioned in the Hebrew Bible, suggesting that it was a fairly common name

**HEBREW TITLE**: *Zephaniah* (YHWH protects)

**DATE**: The superscription sets the Prophet's activity in the reign of Josiah, king of Judah (640–9BCE). The religious abuses described in the book suggest a time early in Josiah's reign and show why many must have considered his religious reforms (2 Kgs. 22–23) to be necessary

**AUTHORSHIP**:
Nothing is known of the Prophet despite the four-generation genealogy given to him. If the "Hezekiah" mentioned was the king of that name, Zephaniah was of royal descent, but that did not stop him from attacking the religious and royal "establishment" of his day

## THE CONTENTS

**CHAPTER 1**
Editorial superscription. The Day of God's judgment against Judah, Jerusalem, and all people

**CHAPTER 2**
Call to repentance. Oracles against foreign nations

**CHAPTER 3**
Additional charges against the Jerusalem leaders. Salvation for Judah and the nations and God's reign as universal king

## KEY THEMES

*The humble to put their trust in God as they wait for divine action*

•

*The Day of the LORD*

For further reading see bibliography numbers: 420, 447, 525, 652, 653, 772, 779

# THE BOOKS OF
# HAGGAI &
# ZECHARIAH

*After the Babylonian Exile, Haggai and Zechariah provided leadership and a
vision for the future reorganization and rebuilding of the community in Jerusalem.*

THE Prophets Haggai and
Zechariah are unique in
already being bracketed
together in the Hebrew
Bible itself (Ezra 5:1; 6:14).
Other Prophets may have been
contemporary with one another
(Jeremiah and Ezekiel) or shared
the same concerns (Amos and
Hosea), but they are never linked
in a comparable way. Haggai and
Zechariah were active when the
Jerusalem community was under
Persian rule, and they or their
editors found no difficulty in
dating them according to the
Persian ruler of the day (Hag.
1:1; Zech. 1:1).

## TWO BOOKS

The name Haggai means "festivals."
The main concern of this book
was the rebuilding of the Temple:
construction had been authorized
by the Persians, but the building
was still in disrepair (Hag. 1:4).
Only when the Temple was rebuilt would present troubles
cease and divine favor return. It would be manifested through
the rule of Zerubbabel, governor of Jerusalem and a descendant of King David (Hag. 2:20–23). Whatever the hopes
for Zerubbabel may have been, they came to nothing.

Zechariah is a more complex book, and its use of visions
(Zech. 1–6) points to the world of the apocalypses. The
significance of several of these visions is now uncertain;

**MULTILAYERED PAPER-CUT OF ZECHARIAH'S VISION**
*This elaborate Turkish paper-cut illustrates Zechariah's vision
(Zech. 4:1–7). The menorah in the center is inscribed with Psalm 67.*

they seem to reflect divisions
within the Jerusalem community
itself, but they also offer hopes
of a better future. In comparison
to Haggai, the book of Zechariah
gives greater emphasis to the
priestly role in leading the Jerusalem community. The book ends
with a vision of restored harmony,
with Jerusalem, the Jews, and their
God as the focus of universal
praise (Zech. 8:20–23).

## THE ORACLES

Zechariah 9–14 consists of
oracles about Israel's enemies and
the coming of Zion's king and
shepherd. Where chapters 1–8
focus on immediate needs and
problems, the oracles look to
a more distant horizon. It is by
no means clear to what circumstances the oracles point – at
least 30 different identifications
of the shepherds in chapters
11:4–7 alone have been made.

Jerome, who completed the first Latin translation of the
Bible, referred to this as "the most obscure book in the Bible."
Because of differences of style and content, the oracles
have been regarded as an addition to the original book.

These chapters clearly influenced the early Christian
community, and important events in the life of Jesus were set
out in the Gospels as the fulfillment of what had been written
in these chapters: the entry into Jerusalem (Palm Sunday)

refers to 9:9; the *"thirty pieces of silver,"* wrongly attributed to Jeremiah in Matthew 27:9, are mentioned in Zechariah in 11:12ff; the scattering of the sheep (Zech. 13:7) is echoed in the disciples' abandonment of Jesus (Matt. 26:31).

## A PERIOD OF TRANSITION

The two books of Haggai and Zechariah stand at the moment of transition from the pre-exilic to the post-exilic period. Haggai resembles the prophets of old, but his oracles are set in a narrative framework – he is referred to in the third person. It may be that the oracles were collected by a later editor. Haggai expresses a hope focused on Zerubbabel, the governor of Jerusalem appointed by the Persians. The terms that he uses are reminiscent of hopes focused on the Messiah, the anointed king descended from King David (2:20–23), but the main interest is in the rebuilding of the Temple. In the period after the Babylonian Exile, the Temple and its priests increasingly took over responsibility for guiding the nation. Haggai presents the challenge of removing the contamination to the Israelites' holiest shrine, which had been caused by heathen defilement during the Exile. He states that sacrificial offerings are not enough, and stresses the importance of repentance.

In the book of Zechariah, the shift to the new situation on the return from Exile is even more pronounced. In the first half of the book, the word of God comes to Zechariah in classical style, but the oracles are already moving toward visions of the future. Prophets of the old style were able to appeal directly to God (*"Thus says the LORD"*), and might contest how the priests were interpreting the covenant laws and what was going on in the Temple, as they had done in the past (*see pp.196–97*). Zechariah, on the other hand, seems to ally himself with such priestly attitudes. For the priests, it was vital that another catastrophe like the Exile should be avoided and that meant faithful obedience to the Law. Eventually it was claimed that the spirit of prophecy had been withdrawn at the time of the Exile as part of God's punishment. Into the gap of commentary on current affairs came Apocalyptic, the unveiling (Greek *apokalupsis* – unveiling, hence "revelation" – *see pp.260–61*) of God's purpose and plan, and thus also of the future.

## TWO MESSIAHS

Equally striking is the way in which Zechariah keeps alive the old hope based on the ruling figure and makes reference to Zerubbabel (4:8–10), but immediately afterward he states that there are to be two Messiahs, i.e. two anointed figures. One anointed figure in Israel is the king; the other is the High Priest. Both will share the same throne: *"Then I said to him 'What are these two olive trees on the right and the left of the lampstand?' … he said 'These are the two anointed ones who stand by the Lord of the whole earth'"* (Zech. 4:9–14).

## THE BOOKS

**TITLES**: Haggai and Zechariah

**HEBREW TITLES**: *Haggay* and *Zecharyah*

**DATE**: The Prophets were active c.520BCE, but the date when their words were compiled is uncertain. Zechariah 9–14 are held by many to be from a different author and date

**AUTHORSHIP**: The oracles of the two Prophets have been placed in an editorial framework, perhaps by those who also compiled the books of Chronicles

## THE CONTENTS

**HAGGAI CHAPTERS 1–2**
A series of short oracles encourages the Jerusalem community to rebuild the Temple. Their leader, Zerubbabel, is to be given special status

**ZECHARIAH CHAPTERS 1–6**
Zechariah has a series of eight visions setting out the future state of Jerusalem, the role of Joshua the priest, and related cultic issues

**ZECHARIAH CHAPTERS 7–8**
Detailed oracles spell out what is required of the Jerusalem community

**ZECHARIAH CHAPTERS 9–14**
Each headed "an oracle," these chapters describe in visionary, but very obscure, terms the future of the community

## KEY THEMES

*The rebuilding of the Temple*

•

*The continuation of David's line in Zerubbabel*

•

*The coming Day of the LORD*

•

*The future glory of Jerusalem*

For further reading see bibliography numbers: 2, 96, 196, 370, 523, 615

# THE BOOK OF
# MALACHI

*This book, written after the Jews had returned from exile, is a call to the people to change their ways. It condemns the offering of polluted sacrifice and mixed marriage. In return for repentance, it promises the enduring protection of God.*

MALACHI'S prophecy is expressed in the unusual form of six question-and-answer dialogues. For much of the book, the verses begin with a theological statement from the Prophet, met by a question from the hearers, to which the Prophet's reply expounds his major theme. It is probably a rhetorical device rather than a secretary's report of an actual dialogue, but it clearly engages with real questions of the time and may well reflect some of the teaching and preaching methods of the Second Temple. This is an insight far truer to the nature of religion in the prophetic period than is the claim that "the Law" and "the Prophets" are opposed to each other, as being the legalistic set against the ethical (*see pp.226–27*).

## GOD'S COVENANT OF LOVE

Malachi speaks of God's covenant with the Levitical priesthood (2:8), of marriage as a covenant between two people before God (2:14), and of God's sending a *"messenger of the covenant"* (3:1), i.e., of the Covenant between God and all the people. God's love for the people is stressed in 1:2–5. This might seem strange in view of the strong charges that God is to bring against many of them, but it shows that the Covenant into which the people enter with God and the love that it brings also require obedience (*cf.* Amos 3:1–2). The dismissal of "Esau" (=Edom) is strange in view of what looks like an almost universalistic outlook in 1:11: *"From the rising of the sun to its setting my name is great among the nations, and*

EGYPTIAN SILVERSMITHS
*The book of Malachi describes God as one who will "sit as a refiner and purifier of silver, and he will purify the descendants of Levi and refine them like gold and silver, until they present offerings to the LORD in righteousness" (Mal. 3:3).*

*in every place incense is offered to my name, and a pure offering; for my name is great among the nations, says the LORD of hosts."* The text here appears to be saying that, in contrast to the faithlessness of Israel's priests, genuine worship by other people (wherever and by whomever it is offered) is acceptable to God. Many have found such an idea difficult to accept. Jewish commentators have taken this to refer to the worship of the Jewish Diaspora or to Gentiles converted to Judaism. Others have seen it as a future promise that one day, all people will worship the one true God. The echo here of Psalm 50:1 (*"The mighty one, God the LORD, speaks and summons the earth from the rising of the sun to its setting"*), a psalm that calls for true obedience to God rather than merely performing animal sacrifice, may suggest that this is the message that Malachi wants to drive home.

## THE RESPONSIBILITIES OF THE COVENANT
In the light of the three covenants mentioned, different groups are called to special responsibilities. The priests are expected to show a proper reverence and zeal in their worship in the Temple (1:6–2:9). Married people are expected to show loyalty and faithfulness to each other (2:10–16). All Israelites should honor God, and the payment of tithes is an outward sign of this duty (3:6–12). God is to be trusted. The time of the Prophet Malachi, shortly after the return from exile in Babylon in the period of the Second Temple, was clearly one of great difficulty and disillusion for his contemporaries in Judah. Twice he echoes the resigned complaints of those who feel God no longer cares about them, or is no longer able to do anything for them (*"What do we profit by keeping his command or by going about as mourners before the LORD of hosts? Now we count the arrogant happy; evildoers not only prosper, but when they put God to the test they escape,"* 3:14–15; see also 2:17). Each time Malachi answers by pointing them to the faithfulness of God and the sure fulfillment of the covenant promises in the future.

## THE MOSAIC LAW
This, the last Prophetic book of the Hebrew Bible, ends with a call to keep the Mosaic Law – *"Remember the teaching of my servant Moses, the statutes and ordinances that I commanded him at Horeb for all Israel"* (4:4) – a call that thus links Prophets and the Torah and gives them equal authority in the canon of Scripture. It also contains a promise that God will renew the prophetic succession, symbolized by the return of Elijah, the first of Israel's Prophets: *"He will turn the hearts of parents to their children and the hearts of children to their parents, so that I will not come and strike the land with a curse"* (4:6). Tradition recalled Elijah as being taken up to heaven rather than dying (2 Kgs. 2:11–12). The promise was still remembered much later (*see* Sir. 48:10; Mark 6:15; 15:35).

# THE BOOK

TITLE: Malachi

HEBREW TITLE: *Malachi*. In Hebrew the title means "my messenger," which may therefore be the personal name of the Prophet or a title used to describe him, perhaps based on 3:1

DATE: Fifth century BCE, the book is clearly post-exilic. It refers to the "governor" rather than a king; the Temple has been rebuilt and is again in use (it was completed by 515BCE); and the situation presupposed in the book seems to predate the return of Nehemiah to Jerusalem in 445BCE

AUTHORSHIP: *See* Hebrew Title *above*

# THE CONTENTS

**CHAPTERS 1–2:9**
1:1 Superscription
1:2–5 God's love for Israel
1:6–2:9 Charges against the priests

**CHAPTERS 2:10–3:5**
2:10–16 Divorce and interracial marriage
2:17–3:5 The Day of the LORD a refining judgment

**CHAPTER 3:6–4**
3:6–12 A call to pay tithes
3:13–4:3 Assurances to the disheartened
4:4–6 Two short additions calling for obedience to the Mosaic Law and promising the return of Elijah

# KEY THEMES

*Calls to repentance*

•

*The coming Day of the LORD*

•

*The return of Elijah*

For further reading see bibliography numbers: 196, 523

# THE GREEK EMPIRE

*The establishment of a Greek-based empire in Asia Minor began with Alexander the Great (336–23BCE). The influence of Greek culture and ideas was felt far beyond the strict boundaries of the Greek empire. This is known as Hellenization.*

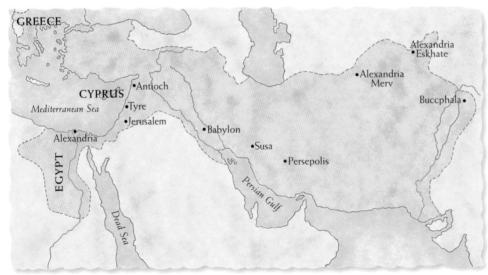

**APHRODITE**

The Greek goddess of love and beauty, Aphrodite was probably a fertility goddess in origin and may have originated in Phoenicia. She was related to the Assyro-Babylonian goddess Ishtar and the Syro-Phoenician goddess Astarte (*see p.141*).

CLASSICAL Greece was organized into city-states that formed defensive coalitions – especially the Delian League, which under Athenian and Spartan leadership drove back Persian invaders in the fifth century BCE. Macedonia, to the north of Greece, was a series of kingdoms finally united under one monarch, Philip II (359–36BCE). He went on to take the rest of Greece and form the first united Hellenistic kingdom.

Kingship, as opposed to coalition, was better suited to expansion, and when Alexander the Great succeeded his father, Philip, he set about extending the empire. Having won over Tyre, Egypt, and the Persian empire, Alexander continued east as far as the Indus until all of the known world was under his control, but he died in Babylon shortly afterward, leaving no clear successor.

By 275BCE, the empire was divided among the three dynasties of Alexander's generals: Ptolemy, Antigones, and Seleucus. Ptolemies reigned in Egypt until the death of Cleopatra (30BCE), the last of that line. Macedonia and

Greece went to Antigones, until they were annexed by Rome in 148 and 146BCE, respectively. Seleucus took the largest part of Alexander's former empire, eastern Mesopotamia, for his dynasty. Judea in particular was fought over by Ptolemaic and Seleucid kings, until Pompey took Jerusalem in 63BCE.

## THE SPREAD OF HELLENISM

Hellenism, the culture of the Greek empire, spread throughout the Mediterranean and up into Mesopotamia; it left a lasting impression. Koine, a Greek dialect, replaced the Aramaic of the Persian empire, and remained the *lingua franca* until the time of Constantine (fourth century CE). New settlements were an essential element in the spread of language and culture throughout the empire: new cities such as Alexandria, Antioch, and Seleucia, often built on or near the site of existing towns and capitals, imposed Hellenistic dominance on the regions. Greek ideas (the constitutions, the establishment of *gymnasia*, etc.) and philosophy presented a great dilemma for the Jews: should they welcome Greek ideas or reject them as being hostile to Torah? Varying answers were given at different times and in different

**THE GREEK EMPIRE**
*Under the leadership of Alexander the Great in the fourth century BCE, Greek influence spread from a base in the Peleponese into Asia Minor and then, with the collapse of the Persian empire, farther east across Asia as far as India. Alexander encouraged Greeks to marry with foreign peoples, thus forestalling the possibility of revolt.*

**TEMPLE OF APOLLO, DELPHI**
*Situated at the heart of the Sacred Precinct at Delphi, the Temple of Apollo has stood on this site since the sixth century BCE. Delphi was the center of Greek prophecy, where the incantations of the Pythia, a type of soothsayer, were interpreted by priests.*

areas where Jews lived. Hellenism was both rejected and assimilated (as, for example, in Egypt, which produced Philo; *see also* the *Letter of Aristeas*, which is an argument for Judaism). This explains the balance of Greek and Hebrew thought found in different expressions of the Jewish faith, and in the early Christian Church and the New Testament. Most Palestinian Jews fought hard in their resistance to Hellenization. Attempts by the Seleucid rulers Antiochus III and Antiochus IV Epiphanes to replace Jewish ways and religion with the culture and religion of the empire were met with fierce opposition, described in the books of the Maccabees (*pp.250–51*).

## EFFECTS ON THE JEWS
Jews in the Diaspora formed important colonies in Egypt at Elephantine (*see right*), Memphis, and Alexandria. Greek replaced Aramaic in the Alexandrian community, which sponsored the translation of the Hebrew Bible – now known as the Septuagint and abbreviated LXX. Not all Jewish writers would have followed Philo (20BCE–50CE) in detecting Stoic and Platonic thought in the Bible, but most early Christians used the Septuagint as their text of the Bible.

Few would have been familiar with Hebrew. A dispute between the "Hellenists" and the "Hebrews" among early Jewish Christians (Acts 6:1) may reflect continuing differences between Jews who spoke Greek and those who spoke Aramaic (*see pp.388–89*).

## THE NEW TESTAMENT
Most of the New Testament authors were Jews by birth, but they wrote in Greek. The worlds of Palestinian Judaism and Hellenism cannot easily be separated or distinguished. It seems probable that many Jews were bilingual and, to some extent, felt at home in both worlds. Their decision to use the Greek language reflected the ease with which this language was read and understood across the world. Paul, for example, claimed to be "Hebrew of Hebrews" (Phil. 3:5), yet showed himself to be an able writer in Greek. Gentile Christians, such as those in the new church at Corinth, would undoubtedly have faced early difficulties as they sought to reconcile their new faith with their purely Hellenistic philosophical and religious inheritance, as the epistles bear witness. The New Testament also occasionally uses "Greeks" to refer to Gentiles, apparently a common usage with no hidden connotation.

**PAINTED PLATE**
Greek art and sculpture reached a new level of sophistication. As a result, the Greeks had a profound influence on the advancement of cultural life in the ancient Near East. The spread of the empire compounded Greek influence already prevalent in the area from trade with the peoples of the coastal areas, such as the Philistines and the Phoenicians.

For further reading see bibliography numbers: 107, 391, 392, 394, 426, 502, 668

# AFTER ALEXANDER

*The period between the rise of Alexander (356–23BCE) and the coming of the Romans was a time of great importance in the emergence of what became Judaism. Despite this there are few surviving records of religion and life in Palestine.*

## ALEXANDER

Alexander's campaign against the Persians in 336BCE resulted in the overthrow of the Persian empire. Originally the king of Macedon, his own conquests stretched as far as India, and he built the greatest empire then known in the world on a policy of cooperation with other peoples. This led to the Hellenization of much of Asia and the influence of Greek thought on both Judaism and Christianity.

RELIGIOUS belief and practice during this period continued to concentrate on the keeping of the covenant conditions in Torah, for which the Temple and the priests were central. However, Jews were now dispersed into other countries, facing the questions of how to live as a Covenant People far from the Temple with non-Jews all around them. This led gradually to the emergence of the pre-rabbis (also known as the Pharisees) and of rabbinic Judaism, which was primarily concerned with how to apply Torah to life in new circumstances. There also emerged a recurring division of opinion, not only in the Diaspora but in Jerusalem itself: should the Jews be more or less like the nations around them? Already by the fifth century BCE a pattern of deep division existed between those who favored greater links with other nations and those who clung to the marks of religious and cultural identity, evident from action taken by both Ezra and Nehemiah (*see pp.160–63*) against mixed marriages in the Judean community. There was tension between those, often the upper classes, who embraced Hellenism and others who rejected it as a threat to their Jewish integrity. However, even those Jews who professed opposition to the new ideas of the Greek world were unable to avoid their influence.

## THE DIVIDED EMPIRE

Alexander died in 322BCE; there followed 20 years of struggle between four of his generals for control of his empire. Palestine was taken in 301BCE by Ptolemy, the general who had gained Egypt as his share of Alexander's empire. Ptolemaic rule in Palestine lasted for a hundred years, generally a time of peace and stability. However, the issue of rapprochement, or of separatism, remained. The Ptolemies encouraged the aristocracy to collect taxes for them: the opportunity to get rich by taking a cut of the taxes was an incentive to loyalty. But it also meant very heavy tax burdens on the people, creating dissatisfaction elsewhere in society. As for religious matters, it seems that the High Priest paid an annual tribute to the Ptolemaic king, but the Jews were free to follow their ancestral faith.

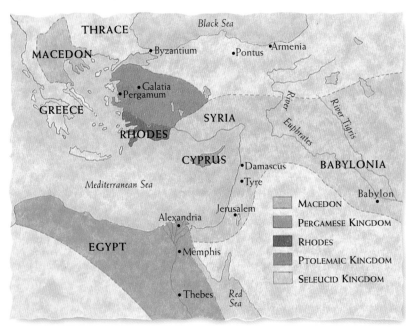

MACEDON
PERGAMESE KINGDOM
RHODES
PTOLEMAIC KINGDOM
SELEUCID KINGDOM

**DIVISION OF THE GREEK WORLD**
*After the Battle of Ipsus in 301BCE, three main power blocs emerged in the ancient Near East: one in Macedon and Greece; another in Syria and Mesopotamia, with its capital at Antioch; the third in Egypt from where the Ptolemaic kings ruled.*

THE LIGHTHOUSE, ALEXANDRIA
*Jewish tradition states that the Greek translation of the Hebrew Scriptures was produced in Alexandria with Ptolemy II's support, indicating the extent of Greek influence even in religious circles.*

## RULING FAMILIES

Two important families who came to prominence during the Ptolemaic period were the Oniads and the Tobiads. The Oniads were the official high priestly family, and tended to be more conservative in their attitude to Hellenism. By contrast, the Tobiads were an aristocratic, moneyed family who embraced Hellenism and were quite lax toward the Jewish Law. The two families came into conflict on several occasions over the next few decades, most famously in

245BCE when the High Priest Onias II angered Ptolemy III by withholding tribute; but Joseph the Tobiad pacified the king and gained his favor, along with extensive tax-collecting rights in Palestine.

## THE SELEUCIDS

In 198 BCE Ptolemaic rule gave way to Syrian-based Seleucid rule (so called from Seleucus I, who had ruled from 312–281BCE) when the Seleucid king Antiochus III captured Palestine. Initially, the Jews were allowed to retain their native laws and customs. But under the later Antiochus IV (175–64BCE), Jason, the brother of the then-serving High Priest Onias III, offered money to the Seleucid king in exchange for the high priesthood and permission to introduce Greek institutions into Jerusalem. Antiochus accepted Jason's proposal, but Jason was soon outbid and deposed by the even more extreme Hellenist Menelaus, who was supported by the Tobiads. Jason tried to regain the high priesthood from Menelaus by force.

Antiochus interpreted Menelaus' actions as a revolt against his own authority, and in 168BCE took action to break what he saw as the resistance to his power. He pulled down Jerusalem's walls and built an armed citadel overlooking Mount Zion; also, probably on the advice of Menelaus, he desecrated the Temple altar and forbade the Jewish Law on pain of death. Instead, he ordered illegitimate sacrifices. This is the scenario that is addressed by the book of Daniel and that proved to be the catalyst for the Maccabean rebellion (*see pp.250–51*).

PTOLEMY I
After the death of Alexander, Ptolemy, one of Alexander's generals, had himself recognized as satrap (commander) of Egypt, while outwardly supporting the accession of Alexander's son. When the boy Alexander was killed in 310BCE, a struggle for control of the empire took place, with Ptolemy capturing Egypt and Palestine. He took the title of king and reigned until 285BCE.

# THE SELEUCID KINGS

| 320BCE | 300BCE | 280BCE | 260BCE | 240BCE | 220BCE | 200BCE | 180BCE | 160BCE |
|--------|--------|--------|--------|--------|--------|--------|--------|--------|

Seleucus I Nicator (311–280BCE)

Antiochus II Theos (261–46BC)

Seleucus III Soter (225–23BCE)

Seleucus IV Philopator (187–75BCE)

Antiochus V Eupator (163–62BCE)

Antiochus I Soter (280–61BCE)

Seleucus II Callinicus (246–25BCE)

Antiochus the Great (223–187BCE)

Antiochus IV Epiphanes (175–64BCE)

**For further reading see bibliography numbers:** 131, 344, 392, 402, 426, 559

# THE MACCABEES

*During the second and first centuries BCE the Maccabeans successfully opposed
the desecration of Jewish holy places and forged an effective resistance to their
Greek overlords. This period was the peak of Jewish independence after the Exile.*

## THE SELEUCID RULERS

The Seleucids were the
dynasty of Greek rulers
who controlled Syria and
Mesopotamia from the late
fourth century to the mid-
first century BCE. Their
founder, Seleucus, was a
general under Alexander
the Great. In 198BCE, the
Seleucid king Antiochus III
captured Palestine from the
Ptolemies but was later
killed while robbing a
temple in order to pay a
15,000-talent fine imposed
by the Romans. His
successor, Seleucus IV,
increased taxation and
tried to rob the Jerusalem
Temple in order to meet
the payments. After the
assassination of Seleucus
IV in 175BCE, the son of
Antiochus III – Antiochus
IV – (see box, opposite)
seized power.

THE Hasmoneans were a family of
Jewish priests who led the Maccabean
rebellion against the anti-Judaism
measures imposed by Antiochus IV (*see
opposite*). They subsequently established
an independent Jewish nation and became its
rulers, forming the Hasmonean dynasty. The
name "Hasmonean" perhaps comes from their
supposed ancestor Hasmonai, and the term
"Maccabean" comes from the nickname
Maccabaios ("Hammer") given to Judas, who
initially led the revolt.

## THE MACCABEAN REVOLT

The story of the revolt is found in the
Apocrypha in the first book of Maccabees.
It began when a Maccabean priest Mattathias
killed a Jew and a royal officer who were
involved in offering the offensive sacrifices
demanded by Antiochus' decree (*p.249*).
Mattathias then fled to the hills with his five
sons and some other supporters. Under the
leadership of Mattathias' son Judas, this group
waged a guerrilla war against the Seleucids, the
Greek rulers of Palestine. Their success resulted
in the decree against Judaism being revoked in
164BCE. That same year the Temple was purified
and rededicated, an event that is still commemorated annually by the feast of Hanukkah.

Although they had originally intended
simply to restore religious freedom, the
Maccabees now began to fight for political
independence. Judas continued as their leader
until he was killed in action in 161BCE.

**THE JUDEAN HILLS**
*During the Maccabean revolt, the Judean Hills
became a center for opposition to Greek rule: "many who
were seeking righteousness and justice went down to the
wilderness to live there ... because troubles pressed heavily
upon them" (1 Macc. 2:29–30).*

**MATTATHIAS KILLS THE APOSTATE**
*Mattathias and his sons were forced to take part in a sacrifice to
the Greek god Zeus. Outraged by this desecration, Mattathias
"gave vent to righteous anger; he ran and killed him on the
altar ... he killed the king's officer who was forcing them
to sacrifice, and he tore down the altar" (1 Macc. 2:24–25).*

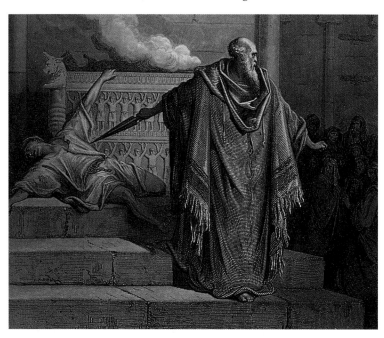

**MACCABEAN GRAVES**
*The hills of Judaea became a center of guerrilla resistance and also the center of the rebel community. Here the Jews brought "their sons, their wives, and their livestock" (1 Macc. 2:30).*

At this point, his brother Jonathan took over. After initial engagements with the Seleucids and a period of stalemate, Jonathan exploited a leadership dispute in the Seleucid empire to have himself nominated first as High Priest (152BCE) and then as general and governor of the province (150BCE). He also managed to gain concessions of both tax and territory from the Seleucid king Demetrius II, but he was eventually captured and killed in 142BCE by Trypho, a pretender to the Seleucid throne.

## SIMON BECOMES LEADER

The last surviving Maccabean brother, Simon, then took up the leadership and high priesthood. Because of leadership struggles in the Seleucid empire he was able to elicit from Demetrius II complete freedom from Seleucid taxation for the Jews, thereby confirming their independence (1 Macc. 13:41). On the strength of this, the Jews passed a decree eulogizing Simon and making him their hereditary leader and High Priest, but the tell-tale qualifying clause, *"until a trustworthy prophet should arise"* (1 Macc. 14:41), shows that there were some reservations about establishing a high priesthood *not* of the traditional line of Zadok *(see pp.64–65)*.

## INDEPENDENCE FOR THE JEWS

Simon was murdered by his own ambitious son-in-law in 134BCE, and Simon's son John Hyrcanus succeeded him as leader and High Priest of the newly independent state. John made considerable territorial gains and was a conscientious and generally respected High Priest, but his successors were somewhat less illustrious.

After John's death in 104BCE, his son Aristobulus seized power by imprisoning his brothers and starving his mother. Aristobulus died in 103BCE, and was succeeded by his brother Alexander Jannaeus, who was notorious for his ruthless cruelty and his contempt for the Torah, even though he was High Priest. Jannaeus was succeeded in 76BCE by his widow, Salome Alexandra, under whom the lay religious group known as the Pharisees *(pp.288–89)* became very influential. On Salome's death in 67BCE, her younger son Aristobulus II seized power instead of the legitimate successor, the older brother Hyrcanus II. Aristobulus spent the next four years fighting Hyrcanus, until the Romans conquered Judea in 63BCE, thereby ending the brothers' power struggle and Jewish independence.

The last two Hasmonean rulers, Hyrcanus II (63–40BCE) and Antigonus (40–37BCE), were puppets of the Romans, with no real political power. Antigonus' execution by the Romans in 37BCE was a sorry end to the dynasty that had started off with such high ideals.

**ANTIOCHUS IV**
Known as Antiochus Epiphanes, "manifest" or "splendid," Antiochus IV was in conflict with Egypt and needed control of Judea. He was an ambitious ruler who was greatly influenced by Greek culture and religion, hence his openness to those in Jerusalem who asked for Hellenization *(see pp.246–47)* and promised him money that would fund his campaigns. His subsequent persecution of the Jews was probably intended to quell perceived unrest in Judea after his recent defeat in nearby Egypt. He died of illness in 164BCE while campaigning in the east.

# THE HASMONEAN RULERS

| | Jonathan (152–42BCE) | John Hyrcanus (134–4BCE) | Alexander Jannaeus (103–76BCE) | Aristobulus II (67–63BCE) | Antigonus (40–37BCE) |
|---|---|---|---|---|---|

| 160BCE | 150BCE | 140BCE | 130BCE | 120BCE | 110BCE | 100BCE | 90BCE | 80BCE | 70BCE | 60BCE | 50BCE | 40BCE |
|---|---|---|---|---|---|---|---|---|---|---|---|---|

| | Simon (142–34BCE) | | Aristobulus I (104–3BCE) | Salome Alexandra (76–67BCE) | Hyrcanus II (63–40BCE) |
|---|---|---|---|---|---|

For further reading see bibliography numbers: 334, 344, 394, 426, 474, 559, 641

# THE
# APOCRYPHA

The Apocrypha (from the Greek meaning "hidden" or "secret") is a collection of books found in many Christian Bibles, but not in the Jewish canon. They form part of the Septuagint, the Greek translation of the Hebrew. They appear in Roman Catholic Bibles as a result of their inclusion in Jerome's translation of the Bible into Latin (the Vulgate), and are called "deutero-canonical" (works that are secondary or of later date). Some other works of the Apocrypha appear in Bibles of the Orthodox Church. Fourteen books are added to Protestant Bibles as the Apocrypha. Since they are not in the Hebrew Bible, Judaism does not refer to these books collectively, though it knows of "Outside Books," *Hishonim*. There are other apocryphal books, both Jewish and Christian, not included in any canon (e.g., there are apocryphal gospels: *see* bibliography 718, 854).

The works in the Apocrypha were composed mostly between the second century BCE and the second century CE, and did not exist as a defined corpus. In the Roman Catholic Bible, they are found scattered throughout the Bible, often attached to books with which they were thought to be connected. Most survive only in translation, some in more than one version. Many are incomplete; some exist only as fragments.

The issue of these books' status came to a head in 382CE, when Jerome began to make his translation. Believing that only the Hebrew text had authority, he rejected the Greek books, calling them "apocrypha" – probably he meant "hidden" or "secret." However, the books went into the canon of Christian Scripture (until the Reformation reopened the questions about them). The books of 1 and 2 Esdras and the Prayer of Manasseh are not included in Roman Catholic Bibles, but the following works are found in the Protestant Apocrypha: 1 and 2 Esdras, Tobit, Judith, Additions to the book of Esther, Book of Wisdom, [Wisdom of Jesus ben] Sirach (or Ecclesiasticus), 1 Baruch, Letter of Jeremiah, Additions to the book of Daniel, Prayer of Manasseh, and 1 and 2 Maccabees. The official text of the Old Testament of the Orthodox Churches includes 1 Esdras, Tobit, Judith, Book of Wisdom, Sirach, Baruch, 1–3 Maccabees, and the Letter of Jeremiah; the Additions to Daniel are included in the book itself.

# APOCRYPHA
# FICTION

*In the stories of Judith, Susanna, Bel, and Tobit, God opposes idolatry and vindicates the righteous. Although not considered canonical in Protestant and Hebrew Bibles, these books have profoundly inspired Jews and Christians alike.*

APART from Tobit, the earliest copies of the fictional works in the Apocrypha are in Greek, although each narrative could have originated from a Semitic language. Some scholars contend that these stories have roots in historical personages. The stories of Susanna and of Bel and the Dragon are additions to the book of Daniel.

## THE BOOK OF JUDITH

The Assyrian king, Nebuchadnezzar, directed the commander of his army, Holofernes, to conquer Judea and its surrounding region. Achior the Ammonite reported to the skeptical Holofernes of the powerful God who would defend the Judeans as long as they did not sin against their God. Judith, a virtuous and devout heroine, entered the Assyrian camp, and falsely told of the Israelites' sin. Captivated by Judith's beauty, Holofernes invited her to dine privately with him. When he became drunk, Judith decapitated him and returned to the Israelite camp with his head. The Israelites then regained their confidence and routed the Assyrians.

The significant historical difficulties in Judith do not mar the wonderfully ironic quality in the narrative. Judith's conspiracy employs extensive double entendre and possibly some

**JUDITH SLAYING HOLOFERNES**
*This 17th-century painting by Artemisia Gentileschi (1593–c.1652) depicts Judith killing the Babylonian commander Holofernes.*

outright lies (*see* 11:12–14, 18–19). Nevertheless, her speeches testify to a deep belief in God's sovereign and saving hand. Several medieval Jewish *Midrashim* also recount this tale.

## THE STORY OF SUSANNA

Although it sometimes precedes the book of Daniel, the story of Susanna was added to Daniel in most Greek and Latin texts.

While in her garden, Susanna, *"a woman of great refinement and beautiful in appearance"* (Sus. 1:31), attracted the attention of two wicked elders. When she refused to have sex with them, they falsely accused her of adultery. After her prayer to God, the young Daniel accused the elders of having *"given false evidence against her"* (Sus. 1:49). When she returned to court, it became obvious that the elders had lied. Susanna's honor was vindicated by God, and Daniel emerged as a hero.

There are two versions of Susanna; they are known as the Septuagint and the Theodotion accounts. The Septuagint version is an older and shorter story; it draws the moral that young people are beloved. The Theodotion account is the more popular form – it includes brilliant narrative touches and emphasizes Daniel's fame (v.64).

## ADDITIONS TO EXISTING BOOKS

Three small books in the Apocrypha are additions to existing books. The Prayer of Manasseh derives from 2 Chronicles 33:18*ff.*, which mentions "his prayer to God" being preserved in the chronicles of the kings of Israel; a later writer has produced this prayer. The Prayer of Azariah and the Song of the Three Young Men is an addition to the book of Daniel in the Septuagint, and between Daniel 3:23 and 3:24 supplies a prayer suitable for the persecuted, and a hymn of praise sung by the three in the fiery furnace. Bel and the Dragon is another addition to Daniel in the Septuagint. It consists of two stories, modifications to the account of the lions' den in Daniel 6, and tells how Daniel scoffed to the Persian king about the lifelessness of the idol "Bel." The king retorted that Bel was a living god who devoured offerings every night, but Daniel told him he had been deceived. The king called the priests of Bel and told them: *"if you do not tell me who is eating these provisions you shall die. But if you prove that Bel is eating them, Daniel shall die because he has spoken blasphemy"* (Bel & Dr. 1:8–9). That evening Daniel spread ashes on the floor of the temple of Bel. The next morning, footprints in the ashes proved that Bel's priests and their families had entered the temple and consumed the offerings. The king was enraged and slew the priests. Daniel destroyed the idol.

Then Daniel prevented further worship of a living dragon by killing it with poisoned cakes. The Babylonians reacted by throwing Daniel into the lions' den. But he was protected by an angel who sent the Prophet Habakkuk to Daniel with food.

Similar to episodes in the canonical book of Daniel, Bel and the Dragon displays God's power over Babylonian deities and heightens Daniel's status as a Prophet of the only living God. Like Susanna, the book exists in two Greek versions.

## THE BOOK OF TOBIT

A righteous exile in Nineveh, Tobit was blinded and could no longer work. Ultimately, he prayed to God for relief through death. At the same time, Sarah, a young woman living in Media, whose previous seven husbands had each been killed by the demon Asmodeus, prayed for death. Tobit sent his son Tobias to collect money stored in Media. Tobias was guided by the angel Raphael, disguised as a man, to collect the money. Along the way, he married Sarah, defeated Asmodeus, and acquired balm for his father's eyes. Upon Tobias' return, and Raphael's revelation of his angelic status, Tobit gave thanks to God. The book closes after Tobit has predicted the destruction of Nineveh and the rebuilding of Jerusalem.

The central theme of the book of Tobit is God's providential care over righteous Israelites. Tobit emphasizes angels and demons, and the practical reward received from righteous acts such as prayer, ritual burial, and especially almsgiving. Hebrew and Aramaic copies at Qumran testify to Tobit's influence in early Judaism. Medieval *Midrashim* also contain versions of this story.

### JUDITH

King Nebuchadnezzar defeats the Medes and then sends his general Holofernes to punish the Israelites for refusing to support him. The general lays siege to the town of Bethulia, among whose citizens is the devout widow, Judith. She leaves the town and enters the enemy camp, offering to help Holofernes defeat the Israelites. When he is drunk, however, she decapitates him and runs back to the town, rousing the Israelites who defeat the Assyrians in a surprise attack.

### SUSANNA

Two respected elders attempt to rape a beautiful and virtuous woman. When she refuses them, she is accused of adultery and brought to public trial on the false charges. She is sentenced to death, but Daniel intervenes and proves that the evidence is false. As a result, the elders are put to death in her place.

### BEL AND THE DRAGON

Daniel mocks the statue of Bel that is said to consume food and drink daily. He proves that the food and drink are consumed by the priests and not by the statue. King Cyrus has the priests executed. Daniel also destroys a dragon worshiped by the Babylonians; as a result, the mob demands that Daniel be sent to the lions. But he remains unharmed and is freed by Nebuchadnezzar, who throws Daniel's enemies to the lions, and they are instantly devoured.

### TOBIT

Tobit, a devout man, has been blinded by an act of kindness. His son Tobias is assisted by the angel Raphael, who is disguised as Azariah, and marries Sarah. Tobias exorcises a demon, Asmodeus, from Sarah who has killed each of her previous husbands on her wedding night. Tobit regains his sight and dies a rich and happy old man.

**For further reading see bibliography numbers:** 224, 448, 481, 488, 552, 566, 591, 718, 733, 814, 854

# APOCRYPHA
# WISDOM

*Wisdom books became increasingly popular in the intertestamental period,
and two major examples appear in the Apocrypha, the Book of Wisdom
and Sirach, along with one smaller example, Baruch.*

W ISDOM literature
(*see pp.170–71*) reveals
the Jews exploring the
ways of God in the
world and in creation. Where early
wisdom works had said little of the
covenant history of Israel, the later
works of the Apocrypha make this
an important part of their search
for the truth of God. The two major
wisdom works in the Apocrypha
are the Book of Wisdom, often
known as the Wisdom of Solomon,
and Ecclesiasticus, or the Wisdom
of Jesus, son of Sira, often
known as Sirach or ben Sira.

## THE BOOK OF WISDOM

The Book of Wisdom was written
in Greek by a Hellenistic author,
possibly from Egypt: the writer
quotes from the Septuagint (the
Greek translation of the Bible), not
from the Hebrew. Because the book
itself was included in the Septuagint, where it appears after
the book of Job, it appears also in the Vulgate (the Latin
version of the Bible based on the Septuagint), and thus
appears in the canon of Roman Catholic and most Orthodox
Churches. It is not in the Hebrew Bible or the Protestant
Bible (*see pp.252–53*). It was written some time between
100BCE and 100CE.

The themes of the book are skillfully interwoven, but
a progression of ideas is discernible. Chapters 1:1–5:23 urge
the readers of the book to seek that divine righteousness
which is immortal. There is a strong emphasis on immortality
and on the final reward of the just (*see especially 3:1–4ff:
"But the souls of the righteous are in the hand of God, and no torment*

**SOLOMON**
*Although the Book of Wisdom is also called the Wisdom of
Solomon, it was probably composed centuries after his death.*

*will ever touch them … For though in the
sight of others they were punished, their
hope is full of immortality"*). Chapter
6 begins with a rhetorical appeal
to the kings of the world to recognize where their power and
authority come from, and to
understand that they must rule
by wisdom that comes from God.
Chapters 6:12–9:18 become a
series of celebrations of Wisdom
as a bride of great beauty, worth
pursuing without fail – *"She is more
beautiful than the sun, and excels every
constellation of the stars"* (7:29). Part
of this praise is expressed in
strongly Hellenistic terms (e.g.,
*"There is in her a spirit that is intelligent,
holy, unique, manifold, subtle, mobile,
clear, unpolluted, distinct, invulnerable,
loving the good, keen, irresistible,
beneficent, humane, steadfast, sure, free
from anxiety, all-powerful, overseeing
all, and penetrating through all spirits
that are intelligent, pure, and altogether
subtle …"* 7:22b–23 *ff.*); some scholars have claimed that
other parts have been drawn from Egyptian praises of Isis.

Wisdom is not identified with Torah, as she is in Sirach
and Baruch, but the presence of Wisdom at creation and
the role of Wisdom as God's agent and instrument are
close to Proverbs 8 and Sirach 24. Chapters 10–12 turn to
the theme of Wisdom in history, while 13–15 point out the
grievous consequences of ignorance and error. Chapter 16
to the end reverts to the Exodus narrative and shows how
all creation works together with God in bringing about
God's purposes (*"For creation, serving you who made it, exerts
itself to punish the unrighteous, and in kindness relaxes on behalf of
those who trust in you,"* 16:24).

## THE BOOK OF SIRACH

Sirach or Ecclesiasticus tells us the name of its author (*"I have written in this book, Jesus, son of Eleazar son of Sirach of Jerusalem, whose mind poured forth wisdom,"* 50:27). According to his grandson, he arrived in Egypt *"in the thirty-eighth year of the reign of Euergetes and stayed for some time."* That would give a date for Sirach of c.180BCE. This agrees with the fact that 50:1–21 is a poem in praise of Simeon II, who was High Priest from 219 to 196BCE, implying that Simeon had been dead for some years (for the history of the Maccabees, *see pp.250–51*)

The book is written in Greek, but Hebrew manuscripts of about two-thirds of it have survived. Because this book is in the Septuagint, it appears in Orthodox and Roman Catholic Bibles (*see pp.252–53*). Although it is not in the Hebrew Bible, it was often quoted by rabbis as though it had authority. The book is made up of a wide variety of different material. In general it follows the line of thought and theology later associated with the Sadducees. It stays close to the biblical texts that precede it (but to what extent these texts were, at this date, regarded as "the Bible" is unknown; *see pp.474–75*). It looks to the past for examples and inspiration. For that reason the author exhorts his readers, "Let us now sing the praises of famous men, the heroes of our nation's history," and follows this with a long recital of those who have exemplified the right and wrong ways to live (chs.44–49), followed by the praise of Simon. Unlike the Book of Wisdom, Sirach does not pursue speculations about life after death, but claims instead that the pursuit of wisdom and the service of God are their own reward. For that reason, the book is distinctly Deuteronomistic (*p.105*) in its outlook.

## OTHER WISDOM BOOKS OF THE APOCRYPHA

The one or two smaller wisdom books in the Apocrypha are associated with the Prophet Jeremiah. Baruch claims to be the work of Jeremiah's secretary and friend (Jer. 32:12–16; 36:4ff.). It is in three dissimilar parts. Chapters 1:1–3:8 are in prose, telling the conquered people how the book came into being and how it is to be used. Chapters 3:9–4:4 are a poem in the style of wisdom literature, speaking of Wisdom as belonging to Israel (*"She has not been heard of in Canaan, or seen in Teman,"* 3:22). Wisdom is equated with *"the book of the commandments of God, the law that endures for ever"* (4:1), and Israel is reproached for having abandoned her (*"For you provoked the one who made you by sacrificing to demons and not to God. You forgot the everlasting God, who brought you up, and you grieved Jerusalem, who reared you. For she saw the wrath that came upon you from God ..."* 4:7–9). The third part (4:5–5:9) is more in the style of Isaiah 40–66 (*see pp.202–3*) and appeals to the people to have courage and to not lose faith. The Letter of Jeremiah forms chapter 6 of this book in the Vulgate, although it is clearly a separate composition criticizing idolatry.

## THE BOOK OF WISDOM

Chapters 1:1–6:11 contrast the lives of the ungodly with the righteous who put their trust in God. They describe how the righteous will triumph and the Final Judgment. Chapters 6:12–9:18 describe Wisdom personified as a woman, her many attributes and virtues. Chapters 10:1–19:21 describe how Wisdom and God have worked through Israelite history. The text then describes the folly of idolatry, which will be punished, narrating specific events in the Israelites' wilderness experience: the manna; the terror of the Egyptians; and the death of the Egyptian firstborn. Chapter 19 describes the Israelites' deliverance and the new creation.

## SIRACH

The opening chapters (1–24) are a series of precepts and proverbial advice for living a devout life. These include proper behavior toward parents, the poor, friends, and relationships with others in general. Much of the advice is miscellaneous (e.g., ch.7). Other themes include pride and the need for humility, relations between rich and poor, the need for self-control in speech and conduct with others (18:30–20:20). The section ends with an address by Wisdom herself (24:3–25:2). The following section deals with social behavior, behavior in commerce, family life, and the glory of God (25:3–43:33). Additional chapters (44:1–50:26) relate stories of the famous men of Israel, the Patriarchs, the Prophets, and kings of Israel. The book closes with an autobiographical note, once again praising Wisdom (50:27–51:30).

## BARUCH

Early verses describe the historical setting, around the time of Jeremiah, to whom Baruch was secretary. Chapters 1:15–3:8 describe the people's sin in a prayer addressed to God. A prayer to Wisdom follows (3:9–4:5). The book concludes with verses to console and encourage those in exile (4:5–5:9).

**For further reading see bibliography numbers:** 180, 448, 481, 488, 552, 591, 638, 703, 713, 718, 733, 817, 854

# APOCRYPHA
# HISTORY

*The purpose and protective care of God continued to be seen in history, and books were written to tell this story. Three historical books appear in the Apocrypha, together with the Additions to Esther.*

THE works in the Apocrypha were composed mainly between the second century BCE and the second century CE. The earlier part of this period is known as the Hellenistic period of Jewish history, when Greek rule and culture extended over the whole of the Near East (*see pp.246–47*). The three historical books in the Apocrypha, i.e., that were not accepted into the Jewish canon of Scripture, are 1 Esdras, and 1 and 2 Maccabees (3 Maccabees is in Greek and Slavonic Bibles, and 4 Maccabees is an appendix to the Greek Bible). Together they cover the period from the Exile to the beginning of the time of John Hyrcanus (*see p.251*). They are, however, very different from one another.

## BOOK OF 1 ESDRAS
In the Apocrypha, the book of 1 Esdras has no connection with 2 Esdras, beyond the fact that Esdras (the Greek form of Ezra, *pp.160–61*) is the central character in both. The book of 1 Esdras begins with King Josiah celebrating the Passover in Jerusalem, in a way not seen since earlier times: *"No passover like it had been kept in Israel since the times of the prophet Samuel"* (1 Esd. 1:20). The story continues into the Exile, following the narrative of 2 Chronicles 35:1–36:21, but then switches to Ezra 1: the decree of Cyrus that allowed the Jews to return and rebuild the Temple (1 Esd. 2:1–15).

The opposition of Persian officials is recorded in 1 Esdras 2:16–30 (*cf.* Ezra 4:7–24). The book then moves to new ground with a debate between the three bodyguards of King Darius about the three greatest powers or forces in the world (1 Esd. 3:1–5:6). The competition was won by Zerubbabel,

when he corrected his first suggestion of *"Women are strongest"* (1 Esd. 3:12) to *"Great is truth, and strongest of all"* (1 Esd. 4:41). The remainder of the book then follows the narrative of Ezra, with only minor variations. The most important of these is that all mentions of Nehemiah (*see pp.154–55*) is omitted, and nothing from the book of Nehemiah is included.

Although many suggestions have been made, it is not possible to say why this Greek version of the Hebrew text of Ezra was written, introducing the variants that it does. The story of the debate, which culminates in truth being recognized as the strongest force in the world, had immense consequences in the Western world. It authorized the pursuit of truth as the highest human good – *magna est veritas et praevalet* (great is the truth and it prevails).

**JONATHAN AND APOLLONIUS**
*This 19th-century engraving by Gustave Doré depicts Jonathan in the presence of the army of Apollonius (1 Macc. 10:67–82).*

## BOOKS OF 1 AND 2 MACCABEES
The books of Maccabees show the brilliance of the religious imagination of the Jews. They take the same basic stories and show how they point to different truths about God and human conduct. Both 1 and 2 Maccabees should be read in conjunction with 3 and 4 Maccabees (not in the Apocrypha).

The book of 1 Maccabees is a straightforward celebration of the Hasmoneans – the family name of the Maccabees, and the name given to the Judean dynasty that descended from them (*see pp.250–51*) – which justifies the way they took power. Their success was founded on the way in which the priest Mattathias and his son refused to abandon Torah and the Covenant, and resisted the attempt of the Seleucids and their Jewish supporters to introduce Greek ideas and practices into Jerusalem. The book follows the story of the Hasmoneans, and places particular emphasis on Simon (142–34BCE), describing him in terms that are overtly Messianic (1 Macc. 14:8–15). The book draws on public and official documents and is written in a style reminiscent of the books of Samuel and Kings.

The book of 2 Maccabees concentrates on the early events of the Maccabean revolt, prefacing the account with two letters that urge the Jews in Egypt to celebrate the purification of the Temple (2 Macc. 1:1–9; 1:10–2:18). The book uses the story of the successful revolt of Judas to emphasize central truths of Jewish faith – the Torah, observance of the Sabbath, the Temple, the importance of keeping faith (even under persecution), and, above all, the faithfulness of God to those who keep faith themselves. It may be that the writer of 2 Maccabees was an opponent of the later Hasmoneans, who had betrayed the purer faith of Judas. Thus the book may have been written at the time of the Hasmonean ruler Alexander Jannaeus (103–76BCE).

## BOOKS OF 3 AND 4 MACCABEES

The book of 3 Maccabees, a later composition from the first century BCE or CE, is concerned with the fate of the Jewish people in Egypt. The writer seems to be familiar with the book of Esther and *The Letter of Aristeas* (a fictional account of the origin of the Greek translation of the Bible – the Septuagint [LXX] – and a plea for the wisdom of Judaism that makes it a partner of Greek philosophy). However, the book is far more anti-Gentile than *Aristeas*. It tells of the intention of Ptolemy, the Egyptian ruler, to desecrate the Holy of Holies and to destroy the Jews of Alexandria. In the end, the Jewish people are vindicated, and the Egyptian ruler acknowledges God.

The book of 4 Maccabees was written by a Jew much influenced by Greek Stoic philosophy. It opens with a defense of reason and of the classic virtues (4 Macc.1:18), showing how biblical figures such as Joseph and Moses ruled themselves by reason, which is expressed in Jewish law. Chapters 5–12 draw on 2 Maccabees 3–4 to retell the story of Eleazar, son of Aaron, and of the mother and the seven brothers, all of whom are martyred. In contrast to 2 Maccabees, where the emphasis is on discipline and patience, the book of 4 Maccabees emphasizes the sacrificial importance of martyrdom.

## ADDITIONS TO ESTHER

Among the Historical books of the Apocrypha may be included the Additions to Esther. These 107 verses that Jerome found in his Greek text, but not in the Hebrew, are not continuous and appear to come from different writers and different times. They make the book far more explicitly religious and stress the rewards of devotion to God.

## 1 ESDRAS

### BOOK OF 1 ESDRAS

Josiah celebrates the Passover (ch.1). Zerubbabel attempts to rebuild the Temple (chs.2–7). The exiles return to Jerusalem (chs.8–9).

## ADDITIONS TO ESTHER

Various additions to the book telling of the Jewish heroine and her defeat of the Jews' enemies (*see pp.166–67*). These add a far more theological aspect to the story than in the canonical book.

## 1 & 2 MACCABEES

### BOOK OF 1 MACCABEES

Mattathias and the uprising (chs.1–2). The campaigns of the Hasmonean kings: Judas Maccabeus (chs.3–9); Jonathan Maccabeus (chs.10–12); Simon Maccabeus (chs 13–16).

### BOOK OF 2 MACCABEES

Introduction (chs.1–2). Events leading to the Maccabean revolt (chs.3–5). The Martyrdom of Eleazar and the Seven Brothers (chs.6–7). The revolt of Judas Maccabeus (chs.8–15).

For further reading see bibliography numbers: 334, 335, 344, 448, 481, 552, 591, 718, 733, 854

# APOCALYPTIC

*Apocalyptic writings are those that reveal and make known things
that would otherwise remain hidden. As prophecy ceased in Israel,
so Apocalyptic became increasingly important.*

THERE is only one long apocalyptic work in the Apocrypha, 2 Esdras. As it stands, it is a Christian work, but it incorporates a Jewish apocalyptic work. The words "apocalypse" and "apocalyptic" come from a Greek word meaning "to uncover or reveal." These terms have come to be used of writings that began to appear in the centuries after the Exile, and continued until about the third century CE. They were both Jewish and Christian. Many different kinds of writings have been called "apocalyptic": what they have in common is that they claim to be a record of disclosures or revelations from God, often mediated, through angels, visions, and dreams. Some of them are guided tours of the heavenly realms; others are maps of the future. They trace the course of history in stages down to the time of the writer, often in the form of prophecies of the future, and then reveal what is about to happen next – usually a final end (they are eschatological, dealing with last things). Evil forces and hostile enemies are defeated, the wicked are judged, and God is the victor in triumph.

## HISTORICAL ORIGINS

Apocalyptic became prominent in the centuries following the Exile. After the Exile, there was a strong move to make sure that such a catastrophe should never happen again. The Prophets had repeatedly warned the people that their lawless and wayward behavior would bring disaster upon them. After the disaster had happened, those at the

THE FOUR BEASTS
*This 12th-century manuscript shows Daniel's vision of
God enthroned above the four beasts of the Apocalypse.*

center of power, in state and the rebuilt Temple, attempted to make sure that in the future all people would know exactly what was expected of them. Chapters 8–10 of the book of Nehemiah (*pp.162–63*) record how Ezra read the Torah to the assembled people, and how they gave their consent to the Torah, saying "Amen and Amen." Even if this is an idealized picture, it summarizes how important the Torah now became as the guide to right behavior, behavior that would make sure the catastrophe of Exile would never happen again.

## THE DECLINE OF PROPHECY

The Prophets might have been expected to reinforce the central importance of Torah, and prophecy certainly continued after the Exile. However, the Prophets were also unpredictable. They were speaking with the direct authority of God, using the phrase *koh amar Adonai* ("Thus says the LORD … "). This meant that the priests or other authorities could not control what the Prophets were saying. Prophets were therefore somewhat ignored, and the word of God came directly from Torah, mediated through the priests. Even so, Prophets continued with their predictions: Agabus, in the book of Acts, performed a prophetic action that any of his distant predecessors would have recognized (Acts 21:10*ff.*).

But the Prophets had always been concerned with the future, with pointing out the consequences, both for good and for ill, of what people were doing in the present. The gap left by the disappearance of this mystic knowledge was increasingly filled by Apocalyptic. Although Apocalyptic was an important form of religious encouragement, it was not endorsed by mainstream religion. Here, the emphasis remained on the keeping of Torah and working out the ways that Torah could be brought to bear on the ever-changing circumstances of Jewish life. The tendency to move toward Apocalyptic can already be seen in some of the Prophetic books: for example, Isaiah 24–27; Ezekiel 38–39; Zechariah 12–14; and Joel 3. They give hope to people in times of crisis, reassuring them that God is on their side. In the Bible as a whole, the two major books of Apocalyptic are Daniel (*pp.216–17*) and Revelation (*pp.468–69*), and in the Apocrypha, 2 Esdras.

Common themes in Apocalyptic are:
• History moves to a purpose under the control of God: the calculation of times and seasons is revealed.
• History is moving to a final climax, when the enemies of God and of Israel will be defeated.
• Cosmic powers, as well as earthly enemies, pit themselves against God and the people of faith, but they are defeated.
• The faithful people of God will be rewarded – this means that God has the power to restore them to life after death.
• Suffering and trouble in the present are the birth pangs of a new age in which the Messiah will come and rule.
• The coming kingdom and the reward of the faithful (and the punishment of the wicked) are described.

## SECRET CODES OF APOCALYPTIC

Much of Apocalyptic is written in code, especially those works that deal with the course of history moving to a final climax in which the wicked are destroyed and God's final triumph is inaugurated. Thus the four beasts in Daniel (chs.7–8) stand for successive kingdoms. In Daniel, they represent a sequence that comes down to the period in which Antiochus Epiphanes was making his attack against the Jews. In 2 Esdras, the same code is used, but the fourth beast has been updated, and becomes an eagle, i.e., Rome.

This is a reminder that while it is often possible for us to decipher the codes and to identify what the original writer had in mind, the codes are sufficiently vague (or obscure) for others to believe that they apply to their own times. That is why endless claims are made, usually by religious enthusiasts, that the true meaning of the codes in Daniel or in Revelation has been discovered, and that the end of the world is at hand. Perhaps it is, but not because apocalyptic works have predicted it. Apocalyptic should be read for what it is, a way in which the persecuted faithful were encouraged to stand firm: the encouragement is coded, so that the persecutors have no access to it.

# THE BOOK

**TITLE**: 2 Esdras (Greek) or 4 Ezra (from the Latin). 1–2 and 13–14 are sometimes called 5 and 6 Esdras

**DATE**: The book is composite, coming from different dates: chapters 1 and 2 are Christian, from after the fall of Jerusalem (70CE). Chapters 3–12 and 13–14 are a Jewish work, possibly from about 100CE

**AUTHORSHIP**: Unknown, but attributed to Ezra

# THE CONTENTS

**CHAPTERS 1–2**
A Christian Apocalypse dealing with the rejection of Israel and the inclusion of Gentiles in the Kingdom

**CHAPTERS 3–14 (4 EZRA) SEVEN VISIONS**
3–5:19 Vision1: Ezra and Uriel debate God's justice and the way sin goes back to Adam
5:20–6:34 Vision 2: Debate about the choice of Israel and its suffering
6:35–9:25 Vision 3: Debate concerning creation, the Messianic age, and the coming judgment
9:26–10:59 Vision 4: Zion mourns for her dead son
11–12 Vision 5: The eagle representing Rome
13 Vision 6: The man from the sea
14 Vision 7: The story of Ezra and the restoration of Scripture
15–16 The tribulations at the end of history

# KEY THEMES

*Visions that give the meaning of history*

•

*The Messiah will bring deliverance*

•

*The meaning of Israel's suffering*

**For further reading see bibliography numbers:** 201, 370, 448, 481, 552, 591, 664, 667, 669, 718, 733, 734, 854

# ESCHATOLOGY

*Eschatology is "that which concerns the last things." Eschatological questions that deal with final or last events include whether time or history lead to a final point or purpose, and how the promises and threats of God will be fulfilled.*

T HE word "eschatology" (from the Greek *eschata*, "last things") has come to refer to the end of time, and of history itself. In the period of the Hebrew Bible, the emphasis on a final judgment at the end of time is relatively late, so that considerations of judgment after death, or of Heaven and hell, scarcely appear. Humans are responsible for their actions, and God weighs them and brings them to judgment; reward and punishment are, generally speaking, received in this life. But is it true that the wicked are punished and the good are rewarded here and now (*see pp.174–75*)? If not, perhaps judgment is applied to the nation and to those who live later, and not necessarily to those engaged in good or evil acts at the present time. This is the first step toward eschatology in its strong, futuristic sense. In Christianity, eschatology is applied to the four last things: death, the final judgment, Heaven, and hell.

## THE ROLE OF THE PROPHETS

The Hebrew Bible is set within a framework of the good and ideal situations from which humans have come, and to which they are invited to return. The story of Genesis is one, not of a fall into original sin but a departure from Eden into new responsibilities (*see pp.30–31*). Genesis displays the evil consequences of the choices that some humans make, and records how God began the work of repair, eventually calling a whole people into a divine covenant. Once the Covenant had been undertaken, the responsibilities of the people became clear, and the consequences of reward and punishment could be stated with conviction.

On this basis, the Hebrew Bible moved toward eschatology, which takes the judgment to a final day. Important in this move were the Prophets (*see pp.196–99*), who understood the way in which the Covenant invited people to return to

**DAWN OF A NEW ERA**
*The Second Letter of Peter described the Day of the LORD as a time when "the heavens will be set ablaze and dissolved, and the elements will melt with fire" (2 Pet. 3:12). Peter believed that out of God's judgment would emerge a universe with "new heavens and a new earth, where righteousness is at home" (3:13).*

the close relationship with God that was prefigured in Eden. The Prophets explored what that return would mean: Israel would be secure on its land; the nations would join Israel in the worship of the one God; and justice and peace would prevail among all the nations. The tense is future: these things "will" come to pass. Thus the move to eschatology is already under way. In the earlier Prophets, the *eschaton* (future state) is not far removed. The Messiah, for example, was not originally a future figure: he was the present king or the newborn royal heir, and the return of the ideal state might perhaps come into reality in his lifetime. Later, after kings had repeatedly disappointed their people, the hope was transferred into the future, and seemed to require an even more cataclysmic intervention of God to bring it about.

THE ETERNAL FIRE
*The lake of fire and brimstone, "the second death," is the place of punishment for specific offenders in Revelation 21:8.*

## THE DAY OF THE LORD

The same shift from near-present to future can be seen in the idea of the Day of the LORD (*p.241*) – the moment when God's judgment would come to be applied. It could be understood as about to happen in the immediate future – often associated with military victories over Israel's enemies – or as something that might happen in a more distant future. The former was taken by some to be a guarantee that God would defeat the enemies of Israel, and it is against this arrogant attitude that Prophets such as Amos fought (Amos 5:18–24).

In Zephaniah 1:14–16, the Day of the LORD is depicted as a battle in which the *"trumpet blast and battle cry"* are heard, and the fortified city with its battlements is threatened. Isaiah uses a similar image (Isa. 2:15) and suggests that the Day of the LORD involves contemporary armies (Isa. 7:18–20). The aftermath of war is depicted at Joel 1:15 and the victory celebration at Zephaniah 3:15–20. This links the Day with the many victories of Israel ascribed to God: against Pharaoh (Exod. 14:14)

> 66 *Why do you want the day of the LORD? It is darkness, not light; as if someone fled from a lion, and was met by a bear; or went into the house and rested a hand against the wall, and was bitten by a snake. Is not the day of the LORD darkness, not light, and gloom with no brightness in it?* 99
>
> (Amos 5:18–20)

and the Midianites (Judg. 7:2–23). It suggests the Day of the LORD is a historical event, part of the ultimate divine victory. Other pictures associated with the Day are reminiscent of a festival. Zephaniah 3:17c–20 continues: *"He will exult over you with loud singing as on a day of festival."* Zechariah 14:16 brings the events to a climax in the festival of Sukkot, linked in Deuteronomy 31:11 with the reading of the Law, and with light. Ancient parallels with that festival celebrated divine victory over chaos and disaster (*see* Ps. 98; Isa. 5:1–30). However, the most striking references to the Day of the LORD concern God's wrath against Israel and Judah for injustice, idolatry, and dishonest worship (Amos 5:18–24; *cf.* Isa. 2:5–22).

## ESCHATOLOGY IN THE NEW TESTAMENT

In the New Testament, God's action was seen in relation to Jesus' life, work, death, Resurrection, and Ascension. Although this inauguration of the kingdom of God was realized in the present (realized eschatology), many Christians also recognized that much remained to be accomplished (future eschatology). Both are found in the teachings of Jesus: some sayings suggest an immediate vindication (Mark 9:1), others that vindication will happen unexpectedly (Mark 13:32). This led to uncertainty among early Christians, who asked if those members of their fellowship who had died had missed the chance of sharing in Christ's time of victory. Paul depicted a sequence of future events whereby all those who belonged to Christ would share in the final victory with him (1 Thess. 4:13–18).

Just as the writers of the Hebrew Bible began to systematize the pictures and the imagery of God's coming victory (Zech. 9–14), so the New Testament writers began to do the same in relation to the cross and the Resurrection of Jesus, often using pictures and imagery from Jewish tradition (Heb. 12:26–29; Rev. 20:7–8).

For further reading see bibliography numbers: 65, 133, 205, 343a, 370, 521, 664, 669

# PLANTS

## IN THE BIBLE

*Plants were a vital source of food, fuel, and building materials in ancient Israel.*
*Some were used in the preparation of medicines and during Temple worship; others*
*had symbolic importance and later became national symbols.*

THE Bible refers to more than 100 species of plant by name. Some of these are well known, but others are more difficult to identify from their Hebrew names. For instance, the *"lily"* of the Song of Songs (2:1–2; 6:2–3) could be one of several flowers, and *"the lilies of the field"* (Matt. 6:28) may simply be a wild flower, such as the daisy.

## SOURCES OF FOOD

Such plants as the date palm, vine, fig, and olive were valuable sources of food in biblical times.

The date palm is a tall, straight tree, topped by foliage where dates grow in clusters. These trees were common in ancient times and can still be found in parts of Palestine and the Sinai. Grapes were another important fruit

crop. Moses' spies returned from the Promised Land with bunches of grapes as a sign of its prosperity (Num. 13:23). Grapes were eaten fresh, made into raisin cakes, or trodden to make wine.

Fig trees are slow growing but bear fruit for much of the year. The large leaves were used to wrap objects, while the figs provided an excellent source of nutrition. The tree that Zacchaeus climbed to get a better view of Jesus was a type of fig tree (Luke 19:4).

Olives were another major tree crop. They were harvested in November, and the berries were either eaten or pressed for their valuable oil.

As well as being an edible fruit, the pomegranate was used for decorative purposes. Its image was embroidered on the priest's robe (Exod. 28:33), and also carved into the stone pillars at

**IVORY POMEGRANATE**
*This pomegranate dates from the mid-eighth century BCE, and may have decorated Solomon's Temple.*

**TREE CROPS**
*Olives were either eaten pickled or crushed to produce oil for cooking, lamp fuel, and anointing.*

**AROMATIC RESIN**
*Myrrh was one of the gifts given to Jesus by the Wise Men. It was used as a spice, a medicine, and holy oil for burning during Temple worship.*

**SYMBOL OF PEACE**
*"… but they shall all sit under their own vines … and no one shall make them afraid" (Mic. 4:4). This vine was a symbol for the Hebrew people. Jesus described himself as the true vine on which the branches depend (John 15:1–5).*

Solomon's Temple (1 Kgs. 7:20). Almonds were a favorite source of food and could also be crushed to make oil. Aaron's rod *"produced blossoms, and bore ripe almonds"* overnight (Num. 17:8).

## STAPLE CROPS

Major crops in biblical times included grains, beans, and lentils. Other staple plants, such as flax and papyrus, had practical uses.

Grains were a chief component in the diet of the people of ancient Israel. Wheat was used to make good-quality bread, in particular the bread that the priests offered to God. Barley was used mainly by the poorer peasants. When the barley crops were ruined by the plague of hailstorms, the wheat crop was saved (Exod. 9:31–32).

The blue-flowered flax plant was used to make clothing and sails. The stems of the plant were soaked in water, allowing the fibers to be separated for weaving (Exod. 26:1).

Papyrus, a variety of the grasslike sedge, grew to a height of ten feet (three meters) in the Nile delta and can still be found in northern Israel. The triangular stems were cut into thin strips and joined together in layers to make sheets of paper. It was also used to make baskets, ropes, and sandals. Much of the Bible might have been written on papyrus.

**FORBIDDEN FRUIT**
*The fruit in Genesis 3:2 is not named, but Latin* malum *translates as both "evil" and "apple."*

## MEDICINES AND PERFUMES

Frankincense and myrrh were two of the gifts given to Jesus by the Wise Men. The thin bark of the frankincense tree was peeled back and an incision made into the trunk. Aromatic resin could then be collected and used as incense during Temple worship (Lev. 2:1). The gum from myrrh was obtained in a similar way; it was mixed with a drink and offered to Jesus as a painkiller when he was on the cross. His body was later embalmed in myrrh and aloe (John 19:39–40).

"Hyssop" (probably modern-day marjoram or caper) was used in the sprinkling of sacrificial blood (Exod. 12:22). Jesus was given vinegar on a sponge as he hung from the cross; this was passed to him on a branch of hyssop (John 19:29).

**NATIONAL SYMBOL**
*The cedar of Lebanon is famed for its beauty. Cedar wood was transported to Jerusalem and used to build and decorate King Solomon's Temple (1 Kgs. 5:6–10).*

## PLANTS AS SYMBOLS

Trees were a symbol of strength (Ps. 1:3). The cedar of Lebanon is mentioned more than 70 times in biblical passages. Huge quantities of cedar wood were floated down the coast of Palestine and then transported to Jerusalem for use in building projects. Although it is still the national symbol of Lebanon, only a few trees now remain.

In Israel, the palm became an emblem of victory. People waved palm leaves as Jesus rode into Jerusalem (John 12:13); the palm leaf was also used in decorative carvings. The grapevine came to represent peace and prosperity for the Hebrew people; it was also a national emblem in Israel. After the Flood, a dove returned to the Ark carrying an olive leaf in its beak. The olive branch later became a symbol of peace.

**STAPLE CROPS**
*Flax was an important crop in biblical times. The stems, which grew to a height of 18in (45cm), were made into string, nets, and lamp wicks, or woven into linen for clothing and sails.*

For further reading see bibliography numbers: 114, 401, 425, 844

# BIRDS

## IN THE BIBLE

*The Bible mentions many different kinds of birds, although it is difficult to identify some exact species from their Hebrew names. They fall into three main categories – birds of prey, birds used for food and sacrifice, and migrant species. Birds play a vital role in many Bible stories.*

PALESTINE offers a variety of habitats, from semitropical to desert, and is very rich in bird life. The region is situated on a major migration path from Africa to Europe, so the great variety of bird life consists of both indigenous and migrant species. There are strict dietary laws describing which birds cannot be eaten (Lev. 11:13–19; Deut. 14:11–20). God's advice to Moses and Aaron includes a list of birds: *"These you shall regard as detestable among the birds. They shall not be eaten; they are an abomination"* (Lev. 11:13).

Birds in the Bible fall into three main categories – the most common species of each category are featured here.

**BARN OWL AND TAWNY OWL**
*Many species of owl are well known in Israel, including the eagle owl, tawny owl, barn owl, and scops owl. This detail from a stained-glass window depicts the barn owl and the tawny owl.*

The most usual Hebrew word for "bird" is *'oph*, which can be used for any flying creature, including insects. A second word, *tsippor*, usually refers to game birds but is sometimes translated as "sparrow" (Ps. 84:3; Prov. 26:2). In the New Testament, the usual Greek word for "bird" is *peteinon*, but when Jesus taught about the value of a sparrow (Matt.10:29–31; Luke 12:6–7), the word is *strouthion*.

## BIRDS OF PREY

The most common birds of prey in the Bible are the eagle, vulture, and owl. Hebrew *nesher* is often translated as "eagle," but also as "vulture." The Palestinian eagle was noted for powerful flight (2 Sam. 1:23; Jer. 4:13) and care of its young (Exod. 19:4; Deut. 32:11). The eagle came to symbolize powerful figures (Ezek. 1:10; 10:14; Rev. 4:7; 8:13). The forces of Rome are described as vulturelike as they waited for Jerusalem to fall: *"Wherever the corpse is, there the vultures will gather"* (Matt. 24:28).

Owls are depicted as the inhabitants of desolate places: *"There shall the owl nest and lay and hatch and brood in its shadow"* (Isa. 34:15). These nighttime hunters are among those birds regarded as unclean and were therefore not permitted to be eaten (Lev. 11:17).

**BIRD OF PREY**
*Traditionally thought of as the king of birds, the eagle is a symbol of power and strength. The symbol was used by Roman legions in New Testament times.*

After the Flood, the raven was the first bird sent by Noah from the Ark to see if the floodwaters had receded: *"At the end of forty days Noah opened the window of the ark that he had made and sent out the raven; and it went to and fro until the waters were dried up from the earth"* (Gen. 8:6–7). Ravens also fed Elijah when God instructed him to hide in the desert during the famine: *"You shall drink from the wadi [valley], and I have commanded the ravens to feed you there"* (1 Kgs. 17:4).

**THE RAVEN**
*The raven is the first bird to be mentioned in the Bible. Noah released a raven from the Ark to see if the waters of the Flood had receded. The term "raven" also refers to other black, flesh-eating birds such as the crow and the rook.*

## BIRDS FOR FOOD AND SACRIFICE

Birds used for food and sacrifice in biblical times included doves and pigeons (*see box, right*), chickens and hens, sparrows, quail, and partridge. Domestic fowl in particular were an important part of everyday life.

Perhaps the best-known reference to the cock is made following the betrayal of Jesus as Peter remembered Jesus' words: *"Before the cock crows, you will deny me three times"* (Matt. 26:75). Jesus also used the hen figuratively when speaking

# DOMESTIC BIRDS

Doves and pigeons are the most common of the birds in the Bible They were kept as domestic birds for food, bartering, message-carrying, and sacrificial offering (Lev. 1:4; *cf.* Num. 6:10). Many people were unable to afford a sheep or goat to sacrifice and would offer two pigeons or doves instead. After the Flood, Noah sent a dove from the Ark in search of dry land (Gen. 8:8). In the New Testament, the dove is a symbol of the Holy Spirit, following the baptism of Christ by John the Baptist (Luke 3:22). In contrast to the raven, the dove has become a symbol of peace, purity, and innocence.

**THE CROWING OF THE COCK**
*Domestic fowl were common in biblical times. The cock's crow has long been used as a timekeeping device, especially in rural communities. Jesus refers to four night watches, including "at cockcrow" (Mark 13:35).*

of his love for Jerusalem: *"How often have I desired to gather your children together as a hen gathers her brood under her wings"* (Matt. 23:37).

Large numbers of quail were found in Palestine, crossing the route taken after the Exodus. This migratory bird flies only several feet above the ground, and was an important source of food for the Israelites because it could be easily caught (Num. 11:31).

Jesus referred to the sparrow when describing God's love for his creatures, even the smallest birds: *"Are not five sparrows sold for two pennies? Yet not one of them is forgotten in God's eyes"* (Luke 12:6).

The Bible refers to rock, desert, and black partridge. David described himself as being hunted like *"a partridge in the mountains"* (1 Sam. 26:20) when being pursued by Saul.

## MIGRANT SPECIES

Palestine is situated on one of the main migration paths. Many species of birds pass through the country as they travel north in summer and south in winter. Their route from Africa into Europe and western Asia extends from the north end of the Red Sea through much of Israel. The most common migrant species are the stork, crane, and quail.

Both black and white storks travel north from Africa along the Jordan Valley: *"Even the stork in the heavens knows its times; and the turtledove, swallow, and crane observe the time of their coming"* (Jer. 8:7). Many other birds were present in biblical times, introduced from farther afield, brought through the trade routes that crisscrossed the area.

**THE CREATION**
*This 12–13th-century CE mosaic from Monreale Cathedral, Sicily, depicts God creating the fish and the birds: "And God said, '… let birds fly above the earth across the dome of the sky'" (Gen. 1:20).*

For further reading see bibliography number: 308

# ANIMALS

## IN THE BIBLE

*There are many references in the Bible to animal life. In addition to playing an important role in everyday life, both domestic and wild species had symbolic importance and were often the subject of vivid imagery.*

ALTHOUGH it is difficult to translate exactly some of the Hebrew names used for animals in the Bible, ancient manuscripts, archaeological findings, and stone carvings have provided important clues. In the Hebrew Bible animals are divided into the "clean" and the "unclean" (*see pp.62–63*). Only the clean can be eaten and used in ritual, especially in sacrifice. The clean and unclean are listed in Leviticus 11:1–47 and Deuteronomy 14:3–21a.

**NOAH'S ARK**
*This detail from a 17th-century stained-glass window shows the animals entering the Ark: "two and two, male and female, went into the ark with Noah" (Gen. 7:9). Seven pairs of "clean" animals went into the ark (Gen. 7:2).*

The one-humped Arabian camel, or dromedary, provided a valuable source of transport for desert nomads. Camels in the stories of Abraham and Jacob (Gen. 12:16; 30:43) may be anachronistic. Archaeological evidence suggests that domesticated camels were found in Iran and Oman during the third millennium BCE but not in general use before the end of the second millennium BCE. Jesus used the camel metaphorically when speaking to the rich young man (Matt. 19:24).

## DOMESTIC ANIMALS

For the people of ancient Palestine, domestic animals were both a valuable commodity and an important source of food. Common species included the sheep, goat, donkey, mule, camel, horse, and cattle.

Sheep and goats were well suited to the rocky hillside pastures of Palestine. Shepherds often tended mixed flocks, protecting them from attack by wild animals and leading them to new areas of grazing (Gen. 27:9; cf. Matt. 25:32). Both animals were killed in Temple sacrifices. The tanned skins of sheep were used to make clothing and for the inner covering of the Tabernacle.

Surefooted donkeys and mules were able to carry heavy loads and were more suited to living in rough country than horses. Mules were probably imported into the region, as breeding between species was specifically forbidden (Lev. 19:19). Donkeys feature in many Bible stories, including the story of Balaam (Num. 22:22–35), the first meeting between Samuel and Saul (1 Sam. 9:1–14), and Jesus' arrival in Jerusalem on Palm Sunday (Matt. 21:1–11).

**THE GOOD SHEPHERD**
*Shepherds and nomads have long been dependent on their flocks for the provision of meat, milk, and materials for clothing. This detail from a fourth-century CE mosaic pavement depicts the Good Shepherd with his sheep.*

# IMAGERY IN THE BIBLE

*Throughout the Bible, animals appear consistently in vivid imagery.*
*Both domestic and wild species were metaphorically significant.*

**PACK ANIMALS**
*Donkeys and mules were used as pack animals and for riding. They were vitally important to the nomadic people of the ancient Near East and often provided their only source of transportation.*

Animals that are the subject of biblical imagery include the sheep, wolf, horse, lion, leopard, and gazelle. Isaiah describes a peaceful kingdom where *"the wolf shall live with the lamb, the leopard shall lie down with the kid, the calf and the lion and the fatling together, and a little child shall lead them"* (Isa. 11:6). There are repeated references to wolves – Matthew warns *"Beware of false prophets, who come to you in sheep's clothing but inwardly are ravenous wolves"* (Matt. 7:15). The strength and courage of the lion made it a symbol of power and strength; for this reason lions were often hunted by kings and noblemen. The graceful, fast-moving gazelle served as an image of gentleness and beauty (S. of S. 2:8–9).

Many biblical animals have metaphorical significance. For instance, the sheep is consistently used to portray humans – easily lost or led astray, unable to fend for themselves, and often depicted as part of a scene with the shepherd leading his flock (Isa. 53:6). Wolves are used as a metaphor for people in authority who are abusing their position of power (Zeph. 3:3), and the leopard stalking its prey is a metaphor for menace (Jer. 13:23).

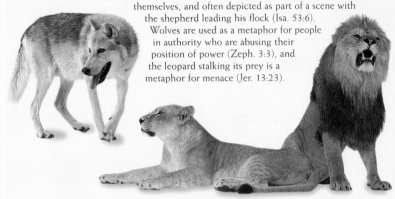

The Pharaoh's horses pursued the Israelites as they crossed the Red Sea (Exod. 14:23). Horses were not kept in Israel until the reign of David and were often associated with war (Josh. 11:4).

Cattle were valuable producers of milk, meat, and leather. A man's wealth was often determined by the number of cattle he owned. Oxen were used by farmers to pull plows, and could also be harnessed to wagons and carts.

## WILD ANIMALS

In biblical times, wild animals were a threat to the Israelites and their livestock. Commonly observed species included the lion, leopard, wolf, jackal, and Syrian brown bear.

Lions roamed the Jordan Valley. They are mentioned many times in the Bible but were quite rare in Israel by the time of the New Testament. The leopard, famed for its camouflage (Jer. 13:23) and more feared than the lion because of its nocturnal habits, was also well known in ancient times.

Wolves and jackals regularly attacked deer, sheep, and cattle, as well as smaller animals. The jackal, a nighttime hunter and descendant of the wolf, is referred to as a scavenger. In the story of Samson burning the Philistine cornfields, the *"three hundred foxes"* (Judg. 15:4) were probably jackals.

The Syrian brown bear was common in the wooded and hilly areas of Palestine. David had to protect his flock from bears (1 Sam. 17:34–36); bears also attacked a group of people who were jeering at the Prophet Elisha (2 Kgs. 2:24).

Other wild animals included fallow and roe deer, gazelle, and the Nubian ibex – a form of wild mountain goat whose meat was very highly regarded.

The elephant was already being exploited for its valuable ivory and was also used in times of war, for instance, during the attack on the Jews by the forces of Antiochus V (1 Macc. 6:30).

**SHIP OF THE DESERT**
*Camels were well adapted to life in the desert. They could go without food or water for long periods, and, in addition to passengers, were able to carry heavy loads over long distances – on average 28 miles (45km) a day.*

For further reading see bibliography numbers: 114, 153, 294

# THE
# NEW
# TESTAMENT

# THE NEW TESTAMENT

| Map of the Eastern |     |
| Mediterranean | 274 |
| Jerusalem | 276 |
| Procurators & Kings | 278 |
| Judaism at the Time of Jesus | 280 |
| Everyday Life for Jews | 282 |
| Everyday Life in the |     |
| New Testament | 284 |
| The Temple | 286 |
| Jewish Groups | 288 |
| The Dead Sea Scrolls | 290 |
| The First Jewish War | 292 |
| Masada | 294 |

## THE LIFE OF JESUS

| Map of Palestine | 298 |
| The Gospels | 300 |
| Synoptic Gospels | 302 |
| Studying the Gospels | 304 |
| **The Gospel According** |     |
| **to Matthew** | 306 |

| **The Gospel According to Mark** | 308 |
| **The Gospel According to Luke** | 310 |
| **The Gospel According to John** | 312 |
| The Importance of Jesus' Family | 314 |
| Mary, Mother of Jesus | 316 |
| The Stories of the Annunciation |     |
| & Nativity | 318 |
| Bethlehem & Nazareth | 320 |
| Education | 322 |
| The Work of John the Baptist | 324 |
| The Story of Jesus' Temptations | 326 |
| The Stories of Jesus Calling |     |
| his Disciples | 328 |
| The Twelve Disciples | 330 |
| Jesus' Teachings | 332 |
| The Teaching of the Sermon |     |
| on the Mount | 334 |
| Parables | 336 |
| Jesus' Parables | 338 |
| Galilee | 340 |
| Miracles | 342 |
| Jesus' Miracles | 344 |
| "Jesus the Messiah" | 346 |

| The Accounts of Jesus' |     |
| Entry into Jerusalem | 348 |
| The Accounts of the Last Supper | 350 |
| The Accounts of Jesus' |     |
| Betrayal & Arrest | 352 |
| The Accounts of the Trial of Jesus | 354 |
| The Trial of Jesus | 356 |
| The Accounts of |     |
| Jesus' Crucifixion | 358 |
| Historical Sites of the Passion | 360 |
| Burial Practices | 362 |
| The Accounts of |     |
| Jesus' Resurrection | 364 |

## THE BEGINNINGS OF CHRISTIANITY

| Map of the Roman Empire | 368 |
| Trade & Travel | 370 |
| The Structure of Roman Society | 372 |
| Marriage & Family | 374 |
| Traditional Religions & Cults | 376 |
| Magic in the Bible | 378 |

Justification by Grace
  through Faith   426
**The Letter to the Ephesians**   428
Unity of Jew & Gentile   430
**The Letter to the Philippians**   432
House Churches   434
Women's Ministry
  in the Early Church   436
**The Letters to the Colossians
  & Philemon**   438
Slavery   440

Acts of the Apostles   380
The Account of
  Jesus' Ascension   382
The Account of Pentecost   384
The Mission of Peter   386
Hebrews & Hellenists   388
The Account of
  Saul's Conversion   390
Breakthrough at Antioch   392
The Jerusalem Council   394
The Account of Paul's Missions   396
Ephesus   398
The Account of Paul's
  Final Years   400
Christianity in Rome   402

## THE LETTERS

Letters in the Bible   406
Paul's Teaching   408
**The Letter to the Romans**   410
"Jesus is Lord"   412
**The First Letter to
  the Corinthians**   414
The Holy Spirit   416
The Sacraments of Baptism
  & the Lord's Supper   418
**The Second Letter to
  the Corinthians**   420
Atonement in Paul's Teaching   422
**The Letter to the Galatians**   424

**The Letter to the
  Thessalonians**   442
The Coming Kingdom   444
**The Letters to
  Timothy & Titus**   446
Ministry   448
**The Letter to the Hebrews**   450
Philosophies   452
**The Letter of James**   454
**The First Letter of Peter**   456
Persecutions   458
**The Letters of
  2 Peter & Jude**   460
Pseudipigrapha in the Early
  Christian Period   462
**The Letters of John**   464
Christian Ethics   466
**The Book of Revelation**   468
Apocalypses   470
Heaven & Hell   472
The Emergence of the Canon   474

**ITALIA**

Roma•

•Apollonia

Thessalonica• •Philippi
•Neapolis

**GREECE**

Troas• •Assos

*Aegean
Sea*

Pergamum†

**SICILY**

Thyatira†

Corinth• •Athens
Cenchreae•

Smyrna†

Sardis†

# EASTERN
# MEDITERRANEAN

Miletus•
Ephesus†

**RHODES**

*The New Testament is set in the period
when the eastern Mediterranean was
under Roman rule. Herod the Great
was the local ruler, or client king, of
Palestine when Jesus was born, while
the whole empire was ruled over by
emperor Augustus Caesar. The main
events in Jesus' life took place in
Palestine, around Galilee and Judea.
After his Ascension, Jesus' Apostles
took the Gospel far afield, spreading
the good news throughout the Mediterranean and establishing many early
Christian churches. Their mission was
greatly aided by the vastly extended
Roman roads and ports.*

**CRETE**

*Mediterranean Sea*

† **The Seven Churches of Asia**
• **Major Cities**

# BIBLICAL HISTORY

| | | | | Archelaus, King of Judea (4BCE–6CE) | | | | | | | Siege of Jerusalem (66CE–70CE) |
|---|---|---|---|---|---|---|---|---|---|---|---|

Herod King of Judea (40BCE–4BCE)

Annas, High Priest (6CE–15CE)

Pontius Pilate, prefect (procurator) (26CE–36CE)

| 40BCE | 30BCE | 20BCE | 10BCE | 0CE | 10CE | 20CE | 30CE | 40CE | 50CE | 60CE | 70CE |
|---|---|---|---|---|---|---|---|---|---|---|---|

Herod Antipas, Tetrarch of Galilee (4BCE–39CE)

Caiaphas, High Priest (18CE–36CE)

Jesus (?6BCE–?30CE)

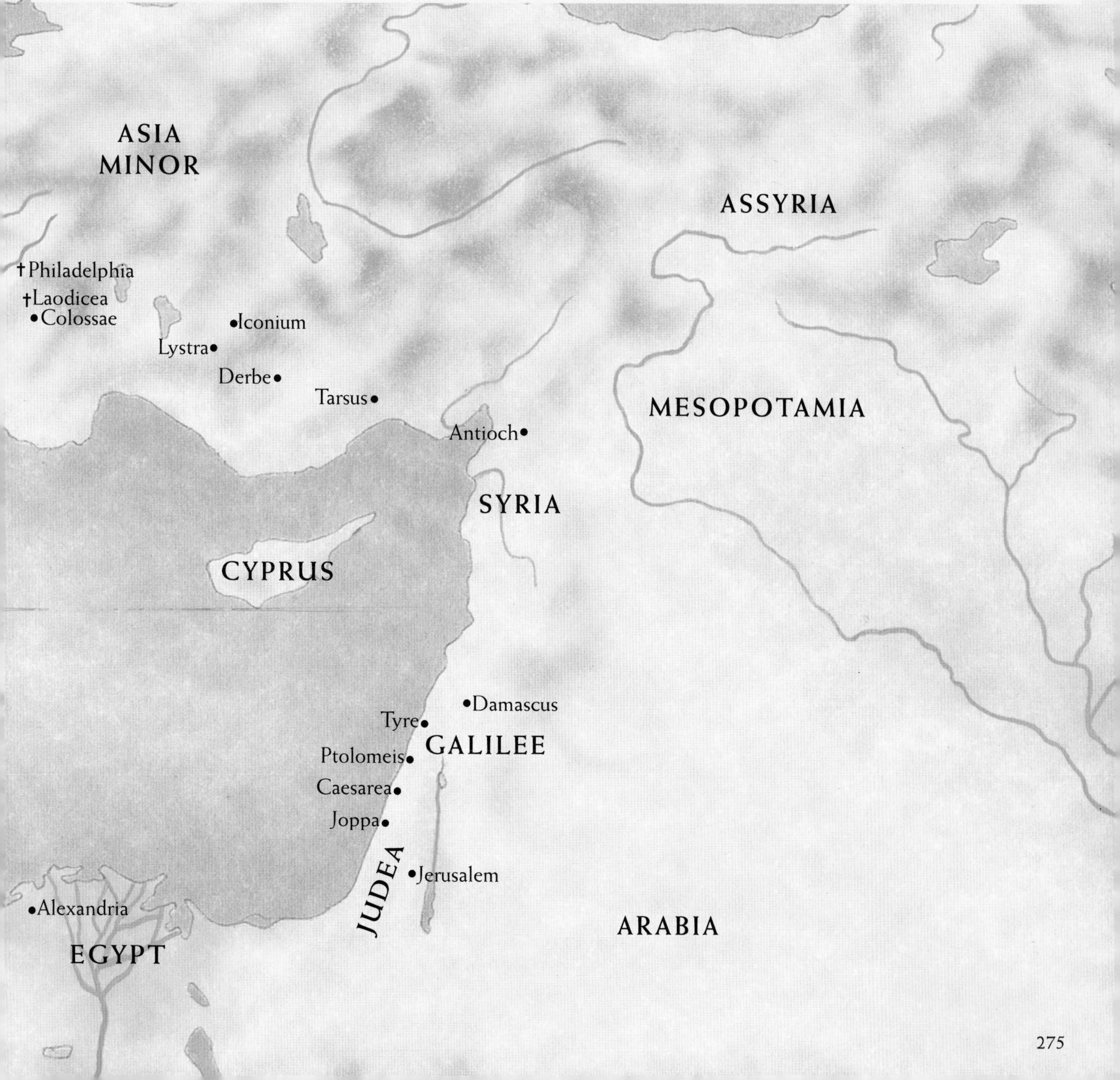

ASIA MINOR

ASSYRIA

†Philadelphia

†Laodicea

•Colossae

•Iconium

Lystra•

Derbe•

Tarsus•

MESOPOTAMIA

Antioch•

SYRIA

CYPRUS

•Damascus

Tyre•

Ptolomeis•

GALILEE

Caesarea•

Joppa•

JUDEA

•Jerusalem

ARABIA

•Alexandria

EGYPT

275

# JERUSALEM CITY

*The city in which the Temple was built is at the heart of the Jewish world.*
*The hope of a return to Jerusalem is kept alive for Jews in their liturgy, especially*
*at Passover: "Next year in Jerusalem!"*

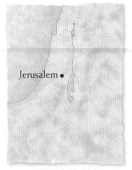

### JERUSALEM

The city of Jerusalem lies approximately 2,599ft (700m) above sea level in the Judean hills and is inaccessible by river. The ground drops away steeply on all sides, except at the northern end. A valley running between two hills cuts through the city, dividing the Temple area and city of David from the upper, western section.

BY the first century CE, Jerusalem was a busy cosmopolitan city of about 30,000 people, filled with inhabitants from all over the known world. Although the Romans moved their provincial capital from Jerusalem to Caesarea in 6CE, the city remained of paramount importance to Jews. The psalmist in exile in Babylon (*pp.146–47*) had cried out, *"If I forget you, O Jerusalem, let my right hand wither!"* (Ps. 137:5), and this loyalty endured.

Access to the city was difficult, with the surrounding hills providing cover for bandit gangs. Trade was brisk, although there were few local raw materials and no natural trade routes in or out. Some complained of corruption among Temple authorities and transferred their allegiance away (*see p.291*). Nonetheless, for most Jews, Jerusalem was "the center of their affections and the navel of the earth" (*Jubilees 8:19*; Josephus, *The Jewish War 52*).

## JERUSALEM IN HEROD'S TIME

Herod the Great, king of Judea c.40–4BCE (*p.279*), undertook major building projects in Jerusalem, including rebuilding the Temple on a far grander scale than ever before (*pp.286–87*). Only the base of the Western Wall remains today, the site for Jewish prayer, also known as the Wailing Wall. For his own safety, Herod built the Fortress Antonia, where Paul was imprisoned (Acts 21:27–22:30). When the Romans took control of Judea in 6CE, Herod's palace became the residence of the procurators (*p.279*); it was here that Pontius Pilate judged Jesus (John 18:28). Jerusalem fell to the Romans in 70CE at the end of the First Jewish War (*pp.292–93*) and was leveled to the ground at the orders of the emperor, Titus. After the second war in 135CE, Hadrian rebuilt the city as Aelia Capitolina, erected a temple to Jupiter, and forbade circumcised people, which included Jews, to enter the city at all.

**JERUSALEM TODAY**
*Jerusalem now extends far beyond its first-century temple site and boundary city walls. The Dome of the Rock now occupies part of the temple area.*

# HEROD'S TEMPLE

*The central focus for Jews in Jerusalem was the Temple, situated on the eastern hill of the city.*

Pilgrims gathered at the Temple for the pilgrimage feasts of Passover, Pentecost, and Tabernacles. Here, once a year, at Yom Kippur, the High Priest entered the Holy of Holies (the innermost sanctuary) to offer prayers for the people. Mary and Joseph came to the Temple for Jesus' presentation (Luke 2:22ff.), and when Jesus was 12 he was brought there for the annual pilgrimage at Passover (Luke 2:39ff.). At this time of year, the city's population increased to almost 200,000, with pilgrims staying in tents and nearby villages such as Bethany, where Jesus' friends, Mary, Martha, and Lazarus, lived. The presence of the Temple ensured enormous revenues generated through the purchase of animals for sacrifice and by pilgrims spending money while in Jerusalem – the so-called "second tithe," which had to be spent in the city. In addition, male Jews, wherever they lived, were required to pay an annual tax to the Temple of a didrachma, or half-shekel; Jesus and his followers maintained this loyalty (Matt. 17:24). In the end, it was Jesus' claim to destroy the Temple and rebuild it in three days that was used against him by the Jewish ruling council based in Jerusalem, which led to his death (Mark 14:58).

**Model of the Temple of Jerusalem**
*Rather than tear down the existing Temple, Herod rebuilt and refurbished it without disturbing the original building.*

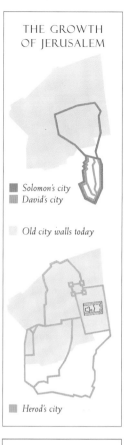

**THE GROWTH OF JERUSALEM**

■ Solomon's city
▨ David's city

Old city walls today

■ Herod's city

## JERUSALEM IN THE NEW TESTAMENT

Jerusalem plays an especially important part in the Gospels of Luke and John. In John, Jesus is often in Jerusalem in confrontations with the authorities. Many of the well-known parables in Luke's Gospel, such as the Good Samaritan (Luke 10:30ff.) and the Pharisee and the Tax Collector (Luke 18:10ff.), relate to the Temple or to city life and its environs. Jesus knew that any claim to be an authentic teacher could be tested only in Jerusalem – judgment had to come from the ruling spiritual authorities there. If Jesus had remained in Galilee, he would not have been crucified; the Gospels show Jesus moving inexorably toward Jerusalem for a final confrontation with the authorities – a confrontation that led to his death (pp. 354–57).

The significance of Jerusalem went far beyond its geographical site. For Jews and Christians alike it symbolized a place of hope, where God and humanity would dwell together. Isaiah 2 promises a restoration of the city when the world will stream to Mount Zion – a reference to the hill south of the old city walls. Paul compares the earthly city with a heavenly Jerusalem representing those who are part of the Covenant that God makes with humans through God's son, Jesus Christ (Gal. 4:23ff.; cf. Heb. 12:22; Rev. 21).

**THE WESTERN WALL**
*Jews come to pray and lament the destruction of the Temple at the only part of the building still in existence.*

For further reading see bibliography numbers: 21, 28, 38, 429, 632, 673, 702, 806, 836, 877

# PROCURATORS & KINGS

*From 37BCE to 66CE Judea and Samaria were ruled by procurators, while the Herod family ruled as client kings in Galilee and other parts of Palestine.*

To Archelaus (4BCE–6CE); under
Roman procurators (6–66CE)
To Herod Agrippa I (41–44CE)

To Herod Antipas (4BCE–39CE)
To Herod Agrippa I (41–44CE)

To Philip (4BCE–34CE)
To Herod Agrippa I (37–44CE)

## THE LAND OF THE HERODS

Herod the Great ruled over Judea and Idumea in the south, Perea and Jaffa, Galilee in the north and, later, Samaria. In his will he divided his kingdom between his three sons: Archelaus, Philip, and Antipas. Archelaus ruled Judea and Samaria, Philip ruled the land east of Galilee, and Antipas ruled over Galilee and Perea.

$P$ALESTINE became part of the Roman empire in 64BCE, and for much of the period between 4BCE and 66CE Judea and Samaria were ruled by Roman governors, known as procurators. Anxious not to offend local religious sensibilities, the Romans had the Herods rule as client kings in Galilee and other parts of Palestine. It was believed that their understanding of Jewish customs (Herod the Great's father had been an Idumaean Jew) would be useful in keeping the peace.

## THE HEROD FAMILY

By the time of his death in 4BCE, Herod the Great (*see panel, right*) ruled over all of Palestine. In accordance with his will, the land was divided between his three sons: Archelaus,

**"GIVE ME ... THE HEAD OF JOHN THE BAPTIST"**
*Herodias' anger against John was so great that she used her daughter Salome to trick Herod Antipas into having John beheaded and delivered to her on a platter (Mark 6:24–28).*

Philip, and Antipas. Archelaus was a tyrannical ruler, and when the Jews could bear his cruelty no longer, they appealed to the emperor in 6CE to be administered by a Roman governor. Philip ruled the land east of Galilee and was the least ambitious of the three sons, but he governed adequately until his death in 34CE.

Antipas ruled over Galilee and Perea from 6BCE until 37CE, and he appears in the Gospels. He is most noted for his confrontation with John the Baptist, after Antipas became infatuated with his brother's wife, Herodias. She insisted he divorce his first wife, a Nabatean princess, to marry her. John denounced Antipas for violating the prohibition in Leviticus 20:21 on marrying a brother's wife. John was arrested and beheaded as a favor to Salome, Herodias'

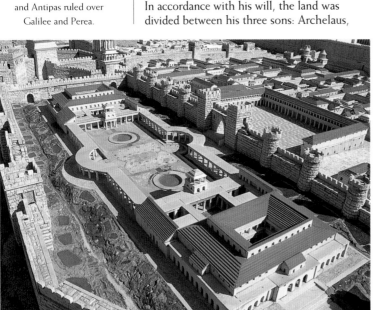

**THE MASTER BUILDER**
*As part of his extensive building plan, Herod the Great had many splendid and luxurious buildings constructed. Apart from his palace in Jerusalem (left), he is famous for his complex in Masada, the port of Caesarea, and the magnificent Herodium.*

daughter. Jesus rebuked Antipas as "that fox" (Luke 13:31–33), and later appeared before him during his trial (Luke 23:6–16; *pp.356–57*).

Herod Agrippa, grandson of Herod the Great, showed great piety and observance of Jewish customs when in Palestine. He promoted the Pharisees, he was responsible for the death of James the son of Zebedee, and for early persecution of the people of "the Way."

## THE PROCURATORS

From 6CE, Rome ruled Judea and Samaria through a number of procurators. Although the governor of Syria exercised overall control of the region, he rarely exercised his authority, and hence the Judean procurators had military, financial, and judicial powers over the region. They also had the power to appoint the High Priest.

The best known of the procurators was Pontius Pilate, who is shown trying to find a middle way at the trial of Jesus. But Jewish writers (Josephus and Philo), attempting to excuse Jewish unrest, portray Pilate in the worst light: he unlawfully took money from the Temple treasury to pay for an aqueduct system, and he killed many Jews when they protested. Luke 13:1 records an incident when he killed a number of Galilean pilgrims. On another occasion, Pilate tried to bring Roman banners bearing pagan images into Jerusalem and backed down only when it became clear that the Jews would rather be

**INSCRIPTION BEARING PILATE'S NAME**
*Discovered in 1961 in Caesarea, this inscription shows Pilate's correct title of "prefect" rather than "procurator."*

killed than allow the banners to remain. He was dismissed in 36CE after killing a number of Samaritan pilgrims.

Apart from the period 37–44CE, when Caligula appointed Herod Agrippa as king, Judea remained under procuratorial rule until 66CE. Acts mentions Paul meeting two procurators: Felix, a freedman, of whom Tacitus wrote as "Practicing every kind of cruelty and lust, he wielded power with the instincts of a slave"; and his successor, Festus, who died in office. The conduct of the procurators led some Jews to revolt (Josephus comments that the two final procurators, Albinus and Florus, "did everything in their power to inflame the situation"), and in 66CE the First Jewish War began (*pp.292–93*).

### HEROD THE GREAT

The first of the client kings, Herod the Great was an outstanding figure in this period of history, rebuilding and establishing great edifices all over his realm (*see also pp.294–95*). Herod was a character who suffered from an extremely suspicious nature, and three of his sons were executed for supposedly plotting against him. Despite his rebuilding of the Jerusalem Temple (*p.277*) and his understanding of Jewish laws, Herod never became popular with the Jewish people. After his death, Herod was remembered more for his repressive policies and extreme outbursts of anger.

# PROCURATORS AND KINGS 37BCE – 66CE

| CLIENT KINGS | | | | | | | | | | | | | | | |
|---|---|---|---|---|---|---|---|---|---|---|---|---|---|---|---|
| | | Archelaus (4BCE–6CE) | | | | | | Herod Agrippa I (37–44CE) | | | | | | | |
| | | Herod Philip (4BCE–34CE) | | | | | | | | | | | | | |
| Herod the Great (37BCE–4BCE) | | Herod Antipas (4BCE–39CE) | | | | | | | Herod Agrippa II (53–100CE) | | | | | | |
| 40BCE | 30BCE | 20BCE | 10BCE | 0CE | 10CE | 20CE | 30CE | 40CE | 50CE | 60CE | 70CE | 80CE | 90CE | 100CE | |
| | | | | | | | | I | K | O | | | | | |
| PROCURATORS | | | A B C D | | E | | F,G,H J | L | N | | | | | | |
| | | | | | | | | | | M | | | | | |

A Coponius (6–8CE)
B Marcus Ambivius (9–12CE)
C Annius Rufus (12–15CE)
D Valerius Gratus (15–26CE)
E Pontius Pilatus (Pilate) (26–36CE)

F Marullus (37CE)
G Herennius Capito (37–41CE)
H King Herod Agrippa I ruled (37–44CE)
I Cuspius Fadus (44–46CE)
J Tiberius Alexander (46–48CE)

K Ventidius Cumanus (48–52CE)
L Marcus Antonius Felix (52–60CE)
M Porcius Festus (60–62CE)
N Clodius Albinus (62–64CE)
O Gessius Florus (64–66CE)

For further reading see bibliography numbers: 344, 411, 412, 426, 702, 706, 729, 730, 877

# JUDAISM
## AT THE TIME OF JESUS

*Although there were differences among Jews throughout the Mediterranean world in the first century CE (see also pp.288–89), they shared many common practices and beliefs, and recognized the difference between themselves and non-Jews (Gentiles).*

JEWS share the belief that God has created all things and called their ancestors into a special covenant relationship of trust and obligation. Its principles are laid out in Torah (*pp.24–25*), which includes the laws that Jews must keep. It is also summed up in the Shema (*pp.82–83*) and in God's promise to give the Jews the Promised Land. At the heart of the Jewish faith is the belief that God, as revealed to his Covenant People, is the only God, and that other claimed gods are false.

In Jesus' time, Judaism attracted many people in the Mediterranean world to practice the ethical monotheism of the Jews, and this increased Jewish diversity, especially in Roman Palestine itself. Such diversity of the Jewish faith and its practice was increased by the Jewish Diaspora (*see opposite*).

## INTERPRETING TORAH

Keeping Torah was important, not simply to give obedient praise to God but also because of the promise of a Messiah (*pp.123, 346–47*): if Jews were to live in harmony with Torah, perhaps this would lead to the coming of a Messiah. But how should Torah be applied to life in the first century CE? It had been entrusted to Moses so many centuries before that its stories and commands could not possibly deal with every later circumstance. And in the face of disagreement, who was to decide the true meaning of Torah? Jews gave different answers to these questions (*see Jewish*

Aedicula (*storage place for scrolls*)

Courtyard

RABBIS AT PRAYER
*It has always been part of the Jewish tradition for rabbis to pray, study (with prayer and study tending to flow into one another), and then interpret Torah in terms of its relevance to contemporary issues. Many Diaspora communities thus developed their own interpretations of Judaism.*

## THE SYNAGOGUE

*This artist's impression of a fourth-century CE synagogue at Horbat Shema', in Galilee, is similar to many in existence in Roman Palestine by the first century CE.*

Entrance to prayer hall

Prayer hall

Side entrance with stone relief above the doorway showing a menorah

Portico

built outside Judea as alternatives to the Temple in Jerusalem. This led to different interpretations of what Torah should mean in Jewish people's lives. Early Christianity emerged as one such interpretation. Although Jewish groups were often in conflict, they did share common beliefs and practices, especially circumcision and observing the Sabbath (*see boxes*), which identified them as the Covenant People. After the Temple was destroyed in 70CE, rabbis became the principal exponents of Torah, and each synagogue became a center for the local Jewish community, sustaining worship, education, and hospitality.

### DIASPORA JEWS

Following the first dispersion after the Assyrian conquest of the northern kingdom of Israel in 722BCE (*p.143*), many Jews had moved to live all over the Mediterranean world. They had settled as far as Babylon and Rome, where a Hellenistic lifestyle (derived from Greek practices and customs) prevailed. This could conflict seriously with Torah (hence the Maccabean Revolt, *pp.250–51*), but for some Jews it was an attractive way of life. To survive as faithful Jewish communities, Diaspora (Greek, "dispersion") Jews depended on their organization, leaders, and on the practice, as in the Holy Land, of regular Sabbath services in synagogue assemblies. Their fulfillment of the Law included paying taxes to the Temple and making regular journeys to the city for different religious festivals.

Groups, *pp.288–89*). While the Temple still stood, the final authority rested there. The Jewish historian, Josephus, wrote: "The ancestral custom is to obey the priest of the God whom we worship" (*Antiquities* 18:11–23). But while the Temple with its sacrifices and liturgy was indeed central to the religion, many disagreed with the way it was run. On occasion, temples were

### JEWISH ASSEMBLY

*Since the late first century CE, synagogues have been used not just for worship and education but also for political meetings, charitable activities, social gatherings, and as courts and hostels.*

## THE SABBATH

Derived from the Creation narrative, the Sabbath was given special emphasis during and after the Exile, and during the revolt against Antiochus Epiphanes (*p.251*). There was much discussion of what "work" and "rest" mean in practice, and this is reflected in the New Testament and in Jesus' ministry. Jewish authorities later classed 39 primary activities as "work" not permitted on the Sabbath.

## CIRCUMCISION

The Bible associates the act of circumcision with God's covenant with Abraham (*pp.60–61*). Jewish males are circumcised eight days after birth according to Genesis 17:10–12. In Jesus' time, it was essential for every male child to be circumcised as a sign of belonging to the Covenant People (*see also Paul's Teaching, pp.408–9*).

**For further reading see bibliography numbers:** 45, 132, 362, 391, 426, 491, 495, 496, 673, 679, 702, 706, 754, 877

# EVERYDAY LIFE
## FOR JEWS

*The everyday life of Jews varied enormously: some were rich, many more were poor; some were priests or were attached to the Temple, others worked on the land; some lived in towns, others in the country. Jesus moved within all these different worlds and applied his teaching to them.*

JEWISH life in New Testament times varied in many different ways. Some of the wealthy took advantage of the influence of Hellenism, the rule of the Romans, and the Herod family in Palestine to adopt a more cosmopolitan lifestyle. Among the relatively poor, some absorbed many folk elements into their religious life (e.g., charms and amulets, consulting the stars, magic, and cures).

Occupying the middle ground were many Jews trying to live in a way that was faithful to Torah and the Covenant with God. Even then, there was a variety of ways in which they could do this (*see Jewish Groups, pp.288–89*). The New Testament reflects some of these many different aspects of everyday religious life.

## DOMESTIC LIFE

For Jews, the home was central to nurturing beliefs, traditions, and values, and for maintaining the link between faith and ethnicity: "He who maintains peace at home maintains it in Israel … Everyone is king in his own home" (*Aboth deRabbi Nathan* 28). To be Jewish was to be distinctive, reciting the Shema and teaching the Commandments to all the family (*see box, below*).

Observing Torah governed life both at home and in public, especially in relation to marriage, children, and the maintenance of family ties. Food preparation and the observance of dietary regulations were integral to

**MORNING PRAYER**
*Apart from the Shema, Jews recite the Amidah, or "Standing Prayer" in the morning, afternoon, and evening. It is one of the few occasions when Jews are required to stand while praying.*

the proper functioning of family life. The rhythm of everyday domestic life and work was governed by the Sabbath and festivals (especially Passover, with the role the family played in instructing children), the Day of Atonement (with

**RELIGIOUS LIFE IN THE HOME**
*The Jewish year includes seven major festivals, all of which are family occasions either seeking God's forgiveness or cleansing, or celebrating God's gifts and provision for his people, such as Hanukkah (see above). Involving children at a young age in such festivals is an important means of religious education.*

## FOOD LAWS AND PRAYER

The "dietary laws" (*kashrut*) are a term for the laws and customs that detail which animals, birds, and fish may be eaten and how they should be prepared (Lev. 11; Deut. 14:3–21). The laws state that meat and milk products should not be prepared and eaten together. In the New Testament these laws were significant in the Gentile mission (e.g., Acts 10:10–15) and in table fellowship (e.g. Gal. 2:12–14). Paul accordingly argued strongly that table fellowship could not be idolatrous (1 Cor. 8:4–6) (*see pp.394–95*).

The Shema, so-called because it derives from the first word of Deuteronomy 6:4 – "*Hear [shema] O Israel, the LORD is our God, the LORD alone*" – is the Jewish declaration of faith (*pp.82–83*). Jews were, and still are, required to say the Shema each morning and evening and on other occasions, such as when the Torah Scroll is taken from the Ark on Sabbaths and festivals. In Jesus' teachings, the act of reciting the Shema is linked to the second great commandment of loving a neighbor (Luke 10:25–28), a point also reflected by Paul in establishing the unity of the church at Corinth (1 Cor. 8:4–6).

its sense of solemnity), and Tabernacles (with its celebratory significance; *pp.116–17*). This way of life was strengthened by regular attendance at the synagogue and the obligatory payment to the Temple of a half-shekel tax.

## WORK AND PLAY

In general, Jews worked in almost all occupations, earning a wide range of incomes, with farming accounting for a high proportion. In the largely agrarian region of Palestine, crop growing, animal husbandry, and fishing were key elements of the rural economy. Savage conflicts sometimes emerged between the peasants working the land and their landlords (e.g., the parable of the Tenant Farmers, Matt. 21:33–41), which was exacerbated by the heavy taxation system. People also worked in a wide range of cottage industries, notably weaving, pottery, leather working, glass, and stone carving.

The majority of the Palestinian population lived and worked in small towns and villages, despite the fact that the cities of Jerusalem, Sepphoris, Tiberias, and Caesarea were important administrative and economic centers

and places of Hellenistic cultural influence. Thus, Jesus' parables reflect the social circumstances and economic hardships of this rural Palestinian existence, rather than the cosmopolitan lifestyle of Jews in Greco-Roman society.

Leisure activities in these communities revolved around such social events as weddings, religious festivals, or, in some cities, sacred games. Religious, economic, or social voluntary associations were common and provided a variety of ways in which the importance of belonging to a community could be celebrated and affirmed.

## RELATIONS WITH NON-JEWS

With its disciplined lifestyle and lack of exoticism, Judaism came to be admired and many Gentiles became proselytes, or converts. Some non-Jews were benefactors of synagogues and

**AGRARIAN LIFE**
*Most Jews worked on the land or were involved in some type of farming or animal husbandry. However, apart from the coastal areas, the land in Palestine was difficult to farm. It was usually managed on a basis of employed tenants, hired day laborers, and slaves.*

became "God-fearers" or "sympathizers," for example, Cornelius (Acts 10:2), Sergius Paulus (Acts 13:7), and Lydia (Acts 14:4). There was, then, a welcome, if passive, acceptance by Jews of the goodwill of Gentiles.

Contacts with non-Jews could raise sharp issues of ritual cleanliness, especially where food and meals were concerned (see *Jerusalem Council, pp.394–95*). However, some Jews had no hesitation in seeking benefactors in ways that were related to the system of patronage in the cities of the Gentile world. This would also have been aided by the privileged legal status that was granted to the Jewish religion by Rome (*p.458*).

**THE PASSOVER MEAL**
*Annual feasts such as Passover are important family occasions. An animal is sacrificed for the meal and the cooked meat is eaten with a variety of herbs and unleavened bread. Four cups of wine are drunk and psalms are sung in celebration.*

For further reading see bibliography numbers: 98, 114, 132, 225, 290, 362, 414, 429, 451, 452, 491, 495, 496, 515, 584, 662, 673, 702, 727, 754, 766, 877

# EVERYDAY LIFE
## IN THE NEW TESTAMENT

*The New Testament provides us with many glimpses into everyday life at that time. We gain an insight into family life and family relations, customary occupations, and some of the more common trades practiced within Jewish and Gentile communities.*

AS in all societies, birth, marriage, and death were, in the world of the New Testament, of paramount importance as occasions for family gatherings or celebration. However, these events aside, day-to-day living for the majority of people could be one of great hardship and poverty, exacerbated by taxation under Roman rule.

### THE YOUNGER GENERATION

Children were important primarily for hereditary reasons, but apart from some traces of the games they played, and a distant echo of children at play in Matthew 11:17, the New Testament offers little access to their experiences.

Parents' wishes to have their young blessed (Mark 10:13; *cf.* Luke 18:15) had their roots in natural folk belief in seeking the best for their children and in warding off harm. The dependent and trusting status of children was used by Jesus to describe believers (Mark 10:13–16). Contemporary child rearing practices mentioned in the New Testament include swaddling (Luke 2:7) and breast-feeding (Luke 11:27).

Exposing children (especially girls) to let them die was an acceptable practice in the Roman world; Judaism and Christianity expressly forbade it (for the wonder of birth, *see* Ps. 139:13–16).

### WEDDINGS AND WAKES

Marriage was a significant rite of passage (*see pp. 374–75*) and its social importance is reflected in the way it is a recurring theme in Jesus' parables. It was generally expected that people would marry with the explicit intention of having children (Mark 12:19–22). In both Gentile and Jewish custom, the bride was conducted amid celebrations to the bridegroom's house by torchlight on the eve of the wedding (Matt. 25:1ff.).

**PREPARING FOR PUBLIC APPEARANCES**
*Unlike Jewish and early Christian girls, young Roman females had far more freedom and were allowed to be seen (and admired) in public. The more affluent girls had their servants apply makeup when going out to such occasions as weddings.*

The marriage itself involved various obligations as a form of legal contract between the two families. Divorce, however, required little legal formality. Indeed, the Law of Moses made it very easy for a man to end his marriage by simply writing a letter of dismissal to his wife (Mark 10:4).

**THE BLESSING**
*It was customary for Jewish children to be blessed by the rabbi. In Jesus' time many hoped the rabbi would lay his hands on the child to be blessed (Matt. 19:13).*

Funeral customs included burial on the day of death, with hired mourners and musicians processing through the streets (Mark 5:38–39; Matt. 9:23; *see also pp. 362–63*). While cremation was a common practice among Gentiles, the Jewish custom was to wrap the deceased in a linen shroud and leave the body in a tomb and, later, an ossuary.

These rites of passage served both a public and social purpose and, although infrequent, provided welcome opportunities for leisure. It was only among the wealthy that time for extended leisure would have been found in frequenting the baths and gymnasia, or in feasting.

**A SOCIAL OCCASION**
*For Jews, weddings provided a wonderful opportunity for gathering together family and friends. It was at a wedding that Jesus performed his first miracle (John 2:1–11).*

## TRADES, OCCUPATIONS, TAXES

A wide range of trades and occupations is mentioned in the New Testament, which follows the usual social custom of identifying people with the trade they followed (Mark 6:3; cf. Matt. 13:55). For example, we learn of "a tanner named Simon" (Acts 9:43), and Paul is known by his profession, that of a tentmaker: *"Paul went to see [Aquila and Priscilla], and, because he was of the same trade, he stayed with them, and they worked together – by trade they were tentmakers"* (Acts 18:3). Acts 19:24 also mentions that the riots in Ephesus were incited by the "silversmith named Demetrius." A glimpse of merchant life in New

Testament times is provided in Revelation 18:11–19, and James 4:13 warns against the material enticements of commerce. It is significant that in all his teachings, Jesus spoke only once of a merchant (Matt. 13:45–46). In general, Jesus' parables reflected the daily life of Palestine with its socio-political-economic system of wealth concentrated in the hands of a ruling elite, while the wider peasant group of tenant farmers, laborers, and slaves were forced to struggle with life's day-to-day necessities and demands.

As part of the demands of everyday life, having to pay taxes was for most people an inescapable duty. For instance, the annual payment of the half-shekel to the Temple was collected by officials who traveled throughout Palestine (Matt. 17:24). The Herod rulers also levied taxes, as did Rome, and censuses were taken to determine the number of people to be

taxed (Luke 2:1–5). The payment of taxes to Rome caused great resentment among people, eventually leading to the First Jewish War in 66CE (*pp.292–93*) – and to the question demanded of Jesus: *"Is it lawful to pay taxes to Caesar or not?"* (Mark 12:14). Not surprisingly, tax collectors were very unpopular, making Jesus' accepting attitude toward them all the more remarkable.

## CHURCH AND SOCIETY

Later, as the Christian Church took root in cities, it continued to encounter social divisions in an urban system of patronage. For instance, wealthy people were inclined to despise manual work and view it as slavish. Yet Jesus exemplified the role of serving others, and this helped transform people's attitudes toward work and slaves (*see pp.440–41*); Paul took pride in supporting himself in ways that others might have regarded with disdain (1 Cor. 4:11–13). Nevertheless, the Church succeeded in establishing itself in urban settings and in drawing on a wide cross-section of society: *"There is no longer Jew or Greek, there is no longer slave or free, there is no longer male and female; for all of you are one in Jesus Christ"* (Gal. 3:28).

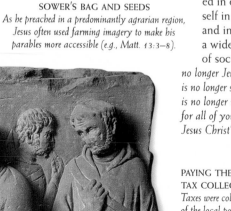

**SOWER'S BAG AND SEEDS**
*As he preached in a predominantly agrarian region, Jesus often used farming imagery to make his parables more accessible (e.g., Matt. 13:3–8).*

**PAYING THE TAX COLLECTOR**
*Taxes were collected by a member of the local population on behalf of the Romans. Tax collectors were one of the most despised members of society, yet Matthew, a tax collector, became one of Jesus' disciples (Matt. 9:9).*

For further reading see bibliography numbers: 18, 225, 280, 290, 429, 514, 515, 544, 577, 662, 722

# THE TEMPLE

*In 19BCE Herod the Great began enlarging the Jerusalem Temple to gain favor with the Jews. His popularity did not increase, but the Temple remained central to Jewish life. It was built to lead, through stages, closer to the holiness of God.*

Jerusalem •

## A FOCUS FOR JEWS

The presence of a temple in Israel's capital, Jerusalem, signified the presence of God among the Israelites. From all parts of the Diaspora (p.281) Jews came to worship here, the most sacred site of Judaism. At one time the wandering Israelites had only "a tent of meeting" in which to worship God, but from the age of Solomon and the building of the First Temple in Jerusalem, the Temple was the center of Jewish worship.

**THE WESTERN (WAILING) WALL**
*This wall is all that remains of the Second Temple complex. At 59ft (18m) high, the stone wall has become the holiest site for Jews, with many bringing their 13-year-old sons here to celebrate their bar mitzvah.*

ACCORDING to the list of holy places cited in the *Mishnah*, the Temple contains the holiest place on earth: starting from the land of Israel as being holier than any other land, the list moves through to the Temple and through the Temple courts to the porch and altar: "Between the Porch and the Altar is still more holy, for none that has a blemish or whose hair is unloosed may enter there; the Sanctuary is still more holy because none may enter there with hands or feet unwashed; the Holy of Holies is still more holy because none may enter there except the High Priest on the Day of Atonement" (*Mishnah Kelim* 1:9). It is true that God cannot be contained in any building, but the Temple was the meeting point between God and the people – the point where mercy and forgiveness could be found, and worship and thanksgiving were offered.

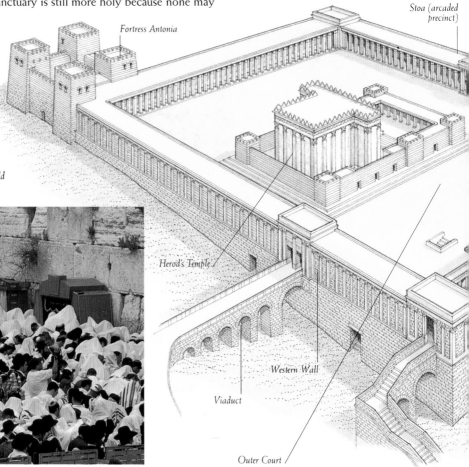

Fortress Antonia

Stoa (arcaded precinct)

Herod's Temple

Western Wall

Viaduct

Outer Court

# FROM PRIESTS TO RABBIS

Chief among the priests who officiated at the Temple, the High Priest was distinguished in a number of ways: he wore additional garments (*see box, p.65*); he was permitted to marry only a virgin; and only he was allowed into the "Holy of Holies" on the Day of Atonement. Initially the position was hereditary but during the Hasmonean period (second–first centuries BCE) the rulers took over as high priests, causing conflict; with the arrival of the Romans, the position was by appointment. After the destruction of the Temple in 70CE the office of high priest disappeared from Jewish life, and the role of interpreting Torah was taken over by the rabbis.

**Rabbis with Torah scrolls.**

## EARLY CHRISTIANS AND THE TEMPLE

The early Christians viewed the destruction of the Temple differently from the Jews. It was understood as the fulfillment of Jesus' prophecy (Mark 13) against the backdrop of the belief, explicitly expressed in the Letter to the Hebrews, that in Jesus the whole sacrificial system – and even the Temple itself – had been fulfilled and replaced (*cf.* the speech of Stephen, Acts 7).

The First Temple of Solomon (*pp.132–33*) had been destroyed by the Babylonians in the time of the Exile and later rebuilt under the leadership of Zerubbabel. It was then known as the Second Temple (*pp.158–59*) and was far less ornate in its design. Captured by the Romans under Pompey in 63BCE, the Second Temple was later rebuilt by Herod the Great (*pp.278–79*) as part of his extensive building plan. The inner sanctuary was built in about 18 months, but the whole temple complex was not completed until many years after Herod's death (*cf.* John 2:20). This, then, was the Temple of the New Testament period, the one known to Jesus.

### THE POST-TEMPLE ERA

The successive Temples were all built on the same site, the one acquired by David (2 Sam. 24:18–25). There was thus an element of continuity beyond the changing faces of the edifice erected on the site. While it stood, the Temple played a major part in the religious life and understanding of the Jews, but after its ruin in 70CE (*see p.293*) it was never rebuilt. Despite this, Jerusalem and its Temple remained in the heart of Jews, and the early rabbis continued to work on the ways in which Temple life, with its worship and sacrifices, should be conducted. The Judaism of the post-70CE era was, without the physical building of the Temple, a different entity but the continuity in prayer and imagination has never been lost.

*Double Gates*

*Royal Basilican*

## HEROD'S TEMPLE MOUNT
*When Herod rebuilt the Second Temple, he enlarged the platform on which the Temple was built (the Temple mount). The resulting edifice was grand both in size and in opulence, incorporating an elaborate series of courts and porticos.*

# FESTIVALS

Feasts, or festivals, were a central part of Jewish life and worship. As expressions of community life, they were occasions of celebration. Some festivals were tied in with the agricultural calendar, while others had specific historical associations (Passover and Purim), yet all were acts of commemoration, acknowledging God's provision for the people or God's powerful intervention on their behalf. Regular observance of these festivals provided continuity of tradition within the religious experience of Israel and the Jews.

Festivals bring happiness and celebration into the center of family and community life, or, as in the case of Yom Kippur, they offer time for repentance. Today Jewish festivals are known by their Hebrew name of *yom tov*, a good day (*see further pp.68–69*).

**Celebrating the Feast of Purim.**

For further reading see bibliography numbers: 38, 58, 325, 381, 506, 535, 702, 877

# JEWISH GROUPS
## IN NEW TESTAMENT TIMES

*Judaism at the time of Jesus was not a single, unified religion. Much was held in common by all Jews (see also pp.282–83), but there were major disagreements among the various groups about the meaning and practice of being Jewish.*

ACCORDING to Josephus, the Jewish historian, "The Jews ... had three philosophies ... that of the Essenes, that of the Sadducees, and, thirdly, that of the group called the Pharisees" (*Jewish Antiquities* XVIII.11). He also mentions another group, the Zealots. There were other interpretations of what it meant to be a Jew faithful to God and Torah, but these groups or movements were the prominent ones.

viduals. They were prominent until the destruction of the Temple in 70CE, when they lost their power. The Sadducees firmly believed that the Laws of Torah should be adhered to as strictly as possible, but that must have been impossible for ordinary people in everyday life. As text literalists, they rejected speculations about life after death (because it was not sanctioned in the biblical texts, *pp.178–79*), but cooperated with the Roman authorities (because this <u>was</u> sanctioned, as, for example in Jeremiah, *pp.206–7*). Believing in free will and resisting determinism, they advocated individual responsibility along with loyalty to the state, the Temple, and the Jewish Law.

of Judaism as it survived the failure of the Jewish revolts against Rome (pp.292–93). Eventually, some of them became extreme in their insistence on keeping the Law in every detail, and later rabbis criticized "Pharisees" (as they were called) as strongly as Jesus did.

By applying written Torah to daily life (their accumulating decisions became known as *Torah she be'al peh*, oral Torah), the Pharisees made Jewish faith and practice possible, not only after the fall of Jerusalem but in places far from that city. Faith was centered in the home and synagogue. On the basis of Scripture (more generously interpreted than by the Sadducees), they extended belief in such matters as angels and demons, life after death, final judgment, and resurrection of the dead. Of all groups, they were closest to Jesus and his followers, although Jesus went far beyond them in questioning, for example,

**THE TEMPLE IN JERUSALEM**
*Until the destruction of the Temple in 70CE, the majority of priests were Sadducees. The party died out when the Temple was destroyed.*

## PHARISEES
The Pharisees were a group that interpreted Torah so that its meaning could be applied to everyday life. Their name means "interpreters," but it can also mean "separatists," and they were called that by their opponents. The Pharisees were the forerunners of the rabbis, and

## SADDUCEES
By New Testament times the Jerusalem Temple had been taken over by the Sadducees, perhaps so-called because they claimed descent from Zadok, chief priest under David and Solomon (2 Sam. 8:17; 1 Kgs. 2:35). Sadducees were a patrician party made up of members of the high priestly families, the landed aristocracy, and other wealthy indi-

**SADDUCEE**
*Members of the Sadducean party included aristocratic priests and wealthy landowners. They believed themselves to be descended from Zadok, the priest who served in the Temple at the time of David (1 Kgs. 2:35).*

## STUDYING TORAH

*An important aspect of Judaism for both Sadducees and Pharisees was the study of Torah. However, whereas the Sadducees emphasized the importance of the Pentateuch (pp.22–23), the Pharisees accepted the whole of the Bible as authoritative. Furthermore, they attempted to give the Scriptures a fresh relevance so that they could be applied to the challenges faced by the majority of Jews in everyday situations.*

Torah scroll.

## PEOPLE OF THE LAND

Despite the presence of these Jewish groups, the majority of Jews did not belong to them. As part of a largely poor, rural, peasant, or artisan class, few Jews had time for such close observance of Torah. Most lived a simpler religion, which often incorporated magic and charms to help them through the trials of everyday life. These semi-observant masses were called *'am ha'arez*, "the people of the land," but that term has several different meanings. In biblical times, it could refer to the native population, to non-Jews living in the Jewish homeland, to the common people as opposed to kings, royal officials or priests, or to the property-owning and politically influential (male) citizens of a specific territory. In rabbinic literature, *'am ha'arez* refers specifically to those who did not observe the Jewish Law (especially the Laws of ritual purity) as opposed to the rabbis who did. Consequently, it became a term of abuse for those who were regarded as lax or ignorant in matters of morality or religion. It is with such people, the "sinners," that Jesus is said to have freely associated, giving rise to the Pharisees' criticism of him (e.g., Luke 15:1–2).

the need for ritual purity and tithing. Lay scholars rather than priests, they attempted to apply the laws of Temple purity to everyday life. Although separated in religious terms from the *'am ha'arez* or "people of the land," they exhibited democratic tendencies, frequently emerging as protectors of the people's rights versus the government.

## ESSENES AND ZEALOTS

Known from Pliny the Elder, Philo, and Josephus, and now (possibly, with caution) from the Dead Sea Scrolls (pp.290–91), the Essenes are not mentioned in the New Testament, although some claim that John the Baptist was an Essene. They were a group that endeavored to obey the command "Be holy" in a radical and ascetic way, seeking to avoid contamination from the world.

The Zealots were a first-century religio-political party characterized by zeal for God, a desire for the autonomy of the land of Israel (*eretz Israel*), a refusal to submit to Rome, and a willingness to suffer for its beliefs. The New Testament makes little mention of them, and the claim that Jesus was connected with them, through, for instance, his association with Simon "the Zealot," his "cleansing" of the Temple, and his death by crucifixion, is far-fetched (although Paul refers to himself as "zealous" in Gal. 1:14). Jewish history abounds with "zealots," activists who, in their "zeal" for the God of Israel, believed themselves to be God's agents for judgment or liberation (e.g., Phinehas, Num. 25:10–30; the Maccabean rebels, *see pp. 250–51*), so whether the Zealots formed a party rather than a recurrent tendency is uncertain, despite Josephus' references to them as "brigands," "the fourth philosophy," *Sicarii* or "dagger-men," and "Zealots." However, they certainly played an important part in the struggles against Rome.

### JEWISH FAITH FOR THE MAJORITY
*Most Jews were not members of any religious party. They worked the land and lived a far simpler life than that followed by those in religious movements.*

For further reading see bibliography numbers: 132, 344, 397, 398, 426, 673, 679, 702, 706, 877, 880, 882

# THE DEAD SEA SCROLLS

*Ancient manuscripts and fragments, first discovered in 1947, have revealed a fascinating insight into life and beliefs before and during the time of Jesus Christ.*

## QUMRAN

Northwest of the Dead Sea, Qumran lies roughly 10 miles (16km) south of Jericho. Before the Essene community occupied the site, it is believed that Qumran had once been one of the frontier posts of the tribal territory of Judah in the period of the Judean Monarchy and was known as the "City of Salt." Scrolls were also found at sites farther into the Judean Desert at Masada (*pp.294–95*), Seelim, and Murabba'at.

THE Dead Sea Scrolls are manuscripts, or fragments of manuscripts, that were found in caves near the Dead Sea between 1947 and 1956. Some appear to come from a sect or sects based at Qumran sometime before the last settlement there was destroyed by Romans toward the end of the First Jewish War (*pp.292–93*). They contain a wealth of Jewish literature written during the period from before and about the time of Jesus, without later revision, adaptation, or censorship. While the scrolls are all now publicly accessible, some await official editing and translation. Among 11 almost complete ancient Jewish scrolls and the thousands of fragments, there are biblical manuscripts in various Hebrew text forms, covering all books except Esther and Nehemiah, and parts of the Hebrew Bible in Greek. The noncanonical, or unofficial, works comprise some previously known texts such as *Sirach*, *Tobit*, *1 Enoch*, and *The Testament of Levi*, together with many previously

### EXCAVATING THE EVIDENCE
*Many scrolls were discovered stored inside terra-cotta scroll jars, ink pots, lamps, and other pottery items were also found in the caves.*

unknown ones. These include commentaries on various biblical Prophets and Psalms, non-canonical psalms and prayers, rules for an ascetic community, and legal and mystical texts.

## WHO WROTE THEM?

Many questions about the identity and significance of these texts are still unanswered. Based on descriptions by the first-century Jewish writers Philo and Josephus, and by the Roman author Pliny the Elder, many Qumran scholars believe that the sectarian scrolls are probably related to the desert branch of the Essene sect (*p.289*). Problems with this view include:
• How to assess the many nonsectarian documents.
• Whether scrolls from more distant caves really belonged to the settlement of Qumran.
• Whether a small desert community could realistically be assumed to have needed and produced such a large library of manuscripts. Perhaps, instead, Qumran was a refuge for diverse dissidents from Jerusalem so that the caves contained manuscripts stored for safekeeping by different people, not least just before or during the First Jewish War of 66–70CE.

Regardless of the answers to these questions, the Dead Sea Scrolls constitute an invaluable resource for our understanding of Jewish practices and beliefs around the first century CE.

### DETAIL OF THE TEMPLE SCROLL
*Over 26ft (8m) long, and with 66 columns, this scroll is one of the longest discovered. It covers such subjects as the proposed rebuilding of the Temple and includes instructions on feasts and the laws of sacrifice.*

# THE SECT AT QUMRAN

*Evidence suggests that the group behind the sectarian scrolls began as a priestly group in the Maccabean period (pp.250–51), which practiced an ascetic and heavily regulated lifestyle.*

Reacting against political and Temple developments, a group led by a priestly figure, "The Teacher of Righteousness," abandoned the corrupt Temple in Jerusalem in c.152BCE for the desert. The sect believed they embodied the new Covenant of Jeremiah 31 as well as the true Temple. The sectarian scrolls reveal their strict study and observance of the Law and the Prophets, which dictated their distinctive views on such practical issues as a separate solar calendar, purity regulations, sacrifice, and the end-time, which was their anticipation of the imminent arrival of the Messiah to lead his people in victory against the Romans and other infidels. Community members led a life of simplicity without private property. They were apparently unmarried, although a few separate tombs of women and children have been found at the Qumran burial site. During the First Jewish War some may have joined the rebels' last stand at Masada, where scrolls have been discovered.

**Khirbet Qumran**
*From the second century BCE to the first century CE, Khirbet, or "ruin" of Qumran, was probably the sect's communal site.*

## LINKS WITH THE NEW TESTAMENT

Like certain New Testament books, the sectarian scrolls show an avid interest in revelation and participation in heavenly worship (1 Cor. 11:10; 13:1), a view of the community as a living temple (2 Cor. 6:16), and, like the earliest church in Jerusalem, the sharing of all property. The texts have important similarities and contrasts with Paul's doctrines, particularly justification (4QMMT). The cosmic warfare of light versus darkness (mentioned in Ephesians, Colossians, and John's Gospel) is also discussed in several of the scrolls. These passages anticipate a final conflagration in which the promised Davidic Messiah will come and lead his people to victory, preach good news to the poor, and raise the dead (4Q521). Claims that 7Q5 (a tiny fragment) is from Mark 6:52–53 are unlikely: too few letters survive.

**THE CAVES AT QUMRAN**
*Most scrolls were excavated from caves located in the cliffs of a wadi (dried-up riverbed) at Qumran. Approximately 190 biblical scrolls were found altogether. The hot, dry, desert climate helped preserve the parchment, which has since been dated between 250BCE and 70CE.*

For further reading see bibliography numbers: 30, 298, 319, 762, 770, 877

## THE SCROLL REFERENCES

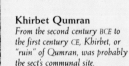

*Abbreviation of document name*

**4QFlor 1.11**

*Number and location of cave where document found*

*Particular section and line referred to*

Individual scrolls are identified first by a number indicating the cave in which the document was found. This is followed by a capital letter indicating the area, so 4Q is the fourth cave at Qumran. An abbreviation of the document name follows this. For example, 4QFlor is the text known as *Florilegium* (Eschatological Midrashim), and 1QpHab is the commentary (Hebrew *pesher*) on Habakkuk. Finally, a series of numbers indicates the specific section and/or line referred to.

## COMMON ABBREVIATIONS

1QapGen (*Genesis Apocryphon*)

1QH[odayot] (*Thanksgiving Hymns*)

1QS[erek hayyahad] (*The Rule, or Manual of Discipline*)

4QMMT (*Works of Torah*)

1QM[ilhama] (*The War Scroll*)

4QPr[ayer of] Nab[onidus]

4QTLevi (*Testament of Levi*)

11QT[emple Scroll]

11QMelch[izedek]

11QJub[ilees]

11QtgJob (*Targum of Job*)

# THE FIRST JEWISH WAR

*The First Jewish War, or Revolt, against Rome was one of the most catastrophic events for Jews in antiquity. Lasting from 66 to 70CE, the conflict came to a violent conclusion with the destruction of the magnificent Temple in Jerusalem.*

### JUDEA
The war finally ended when the besieged city of Jerusalem fell to Titus and his army in 70CE. After five months of siege few escaped, but those who did managed to reach Jewish garrisons at Herodium, Machaerus, and Masada.

JEWISH clashes with Rome broke out repeatedly during the first century CE, but they were mostly on a local scale. Apart from social gangs who made a practical protest against injustice and poverty, there were messianic claimants, revolutionary and popular prophets, apocalyptic preachers who foresaw the imminent end of the world, assassins known as *Sicarii* (from the type of dagger they carried), and Zealots (sometimes identified with the *Sicarii* but probably distinct). Jews could well remember the success of the Maccabean Revolt (*pp.250–51*) and the ensuing period of Jewish independence, and some at least could equate faithfulness to God with success in re-creating an independent and Torah-obedient state. This background of unrest and Jewish independence was evident in the society Jesus lived in.

Such attitudes gained momentum because of the growing corruption and insensitive administration of Roman procurators (44–66CE, *pp.278–79*). According to the Jewish historian, Josephus, the immediate cause of the First Jewish War was the mismanagement of Judea

### RETURNING IN TRIUMPH
*This panel from the Titus Arch shows Roman soldiers parading their sacred spoils, including the seven-branched ritual candlestick (menorah), from the Jerusalem Temple.*

### ARCH OF TITUS
In 71CE, to commemorate Titus' victory in the First Jewish War, the Roman Senate declared a triumphal procession to pass through the streets of Rome. A Triumphal Arch of wood and stucco was erected, through which the victorious Roman generals paraded with their Jewish prisoners. In 81CE the arch was replaced with one of marble and bronze (*above*).

by the procurator Gessius Florus. In addition to plundering towns under his jurisdiction and allowing banditry in exchange for a share in the spoils, Florus attempted to rob the Temple treasury. When Jews protested, he tried to force their submission in Jerusalem with 1,200 soldiers. After a fierce battle, Florus and the soldiers withdrew. An armed conflict then ensued, which lasted four years.

## THE FOUR PHASES OF THE REVOLT

• 66CE: early Jewish successes and organization of resistance. During the first year of the revolt, the Jewish effort met with some success. Having marginalized the influence of moderate voices wishing to end the conflict peacefully, those insisting on violent means organized the revolt. The Jews routed an army of 20,000 soldiers who had been sent from Syria to put down the revolt. Inspired by this, they set up defenses and organized armies in Jerusalem, Judea, and Galilee.

• 67CE: Jewish Galilean resistance crushed. Vespasian was appointed by the emperor Nero to head an army of 60,000 soldiers, which he brought to Galilee. It was here and in Gaulanitis that the war was fought, and the Jewish resistance was soundly crushed. While Josephus defected to the Roman side, other leaders more radically committed to the conflict escaped to Jerusalem. Among the latter was John of Gischala, who gained a foothold for power in Jerusalem by murdering the High Priest there.

• 68–69CE: the Roman campaign in Palestine and infighting in Jerusalem. As Vespasian's army gained control of remaining parts of Palestine, more Jews fled to Jerusalem. This influx resulted in the formation of another radical party, led by Simon Bar-Giora, who vied with John of Gischala for power. In the meantime, Vespasian became emperor and left his son, Titus, in charge of the Roman army.

• 70CE: the Roman capture of Jerusalem. Under Titus the Romans laid siege to Jerusalem. Taking advantage of bitter infighting among the Jewish parties and of the worsening conditions and starvation within the walled city, Titus had ramparts built on

**THE MIGHTY ROMANS**
*Nero (top) sent Vespasian to quell the rebellion in Judea. But it was Titus (left), Vespasian's son, who led his soldiers into Jerusalem and burned the Temple.*

the north side. After five months the Roman forces finally captured the city and destroyed much of the Temple. The leaders of the revolt, including John and Simon, were taken prisoner along with 700 others and brought to Rome for a humiliating triumphal procession. The final subjugation occurred at Masada in 73CE (pp.294–95).

After the war, Judea was placed more directly under Roman rule. Deprived of the Temple sacrificial cult, the Jewish priesthood was effectively dispossessed. As a result, leadership gradually passed to the rabbis, known for their skill in applying Torah to daily life. Since the Jewish Christian community did not participate in the war effort, the First Jewish War contributed to the growing breach between Judaism and emerging Christianity, which was inclined to interpret the disaster as the judgment of God.

For further reading see bibliography numbers: 1, 45, 325, 344, 397, 398, 418, 426, 441, 442, 645, 673, 706, 877

### JEWISH COINS
During the revolt the Jews minted their own silver and bronze coins bearing Hebrew inscriptions and symbols as a further stand against Rome.

# MASADA

*In 36BCE the innovative builder, Herod the Great, transformed the rock of Masada into a magnificent mountain-fortress, its great fortifications later providing Jewish rebels with the protection they needed in their last stand against the Romans.*

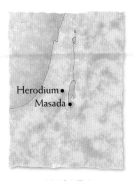

## MASADA

Situated on top of a steep-sided, diamond-shaped mesa, on the rock *es-Sebba* in the Judean Desert, the palace-fortress of Masada overlooks the western shore of the Dead Sea. It rises 800ft (240m) above the desert and is located about 10 miles (16km) south of En-gedi.

JOSEPHUS, the first-century Jewish historian, records that Jonathan, the High Priest and brother of Judas Maccabeus (161–143BCE), first erected a fortress on this great rock in the Judean Desert and called it Masada. However, a majority of scholars now attribute the first buildings to the time of Alexander Janneaus (103–76BCE). During the Hasmonean period, the existing paths to the summit were built, as were the Western palace, three smaller centrally located palaces, cisterns, towers, a pool, and other buildings with administrative, living, and storage facilities.

In 36BCE Herod the Great visited the site and added to the existing buildings, turning ' Masada into one of his spectacular rocky fortress palaces (*see box, right*).

Masada came to prominence again in the summer of 66CE, when Gessius Florus governed Judea. During his turbulent administration, Masada was overrun by Jewish rebels, or *Sicarii*, who slew the Roman guards and put a garrison of their own in their place (*see The First Jewish War, pp.292–93*). They remained in control of the fortress for the next eight years. After Jerusalem fell to the Romans in September 70CE, and after the fortresses of Herodium and Macherus had also fallen, only Masada remained defiant.

## THE ROMAN ATTACK

However, in late 73CE, the Roman general Flavius Silva finally managed to subdue the district. He established garrisons and built a perimeter wall around the base of Masada. He set up nine camps and built an earth ramp to the wall, up which a tower and a ram were hauled to effect a breach.

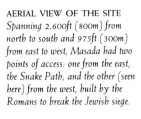

**AERIAL VIEW OF THE SITE**
*Spanning 2,600ft (800m) from north to south and 975ft (300m) from east to west, Masada had two points of access: one from the east, the Snake Path, and the other (seen here) from the west, built by the Romans to break the Jewish siege.*

# SITE PLAN OF MASADA

*Having twice previously visited the rocky fortress of Masada, Herod the Great then built extensively on the summit, attracted by the virtual inaccessibility of the site to intruders from the surrounding Judean Desert.*

Herod enclosed the entire summit with a wall of white stone 4,593ft (1,400m) long, 20ft (6m) high, and 13ft (4m) wide and then built more than 30 towers on it, from which there was access to apartments constructed on the inside of the wall. He also built a palace on three levels on the northern end of the rock and equipped the fortress to withstand siege conditions. To this end he made the approaches to the fortress even more difficult, established a large armory, and ensured ample supplies of food and water by cultivating the plateau and by cutting 12 large water reservoirs out of the rock.

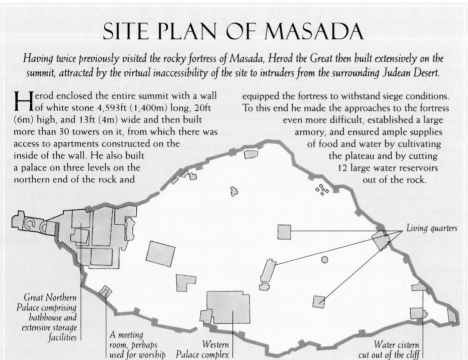

Living quarters

Great Northern Palace comprising bathhouse and extensive storage facilities

A meeting room, perhaps used for worship

Western Palace complex

Water cistern cut out of the cliff

## HERODIUM
One of Herod's most spectacular, and perhaps strongest projects, the fortress of Herodium was built on an artificially raised hilltop 8 miles (12km) south of Jerusalem. Enclosed within high, circular walls stood a luxurious royal villa with a pillared courtyard, garden, richly decorated bathhouse, and a Roman-style pool. Yet Herodium was not simply a fortress incorporating a palace of leisure and luxury; Herod's intention was that it should also serve as his burial place, although a tomb has never been found.

At this point sources differ. Josephus writes, concerning the night before 15 Xanthicus (May 2) 74CE, that the *Sicarii* leader, Eleazar, son of Jairus, appealed to the defenders to end their own lives and those of their families because God had deserted them on account of their sin. He said that it was better they should die at their own hands than at the hands of the enemy. His entreaty ultimately succeeded. The women and children were slaughtered, the remaining stores and valuables burned, and the men were then killed in accordance with a lottery contrived by Eleazar. At daybreak, silence greeted the Romans. Before them lay the dead bodies of 960 men, women, and children. Two women and five children survived to tell this story, having concealed themselves in an underground cistern.

Much of Josephus' account is rendered implausible by archaeological evidence that suggests that only some of the *Sicarii* killed their families, burned their possessions, and set fire to the public buildings before ending their own lives, while others fought the Romans to the death or even tried to hide or escape. Between 1963 and 1965, when the site was extensively excavated under the direction of Israeli archaeologist Yigael Yadin, the remains of only 25 bodies were uncovered; how they died could not be ascertained. Recent excavations in 1997 found pig bones among some of the buried bones. Because of the ban on eating pork, these pig bones would not have been buried with Jewish bodies. It appears then that these bodies must have been the remains of Roman soldiers.

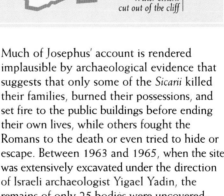

REMAINS OF HEROD'S PALACE
*Herod's luxurious "hanging palace" was built on three natural rock terraces, each one providing a breathtaking view of the Judean Desert.*

For further reading bibliography numbers: 1, 199, 325, 344, 441, 442, 645, 837

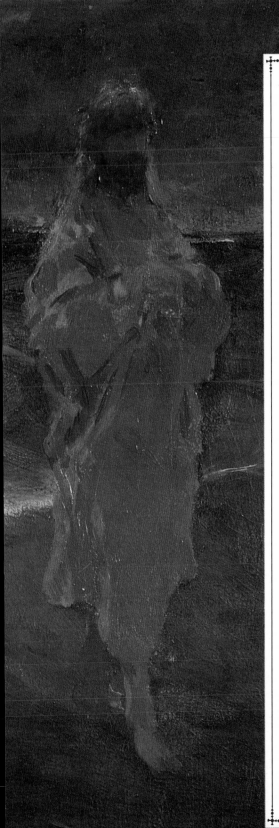

# THE LIFE OF
# JESUS

Jesus' life is known almost entirely from the four Gospels, which concentrate on Jesus' life from the beginning of his ministry to his Passion, death, and Resurrection. Each Gospel tells Jesus' story in its own way, but the outline of events is clear.

Two of the Gospels record the events surrounding Jesus' birth, but little is said of his childhood. The main story begins with Jesus' baptism, his time of testing in the wilderness, and then his role as an itinerant teacher in the northern region of Galilee. He also called 12 particular disciples to be with him and gradually prepared them to understand the purpose of his mission and ministry. Jesus' message was simple but urgent: *"The time is fulfilled, and the kingdom of God has come near; repent, and believe in the good news!"* (Mark 1:15). According to Luke 4:16–30, Jesus saw himself as fulfilling the yearning prophecy of Isaiah 61:1–2. Not only was his teaching vivid and memorable but he acted in ways that met people's needs, in healing, in forgiveness, and in miracles. Crowds began to come to him, some enthusiastically, believing it was God's power at work among them. Others were deeply opposed to Jesus and considered that he questioned God's Law. How could this ordinary man, whose family was well known, speak with such authority, and do these amazing things? Jesus insisted that his authority came from God. The Gospels record the difficulties the disciples had in understanding Jesus' mission. A decisive moment came at Caesarea Philippi (Matt. 16:1–23ff.), when they were challenged and made to realize that Jesus must go to Jerusalem in order to suffer death there.

Jesus arrived in Jerusalem at Passover knowing that he would soon die, and the story moves to his Passion – his suffering in the last week of his life. As he celebrated the Passover with his disciples, he made his last supper with them memorable through his actions, pledging that his presence would remain with the disciples even after his death. Later that night, he was betrayed and arrested, then taken for investigation, tried before the Romans, and crucified. On the third day after his Crucifixion, his followers, knowing that he had died, were astounded to find out that he was alive again.

# PALESTINE

In the first century CE, Palestine was divided into three provinces – Judea, Galilee, and Samaria – all of which were under Roman rule (pp.278–79). Geographically, the whole region is diverse, with deserts, mountains, valleys, plateaus, and plains. Jesus' ministry took place mainly in Galilee and Judea, and the rural settings of Jesus' parables reflect the everyday life of Jews at this time. Most people worked on the land or earned their living by fishing in the Sea of Galilee, an important source of employment. As the Romans became more established in the region, roads and ports were improved, and Palestine was opened up to international trade.

### JEWISH GROUPS
Evidence, such as these sandals, survives of independent Jewish groups living in the Judean Desert around the time of Jesus (pp.288–89).

### JERUSALEM
The Temple in Jerusalem was the spiritual focus for Jews (pp.276–77, 286–87). Jesus came to the city to face the Temple authorities, knowing that he would soon be put to death (pp.348–59).

### BETHLEHEM
The hill town of Bethlehem lies southwest of Jerusalem. The Hebrew prophet Micah foretold the birth of a Messiah in Bethlehem who would deliver the people from oppression and injustice. Matthew's and Luke's Gospels both mention that Jesus was born in Bethlehem (pp.320–21).

Ptolemais (Acre)

Sepphoris

Caesarea

*Mediterranean Sea*

Samaria (Sebaste)

**SAMARIA**

Antipatris

Joppa

Lydda

Emmaus

Jerusalem

Bethlehem

Herodium

Bethphage

**JUDEA**

**IDUMEA**

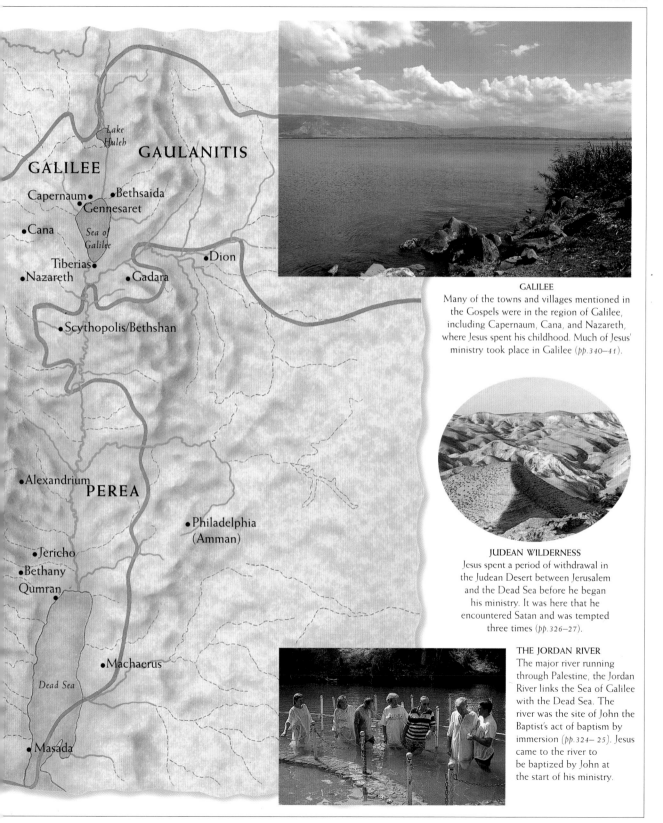

**GALILEE**
Many of the towns and villages mentioned in the Gospels were in the region of Galilee, including Capernaum, Cana, and Nazareth, where Jesus spent his childhood. Much of Jesus' ministry took place in Galilee (*pp.340–41*).

**JUDEAN WILDERNESS**
Jesus spent a period of withdrawal in the Judean Desert between Jerusalem and the Dead Sea before he began his ministry. It was here that he encountered Satan and was tempted three times (*pp.326–27*).

**THE JORDAN RIVER**
The major river running through Palestine, the Jordan River links the Sea of Galilee with the Dead Sea. The river was the site of John the Baptist's act of baptism by immersion (*pp.324–25*). Jesus came to the river to be baptized by John at the start of his ministry.

# THE GOSPELS

*These books contain accounts of the life and ministry of Jesus and tell of his death and Resurrection. Three (those "according to Matthew, Mark, and Luke") are related to each other and are called "the Synoptic Gospels" (pp.302–3). The Gospel "according to John" is also called the Fourth, or Last, Gospel.*

THE word *gospel* means "good news." Its Christian usage probably derives from the early belief that Jesus filled the role spoken of in Isaiah 52:7 and 61:1 – he "preached good news" (Luke 4:16–21). In Paul's letters (written before the Gospels), "good news" had already become established as a technical term for the message that he and the other earliest missionaries preached, focusing particularly on Jesus' death and Resurrection (1 Cor. 15:1–7). This was the usage that Mark picked up at the beginning of his Gospel (Mark 1:1). It was probably from this usage that the word *Gospel* was transferred to the actual writing itself, as in the Gospel according to Mark.

The name is traditionally associated with the four Gospels in the New Testament – Matthew, Mark, Luke, and John. Strictly speaking, they are referred to not as the Gospel *of* Matthew, etc., but the Gospel *according to* Matthew, etc. The implication is clear: these were not different Gospels, but one and the same good news in different versions.

## PASSION NARRATIVES

The origin of the word *gospel* helps explain the character of the canonical Gospels. In each case, the Gospel builds up to the climax of Jesus' Passion and Resurrection, or "Passion narratives with extended introductions," to cite a famous

**SCENES FROM THE LIFE OF JESUS**
*Together, the four canonical Gospels provide us with the most knowledge we have of Jesus and his life and ministry.*

66 *I too decided, after investigating everything carefully ... to write an orderly account for you ... so that you may know the truth ...* 99

(Luke 1:3–4)

description (Martin Kahler). This helps explain why other claimants to the title "Gospel" – known as "apocryphal gospels" – did not become established or widely accepted as part of the New Testament canon (pp.474–75). The most famous of these today is the one known as the *Gospel of Thomas*, a collection of sayings of Jesus well regarded in Gnostic circles in the second and third centuries CE (*see box*). However, Mark had evidently established the Passion framework for a written "Gospel," and collections of sayings as such did not fit within that definition.

## GOSPELS AS BIOGRAPHIES

"Gospels" are unique documents in the ancient world. This has often been taken to mean that they cannot be classified as biographies. Certainly they do not share the interest of modern biographies, which follow the subject's history from birth and trace the development of his or her character and self-awareness.

The Gospels do, however, share much of the character of ancient biographies – that is, they portray the character of the subject by telling stories about, and recalling sayings of, the subject. They present the essentials of the good news and show how this is related to, and arises out of, the life of Jesus. In this respect the New Testament Gospels can be compared with ancient biographies

# OTHER GOSPELS

*Approximately 24 other documents from the early world also lay claim to the word* Gospel.
*These are usually called "Apocryphal gospels."*

Most Apocryphal gospels are dated later than those according to Matthew, Mark, Luke, and John – approximately the second century CE onward. The Apocryphal Gospels are of value for early Church history but not for the life of Jesus. Some follow the form of the New Testament Gospels but most do not, such as those with sayings attributed to Jesus. Some are attributed to people like Peter, Thomas, and Nicodemus. In recent years, some people have claimed that a few give us authentic information about Jesus – for example, the *Egerton Gospel* and some sayings in the *Gospel of Thomas* (p.463).

The *Gospel of Peter*, supposedly written by Simon Peter, the chief Apostle, is a retelling of the Gospel account of what happened from the end of Jesus' trial to his Resurrection appearances. Part of a longer work, it seems to date from about the second century CE. The *Egerton*

*Papyrus 2*, a tiny document on papyrus, contains sayings similar to some of those in the Gospels, and otherwise unknown material. The *Gospel of Thomas* includes 114 sayings attributed to Jesus. Some are almost identical to Jesus' sayings in the Gospels; others are related to known sayings but developed into different points. Much of it is unfamiliar. The *Gospel of Thomas* and others are clearly Gnostic interpretations of Jesus, claiming knowledge of spiritual mysteries; the *Gospel of Thomas* has been identified with the Gospel used by the Naasene Gnostics. The American book *"The Five Gospels: The Search for Authentic Words of Jesus,"* which published the four Gospels with Thomas, concluded that only five sayings in the *Gospel of Thomas* can reasonably claim to be authentic. Claims that the authentic Jesus can be found as much outside as inside the canonical Gospels are unwarranted.

---

such as Philostratus' *Life of Apollonius of Tyana*, and Xenophon's *Memorabilia*. This also means that the Gospels cannot be dismissed as merely propaganda documents lacking any historical substance. On the contrary, they reflect something of the curiosity that early Christian preaching must have stimulated: "Who was this Jesus?" And for the most part the Gospels evidently contain memories of those who first followed Jesus and who became the first Christians. The forms in which the evangelists transmitted such records often indicated grouping of material for ease of teaching or learning, for example, the Sermon on the Mount and the collections of parables.

## THE INTERRELATIONSHIPS BETWEEN THE GOSPELS

The first three Gospels share the same character and much of the same material. Because they can be looked at together (synopsis), they are usually known as "the Synoptic Gospels," or alternatively called the "Synoptics" (pp.302–3).

Much of the content of Mark appears also in Matthew, and in the parallel passages it often seems that Matthew and also Luke have abbreviated and polished the rougher style of Mark. In places, all three Synoptic Gospels carry exactly the same verses, almost word for word. Most people

SCENES FROM JESUS' CRUCIFIXION
*All four Gospels include the Passion narrative, a term referring to Jesus' suffering in the final days and his death.*

therefore conclude that Mark is the earliest of the Gospels and that Matthew and Luke used Mark as one of their principal sources (pp.302, 308).

In addition to the links with material in Mark's Gospel, Matthew and Luke often contain additional material that is very similar or identical, therefore leading most people to conclude that Matthew and Luke had a second source (usually known as Q). Q would have been a collection of sayings of Jesus, so it is of interest to note that Q was not retained as such by the early Christians, but only as incorporated into the Gospel (Passion) framework supplied by Mark.

## THE FOURTH GOSPEL

John's Gospel is very different from the other three Gospels. However, it does retain the basic Gospel structure and may well contain historical traditions unknown to, or passed over by, the other Gospel writers, for example, the early links between the missions of John the Baptist and Jesus. John's Gospel clearly has its roots in Synoptic-like tradition, but most scholars think that John's Gospel was written late in the first century CE as a kind of extended meditation or reflection on what Jesus had said and done and the fuller significance of these events.

For further reading see bibliography numbers: 86, 151, 609, 724, 725, 726, 727, 861, 870, 876

# SYNOPTIC GOSPELS

*The Synoptics are the three Gospels that can be looked at side by side and compared in order to show the relationship between them.*

THE word "synoptic" comes from the Greek *synopsis*, meaning "things can be seen together." The Gospels of Matthew, Mark, and Luke can be printed as a synopsis because they share material. These extracts (*right*) recount the story of the Transfiguration, and of Jesus' agony in the Garden of Gethsemane (in part). They show why the majority of scholars think that Mark was the first of the Gospels and that it was used by Matthew and Luke in different ways (e.g., note the different title for Jesus in Mark 9:5). Matthew and Luke sometimes agree with each other but not with Mark. Did one of these evangelists also know and use the other's work? Matthew and Luke also contain original material, part of which they share (so perhaps it belonged to a lost source known as Q, *see p.301*), and part of which is uniquely their own (e.g., their infancy narrative and Luke 9:51–18:14, of which only some of the material is included in Matthew).

## INTERRELATIONSHIPS BETWEEN THE GOSPELS

*There is no certainty of knowing how the Gospels relate to each other, but this diagram shows the most commonly held view.*

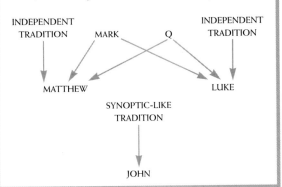

## MATTHEW

### THE TRANSFIGURATION, 17:1–9

MATT. 17:1  Six days later, Jesus took with him Peter and James and *his brother* John and led them up a high mountain, by themselves.

MATT. 17:2  And he was transfigured before them, and his face *shone like the sun*, and his clothes became dazzling white.

MATT. 17:3  Suddenly there appeared to them Moses and Elijah talking with him.

MATT. 17:4  Then Peter said to Jesus, "*Lord*, it is good for us to be here; *if you wish, I will* make three dwellings here, one for you, one for Moses and one for Elijah."

MATT. 17:5  While he was still speaking, suddenly a bright cloud overshadowed them, and from the cloud a voice said, "This is my Son, the Beloved; *with him I am well pleased*; listen to him!"

MATT. 17:6  *When the disciples heard this they fell to the ground and were overcome by fear.*

MATT. 17:7  But Jesus came and touched them, saying, "Get up and *do not be afraid.*"

MATT. 17:8  *And* when they looked *up*, they saw no one *except* Jesus *himself alone.*

MATT. 17:9  As they were coming down the mountain, *Jesus* ordered them, "Tell no one *about the vision* until after the Son of Man has *been raised* from the dead."

### JESUS' AGONY IN THE GARDEN, 26:36–39

MATT. 26:36  *Then* Jesus went *with them* to a place called Gethsemane; and he said to his disciples, "Sit here while I *go over there and* pray."

MATT. 26:37  He took with him Peter and *the two sons of Zebedee,* and began to be *grieved* and agitated.

MATT. 26:38  *Then* he said to them, "I am deeply grieved, even to death; remain here, and *stay* awake *with me.*"

MATT. 26:39  And going a little farther, he threw himself on the ground and prayed, "*My* Father, *if it is* possible, *let this cup pass* from me; yet not what I want but what you want."

*Note: Material unique to each Gospel is in italics.*

# MARK

## THE TRANSFIGURATION, 9:2–9

*MARK 9:2*  Six days later, Jesus took with him Peter and James and John, and led them up a high mountain *apart*, by themselves.

*MARK 9:3*  And he was transfigured before them, and his clothes became dazzling white, *such as no one on earth could bleach them.*

*MARK 9:4*  And there appeared to them Elijah with Moses, who were talking with *Jesus.*

*MARK 9:5*  Then Peter said to Jesus, "*Rabbi*, it is good for us to be here; let us make three dwellings, one for you, one for Moses, and one for Elijah."

*MARK 9:6*  *He did not know what to say for they were terrified.*

*MARK 9:7*  *Then* a cloud overshadowed them, and from the cloud there came a voice, "This is my son, the Beloved; listen to him!"

*MARK 9:8*  *Suddenly* when they looked around, they saw no one *with them any more,* but only Jesus.

*MARK 9:9*  As they were coming down the mountain, *he* ordered them *to* tell no one about what they had seen, until after the Son of Man had *risen* from the dead.

## JESUS' AGONY IN THE GARDEN, 14:32–36

*MARK 14:32*  *They* went to a place called Gethsemane; and he said to his disciples, "Sit here while I pray."

*MARK 14:33*  He took with him Peter and *James and John,* and began to be *distressed* and agitated.

*MARK 14:34*  *And* he said to them, "I am deeply grieved, even to death; remain here, and *keep* awake."

*MARK 14:35*  And going a little farther, he threw himself on the ground and prayed *that, if it were possible, the hour might pass from him.*

*MARK 14:36*  He said, "*Abba*, Father, *for you all things are* possible; remove this cup from me; yet, not what I want, but what you want."

# LUKE

## THE TRANSFIGURATION, 9:28–36

*LUKE 9:28*  *Now about eight days after these sayings* Jesus took with him Peter and John and James, and *went up on the mountain to pray.*

*LUKE 9:29*  *And while he was praying, the appearance of his face changed,* and his clothes became dazzling white.

*LUKE 9:30*  Suddenly *they saw two men,* Moses and Elijah, talking to him.

*LUKE 9:31*  *They appeared in glory and were speaking of his departure, which he was about to accomplish at Jerusalem.*

*LUKE 9:32*  *Now Peter and his companions were weighed down with sleep; but since they had stayed awake, they saw his glory and the two men who stood with him.*

*LUKE 9:33*  *Just as they were leaving him,* Peter said to Jesus, "*Master,* it is good for us to be here; let us make three dwellings, one for you, one for Moses, and one for Elijah" – *not knowing what he said.*

*LUKE 9:34*  *While he was saying this,* a cloud came and overshadowed them; and they were terrified *as they entered the cloud.*

*LUKE 9:35*  Then from the cloud came a voice *that said,* "This is my Son, *my Chosen;* listen to him!"

*LUKE 9:36*  *When the voice had spoken, Jesus was found alone. And they kept silent and in those days told no one any of the things they had seen.*

## JESUS' AGONY IN THE GARDEN, 22:39–44

*LUKE 22:39*  *He came out and went, as was his custom, to the Mount of Olives; and the disciples followed him.*

*LUKE 22:40*  *When he reached the place, he said to them, "Pray that you may not come into the time of trial."*

*LUKE 22:41*  *Then he withdrew from them about a stone's throw, knelt down,* and prayed,

*LUKE 22:42*  "Father, *if you are willing,* remove this cup from me; yet, not *my will but yours be done.*"

*LUKE 22:43*  *Then an angel from heaven appeared to him and gave him strength.*

*LUKE 22:44*  *In his anguish he prayed more earnestly, and his sweat became like great drops of blood falling down on the ground.*

For further reading see bibliography numbers: 5a, 605a, 748a, 876

# STUDYING THE GOSPELS

*The Victorian portrait painter Henry Richmond was once asked whether he tried to paint his portraits truthfully. "Yes," he said, "The truth. But the truth lovingly told." The Gospels also tell the truth about Jesus, but the truth lovingly, and thankfully, told.*

FROM the second century CE, people tried to consolidate the Gospel narratives in order to obtain a single complete account of Jesus, but it has since been accepted that the Gospels are all different. Not only are Mark, Matthew, and Luke – the Synoptic Gospels – different from that of John, they each give a distinctive picture, which a Gospel consolidation would destroy. It should be understood, therefore, that although each Gospel is complete in itself, the picture they give when studied as a whole is all the richer for the different individual emphases.

## HISTORICAL CRITICISM

For more than two hundred years, a major concern of Gospel study has been historicity: to what extent is it possible to demonstrate how accurate the Gospels were in recording what Jesus said and did, and how far can we reconstruct the process that led to the present Gospels? This historical emphasis has given rise to different kinds of Gospel criticism:

• **Source Criticism.** This involves trying to go behind the Gospels to the earliest pre-Gospel sources, closer in time to the historical Jesus. There may have been no written Gospel until about 30 years after his death.

• **Form Criticism.** If the earliest traditions were passed on orally, useful information might be learned from the forms of transmission – parables, miracle stories, legal sayings, etc. – and their function in the earliest communities. Scholars have looked for the "setting in life" of each form and of each saying or story. A story, for example, might gain a different meaning taken out of the context of Jesus in Palestine into that of a Hellenistic community of an early church. Thus, attention shifted to the earliest communities and to the disciplines of sociology and social history. However, recognizing sources and community influences requires much guesswork since there is virtually no direct evidence.

• **Redaction Criticism.** Source and Form criticism treat the evangelists as essentially compilers of earlier traditions, but the way they redact, or edit, their sources may give clues to the compilers' own theology and intentions as authors. This is solidly based only if the source being used is extant, as is probably the case with Matthew and Luke in their use of Mark.

## BEYOND HISTORICAL CRITICISM

In recent years, the emphasis on recovering the history of Jesus through the Gospels has been questioned. Historical research remains essential for the whole Bible because it is

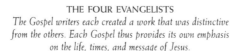

THE FOUR EVANGELISTS
*The Gospel writers each created a work that was distinctive from the others. Each Gospel thus provides its own emphasis on the life, times, and message of Jesus.*

rooted in events. But the texts that bear those events to the reader take many different forms. Attempts have been made, therefore, to gain fresh insight into the Gospels by looking at the following issues:

• The effect they have on readers, and the way readers discern meanings in the text (reader-response criticism).

• The way the Gospels are structured to convey their meaning (structuralist criticism).

• The extent to which the Gospels were written to achieve a reaction from readers, much as a speech is written and delivered to move the hearers (rhetorical criticism).

• The impact on the Gospel narratives of the particular interests of those who wrote them and of the social and religious world in which they lived. For example, society at the time was a patriarchal one controlled by men, especially in the family. What has the consequence been of texts written from a masculine point of view (feminist criticism)? More broadly, this is known as ideological criticism.

• The importance of the story and narrative format and the part that literary design has played in shaping the Gospels (narrative criticism).

## A DEEPER UNDERSTANDING

These ways of deepening our understanding of the Gospels reflect the way in which literary critics deepen and enrich our understanding of books or poems written in the past. There is no final "meaning of the text"; there are only ways of discerning new and important layers of meaning, but meanings that are nonetheless controlled by the text itself. They are a reminder that the worth of the Bible does not depend on the extent to which it is a good or bad history book. Truth about God and about human beings can be found just as much in fiction as in fact, in a poem as in prose, in a novel as in a scientific paper. The study of the

> *" ... many have undertaken to set down an orderly account of the events that have been fulfilled among us. "*
>
> (Luke 1:1)

THE GOSPELS: A SOURCE OF PRAYER
*The four Gospels are not simply the story of past events: they lead to an encounter with Christ in prayer (see Introduction, p.11).*

> *" These [signs] are written so that you may come to believe that Jesus is the Messiah, the Son of God, and that through believing you may have life in his name. "*
>
> (John 20:31)

Gospels is moving away from its long preoccupation with historicity and into exciting new areas. History remains indispensable, but each Gospel can be studied as a literary whole, especially in the light of additional ancient writings and the other writings in the Bible. All these different approaches, including the historical, bring the words and messages of the Gospels closer to the everyday lives of people.

## WAYS OF APPROACH

The four Gospels, though not biographies in the modern sense, all fit into the ancient category of *bioi* (Greek, lives). They have a genuine historical base on which material has been used to bring out the importance and character of Jesus, just as a good portrait does of a person, much more so than a photograph. This is particularly true of the Passion narrative, which is the climax of each Gospel. Here there is a dramatic switch from "action," where Jesus dominates the story in word and deed, to "passion," where silence, and suffering, passivity and pain and, in John, love dominate. But in his weakness the defendant is seen to be the judge, his accusers condemn themselves, and in John's Gospel the victim "reigns from the tree." From this vantage point one can see that irony with hindsight pervades the whole story.

The Gospels were working texts to serve Christian communities, and the story has two levels: behind the descriptions of Jesus in Palestine can be glimpsed the needs and experiences of those communities (e.g., Matt. 10). An awareness of the historical context and of community dynamics will help illuminate the message of the Gospels.

All four Gospels emphasize fulfillment, the continuity of God's work in Israel, in Jesus, and in the Church. Thus they tell the story so as to echo the Scriptures, with explicit quotations and allusions, which those familiar with the Scriptures would be able to recognize.

For further reading see bibliography numbers: 11, 26, 27, 55, 135,151, 200, 203, 562, 670, 671, 677, 684, 724, 726, 727, 845, 861, 870, 876

# THE GOSPEL ACCORDING TO

# MATTHEW

*Matthew's Gospel is one of four Gospel accounts in the New Testament of Jesus and his life. Jesus is the fulfillment of everything the Jews believed in and expected but his message and teaching is for everyone.*

THE Gospel of Matthew was long thought to be the earliest Gospel and thus to have been used by Mark and Luke, but only a few scholars now maintain this view. More probably, Matthew used Mark, having the same outline of events but adding accounts of Jesus' birth and Resurrection appearances and a fuller selection of Jesus' teaching. Matthew's Gospel has frequently been quoted and used in the liturgy of the Christian Church from its earliest days.

## MATTHEW'S AIMS

Matthew was probably written at a time when divisions between Jews and Christians were solidifying, perhaps after the destruction of Jerusalem in 70CE and when Gentile Christians were distancing themselves from Judaism. At the outset, most Christians were Jews, but by the end of the first century CE the balance was changing. Matthew addresses both groups: to Jews it declares that Jesus was indeed the Messiah the biblical Prophets had predicted (p.346); to Jewish and Gentile Christians, God's Law and promise have been widened to include all nations. For Matthew, the truth that Jesus was the Messiah is of urgent importance. Matthew emphasizes the penalty for those who failed to live as the kingdom of God demands, using the phrase "weeping and gnashing of teeth" five times (8:12; 13:42; 22:13; 24:51; 25:30).

**MATTHEW**
*The Gospels and their writers are sometimes represented symbolically as in these English medieval manuscripts (cf. pp.308, 310, 312), where Matthew's sign takes the form of a human face or figure.*

## JESUS THE JEW

Matthew's Gospel emphasizes the way in which Jesus had not betrayed the Jewish heritage and Law, but widened and deepened it to become God's Law for all nations: Jesus completed and fulfilled Hebrew Scriptures. The Gospel begins with the words, *"An account of the genealogy of Jesus the Messiah, the son of David, the son of Abraham."* This genealogy of Jesus' descent from Israel's king David, and forefather Abraham, was an important form of legitimation at that time. Women occasionally appear in genealogies, but in Matthew there are four – Tamar, Rahab, Ruth, and "the wife of Uriah" – who are morally or ethically dubious, a warning that the fulfillment of God's promises will be contrary to normal expectations.

## MATTHEW'S MESSAGE

Matthew's Gospel is bracketed by two passages (1:23; 28:18–20) that show how closely Jesus is related to God – "God is with us." There is much that is distinctive in Matthew:
• Matthew alone tells of the visit of the Magi (wise men, or ritual experts, p.379): the event is significant for all people.
• Characteristically, Matthew shows how events in the life and ministry of Jesus were foretold in Hebrew Scriptures (2:17; 2:23; 8:17; 12:17; 13:35; 21:4; 26:54, 56; 27:9, 35).
• This Gospel has the largest collection of Jesus' sayings. He is presented as a great teacher who gives instruction for the

new Israel. His main teaching occurs in his Sermon on the Mount (*pp.334–35*), where he focuses on the "kingdom of God," or the "kingdom of Heaven."
• Matthew's account of Jesus' death and Resurrection follows the same outline as that of Mark's Gospel, but Matthew describes a number of miraculous occurrences to stress that the Resurrection was no ordinary happening.
• Matthew stresses that Jesus endorses the Law (5:17–20). This is to show that God's purpose cannot be defeated, and neither the new Law nor Jesus' words can pass away (24:35).
• Matthew stresses what it means to be a disciple of Jesus, who demands radical obedience to his teaching.

## ECCLESIASTICAL GOSPEL

Matthew wrote for the new community of Jewish and Gentile Christians, and he is the only evangelist to mention the Church, its role, and its authority to make doctrinal and disciplinary decisions (16:18–19; 18:15–18). Seeking to unify its moral and religious discord, Matthew also includes some warnings to the Church, of judging without mercy (18:21–35), and of needing to be like humble children (18:1–14).

Matthew seeks to show how Jesus is the fulfillment of God's promises to the Jews and thus through them to all nations. Jesus' final instruction to his disciples is, *"Go therefore and make disciples of all nations"* (28:19).

## THE DISCOURSES

The writer of Matthew had clear theological intentions and used a systematic arrangement in his Gospel. There are three main sections of birth stories, teaching, and death and Resurrection. He included five large discourses, or blocks, of Jesus' teaching, each with its own theme, perhaps echoing the five books of Moses. The structure below, in which things are arranged in an *a b c b a* pattern, was common in ancient writings. The first block reflects the last, the second the fourth, and the middle is the pivotal point of the whole construction.

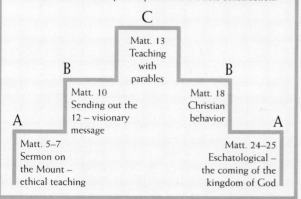

C
Matt. 13
Teaching
with
parables

B
Matt. 10
Sending out the
12 – visionary
message

B
Matt. 18
Christian
behavior

A
Matt. 5–7
Sermon on
the Mount –
ethical teaching

A
Matt. 24–25
Eschatological –
the coming of the
kingdom of God

## THE BOOK

TITLE: The Gospel According to Matthew

DATE: c.85–90CE. Sensational claims in 1994 that P64 (fragments of Matthew) were written before 70CE were false

AUTHORSHIP: Traditionally by Matthew the tax collector (10:3), but many now think that the author may have lived in Antioch toward the end of the first century CE (if the event in Matt. 22:7 refers to the fall of Jerusalem), knew Greek well, and received some rabbinic training. If Mark's Gospel came first and was expanded a generation later, the author could not have been one of the original 12 disciples. Perhaps Matthew the tax collector was the source for the material not included in Mark? Much material in this Gospel has parallels in Luke and may stem from a lost source, Q

## THE CONTENTS

CHAPTERS 1–4
Jesus' birth, baptism,
and temptation

CHAPTERS 5–7
First Discourse: the
Sermon on the Mount

CHAPTERS 8–9
Ten miracles

CHAPTER 10
Second Discourse: the
12 disciples are sent out

CHAPTERS 11–12
Questions and controversies

CHAPTER 13
Third Discourse: parables
about God's kingdom

CHAPTERS 14–17
Miracles and teaching

CHAPTER 18
Fourth Discourse:
Church discipline

CHAPTERS 19–20
On the road to Jerusalem

CHAPTERS 21–22
Jesus in the Temple

CHAPTERS 23–25
Fifth Discourse:
eschatological warnings

CHAPTERS 26–28
Jesus' betrayal, arrest, trial
and Crucifixion; Resurrection
and great commission

## KEY THEMES

*Jesus is the Messiah with God's authority,*
*who fulfills prophecies*

•

*Jesus inaugurates the kingdom of God*

For further reading see bibliography numbers: 88, 233, 356, 387, 435, 436, 439, 493, 649, 738, 821

# THE GOSPEL ACCORDING TO
# MARK

*Mark is the shortest of the four Gospels and perhaps the earliest.*
*Its simple structure of short sayings and its fast, episodic*
*narrative provide a powerful account of the life of Jesus.*

THROUGHOUT history, Mark's Gospel was used less by the Church than were those of Matthew and Luke: until about 150 years ago, it was assumed that Mark had abbreviated Matthew's Gospel, which contains almost all Mark's material. Most, although not all, scholars now think that Matthew expanded Mark, as did Luke. Mark, as a result, has taken on new value as being closest in time to the historical Jesus (*see column, opposite*).

## MARK'S AIMS

Looking at first like an artless string of loosely connected anecdotes, written in vivid and sometimes rugged language, Mark has a structure that conveys a strong theology, supported by scriptural allusions. Mark is now recognized as having written a highly organized account, weaving together the stories that he heard through oral tradition (*p.109*). The writer often used the word *immediately* to give pace to his narrative.

The beginning of chapter 1 identifies Jesus as the Son of God (*cf. 9:7*), who fulfills the Scriptures and who receives the Spirit, and in whose power he confronts Satan proclaiming that the kingdom of God has come near: *"The time is fulfilled, and the kingdom of God has come near; repent, and believe in the good news"* (Mark 1:15). The rest of the Gospel displays the meaning of the kingdom in the ministry of Jesus, and yet it also unfolds how, paradoxically, this leads to the Passion.

MARK

*Mark's sign is a lion. The tetramorphs ("four signs") of the Gospels are taken from Ezekiel 1:4–10 and Revelation 4:6–7.*

## MARK'S MESSAGE

Unlike Matthew and Luke, Mark says nothing about Jesus' birth; two other vital events enclose the main narrative. It begins with Jesus' baptism and the opening of the heavens: *"And just as he was coming up out of the water, he saw the heavens torn apart and the Spirit descending like a dove on him. And a voice came from heaven, 'You are my Son, the Beloved, with you I am well pleased'"* (1:10–11). It effectively ends with Jesus' death and the rending of the Temple curtain: *"And the curtain of the temple was torn in two, from top to bottom. Now when the centurion, who stood facing him, saw that in this way he breathed his last, he said, 'Truly this man was God's Son'"* (15:38–39). Everything that Mark describes within these two events signifies God's act of breaking down the barriers between Heaven and earth through God's Son, Jesus Christ, through Jesus' healing power and, above all, through Jesus' "Passion," his suffering in the last few days of his life.

The first half of Mark's Gospel consists of a series of triumphant encounters with Satan in the form of demon possession, sickness, and storm (at 4:39 Jesus addresses the storm like the "unclean spirit" in 1:25), and in the form of opposition from the religious leaders and from his own disciples. This reaches a climax at Caesarea Philippi: Peter hails Jesus as Messiah, Jesus explains his way of messiahship – the Son of Man must be rejected and suffer – Peter demurs and is himself addressed as Satan (8:22–33).

The second half of the Gospel is an increasingly somber account of Jesus' road to rejection, with the Transfiguration confirming that he is God's Son (9:7; cf. 1:11; 15:39) and that this is all God's will. This technique of bracketing narrative material occurs within examples. The most obvious example is Jesus' cleansing of the Temple, enclosed within the story of the barren fig tree: both are fruitless and therefore doomed (11:12–23). This act may be illuminated by Ezekiel 47, where the Temple river is the source of many trees bearing fruit all year round.

## SECRET MESSIAH

Jesus said and did much that made many people think he might be the promised Messiah. But Jesus was very cautious about this, as though the title might be misleading or misunderstood: *"Immediately the leprosy left him, and he was made clean. After sternly warning him he [Jesus] sent him away at once, saying to him, 'See that you say nothing to anyone …'"* (1:42–44). It is also worth noting Jesus' response to Peter's question of whether he was the Messiah: *"he sternly ordered them not to tell anyone about him"* (8:30). This suggests that Jesus was avoiding any interpretations that connected him to God in the wrong way (8:28). Rather than identify with the popular understanding of "Messiah" (pp. 346–47), Jesus used the phrase "the Son of Man" to signify his role as one who was not a supernatural figure like an angel, but one who, like all people, was bound to die and, as described in Daniel 7, will be vindicated by God beyond death.

Chapter 13 is often called "the Markan Apocalypse" because it deals with the unfolding of God's purpose. This theme does occur throughout the Gospel and is connected with the messianic secret. God's purpose is disclosed only to Jesus' followers (4:11–34); parables or riddles are used to tell things to outsiders (8:14–21).

## THE ENDING OF MARK'S GOSPEL

In the earliest manuscripts from the fourth century CE, Mark's Gospel ends at Chapter 16:8: *"they said nothing to anyone, for they were afraid."* The ending is abrupt and surprising. Many manuscripts have the so-called "Longer Ending" (16:9–20), and there are also other additions, all in a very different style, but these are not included in the NRSV. Matthew and Luke follow Mark up to 16:8, but then go their separate ways, probably finding this ending unsatisfactory. Did Mark die before finishing? Did the last page get lost? Certainly any attempts to supply an ending were difficult, since there was no memory of an ending to rely on, and the endings varied so much. Did Mark intend to end here, perhaps recalling how Daniel reacted to his vision (Dan. 10:7–12)? At least the abrupt ending is consistent with Mark's emphasis on the frailty of humans, who are nevertheless called to follow Jesus.

# THE BOOK

**TITLE:** The Gospel According to Mark.

**DATE:** Probably 65–75CE

**AUTHORSHIP:** According to Papias, the Gospel was written by "Mark, the interpreter for Peter" (cf. 1 Pet. 5:13). Traditionally Mark has been identified with John Mark, nephew of Barnabas, although he was associated with Paul rather than Peter. If, as Papias suggests, Mark was close to Peter and acted as his interpreter, Mark could be even more important as being the closest to the historical Jesus. However, this is uncertain and the Greek *hermaeneutes* may mean that Mark acted as interpreter for Peter, not that he interpreted Peter's reminiscences of Jesus.

# THE CONTENTS

**CHAPTER 1:1–13**
Jesus' baptism and temptation

**CHAPTERS 1:14–3:35**
Initial opposition to Jesus' teaching in Galilee

**CHAPTER 4:1–34**
Jesus teaches using parables

**CHAPTERS 4:35–8:26**
Jesus performs miracles and healings amid growing opposition to his work

**CHAPTER 8:27–38**
Peter's confession; the cost of discipleship

**CHAPTER 9:1–13**
The Transfiguration

**CHAPTERS 9:14–10:52**
Jesus teaches and prepares his disciples

**CHAPTERS 11:1–12:44**
Jesus enters Jerusalem, cleanses the Temple, and engages in argument

**CHAPTER 13**
Jesus teaches of future events ("the Markan apocalypse")

**CHAPTERS 14–15**
The Last Supper; Jesus' arrest, trials, and crucifixion

**CHAPTER 16:1–8**
Empty tomb (original ending)

**CHAPTER 16:9–20**
Resurrection appearances

# KEY THEMES

*The good news is Jesus Christ*

•

*The authority of Jesus in healing and teaching that comes from God*

•

*Suffering and discipleship*

For further reading see bibliography numbers: 83, 85, 396, 417, 435, 449, 459, 460, 595

# THE GOSPEL ACCORDING TO

# LUKE

*Luke shows Jesus as a man with compassion for all people, "a light for revelation to the Gentiles, and glory to your people Israel." Together, Luke and Acts form two volumes telling Jesus' story and the beginnings of the Christian Church.*

LUKE'S Gospel, like that of Matthew, is now generally agreed to be dependent upon Mark's outline, but Luke omits Mark 6:45–8:26 and inserts instead what is called the "travel narrative," describing Jesus' journey from Galilee to Jerusalem (*see right*). Much of Luke's material not based on Mark has parallels in Matthew. Some scholars think that Luke had access to Matthew's work, but the majority holds that Luke and Matthew drew independently on an earlier source, or sources, known as Q (*p.301*).

## LUKE'S AIMS

Both Luke and Acts were written by the same author and dedicated to Theophilus, a Greek, about whom little is known. Luke set out his intentions clearly at the beginning of his historical work: *"Since many have undertaken to set down an orderly account of the events that have been fulfilled among us, just as they were handed on to us by those who from the beginning were eyewitnesses and servants of the word, I too decided, after investigating everything carefully from the very first, to write an orderly account ..."* (Luke 1:1–4). In writing about a new movement that seemed to be both heretical and subversive, Luke needed to present it as the fulfillment of God's plan for the world: to the Romans and Greeks, he wrote to distance Jesus from Israel's political aspirations; to the Jews, he wrote that Jesus' messiahship was in accordance with the Scriptures. Like the biblical histories,

**LUKE**
*Luke's sign is a winged ox. He was probably the author of the Gospel according to Luke and the Acts of the Apostles.*

Luke told the story in order to show God at work in history, and he emphasized how important the work of the Holy Spirit is.

Luke was concerned to make God's plan of salvation (a key term in Luke/Acts) evident to Theophilus and to his other readers. Central to this plan were the life, death, Resurrection, and Ascension of Jesus – which have brought new hope to the poor and needy – and the offer of God's powerful blessings and the beginning of a new age to those who are spiritually humble. Luke also wanted to draw a picture of the new community in the kingdom of God, beginning with the twelve (*pp.328–331*), extending into the mission of "the seventy," and continuing into the Church (Luke 10:1–17).

## LUKE'S MESSAGE

Luke's Gospel begins and ends in Jerusalem. It stresses Jesus' Davidic descent, but it also points to the universal scope of God's work by extending the genealogy back to Adam, the father of all humanity (3:38). In contrast to Mark 6:1–6, Luke placed Jesus' sermon at Nazareth at the start of his ministry, as it includes the main themes of both Luke and Acts: the Holy Spirit, healing the poor and oppressed, preaching, and God's activity outside Israel (4:16–30). The murderous rage that this caused points forward to the Crucifixion. Luke emphasized the role of the Holy Spirit in Jesus' ministry. John the Baptist and his parents were filled with the Holy Spirit (1:15, 41, 67), as was Simeon at Jesus' presentation. Jesus began his ministry "filled with the power of the Spirit" (4:14) and predicted the descent of the Spirit on his own disciples (12:12).

Luke's selection of parables reveals Jesus' vivid interest in humanity and illustrates some of his concerns, including the poor and the marginalized (women, children, outcasts, and cripples), and the dangers of wealth. These stories reverse normal assumptions about blessedness, such as a despised tax collector who is closer to God than a self-righteous Pharisee (18:9–14), a disgraced son who is nearer to his father's heart than his model elder brother (15:11–32), a rich man unaware of Lazarus starving at his door (16:19–31), and a rich fool who in God's sight has nothing (12:13–21).

Luke's Gospel, like Acts, begins in prayer (1:10; cf. Acts 1:14) and shows Jesus praying at critical moments: "Now during those days he went out to the mountain to pray; and he spent the night in prayer to God" (6:12; cf. 3:21; 5:16; 9:18, 28; 11:1). Only Luke uses the word agony of Jesus' prayer in Gethsemane (22:44). Yet prayer in Luke's Gospel also includes thanks and praise, such as the songs of Zechariah, Mary, and Simeon featured at the beginning of the book.

## JOURNEYS

Luke's main addition to Mark is a travel narrative of Jesus' journey from Galilee to Jerusalem (9:51–18:14), a journey of more than just geographical importance, with its echoes of Moses and Israel in the desert. Before Jesus began his journey, Moses and Elijah appeared at his Transfiguration, "speaking of his departure, which he was about to accomplish in Jerusalem" (or more literally, "the exodus [of redemption] he was to fulfill"). The Greek for "go" (poreuesthai) occurs 22 times in these chapters, and also in the double meaning of Jesus' death mentioned in Luke 13:33: "Yet today, tomorrow, and the next day I must be on my way, because it is impossible for a prophet to be killed outside of Jerusalem." Like Paul, Luke's Gospel presents Jesus' death as the new Passover and Exodus, with Christians symbolizing Israel journeying through the desert to the Promised Land (1 Cor. 5:7; Luke 10:1–13). Luke's final journey story, of the disciples on the road to Emmaus, describes Jesus revealing himself to his disciples after the Resurrection: "He took bread, blessed and broke it, and gave it to them. Then their eyes were opened ..." (24:30–31).

Luke extended his journey theme to steer Christian eyes away from the hoped-for return of Christ and toward the present day-to-day task of discipleship and witnessing: Christians are to "take up their cross daily" and ask "each day [for] our daily bread." Their salvation lies not in the days ahead, but "today," as Jesus says in his sermon in Nazareth: "Today this scripture has been fulfilled in your hearing" (4:21). Luke has a universal perspective, and his Gospel points forward to a universal salvation.

# THE BOOK

TITLE: The Gospel According to Luke

DATE: Not given. If Luke used Mark, c.80CE

AUTHORSHIP: Traditionally thought to be Luke, "the beloved physician," companion of Paul (Col. 4.14; Philem. 24; 2 Tim. 4.11). Acts 1:1 tells Theophilus that this book follows the first (cf. Luke 1:3), and it is generally agreed that Luke and Acts are by the same author

# THE CONTENTS

**CHAPTERS 1–2**
Births of John the Baptist and Jesus; Jesus' childhood

**CHAPTER 3**
John the Baptist's ministry; Jesus' baptism

**CHAPTER 4:1–13**
Jesus' temptations

**CHAPTERS 4:14–6:11**
Jesus' ministry

**CHAPTER 6:12–16**
The 12 disciples

**CHAPTER 6:17–49**
The Sermon on the Plain

**CHAPTERS 7:1–9:50**
Jesus' ministry continues; feeding of the 5,000; the Transfiguration

**CHAPTERS 9:51–19:27**
Increasing opposition to Jesus; Jesus teaches with specific instructions and predicts his death and Resurrection

**CHAPTERS 19:28–23:56**
Entry into Jerusalem; ministry and teaching in Jerusalem; the Last Supper; Jesus' arrest, trials, and Crucifixion

**CHAPTER 24**
Resurrection appearances; the Ascension

# KEY THEMES

*Jesus as a compassionate man, caring for the poor and the oppressed, fulfilling Scripture (4:18–21)*

•

*The activity of the Holy Spirit in Jesus' work*

•

*The good news is for those who were not highly regarded – tax collectors, Samaritans, Gentiles, and women*

For further reading see bibliography numbers: 117, 152, 279, 282, 321, 436, 443, 518, 519, 610, 742, 758, 760, 815, 821

# THE GOSPEL ACCORDING TO

# JOHN

*The fourth Gospel reveals the glory and majesty of God being brought visibly into the world. It emphasizes the meaning of Jesus' life, death, and Resurrection, and is often referred to as the "spiritual Gospel."*

Echoing Genesis 1:1, John's Gospel opens with the tremendous claim: *"In the beginning was the Word, and the Word was with God, and the Word was God."* This Gospel, with its longer discourses and emphasis on dramatic signs, shows the truth made manifest in Jesus and its importance for the world.

## JOHN AND THE SYNOPTICS

John's Gospel tells the same story of Jesus as the Synoptics, but in a different way and often with added detail. Unlike Mark's Gospel (*p.309*), John does not conceal Jesus' identity but draws attention to him as a mediating agent between Heaven and earth (1:51). In contrast to the three Synoptics, Jesus speaks not of "the kingdom of God" (*except* 3:3, 5; *note* 18:36) but of "eternal life," and Jesus' ministry covers not one Passover but three (2:23; 6:4; 11:55). John also contains longer theological reflections in the form of discourses than the Synoptics do, although it does not include any parables or the Lord's Prayer.

## JOHN'S MESSAGE

Important themes that John includes:

• **Prologue** (1:1–18): Jesus is identified as the *Logos*, the divine "Word" that exists with God and comes into the world uniquely in Christ. The word that is God's is not in Jesus as a verbal

**JOHN**
*John's sign is an eagle. Traditionally he has been identified as the "beloved disciple" (see panel, right).*

message; it comes fully into human life. Jesus is also identified in chapter 1 as "Son," "Christ," "Son of God," "King of Israel," and "Son of Man." Son of God could refer to Israel as God's child (Hos. 11:1) or God's Messiah, King of Israel (Ps. 2:7; 2 Sam. 7:4–17; John 1:41, 49). In John's Gospel this term associates Jesus with God in a unique way.

• **Signs**, chapters 2–12: John gives the purpose of his Gospel in 20:30–31, explaining that in recording the signs, or miracles, that Jesus performed, people would continue to believe in him as the Messiah. John records seven of these signs, echoing God's work in Creation, each one followed by a discourse in which Jesus explains the meaning of his actions and his mission. These signs are: turning water into wine (2:1–11); the official's son (4:46–54); the sick man (5:1–9); the feeding of the 5,000 (6:5–13); walking on water (6:16–20); the man born blind (9:1–7); and the raising of Lazarus (11:1–44). Perhaps they echo the seven days of Creation, with Jesus' death and exaltation as the climactic sign (12:31–33; *cf.* 3:14), the first day of the New Creation (20:1).

• **The Passion**, chapters 13–20: recounting Jesus' entry into Jerusalem, arrest, trial, Crucifixion, and Resurrection. The Jesus John describes is in control of his destiny, and not at the mercy of his enemies. There is no secret as to what Jesus' purpose is (19:36–20:29, 35; *cf. p.309*).

• **Epilogue**, chapter 21: this is thought by many to be a later addition as it concerns an additional Resurrection appearance and the fate of Peter. Perhaps it was added when there was concern over the death of John, the "beloved disciple" (21:23). This passage associates John with the traditions underlying the Gospel but does not identify him.

Throughout his Gospel, John makes it clear that to believe Jesus is Christ involves abiding in his "word" – his whole life and teaching – summed up by his command to love (15:12, 13). John also identifies the immediacy of Jesus' contact with God, as do the Synoptics (usually in a less overt way) and finds it the reason for the essential conflict between Jesus and his contemporaries.

## JUDAISM IN JOHN'S GOSPEL

Allusions to Scripture and to Jewish institutions punctuate the Gospel, as in the Synoptics, showing how Jesus fulfilled and transcended them. To explain the agonizing rejection of Jesus and of his followers, John's Gospel recalls the accusations made against the rulers of Israel by Prophets, especially Isaiah (12:38–42). The Jews are viewed as being open to Jesus but repeatedly divided in their assessment of him. The Gospel also records Jesus' condemnation of those who opposed him, usually designated in a kind of code as "the Pharisees." John remained certain that "salvation is from the Jews" (4:22).

John's Gospel also records Jesus' visits to the Temple for the festivals, above all at Passover. Jesus fulfills the Temple, for he himself is the place where God is present (2:21). He dies as the Lamb of God at the same time the Passover lambs are killed, not the day after as in the Synoptics (1:29, 35).

## THE "I AM" SAYINGS AND PARACLETE

John records a number of Jesus' sayings stating "I am." They appear with and without modifiers. Those with modifiers include: bread of life (6:35); light of the world (8:12); gate for the sheep (10:7); good shepherd (10:11, 14); Resurrection and Life (11:25); way, truth, and life (14:6); true vine (15:1). These are traditional Hebrew metaphors for salvation. John presents Jesus as the reality, or way to the reality, to which they point. Those without modifiers generally infer "I am the one you are speaking of" (e.g., 6:20; 9:9; 18:5). Yet the "I am" sayings of Jesus are unlikely to have been a claim that he was God, as some argue with reference to the Greek translation of *ego eimi* (I am) in Exodus 3:14. *Ego eimi* is not the name of God.

Paraclete, translated as "one called alongside [to help]," comes from the Greek *parakletos*. The word can mean comforter, counselor or teacher, advocate, and mediator – all functions Jesus fulfilled with his disciples. In John's Gospel Jesus promises "another paraclete," the Holy Spirit: *"And I will ask the Father, and he will give you another Advocate, to be with you forever"* (John 14:16, 26; 15:26; 16:7 cf. 1 John 2:1).

# THE BOOK

**TITLE**: The Gospel According to John

**DATE**: It is thought by some to be the latest of the Gospels (written at the end of first century CE). John 9:22 and 16:2 may refer to the exclusion, in c.85–90CE, of heretics from synagogue worship. Yet its independence from the Synoptics, combined with its attentive historical details, has led others to think of John's Gospel as an early way of telling the Gospel story in order to draw out the ways in which, through Jesus, God was able to bring his Word, Light, Glory, Truth – all words characteristic of John's writing style – into the world. The theory that it must be a later reflection on a simpler story is an assumption. John 21:22 suggests that at least one of the early followers was still alive awaiting the return of Jesus.

**AUTHORSHIP**: Not mentioned. Traditionally, "the beloved disciple," mentioned repeatedly in this Gospel, has been assumed to be John, son of Zebedee (Mark 1:19; 9:2; 14:33), and has been identified as the author.

# THE CONTENTS

**CHAPTER 1**
Prologue: the meaning of the story; major protagonists (Jesus, John, the call of the disciples); the Spirit descends on Jesus

**CHAPTERS 2–12:11**
Seven signs and discourses in Judea, Samaria, and Galilee

**CHAPTERS 12:12–17:26**
Triumphal entry; the Last Supper and discourses; Jesus instructs his disciples on the way to the garden

**CHAPTERS 18:1–19:42**
Jesus' arrest, trials, Crucifixion, and burial

**CHAPTER 20**
Resurrection appearances

**CHAPTER 21**
Epilogue

# KEY THEMES

*Jesus Christ is identified as the eternal Word (Logos) of God*

•

*He is the true source of eternal life*

•

*The seven signs and discourses and "I am" sayings*

For further reading see bibliography numbers: 22, 55, 137, 138, 149, 242, 243, 253, 289, 393, 435, 500, 656, 747, 839

# JESUS' FAMILY

*Jesus' family plays a specific part in the New Testament and was well known in Nazareth. When Jesus taught in the synagogue there, people were astounded at his wisdom: "Isn't this Mary's son and brother of James, Judas, Joses, and Simon? Aren't his sisters here with us?"*

CONSIDERING the central importance of Jesus in the New Testament, and of his mother Mary in later Christian devotion, the Bible reveals little about his family origins and its individual members.

Outside Luke and Matthew's infancy narratives, the Gospels mention Jesus' relatives only in passing and in largely ambivalent roles. Acts records Jesus' mother and brothers as part of the earliest church in Jerusalem, but it shows a sustained interest only in the role of his brother James. Apart from fleeting remarks, the Epistles – even those ostensibly written by Jesus' brothers, James and Jude – never identify his relations at all. With the exception of Mary's story in Luke's Gospel, Jesus' family has no theological status or privileges in the New Testament. At the same time, three important family issues do emerge in the New Testament: that of Jesus' Davidic descent, his family's rejection of his earthly ministry, and their subsequent role in the early Christian Church.

## JESUS' DAVIDIC DESCENT

Tribal and family descent were profoundly important in post-exilic Jewish culture, not only for priests and Levites but also for Benjaminites such as Paul. Luke and Matthew trace the genealogy of Jesus back to King David, who reigned over Israel in the tenth century BCE, (*pp.124–25*). This might seem common of messianic expectation based on formative biblical texts, but some scholars regard it as an early Christian apologetic fiction to underpin the claim of Jesus' messianic status. Yet Jesus' descent from the royal line is assumed to be uncontroversial in the Gospels (Matthew and Luke trace it through different sons of David) and in Paul's letters. Jewish polemic, echoed in the New Testament, seems not to question his Davidic descent, and a widespread later charge of Jesus' illegitimacy seems designed to counter the claim of virgin birth rather than that of Davidic descent. The New Testament writers, especially Matthew, see this descent as central to Jesus' fulfillment of the messianic line of promise.

ACTS 1:14

ACTS 15:13–21

GAL. 1:19
1 COR. 9:5

MARY'S STORY

LUKE 1:26–56

ROM. 11:1

PHIL. 3:5

MATT. 1:1–6
LUKE 3:23–38

2 SAM. 7
PS. 89
MIC. 5:2
ISA. 11:1
JER. 23:5; 33:15

MATT. 1:3
LUKE 3:31

ROM 1:3
cf. 2 TIM. 2:8

A 19th-century depiction of Jesus surrounded by his family in Joseph's workshop.

## FAMILY REJECTION

The Gospels suggest that at first Jesus' public ministry was not accepted by his family, who, like others in Nazareth, may have sought to stop his controversial activity: *"When his family heard it, they went out to restrain him, for people were saying, 'He has gone out of his mind'"* (Mark 3:21, 31–35). This episode has often been thought to imply rejection, since Jesus changed family obligations (Matt. 8:22; Luke 14:25–26ff.). Yet other statements are more positive about honoring parents, and John's Gospel assumes frequent interaction between Jesus and his mother and brothers (John 2:1–5, 12; 7:3–6; 19:25–27).

Joseph and Jesus.

## JESUS' FAMILY IN THE CHURCH

Jesus' family, above all Mary and James were prominent in the earliest Church. They were held in high esteem – a fact which Luke's infancy narratives, Acts, and the letters of James and Jude all mention. Even Paul, despite his tensions with the Jerusalem church (pp.394–95), did not hesitate to identify James unambiguously as "the brother of the Lord." Interest in descendants of Jesus' relatives (Jude's grandsons, for instance) continued for several centuries.

A combination of reverence for Jesus' relatives (echoed in classic icons of the Madonna and child), and their obscurity in the Bible, reflects the unique role of this wholly human family in welcoming and nurturing Jesus in the world. Such obscurity, however, is penetrated by poets, including the English 20th-century poet Ruth Pitter, who describes the way Jesus' family protected him:

> *"Perhaps the thoughts that ebb and flow*
> *In that, his human home*
> *May blow to brightness the small spark*
> *They carry through the vasty dark."*

*1 COR. 15:7*

*JESUS' BROTHER JAMES GAL. 1:19*

# JOSEPH

*Despite being Jesus' legal father, Joseph has a surprisingly low profile in the New Testament and in Christian tradition.*

The New Testament reveals little about Joseph beyond the fact of his profession as a carpenter of modest means. Joseph is not mentioned outside the infancy narratives of Matthew and Luke, although in three of the four Gospels, Jesus is referred to as Joseph's son (Matt. 1:23–25; 13:55; Luke 3:23; 4:22; John 1:45; 6:42; cf. Mark 6:3). Additional details on Joseph are few: Matthew and Luke's infancy narratives trace Joseph's Davidic descent through different sons of David (Matt. 1:6; Luke 3:31); before Jesus' birth, Joseph, in Matthew, seems to be a resident of Bethlehem (p.320), but in Luke, a resident of Nazareth (p.321). Although there is an assumption that Joseph's paternity is straightforward (Matt. 13:55), the Gospel writers maintain a guarded ambivalence that suggests mystery surrounding the human origins of Jesus, but which remains in keeping with Matthew and Luke's claim of a virginal conception (1:34–37). Joseph's role is confined to that of a supporting actor, a perplexed bystander, the main observer of unfolding events – and yet one whose faithfulness and conquered hesitations are instrumental to God's saving design in the Incarnation.

# JESUS' SIBLINGS

*The New Testament indicates that Jesus had at least four brothers and two sisters.*

The names of Jesus' brothers are given as James, Joses (Yose, short for Joseph), Judas (commonly known as Jude), and Simon (Matt. 13:55; Mark 6:3); a variety of apocryphal Christian sources refers to his sisters as Salome and Mary. Of these, James and Jude are best known – a letter was attributed to each. James became the leader of the early Christian community until his martyrdom in Jerusalem in 62CE. The term "brothers of the Lord" (Gal. 1:19; 1 Cor. 9:5) has long been disputed as to whether it refers to full blood brothers, half-brothers born to Joseph from an earlier marriage, or cousins or other relatives. On the simplest historical reading, the first of these (held by the majority of scholars) seems the most plausible: the Gospels do not contradict the view that Jesus' brothers and sisters were born to Joseph and Mary. The second definition has the support of a widely held tradition, attested since the second century CE, that Joseph was a widower with children from a previous marriage. It is unclear whether this latter tradition gave rise to the view of Mary remaining a virgin, or vice versa. The third interpretation, still supported by many Christians, is difficult on philological grounds since Jesus' relationship with these "brothers" is not described in any other terms, although words for "cousin" existed.

For further reading see bibliography numbers: 69, 70, 81, 109, 136, 436, 547

# MARY, MOTHER OF JESUS

*Mary is honored widely in the Christian Church as the mother of Jesus. She had a
unique relationship with God and was a great servant of God, not only in
giving birth to Jesus and rearing him but in helping to establish the early
Church with Jesus' brothers after his death.*

MARY was close to Jesus, not
simply as his mother but also
as a follower throughout Jesus'
ministry. She was among the group of
Apostles, which included Jesus' brothers
and some other women, that prayed
together in Jerusalem after the
Ascension (Acts 1:14; *pp.382–83*).

**❝** *The angel said to her, 'Do not
be afraid, Mary, for you have
found favor with God. And now,
you will conceive in your womb
and bear a son, and you will
name him Jesus.'* **❞**

(Luke 1:30–31)

## MARY IN THE GOSPELS

The earliest Gospel, Mark, has little to
say specifically about Mary. While Jesus
was teaching his disciples, she and the rest
of his family sought him out: *"Then his
mother and his brothers came; and standing outside,
they sent to him and called him. A crowd was
sitting around him; and they said to him, 'Your
mother and your brothers are outside, asking for
you.' And he replied, 'Who are my mother and
my brothers?' And looking at those who sat
around him, he said, 'Here are my mother and
my brothers! Whoever does the will of God is
my brother and sister and mother'"* (Mark
3:31–35). Jesus' own family seemed
not to appreciate his teaching (*p.315*),
in contrast to his disciples, who "hear
the word of God and keep it."

Matthew's Gospel states that Mary
was betrothed to Joseph, a descendant
of David but conceived her Son
"through the Holy Spirit" (Matt. 1:18).
Girls at that time were often betrothed
as young as 12 years old, but it is not
actually stated in the New Testament that
she was, in fact, that young. Hearing that
Mary was pregnant, Joseph wanted to break
the engagement quietly, but instead he
received a divine message that her conception
was the fulfillment of a prophecy from Isaiah,
*"Look, the young woman is with child and shall bear a*

**THE VIRGIN MARY**
*Mary is held in high esteem
throughout the world. This is a
contemporary Mexican image.*

*son, and shall name him Immanuel"* (Isa. 7:14).
Matthew's version of the passage is taken,
not from the Hebrew but from the Greek,
which uses the word *virgin*. Joseph was
told that he was to marry Mary and adopt
her son into the royal house of David.

Integral to the birth narratives of
both Matthew and Luke is that Jesus
was "born of a virgin." In Israel, virginity
has always been the symbol of fidelity:
insofar as Israel is faithful to God,
she is represented as the virgin daughter
of Zion. On the issue of whether Mary
had other children, *see p.315*.

## SERVANT OF THE LORD

In contrast to the emphasis on Joseph
in Matthew's birth narrative, Luke's
Gospel presents a more developed
picture of Mary as a betrothed woman
called upon by God. The angel Gabriel
greeted Mary as favored by God; he
announced to her that the Holy Spirit
would come upon her and she would
bear a son, the fulfillment of the
promises made to his ancestor,
David, who "will reign over the
house of Jacob forever" (Luke 1:33).

Unlike Zechariah, who doubted
God's message that he would father
John the Baptist, Mary responded to
God in obedient acceptance,
proclaiming herself "the servant of the
Lord." Her song, the Magnificat (Luke
1:46–55), which she sings when she visits
Elizabeth, is a triumphal song, like that of
Hannah in 1 Samuel 2:1–10. It rejoices in
the way in which God reverses fortunes on
earth and is, in this case, more appropriate for
Elizabeth than Mary: *"My soul magnifies the Lord,*

*and my spirit rejoices in God my Savior, for he has looked with favor on the lowliness of his servant. Surely from now on all generations will call me blessed; for the Mighty One has done great things for me, and holy is his name"* (Luke 1:46–49). Through the ages the Magnificat has been a favorite prayer for Christians, and its perceived subversive message has reinforced Christian commitment to the poor.

Much has been inferred about Mary from the Magnificat: for example, that she is poor and embodies the neglected and the marginalized. But nowhere in the New Testament is it stated that she was in fact poor (although Luke 2:24 and Lev. 12:8 suggest poverty) or that she was particularly marginalized. The reversals, however, of the Magnificat are already apparent in the birth of Jesus (greeted on earth by poor shepherds, yet acclaimed by angels in Heaven) and in the status of Mary (giving birth to her son in a strange town in humble circumstances, yet the mother of "a Savior, who is Christ the Lord").

## MARY AND JESUS IN LUKE

Luke suggests that Mary's relations with Jesus may not have been easy; he alone tells of the anxiety Jesus caused his parents during a visit to Jerusalem: *"Child, why have you treated us like this? Look, your father and I have been searching for you in great anxiety."* He also recounts that Jesus gave Mary much to think about, which she treasured (Luke 2:41–51). When she presented her son in the Temple for circumcision eight days after his birth, the prophet Simeon told Mary that a sword would pierce her soul, meaning, in the context, that she too would have to decide for or against Jesus, and that family ties do not create faith (Luke 2:33–35).

When Jesus' family came to him while he was preaching, both Matthew (Matt. 12:46–50) and Mark (Mark 3:31–35) make it clear that his "family" is made up of those who carry out the will of God. Luke 8:21 makes his family those who hear the word of God and do it, as in 11:27ff. Luke mentions Mary waiting and praying with the other

**MADONNA AND CHILD**
*This 20th-century sculpture of Mary and Jesus provides a powerful modern interpretation of a traditional image.*

disciples after the Ascension (Acts 1:14). The special attention paid to Mary in Luke's writings has given rise to the assumption that he was associated with Mary at Ephesus (*pp.398–99*).

## MARY AND THE CHURCH

In John's Gospel, Mary appears only twice, at the beginning and at the end of Jesus' ministry. She instigated his first miracle at the wedding at Cana, even though his "hour had not yet come" (John 2:4), and took her place beside her dying son at the foot of the cross, where Jesus commended her and "the disciple whom he loved" to each other's care as mother and son (John 19:26–27). To some, this moment is the birth of the Christian Church, with Mary as the mother of the Church and the Beloved Disciple representing all those whom the Lord loves.

Accordingly, the woman in the book of Revelation (Rev. 12:1–6) standing on the moon and robed with the sun, who is pursued by the great red dragon as she gives birth to a royal son, has traditionally been interpreted as Mary, mother of the Messiah and of his people: *"And she gave birth to a son, a male child, who is to rule all the nations with a rod of iron."* The development of this into devotion to Mary, and into the affirmation of her Immaculate Conception and of her assumption into Heaven at the time of her death, belong to Church history rather than to the New Testament.

What does belong to the New Testament, however, is the way that Mary bore Jesus into life and then into death, as one of the group of women followers who watched him die on the cross. At that point, Mary had no clear idea why Jesus had lived in such a way that his life had come to this conclusion. Yet, even in pain and after words of apparent rejection from him, Mary never gave up on Jesus, remaining with him to the end and becoming prominent in the earliest church in Jerusalem. And, if speculation is allowed, from whom else is Jesus, in such a masculine society, likely to have learned to welcome the worth of women in the way that he clearly – and frequently – did?

> ❝ When Jesus saw his mother and the disciple whom he loved standing beside her, he said to his mother, 'Woman, here is your son.' Then he said to the disciple, 'Here is your mother.' ❞
>
> (John 19:26–27)

For further reading see bibliography numbers: 136, 139, 140a, 436

# THE STORIES OF THE
# ANNUNCIATION & NATIVITY

*The stories of Jesus' conception and birth are recorded only in the Gospels of Matthew and Luke, and each clearly uses different sources. The supernatural nature of Jesus' conception is a dramatic contrast to the humble circumstances of his birth.*

## MATTHEW'S STORY

MATT. 1:18    Mary found that she was *"to be with child from the Holy Spirit"* after she had become engaged to Joseph but before they were married. Joseph, worried about the public disgrace she would face as an unmarried mother, decided to break the engagement. Then an

MATT. 1:20–23    angel appeared to him in a dream. The angel told him Mary would be his wife and the baby would be called Jesus.

MATT. 2:1–2    After Jesus' birth, three wise men, or magi, from the East were led by a star to Jerusalem in

MATT. 2:3    search of *"the king of the Jews."* Herod heard that they had come to publicly acknowledge the Messiah, and he grew afraid of such a threat to his kingship. The magi went to

MATT. 2:11    Bethlehem and offered their gifts of gold, frankincense, and myrrh to Jesus. Then they

MATT. 2:12    left for their own country after a dream warned them not to return to Herod. When Herod

MATT. 2:16–18    ordered all the children who were two years old or under in Bethlehem to be killed, Joseph and his family escaped to Egypt until Herod died, and they then returned to Nazareth.

Jesus' birth in Bethlehem.

## LUKE'S STORY

LUKE 1:26–38    An angel came to Mary in Nazareth to tell her that she had *"found favor with God"* and would bear a son conceived by the Holy Spirit.

LUKE 1:46–56    Mary praised God for being so blessed.

LUKE 2:1–3    When a new decree went out from Emperor Augustus that everyone should be registered,

LUKE 2:4–5    Joseph took Mary to his hometown, Bethlehem. There Mary gave birth

LUKE 2:5–7    to her son and laid him in a manger as there was *"no room at the inn."*

LUKE 2:8–9    That night an angel appeared to shepherds outside Bethlehem. The angel said that he

LUKE 2:10–12    had *"good news,"* that a baby born that day

LUKE 2:13–14    was *"a Savior, who is the Messiah."* A multitude of angels appeared, praising God. When they

LUKE 2:15–20    had gone, the shepherds went to Bethlehem to find Jesus and spread the news.

LUKE 2:21–24    When he was eight days old, Jesus was circumcised, then presented to God in the

LUKE 2:25–38    Temple. There Simeon, an old man, and Anna, a prophetess, praised God publicly for sending

LUKE 2:39    Jesus to redeem Israel. Then his parents took Jesus back to their home in Nazareth.

## COMPARING THE STORIES

The stories of Matthew and Luke have much in common: the birth is foretold by an angel; the baby is conceived by the special action of the Holy Spirit; he is born to a virgin in Bethlehem in the days of King Herod. However, there are also great differences between the two versions. Matthew alone has wise men and a star and the hurried escape to Egypt, when King Herod tries to kill all the baby boys in Bethlehem. Luke includes a Roman census, a manger, shepherds, an angel choir, and an encounter in the Temple with the prophetic figures Simeon and Anna. Luke also recounts the birth of John the Baptist before beginning his story of the Annunciation and Nativity.

## THE MEANING

To understand these stories, we need to recognize the many biblical associations in the two accounts. Matthew's birth narrative is sprinkled with "fulfillment texts" (Matt 1:23; 2:6; 15, 18, 23), stating that the birth of Jesus has realized a host of ancient prophecies. In Matthew's story, Jesus traces the footsteps of Moses: his life is threatened by an evil king; he spends time in Egypt; and then comes through water and desert to bring his teaching to Israel from a mountain (Matt. 3–5). Obviously the birth stories contribute to the picture of Jesus taking up the mantle and ministry of Israel's great lawgiver. The connecting thread between them is formed by the dreams Joseph has, in which he is led to do God's will; Joseph is portrayed as a typical Patriarch.

In Luke's account, Jesus combines the figures of prophet and king – another Samuel and a new David. Comparing Luke 2:52 with 1 Sam. 2:26 gives a prime clue, and there are other links: Mary's Magnificat is like Hannah's song (Luke 1:46–55; 1 Sam 2:1–10); the child in the Temple knows the mind of God (Luke 2:41–52; 1 Sam. 3). The Holy Spirit, mentioned so often in the early chapters of Luke, is a feature of prophetic and royal service, showing Jesus as a messenger and a national leader from God. A connecting thread is formed by Mary as a type of biblical prophetess and as a model disciple.

## THE MESSAGE

The purposes of the birth narratives in Matthew and Luke are clear and deeply rooted in Scripture and in the fulfillment of the purposes of God: the initiative comes from God, working through the lives of people and the circumstances of the time.

For some Christians, this is enough: the view that such writing has worth only if it can be demonstrated to be historically and descriptively accurate is not acceptable. For others, the writing seems to be making claims about "what actually happened." The various problem issues – the date of

**THE VISIT OF THE THREE MAGI**
*Magi were Zoroastrian ritual experts, and thus regarded as "wise men." According to Matthew, the magi from the East traveled to pay their homage to Jesus some time after his birth. They journeyed first to Jerusalem to Herod's court before going to Bethlehem. Matthew may have included them to stress the importance of Jesus' birth.*

the census and of Herod's death, the astral phenomena and the visit of the magi, the place of birth, the otherwise unmentioned massacre of the children – are dealt with in different ways in order to test their historicity.

There are different understandings of Matthew's and Luke's account of the virginal conception and birth (*see left;* the idea that Mary remained a virgin *after* the birth, is later, from about the fourth century CE onward). Might the story of a virgin birth have been shaped by Isaiah 7:14: "*Therefore the Lord himself will give you a sign. Look, the young woman is with child and shall bear a son and shall name him Immanuel*"? This statement seems to prophesy a virgin-born Messiah, but it may come from the Greek, not the original Hebrew. 'Almah, Hebrew for young woman, was translated *parthenos*, Greek for virgin. The text from Isaiah seems not to have been used in Judaism to predict a virgin-born Messiah, so perhaps nobody thought of reading the text in this way until the event happened. Yet that, in its own way, supports the view that it did actually happen.

What is clear is that the narratives of Luke and Matthew (and the prologue of John) point to the way in which God, through the birth of Jesus, took the initiative to come into the human situation and make a new start of repair and renewal. In their own way, therefore, the narratives initiate the entire witness of the New Testament, that God was uniquely present in and through the person of Jesus without destroying or compromising his real humanity. Jesus brings in the kingdom of God: what this means he made clear in his own life, in both actions and words (*pp.332–45*).

For further reading see bibliography numbers: 136, 139, 484, 831

### BETHLEHEM AND NAZARETH

Bethlehem was a small village in the hills 5 miles (8km) south of Jerusalem, in the region of Judea. It was situated along the ancient main road from Jerusalem to Hebron and Egypt. The relatively obscure first-century CE village of Nazareth was located in the region of Galilee, in a secluded valley 16 miles (25km) west of the Sea of Galilee and 5 miles (8km) west of Mount Tabor.

# BETHLEHEM & NAZARETH

*Christian tradition, based on Matthew and Luke, has always identified Jesus' birthplace as Bethlehem, in fulfillment of the prophecy in Micah, and the town where he grew up as Nazareth.*

BETHLEHEM was in biblical times a small and politically insignificant village. Its religious importance was due to Micah, the Prophet, who connected it symbolically with a future rule of peace under a royal deliverer from David's line (Mic. 5:1–4).

Aside from a passing reference in John's Gospel (John 7:40ff.), the New Testament mentions Bethlehem only in the birth narratives of Matthew and Luke. Some scholars see this reference as an apologetic allusion to Jesus' messianic status in fulfillment of Micah's prophecy, despite his origins in Nazareth. In Luke, Joseph and Mary travel to Bethlehem from Nazareth to register for a census under the governor of Syria, Quirinius. However, Quirinius became governor in 6CE, about 10 years after Jesus' birth, so Luke 2:2 could be referring to "the census before the one under Quirinius." A Roman census would not require people to travel from their place of residence: a journey

**THE ROAD TO BETHLEHEM**
*Traveling by road was arduous. Luke describes a pregnant Mary visiting her relative, Elizabeth, in the Judean hills – 75 miles (120km) or more on foot (Luke 1:39). He also mentions that once Mary and Joseph reached Bethlehem, they stayed for at least five weeks after Jesus' birth before journeying back to Nazareth.*

**BETHLEHEM'S SIGNIFICANCE**
*A sustained Christian influence grew in Bethlehem in the fourth century CE. Pilgrimages there increased after the emperor Constantine built a church in c.338CE and St. Jerome founded a monastery.*

**JESUS' HOME TOWN**
*In the first century CE, the small town of Nazareth was over-shadowed by two nearby towns: Japha, 2 miles (3km) to the southwest, was the largest village in Galilee; and just over an hour's walk away was Sepphoris, the largest city in the region.*

BETHLEHEM AND
NAZARETH IN THE
SCRIPTURES
The first biblical mention of Bethlehem occurs in connection with the burial of Rachel on the road to *"Ephrath, that is, Bethlehem"* (Gen. 35:19). In addition to two obscure stories in the book of Judges (17, 19), several familiar episodes involve Bethlehem. Ruth moved to Naomi's hometown of Bethlehem and married a local landowner named Boaz; her great-grandson was King David, born in Bethlehem and anointed there by Samuel (*p.114*). After a Philistine garrison held Bethlehem at the time of David (2 Sam. 23:14), his grandson Rehoboam fortified the site to guard the approach to Jerusalem (2 Chr. 11:5*ff*). Other than the New Testament and early Christian sources, Nazareth is not attested before c.300CE, when it occurs in an inscription from Caesarea listing priestly courses in Galilee.

from Nazareth to Bethlehem would make sense only if Joseph was in some significant sense already resident there. The Greek phrase translated in Luke as "there was no room at the inn" (Luke 2:7) could also be interpreted as meaning there was not enough space for Mary and Joseph in their extended family's "living room," so Mary laid Jesus in a food trough for animals, which were sometimes kept near the entrances of first-century CE cave dwellings found in Bethlehem and in other Palestinian cities.

In Matthew, Mary and Joseph appear to live in Bethlehem in a house (Matt. 2:11). After Jesus' birth they seem to stay on for perhaps as much as two years before escaping Herod's wrath by fleeing from Jerusalem to Egypt until his death (*p.318*), when they move north to live in Nazareth (Matt. 2:13–23).

## NAZARETH

Jesus' hometown was Nazareth. He remained known as "Jesus of Nazareth" even when he moved to Capernaum (Matt. 4:13), and members of his family were resident in the area until at least the third century CE. Matthew regards Jesus' living in Nazareth

as a fulfillment of an unspecified Hebrew quotation: *"He will be called a Nazorean"* (Matt. 2:23). The source of this quotation and its connection with Nazareth are not obvious, but it has been associated with biblical messianic prophecies involving the Messiah as a "Branch" (Hebrew, *nezer*, Isa. 11:1) or, less plausibly, as a Nazirite.

Nazareth assumes a unique importance in Luke, where Jesus gives his sermon in the synagogue there and describes his ministry as fulfilling the prophecy of Isaiah, and to bring *"good news to the oppressed, to bind up the broken hearted, to proclaim liberty to the captives, and release to the prisoners; to proclaim the year of the Lord's favor"* (Isa. 61:1–2). The themes of this messianic manifesto are distinctively developed in Luke's Gospel.

In Jesus' time, Nazareth was a tiny, culturally and politically insignificant rural village. It is perhaps this undistinguished ordinariness, rather than any particularly odious connotation, that lies behind Nathanael's first reaction to Jesus in John 1:46: *"Can anything good come out of Nazareth?"*

**THE MARKETPLACE IN NAZARETH**
*After the Roman general Varus destroyed Sepphoris in 3BCE, Herod Antipas reconstructed it in Hellenistic style. This benefited the surrounding area, including the village of Nazareth, which received an economic boost.*

For further reading see bibliography numbers: 109, 136, 484, 548, 579, 736

# EDUCATION

## IN THE NEW TESTAMENT

*The New Testament reveals a world where children were valued, and where learning in one form or another was of importance, whether in the home, synagogue, or at school.*

EDUCATION as depicted in the New Testament reflects characteristics of a patriarchal society (Matt. 10:35). We know little of Jesus' upbringing, apart from the conventional path of learning a family trade, but Luke suggests how this nurtured his faith: *"The child grew and became strong, filled with wisdom, and the favor of God was upon him"* (Luke 2:40). Jesus would have learned about the Bible and key social values derived from it. In his later teachings he upheld the filial duty of respect for parents along with reciprocal parental affection.

According to Luke's Gospel, the 12-year-old Jesus was found preaching in the Temple where he gave a youthful hint of the emerging sovereign claim of the kingdom of God and of an acquired depth of learning: *"... they found him in the temple, sitting among the teachers, listening to them and asking them questions. And all who heard him were amazed at his understanding and his answers"* (Luke 2:46–47). The Gospels record Jesus in his ministry as having a good knowledge of the Scriptures and of being aware of the current divisive issues between Pharisees and Sadducees (see pp.288–89). Specific educational practices, recalling the method of learning to write by following a faintly outlined letter, may be reflected in 1 Peter 2:21, and Galatians 3:24 refers to a slave

**THE YOUNG JESUS IN THE TEMPLE**
*Jewish boys, considered adults at 13, were allowed into the "inner court" of the Temple. Jesus' parents once found him here conversing with teachers of the Law.*

taking care of a school child. Education in the synagogue was mainly, but not exclusively, for boys, whereas girls were taught how to read and given basic moral and religious instruction by their mothers.

In the Jewish Diaspora (p.281), little information has survived about the patterns of education in synagogues, but the fact that children and proselytes (the newly converted) received instruction (Rom. 2:19–21), and that the writings of the New Testament were addressed to congregations that included Jews, presupposes a measure of education through Jewish texts and of literacy.

## THE ORAL TRADITION

Among rabbis and their pupils, a strong emphasis was placed on learning by memorization. In this way the oral tradition was faithfully transmitted and extended. This oral history was eventually gathered into the *Mishnah* and the *Talmuds*, and into a number of

**RABBI/TEACHER**
*From the age of six, Jewish boys were sent to the synagogue to be taught the rudiments of language, grammar, history, and geography.*

**A PLACE OF LEARNING**
*For the adult Jew the synagogue continued to be a place of religious instruction and learning, where Scripture was read aloud and carefully studied.*

other supplementary texts. Some have suggested that Jesus gathered his disciples into a formal group of this kind so that his own teaching would be carefully transmitted, expressed in such powerful sayings as, *"Heaven and earth will pass away, but my words will not pass away"* (Matt. 24:35). There is, however, no direct evidence of that being done.

## HELLENISM AND CHRISTIANITY

In Hellenistic society, education for both boys and girls was of central importance and took place in a *gymnasium*. Teachers were paid by the parents or at public expense. A core curriculum based on classical epic drama and orations gave education a broad uniformity whereby people could have been familiar with Paul's allusions to Greek poets such as Menander (1 Cor.

15:33), and Epimenides (Tit. 1:12). Higher education involved the study of rhetoric, or skillful verbal communication, and it is likely that the Apostle Paul was judged according to his rhetorical ability (1 Cor. 2:2–4).

Since the early Christian Church met in individual households, it would be natural for teaching to be provided within the context of family life. Unlike Judaism, however, the early Church transcended ethnic boundaries; in making converts within Greco-Roman families, it also disturbed their traditional family ties. The Domestic Codes (also known as Household Tables, *see p.375*) presuppose a framework of education, but these rules also reflect the awareness of change occasioned by faith. Taking as an example Timothy, whose mother and grandmother were Christians but whose father was not (2 Tim. 1:5), the education of children in the Christian faith could become

**THE PRIVILEGED ONE**
*Only in Greco-Roman society were girls fortunate enough to receive a full education, either at a gymnasium or through their own private tutor. Most Jewish girls stayed at home with their mothers.*

**WRITING TABLET**
*This first-century CE wooden tablet was coated with wax, which could be easily written on with a pointed instrument.*

a delicate matter within a patriarchal family structure. It may well be intentional that in the Domestic Code in 1 Peter 3:1*ff.*, a significantly longer exhortation is addressed to wives than to husbands, reflecting a search for a way of serving God within the changed circumstances that conversion would bring (*cf.* 1 Cor. 7:12–16). Here as in other ways, the link between learning and serving in the teaching of Jesus, in its unique use of the image of the child as an exemplar of humility (Matt. 18:1–4), no doubt continued to inform the particular connection between education and discipleship, relevant for all believers irrespective of age.

For further reading see bibliography numbers: 26, 48, 292, 306, 517, 737, 783, 877

# THE WORK OF
# JOHN THE BAPTIST

*John the Baptist was a Jewish prophet who preached and practiced a baptism of repentance in anticipation of Jesus' ministry. The Gospels note that "all" came to hear him, such was the appeal of his message and act of baptism.*

*LUKE 1:5–80*

*BIRTH OF JOHN: LUKE 1:5–8*

JOHN the Baptist, a cousin of Jesus (Luke 1:5–30), was miraculously born to Zechariah, an elderly priest, and Elizabeth, his wife. Prior to his ministry, John *may* have belonged to the community at Qumran in the Judean Desert (*p.291*). In common with community members, John had priestly connections, believed in imminent divine judgment, opposed Jerusalem and the Temple, and used water in a ritual way. The words of Isaiah, *"A voice cries out: 'In the wilderness prepare the way of the Lord,'"* both gave the community its rationale for being in the desert, and supplied the evangelists with their introduction to John's ministry. But the links between the community and John are not strong, and the Gospels portray him operating independently of any group.

*MATT. 3:3 ISAIAH 40:3*

*MARK 1–3*

## JOHN'S MINISTRY

John's work anticipated and overlapped with that of Jesus. His public ministry, which began c.28CE, was a passionate cry, associated with baptism, to people to repent before the wrath to come overwhelmed them. Once he had received his prophetic calling from God

*LUKE 3:1*

*JOHN URGES THE PEOPLE TO REPENT: LUKE 3:8*

in the desert area along the Jordan Valley, John dressed in a prophet's attire of camel hair clothes, with a leather belt around his waist, and subsisted on locusts and honey.

The location of John's ministry is significant. The wilderness (*p.73*) was a place of new beginnings away from Jerusalem and the Temple: *"And people from the whole Judean countryside and all the people of Jerusalem were going out to him, and were baptized by him in the river Jordan, confessing their sins."* John's teaching of forgiveness through baptism rather than by making Temple sacrifices only increased the distance between John and official Judaism. John saw himself as the precursor of *"one who is more powerful than I,"* his act of baptism anticipating the coming baptism with the Holy Spirit and fire (*pp.384, 417*). John called for repentance based on the broad principles of the Jewish Law, rather than the narrow concerns of the separatist Essenes (*p.289*) and Pharisees (*p.288*). Unlike these and other Jewish groups of the time, John was not impressed by racial or national identity: *"God is able from these stones to raise up children to Abraham."*

*HOSEA 2:14*

*JOHN BAPTIZING: MARK 1:5*

*MARK 1:4*

*JOHN PREPARES THE WAY FOR JESUS: MATT. 3:11*

*MATT. 3:16*

*LUKE 3:8*

John the Baptist.

## JESUS AND JOHN

Among those drawn to John was Jesus, whom John baptized in the Jordan River. Luke's opening chapter strengthens the links between them, yet only in John's Gospel do they work together for a while as members of the same renewal movement, where Jesus meets his first followers. Popular opinion also connected Jesus with John, although John's initial expectations were disappointed: perhaps John had expected Jesus to emphasize judgment rather than salvation in his teachings. After his imprisonment by Herod Antipas (*see below*), John even sent some of his disciples to Jesus to ask directly if Jesus was the expected Messiah.

In contrast, Jesus had no doubts about John's importance: his ministry marked a transition between the old age and the new. For Jesus, John the Baptist was the greatest Prophet – perhaps even the Elijah, whose return would herald the Lord's coming: *"Truly I tell you ... no one has arisen greater than John the Baptist; yet the least in the kingdom of heaven is greater than he ... and if you are willing to accept it, he is Elijah who is to come"* (*pp.139, 245*).

*JOHN 3:22*

*JOHN 1:35ff.*

*MARK 6:14ff.*
*MARK 8:28*

*MATT. 11:2–6*

*JOHN AND ELIJAH:*
*MATT. 11:7–19*

## THE DEATH OF JOHN THE BAPTIST

John later taught in the region of Galilee, where he was arrested by the client ruler, Herod Antipas (*p.278*), and then executed for publicly criticizing Herod's marriage to his sister-in-law. (Josephus, the Jewish historian, wrote that Herod feared a riot by John's mass following.) Matthew and Mark draw parallels between John's execution – after a rash promise made by Herod at a drunken party – and the Passion of Jesus (*pp.358–59*). John prepared the way for the Messiah by paying the ultimate price for speaking out against the authorities. John's influence outlived him: Paul met disciples of John the Baptist in Ephesus, a city traditionally linked to John's Gospel (*pp.312–13*). Even today, there are some (the Mandaeans, a Gnostic sect, surviving in Iraq) who revere John as a priest of their tradition.

*MARK 6:14–29*

*JOHN'S*
*FOLLOWERS:*
*ACTS 19*

*JOHN 1:8, 19*
*JOHN 3:30*

## THE BAPTISM OF JESUS IN THE GOSPELS

The Synoptic accounts of Jesus' baptism by John, with Jesus being addressed with words from Scripture (Ps. 2:7; Isa. 42:1), reveal God's call: Jesus is to begin his messianic work in the power of the Holy Spirit.

All the evangelists' stories of Jesus' baptism reflect their own concerns without losing sight of the historical Jesus. Mark's Gospel is the most straightforward: the voice is addressed to Jesus alone: *"You are my Son, the Beloved; with you I am well pleased"* (Mark 1:9–11). Matthew turns Jesus' personal experience into a public proclamation: *"This is my Son, the Beloved ..."* He also has John hesitate, for why would Jesus repent? *"I need to be baptized by you, and do you come to me?"* (Matt. 3:13–17); Jesus' insistence overcomes John's reluctance to baptize him. Luke 3:21–22 separates Jesus' baptism from the descent of the Spirit and heavenly voice; these come later, as he is praying. Luke also refers to the "bodily form" of the Spirit – typical of his way of stressing the reality of spiritual experience. Perhaps Luke wanted to distinguish John's ministry from the coming of the Spirit (*p.384*). John's Gospel takes these reservations about John the Baptist even further, by not actually saying that John baptized Jesus. In a flashback, John testifies to God telling him: *"'He on whom you see the Spirit descend and remain is the one who baptizes with the Holy Spirit.' And I myself have seen and have testified that this is the Son of God"* (John 1:33–34). In the Bible, John the Baptist is the supreme witness to Jesus as the Messiah and the Lamb of God.

**JESUS' BAPTISM**
*The Gospels describe Heaven opening, the Holy Spirit descending on Jesus like a dove, and a heavenly voice addressing him in words from the Scriptures.*

For further reading see bibliography numbers: 30, 469, 553, 677, 698, 816

# THE STORY OF
# JESUS' TEMPTATIONS

*The story of Jesus' great conflict with Satan is one of the major themes of the Synoptic Gospels. To each temptation, Jesus replies with words quoted from the Bible, proving his total devotion to God and his rejection of temptation.*

*MATT. 4:1*
*MARK 1:12–13*
*LUKE 4:1*

AFTER his baptism by John the Baptist (*p.325*), Jesus had a strong sense of being led, or driven, by the Holy Spirit into the wilderness. Here, where John the Baptist had called for repentance, Jesus was tested by Satan. Satan had appeared before to test Job (*p.175*), but now he was a more distinct figure attempting to turn Jesus away from his 40-day fast and thus away from his commitment to God. Satan tempted Jesus to perform a miracle, *"If you are the Son of God, command these stones to become loaves of bread,"* but Jesus answered him with a text from Hebrew Scripture: *"One does not live by bread alone, but by every word that comes from the mouth of God."* Taking Jesus to the

*MATT. 4:3*
*LUKE 4:3*

*DEUT. 8:3*
*MATT. 4:4*
*LUKE 4:4*

pinnacle of the Temple in the Holy City, Jerusalem, Satan started to quote Scripture himself, *"If you are the Son of God, throw yourself down from here, for it is written, 'He will command his angels concerning you, to protect you.'"* Jesus replied: *"Again it is written, 'Do not put the Lord your God to the test.'"* Finally Satan offered Jesus the kingdoms of the world and the glory of them, as though they were his to give away, if Jesus would turn from God: *"All these I will give you, if you will fall down and worship me."* Again Jesus replied to Satan with a biblical verse: *"'Worship the Lord your God, and serve only him.'"* Hearing this the devil finally left Jesus, and suddenly God's angels came and waited on Jesus instead.

*LUKE 9:9–11*
*MATT. 4:5–6*
*PS. 91:11*

*MATT. 4:7*
*LUKE 4:12*
*DEUT. 6:16*

*MATT. 4:9*
*LUKE 4:7*

*MATT. 4:10*
*LUKE 4:8*
*DEUT. 6:13*

*MATT. 4:11*
*LUKE 4:13*

Satan tempts Jesus three times: to turn stones into bread; to jump from the top of the Temple; and to worship him instead of God.

## THE SYNOPTIC ACCOUNTS

In the Synoptic Gospel accounts, Jesus' baptism by John gives way to a time of testing by the devil in the Judean wilderness, a location that was popularly regarded as the dwelling-place of demons. Jesus' 40 days of fasting echoes Israel's 40 years in the wilderness, and the devil's probing of Jesus' loyalty to God has some parallels with Job's testing. By overcoming the devil's temptations, Jesus proves faithful to his baptismal experience and ready to begin his public ministry as God's Son and Israel's Messiah.

Each Gospel narrative has its own distinctive features. Mark's brief account makes no mention of each specific temptation; the only indication of the outcome of Jesus' trials is given in its enigmatic ending: *"and he was with the wild beasts, and the angels waited on him."* Allusions abound to Israel's creation stories and to hope: notably the prophetic longing in Isaiah 11:1–9 for creation to be restored to its primeval harmony by a Spirit-anointed descendant of David, and beliefs about angels ministering to Adam and Eve in the Garden of Eden. The victory of Jesus, the Spirit-anointed Son of God, reverses Adam's disobedience and renews the ideal order of Creation.

Matthew and Luke expand Mark by referring to three specific temptations; the degree of overlap between their narratives makes it likely that they are based on a common source. Matthew's first two temptations, with their introductory *"If you are the Son of God,"* hark back to Jesus' baptism. *"Command these stones to become loaves of bread"* fastens onto Jesus' hunger during his 40-day fast and invites him to use his spiritual power to satisfy his own needs. *"Throw yourself down [from the pinnacle of the Temple]"* calls Jesus to test his trust in God's providential care, on the basis of Psalm 91:11ff. Matthew's third temptation has the devil showing Jesus *"all the kingdoms of the world and the glory of them"* from a great height, and promising them to him in exchange for the honor due only to God. In each case Jesus counters the devil by quoting Scriptural texts, drawn from Moses' appeal for Israel's loyalty once they entered the Promised Land. Jesus' allegiance to God emerges undiminished after his desert ordeal, unlike Israel of old, whose faithfulness failed when it put God to the test: *"Remember the long way that the LORD your God has led you these forty years in the wilderness, in order to humble you, testing you to know what was in your heart, whether or not you would keep his commandments,"* (Deut. 8:2; cf. 6:16). Jesus, by contrast, is God's faithful Son, the true Israelite. Luke differs from Matthew in the order in which he places the second and third temptations. Luke's account reaches its climax

THE WILDERNESS
*Situated between Jerusalem and the Dead Sea, the "wilderness of Judea" was an arid, stony, hilly setting for Jesus' preparation of his ministry.*

with Jesus in Jerusalem, on the pinnacle of the Temple, just as his Gospel also culminates in the Temple (Luke 24:52–53). Luke makes no mention of the angels ministering to Jesus, remarking only that *"the devil departed from [Jesus] until an opportune time"* – a reference, perhaps, to the return of Satan as Jesus' Passion approaches (Luke 22:3; cf. Luke 22:31).

## TESTING ISSUES

Some modern commentators see the journeys of ascent – to a high mountain and the pinnacle of the Temple – as suggestions of visionary experience, with scriptural quotations and allusions dramatizing Jesus' struggles and their significance. The temptation stories are pointers, not only to a period of testing prior to Jesus' ministry but also to his continuing fight to be faithful to God as his ministry progressed. The temptations are economic, religious, and political, and these issues recurred. Jesus repeatedly faced choices in living out his divine vocation and in using his messianic power. What would be his response to the political pressures he faced (John 6:15)? What was he to make of his critics' expectations or even those of his closest followers (Mark 8:11, 33)? What kind of power would he use to confront those whom he saw as the enemies of God's kingdom, the leaders in Jerusalem (Matt. 20:17ff.)? Could he trust in God's providential care when his life was about to be taken from him (Matt. 26:39)? That his loyalty to God emerged intact enabled the writer of Hebrews to commend his example to those whose faithfulness was also on trial (Heb. 2:18; 4:15ff.).

For further reading see bibliography numbers: 85, 232, 282, 529, 761

## THE STORIES OF

# JESUS CALLING HIS DISCIPLES

*After Jesus had begun his ministry, he chose 12 men to live and work with him as his close disciples. There were also women followers and disciples who went with Jesus in Galilee and on to Jerusalem.*

ANDREW:
JOHN 1:40

SIMON PETER:
JOHN 1:41

JOHN'S Gospel recounts how Jesus met Andrew while he was still a disciple of John the Baptist. As Jesus walked by, John told him who he was. Andrew told his brother, Simon Peter, that they had "found the Messiah" and the brothers became "disciples" (Latin *disco*, "I learn"). The next day, Jesus went to Galilee and called Philip to follow him. Philip told Nathanael, who mocked him, but he also became one of Jesus' disciples.

MATT. 4:18–20
MARK 4:16–18
JOHN 1:43

PHILIP AND
NATHANAEL:
JOHN 1:45–49

Jesus' first disciples were fishermen whom he met on the shores of the Sea of Galilee.

## JESUS AND THE FISHERMEN

The Synoptics describe Jesus calling his first disciples, Simon, Andrew, James, and John, from among the fishermen working the lake in Galilee. Jesus was walking by the Sea of Galilee when he saw Simon and Andrew fishing. He challenged them to come and be fishers for people. Luke adds a longer story that Jesus got into one of the boats to teach the crowds, and then instructed Simon to push the boat out and for the fishermen to cast their nets again for fish. Simon replied that they had toiled all night and caught nothing. Nevertheless, at his command they would try again. This time, the nets nearly burst with fish. Back on land, Simon fell down before Jesus and said, *"Go away from me Lord, for I am a sinful man!"* Jesus invited Simon to be a disciple and a fisher for people. Matthew and Mark stress the immediacy of these disciples' response to Jesus' call to "follow me" – an example of the repentance Jesus demands in the name of God's kingdom.

*MATT. 4:18–22*

*MARK 1:16–20*

*LUKE 5:2–11*

## DISCIPLESHIP

As Jesus began teaching, many disciples gathered around him. Later, after his first healings and teachings, they were narrowed down to an inner group of 12. Matthew became a disciple after Jesus walked past him in his tax collector's booth and asked him also to become a follower. The Gospels also make it clear that women were extremely important as disciples of Jesus – a highly unusual welcome of women at that time. Some of them accompanied Jesus on his journeys. They went with him to Jerusalem, attended the Crucifixion, and were the first to arrive at the empty tomb. Luke mentions a group of women who accompanied Jesus and the twelve, providing financial support.

Jesus called his disciples to be "with him," to abandon their homes, possessions, and economic ties, and to join him in his itinerant ministry. Whatever the cost, their discipleship came first. Such an attitude went beyond a normal teacher-pupil relationship and gave the word *disciple* a new meaning. Jesus gave these disciples authority to preach, heal, and exorcize, and so they continued and extended his work.

*JOHN 6:60*

*MARK 3:14*
*MATT. 10:1*
*LUKE 6:13*

*MATTHEW, THE TAX COLLECTOR*

*WOMEN DISCIPLES*

*LUKE 8:1–3*

## DISCIPLE GROUPS

When viewed against the backdrop of the Hebrew Bible and contemporary culture, it is not surprising that the Gospels depict Jesus in the company of disciples. In Israelite society, master-disciple relationships could be found wherever divine revelations were interpreted and communicated: among Prophets (Isa. 8:16), scribes (Ezra 7), and teachers (Prov. 1).

The Greek understanding of disciples (those who attached themselves to teachers in order to learn from them) already existed in the Judaism of Jesus' day. A broad spectrum of Jewish movements – philosophical, legal, sectarian, and revolutionary – each had its own disciples, a situation that was reflected in the evangelists' references to disciples of the Pharisees, John the Baptist, and Moses (Mark 2:18; John 9:28).

## THE TWELVE

Traditionally, all Israelites believed that they were descended from Jacob's 12 sons, the Twelve Tribes that ruled "all Israel" *(pp.102–3)*. The specific number of Jesus' disciples suggests that they symbolize the nucleus of a renewed Israel. Common to all the Synoptic stories is Jesus' call to renounce a livelihood and follow him: *"Follow me, and I will make you fish for people"* (Mark 1:17ff.; cf. Jer. 16:16ff.). John's Gospel sees the fruit of Jesus' call more in terms of people coming to believe in him as the Messiah: *"Nathanael replied, 'Rabbi, you are the Son of God! You are the King of Israel!'"* (John 1:49; 1:41).

Luke 6:13 and Matthew 10:2 underline Jesus' commissioning of those he calls: they are his "apostles" (Greek *apostello*, "send"). John's Gospel gives the impression that there is a degree of self-selection about the formation of this nuclear group's difficulties with Jesus' teaching meant that *"many of his disciples turned back and no longer went about with him"* (John 6:60, 66). But the emphasis throughout these accounts is on Jesus' initiative: *"Did I not choose you, the twelve?"* (John 6:70; 15:16) – a factor distinguishing Jesus' followers from those disciples who choose their own master.

The twelve are not the only disciples of Jesus mentioned in the Gospels. In Mark 9:38, John complains of someone exorcizing in Jesus' name, Luke 10:1–17 describes the mission of "the seventy", and Matthew's Gospel refers to a wider circle of disciples, including Joseph of Arimathea (Matt. 8:19ff.; 27:57). But Jesus' calling of the twelve focuses the nature of discipleship. Discipleship is always costly but not without its rewards (Mark 8:34ff.; 10:28ff.). It expresses itself in its devotion to the cause of Jesus and through its conformity to Jesus' way (Mark 10:32–45ff.; John 12:24ff.). The fundamental relationship between the master and his disciples can never be outgrown (Matt. 23:8–12).

For further reading see bibliography numbers: 83, 84, 112, 258, 389

# THE TWELVE
# DISCIPLES

*Once appointed by Jesus, the 12 disciples were empowered to heal, to cast out demons, and to convey Jesus' message to a wider audience. As his representatives, Jesus tried to prepare them for the hardships this role could bring them after his Resurrection.*

THE 12 disciples are listed at four points in the New Testament: Matthew 10:2–4; Mark 3:16–19; Luke 6:13–16; and Acts 1:13 (*see box, below right*). Except for Judas Iscariot, the list of names in Luke and Acts correspond, although not in the same order, and Matthew follows Mark in the same way. Thaddeus could be Luke's Judas, son of James (perhaps Thaddeus was a nickname), while in Luke Simon the Cananean ("man of zeal") has a Greek rather than Aramaic surname. John's Gospel refers to "the twelve" without listing them, but is unique in its mention of the anonymous "beloved disciple" (*see p.313*). However, it makes no reference to Matthew the tax collector, Simon the Cananean, James the son of Alphaeus, or Bartholomew, whom Christian tradition has identified with Nathanael, one of the disciples found only in John's Gospel.

## A HIERARCHY

Simon Peter appears at the head of all the lists, reflecting his prominence in the early Church. He often acts as spokesman for the twelve, and in Matthew 16:16ff. he articulates the faith on which the Church is built by saying to Jesus: *"You are the Messiah, the Son of the Living God."* Philip and James, sons of Alphaeus,

always appear in fifth and ninth places, respectively. This may indicate that the twelve were subdivided into groups of four, led by these three who, with Andrew, constituted an "inner circle" within the twelve. Occasionally Jesus took the three apart from the rest to teach them. They accompanied him, for example, on his visit to Jairus' house (Mark 5:37), to the mount of

the Transfiguration (Mark 9:2), and into the Garden of Gethsemane where Jesus pleaded with them to stay awake while he prayed (Mark 14:33). According to Mark 13:3–4, only Peter, James, John, and Andrew heard Jesus' final discourse.

## WHY THESE TWELVE?

Although we know little, if anything, about most of the disciples, the information we do have reveals that they were a diverse group. As a tax collector, Matthew collaborated with the Romans, while Simon (if a Zealot) would have resented the presence of foreigners on Jewish soil. In view of the symbolic significance of their number (i.e., the Twelve Tribes of Israel), it seems likely that Jesus saw the

**TAX COLLECTOR**
*Matthew, also called Levi, followed Jesus immediately when called. Some were appalled that Jesus mixed with tax collectors (Matt. 9:11).*

**BEARING WITNESS**
*Jesus deliberately chose 12 men among his many followers to bear witness to the kingdom of God.*

disciples as the nucleus of a restored Israel. He deliberately chose people unlikely to have been admitted to movements such as the Pharisees or the Essenes (*see Jewish Groups, pp.288–89*) in order to indicate the inclusiveness of his vision of the kingdom of God.

## THE ROLE OF THE DISCIPLES

Mark's relatively brief account of the selection and commissioning of the twelve (Mark 3:13*ff.*) is expanded by Matthew and Luke, who refer to them as "apostles" (Matt. 10:2; Luke 6:13). The disciples were authorized and "sent away" (the root meaning of apostle) to extend Jesus' work of preaching the coming of God's kingdom, healing, and exorcism (Matt. 10:1–16), sustained only by trust in God and others' hospitality. Matthew 10:5*ff.* restricts their work to *"the lost sheep of the house of Israel,"* for it is only <u>after</u> the Resurrection that their role is broadened (Matt. 28:19*ff.*).

The disciples are promised a share in the coming judgment (Matt. 19:28; Luke 22:30), but Jesus warns them of the potential hardships they are likely to face first: *"I am sending you out like sheep into the midst of wolves … they will hand you over to councils and flog you in their syna-gogues; and you will be dragged before governors and kings because of me, as a testimony to them and the Gentiles"* (Matt. 10:16–18*ff.*). According to Acts 12:2, James, the brother of John, was the first of the twelve to be martyred as part of the severe persecution suffered by the early Church in Jerusalem (*pp.458–59*).

The number 12 continued to be significant for the first Jewish Christians in Jerusalem, as Judas' replacement by Matthias shows (Acts 1:21–26). We know nothing of Matthias' ministry, nor that of most of the twelve Apostles after Pentecost. However, with the spread of apostolic authority from the second century CE onward, Matthew and John became associated with the first and fourth Gospels, and Peter (as Mark's mentor) with the second.

**CASTING OUT NETS**
*Simon Peter, Andrew, James, and his brother John were all fishermen whom Jesus called to abandon their nets and "fish for people."*

**BRONZE FISH HOOK**
*This first century CE fish hook is typical of those used in the rivers of Palestine at that time.*

## STRENGTHS AND WEAKNESSES

The way the evangelists present the disciples as role models, both positive and negative, is important. They confess faith and profess loyalty toward Jesus, but they also betray, deny, and desert him. Mark's picture has the darkest hues: the twelve never overcome their habitual misunderstanding of Jesus, particularly as he moves toward his Passion. The Fourth Gospel almost makes a virtue out of their confusion, using it to draw further explanations from Jesus about his teaching (e.g., John 14:8*ff.*).

Luke tends to play down their shortcomings, and Matthew lightens Mark's somber tones with his depiction of the twelve as *"men of little faith"* (8:26; 14:31; 16:8; 17:20), under-lining the potential for growth.

Ultimately, the story of the disciples demonstrates the triumph of Jesus' faith in them. The women who come to Jesus' tomb are told: *"Go, tell his disciples and Peter that he is going ahead of you to Galilee; there you will see him, just as he told you"* (Mark 16:7). Peter is called away from his fishing in Galilee to a pastoral leadership fashioned by the cross (John 21: 15–19) – the way of all discipleship (*"If any want to become my followers, let them … take up their cross and follow me"* Mark 8:34).

# THE CHOSEN TWELVE

*Jesus chose a core group of 12 disciples from the larger company of his followers. Their names are listed in four different books in the following sequence:*

| MATT. 10:2–4 | MARK 3:16–19 | LUKE 6:13–16 | ACTS 1:13 |
|---|---|---|---|
| Simon, called Peter | Simon, called Peter | Simon, called Peter | Peter |
| Andrew | James and John, | Andrew | John |
| James and John, | sons of Zebedee | James | James |
| sons of Zebedee | Andrew | John | Andrew |
| Philip | Philip | Philip | Philip |
| Bartholomew | Bartholomew | Bartholomew | Thomas |
| Thomas | Matthew | Thomas | Bartholomew |
| Matthew | Thomas | Matthew | Matthew |
| James, son | James, son | James, son | James, son |
| of Alphaeus | of Alphaeus | of Alphaeus | of Alphaeus |
| Thaddeus | Thaddeus | Simon the Zealot | Simon the Zealot |
| Simon the Cananean | Simon the Cananean | Judas, son of James | Judas, son of James |
| Judas Iscariot | Judas Iscariot | Judas Iscariot | [Matthias, 1:26] |

For further reading see bibliography numbers: 84, 258, 389

# JESUS' TEACHINGS

*The main themes of Jesus' teaching can be summed up by the announcement he made in Galilee at the start of his ministry: "The time is fulfilled, and the kingdom of God has come near; repent, and believe in the good news" (Mark 1:15). Jesus lived and taught this message.*

MUCH of Jesus' teaching can be paralleled in other Jewish teaching of the time, but Jesus combined it in a unique way with his own enacted ministry. He claimed God's authority to define the nature of God's kingdom and the response God expected from the Covenant People at the beginning of a new chapter in their history.

> **" *Father, hallowed be your name. Your kingdom come. Give us each day our daily bread. And forgive us our sins, for we ourselves forgive everyone indebted to us. And do not bring us to the time of trial.* "**
>
> (Luke 11:2–4)

## THE COMING KINGDOM

Jesus applied the core meaning of "the kingdom of God" – the coming of God in power to redeem Israel and transform the world – to the events taking shape through him and around him (*pp.444–45*). In one sense, the kingdom of God had already arrived – "the kingdom of God is among you" (Luke 17:21) – but Jesus encouraged his followers to pray for its coming (Matt. 6:10).

Overall, Jesus' teaching gives the impression that he expected the kingdom of God to appear in a series of events, beginning with his own ministry and stretching into the future (Mark 9:1; 14:25). He did not share a popular expectation that the Jews would usher in God's kingdom by defeating their Gentile enemies, removing them from their ancestral lands, and assuming political and religious supremacy in the world. Instead, he spoke of God's indiscriminate grace and compassion (e.g., Matt. 5:45; Luke 6:35–38; 15:11ff.). To <u>this</u> Israel, all

those open to God in faith and life can belong (Luke 14:12ff.). His teaching about God's kingdom found practical expression in his table fellowship with outcasts, and in a healing ministry that crossed social and religious boundaries. To those people who expected a military victory, the kingdom according to Jesus would have appeared small and trifling, but like seed and yeast, its impact was undeniable (Mark 4:26ff.; Matt. 13:33).

Jesus called his hearers to God's kingdom, painting impressionistic pictures in parables (*pp.336–39*) to explain what this entailed: alertness, responsibility, prayer, faith, generosity, humility, and forgiveness. This teaching is rooted in Torah and Scripture (especially in Matt 5:17ff.), and also Jesus' appeal to the Ten Commandments (Mark 10:19ff.). But where some thought that the strict observance of Torah ("Build a fence around Torah!"; *cf. right box, p.431*) was the condition of God sending the Messiah, Jesus said that the true condition of God's action is the faith that it actually exists without conditions. Among outsiders, even Gentiles, Jesus found greater faith than in Israel.

His question to the lawyer in Luke 10:26 shows that Jesus recognized more than one way of reading the Law. He resisted the way some religious authorities appealed to Moses to sanction sectarian views of holiness, which were dangerous in a deeply

**TEACHING ABOUT GOD'S KINGDOM**
*Jesus called his listeners to repent by embracing his vision of God's kingdom wholeheartedly. The kingdom of God, or of Heaven, is the universal rule of God, not limited to one people or one land.*

# THE LORD'S PRAYER

*The Lord's Prayer resembles the Qaddish, a Jewish prayer that Jesus may have known.*

The Gospels have two versions. Matthew 6:9–13 exemplifies how to pray, while Luke 11:2–4 is a model prayer. Matthew's longer version may reflect use in worship. Both address God as "Father" and introduce Jesus' disciples into his relationship with God. Matthew's additional "in heaven" emphasizes God's transcendence. "Hallowed be your name" shows God worthy of the highest honor. "Your kingdom come" is the main theme of the prayer. Matthew's expansion, "Your will be done," understands this as earth governed by the ways of Heaven. "Daily bread" probably means "bread for the coming day," appropriate for a prayer said at the start of each day. Matthew's "this day" asks God to "let your kingdom come now"; Luke's "each day" wants a daily gift of enough to eat. Matthew's "forgive us our debts" reflects the Aramaic euphemism for sins. "As we ourselves forgive/have forgiven" reflects Jesus' insistence on this theme. "Temptation" may mean "spare us from temptation," or "do not bring us where we will be tempted," or "do not cause us to enter into testing by evil" (or "the evil one" in Matthew). Matthew's longer ending, "For yours is the kingdom, the power and the glory forever" is not in all manuscripts.

# A COMMAND TO LOVE

*Rabbis were often asked which of the Law's 613 precepts summed up the whole. When asked, Jesus combined two passages.*

The passages that Jesus brought together from the Law as "the great commandment" comprise: *"... The LORD is our God, the LORD alone. You shall love the LORD your God with all your heart, and with all your soul, and with all your might"* (Deut. 6:4–5) and *"You shall love your neighbor as yourself"* (Lev. 19:18). In Matthew 22:34–40 and Luke 10:25–28, an expert in the Law tests Jesus; in Mark 12:28–34 it is a scribe. He repeats Jesus' answer, adding that love for God and a neighbor is more important than the Temple cult. Jesus commends him. Luke's lawyer asks about inheriting eternal life and Jesus asks him about the Law: "How do you read?" implies more than one way of grasping the central message. The lawyer's next question, "Who is my neighbor?" leads to the parable of the Good Samaritan. Jesus may have been the first to join love for God and neighbor so explicitly. Each evangelist finds a particular significance in this: in Matthew Jesus' statement echoes his claim to fulfill the Law in the Sermon on the Mount (Matt. 5:17–20; 7:12); Luke suggests that loving the God of mercy means living mercifully (Luke 6:36). Mark's lawyer makes the point that without love for God and neighbor, religious ritual is empty.

---

divided society. Purity, he argued, should not be understood in terms of separation from anything or anyone considered "unclean"; defilement comes "from within" (Mark 7:1ff.). He defined God's call to holiness in terms of the "weightier matters of the Law" – justice, mercy, and love (Matt. 23:23), which he used as keys to unlock the meaning of the tradition of Moses. So justice is the arbiter of true religion (Mark 11:15ff.), mercy has priority over sacrifice (Matt. 9:13), and love for the needy takes precedence over Sabbath observance (Luke 6:1ff.). Jesus' reading of the Law also led him to reverse many of the values of traditional Jewish wisdom, with its teaching about the place of family, wealth, and honor (Matt. 12:46ff.; Mark 10:1ff.; Luke 14:7ff.).

## TEACHING ABOUT THE APOCALYPSE

A note of urgency permeated Jesus' teaching as he called Israel to choose destruction or life: *"Enter through the narrow gate; for the gate is wide and the road is easy that leads to destruction, and there are many who take it. For the gate is narrow and the road is hard that leads to life, and there are few who find it"* (Matt. 7:13–14). Did

Jesus expect the world to end? Should his call go unheeded? Cosmic imagery and judgment day scenarios are certainly found in his sayings and stories (Matt. 25:31ff.; Luke 17:20ff.). There is evidence, though, that he expected the world to continue for some time (Matt. 25:1ff.), and this suggests an alternative way of interpreting his "end of the world" language. Like the Prophets before him *(pp.196–99, 324–25)*, Jesus called his hearers to change their perceptions and behavior or face the "earth shattering" consequences of their impenitence in their own generation. The rising tide of violence would threaten even those who lived by Jesus' teachings, culminating in the destruction of so much that was held dear, including their Temple in Jerusalem. When Jerusalem fell to the Romans *(pp.292–93)*, this and the ruined Temple served to vindicate Jesus' teaching (Mark 13).

In all Jesus' teaching, his own experience of God was paramount. He addressed God as *Abba, Father,* a child's word of respect for a parent who sustains and cares for his family in every detail. As he prayed often himself, so he taught his followers much about prayer and its absolute importance in Christian life.

For further reading see bibliography numbers: 55, 75, 109, 112, 122, 166, 222, 257, 430a, 501a, 547, 548, 553, 574, 612, 616a, 648, 677, 678, 759, 783 ; 833,

# THE TEACHING OF THE
# SERMON ON THE MOUNT

*As Jesus traveled through Galilee preaching, crowds began to come to listen to him.*
*Some of his most memorable teaching has been gathered together in a single "sermon"*
*that has become one of the most influential parts of the New Testament.*

*MATT. 4:23–25*

WHILE Jesus had been teaching in the synagogues and healing sick people throughout Galilee, his fame grew and large crowds began to follow him. According to Matthew's Gospel, when Jesus saw the crowds that had gathered, he went up on a mountainside to speak to his disciples. Luke's Gospel recounts that Jesus stood *"on a level place, with a great crowd of his disciples and a great multitude of people."* Jesus began to teach, starting with a series of blessings, or Beatitudes *(see box, opposite)*, and then turned to the issue of human conduct. He taught the Lord's Prayer *(p.333)* and then ended, using dramatic language, by contrasting different ways of living *(pp.336–39)*.

*MATT. 5:1–2*

*LUKE 6:17–19*

*MATT. 5:3–12*
*LUKE 6:20–25*

*MATT. 5:13–7:29*
*LUKE 6:26–49*

Matthew recounts that Jesus sat down when speaking to his disciples, a typical Jewish position for teaching.

## THE MESSAGE OF THE SERMON

Known as The Sermon on the Mount since St. Augustine's commentary of 396CE, this is the first of five blocks of Jesus' teaching detailed in Matthew's Gospel (*pp.306–7*). A shorter version following the same order appears in Luke, which is often called The Sermon on the Plain (Matthew has more than 100 verses; Luke has 30: Matt. 5–7; Luke 6:17–49).

Matthew was probably responsible for the present form of the Sermon and may have seen parallels between Jesus and Moses, who also taught from a mountain. Throughout the Sermon, Jesus aims for an integrity that holds together attitude and action, belief and behavior. The Beatitudes are a great charter for human freedom set apart from selfishness and greed, with the promise of God's blessing (*see box, right*).

The Sermon's central section (Matt. 5:17–7:12) presents Jesus' interpretation of "the Law and the prophets," although he stresses that the authority of the Law remains, down to every letter and pen-stroke. Unlike the scribes and Pharisees, Jesus fulfills the Scriptures and draws out their true meaning (Matt. 5:21–48). Despite his – *"you have heard that it was said ... but I say to you"* – Jesus does not so much contrast his teaching with that of Moses as address problematic attitudes that hide behind supposedly righteous behavior: it is not enough to live within the laws regulating killing, adultery, divorce, oaths, or retribution. The spirit of the Beatitudes demands a more radical approach, with no place for inner dispositions that breed violence or injustice. These are entirely at odds with the indiscriminate generosity of God, whose perfection is the model for the righteousness that Jesus demands: *"Be perfect therefore, as your heavenly Father is perfect"* (Matt. 5:48; 6:1–8).

Jesus goes on to criticize the hypocrisy that can be masked by traditional piety: if almsgiving, prayer, and fasting are intended only to enhance an individual's reputation and honor, then that is the reward he will receive and nothing more. By contrast, purity of heart will find its own reward in secret generosity, prayers offered privately and simply, and unostentatious fasting. Jesus follows with a warning against relying on "treasures on earth," whose vulnerability makes them unworthy of ultimate trust (6:19–34); a pure heart, totally trusting, seeks *"first God's kingdom and his righteousness."*

Jesus words on judgment (Matt. 7:1–5) echo his warnings about hypocrisy. However, there is a kind of judgment he does commend in appealing to commonsense wisdom (v.6): just as no Jew would put anything holy in the way of unclean animals, so Jesus calls his listeners to practice discernment according to the values of the kingdom of Heaven. God's indiscriminate kindness provides for all God's children and offers a model for human conduct. Jesus uses the "golden rule" (v.12) to sum up the teaching of the Law and the Prophets, and thereby fulfill them. The sermon concludes with a series of warnings, set out in four contrasts between life and death, good and bad fruit, true service and lip-

# THE BEATITUDES

*Matthew and Luke introduce their collections of Jesus' teaching with the Beatitudes, which promise the blessings of God's kingdom.*

**The site of Jesus' teaching.**
*Matthew mentions Jesus teaching the Beatitudes on a mountain, thought by some to be Mount Tabor. Luke refers to a level place, which may have been by the Sea of Galilee.*

While there is common ground in Matthew 5:3–12 and Luke 6:20–26, there are significant differences. Matthew has nine Beatitudes, Luke four, including four "woes" not found in Matthew. Matthew recounts the Beatitudes (except for the last) in the third person, Luke in the second. Matthew's version is concerned with attitudes and behavior appropriate to God's kingdom; Luke's expects the reversal of distressing material conditions in the age to come. It is difficult to say which set of Beatitudes is closer to Jesus' teaching because each reinforces the message of the Gospel to which it belongs. Matthew stresses the integrity of inner dispositions and behavior. Luke's emphasis on reversal is one of his major themes (e.g., 1:46–55). It is likely that both adapted Jesus' sayings, and that Matthew probably composed some Beatitudes (e.g., 5–10) based on the material available to him. Both accounts challenge the prevailing wisdom of their day, calling into question any easy identification of divine blessing with worldly well-being.

# THE FOOLISH BUILDER

Both Matthew and Luke end their accounts with the parable of wise and foolish builders – with only one of them building his house on foundations firm enough to withstand the elements. The parable warns that those who hear Jesus' teaching without letting his message become the foundation of their lives will likewise face disaster. Luke applies the parable to Jesus' teachings in general, while Matthew applies it specifically to the Sermon on the Mount: *"everyone who hears these words of mine and does them ..."* As the climax of a series of warning contrasts, Matthew elevates the significance of the foolish builder's actions: his ruin is not merely a house reduced to rubble but the prospect of unfavorable judgment on the last day.

**For further reading see bibliography numbers:** 88, 356, 387, 439, 724, 738

# PARABLES

*Of all the aspects of Jesus' life and ministry, his parables are the most accessible. Yet these stories raise many questions, including the challenge to decide about Jesus and his mission, and Jesus' own reported insistence that he told them in order not to be understood.*

JESUS' teaching was characterized by his use of parables. The word *parable* is derived from the Greek *parabole*, which means the placing of two things side by side for the sake of comparison. In this sense, almost all of Jesus' teachings are "parabolic," explaining, for instance, the kingdom of God. Strictly, the word *parable* should be used of sayings that begin, "The kingdom of God/Heaven is like …," but usually the word *parable* is applied far more freely, even to stories that offer examples of how to live, such as that of the Good Samaritan (Luke 10:30–37) and the Faithful Steward (Luke 12:42–48).

## WHAT IS A PARABLE?

In Hebrew, the word *mashal* translates the Greek *parabole*. *Mashal* may refer to a puzzling saying intended to provoke thought, but it is more commonly used for a story told by a rabbi to make his teaching clear and intelligible. There are, in fact, many surviving parables told by rabbis. The form and nature of rabbinic parables indicate that, although Jesus' parables have been included by the evangelists to serve the purpose of each Gospel, there is no need to suppose (as was done until recently) that they have been removed from the context in which Jesus first spoke them. This view is

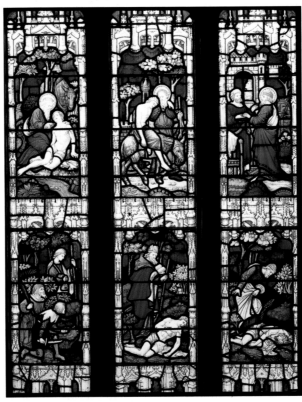

**THE GOOD SAMARITAN**
*This stained-glass window depicts the parable of the Judean man in need, who, although ignored by a priest and a Levite, was helped by a Samaritan (see overleaf).*

> **❝** *They may indeed look, but not perceive, and may indeed listen, but not understand; so that they may not turn again and be forgiven.* **❞**
>
> (Mark 4:12)

reinforced by the fact that the parable stories reflect daily life in Palestine, and certain everyday settings, objects, events, and characters were included to highlight the main point of Jesus' preaching: the proclamation of God's kingdom.

## THE PURPOSE OF PARABLES

Jesus told parables in different contexts and for a variety of purposes. In his conflict with some Pharisees (*pp.288–89*), Jesus challenged their complacency and their opposition to him. Surrounded by controversy, Jesus explained his authority and actions. Through his parables, Jesus gave his understanding of God's kingdom, and he urged his listeners toward repentance.

In the Gospels, the word *parable* is used to describe a riddle (Mark 3:23), a proverb (Luke 4:23), a contrast (Luke 18:1–8), and a comparison (Matt. 13:33). It is used for both simple and complicated stories (Luke 13:6–9; *cf.* Matt. 22:1–14). In all three Synoptics, one parable, that of the Sower (Matt. 13:3–8; Mark 4:3–8; Luke 8:5–8), is followed by an explanation of Jesus' purpose in teaching in this way. This story could well be called the parable of the Ground, since the sower does not appear after the first sentence, and the parable tells of the different ways in which people hear and respond to the teaching of the Word. Jesus tells the disciples that they have been given the mysteries of the kingdom of God, but that others receive parables *"so that they may not look with their eyes, and listen with their ears, and comprehend with their minds, and turn and be healed"* (Isa. 6:10). Some people argue that Jesus taught in this way "with the consequence that" (Greek, *hoste*) some listeners would understand and some would not, but the Greek explicitly states that he taught with that "purpose" (Greek, *hina*). It seems to be a harsh saying. The later Jewish tradition interpreted the passage from Isaiah in the same way: it understood the purpose of God's message through Isaiah as intended, for finding good ore in the midst of useless material by repeated smelting – trial after trial by fire – until only the good remnant remained. Jesus' parables were, therefore, intended to make clear who does, and who does not, belong within the kingdom of God.

> ❝ *Then his disciples asked him what this parable meant. He said, 'To you it has been given to know the secrets of the kingdom of God; but to others I speak in parables.'* ❞
>
> (Luke 8:10)

## THE PARABLES AND TEACHING

Parables are often classified into four main groups according to the different styles or forms in which they appear. While the distinctions are not precise, they draw attention to important differences of form. For instance, similitude stories make comparisons (*x* is like *y*); example stories offer positive or negative models and lead to the statement, "Go and do, or do not do, likewise." Some parables offer an extended metaphor, such as the parable of the Banquet (Luke 14:16–24), and others are allegorical, offering a series of related metaphors, such as the story of the Sheep and the Goats (Matt. 25:31–46).

Jesus' parables concentrate on the kingdom of God, or of Heaven, either at present or as yet to come. Other common themes include discipleship, prayer, and the right use of possessions. Jesus' vivid parables captured attention, challenged assumptions, invited audiences to see reality from a different perspective, and provoked further reflection.

# PARABLES TOLD BY JESUS

*These are some of many sayings and stories that Jesus told in order to explain the kingdom of God.*

| | MATTHEW | MARK | LUKE | | MATTHEW | MARK | LUKE |
|---|---|---|---|---|---|---|---|
| A Lamp under a Bushel: | 5:14–15 | 4:21–22 | 8:16;11:33 | The Talents (Matthew); The Pounds (Luke): | 25:14–30 | | 19:12–27 |
| Houses on Rock and on Sand: | 7:24–27 | | 6:47–49 | Sheep and Goats: | 25:31–46 | | |
| New Cloth on an Old Garment: | 9:16 | 2:21 | 5:36 | Seedtime to Harvest: | | 4:26–29 | |
| New Wine in Old Wineskins: | 9:17 | 2:22 | 5:37–38 | Creditors and Debtors: | | | 7:41–43 |
| The Sower: | 13:3–8 | 4:3–8 | 8:5–8 | The Good Samaritan: | | | 10:30–37 |
| Mustard Seed: | 13:31–32 | 4:30–32 | 13:18–19 | A Friend in Need: | | | 11:5–8 |
| Wheat and Tares: | 13:24–30 | | | A Rich Fool: | | | 12:16–21 |
| Leaven (yeast): | 13:33 | | 13:20–21 | Alert Servants: | | | 12:35–40 |
| Hidden Treasure: | 13:44 | | | A Faithful Steward: | | | 12:42–48 |
| A Pearl of Great Value: | 13:45–46 | | | A Fig Tree Without Figs: | | | 13:6–9 |
| The Great Net: | 13:47–48 | | | Places of Honor at the Wedding-feast: | | | 14:7–14 |
| Lost Sheep: | 18:12–13 | | 15:4–6 | A Great Banquet and Reluctant Guests: | | | 14:16–24 |
| Two Debtors (unforgiving servant): | 18:23–34 | | | Counting the Cost: | | | 14:28–33 |
| Workers in a Vineyard: | 20:1–16 | | | A Lost Coin: | | | 15:8–10 |
| Two Sons: | 21:28–31 | | | The Prodigal Son: | | | 15:11–32 |
| Tenant Farmers: | 21:33–41 | 12:1–9 | 20:9–16 | Dishonest Steward: | | | 16:1–8 |
| An Invitation to a Wedding Feast; a Man Without a Wedding Garment: | 22:2–14 | | | A Rich Man and Lazarus: | | | 16:19–31 |
| The Fig Tree as Herald of Summer: | 24:32–33 | 13:28–29 | 21:29–32 | A Master and his Servants: | | | 17:7–10 |
| Ten Bridesmaids: | 25:1–13 | | | A Persistent Widow and an Unrighteous Judge: | | | 18:2–5 |
| | | | | A Pharisee and a Tax Collector: | | | 18:9–14 |

For further reading see overleaf

## THE IMPACT OF THE PARABLES

Although it is now generally recognized that there is no single "correct" interpretation of the parables, some traditional interpretations of Jesus' stories are discussed below; the impact that the parables made on the earliest listeners ensured that they were preserved in that tradition.

Jesus controversially mixed with those despised by the "righteous" as "sinners," and with tax collectors regarded as agents of the Roman rulers. To those who were angered by this, he told the parable of the Prodigal Son (*see right*). Each of the characters in this parable has significance: the younger son represents sinners; the father exemplifies God's compassionate response to those who are repentant; the older son embodies the self-righteous attitude of those who want to keep their good things for themselves, such as the religious leaders – chief priests, scribes, and elders – and their false piety. The parable can be seen as both a reproach and an appeal to people to think again.

By telling the parable of the Sheep and the Goats (*see right*), Jesus asked his listeners to consider the criterion of judgment. He asked them to do all they could to help those in need since, whatever they did, they did for Jesus himself. Those who had served the needs of others would be rewarded with eternal life in God's presence; those who failed God's judgment would be condemned.

The characters in the parable of the Pharisee and the Tax Collector (*see right*) are approaching caricature. Through the story, Jesus attacks the self-righteousness of the Pharisee for believing himself to be virtuous and for regarding others, including the tax collector, with contempt. Jesus declares that God welcomes the humble sinner but rejects anyone who is proud.

The parable of the Tenant Farmers (*see right*) is a thinly veiled attack on the religious leaders who refused to accept Jesus' authority (*cf.* Mark 11:27–28). The tenants' stubborn indifference to the claims of the landowner, culminating in his son and heir being killed, is indefensible. Their action prompts the question, *"when the owner of the vineyard comes, what will he do to those tenants?"* (Matt. 21:40). God will punish them and others will take their place. Although the leaders of Israel recognized this stinging indictment of them (Mark 12:12), they failed to heed the parable's warning.

The setting for the parable of the Good Samaritan (*see right*) was a dialogue between Jesus and a lawyer about the Law. Jesus congratulated the lawyer on being able to cite the commandments to love God and love your neighbor as the heart of the Law. However, the lawyer then probed further into the issue about who should be included in the term "neighbor." Jesus interpreted the word to include everybody in need, rather than just "fellow countrymen," and also attacked the long-standing Jewish prejudice against the Samaritans.

# JESUS'
# PARABLES

### THE PRODIGAL SON

*LUKE 15:11–32*

The parable of the Prodigal Son begins with a man who had two sons. The younger son asked for his share of the inheritance – tantamount to wishing his father dead – and traveled to a far country where he wasted his money on dissolute living. The country was struck by a severe famine, and the son ended up in the desperate situation of feeding pigs. Tired and hungry, he returned to his father and offered to work as a slave. His father, instead of reacting with anger, welcomed his son back into the family and gave him the best robe (a symbol

*LUKE 15:12*

*LUKE 15:13*

*LUKE 15:15*

*LUKE 15:20*

*LUKE 15:22–24*

A 19th-century Chinese interpretation of the Prodigal Son.

LUKE 15:29

LUKE 15:32

of honor), a ring, and sandals (the mark of a free man), and held a feast to celebrate his return. However, the older son complained that he had been unfairly treated, for, unlike his brother, he had never disobeyed his father. Despite the older son's protestations, the father forgave his younger son.

## THE SHEEP AND THE GOATS

MATT. 25:31–46

MATT. 25:31

MATT. 25:32

MATT. 25:35

MATT. 25:41

This parable envisages a time after Jesus' Resurrection *"when the Son of Man comes in his glory"* to judge the nations. Jesus tells his disciples that God will separate people from one another *"as a shepherd separates the sheep from the goats."* Those who had offered food, water, clothing, care, and shelter to Jesus in his time of need would be granted eternal life; those who had not offered help would be sent into eternal

MATT. 25:40, 45

punishment: *"Truly I tell you, just as you did it [or did not do it] to one of the least of these, you did it [or did not do it] to me."*

## A PHARISEE AND A TAX COLLECTOR

LUKE 18:9–14

LUKE 18:11

LUKE 18:13

LUKE 18:14

In this parable, a Pharisee and a tax collector went to the Temple to pray. The Pharisee, a strict adherent to the Law, paraded his piety by thanking God that he was not like other people. The tax collector worked for the Romans and was classified with sinners as one who flouted the Law. He admitted that he had sinned, but displayed humility by asking God to be merciful. Confounding the audience's expectation, it was the tax collector who was forgiven his sins.

## THE TENANT FARMERS

MATT. 21:33–41

LUKE 20:9–16

MARK 12:1–9

MARK 12:1

MARK 12:2

MARK 12:3–5

MARK 12:6

MARK 12:8

In the parable of the Tenant Farmers, Jesus told a story about a vineyard. The vineyard owner traveled to another country, leaving it in the hands of tenants. At harvest time, the owner sent successive servants to collect his share of produce from the vineyard. The first servant was beaten, the second beaten and insulted, and the third killed. Finally, the landowner sent his son to the vineyard, believing that he would win the respect of the tenants. However, they refused to accept his authority and, realizing that he was the heir to the vineyard and that they could claim his inheritance, they killed him too.

## THE GOOD SAMARITAN

LUKE 10:30–37

LUKE 10:30

LUKE 10:31–32

LUKE 10:33–35

In this parable, a man from Judea was traveling on the long descent from Jerusalem to Jericho, a route notorious for robbers. He was attacked, beaten, and left by the road. Both a priest and a Levite passed by him on the other side of the road without stopping. In contrast, a Samaritan, a traditional enemy of the Jews, demonstrated compassionate love by helping the man in his need. The Samaritan attended to his wounds and took him to a nearby inn to recuperate for the night, even paying for the room himself.

For further reading see bibliography numbers: 32, 33, 106, 119, 244, 386, 430, 714, 833, 840

# GALILEE

*Jesus spent most of his life and his years of public ministry in Galilee. Many of his best-known miracles, such as the feeding of the 5,000 and the changing of water into wine, took place in this region.*

### GALILEE
Divided into Upper and Lower Galilee, this Jewish region was surrounded on all sides by non-Jewish territory – Greek cities such as Caesarea Philippi and Tyre. The Sea of Galilee, a large freshwater lake 12½ miles (20km) long by 7 miles (11km) wide, gave the region natural protection from these largely Gentile areas.

GALILEE was the northernmost region of Palestine in Jesus' time. He grew up here in the town of Nazareth, before moving to Capernaum on the northern shore of the Sea of Galilee for his public ministry.

Josephus, the Jewish historian who became governor of the region in 66CE, records 204 villages and towns in Galilee, making it a densely populated area. He also remarks on the richness of the soil and that most people lived in villages and worked the land. Jesus is never recorded as going into Galilean cities; until he goes to Jerusalem, all his teaching is in a rural setting. Many of his parables, such as that of the Sower, or the Lost Sheep, are set in this rural environment, enabling his teaching to be accessible to his listeners.

Fishing on the Sea of Galilee was a vital source of employment for many; Jesus' disciples Peter, James, and John all worked as fishermen before meeting Jesus. The Gospels portray a lake capable of producing terrifying storms (Luke 8:22–25) and abundant provision through an outsize catch of fish (John 21).

### LOWER AND UPPER GALILEE
*Lower Galilee was dominated administratively by Sepphoris and Tiberias, while Upper Galilee retained a largely independent rural village culture. Jesus moved between a few minor towns and the country-side, preaching to those who had left the cities to follow him.*

### THE SEA OF GALILEE
*Described as the Sea of Galilee by Mark and Matthew, Luke gives it its original name, Lake Gennesaret. It was also called the Sea of Tiberias and the Lake of Tarichaeae after two of the more important towns on its shores.*

# GALILEAN LIFE

**Most Galileans earned their living by fishing, farming, or tending animals.**

Although both Josephus and Pliny mention the fertility of the land and describe the variety of agricultural produce and plentiful supply of fish, many people worked as poor tenants and sharecroppers. Poverty drove many to the towns in the hope of a better life. Galileans were later reported as being ignorant country peasants who did not observe the Law and were not good Jews.

John's Gospel seems to confirm this view: for example, the Jewish leaders mock the Pharisee Nicodemus for thinking that a prophet could possibly come from Galilee. One rabbi, who spent 18 years in Galilee, is reported as saying, "Galilee, Galilee, you hate the Torah." Yet recent studies have shown that Galileans were noted for their attachment to Jerusalem and the Temple.

## UNDER ROMAN RULE

At the time of Jesus, Galilee was governed by Herod Antipas, who ruled from 4BCE to 39CE (p.279). Herod's main city was that of Sepphoris, 3 miles (5 kilometers) north of Nazareth, though he later moved to Tiberias, a town he started to build in 19CE on the shores of the Sea of Galilee. Towns such as Sepphoris and Tiberias would have had a strong Greek influence, but to Jews in Galilee living outside the cities, their own Jewish culture was more important. Although they were physically cut off from Judea by Samaria, the Galilean Jews continued to travel to Jerusalem for the pilgrimage at Passover (Luke 2:41–52). There were many synagogues throughout the region, and the Pharisees who lived in the area would have been meticulous in their observance of the Torah and written traditions.

## THE POST-BIBLICAL ERA

In post-biblical times Galilee remained a Jewish stronghold, and many Jews fled Judea to Galilee after the Second Jewish Revolt failed in 135CE. The academy of Jamnia, where prominent rabbis gathered, moved close to Haifa, and many important Jewish texts, such as the Palestinian Talmud, were produced there. A Christian presence continued in Galilee until its sixth-century CE conquest by Arabs, but despite Jesus' ministry there, it has been less significant to Christians than Jerusalem.

### GALILEE IN THE JEWISH SCRIPTURES

According to the book of Joshua, this region was divided up among five tribes of Israel. Many of the original occupants continued to live there. The prophet Isaiah referred to it as *"Galilee of the nations"* (Isa. 9:1), many years before much of the Northern Kingdom and most of its inhabitants were taken into exile (pp.146–47). The countryside through Galilee also inspired many of Israel's poets and prophets. The mountains of Hermon and Tabor praise God in Psalm 89:12, while Mount Carmel in the west of Galilee, near the Mediterranean, and the area of Bashan join in the mourning after the conquest of the invading Assyrians described in Isaiah 33:9. Mount Carmel was also the scene of confrontation between Elijah and the prophets of Baal, recorded in 1 Kings 18.

# CAPERNAUM

*A place of some significance in Jesus' day, Capernaum became, for a time, Jesus' home, and he performed many reported miracles there.*

Located on the northern shores of the Sea of Galilee, Capernaum was the fishing village where Jesus is said to have preached more sermons and performed more miracles than in any other place (e.g., Matt. 8). The remains of a synagogue visible today date back to the early fourth to fifth centuries CE, but there is also evidence of an earlier building beneath these ruins, possibly dating from the first century CE. Although archaeological work on this smaller building is still in progress, it is thought that it was in this synagogue that Jesus taught and mixed with other Jews (Mark 1:21–28; Luke 4:33–37).

**The ruined synagogue at Capernaum.**

For further reading see bibliography numbers: 310, 568, 579, 644, 672

# MIRACLES

*In biblical times, miracles were understood as "deeds of power" by God, anticipating God's coming in strength to overthrow evil. This power of God is the foundation for the many stories of Jesus performing miracles.*

IN the Hebrew Scriptures and in biblical times, miracles were understood as special signs of God's presence as savior or judge, rather than divine interruptions of the laws of nature. The important question was not whether a miracle had happened, but what such an astonishing event meant in relation to God's purposes. The miracles were intended to show how God would, one day, restore the blessing of peace in Israel and among the nations. In the New Testament, Jesus' miracles demonstrated that he was the expected Messiah, and that God's promise of a new kingdom is about to dawn.

## JESUS THE HEALER

One of the surest details we have concerning Jesus is that he performed acts of power, healing those with faith – Jews and Gentiles, men and women, rich and poor. Jesus cured many conditions, including fevers (Mark 1:30), paralysis (Mark 2:3), blindness (Mark 8:22), deafness, and speech impediments (Mark 7:32), together with various anatomical (Luke 13:11), dermatological (Mark 1:40), and gynecological complaints (Mark 5:25). The evangelists distinguished between these cures and exorcisms, where restoration to health required the expulsion of evil spirits. In addition, resuscitations were recorded (Mark 5:21–43).

> **" The blind receive their sight, the lame walk, the lepers are cleansed, the deaf hear, the dead are raised, and the poor have good news brought to them. "**
>
> (Matthew 11:4–5)

Although scientific knowledge can now explain how some of these cures came about, this does not affect Jesus' effectiveness as a healer, which resulted from his ability to communicate power directly from God through himself, thus effecting release from disease and restoration to wholeness. Words of healing and physical touch were his usual means of action (Mark 1:25, 41; 2:10–11; 5:41), although he also used substances (e.g., spittle; Mark 7:33; 8:23; John 9:6).

Faith, whether the expectant trust of patient and supporter (Mark 2:5; 5:36; 9:24), or the doubt-free conviction of Jesus himself (Matt. 17:14–20; Mark 11:22–24), was also vital and often stressed as the reason for the return to health (Mark 5:34; 10:52). The sick were often found on the margins of society in quarantine: laws of purity rendered many sick people unclean, preventing them from being able to participate in public worship (Mark 5:1–5; 10:46). Restoration to health was vital, therefore, if they were to be reintegrated into community life.

For Jesus, as in the Bible, God was the source of all well-being (Exod. 4:1–9; 2 Kgs 5:7; Job 5:18; Eccles. 38; cf. John 20:30–31; Acts 2:22). So thanksgiving to God for healing was a normal response (Ps. 30; Luke 17:11–19). It was believed that disease resulted from sin, whether as a consequence of sinful action or as a punishment from God (cf. Luke 13:10–17;

**HEALING OF THE PARALYZED MAN (LUKE 5:18–25)**
*Jesus often healed through forgiveness. In Capernaum he told a paralyzed man to stand up and walk, for his sins had been forgiven (see overleaf).*

# JESUS' MIRACLES IN THE GOSPELS

*Works of power (Greek, dunamais) that point to God are also called signs (especially in the Gospel of John) and wonders (especially in Acts).*

| | MATTHEW | MARK | LUKE | JOHN |
|---|---|---|---|---|
| **HEALINGS** | | | | |
| A Leper: | 8:2–3 | 1:40–42 | 5:12–13 | |
| A Centurion's Servant: | 8:5–13 | | 7:1–10 | |
| Peter's Mother-in-Law: | 8:14–15 | 1:30–31 | 4:38–39 | |
| Two Gadarenes: | 8:28–34 | 5:1–15 | 8:27–35 | |
| A Paralyzed Man: | 9:2–7 | 2:3–12 | 5:18–25 | |
| A Woman with a Hemorrhage: | 9:20–22 | 5:25–29 | 8:43–48 | |
| Two Blind Men: | 9:27–31 | | | |
| A Man Dumb and Possessed: | 9:32–33 | | | |
| A Man with a Withered Hand: | 12:10–13 | 3:1–5 | 6:6–10 | |
| A Man Blind, Dumb, and Possessed: | 12:22 | | 11:14 | |
| A Canaanite Woman's Daughter: | 15:21–28 | 7:24–30 | | |
| A Boy with Epilepsy: | 17:14–18 | 9:17–29 | 9:38–43 | |
| Bartimaeus, and another Blind Man: | 20:29–34 | 10:46–52 | 18:35–43 | |
| A Deaf and Dumb man: | | 7:31–37 | | |
| A Man Possessed at the Synagogue: | | 1:23–26 | 4:33–35 | |
| A Blind Man at Bethsaida: | | 8:22–26 | | |
| A Woman Bent Double: | | | 13:11–13 | |

| | MATTHEW | MARK | LUKE | JOHN |
|---|---|---|---|---|
| A Woman with Dropsy: | | | 14:1–4 | |
| Ten Lepers: | | | 17:11–19 | |
| Malchus' Ear: | | | 22:50–51 | |
| An Official's Son at Capernaum: | | | | 4:46–54 |
| A Sick Man at the Pool of Bethesda: | | | | 5:1–9 |
| A Man Born Blind: | | | | 9 |
| **NATURAL MIRACLES** | | | | |
| Calming the Storm: | 8:23–27 | 4:37–41 | 8:22–25 | |
| Walking on Water: | 14:25 | 6:48–51 | | 6:19–21 |
| Feeding the 5,000: | 14:15–21 | 6:35–44 | 9:12–17 | 6:5–13 |
| Feeding the 4,000: | 15:32–38 | 8:1–9 | | |
| Coin in a Fish's Mouth: | 17:24–27 | | | |
| A Fig Tree Withered: | 21:18–22 | 11:12–26 | | |
| A Catch of Fish: | | | 5:1–11 | |
| Water Turned into Wine: | | | | 2:1–11 |
| Another Catch of Fish: | | | | 21:1–11 |
| **RAISING THE DEAD** | | | | |
| Jairus' Daughter: | 9:18–25 | 5:22–42 | 8:41–56 | |
| A Widow's Son at Nain: | | | 7:11–15 | |
| Lazarus: | | | | 11:1–44 |

John 9:1–3), so that healing and forgiveness were intimately linked (Ps. 32:3–5; Mark 2:1–12). Comparable acts of healing were attributed to such figures as the Jewish charismatic Hanina ben Dosa and the Greek philosopher Apollonius of Tyana, both of whom lived in the first century CE. But Jesus' acts of healing were different. They were a fundamental expression of the good news of God's liberating presence among people.

## THE SIGNIFICANCE OF THE MIRACLE STORIES

Each miracle story in the Gospels is important far beyond the question of "what exactly happened." In a strict sense, we can never know the answer to that, because we have no other accounts beyond those of the Gospels, and it is clear that whatever the original event may have been, the Gospel writers told the stories to draw out the meaning of what happened. An example is the feeding of the 5,000 (*see overleaf*). While Mark and Matthew attribute to Jesus the miraculous feeding of crowds of both 5,000 and 4,000 (Mark 6:35–44; 8:1–9; Matt. 14:13–21; 15:32–38), Luke

and John concentrate on the story of the feeding of the 5,000 alone (Luke 9:12–17; John 6:5–13). The stories resonate with the biblical accounts of the miraculous feeding of the Israelites by God through Moses in the wilderness (Exod. 16), and of the band of 100 prophets at Gilgal by Elisha (2 Kgs. 4:42–44). Jesus is portrayed not just as a great prophet like Moses and Elisha; but even greater the fulfillment of all God's saving actions on behalf of the people.

Thus the story is not just an attempt to prove Jesus' divinity in the style of certain kinds of apologetics. Nor is it one of a morally improving kind about the example of Jesus in feeding the poor. Much more, it is a narrative of messianic significance. The feeding is a sign that the cries of God's leaderless people have been heard, and that the messianic shepherd-king Jesus has come to rescue them. Jesus knows that this rescue will cost him his life. This is why in John's version Jesus identifies the bread as his own flesh, and why the miraculous feedings soon came to be interpreted in Eucharistic terms (cf. John 6:52–58). Another example of messianic significance is the miracle of Jesus walking on water (*see overleaf*).

For further reading see overleaf

*(Cont.)* The miracle of Jesus walking on water follows immediately after the miraculous feeding and ends with a comment that links the two episodes together: *"They were utterly astounded, for they did not understand about the loaves"* (Mark 6:51–52). Jesus is revealed to the terrified disciples in the boat on the stormy sea as a divine being, one who stills storms (4:35–41) and walks on water (6:45–52). Therefore they need not be afraid. The master who called them to follow him has the power to deliver them in time of need and adversity. The background is once again biblical: God, the creator of land and sea, is the One who *"trampled the waves of the Sea"* (Job 9:8) and gave Israel safe passage through it (Exod. 14–15; Ps. 107:23–32). Now God has sent the Son, the Messiah, to deliver Israel once again. The story is a revelation of Jesus' divine authority and a summons to faith: *"Take heart, it is I; do not be afraid"* (Mark 6:50).

## THE PURPOSE OF THE MIRACLE STORIES

Some miracles (those which apparently suspend the laws of nature on which the universe depends) may seem problematic if one considers that Jesus mediates the effect and consequence of God through his own, unequivocally human, life. Without commenting on what God can and cannot do in the created order, the Incarnation (*pp.412–13*) is contradicted if the universe is put on hold for some particular incidents. But to assume this may miss the point of what the Gospel writers were doing. They used the stories available to them, not to reconstruct the life of Jesus but to reconstruct the lives of those who need the effect of God, now as much as then, for their healing, forgiveness, and encouragement. Whatever originally happened, the miracle stories point beyond themselves to the meaning of Jesus in the purposes of God. Thus the writers do not use the stories to prove "the truth of Jesus," because Jesus refused to perform supernatural feats to authenticate his credentials (Matt. 12:38–39).

Their truth is in revealing the power of God in the present, as much as in the past. When the Israelites needed to be delivered from slavery in Egypt, and God's overriding purpose was marked in signs and miracles, so Jesus' acts of power demonstrate God's overriding command of all things. As such, miracles form a part of his proclamation of the kingdom of God – in John, they are called "signs." In addition, while Jesus' exorcisms demonstrate the outworkings of God's victory over the forces of evil, his acts of healing realized Jewish hopes that God would intervene once more in history to restore God's people to wholeness and peace. As a result, Jesus gave his disciples the authority to perform miracles after his death, and Acts 2:43 records that *"many wonders and signs were being done by the apostles"* as part of the early Church's pattern of evangelism.

# JESUS'
# MIRACLES

## FEEDING OF THE 5,000

The Gospels describe many of the different miracles Jesus performed: the casting out of evil spirits; healing the sick; raising the dead; and having power over the forces of nature.

*MATT. 14:15–21*
*MARK 6:35–44*
*LUKE 9:12–17*
*JOHN 6:5–13*

One of the best known of Jesus' nature miracles is the feeding of the 5,000 on the shores of Lake Galilee. (Matthew and Mark's Gospel include the feeding of the 4,000 as well as the 5,000, whereas Luke and John concentrate on the feeding of the 5,000 alone; *see p.343.*)

*LUKE 15:20*

Jesus had gone to Lake Galilee to be alone, but the people flocked from the towns and villages to meet him. When Jesus saw them, he had compassion for them and healed the sick, talking to them and answering their questions. When evening came the disciples went to him and said, *"This is a deserted place, and the hour is now*

*MARK 6:35*

*late; send the crowds away so that they may go into the villages and buy food for themselves."* But Jesus told the disciples that the people could stay and be fed there. The disciples could not understand this because the only food the people had were five loaves and two fish. Jesus ordered the

*MARK 6:41*

disciples to organize the people into groups of hundreds and fifties and then *"taking the five*

Jesus calms the storm.

*loaves and the two fish, he looked up to heaven, and blessed and broke the loaves, and gave them to his disciples to set before the people; and he divided the two fish among them all."* The crowd ate its fill and the disciples were astonished to find that 12 baskets of food were collected as remainders.

MARK 6:43

## CALMING STORMS

Jesus' control over the forces of nature is further exemplified by his ability to calm storms and still the waves. When Jesus was out in the boat with his disciples a fierce storm arose on the sea. The frightened men woke Jesus saying, *"Lord, save us! We are perishing!"* Jesus rebuked them for their lack of faith, then he spoke to the waves and the wind and calmed the storm. They could not believe their eyes and said to themselves, *"What sort of man is this, that even the winds and the sea obey him?"*

MATT. 8:23–27
MARK 4:37–41

MATT. 8:25

MATT. 8:27

Another time, the disciples were out alone in their boat when night fell and a strong wind blew up. They became afraid as their boat was tossed around in the stormy sea. Jesus, who had stayed behind to pray, knew that they were distressed and he went toward them, walking on the surface of the water. The disciples were amazed at what was happening, believing that they were seeing a ghost. But Jesus reassured them saying, *"Take heart, it is I; do not be afraid."* The disciples took him into the boat, and the strong winds died down.

MATT. 14:22–27
MARK 6:47–51

MATT. 14:25–26

MATT. 14:27
MARK 6:50

## JESUS HEALS THE PARALYZED MAN

When Jesus was staying in Capernaum, the crowds at his door were so great that four men carrying a paralyzed man on a stretcher found themselves unable to reach him. So they made

LUKE 5:18–25
MARK 2:3–12

A modern reconstruction of the distribution of the loaves and fishes.

a hole in the roof of the house and lowered the paralyzed man gently down into the room. When Jesus saw him he said, *"Son, your sins are forgiven."* In spite of the disapproval from the Jewish leaders and the Pharisees, who believed that only God had the power to forgive sins, Jesus turned to the paralytic and said, *"I say to you, stand up, take your mat and go to your home."* The crowds were amazed to see the man get up and walk.

MARK 2:5
LUKE 5:20

MARK 2:11

## THE RAISING OF JAIRUS' DAUGHTER

Jairus, the head of a local synagogue in Galilee, pleaded with Jesus to return to his home and heal his dying daughter. When Jesus reached the house he saw people wailing and crying and said to them: *"Why do you make a commotion and weep? The child is not dead but sleeping."* They laughed at him, but Jesus went inside with Peter, James, John, and the girl's parents, took the girl's hand, and said to her: *"'Talitha cum,' which means, 'Little girl, get up!'"* and she got up. Jesus ordered the onlookers not to tell anyone what they had seen.

MARK 5:22–42
MATT. 9:18–25

MARK 5:39

MARK 5:41

For further reading see bibliography numbers: 134, 268, 273, 275, 385, 451, 452, 466, 504, 548, 608, 745

# "JESUS THE MESSIAH"

*In Hebrew Scripture, mashiach ("messiah") means "anointed one." It was a sign of divine commissioning and authorization, and kings, priests, and sometimes prophets were anointed. Christians believe that Jesus is the answer to messianic expectations, the longed-for savior.*

WAS Jesus the Messiah of Jewish expectations? One messianic hope was the Jewish belief that God would send a divinely commissioned figure to deliver the Israelites from the oppression of other nations: such was the experience of the small nation of Israel throughout much of its history. There was, however, no single, clearly defined Jewish messianic hope, and there were other visions of a new age that featured no messianic figure at all.

## THE DAVIDIC DYNASTY

In Jewish tradition, the most important of the anticipated messianic figures was that of a royal Messiah, another David: *"A shoot shall come out of the stump of Jesse, and a branch shall grow out of his roots. The spirit of the LORD shall rest on him, the spirit of wisdom and understanding, the spirit of counsel and might, the spirit of knowledge and the fear of the LORD"* (Isa. 11:1–2; cf. 2 Sam. 7:12–14; Ezek. 34:24; 37:25; Jer. 23:5; for this belief, based on the undertaking in Jewish Scripture that the dynasty of David would continue forever, *see p.123*). For Jews, the word *Messiah* became almost synonymous with the notion of a king and was eventually applied to the idea of a future king, whose reign would

**THE RISEN MESSIAH**
*This 19th-century Ethiopian reliquary depicts the disciples' realization of who Jesus really was after his Resurrection.*

❝ The days are surely coming, says the LORD, when I will raise up for David a righteous Branch, and he shall reign as king and deal wisely, and shall execute justice and righteousness in the land. ❞

(Jeremiah 23:5)

be characterized by everlasting justice, peace, and security. It included the expectation that the Roman oppressors of the Jews would be driven from Israel and that the kingdom of God would be fully reestablished by military means. The Gospels link Jesus to the fulfillment of the prophecy for a hoped-for royal leader through his claimed descent (Matt. 1:1–16; Luke 3:23–37; *see right*). Such hope for a son of David features in the Psalms of Solomon 17, the collection of hymns from the first century BCE, and also in some Dead Sea Scrolls from Qumran (1QSa. 2:12; 14:20; 4QFlor. 1:10–13; *pp.290–91*).

Since priests were commissioned by anointing, messianic hope often included a priestly figure (Zech. 4); the priestly sect located at Qumran was searching for a priestly Messiah (1QS 9:11). Jesus was not from the tribe of Levi (*pp.102–3*), so the issue of Jesus as a priestly Messiah is never raised. Hebrews argues for a different kind of priesthood for Jesus: *"a high priest, one who is seated at the right hand of the throne of the Majesty in the heavens"* (Heb. 8:1). Less well-defined were various expectations of the arrival of a future prophet: the return of Elijah (Mal. 4:5); or a "prophet like Moses" (Deut. 18:15, 18); or an unnamed prophet, as in Isaiah

61:1–2. Whether the figure "like a Son of Man" mentioned in the vision in Daniel (7:13–14) is related to these expectations is unclear. It is debatable whether this was a specific angelic figure or a more general symbol of the faithful being vindicated beyond death. Jesus called himself Son of Man, but not as a messianic title (p.348).

## JESUS IN THE GOSPELS

The Gospels show that, at the time of Jesus, there was a sense of heightened expectation of the Messiah's arrival: Luke and John both record the questioning of whether John the Baptist was the Messiah (Luke 3:15–17; John 1:20–21). Matthew's Gospel opens with *"an account of the genealogy of Jesus the Messiah, the son of David, the son of Abraham"* (Matt. 1:1); Luke's Gospel traces Jesus' genealogy back through King David to Adam himself (Luke 3:23–38). The Gospel writers also echo biblical references to a messianic figure: the feeding of the 5,000 in Mark 6:32–44, and Jesus' entry into Jerusalem (Mark 11:1–11). In Greek, the language of the New Testament, *Christos* means Messiah. By calling Jesus "Christ," his followers showed that they had accepted him as Messiah.

In the only recorded conversation referring explicitly to messiahship, the implication of Jesus' response to the question of whether he was the Messiah was that he did not welcome the title: *"'But who do you say that I am?' Peter answered him, 'You are the Messiah.' And he sternly ordered them not to tell*

> **❝** So the Jews gathered around [Jesus] and said to him, 'How long will you keep us in suspense? If you are the Messiah, tell us plainly.' Jesus answered, 'I have told you and you do not believe.' **❞**
>
> (John 10:24–25)

*anyone about him"* (Mark 8:29–30). He was probably unwilling to be categorized as the hoped-for royal military leader. In his interview with Pilate, he evaded the suggestion that he was the king of the Jews. The idea that Jesus was a prophet, fulfilling the longing that the drought of prophecy might be ended, was popular but was not given much prominence in the records. But Jesus himself seems to have drawn on at least one messianic passage from Isaiah 61:1 to interpret his own mission (Luke 4:18–19; cf. Matt. 11:5; Luke 6:20).

## JESUS AND THE JEWS

For Jews, the claim to be the Messiah depends on whether signs in Scripture of the proposed Messiah exist. The Christian claim that Jesus was Israel's expected Messiah focuses primarily on his death and Resurrection. The early Christians pointed to texts that could be applied to the Messiah's sufferings, as in Psalms 22, 55, 69, and 88, and in the Suffering Servant of Isaiah 53. That Jesus was "Christ crucified" and had "died for our sins in accordance with the Scriptures" (1 Cor. 1:3 and 15:3) was among the earliest Christian preaching. By the time Paul wrote his letters to the different churches within 20 to 30 years of the Crucifixion, the title "the Christ" had already become more or less a proper name: "Jesus Christ." This suggests that the claim that Jesus was the Messiah quickly became established among the first Christians.

# MESSIANIC CLAIMS

*It is possible that there were several others at or near the time of Jesus who claimed to be a messiah, or even the Messiah, the Christ.*

The Dead Sea Scrolls (*see main text*) envisage a "messiah of Aaron" (a priestly figure) and a "messiah of Israel," but no one is claimed as either of those figures. The Jewish historian Josephus (*Antiquities* 14:159) records the success of Ezekias (Hezekiah) in leading a large troop to military success on the borders of Syria (until captured and executed in 49CE), and some have seen Ezekias as a messianic claimant, but Josephus calls him simply "a leader of robbers." However, that was Josephus' way of describing any activists against Rome (since he wrote his work to help Romans understand the troubles that led to the First Jewish War).

Josephus knew very well that there were many, whom he dismissively called "impostors and deceivers," who induced the mob to follow them promising "unmistakable marvels and signs." One was an Egyptian prophet who, declaring that he was a prophet, summoned the people to the Mount of Olives and promised that he would cast down the walls of Jerusalem (*Antiquities* 20:167ff.). Acts 5:36ff. mentions Theudas and Judas, who led rebellions and were executed, but again, nothing is said about their being messianic claimants, although Theudas, it is said, "claimed to be somebody." Josephus (*Antiquities* 20:97ff.) also mentions "a certain worker of magic [or "impostor"] named Theudas," who claimed to be a miracle-working prophet and was executed, but it is not clear if Josephus is talking about the same person.

During the Second Jewish War against Roman rule in 132–135CE, the claim of messiahship became a divisive issue. The leader of the revolt, Simon Bar Kokhba, was hailed as the Messiah by Rabbi Akiba, one of the leading rabbis of the day. Christian Jews were placed in the position of having to choose between Jesus as the Messiah and the national religious hero, Bar Kokhba. The parting of the ways thus became inevitable.

**For further reading see bibliography numbers:** 109, 138a, 172a, 395a, 553, 876

## THE ACCOUNTS OF JESUS'

# ENTRY INTO JERUSALEM

*The Gospels describe Jesus' entry into Jerusalem, for what proved to be the last time, with a strong note of celebration. Jesus continued his ministry in the city, driving buyers and sellers out of the Temple, knowing that it would all lead to a testing encounter with the authorities.*

*JESUS HEALS AND TEACHES: MARK 10*

LEAVING Galilee, Jesus traveled with his disciples through Judea to Jerusalem, teaching and healing as he went. He knew (and the crowds saw) that, through his ministry, he was bringing the power and effect of God to bear on many lives in need of healing and forgiveness. He also knew that he had go to Jerusalem (the Greek in the Gospels uses a strong word, *dei*, "it is necessary"), because only there could a decision be made by the authorities as to whether he was truly a teacher of God's word (*see p.356*). Jesus knew what the outcome of that inquiry was likely to be. He was aware that he, as much subject to death as anyone else, had to suffer, and he predicted this three times. Yet he believed that he would be vindicated by God, so he called himself the Son of Man. In the Bible this means "humans subject to death" and also "the faithful who will be vindicated by God beyond death" (Dan. 7). Jesus put both together: he would be put to death but had faith that he would be vindicated. So, in what proved to be the last week of his life, Jesus approached the city

*JESUS' PREDICTIONS: MATT. 17:23*

*MATT. 20:18*

*MARK 7:31–33*

*MARK 9:31*

*MARK 10:32–4*

*LUKE 9:22, 44*

*LUKE 18:31–33*

Crowds celebrated as Jesus rode into Jerusalem.

just before Passover began. When they reached Bethphage and Bethany, near the Mount of Olives in Jerusalem, Jesus sent two of his disciples to a nearby village to fetch a colt. They did as he asked, and Jesus rode into Jerusalem. Excited crowds celebrated and spread their cloaks on the road before him (in John they spread palm branches). They knew what Jesus had done: even as he left Jericho, Jesus healed a blind man (known as Bartimaeus in Mark's Gospel).

*JESUS ENTERS JERUSALEM: MATT. 21:1ff. MARK 11:1ff. LUKE 19:28ff. JOHN 12:12ff.*

*MARK 10:46–52*

## CLEANSING THE TEMPLE

Jesus entered the city amid scenes of shouting and singing. Then he went into the Temple to carry out a public demonstration: he began to drive out those who were buying and selling things, quoting from Hebrew Scriptures. The meaning of his symbolic actions (*see opposite*) is drawn out in the way the Gospels tell the story. (For theological reasons, John placed Jesus' cleansing of the Temple earlier in his Gospel.) Every day after that, Jesus taught in the Temple, and the crowds there were amazed by his teaching.

*ISA. 56:7 JER. 7:11*

*JOHN 2:13ff.*

*JESUS TEACHES IN THE TEMPLE: LUKE 21:37–38*

## FULFILLING THE PROPHECY

The Gospels all portray Jesus' entry into Jerusalem as the fulfillment of a biblical prophecy. In John's Gospel, Jesus finds a young donkey and rides it; only later do the disciples reflect and connect this incident with Zechariah 9:9: *"Lo, your king comes to you; triumphant and victorious is he, humble and riding on a donkey, on a colt, the foal of a donkey."* In the Synoptic accounts, Jesus is more deliberate and exercises what seems to them to be the right of a ruler to requisition transportation. This hint of Jesus' authority is made explicit by Matthew's quotation of Zechariah (Matt. 21:5); in his very literal sense of fulfillment Jesus rides both the ass and her colt! John quotes a shorter version of this text, while Mark and Luke only allude to it.

## CLOTHES AND BRANCHES

In the Synoptics the crowds spread their cloaks on the road out of respect for Jesus. John alone refers to palm branches. Luke does not mention any branches, but Matthew and Mark describe the crowds also spreading cloaks and branches on the road. This recalls the Maccabean stories of the purification of the Temple in 167BCE and its cleansing in 141BCE: on both occasions palm branches were carried in celebration (2 Macc. 10:6–7; 1 Macc. 13:51).

## THE ACCLAMATIONS.

As Jesus rode by, the crowds shouted "Hosanna" ("save us") and "Blessed is he who comes in the name of the Lord," phrases taken from Psalm 118 (vv.25–26), which were sung in processions at Jewish festivals. The evangelists' additional references to Jesus as the "son of David" and "King of Israel" bring out the messianic significance of Jesus' arrival in Jerusalem at a time when popular hopes for liberation ran high. In the way that the evangelists tell the story, Jesus deliberately staged this symbolic act (*pp.198–99*). As part of a pilgrim procession it was probably low-key, but for those with eyes to see, it revealed the nature of Jesus' authority as Israel's Messiah and his desire to reclaim Jerusalem for God.

## JESUS' ACTION IN THE TEMPLE

Jewish expectations about the future of the Temple provided the backdrop for Jesus' demonstration inside the Temple grounds. The Prophets foresaw a day when traders would be removed from the Temple (Zech. 14:21) and its priesthood purified (Mal. 3:1ff.). Some contemporary Jewish groups expected the Messiah to restore the Temple, while others anticipated an entirely new structure. Jesus is unlikely to have cleared the Temple of every last trader. His action against those who sold sacrificial animals to the pilgrims and exchanged Temple coinage cannot be called a total

---

# THE MOUNT OF OLIVES

*This hillside is mentioned in the New Testament as a place of significance in the last week of Jesus' life.*

The Mount of Olives today.

A thickly wooded hillside in Jesus' day, the Mount of Olives runs parallel to the east side of Jerusalem, a short distance from the city. According to Zechariah 14:4, God would arrive there at his coming to liberate Jerusalem. The Mount would split, and the time of salvation would then be inaugurated and Israel's enemies defeated. So the Mount of Olives was an eschatological symbol (i.e., concerned with final events).

Jesus' entry into Jerusalem from the Mount of Olives heightened the messianic significance of what followed (Mark 11:1ff.). The enigmatic saying in Mark 11:23 may have alluded to the splitting of the Mount: *"Truly I tell you, if you say to this mountain, 'Be taken up and thrown into the sea ...'"* Jesus' discourse about the future was delivered from the Mount of Olives, as if to invite his disciples to see the coming of God in the distressing and destructive events that lay ahead (Mark 13:3ff.). After his arrival in Jerusalem, Jesus spent every night before his arrest on the hillside (Luke 21:37). His ascension into Heaven from the Mount of Olives (Acts 1:12) stresses the eschatological significance of his Passion, Resurrection, and the coming of the Spirit.

---

"cleansing" since the system of sacrifice was deeply embedded in what God commanded. Jesus' words draw on Isaiah 56:7, *"... their burnt offerings and their sacrifices will be accepted on my altar; for my house shall be called a house of prayer for all peoples"* and Jeremiah 7:11, *"Has this house, which is called by my name, become a den of robbers in your sight?"* and thus connect his symbolic action with his prediction of the Temple's destruction in Mark 13:2: *"Not one stone will be left here upon another; all will be thrown down."* As with Prophets of old, especially Jeremiah, this was but one instance of an institution that would fall under God's judgment, to be replaced by an entirely new kind of Temple: *"We heard him say, 'I will destroy this temple that is made with hands, and in three days I will build another, not made with hands'"* (Mark 14:58; John 2:19–21).

For further reading see bibliography numbers: 58, 85, 553, 678, 833

## THE ACCOUNTS OF THE

# LAST SUPPER

*The night before he died, Jesus shared a final meal with his disciples. This Passover seder, which Jesus invested with special meaning, led to the Christian practice variously described as "the Lord's Supper," "the breaking of bread," or "the Eucharist."*

PREPARATIONS FOR
THE MEAL:
MATT. 26:17–19
MARK 14:12–16
LUKE 22:7–13

MATT. 26:20–21
MARK 14:18
LUKE 22:14–16

BREAKING THE BREAD:
MATT. 26:26
MARK 14:22
LUKE 22:19

SHARING THE WINE:
MATT. 26:27
MARK 14:23–25
LUKE 22:20

A S the Passover approached, Jesus sent two disciples to prepare an upper room where they could eat the Passover meal together. He knew that his way of living and teaching had put his life in danger, and at this seder with his disciples he made it clear that he did not expect to eat with them again on earth. He foretold that one of his disciples would betray him; then he took the bread, blessed it, broke it, and gave it to them saying *"This is my body"* (*see also box, right*). Then he took a cup of wine, gave thanks, and gave it to them as the blood of a new Covenant (*see right*). Jesus told them that he would not drink wine again until the coming of the kingdom of God (*pp.332–33*). After the meal they went out to the Mount of Olives (*pp.352–53*). According to the Synoptic Gospels, the Last Supper was a Passover meal, the annual commemoration of liberation from slavery in Egypt and of the covenant relationship with God (*pp.60–61*). Unlike the Synoptics, John places the "Last Supper" a day earlier than the Passover feast: this means that Jesus is crucified (according to John) as the Passover lambs are being slaughtered. None of the Gospel accounts mention the foods essential for Passover (*pp.68–69*) and John has no mention of the bread and wine; Jesus teaches about his flesh and blood after feeding the 5,000. John's account shows Jesus as a servant who washes his disciples' feet and teaches that his death is a gateway to eternal life.

MATT. 26:30
MARK 14:26
LUKE 22:39

JOHN 13:1; 18:28

JOHN 6:48–58

JOHN 14–17

This Passover meal was the final time that Jesus shared a fellowship meal with his disciples before his Crucifixion.

# JESUS' WORDS

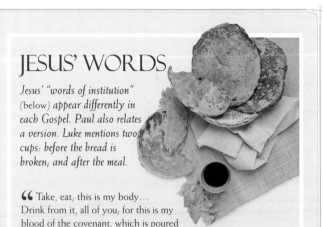

*Jesus' "words of institution" (below) appear differently in each Gospel. Paul also relates a version. Luke mentions two cups: before the bread is broken; and after the meal.*

66 Take, eat; this is my body… Drink from it, all of you; for this is my blood of the covenant, which is poured out for many for the forgiveness of sins. 99 *Matt. 26:26–28*

66 Take; this is my body … This is my blood of the covenant, which is poured out for many. Truly I tell you, I will never again drink of the fruit of the vine until that day when I drink it new in the kingdom of God. 99 *Mark 14:22–25*

66 Take this [cup] and divide it among yourselves; for I tell you that from now on I will not drink of the fruit of the vine until the kingdom of God comes … This is my body, which is given for you. Do this in remembrance of me … This cup that is poured out for you is the new covenant in my blood. 99 *Luke 22:17–20*

66 This is my body that is for you. Do this in remembrance of me … This cup is the new covenant in my blood. Do this, as often as you drink it, in remembrance of me. 99 *1 Cor. 11:24–25*

## WHAT DID THE LAST SUPPER MEAN?

In biblical times, meals meant more than just eating food: they were important in Jewish life, and in Jesus' ministry as a celebration of God's sustenance and saving presence (Mark 2:18–20; 6:31–44; 8:1–10; Luke 7:31–35). Meals were also seen as a tangible demonstration of God's acceptance of and reconciliation with humankind, and they signified a foretaste of the abundant blessings that communion with God would one day yield. His "feasting rather than fasting" approach to life and his willingness to eat with outcasts and those on the margins of society, were distinctive characteristics of Jesus. This "Last Supper" also anticipated the eschatological banquet mentioned in Old Testament passages. The four Gospels and 1 Corinthians each draw out different themes. As a result, various interpretations, from the sacrifice of the Mass to a memorial meal, continue today in different denominations of the Christian Church (*cf. pp. 418–19*).

## INTERPRETATIONS OF JESUS' WORDS AND ACTIONS

Some Christians understand Jesus' words as identifying his body and blood with the bread and wine, and thus interpreting his forthcoming death as a new Passover sacrifice. In this sense, Jesus bequeathed to his followers a way of enabling them to participate in his new act of salvation.

Other Christians believe that Jesus intended the bread and wine to *represent* his body and blood, not to actually *become* them: the prospect of drinking blood would be abhorrent to a Jew (Deut. 12:15–28); to the Jewish mind, the word "body" would not refer to a part of Jesus (in contrast to his blood) but to the entire person. Jesus may well have wished to associate "wine" with "covenant" and only indirectly with "blood" (*cf. "This cup is the new covenant in my blood"*). From this viewpoint, Jesus' words and actions associated with the bread become a commissioning of the disciples and an entrusting to them of his vocation (i.e., his life). His words and actions associated with the wine celebrate a new relationship with God shared by Jesus and his disciples (and soon to be ratified by his death) – a relationship expressed in their common meals during Jesus' ministry and one that he would not share with them again until their reunion in God's kingdom (Mark 14:25).

Whatever the different understandings of the Last Supper, it is clear that these were solemn actions and words from one on the edge of death. In this sense, Jesus' actions seem to resemble those of the Prophets, who put their most urgent and important messages into acted form (*pp. 196–97*). In the most dramatic way possible, Jesus gave himself to the continuing lives of his disciples and for "many" (*see box*), a countless multitude of believers, to be with them to the end of time.

For further reading see bibliography numbers: 178, 403, 405, 428, 554

THE ACCOUNTS OF JESUS'

# BETRAYAL & ARREST

*The Gospel accounts of the betrayal and arrest of Jesus are full of drama, and they set the scene for Jesus' subsequent interrogation and Crucifixion. The key figure in the story is Judas Iscariot, identified as "one of the twelve," who agreed to betray Jesus.*

As Judas betrays Jesus with a kiss, one of the disciples, attempting to defend him, slices off the ear of the High Priest's slave.

*JUDAS AND THE*
*CHIEF PRIESTS:*
*MATT. 26:14–16*
*MARK 14:10–11*
*LUKE 22:3–6*

AS the Gospels tell the story, Judas had previously approached the chief priests to see what they would offer him if he were to betray Jesus to them. His arrangement with them was reached just before Passover. So the Passover meal that Jesus shared with his disciples was fraught with foreboding: Jesus already knew who would betray him and who would deny him.

*MATT. 26:30*
*MARK 14:26*
*LUKE 22:39*

After the meal and a hymn, Jesus and his disciples went out to Gethsemane, on the Mount of Olives. There Jesus told them that they would all desert him that night. Although Peter refuted Jesus, saying he would never desert him, Jesus told him that before the cock crowed the next morning, Peter would deny him three times.

*MATT. 26:33–35*
*MARK 14:27–31*
*LUKE 22:31–34*
*JOHN 13:36–38*

## JESUS PRAYS

Telling his other disciples to sit and wait in the Garden of Gethsemane, Jesus took Peter, James, and John aside and asked them to stay awake and sit near him while he prayed.

*MATT. 26:36–38*
*MARK 14:32–35*

Having struggled with the disciples at the meal, Jesus now struggled with God in prayer, preparing himself for what was to come. He pleaded that if it was God's will, the burden of what was about to happen might be taken away from him. Then he saw the disciples sleeping and admonished them. Again he prayed and again found them asleep. After praying for a third time, he woke them once again.

*JESUS PRAYS:*
*MATT. 26:39*
*MARK 14:35–36*
*LUKE 22:41–42*

*MATT. 26:40–46*
*MARK 14:37–42*

## JESUS' ARREST

As Jesus was speaking to the three disciples, Judas appeared leading an armed crowd. These were presumably members of the chief priests' Temple guard, although John implies that Roman soldiers were present as well. According to the Synoptics, Judas singled Jesus out with the prearranged signal of a kiss.

*MATT. 26:47–49*
*MARK 14:43–46*

*JOHN 18:3*

As Jesus was seized, one of his followers attempted armed resistance and struck the slave of the High Priest with his sword, cutting off his ear. John identifies the disciple as Simon Peter and the slave as Malchus. Jesus, however, turned to Simon Peter and told him to put his sword away. Luke adds the detail that Jesus then touched the ear of the wounded slave and healed him. Jesus also reprimanded the crowd of captors for using their swords and clubs as if he were a robber, and he stressed that his way was not that of violence.

*JESUS IS ARRESTED:*
*MATT. 26:51–56*
*MARK 14:47–50*
*LUKE 22:47–48*

*JOHN 18:10–11*

*LUKE 22:51*

## THE YOUNG DISCIPLE

According to Mark and Matthew, the disciples took flight and left Jesus to his fate. However, Mark narrates the curious incident of a young disciple who followed Jesus, was seized by the guards, and escaped naked, leaving behind his only covering, a "linen garment." Perhaps this disciple symbolizes all the disciples, his nakedness a sign of their shame in abandoning Jesus. Jesus was now alone (later we read that Peter followed at a distance) and was taken to be interrogated first by Caiaphas and the Council of the elders.

*MATT. 26:56*
*MARK 14:50*

*MARK 14:51–52*

# THE PAVEMENT

According to John's Gospel, Jesus' trial before Pilate (p.355) reaches a climax when the Jews refuse to accept Jesus' release. They even make an implied threat against Pilate, effectively forcing his hand, accusing him of not acting as a "friend of Caesar" in wanting to let Jesus go: *"When Pilate heard these words, he brought Jesus outside and sat on the judge's bench at a place called The Stone Pavement, or in Hebrew Gabbatha"* (John 19:13). About to pass sentence, Pilate sits on the judgment seat to make the action official. The importance of the event is indicated by the specified time and place: the time is noon on the day of preparation before Passover when lambs were sacrificed; the place is the Pavement. Some think this is a pavement of massive stone slabs in the area of what was the Fortress Antonia. Others think Pilate's praetorium, tribunal, and the Stone Pavement were all in King Herod's palace on the western hill of Jerusalem (pp.360–61).

## JUDAS THE BETRAYER

The most dramatic aspect of Jesus' arrest is the fact that one of those closest to him played a leading role in bringing about his death. That Jesus anticipated this is clear from his words at the Last Supper: *"Truly, I tell you, one of you will betray me, one who is eating with me"* (Mark 14:18). Jesus' enemies were not just his opponents – the Herodians, Pharisees, chief priests, and Romans – they were among his own supporters as well.

Why Judas took the initiative to act as an agent of the chief priests and elders in arranging Jesus' arrest is never fully explained. Mark's Gospel implies that Judas' action was precipitated by an incident at Bethany, when Jesus was extravagantly anointed by a woman: *"But some were there who said to one another in anger, 'Why was the ointment wasted in this way?'"* (Mark 14:3–9).

For Matthew, the motive was greed: *"What will you give me if I betray him to you?"* (Matt. 26:15; cf. Mark 14:11; John 12:4–6). Luke and John both attribute Judas' action to demonic possession: *"Then Satan entered into Judas"* (Luke 22:3; cf. John 13:27). Judas gets caught up in the battle between God and Satan and thus becomes an instrument of Satan. We are not told why it is Judas who gets taken over like this, but the idea of his greed may be a clue: John 12:6 says he was in charge of the common purse, but stole from it. Others have suggested that Judas wanted to provoke a revolutionary act against the Romans. "Iscariot" may mean "of the Sicarii" (an assassin, p.289), but it may also mean "from Kerioth." Judas is the only disciple who was not a Galilean.

Matthew reports that Judas received his 30 pieces of silver, then repented, returned the money, and hanged himself. Acts 1:18–19 records that he bought a "Field of Blood" and died after a fall when "all his bowels gushed out."

For further reading see bibliography numbers: 67, 85, 254, 323, 366, 453, 526, 614a

# THE ACCOUNTS OF THE
# TRIAL OF JESUS

*The Gospels record two main interrogations, one by Jewish authorities, the other by Pontius Pilate.*
*That Jesus was taken to his execution after some kind of process is clear, but the process itself is not: the*
*Gospels do not tell the same version of events. The following narrative amalgamates the accounts.*

JESUS IS SENT TO
CAIAPHAS' HOUSE:
MATT. 26:57
LUKE 22:54
MARK 14:53

JOHN 18:13—14,
19—24

JESUS knew that his arrival in Jerusalem would bring the issue of the authority of his teaching to a head and could lead to his death. After his arrest and the flight of his disciples, and while it was still night, Temple priests began to investigate Jesus' teaching on the grounds that it threatened the authority of the Temple. According to John, there was a hearing before Annas, a former high priest (6–15CE); Jesus was then sent on to the High Priest Caiaphas.

Peter had halted his flight and came back to see what was happening. About three o'clock in the morning (the time of the cockcrow in Jerusalem in April), bystanders asked Peter three times if he knew Jesus, and three times he denied it, despite being recognized.

The night investigation was not a trial but a way of establishing that Jesus refused to acknowledge the authority of the High Priest in matters of teaching and Torah (*see also p.356*). Jesus remained silent before Caiaphas, making

PETER'S DENIALS:
MATT. 26:69—75
MARK 14:66—72
LUKE 22:55—62
JOHN 18:15—18,
25—27

Jesus was interrogated by Caiaphas, the High Priest, before he went before the Roman governor.

it obvious that he did not accept the High Priest's authority. Caiaphas asked Jesus: *"Are you the Messiah, the Son of the Blessed One?"* Jesus replied, *"I am; and you will see the Son of Man seated at the right hand of the Power and 'coming with the clouds of heaven.'"* Caiaphas tore his own clothes, calling it a blasphemous claim.

*JESUS BEFORE THE HIGH PRIEST: MATT. 26:59–68*

*MARK 14:55–63*

Although the Council condemned Jesus as worthy of death, there was one other possible source of authority for Jesus' teaching: that he might be directly inspired as a prophet. They tested him by demanding that he prophesy, but Jesus remained silent.

*MARK 14:64*

*MARK 14:65 LUKE 22:63–65*

## JESUS BEFORE PILATE

According to Luke, the next morning there was a full session of the Council of the elders – the chief priests and teachers of the Law – although Matthew and Mark say that it was an informal meeting to decide what to do next. They decided to take Jesus to Pontius Pilate, the Roman governor, accusing Jesus of stirring up seditious trouble against Rome. Matthew adds an account of the death of Judas. Then proceedings began before Pilate as to whether Jesus was king of the Jews.

*LUKE 22:66–71*

*MATT. 27:1–2 MARK 15:1 JOHN 18:28*

According to Luke, Pilate realized that Jesus came from Galilee and was thus under the jurisdiction of Herod. Pilate sent Jesus to Herod. Again Jesus remained silent.

*LUKE 23:6–12*

According to John, Jesus entered into serious discussion with Pilate about the nature of God's kingdom. Pilate sought to exercise his privilege of releasing a prisoner at Passover. He asked a crowd that had gathered whether they wanted him to release *"the king of the Jews"*; they demanded instead that Pilate release Barabbas, a rebel who had committed murder. Pilate's wife, Matthew says, sent a message imploring him, as the result of her dream, not to execute a just man. Pilate publicly washed his hands of the crowd's decision. According to John, Pilate made a further attempt to release Jesus, which was met with cries that Jesus should be executed. He made a final appeal to Jesus but then handed him over. Jesus was crowned with thorns as king of the Jews and mocked by the soldiers, then led away to be crucified.

*JOHN 18:29–40*

*PILATE TALKS TO THE CROWDS: MATT. 27:11–26 MARK 15:2–15 LUKE 23:13–25*

*JOHN 19:13–16*

## THE SANHEDRIN

The word *"sanhedrin"* means "council," either a local council (Matt. 5:22; 10:17; Mark 13:9; Acts 22:5), or the supreme council, which was located in Jerusalem, the capital (Matt. 26:59ff.). Sanhedrins were used extensively by the Romans as ruling councils. Thus the council investigating Jesus may have been more a political than a religious body. Later Jewish sources speak of a more religious court of 70 or 71 Jewish elders, which they regarded as the predecessor of the rabbinic Bet Din (a "house of judgment," or a court). This religious court decided major cases and disputed points of law. But the accounts of this body (notably in the *Sanhedrin* tractate of the *Mishnah*) were written much later: the *Mishnah* was written down and codified in c.200CE, although it conserved past traditions. There are major discrepancies between the later (Mishnaic) Sanhedrin and the Gospel accounts.

Using Mark's story as an example:
• Jesus was tried by night before the High Priest and the Sanhedrin (Mark 14:53–15:1); the *Mishnah Sanhedrin* 4:1 specifies that trials by night are illegal. In Luke, the proceedings begin during the day (Luke 22:66).
• Mark mentions that Jesus is tried in the High Priest's house; the *Mishnah Sanhedrin* 11:2 states that trials should take place in the Sanhedrin's official chamber, the Hall of Hewn Stones. Luke's account, however, leaves this possibility unspecified.
• Jesus was tried on the eve of Passover (cf. Mark 14:1–2, 12ff., 15:6; John 18:28); *Mishnah Sanhedrin* 4:1 specifies that trials cannot take place before a festival.
• The Jewish charges against Jesus seem ambiguous: charges of blasphemy (for which the traditional penalty was stoning) were added to the initial crime of speaking out against the Temple, making messianic claims (which Jewish Law did not recognize as a crime), and being a false prophet.
• The High Priest seeks to get Jesus to incriminate himself; in the *Mishnah* this is illegal, the judge being the counsel for the defense.
• And finally, Jesus is condemned at the first session of the Sanhedrin, despite the *Mishnah* stating that the verdict in capital cases must be delivered in a statutory second session.

From this, it seems likely that there was no formal "trial" of Jesus but rather an investigation of Jesus by a council working with the Romans. It cannot be read as "the Jews" or "Judaism" condemning Jesus. In fact, the Gospels make it clear, by the way they tell the story, that if there was a trial going on, it was not really Jesus who was on trial, but those who accused him and those (the Romans) who implemented the sentence. Indeed, in John's Gospel (pp.312–13) it is the world itself that is on trial.

For further reading see overleaf

# THE TRIAL OF JESUS

*The trial(s) and death of Jesus are matters of fact better attested than any other events*
*like them in the ancient world. The basic record in Mark and Matthew is*
*supplemented in Luke and John.*

AFTER the investigation by members of the Sanhedrin (*p.355*), Jesus was taken before Pontius Pilate. He was sentenced to death and crucified by the Romans on a political charge of sedition.

The Temple authorities had investigated whether Jesus' teaching had authority or not, as they did in the only other case of execution in the early Church, of which some record survives (Stephen in Acts 6:8ff.). According to Deuteronomy 17:8–13, which specifies that anyone who refuses the judgment of the High Priest on disputed matters must be executed, the Temple authorities were bound to carry out an investigation. To have discordant teaching on matters of Torah would destroy Israel, and that was why Jesus was questioned repeatedly when he came to Jerusalem for the last time.

In both Jesus' case and that of Stephen, the charge against them was that they or their teachings were threatening the Temple. On that basis, it would be wrong to speak of a "trial" of Jesus by the Jews. There was only an investigation by members of a council to see whether Jesus was indeed refusing the authority of the High Priest. By remaining silent, Jesus did so. They invited him to show independent authority by acting as a prophet, but again Jesus remained silent.

Capital punishment may not have been a prerogative of the Temple authorities at this time (John 18:31), so the Roman authorities had to be involved. On this account it was not "the Jews" who executed Jesus: the Temple authorities, against whom many other Jews protested greatly (*see pp.288–89, 291*), took action to deal with a resistant teacher who insisted on his own authority from God against the High Priest. From

**JESUS BEFORE THE CROWDS**
*This 19th-century painting depicts the moment when, according to the Gospel accounts, Pilate asked the crowd whether Jesus should be released. The crowds cried out instead for the release of Barabbas, a notorious prisoner. When Pilate asked the people what he should do with Jesus, they answered that he should be crucified. When Pilate asked what "evil" Jesus had done, they "shouted all the more, 'Let him be crucified!'"*

# THE ROMAN TRIAL

*After his interrogation by the Sanhedrin (pp.354–55), Jesus was brought to trial before the Roman governor of Judea.*
*This trial was the climax of the opposition to Jesus that had been been growing throughout his ministry.*

Pontius Pilate was governor of Judea under the emperor Caesar from 26–36CE. As procurator, he was in charge of the large Roman army based at Caesarea and a detachment garrison at the Fortress Antonia in Jerusalem. He had power to appoint high priests and overturn capital sentences passed by the Sanhedrin, which then had to be submitted to him for ratification.

Like the Jewish hearing, the Gospel accounts of Jesus' trial before Pilate raise several issues:
• Jesus' trial before Pilate presupposes that although the Sanhedrin could condemn Jesus worthy of death, it could not carry out the sentence (John 18:31). Some scholars have questioned this assumption and offered examples of Jewish authorities exercising capital punishment, such as the execution of Gentiles who violated the Temple, or the stoning of Stephen in Acts 7:54–60.
• The Gospels describe Pilate taking a personal interest in his prisoner and, convinced of Jesus' innocence, acting only reluctantly as his executioner.

This portrait clashes with the insensitive and brutal figure depicted by Philo (*Legation to Gaius*, 299–305) and Josephus (*Antiquities*, XVIII 56–62).
• According to the evangelists, it was Pilate's custom at Passover to release any prisoner nominated by the people. However, no other evidence exists for this act of clemency.

In reply, it is argued that the examples offered by those questioning this assumption were exceptional. Jurisdiction over capital cases was jealously guarded by the Romans; it is claimed that in Palestine this jurisdiction was almost exclusively theirs for the first half of the first century CE. The portrait of Pilate that Philo and Josephus painted may be equally tendentious, and the lack of corroborative evidence for the privilege Pilate was reputedly allowed to exercise does not necessarily overrule evidence in John's Gospel.

**Pilate questions Jesus**
*Pilate's question, "Are you the king of the Jews?" is the central focus of the Gospel accounts.*

their point of view, the Temple authorities had no option, since the words of Deuteronomy required them to take action. Jesus' activity as an eschatological prophet and his proclamation of the coming kingdom of God challenged both the Temple (Sadducean) and the Roman authorities. This threat might have been even graver if Jesus' mission were seen – by himself and/or his followers and/or the Jewish masses – as having messianic implications (*cf. pp.346–47*). When Jesus cleared the traders from the Temple, this act may indeed have been the decisive factor that provoked the Temple authorities to act in complicity and have Jesus speedily removed from the scene.

## THE RELIABILITY OF THE SOURCES

Jesus' execution is mentioned in various sources: in the Roman historian Tacitus' *Annals*; in Josephus' *Antiquities* (the *Jewish War*, and Slavonic Additions were almost certainly added later by Christians); in the Jewish medieval *Toledoth Jeshu*; in a Syrian letter of Mara bar Serapion; and in Christian sources, above all the New Testament. The four Gospels

share common material, mainly following the order of Mark, but each other Gospel has variations and some additions, such as Pilate's wife and the death of Judas in Matthew, Jesus before Herod in Luke, and Jesus speaking with Pilate in John.

How, then, are the Gospel accounts related? One view is that Mark is the primary account and that Matthew, Luke, and John added variations. This could be either because the latter, especially Luke and John, had additional information of historical worth, or because they had a point to make about the reasons for Jesus' death. However, apparent discrepancies in the Gospel accounts, while important, do not rule out these accounts as historically suspect. Together, the Gospels agree in showing that some Temple authorities failed to recognize Jesus' true, that is, divine status, and that they involved the local Roman authorities in dealing with him. The Gospels show the connections between particular prophecies and the Passion, but that does not mean events were "invented" to fit the prophecies. It is because of these events that Christians saw their anticipation in the Bible. The Bible has influenced the Gospels or their sources, but it did not create them.

For further reading see bibliography numbers: 44, 45, 127, 169, 351, 366, 411, 453, 526, 818

# THE ACCOUNT OF JESUS'
# CRUCIFIXION

*The Gospels portray the full horror of Jesus' Crucifixion and death. Crucifixion was*
*a Roman punishment, the usual method of execution for*
*slaves or rebels.*

MATT. 27:27–32
MARK 15:16–21
LUKE 23:26–32
JOHN 19:16–17

AFTER Pilate had sentenced Jesus, the Roman soldiers stripped him, put a robe on him, a crown of thorns on his head, and a reed in his right hand. They spat on him and mocked him as "King of the Jews." Then they put his own clothes on him again and led him away to be crucified. As they went out they

SIMON OF
CYRENE CARRIES
JESUS' CROSS

came across a man called Simon, from Cyrene, and forced him to carry Jesus' cross (the Romans usually forced the convicted man to carry his own wooden beam, as John's Gospel records).

## JESUS CRUCIFIED

AT GOLGOTHA:
MATT. 27:33–37
MARK 15:22–32
LUKE 23:33–43
JOHN 19:18–24

When they reached the place called Golgotha, meaning "Place of a Skull," on a hill outside Jerusalem, the soldiers crucified Jesus. Then they divided his clothes between them by casting lots, thus

PS. 22:18

fulfilling a prophecy. Afterward, they nailed a board above his head that read: "This is Jesus, the King of the Jews" (John states that Pilate arranged the inscription). The soldiers then sat and kept watch over Jesus. Two bandits were also crucified that day, one on either side of Jesus. People who passed by

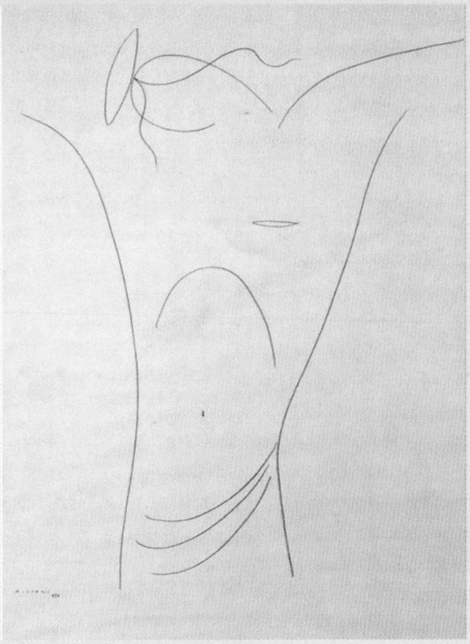

The crucified Jesus.

Jesus mocked him for claiming he would destroy the Temple and build it again in three days. The bandits also began to taunt him. According to Luke, only one of the bandits mocked Jesus; the other rebuked his fellow criminal and said to Jesus, "*Jesus, remember me when you come into your kingdom.*" Jesus assured him that he would be with him that day in Paradise.

LUKE 23:40–43

## JESUS' DEATH

According to Mark's Gospel, Jesus was crucified at nine o'clock in the morning. The Synoptics record that at noon the sky went dark until three in the afternoon. Then the Temple curtain was torn in two, and Jesus cried out to God as he died. Matthew describes how at this point the earth shook, rocks split, and the resurrection of the dead occurred. John recounts that Jesus died before the soldiers could break his legs and hasten his death, fulfilling the Hebrew Scripture that "*none of his bones shall be broken.*" The crowd that had gathered went home in anguish, leaving the women among Jesus' disciples to watch him being let down from the cross.

MATT. 27:45–61
MARK 15:33–47
LUKE 23:44–55

THE TEMPLE
CURTAIN SPLITS

MATT. 27:51–53

JOHN 19:31–37

EXOD. 12:46
NUM. 9:12
PS. 34:20

**THE PIETA**
*This 20th-century Japanese painting shows Jesus being received from the cross after his death, attended by his mother, Mary, and Mary Magdalene – two of the women who watched him die.*

## CRUCIFIXION IN THE ANCIENT WORLD

Crucifixion was widely used in the ancient world as a method of execution. It was common in the Greek empire from the late fourth century BCE and was first mentioned in Roman sources around 200BCE.

Roman rule extended crucifixion into Palestine in the first century BCE: the Roman governor of Syria had 2,000 Jews crucified in 4BCE. There is evidence from the Dead Sea Scrolls that some Jews occasionally used crucifixion; the Temple Scroll, 11QT (*p.290*), makes it part of the covenant legislation of Moses. In 4Q169, the Commentary on Nahum, "hanging" is probably a synonym for crucifixion. The Romans used crucifixion to control their subjects. It was reserved for the lower classes, particularly slaves, criminals, and foreigners, although there is some evidence that on rare occasions Roman citizens found guilty of high treason were crucified. By enforcing the rule of law, crucifixion proved to be an effective weapon against resistance, and in Palestine it was used to keep Jewish nationalism in check.

Descriptions of actual crucifixions are rare, which is not surprising in view of the widespread abhorrence of the practice. Compared to other contemporary reports, the brief and restrained accounts of Jesus' Crucifixion in the Gospels are relatively full and provide important historical evidence for some of the details of crucifixion. The Romans had their victims stripped and flogged before being crucified in a public place, where they were ridiculed by spectators. Because crucifixion neither damaged internal organs nor resulted in excessive bleeding, death was slow and painful. Breathing became increasingly difficult, and the victims eventually died through a combination of asphyxiation, shock, hunger, and thirst *(see box)*. Sometimes they were

left unburied, and their bodies fell prey to birds and animals. The Jews found crucifixion particularly horrifying in view of Deuteronomy 21:23: *"anyone hung on a tree is under God's curse."* Although this originally referred to the practice of hanging a dead criminal on a tree, by the first century CE it was applied to the victims of crucifixion, as Paul recognized in Galatians 3:13. Crucifixion was so shameful that it never became a symbol of martyrdom and resistance among Jews.

Yet from the earliest records onward in the New Testament, Jesus' death on the cross was not seen as a disgrace. It was seen as the purpose and direction of his life, and it was interpreted as an atoning sacrifice, reconciling humans with God. What Jesus did during his life, in his work of reconciliation, is now made possible for all. Jesus' final utterances on the cross are known as the "Seven Last Words":

*"'Eli, Eli, lema sabachthani?' that is, 'My God, my God, why have you forsaken me?'"* (Matt. 27:46=Mark 15:34)

*"Father, forgive them, for they know not what they are doing."* (Luke 23:34)

*"Truly I tell you, today you will be with me in Paradise."* (Luke 23:43)

*"Father, into your hands I commend my spirit."* (Luke 23:46)

*"'Woman, here is your son,' and to the disciple, 'Here is your mother.'"* (John 19:26)

*"I am thirsty ... It is finished."* (John 19:28, 30)

## CRUCIFIXION

There were several different methods of crucifixion. Victims might be impaled on, or hung from, a wooden stake; in mass executions, several beams were attached to a scaffold of vertical wooden planks. Often the convicted men were bound and nailed with hands extended over their head. Those convicted were not always crucified upright. When they were, the beam was raised on wooden forks and slotted into a groove, cut either into the top of the upright forming a t-shape, or lower down creating a cross-shape. Once crucified, the victim's feet might be no more than 12in (30cm) from the ground. John's Gospel records that the Romans sometimes broke a victim's legs after a certain period in order to restrict breathing even further and hasten death (John 19:31–32). Sometimes a small wooden crossbar was fixed to the upright beam for the crucified man to sit on. While this gave support and enabled him to breathe, it also prolonged the agony by preventing the collapse of his lungs.

In 1968, the bones of a man in his late 20s, who was crucified before 70CE, were found in an ossuary in Jerusalem (cf. p.363). An iron nail was still in place through his right heel, and although the evidence is difficult to interpret, it suggests that his feet were nailed to either side of the upright stake. The bones of his hands and forearms were undamaged, implying that the victim's arms were actually tied to the crossbeam.

For further reading see bibliography numbers: 85, 351, 390, 526

# HISTORICAL SITES OF
# THE PASSION

*For Christians, the death and Resurrection of Jesus are so important that many attempts have been made to identify the sites where all these events took place. Locating these sites with any certainty, however, is a difficult, if not impossible, task.*

WINDING through Jerusalem is the Via Dolorosa (The Way of Sorrows). It traces Jesus' journey to the cross, and along its route 14 episodes are identified, displayed in some churches as the "Stations of the Cross" *(see box, right)*. However, it is unlikely that this was the same route as that taken by Jesus, and although this does not affect the intention and devotion of pilgrims, it summarizes the difficulties involved in identifying the places associated with his last days. While general areas are often clear, exact identifications are usually impossible to make.

## GETHSEMANE

According to Mark 14:32 and Matthew 26:36, Jesus prayed in Gethsemane before his arrest. According to Luke 22:39, Jesus' arrest took place on the Mount of Olives (east of Jerusalem, *p.349*), while in John 18:1, it took place in the Kidron Valley. Gethsemane is Hebrew for "oil-press," so it would have been closely associated with the Mount of Olives. Several sites are claimed for Gethsemane, but none of them is earlier than the fourth century CE.

## GABBATHA
(THE PAVEMENT)

This word appears in John 19:13 as the place where Pilate examined Jesus: "[Pilate] sat on the judge's bench at a place called *The Stone Pavement, or in Hebrew Gabbatha.*"

**GOLGOTHA**
*It is impossible to determine the exact place of Jesus' Crucifixion, but this hill is one of the sites thought to be where Jesus died.*

**GARDEN TOMB**
*One of the traditional sites of Jesus' burial place has been allotted to this garden tomb found in the 19th century.*

**PILGRIMS AT THE FOURTH STATION**
*According to tradition, Jesus encountered his mother along the route before he was helped by Simon of Cyrene.*

The Aramaic word is the equivalent of the Greek *Lithostroton*. The Jewish historian, Josephus, refers to a paved court adjoining Herod's palace where trials were held, but this has not yet been uncovered by archaeologists. Others have placed the scene in the Fortress Antonia, a Hasmonean stronghold rebuilt by Herod. An extensive pavement was uncovered here (*see also p.353*), including a games board scratched into a flagstone by Roman soldiers (*cf.* Matt. 27:35). But the pavement beneath the convent of Notre Dame de Sion in Jerusalem, once claimed as the Pavement, has since been dated to the second century CE, when Hadrian rebuilt Jerusalem.

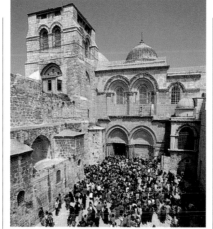

**FORTRESS ANTONIA**
*The Ecce Homo arch of the Fortress Antonia may have been where Pilate examined Jesus.*

debate about the exact line of the city walls at that time. A different site was identified by the British soldier, General Gordon in the 19th century (and is sometimes known as Gordon's Calvary). It lies northeast of the Damascus Gate, on a slight rise that bears a vague resemblance to a skull. This was certainly outside the city walls, but fewer people now support this identification.

## THE TOMB

According to John 19:41, the entombment was close to the place of crucifixion, and there is no reason to question this. So, the two claimed sites for the Crucifixion (*above*) are also said to contain the tomb. The tomb near Gordon's Calvary was discovered in 1867 and is known as the Garden Tomb. This has outside it (as also do other tombs) a groove in which a wheel-like stone might have been rolled to seal and open it (Matt. 27:60; 28:2). But there can be no certainty, especially since Jesus' body was placed hastily in an unprepared tomb. In any case, the tomb was a new one (Matt. 27:60), and it would therefore not have had any established marks identifying it with the family of Joseph of Arimathea.

## GOLGOTHA

The site of Jesus' Crucifixion is named as Golgotha in Matthew 27:33, Mark 15:22, Luke 23:33, and John 19:17. The Aramaic, *gulgalta* (Hebrew, *gulgolat*) means "a skull." The name Calvary comes from the Latin translation of Golgotha, *calvaria*. John 19:20 confirms the custom that executions took place outside the city. Matthew 27:39 suggests that it may have been near a road. The Church of the Holy Sepulchre is built over the place claimed as the site since the fourth century CE. Whether that site was inside the city walls depends on continuing

**GARDEN OF GETHSEMANE**
*It was here, where Jesus prayed after the Last Supper (Matt. 26:36), that Judas betrayed Jesus with a kiss – the signal to the authorities that this was the man who they were seeking to arrest.*

# 14 STATIONS

1 Jesus is condemned to death
2 Jesus bears the cross
3 Jesus falls for the first time
4 Jesus meets his mother
5 Jesus is helped by Simon of Cyrene to carry the cross
6 Veronica wipes Jesus' face
7 Jesus falls for the second time
8 Jesus consoles the daughters of Jerusalem
9 Jesus falls for the third time
10 Jesus is stripped of his clothes
11 Jesus is nailed to the cross
12 Jesus dies
13 Jesus' body is taken from the cross
14 Jesus is laid in the tomb

For further reading see bibliography numbers: 468, 579, 662

# BURIAL PRACTICES

*Rabbi Akiba, martyred in 135CE, said: "Deal graciously with the departed, that you may be dealt with graciously: mourn, bury, and accompany the deceased to the grave." The Jewish way of "dealing graciously with the dead" is reflected in New Testament burial practices.*

WASHING the body of a dead person in preparation for burial was standard practice for both Jew and Gentile; the body could also be displayed (Acts 9:37). According to John 19:40, Jesus was buried "in the burial custom of the Jews," which consisted of washing the body, anointing it with oil or spices, and wrapping it in linen cloths. In the case of Jesus, the Sabbath disrupted some of these preparations (Mark 16:1; Luke 23:56), even though the rabbis permitted preparation of a body on the Sabbath (Mish. *Semahot* 23:5).

As part of the burial procedures, it was usual for mourners, perhaps accompanied by hired pipers, to lament the death of a person (Matt. 9:23; Mark 5:38–39; John 11:19, 33; Acts 8:2). As in the second century BCE, the normal period of mourning in Jesus' time was apparently seven days; John's Gospel describes the mourning continuing four days after the burial of Lazarus (John 11:17–19).

EMBALMMENT
*A body was traditionally prepared for burial by being washed and then wrapped in linen bandages or a sheet, which usually contained aloes and myrrh.*

THE BURIAL AND RAISING OF LAZARUS
*Lazarus, the brother of Martha and Mary, had died and had already been buried for four days when Jesus asked Mary to show him the rock tomb where he was laid. Jesus then raised Lazarus to life as a sign that he had power over death: "...[Jesus] cried with a loud voice, 'Lazarus, come out!' The dead man came out, his hands and feet bound with strips of cloth and his face wrapped in a cloth. Jesus said to [the mourners] 'Unbind him, and let him go'" (John 11:43–44).*

## JEWISH AND ROMAN CUSTOMS

The bodies of Jewish people were buried, not cremated, with the emphasis on a rapid burial. Tacitus, the Roman senator and historian born in c.56CE, relates that it was the Roman custom in the first century CE to cremate the dead, even though burial had been the preferred practice. By the late fourth century CE, burial would again become the custom. The Jewish custom of a rapid burial was based on a command in Deuteronomy 21:22–23 not to leave the body of an executed person overnight upon a tree. Reinforced by the fear of defilement, the burial of Ananias took place within three hours (Acts 5:6–10). The funeral usually took place on the day of death, with the body carried from the home to the burial place on a bier, or frame, rather than in a coffin (although the archaeological evidence from Qumran, for instance, shows that coffins were,

# OSSUARIES

The practice of two burials was widespread in Roman times. The first burial stage was complete once the embalmed body had been laid inside the tomb. Relatives waited for the flesh to decay before collecting the bones into a receptacle known as an ossuary, a short stone coffin 31in (80cm) long. This kept the bones of the dead person together, probably in preparation for the resurrection of the body, although the practice also saved space.

in fact, used). As in the funeral of the boy from Nain described in Luke's Gospel, the bier was followed by the mourning family and others from the town who, if passing a funeral, were expected to join the procession (Luke 7:11–17).

## THE BURIAL PLACE

Bodies were buried according to normal Semitic practice, either in the ground or in rock tombs (Acts 5:6, 9–10; 8:2).

**FUNERAL FLUTE**
*Jewish custom expected that whoever could afford it should hire professional mourners and musicians.*

Having two burials was common practice (*see box, above*). Lazarus' rock tomb was an existing cave with a stone lying against the entrance, but Jesus' tomb was newly hewn and of a type the rich presumably provided for themselves. Archaeological evidence from Jerusalem and Jericho indicates that such rock tombs of the period were of two types: *loculi*, with several niches for bodies hewn from rock around three walls of a chamber (which often also contained a pit); and *arcosolia*, with a bench hewn out of the rock on which the body was placed. Hints in the Gospels indicate that Jesus' tomb was an arcosolium.

## THE UNBURIED DEAD

All cultures placed a high value on the proper disposal of the dead. This was considered to be an act of piety, not exclusively but perhaps especially among the Jews, whereas refusing to bury someone could be the last act of contempt for an enemy, and the lack of burial could feature as one component of a curse. There

**FAMILY ROCK TOMB**
*This family burial cave (1BCE–1CE) is located in Sanhedriya, Jerusalem. It was usual for Israelites to be buried in a tomb that one of their ancestors had acquired generations earlier.*

was a fear of remaining unburied that led in turn, for example, to a fear of being shipwrecked, as Paul was to experience on his voyage to Rome (*pp.400–1*). A death at sea would prevent a proper burial altogether or, at best, entail burial by strangers rather than by relatives.

## MAGICAL RITES

As in many civilizations, there is evidence that some people believed that the unburied dead would be in distress and might therefore disturb the living until they were properly cared for. A proper burial helped protect the living from such threats. The belief that certain people were likely to become restless ghosts, who could then be manipulated by magical means, led to the use of magic and

**ARCOSOLIUM TOMB**
*This well-preserved tomb with a rolling stone is thought to be of the type Jesus was buried in.*

magical rites in connection with burials. One widespread practice was that of depositing "curse tablets," usually made of lead, in graves, in an effort to bring harm to their intended victims. To those aware of such practices, almost any of the different illnesses suffered by various minor characters in the Gospels (*e.g., pp.342–45*) might have come under suspicion of using the dead to harm the living.

For further reading see bibliography numbers: 317, 556, 557, 596, 666, 892

# THE ACCOUNTS OF
# JESUS' RESURRECTION

*Belief in Jesus' Resurrection is the foundation of the Christian faith, the reason why, among the many interpretations of what Jewish faith and practice might be (pp.281, 288–89), Christianity became a new and different religion.*

THE belief that Jesus died on the cross and yet was alive after his death is the reason why the New Testament books were written and why Christianity exists. Although no one witnessed the Resurrection, the event is as real to the New Testament writers as the Crucifixion was.

MARK 16:9–18

Apart from Mark's Gospel, which has no post-Resurrection appearance stories (the original Gospel stops at 16:8), the post-Resurrection stories recorded in the other Gospels complement one another.

MATT. 27:62–66

Matthew's Gospel describes how guards were placed by the tomb after Jesus' burial so that his disciples could not steal Jesus'

MATT. 28:1–7

body. As the first day of the week dawned, Mary Magadelene and the "other Mary" went to the tomb. Suddenly there was an earthquake and an angel appeared, terrifying the guards. The angel

THE WOMEN AT THE TOMB

said that Jesus had been raised from the dead and that the women should tell Jesus' disciples to meet him in Galilee. The Gospel ends with

MATT. 28:16–20

Jesus meeting the disciples in Galilee and commissioning them to teach and baptize

Mary Magadelene mistakes Jesus for a gardener.

throughout the world. In Luke's Gospel, the women went to the tomb and were met by two men "in dazzling clothes," who told them that Jesus had risen. The women returned to the disciples to tell them the news, and Luke adds the account (in some manuscripts) of Peter going to the tomb to verify that it was empty.

LUKE 24:1–12

ON THE ROAD TO EMMAUS

Jesus then appeared to two disciples on the road to Emmaus. When Jesus blessed and broke bread at supper, the disciples realized who he was, and Jesus then vanished from their sight. He later reappeared, invited them to touch him, and then ate some food, instructing the disciples to eat also.

LUKE 24:13–43

John's Gospel describes the story of the two women, Peter, and the "disciple whom Jesus loved" all visiting the tomb; John adds that when Jesus appeared to Mary, she

JOHN 20:1–18

initially mistook him for a gardener. Jesus appeared to his disciples, commissioned them with the gift of the Holy Spirit and convinced Thomas that he was indeed alive. He last appeared to them on the shores of Lake Tiberias.

JOHN 20:19–29

JOHN 21

**SUPPER AT EMMAUS WITH THE DISCIPLES**
*It was only when Jesus blessed and broke bread during supper in the village
of Emmaus that his disciples connected his actions with the Last Supper and
realized who he really was.*

## POST-RESURRECTION APPEARANCES

The earliest recorded claims (pre-55CE) to post-Resurrection
appearances are mentioned by Paul (1 Cor. 15:1*ff.*) in list form.
Mark's Gospel presents the first clear evidence of an empty
tomb story, but the most reliable manuscripts, which
end abruptly at Mark 16:8, give no post-Resurrection
appearances. Later scribes supplied additional textual
endings (Mark 16:9–20 *et al.*), but these are, for the most
part, a summary of appearance stories drawn from the
other Gospels. Separate narrative accounts were added
by Matthew (ch.28) and Luke (ch.24) to Mark's ending.
John's Gospel has additional stories in its concluding
chapter (ch.20) and epilogue (ch.21).

Because of the variety of the Gospel accounts, and
because it is difficult (but not impossible) to reconstruct a
continuous narrative of what happened from the Gospels,
some have argued that claims of the Resurrection were a
way of affirming that the spirit of Jesus was still alive, that
people grieving for Jesus were overcome by mass
hallucination, or that Jesus did not die on the cross but
had fainted and was then revived. However, these views are
far removed from what the New Testament actually says.
People who had no doubt that Jesus had died, and who had
been overwhelmed with grief, were equally overwhelmed by
the realization that he was alive once more. Jesus appeared
to them again in a bodily form that they could identify as
his, but it was not exactly the same body as in his earthly
life. In other words, he had not simply been revived but had
died and risen again.

The fact that the Resurrection happened is supported by
four main areas of evidence or argument: the reliability
of the empty tomb story; the multiple witnesses to post-
Resurrection appearances, which retain a note of total surprise;
the experience of the Christian Church – its very existence
being a major part of the evidence of the Resurrection; and
an absence of satisfactory alternative explanations.

## CONTEMPORARY BELIEFS

The extraordinary nature of the Resurrection can be seen
in the ways in which the New Testament accounts, at that
time, differ from other beliefs in life after death. Such
beliefs were relatively common in the world of the first
century CE, but they were by no means uniform. Greeks
and Romans emphasized the immortality of the soul, while
those who believed in "mystery" religions (*see also pp.376–77*)
invested their faith in gods such as Osiris, Attis, and Adonis,
who, following the cycle of death in winter to new life in the
spring, died and rose again after two or three days. Powerful
individuals, such as the emperor Nero, were also expected to
return from the dead or be reincarnated. Restoring the dead
temporarily to life had been attributed to philosopher-healers
such as Apollonius of Tyana. But none of these resembles the
phenomenon of Jesus being alive after death – an experience
that underlies other New Testament accounts of the
Resurrection as a fact (but without detail), especially in Paul.

Pharisees, but not Sadducees, believed in the resurrection
of the body at the end of time, but this was a relatively
recent tenet. Restoring dead people to life (e.g., Lazarus
in John 11) was attributed to Elijah and Elisha. Elijah was
exempted from death and literally taken up to the sky
(2 Kgs. 2:11). The notion that the dead would rise and
that Elijah, Enoch, or Moses would reappear is found in
apocalyptic literature (*pp.260–61*). Consequently, some
believed that John the Baptist was Elijah *redivivus* (Latin, "
living again"). Others wondered if Jesus might have been
John the Baptist *redivivus*.

Resurrections of the dead were attributed to Jesus and to his
disciples. Among early Christians, the restoration of the dead
to life was seen as a sign that God's kingdom was imminent.
Jesus' Resurrection as "firstborn of the dead" was regarded
as the harbinger of the general resurrection to follow (1 Cor.
15:20). There were, therefore, varied beliefs about the dead
living again. The New Testament record of Jesus' Resurrection is different from them all. It points to the most amazing
event of human history, that Jesus' death is the beginning
of life, not just for himself but for those who are brought
into his body through baptism and faith. From the earliest
records in the New Testament onward, Jesus, a man recently
crucified, is associated with God in such a way that he can
only properly be thought of and approached in ways that
rightly belong to God.

For further reading see bibliography numbers: 10, 68, 111, 118, 121, 139, 350, 373, 606, 614, 790, 883

# THE BEGINNINGS OF
# CHRISTIANITY

The account of the beginnings of Christianity is described mainly in the book of Acts, although Paul's letters also convey some details, not all of which can easily be reconciled with Acts.

The first part of Acts highlights the great diversity of the earliest stages of Christianity after the Ascension of Jesus and the gift of the Holy Spirit coming upon his disciples at Pentecost. The disciple Peter is a dominant figure in the opening chapters. He taught and healed, arousing strong opposition, which resulted in his imprisonment. A dispute between the Hebrew and Hellenist Christians in Jerusalem led to the growth of Christian missions outside Israel, such as Philip's mission to Samaria where he performed acts of healing. The importance of the Apostles, not only in their acts of healing but also in the process of conversion, was vital: in Acts 8:14–24 the first converts had been baptized, but they did not receive the Holy Spirit until Peter and John were sent by the Apostles to lay hands on them. The final episode in this important sequence of events describes the conversion and baptism of the Ethiopian eunuch by Philip.

From chapter 9 onward Paul emerges as the central figure in Acts, following his dramatic conversion. Paul became involved in the major issue of whether Gentiles should be accepted into the Christian community without keeping Torah or being circumcised. Peter, initially adverse to accepting non-Jews into the Church, was compelled, through a vision, to change his mind on this issue, and went on to convert a Gentile named Cornelius. However, to the end Peter equivocated on this matter, whereas Paul was adamant that the Gentiles should be admitted without first being required to keep the Law. The compromise reached is recorded in Acts 15, but the issue was not settled. The last part of Acts describes Paul's pioneering missionary work in the Mediterranean and his imprisonment in Rome.

# ROMAN EMPIRE

*The Roman empire arose from a policy of gradual territorial expansion. By the time of the emperor Trajan's death in 117CE, the empire had grown to its greatest size, encompassing 40 provinces and almost 2 million square miles (3.6 million square kilometers), half the size of modern-day China. Aqueducts, roads, theaters, amphitheaters, temples, and villas were built, and a single currency, a code of laws, and an elaborate tax system were implemented, all under the authority of the emperor. With the idea that cooperation was more beneficial than conflict, the defeated provincials were allowed to become Roman citizens and thus gained protection from the empire's great army.*

**ROMAN ROAD, POMPEII (ITALIA)**
Roads were constructed by the Roman army and, although useful to commerce, were primarily built to allow the legions easy access within the conquered territories. Most roads had a camber (hump), so that water could drain away.

**AQUEDUCT, SEGOVIA (HISPANIA)**
The engineering skills of the Romans are best exemplified by the huge aqueducts built to bring supplies of water into towns. A Roman official boasted: "Will anybody compare the idle Pyramids … to these aqueducts, these many indispensable structures?" This stone aqueduct probably dates from the time of Augustus (63BCE–14CE).

BRITANNIA

Oceanus Atlanticus
(Atlantic Ocean)

GALLIA

REATIA

NORICUM

PANNONIA

HISPANIA

ILLYRICUM
DALAMATIA

ITALIA
Roma•

MAURETANIA

AFRICA

## THE FORUM, ROME

The political heart of the Roman empire, the forum in Rome contained temples, basilicas, triumphal arches, and courts of law. It was once teeming with citizens hoping to catch a glimpse of the emperor as he rode past in his chariot, with priests offering sacrifices to the gods and orators proclaiming the news of the day.

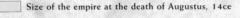

☐ Size of the empire at the death of Augustus, 14ce

☐ Land gained between Augustus' and Trajan's reign, 14-98ce

☐ Land gained under Trajan, 98-116ce

DACIA

MOESIA

THRACIA

MACEDONIA

*Pontus Euxinus*
*(Black Sea)*

BITHYNIA & PONTUS

ASIA

GALATIA

CILICIA

CAPPADOCIA

ARMENIA

ASSYRIA

MESOPOTAMIA

LYCIA

CYPRUS    SYRIA

*Mare Caspian*
*(Caspian Sea)*

*Mare Internum*
*(Mediterranean Sea)*

JUDEA

ARABIA

CYRENE    AEGYPTUS

### HADRIAN'S TEMPLE, EPHESUS (ASIA)

Many Romans actively participated in the imperial cult, whereby the emperor was honored as a deity. All over the empire, temples were dedicated to Roman emperors such as Domitian, Trajan, and Hadrian.

### THEATER, CAESAREA (JUDEA)

Built by Herod the Great to adorn his new city, this impressive theater dates back to the first century CE. Herod completely rebuilt Caesarea, adding to it not only this theater but also an immense harbor (his largest engineering work after the Jerusalem Temple), a hippodrome, and a palace.

**For further reading see bibliography numbers:**
59, 73, 108, 140, 159, 252, 320, 338

# TRADE & TRAVEL

## IN NEW TESTAMENT TIMES

*The Roman invasion of Palestine brought about a peace that allowed merchandise from all over the empire to be traded in and around the region. The Romans built roads and developed great ports that aided international and local trade and allowed people easier travel within the country.*

BY the first century CE international trade in the Mediterranean was firmly in the hands of the Romans. Palestine, a region with limited food produce (its main exports being olive oil and salt mined from the Dead Sea), was opened up to goods from all over the empire and beyond as merchant shipping developed and travel inland became much safer.

Spices, perfumes, grain from Egypt, Italian wines, cottons, silks, and ceramics were only a few of the items that crossed land and sea along the main trade routes and ended up at the principal market centers. In Jerusalem over a hundred different kinds of luxury goods were sold at the market there.

### PRESTIGIOUS PURPLE
*The Phoenicians were renowned for trading an expensive purple-dyed cloth, the color of which was obtained from murex shells. Eventually, the cloth became so highly prized it could be worn only by the emperor himself.*

### THE MARKETPLACE

In the local markets, strict regulations on buying and selling were drawn up to discourage any false dealings, and there were even market inspectors to make sure these rules were carried out. Local currencies, banking systems, and money changers were available for those who arrived from other countries or for the Jews who came to pay their annual Temple tax in Jerusalem.

Special dealers controlled particular products in local areas to operate their own markets, and a trader such as Lydia, mentioned in Acts 16:14 as a "dealer in purple cloth," might have been one of these dealers. She came from Thyatira in Asia Minor, a thriving center of trade and commerce. Archaeological evidence shows that wood and leather workers, tanners, potters, bronze-smiths, and even slave traders were

### AN ESSENTIAL OIL
*Olive oil was a popular trade commodity and the Palestinian region's main export. It was used not only in food preparation but also as a medicine, for applying to hair, and as a base for various lotions. It was also sold as a fuel for lamps.*

### APPIAN WAY
*The Appian Way was the main road that led to Rome from southern Italy. Paul would have traveled along here to reach Rome on his final journey.*

active there, as well as linen workers and dyers. The purple dye they produced came from the madder root, a less expensive version of the purple dye traded by the Phoenicians (*see left*).

Many of the trade activities were organized through trade guilds, most of which were under the patronage of pagan deities. It therefore became very difficult for the Jews and early Christians to trade successfully. Both religious groups faced much opposition from these guilds, since their beliefs conflicted with the markets of certain tradespeople. For example, the silver-smiths of Ephesus relied on selling cult objects and souvenirs to pilgrims at the shrine of Artemis. They found their livelihood threatened by Paul and

# MONEY & MEASUREMENTS

*Three different currencies co-existed in the area around Palestine, while new Roman measures were added to existing ones found in the Hebrew Bible.*

The most common metals used for coinage were gold, silver, copper, bronze, and brass. Most Jewish coinage was bronze, e.g., the *lepton* (Mark 12:42), although at the time of the First Jewish War (*see pp.292–93*) Jews were able to issue their own silver coin, the *shekel*, with which to pay their Temple tax, instead of having to change their money into Tyrian coinage. Greek coins included the silver *drachma* and the *tetradrachma*. Roman coinage was the official imperial money and included the bronze *as*, the silver *denarius*, and the golden *aureus*. The *talent* (Matt. 25:14–30) was not a coin but a unit of weight (approximately 66lb or 30kg) and represented about 3,000 shekels or 12,000 denarii.

Units of length included the *cubit* (20⅞in/530mm), the *orgyria* or *fathom* (6ft/1.85m), and the *stadion* or *furlong* (4849ft/1478m). The Roman *milion* (mile) was measured at a thousand paces and was about 4855ft (1480m) long. Units of capacity included the *quart* (Rev. 6:6), which was about 32oz (905g), and the *bushel* which was equivalent to about eight quarts. In addition to the talent, there was the *litra* (12oz/340g), a unit of weight.

1,000 paces to record the distance from the nearest city. Many of the major roads were also carefully policed, so for the first time people could travel in relative safety. However, it was still hazardous for those traveling in the less populated areas, as seen, for example, on the road from Jerusalem to Jericho in Jesus' parable of the Good Samaritan. Most people traveled on foot, although light carriages (pulled by mules or horses) and heavier ox wagons were also used. Donkeys carried goods as well as people and horses were essential as a swift means of transportation for messengers and soldiers.

At sea and in the more remote mountain and plateau areas, travel was far more difficult and was limited, or ceased completely, during the winter months.

his Christian teachings and were able to exert sufficient pressure to end his ministry there (Acts 19:23–41). The guild of butchers was also affected when it found that sales of animals for sacrificial offerings were diminishing.

## OVER LAND AND SEA

By the first century CE the Romans had set up a comprehensive road system, making travel relatively easy in many parts. Roads ran as straight as possible, were often paved, and had proper drainage. Surveyors were appointed to oversee road-building projects, and milestones were set at

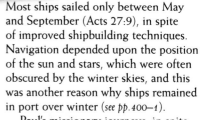

**IMPORTS AND EXPORTS**
*The Romans virtually eradicated piracy at sea, allowing merchant shipping to become more reliable and passage more frequent. Trading ships could be used by travelers, and Paul himself made great use of them on his missionary journeys, undeterred by his three shipwrecks (2 Cor. 11:25).*

**OPEN CART, 1ST CENTURY CE**
*Donkeys or horses were attached to a light cart (either open or covered) and could cover a distance of about 25 miles (40km) a day. They were often used for transporting goods or as a courier service, and traveling on them became easier as the Roman road system developed.*

Most ships sailed only between May and September (Acts 27:9), in spite of improved shipbuilding techniques. Navigation depended upon the position of the sun and stars, which were often obscured by the winter skies, and this was another reason why ships remained in port over winter (*see pp.400–1*).

Paul's missionary journeys, in spite of his shipwrecks, show us that crossing the seas and traveling from country to country was possible and perhaps not even unusual during this period. Improved traveling conditions were in part responsible for helping Christianity spread beyond Palestine to the distant shores of the Roman empire.

**For further reading see bibliography number: 853a**

# STRUCTURE OF ROMAN SOCIETY

*By the first century CE, the Roman empire was nearing the height of its power, its society firmly set into identifiable classes and social ranks. As Christianity spread, so its own structures were influenced by Rome.*

## THE POWER OF ROME

The heart of Roman government was the Senate. Based in Rome, it was presided over by the emperor and was made up of consuls, magistrates, and provincial governors. Outside Rome, the emperor's procurators and governors ruled the provinces (*see pp.278–79*), enforcing Roman law and perpetuating the Roman class system.

ROMAN society consisted of several identifiable social classes (*ordines*). It was a nonegalitarian society based on a system of patronage whereby power and wealth were generally concentrated in the hands of an elite minority. Key values reflected the bestowal of honor and the avoidance of shame.

## SOCIAL RANKING AND MOBILITY

At the upper level of society were the senators, their number fixed by the emperor Augustus at 600. Originally members of the ancient Roman ruling aristocracy, they were recognizable by the broad purple stripe on their togas and their prominence at religious and public ceremonies. The senatorial rank governed the most important provinces and held senior posts in the army. Their backgrounds lay essentially in landownership and farming. Nonetheless, the increasing concentration of power vested in the emperor eventually led to bitter conflicts and the severe reduction of the old senatorial aristocracy during the Julian-Claudian dynasty (Tiberius, Caligula, Claudius, and Nero). Gradually, senators of non-Roman and non-Italian origin emerged, with consequent changes in a broadening of cultural outlook. Just below the senatorial order were the equestrians, or knights. These were not limited in number and historically represented those landowners who could afford to ride into battle on horseback. An equestrian could be so designated if he was of free birth and had a registered income above a certain level. The equestrian order represented an intermediate elite whose careers spanned modest commands in the army, positions of financial administration, and the governorship of minor provinces (e.g., Judea).

ROMAN PALACE AND FORUM IN JERUSALEM
*By the time the Roman governor Pontius Pilate presided over Jesus' trial, Rome's political power had been firmly established in Jerusalem.*

**THE EQUESTRIAN ORDER**
*These knights usually came from rich backgrounds and served in the army or in administration. It was possible for them to rise in social rank and become senators.*

Members of local municipal bureaucracies in the provinces were also a part of the ruling aristocracy. These people had gained their positions of wealth in political and business life. They provided important functions in the ordering of public affairs, the maintenance of buildings, including markets and harbors, and the diplomatic work of embassies. Beneath the aristocracy was the large, amorphous category of freeborn citizens (*plebs*). Having little income, much of the plebeian class fell into poverty, becoming dependent on dole provision of grain and other forms of subsidized state provision, or eking out a marginal existence as day laborers or in the service of wealthier patrons. Despite being freeborn, they had little political importance.

Slaves were the lowest point in the social scale (*see pp.440–41*) and were not permitted any legal rights. It was possible, however, for them to be granted freedom as a reward for service or as a means whereby a patron could retain loyal dependents. Having acquired the status of freedmen, some slaves advanced to high rank. One such freedman was Felix, governor of Judea (Acts 23:26; *see p.279*). Generally, however, social mobility was restricted and the privileges of the aristocracy were closely guarded. Luke 16:19–31 reflects on the wide gulf that was fixed between the wealthy and the poor.

## THE CHRISTIAN HIERARCHY

In the New Testament only Paul is called a Roman citizen (Acts 22:29), but there are several people with Roman names: Achaicus, Fortunatus, and Lucius at Corinth (1 Cor. 16:17; Rom. 16:21), where Gaius seems to have been rich enough to entertain not only Paul but the whole local church (Rom. 16:23).

A major consequence of these structures for Christianity was a shift in the understanding of the Church from being a body – in which all parts are equal under the headship of Christ ("*... you are the body of Christ and individually members of it*" 1 Cor. 12:27) – to one in which hierarchy and the exercise of authority became paramount. By the turn of the first century CE, the model of Christian organization had become quite similar to that of the Roman army, with ministers in ranks from the bishop downward.

### A WOMAN'S STATUS
High-ranking women in Roman society were meant to serve as models of domesticity, through arranged marriages to managing the household, and subject to the authority of their husbands. On the other hand, women wielded considerable influence, and some had wealth, ability, and business acumen in their own right (Acts 16:14; 18:3). The first-century CE fresco above shows a banqueting couple with their female slave – a clear indication of the extreme ends of the social scale a woman could occupy in Roman society.

# 1ST CENTURY-CE ROMAN EMPERORS

*In Roman society, the emperor rose high above the other social classes. Augustus was the first emperor responsible for bringing stability and prosperity to the Greco-Roman world and was also ruler at the time of the birth of Jesus.*

| | | | | | | | | | | Galba, Otho, Vitellius (68–69CE) | | | |
| --- | --- | --- | --- | --- | --- | --- | --- | --- | --- | --- | --- | --- | --- |
| | | | | | | | Tiberius (14–37CE) | | Gaius (Caligula) (37–41CE) | | | Titus (79–81CE) | |
| 30BCE | 20BCE | 10BCE | 0CE | 10CE | 20CE | 30CE | 40CE | 50CE | 60CE | 70CE | 80CE | 90CE | 100CE |
| Augustus (27BCE–14CE) | | | | | | | Claudius (41–54CE) | Nero (54–68CE) | | Vespasian (69–79CE) | Domitian (81–96CE) | | |

For further reading see bibliography numbers: 59, 73, 108, 159, 252, 290, 320, 338, 514, 544, 642

# MARRIAGE & FAMILY
## IN NEW TESTAMENT TIMES

*How important was marriage in early Christianity, and how vital was it to make the family the focus of religious life, as in Judaism? A variety of attitudes emerges from different New Testament texts, implying that there was no single view on the matter.*

**HOME LIFE**
*The home was the domain of most first-century women, since they were denied much public freedom.*

EARLY Christian attitudes to marriage and family appear to have been both socially conservative and also somewhat radical. However, such attitudes need to be viewed against their contemporary backgrounds, which were not simple: the Jewish, Hellenistic, and Roman cultures were all very different, and even within each culture the understanding and practice of marriage and the family appear to have varied greatly.

## JUDAISM

Marriage and the procreation of children were of central importance in first-century CE Judaism (*pp.282–83*). The home was the one significant sphere of influence for women, who exercised very limited public religious roles (the extent of which is disputed), and were for the most part economically dependent on fathers or husbands. They had little control over marriage or divorce, the latter being reasonably easy for men to obtain.

## HELLENISTIC SETTINGS

Within the Hellenistic, or Greek, world a great diversity of arrangements for marriage and family existed, all of them to a greater or lesser extent patriarchal. In Athens, there was a partial separation of domestic duties, sexual roles, and intellectual companionship: women might be wives, concubines, or companions. In Sparta, men's and women's roles within marriage and the family were shaped by a concern for the birth and up-bringing of soldiers. In Macedonia and Asia Minor, wealthier women enjoyed greater freedom than in other parts of the Hellenistic world, both in the home and in public; one such woman was Lydia, the dealer in purple cloth, who is mentioned in Acts 16 (*see also p.370*).

## ROMAN BACKGROUND

In general, the structures of family life in Roman society were freer than in the Greek or Jewish cultures, at least for the aristocratic class, for which we have the most evidence. Divorce was easy for both men and women (life-long marriage was unusual). Women had greater parity in education and property rights, and they had more political influence than elsewhere. However, even for Roman women the main sphere of influence was still the home – for aristocratic women this would mean a household that included slaves – and there was a strong conservative tendency in Roman society, encouraged by Augustus, who was proclaimed emperor in 27BCE.

**JEWISH WEDDING**
*A Jewish wedding service evokes Jeremiah's vision of a restored Jerusalem, rejoicing at "the voice of the bridegroom and the voice of the bride" (Jer. 33:11).*

## JESUS' TEACHING

Early Christian practice in matters of marriage and family was inevitably rooted in Jesus' own example and ministry. His teaching affirms the worth of marriage and family, with emphasis on his condemnation of adultery and opposition to divorce (Matt. 5:27–28, 31–32), his advocacy of honor and

**RELIGIOUS HOUSEHOLDS**
*In Hellenistic cities, the household was important in establishing early Christian churches. For Jews, the family link was so strong that Acts mentions fathers bringing their entire family to convert to Christianity.*

support for parents (Mark 7:9–13), and his positive attitude toward children (Mark 9:33–7; 10:13–16).

However, both Jesus' own status as a single person and his teaching that the demands of family remain relative to the demands of God's kingdom (Luke 9:61–62) have been seen as a call to a way of life higher than that of the family. This seems to be reflected in Jesus' own, apparently ambivalent, attitude to his immediate family: *"Here are my mother and my brothers! Whoever does the will of God is my brother, and sister, and mother"* (Mark 3:31–35; p.315). The state of singleness is also discussed in 1 Corinthians 7, where both marriage and singleness are gifts from God: it is not freedom from sexual relations that is the issue but freedom from anxiety and freedom to serve God. An emphasis on celibacy developed in

the Christian Church later on. Insofar as it is present in the New Testament, it clearly owes something to Jesus' lifestyle, reinforced by his teaching that *"when they rise from the dead, they neither marry nor are given in marriage, but are like angels in heaven"* (Mark 12:25). Christian hope in the "resurrection of the dead and the life everlasting" challenged the view that procreation was a means of ensuring a future community, which was prevalent in most societies including those within which Christianity grew.

## PAUL'S TEACHING

Paul has praise for those who are single but also teaches positively about marriage, condemning adultery and encouraging couples not to divorce, even when one is a believer and the other not (1 Cor. 7:10–16). His hierarchical view of the husband as the head of the wife (1 Cor. 11:3) is balanced by his radical view of equality in marriage as regards sexual relations: *"The husband should give to his wife her conjugal rights, and likewise the wife to her husband. For the wife does not have authority over her own body, but the husband does; likewise the husband does not have authority over his own body, but the wife does"* (1 Cor. 7:3–4).

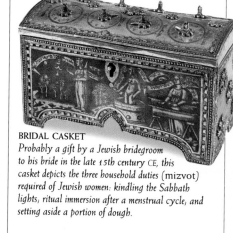

**BRIDAL CASKET**
*Probably a gift by a Jewish bridegroom to his bride in the late 15th century CE, this casket depicts the three household duties (mizvot) required of Jewish women: kindling the Sabbath lights; ritual immersion after a menstrual cycle; and setting aside a portion of dough.*

## CHRISTIAN HOUSEHOLDS

Several of the letters in the New Testament contain examples of "Domestic Codes," or "Household Tables," outlining appropriate behavior and relationships within Christian households (Col. 3:18–4:1; Eph. 5:22–6:9; 1 Tim. 2:8–15; 6:1–2; Tit. 2:1–3:8; 1 Pet. 2:13–3:7). The term "household" included slaves, as well as parents and children. These Codes were generally conservative, reinforcing a patriarchal model of the household within society and the Church, but they also emphasized Christian virtues of kindness and self-control. Whether these Codes have a background in Greek or Hellenistic thought is disputed by some scholars.

## THE MARRIAGE AT CANA

According to John's Gospel, Jesus performed his first miracle at a wedding feast at Cana in Galilee (pp.340–41), to which he, his mother, and his disciples had all been invited. The start of Jesus' public ministry is played out in a personal setting among his family and friends. When the wine runs out Mary tells her son, not expecting that he will perform a miracle by turning water into wine and repaying the wedding host's hospitality (John 2:1–11). The enormous quantity of wine Jesus produces from water intended for Jewish purification rites shows that he is the bringer of new life, turning scarcity into abundance through his miraculous act.

**Terra-cotta jars for storing water.**

For further reading see bibliography numbers: 26, 66, 292, 368, 483, 577, 642, 825, 838

# TRADITIONAL
# RELIGIONS & CULTS

*Pagan worship took many forms in the Roman empire, and the cultic religions from Egypt and Asia were very popular. Christianity came into conflict with some of these religions but also made use of certain aspects of their features.*

LED by the priests of Zeus with their oxen and garlands, the pagan procession described in Acts 14:13 reveals important aspects of traditional religion in the first century CE. As part of a complex sequence of symbolic actions, such a procession would culminate in a sacrifice. The animal would be struck down and its blood collected and poured over an altar as an act of exchange between the people and the gods. The dead beast would then be ritually carved by a civic functionary, the bones wrapped in fat to be burned as the portion for the gods, and the cooked viscera eaten by an elite few. Everything in this cultic welcome for Barnabas and Paul, identified with the gods Zeus and Hermes, would have reinforced

TEMPLE OF APOLLO, CORINTH
*The siting of temples and shrines on an elevated part of the city made them a focus for local inhabitants.*

the structures that bound together society in Lystra. Like the great religious festivals, the cultic acts would have reinforced the society's dependence on the sequence of sowing, watering, growing, and harvesting associated with the gods. Barnabas and Paul insisted that all this comes from God alone and denied that they were Zeus and Hermes (Acts 14:17–18).

In a similar way, the formal worship of a pagan god such as Apollo, which some Corinthian Christians may have attended (1 Cor. 10:23), could have been viewed by them more as a social

SACRIFICIAL OX
*After taking part in a sacrificial procession an ox was ritually killed and offered up to a god.*

occasion or a fraternal organization based on civic ties. A private meal might have been given by a friend who had made a personal sacrifice to fulfill a vow, to celebrate success, or to avoid bad luck (1 Cor. 10:27). The common factor of all such meals in Corinth would have been that no meat was eaten that had not first been sacrificed.

## WORSHIP AND RITUAL

Altars, such as the one interpreted by Paul in Acts 17:22–23 as a sign of extreme religiousness, were common. All over the Roman empire numerous temples and shrines were dedicated to gods. The greater gods had their own favorite haunts, identified in ancient myths and stories. Presumably the inscription *"To an unknown God,"* found by Paul on the altar, was an honest admission that the identity of the god controlling that locality was unknown.

The invocation of gods by name has always been a central feature of prayer and magic. In Roman and Greek religion it was essential to discover the name of the god and to invoke that name, or to find some kind of blanket expression to cover all eventualities. Reciting the correct formula or performing the designated action was also important. Ascertaining the will of the gods was another essential part of traditional religion. This might be achieved at a center like Delphi, through astrology (Matt. 2:2), or by various forms of divination and the noting of strange omens (Luke 21:11).

Some cultic activities would have been associated with specific myths such as those of Asclepius or Artemis (p.399). But among the most popular myths were those of the Egyptian cult of Isis and the Persian Mithra cult. Unlike many of the Greek deities who penetrated the Roman world, these cultic gods retained their original personalities, functions, and rites.

## THE GODDESS ISIS

Isis was an important goddess in Egypt from the seventh century BCE until the time of Christianity, by which time her cult had spread to the Roman empire. She was the wife of Osiris, ruler of the underworld, and was worshiped as a life-giver and mother-figure dealing with people rather than crops. In Alexandria she became the

**THE THRONED MOTHER GODDESS**
*Originally, the Egyptian goddess Isis was represented with the hieroglyphic sign of the throne on her head, either seated alone or with her son Horus on her lap.*

**PRIEST OF ISIS**
*Among the functions the priest of Isis had to perform was to hear confessions from any new candidates and to conduct specific purification rituals, which were all part of the various preparations for the initiation ceremonies.*

patroness of seafarers, and it was from here that her cult reached the shores of the Mediterranean. From there it was brought to Rome by Italian merchants. In Rome Isis was often worshiped together with the god Serapis (a Hellenization of the Egyptian Osiris), and their cult was connected with the cycle of life, death, and rebirth, giving worshipers comfort and hope for the afterlife.

According to Plutarch's description of the myth of Isis, Osiris became the lord of souls once they were freed from the body and its emotions. This helps illustrate how the relationship of worshipers to their lord was understood during this period. There is also evidence of a priest of Capitoline Isis in Rome, although the favors shown to the Egyptian cult in Rome fluctuated with Rome's attitude toward Egypt.

## THE MITHRA CULT

Mithra, or Mithras, was the Persian god of light. He became known as the creator of life after killing the sacred bull from which the sky, earth, animals, and plants were born. According to the myth, Mithra was born of a rock and armed with a knife and a torch. As a warrior deity he was particularly suited to soldiers and the imperial officials, and many Mithraic monuments have been discovered at military borders.

The Mithraic liturgy was celebrated in caves at the far end of which was a picture of the god about to sacrifice the sacred bull. Mithra was also associated with the planets and stars, as surviving

**ROMAN MITHRAIC MARBLE RELIEF**
*This relief shows a young divinity, probably Aion, god of Time, surrounded by signs of the zodiac. Mithra was believed to have created day and night, the seasons, and time. Other gods associated with Mithraism could be found on such cultic reliefs.*

frescos and mosaics show. The *Mithraeum* in Ostia, near Rome, has a mosaic pavement showing an eight-rung ladder with symbols between each of the rungs. The initiate hoped to pass through the seven planetary spheres to a home in the stars.

In one so-called Mithraic Liturgy there is a reference to a cultic ceremony of death leading to a vision of salvation. The worshiper passes through the inexorable necessity of death; from there the soul's progress is compared with that of an initiate who passes through terror into a land of light and into the company of pure and holy men.

The cults were thus varied: that of Isis, as described in Apuleius' famous *The Golden Ass*, is far from the ascetic discipline of Mithraism. Christianity displaced the cults by relating salvation to the historical Jesus.

For further reading see bibliography numbers: 709, 784

# MAGIC
## IN THE BIBLE

*Magic involves the search for help in dealing with life's problems and uncertainties.*
*Magic takes many forms, and the Bible condemns any of these alternatives*
*if they imply a lack of trust in God.*

THE term "magic" comes from the Greek *mageia* and is often used to describe the attempt by humans to harness or control the powers of a deity, or deities, for a desired effect. It is found in all religions and, judging from archaeological finds, was popular with some Jews. In a narrow sense, magic may refer specifically to the practices of a "magician," but in a broader sense it may be related to a wide range of activities, such as divination, necromancy, exorcism, witchcraft, and astrology. The Hebrew Scriptures contain a number of expressions for these practices and for those people who engaged in them. In some cases

**MAGIC AND CHAOS**
*Turner's mid-19th century painting "Sunrise with Seamonsters" reflects how the sea in the Bible is the chaos against which magic fights (see also p.472). Yet magic, as used by evil agents, is itself contested in the Bible.*

the original meanings for such terms remain obscure, and precise definitions for what should properly be called "magic," as opposed to "religion" or "faith," are elusive.

The basic point is that any practices associated with magic are condemned if they detract from trust and faith in God. There are a number of stories in which God's servants defeat the magic of others, or simply do it better because God is the power behind it. This is especially true of healings (Num. 21:4–9; 1 Kgs. 17:17–24; Mark 7:33; Acts 5:15; 13:6–11). But practices connected with magic are strongly condemned (Exod. 22:18; Lev. 19:31; Deut. 18:9–12; Acts 19:19–20; Gal. 5:20; Rev. 21:8). The tension generated by magical practices can be clearly seen in 1 Samuel 28 when Saul, having expelled mediums and wizards (v.3), nevertheless visits "the woman who is a medium" (v.7) at Endor because Saul wanted advice from Samuel. The advice he receives is far from comforting, and Saul remains uneasy about having gone to the woman. However, the story makes it clear that Samuel's advice was real and genuine.

The words "witch" and "witchcraft" in earlier English translations of the Bible have nothing to do with the later medieval concept of witches. In a biblical context these words (e.g., *kashaph, qesem, pharmakei*)

## SIMON MAGUS

A popular magician, Simon Magus is introduced in Acts 8:9 as one who amazed the Samaritans with his magical arts. He became a Christian and was baptized after hearing Philip preach (*see p.389*). However, his basic attitude was still that of a magician. He was so impressed by Peter's bestowal of the Holy Spirit that he attempted to buy the power from him. Simon was immediately condemned by Peter, who charged him with greed (*see also Acts 1:18; 5:1–11*). The term for the offense of "Simony" derives from this particular magician.

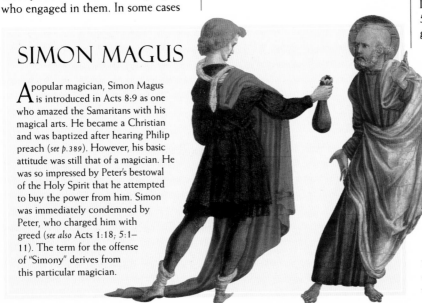

# BAR-JESUS

Described in Acts 13:6 as a *magos* and "false prophet," Bar-Jesus was associated with Sergius Paulus, the Roman proconsul of Cyprus. When Paul arrived on the island, Bar-Jesus tried to turn the proconsul away from the Apostle's preaching and was struck blind by the Holy Spirit. It is likely that the author of Acts intended this blindness to signify a condition appropriate to the magician's spiritual state (Acts 13:11). His other name, "Elymas" (from the Aramaic *powerful*), means a wonder-worker.

describe different ritual specialists, such as mediums or those trying to effect cures or divining. Women may have been particularly involved in these activities because they were excluded from the official cult. They are better regarded as "skilled women."

## WISE MEN AND MAGICIANS

In several traditions, practitioners of "magic" are assigned to the wise courtiers of a foreign king. The biblical authors stress the superiority of God's special representatives over such groups, who were associated with those opposed to God's people. Thus Joseph (*pp.44–45*), not the wise men or the magicians of Egypt, is the one able to interpret Pharaoh's dreams (Gen. 41:8, 24). During the episode of the plagues in Egypt, Pharaoh's magicians cannot reproduce some of the miracles performed by Moses and Aaron. Instead, their capacities are ultimately shown to be inferior. Daniel's reliance on God's wisdom for the interpretation of dreams and signs (*pp.216–17*) is contrasted with the vain efforts of the magicians and diviners in the courts of

Nebuchadnezzar and Belshazzar. Similarly, the author of Acts describes encounters in which the Apostles, as representatives of the Gospel, emerge triumphant over opponents of their mission (*see boxes*).

Nevertheless, these stories do not prevent the biblical authors from admitting that magical practices, popular in antiquity, wielded a certain amount of influence on the faithful. Wherever these activities are labeled as "magic," "witchcraft," or "sorcery," they are usually related to the deception

**INTERPRETING THE PHAROH'S DREAMS**
*Joseph was summoned by the Pharaoh to interpret his dreams for him (Gen. 41:8); a function usually carried out by wise men and magicians.*

and misfortunes of God's people (1 Sam. 28:7; 2 Kgs. 9:22; Jer. 27:9; cf. Acts 13:10). Practitioners of such activities will be subject to divine judgment (Mic. 5:12; Mal. 3:5; cf. Rev. 21:8; 22:15). It is therefore not surprising that these terms do not always describe a particular practice of magic; rather, they could function as a rhetorical way of singling out an unacceptable form of behavior (1 Sam. 15:23; Isa. 57:3).

**WARDING OFF EVIL**
*Amulets were carried by some Jews in the belief that they could protect them from evil. They were usually in the form of a scroll containing biblical text.*

# THE BOOK OF SPELLS

Literary sources from antiquity bear witness to the existence of magical books containing collections of spells. In Acts, the effect of the Gospel on the city of Ephesus is described by referring to the public burning of such books by the practitioners of magic (19:19). This episode is reminiscent of a decree by the Roman emperor Augustus, who is said to have had some 2,000 such scrolls destroyed by fire during the year 13 BCE (Suetonius, *Augustus* 31:1). The writer of Acts uses this story to illustrate the visible superiority of the Gospel over evil. Furthermore, given the general suspicion in the Roman empire that practitioners of magic were prone to secrecy and subversion, Acts attempts to show how the Christian faith may be regarded as consistent with a sense of public responsibility.

For further reading see bibliography numbers: 19, 20, 317, 321, 451, 466, 584, 877

# ACTS OF THE
# APOSTLES

*Acts of the Apostles draws together stories of the beginning of the Christian Church
with a storytelling skill that makes it one of the most gripping of New Testament
books. The driving force of its narrative can be compared with that of Mark's Gospel.*

THE Acts of the Apostles, thought to have been written by Luke, records the impact that Jesus' Resurrection had on his followers. Whereas before his death, Jesus' disciples had deserted him when he was arrested; after his Resurrection they became changed people, receiving the Holy Spirit and risking beatings and death to spread the gospel *(for the stories from Acts, see pp.382–87, 390–93, 396–97, 400–1).*

## LUKE'S AIMS

Why was the book of Acts written, and what did Luke hope to achieve by it? There is more than one answer to those questions. Luke's fundamental concern seems to have been to identify the movement whose early history he describes as clearly as possible by its reference to Jesus – Christianity: *"So it was*

*that for an entire year they met with the church and taught a great many people, and it was in Antioch that the disciples were first called 'Christians'"* (11:26). Christians are the people who revere the name of Jesus (4:12) and who follow "the Way" of Jesus (8:36; 9:2; etc.), the "sect of the Nazarenes" (24:5; 28:22, see p.321).

More clearly visible is Luke's intention to describe the spread of the movement and the success of its evangelism in the power of the Spirit: *"But you will receive power when the Holy Spirit has come upon you; and you will be my witnesses in Jerusalem, in all Judea and Samaria, and to the ends of the earth"* (1:8 – the "acts" of the Holy Spirit). Equally evident is the deliberate apportioning of the book between the acts of Peter in chapters 1–12 and the acts of Paul in chapters 13–28. These correlate with accounts of the growing schism with "the Jews" (6:8–8:1; 13:44–50; 18:5–7), the justification of the development of

PETER AND PAUL
*As the Gospel was preached across the Roman empire, Luke's attention shifted from Peter, one of Jesus'
original disciples, to Paul, who became a leading figure in taking the Gospel around the world.*

the Gentile mission (Paul here is the real hero – his conversion is narrated in chapters 9, 22, 26), and the sustained attempt to display the unity of the new movement despite certain disputes (particularly 15:1–35). Not the least of Luke's concerns was to demonstrate that Christianity was no threat to Roman power and that it regularly received favorable treatment from the Roman authorities (e.g., 16:35–39; 18:12–17).

## LUKE'S MESSAGE

That Luke is the author of Acts is indicated by one strong clue: the presence of first person ("we/us") narratives in the second half of the book (16:10–17; 20:5–15; 21:8–18; 27:1–28:16). A strong body of scholarly opinion supports the view that the narrative feature is merely stylistic. The more obvious inference is that the author was personally present and involved in the events described, in which case he drew on eyewitness memories of most, if not all, of the stories he told.

Acts can be called a history book, as long as it is not judged by the methods of modern historiography. It was written on the basis of careful research (Luke 1:1–4), but Luke did not hesitate to gloss over less positive features of the early Christian mission (such as those we read about in Gal. 1:6–7 and 2:11–14). Luke no doubt followed the conventions of the time in regard to some of the speeches in Acts (*see p.385*): where he could draw on tradition he did so, but he did not hesitate to compose a speech when he thought it was appropriate to the occasion. His practice was to present little cameo speeches, each of which lasts only three or four minutes (e.g., 2:14–36; 17:22–31).

Luke's key themes include the sovereign purpose and providence of God (e.g., 4:27–28; 14:15–17), the Christian mission as "bearing witness to Jesus" and preaching "salvation" (1:8; 2:21, 47; etc.), and the empowering by the Spirit (e.g., 2:38–39; 10:44–48). Some have taken the references to "the Jews" too casually and accuse Luke of anti-Semitism. A more careful reading indicates the importance, for Luke, of understanding Christianity as a movement composed of Jews and Gentiles that thereby fulfills God's purpose for Israel (e.g., 15:14–17; 28:20). Luke, therefore, cites more than 40 direct quotations from the Scriptures (or Hebrew Bible).

Among major subthemes are Luke's delight in recounting tales of visions and miraculous events (5:15; 10:10–14), of Christianity's triumphs over magic (13:4–12; 19:13–20), that with Christianity prophecy had been recovered (2:16–21), and his concern to portray the church as well organized around Apostles (6:2) and elders (14:23).

Another title for Acts would be "How the good news came from Jerusalem to Rome." Jerusalem symbolizes the history of Israel and reminds the reader of where Christianity comes from. Rome symbolizes the wider world and reminds the reader of the universality of Christianity.

## THE BOOK

TITLE: Acts of the Apostles

DATE: Most scholars think it was written in approximately 80CE, although some would argue that the lack of mention of Paul's death points to a date in the early 60s

AUTHORSHIP: Luke's Gospel and Acts are both written by the same author and addressed to Theophilus – a man of some rank and influence – but we may presume it had a wider audience in view, with Theophilus as its sponsor. The author is traditionally identified as Luke, "the beloved physician" (Col. 4:14)

## THE CONTENTS

CHAPTERS 1–2
Jesus' resurrection appearances, and Ascension; Pentecost; first preachings

CHAPTERS 3:1–4:31
Peter and John arrested and brought before the Sanhedrin; their release

CHAPTERS 4:32–7:60
Ananias and Sapphira lie; Apostles perform miracles and are persecuted; deacons appointed; Stephen martyred

CHAPTERS 8:1–9:31
Philip's mission to Samaria; Saul is converted, preaches at and escapes from Damascus

CHAPTERS 9:32–11:18
Peter's mission to Lydda and Joppa

CHAPTERS 11:19–12:25
Barnabas sent to Antioch; persecution by King Herod

CHAPTERS 13–14
Saul and Barnabas sent from Antioch on their first mission to Cyprus, Antioch in Pisidia, Iconium, Lystra, and Derbe

CHAPTER 15:1–35
The Jerusalem Council

CHAPTERS 15:36–18:22
Paul and Barnabas disagree; Paul travels independently to the Galatian churches, Macedonia, and Greece

CHAPTERS 18:23–21:16
Paul travels back to Galatia, Phrygia, Ephesus; travels to Macedonia where he hears of the plot against him and goes instead to Miletus and on to Caesarea and Jerusalem

CHAPTERS 21:17–28:31
Paul arrives in Jerusalem, is arrested, detained, and sent on his final journey to Rome

## KEY THEMES

*Pioneer missionary outreach preaching the Gospel*

•

*The Holy Spirit, mentioned nearly 60 times in the book*

For further reading see bibliography numbers: 143, 167, 256, 275, 279, 321, 365, 367, 388, 434, 443, 610, 742, 760, 808, 814a, 822

# THE ACCOUNT OF JESUS'
# ASCENSION

*The Ascension is one of the most important New Testament themes. Its writers are united in their conviction that the crucified and risen Jesus has been "exalted to the right hand of God," the place of supreme authority. Luke records the events in his Gospel and Acts.*

THE word "ascension" is a way of describing what the first Christians believed had happened to Jesus after his death and Resurrection, using the imagery of Heaven as "above."

ACTS 1:3

According to Luke, Jesus' Ascension took place 40 days after his Resurrection. Luke's Gospel records that during the time Jesus spent with his disciples after the supper at Emmaus and before the Ascension took place, he helped them understand the meaning of certain passages in the Scriptures concerning himself. Jesus stated plainly to his disciples that they should wait in Jerusalem until they had been clothed with power from on high.

WITH THE DISCIPLES AT EMMAUS: LUKE 24:36–46

LUKE 24:47–49
ACTS 1:4–5

They were to be his witnesses in Jerusalem, Judea, Samaria, and *"to the ends of the earth."* He then led them as far as Bethany, by the Mount of Olives, blessed them, and parted from them (some texts add "and was offered, or carried up, into heaven"). Acts records how Jesus was raised to a higher point until a cloud hid him. Two men in white robes stood beside them and said *"This Jesus, who has been taken up from you into heaven, will come in the same way as you saw him go into heaven."* The Ascension marks the separation of Jesus' earthly life from his heavenly life, while also making the two inseparable, and thus holds the history of Jesus and the Christ of faith together.

LUKE 24:47
ACTS 1:8

LUKE 24:50–51

ACTS 1:9

JESUS ASCENDS INTO HEAVEN

ACTS 1:10–11

"As they were watching, he was lifted up, and a cloud took him out of their sight" (Acts 1:9).

## CORONATION PSALMS

Jesus' ascension into Heaven marked his "coronation," or exaltation, and it is one of the most important themes in the New Testament. Behind much of the language of the Ascension lies Psalm 110:1, often regarded as a Coronation Psalm: *"The LORD says to my Lord, 'Sit at my right hand until I make your enemies your footstool.'"* The Coronation Psalms, which include Psalms 24, 47, 68, and 118, are sung at Rosh Hashanah (*pp. 68–69*), the festival of the Jewish New Year, to celebrate the enthronement of God as a universal king. In Psalm 110 the first "Lord" is Yahweh; the second was interpreted by some contemporary Jewish groups as the Messiah. Early Christian belief in Jesus as Messiah, confirmed by the Resurrection, meant that this verse could readily be applied to him.

## THE MANNER OF JESUS' DEPARTURE

A brief survey of the books of the New Testament shows that there were different ways of linking Jesus' exaltation to his death and Resurrection. In the Pauline letters the Resurrection is sometimes mentioned (e.g., 1 Thess. 1:10; Eph. 1:20), but elsewhere only Jesus' Crucifixion is mentioned (e.g., Phil. 2:9). In 1 Timothy 3:16 there is no direct reference either to the Crucifixion or the Resurrection preceding exaltation. Romans 8:34 has Jesus' death, Resurrection, and exaltation in sequence and sees his heavenly ministry in terms of priestly intercession: *"Who is to condemn? It is Christ Jesus, who died, yes, who was raised, who is at the right hand of God, who indeed intercedes for us."*

This image is developed further in Hebrews, which shares the contemporary Jewish belief in a heavenly sanctuary, of which the Jerusalem Temple is a copy. Rejecting the idea that the earthly sanctuary connects worshipers with the heavenly, Hebrews insists that access to the presence of God comes through Jesus alone because he has been exalted through his death into the heavenly sanctuary itself. Now that he has completed his priestly work of offering sacrifice, he represents all humanity before God.

## JOHN'S GOSPEL

Like Hebrews, John's Gospel sees Jesus moving from earth to Heaven via his Crucifixion. Having descended from Heaven, Jesus returns to the Father's glory through his "lifting up" on the cross (John 3:13–14; 12:32–34). So important is the Crucifixion in restoring Jesus to "the bosom of the Father" (John 1:18) that it is referred to as his glorification (John 17:5). John's account follows the sequence of death, resurrection, and ascension. He includes resurrection narratives, and the words of the risen Jesus to Mary suggest a time interval between the Resurrection and Ascension: *"Do not hold on to me, because I have not yet ascended to the Father"* (John 20:17).

## LUKE'S ACCOUNTS

Luke links Jesus' Ascension with his Crucifixion (Luke 24:26) and Resurrection (Luke 24:50–51; Acts 2:32–36). He is the only New Testament writer to mention an interval between Jesus' Resurrection and Ascension. In Acts 1:3 it becomes a 40-day period of Resurrection appearances, after which Jesus ascends into Heaven (Acts 1:3, 9–11; Paul also suggests a limited period of Resurrection appearances in 1 Corinthians 15:5–9). Why did Luke write in this way?

• It allows Luke to show that Jesus had time to prepare all his disciples for their future work, just as he had prepared for his ministry during his 40-day fast in the wilderness (Acts 1:3–5; Luke 4:1–13).

• It allows him to address uncertainties about Jesus' status following his shameful execution. He does this by comparing Jesus with Elijah (*pp. 138–39*), Israel's most celebrated Prophet, who also ascended into Heaven (2 Kgs. 2:9–13; Sir. 48:9–12). Popular belief held that Moses also ascended into Heaven, and Moses and Elijah appeared with Jesus at the Transfiguration (Luke 9:28–35).

• It allows him to demonstrate how the early Christians used the Hebrew Scriptures to work out the way Jesus' Resurrection led to his exaltation. In Luke's scheme, Jesus' Ascension preceded Pentecost. Peter's speech on the day of Pentecost moves from the gift of the Spirit to its giver: Jesus can give the Spirit from Heaven only because he has received the Spirit in Heaven, when he was installed as Messiah by virtue of his Resurrection (applying Psalm 16:8ff. in Acts 2:25–32). If Jesus is Messiah, then he is Lord: this can only mean that he has been exalted to the right hand of God (applying Psalm 110:1 in Acts 2:33–36).

• It allows him to describe the nature of the authority exercised by the ascended Jesus. He ushers in "the last days," by pouring out the Spirit and thereby restoring and refreshing Israel. Though removed from human sight, Jesus is present through his Spirit and directs his Church from Heaven in its universal mission.

• It allows him to show that Jesus was not just a resuscitated body. Although Luke makes it clear that his resurrected body is palpable (as does John), nevertheless it is not one body that remains on earth. It is truly a body in the sense that it presents the reality of Jesus in continuity from the body that was crucified and died. Otherwise, Jesus could not have been recognizable, startling though it was, but it is not the same as a human body that has yet to die.

Luke's approach to the Ascension accords well with the glory of Jesus found elsewhere in the New Testament. As part of the narrative of a new Church, it has the particular power of a story to communicate its exalted message.

For further reading see bibliography numbers: 232, 256, 377, 423, 610

THE ACCOUNT OF

# PENTECOST

*Sukkot, or Pentecost (50 days after Passover), was a Jewish harvest festival when first fruits were offered to God, later celebrating the renewal of God's Covenant. In Acts, the gift of the Holy Spirit was the beginning of the Church: Augustine (p.335) called it* dies natalis, *or birthday.*

LUKE'S account of the dramatic events experienced by Jesus' disciples at the first Pentecost after Jesus' death forms the basis of his narrative in Acts, which tells of the extension of the Church from its origins in Jerusalem to the Roman world.

*THE DISCIPLES WAIT IN JERUSALEM ACTS 2:1*

A group of about 120 people, including the 12 disciples, Jesus' mother, Mary, and his brothers, were together in a house in Jerusalem, waiting for Jesus' final promise to be fulfilled.

*LUKE 24:49 ACTS 1:4–8*

The event happened on the day of Pentecost, when those gathered together suddenly heard a sound like a strong wind fill the house and saw tongues like fire resting upon each of them. The language reflects biblical stories of God's appearance and picks up on John the Baptist's expectation that Jesus would *"baptize you with the Holy Spirit and fire."*

*ACTS 2:1–2*

*EZEK. 13–13 EXOD. 19:18*

*LUKE 3:16*

Filled with the Spirit, the group of disciples began to speak in "other tongues": *"All of them were filled with the Holy Spirit and began to speak in other languages, as the Spirit gave them ability."* The noise attracted a crowd of Jews drawn from "every nation under heaven," who were living in Jerusalem at that time. Each heard his own native language and were amazed and astonished: *"Are not all these who are speaking Galileans?"* But others sneered, and dismissed the disciples' noise as drunkards' babble.

*THE DISCIPLES SPEAK IN TONGUES ACTS 2:4*

*ACTS 2:7*

Tongues like fire rested on the disciples.

## FULFILLING THE PROPHECY

Peter, standing with the other 11 disciples, addressed the crowd before him. He interpreted the tongues as the fulfillment of God's promise, described in Joel, of the renewal of "all flesh" by the Spirit: *"I will pour out my Spirit upon all flesh, and your sons and your daughters shall prophesy."* The gift of prophecy had returned as a sure sign of the "last days," and its source was Jesus, now ascended to Heaven as Israel's Lord and Christ.

*PETER'S SPEECH: ACTS 2:14*

*ACTS 2:17–21*

## THE FIRST CONVERTS

After giving his message, Peter persuaded about 3,000 people to be baptized that day. They joined the company of believers as the first fruits of a renewed Israel, which now had the potential to cross all cultural boundaries.

*3,000 ARE CONVERTED*

*ACTS 2:42–47*

## THE UNFOLDING OF GOD'S PURPOSE

The story of Pentecost is described only in Acts, although John tells of another occasion when the Spirit came upon the disciples in a way that initiated their mission (John 20:19–23; cf. 14:16–17). The Ascension (pp.382–83) opened the way to the presence of God among the faithful in the gift of the Holy Spirit (see also Eph. 4:1–13), and Pentecost initiated a new stage in the unfolding of God's purpose, as Peter's speech makes clear (Acts 2:14–36).

Acts makes it clear that the events at Pentecost were the fulfillment of promises in Scripture, especially that of Joel 2:28–32. Fire and wind are familiar biblical signs of God's presence and activity: there was a sound "like the rush of a violent wind" (Acts 2:2), and "divided tongues, as of fire" (Acts 2:3). As with the Resurrection, unique events defy exact description. Isaiah 66:18 had promised, *"I am coming to gather all nations and tongues,"* and this is seen as being fulfilled, but Acts is cautious about saying exactly what happened. Was it the kind of "speaking in tongues" of 1 Corinthians 12 and 14, which was made intelligible through a miracle of hearing? Or was it a speaking of many different languages (vv.4, 5–11; *xenolalia*)? The report that other people heard the same sounds differently supports the idea of a miracle of hearing, and some have argued that the idea of different languages comes from a desire to show that the confusion following the Tower of Babel (p.33) had been reversed. But others have argued that Acts has interpreted the original "many languages" in terms of *glossolalia* (p.417), because that particular aspect was becoming familiar in the Church.

These arguments show how difficult historical judgments are. Often we are left with a balance of probabilities: we can be certain that some suggestions are wrong (e.g., that Acts is a complete invention written in the 19th century), but we cannot always be certain which of the several suggestions is right. This weighing of evidence and argument applies equally to the speeches in Acts, of which Acts 2:14–36 is the first example. Some scholars have argued that the writer has followed the example of the Greek historian Thucydides (c.455–c.400BCE) who, when he had no record of a speech, supplied what he thought the speaker might have said. Is that what Luke did? The speeches in Acts are in the same style and are sometimes extremely short for the occasions described. In Peter's speech, it is pointed out that the Bible quotations are from the Greek translation (the Septuagint), not from the original Hebrew. Could Peter, who spoke Aramaic or Hebrew with an accent that betrayed him as a Galilean (Matt. 26:73), and who is described in Acts 4:13 as "uneducated and ordinary," have spoken in this way? There is no certain way of resolving this argument, since we have no other record than that of Acts. Where does the balance of probability lie? If, as most agree, Luke wrote Acts, it is important to remember that he claimed to be making a careful record (Luke 1:1–4), and that when he used Mark

## SHARING POSSESSIONS

*Twice Luke records that the life of the earliest Christian community in Jerusalem was characterized by the sharing of all its possessions.*

Peter and John distribute money to the poor.

Acts 2:44 and 4:32 describe how those who owned goods and property sold them and how the Apostles took responsibility for distributing the proceeds to the needy in the community. This sharing of things was no doubt fed by the expectation that Jesus would soon return from Heaven. But it also reflected the fact that wealth was increasingly concentrated in the hands of a relatively small proportion of the population. Other Jewish renewal movements also held possessions in common. In *The Jewish War* Josephus writes of the Essenes that "they despise riches, and their community of goods is truly admirable; you will not find one among them who has more possessions than another. They have a rule that anyone who wants to enter the sect must hand over his property to the community."

There were problems, however, in Jerusalem. Not all members of the community were honest in their generosity: Ananias and Sapphira, who secretly retained some money they had received from selling property, were struck dead (Acts 5:1–6). Neither was the distribution always fair: Greek-speaking Christians, probably wealthier than their Jewish brothers and sisters, complained about the neglect of their widows in the distribution (Acts 6:1; see p.388). The selling of property may have contributed to the difficulties experienced by the Jerusalem church during the empire-wide famine in 46–47CE, when it needed help from outside (Acts 11:28ff.). Paul's collection for the "poor" church in Jerusalem (Gal. 2:10; Rom. 15:26) may also have been an indication of its economic distress.

as a source, while he treated it with enough freedom to integrate it into his own account, he was also very careful with it. Thus the probability is that Luke made a summary or paraphrase of speeches, accurately conveying their contents and translating some of them from Aramaic.

Luke's account of Pentecost shows the Church rooted in the powerful activity of the Holy Spirit. The disciples, who had previously found Jesus so hard to understand, now had a firm grasp of what he intended and the truth of his teaching.

For further reading see bibliography numbers: 143, 257, 443, 450, 759, 760

# THE MISSION OF

# PETER

*Peter is a central figure of the early Christian movement. Originally called Simon, Jesus changed his name to Peter, the Greek translation of the Aramaic "rock," in anticipation of his role as leader of the disciples and of the first church in Jerusalem.*

BEFORE receiving Jesus' call to become one of his disciples, Peter worked as a fisherman in Galilee. He was the brother of Andrew and was married; his wife later accompanied him in his work. Peter, together with the brothers James and John, formed an inner circle of three close disciples. These three were near Jesus at the most important moments of his life (*see p.330*).

*MATT. 4:18*

*1 COR. 9:5*

Peter is recorded as having been a willing disciple who nevertheless struggled with his faith, admitted his unworthiness, and took the lead in asking questions. When he argued with Jesus at Caesarea Philippi, Jesus identified him with Satan for his worldly preoccupations. He was present with James and John at the Transfiguration and was the first male disciple to see Jesus after the Resurrection, yet at the time of testing, Peter denied knowing Jesus while he was being examined by the Jewish Council (*p.355*). According to a graphic story recounted in John's Gospel, Peter was told the kind of death he would suffer; according to tradition, his martyrdom occurred in Rome.

*MATT. 14:28*
*LUKE 5:8*
*MATT. 15:15*
*LUKE 12:41*
*JOHN 13:24, 36*
*MARK 8:27–31*
*MATT. 17:1–8*
*MARK 9:2–8*
*LUKE 9:28–36*
*JOHN 21:1–23*

Peter's shadow heals a cripple.

## CHURCH LEADER

Although considered by his opponents to be "an uneducated and ordinary man," Peter emerged from the start as the first acknowledged leader of the earliest Jerusalem church, partly because he had been the chief figure among Jesus' three closest confidants and partly because the risen Jesus appeared to Peter first out of all the 12 disciples (*see also p.364*). Perhaps it was also because Peter was a born leader. Initially, however, his leadership seems to have been confined to establishing the first infant church in Jerusalem itself, with no thought of any other missionary work beyond the city.

*ACTS 4:13*

*PETER BECOMES LEADER OF THE JERUSALEM CHURCH*

*1 COR. 15:5*

*ACTS 2–5*

## THE WIDER MISSION

When and why Peter began his wider mission is unclear. According to Acts, his first substantive outreach beyond Judea was in confirming the mission of Philip in Samaria (*see also p.389*). It is not said if this was a turning point for Peter, but Luke reports that he and John returned to Jerusalem proclaiming the good news to many Samaritan villages.

*PETER'S FIRST MISSION*

*ACTS 8:14–24*

*LUKE 8:25*

## PETER AND CORNELIUS

Peter's first mission is recalled as his tour of "going here and there" among newly established groups of believers on the Mediterranean coast in Acts 9:32–43. A hint is given that his perspective was opening outward when Luke notes that in Joppa he stayed with Simon, a tanner (an "unclean" trade).

Statue of Peter in St. Peter's, Rome.

However, this was all pre-liminary to the most decisive episode of Peter's mission-ary career. It is usually described as the "conver-sion of Cornelius" (*see right*). But Luke's account is better termed "the conversion of Peter and the acceptance of (the Gentile) Cornelius."

*ACTS 10:1–11:18*

## PETER'S LATER WORK

Thereafter, Peter disappears from sight in Acts, having played out his key role in the narrative. We hear no more of Peter's mission as such from then on, but there are various indications that he was known to have been active in mission. The most explicit of these are in 1 Corinthians. Paul refers to Cephas (Peter) embarking on what were presumably missionary or apostolic journeys, accompanied by his wife. The earlier references to Cephas could well mean that Peter himself or his associates had visited the church in Corinth following its establishment by Paul.

*1 COR. 9:5*

*1 COR. 1:12*
*1 COR. 3:22*

Peter is also prominent in Matthew's Gospel: the specific role and commission given him in Matthew 16:17–19 may well reflect a recognized church-founding role in which he was very successful. The fact that 1 Peter is written to a wide range of churches in what is now present-day Turkey suggests that he had an active missionary role. And the ancient, though not New Testament, tradition that Peter founded the church in Rome may be based on a memory of at least some kind of missionary work he conducted while in that city (*see also p.403*).

*PETER'S CHURCH-FOUNDING ROLE*

## THE CONVERSION OF CORNELIUS

Cornelius was a Roman centurion, "a devout man who feared God." One afternoon he had a vision and saw an angel who told him to send for Peter, who was lodging with Simon the tanner in Joppa. When Peter and Cornelius met and talked, Peter understood the meaning of his divine prompting (Acts 10:11–16). When Cornelius and other people in his house received the Holy Spirit and began talking in tongues, Peter baptized them (Acts 10:1–48).

As Luke recounts it, Peter was initially presented as still very traditional in avoiding both unclean food and unclean people: *"Then he heard a voice saying, 'Get up Peter; kill and eat.' But Peter said, 'By no means, Lord; for I have never eaten anything that is profane or unclean'"* (Acts 10:13–14). It was only when he experienced obvious marks of divine approval – visions, the Spirit prompting, and the Spirit falling on Cornelius – that Peter was moved to accept the Gentile into the Christian faith (Acts 10:28). Peter also acknowledged God's acceptance of Cornelius even without his becoming a proselyte (Acts 10:44–48).

## PETER, PAUL, AND THE GENTILES

This was a decisive event for the course of the Christian movement: Peter's change of heart regarding Gentile acceptance became critical in persuading some early Jewish believers to accept such a breakthrough to the Gentiles (Acts 11:18). According to Acts, the precedent was crucial in the first Jerusalem Council (Acts 15:6–11; *pp.394–95*), at which a mission to the Gentiles was ratified that did not require the Gentiles to be circumcised and thus keep the Law of Moses (Acts 15:22–29).

According to Paul, the agreement at Jerusalem was that the main thrust of missionary outreach should be divided: Cephas (Peter) entrusted with "the gospel for the circumcised"; Paul for the uncircumcised (Gal. 2:7–9). In Galatians 2:11–14, we hear of Peter in Antioch, enjoying a meal with Gentile believers, then withdrawing from such fellowship as a result of more traditional Jewish believers from Jerusalem visiting Antioch. In this argument, Peter may have been trying to hold both sides together, but the surviving evidence shows him to be inconsistent and changing his mind. In contrast, Paul remained clear that to be a member of the people of God is through Jesus Christ, and that to require – as of necessity – anything further is to challenge the sufficiency of Jesus.

However, Peter is also remembered as being the first among Jesus' disciples (Matt. 10:2), and as the rock on whom the Church would be founded: *"I will give you the keys of the kingdom of heaven and whatever you bind on earth will be bound in heaven, and whatever you loose on earth will be loosed in heaven"* (Matt. 16:19).

For further reading see bibliography numbers: 140b, 388, 749a

# HEBREWS & HELLENISTS

*Since its very beginning, the Church has been full of argument and disagreement. The dispute between Hebrews and Hellenists was of great importance in the early Church, but who were the two protagonist parties?*

### SPREADING THE GOSPEL

The persecution of the Christians in Jerusalem brought about a great dispersion of the Hellenist members of the early Church. Many were forced to flee northward from Jerusalem up the Syrian and Phoenician coast. Some settled in Samaria, others in Caesarea and in Antioch, where they spoke of Jesus and his teachings. It was at Antioch that the Gospel was first preached to Gentiles as well as Jews. From here, Paul departed on his first missionary journey to Cyprus.

THE word "Hellenist" means basically "Greek-speaker," so "Hebrew" may mean "Hebrew-speaker," or, more precisely, "Aramaic-speaker" (Acts 21:40). Greek was the most common language of the whole Mediterranean region, so most native Aramaic speakers would also have spoken some Greek. What can be deduced, therefore, is that the Hellenists were so called because their most distinctive feature was they could speak *only* Greek. It follows that the Hellenists were unlikely to have been native to Judea and must have been part of the Jewish Diaspora (*see pp. 280–81*), where Greek would have been the language of most residents in large cities. In contrast, Paul called himself "a Hebrew born of Hebrews" (Phil. 3:5), presumably because, though born in Greek-speaking Tarsus and a Greek speaker, Paul had been brought up as a faithful Jew and so taught to speak Hebrew and Aramaic from his youth. Furthermore, if the Hellenists could speak and understand only Greek, their culture and thought processes must also have been Greek. For example, Hellenists may well have met and worshiped separately, and such factors would have clearly marked them out within Jerusalem and the Jerusalem church.

## OPPOSING SIDES IN JERUSALEM

The "Hebrews" and the "Hellenists" appear briefly in Acts 6:1 at an important developmental stage of the earliest church in Jerusalem. In Acts 2 the two groups are introduced abruptly, "the Hellenists" being the aggrieved party who complained against "the Hebrews" as Hellenist widows were being neglected in the daily distribution of food from the common funds. (Funds had been set up to cope with the growing number of church members, many of whom were very poor.) In the light of the fact that the Jerusalem believers held everything in common (Acts 4:32–37; *p. 385*), and that many women were left widowed, the problem is clear: the basic organization of distribution had broken down.

**PAUL WITH THE JEWS AND GREEKS**
*Paul was able to communicate with both his fellow Jews and Greeks. This would have helped greatly on his Gentile missions.*

SAMARIA
*Philip, one of the Christian Hellenists, came to Samaria where he preached, baptized, and converted the people. It was here too that the magician Simon Magus attempted to buy the power of the Holy Spirit from Peter (see p.378).*

PHILIP THE "EVANGELIST"
Philip was one of the "Seven" appointed as officials by the Jerusalem Church in response to the Hellenists' complaint (Acts 6:5). After the martyrdom of Stephen, Philip was forced to flee Jerusalem and took the traditions about Jesus and the Gospel to Samaria. Known as the "evangelist," he baptized people and preached the Gospel. Acts 8:26–40 recounts Philip's meeting with a devout Ethiopian eunuch (who was reading the Prophet Isaiah at the time). Eunuchs were usually excluded from Jewish worship. Philip told the eunuch about Jesus, and he was so impressed by Philip's words that he asked to be baptized. This account is a significant demonstration of how forward-thinking Philip was in his teaching and practice, and was therefore convinced that there should be no barriers in the Christian Church to those who believed. Acts 21:9 offers a further glimpse of this: Philip had four daughters who exercised the ministry of prophecy.

The immediate problem of the Hellenist widows was resolved easily enough by the Apostles choosing "seven men of good standing" to supervise the distribution of food (Acts 6:2–6). But the evangelistic work of one of the leading Christian Hellenists, Stephen, created further unrest, this time within the larger community of Diaspora Jews in Jerusalem. It resulted in Stephen's martyrdom, on exactly the same grounds on which Jesus had been crucified: both had threatened the authority of the Temple (Deut. 17:9; see also p.356). For the Hebrew Christians still attached to the Temple, this might have created uncertainty at the very least, but what they thought of Stephen and his Hellenist supporters is unclear. After Stephen's death, Christians, and some Hellenists probably came under attack, forcing many to flee northward from Jerusalem (Acts 8:1).

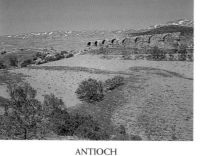

ANTIOCH
*It was in this Syrian city that the Christian Hellenists first brought the Gospel to the Gentiles.*

## HELLENIST PROGRESSIVENESS

The Hellenist Christians could be considered unsung heroes of the earliest Christian mission and theology as indicated by the following:
• Within the first few years of Jesus' death, the traditions about Jesus and the Gospel were being passed on in Greek.
• The Hellenists broke with the Hebrew tradition of remaining focused on the Jerusalem Temple.
• They were evidently the first people to take the Gospel beyond Jerusalem and Judea: first to Samaria (Acts 8) and then to Syrian Antioch. When news of the many conversions "came to the ears of the church of Jerusalem," they sent Barnabas to Antioch: *"When he came and saw the grace of God, he rejoiced, and he exhorted them all to remain faithful to the Lord with stead-fast devotion ... And a great many people were brought to the Lord ... [and] ... it was in Antioch that the disciples were first called 'Christians'"* (Acts 11:23–26).
• It was the church at Antioch that first commissioned Paul as a missionary (Acts 13:1–3) and from where he left on his first mission, traveling to Cyprus and modern-day Turkey.

For further reading see bibliography numbers: 256, 388, 392, 406, 877

# THE ACCOUNT OF

# SAUL'S CONVERSION

*Saul was a zealous young Pharisee who had been strongly opposed to Christianity when it came to prominence in Jerusalem. Yet he became an enthusiastic Christian, the founder of churches in the Mediterranean world, and writer of New Testament letters.*

*ACTS 7:58*

*ROM. 11:1*
*PHIL. 3:5*

S AUL was born a Jew in Tarsus, Cilicia (southern Turkey), and is called "a young man" at the time of Stephen's stoning and martyrdom (*see below*). Thus, Saul may have been about ten years younger than Jesus. He was also born a Roman citizen, in a family that could trace its descent to the tribe of Benjamin. He is first called Paul in Acts 13:9, but may always have had the two names.

## SAUL THE JEW

*SAUL'S BACKGROUND*

*ACTS 26:5*
*PHIL 3:5*

*THE PERSECUTION OF STEPHEN:*
*ACTS 7:58–8:1*

Saul was a well-educated man, receiving instruction from the eminent Rabbi Gamaliel in Jerusalem and then rising to a position of eminence as a Pharisee. His confident knowledge of Hebrew Scripture is reflected in his New Testament letters, which contain 200 quotations or allusions. Saul, therefore, understood well the dangers of the new movement among Jews in Jerusalem, which claimed that Jesus was the Christ (i.e., the Messiah). Saul is recorded as being present at Stephen's death: *"They dragged him out of the city and began to stone him, and the witnesses laid their coats at the feet of a*

*young man named Saul"* (*see also pp.356, 389*), and he became a vehement persecutor of Christians. He was even prepared to take personal responsibility for ensuring the extermination of the new movement. It was in pursuit of Christians to arrest that he set out for Damascus, in Syria.

*ACTS 8:1*

*ACTS 9:1–2*
*1 COR. 15:9*
*GAL. 1:13*

Scenes from the conversion of Saul.

## SAUL'S CONVERSION

What happened to Saul on the road to Damascus is described in three places: once in the narrative of Acts, and twice in speeches by Paul. There are additional recollections in Paul's letters to the Corinthians and to the Galatians (*see also right*). There are slight differences in the accounts of Saul's vision as he traveled to Damascus, but common to them all is the overwhelming sense that Jesus had challenged Saul and had spoken to him: *"He asked, 'Who are you Lord?' The reply came, 'I am Jesus, whom you are persecuting.'"* Saul's life was changed by this experience of coming under the command of Christ. The brilliant light of the vision had blinded Saul, and he had

*ACTS 9:1–19*

*ACTS 22:3–16*
*ACTS 26:9–17*

*1 COR. 9:1*
*GAL. 1:11–17*

*SAUL'S VISION:*
*ACTS 9:4–6*

to be led by his companions to Damascus, where he waited for three days without seeing, drinking, or eating. A Christian in Damascus, Ananias, also had a vision from the Lord, who told him to go to Judas' house on the street called Straight to find Saul. Knowing that Saul was a persecutor, Ananias did as he was told and went and laid hands on Saul. As soon as Saul received the gift of the Holy Spirit, *"something like scales fell from his eyes,"* his sight was restored, and he was baptized as a Christian.

## SAUL'S ESCAPE FROM DAMASCUS

Uncertainty remains over Saul's movements from this point on, because the account in Acts and the references in his own letters do not seem to correlate easily. According to Acts, he spent several days with the disciples in Damascus after his conversion and immediately began to preach in the synagogues there. He not only proclaimed that Jesus was the Messiah but that Jesus was the Son of God. Everyone who heard Saul speak was amazed at his conversion from a persecutor to a believer. Saul's powerful arguments led to a plot by the Jews to kill him. Saul heard of the plot, so his disciples helped him to escape from the city at night by lowering him through an opening in the city walls in a basket. Saul escaped to Jerusalem, after which he began to preach more widely. He continued to be called Saul until he reached Cyprus on his first mission (*p.393*), when he is first described in the middle of Acts as *"Saul, also known as Paul."*

However, in his letter to the Galatians, Paul states that he did not consult with anyone after his vision, nor did he go to Jerusalem once he had been converted. He states instead that he went at once to Arabia, then back to Damascus, and only after three years did he finally go to Jerusalem.

Saul is lowered through the city walls in a basket.

ACTS 9:19–22

SAUL'S ESCAPE
ACTS 9:23–25

ACTS 9:26

ACTS 13:9

GAL. 1:17–18

## SAUL'S VISIONS

That Saul should have seen a vision as he traveled to the city of Damascus is not surprising: he saw several visions during his life, and as a well-educated Jew it seems likely that he had been instructed in the advanced Jewish practice of "chariot mysticism" (*merkabah* mysticism). This was often practiced (usually on journeys) by visualizing the chariot chapters from the book of Ezekiel (*pp.214–15*) until a visionary state was achieved.

Saul/Paul was certainly given to visionary states: at least eight are recorded or alluded to in connection with him. In addition to Paul's vision on the road to Damascus and Ananias' vision (Acts 9:12), we know of Paul's vision of the Macedonian man (Acts 16:9–10), his vision of the Lord giving him assurance in a dream, while staying in Corinth (Acts 18:9–10), Jesus telling him to escape from Jerusalem as he prayed in the Temple there (Acts 22:17–21), Jesus telling him one night to witness in Rome (Acts 23:11), and the angel telling him that he would survive a shipwreck (Acts 27:23–26).

In addition, Paul describes an experience in 2 Corinthians 12:2 of being "caught up" into the third heaven. In Jewish accounts it is to the third heaven that other practitioners of chariot mysticism are caught up. There are surviving records of the experience of Rabbi Johanan ben Zakkai, the great contemporary of Paul, to whom the recovery of Judaism after the First Jewish War (*pp.292–93*) owed so much. The resemblances between those records and the descriptions of what happened to Saul on the road to Damascus are sufficiently close to make it possible that Saul was engaged in this visionary practice during his journey. What remains extraordinary is Saul's shattering and absolute certainty that it was Jesus who spoke to him. The fact that we can place Saul's vision in a practice open to well-trained Jews as part of their "further education" makes it all the more remarkable that Saul had no doubt that it was Jesus who confronted him in this way.

## PAUL AS A MISSIONARY LEADER

Paul's conversion led him to become leader of an extensive mission, making journeys in the regions around the eastern Mediterranean and establishing churches in many places (*see pp.392–93, 396–97*). He was certain that the Gentiles were invited to become members of the people of God.

In his second century CE work, *Acts of Paul and Thecla*, the Roman writer Onesiphoros described Paul as being: "rather small in size, bald-headed, bow-legged, with eye-brows that met, and with a large, red, and rather hooked nose. Strongly built, he was full of grace, for at times he looked like a man, at times like an angel." Frescos of Paul in the catacombs at Rome resemble that description very closely (*see p.463*).

For further reading see bibliography numbers: 122, 143, 360, 395, 399, 431, 696, 699, 834

# BREAKTHROUGH AT
# ANTIOCH

*The church in Antioch was the first center of Gentile Christianity. As a result of the successful preaching of unnamed Jewish believers, many Greeks converted, and the first Gentile church was born.*

THE Antioch church became the main base for the Gentile mission of Paul and other preachers who traveled across the northern Roman empire. Subsequently, it was in the uneasy relationship between the churches in Antioch and Jerusalem that problems over the inclusion of Gentile believers into the early Church were hammered out.

Syrian Antioch (modern Antakya in Turkey) lay 300 miles (485 kilometers) north of Jerusalem. By the first century CE it had become the third largest city in the Roman empire. With a population of about 500,000, Antioch's substantial Jewish population made it the natural place for Jewish Christians to escape to when the Jerusalem church was first persecuted following the martyrdom of Stephen. While most of those who fled the persecution proclaimed Christ only to Jews, Luke tells us that some unnamed Jewish believers in Antioch *"spoke to the Greeks also ... and a great number became believers and turned to the Lord."* When the news of the conversion of Greeks in Antioch reached Jerusalem, the church there sent Barnabas to investigate: *"when he came and*

An early Christian church in Antioch.

*saw the grace of God, he rejoiced."* Subsequently, according to Acts, Barnabas brought Paul from Tarsus to Antioch. Together they taught the Gospel for a year before traveling back to Judea with famine relief for the church elders to distribute among the believers.

## A GENTILE CHURCH

Although Luke's account is brief and lacks many details, he was in no doubt about the significance of the breakthrough made by the conversion of Greeks in Antioch. The account follows immediately after the story of Peter's explanation of the conversion of Cornelius, the first Gentile believer (*p.387*), to some sceptical Jewish believers in Jerusalem. Thus, the story of the founding of the first Gentile Church follows the account of the conversion of the first Gentile household. Like the conversion of Cornelius, the breakthrough in Antioch happened independently of the Jerusalem church, but in each case the events were followed by ratification by the church elders.

The first Gentile converts in Antioch may, like Cornelius, have been from among those Gentiles who were attracted to Judaism. However, there is no doubt that the inclusion of

*ACTS 11:25–26*

*ACTS 11:27-30*

*ACTS 10:1–11:18*

*ACTS 11:3*

*ACTS 11:19*

*GREEKS ARE CONVERTED*
*ACTS 11:20-21*

*ACTS 11:23*

many Greeks meant a decisive turn for the new movement. It could no longer be understood as an entirely Jewish organization; it now became one that had a strong and somewhat independent Gentile focus in the Antioch church.

Despite the decisive breakthrough in Antioch, not all problems were resolved. Differences arose that prompted not only the Jerusalem Council (pp.394–95) but the later conflict between Peter and Paul in Antioch. It was not easy to work out exactly what behavior was to be expected of Gentile believers, nor how to operate a culturally mixed church of Jews and non-Jews. Resolving these difficulties involved uneasy negotiations and sharp disagreements between the most significant leaders and churches of earliest Christianity.

*PROBLEMS AND CONFLICTS*

*ACTS 15*

*GAL. 2:11–14*

## PAUL'S FIRST JOURNEY

Antioch's geographical position made it the ideal place for the Gospel to spread to Asia Minor and Greece, and the city soon became the center of missionary activity to these Gentile areas. It is therefore not surprising that it became the place where Paul's first journey began and ended. He and Barnabas were commissioned by the church in Antioch and "sent out by the Holy Spirit." They traveled first to Cyprus by sea, and from there went to Perga in Pamphylia (southwest Turkey). From Pamphylia they traveled through four towns in Pisidia (central southern Turkey) – Antioch, Iconium, Lystra, and Derbe – before making their way back to Antioch.

*SPREADING THE GOSPEL*

*ACTS 13–14*

*ACTS 13:4*

*ACTS 13:13*

Although Paul and Barnabas began their work visiting the Jewish synagogues, their main successes were among the non-Jews. In Luke's account, they performed miracles and preached about Christ, finding themselves enthusiastically welcomed by many Gentiles but bitterly opposed by some of the local Jews (at Lystra Paul was stoned and left for dead). Despite such difficulties, Paul and Barnabas courageously returned to the coast along the route by which they had come, encouraging and organizing the new groups of believers to whom Paul would return on his later travels.

## "IT WAS IN ANTIOCH THAT THE DISCIPLES WERE FIRST CALLED 'CHRISTIANS'"

According to Acts 11:26, believers in Jesus were first given the name "Christians" in Antioch. Although there is no mention of when and why this new name emerged, the context of the comment is meant to suggest that the name was coined during Paul and Barnabas's ministry in the city. Up until this point adherents of the new faith were simply known as "disciples," "believers," or "followers of the Way," and knew each other as "brother" and "sister." The Latin term *Christiani* was equivalent to "Christ-ones" and was a nickname given to believers in Jesus by those outside the early Church, perhaps even by the civil authorities in Antioch when they became aware of the emergence of the new movement. That this term was coined indicates that the believers in Jesus were developing their own identity, which distinguished congregations from among the other religious and ethnic groups in Antioch.

## FROM NICKNAME TO CHOSEN TITLE

Although the early Christians might have looked like a Jewish group to many pagans and only partially Jewish to many Jews, their allegiance to Jesus Christ had become a sufficiently well-known factor in their faith for them to be identified as devotees of Christ. In the New Testament, the term "Christian" is found only in Acts 11:26, 26:28, and 1 Peter 4:16, but by the second century CE it came to be used as a self-description by believers in Jesus. Like many religious movements (e.g., Methodists, Anabaptists), a term that was initially a nickname given by outsiders gradually became the preferred name of the movement itself.

Paul's first mission.

For further reading see bibliography numbers: 140, 256, 814a

# THE JERUSALEM COUNCIL

*The "Jerusalem Council" is the name given to the meeting of important figures of the early Church. The council convened to discuss problems that had arisen as a result of converted Gentiles being included in the Church.*

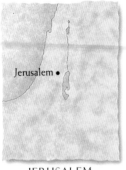

## JERUSALEM

Disturbed by the news of the spread of the Gospel by Paul and Barnabas among Gentile communities in Antioch (Acts 11:19*ff.*), Cyprus, and Asia Minor (Acts 13:4–14:26), conservative Jewish believers in Jerusalem sent for Paul and Barnabas to return from Antioch. A council was then set up by the elders of the Jerusalem church to seek agreement on whether Gentile converts should become proselytes (by undergoing circumcision).

THE problem facing the early Church leaders in Jerusalem was to know what was required of converts to Christianity. If Christianity was understood as the fulfillment of God's promises within Judaism, then converts should be compelled to keep the commands of Torah, including the requirement – in the case of men – of circumcision. But if Jesus had thrown open reconciliation with God to all people, then the requirements of Torah (including circumcision), did not apply. The result of the meeting was the agreement by the Apostles that Gentile believers could be Christians without having to be circumcised, although they were required to keep certain rules that would, if broken, have been deeply offensive to those from Jewish backgrounds.

**CIRCUMCISION: A DIVIDING ISSUE**
*Initially, the church elders in Jerusalem believed that if the Gentiles were to become members of the new Church they should first undergo conversion to the Jewish faith. One of the demands was that a male proselyte should be circumcised.*

## REASONS FOR THE COUNCIL

Understanding both the events and results of the Jerusalem Council is made more difficult by the fact that there are two biblical accounts of the event. The Council is described in Acts 15, but it may also be described in Paul's letter to the Galatians (2:1–10), yet the latter could be of a different visit Paul made to Jerusalem (*see panel, right*). However, although the details do not always agree, the central points appear to be clear.

The council met because some Jewish believers had arrived in Antioch insisting that Gentiles who believed in Christ should be circumcised and keep the Jewish customs based on the Law of Moses in order to be members of the people of God. Such a view implied that the Gentiles could become members of the people of God only by becoming Jews, which would have resulted in the new "Christ" movement remaining a sect within Judaism. Paul, however, maintained the view

**PAUL AND BARNABAS IN ANTIOCH**
*When news reached Jerusalem that Paul and Barnabas were converting Gentiles in Antioch, the leaders of the early Church assembled to discuss what should be done.*

that Gentiles could be included without having to keep Jewish customs. Believing he had been commissioned to preach this Law-free Gospel to the Gentiles by the risen Christ, Paul traveled with Barnabas to Jerusalem ready to defend this revelation.

In Jerusalem, Paul and Barnabas met with Peter, John, Jesus' brother James, and other leaders of the Jerusalem church. The Jerusalem Apostles heard the ways in which the work of God had been evident in Paul's preaching of the Law-free Gospel among the Gentiles. They came to the conclusion that the Gentiles did not have to be circumcised and keep the Jewish Law in order to become members of the people of God. Paul had taken with him his companion Titus, who provided a test case since he was a Greek believer, but in the event he was not required to be circumcised (Gal. 2:3).

Paul was no doubt aware of the disruptive effect that an adverse decision would have had on his work. But Paul and Barnabas were not disappointed; their Law-free gospel to the Gentiles was vindicated. The Jerusalem Apostles gave them "the right hand of fellowship" to confirm them in their preaching to Gentiles, while agreeing to confine their own mission activity to Jews.

## THE APOSTOLIC "DECREE"

The Council had made its most important decision, yet it also imposed four additional requirements of an "Apostolic Decree" on the Gentiles. The exact nature of this decree is made uncertain by variations in the texts of Acts. In one group, the decree has to do with fundamental laws regarding food and (probably) marriage. In another the decree is concerned with basic morality.

• The majority of texts give it in a fourfold form: *"... but we should write to them to abstain only from things polluted by idols and from fornication and from whatever has been strangled and from blood"* (Acts 15:20). These may reflect laws concerning food and sexual relations in Leviticus 17–18, which are binding on non-Israelites dwelling in the Land ("aliens") as well as Israelites. These conditions would refer to the minimal conditions that might allow those who were sensitive to the demands of Torah to share meals with others who were not.

**TAKING FOOD TOGETHER**
*Sharing food is an important part of participating in any religion, yet in the early Church strict Jewish food laws excluded the converted Gentiles from eating with the Jews.*

• Some Latin texts and the major variant text of Acts, known as D or the Western Text, omit *"whatever has been strangled"* and have instead *"whatever you do not wish to be done to you, do not do to others,"* thus recording the decree as concerned with general morality. An early papyrus and some other texts omit "fornication." Some have regarded the moralizing version as original, mainly on the grounds that Paul never subsequently mentioned the rules in his letters, even when, in the midst of his argument regarding food laws, it would have been to his advantage to do so.

At the Jerusalem Council, therefore, the new direction set out by the early Church in admitting Gentiles was severely tested. The outcome, vindicating Paul, was the crucial decision that salvation did not involve keeping the Jewish Law. Thus Gentiles could be part of the people of God without becoming Jews, and Christianity was allowed to continue along the path to becoming the largely Gentile faith that it is today.

For further reading see bibliography numbers: 256, 360, 431, 503, 505, 814a

## PAUL'S VISITS TO JERUSALEM

The early history of this period is difficult to reconstruct because it is not certain how Paul's visits to Jerusalem recorded in Galatians relate to those recorded in Acts.

There are two visits in Galatians and five in Acts:

(1) Galatians 1:18
(2) Galatians 2:1–11
(A) Acts 9:26–28
(B) Acts 11:30; 12:25
(C) Acts 15:1, 5
(D) Acts 18:22
(E) Acts 21:17–25:12

The main ways in which these accounts might be related are:

(2)=(B);
(2)=(C);
(2)=(B)+(C), Acts recording it twice, or splitting one visit into two separate visits;
(2)=(D);
(2)=(A);
(2) is not recorded in Acts at all.

## RELIGIOUS SYMBOLS

The issue of the relation between symbols in an existing religion and those of Christianity remains to the present day. The voodoo cross (*see below*) shows the two united.

# PAUL'S MISSIONS

*In a kind of obituary written before his death, Paul described the rigors of his mission to share the new freedom in Christ given by God: "… on frequent journeys, in danger from rivers, danger from bandits … danger in the wilderness, danger at sea" (2 Cor. 11:21–33).*

*1 COR. 9:1,*
*15:8–10*
*GAL. 1:15–16*
*ROM. 11:13*

**P**AUL regarded his conversion (*pp.*390–91) as his apostolic commission, "apostle" meaning "emissary" or "missionary." For Paul, that meant "apostle to the Gentiles." The accounts of Paul's conversion in Acts reflect the same emphasis – that he was chosen to bring the name of Jesus to Gentiles and was sent to bring them from darkness into light.

*ACTS 9:15*
*ACTS 22:21*

*ACTS 26:18*

*PAUL'S EARLY*
*WORK*

*GAL. 1:21–23*

If Paul began his missionary work during his three years in Arabia, no trace survives. The earliest recorded phase of the mission is in Galatians: he preached in his native province of Cilicia. He also refers to Syria, the main city of which was Antioch. So at some point Paul made Antioch the base of his work. Of this period too, no trace of his work survives.

## MISSIONARY OUTREACH

*ACTS 11:25–26*

From Antioch, where he spent at least five years, Paul was commissioned by the Church for missionary outreach with Barnabas in approximately the mid-40s CE. During this so-called "first missionary journey," through Cyprus and south-central Anatolia (south Galatia), Paul emerged as a leader and established his strategy: first, he would go to the Jewish synagogue, attracting in particular those Gentiles sympathetic to Judaism (God-fearers, who were to be found in most Diaspora synagogues). According to Acts, it was only when tension with more traditional Jews became too extreme that Paul focused his mission more directly on Gentiles. But "Jew first and also Gentile" remained a theological principle of primary importance for Paul's mission, since he saw Gentiles included in God's people. After the Jerusalem Council approved his mission among the Gentiles, Paul extended his work further, perhaps because, after his confrontation with Peter at Antioch (*p.*387), he saw Peter's behavior as threatening the Gospel as he understood it. A split followed with Barnabas and perhaps also with the Antioch church. Thereafter, Paul continued his work independently.

The Aegean Mission lies at the heart of Paul's mission work (*see also,*

*PAUL'S FIRST*
*MISSION:*
*ACTS 13:1–3*

*ACTS 13–14*

*ROM. 1:16*

*ACTS 15*
*GAL. 2:1–10*

*GAL. 2:11–21*

*ACTS 15:36–41*

*ACTS 16–20*

Paul preaching in Athens.

*right*). This phase is usually described as the "second and third missionary journeys," that is, journeys starting from and returning to Jerusalem. But what Acts actually describes is a sustained mission, lasting about eight years in all, around the coasts of the Aegean Sea, with only a briefly described visit to Jerusalem in the middle. It began with divine prompting and an initial circuit of the northern and western side of the Aegean Sea, and ended in a moving speech (virtually Paul's last will and testament) and farewell circuit. In between, Paul spent lengthy periods based in cities: at Corinth, on the west side of the Aegean, for 18 months or more; and at Ephesus, on the east of the Aegean, for two more years.

Although having previously acted on behalf of the church in Syrian Antioch, the Christianity Paul brought to Europe now had less direct ties to the Jerusalem and Judean churches. His previous disagreements made Paul sensitive to the need to safeguard his mission from those churches, which interpreted the Gospel in more traditionalist Jewish terms. Paul was cautious about getting caught in a web of patronal support, which might have demanded favors from him. This would have limited his freedom of movement and authority. As a result, he chose to work to support himself, even though the time spent earning a wage must have been considerable. His anger when those churches tried to encroach on his work is indicated in 2 Corinthians and Philippians. Paul concentrated his work on the major cities on coast or trade routes. It was probably from his headquarters at Corinth and then Ephesus that missionary teams spread to other cities, such as Colossae. In this more settled phase, he developed his ministry as pastor and letter writer.

Throughout his ministry endeavor, Paul saw himself extending the work begun in Christ. It is not too much to claim that Paul's missions fundamentally transformed emerging Christianity from a Jewish sect to a religion less tied to its ethnic roots but capable of challenging the world as a whole to come to faith in Jesus Christ.

*EIGHT-YEAR MISSION*

*ACTS 18:22–23*
*ACTS 16:6–9*
*ACTS 16–17*

*ACTS 20:18–35*
*ACTS 20:1–6*

*ACTS 18*
*ACTS 19*

*ACTS 13:3*

*2 COR. 12:11–13*
*PHIL. 3:2*

*2 COR. 5:9–20*

## THE AEGEAN MISSION

The Aegean mission was one of the most formative and influential in the history of Christianity. Its importance for Paul was considerable on several counts:
• Its success confirmed his stand at Antioch – that Gentile believers should not be expected to undergo circumcision or to adopt a Jewish way of life.
• Apart from Galatians and Romans, all the letters written by Paul (or in his name) were to churches founded in this period: Philippi, Thessalonica, Corinth, Ephesus, and also Colossae, all only 100 miles (160 kilometers) or so from the Aegean coast.
• More important, almost all Paul's letters were written during this period from his Aegean bases. Only the so-called "Prison or Captivity Epistles" – namely Ephesians, Philippians, Colossians, and Philemon – may have been written from Rome at a later date.
• It was thus in this period that he wrote within a few years his four greatest letters: Romans, 1 and 2 Corinthians, and Galatians. Romans, written toward the end of the Aegean mission, was his attempt to express and defend the Gospel for which he had worked so selflessly (Rom. 15:18–21).

Several themes are also prominent in Acts:
• Paul's mission is attended by regular signs of divine approval (Acts 16:1–10; 18:9–10; 19:11–12).
• The Gospel triumphs over other spiritual forces (e.g., 16:16–18; 19:11–20) and other philosophies (17:22–31).
• The new movement and its missionaries pose no threat to civil authorities and should be treated with respect (16:35–39; 18:12–17; 19:23–41).

The Aegean Mission.

For further reading see bibliography numbers: 113, 143, 360, 399, 431, 505, 580, 699

# EPHESUS

*In the two centuries prior to the time of the New Testament, Ephesus had grown into one of the greatest commercial cities in the eastern Mediterranean. After the arrival of Paul, it became a key center in the establishing of Christianity in Asia Minor.*

### EPHESUS
The city once stood at the mouth of the Cäyster River on the Aegean Sea. Perfectly situated at the center of many trade routes into Asia, its great harbor served as a natural landing point from Rome. Today, the coast lies about 6 miles (10km) away, due to the silting up of the port that has occurred over the centuries.

THE now-uninhabited city of Ephesus is one of the most impressive ruined sites of Roman Asia Minor. Originally an ancient Ionian Greek city, it became part of the kingdom of Pergamum before it was bequeathed to Rome by Atalus III in 133BCE. Situated on the mouth of the Cäyster River on the Aegean Sea (the west coast of present-day Asiatic Turkey), Ephesus provided a natural landing point for seafarers and convenient access to the extensive Asian trade routes.

Within the walled city itself, grandeur advertized the importance of Ephesus. Stately columns lined either side of the 7-foot-wide road that ran down to the harbor. Its great theater is estimated to have had a maximum capacity of 24,000 people;

and it enjoyed the luxuries of baths, temples, fountains, gymnasia, a stadium, and (by the second century CE) an extensive library.

Aside from its commercial and political importance, the city's ancient fame had much to do with the fact that the main temple of the Greek goddess Artemis was based here (*see panel, opposite*). By New Testament times, the people of Ephesus also actively participated in the Roman imperial cult, and some of its temples and fountains became associated with the names of various Roman emperors of the first and second centuries CE, such as Domitian, Trajan, and Hadrian.

### THE LUXURY OF EPHESUS
*Many of the splendid Greek and Roman buildings, uncovered since excavations first began in the 19th century, have been extensively restored. The remains of the Temple of Hadrian (above) stand on the marble-laid street that leads to the great theater.*

### THE ROMAN THEATER
*The great theater is situated in the center of the city. Built into Mount Pion, it was completed in its present form under the emperor Trajan. It was in this theater that the silversmiths staged their famous protest against Paul and his Christian preachings.*

## PAUL IN EPHESUS

Christianity spread to Ephesus with the arrival of Paul in c.52CE. Acts 18:18–21 records Paul remaining there at this time (probably in the spring), and leaving behind his companions, Aquila and Priscilla, when he left. He later returned for at least two years, initially speaking "for three months" in a synagogue (a large number of Jews enjoyed a privileged position under Roman rule in Ephesus at this time). From here, Christianity extended to nearby cities, such as Colossae (Col. 1:1–2) and Laodicea (Col. 4:16).

Paul's ministry is closely associated with Ephesus, but he did experience complications while living there (cf. Acts 19:23–41). When writing his letters to the Corinthian Christians, Paul spoke of having "many adversaries" in Ephesus (1 Cor. 16:8–9), of being "in peril every hour," of dying "every day," and of having "fought with wild beasts at Ephesus" (1 Cor. 15:30–32). This last statement was perhaps a metaphorical expression referring to some form of extreme opposition to his ministry. He probably wrote his letters to the Corinthians from Ephesus (cf. 1 Cor. 16:8). Some have also maintained that Paul's so-called "Captivity Epistles" (see pp.405, 428–29, 432–33, 438–39) were written from an Ephesian rather than Roman prison.

## OTHER CHRISTIAN INFLUENCES

There is evidence to suggest that John the Baptist may have been held in high regard by some Ephesians in the New Testament period (see also p.325). Apollos (Acts 18:24–28) taught accurately of Jesus but knew only the baptism of John. In Acts 19:1–7 we hear of 12 recent Christian converts who had been baptized "into John's baptism."

**PAUL'S SUCCESS IN EPHESUS**
*Despite initial opposition, Paul met with success in Ephesus, his Christian preachings inducing those who practiced sorcery to burn their scrolls publicly.*

According to early traditions (i.e., Irenaeus and Eusebius), Ephesus was also the center for the ministry of the Apostle John. The John who wrote Revelation was exiled to the island of Patmos and addressed the church of Ephesus as the first of the seven churches of Asia Minor (Rev. 2:1–7). He found, however, that the church at Ephesus had lost the freshness of its original devotion. It may have been exposed to the teachings of the pagan "Nicolaitans," who seem to have encouraged compromise with the heathen environment, perhaps participating in the imperial or Artemis cults.

After the New Testament era, Ephesus was identified by Ignatius as a Christian center of repute for its faithfulness (Eph. 8–9). The city was destroyed by the Goths in 262CE, but continued to be an important center in the early history of Christianity. According to local tradition, Ephesus was also the last home of Jesus' mother, Mary, who was brought there by John.

For further reading see bibliography numbers: 19, 499, 658, 754

## THE TEMPLE OF ARTEMIS

The Greek goddess, Artemis, (known in other traditions by the name Diana) was associated with fertility and nurture, and was usually represented as a many-breasted figure. Her temple, the *Artemesium*, was acclaimed as one of the seven great wonders of the world and became a great pilgrimage center. Silver images of Artemis and the temple were sold, and Acts 19:23–24 tells of the riot that broke out in defense of Artemis when the silversmiths saw their livelihood threatened by Paul's preaching.

Symbol of fertility.

# PAUL'S FINAL YEARS

*After a riot in Jerusalem, Paul was taken into Roman custody. As a Roman citizen, he appealed to the emperor, and after being imprisoned for two years he was then sent on a perilous sea journey to Rome to appear before Caesar.*

ACTS 21:17

ACTS 21:21

ACTS 21:27

PAUL arrived in Jerusalem again in 57CE with a collection for the poor from his predominantly Gentile congregations. The church leaders were nervous about Paul's coming; they were not sure what would be the attitude to Paul of the local (Jewish) Christians there who continued to keep the Jewish Law. When some Jewish pilgrims accused Paul of bringing Greeks into the Temple, a riot began and Paul was rescued by Roman soldiers and taken into custody.

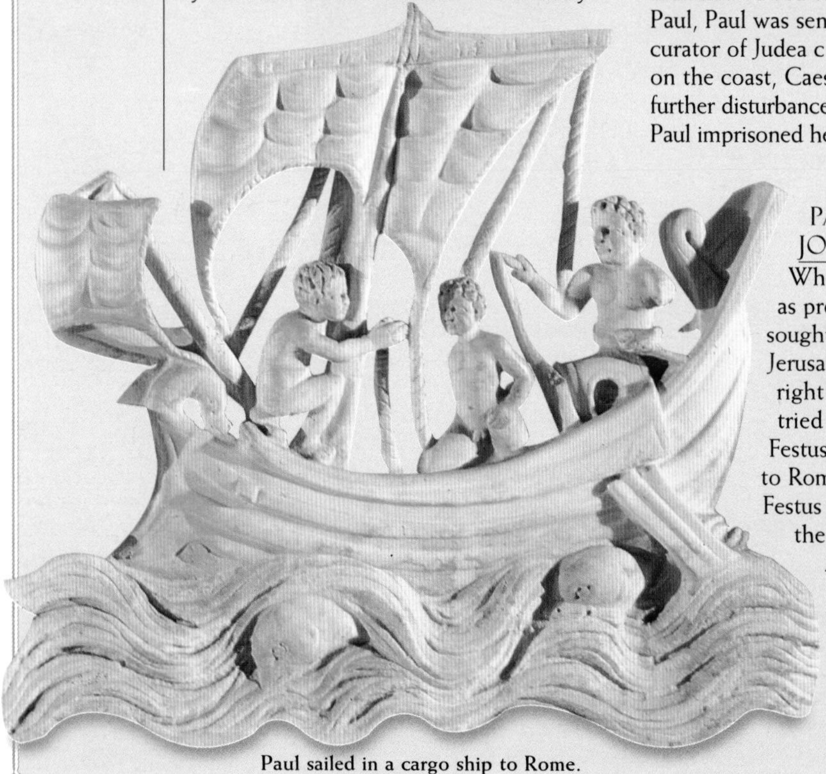

Declaring that he was a Roman citizen, Paul was allowed to speak to the rioting crowds, who eventually shouted him down, and he was taken away to the Fortress Antonia overnight. The next day Paul appeared before the Sanhedrin (*p.355*) and divided his opponents by stating his belief in the hope of resurrection (*see also opposite*). Paul was returned to the fortress, but when the commander of the garrison heard that 40 men had vowed to fast until they had killed Paul, Paul was sent under guard to Felix, procurator of Judea c.52–c.59CE, at his capital on the coast, Caesarea. Anxious to avoid any further disturbance among the Jews, Felix kept Paul imprisoned here for two years (57–59CE).

ACTS 21:37–22:24

ACTS 22:30–23:1–10

ACTS 23:12–22

ACTS 23:23–35

ACTS 24:25–26

## PAUL'S FINAL JOURNEY BY SEA

When Festus succeeded Felix as procurator, the Jewish leaders sought to bring Paul to trial in Jerusalem. Paul exercised his right as a Roman citizen to be tried before the emperor, so Festus was obliged to send him to Rome under escort. When Festus sought clarification of the charges from Herod Agrippa II (king of parts of Palestine 50–c.100CE) first, Agrippa responded to Paul's speech by saying, "So soon you persuade me to be a Christian!" He also stated

ACTS 24:27

ACTS 25:14–22

ACTS 26:1–29

Paul sailed in a cargo ship to Rome.

that Paul should have been freed had he not already appealed to the emperor, Caesar.

In the autumn of c.60CE, Paul and other prisoners were put on board a ship sailing for Rome. Caught in a violent storm, the ship was wrecked off the coast of Malta (this was Paul's fourth shipwreck). The ship broke to

**Paul and the serpent.**

pieces, but the passengers were saved – an event Paul had foretold after claiming to have received a vision from God. Once, as he picked up firewood while the passengers wintered in Malta, Paul was bitten by a snake. When no harm came to him, people imagined him to be a god. When he healed the father of a public figure, others were brought to him for healing, and he won favor with the Maltese people. After three months, Paul boarded another ship, landed at Puteoli, Italy, and went on to Rome by foot. Christians came out to meet him at the Appian market and accompanied him along the final stage.

*ACTS 27:23–26*

*ACTS 28:3–6*

*ACTS 28:7–9*

*ACTS 28:13–16*

## AN UNCERTAIN END

In Rome, Paul was kept under house arrest for two years, but he was allowed to receive visitors. Here he may have written the letters known as the Captivity Epistles (*see right*). The end of his life is uncertain: it is not known if his case ever came to trial, or if it did, what its outcome was. Did he ever make the journey to Spain that he had hoped for? If he wrote the Pastoral Epistles from Rome (*pp.446–47*) then he also made journeys into Asia Minor. One Church historian, Eusebius (fourth century CE), states that Paul was executed in Rome during a period of Christian persecution by the emperor, Nero (54–68CE); Tertullian (second century CE) claims he was beheaded, and others add that the execution site was on the road to Ostia, 3 miles (5 kilometers) outside the city of Rome.

*ROM. 15:24*

## THE BACKGROUND TO THE STORY

Paul called the collection for the poor "a generous gift" of service and fellowship. It preoccupied him as a matter of great importance, an importance that lay not only in a simple obedience to Jesus' example and command but also in demonstrating the unity of the growing Church, in spite of the divisions between those converts who still kept the Law of Moses and those who did not.

Paul's last voyage has been compared to the final journey of Jesus, his own "Via Dolorosa" (*p.360–61*). Here, Paul's faith is unmistakable. His journey to Rome, under the constant supervision of a Roman guard, is recorded in the first person plural, "we," in Acts 27:1–28, possibly because the writer of Acts, Luke, had been present himself, or because he had access to the diary of someone who had.

The Captivity Epistles would throw great light on Paul's faith during his captivity, but there are problems. It is not certain if the captivity to which Paul refers is in Rome or Caesarea. Some scholars also question the authorship of all letters attributed to Paul, which may include Philippians, Philemon, and perhaps Colossians and Ephesians (*pp.432–33, 438–39, 428–29*). Colossians 4:16 mentions a letter to the Laodiceans, now lost or included with another letter.

**Paul's last journey.**

## THE QUESTION OF RESURRECTION

The way in which Paul divided the Pharisees and the Sadducees over the question of the resurrection (Acts 23:6ff.) exploited a basic division over the status of Scripture: Sadducees adhered to the basic text of Torah and could find no text that spoke unequivocally of the resurrection of the dead (*see pp.178–79, 288*). Pharisees were prepared to look at the text and by exegesis to take up indications (e.g., Ezek. 37) that God would indeed re-create human lives after death. This is one of many disputes dividing the Pharisees from the Sadducees. Almost all of these dissensions stem from one basic issue: how literally must the text of Torah be taken?

For further reading see bibliography numbers: 360, 431, 505, 580, 592

# CHRISTIANITY IN ROME

*"There has never been anything more remarkable in the whole world,"*
*wrote Pliny the Elder in reference to Rome and its great empire.*

## CAPITAL OF THE EMPIRE

Rome's strategic location on the Tiber River allowed easy access to the Mediterranean basin, about 17 miles (28km) away. Rome's main port was that of Ostia, which lay on the mouth of the Tiber and to which ships from all over the empire arrived bearing food and luxury goods for the city. Situated on seven hills, Rome had the added advantage of being provided with a fortresslike protection in times of conflict.

THE Roman empire was an impressive achievement, with its boundaries spreading far beyond the Mediterranean world. Its building projects and roads, its army, and its law and administration created a *Pax Romana*, a condition of security that many were glad to live in.

By the first century CE, the ancient city of Rome had a population of approximately one million. It was a city without equal and one that required extraordinary administrative oversight. An elaborate road system was developed to connect Rome's empire and extensive building projects were undertaken: temples, palaces, aqueducts, baths, fountains, and theaters, many of which can still be seen and admired today.

The spread of Christianity to Rome may have taken place soon after Jesus' ministry ended, and it seems to have developed largely within the matrix of the Jewish religion already established at Rome. In the first century CE, there were about 40,000–50,000 Jews in Rome. Most came from the lower classes and were probably brought to Rome as slaves. We know of 10 to 13 independent synagogues in existence in Rome at this time, and of Jewish catacombs, although there is little evidence to indicate a coordination of authority across the Roman Jewish constituency. Since much of the early

### REMAINS OF THE FORUM
*As the center of ancient Rome's political, commercial, and judicial life, the forum once teemed with lawyers, bankers, brokers, and shopkeepers.*

### THE COLOSSEUM
*Commissioned by the emperor Vespasian in 72CE, Rome's great amphitheater, the Colosseum, was one of the most impressive and beautifully designed buildings in the city. It may have been a site of persecution for many Christians.*

Christian mission was among Jews, Christianity probably took root in Rome by the conversion of Jews and God-fearers associated with the synagogues.

Not all sectors of Roman Jewry came into contact with early Christianity, although Acts 28:22 suggests that some Jewish leaders in Rome claimed to have knowledge of Christianity (59–60CE). Perhaps the early Christian house churches of Rome arose in connection with Jewish synagogues, but they may also have been established by Gentiles who had no connection with the synagogue.

JEWISH WORSHIP IN THE CITY
*One of the oldest known synagogues in the ancient Jewish ghetto of Rome.*

## THE CHRISTIAN EXPULSION

If there was a connection between the synagogue and the founding of house churches, it might account for the situation described in Acts 18:2. Aquila, a Jew, and his wife, Priscilla, seem to have already been Christians when they met Paul in Corinth, but they had been forced to leave their home in Rome because of Claudius' edict in 49CE to expel all Jews from the city. The Roman historian Suetonius speaks of the same expulsion and attributes it to Jewish "disturbance at the instigation of Chrestus" (*Claudius* 25:4). Many think this a confused reference to the founder of Christianity, thereby indicating that controversy had arisen within Jewish ranks concerning the Messianic credentials of Jesus.

This identification cannot be certain, however, nor can it be the case that all ethnic Jews were expelled. Nonetheless, the deportation of Jewish Christians would have increased the number of Gentile Christians within Roman Christian circles. This may have fostered some forms of ethnic tension within Christian circles (*cf.* Rom. 11:17–21), especially upon the return of Jewish Christians after the edict had been repealed by the death of Claudius in 54CE.

If some Roman Jews had no knowledge of Christianity by 60CE, this was certainly not the case after 64CE, the date when Rome was severely damaged by fire. The emperor Nero placed the blame for this event on the Christians who were, by now, an identifiable group that could be distinguished from its parent group associated with the synagogues. The Roman historian Tacitus records how the Christians in Rome were loathed for their "hatred of the human race," and many were subject to horrific persecutions (*Annals* 15:44; *see also pp.458–59*).

PETER AND ROME
The tradition that Peter was in Rome at the same time as Paul first appears in the late second century CE. Like Paul, Peter is believed to have worked in the city. He may have been martyred during the Neronian persecutions of c.64CE. Later, in the fourth century CE, the claim that Peter had been the first bishop of Rome appears. Despite a lack of any specific evidence in the New Testament, the link between Peter and the founding of the papal seat in Rome has become an accepted part of Roman Catholic tradition.

# CHRISTIAN ATTITUDES TO ROME

*Paul was eager to visit the Roman empire's great capital city in order to spread the word of God, yet for those who refused to acknowledge the imperial cult, it was a time of danger and persecution.*

In his letter to the Roman Christians, Paul presents himself as eager to get to Rome (Rom. 1:10–15; 15:23), evidently as a means of furthering his ministry westward (Rom. 15:23–24). The Acts of the Apostles depicts the spread of Christianity from its Jewish cradle to the center of the Greco-Roman world, represented by Jerusalem and Rome respectively. Jesus' statement about paying taxes to Caesar (e.g., Mark 12:13–17) has often been interpreted to mean that the "state" (Rome) is a divinely ordained feature of social life, an interpretation evident in Paul's advice to the Roman Christians and elsewhere (e.g., Rom. 13:1–7). Nonetheless, early

Christians also proclaimed the politically charged message that "Jesus is Lord" and found him alone to be worthy of devotion (Phil. 2:9–11).

Consequently, many Christians were prepared to face extreme forms of persecution rather than join the majority of their contemporaries in the worship of Rome's emperor as divine. In a context such as this, the author of Revelation provides the most devastating critique of Rome's political, religious, and economic condition (Rev. 12–19), finding it to be not the instrument of the divine nor the means of stability, security, and peace (the *Pax Romana*), but instead the incarnation of evil.

**For further reading see bibliography numbers:** 143, 491, 496, 544, 642, 709

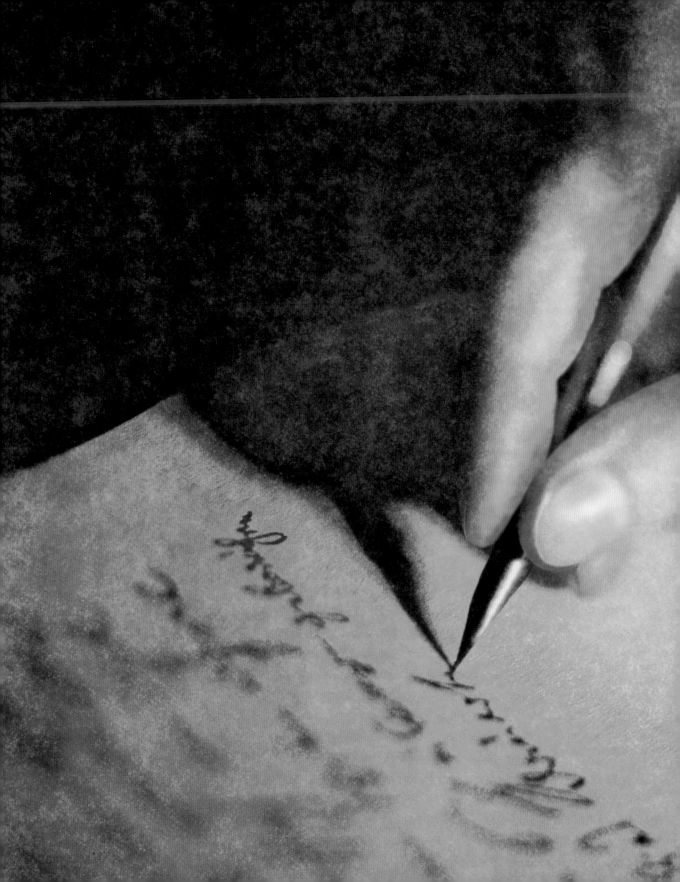

# THE
# LETTERS

The New Testament contains 21 letters, or Epistles, which were sent out by different people, evidently early Church leaders, to individuals or to Christian communities throughout the Mediterranean. These letters were sent partly as a means of communication and partly as a form of teaching and imparting advice to new Christians.

Strictly speaking, the number of letters included is uncertain because some of them may contain more than one original letter (more than one letter may have been linked to make the present document). Some of the letters originally may have been forms of public teaching (particularly Hebrews), and the uncertain authorship of others left their canonical authority in doubt for many years in the first centuries.

Of the full list, the following documents are attributed to Paul (for the questions raised by some scholars covering this, see the panel on authorship for each letter):
Romans, 1 & 2 Corinthians, Galatians, Ephesians, Philippians, Colossians, 1 & 2 Thessalonians, 1 & 2 Timothy, Titus, and Philemon. Of these, Philippians, Colossians, Philemon, Ephesians, and 2 Timothy are sometimes referred to as "the Captivity Letters," because they were written from prison.
1 & 2 Timothy and Titus are often called "the Pastoral Letters" because of their subject matter on the pastoral care of communities and on Church life and practice.

James, 1 & 2 Peter, 1, 2, & 3 John, and Jude are known as "catholic letters," from the Greek *katholikos*, meaning "universal." These letters were not addressed to any specific community, as were Paul's letters, but were understood as being addressed to the Church as a whole. The remaining letter of the 21 is that to the Hebrews.

# LETTERS
## IN THE BIBLE

*As Christianity spread, maintaining contact with widespread communities became increasingly important. Christian leaders, such as Paul, used letters to encourage and instruct other Christians. Therefore, many of the New Testament letters are lengthy.*

MANY letters from the ancient world still survive. They range from the most informal "to do" lists and personal letters involving intimate family matters, to official communications and formal treatises presented as literary letters, such as the letters of Cicero or Seneca. In every culture, the letter is regarded not only as a form of communication but as a substitute for the direct encounter between two parties, whether individuals or groups. Thus, in a real sense, the letter represents the absent person. This is true of the Hellenistic letter and is an especially strong aspect of Paul's letters.

There are 22 documents of the New Testament that can be classified as letters. However, a few of these, such as Hebrews and 1 John, are more like formal treatises or tractates written in a quasi-letter form than actual personal letters. While the letters of the New Testament occasionally contain personal elements, they are not private documents.

## PAUL'S LETTERS

Paul usually wrote for his churches and expected his letters to be read publicly and received as authoritative.

There are clear differences between Paul's letters and a typical personal Hellenistic letter.

First, Paul's letters tend to be much longer (with the exception of Philemon). Their length is the direct result of their being public teaching documents. Second, a number of Paul's letters are written in more than one name. Third, Paul's letters are usually addressed to more than one individual, as, for

**ANCIENT PAPYRUS**
*This letter was written by the scribe Butehamun and dates back to the Rameses period, c.1200BCE.*

**PROFESSIONAL WRITERS**
*Letters were usually written by scribes who were well respected by society. This scribe sits in the traditional position for writing.*

example, *"to the church of God that is in Corinth"* (1 Cor. 1:2; 2 Cor. 1:1). This points to the public, corporate, or churchly aspect of Paul's letters.

## FORM AND STYLE

The form of the Hellenistic letter was highly stylized. Ancient handbooks reveal that formal training in letter-writing was available in schools. There, one could obtain not only instruction in writing different types of letters but also in the formal aspects of letters. The standard form of a letter consisted, in its simplest version, of a prescript or opening, "A to B, greetings" – thus leaving no doubt from the very beginning about the identity of the author. This greeting was followed by the body of the letter, which contained its main concern, and the formal closing, also known as the "farewell." This form would often be expanded to include a wish for health, which followed the prescript and to which was sometimes added a prayer or thanksgiving.

The New Testament letter writers adopted this form of letter writing, which they modified somewhat for their own purposes and which they used consistently to articulate their Christian perspective. The most remarkable contrast with the Hellenistic form

# WRITING IMPLEMENTS

*Many writings of the Bible, like virtually all literature of antiquity, were written on papyrus, made from the flattened stems of the papyrus plant.*

Specially prepared animal skins, known as vellum or parchment, increasingly replaced the use of papyrus in literary works from the second century CE. Paper, invented in China, did not come to the West until the end of the eighth century CE. Primitive pens were made from reeds or metal, and a pigment made from the carbon produced by lamps was used as ink on papyrus and vellum.

**Pens and styli.**

Letters could be written on individual sheets of papyrus, but longer works meant that sheets had to be glued together to make rolls. Luke's Gospel and the book of Acts would have required rolls of over 30 feet (9m) in length. Christians therefore began to use the Codex – sheets of papyrus bound together as pages and placed between two blocks of wood or tablets – allowing both sides of a sheet to be used. This enabled the four Gospels to be bound together from the start and was thus vital for Christian history and the development of the canon (*see p.474*), for it made biblical texts more accessible.

is that the last main section of the body is frequently devoted to ethical exhortation (also known as *paranesis*). It was also common for New Testament letter writers to alter the traditional farewell into a concluding benediction or doxology (a public form of praise to God). The letter writers of the New Testament, in short, Christianized the secular Hellenistic letter form. They missed no opportunity to enrich their readers with spiritual knowledge and a sense of worship. In doing so, they may well have had in mind the fact that their letters would be read in a setting of corporate worship.

## WRITING SKILLS

The letters of the New Testament often employ rhetoric, the persuasive language of effective communication. Rhetoric was a standard element in the curriculum of Greco-Roman schools. The study of rhetoric shows how intimately form and content are related. It would have been natural for New Testament writers to make use of the formal elements of rhetoric in their desire to communicate effectively. Paul may have received training in rhetoric; the structure of his letters occasionally bears the marks of formal rhetoric of the ancient schools (*cf.* 2 Cor. 10:10, where even Paul's opponents admit that *"his letters are weighty and strong"*). Paul employed a large variety of rhetorical devices or techniques. He used "diatribe," which is the device of discussion with an imaginary opponent who is allowed to object and cross-examine (*see* Romans). He made use of different kinds of liturgical elements from church worship, such as hymns, confessions, credal

### WRITING SURFACES
*Before papyrus became widely available, clay tablets were used as a writing surface. Zechariah used one on which to write the name of his son, John (later John the Baptist), while he was temporarily mute.*

fragments, prayers, benedictions, and doxologies. He quoted or alluded to the Scriptures to substantiate an argument or otherwise to win over his readers. All of this has to do with persuasive, effective communication and was part of Paul's rhetorical strategy.

The great importance for Paul of *paranesis* is made conspicuous by its comparison with the rhetoric of the ancient world. In his *paranesis*, Paul made use of much traditional material, including Jewish matter from the Hebrew Bible, the teachings of Jesus, Greco-Roman (e.g. Stoic) ethics, and vice-and-virtue catalogs. But the influence of the letter form and the canons of rhetoric are evident in many of the New Testament writers.

### INKPOTS
*Making decorative inkpots, usually from faience, a glassy material (above), or bronze (right), allowed craftsmen to display their skills.*

### PAPYRUS PLANT
*This triangular-stemmed reed grew along the banks of the Nile. It reached heights of 13ft (4m) and was used to make baskets and sandals as well as writing materials.*

For further reading see bibliography numbers: 26, 27, 246, 507, 798

# PAUL'S TEACHING

*Paul was a deeply religious and well-educated man. In his letters, he produced brilliant and searching insights into the nature of God and God's actions in relation to the world. He applied these to a vision of what makes us the kind of people we are and can become, both within ourselves and with others.*

AUL'S imagination, deeply rooted in faith and prayer, was so prolific in ideas that they cannot be compressed. Moreover, in his letters we never see him present his thought as a unified whole. Instead, we see individual aspects of it applied to particular situations. There has been much debate as to how different aspects of Pauline theology should be related to each other. In addition, there is an ongoing scholarly debate on which letters Paul actually wrote. The central tradition of "Pauline teaching," however, accepts the 13 letters attributed to Paul as representing his teaching. Vital themes are scattered throughout Paul's letters (relevant readings are suggested at the end of each section below):

## GOD AND HUMAN NATURE

• **God**: From Paul's experience of the Jewish faith, he knew well the majesty and transcendence of God. He also knew that God acts in the world, especially in the people of Israel. God acts also in Christ, who, leading on from Moses, brings to completion God's purpose in choosing the Jewish people, "confirming the promises given to the patriarchs" (Rom. 15:8); Christ does not introduce a new religion. See Romans 11.

• **Jesus Christ**: God's action in Jesus Christ is particularly dramatic and amazing: in Jesus' life, death, and Resurrection God has done for people what they cannot do for themselves – a "rescue mission" from a hopeless situation. Jesus Christ, who was crucified but who has now been raised from the dead, as many including Paul have witnessed, has transformed life and death. He is associated so closely with

God that he shares in the honor and worship due to God. This is the most extraordinary fact: this recently executed individual, still referred to by his human name, is known to be alive and present, not just by Paul and a few others but wherever people meet in his name (*see* Rom. 8; 1 Cor. 2; Col. 1; Phil. 2:1–13).

• **Human nature**: What is there about people that made God's rescue mission necessary? Our human nature (Greek, *sarx; see box opposite*) betrays us, leading us into actions we know are wrong, then locking us into death; our frail state is summarized in our sin and death. Yet we know that we are more than our worst moments, we are spirit and soul as well. See Romans 1:1–3:26; Ephesians 2:1–10.

COMMUNICATING THE GOSPEL
*Paul's letters were a vital way of communicating his teaching and giving encouragement to those Christians he could not personally visit.*

## SALVATION

• **Rescue**: Caught in a trap of good intentions but of bad thoughts and actions, humans cannot repair themselves and the world. God acted in Christ to make that act of repair. Paul used the story of Adam, representing man/humanity, to show that humans are all gripped by sin and death in an unmovable vice. Jesus is the second Adam who breaks that grip and sets them free. How did he do this? Paul used different metaphors to illustrate this: of slaves being ransomed; of charges being canceled in a law court; through the shedding of blood that marks both Passover and the making of a covenant; through a victory over the powers of evil. In effect, it is a transfer from death into the risen life of Christ; it is a genuine participation in him. Consequently, the barriers that divide human beings are broken down (Gal. 3:28). See Romans 5–6.

# HUMAN NATURE

*The New Testament writers drew much of their understanding of human nature from the Hebrew Bible, but it was transformed by their belief, not only that Jesus the man had risen from the dead, but that he offers the way to new life for others.*

There is no single or unified account in the New Testament of what makes up a human being, but certain features recur, with many of them given their fullest expression in Paul's teaching. People are always creatures before God (created by God and standing within God's purposes). They are embodied, but the body is not just the physical appearance. The body (Greek, *soma*) is the whole reality of a person gathering different functions into one (Matt. 5:25, 30; Rom.12:4–8; 1 Cor. 12:12–26).

Future human existence is thus unimaginable without a body, but after death it is of a spiritual kind (1 Cor. 15:35–49; Phil. 3:21). The spirit (Greek, *pneuma*, the source of life) and soul (Greek, *psyche*, the principle of life within) are not parts of a person. They only represent the living person (Matt. 10:28; 16:26; Luke 9:56; 12:20; John 12:27; 2 Cor. 1:23; 12:15; Phil. 1:27; 1 Thess. 2:8), especially with consciousness and will, deriving life from God (Matt. 6:25ff.). Humans have intelligence (Greek, *nous*, Rom. 7:23; 12:2; 14:5; 1 Cor. 1:10) and emotions and commitments, summarized as "heart" (Greek, *kardia*, Matt. 6:21; 15:8; Luke 2:19; 8:15; John 12:40; Rom 2:14; 6:17; Phil. 1:7; Eph. 3:7). The whole person is made up of "flesh" (Greek, *sarx*), which is more than the substance that constitutes a bodily being. It is the person in weakness and dependence on God, subject to sin and to death (note especially Rom. 7). "Flesh" thus signifies human beings in their weakness, living "after the flesh" or "according to the flesh" (Rom. 1:3; 8:13; 9:5; 1 Cor. 1:26; 10:18; 2 Cor. 5:16; 11:18; Gal. 2:20; 3:3; Phil. 1:22, 24), and thus under the dominion of its demands (Rom. 8:1–9). It is possible, therefore, to see human life as warfare between the flesh and the Spirit (Gal. 5:13–26). In this conflict, Christ is already the victor, who took "his fleshly body" (Col. 1:22) and won the victory in it. People become a part of that victory by being taken through baptism into Christ and his conquest of death (Rom. 6:1–10). A different seed is sown and a new life begins (Gal. 6:8), enhanced by the gifts of the Spirit.

• **New life**: A new life in Christ begins when people are baptized, for then they are made a part of Christ's death and Resurrection: *"You have died, and your life is hidden with Christ in God"* (Col. 3:3). The Lord's Supper sustains this union during life on earth. To be "in Christ" is the new life that Paul experienced for himself. For Jews, membership as God's people is initiated by birth (less often by conversion) and secured by the conditions of the Covenant, such as circumcision, food laws, and the Sabbath. For Christians, membership and participation are initiated and secured "by faith alone." See Ephesians 1; Romans 8: 28–39; 2 Corinthians 5:16–21.

• **Holy Spirit**: Paul also experienced the firework brilliance of God in the continuing work of the Holy Spirit. The Spirit of God, present to all people, was already well known to Jews, but for Paul the experience of the Holy Spirit formed the bond with Christ and the bond between believers, granting them his gifts and graces. The Spirit is the sign and confirmation that the new creation has already begun. See 1 Corinthians 12:1–11; Galatians 5:13–26.

## THE CHURCH AND CHRISTIAN LIFE

• **The Church**: the Spirit's gifts to each individual cannot be in competition with one another. They should constitute a whole, just as the feet, legs, and other parts are all equally required for a whole body. The body, with Christ as the head, is the beginning of the Church. See 1 Corinthians 12:12–31; Ephesians 4:1–16.

• **Behavior**: Paul sometimes wrote as though he were laying down the law for the new churches he had helped to found. Certainly he gave clear guidance and instruction. But he applied the more general principle, exactly as Jesus had himself stated it, that all behavior must arise out of love (Greek, *agape*): this is the more excellent way of 1 Corinthians 13. There is no new "law," only the application of the controlling principle of love. Here, as elsewhere, Paul remained close to all that Jesus lived and taught. Paul rarely quoted the Gospel story, but constantly applied its implications. See 1 Corinthians 13:1–11; 1 Thessalonians 4:1–11; Colossians 3:1–4:1.

• **Grace and faith**: How does all this come about? Not by birthright or belonging to a particular race or nation, nor by keeping rules and laws in order to earn or retain God's favor. In all cases the initiative is God's. People are called, or invited, to serve God and shown how to live. Yet God also makes provision for covering human failure, for repentance, and for forgiveness. Paul believed that God had, in Jesus, drained the poison of sin and the power of death. In the Holy Spirit, God had given a power that would overcome the weakness of human nature. The primary response that God looks for is faith, that is, acknowledging God and living in trust and thankfulness. See Romans 8; Galatians 3.

> **❝** *There is therefore now no condemnation for those who are in Christ Jesus. For the law of the Spirit of life in Christ Jesus has set you free from the law of sin and of death.* **❞**
>
> (Romans 8:1–2)

For further reading see bibliography numbers: 56, 77, 113, 155, 261, 316, 350, 373, 407, 472, 497, 505, 554, 580, 646, 680, 681, 682, 699, 832, 834, 842, 886

# THE LETTER TO THE

# ROMANS

*Romans is the most important letter written by Paul, and possibly the most important letter ever written by a Christian. It provided a fundamental statement of Christian thought and became the basis of influential restatements of theology throughout Christian history.*

PAUL wrote his letter to the Romans almost certainly from the city of Corinth, Greece, sometime between 55 and 57CE. He wrote for several reasons:

• He had completed his missionary work in the eastern Mediterranean and was looking for new mission fields in the West; Rome would provide an invaluable support base: *"Now, with no further place for me in these regions, I desire, as I have for many years, to come to you when I go to Spain. For I do hope to see you on my journey and to be sent on by you, once I have enjoyed your company for a little while"* (15:23–24ff.; 15:14–22).

• He wanted to expound the Gospel that he had been preaching in order to avoid any misconceptions and to clear up any mis-understandings (e.g., 3:1–8; 6:1; 7:7; 9:6; 11:1; 14:1). This was important because he was about to take the collection for the poor Christians in Jerusalem that he had made among his (Gentile) churches to the mother church there and was fearful of the outcome of this action (15:25–32; pp.400–1).

• He was anxious to bring spiritual blessings to the Christian congregations in Rome (1:8–15), and to counsel them on various matters of their common life within the threatening environment of the capital city of the empire (12:1–15:7).

• He wished to commend Phoebe, a deacon and a patron of the nearby church in Cenchreae, to the Roman believers. Paul's letter was probably carried by her (16:1–2).

**"WHO WILL SEPARATE US FROM THE LOVE OF CHRIST?"**
*One of the most famous passages in Romans is chapter 8: "For I am convinced that neither death, nor life, nor angels, nor rulers, nor things present, nor things to come, nor powers, nor height, nor depth, nor anything else in all creation, will be able to separate us from the love of God in Christ Jesus our Lord" (8:38–39).*

## BEGINNINGS OF CHRISTIANITY IN ROME

The origin of the Christian churches in Rome is unclear. Although Peter and Paul are traditionally credited as the church's founding Apostles, there were clearly churches meeting there before Paul arrived, but there is no mention of Peter's presence there at that time. The only Apostles mentioned are Andronicus and (his wife?) Junia (16:7). Christianity in the city may have emerged as teaching about Jesus the Messiah within the Roman synagogues. As much is suggested by the Roman historian Suetonius in his report describing the emperor Claudius expelling Jews from Rome in 49CE "because of ... Chrestus" (presumably Christ).

The evidence from Acts 28, which does not sit easily with inferences drawn from the letter to the Romans, also suggests a Christianity that began in internal dialogue within the large Jewish commu-nity in Rome. If many – or most – of the Christian Jews had been expelled within the decade before Paul wrote to the Romans, this may explain why his letter was addressed primarily to Gentiles: *"Now I am speaking to you Gentiles. Inasmuch then as I am an apostle to the Gentiles, I glorify my ministry in order to make my own people jealous and thus save some of them"* (11:13ff.; 1:5–6). The return of Jewish "exiles" to predominantly Gentile churches may be implied in 14:1: *"Welcome those who are weak in faith, but not for the purpose of quarreling over opinions."*

## THE GOSPEL ACCORDING TO ROMANS

The context just described may help explain the principal thrust of this letter to the Romans: it sets out to expound the Gospel of God's righteousness (that is, God's self-chosen obligation to save those who trust in him), as an obligation to "Jew first but also Greek/Gentile" (1:16–17). This involves a recognition from the Jews that not just Gentiles have fallen away from God's intended dependence of "creature on Creator." Jews too, despite being chosen as God's own people, continue to fall short of God's standards and need his forgiveness and salvation (1:18–3:20).

For Paul, God's saving outreach had come through Christ, and particularly through his death and Resurrection: *"But now, irrespective of the law, the righteousness of God has been disclosed, and is attested by the law and the prophets, the righteousness of God through faith in Christ Jesus for all who believe. For there is no distinction, since all have sinned and fall short of the glory of God; they are now justified by his grace as a gift, through the redemption that is in Christ Jesus"* (3:21–24ff.). This confirms that Jews, as well as Gentiles, need to rely on the justifying grace and power of God, which has been foreshadowed in the archetypal case of Abraham (3:27–4:25; *pp.38–39*) and is now demonstrated by Christ. The result extends beyond Abraham and the Jew/Gentile division of humanity: in Christ, God has reversed the state of affairs that Adam's, meaning humanity's, disobedience had set in motion (ch.5).

Paul then proceeds to spell out the corollaries of this exposition of the Gospel: for the powers of sin and death – believers can be freed from them by grace (ch.6a); for the function of the Law – as a power for death or a power for life? (ch.7); for the weakness of the all-too-human flesh – which can now be overcome by the Spirit of God (8:1–30). Thus, believers can be wholly confident in this God (8:31–39).

But this affirmation raises the question of God's faithfulness to his people Israel. Why have they not accepted this Gospel? Has God's word and purpose failed (9:6–8)? Paul attempted to answer by pointing out that "Israel" is defined by God's call to individuals, rather than by physical descent or religious practice: *"For not all Israelites truly belong to Israel, and not all of Abraham's children are his true descendants; but 'It is through Isaac that descendants shall be named after you.' This means that it is not the children of the flesh who are the children of God, but the children of the promise are counted as descendants"* (9:6b–8ff.). The recognition that God's choice of some implies rejection of others (9:19–23) is qualified in several ways: the rejection first of all is the rejection of Israel "in part"; and God's overarching purpose is one of mercy to all, to Jews as well as Gentiles, to all Israel (9:24–11:36).

The rest of the letter deals with exhortations on how the Christian community should function as the body of Christ (12:1–8), how it should live within a hostile society (12:9–13:14), and how it should handle its internal disagreements (14:1–15:6).

## THE BOOK

**TITLE:** The Letter of Paul to the Romans

**DATE:** Probably c.56CE

**AUTHORSHIP:** Paul

## THE CONTENTS

**CHAPTER 1:1–17**
Address, greeting, thanksgiving, and theme

**CHAPTERS 1:18–3:20**
Indictment of humanity, Jew first but also Greek

**CHAPTERS 3:21–5:21**
The Gospel's response – God's saving righteousness

**CHAPTERS 6–8**
How grace answers the problems of sin and death, of the Law, and the weakness of the flesh

**CHAPTERS 9–11**
What the Gospel means for Israel

**CHAPTERS 12:1–15:13**
How Christians should conduct themselves in the face of others and among themselves

**CHAPTER 15:14–32**
Travel plans and hopes

**CHAPTER 16**
Personal greetings and final exhortation

## KEY THEMES

*The Gospel as God's means to salvation; justification by faith*

•

*Who is Israel and how shall Israel be saved?*

•

*The problem of the Law and the power of the Spirit*

•

*Love as the key to positive relationships*

For further reading see bibliography numbers: 111, 435, 570, 657, 843

# "JESUS IS LORD"

*The statement that "Jesus is Lord" is the foundation of the Christian Church, acknowledging that Jesus lived, died, and rose again, exalted by God as Lord of Heaven and earth.*

P AUL wrote in Romans 10:9: *"If you confess with your lips that Jesus is Lord and believe in your heart that God raised him from the dead, you will be saved."* He wrote in 1 Corinthians 12:3: *"No one can say 'Jesus is Lord' except by the Holy Spirit."* This confession that "Jesus is Lord" has been acknowledged by Christians since the earliest times. But what does it mean?

## THE MEANING

The Greek *kurie* ("sir") is a form of address usually directed to another person, as is the Aramaic equivalent *mar*, or *mareh*. But it may also be used to address God as Lord. The Aramaic is found in Daniel (2:47; 5:23) and the Greek form, *Kurios*, is found in the Septuagint as Lord God, and also in other Jewish texts. Thus both words (Greek and Aramaic) could be used for God and for a human. Which of the two meanings did early Christians have in mind? Were they addressing Jesus respectfully as "Sir," "Master," or "Teacher," or were they associating Jesus with God?

Some have argued that Jesus was first called Teacher, or Sir, and that only later was he called Lord. However, in some of the earliest New Testament passages Jesus is clearly thought of as more than a man and a teacher. An example is the early hymn, written or quoted by Paul: *"so that at the name of Jesus every knee should bend, in heaven and on earth and under the earth, and every tongue confess that Jesus Christ is Lord"* (Phil. 2:6–11; cf. Isa. 45:23). Likewise the prayer *maranatha*, Aramaic for *"Our Lord, come!"* (1 Cor. 16:22), is looking for more than the return of a great teacher.

## LORD OF LIFE AND DEATH

In light of their belief that Jesus was risen from the dead (Acts 2:32–36), it seems clear from the start that those believers who accepted Jesus as Christ also associated him with God as Lord. The Resurrection not only demonstrated that God was able to overcome death but also vindicated Jesus and his message as truly of God. Some passages in the Bible that unmistakably apply to God are also applied to Jesus, such as the reference to Psalm 102, in Hebrews 1:10–12, and the affirmation of Jesus' lordship over the cosmos described in 1 Corinthians 8:6 and Colossians 1:15–20 (cf. below). Because Jesus is risen from the dead, he is the one who has control over life and death (Rom. 14:9).

## LORD OF THE CHURCH AND LORD OF CREATION

Jesus is also recognized as Lord of the Church. He is the one who brings salvation, sends the Holy Spirit to empower the Church for mission, and gives gifts to the Church for its expansion.

Jesus is the judge not only of the Church but of all people, the Lord of Creation through whom everything was created and in whom everything holds together. In his call to his disciples to go and preach the Gospel throughout the world, Jesus' authority is named as universal: *"All authority in heaven and on earth has been given to me. Go therefore and make disciples of all nations, baptizing them in the name of the Father and of the Son and of the Holy Spirit, and teaching them to obey everything that I have commanded you"* (Matt. 28:18–20).

**JESUS AS LORD**
*As Lord, Jesus reigns over Heaven and earth: "I am alive forever and ever; and I have the keys of Death and of Hades" (Rev. 1:18).*

# THE TRINITY

*Although the word "Trinity" is not found in the Bible, it is a central doctrine of Christianity: Father, Son, and Holy Spirit,*
*three persons as one Godhead. The term evolved in the fourth century CE after a long series of Christian debates.*

The first Jewish Christians came from a deeply monotheistic tradition of belief in One God. It is all the more remarkable then, that they associated Jesus with God as Lord in a way that led to the realization that Jesus *is* God. Their experience of the Holy Spirit (*pp.416–17*) made clear to them that God is always present, even to Jesus during his life (e.g., at Jesus' baptism, *p.325*). Thus God is present in the world and yet apart from it.

This meant that, while the Jewish belief in the Spirit of God present among God's people remained unimpaired, the earliest Christians' experience of Jesus (reflected in Paul's letters) compelled them to believe that Jesus embodied the presence of God and brought into their midst what Judaism attributed to God: Creation, conviction of sin, forgiveness, redemption from evil and from death, new life, and hope. Jesus, still recognized and remembered as a human individual of recent history, was also greater than that – his power was universal and cosmic, for he shared the very being, or reality, of God. Such convictions cannot be explained by the view (held by some scholars) that Jesus was "promoted" from an impressive teacher to being God. The early Christians based their evidence on the fact that Jesus was who he was and did what he did because of his relationship to God. That they held such convictions is powerful evidence for Jesus' Resurrection, since without the Resurrection it is impossible to account for these extraordinary beliefs. This early Christian belief was not an alternative to the Jewish belief in the Spirit of God, but a new, decisive experience of the Holy Spirit, leading to a profound exploration of the mystery of God as "Father, Son, and Holy Spirit."

### Three in One
*This Greek Orthodox icon depicts God's encompassing relationship of love, communication (the Holy Spirit in the form of a dove), and self-giving (Jesus). The full understanding of the Trinity is not explicit in the New Testament, but it does indicate threefold formulas, as in 2 Corinthians 13:13.*

## THE SON OF GOD

In recognizing Jesus as Lord, the early Christian Church clearly believed that he was more than a teacher. Yet the New Testament also points to Jesus' humanity: he was born, ate, slept, was tired, wept, was crucified, and died. He was tempted and so is able to sympathize with human weaknesses (Heb. 4:15).

However, the New Testament writers also emphasize what is different about Jesus. In the Gospels, Jesus is presented consistently as one who exercises power (Greek, *dunamis*), authority, and wisdom. For example, Mark 6:2 describes how, when Jesus began to teach in the synagogue at Nazareth, those people who witnessed the radicalism of Jesus' words and actions asked a fundamental question, *"Where did this man get all this? What is this wisdom that has been given to him? What deeds of power are being done by his hands! Is not this the carpenter, the son of*

> **66** *Yet for us there is one God, the Father, from whom are all things and for whom we exist, and one Lord, Jesus Christ, through whom are all things and through whom we exit.* **99**
>
> (1 Corinthians 8:6)

*Mary ... ?"* They knew that Jesus was human; they had seen him grow up, so they wondered "how can these things be?" Jesus pointed to God as the source of all he did. That, essentially, is why the early Church associated Jesus with God as Lord: through Jesus, the power, authority, and wisdom of God are alive among all believers.

There are various descriptions in the New Testament illustrating the origin of Jesus' close relationship with God. The Gospels of Matthew and Luke tell the story of Jesus' miraculous birth from a virgin through the power of the Holy Spirit. The Spirit is also seen coming upon Jesus at his baptism in the form of a dove (*p.325*). In Romans 1:4, Paul links Jesus' Resurrection to his special "sonship" with God, while the Gospel of John opens with a prologue that explains the true identity of Jesus Christ as the "Word" (*Logos*), or God taking the human form of a man (John 1:1–18).

**For further reading see bibliography numbers:** 109, 121, 136, 138a, 377, 423, 538, 575, 576, 647, 833, 870

# THE FIRST LETTER TO THE
# CORINTHIANS

*One of the earliest parts of the New Testament, 1 Corinthians was addressed to newly converted Christians living in the rich, cultured city of Corinth. It deals with many specific problems, and points to Christian love as a "more excellent way" to live.*

PAUL'S first letter to the Corinthian church was his response to a verbal report and a letter sent from Corinth about developments there since his departure three years previously. Dispelling any idealized images of early Christianity by revealing a church with many problems, Paul wrote to the Christian believers there to correct nearly a dozen different areas of behavior and belief. As well as revealing Paul's understanding of the cross and the Resurrection of Christ, this letter develops Christian sexual ethics, provides unique insights into early Christian worship, and contains Paul's famous eulogy on Christian love.

## A DIVIDED CHURCH

Sitting astride the isthmus – the narrow piece of land that connects the Greek mainland and the Peloponnese – first-century Corinth was a busy, cosmopolitan trading port. Paul had founded the church there during an 18-month stay in 50–51CE. Although the church included some highborn individuals, it was composed mainly of ordinary people such as artisans, freedmen, and slaves. The message and letter received by Paul from Corinth indicated both that some people were engaging in unacceptable behavior, and that the church was dividing into factions. Some, perhaps the richer and better-educated members of the church, were claiming superior wisdom, spiritual insight,

and status. This supposed superiority allowed them to engage in immorality and idolatry, and caused them to despise the less-sophisticated believers as foolish and weak in their faith. It was also dividing the church. Some were associating with prostitutes, others falling out badly enough to take each other to court (ch.6), some were participating in idolatrous feasts (chs.8 and 10), and at the Lord's Supper the rich were eating all the food and leaving the poorer believers to go hungry.

**TEAM-BUILDING**
*Paul sought to dispel any discordant or incorrect beliefs among the Christian believers of the Corinth church, and to unite them as members of one body under Christ.*

## CHRISTIAN BEHAVIOR (CHAPTERS 1–10)

In his letter, Paul asserted his right as the founder of the church at Corinth, and as an Apostle commissioned by the risen Christ, to oppose vigorously the immoral behavior in the church. For Christian believers, true wisdom and divine power are found not in the arrogance of human "wisdom" or "knowledge," but in the apparently weak and foolish message of a despised and crucified Savior. True spirituality is knowing the crucified Christ and following the way of love (1 Cor. 2).

In the central chapters of the letter (5–10), Paul confronts head-on the behavior of the Christian believers in Corinth. He instructs them to shun an unrepentant believer who is living with his father's wife (ch.5). He reprimands believers for going outside the church to settle their disputes: "it would be better to be wronged or defrauded than to do this" (6:7).

While he agrees with those who do not think idols exist, Paul does not agree with their conclusion that participating in idolatrous meals is unimportant. Some believers have not yet realized that idols are unreal, so to treat idolatrous meals as having no significance might lead those believers inadvertently into conflict with demonic forces behind idol worship.

In chapter seven Paul sketches out a Christian sexual ethic that is a combination of clear principle and honest realism. While he encourages the single life as providing greater freedom to serve God, he recognizes that this is not a practical option for many. He sees sexual relations as essential to marriage and rejects the separation of Christian partners except where it takes place at the initiative of a nonbelieving spouse. Despite his strong words Paul prefers to appeal to the Corinthians and persuade them to adopt his point of view. Throughout this central section of the letter, Paul uses a combination of the Jewish Scriptures, Jesus' teachings, and his own theological arguments to promote his vision of acceptable Christian behavior.

## INSTRUCTING THE CHURCH (CHAPTERS 11–15)

In later chapters, Paul gives instructions about the orderly conduct of Christian worship. He instructs both men and women on appropriate demeanor in worship (11:1–16). He recounts the words of institution of the Last Supper *(p.351)* and argues that a true appreciation of the body and blood of Christ implies showing consideration, not contempt, for fellow Christians (11:17–34). Paul teaches that the congregation is the "body of Christ," a mutually interdependent community of believers. They all need one another and the different gifts and ministries that God has given to each person. In worship gatherings, the verbal contributions of the worshipers are to be ordered, readily understood, and offered in a spirit of love and mutual consideration so that the church is edified. Any conflicts can be resolved by following the more excellent way of Christian love (ch.13).

In chapter 15, Paul confronts those influenced by Greek philosophical teaching who did not believe that postmortem existence could be in bodily form. In beginning his argument with a list of some of the first eyewitnesses to the risen Christ, Paul incidentally provides us with the earliest written evidence for the Resurrection of Christ. Paul argues that Christ's Resurrection was both the model and the guarantee of the resurrected body that Christians will share at Christ's coming. This resurrected body will not be merely the physical body revived but a transformed and glorious immortal body. In proposing such a view of future life, Paul maps a careful path between two extremes: understanding the Resurrection as mere resuscitation of a corpse, and interpreting it as simply a spiritual "idea." *"We will not all die, but we will all be changed, in a moment, in the twinkling of an eye, at the last trumpet"* (15:51b–52a).

## THE BOOK

TITLE: The First Letter of Paul to the Corinthians

DATE: c.55CE

AUTHORSHIP: Paul

## THE CONTENTS

### CHAPTERS 1–4
Paul's response to reports of divisions within the church in Corinth: the reasons for the divisions are a misunderstood message, a misunderstood messenger, and a misunderstanding of Paul's ministry

### CHAPTERS 5–10
Paul addresses problems of Christian behavior in the world: sexual immorality, lawsuits among believers, marriage, the unmarried, sacrificed food, forfeiting liberty, the dangers of complacency

### CHAPTERS 11–15
Paul gives instructions on worship and doctrine: public prayer, the Lord's Supper, spiritual gifts, love, prophecy and tongues, the Resurrection of Christ and of the dead

### CHAPTER 16
Collection for the saints at Jerusalem, travel plans, greetings, and farewell

## KEY THEMES

*The power of the cross and the Resurrection of Christ*

•

*Correcting Christian behavior and instructing Christian worship*

•

*The importance of Christian love*

**For further reading see bibliography numbers: 111, 166, 259, 287, 379, 819, 823**

# THE HOLY SPIRIT

*For the early Christians, the Holy Spirit was a conscious and living force in the lives
of individual believers and in Christian communities. The Spirit is God's
presence among believers.*

WHAT was strikingly characteristic of the early Christians was their sense of empowerment by God after receiving the Holy Spirit, which transformed their lives. Paul wrote of gifts received (Rom. 12:6–8; 1 Cor. 12–14) and of the fruits of the Holy Spirit (Gal. 5:16–26), characteristics that persist in Christian life today. The Spirit brought a new awareness of God and an experience with the risen Jesus, strengthening and empowering them in their Christian lives. The early Church experienced the Holy Spirit in its worship and mission, and it looked forward with hope, inspired by the Spirit, to the new life of the Resurrection and of the world to come *(pp.444–45)*.

## THE SPIRIT OF GOD AND OF CHRIST

For Paul, the Holy Spirit was understood to be the Spirit of God, that is, God's presence and power, active and effective among the people. The Spirit stands with God the Father and Jesus Christ as the source of life and blessing for the Church: *"Now there are varieties of gifts, but the same Spirit; and there are varieties of services, but the same Lord; and there are varieties of activities, but it is the same God who activates all of them in everyone"* (1 Cor. 12:4–6; 2 Cor. 13:13).

But more often Paul refers to the Holy Spirit as the effective working of God in the lives of believers, the means by which God's purpose is communicated and effected in the world. Because God's work of human salvation was effected through Christ, the Holy Spirit is also

**SYMBOL OF THE SPIRIT**
*At the time of Jesus' baptism, "the Holy Spirit descended upon
him in bodily form like a dove" (Luke 3:22). The dove has
become a symbol for freedom, which only God can give.*

the Spirit of Christ, so that by God's Spirit the benefits of salvation are received and the life and character of Christ are formed in believers: *"But when the fullness of time had come, God sent his Son, born of a woman, born under the law, in order to redeem those who were under the law, so that we might receive adoption as children. And because you are children, God has sent the Spirit of his Son into our hearts, crying, 'Abba! Father!' "* (Gal. 4:4–6; Rom. 8:5–17).

The coming of the Holy Spirit upon believers at the beginning of their Christian lives marks a crucial transformation: it is by the Spirit that believers confess Jesus as Lord *(pp.412–13)*. From then on, the Holy Spirit dwells in those believers who live lives that owe allegiance to Jesus Christ. Living life in the Spirit means no longer being enslaved to selfish values and desires but being free to live a life that reflects the holy character of God and produces spiritual fruits: *"The fruit of the Spirit is love, joy, peace, patience, kindness, generosity, faithfulness, gentleness, and self-control"* (Gal. 5:22).

> **❝ The grace
> of the Lord Jesus
> Christ, the love of God,
> and the communion
> of the Holy Spirit
> be with all
> of you. ❞**
>
> (2 Corinthians 13:13)

## THE SPIRIT AND HISTORY

The Spirit also has a historical dimension for Paul. The new Covenant in Christ is the Covenant enacted by the Spirit, in contrast to the old Covenant of the Law: *"Surely we do not need, as some do, letters of recommendation to you or from you, do we?... You show that you are a letter of Christ, prepared by us, written not with ink but with the Spirit of the living God, not on tablets of stone but on tablets of human hearts ... [God] has made us competent to be ministers of a new covenant, not of letter but of spirit; for the letter kills, but the Spirit gives life"*

(2 Cor. 3:1–6). But more than this, the work of the Spirit in Christians anticipates the kingdom to come when, at the Resurrection, believers will have "spiritual bodies," that is, bodies made alive in the Spirit (1 Cor. 15:44). The Spirit's work now is an anticipation of this future life, the down payment or first installment of what is to come: *"He who has prepared us for this very thing is God, who has given us the Spirit as a guarantee"* (2 Cor. 5:5; cf. 2 Cor. 1:21–22; Eph. 1:14; Rom. 8:18–27).

> 66 *It is God who establishes us with you in Christ and has anointed us, by putting his seal on us and giving us his Spirit in our hearts as a first installment.* 99
>
> (2 Corinthians 1:21–22)

of different gifts, or *charisms* (Greek "gift"), to the Church. These various charisms, such as teaching and healing (prophecy and glossolalia, *below*, are only two among many), contribute to the life and worship of the Church. Distributed by the Holy Spirit to the members of the Church, the charisms help to bring the Church to maturity, when each believer exercises his or her gifts in love, and to build one another up: *"To each is given the manifestation of the Spirit for the common good. To one is given through the Spirit the utterance of wisdom, and to another the utterance of knowledge according to the same Spirit, to another faith by the same Spirit, to another gifts of healing by the one Spirit, to another the working of miracles, to another prophecy, to another the discernment of spirits, to another various kinds of tongues, to another the interpretation of tongues. All these are activated by one and the same Spirit who allots to each one individually just as the Spirit chooses"* (1 Cor. 12:7–11).

## THE SPIRIT AND THE CHURCH

The work of the Spirit was and is evident in the Church and its worship. The Church is one because all are baptized in one Holy Spirit (1 Cor. 12:13). All Christian believers share *koinonia* (Greek "participation") in the Spirit (Phil. 2:1). When Christian believers gather together for worship, they do so in the unity of the one Spirit who distributes a variety

# PROPHECY

*Prophecy is speaking directly for God. In the New Testament it has its source in the Spirit of God.*

Prophecy would have been familiar to the first Christians, from the biblical Prophets *(pp. 196–97)*, from Agabus (whose prophecy of a famine in Acts 11 resulted in the collection for the poor that Paul took to Jerusalem, *p. 400*), and from John the Baptist. Jesus himself was seen as a prophet. Paul experienced the ministry of prophets in the church in Antioch: *"At that time prophets came down from Jerusalem to Antioch. One of them named Agabus stood up and predicted by the Spirit that there would be a severe famine all over the world; and this took place in the reign of Claudius"* (Acts 11:27–28). Some prophecies were predictions of future events, and others were simply understood as revelations from God given through human messengers.

Paul described prophetic utterances as *charismata*, gifts from God, inspired by the Holy Spirit. Among the other charisms, prophecy was regarded as important for building up the Church. Paul taught that the inspiration of prophets was under their own control and so prophesying should be done in a responsible and orderly way during worship. Prophecy was not to be despised but tested (1 Thess. 5:19–22). Only two or three prophets were allowed to speak during any given session and each had to take an orderly turn. The discernment of the congregation was to be used to test their messages so that the good could be retained and the prophecies would result in the strengthening of the Church: *"When you come together, each one has a hymn, a lesson, a revelation, a tongue, or an interpretation. Let all things be done for building up ... For you can all learn prophecy one by one, so that all may learn and all be encouraged"* (1 Cor. 14:26–33). In this way, Paul intended to ensure that the prophetic messages of those speaking in God's name were subject to the considered judgment of the worshiping congregation.

# GLOSSOLALIA

*"Speaking in tongues," or glossolalia, comes from the Greek, glossa, meaning "tongue," and lalia, meaning "speech."*

Speaking in tongues was a feature of worship and prayer in the early Church, as it has been in various movements in the history of the Church ever since. The book of Acts describes the very first believers speaking in tongues on the day of Pentecost: *"Divided tongues, as of fire, appeared among them, and a tongue rested on each of them. All of them were filled with the Holy Spirit and began to speak in other languages, as the Spirit gave them ability"* (Acts 2:3–4). Acts also gives other instances of new converts speaking in tongues when the Holy Spirit came upon them. Whereas in prophecy a member of the worshiping congregation would give a message to the church from God, speaking in tongues was a form of prayer or praise addressed to God.

1 Corinthians 12 and 14 contain Paul's practical instructions to the Corinthian church about glossolalia. Paul tells us that he himself spoke in tongues but thought little of the gift. He taught that glossolalia had a place in congregational worship only if it were followed by an interpretation in the vernacular so that the rest of the congregation could understand. Only when those who were listening could understand what was being said could they be edified and say "Amen." If there was no one in the church to interpret, and the speakers could not do so themselves, then the gift of tongues was to be reserved for private prayer to God: *"Those who speak in a tongue do not speak to other people but to God; for nobody understands them, since they are speaking mysteries in the Spirit ... Those who speak in a tongue build up themselves, but those who prophesy build up the church ... If anyone speaks in a tongue, let there be only two or at most three, and each in turn; and let one interpret. But if there is no one to interpret, let them be silent in church and speak to themselves and to God"* (1 Cor. 14:1–28).

For further reading see bibliography numbers: 257, 287a, 520d, 575, 759, 760

# THE SACRAMENTS
## OF BAPTISM AND THE LORD'S SUPPER

*Sacraments are important truths put into enacted form. Baptism and the Eucharist were instituted during the New Testament period and, because they are connected directly with Jesus, they are often known as "Dominical" sacraments.*

T HE word *sacrament*, understood as an outward and visible sign pledging an inward and spiritual grace, comes from the Latin translation of the New Testament, where *sacramentum* was used to translate the Greek *mysterion*, or mystery. The seven sacraments, or ceremonies, that came to be recognized in both Eastern and Western Christianity are baptism (*see pp.324–25*), confirmation, the Lord's Supper (*pp.350–51*), penance, extreme unction (anointing of the sick; *see also p.454*), ordination, and marriage. Some of these, such as confirmation and penance, were not, as far as we can tell, practiced during New Testament times in the forms known today. Thus for some Christians, baptism and the Lord's Supper are the only sacraments,

**NEWLY WEDS, ERITREA**
*In the Bible, marriage customs involve two events – the betrothal and the wedding ceremony.*

because only they can be derived directly from Jesus. He instituted the commemoration of the Last Supper, and John's Gospel records that he himself practiced baptism (John 3:22). He also commanded his disciples to go and baptize all nations (Matt. 28:19). The practice of putting important truths into enacted form is deeply embedded in the Hebrew Bible, above all in prophetic actions (*pp.198–99*), and it may be that this is the background to the sacraments – one marking initiation, the other continuation in the grace of God.

**HOLY WATER**
*After Jesus' Resurrection, baptism became an important element in the early Church's process of conversion. Acts 2:38 recounts Peter's words: "Repent, and be baptized ... so that your sins may be forgiven; and you will receive the gift of the Holy Spirit." Today, the many different Christian denominations have their own traditions of baptizing initiates, either by the anointing of water or by total submersion. Here, a member of the Russian Orthodox Church is submerged in the holy water of a consecrated ice-hole.*

## BAPTISM

From a New Testament perspective baptism has a five-fold symbolism:
• It is a declaration of union with Jesus, expressing solidarity with the crucified and risen Jesus (Rom. 6:3–4).
• It is a sign of cleansing – a "bath" in which sins are "washed away" (Acts 22:16; Eph. 5:25–27; Tit. 3:5).
• It is a confession of faith, where Jesus is declared as Lord (1 Tim. 6:12).
• It is a rite of initiation into the Church (1 Cor. 12:13; Gal. 3:26–28).
• It is a sign of the Spirit's presence, where God's mark of ownership is stamped on the baptized (Eph. 1:13–14).

Christian baptism has its roots in the "Great Commission." Before the Ascension (*pp.382–83*), Jesus is described as commanding his disciples to *"go ... and make disciples of all nations, baptizing them"* (Matt. 28:19). It follows the example of Jesus' baptism (Matt. 3:13–17; Mark 1:9–11; Luke 3:21–22), and, according to John 3:22, of Jesus

**THE EUCHARIST**
*The breaking of bread and the drinking of wine is celebrated by worshipers during Church services in order to commemorate Jesus' last supper with his disciples, and to receive him in the way that he himself promised.*

# BAPTISM OF THE DEAD

In Paul's letter to the Corinthians there is a puzzling verse: *"Otherwise, what will those people do who receive baptism on behalf of the dead? If the dead are not raised at all, why are people baptized on their behalf?"* (1 Cor. 15:29). It is inconceivable that Paul could ever have approved of Christians being baptized on behalf of those who had died without believing in Jesus. A clue may be found in a description of Marcionite practice (*p.475*): "When a catechumen among them dies, they hide a living man under the dead man's bed, approach the dead man, speak with him, and ask if he wishes to receive baptism; then when he makes no answer the man who is hidden underneath says instead of him that he wishes to be baptized, and so they baptize him instead of the departed." It is possible, therefore, that Paul's obscure verse refers to a group of Christians who practiced baptism on behalf of those who had died believing, but before baptism. Without giving approval to this practice, Paul used it as an argument for believing in the Resurrection.

baptizing others. Although the parallel between Jesus' baptism and Christian baptism is not exact – because Jesus in his baptism identified himself with the sinfulness of humanity, whereas Christians identify themselves with Jesus who overcame sin – there is a common theme of obedience (*see* Matt. 3:15). In the early Church, baptism was an integral part of the conversion process.

## THE LORD'S SUPPER

From a New Testament perspective the Lord's Supper also has a five-fold symbolism:
• It is a meal for believers to remember the death of Jesus during which his enacted sign (*p.351*) is

made of real and repeated effect (1 Cor. 11:24*ff*.).
• It is an occasion when the Church remembers how the risen Jesus broke bread with his disciples (Luke 24:30–31), and how the Church "feeds" on him by faith and so has communion with Jesus.
• At the Lord's table the Church looks forward to Jesus' return (1 Cor. 11:26) and so anticipates Heaven itself.

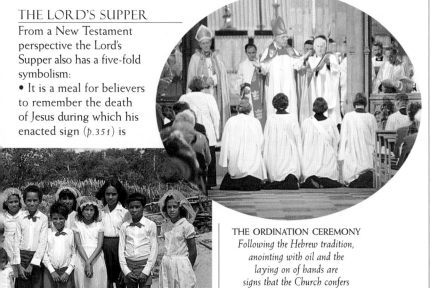

**THE ORDINATION CEREMONY**
*Following the Hebrew tradition, anointing with oil and the laying on of hands are signs that the Church confers authority on its ministers.*

**CHILDREN AT CONFIRMATION**
*Confirmation is a time when the baptismal vows are renewed. Some link it to the laying on of hands (Acts 8:14–17; 19:1–7), others to Pentecost.*

• It is an expression of fellowship. The bread symbolizes oneness in Jesus, and so to eat the bread or drink the cup "in an unworthy manner" is to fail to discern the Body of Christ (1 Cor. 11:27–28).
• The "new Covenant" is made real every time the bread is broken and the wine, or juice symbolizing wine, is drunk. By implication, the Lord's Supper is the place where baptismal vows are renewed.

The Lord's Supper is rooted first and foremost in the Last Supper, where Jesus, as he the broke bread and poured out the wine, commanded his disciples to "do this in remembrance of me" (*see pp.350–51*). It also has its roots in those occasions when the risen Jesus invited his disciples to share with him in the "breaking of bread" (Luke 24:30). It became very much the practice of the early Church, as in Jerusalem, for example, where the first Christians met daily to "break bread" (Acts 2:42, 44); at Troas they did so weekly (Acts 20:7).

For further reading see bibliography numbers: 54, 74, 428, 508, 784

# THE SECOND LETTER TO THE
# CORINTHIANS

*2 Corinthians is a deeply personal letter by Paul, reestablishing his relationship
with the church at Corinth after a series of difficulties
and misunderstandings.*

PAUL'S second letter to the Corinthians is an
emotional, staccato letter of deep pastoral concern
and love. It was probably sent from Macedonia
(Acts 20:1) to the church Paul had founded in
Corinth, and was written to repair a damaged relationship.
After Paul had left Corinth, newcomers to the city attracted
local Christians to a style of faith that Paul considered to
be a serious distortion of the Gospel. He wrote to defend
the integrity of his own ministry, to explain how the
message of Christ's cross
should influence the lifestyle
of those who preach it, and
to win the Corinthians back.

## COUNTER-MISSIONARIES

Corinth had proved a difficult
place for the Christian faith
to take root. Paul's first letter
to the Corinthians (*pp.414–15*)
had addressed a host of
problems in the church
there. Some of those
problems had arisen from the
pride and elitism that were
part of the city's culture. The
Corinthians were confident
and authoritarian, they spoke
about their own credentials
and spiritual gifts, and they
deplored what they saw as
Paul's weak apostleship.

Paul's assertive leadership
in his first letter impressed at
least some of the Corinthians.
They appreciated rhetorical
polish and were prepared to
pay for cultured preaching.

Some of them, however, may have resented Paul and would
have been glad to find other leaders. A visit that Paul made
(probably from Ephesus, *see* Acts 19:10) had led to an
awkward clash. He fretted that his converts were being
duped by a shallow and unsatisfactory version of Christianity.

## MANY LETTERS, ONE EPISTLE?

It is possible that 2 Corinthians, as we now have it, might
be a composite of two or
three shorter letters. There
are some abrupt changes of
subject in the earlier chapters
of the Epistle. Could these
chapters have been made by
merging two or more original letters? Many modern
readers of this letter, or
Epistle (Greek, "send news"),
find the change in tone at
the start of chapter 10 –
from conciliation and appeal
to protest and challenge –
jarring and unnatural. Might
chapters 10–13 once have
formed a separate letter,
written after the earlier
portion, when the situation
in Corinth had deteriorated?

However, the letter can
also be seen as a whole. Its
pattern follows that of Greek
letter writing (*pp.406–7*) and
deals with similar themes
from beginning to end. Its
sharp changes in tone and
direction might have been
caused by Paul's strong
emotions when he wrote it.

**THE CROSS OF CHRIST**
*Paul understood that human suffering and weakness reveals the greatness
of God's power, shown by Christ's suffering and his resurrection from death.*

## THE CROSS OF CHRIST (CHAPTERS 1–7)

Paul writes first of his own honesty, and of the consistent care he has always shown for the church in Corinth (chs.1 and 2). He is conscious of God's presence in his life, and that gives him a sense of strength and hope when his calling leads to hardship and suffering. He states that ministers of Christ may expect to suffer, for they serve a God who saves from a cross (ch.4). Yet that cross is the basis of a Christian's relationship with God (ch.5), so Paul appeals to the Corinthians to come back to a faith in which Christ's death takes a central place (ch.6).

## MONEY MATTERS (CHAPTERS 8–9)

Although this section is an aside to the main line of argument, it shows one reason why Paul wanted to regain the Corinthians' trust. A number of passages in the Epistles and Acts mention Paul collecting money from his Gentile churches for needy Christians in Jerusalem (*pp.401, 410*). Romans 15 outlines the significance of this gift of money in relation to Paul's wider vision. Yet these two chapters in 2 Corinthians give the most sustained account anywhere in the Bible of the many proper motives for Christian charitable giving.

## CONTRAST OF STYLES, CONFLICT OF SUBSTANCE (CHAPTERS 10–13)

The newcomers (*p.420*) have boasted about their power and their record. Paul calls them deceivers and cheats. Then he turns their way of thinking upside-down: he lists the weaknesses and woes of his career as signs that he is an authentic servant of Christ. Even the mysterious "thorn in the flesh" (12:7), whatever impediment that may have been, he now welcomes as a blessing: *"for whenever I am weak, then I am strong"* (12:10). There have been many attempts to guess what this "thorn" might be, ranging from persecution to physical illness. Whatever its nature, this and other forms of suffering are deeply important to Paul because they demonstrate the absolute priority of his life: in the greatest weakness, as in the death of Christ, God's power to overcome all things is made clear. Paul believes that suffering does not question his status as an Apostle of Christ; rather it confirms his faith, for that is where the true power of Christ lies.

## SUFFERING

The theme of sharing in the suffering of Christ is of paramount importance in 2 Corinthians: *"For while we live, we are always being given up to death for Jesus' sake, so that the life of Jesus may be made visible in our mortal flesh"* (4:11). Suffering is not a sign of failure: the God of the cross is present and involved in suffering. People who suffer are sometimes the most effective ambassadors of Christ.

# THE BOOK

TITLE: The Second Letter of Paul to the Corinthians

DATE: Probably 55 or 56CE

AUTHORSHIP: Paul

# THE CONTENTS

### CHAPTERS 1–2:13
Personal background: a reminder of Paul's own conduct

### CHAPTERS 2:14–5:10
A description of what true Christian ministry should be like – when it is shaped by the cross of Christ

### CHAPTERS 5:11–7:4
An appeal to the Christians at Corinth to be reconciled to God

### CHAPTER 7:5–16
News from Corinth of a trouble resolved

### CHAPTERS 8–9
Collecting money for distant Christians

### CHAPTERS 10–13
About Paul's coming visit: intruders at Corinth; a church deceived; the signs of a true Apostle; a call to be ready

# KEY THEMES

*Paul's defense of his apostolic credentials and authority*

•

*Teaching on Christian ministry*

•

*Christ's death and suffering as central to the Christian faith and understanding of others' weakness and suffering*

For further reading see bibliography numbers: 50, 57, 581, 823

# ATONEMENT
## IN PAUL'S TEACHING

*Paul wrote very little about Jesus' life and much about his death. He knew that all people,
including himself, needed help and rescue from the predicament they were in.*

THE death of Jesus lies at the center of Paul's teaching about the Christian faith: *"For I handed on to you as of first importance, what I in turn had received: that Christ died for our sins in accordance with the Scriptures"* (1 Cor. 15:3). Paul learned this teaching from others who were Christians before him (*"I handed on to you ... what I also received"*), yet he also made it his own, both by the emphasis he gave it – Jesus' death on the cross takes a prominent place in all the main Pauline letters – and through the ways he explained and used it.

## DEALING WITH SIN

The cross of Christ stands between human wrongdoing and God's judgment. Christ did not intervene to save people from God's wrath, but rather God in Christ made expiation for all that has gone wrong and brings about reconciliation. This is the pivot of Paul's long argument in the early chapters of Romans: *"But God proves his love for us in that while we were still sinners Christ died for us"* (Rom. 5:8). Rather than people enduring God's wrath, God has taken the initiative, through Jesus' death, to forgive them and put them right (*see also pp.426–27*).

"Forgiveness" is not a word commonly used in Paul's letters. Instead, the reason for Christ's death is spelled out in a variety of different ways:

• **Expiation**, which means the covering up or wiping away of sin. Paul means that human guilt is blotted out by Jesus, *"whom God put forward as a sacrifice of atonement by his blood,*

JESUS' SACRIFICE OF ATONEMENT
*God forgives people's sin because of Jesus' death on the cross. Paul constantly returns to focus on this theme in his preaching (1 Cor. 2:2).*

*effective through faith"* (Rom. 3:25). In the face of God's legitimate anger (Rom. 1:18ff.) stands Christ as the place (perhaps "mercyseat," Lev. 16:13–16) where mercy and justice meet. God's love removes the sting of judgment.

• **Redemption**, which means being rescued from sin and damnation: *"Since all have sinned and fall short of the glory of God, they are now justified by his grace as a gift, through the redemption that is in Christ Jesus"* (Rom 3:23–24). This recalls the great act of rescue in Exodus (*pp.48–49*), of people caught as slaves to wrongdoing being set free to do right (Rom 6:17–23).

• **Reconciliation** is used by Paul to mean the restoring of a relationship. Enemies become friends again, just as people who once lived in opposition to God are brought back to enjoy God's love: *"In Christ God was reconciling the world to himself, not counting their trespasses against them, and entrusting the message of reconciliation to us"*, (2 Cor. 5:19; cf. Rom. 5:10)

• **"Justification"** is a key term for Paul (*pp.426–27*). It is a metaphor drawn from the law court, and he uses it to explain the Gospel as God's offer to acquit those who have done wrong; the charge has been cancelled for those who trust in God through Jesus Christ: *"Therefore, since we are justified by faith, we have peace with God through our Lord Jesus Christ"* (Rom 5:1; 3:24).

For Paul, Christ's death is not just a past event; it leads on to become a personal experience. Christians are drawn into, included in, what happened to Jesus – his death on the cross and Resurrection. One way of life comes to an end, *"our old*

# SACRIFICE

*What led Paul to shape his interpretation of Jesus' death in the way that he did? He drew on anything around him or from his own experience that might help others understand the breathtaking fact of what God has done to rescue people from their sins.*

Paul used many analogies and metaphors to bring the consequence of Jesus' death home: walls of division are broken down (*p.431*); slaves and prisoners are set free because the ransom price has been paid; victories are won; covenants are renewed; enemies are reconciled to each other.

Possibly Paul looked back to stories of Jewish martyrs of the Maccabean period (*pp.250–51*), reflecting the idea of a "noble death" in Greek and Roman philosophical writings. Perhaps he knew of various scapegoat rituals. Certainly he knew of the sacrificial system of the Hebrew Bible and of the Temple, and this also played a part in his attempt to convey the meaning of Christ's death and Resurrection. Thus when he writes, *"Christ Jesus, whom God put forward as a sacrifice of atonement by his blood, effective through faith"* (Rom. 3:25), of God *"sending his own Son ... to deal with sin"* (Rom. 8:3), and of Christ, *"who knew no sin"* being made *"to be sin"* (2 Cor.

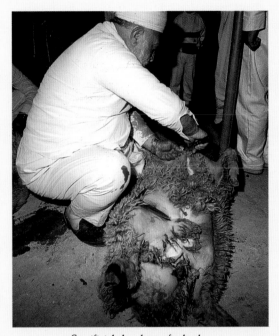

**Sacrificial slaughter of a lamb.**

5:21), he is using language that recalls the sin-offerings of Israel (Lev. 4) to explain the death of Jesus. The sacrificial animal represented the guilty person; hands were laid on its head to indicate the transfer of sin to the animal. Then the animal's blood both showed and symbolized the ending of a life in death.

For Paul, Jesus had drawn the whole significance of the ancient sacrificial system into his own death, bearing in his sinless self the guilt of others and so bringing to them the forgiveness of God. The death of Christ was unique. Yet the total giving of sacrifice is mirrored in the Church's response. In gratitude for "the mercies of God," Christians are inspired to offer themselves in service "as a living sacrifice" (Rom. 12:1). In Paul's own missionary work, he thought of the Gentile churches as a kind of sacrificial offering to God, won by Christ through Paul's ministry (Rom. 15:16).

self was crucified with him" (Rom 6:6), and another kind of living begins, *"no longer for themselves, but for him who died and was raised for them"* (2 Cor. 5:15). Jesus models a personal history that also becomes true for his followers: Christians are "alive to God in Christ" (Rom 6:11) and are set on a path of right and holy living. The first Adam introduced sin and death (Gen. 3); the second Adam brings forgiveness and new life (Rom. 5:12–21; 1 Cor. 15:20–28, 42–49).

## TURNING POINT

The cross and the Resurrection (the two cannot really be separated) marked a climactic moment in God's dealings with the world. Jesus *"gave himself ... to set us free from the present evil age"* (Gal. 1:4). Through his death, God defeats and disarms those spiritual powers that limit human living (Col. 2:15), opening new hopes and possibilities to the world. On the cross

> **❝ But God proves his love for us in that while we were still sinners Christ died for us. Much more surely then, now that we have been justified by his blood, will we be saved through him from the wrath of God. ❞**
>
> (Romans 5:8–9)

Jesus died as a man under a curse. Yet in the divine exchange of his death, people are released from the "curse of the law" (Gal. 3:13). As the Law no longer determines human identity, so God breaks the boundary separating Gentile nations from God's grace (Eph. 2:14). The Church that looks to the cross is an international community united in Christ (Gal. 3:28), Jew and Gentile together.

Paul wrote of the cross as an example for Christian behavior: to motivate his readers to show humble concern for one another (Phil. 2:6–11); and as a pattern for faithful ministry in spite of suffering (2 Cor. 4:7–12). Confronted by opposition and misunderstanding of Jesus' sacrifice of atonement on the cross, Paul explained that it remained a mystery, "a stumbling block" to the world's expectations (1 Cor. 1:22–25). Yet one man's death proved itself to be God's power to make human lives new again.

For further reading see bibliography numbers: 212, 261, 388a, 571

# THE LETTER TO THE
# GALATIANS

*Galatians is a strong letter, dealing with controversial matters. At its heart lies Paul's own commitment: "May I never boast of anything except the cross of our Lord Jesus Christ, by which the world has been crucified to me, and I to the world."*

G ALATIANS is probably among the earliest of Paul's letters, written to churches he himself had established in the central-southern heartland of modern-day Turkey *(see map, pp.274–75)*. Paul had visited the region during his first missionary journey, for which he had been commissioned by the church in Syrian Antioch (Acts 13:13–14:23), and he passed through the region again at least twice (Acts 16:1–6; 18:23). The main theme is the threat posed by the appearance of a group of people who held that Christians must keep Jewish Law, and Paul's response to this *(see pp.387, 394–95)*.

## COUNTERING THE "TROUBLEMAKERS"

On his first visit to the region, Paul had obviously been successful in his preaching. Many native Galatians believed Paul's preaching, and their lives displayed clear signs that God's spirit was at work in them (3:1–5). The reason why Paul now wrote is made clear from the opening paragraphs of this letter. Other missionaries had arrived in Galatia and were telling the new Gentile converts that, if they wanted to share in the blessings promised to Abraham and his descendants, they had to be circumcised and keep the Jewish Law. Who precisely these other missionaries were is not clear. Paul calls them "troublemakers" or "agitators" (1:7; 5:10, 12). But almost certainly they were Jews who were also Christians,

**FREEDOM FROM BONDAGE**
*Through Christ's death, Christians are set free not only from the bondage of the Law but also from the bondage of sin.*

that is, those who accepted that Jesus was the Messiah, or Christ, and who believed that this belief should lead to a better keeping of Jewish ritual Law, not an abandoning of it.

It is important to remember that at this stage the term "Christianity" had not yet been coined. The movement that Paul represented was still a "sect of the Nazarenes" within first-century Judaism. It was taken for granted in most cases that the first Gentiles converted were converted to a form of Judaism. Usually this would mean that the convert became a proselyte, being circumcised (if a male) and taking on the yoke of Torah. However, clear evidence that Gentiles were experiencing the grace of God freely, and without circumcision (2:7–9; 3:1–5), was causing a radical rethinking of the question. Paul himself recalls the discomfort and debates on the issue and its ramifications in chapter 2 of Galatians.

## A CLEAR ISSUE (CHAPTERS 1–2)

For Paul, the issue was clear. He was enraged that the Galatians, who had been converted from paganism, had then apparently been swayed by those who argued for circumcision and for keeping the Jewish Law. In his letter he argues that to impose the Law upon Gentile converts is to say that faith in Christ is not sufficient and that only those willing to become Jews can belong to God's people. Paul and his Gospel were under threat, and he mounts a sustained and powerful defense in chapters 1 and 2. He argues cogently, defending his own authority, which seems also to have been questioned by his opponents. Paul claims God's divine authority in preaching to the Gentiles (1:15–17), which had been acknowledged by the church in Jerusalem (2:7–8). He draws on the Scriptures and cites the Galatians' experience in order to convince them that faith alone is needed to restore an individual's relationship with God and thus become one of God's people: *"We ourselves are Jews by birth and not Gentile sinners; yet we know that a person is justified not by the works of the law but only through faith in Jesus Christ"* (2:15–16).

## FAITH, THE LAW, AND GOD'S PROMISE (CHAPTERS 3–4)

In chapter 3, Paul argues that Abraham himself provided the great precedent of being justified by his faith and trust in God. God's promise to Abraham was to bless the nations – presumably following that precedent (3:6–9; *see p.39* for God's covenant with Abraham). The Law, which came later, did not change these basic terms of God's promise. The Gentiles, already experiencing God's blessing so freely and directly, simply confirm the character of Abraham's heritage. This argument is the central thrust of the whole letter.

In chapter 4, Paul continues his argument, explaining that people are restored to a relationship with God by having faith in Christ Jesus. Thus, there is no need for Gentiles to be required to keep the Law and be circumcised *(see also pp.60–61, 281)*. If the Galatians choose the Law, Paul writes, they will forgo their position as the true descendants of Abraham by faith and lose their new-found freedom in Christ. He uses the allegory of Hagar, the slave, and Sarah, the freed woman, to make his point about the two covenants: *"So then, friends, we are children, not of the slave but of the free woman. For freedom Christ has set us free. Stand firm, therefore, and do not submit again to a yoke of slavery"* (4:31–5:1).

## FREEDOM IN CHRIST (CHAPTER 5)

Paul tells the Galatians to reject "the flesh" and to live and walk "by the Spirit" in chapter 5. They are to serve one another in love, restore those who have sinned, and "bear one another's burdens." For Paul, circumcision is irrelevant: to be in Christ is to be a new creation (6:15). Paul also lists "the fruits of the Spirit" (5:22–23), the closest rival to his majestic passage to the hymn of love in 1 Corinthians 13.

As well as being valuable for its information on Paul's conversion and early ministry (chs.1–2), Galatians provides the earliest, and fiercest, statement of "justification by faith" (1:6–9; 5:2–12; *pp.426–27*).

## THE BOOK

TITLE: The Letter of Paul to the Galatians

DATE: Probably one of the earliest of Paul's letters, written in the early 50s CE

AUTHORSHIP: Paul

## THE CONTENTS

**CHAPTER 1:1–9**
Greetings. Paul expresses concern that the Galatians are so quickly departing from the Gospel that brought them salvation

**CHAPTERS 1:10–2:21**
The Gospel to Gentiles commissioned by God and recognized by the Apostles

**CHAPTER 3**
The relations between faith, Law, and the Gospel exemplified in Abraham

**CHAPTER 4**
Christian believers have inherited the promise as free children, not slaves, exemplified in the contrast between Hagar and Sarah

**CHAPTER 5**
The character of Christian freedom and of life in the Spirit

**CHAPTER 6**
Practical application and conclusion

## KEY THEMES

*Jews and Gentiles are justified before God by faith alone, not by the Law and not dependent on circumcision*

•

*The power of the Spirit dwelling in Christians and the fruit of the Spirit*

•

*The example of Abraham*

For further reading see bibliography numbers: 141, 256a, 503, 520b, 680, 842

# JUSTIFICATION BY GRACE THROUGH FAITH

*Central to Paul's teaching is his understanding of the way God rescues all humans and sets them free from sin and death: "since all have sinned and fall short of the glory of God; they are now justified by his grace as a gift, through the redemption that is in Christ Jesus."*

PAUL held a realistic view of human nature. He knew well, not least in his own case, how much people are caught up in wrong thoughts and actions and that sinfulness is plentiful and characteristic of everyone: *"Therefore, just as sin came into the world through one man, and death came through sin, and so death spread to all because all have sinned ..."* (Rom. 5:12; cf. 3:9). In other words, this situation would result in death for all people, were it not for the fact that God has taken the initiative to put things right for the whole cosmos, and in particular for those who put their faith in Christ. Human dependency upon God is honored and people are set right again with God. To use Paul's language, God "justifies" people by their faith, so that they are "righteous" in God's sight. *"For I am not ashamed of the gospel; it is the power of God for salvation to everyone who has faith, to the Jew first and also to the Greek. For in it the righteousness of God is revealed through faith for faith; as it is written, 'The one who is righteous will live by faith.'"* (Rom. 1:16–17; cf. 3:22; the Greek word underlying "justify" or "justification" and "righteousness" is the same).

This means that, instead of enduring God's wrath, those who have faith in Christ have peace with God: *"Therefore, since we are justified by faith, we have peace with God through our Lord Jesus Christ through whom we have obtained access to this grace in which we stand"* (Rom. 5:1–2; cf. 8:1). If one thinks in

terms of a court of law, "justification" is not a matter of God deciding that, although people are guilty as charged, God will pronounce them innocent. It is, in Paul's far more dramatic understanding, that God decides to cancel the charge against them altogether.

THE MEANING OF JESUS' DEATH AND RESURRECTION
*Jesus' death and Resurrection liberate those who believe in him from the oppression of death and sin: the fear of death is broken, and sin is confronted and defeated. Paul makes the point that those who have faith in Jesus will be raised in him to glory.*

## THE IMPLICATIONS OF PAUL'S MESSAGE

Paul's message turned out to be a controversial one. What made it so was Paul's claim that all this can occur "irrespective of the law" (Rom. 3:21), by which he meant the legal parts of Torah (*pp. 84–85*) as well as the natural law (i.e. what non-Jews recognize as right and wrong). Since no one is able to live consistently by the Law, then the Law is impotent to deliver people into a good life, although it does emphasize to what extent people have failed to live as they should.

Since the Law served as a guide for proper behavior, some people thought that Paul's claim implied that Christianity put no restrictions on an ethical lifestyle. While some people might have found such a suggestion attractive and others found it abhorrent, Paul repeatedly rejected this implication as a distortion of his message: *"What then are we to say? Should we continue in sin in order that grace may abound? By no means! How can we who died to sin go on living in it?"* (Rom. 6:1–2; cf. Rom. 3:8; 15; 1 Cor. 6:12; 10:23; Gal. 2:17). Instead, Paul claimed that the kind of lifestyle envisaged within the Law actually came to life in Christian love under the direction of God's Spirit: *"For God has done what the law, weakened by the flesh, could not do: by sending his own Son in the likeness of sinful flesh, and to deal with sin, he condemned sin in the flesh, so that the requirement of the law might be fulfilled in us, who walk not according to the flesh but according to the Spirit"* (Rom. 8:3–4; cf. Gal. 5:13–14; Rom. 13:8–10).

> 66 *There is now no condemnation for those who are in Christ Jesus. For the law of the Spirit of life in Christ Jesus has set you free from the law of sin and of death.* 99
>
> (Romans 8:1–2)

## JUSTIFICATION AND THE LAW

Another implication of Paul's message of justification through faith apart from the Law was just as controversial, but he defended it fully. If the means of the justification is faith alone, then by definition no other kind of qualification is acceptable before God. There is nothing one can do to acquire God's favor, since sinfulness is pervasive within one's own activity. This means that *"a person is justified not by the works of the law but through faith in Jesus Christ. And we have come to believe in Christ Jesus, so that we might be justified by faith in Christ and not by doing the works of the law, because no one will be justified by the works of the law"* (Gal. 2:16; cf. Rom. 3:20, 28). But that claim would seem to run contrary to one of the central convictions of the Hebrew Scriptures: and they surely make it clear that God has chosen Israel to be God's people and requires them to observe the practices prescribed in the Scriptures in order that they might "live": *"My ordinances you shall observe and my statutes you shall keep, following them: I am the LORD your God. You shall keep my statutes and my ordinances; by doing so one shall live: I am the LORD"* (Lev. 18:4–5).

Paul did not question the fact that the Law has played a vital part in the purposes of God, not did he expect that his Gentile converts would actually become "unlawful," but he argued that the Law alone was not able to deliver people into goodness. Thus, Paul did not doubt that Israel held a special place in God's dealings: *"Then what advantage has the Jew? Or what is the value of circumcision? Much, in every way. For in the first place the Jews were entrusted with the oracles of God"* (Rom. 3:1–2; cf. 9:1). He even described Gentile Christians as sharing in the spiritual blessings that belonged to the people of Israel. They were wild olive shoots grafted onto the olive tree (Rom. 11:17) and shared in the same blessings (Rom. 15:27), the "rich root of the olive tree."

However, Paul denied that Christians needed to observe the Law in order to be justified. Even Jewish Christians

> 66 *You have died to the law through the body of Christ, so that you may belong to another, to him who has been raised from the dead in order that we may bear fruit for God.* 99
>
> (Romans 7:4–5)

could take the prescriptions of the Law lightly if they so desired, although Paul had no qualms about Jewish Christians practicing the Law as a matter of cultural and ethnic identity, as long as such practices were not thought to have status or significance in terms of salvation: *"However that may be, let each of you lead the life that the Lord has assigned, to which God called you. This is my rule in all the churches. Was anyone at the time of his call already circumcised? Let him not seek to remove the marks of circumcision. Was anyone at the time of his call uncircumcised? Let him not seek circumcision. Circumcision is nothing and uncircumcision is nothing; but obeying the commandments of God is everything. Let each of you remain in the condition in which you were called"* (1 Cor. 7:17–20; cf. Rom. 14–15.6).

## GOD'S GRACE FOR ALL

Some of Paul's contemporaries were convinced that Gentile Christians needed to become circumcised and observe other prescriptions of the Law in order to protect their salvation in Christ. This conviction was not fostered by a legalistic motivation, whereby salvation is earned by obedient works, but was fostered by the belief that scriptural regulations, such as circumcision (cf. Gen. 17), were ordained by God and were therefore applicable to the people of God.

Paul argued against restricting the people of God to an ethnic group, since God is the God of both Jews and Gentiles: *"Is God the God of Jews only? Is he not the God of Gentiles also? Yes, of Gentiles also, since God is one; and he will justify the circumcised on the grounds of faith and the uncircumcised through that same faith. Do we then overthrow the law by this faith? By no means! On the contrary we uphold the law"* (Rom. 3:29–31). Paul conceded that Abraham was the forefather of the Jewish people but maintained that Abraham's primary significance is as a figure of faith: *"Just as Abraham 'believed God, and it was reckoned to him as righteousness,' so, you see, those who believe are the descendents of Abraham. And the scripture, foreseeing that God would justify the Gentiles by faith, declared the gospel beforehand to Abraham, saying, 'All the Gentiles shall be blessed in you.' For this reason, those who believe are blessed with Abraham who believed"* (Gal. 3:6–9; Rom. 4). Those who believe in Jesus Christ are rightly identified as the descendants of Abraham, whether they are Jews or Gentiles. God's grace is available to all people, both "circumcised" and "uncircumcised," on the basis of their faith alone (Rom. 3:30; cf. Gal. 5:6).

For further reading see bibliography numbers: 261, 538a, 669a, 832, 886

# THE LETTER TO THE
# EPHESIANS

*The letter to the Christian community at Ephesus – one of the most important Mediterranean bases in the development of Christianity from Palestine – is concerned with uniting the church as a fellowship, and it discusses life as it should be lived within that fellowship.*

EPHESIANS is one of the boldest statements of the Christian message in the New Testament: Christ makes known the mystery of God's purpose. His Resurrection and exaltation demonstrate God's power over all that claim authority. Christians share in this power through the Holy Spirit and are also told how they should live as Christians.

## WHAT KIND OF LETTER?

Ephesians has been called "the quintessence of Paulinism," with its emphasis on the grace of God in Christ, the Church of Jews and Gentiles, and the power and gifts of the Spirit. But uncertainty surrounds its authorship. The letter is written in a more complex style than Paul's other letters; it includes no personal references (although Paul founded the church at Ephesus, the author seems not to have visited the Christian community there); and Pauline themes are extensively developed rather than expressed, as in Paul's other letters. Among the main themes developed in Ephesians are the following:

• Ephesians distinguishes between the body of Christ and its head (4:15–16), unlike 1 Corinthians 12.
• Believers have already been raised with Christ (2:6), whereas Paul, earlier, awaited the resurrection of the dead (Phil. 3:11).

• Ephesians looks forward to the whole creation being united in Christ (1:10), rather than Christ coming from Heaven (1 Cor. 15:23).
• There is a stronger emphasis on the Church (the Greek, *ekklesia*, refers to local assemblies in Paul but to the whole association of Christians in Ephesians) and a stress on tradition rather than on grace and life controlled by the principle of love.
• Ephesians deals at length with the inclusion of the Gentiles (2:11–22), but the mixed-race Church is not so much the grafting of a Gentile olive shoot onto a Jewish olive tree (Rom. 11:17*ff.*) as an entirely "new humanity" (2:15*ff.*), perhaps reflecting the increasingly Gentile nature of the Church. For some scholars, this suggests that Ephesians was actually written by a disciple of Paul in order to apply his teaching to new circumstances that were developing in the period c.80–90CE. Others see the letter

**A NEW HUMANITY**
*Ephesians discusses the mystery of God's plan in bringing together Jews and Gentiles, of reconciling previously hostile groups – perhaps echoed in the recent dramatic fall of the Berlin Wall.*

as a mature reflection on Paul's part while in prison: *"This is the reason that I Paul am a prisoner for Jesus Christ for the sake of you Gentiles"* (3:1, 2–13; 1:1; 6:19–22). Perhaps it was intended to be passed around as a circular letter (the earliest manuscripts omit the word "Ephesians" from the title). However, since it is so typical of Paul's other letters, it seems simpler to regard it as being written by Paul.

The teaching in Ephesians is shaped by its stated purpose to "encourage your hearts" (6:22). The popular belief that the world was ruled by spiritual forces (the "principalities and powers") gave credibility to magic (pp.378–79), astrology, and religious ritual as means of spiritual control. Their prevalence around the city of Ephesus would have challenged confidence in the Christian Gospel.

## BELIEVERS "IN CHRIST" (CHAPTERS 1–3)

The first three chapters use the language of praise and prayer to renew the believers' vision of God and their understanding of their own status. Believers are "in Christ," secure in the eternal purposes of God which have now been revealed in the apostolic Gospel (1:3–9). They already share in Christ's victory over sin and principalities and powers (1:20–2:8). The indwelling Spirit acts as the guarantor of their inheritance (1:13–14), and even now gives them access to the resurrection power of God (3:16). They are full and equal members with Jewish Christians of the new humanity, God's household (2:11–22). The example of the imprisoned Paul shows that suffering for the sake of the Gospel need not impede the flow of God's grace (3:1–13). So Ephesians insists on the sufficiency of spiritual resources available to these believers – what they need is greater insight into God's blessing and promise (1:17–19; 3:14–21).

## THE BODY OF CHRIST (CHAPTERS 4–6)

The second half of the letter encourages everything that sustains the life of the body of Christ. The Ephesians need to maintain their common life, because loss of confidence threatens a church's cohesion and identity. The Church walks on the ground of the one apostolic faith (4:4–6). Christ's gift of grace "equips the saints for the work of ministry" to build up the body of Christ, the head who directs bodily life (4:7–16). Because each is a member of the other, the body as a whole walks in the way of forgiveness and love, imitating God and Christ (4:25–5:2). Christlike love – energized by the indwelling Spirit (3:16–17) – shapes the Christian household, where every relationship is modeled on Christ (5:21–6:9).

By contrast, Christian believers are to avoid walking as the Gentiles do. By describing their ways as futile, dark, shameful, and foolish (4:17–19; 5:3–18), the letter adopts Jewish stereotypes of Gentile life in order to ward off those converts who might still be attracted by their former way of life. The values and behavior of a corrupt and unredeemed world imperil the distinctive walk of the Church, not least because they embody the powers of evil. Believers are to resist these temptations, walking with the full protection of God's power: *"Put on the whole armor of God, so that you may be able to stand against the wiles of the devil"* (6:11).

# THE BOOK

TITLE: The Letter of Paul to the Ephesians
(The word "Ephesians" is missing from some early manuscripts)

DATE: c.60CE (if by Paul)

AUTHORSHIP: Paul, although some scholars have questioned this (*see text*)

# THE CONTENTS

**CHAPTER 1**
Greetings; praise for God's blessings; prayer for greater insight

**CHAPTER 2**
Being made alive in Christ; Jews and Gentiles made one in Christ

**CHAPTER 3**
The mystery made known; the power of grace; a prayer for his readers

**CHAPTER 4**
Unity in the body of Christ, and living as children of light

**CHAPTERS 5–6**
Regulations for households and the armor of God; final greetings

# KEY THEMES

*Building the body of Christ*

•

*Christian practice (unity, holiness in life, responsibilities in the household)*

For further reading see bibliography numbers: 19, 154, 155, 498

# UNITY OF
# JEW & GENTILE

*The early Christian Church witnessed discord between circumcised Jewish Christians, still obedient to Torah, and uncircumcised Gentile Christians, who felt liberated from the Law. Paul believed that Jews and Gentiles alike were members of the true Israel.*

THE Jerusalem Council (*pp. 394–95*) shows how difficult it was for Jewish Christians to accept Gentile converts without the converts having first accepted the Law. In Galatians, Paul argues that the converts are already children of Abraham (Gal. 3:7, 13–14), so that if they observe Torah, they are in effect denying what God had done for them, and thus are denying Christ (Gal. 5:4). Jew and Gentile alike are members of the true Israel (Gal. 3:27–29; Rom. 3:29–30). In Ephesians, the relations between Jews and Gentiles are placed in the larger framework of God's purposes for all Creation. Ultimately God intends to *"gather up all things … in heaven and … on earth"* (Eph. 1:10). Paul's ministry was directed toward the creation of a church of Jews and Gentiles, drawn together by their common faith in Jesus. This mixed community was nothing less than a public demonstration of the purposes of God the Creator (Eph. 3:4–9).

The significance of this unity is brought out in Ephesians by the juxtaposition of first- and second-person pronouns:
• Chapter 1:12–14 sets "we who were the first to set out hope in Christ" (i.e., Jewish believers) alongside "you also, when you had heard the word of truth … and had believed in him."

**TOLERATING THE BELIEFS OF OTHERS**
*This 20th-century work is titled* The Golden Rule, *which is a statement of the most important requirement of human behavior: to "do to others as you would have them do to you." The painting encapsulates a sense of diversity in unity across all religions.*

Gentiles, too, have been sealed by the Spirit as a pledge of the inheritance that was promised to Abraham's offspring (i.e., God's universal blessing).
• In chapter 2:1–6, "you" Gentiles and "we" Jews once walked in the ways of disobedience and self-centeredness under the sway of evil powers and were destined for God's judgment. But now both have been delivered from this living death by God's grace in Christ: you he made alive (2:1) and "God … made us alive together with Christ" (2:5), so that Jew and Gentile share the ascended life of Christ.
• In chapter 2:11–22, the contrast between "you" and "we" is at its most marked: *"So then, remember that at one time you Gentiles by birth … were at that time without Christ, being aliens from the commonwealth of Israel, and strangers to the* covenants of promise, having no hope without God in the world. [But Christ] is our peace; in his flesh he has made both groups into one" (2:11–14). In an Israel-centered worldview, Gentiles are outside the promises to the Covenant People. But now all this has changed, and the new situation brought about by Jesus Christ is interpreted by bringing together two biblical texts. In Isaiah 52:7, the herald of good tidings "announces peace," which in Isaiah 57:19 is proclaimed

to "the far and the near." In the light of Jesus Christ, the "near" are the Jews and the "far" the Gentiles. "Peace" is both reconciliation with God and between those divided by hostility, and its herald is Jesus Christ.

## IMAGES OF UNITY

In his ministry, and supremely in his death, Jesus broke down the walls of hostility that kept Jews and Gentiles separated. "You" and "we" have become "us both … we both." Five distinct images are used to convey this sense of unity:
• First, unity is seen as a body: Christ is the head, reconciling "both groups to God in one body" (Eph. 2:16; cf. 4:4, 16).
• Second, the Christian Church is seen as a single new humanity, where Gentiles neither become Jews nor, as Paul had suggested in Romans, are grafted like a wild olive shoot

> **❝** *For [Christ] is our peace; in his flesh he has made both groups into one and has broken down the dividing wall, that is, the hostility between us.* **❞**
>
> (Ephesians 2:14)

onto the Jewish olive tree: *"He has abolished the law with its commandments and ordinances, so that he might create in himself one new humanity in place of the two, thus making peace"* (Eph. 2:15; cf. Rom. 11:17ff.).
• Third, this sense of unity is a nation in which Gentiles are no longer outside Israel like strangers and sojourners but are full and equal members of God's people, "citizens with the saints and also members of the household of God" (Eph. 2:19).
• Fourth, it is God's household, a structure built on the foundations of the Apostles and Prophets and held together by Jesus Christ (Eph. 2:19–20).
• Fifth, Christian unity is like a holy temple, a community rather than a building (as in 1 Peter 2 and the Dead Sea Scrolls). The Temple is as yet unfinished, but in this growing community of different races and cultures, God is very much at home in the one Spirit.

## JESUS AND THE GENTILES

*The distinction between Jews and Gentiles was profound, but Jesus was moved by their persistence and faith.*

Jesus understood his mission to be primarily to the Jews. According to Matthew 10:5–6, he prohibited missionary work among the Gentiles and shared the common view that Gentiles were sinners or far from God (Matt. 5:47; 6:7). Jesus did not seek Gentiles out: he initiated a conversation with a Gentile only in the case of the Samaritan woman (John 4:1–42). But Gentiles followed him (Matt. 15:29–31; Mark 3:7–12;), and he ministered to them (Matt. 8:5–13; Mark 5:1–20; 7:24–30; Luke 7:1–10). He found that Gentiles might have far greater faith than he found in the house of Israel. Attempting, at first, to put off a Syro-Phoenician woman, Jesus then acceded to her persistence (Mark 7:24–30), just as he did in the case of the centurion pleading for his son (Matt. 8:5–13; Luke 7:1–10). It is to the centurion that Jesus said, *"Truly I tell you, in no one in Israel have I found such faith."*

Jesus seems, therefore, to have shared the biblical view that the conversion of Israel to the true worship and service of God would lead the way for the Gentiles to come to worship God (Isa. 19:23; Hab. 2:14; cf. Isa. 11:9; Jer. 3:17; Zech. 8:20–23). But the way in which the Gentiles were already pressing upon him in faith and trust showed that the kingdom of God (pp.332–33) did not lie in some distant future, but was already breaking in upon the world. In practice, Jesus' life enacted the breaking down of barriers that was so important for Paul – as he did also in the way in which he accepted and affirmed the ministry of women (pp.436–37) and shared the lives of those regarded as outside the norms of society.

## THE "DIVIDING WALL OF HOSTILITY"

*Paul's phrase "dividing wall of hostility" refers to Jesus breaking through the hostile divisions between people to bring peace.*

Two possibilities have been suggested for the metaphor of a dividing wall of hostility, which, in Ephesians 2:14, Jesus is said to have broken down.

The first is that it refers to the wall that divided the Court of Gentiles from the inner courts and the sanctuary of the Temple in Jerusalem. The architecture of the Temple enshrined an understanding of holiness that separated God's holy people from those outside the Covenant. By breaking this down, Jesus brought together those who were formerly kept apart. The main difficulty with this interpretation is that it depends on the Gentile readers' familiarity with the details of the Jerusalem Temple. If Ephesians (pp.428–29) dates from a later period, the Temple, which was destroyed by the Romans in 70CE, may not have been standing by the time the letter was written.

The second possibility is that it refers to the Jewish Law itself. "He has broken down the dividing wall of hostility" is paralleled in Ephesians 2:15 where he "abolished the law with its commandments and ordinances." Jewish writers referred to the Law of Moses as a fence around Israel creating an enclave of holiness. The Law forbade eating with non-Jews and inter-marriage between Jews and Gentiles. The Gentiles have their own status (see the covenant with Noah, p.33), but the apparent exclusiveness of the Jewish vocation evoked Gentile hostility toward Jews. Jesus' death broke down the dividing wall of the Law by bringing to an end the era in which the Law, with its power to separate and exclude, held sway.

For further reading see bibliography numbers: 497, 722, 778a, 814a

# THE LETTER TO THE
# PHILIPPIANS

*Philippians was written by Paul to Christians living in Philippi, Greece, while he was in prison. Paul was concerned that the Philippians' faith and their love for one another should not fail, as they too may have been facing persecution.*

PHILIPPIANS is a letter of cordial Christian friendship to a church that Paul had founded and that had supported his continuing missionary work with gifts of money. The letter is full of gratitude and encouragement but also shows a sober awareness of opposition and danger. Paul was in prison "for Christ" (1:13), and his life was at risk. Paul, however, does not say where he is in prison in chapter 1. The later chapters of Acts mention his long confinements in the Palestinian coastal city of Caesarea and then in Rome. But this letter may be earlier; it cannot be dated precisely.

## STANDING FIRM (CHAPTERS 1–2)

The prison setting flavors much of the opening chapter; Paul faces possible martyrdom. He writes positively of being "with Christ" beyond death (1:23), yet he feels that he still has important work to do among the churches that depend upon him.

The final few verses of chapter 1 summarize this letter and its message: the church must "stand firm" as a united fellowship, persistent in its faith even when Christian believers come into conflict and suffering. The unity of the church will be sustained only by patient and humble care (2:1–4), and Paul urges the Philippians to copy the attitude of Jesus as shown in the "Christ hymn" of 2:6–11: *"[Christ] emptied himself, taking the form of a slave, being born in human likeness. And being found in human form, he humbled himself and became obedient to the point of death – even death on a cross"* (2:7–8). This passage stands

**IMITATING CHRIST'S HUMILITY**
*Paul urged the Philippians to act humbly toward one another in a spirit of love and to do nothing out of selfish ambition or conceit.*

out; for the eloquence of its language and for the far-reaching claims about Jesus Christ: Jesus is so closely associated with God that, in worshiping him, believers in effect worship God. It may have originally been a poem, a hymn, or a creed, known already in the churches and quoted by Paul. It certainly contains some of the most profound words of praise and faith in the whole of the New Testament.

The hymn probably presents a contrast between Jesus and the disobedience of Adam, who, though in the form of God (Gen. 1:26), sought equality with God (Gen. 3:5). Instead of such "grasping," Christ accepted the lot of humanity and became obedient to death, even death on a cross. "Therefore God also highly exalted him" (2:9), and Creation will one day recognize him as Lord (2:11). This model of humility and triumph is offered to oppressed and distressed Christians for them to copy and to trust.

## PRESSING TOWARD THE GOAL (CHAPTERS 3–4)

The word "finally" (3:1), so long before the letter ends, seems odd, as does the sharp change of tone from friendship to bitter warning at 3:2. Was the Epistle written in this form? Are several original letters combined here? Various theories have been tried, but perhaps they are not needed: "finally" might equally be translated "furthermore." The positive advice in chapter 2 and warnings of danger in chapter 3 (with significant parallels of wording and ideas linking 2:6–11 with 3:4–11) give the letter form and integrity as it now stands. Paul's warning is against "dogs," "evil workers," and those who "mutilate the flesh" (3:2). He probably meant those groups that drew Christians into the rituals of Judaism – possibly Jewish Christian preachers of the type encountered in Galatians (pp.424–25). As he considers their aims, Paul reflects on his own change of direction, from Pharisaic zeal to Christian faith (pp.390–91). Paul values knowing Jesus above everything else in life, and he presses forward to eternal hope. Perhaps deliberately, this account of Paul's own pilgrimage matches what was said about Jesus, that glory comes through sacrifice: *"I want to know Christ and the power of his resurrection and the sharing of his sufferings by becoming like him in his death"* (3:10).

In chapter 4, the warmth of the pastoral relationship returns. The main command to stand firm is reemphasized (4:1). Paul urges that peace should reign, both in the Philippians' dealings with one another and in their hearts (4:2–9). Finally, he remembers this church's gifts of money and friendship during his troubles (4:10–20), and thanks them more fully for their "partnership in the gospel" that he first mentioned in chapter 1.

# PAUL'S FIRST CHURCH IN EUROPE

*Paul had a special relationship with the church at Philippi, and it played an important part in helping to spread the Gospel.*

Philippi, a city in the Roman province of Macedonia, had the special status of being a colony. The city governed itself according to Roman law as an outpost of the imperial capital and enjoyed certain financial privileges.

In about 49CE, Paul and his companions crossed the Aegean Sea to Macedonia (Acts 16:9–11) and then traveled inland to Philippi. The church was the first that Paul founded in Europe, through his preaching to a group of praying women (Acts 16:13–15). Lydia, a cloth merchant, was the first convert. At Philippi, these women converts worked to spread the faith; Paul names two women as valued Gospel workers (Phil. 4:2–3). Trouble in the church came early, when Paul exorcised a spirit from a slave girl. Her owners were angry to lose the profit her mystical powers had earned them. This exorcism may also have been seen as a public religious challenge, attacking the prophetic powers associated with the Greek god Apollo – even threatening the worship of the Roman emperor. Paul and his companion, Silas, were beaten and jailed, and later released when their status as Roman citizens became known (Acts 16:16–40).

Perhaps above all others, this church cared for Paul in his later travels and sufferings (Phil. 4:10–18); it had seen how much his missionary commitment could cost him. Paul saw that the church, in a colony of Rome, was also an outpost of God's heavenly kingdom, to which the Christians belonged, and to which they must be loyal and faithful despite pressure from their opponents (Phil. 1:28).

## THE BOOK

TITLE: The Letter of Paul to the Philippians

DATE: Between 53 and 62CE

AUTHORSHIP: Paul

## THE CONTENTS

**CHAPTER 1:1–11**
Greetings and prayers of thanksgiving

**CHAPTER 1:12–26**
Paul's own situation and outlook

**CHAPTER 1:27–30**
An appeal for steadiness and unity

**CHAPTER 2:1–18**
Call for humility: the example of Christ

**CHAPTER 2:19–30**
News of faithful friends

**CHAPTERS 3:1–4:1**
Warning against opponents: Paul's own example

**CHAPTER 4:2–9**
Appeal for peace and goodness

**CHAPTER 4:10–23**
Gratitude for the church's help; final greeting

## KEY THEMES

*The need for Christian unity and partnership in spreading the Gospel*

•

*Confidence in Christ, and humility*

•

*Gratitude for the Philippians' support*

For further reading see bibliography numbers: 245, 517a, 520c, 824

# HOUSE CHURCHES

*House and home were extremely important in the Roman empire.
As Christianity spread, its organization, and its ideas about organization
were based not so much on the synagogue as on the household.*

## "HOUSEHOLD OF GOD"

Because of the importance of the household, it was natural to describe the Church as "the household of God" (1 Tim. 3:14), much as the Roman emperor was regarded as the father of his household (the state). To become a Christian is to join "the household of God" (Eph. 2:19), or "the household of faith" (Gal. 6:10). The family of God must live together in one household and for that reason it was natural for household codes (*p.375*) to be adapted to give guidance on what this means in practice.

THE first identifiable church buildings do not appear until around 200CE, when many of the earliest Christians gathered together in each other's homes. There were gatherings, especially for prayer and worship, outside the home, but the foundations were established in the household. The pattern is already set in Acts 2:46: *"they broke bread at home and ate their food with glad and generous hearts, praising God and having the goodwill of all the people."*

Initially, the established patterns of Jewish worship were followed in daily attendance, for those in Jerusalem, in the Temple. But the first believers also met in each other's homes to share common meals and also, no doubt, for

teaching from Scripture, to recall what Jesus said and did, and to sing and pray (Acts 12:12–27; 20:7–12). The pattern became established as Christianity spread farther afield. The Gospel (concerning, as it did, the Messiah whom Jews were expecting) would be preached first in the local Jewish synagogue, which was the most obvious means of reaching

**CORNELIUS' HOUSE**
*After Peter had been sent for to preach in Caesarea, he spoke to Cornelius, a devout centurion, in whose home expectant friends and family had gathered to listen to Peter's words (Acts 10:27–29).*

**PETER'S HOUSE, CAPERNAUM**
*These are believed to be the remains of Peter's house, where Jesus stayed and performed miracles, including the healing of Peter's mother (Mark 1:29–32). The house was gradually enlarged, and by the end of the second century CE it had become one of the first Christian churches.*

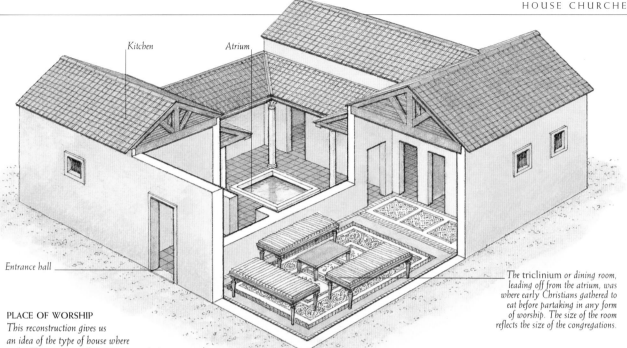

Kitchen

Atrium

Entrance hall

The triclinium or dining room, leading off from the atrium, was where early Christians gathered to eat before partaking in any form of worship. The size of the room reflects the size of the congregations.

**PLACE OF WORSHIP**
*This reconstruction gives us an idea of the type of house where early Christians may have congregated. At a time when Christians were being persecuted and discretion might be essential for survival, gathering together in someone else's home attracted far less unwanted attention.*

the Jews as well as the Gentile adherents who had attached themselves to the Jewish community. However, the distinctive emphases and practices of the new movement could not be carried on in the synagogue itself. More usual would be the move away from the synagogue to a private house, with the house group – or breakaway house group of the local synagogue (Acts 18:7) – serving as the church.

## TYPES AND SIZES
Paul speaks of several house churches – those that met in the homes of Priscilla and Aquila (Rom. 16:5), of Nympha (Col. 4:15), and of Philemon (Philem. 2), for example. Given the archaeological evidence regarding the size even of well-to-do homes, this suggests that most of the first churches were small enough to meet in a home, that is, typically 20–30 people and 40–50 at the most. The house of Gaius was large enough to host "the whole church" in Corinth (Rom. 16:23). But unless Gaius had an enormous mansion, this must have meant that the arguments and splinter-ing of the Corinthian church (as pointed out in much of 1 Corinthians) were happening in

a relatively small group. At the other end of the housing scale, we probably have to envisage many of the first Christian churches meeting in much more cramped spaces, the equivalent in size of small apartments today.

## WORSHIP AND AMBIGUITY
Apart from sharing a meal, worshipers could each participate in the service by teaching, "speaking in tongues," or singing hymns of praise (cf. 1 Cor. 14:26–31). Paul tells the church in Colossae to *"teach and admonish one another in all wisdom; and with gratitude in your hearts sing psalms, hymns, and spiritual songs to God"* (Col. 3:16). The legal status of gatherings such as these may have been a factor in early Christian worship being held in the home. The Roman author-ities were always suspicious of unauthorized sects and group meetings, and the private nature of the early Christian churches may have helped protect them from unwelcome police attention. It would not have been clear whether they were part of the synagogue, a friendly society, a religious cult, or simply the host's social circle.

## BREAKING BREAD TOGETHER
Paul was concerned that when people came "together as a church" (1 Cor. 11:18) they should behave properly in their sharing of a meal. This was connected with the Lord's Supper (1 Cor. 11:23–29). It probably took the form of a potluck supper, where people brought food to share and the householder acted as host. The third century CE wall painting below depicts a meal shared by Christians.

Christians sharing a meal.

For further reading see bibliography numbers: 46, 257, 514, 544, 722

# WOMEN'S MINISTRY
## IN THE EARLY CHURCH

*What ministerial roles did women play in the early Church? Did they hold "official"offices?*
*Did they minister to both men and women? Such questions have become important as argument*
*has raged concerning the appropriate ministry for women to exercise in the Church today.*

THE Gospels tell the story, not only of 12 special male disciples, but also of the numerous women and men, named and unnamed, who were deeply involved in Jesus' ministry. Some women are named – for example, Mary the mother of Jesus, Mary and Martha, Mary Magdalene, and Joanna and Susanna. Luke tells how these last two went around with Jesus and his disciples and *"provided for them out of their resources"* (Luke 8:3).

Women are prominent in the account of Jesus' Crucifixion, where their faithfulness appears in stark contrast to the desertion of the male disciples (Mark 15:40–41). Similarly, women are the first to witness Jesus' resurrection from the dead, yet when they recount their experiences the 11 disciples refuse to believe them, and the women's words are dismissed as "nonsense" (Luke 24:11).

### EARLY PUBLIC MINISTRY

The book of Acts and the letters of the New Testament give further evidence of women's ministry in the early Church. Women are seen working in close partnership with men as, for example, Priscilla and Aquila (Acts 18:1–3, 26;

1 Cor. 16:19; Rom. 16:5). Women are also seen working individually as apostles (Rom. 16:7), in prophecy (1 Cor. 11:2–16), as "deacon" (Rom. 16:1), and "fellow-workers" (Rom. 16:12). Other ministries are mentioned that were probably taken up by both men and women; for example, teacher, evangelist, and "speaker in tongues."

In general, Paul appears to have welcomed women's ministry (*see also* Phil. 4:2–3). Two passages seem to set a limit: 1 Corinthians 14:34–36, although this may be restricted to asking questions; and 1 Timothy 2:9–15, thought by many not to have been written by Paul (*see pp.446–47*), which addresses specific issues for men, then women. Neither of these passages calls into question the affirming openness of Jesus to women. Nor do they reflect the positive welcome of women's ministry in the early Church. From the New Testament, it is clear that the early Church was founded upon apostolic witness, and this was certainly not confined to men still less to the 12 disciples. All Christians, women as much as men, received the Holy Spirit, and were thus empowered for ministry (Rom. 12:6*ff.*; 1 Cor. 12:4–11; Eph. 4:11*ff.*).

**PAUL WITH PRISCILLA AND AQUILA**
*Priscilla was the Roman wife of Aquila and both became close friends of Paul. Together they helped Paul in his ministry.*

### INTERPRETING THE EVIDENCE

Traditional interpretation was inclined to limit women's ministry in the earliest churches claiming that:
• It was originally conducted in the private sphere of the home or in a house church (*pp.434–35*).
• It was primarily addressed to other women.

**MARTHA AND MARY**
*These two sisters are mentioned in the Gospels as providing Jesus with much hospitality and love whenever he visited their home. Jesus brought their brother Lazarus back from the dead (John 11:1–44).*

# PHOEBE, THE FIRST DEACON

*Phoebe is the first person in Christian history to be designated "deacon," although the role of deacons in the early years is unclear (Acts 6:2; Phil. 1:1; 1 Tim. 3:8–13).*

Phoebe is commended by Paul in his letter to the Romans (16:1), where he describes her as a *diakonos* and a *prostatis*. The Greek *diakonos* is translated to the English word "deacon." The meaning of the word *diakonos* is not immediately identifiable with any of the specific offices of deacon in modern denominations but clearly refers to a ministry of service to the community (*cf.* Acts 7; 1 Tim.). Paul's reference to a "deacon of the church" here would seem to indicate some sort of official title and office. It was open to women as well as men to be deacons, as the mention of Phoebe here shows (*cf.* 1 Tim. 3:11). Phoebe is further described as a *prostatis*, which would probably be understood in the sense of "patron, benefactor," that is, a person of substantial means who used her resources and influence in the service of the church. Paul put Phoebe into that wide group of men and women who had been his helpers and co-workers. Priscilla, the high-ranking Roman wife of Aquila, was among this group. As part of a well-loved couple in the Gentile church, she played an important role in helping Paul with his ministry (*cf.* Rom. 16:3).

**WOMEN'S LEADERSHIP TODAY**
*Only recently has the ordination of women been accepted by many Christian denominations.*

• It was not included in the subsequent mainstream development of the three offices in the Church, those of bishop, priest, and deacon.

Much recent scholarship has called these arguments into question, recognizing the strong affirmation of women in a way unusual for that time, and drawing attention to the following points:

• There was clearly dispute over women's ministry in the earliest churches; proscriptions of certain activities for women probably indicate disagreement and diversity of practice.

• Much of the New Testament is written in generic language, i.e., using "he" for both men and women with the result that women may often become "invisible" in the text. It must therefore be assumed that women are present even when they are not explicitly mentioned.

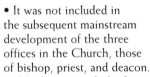

**MOTHER OF JESUS**
*Mary, the mother of Jesus, is mentioned in Acts as joining the Apostles and brothers of Jesus in prayer after the Resurrection (1:14).*

• Women did exercise official ministry within the churches; a presupposition that they did not distorts a proper understanding of the biblical text. For example, in Romans 16:7 the far less probable reading deriving from *Junias* (male) has been suggested instead of *Junia* (female) because traditionally it was not thought possible that women could be apostles.

Generally, the New Testament presents a very diverse picture of the kinds of ministerial roles offered by women, which includes both the public and the private, the "ad hoc," and the undeveloped "official."

For further reading see bibliography numbers: 18, 54, 132, 135, 179, 202, 292, 293, 514, 613, 665, 697, 722, 749, 786, 819, 825, 871

# THE LETTERS TO THE
# COLOSSIANS
# & PHILEMON

*These letters are closely connected. In Colossians, Paul deals with a crisis in the church, although he takes the opportunity to deal with other important matters. Philemon, though short, throws engaging light on Paul's work and his understanding of it.*

THE church at Colossae, in modern-day Turkey, had been founded by Epaphras, Paul's co-worker and fellow-prisoner (1:7; 4:12). Paul did not know the church personally (2:1) and had never visited the Christian community there. Hearing a report that opposition was threatening the growth of the church, a letter to the Colossians was sent by Paul and Timothy from prison, probably in Rome. It was entrusted to Tychicus and Onesimus (4:7–9) on the understanding that it would also be read out to the church in nearby Laodicea (4:16).

## A RIVAL PHILOSOPHY

What had undermined confidence among the Colossian believers was the challenge of a rival philosophy: *"See to it that no one takes you captive through philosophy and empty deceit, according to human tradition, according to the elemental spirits of the universe, and not according to Christ"* (2:8; 1:23; 4:12). The outline of the philosophy – "spirituality" is a better term because it was more than a set of ideas – is apparent in chapter 2:8–23. It seems to have been based on Judaism, with a strong emphasis on diet and holy days. Its spiritual disciplines led to visionary experiences, which supposedly gave access to

THE PREEMINENCE OF CHRIST
*Colossians centers on the preeminence and sufficiency of Christ; Philemon, on his forgiveness and love.*

the angels' worship of God in Heaven. This ascetic mysticism claimed to offer a "fullness" (the word occurs twice in Colossians) to which faith in Christ was, at best, an introduction. However, it left Christian believers with a sense of inadequacy.

## THE SUPREMACY OF CHRIST

The appeal of this rival spirituality lay in its offer of power over the invisible forces thought to govern the world. Paul countered this by emphasizing the supremacy of Christ over the whole created order – spiritual and temporal powers, the Church, and even death: *"He is the image of the invisible God, the firstborn of all creation; for in him all things in heaven and on earth were created, things visible and invisible, whether thrones or dominions or rulers or powers – all things have been created through him and for him. He himself is before all things, and in him all things hold together. He is the head of the body, the church; he is the beginning, the firstborn of the dead, so that he might come to have first place in everything"* (1:15–18). Paul called on believers to realize what was already theirs on the basis of their baptism. Faith in Christ effects a genuine participation in his whole being and in the fruits of his work: it brings deliverance from the realm of evil to the rule of Christ; forgiveness of sins (1:13–14); a wealth of understanding from the treasury of wisdom and knowledge (1:9; 2:2–3); reconciliation with God through the death of Christ (1:20, 22); entry into "fullness" of life through Christ, who is the "fullness of God" (1:19; 2:9–10); a share in the victory of his Resurrection (2:12–13); access to the hidden qualities of Heaven (2:1–3); and hope for the age to come (1:27; 2:4).

Paul also engaged in a fierce polemic against the rival teachers and their spirituality. Their teaching was an empty human invention, demonic rather than divine. Their ascetic practices enslaved people rather than liberated them. They delivered shadows, not the substance of divine fullness. Their supposed spiritual maturity bred an arrogant self-regard and contempt for others. What they delivered was part of the human problem – the pursuit of self-interest at all costs ("self-indulgence" in 2:23) – rather than its solution.

For Paul, spiritual maturity is not achieved through the rigors of personal discipline or the intensity of spiritual experience, but by growth into Christ, who bears the image of the Creator (3:10). This shows itself in its capacity to transform the mundane realities of a world divided by race and status (3:11). Where people are clothed with the "new nature" of Christ, forgiveness, love, and peace hold sway (3:12–17). In the everyday obligations of the household, rather than the special days of "festivals, new moons and Sabbaths," the fullness of God is seen in the mutual respect and justice that serve and fear the Lord (3:18–4:1).

## PHILEMON

Paul's letter to Philemon is traditionally linked with his letter to the Colossians. They were written in similar circumstances and mention the same people (vv.23–24; cf. Col. 4:10ff.). It appears that a slave, Onesimus, had a grievance against his master, Philemon, and had asked Paul to mediate between them as the Roman law allowed. The situation had become complicated now that Onesimus had converted to Christianity and become a "beloved brother."

In returning Onesimus to his master, Paul appealed to Philemon's love and faith, rather than to his own apostolic authority. He hoped that Onesimus might now be treated as a brother in Christ and allowed to return as one of Paul's co-workers. If Onesimus owed Philemon anything, Paul would repay it: *"So if you consider me your partner, welcome him as you would welcome me. If he has wronged you in any way, or owes you anything, charge that to my account"* (vv.17–18). Would Philemon refresh Paul's heart (vv.7, 20; cf. 12) and benefit from the now useful Onesimus (note the puns: Onesimus in Greek means "useful," "beneficial")? We do not know the outcome, but the letter affords a glimpse of how the statement, *"there is no longer slave and free"* (Col. 3:11) challenged attitudes at least, although slavery would not be abolished until the 19th century.

## THE BOOKS

**TITLES**: The Letter of Paul to the Colossians; The Letter of Paul to Philemon

**DATE**: Colossians: c.60CE (if by Paul); Philemon: c.60CE

**AUTHORSHIP**: Paul, although some scholars have questioned this

## THE CONTENTS

### COLOSSIANS

Chapter 1:1–14: Greetings, thanksgiving, prayer

Chapter 1:15–23: The supremacy of the Son of God

Chapters 1:24–2:7: Encouragement from Paul to know the mystery of God, namely Christ

Chapter 2:8–23: A rival spirituality and its teachers

Chapter 3:1–17: Life above and life below

Chapters 3:18–4:6: Rules for households and for Christian living

Chapter 4:7–18: Closing greetings

### PHILEMON

Verses 1–3: Greetings

Verses 4–7: Thanksgiving and prayer

Verses 8–22: A request for Onesimus

Verses 23–25: Closing greetings and blessing

## KEY THEMES

### COLOSSIANS

*The need to remain faithful in the face of false teaching*

•

*The preeminence of Christ*

•

*Life lived as thanksgiving*

### PHILEMON

*Slavery; all believers are partners*

**For further reading see bibliography numbers:** 60, 126, 245, 497, 520, 616

# SLAVERY
## IN THE NEW TESTAMENT

*Slavery was taken for granted in the ancient world. Slaves had certain rights, but when Jesus
said to his disciples, "I shall no longer call you slaves but friends," he was making
a major statement about the freedom that comes from God.*

SLAVERY was an integral part of
the Roman empire. As many as
one third of those living in the
great Mediterranean cities may have
been slaves, with others having slave
origins. In Rome and Italy the figures
were higher, perhaps as many as
80–90 percent of the population. The
economies of ancient states could not
have run without them. Originally
slaves had been supplied from the
ranks of defeated enemies, but by the
first century CE the main supply came
from children born to slaves.

## A SLAVE'S STATUS
Given the modern
Western abhorrence of
slavery, it is important
to realize that
during this period
slavery was not
thought of as
immoral or as
necessarily degrading.
A slave was simply the
bottom rung of the
economic ladder, doing
the jobs equivalent to
those which, typically
in 19th- and 20th-
century Western
economies, were
undertaken by immi-
grant labor. Slaves were
not always low-born or
completely powerless. For
example, someone of a
higher social stand-
ing but in debt

might sell himself into
slavery as a last resort.
Slaves could be found in
all kinds of occupations
ranging from responsible
posts in administration
and commerce to
working in gangs on
ships, farms, road
building, and in mining.
Some slaves were well
educated, and might
have been responsible
for the education of the
children. Moreover,
most slaves could expect
to be freed by grateful
masters, many of them
before their 30th birth-
day. They were also
allowed to earn money
with which they might eventually purchase their freedom.
    Nevertheless, the distinction
between slavery and freedom was
fundamental to the educated mind
– the slave being defined as "one who
does not belong to himself but to
someone else" (Aristotle), and as
one who "does not have the power
to refuse" (Seneca). Cicero expressed
the contrast powerfully in words
echoed by Paul in his letter to the
Romans (8:21) when he was

**THE HEBREW SLAVES IN EGYPT**
*The Hebrew Scriptures reminded the
Israelites that they had once
been slaves in Egypt, and that,
encouraged by this memory,
they should be merciful.*

**FEMALE SLAVES**
*Once brought into slavery, many women became concubines
to their masters or their master's sons.*

describing the condition of freedom
to which the whole of Creation aspires:
*"Nothing is more foul than slavery, for we have
been born for glory and for freedom."* Not surprisingly, freedom, or manumission (*see
box, opposite*), was every slave's goal. And
this, despite the fact that the freed slave
– freed usually to become the client of
his old master – was often in a more
difficult economic condition as a result.

## THE CHRISTIAN STANCE
Christians also had slaves. In the way
that Victorian households had servants,
their presence was taken for granted,
particularly in Paul's writings, and the
fact of slavery was not regarded as a
matter for objection, either as an issue
of principle, or on Christian grounds.

Those who find this odd should recall that in present-day Western economies, where groups and parties can exercise a political power unthinkable in the ancient world, there is widespread acceptance of the effects of the free market on the bottom end of the labor market.

What is more striking, however, is the fact that slaves are directly addressed in Paul's letters as members of the churches written to. Paul clearly regarded them as full members of these churches. Slaves along with masters are given strong advice, as in Paul's letter to the Colossians (3:22–4:1). This was unusual at that time. In the nearest parallels to such advice, only the masters are addressed. The principle "neither slave nor free" (1 Cor. 12:13; Gal. 3:28) was intended seriously, not in the sense of abolishing the difference and ending slavery, but in the sense of abolishing its significance as far as the relationship with God and with one another was concerned.

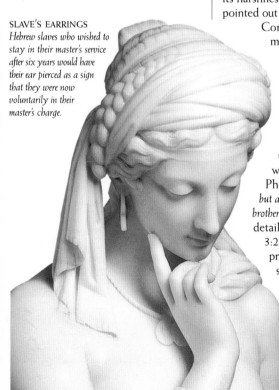

SLAVE'S EARRINGS
*Hebrew slaves who wished to stay in their master's service after six years would have their ear pierced as a sign that they were now voluntarily in their master's charge.*

# MANUMISSION

*"It is a slave's prayer that he be set free immediately" (Epictetus). A slave was an item of property and only on being freed did the slave become a legal citizen.*

Manumission is the setting free of slaves, something that happened commonly. Sometimes an owner liberated his slaves in his will. A slave could be forced by torture to testify against his master, but not a freedman (except in cases of treason). It could be more economical to act as patron to a freedman and thus to command much the same services, than to bear the expense of housing and feeding a slave. A slave could save up enough money and purchase his freedom through the mediation of a local temple. Jewish slaves were subject to the Sabbath-year manumission when the Jewish community could ransom their own people held in slavery by Gentiles after six years. When released, they were provided with enough stock to make a new start in life. In 1 Corinthians 7:21 and Philemon vv.15–16 there is some question as to what Paul was calling for; in the one case, whether to remain as slaves or to take advantage of the opportunity to become free; in the other, whether Paul hoped for Philemon to free his slave, Onesimus, or simply for Philemon to recognize that the relationship between master and slave was bound to be transformed by the fact that they were Christian brothers. Elsewhere, Paul uses the imagery of emancipation as a powerful metaphor for the change of ownership and responsibility to be lived out by Christians (Rom. 6:16–23).

Within the constraints of the social system, Paul's concern was to make sure that the system worked fairly and that its harshness was alleviated by love. He pointed out to believing slaves in the Corinthian church that, far more importantly, slaves and the free all belong to Christ (1 Cor. 7:21). Their relationship with Christ was primary, and it relativized all others. In his letter to Philemon, Paul was concerned to reconcile the offending Onesimus with his aggrieved master Philemon – *"no longer as a slave, but as more than a slave, a beloved brother"* (Philem. 16). In the more detailed advice in Colossians 3:22–4:1, it is clear that the primary relation "to the Lord" should determine everything, both the slave's wholehearted service and the master's treatment of his slaves "with justice and equity."

It should also not be forgotten that Paul found the image of slavery to be a very

SLAVE REVOLTS
*Revolts occurred among prisoners of war who had been forced into slavery by the Romans.*

positive indication of the degree of commitment that Christians owed to their master. The Gospel brought freedom from one slavery, but human beings could only realize their full potential as God's creatures in the relation of absolute dependence on God, which the image of slavery so powerfully expressed.

For further reading see bibliography numbers: 60, 126, 520, 544, 616

# THE FIRST & SECOND LETTERS TO THE

# THESSALONIANS

*The two letters written to the Christians at Thessalonica are among the earliest Christian writings to have survived. They were written to encourage this early Christian community to keep faith even in the face of testing opposition.*

DURING their time preaching in Thessalonica, in the region of Macedonia, Paul and his companion Silas had established the first Christian church there. Paul, writing his first letter to the Thessalonians a few months after their departure, recalled his work among the Thessalonians and wrote to express both his joy at the subsequent growth of their faith and his desire to visit them again. He also addressed the question of what would become of those Christians who had died before Jesus' return.

Paul's second letter to the Thessalonians is thought to have been written a few weeks later, urging the Christian believers there to live holy lives in the light of Christ's coming, and to tell them what to expect before Christ's return. Probably among the earliest of all Christian writings, these two letters are an invaluable insight into the young and joyful faith of an emerging Christian congregation.

## 1 THESSALONIANS

According to Acts (Acts 17:1–9), Paul traveled along the Egnatian Way from Philippi (*pp. 396–97*) to Thessalonica (modern-day Salonika, Greece) and spent a few weeks preaching the Christian Gospel in the Jewish synagogue there. Some of the Jews believed his message, but other Jews stirred up the crowds to oppose him so that he had to escape from the city. This account is largely confirmed by 1 Thessalonians, which was written to a church that *"in spite of persecution … received the word with joy inspired by the Holy Spirit"* (1:6), a church that consisted mainly of converts from paganism who "turned to God from idols, to serve a living and true God" (1:9). After being prematurely ejected from Thessalonica, Paul had repeatedly wanted to return but had been unable to do so because "Satan blocked our way" (2:18). Instead, Paul sent Timothy to return from Athens to

**CHRIST'S COMING**
*Of all the letters attributed to Paul, 1 and 2 Thessalonians contain the most vivid descriptions of Jesus' return, when he will be "revealed from heaven with his mighty angels in flaming fire."*

Thessalonica to see how the believers there were progressing in their new faith. When Timothy returned and caught up with Paul in Corinth, Paul, having heard his good report, sent 1 Thessalonians to express his joy that the faith of the believers there had not only survived but flourished in his absence.

Much of 1 Thessalonians is an encouragement to good behavior: Paul instructs the church to avoid sexual immorality and encourages it to develop a harmonious and lively Christian community. He also deals with one specific question that had been causing concern in Thessalonica: how should Christians feel when their fellow believers die? Paul's explanation is based on his teaching that the risen Christ will come again from Heaven. He explains that they should take comfort from the fact that, like Jesus, dead believers will be raised from death when Christ returns. Both the living and those who have died will "be with the Lord for ever" (4:17). Paul was careful to say that although Christ's return will be a surprising and sudden event for those who are not looking for it, he expects believers to be prepared and to live sober lives in the meantime.

## 2 THESSALONIANS

Some scholars query whether Paul wrote 2 Thessalonians. Much of it is close to 1 Thessalonians, but 1:5–12 emphasizes punishment, and 2:1–12 goes into the kind of apocalyptic detail that is discouraged in 1 Thessalonians. But perhaps Paul wrote like this because his first letter had not had the desired effect. If that is the case, 2 Thessalonians was written just a few months after Paul's first letter to correct a misapprehension among the Thessalonians that "the day of the Lord" had already come (2 Thess. 2:2). The letter tells them that this cannot happen until a "lawless one" (perhaps the Antichrist, *p.445*) has first tried to deceive people with blasphemous claims to be divine. At his return, Christ is expected not only to reward Christian believers and punish those who do not believe but to destroy this self-styled god: *"And then the lawless one will be revealed, whom the Lord Jesus will destroy with the breath of his mouth, annihilating him by the manifestation of his coming"* (2:8). So the Thessalonians are exhorted to live up to their calling, maintain their faith, and live holy lives. As for those who had given up work-ing, perhaps because they expected Christ to return at any minute, they are told to follow Paul's example and earn their bread by hard work.

Nowhere else in his later letters did Paul write in such explicit and vivid language about his expectation of Christ's coming as he did in 1 and 2 Thessalonians. That Christ would return in glory as a savior and judge of the world was an essential part of early Christian belief. These letters show the first Christians grappling from the start with the question of how such beliefs about the future affected their attitudes toward life and death.

## THE BOOK

**TITLES:** The First Letter of Paul to the Thessalonians; The Second Letter of Paul to the Thessalonians

**DATE:** Both letters appear to have been written c.50CE within a few weeks of each another, and sent from Corinth during Paul's stay there

**AUTHORSHIP:** Paul, with Silas (Silvanus) and Timothy. That Paul wrote 1 Thessalonians is beyond serious doubt, but 2 Thessalonians may have been written later by a disciple of Paul (perhaps Silas or Timothy was involved)

## THE CONTENTS

**1 THESSALONIANS**

Chapter 1: Greetings and thanksgiving for the Thessalonian church

Chapter 2:1–16: Defense of Paul and his companions, and further thanksgiving

Chapters 2:17–3:13: Paul's care and a prayer

Chapter 4:1–12: Encouragement to holy living

Chapters 4:13–5:11: Concerning Christians who have died and the coming of Christ

Chapter 5:12–28: Obedience and church life; final blessings

**2 THESSALONIANS**

Chapter 1:1–4: Greetings and thanksgiving for the Thessalonian church

Chapter 1:5–10: God's vindication

Chapter 1:11–12: A prayer

Chapter 2:1–12: The man of lawlessness

Chapters 2:13–3:5: Thanksgiving and a prayer

Chapter 3:6–15: Discipline for the idle

Chapter 3:16–18: Final greetings and blessing

## KEY THEME

*Holiness in expectation of Christ's coming*

For further reading see bibliography numbers: 432, 776

# THE COMING KINGDOM

*Jesus lived and taught that the kingdom of God is in the world even now. Yet it is not fully here in the present. The early Christians looked for the completion of God's kingdom by Jesus in the future, an event called his "Second Coming."*

JESUS did not end with his death. He had indeed died upon the cross but afterward he was known to be alive. He belongs, therefore, to the past, but even more to the present and the future. In Jesus' teaching the kingdom of God is close at hand, the world order where God is paramount, and where a true relationship with God (with all its consequences) is established. Jesus' life and actions demonstrated both in practice and effect what God's kingdom means: *"If it is by the Spirit of God that I cast out demons, then the kingdom of God has come to you"* (Matt. 12:28; Luke 11:20). Resisting any speculation about when the final and cataclysmic intervention of God might be expected, Jesus said, *"In fact, the kingdom of God is within you"* (Luke 17:21; the translation "among you" is also possible).

## THE PRESENT AND THE FUTURE

Those parables describing the kingdom of God (*see pp.336–37*) pointed to the differences that it made to people's lives at the time. Instead of fighting Romans and looking for violent solutions, Jesus taught that people should live and work in the transforming power of the kingdom. When Jesus taught his disciples to pray, "Your kingdom come, Your will be done," there is a sense that their prayer, and the prayer of countless Christians after them, has already been answered: the sovereignty of God has been established and made actual through the work of the Spirit, and is now made actual in Christian believers.

And yet there is a sense in which the kingdom is still to come in the future, at least in all its fullness. The recognition by Christians from the earliest days of Jesus as Lord (*pp.346–47, 412–13*) meant that he is as much at the center of the kingdom in the future as he was in the past. Even so, in the Bible the coming of the kingdom is not usually described strictly as a "second coming" of Jesus (*except* Heb. 9:28). Instead, the advent or coming of the kingdom in a final and complete way is known as *Parousia* (Greek for presence, advent, coming). The Parousia "of the Lord" (Jas. 5:9) may mean God, but because Jesus was, from the start, associated closely with God, the Parousia and completion of the kingdom are more often associated with him.

THE COMING OF CHRIST
*Jesus taught that one day "he will come again to judge the living and the dead" – a longed-for time of salvation by his disciples.*

## THE SECOND COMING

Jesus, who lived the kingdom of God in his own person as well as teaching about it, clearly looked for the full coming of the kingdom in its completeness. Insofar as the kingdom of God in Heaven has already come in the life and death of Jesus (e.g., Matt. 11:5–6; 12:28; Mark 1:15; Luke 4:16–30; 7:22–23; 11:20), the future completion of the kingdom of God on earth is all the more certain.

Many of Jesus' parables referred to a returning Lord, such as the parables of the Ten Bridesmaids (Matt. 25:1–13) and of the Talents/Pounds (Matt. 25:14–30; Luke 19:12–27). The parable of the Burglar (Matt. 24:43–44; Luke 12:39–40) emphasizes the unexpectedness of the Son of Man's coming.

# THE ANTICHRIST

*The recurring New Testament figure of the Antichrist has given rise to many interpretations. It has been taken to refer to particular persons or institutions (such as the Roman empire), or to be a personification of evil forces that wage war against God.*

The Pope, Napoleon, Hitler, Mussolini, and Stalin have all been identified with the Antichrist. But who is the Antichrist? In the New Testament, the term *antichrist*, meaning "one who opposes Christ," is found only in the letters of John (1 John 2:18, 22; 4:3; 2 John 7), but the comparable figures are also found elsewhere in the New Testament:

• In his teaching on the end-time, Jesus drew upon imagery from the book of Daniel (9:27; 11:31; 12:11) to describe one who would, like Antiochus Epiphanes in 169BCE (*p.251*) – as "the abomination of desolation" – violate the Temple (Mark 13:14: *also* Matt. 24:15; Luke 21:20 does not have the Danielic figure). This Antichrist figure would seek to supplant the worship of the true God.

• Paul in 2 Thessalonians refers to a "man of lawlessness" (2:3) who immediately before the day of visitation would oppose the worship of God by exalting himself and "proclaiming himself to be God" (2:4). In Revelation the figure is probably the Roman emperor, worshiped as "Lord and God."

• John sees "the Antichrist who is coming" (1 John 2:18) already at work in the activities of false teachers, themselves termed "antichrists," for they deny that Jesus is God's Son who came as a real human being, "in the flesh" (1 John 4:3; 2 John 7). There are two threads of thought running through all these passages. First, a conviction that the end-time will be marked by an explosion of evil, when many will be deceived and which will issue in an epic battle where evil will be defeated. And second, a willingness to see the evil of the end-time already anticipated in the present.

---

But sayings about the Son of Man coming in the future are linked to Daniel (*see p.216*), and therefore have more to do with the inauguration of the kingdom of God in the vindication of Jesus beyond death than to do with a Second Coming as the inauguration of the final kingdom of God. At the hearing before the High Priest just before his Crucifixion (*pp.354–55*), Jesus drew upon the imagery of Daniel 7:13 to speak of his "coming with the clouds of heaven" as the glorified, and therefore vindicated, Son of Man (Mark 14:62; Luke 22:69). Jesus spoke also of the final verdict being tied to the vindicated Son of Man (e.g., Matt. 10:22; 25:31–46; Mark 8:38; Luke 9:26).

Insofar as Jesus looked to a coming vindication, he linked it to his foretelling of the destruction of the Temple in Jerusalem (Matt. 24; Mark 13; Luke 21), which he regarded as a sign of the end-time, and which was the substance of the charge against him in Jerusalem. Although Jesus believed the end-time to be very near (Mark 13:30; *see also* Matt. 16:28; Mark 9:1; Luke 9:27), he made it clear that he himself did not know the exact timing – hence the need for watchfulness (Mark 13:32–37). Further substantial teaching is found in the so-called "apocalypse" of Luke's Gospel (Luke 17:22–37). Linked as it is to the destruction of the Temple, the purpose of the Coming is for judgment, and as such is a dreadful day to be associated with "weeping" and "gnashing of teeth." However, it is also a good day, because it is for salvation. Sayings about feasting together in the kingdom of God emphasize the happiness of the occasion (Matt. 8:11–12; 26:29; Mark 14:25; Luke 13:28–29; 22:15–18).

> **❝** All the tribes of the earth will mourn, and they will see the Son of Man coming on the clouds of heaven with power and great glory. And he will send out his angels with a loud trumpet call. **❞**
>
> (Matthew 24:30–31)

## THE HOPE OF THE EARLY CHURCH

The early Christian communities looked forward eagerly to the day of visitation or judgment: *"Be patient, therefore, beloved, until the coming of the Lord. The farmer waits for the precious crop from the earth, being patient with it until it receives the early and the late rains. You must also be patient. Strengthen your hearts, for the coming of the Lord is near. Beloved, do not grumble against one another, so that you may not be judged. See, the judge is standing at the doors!"* (Jas. 5:7–9; 1 Pet. 1:7; 2:12; 1 John 2:28; 4:17). Paul expected the coming of the kingdom, perhaps in his lifetime (e.g., 1 Cor. 15:50–52; 1 Thess. 2:19; 3:13; 4:13–17; 5:23), but in 2 Corinthians 5:1 he clearly envisaged the possibility of death before it would happen. The Day of the Lord will be as unexpected as the coming of a thief (1 Thess. 5:2) and as unavoidable as the birth of a child once a woman has gone into labor (1 Thess. 5:3). Although the vividness of some of the apocalyptic imagery of 2 Thessalonians (1:5–2:12) is not found in Paul's later letters, the hope of the Lord's return remains undiminished (*cf.* Rom. 13:11–14; Phil. 2:16; 3:20). However, the Aramaic phrase *maranatha* (1 Cor. 16:22) and its equivalent in Greek, *kurios* (Rev. 22:17–20; *see also p.412*), both of which are often translated as though they are a prayer for the Second Coming ("Our Lord, come"), may be, in the context, an invocation to enforce an excluding ban or warning. The apparent delay of the return of Jesus caused problems in the early Church. This is clear in 2 Peter, where the writer emphasizes that God's ways of measuring time are of another order than ours (3:8), and that God is simply being patient rather than slow (3:9).

For further reading see bibliography numbers: 55, 75, 133, 499, 574, 654, 655, 753, 833, 870

# THE LETTERS TO
# TIMOTHY
# & TITUS

*These three letters, addressed to two church leaders, deal with issues that concern the organization of early Christian communities and the care of people in the churches.*

THE two letters written to Timothy and one to Titus have been known collectively as "the Pastoral Epistles" since the 18th century, since they are concerned with the pastoral care of communities and church life and practice. They are addressed to Paul's companions, Timothy and Titus, who were acknowledged leaders in churches that Paul had established on his travels. Although addressed to two individuals, these letters provide guidance for the whole church community and address the issue of the appointment of church leaders.

Whether Paul wrote all these letters is now disputed. It is unlikely he wrote them during the period covered in Acts, at the end of which he was in prison before his death (*p.401*). It is possible that he was released and went on another missionary journey in Asia Minor and Macedonia some time between c.63 and 66CE. If that was so, Paul may have written 1 Timothy and Titus during this time. On his return to Rome, he would then have been rearrested and sentenced to death. He could have written 2 Timothy, recognizing that death was imminent: *"as for me, I am already being poured out as a libation, and the time of my departure has come"* (2 Tim. 4:6). However, questions are raised about this view (*see panel, opposite*).

**PASTORAL CARE AND LEADERSHIP**
*1 & 2 Timothy and Titus provide Christian leaders with important examples of sound doctrine to care for congregations and counter false teaching.*

## TIMOTHY AND TITUS

Timothy emerges from the New Testament as one of Paul's closest companions. He came from Lystra, in Asia Minor, and after his conversion accompanied Paul on many of his journeys. Often he would go on ahead of Paul to a place or remain there after he had left (e.g., 1 Cor. 16:10–11; 1 Tim. 1:3). Five of Paul's other letters are said to have come from him as well (*see* 1:1of 2 Corinthians, Philippians, Colossians, 1 Thessalonians, and 2 Thessalonians). Paul looked upon Timothy as a son, describing him as his beloved and faithful child (1 Cor. 4:17). Timothy became a church leader in Ephesus, and Paul addressed his letters to him there (1 Tim. 1:3).

Titus we know less about. He is mentioned in Acts, but Paul also referred to him in a number of his letters. Titus accompanied Paul on an early journey up to Jerusalem, recounted in Galatians 2, and worked alongside him in Corinth (2 Cor. 8:23). At the beginning of this letter, Titus is described as leading the church on the island of Crete: *"I left you behind in Crete for this reason, so that you should put in order what remained to be done, and should appoint elders in every town, as I directed you"* (Tit. 1:5).

## WHY THE LETTERS WERE WRITTEN

In the years since Paul had first established the churches in Ephesus and on Crete, they had grown and were now becoming a more accepted part of society. Church leaders were anxious to lay down guidelines to enable Christians to live according to rules that conformed more to the general pattern of behavior in first-century CE society.

There was also a number of false teachers saying that marriage was forbidden and that certain foods were to be avoided (1 Tim. 4:3). It seems that the teaching was especially popular among women, and that they were exercising leadership and teaching others to an extent that the traditional society of the Roman empire could not countenance.

1 Timothy 3 states the reason for the letter: that *"you may know how one ought to behave in the household of God, which is the church of the living God"* (1 Tim. 3.15). The Roman ideal of godliness or piety is prized as the highest virtue in a number of verses: *"Have nothing to do with profane myths and old wives' tales. Train yourself in godliness, for, while physical training is of some value, godliness is valuable in every way, holding promise for both the present life and the life to come* (1 Tim. 4:7–8; cf. 2:2; 2 Tim. 3, 5; Tit. 1:1).

## CARE FOR THE CHURCHES

All three letters emphasize faith and sound teaching, and false teaching is vigorously attacked. They show a great concern for the life of the churches, but they achieve this in different ways. 1 Timothy contains specific instructions: it deals with prayer (1 Tim. 2:1); the role of women in liturgical assembly (1 Tim. 2:8–15); the qualifications for bishops, deacons, and women deacons (1 Tim. 3:1–11); the care of widows (1 Tim. 5:3–16); the payment of elders and the handling of charges against them (1 Tim. 5:19–22); and the attitude of slaves (1 Tim. 6:1–2) and the rich (1 Tim. 6:17–19).

In 2 Timothy, the emphasis is on example (and is therefore sometimes called a "paranetic letter" from the Greek letters written to exhort someone to pursue a good way of life). Paul is offered as a model for Timothy in teaching and suffering (2 Tim. 1:8–14; 3:10–16; 4:6–18), and Timothy is told how to resist the false teachers that surround him (2 Tim. 2:14–4:5). Titus also contains instructions (Tit. 2:1–13) summed up as the doing of good deeds (Tit. 2:14; 3:8, 14). The major threat posed by the false teachers in the Christian communities (*see above*) is countered in 1 and 2 Timothy by the supreme fact of Jesus <u>as he is remembered</u>, as a control and a guide when dealing with the false teaching of new and strange ideas: *"Remember Jesus Christ, raised from the dead, a descendant of David – that is my gospel"* (2 Tim. 2:8).

These letters are important in providing one example of early Church leadership structure. Their significance has increased in the 20th century as ecumenical discussions between different church denominations have sought to find guidance from the New Testament for models of leadership today.

## THE BOOK

**TITLES:** The First Letter of Paul to Timothy; The Second Letter of Paul to Timothy; The Letter of Paul to Titus

**DATE:** Debated (*see below*)

**AUTHORSHIP:** The first verse of the first chapter of each book ascribes each letter to Paul. However, some believe them to be pseudonymous and think that they were written after Paul's death by a follower of his. If this is correct, they could be as late as the beginning of the second century CE, although c.85CE is more realistic. The vocabulary and style are different from Paul's other letters, reflecting a more sophisticated, literary Greek. The emphasis on church order points to a community institutionalized to an extent that would have been unlikely by the 60s. Very few of Paul's great theological themes, such as the Holy Spirit or believers living in Christ, appear. It may, however, be a mistake to call the letters "the Pastorals" and treat them as one. There is a case for Paul writing 2 Timothy and for 1 Timothy, which is far less Pauline, being based on it. Titus appears to be a genuine piece of correspondence but difficult to associate with Paul's known life (or style). The letters are not mentioned by Christian writers until the second half of the second century CE, supporting the view that they were written after Paul died

## THE CONTENTS

### 1 TIMOTHY

Chapters 1–4: Instructions for teaching, worship, appointment of leaders; false teaching condemned
Chapters 5–6: Instructions for members of the community and against false teachers

### 2 TIMOTHY

Chapters 1–4: Paul as an example to follow; against false teachers

### TITUS

Chapter 1: Instructions for appointment of leaders
Chapters 2–3: Instructions for the members of the community and against false teaching.

## KEY THEMES

*Pastoral care and leadership for the community*

•

*Church life and practice*

For further reading see bibliography numbers: 234, 288, 419, 841

# MINISTRY

*Everyone needs help from others, and society needs people in different positions to make decisions and undertake different tasks. And so it was in the early Church, where varying patterns of service and ministry emerged.*

IT is easy to look back on the churches of the New Testament period and think that they must have been organized in the same way as the churches of today, with (in most cases) bishops, priests, and deacons. But a structured ministry did not emerge until, at the earliest, the end of the New Testament period. From the outset, ministry was the service of people by one another, following the example of Jesus himself. The emphasis is on the ministry of the whole people of God, called in 1 Peter 2:5–10 "a holy and a royal priesthood."

In Paul's writings, believers made up the Body of Christ, in which they shared with each other the various gifts they received from the Holy Spirit (*p.417; cf.* 1 Pet. 4:10–11). As Paul makes clear in Romans 12:14–18 and 1 Corinthians 12:4–12, all God's people are gifted for ministry. In that sense of being "gifted" (Greek, *charisma*), God's people are "charismatic" (*see also* Rom. 12:4–8). Pastoral care, therefore, is not the preserve of the few but the responsibility of all: "*But God has so arranged the body, giving the greater honor to the inferior member, that there may be no dissension within the body, but the members*

> **❝** *For who is greater, the one who is at the table or the one who serves? Is it not the one at the table? But I am among you as one who serves.* **❞**
>
> (Luke 22:27)

*may have the same care for one another. If one member suffers, all suffer together with it; if one member is honored, all rejoice together with it"* (1 Cor. 12:24–26). All God's people are called to serve one another by, for example, bearing one another's burdens (Gal. 6:1–2), speaking the truth in love (Eph. 4:15), encouraging one another (1 Thess. 5:11), and praying for one another (Jas. 5:16).

In the New Testament there is no set pattern of ministry, nor is there an inherited priesthood passed on in families. There are, however, certain figures who emerge with particular roles:
• Ephesians 4:11–12 mentions apostles, prophets, evangelists, pastors, and teachers, whose roles were to support the ministry of all and "to equip the saints for the work of ministry."
• At the church in Philippi there were "overseers and deacons" (*episkopoi* and *diakonoi; see* Phil. 1:1). The word *episkopos* used to be translated as *bishop*, hence the English word *episcopacy*, but it means simply *overseer*. The word *diakonos* underlies the English word *deacon*: it means one who mediates between one party and another, as a waiter

**PETER'S MINISTRY**
*This 15th-century Italian fresco shows Peter, one of the first leaders of the early Christian Church, raising Tabitha from the dead (Acts 9:36–42) and healing a cripple. In raising Tabitha from the dead, Peter followed Jesus' example of raising Jairus' daughter, at which Peter was present (Mark 5:35–43).*

"mediates," or goes to and fro between kitchen and table. Hence the word came to mean *servant*. In Acts 6:1–7, seven deacons were chosen to wait on tables in order to set the 12 Apostles free for "prayer and serving the word."

• At the church in Jerusalem, elders were linked with the Apostles as having the authority to discuss an issue of "dissension and debate" (Acts 15:2).

• At Lystra, Iconium, and Pisidian Antioch, Paul and Barnabas appointed "elders" in each church (Acts 14:23).

• Paul commended to the church at Rome "our sister Phoebe, a deacon of the church at Cenchreae" (Rom 16:1). Phoebe was a benefactor (Rom 16:2), but to what extent her generosity was linked with her role in the church remains uncertain (*p.437*).

• At Ephesus there were overseers (perhaps identical with the elders who are also mentioned) and deacons (1 Tim. 3:1–13), but apart from the fact that the overseers, or bishops, had to be "apt teachers" (1 Tim. 3:2), nothing is said about their differing roles.

**LEADING BY EXAMPLE**
*Jesus' example of servant ministry – here washing the feet of his disciples – is commemorated annually in different ceremonies.*

New Testament Church there was always a plurality of gifts and ministries: *"After they had appointed elders for them in each church, with prayer and fasting they entrusted them to the Lord"* (Acts 14:23; cf. Acts 13:1; 15:23; 20:17, 28; Phil. 1:1). The only example of one-man ministry in the New Testament is found in 3 John 9, where Diotrephes, "who likes to put himself first," was not recommended as an example to be followed. Outside the Church, there are passages commending supreme leaders in the state (Rom. 13:1; 1 Pet. 2:13ff., 17; 1 Tim. 2:1ff.).

## SERVANT MINISTRY

In the New Testament, leaders were normally appointed with prayer and with the laying on of hands: *"While they were worshiping the Lord and fasting, the Holy Spirit said, 'Set apart for me Barnabas and Saul for the work to which I have called them.' Then after fasting and praying they laid their hands on them and sent them off"* (Acts 13:2–3; cf. Acts 16:1–6; 14:23; 1 Tim. 4:14; 2 Tim. 1:6). In the light of rabbinic parallels, it would appear that such a ceremony conveyed not just blessing but also the delegation of authority to discharge one's duty. However, while church ministries may have had authority (1 Thess. 5:12; 1 Tim. 4:11; 5:17; Heb. 13:17), they were not free to be authoritarian. Christian leadership exhorts, rather than coerces (1 Tim 5:1).

As Jesus made clear on more than one occasion, it is the servant who is the true leader: *"Whoever wishes to become great among you must be your servant, and whoever wishes to be first among you must be slave of all"* (Mark 10:43; Matt. 20:25–27; cf. Luke 22:24–26); *"Whoever wants to be first must be last of all and servant of all"* (Mark 9:35; Luke 9:48). A true Christian leader follows the example of Jesus, who washed his disciples' feet: *"If I, your Lord and Teacher, have washed your feet, you also ought to wash one another's feet. For I have set you an example, that you should do as I have done to you"* (John 13:14–15). With Jesus' example in mind, Peter ruled out leaders "lording" it over others (1 Pet. 5:2–3). Paul expanded the same theme, saying that servant ministry is never from "above," it is always from "below" (1 Cor. 16:15–16). Servant ministry by definition is noncoercive.

## LEADERSHIP

Being leader and Lord belongs to God (1 Tim. 6:15–16) not to humans, as Paul realized: *"I do not mean to imply that we lord it over your faith; rather, we are workers with you for your joy, because you stand firm in the faith"* (2 Cor. 1:24). Authority is derived from God through Christ, who is the head of the whole body of the Church, and from who the body grows in love: *"Speaking the truth in love, we must grow up in every way into him who is the head, into Christ, from whom the whole body, joined and knitted together by every ligament with which it is equipped … promotes the body's growth in building itself up in love"* (Eph. 4:4–16). For that reason, leadership is exemplary: *"Remember your leaders, those who spoke the word of God to you, consider the outcome of their way of life, and imitate their faith"* (Heb. 13:7). Then, leadership involved the preaching and teaching of God's Word (Acts 6:4; Eph. 4:11; 1 Tim. 3:2; 4:13; 2 Tim. 2:2, 15; 4:2), the overseeing of God's people (Acts 20:28; 1 Pet. 5:2), and equipping and building up God's people for service (Eph. 4:11–12). Such leadership was always shared. In the

> **66** *Be strong in the grace that is in Christ Jesus; and what you have heard from me through many witnesses entrust to faithful people who will be able to teach others as well.* **99**
>
> (2 Timothy 2:2)

For further reading see bibliography numbers: 54, 61, 202, 352, 613, 697, 722

# THE LETTER TO THE

# HEBREWS

*Hebrews is a finely written statement of the great themes of Christian belief and hope.
It is closely argued and draws contrasts between the old situation under the
Law and the new hope and faith made possible in Christ.*

HEBREWS is a densely argued work. In form, it is not much like a letter but may be closer to a sermon or homily. It is impossible to pick out one part that might stand on its own because the argument is continuous and themes recur to be further developed; it demands being read as a whole. Those to whom the letter was addressed appear to be Jewish Christians who were in danger of turning away from their Christian faith and reverting to Judaism (6:4–6). This letter argues for the supremacy and finality of Jesus and his work, especially in relation to Jewish sacrificial worship in the Tabernacle of Moses (chs.8–9). It argues that Jesus is supreme over the agents of the old Covenant, and his death is the final sacrifice, valid for all time. Therefore, these Christians are not to look back but to persevere, focusing on Jesus who has given them an example of living by faith and who has gone ahead of them into Heaven. They are to follow in faith.

## JESUS IS SUPREME

The author of Hebrews contrasts Jesus with angels, Moses, and the High Priest. He contends that Jesus is superior to the angels, using seven biblical texts to stress Jesus' exalted status in Heaven and to diminish the Jewish Law, which was thought to have been given to Moses by angels (ch.1). He claims that Jesus is greater then Moses by comparing their relative status, emphasizing the inferiority of a servant to a son in the home: *"Now Moses was faithful in all God's house as a*

**FOCUSING ON JESUS**
*Hebrews invites a Jewish Christian community to meet together to affirm its faith in
God's new Covenant through Christ, as opposed to the old Covenant given to Moses.*

*servant, to testify to all the things that would be spoken later. Christ, however, was faithful over God's house as a son, and we are his house if we hold firm the confidence and the pride that belong to hope"* (3:5–6). Jesus is described as the "great high priest" because he is merciful, faithful, and most distinctively, eternal: *"For we do not have a high priest who is unable to sympathize with our weaknesses, but we have one who in every respect has been tested as we are, yet without sin"* (4:15). Also, Jesus is the mediator of a new and better Covenant, defined by a close, immediate relationship with God as prophesied by Jeremiah and thus rendering the old Covenant "obsolete" (8:6–13; cf. Jer. 31:31–34). The author's point is clear: Jesus is supreme.

## THE FINAL SACRIFICE

Whereas the sacrifices for sin under the old Covenant had to be repeated each time the relationship with God was broken, Jesus' death was the final and decisive sacrifice effective for all time. In particular, the author focuses on the annual Day of Atonement (Exod. 30:10; cf. Lev. 16; pp.68–69), the one day each year when the High Priest could go into the most holy place in the Tabernacle to offer a sacrifice for the sins of the people. The Tabernacle was made on earth, but Jesus enters Heaven to appear in the presence of God on behalf of humans: *"For Christ did not enter a sanctuary made by human hands, a mere copy of the true one, but he entered into heaven itself, now to appear in the presence of God on our behalf. Nor was it to offer himself again and again, as the high priest* enters the Holy Place year after year with blood that is not his own; for then he would have had to suffer again and again since the foundation of the world." (9:24–26a). Just as a will cannot come into effect until the person who made it has died, and just as the first Covenant required animal blood to be shed to bring it into effect, so Jesus had to die. Through the blood that he shed, he brought into effect the true and enduring Covenant with God. His sacrificial death seals a new and better Covenant, characterized by a confident approach to God: *"Therefore, my friends, since we have confidence to enter the sanctuary by the blood of Jesus, by the new and living way that he opened for us through the curtain (that is, through his flesh), and since we have a great priest over the house of God, let us approach with a true heart in full assurance of faith, with our hearts sprinkled clean from an evil conscience and our bodies washed with pure water"* (10:19–22).

## WARNINGS AND ENCOURAGEMENT

The author of Hebrews uses warnings, encouragement, and exhortation to motivate this community to continue in their Christian faith. He warns them that if they reject Christ, they risk a punishment more severe than under the Law of Moses, and they will be like those who were led out of Egypt but failed to reach the Promised Land (chs.2–4). The warnings are particularly severe: in chapters 6:4–8 and 10:26–31, the terrifying consequences of turning away after receiving the knowledge of truth are made clear: *"For if we willfully persist in sin after having received the knowledge of the truth, there no longer remains a sacrifice for sins, but a fearful prospect of judgment, and a fury of fire that will consume the adversaries"* (10:26–27). Just as those Israelites who, in rejecting the Law of Moses, died without mercy, then, "on the testimony of two or three witnesses" (10:28), how much more will those who trample the Son of God under foot be punished for their actions?

## PERSEVERANCE

As a result of his view of the urgency of the issues, the author encourages his readers, or listeners, to remember those who have shown a patient faith, citing Abraham and concluding with Jesus as the ultimate example (11–12:2). He urges this Christian community to turn to Jesus and God in times of weakness: Jesus can help these Christians as he faced temptation but did not sin (2:14–18). They can draw near to God for "mercy" and "grace" because Jesus has gone ahead of them into Heaven, where he acts as their "high priest" (4:15–16).

In addition, the members of this Christian community are to meet together for mutual support and encouragement: *"And let us consider how to provoke one another to love and good deeds, not neglecting to meet together, as is the habit of some, but encouraging one another, and all the more as you see the Day approaching"* (10:24–25). This is a time of crisis, and the clarion call is to "persevere" in faith.

# THE BOOK

TITLE: The Letter to the Hebrews

DATE: Probably before 70CE

AUTHORSHIP: Unknown. The author is not named. He was clearly someone with knowledge of the Hebrew Scriptures, who quoted mostly from the Greek (LXX) version, and who assumed that his audience knew the Scriptures equally well. He also had the same interest in Greek thought as Jews living in Alexandria – especially Philo. He used the Platonic distinction between the real world and the ideal world, the real world being less good than the ideal world; Jesus is the ideal in contrast to the old order of religion. Some have thought Apollos (Acts 18:24–28) was the author

# THE CONTENTS

CHAPTERS 1:1–3:6
God's final revelation in his Son; Jesus is greater than the angels and Moses

CHAPTERS 3:7–4:13
The promise of entering into God's rest

CHAPTERS 4:14–5:10
Jesus the Great High Priest

CHAPTERS 5:11–6:20
Human frailty and God's promise

CHAPTERS 7:1–9:28
Jesus is a High Priest like Melchizedek; the High Priest of a new Covenant; worship and sacrifice of the new Covenant

CHAPTERS 10:1–11:40
Christ's sacrifice; call to persevere; examples of faith

CHAPTERS 12–13
God's discipline; final warnings, encouragements and greetings

# KEY THEMES

*The sovereignty and faithfulness of God*
•
*The superiority of Christ to the old order, and his priestly ministry*
•
*The need to persevere*

For further reading see bibliography numbers: 142, 435

# PHILOSOPHIES
## OF THE NEW TESTAMENT PERIOD

*Many schools of philosophy flourished in the Mediterranean world in the first century CE.
Jews had interacted with these schools, especially in Egypt, and Christianity
was soon also to do so.*

ACCORDING to Acts 17:17–18, Paul argued with passersby in the agora (market place) in Athens, where philosophers joined up with him and invited him to the Aeropagus to hear what he had to say.

By the time of Paul's arrival in Athens in the first century CE, the city was still the natural heart of the philosophical world. The history of philosophy in Athens stretched back five centuries to the time of Socrates, Aristotle, and Plato. The excitement generated by the conquest of the eastern Mediterranean by Alexander the Great had brought a new breed of philosophers to Athens. As a result of the city of Alexandria (Alexander's foundation in Egypt)

attracting many of the ancient disciplines of scholarly research, philosophy in Athens narrowed down to something like the specific discipline it is today.

These changes affected Hebrew wisdom as the Jews and their religion moved into the Hellenistic world. The Wisdom of Solomon (7:17–22), which some scholars associate with Alexandria, suggested that God's wisdom provides

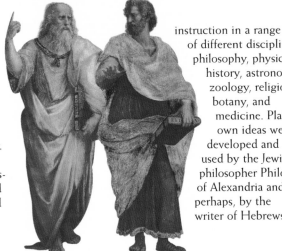

**PLATO AND ARISTOTLE**
*These two philosophers were the most influential of ancient times and their schools subsequently developed their thought.*

instruction in a range of different disciplines: philosophy, physics, history, astronomy, zoology, religion, botany, and medicine. Plato's own ideas were developed and used by the Jewish philosopher Philo of Alexandria and, perhaps, by the writer of Hebrews.

## FATE AND DETERMINISM

By Paul's time, the Platonic tradition had taken on heavily sceptical and critical elements. The new philosophers of the Academy, for example, accepted the argument that there could be no possible criterion for identifying truth. They, along with the Epicureans and Stoics, were also concerned with the question of fate and determinism as were, according to the Jewish historian Josephus, the Pharisees of his day. However, the belief that everything that happens is determined in advance took different forms.

In their different ways, Epicureans, Cynics, and Stoics were all concerned with the relationship between truth and behavior. By New Testament times, contemporary philosophy was thought to have become primarily concerned with the art of living.

## THE CYNICS

The name Cynic probably comes from the Greek for "dog" (*kyon*) and describes those who belonged to a tradition of philosophy going back to Antisthenes and Diogenes (*left*) of the fourth century BCE. Scorning worldly goods and advocating self-control, the Cynics had an uncouth appearance, characterized by dirty clothes, unkempt hair, and a staff. Some have seen similarities between the Cynics and Jesus. For example, the instructions he gives his disciples for their missionary journeys resemble the Cynic patterns of travel. There are also suggestions in the Gospels of an asceticism rooted in the natural sufficiency of the world (Matt. 7:25–34; Luke 12:22–31). However, against this argument is the fact that the first-century CE revival of Cynicism only occurred <u>after</u> the time of Jesus.

## THE EPICUREANS

Epicurus (341–270BCE) established his school in Athens in the Garden between the Academy and the Dipylon Gate. He spelled out a system of thought with such precision that there were relatively few issues for his successors to debate. Essential to that system was an understanding of the cosmos in physical terms, with the result that fear of death and of divine punishment could be eliminated.

Epicurus should not, however, be regarded as a determinist. While he wanted to dissuade people from trying to evade death, he could appreciate the extent to which they were able to establish their own wishes. He should also not be regarded as an atheist, for to him the gods were reflections of one's own ethical goals. He believed that those who were bad chose gods who were power-seeking meddlers like themselves, and that those who were good gained uplift from the supreme tranquillity of divine blessedness. Nor was Epicurus an individualist as his interest in pleasure as the supreme good might suggest. The Garden community anticipated the time when everything would be full of justice and mutual friendship.

Jewish reaction to Epicureanism in the first century CE is illustrated by Josephus and Philo; they strongly denounced its denial of divine providence.

## THE STOICS

Stoics, or "the men from the Stoa," took their name from the colonnade in the market place of Athens where Zeno of Citium taught (c.300BCE). For them, philosophy was composed of three parts: logic, physics, and ethics. Logic made it possible to achieve reliable knowledge of reality; physics established that the world was a uniformly structured physical form imbued with a creative divine power

called "reason"; and ethics enabled them, through this rational outlook, to know how they should act. Furthermore, the Stoics believed that humans were constituted in such a way as to allow virtue to guarantee their happiness, and that they had a pre-ordained part to play in the world, in the city-state, and for the good of the whole. They could live with a "stoical" attitude, even in misfortune. The history of Stoicism moved into a second period with the work of Panaetius of Rhodes (198–185BCE) and his pupil

**THE AGORA, ATHENS**
*Athens' colonnaded market place provided the Stoics with their arena.*

Posidonius (150–135BCE), and into a third period during the Roman empire with Seneca (c.5BCE–65CE), Cicero (106–43BCE), and at the end of the century, Epictetus (c.55–c.135BC) as major influences.

Some Stoics taught an austere form of virtue (see 1 Cor. 9:26–27) with a strict control of sexual behavior through concentration on inner motivations and attitudes. Throughout their history, the Stoics never swayed from Zeno's thesis that a knowledge of the world is possible, and that humans have a natural ability to distinguish truth from falsehood, right from wrong.

Philo drew several ideas from Stoicism, describing the cosmos as the "great city," and expounding on the economy of the city-state and the household as built on marriage. However, on occasion he could blend this with a more contemplative, and perhaps ascetic and Cynic, attitude. Paul, in 1 Corinthians 7:17–31, develops a similar pattern of arguments in a comparable rhetorical form.

## THE BIBLICAL STANCE

At various points the New Testament appears to attack philosophy. But the early Church quickly discovered the value of systematic thought and reflection. It may be that the reference to philosophy in Paul's letter to the Colossians (2:8), which is associated with "vain deceit" and "the elemental powers of the cosmos," is not an attack upon serious forms of classical philosophy but on those forms of teaching that claimed to give precise knowledge of Heaven.

**BACCHUS, GOD OF WINE AND DRUNKENNESS**
*Primarily concerned with living life to the full and not being afraid of death, Epicureans were often associated with imprudent yet passionate actions and were accused, perhaps falsely, of indulging in immoral acts.*

For further reading see bibliography numbers: 502, 507

# THE LETTER OF
# JAMES

*James is the first of the "catholic," or general, Epistles — so-called because they were written to the wider believing community, rather than to a specific congregation. The letter is full of practical advice on how to live as a Christian.*

JAMES, along with the letters of Peter, John, and Jude, is thought to have been addressed to Christians in general, and is therefore named after the letter's author, rather than after a particular church.

## HEIRS OF ISRAEL

James was written to *"the twelve tribes in the Dispersion"* (1:1), presumably Greek-speaking Christians who recognized themselves as the heirs of the traditions of Israel. References to Jesus are made only twice (1:1; 2:1), while there are several biblical quotations or allusions throughout. Jewish heroes such as Abraham, Rahab, Job, and Elijah are given prominence as examples to follow: *"Thus the scripture was fulfilled that says, 'Abraham believed God, and it was reckoned to him as righteousness,' and he was called the friend of God"* (2:23). For these reasons, some scholars have suggested that this letter was originally a Jewish text adapted to Christian use. This view seems too extreme, since it reflects a Jewishness that is also apparent in Jesus' teaching, especially in the Sermon on the Mount (*pp.334–35*). In any case, this letter is an important witness to one strand of first-century CE Christianity that remained rooted in Judaism and stressed the Jewish foundations of Christianity.

**LIVING FAITH**
*James talks of a true faith of commitment to God being reflected in good deeds, rather than in living a worldly lifestyle — exemplified in modern times by the work of Mother Theresa (1910–1997) and her nuns.*

## LIFE AS A CHRISTIAN (CHAPTERS 1–3)

The emphasis of James is on living a life devoted to God. The author uses vivid imagery and powerful contrasts to convey his ideas: *"Be doers of the word and not merely hearers who deceive themselves. For if any are hearers of the word and not doers, they are like those who look at themselves in a mirror; for they look at themselves and, on going away, immediately forget what they were like. But those who look into the perfect law, the law of liberty, and persevere, being not hearers who forget but doers who act — they will be blessed in their doing"* (1:22–25).

The letter goes on to stress that merely having correct belief is not enough; it must be united with an appropriate Christian lifestyle: *"What good is it, my brothers and sisters, if you say you have faith but do not have works? Can faith save you? If a brother or a sister is naked and lacks daily food, and one of you says to them, 'Go in peace; keep warm and eat your fill,' and yet you do not supply their bodily needs, what is the good of that? So faith by itself, if it has no works, is dead"* (2:14–17). The author gives examples — one male, Abraham, and one female, Rahab — to make his point (2:21–26). He also warns of how harmful words can be, and his mention of caring for the sick by anointing them with oil (5:14) is the biblical basis for the Church's anointing with oil in sacramental ceremonies.

## WISDOM (CHAPTERS 4–5)

The most prominent influence from Hebrew Scriptures in James is the Wisdom tradition (*pp.170–71*). The author quotes from Proverbs 3:34 in chapter 4:6, *"God opposes the proud, but gives grace to the humble,"* to stress that wisdom is seen as one of the greatest virtues to be sought: *"If any of you is lacking in wisdom, ask God, who gives to all generously and ungrudgingly, and it will be given you"* (1:5; 2:13, 17). Practical advice, characteristic of Wisdom thinking, appears throughout the letter, as does the theme of the suffering of the righteous, also prominent in Wisdom thinking. Job is seen as one who persevered to the end through suffering: *"We called blessed those who showed endurance. You have heard of the endurance of Job, and you have seen the purpose of the Lord, how the Lord is compassionate and merciful"* (5:11). The summary of the Hebrew Law taken from Leviticus, *"You shall love your neighbor as yourself"* (Lev. 19:18), is described by James as "the royal law" (2:8). This central chapter from Leviticus (*pp.62–63*), with its concern for the poor at the harvest, finds other echoes in chapter 5.

## JESUS' INFLUENCE

Although Jesus is scarcely mentioned in this letter, it is clear that his teaching is known, especially that from the Sermon on the Mount. The verse in chapter 2, *"Has not God chosen the poor in the world to be rich in faith and to be heirs of the kingdom?"* (2:5), expresses a similar sentiment to one of the Beatitudes: *"Blessed are the poor in spirit, for theirs is the kingdom of heaven"* (Matt. 5:3). James' "royal law" harks back to Jesus' teaching, stated in Mark (12:31) and Matthew (22:39).

## DOES JAMES CONTRADICT PAUL?

In its assertion that *"a person is justified by works and not by faith alone"* (2:24), James appears to be in contrast with Paul, who wrote that *"a person is justified by faith apart from works prescribed by the law"* (Rom. 3:28). This contrast of views has led many to regard James with suspicion and not as important for Christian teaching as Paul's letters. The German theologian Martin Luther (1483–1546) described it as "an epistle of straw," and Protestants have been wary of any teaching that goes against justification by faith alone (*pp.426–27*). It may be that early Christians distorted Paul's teaching, saying that conduct did not matter as long as a person believed. It is this distortion that James was anxious to correct. Some second-century CE Christian writings appear to refer to James, but it was not until the following century that it was more widely accepted as ranking alongside Paul's letters. Luther's suspicion of the letter influenced much subsequent Christian thought, but its importance is now recognized as a distinctive voice alongside that of Paul. It provides a positive portrayal of faith lived from day to day and a reminder of Christianity's Jewish inheritance.

# THE BOOK

TITLE: The Letter of James

DATE: Uncertain: possibly mid-50s or early 60s CE

AUTHORSHIP: James (1:1). There are five James in the New Testament, with Jesus' brother, who led the church in Jerusalem (Acts 12:17; 15:13; Gal. 2:9), being the most likely candidate. We have no record of his following Jesus during Jesus' lifetime (and the letter records no detail about Jesus), but Paul records that he was one of those to whom Jesus appeared after the Resurrection (1 Cor. 15:7). If James did not write this letter, the other most likely option is that it is pseudonymous

# THE CONTENTS

CHAPTER 1:1–18
Greetings; facing trials

CHAPTERS 1:19–2:26
True faith is shown in good works

CHAPTERS 3:1–4:12
The dangers of dissension

CHAPTERS 4:13–5:12
The uncertainties of life; warnings and encouragement

CHAPTER 5:13–18
The power of prayer and anointing of the sick

CHAPTER 5:19–20
The importance of persuading sinners to return

# KEY THEMES

*Patience in suffering*

•

*Guarding one's tongue*

For further reading see bibliography numbers: 69, 70, 81, 173, 241, 485, 741

# THE FIRST LETTER OF
# PETER

*The purpose of this letter is summarized in 5:12: "I have written this short letter to encourage you, and to testify that this is the true grace of God. Stand fast in it."*

THE First Letter of Peter is a letter written to Jewish and Gentile Christians scattered throughout Asia Minor against a background of localized persecution. It is a letter with many themes and sections of practical advice for believers. Peter includes more specific references to suffering, trials, and fears than any other New Testament writer and makes three basic points to his readers:

• Suffering should come as no surprise when Christians remember what Christ endured (4:12).

• Suffering should never be as a result of a Christian's anti-social behavior (4:15).

• Much can be learned even in the midst of suffering (1:6, 7).

It is probable that at this stage the "persecutions" referred to were not by the Roman government, whose organized initiatives against Christians came later under the notorious emperors Nero and Domitian. It is more likely that the letter has in mind more local conflicts, for example, at Ephesus (Acts 19): *"But even if you do suffer for doing what is right, you are blessed. Do not fear what they fear, and do not be intimidated"* (3:14).

In a literal sense, 1 Peter is addressed to "aliens and strangers" (displaced persons lacking legal status and security); but also, at a deeper level, to all who felt alienated from the standards, values, and priorities of those around them, and who were targets of sustained local hostility. They are encouraged to stand firm in their faith, not by taking on the attitude of the Stoics (*p.453*), but by remembering the great change brought about in their lives and their new status as children of God: they have new birth, a living hope, a sure inheritance. They are not worthless outsiders but *"a chosen race, a royal priesthood, a holy nation … the people of God"* (2:9–10).

**20TH-CENTURY CHRISTIAN MARTYRS**

**ELIZABETH OF RUSSIA (1864–1918)**
*Now a saint in the Russian Orthodox Church, Grand Duchess Elizabeth was killed by Bolsheviks.*

**MARTIN LUTHER KING JR. (1929–68)**
*A Baptist minister, his nonviolent resistance to racial discrimination in the US led to his assassination.*

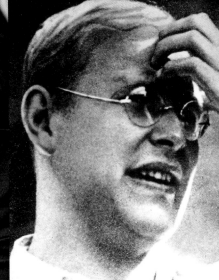

**DIETRICH BONHOEFFER (1906–45)**
*A Lutheran, Bonhoeffer was executed by the Nazis for complicity in the plot against Hitler.*

## PRACTICAL ADVICE TO CHRISTIANS

The letter links the new status of believers to the behavior required in their lives. They are urged to do good, and to let their deeds speak volumes when words fall on deaf ears. They are to imitate God in that most fundamental of Jewish and biblical commands: *"You shall be holy, for I am holy"* (1:16, quoting Lev. 11:44–45; 19:2; 20:7). Because they are now the children of a holy God, their lives must bear the character of holiness. This is not merely an individualistic calling, but a new community of faith, so interpersonal relationships must be characterized by love and mutual respect (1:22*ff.*). Husbands and wives are to complement one another instead of the wife being the "property" of her husband. Christian slaves are to give exemplary service even in distressing circumstances (2:13–3:7). Because Christ did not retaliate, neither should they (2:21*ff.*); gentleness and respect are to be the keys to success in all circumstances.

The connections between the language and ideas of this letter and those of Paul – and also with James – are such that some have argued it is a "general letter" drawing on themes from both men *(see panel, right)*. Yet the "stone" metaphors in 1 Peter link with the Greek word, *Petros*, from the Aramaic, *Cephas*, "rock" – a name that Jesus gave to his disciple, Simon Peter (Matt. 16:18). The message of the letter is that Christ may be a stumbling stone to many, but Christians are to revel in the truth that they are being "built" into the ultimate center of worship: *"Come to him, a living stone, though rejected by mortals yet chosen and precious in God's sight, and like living stones, let yourselves be built into a spiritual house, to be a holy priesthood"* (2:4–5).

OSCAR ROMERO (1917–80)
*Roman Catholic Archbishop Romero was assassinated while saying mass in the cathedral in El Salvador.*

# THE BOOK

TITLE: The First Letter of Peter

DATE: Probably early 60s CE

AUTHORSHIP: The author describes himself as "Peter, an apostle of Jesus Christ." Many accept Peter as author. Others regard it as pseudepigraphical (*pp. 462–63*), mainly because of the strong connections with Paul. In 5:13, Mark is called "my son."

The only known Mark in the New Testament (although a common name) was, on occasion, a companion of Paul (Acts 15:37; Col. 4:10; Phil. 24; 2 Tim. 4:11). In 5:12, the author writes "through Silvanus," or Silas. The only known Silas was even more closely associated with Paul (Acts 15:40; 17:14*ff.*; 18:5; 2 Cor. 1:19; 1 Thess. 1:1; 2 Thess. 1:1). Peter was commissioned to preach to the circumcised; Paul to the Gentiles. Peter, although he recognized that Gentiles could be baptized, continued to vacillate on this issue, yet this letter is written unmistakably to Gentiles. The reference to a direct, eyewitness knowledge of Jesus in 5:1 ("a witness of the sufferings of Christ") is odd if it is understood to refer to the Crucifixion, since Peter did not witness the Crucifixion. The cultured Greek is surprising since Peter was claimed to be uneducated. Some suggest that another, perhaps Silas (1 Pet. 5:12), acted as secretary/editor

# THE CONTENTS

**CHAPTERS 1:1–2:3**
Greetings; the necessity of holiness

**CHAPTERS 2:4–3:7**
The status of believers; submission to authority

**CHAPTERS 3:8–4:19**
The conduct of believers as a result of Christ's example and the present circumstances

**CHAPTER 5**
Specific commands and final greetings

# KEY THEMES

*Suffering for the cause of Christ*

•

*Christian responsibilities and obligations*

For further reading see bibliography numbers: 165, 172b, (173), 191

# PERSECUTIONS

## IN NEW TESTAMENT TIMES

*A common picture of life in the early Church is that Christians were persistently persecuted, usually by being thrown to the lions. More recently, some scholars have suggested that there were only a few localized difficulties. Neither picture is wholly true, as biblical and secular sources show.*

CHRISTIANITY began as one interpretation, among others (*pp.281, 288–89*), of what Jewish belief and practice should be, given that Jesus was accepted as the promised Messiah, or Christ. Jesus was a Jew, and after his death, Resurrection, and Ascension, his followers (for example, Peter and Paul) preached in the Temple and in synagogues. Christians were identified by Roman authorities with the Jews and therefore enjoyed a certain amount of tolerance.

### THE CHRISTIAN EXPERIENCE

Provided religious groups behaved circumspectly, they were left alone in most cases. If there were conflicts, they were confined to isolated incidents. However, after the destruction of Jerusalem in 70CE, Jews became increasingly aware of the ways in which Christians were distancing themselves, and they began to take stronger action against Christians in their midst. The insistence of Christians that Jesus was the promised Messiah, the Christ, led to them being increasingly excluded from synagogues. This is perhaps reflected in John 9:22; 12:42ff.; 16:1ff.

Thus, the status and home base of Christians began to change, and during the first century CE Christianity moved more confidently into the Roman empire. However, this was the period when the successors of Augustus were developing their own ideas of what it meant to be an emperor. From the East came the custom of offering divine honors to any ruler. The conquering Romans found this flattering; gradually emperors began to demand lavish worship as a right as well as a test of loyalty, and for Christians this compromised loyalty to God and Christ. At the same time, it was not altogether clear what this "new

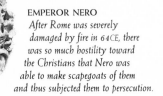

**EMPEROR NERO**
*After Rome was severely damaged by fire in 64CE, there was so much hostility toward the Christians that Nero was able to make scapegoats of them and thus subjected them to persecution.*

religion" actually was, if it was not a form of Judaism. By refusing to worship any God but their own, Christians threatened the favor of the gods who were believed to protect the empire and its affairs, the *pax Deorum*. Christians were regularly accused of atheism because they would not participate in pagan ceremonies.

They were also accused of cannibalism, because they were said to eat the body of Christ, and of orgies, including incest (this was probably a misunderstanding of the kiss of peace and "brother and sister" language used for nonfamily members).

In 106CE, Pliny the Younger wrote to the emperor Trajan after torturing a slave girl. He said that he was punishing Christians, not for being Christians, but for being obstinate and because their secret eucharistic practices encouraged superstition. Pliny's policy was not to seek out Christians specifically, but if people were found to be believers they were executed if they refused to renounce the faith.

**INSIDE ROME'S COLOSSEUM**
*In these underground rooms (excavated in the 19th century) animals were kept caged before being let loose on the Christians in the arena.*

# CHRISTIAN MARTYRS

Although some Christians capitulated under persecution, most did not. For many, martyrdom was seen as part of following Christ and was even welcomed. Ignatius wrote: "I desire to be ground by the teeth of lions to make the finest wheat flour for Christ." When Origen's father was martyred in 202CE, Origen longed to follow his example, so his mother hid his clothes until the opportunity passed. Nevertheless, Origen lived out his life in an "alternative martyrdom" of self-denial and asceticism.

If the effect on the Christian community was to purge it of the fainthearted and lukewarm, the effect on the pagan world was often dramatic too. Emperor Marcus Aurelius admitted that the bravery of Christians in the face of death was praiseworthy. As a consequence of the martyrdom of Perpetua and Felicitas at Carthage, the prison governor was converted; and the sufferings of martyrs at Lyons and Vienne in France in 177CE resulted in many of the bystanders converting to Christianity.

The burning of Christians.

### PETER'S CRUCIFIXION IN ROME
*According to local tradition, when Peter was martyred under Nero in c.64CE he insisted on being crucified upside down since he did not consider himself worthy of dying in the same way as Jesus.*

### THE MARTYRDOM OF PAUL
*The account of Paul's death, like Peter's, stems from local tradition: beheaded with a sword, Paul's head bounced three times on the ground, causing three fountains to spring up.*

## THE SCALE OF PERSECUTIONS

Persecution is mentioned in various New Testament writings, but not always with a specification of what the persecution was (*see 1 Peter, pp.456–57*).

Jesus spoke of persecutions coming on his followers (Matt. 5:10–12), but this may have been domestic and local division (Mark 10:29).

Paul claimed to have persecuted the Church (1 Cor. 15:9) and was himself on the receiving end of local disturbance (Acts 14:19).

Not all Christians suffered persecution, and not all emperors were equally antagonistic toward Christianity. Some attacks did occur (e.g., in Rome in 64CE by Nero), and the descriptions – and the hostility to Rome – in the book of Revelation may reflect Christian persecution in Asia under the emperor Domitian. But persecution did not become widespread and systematic until the rules of the emperors Decius and Diocletian (third–fourth century CE). Diocletian was probably the most antagonistic of all: torture, executions, and mass destruction of church buildings and Scriptures were widespread, especially in the eastern part of the empire.

For further reading see bibliography numbers: 172, 367, 706, 732

# THE LETTERS OF
# 2 PETER & JUDE

*These two letters are warnings against distraction, against being carried away*
*into false teachings, and forgetting that the final judgment*
*belongs to God.*

THE second letter of Peter and the letter of Jude are both catholic, or general, Epistles (*see also pp.446–47*). They were written to voice concerns over the spread of false teaching in early Christian communities, and to counteract its influence. The attacks in both letters are so similar that there is clearly a relationship between the two (*see panel, opposite*) and they are forthright in their condemnation of the false teachers, who are described as perverting the grace of God, and as grumblers and malcontents with hearts trained in greed.

It appears that a group of traveling teachers had joined the Christian fellowships to which these letters were sent. They taught that there would neither be a Second Coming of Jesus as anticipated, nor would there be any future judgment by God; Christian salvation could be fully experienced in this life now. If there was no future judgment, then it did not matter too much how a person behaved. These false teachers do not seem to have set much store by Jesus' teaching, and they scorned any other authority, including angels.

## 2 PETER

This was written as the final letter of a dying man (1:14) encouraging his flock to remain committed to the true faith. For some scholars, this reinforces the case for Peter being the author (1:1, 17*ff.*). Other scholars point out that it was a common literary device in Judaism at this time for people to write what purported to be the final speech of heroic figures, such as Moses, Job, or Enoch. Such speeches would contain ethical warnings and revelations of the future. It

GUERNICA
*2 Peter and Jude warn against believing in false teachers and predict "swift destruction" for these "scoffers": ultimately God's judgment will come. Picasso's*
*Guernica, evoking the horror of the Spanish Civil War, could perhaps find associations with Peter's descriptions of divinely induced catastrophic events.*

may be that a Christian leader adapted this into letter form, writing some time after Peter's death (believed to have taken place around 64CE). The language and use of ideas in 2 Peter seem so different from 1 Peter that few commentators think that both letters could be by the same hand.

## JUDE

This is one of the shortest books of the New Testament. It contains graphic language of angels contending with the Devil and includes quotes from Jewish apocryphal works. (Many of the same ideas appear in 2 Peter.) Jude ends with a glorious song of praise to God, which is often used in Christian liturgies: *"Now to him who is able to keep you from falling, and to make you stand without blemish in the presence of his glory with rejoicing, to the only God our Savior, through Jesus Christ our Lord, be glory, majesty, power, and authority, before all time and now and for ever. Amen"* (vv.24–25).

## TRUE TEACHING AND FINAL JUDGMENT

Both letters point to examples in the Bible, such as Sodom and Gomorrah and Balaam, where God's judgment was shown against those who strayed from the true path. Jude quotes from *1 Enoch*, a Jewish book written between the third and first century BCE *(p.462)*. According to Genesis, Enoch lived in the seventh generation after Adam, and was often held up within Judaism as a hero of the faith. Both 2 Peter and Jude encourage all their readers to avoid any immoral behavior and to hold firm to the true faith and remember the coming judgment. If there is a delay, the author of 2 Peter assures his readers, then it is caused by God's love and patience in allowing as many people as possible to avoid condemnation.

2 Peter makes a particularly strong appeal to the final judgment that God will bring upon the earth. "The scoffers," whom the letter is attacking, say that the world is going along much the same as it always has, and where is this coming Day of the Lord *(pp.444–45)* that is claimed? The answer depends on Scripture: the world does not continue of its own accord, but only because God keeps it in being; as water was essential for its making, so water became an instrument of destruction in the time of Noah (2 Pet. 3:5–7). This time the destruction will be by fire, and the author reminds his readers that God is a free agent: *"But the day of the Lord will come like a thief, and then the heavens will pass away with a loud noise, and the elements will be dissolved with fire, and the earth and everything that is done on it will be disclosed"* (2 Pet. 3:10; cf. Elijah's contest with the prophets of Baal, *pp.138–39*). This leaves 2 Peter with a picture of judgment that goes into much greater detail: it involves the destruction of the earth. There is nothing here of the inauguration of a messianic age *(pp.346–47)*.

## THE BOOK

TITLE: The Second Letter of Peter; The Letter of Jude

DATE: 2 Peter: unknown. Perhaps c.80CE – or maybe well into the second century CE
Jude: unknown. Perhaps 70CE – or as late as the second century CE

AUTHORSHIP: Either one letter is dependent on the other, or they both used a common source. 2 Peter (1:1) is attributed to Peter, but most scholars regard it as pseudonymous. It is unlikely that 2 Peter was written before Peter's death (64CE). The most likely explanation is that Jude was written first, and then the author of 2 Peter used its ideas to address a similar problem. Jude (1:1) may have been Judas, the brother of James and Jesus, although some say this letter is also pseudonymous. Jude was probably written to Jewish Christians living in Palestine in the first century CE. We know that Judas was a leader in the church there. The letter is written in good, literary Greek, which many believe was beyond the competence of a Galilean peasant. However, it is likely that Judas spent some time as a traveling missionary in Asia Minor and Greece, and he may have learned Greek then

## THE CONTENTS

**2 PETER**

Chapter 1: Greetings; making sure of one's welcome in God's kingdom; the certainty of God's promises through prophecy
Chapter 2: Against false teachers
Chapter 3: Christ's return in judgment

**JUDE**

25 verses consisting of a sermon against false teachers and a warning to remain true to the faith

## KEY THEMES

*The threat posed by false teaching*

•

*The destructive nature of sin*

•

*God's final judgment*

For further reading see bibliography numbers: 69, 70, 71, 173

# PSEUDEPIGRAPHA

## IN THE EARLY CHRISTIAN PERIOD

*A pseudepigraphical writing is one that is unlikely to have been written by its named author. Such writings were particularly prevalent among religious groups. Pseudepigraphical works are common outside the Jewish and Christian canons, but some may be found within them.*

PSEUDEPIGRAPHICAL writing may have been an early equivalent to the "ghost writing" that is common today. A "pseudepigraph" (from the Greek for "false writing") means a writing incorrectly attributed to an author. This was a relatively common practice in the ancient world and was often a means of indicating the school or tradition to which a work belonged. According to the fourth-century CE philosopher Iamblichus, it was an honorable act to publish one's own treatise under the name of a venerable teacher such as Pythagoras.

**GHOST WRITING**
*The modern idea of "copyright" did not exist in the ancient world, hence pseudepigraphy became widely practiced and was even regarded as an acceptable literary device.*

### NONCANONICAL WORKS

The term *pseudepigrapha* occurs in Christian literature as early as the second century CE, when the theologian Serapion referred to the Gospel of Peter and other noncanonical claimants to apostolic authorship.

Today the term pseudepigraph is applied to many works outside the Jewish and Christian canons. For example, it is used when referring to works attributed to the biblical character Enoch, who is mentioned in Genesis (*see below*).

**THE LEGEND OF ENOCH**
*According to Genesis 5:22–24, Enoch walked with God for 365 years and then "was no more, because God took him." This was later interpreted to mean that he ascended into Heaven and was witness to divine revelations, which the works claim to convey. They were written between c. third century – first century CE. A complete copy of The First Book of Enoch still survives in Ethiopic (the liturgical language of the Coptic Church of Ethiopia).*

In the past 200 years pseudepigrapha has been used by biblical scholars to describe New Testament documents whose claimed authorship seems doubtful. For example, Ephesians, the Pastoral Epistles, and 2 Peter have all had their authorship questioned in this way.

For some scholars, the possibility that such works are pseudepigraphical calls into question the reliability of the canon itself, since it seems to suggest that those who drew up the canon were taken in and deceived by false claims of authorship. The real problem, however, is caused by the word itself: the word pseudepigraphy carries with it the impression of falseness and deceit, because that is what the underlying Greek, *pseudo*, suggests.

### TRADITION AND AUTHORSHIP

We need to remember that, in Jewish circles, there was a long-established process whereby traditions that began with central figures in Israel's history, such as Moses, David, Solomon, and Isaiah, were elaborated on in the course of transmission before becoming fixed in canonical form. For example, the Pentateuch, the five books of Moses (*pp. 20–21*), are still attributed to Moses, even though it is almost universally recognized that they

## OTHER "GOSPEL" WRITINGS
*From the second to the ninth century CE, many texts were produced by various Christian groups. The works included gospels recounting stories of Jesus' life, acts of the apostles, and apocalyptic writings. One such example is the Egerton Papyrus 2 (left), which contains parts of stories and sayings similar to those found in the Synoptics as well as different material. Other examples include* The Gospel of Thomas *and* The Gospel of Peter *(see also p.301).*

elaborated on, even in the first generation or so after his death. John's Gospel, compared to the other three, shows how extensive that elaboration could be, and yet still be the (same) Gospel according to John. The original titles of *"The Gospel according to ..."* Matthew, Mark, Luke, and John, rather than *"The Gospel of ..."* make the point that it is the same good news in different versions (*see pp.300–1*).

### THE PAULINE LETTERS
Those who see problems in accepting the claimed authorship of particular letters are inclined to set them within this practice of the "living tradition." In the case, for example, of the Pastorals (*pp.446–47*) they would argue of the letters that:
• They were written by someone from within the circle of Paul's immediate co-workers or disciples.
• They were consciously written in the tradition of Paul's own concerns and theology.
These letters would therefore be regarded as an authoritative attempt within the Pauline circle to express Paul's views in situations that developed after his death. In the same way, the Gospel according to John, written at about the same time as these letters, was recognized as an appropriate expression of Jesus'

teaching. In such ways, the vitality of the living tradition was maintained.

All of this is comparable to the way in which, in the studio of a great artist, the brushstrokes were those of unknown disciples, but the inspiration and character was that of the master himself, even if the masterpiece was executed or completed after the artist's death.

However, there is some discussion and disagreement about this view. Where an authorship is explicitly claimed, many scholars see no compelling reasons to regard these and other works as pseudepigraphical but prefer to accept the ascription of authorship in the text. Thus, it is an issue of trustworthiness and truth. Perhaps it would be far less confusing if the word pseudepigraphy were used in a more precise way. The term could be applied only to those documents (such as those mentioned by Serapion) that could not be held to belong to the genuine apostolic tradition. (For the importance of the apostolic tradition in determining the canon, *see pp.474–75.*)

**NEW TESTAMENT AUTHORSHIP**
*The earliest writings in the New Testament were written by Paul (above). However, the authorship of the later writings in the New Testament is not so certain.*

reached their present form at a later date.

Many works are attributed to Solomon because his name stood at the head of the tradition of Wisdom writings (*pp.170–71*). Many scholars recognize at least three different voices behind Isaiah but all keeping the tradition that Isaiah inaugurated. The Gospels themselves demonstrate by their interrelationships how the tradition of Jesus was structured, edited, and

For further reading see bibliography numbers: 5, 260, 400, 484, 543a, 854,

# THE LETTERS OF
# JOHN

*The readers of these three letters are told to guard against false teaching by remembering and living out the central truths of the Gospel.*

O F these three short books, commonly designated as Epistles, only the second and third letters of John actually display the characteristics of letters; 1 John reads more like a homily or a tract. All three letters address conflicts within a specific community of believers and stress the importance of fellowship with God.

## PASTORAL CONCERNS

Each of the letters has a warm, informal, caring tone, and there is a personal concern expressed for those to whom the letters are addressed: in 1 John they are called "dear children," or "dear friends" (1 John 2:1; 4:1; cf. 2 John 1; 3 John 1). At the same time, 1 John is written with an air of authority, as though by one who has responsibility of some kind. Indeed, 1 John has been described as a "pastoral letter," written to one or more congregations (*note* 1 John 2: 12–14); the opening salutations of 2 and 3 John speak for themselves. The twin themes of "truth" and "love" are recurring motifs, finding particular poignancy when combined in the expression, "loving in [the] truth," mentioned in each of the three letters (1 John 3:18; 2 John 1; 3 John 1).

**ABIDING IN CHRIST**
*The three letters of John commend Christians to live in the "light" of Jesus, in "truth" and "love," in order to receive God's salvation. 1 John in particular sets out the basic conditions for Christian living.*

## I JOHN

In its dramatic opening chapter, the author centers his message on Jesus, whom he and others had seen, touched, and heard: *"We declare to you what was from the beginning, what we have heard, what we have seen with our eyes, what we have looked at and touched with our hands, concerning the word of life … we declare to you what we have seen and heard so that you may also have fellowship with us; and truly our fellowship is with the Father and with his Son Jesus Christ"* (1:1, 3). The author is concerned to establish the ways in which true believers can be distinguished from those people who falsely claim to be so. The clearest expression of this desire to know true Christian believers is found in the manifestation of love in chapter 3 (3:11–17; *see also quote, below*).

Much of 1 John focuses on the themes of certainty and assurance. For example, the expression, "we know," is used frequently. Even though a clear sense of authority is conveyed by the author as he writes, his tone is warm, with a strong focus on love: *"We know that we have passed from death to life because we love one another. Whoever does not love abides in death. All who hate a brother or sister are murderers, and you know that murderers do not have eternal life abiding* in them. *We know love by this, that he laid down his life for us – and we ought to lay down our lives for one another"* (3:14–16). Much of 1 John is constructed around the twin attributes of light and love, both viewed as characteristics of God (1:5; 4:16). The author states that these qualities should be the foundation of the understanding and the lifestyle of Christian believers.

The need for the author to emphasize his authority would seem to be necessary in view of the fact that a major problem being faced was heresy, which had sprung up within the community and which eventually resulted in a split (2:19). Evidently, this had led to confusion, hesitancy, and a loss of confidence. This crisis had to be addressed in a caring but authoritative way. Thus as a response, this letter displays a concern for the well-being of the believers at the same time as offering a defense of right belief and practice (orthodoxy and orthopraxy).

The nature of the false teaching being attacked is far from clear (it has to be worked out from the letter itself, since no record of it survives). However, there seem to have been at least two targets:

• First, a separation of religious knowledge from moral action and behavior. The two must belong together: *"If we say that we have fellowship with him while we are walking in the darkness, we lie and do not do what is true"* (1:6; 2:29; 3:6).

• Second, a denial of the truth and reality of the incarnation (note the emphasis in the opening verses). The true believer is one who acknowledges that Jesus is the Christ (2:22), and that Jesus Christ "has come in the flesh" (4:2; cf. 2 John 7).

It may be that the false teaching belonged to some form of pre-Gnosticism or incipient Gnosticism (*p.475*). That is, the letter seems to be confronting some early form of the Gnosticism, which became more fully formulated later in the second century CE.

## 2 JOHN AND 3 JOHN

Two of the shortest books in the New Testament, these letters each consist of only one chapter. They also have a number of parallels: both are written by "the elder"; they share a common structure; and they both conclude with the hope of a personal visit by the author (2 John 12 is virtually identical to 3 John 13–14).

2 John has strong affinities with 1 John in its emphasis on love (2 John 5–6) and its warning against false teaching: *"Many deceivers have gone out into the world, those who do not confess that Jesus Christ has come in the flesh; any such person is the deceiver and the antichrist! Be on your guard, so that you do not lose what we have worked for, but may receive a full reward"* (2 John 7–8).

3 John is concerned with particular individuals within this Christian community who are in rivalry with one another. Both 2 and 3 John are brief, personal letters offering appropriate instruction and encouragement to their recipients.

## THE BOOKS

TITLE: The First, Second, and Third Letters of John

DATE: Dating these letters is a complex matter, bound up with issues that include authorship and their relation to the Gospel of John. The most widely accepted date is the early 90s CE

AUTHORSHIP: No claim is made in the letters about who wrote them. 1 John is anonymous, and 2 and 3 John are both written by "the elder," whose identity was doubtless known to the recipients of the letters but not to us now. The traditional view that 1–3 John were all written by the Apostle John is now not usually held, but there are links of style and thought between the Gospel of John and these letters. Many scholars believe that these documents were produced by (an) unknown author(s) within a community that was also responsible for the Gospel of John: a community that may have had John the Apostle as its founder and figurehead. Nothing in the letters tells us where the recipients lived. Ephesus has early traditions in its favor, but some modern scholars favor Syria

## THE CONTENTS

**1 JOHN**
Chapter 1:1–4: Prologue: the Word of Life
Chapters 1:5–2:11: Walking in the light; the way of love
Chapter 2:12–17: Following God, not the world
Chapter 2:18–27: A warning about antichrists
Chapters 2:28–3:10: Living as the children of God
Chapter 3:11–18: Loving one another
Chapter 3:19–24: Having confidence before God
Chapter 4:1–6: Discerning the spirits
Chapters 4:7–5:4: God's love

Chapter 5:5–12: Faith in Jesus
Chapter 5:13–21: Epilogue: confidence of eternal life

**2 JOHN**
Verses 1–6: Greeting; obedience of love
Verses 7–13: Observance of truth; concluding greeting

**3 JOHN**
Verses 1–8: Greeting; walking in the truth; working for the truth
Verses 9–12: Diotrephes condemned, and Demetrius commended
Verses 13–15: Concluding greeting

## KEY THEME

*The fundamental truths of the Christian faith*

For further reading see bibliography numbers: 137, 138, 149, 705, 708, 735, 748

# CHRISTIAN ETHICS

*The ethical teaching of the New Testament seems straightforward: according to Jesus' teaching it can be summarized as "love God and love your neighbor." But who is our neighbor, and what does "love" mean? The New Testament begins to answer these questions.*

DURING his ministry, Jesus was asked, like other Jewish teachers, to identify one command that contains all the other commands of God. He answered by linking Deuteronomy 6:4–5 and Leviticus 19:18: *"You shall love the Lord your God with all your heart, and with all your soul, and with all your mind"* … *"You shall love your neighbor as yourself"* (Matt. 22:34–38; Mark 12:28–30; Luke 10:25–27). This is not only the foundation of moral life, it is, according to Luke, the way to live in order to inherit eternal life (*note also the Sheep and the Goats, p.339*). This seems to set Christian life free from rules and regulations. Yet, in fact, large parts of the New Testament (e.g., Paul's letters) seem to be doing exactly that: setting down how Christians should behave and what they should do. Does this mean that there is a contradiction between the two views?

**ETHICAL MINISTRY**
*Jesus not only taught about developing right relationships, he actually lived out his ministry by mixing with outcasts and those on the fringes of society, and by caring for the hungry, sick, and oppressed. In doing so, he rejected racial, sexual, and social prejudices.*

commands (i.e., commands relating to particular contexts). Should Christians today continue to observe all the context-dependent commands of the New Testament – for example, should women cover their heads and not speak in church? If a context-dependent command becomes, in practice, a contradiction of Jesus' context-independent command to love God and one's neighbor, then that command should not be obeyed any longer. That is why Christians have, in the past, changed their attitudes and actions on many issues, and why they must and will continue to do so today and in the future. This process may happen slowly, but happen it does and must. Guiding everything, as Paul realized when he dealt with particular issues, is the more excellent way of love (*see also* 1 Cor. 3:12, 13; Rom. 13:8–10).

## APPLYING JESUS' COMMAND

The explanation for this apparent contradiction is simple. Jesus gave what is known as a "context-*independent* command." That is to say, his command applies, not just to one particular issue or context in life, but to all decisions and in all contexts. The New Testament writers (and at times Jesus himself) applied this command to specific contexts and issues. This is why their New Testament writings contain what are known as "context-*dependent*"

> **" *Which of these three, do you think, was a neighbor to the man who fell into the hands of the robbers?' He said, 'The one who showed him mercy.' Jesus said to him, 'Go and do likewise.' "***
>
> (Luke 10:36–37)

## CHRISTIAN LIVING

The New Testament writers never set out their ethics in a systematic, philosophical way. They do not present abstract reflections on the philosophical grounds for moral action. Rather, they invite their readers to a new way of life in general, and in some circumstances, actually say what that means for particular people. There is much context-dependent teaching on particular issues of behavior in the New Testament, which brings to bear on life a radical reinterpretation of the

Scriptures and the story of Israel in the light of the life, death, and the Resurrection of Jesus. Jesus himself made a searching interpretation and application of the demands of God, as can be seen in the Sermon on the Mount (pp.334–35). The specific teaching in the New Testament served the needs of groups of believers seeking to live out their Christian discipleship in various towns and cities of the Roman empire. Thus, New Testament teaching is a body of wisdom and instruction, indebted to the moral traditions of Israel on the one hand and to Greece and Rome on the other. This teaching is all refracted through the lens of the story of Jesus and his teaching, together with the experience of the Spirit, in communal Christian gatherings for worship.

Jesus' teaching is radical indeed: "take up the cross" (Matt. 10:38; 16:24; Mark 8:34; Luke 9:23; 14:27). Christian life "seeks those things that are above," because "you have died, and your life is hidden with Christ in God" (Col. 3:2). This sets all human actions in a kind of reckless context of absolute trust and faith, which brings forth the crop (i.e., the fruit) of the Spirit. Yet what is important is not universal reason but faithful obedience in the life of the Spirit. The exemplary figure here is not the philosopher but the martyr (i.e., a witness).

> 66 Love is patient; love is kind; love is not envious or boastful or arrogant or rude ... It bears all things, believes all things, hopes all things, endures all things. 99
>
> (1 Corinthians 13:4–7)

## PRACTICAL GUIDANCE

What guidance, then, does the New Testament give on how to live? There are a number of different, closely interrelated forms: specific rules, general principles, paradigmatic stories, and a symbolic world portraying how things are between God and his Creation.
• Specific rules: the prohibition of divorce and remarriage in Mark 10:2–12 is a rule, or command. Its intention is to preserve faithfulness and stability in marriage as a sign of the kinds of relationship God intended for humans from the beginning. Typically for Jesus' teaching, it is not a rule that contradicts the Law of Moses. The context-independent command of love takes the issue back behind the Law to its original intent: that marriage must recreate the original condition of harmony of the Garden of Eden. But equally, this command cannot be made into an invariable, context-independent command in itself, as though it applies to situations that Jesus did not imagine, as Paul's own elaboration of Jesus' teaching at this point was soon to show (1 Cor. 7:8–16). This is also true of Jesus' teaching in the Sermon on the Mount.
• General principles: an example of a general principle is

> 66 Whoever does not take up the cross and follow me is not worthy of me. Those who find their life will lose it, and those who lose their life for my sake will find it. 99
>
> (Matthew 10:38–39)

Paul's teaching on exercising Christian freedom in relation to the eating of meat sacrificed to idols (1 Cor. 8–10). What matters most, says Paul, is neither eating nor abstaining but first recognizing that material things, while unimportant in themselves, are a medium through which we form relationships. In this sense we may be giving ourselves to demons – and that is *far* from unimportant: *"What do I imply then? That food sacrificed to idols is anything, or that an idol is anything? No, I imply that what pagans sacrifice, they sacrifice to demons and not to God"* (1 Cor. 10:19–20). Then, behaving in a way that respects the conscience of the "weaker" brother or sister in Christ: *"Do not seek your own advantage, but that of the other ... So, whether you eat, or drink, or whatever you do, do everything for the glory of God. Give no offense to Jews or to Greeks or to the church of God, just as I try to please everyone in everything I do, not seeking my own advantage, but that of many, so that they may be saved"* (1 Cor. 10:24, 32–33). Important in Paul's approach here and elsewhere is the way freedom is distinguished from license and made subordinate to the higher virtue of love.
• Paradigmatic stories (stories that create a pattern or model for their readers): the Gospels are full of paradigms, or examples, on which to model virtuous conduct. The parables have also been understood in this way, although originally many parables were intended to rouse their hearers to accept God's sovereignty in the face of an urgent political crisis in the prelude to the First Jewish War (pp.292–93). Thus, the story of the Good Samaritan (Luke 10:30–37) shows the character of true neighborliness, and the parable of the Prodigal Son (Luke 15:11–32) displays what is meant by true forgiveness. But the Gospel stories as a whole are paradigms, as are the stories about the early life of the Church in Acts and the autobiographical statements of Paul in his letters. They display what it means to "take up the cross daily" and to follow Christ.
• A symbolic world: the symbolic world of the New Testament is fundamental for shaping Christian morality. The characterization of God as love is the warrant for the teaching in 1 John 4:7–11 to "love one another." The Church as the "body of Christ" (1 Cor. 12) is the warrant for avoiding factionalism and living in unity. The image of each individual believer being a temple where God's Spirit dwells (1 Cor. 6:19) is the warrant for living a holy life and avoiding immorality. Finally, the idea that the reign of God is drawing near (Rom. 3:11–14) serves as a powerful justification for repentance, conversion, and living a life according to God's will.

For further reading see bibliography numbers: 96, 250, 261, 316, 361, 376, 380, 545, 546, 604, 722, 769, 838

# APOCALYPSES

*"Apocalypse" (Greek, apocalypsis), means "revelation, unhiding." It describes writings that unveil truths lying beyond immediate knowledge (see also pp.260–61). Apocalypses reveal the true meaning of events or their outcome, or the heavenly reality behind or beyond earthly appearances.*

APOCALYPTIC sayings may have originally been given as individual oracles, or revelations, but of the many sayings that are known now, most all have been gathered into writings or books to form a distinct type of literature known as "Apocalyptic" (pp.260–61) which incorporates recurring features:

- A seer ("one who sees") who has dreams or visions, which are often strange or even puzzling.
- An interpreting angel.
- Ascents to Heaven, with a guided tour of the heavenly regions.
- Lectures on the science of the day, astronomy, meteorology, pharmacology, etc. (there are links with the Wisdom writings attributed to Solomon, pp.170–71).
- Prayers, hymns, laments, and admonitions.

Most typically, there is an unfolding of the destiny of the Covenant People, oppressed by Gentile nations or by Jews who are assumed to be unfaithful or corrupt by the writer and his readers. A catastrophic course of events is described – before divine rule and recompense are reimposed (*see box, opposite*).

In the Bible, the book of Zechariah (pp.242–43) is the earliest example in which apocalyptic visions are gathered together in a single book, but there are apocalyptic passages in Isaiah (24–27; 59–66) and other Prophets. After the Exile, contemporary prophecy was gradually

> ❝ Now the LORD is about to lay waste the earth and make it desolate, and he will twist its surface and scatter its inhabitants ... The earth shall be utterly laid waste ... for the LORD has spoken his word. ❞
>
> (Isaiah 24:1, 3)

discredited (cf. Zech. 13:4). Instead, apocalyptic revelations were attributed to great figures of the past. Examples are the book attributed to Daniel (pp.216–17), a hero of the Exile, and 2 Esdras (i.e., Ezra) in the Apocrypha (pp.258–59).

Outside the canon there are many examples. Some were attributed to Enoch (Gen. 5:24), one of which is regarded in Jude as Scripture (Jude 14). For Christians, perhaps because they were living in the new age of the Spirit, this convention of writing pseudonymous apocalypses did not appeal, and the supreme Christian apocalypse is that of John of Patmos – the book of Revelation (pp.468–69).

**APOCALYPSE NOW**
*The 1979 American film, Apocalypse Now, envisioned the horrors of the Vietnam War as the end-time.*

## APOCALYPTIC ART FORM

At least some of the early apocalyptic writings may have stemmed from marginalized groups in post-exilic Israel, which despaired of the present and looked to the destruction of this evil world and its replacement by a new heavenly order. In contrast, those in power – centered on the Jerusalem Temple and its cult – looked to God's presence there and his rule, or kingdom, in this world. But this kind of writing was not just pessimistic and sectarian, on the edges of mainstream religion. It was an important "art-form," just as operas, novels, or even sitcoms have become in modern times.

# VISIONS OF THE FUTURE

*Behind the fantastic imagery of prophets and apocalyptists, there is a regular pattern of what is called "recapitulation": the end will be as the beginning.*

Visions of apocalypse in the Bible include two areas of cosmic imagery:
• There are cosmic catastrophes: the sun darkened and the moon turned to blood in Joel 2:31; the sky rolled up and the stars fell in Isaiah 34; earthquakes and floods in Isaiah 24:18, 19 – signifying that God is undoing his work in Creation (Gen. 1; cf. Jer. 4:23ff.) – which angels and humans have corrupted: *"All the host of heaven shall rot away, and the skies roll up like a scroll. All their host shall wither like a leaf withering on a vine, or fruit withering on a fig tree"* (Isa. 34:4). There is also social disintegration and conflict: deception, betrayal, murder in Daniel 11:32, 33 and 2 Peter 2, echoing the stories of Eden, Cain, and Sodom (Gen. 3, 4, 19), and a final battle echoing God's primeval victory over the waters of chaos, which to Jews symbolized destructive empires (Gen. 1:2, NRSV only; Dan. 7:2ff.; 2 Esd. 13:2ff.). This is retold in Revelation (e.g., 6:12–14; 13; 19:11ff.).

• Then there are pictures of cosmic renewal: a new heaven and a new earth in Isaiah 65:17 and 2 Peter 3:13; God's glory replacing the lights of Heaven in Isaiah 60:19, 20 and Zechariah 14:6, 7; and living waters in Zechariah 14:8: *"On that day living waters shall flow out from Jerusalem, half to the eastern sea and half to the western see … in summer and in winter."* Likewise, there will be social harmony and fulfillment: Eden restored and the curse healed (Isa. 65:25). Sometimes it is described as a process of an instant, "in the twinkling of an eye" (1 Cor. 15:52), or 40, or 400 (2 Esd. 7:28), or 1,000 years with or without a messianic ruler, but "with the Lord one day is like a thousand years" (2 Pet. 3:8; Ps. 90:4). This, too, is condensed in Revelation (21:1–22:5). These visions express confidence that God will perfect what God has begun, in spite of all corruptions, and they show the end result of present choices, for good or ill.

Apocalyptic literature was a way of bringing heavenly reality to bear on the appearances of this world, whether threatening or seductive, and had its place within the mainstream of Jewish life. It could comfort the afflicted, but also afflict the comfortable, just as the Prophets had savaged the complacent and declared that God would take action to punish injustice within the establishment.

Jesus used apocalyptic language to prepare his disciples for the critical days ahead (Matt. 24; Mark 13; Luke 21), and to warn the Pharisees: *"Those who try to make their life secure will lose it, but those who lose their life will keep it. I tell you, on that night there will be two in a bed; one will be taken and the other left"* (Luke 17:33–34). His "apocalypse" on the Mount of Olives (an apocalyptically significant location, Zech. 14:4) updated Daniel. Paul used apocalyptic language to challenge the Corinthians (1 Cor. 15:20ff.), to comfort the Thessalonians (1 Thess. 4),

and to correct misapprehensions: *"[do not be] quickly shaken in mind or alarmed, either by spirit or by word or by letter, as though from us, to the effect that the day of the Lord is already here"* (2 Thess. 2:2). But Apocalyptic had its dangers in encouraging false hopes of divine intervention, resulting in disastrous Jewish wars against Rome. When rabbis set about making sure of the continuation of Jewish faith and life after Jerusalem and the Temple were destroyed, they abandoned Apocalyptic, and the Christians continued to preserve the tradition.

Its dangers continue into the present for those who take its words as literal predictions of the future. The vague nature of Apocalyptic means that it can be applied to virtually any situation and used to generate fear and enthusiasm. But taken as a language in which warnings are given to those contemptuous of God and fellow humans, and through which encouragement is given to the oppressed and troubled, its voice still speaks.

> **❝** *When you hear of wars and rumors of wars, do not be alarmed; this must take place, but the end is still to come. For nation will rise against nation and kingdom against kingdom.* **❞**
>
> (Mark 13:7–8)

For further reading see bibliography numbers: 111, 133, 153, 664, 718

# HEAVEN & HELL

*In the Hebrew Bible, the heavens are plural. During the biblical period, the heavens became Heaven, the place where God rules in majesty and splendor. Hell is not referred to as part of the original Creation but appears later as a place of punishment for rebels against God.*

THE Hebrews pictured earth as a plate covered by "the heavens," conceived as a tent or a solid dish cover (the "firmament") in which the heavenly bodies are set. Above and beneath the earth are waters (Gen. 7:11), and above the waters is "Heaven," where God is enthroned: *"The LORD sits enthroned over the flood; the LORD sits enthroned as king for ever"* (Ps. 29:10).

> **"** *[The angel] showed me the holy city Jerusalem coming down out of heaven from God. It has the glory of God and a radiance like a very rare jewel, like jasper, clear as crystal.* **"**
>
> (Revelation 21:10b–11)

## HEAVEN AND EARTH

Biblical geography, however, is symbolic and not spatial in the literal sense of traveling through space. The word "above" signifies superiority, authority, and control, while "below" suggests weakness and subjection. God dwells in the high and holy place and also with the contrite and humble (Isa. 57:15). The Bible also talks of gates of Heaven on earth: *"He was afraid and said, 'How awesome is this place! This is none other than the house of God, and this is the gate of heaven'"* (Gen. 28:17). In chapter 4 of Revelation, Heaven is the "place" of both worship and of adoration.

All these images are kaleidoscopic: they can appear together or apart, combined in different patterns of association. "Heaven" can stand for God in sole control and perfect holiness, the place of worship. Or God can be conceived as ruling through

**A NEW HEAVEN**
*Jesus, who has "all authority in heaven and on earth," taught that one day he will return. The prophetic book of Revelation provides graphic descriptions of Christ's final victory over hell, and God's creation of a new heaven.*

"the sons of God," or angels ("messengers"), or through the heavenly bodies that "rule" day and night and the passing of the seasons (Gen. 1:16). The "host of heaven" can be the angels or the stars (Isa. 40:26, 27).

From this point of view, Heaven and earth are not separate but an interlocking whole. Angels or stars stand behind the earthly rulers (Isa. 24:21–23; Ps. 82). God is surrounded by his "sons," like an earthly king by his court. Prophets are like messengers, who attend heavenly cabinet meetings and report back (1 Kgs. 22:19–23). Each nation has its prince (Dan. 10:20, 21); each church and each person, its angel – a spiritual counterpart (Rev. 1:20ff.; Matt. 18:10; Acts 12:15). Heaven can affect earth, such as the destruction of Sodom by angels (or God) (Gen. 19:13), and earth can affect Heaven, as when Abraham argued with God (Gen. 18:22ff.).

From here, it is an easy step to seeing evil or fallen angels behind corrupt earthly powers. Heaven is a place where moral choices have to be made – much as the original Garden of Eden had been. Satan has a place there, but because he has fallen he is also below, in the underworld. Even the heavenly sea is a symbol of disorder and destruction, as with the dragon of chaos (Ps. 74:14; p.28). No wonder Prophets looked for a new heaven as well as a new

# THE DEVIL

*In Hebrew,* satan *means "adversary," often in the legal context of a prosecutor. Originally, an archangel in Heaven,*
*Satan has become the personification of evil, the archenemy of God and humans.*

Originally one of God's archangels, Satan had a place in Heaven as the fault-finder who tested human loyalty (Job 1, 2; Zech. 3:1–2). But then he became a tempter and false accuser (the Greek for devil, *diabolos,* means "slanderer") and then executioner – the enemy of God and humans. After a battle with the archangel Michael, he was expelled from Heaven. The power behind Michael's victory over Satan and his angels is Christ's death: *"Since, therefore, the children share flesh and blood, he himself likewise shared the same things, so that through death he might destroy the one who has the power of death, that is, the devil, and free those who all their lives were held in slavery by the fear of death"* (Heb. 2:14–15; cf. Rev. 5; 12:5–11). Satan became a parody of God, with his own kingdom and host of demons (Mark 3:22ff.). The Bible disallows the equal existence of beings or powers outside of God: Satan was "given" his authority (Luke 4:6), and personifies the usurpation of God-given powers (Rev. 13) and every kind of opposition to God.

Jesus called Peter "Satan" (Matt. 16:23) and the Jewish leaders "children of the devil" (John 8:44). John called hostile Jews in Smyrna and Philadelphia "synagogue of Satan" (Rev. 2:9; 3:9). Early Christians seem to have felt themselves involved in spiritual warfare between God on the one hand and the Devil and spiritual powers of evil on the other. 1 Peter 5 warns that *"Your adversary the devil prowls around, looking for someone to devour"* (1 Pet. 5:8b). Ephesians paints a scene of cosmic battle: *"For our struggle is not against enemies of blood and flesh, but against the rulers, the authorities, against the cosmic powers of this present darkness, against the spiritual forces of evil in the heavenly places"* (Eph. 6:12) The language of warfare against Satan, and against spiritual powers of evil, expresses the way in which many people experience temptation and evil as if they are fighting with a personal enemy or enemies. Through history, those people who have applied such language to those whom they regard as their enemies – such as heretics or witches – have been in error and have made themselves the agents of evil.

earth: *"Then I saw a new heaven and a new earth; for the first heaven and the first earth had passed away, and the sea was no more"* (Rev. 21:1; Isa. 65:17). In Revelation, chapter 5, the death of Christ (the Lamb) is introduced into Heaven to become the key that opens the sealed scroll, or book (*p.469*).

## HELL

Originally the underworld, "Sheol," or the pit, was simply the place of the dead: dark, shadowy, and out of God's sight (Ps. 88:3–5; *pp.178–79*). But for the powerful and arrogant, the descent to Sheol came to be seen as punitive, as in the dirge over the king of Babylon (Isa. 14:12–20). When ideas of resurrection and judgment came about (e.g., Dan. 12:2), Sheol could be thought as divided into different quarters to separate the righteous from the wicked. From this developed the view that the wicked were imprisoned, as probably reflected in 1 Peter 3:19: *"[Christ] also went and made a proclamation to the spirits in prison."*

Fire was an obvious symbol of destruction, but in Luke 16:24 it has become a means of torture. Likewise, the righteous could be seen as in a place of refreshment –

66 *But Abraham said, 'Child, remember that during your lifetime you received your good things, and Lazarus in like manner evil things; but now he is comforted here, and you are in agony.'* 99

(Luke 16:25)

Abraham's bosom, or Paradise (modeled on the Garden of Eden). The fate of the wicked is sometimes extinction (2 Thess. 1:9), sometimes eternal torture, as the lake of fire in Revelation 20:10 suggests, but this is primarily for the Satanic triad – the devil, the beast, and the false prophet – who have deceived the nations. The language of Apocalyptic, as of Jesus' parables, is to enforce the urgency of moral choices here and now. These ideas are in tension with God, who "descends into hell" (Ps. 139:8) not to punish but to redeem. Ephesians 4:9 probably refers to Christ's incarnation, and 1 Peter 3:19 to the universal scope of his death in dealing with sin.

What the New Testament makes clear is that the idea of hell defends the importance of free will, that human choice is real, that it matters, and that it does make a difference. The idea of Heaven defends the equal truth that God's love is absolute and enduring, going to the farthest lengths – the death of Christ – to make itself and its effect known. The tension lies in the never-ending love and the power to reject it, which the Bible came to express in terms of Heaven and hell.

For further reading see bibliography numbers: 20, 82, 133, 155, 350, 478, 654, 888

# THE EMERGENCE OF THE CANON

*The list of books within the New Testament had to be determined by the Churches in the early centuries CE. There was no original, or even early, agreement on the ones to be included, so how did they arrive at the present list?*

## RELIGION OF THE BOOK

During the early centuries CE, the scroll form was gradually replaced by the smaller codex format, which had text on both sides of the sheets. For as long as scrolls remained in use, Christians would have had difficulty collecting their writings; even longer scrolls could contain little more than one large document or several smaller ones. However, the codex made it possible for many writings to be contained in a single book. By facilitating the process of bringing writings together, this development meant that Christians had to decide which documents to include and to determine the order in which they should be arranged.

THE term "canon" is taken from the Greek word *kanon*, meaning "a straight stick." Drawing on the word's metaphorical sense of "standard" or "rule," Athanasius of Alexandria, in his Easter Letter of 367CE, designated as "canon" 27 New Testament works that should be considered authoritative for the Christian Church. However, even after this decisive stage, additional books and letters were being included in New Testament manuscripts (*see below*). Although Roman and Protestant Churches are in agreement on the 27 documents in the New Testament canon, there still remains some variance on the matter among other Church communions. For example, the Syrian Orthodox Church includes only 22 and the Ethiopian Orthodox Church has as many as 35 documents.

## DEVELOPMENTAL FACTORS

To understand the nature and extent of the New Testament canon among these traditions, it is important to consider some of the factors that led Christians to form such a collection during the first four centuries.

• The proliferation of "Gnostic" gospel traditions: By the first century CE, a number of literary sources had emerged that claimed to preserve secret teachings of Jesus or that contained teachings on the nature of God and salvation that many Christians regarded as suspect. Therefore, the need arose to develop clearer criteria for determining which gospels and letters could be deemed authoritative.

• Increasing standardization: The process of canonization among Christians reflected part of a wider movement toward classification and standardization of literature in Greco-Roman antiquity. In centers such as Alexandria, lists of classical works were being drawn up as examples for thought and writing. Jews decided the bounds of their canon (for

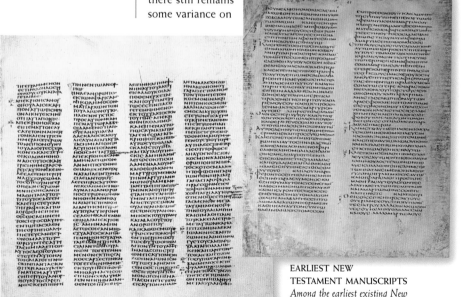

**EARLIEST NEW TESTAMENT MANUSCRIPTS**
*Among the earliest existing New Testament works, these codices include such additional documents as* The Epistle of Barnabas, The Shepherd of Hermas, *and* 1 & 2 Clement.

the forming of the Jewish canon *see p.189*).

• Marcion: Marcion was excommunicated from the church in Rome in 144CE. An influential organizer of the church, he distinguished radically between the judgmental God of the Hebrew Scriptures and the gracious God of Jesus. In accordance with this framework of two gods or aspects of God, Marcion drew up a list of acceptable writings. It may have been his own initiative, or he may have been drawing on existing lists and modifying them. This list, which radicalized the Pauline distinction between faith and works of the law, was limited to only one Gospel (mostly Luke) and ten letters attributed to Paul. Marcion's opponents were soon drawing up lists of their own, which emphasized that the God of Israel and of Jesus were one and the same.

• Montanism: The Cybele priest Montanus founded a movement during the latter half of the second century CE that stressed the inspiration of the Holy Spirit and expected the imminent arrival of the heavenly Jerusalem. Consistent with these emphases was a particular interest in the Gospel of John and the book of Revelation, which, because of the Montanists' perceived abuse of these writings, became suspect in some Christian circles. Given the Montanist's interest in ecstatic prophecy through the Holy Spirit, one may infer that many became increasingly wary of relying on oral tradition. The result was an increased emphasis on written tradition.

• Persecution: During political persecutions in the third century CE, Christians were sometimes required to hand over their precious writings to soldiers. The question arose as to which books could be given up without betraying the faith.

• Preaching and worship: In the first century CE great emphasis was placed on "the living voice," or oral tradition. By the second century CE quotations from written Gospels were already becoming dominant. This enabled them to be read in public worship and to become the basis of preaching and teaching.

In this move toward an agreed canon, the main consideration was reliability: how reliably did any document set forth the original revelation given in Jesus Christ? The issue was not one of inspiration, as though one could determine which books had been written under inspiration and which had not. Far more

**CANON TABLE SHOWING THE FOUR GOSPELS**
*This canon table comes from Jerome's Latin Bible (the Vulgate), which he translated in the fourth century CE.*

important was whether a document could be connected with the Apostles. Also considered were conformity with what was emerging as the agreed faith (in Latin, *regula fidei*, rule of faith). But this did not produce a canon of works that had to be in agreement with each other. There are many obvious differences among the books in the canon, but no attempt was made to include only those that could be harmonized with each other. Indeed, when, in the second century CE Tatian made a harmony of the four Gospels (*see right*), which was used by some Churches instead of the original Gospels, it was rejected.

## TATIAN

Educated in Greek philosophy, Tatian was a second-century CE Christian. He was also an apologist, that is, he wrote an outstanding defense of Christianity.

He wrote the *Diatessaron*, which is a history of the life of Jesus compiled from the four Gospels. Thus, the Church recognized that the variety in the Gospels builds up a more complete picture of Jesus.

For further reading see bibliography numbers: 5, 158, 281, 318, 400, 717, 746, 870

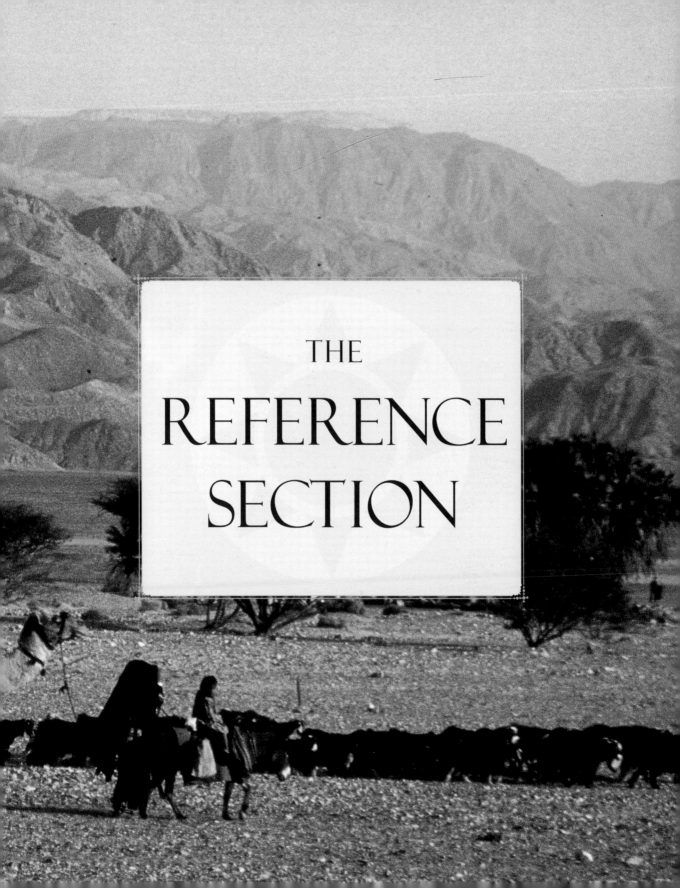

# THE
# REFERENCE
# SECTION

# A-Z OF
# PEOPLE
## IN THE BIBLE

# A

## AARON
Elder brother and spokesman of Moses. He convinced the Israelites that Moses had a special charge from God. He was responsible for the golden calf set up by the Israelites. Israel's first High Priest, he died before the Israelites entered Canaan.
*See p.65*
*Exodus 4–12, 28, 32;*
*Numbers 12; 17; 20:23–29*

## ABEDNEGO
Companion of Daniel exiled to Babylon. Thrown into a furnace on the orders of Nebuchadnezzar, he was protected by God and survived the flames.
*Daniel 1:7; 2:49; 3:13–30*

## ABEL
Second son of Adam and Eve. His offer of an animal sacrifice was preferred to the grain offering of his brother, Cain, who then murdered him.
*See pp.30–31*
*Genesis 4:1–8; Hebrews 11:4*

## ABIATHAR
Son of Ahimelech, priest of Nob who joined David and became joint High Priest with Zadok. On David's death, he supported Adonijah against Solomon and was stripped of his office by King Solomon, and his family was disgraced.
*1 Samuel 22–23; 2 Samuel 8:17; 1 Kings 1–2;*
*1 Chronicles 15:11–15*

## ABIGAIL
Wife of Nabal, later married to David.
*1 Samuel 25; 30:5; 2 Samuel 2:2; 3:3*

## ABIHU
Son of Aaron. With his brother, Nadab, he offered unauthorized fire to God and was destroyed.
*Exodus 6:23; Leviticus 10*

## ABIJAH
• Son of King Jeroboam of Israel, he died according to a prophet's prediction as a sign of God's punishment of his family.
*1 Kings 14*
• Son and successor of King Rehoboam of Judah c.907–06BCE (also called Abijam).
*1 Kings 15; 2 Chronicles 13*

## ABIMELECH
• Name of several Philistine kings of Gerar. Abraham pretended to one Abimelech that Sarah was his sister in order to protect himself. A similar story is told of Isaac and Rebecca.
*Genesis 20; 26:7–11*
• Son of Gideon who murdered all his 70 brothers, with the exception of Jotham.
*Judges 8:31; 9*

## ABINADAB
The man in whose house the Ark of the Covenant was stored between its return from Philistia and its installation at the Temple.
*1 Samuel 7:1; 1 Chronicles 13*

## ABIRAM
Conspired against Moses with his brother, Dathan, and Korah, a Levite, while in Sinai. They, their families, and their cattle were all swallowed up by the earth.
*Numbers 16*

## ABISHAG
Virgin from Shunem who became David's attendant in his old age.
*1 Kings 1, 2*

## ABISHAI
Brother of Joab and one of David's 30 warriors. He urged David to kill Saul, but David refused.
*1 Samuel 26*

## ABNER
Commander of Saul's army, killed by Joab who did not trust his professed loyalty to David.
*1 Samuel 14:50; 2 Samuel 2–3*

## ABRAHAM / ABRAM
First Ancestor of the nation of Israel.
*See pp.38–39*

## ABSALOM
Third and favorite son of David. He murdered his half-brother Amnon, who had raped Absalom's sister Tamar and then fled, fearing his father's anger. David's general, Joab, interceded for Absalom and he was forgiven. Later, Absalom led a rebellion against his father. Despite David's orders to spare him, he was killed by Joab.
*2 Samuel 13–19*

## ACHAN
One of the tribe of Judah who stole from the spoils "devoted" to God when the Israelites conquered Jericho. As a result, the Israelites' attack on Ai failed and Achan was stoned to death.
*Joshua 7*

## ACHISH
King of Gath and one of the leaders of the Philistines with whom David twice took refuge from Saul.
*1 Samuel 21:10–15; 27–29; 1 Kings 2:39–40*

## ADAM
The first man, created by God and given charge of the Garden of Eden.
*See pp.30–31*

## ADONI-BEZEK
Canaanite king who cut off the toes and thumbs of 70 kings. When defeated by Simeon and Judah, the same punishment was exacted on him.
*Judges 1:4–7*

## ADONIJAH
Fourth son of David, who attempted to seize the throne destined for Solomon. He later requested Abishag as a wife but was refused and killed by Solomon.
*1 Kings 1–2*

## ADONI-ZEDEK
Canaanite king of Jerusalem, defeated and killed by Joshua.
*Joshua 10*

## AENEAS
Man from Lydda whom Peter cured of paralysis.
*Acts 9:32–35*

## AGABUS
Prophet who predicted famine at Antioch and Paul's arrest by the Jews of Jerusalem.
*Acts 11:27–30; 21:10–14*

## AGAG
King of the Amalekites, defeated by Saul. His life was spared by Saul, but he was executed by Samuel.
*1 Samuel 15*

## AGRIPPA I SEE HEROD AGRIPPA I

## AGRIPPA II SEE HEROD AGRIPPA II

## AHAB
King of Israel c.873–51BCE who revised the nation's foreign policies and built the new capital of Samaria. He married the Phoenician princess Jezebel, who revived the worship of Baal in Israel, for which he was condemned by the Prophet Elijah. He joined Judah in war against Syria but was killed at Ramoth-gilead.
*1 Kings 16:29–22:53*

## AHASUERUS
Persian king of 127 provinces stretching from Ethiopia to India, probably to be identified with Xerxes I (c.485–65BCE). He made Esther, a Jew, his queen.
*Ezra 4:6; Esther*

## AHAZ
King of Judah c.742–27BCE, son of Remaliah and father of Hezekiah. He introduced pagan worship and took away some of the Temple treasures out of deference to King Tiglath–Pileser of Assyria. He built a copy of the pagan altar at Damascus for the Temple in Jerusalem.
*2 Kings 15:38; 16; Isaiah 7*

## AHAZIAH
• Ahab's son, king of Israel c.851–849BCE. Became a worshiper of Baal like his father.
*1 Kings 22:51–53; 2 Kings 1; 2 Chronicles 20:35–37*
• Son of Jehoram, king of Judah c.843BCE; he was murdered by Jehu.
*2 Kings 8:24–30*

## AHIJAH
Prophet who tore his robe into 12 pieces to show how Solomon's kingdom would be divided. He gave ten pieces to Jeroboam to show that he would rule over ten of the Twelve Tribes of Israel.
*1 Kings 11:29–39; 14:1–18*

## AHIMAAZ
Son of the High Priest Zadok, who passed information to David during Absalom's rebellion and brought news of Absalom's defeat.
*2 Samuel 15:27; 18:19–30*

## AHIMELECH
Priest of Nob, killed for assisting David when he was escaping from King Saul.
*1 Samuel 22:6–18*

## AHITHOPHEL
David's trusted adviser, who betrayed him to support Absalom. He committed suicide.
*2 Samuel 16:5–17:23*

## AMALEK
Grandson of Esau and ancestor of the Amalekites.
*Genesis 36:12; Exodus 17:8–13; Deuteronomy 25:17–19*

## AMASA
Commander of Absalom's army, nephew of David, killed by Joab.
*2 Samuel 17:25; 19; 20:4–13; 1 Kings 2:32; 1 Chronicles 2:17*

## AMAZIAH
Son of Joash, king of Judah c.800–791BCE. Having defeated Edom, he challenged Israel but was routed. He was murdered by his people when exiled to Lachish.
*2 Kings 12:21–14:22; 2 Chronicles 25; Amos 7:10–17*

## AMNON
David's eldest son, who raped Tamar and was killed by Absalom.
*2 Samuel 13*

## AMON
Son of Manasseh and king of Judah c.642–40BCE.
*2 Kings 21:19–26; 2 Chronicles 33:21–25*

## AMOS
Prophet from Tekoa c.750BCE.
*See pp.224–25*

## AMRAM
Father of Moses, Aaron, and Miriam, and father of the Levitical family, the Amramites.
*Exodus 6:18–20; Numbers 3:27; 1 Chronicles 26:23*

## ANAK
Ancestor of a race of giants (the Anakim).
*Numbers 13; Deuteronomy 9:1–2; Joshua 15:14*

## ANANIAS
• Man who sold a piece of property and gave only a part of the promised amount to the Apostles. Challenged by Peter, he died immediately, as did his wife.
*Acts 5:1–11*
• Christian at Damascus, sent to Saul by God to cure the blindness Saul had after his vision on the road to Damascus.
*Acts 9:10–19*
• High Priest in Jerusalem who ordered a guard to strike Paul after his arrest in Jerusalem.
*Acts 23:2–3; 24:1*

## ANDREW
Apostle and fisherman, brother of Peter. The first to be called by Jesus. Told by John the Baptist that Jesus was the "lamb of God," Andrew later told Simon he had found the Messiah. There are post-biblical stories about his martyrdom.
*Matthew 4:18–19; 10:2; Mark 1:16, 3:13–19; 13:3–4; Luke 6:13–16; John 1:35–42; 12:22; Acts 1:13*

## ANNA
• Prophetess in the Temple at the time

that Jesus was presented. She recognized Jesus as the Messiah and told others about him.
*Luke 2:36–38*

• Wife of Tobit, mother of Tobias.
*Tobit 1:9, 20; 2:11*

## ANNAS
Jewish High Priest, father-in-law of Caiaphas before whom Jesus stood trial. Although deposed by the Romans in 15CE, he was still recognized as High Priest by the Jews. He opposed the Apostles in Jerusalem after the Ascension of Jesus.
*Luke 3:2; John 18:12–24*

## ANTIOCHUS
Name of Seleucid kings of Syria in the time between the Hebrew Bible and the New Testament.
*See p.249*

## ANTIPAS SEE HEROD ANTIPAS

## APOLLOS
Learned Jew from Alexandria, instructed in Christianity by Aquila and Priscilla. A powerful preacher and leader of the church at Corinth.
*Acts 18:24–28; 19:1; 1 Corinthians 16:12*

## AQUILA & PRISCILLA
Jewish Christian couple who instructed Apollos and served the Church in various places, including Ephesus and Rome.
*Acts 18:1–3, 18–26; 2 Timothy 4:19*

## ARAUNAH / ORNAN
Man whose threshing floor David bought, and on which David built an altar that later became the site of the Temple.
*2 Samuel 24:16–25; 1 Chronicles 21:18–30*

## ARCHELAUS SEE HEROD ARCHELAUS

## ARCHIPPUS
Christian leader in Asia Minor. Paul addressed him as a fellow soldier.
*Colossians 4:17; Philemon v.2*

## ARISTARCHUS
Paul's companion and fellow worker. He accompanied Paul on his last visit to Jerusalem and Rome. He stayed with Paul when he was imprisoned in Rome.
*Acts 19:29, 20:4, 27:2; Colossians 4:10*

## ARTAXERXES
Name of several kings of Persia. For the identity of the Artaxerxes during whose reign Ezra and Nehemiah returned from exile, see p.161.
*Ezra 4:6–23*

## ASA
Third king of Judah, reigning for 41 years c.905–874BCE. He worshiped YHWH and sought to remove pagan shrines.
*1 Kings 15:8–24; 2 Chronicles 14:1–16:14*

## ASAHEL
David's nephew and one of his 30 warriors. He was killed by Abner.
*2 Samuel 2:18; 23:24; 1 Chronicles 11:26*

## ASAPH
Levite, leader of David's choir. Psalms 50, 73–83 are said to be by him, or for him.
*1 Chronicles 15:17; 16:5, 7, 37; 25:1*

## ASENATH
Joseph's Egyptian wife; mother of their sons Manasseh and Ephraim.
*Genesis 41:50–52*

## ASHER
One of Jacob's 12 sons. His mother was Zilpah, the servant of Leah.
*Genesis 30:13; 35:26; Joshua 19:24–31*

## ASHURBANIPAL
Last of Assyria's great kings 669–c.627BCE.
*Ezra 4:10*

## ATHALIAH
Daughter of Ahab and Jezebel, who married Jehoram of Judah and seized the throne after her son Ahaziah's death. She reigned c.843–37BCE.
*2 Kings 11:1–16; 2 Chronicles 22:10–12*

## AUGUSTUS CAESAR
Roman emperor 27BCE to 14CE, who ordered the census that brought Joseph and Mary to Bethlehem.
*Luke 2:1*

## AZARIAH SEE UZZIAH

# B

## BAAL / BAL / BEL SEE GLOSSARY
Baal means "Lord."   *1 Kings 18*

## BAANAH
Servant of King Ish-bosheth, whom he murdered in the hope of gaining some reward from David.
*2 Samuel 4*

## BAASHA
Man who seized the throne of Israel from Jeroboam's sons; he reigned c.902–86BCE.
*1 Kings 15:16–16:7*

## BAGOAS
Judith's chief eunuch.

## BALAAM
Prophet called on by Balak to curse the Israelites during their time in the wilderness. An angel stopped Balaam on his way to the king and warned him to say only what God told him. Instead of cursing the Israelites, he blessed them three times. He was later killed when the Israelites attacked the Midianites.
*See p.74*
*Numbers 22–24; 31:8; Joshua 24:9; Nehemiah 13:1–3*

## BALAK
Moabite king who hired Balaam to curse Israel.
*Numbers 22–24*

## BARABBAS
Robber released instead of Jesus. Pilate initially tried to release Jesus, but the priests stirred up the crowd against him; Pilate then released Barabbas.
*Matthew 27:15–26*

## BARAK
Deborah's commander in the defeat of Sisera and the Canaanites.
*Judges 4–5*

## BAR–JESUS OR ELYMAS
Jewish sorcerer and false prophet in Paphos, Cyprus, who was temporarily blinded as a punishment for opposing Paul's message.
*See pp.378–79*
*Acts 13:6–12*

## BARNABAS
Originall a Levite from Cyprus, he was commissioned for missionary service with Paul by the church at Antioch. He

sold his land to give the money to poor Christians. He later split from Paul, who refused to allow John Mark, Barnabas' cousin, to accompany them again.
*Acts 4:36; 9:27; 11:22–30; 12:25; 13–15; 1 Corinthians 9:6; Galatians 2:1*

## BARTHOLOMEW
One of the 12 Apostles, possibly "Nathanael" in John's Gospel. Legend has it that he was flayed alive in Armenia.
*Matthew 10:3; Acts 1:13*

## BARTIMAEUS
Blind beggar from Jericho who was healed by Jesus as Jesus traveled to Jerusalem for the Passion.
*Mark 10:46–52*

## BARUCH
Jeremiah's secretary. A book in the Apocrypha is named after him.
*Jeremiah 36; 43:6; Baruch*

## BARZILLAI
Loyal friend of David during Absalom's rebellion.
*2 Samuel 17:27; 19:31–39*

## BATHSHEBA
Wife of Uriah the Hittite, mother of Solomon. David committed adultery with her and later married her.
*2 Samuel 11–12; 1 Kings 1–2*

## BELSHAZZAR
Ruler (coregent) of Babylon.
*See pp.216–17*
*Daniel 5, 7, 8*

## BELTESHAZZAR
Babylonian name given to Daniel.
*Daniel 1:7*

## BENAIAH
One of David's officers responsible for proclaiming Solomon king. He became commander of his army.
*2 Samuel 8:18; 1 Kings 1–2; 1 Chronicles 11:22–25*

## BEN-AMMI
Ancestor of the Ammonites. His half-brother Moab was ancestor of the Moabites. Their lands lay east of the Dead Sea.
*Genesis 19:38*

## BEN-HADAD
Name of three rulers of Syria c.900–800BCE. The name probably means "son of Hadad," who was the Syrian storm god.
*1 Kings 20:1–34; 2 Kings 6:24–8:15; 13*

## BENJAMIN
Youngest son of Jacob; Rachel died giving birth to him. After his brother Joseph's disappearance, he was his father's favorite. Ancestor of the tribe of Benjamin, which became part of Judah in the division of the kingdom.
*Genesis 35:18–20; 43–45*

## BERNICE
Sister of Herod Agrippa II. She was with him when he heard Paul's case at Caesarea.
*Acts 25:13*

## BETHUEL
Father of Laban and Rebecca.
*Genesis 22:22; 24:15–51; 25:20*

## BEZALEL
Craftsman chosen to construct the Tabernacle and its furnishings during the wilderness period.
*Exodus 35:30–36:2; 37:1*

## BILDAD
One of Job's three friends.
*Job 2:11; 8; 18; 25; 42:9*

## BILHAH
Rachel's servant, mother of Dan and Naphtali.
*Genesis 29:29; 30:3–7*

## BOAZ
Landowner in Bethlehem. Became Ruth's husband and great-grandfather of David.
*Ruth 2–4*

## BUZ SEE HUZ

# C

## CAESAR
Title of emperors of Rome. During the reign of Augustus (27BCE–14CE) Jesus was born. Tiberius (14–37CE) followed him. Peter and Paul were probably martyred when Nero was Caesar (54–68CE).
*Mark 12:14–17; Luke 2:1; 3:1; Acts 25:8–21; 26:32*

## CAIAPHAS
High Priest before whom Jesus was interrogated. He found Jesus guilty and sent him to Pilate for sentence. He was also the High Priest mentioned in Acts who persecuted the first Christians.
*Matthew 26:3, 57; Luke 3:2; John 18:13–14; Acts 5:17*

## CAIN
Eldest son of Adam and Eve. He was a farmer, and his brother Abel was a shepherd. His grain offering to God was not accepted. Cain killed Abel and was forced to live the rest of his life as a nomad.
*Genesis 4*

## CALEB
Sent by Moses to spy out Canaan. Of the 12 spies, only he and Joshua believed God would bring them into the Promised Land. Consequently, they were the only two allowed to settle in Canaan, while the others all died in the desert.
*Numbers 13–14; 26:65; Deuteronomy 1:35–36*

## CANAAN
Son of Ham. Because of his disrespect, his grandfather, Noah, cursed him and his descendants.
*Genesis 9:18–27*

## CANDACE
Queen of Ethiopia (Nubia) whose eunuch was baptized by the deacon Philip.
*Acts 8:26–39*

## CEPHAS SEE PETER

## CHEDORLAOMER
King of Elam who headed a punitive raid against Sodom and Gomorrah. He was later pursued and killed by Abraham.
*Genesis 14*

## CLAUDIUS
Roman emperor, reigning from 41 to 54CE. He forced all Jews to leave Rome.
*Acts 11:28; 18:2*

## CLAUDIUS LYSIAS
Military tribune in Jerusalem who took Paul into custody after learning of a plot to kill him.
*Acts 23:19–30*

**CLEOPAS**
One of two who met the risen Jesus on the road to Emmaus after the Crucifixion.
*Luke 24:13–35*

**CORNELIUS**
Roman centurion to whose household Peter was sent to preach the gospel. He was converted, becoming the first-recorded Gentile Christian.
*Acts 10*

**CRESCENS**
Companion of Paul sent to Galatia.
*2 Timothy 4:10*

**CRISPUS**
Ruler of the synagogue in Corinth, who was converted through Paul's ministry.
*Acts 18:7–8*

**CUSHAN-RISHATHAIM**
Mesopotamian king who ruled over the Israelites in the time of the Judges.
*Judges 3:7–10*

**CYRUS THE GREAT**
King of Persia c.559–29BCE who overthrew the Babylonians and allowed the Jews to return from exile and rebuild their Temple in Jerusalem. He returned to them the treasures stolen from the Temple by Nebuchadnezzar.
*2 Chronicles 36:22–23; Ezra 1:1–6:14*

# D

**DAMARIS**
Woman from Athens converted by Paul.
*Acts 17:34*

**DAN**
Son of Jacob, ancestor of the tribe bearing his name.
*Genesis 30:4–6; 35:25*

**DANIEL**
Interpreter of dreams. Taken captive to Babylon c.605BCE as a young man, he became a leading figure at Nebuchadnezzar's court.
*See pp.216–17*
*Daniel 1–12*

**DARIUS**
• Darius the Mede. He is mentioned in Daniel 5:31; 6; 9:1; 11:1; not otherwise known.
*See p.216*
• Darius I, king of Babylon and Persia 522–486BCE. He allowed the returned Jews to rebuild the Jerusalem Temple.
*Ezra 4:5; Haggai 1:1; Zechariah 1:1*

**DATHAN**
Person who rebelled against Moses with Abiram and Korah.
*Numbers 16*

**DAVID**
Shepherd boy from Bethlehem who killed Goliath. He became Israel's second king c.1010–970BCE and founded the royal line from which the Messiah was to be born.
*See pp.124–25*

**DEBORAH**
Prophet in the time of the Judges and wife of Lappidoth. She joined with Barak and his army of 10,000 to overthrow Sisera and the Canaanites.
*See pp.104–107*
*Judges 4–5*

**DELILAH**
Mistress of Samson, who betrayed him to the Philistines after finding that the source of his strength was his hair. She cut off his long hair before he was blinded and enslaved.
*Judges 16:1–22*

**DEMAS**
Paul's fellow Christian worker who was imprisoned with him in Rome. He later deserted Paul and went to Thessalonica.
*Colossians 4:14; 2 Timothy 4:10*

**DEMETRIUS**
• Silversmith at Ephesus who made silver shrines of Diana (Artemis). He stirred up a riot against Paul.
*Acts 19:23–41*
• Christian commended by John.
*3 John 1:12*

**DIDYMUS** SEE THOMAS

**DINAH**
Jacob's daughter, whose rape by Shechem was cruelly avenged by her brothers Simeon and Levi.
*Genesis 34*

**DIONYSIUS**
Member of the Areopagus (a powerful court at Athens set up to hear religious cases) who became a Christian after meeting Paul.
*Acts 17:34*

**DIOTREPHES**
Self-seeking church leader criticized by John for refusing to accept his authority.
*3 John 1:9–10*

**DOEG**
Edomite servant of Saul, who informed him that Ahimelech had helped David in his flight from Saul. As a consequence, Ahimelech was killed by Doeg.
*1 Samuel 22:9–23*

**DORCAS** SEE TABITHA

**DRUSILLA**
Herod Agrippa I's youngest daughter and wife of the procurator Felix, who heard Paul's case.
*Acts 24:24*

# E

**EBED-MELECH**
Ethiopian servant of Zedekiah who saved Jeremiah's life and whose own life was saved by God as a result.
*Jeremiah 38:7–12; 39:16–18*

**EGLON**
King of Moab who defeated the Israelites and ruled over them for 18 years before being killed by Ehud.
*Judges 3:12–26*

**EHUD**
Israelite champion who killed Eglon of Moab. Once Eglon was dead, he freed the Israelites after defeating the Moabites.
*Judges 3:12–30*

**ELAH**
The name of a number of individuals, notably the son of Baasha, king of Israel c.877–76, assassinated by Zimri.
*1 Kings 16:8–14*

**ELEAZAR**
Aaron's third son, who became High Priest after the death of Aaron. He

was put in charge of the Levites and the Tabernacle.
*Numbers 3:2; 20:1–2, 21, 27:22–29; Joshua 14:1*

## ELI
Priest and judge at Shiloh, mentor to the young Samuel. His sons were rebellious and as a result Eli's house was cursed. Both sons were killed in battle against the Philistines, and the Ark of the Covenant was also stolen. When Eli heard the news he collapsed and died.
*1 Samuel 1–4*

## ELIAB
Eldest son of Jesse, and brother of David.
*1 Samuel 16:6; 17:13, 28*

## ELIAKIM
Name of several individuals, most notably the steward of Hezekiah's household, who negotiated with Sennacherib's officers.
*2 Kings 18:18; Isaiah 36:1–37:7*

## ELIASHIB
High Priest who helped rebuild Jerusalem in the time of Nehemiah.
*Nehemiah 3:1; 13:4–9*

## ELIEZER
Abraham's chief servant and adopted heir, who was sent to find a wife for his son Isaac. He found Rebecca in Mesopotamia.
*Genesis 15:2–3; 24*

## ELIHU
The fourth of Job's friends, who points Job to God for an explanation of his suffering.
*Job 32–37*

## ELIJAH
One of Israel's greatest prophets, who lived during the reign of King Ahab (c.873–51BCE) and his wife Jezebel.
*See pp.138–39*

## ELIMELECH
Husband of Naomi. Ruth was his daughter-in-law.
*Ruth 1, 2*

## ELIPHAZ
One of Job's three friends who tried to comfort him.
*Job 2:11; 4–5; 15; 22; 42:9*

## ELISHA
Elijah's successor as prophet of Israel. He carried out the task set by Elijah to anoint Hazael and Jehu as kings-to-be in Syria and Israel. He performed a number of miracles, including bringing the Shunammite woman's son back to life, and healing Naaman, a Syrian general, of his leprosy.
*1 Kings 19:16–21; 2 Kings 2–9; 13:14–20*

## ELIZABETH
Wife of Zechariah, and mother of John the Baptist. She was the cousin of Jesus' mother, Mary, who visited her before the birth of their sons (the Visitation). Elizabeth knew instantly that Mary's child would be the long awaited "Messiah."
*Luke 1*

## ELKANAH
Father of Samuel and husband of Hannah.
*1 Samuel 1*

## ELYMAS SEE BAR–JESUS

## EN–DOR
The skilled woman of En-dor, who raised the ghost of Samuel for Saul. It foretold Saul's coming defeat by the Philistines. Saul fainted in despair, and the woman forced him to eat and regain his strength.
*1 Samuel 28*

## ENOCH
Descendant of Adam's son Seth, who was said to have been taken into God's presence without dying.
*Genesis 5:18–24; Hebrews 11:5*

## EPAPHRAS
Paul's friend and fellow worker who planted the Christian church in Colossae.
*Colossians 1:7–8; 4:12; Philemon v.23*

## EPAPHRODITUS
Christian sent to Paul by the Philippian church, and who brought a gift from the Philippian church to Paul at his Roman prison.
*Philippians 2:25–30; 4:18*

## EPHRAIM
The youngest of Joseph's two sons, who received a greater blessing from his grandfather Jacob than his brother, Manasseh. The tribe of Israel that was named after him was an important one, and the Prophets sometimes use the name Ephraim when referring to Israel.
*Genesis 41:52; 48*

## EPHRON
Hittite from whom Abraham bought the cave of Machpelah at Hebron as a burial place for his wife, Sarah.
*Genesis 23; 25:9; 49; 50:12–14*

## ERASTUS
• Paul's assistant, sent to Macedonia with Timothy.
*Acts 19:22; 2 Timothy 4:20*
• Christian city-treasurer from Corinth.
*Romans 16:23*

## ESARDADDON
He succeeded Sennacherib as king of Assyria. Ruled 680–69BCE.
*2 Kings 19:37; Ezra 4:2*

## ESAU
Son of Isaac and Rebecca and twin brother of Jacob.
*See pp.40–41*

## ESDRAS
Greek for Ezra (*see below*).

## ESTHER
Jewish exile who became the queen of the Persian king Ahasuerus.
*See pp.166–67*

## EUNICE
Jewish mother of Timothy.
*2 Timothy 1:5*

## EUTYCHUS
Young man who fell to his death from a window during Paul's sermon at Troas. Paul restored him to life.
*Acts 20:7–12*

## EVE
The first woman, created by God from Adam's rib.
*See pp.30–31*

## EZEKIEL
Major prophet who lived in Babylon during the Exile.
*See pp.212–15*

## EZRA / ESDRAS
Priest and scribe. He returned to Jerusalem from Babylon with a company of exiles.
*See pp. 54–61*

# F

## FELIX
Roman procurator c.52–60CE who kept Paul in prison at Caesarea for two years.
*Acts 23:24; 24*

## FESTUS
Successor to Felix as procurator of Judea. He heard Paul's case at Caesarea and agreed that Paul was innocent.
*Acts 25–26*

# G

## GABRIEL
Archangel sent to interpret Daniel's vision. He announced the birth of John the Baptist to Zechariah and the birth of Jesus to Mary.
*Daniel 8:16; 9:21; Luke 1:11–20, 26–38*

## GAD
• Son of Jacob and Leah's maid Zilpah; ancestor of a tribe of Israel whose territory lay to the east of the Jordan.
*Genesis 30:10–11; 49:19; Numbers 32*
• Prophet who advised David to leave Moab for Judah.
*1 Samuel 22:5; 2 Samuel 24*

## GALLIO
Proconsul of Achaia 51–52CE (and brother of Seneca, the tutor of Nero), whose decision against the Jews, who wanted to bring charges against Paul, gave the Church new freedom.
*Acts 18:12–17*

## GAMALIEL
Influential Pharisee, rabbi, member of the Sanhedrin, and tutor of Saul of Tarsus (later Paul the Apostle). He advised cautious handling of the Apostles when they were arrested. He suggested that if the Apostles were doing only human work nothing would come of it but if they were doing God's work, opposition would be futile.
*Acts 5:34–39; 22:3*

## GEDALIAH
Governor of Judah, appointed by Nebuchadnezzar. He was assassinated after only a few months.
*2 Kings 25:22–26*

## GEHAZI
Servant of Elisha, punished for seeking reward from Naaman, whom Elisha had cured of leprosy. As a punishment Gehazi caught leprosy himself.
*2 Kings 4–5; 8:4*

## GERSHON
Son of Levi and head of one of the three Levitical families.
*Exodus 6:16–17; Numbers 3:17*

## GESHEM
An Arabian, one of Nehemiah's main opponents to rebuilding the walls of Jerusalem.
*Nehemiah 2:19; 6:1–7*

## GIDEON
Judge of Israel who delivered Israel from the Midianites. He was called to action by an angel, and to guarantee the message was truly from God, he asked for two signs, which he was given. His 300 men attacked the enemy at night, shouting "The sword of the Lord and of Gideon." In their fear, the Midianites turned on each other and then fled the land. Peace reigned until after Gideon's death.
*See pp. 104–07*
*Judges 6–8*

## GILEAD
Son of Manasseh and forefather of the Gileadites, who belonged to the Manasseh tribe.
*Numbers 27:1; 36:1; Joshua 17:1, 3; 1 Chronicles 7:14–17*

## GOG AND MAGOG
The book of Ezekiel describes Gog as the ruler of the land of Magog. In Revelation, Gog and Magog represent those who oppose the rule of Christ.
*Ezekiel 38–39; Revelation 20:7–8*

## GOLIATH
Giant from Gath, killed by a stone from David's sling. David then beheaded him.
*1 Samuel 17:1–51*

## GOMER
Hosea's unfaithful wife.
*Hosea 1–3*

# H

## HABAKKUK
Prophet to Judea during the period of the Babylonian ascendancy.
*See pp. 238–39*

## HADAD
Edomite who fled to Egypt and married the queen's sister. On hearing that both David and Joab were dead, he returned to Edom and harassed Solomon.
*1 Kings 11:14–25*

## HADADEZER / HADAREZER
King of Zobah, defeated by David.
*2 Samuel 8–10; 1 Chronicles 18–19*

## HADASSAH
Esther's Jewish name.

## HAGAR
Egyptian servant of Abraham's wife, Sarah. The barren Sarah gave Hagar to Abraham so that she might bear him a child. Sarah began to treat Hagar so badly that she fled, but the angel of the Lord brought her back, and she gave birth to Ishmael.
*Genesis 16; 21:8–20*

## HAGGAI
Prophet of the sixth century BCE.
*See pp. 242–43*

## HAM
Noah's son, who was the founder of he Hamites, spreading over the northern part of Africa. The Hamites were enemies of the Israelites.
*Genesis 5:32; 6:10; 10:6–20*

## HAMAN
Villain of the book of Esther, who plotted against the Jews because he had been slighted by Mordecai, a Jew. Haman was subsequently hanged when Esther revealed his treacherous plans to the king.
*See pp. 166–67*
*Esther 3–9*

## HAMMURABI
King of Babylon, compiler of a code of laws.
*See p.85*

## HANAMEL
Jeremiah's cousin, who sold him the field at Anathoth during the Babylonian invasion. Jeremiah bought the field as a sign that one day Judah would no longer be under the power of Babylon.
*Jeremiah 32:6–12*

## HANANI
Man who traveled to Susa to tell Nehemiah that despite the return of the exiles, Jerusalem was still in ruins. He was made governor by Nehemiah once the walls of the city had been rebuilt.
*Nehemiah 1:2; 7:2*

## HANANIAH
False prophet denounced by Jeremiah.
*Jeremiah 28*

## HANNAH
Mother of Samuel. Childless for years, she finally bore a son and in gratitude devoted him to God as Eli's servant.
*1 Samuel 1–2*

## HANUN
Ammonite king who shaved off the beards of David's emissaries and cut down their clothes. His army was routed by David's in revenge.
*2 Samuel 10:1–4; 1 Chronicles 19:1–6*

## HARAN
Abraham's brother, who died in Ur before Terah and Abraham migrated out of the city. He had three children, Lot, Milcah, and Iscah.
*Genesis 11:27–31*

## HAZAEL
He seized the throne of Syria after assassinating Ben-hadad following Elisha's prediction. Waged war against Israel and Judah in the ninth century BCE.
*1 Kings 19:15–17; 2 Kings 8:7–9:15*

## HEBER
Husband of Jael. He killed Sisera, the Canaanite general.
*Judges 4:11–21; 5:24*

## HEROD ARCHELAUS
Better known as Herod the Ethnarch.
*See pp.278–79*

## HEROD AGRIPPA I
Grandson of Herod the Great, and ruler of Galilee, Judea, and Samaria.
*See pp.278–79*

## HEROD AGRIPPA II
Son of Herod Agrippa I.
*See pp.278–79*

## HEROD ANTIPAS (HEROD THE TETRARCH)
Son of Herod the Great; he married his sister-in-law, Herodias.
*See pp.278–79, 325*

## HEROD THE GREAT
Ruler of Judea.
*See pp.277, 278–79, 286–87*

## HERODIAS
Wife of Herod Antipas, who brought about the beheading of John the Baptist through her daughter, Salome.
*Matthew 14:3–11; Mark 6:17–29; Luke 3:19*

## HEZEKIAH
One of Judah's great kings c.727–698BCE; contemporary of Isaiah. He succeeded Ahaz, his father. On becoming king, he set out to rid his land of idol worship. He rebelled against the Assyrians, but the constant threat from the north made him realize the possibility of a siege. To ensure Jerusalem's water supply he cut a tunnel.
*2 Kings 18–20; 2 Chronicles 29–32*

## HILKIAH
High Priest at the time of King Josiah. He discovered the Book of the Law in the Temple, which was being repaired.
*2 Kings 22:3–23:4; 2 Chronicles 34:9–22*

## HIRAM / HIRIAM
King of Tyre, who formed an alliance with David and Solomon. He supplied cedar and skilled labor for the Temple, and he joined with Solomon to operate a Red Sea trading fleet.
*2 Samuel 5:11; 1 Kings 5:1–2*

## HOLOFERNES
Captain at the time of Nebuchadnezzar; he was decapitated by Judith.
*Judith 2–7; 10–15*

## HOPHNI
Unprincipled son of Eli. A priest at Shiloh, he was killed when the Philistines captured the Ark of the Covenant.
*1 Samuel 4:4–11*

## HOSEA
Prophet in the time of Jeroboam II.
*See pp.218–19*

## HOSHEA
Last king of the Northern Kingdom of Israel, c.732–23BCE. Hoshea killed King Pekah and appointed himself ruler of the land. He was imprisoned by Shalmaneser, and a few years later Samaria, the capital of Israel, fell.
*2 Kings 17:1–6*

## HULDAH
Prophetess consulted by Hilkiah after he discovered the Book of the Law.
*2 Kings 22:14; 2 Chronicles 34:22*

## HUR
Moses' chief lieutenant after the Exodus. He was involved in the battle against the Amalekites.
*Exodus 17:10–13; 24:14*

## HUSHAI
David's friend, who persuaded Absalom not to take Ahithophel's advice. He undermined Ahithophel's influence after he had deserted David for Absalom. Hushai's misleading advice led to Ahithophel hanging himself and to Absalom marching across the Jordan to his death.
*2 Samuel 15:32–17:15*

## HUZ AND BUZ
Two of the eight children of Nahor, Abraham's brother.
*Genesis 22:21*

## HYMENAEUS
Man disciplined by Paul for unsettling people's faith with false teaching.
*1 Timothy 1:20; 2 Timothy 2:17*

# I

## ICHABOD
The grandson of Eli.
*1 Samuel 4:12–22*

## ISAAC
Son of Abraham, father of Jacob and Esau.
*See pp.40–41*

## ISAIAH
Major Judean prophet.
*See pp.200–05*

## ISCARIOT  SEE JUDAS ISCARIOT

## ISH–BOSHETH / ISHABAAL
Saul's son, made king by Abner. He ruled over much of Israel while David was king of the tribe of Judah. He was finally murdered by two of his generals.
*2 Samuel 2–4*

## ISHMAEL
Son of Abraham and Hagar.
*Genesis 16; 21:8–20*

## ISRAEL
Name God gave Jacob after the encounter at the Jabbok River. The name means "the man who fights with God"; this name was also given to Jacob's descendants.
*See pp.40–41*
*Genesis 32:22–28; 35:9–10*

## ISSACHAR
Son of Jacob and father of one of the Twelve Tribes of Israel.
*Genesis 35:23*

## ITHAMAR
Son of Aaron, a priest of Israel who founded a family of priests.
*Numbers 3:2; 1 Chronicles 24:1*

## ITTAI
Philistine from Gath who stood by David during Absalom's rebellion. As a reward he was made commander of one-third of David's army.
*2 Samuel 15:19–22; 18:5*

# J

## JABAL
Son of Lamech and his first wife, Adah.
*Genesis 4:19–20*

## JABIN
King of Hazor whose army was defeated by Joshua.
*Joshua 11:1–11*

## JACOB
Son of Isaac and Rebecca, and ancestor of the tribes of Israel through his twelve sons.
*See pp.40–41*

## JAEL
Wife of Heber, who killed Sisera, the Canaanite general, with a tent peg.
*Judges 4:17–22; 5:24–27*

## JAIRUS
Ruler of the synagogue at Capernaum, whose 12-year-old daughter was restored to life by Jesus.
*Mark 5:22*

## JAMES
• Son of Zebedee, brother of John, one of the 12 Apostles; known as James the Great to distinguish him from James the Less (*see below*). He and his brother John were nicknamed "men of thunder" by Jesus. He was executed by Herod Agrippa I. Legend has it that he went to Spain, where his shrine at Santiago was popular among pilgrims in the Middle Ages.
*Matthew 4:21; 17:1; Mark 5:37; 10:35; Acts 1:13; 12:2*
• Son of Alphaeus, author of the Apostles called James the Less or James the Younger in Mark 15:40.
*Matthew 10:3; Mark 15:40; Acts 1:13*
• Brother or half-brother of Jesus, who became leader of the Jerusalem church. He was allegedly stoned and clubbed to death for refusing to denounce Jesus.
*See pp.315, 454–55*
*Matthew 13:55; Acts 12:17; 1 Corinthians 15:7; James 1–5*

## JAPHETH
One of Noah's three sons. He survived the Flood to become ancestor of a number of nations.
*Genesis 5:32; 9:18; 10:12*

## JASON
Paul's host, who was held answerable for him at Thessalonica.
*Acts 17:5–9*

## JEDUTHUN
Levite who was appointed by David as one of the leaders of the Temple music.
*1 Chronicles 16:41–42; 25:1; 2 Chronicles 5:12*

## JEHOAHAZ
• Son of Jehu and king of Israel 814–798BCE. He tolerated idol worship, and Israel was oppressed by Syria for part of his reign.
*2 Kings 13:1–9*
• Son of Josiah and king of Judah for three months, c.609BCE. He was captured by Pharaoh Neco II and taken to Egypt. Called Shallum by Jeremiah.
*2 Kings 23:31–34; 1 Chronicles 3:15; Jeremiah 22:11–12*

## JEHOASH  SEE JOASH

## JEHOIACHIM
Son of Josiah, king of Judah c.608–598BCE, placed on the throne by Pharaoh Neco II. He burned Jeremiah's scroll of prophecies and later rebelled against Babylonian control. He died on the way to captivity.
*2 Kings 24:1–7; 2 Chronicles 36:4–8; Jeremiah 22:18; 26; 36*

## JEHOIACHIN
Son of Jehoiachim, king of Judah for three months in 598–97BCE. He was taken to Babylon by Nebuchadnezzar.
*2 Kings 24:8–16; 25:27–30; 2 Chronicles 36:9–10; Jeremiah 52:31–34*

## JEHOIADA
Name of several individuals, notably the chief priest responsible for the coup that dethroned Athaliah and placed Joash on the throne of Judah c.837BCE.
*2 Kings 11–12; 2 Chronicles 23:1–24:15*

## JEHORAM / JORAM
• Son of Ahab of Israel, killed and succeeded by Jehu at the instigation of Elijah (c.849–43BCE).
*2 Kings 3:1–8; 9:14–24*
• King of Judah c.850–43BCE. He died of disease, having reverted to idol worship.
*2 Kings 8:16–24, 2 Chronicles 21:14–20*

## JEHOSHAPHAT
Son of Asa, king of Judah c.874–50BCE, allied by marriage to Ahab of Israel. He fought with Ahab against the Syrians at Ramah-gilead. He discouraged the worship of idols, and made sure that his people learned God's laws.
*1 Kings 22; 2 Kings 3:1; 2 Chronicles 17:1–21:1*

## JEHOSHEBA / JEHOSHABEATH
Princess of Judah and wife of the priest Jehoida, who saved the life of Joash.
*2 Kings 11:1–3; 2 Chronicles 22:11–12*

## JEHU
King of Israel c.843–16BCE, anointed by Elisha to destroy Ahab's line. He killed his predecessor Jehoram, before restoring worship of YHWH and eradicating the worship of Baal.
*2 Kings 9–10*

## JEPHTHAH
One of Israel's principal judges. His vow to God resulted in his daughter's sacrifice.
*See p.107*
*Judges 11:1–12:7*

## JEREMIAH
Major prophet of Judah.
*See pp.206–07*

## JEROBOAM
• First king of the Northern Kingdom of Israel, c.924–03BCE. He rebelled against Solomon and became an exile in Egypt before returning to lead the ten northern tribes after Solomon's death.
*1 Kings 11:26–14:20*
• Jeroboam II, king of Israel c.785–45BCE. He reestablished Israel's political power and material prosperity, but the social evils and empty ritual of his reign were attacked by the prophet Amos, who predicted the fall of Samaria as a result.
*2 Kings 14:23–29; Amos 7:10–11; Hosea 1:1*

## JESSE
David's father, grandson of Ruth and Boaz.
*1 Samuel 16–17*

## JESUS CHRIST
The central person in the New Testament, and the reason why it was written.
*See especially pp.297, 306–65*
*Matthew, Mark, Luke, John*

## JESUS SON OF SIRACH
Greek form of the name of the author of the book of Sirach, Latin name Ecclesiasticus.
*See pp.256–57*
*Sirach*

## JETHRO
Midianite priest and father-in-law of Moses. Sometimes known as Reuel.
*Exodus 3:1; 4:18–19; 18*

## JEZEBEL
Princess of Tyre and Sidon who married Ahab, the king of Israel. She introduced the worship of Baal into the kingdom and was responsible for Naboth's death. Elijah predicted her violent death and, on the orders of Jehu, she was finally thrown from an upstairs window.
*1 Kings 16:31; 18:4, 13, 19; 19:1–2; 21; 2 Kings 9:30–37*

## JOAB
Nephew of David and commander of his army. He helped to reconcile David with his son, Absalom, but later killed Absalom against David's orders. Joab had earlier murdered his army rival Abner, and was put to death by Solomon.
*2 Samuel 2:13–3:31; 10–11; 14; 18–20; 24:1–4; 1 Kings 1:15–34*

## JOANNA
Wife of one of Herod Antipas' officials. She was healed by Jesus and provided for Jesus and the Apostles. She was one of the women who found the tomb of Jesus empty on the morning of the Resurrection.
*Luke 8:1–3; 24:10*

## JOASH / JEHOASH
• Rescued from Athaliah's massacre, he became king of Judah at the age of seven. He ruled c.837–800BCE. Guided by Jehoiada during much of his reign, he repaired the Temple and obeyed God's laws. After Jehoiada's death, he allowed worship of Baal and killed Jehoiada's son. He was finally murdered by his officials.
*2 Kings 11–12; 2 Chronicles 24*
• Son of Jehoahaz. The 12th king of Israel, 800–785BCE. He was aided in territorial battles by Elishah.
*2 Kings 14*

## JOB
Central figure of the book of Job.
*See pp.172–73*

## JOEL
Prophet in the time of Uzziah known only from the book of Joel.
*See pp.220–21*

## JOHANAN
Popular Hebrew Bible name, but the Jewish leader who warned Gedaliah of the plot to kill him is the most notable. He ignored Jeremiah's advice and led the people to Egypt.
*Jeremiah 40–43*

## JOHN (THE APOSTLE)
Son of Zebedee, he was, together with Peter and James, especially close to Jesus. He was present at the Transfiguration, and was in the Garden of Gethsemane just before Jesus' death. After the Ascension, John became a leader of the church in Jerusalem. According to tradition, he moved to Ephesus and has been identified with the author of Revelation; but see p.469.
*See pp.312–13*
*Matthew 4:21; 10:2; 17:1; Mark 3:17; 5:37; 10:35; 14:33; Luke 9:49; John 19:26–27; Acts 3–4; Galatians 2:9; Revelation 1:9*

## JOHN MARK
Cousin of Barnabus who joined Paul and Barnabus in Jerusalem and accompanied them on their missionary journeys. Barnabus left Paul to go his separate way with John Mark after an argument with Paul. It is possible that he was the author of Mark's Gospel.
*Acts 12:12; 13:4; Colossians 4:10; 2 Timothy 4:11; Philemon v.24*

## JOHN THE BAPTIST
Cousin and forerunner of Jesus, who was sent to prepare the people for the coming Messiah.
*See pp.324–25*

## JONADAB
Friend and cousin of David's son Amnon. An evil man who was murdered by Tamar's brother Absalom.
*2 Samuel 13*

## JONAH
Prophet whose mission to Nineveh is recounted in the book bearing his name.
*See pp.230–31*

## JONATHAN
• Saul's son, who became a great friend of David. He was a brave warrior who fought against the Philistines and saved David from being killed by Saul. Together

with Saul, he was killed when the Israelites were defeated by the Philistines.
*1 Samuel 13–14; 18–20; 23:16–18; 31:2; 2 Samuel 1*

• Son of Abiathar the priest. He delivered vital information to David that helped David in his feud with Absalom.
*2 Samuel 15:36*

• Brother of Judas Maccabeus.
*1 Maccabees 9:19–13:25; 2 Maccabees 8:21–22*

### JOSEPH

• Eleventh son of Jacob.
*See pp.44–45*

• Husband of Mary, mother of Jesus. An angel told him not to divorce his pregnant fiancée and that his child would be called Jesus. He fled with his family to Egypt after hearing of Herod's plans to murder newborn Hebrew boys. He later returned to work as a carpenter in Nazareth.
*See p.315*
*Matthew 1–2; Luke 1–2; John 6:42*

• Joseph of Arimathea, secret disciple of Jesus. After the Crucifixion, Joseph asked Pilate for Jesus' body, which he wrapped in a cloth and placed in a new tomb.
*Matthew 27:57–60; Luke 23:50–55; John 19:38–42*

### JOSEPH BARSABAS

Candidate to fill the place of Judas Iscariot as one of the 12 Apostles. Matthias was chosen instead.
*Acts 1:23*

### JOSES / JOSEPH

A brother or relative of Jesus.
*Mark 6:3*

### JOSHUA

• Succeeded Moses as leader of Israel and led the Israelites into Canaan. He had been one of the original spies who believed conquest was possible. He directed the military campaign and demanded strict adherence to the Law of Moses. Joshua divided the Promised Land among the Twelve Tribes of Israel. Before his death, he reminded the Israelites of God's love for them in a renewal of the Covenant at Shechem.
*See pp.92–103*
*Exodus 17:9–13; Numbers 13–14; Joshua 1–24*

• High Priest of the 537BCE restoration, under whom the altar was rebuilt, and the Temple was dedicated.
*Zechariah 6:12*

### JOSIAH

King of Judah c.639–09BCE.
*See pp.144–45*

### JOTHAM

Son of Uzziah, king of Judah. Defeated the Ammonites.
*2 Kings 15:32–38; 2 Chronicles 27:1–9*

### JUBAL

Lamech's son by his first wife, Adah. The ancestor of those who make music and musical instruments.
*Genesis 4:21*

### JUDAH

Jacob's fourth son by Leah, who became the ancestor of the royal tribe of Israel. Judah convinced his brothers to sell Joseph to merchants on the way to Egypt rather than have him killed. Eventually the territory of Judah became the Roman province of Judea.
*Genesis 29:35; 37:26–27; 38; 49:8–10*

### JUDAS

• Brother of Jesus, to whom the letter of Jude is attributed.
*See p.315*
*Matthew 13:55*

• "Son of James," one of the 12 Apostles. Known thus in Luke's Gospel and Acts; called Thaddeus in Mark and Matthew. John's Gospel does not name him.
*Matthew 10:3; Mark 3:18; Luke 6:16; Acts 1:13*

### JUDAS BARSABAS

Sent to Antioch by the Christians, together with Silas, Paul, and Barnabas. After a time he returned to Jerusalem.
*Acts 15:22*

### JUDAS ISCARIOT

Disciple who betrayed Jesus.
*See p.353*
*Matthew 10:4; 26:14; 27:3–5; John 12:4–6; 13:21–30; Acts 1:18–19*

### JUDAS MACCABEUS

The most important member of the Maccabeus family (Hasmonedus; see pp.250–51), which created the independent state that lasted for a hundred years before the arrival of the Romans.
*See pp.250–51*
*1 Maccabees 3–9; 2 Maccabees 2:19; 5:27; 8; 10–15*

### JUDITH

Widow from Judah who cut off the head of Nebuchadnezzar's general, Holofernes. She decapitated him with his scimitar.
*See pp.254–55*
*Judith 1:16*

### JULIUS

Roman centurion charged to take Paul to Caesarea from Rome.
*Acts 27:1, 3, 42–44*

### JUSTUS

Man who Paul stayed with in Corinth.
*Acts 18:7*

# K

### KETURAH

Abraham's second wife, after Sarah's death.
*Genesis 25:1*

### KISH

Father of King Saul.
*1 Samuel 9:1*

### KOHATH

Son of Levi. He was the ancestor of Moses.
*Exodus 6:16; Numbers 3:17*

### KORAH

• Levite who with Dathan and Abiram conspired against Moses and Aaron. He died because of his rejection of God's chosen leaders.
*Numbers 16*

• Son of Levi, whose descendants were singers in the Temple.
*1 Chronicles 6:37; Psalms 44–49*

# L

### LABAN

Rebecca's brother and Jacob's uncle, who tricked him into marrying his elder daughter Leah, instead of Rachel. Jacob was later able to cheat his uncle, with the result that his own flock of sheep and goats became larger and stronger

than his uncle's. When Jacob secretly left for Canaan, Laban gave chase but God warned him in a dream not to harm Jacob. They reconciled their differences and went their own ways.
*Genesis 24:29; 29–31*

## LAMECH
• Descendant of Cain.
*Genesis 4:18–24*
• Noah's father.
*Genesis 5:28–31*

## LAZARUS
• Brother of Martha and Mary, whom Jesus raised from the dead. His body had been in the tomb for four days when Jesus commanded the onlookers to roll away the stone in front of it. Lazarus walked free from the cave tomb.
*John 11:1–12:11*
• Beggar in Jesus' parable of the rich man and the beggar at his gate.
*Luke 16:19–31*

## LEAH
Elder daughter of Laban, who became Jacob's first wife and mother of six of his sons and his daughter, Dinah.
*Genesis 29:16–35*

## LEVI
• Third son of Jacob and Leah. He was cursed by his father for attacking the city of Shechem with his brother, Simeon, and for killing the male inhabitants.
*Genesis 29:34; 34:25–26*
• *See* MATTHEW

## LOT
Abraham's nephew, who chose to live in Sodom after parting from Abraham. Later, when Sodom was destroyed, Lot escaped but his wife looked back at the city and was turned into a pillar of salt. Lot went to live in a cave with his daughters who, afraid of never finding husbands, seduced their father and bore him sons.
*Genesis 11:31–14:16; 19*

## LUKE
Greek author of the third Gospel and Acts. He is thought to have accompanied Paul on his missionary journeys.
*See pp.310–11*
*Luke 1–24; Colossians 4:14; 2 Timothy 4:11; Philemon v.24*

## LYDIA
Businesswoman from Thyatira (in modern Turkey), converted at Philippi.
*Acts 16:14–15, 40*

# M

## MAACAH / MAACHAH
Common Hebrew Bible name, used for both men and women.

## MAGDALENE  SEE MARY

## MAHER–SHALAL–HASH–BAZ
Son of the Prophet Isaiah.
*Isaiah 8:3–4*

## MALACHI
Author of the book of Malachi; the name may simply mean "my messenger."
*See pp.244–45*

## MALCHUS
Servant of the High Priest. Peter cut off his ear as Jesus was arrested in the Garden of Gethsemane. According to Luke, Jesus then healed his ear.
*John 18:10*

## MANASSEH
• Joseph's son, and ancestor of one of the tribes of Israel.
*Genesis 41:51; 48:1*
• Son of Hezekiah, king of Judah c.697–42BCE. He encouraged pagan worship and persecuted prophets, but 2 Chronicles records his repentance.
*2 Kings 21:1–18; 2 Chronicles 33:1–20*

## MAMRE
Amorite friend of Abraham. It was also the name of the place in Hebron where Mamre lived.
*Genesis 14:13, 24; 18:1*

## MANOAH
Father of Samson, told by an angel that his barren wife would bear him a son.
*Judges 13*

## MARK
Author of the second Gospel. The Mark named is not further identified. It was a common name: there is a Mark in 1 Peter, and a John Mark in Acts, but the author of the Gospel may

be different from these.
*See pp.308–09*
*Mark 14:51–52; Acts 4, 12, 13; Colossians 4; Philemon; 2 Timothy 4*

## MARTHA
Sister of Mary and Lazarus in whose house Jesus stayed in Bethany. Jesus restored her brother Lazarus to life.
*Luke 10:38–42; John 11:1–12:2*

## MARY
• Mother of Jesus and wife of Joseph.
*See pp.316–17*
• Sister of Martha and Lazarus who anointed Jesus.
*John 11:1–44, 12:1–8*
• Mary Magdalene, who was healed by Jesus and was first to see him after his Resurrection.
*Luke 8:2; 10:42; John 11:2; 20:11–18*
• Mother of Mark.
*Acts 12:12*
• Mother of James; wife of Clopas, who are probably the same person.
*Matthew 27:56; 28:1, Mark 16:1; John 19:25*

## MATTATHIAS
Founder of the Maccabean dynasty; also known as the Hasmonean dynasty.
*1 Maccabees 2*

## MATTHEW
• Son of Alphaeus, also called Levi. Matthew was a tax collector and became one of the 12 Apostles.
*Matthew 9:9, 10:3; Luke 5:27–32;*
• Author of the first Gospel, whom some have identified with the Matthew above.
*See pp.306–07*

## MATTHIAS
Chosen to take the place of Judas Iscariot as the twelfth apostle.
*Acts 1:21–26*

## MELCHIZEDEK
Priest and king of Salem, who met and blessed Abraham. He is mentioned in the New Testament when Jesus is described as a High Priest and king like Melchizedek.
*Genesis 14:18–20; Psalm 110:4; Hebrews 5:6–10*

## MENAHEM
One of the last kings of Israel c.745–36BCE, who approved idol worship. When Assyria invaded, he paid the

Assyrian king a large sum of money
to remain in power.
*2 Kings 15:14–22*

MEPHI-BOSHETH
Grandson of Saul and son of Jonathan,
who was honored by David for
Jonathan's sake.
*2 Samuel 4:4; 9; 16:1; 19:24–30; 21:7*

MERAB
Saul's daughter, promised to David but
given to another man instead.
*1 Samuel 14:49; 18:17–19*

MERARI
One of Levi's sons. He went on
to form one of the three groups of
Levites, the Merarites.
*Exodus 6:16; Numbers 3:17, 33–37*

MESHACH
One of Daniel's three companions
in exile at Babylon who was thrown
into the furnace but remained
unharmed.
*Daniel 1:7; 2:49; 3:13–30*

METHUSELAH
Long-lived (969 years) grandfather of
Noah.
*Genesis 5:22–27*

MICAH
Prophet in Isaiah's time.
*See pp.234–35*

MICAIAH
Prophet who was summoned by Ahab
for prophesying the King's defeat by
the Assyrians. Ahab threw Micaiah into
prison, but the prophet's words came true.
*1 Kings 22:9–28; 2 Chronicles 18:7–27*

MICHAEL
Archangel described in Daniel as being
the guardian of the Jewish people.
*See pp.42–43*
*Daniel 10:21; 12:1; Jude 1:9; Revelation 12:7*

MICHAL
Saul's daughter, the wife of David, who
helped him escape Saul, but disapproved
of him dancing before the Ark. She
was condemned never to have a child.
*1 Samuel 14:49; 18:20–29; 25:44;*
*2 Samuel 3:13–14; 6:16–23*

MILCAH
Daughter of Haran, who married her
uncle, Nahor. Rebecca was her
granddaughter.
*Genesis 11:29; 22:20; 24:24*

MIRIAM
Elder sister of Moses and Aaron. She
sang in triumph at the crossing of the
Red/Reed Sea when the Israelites left
Egypt. She became jealous of Moses
and was temporarily punished with a
skin disease for rebellion against Moses,
who asked God to forgive and heal her.
*Exodus 15:20–21; Numbers 12; 20:1*

MOAB
Lot's son, the ancestor of the Moabites.
*Genesis 19:36–37*

MORDECAI
Uncle to Queen Esther, who prompted
her to act and save the Jewish people
from massacre after he had heard of a
plot to kill them.
*Esther 2:5–10:3*

MOSES
Great leader and lawgiver of the Jewish
people.
*See pp.50–51*

# N

NAAMAN
Syrian army commander healed of
leprosy by Elisha after his king sent him
to Israel to find a cure.
*2 Kings 5*

NABAL
Husband of Abigail, the landowner who
refused David's request for hospitality.
David planned to punish him, but
Abigail appeased him. Nabal died soon
after, and Abigail became David's wife.
*1 Samuel 25*

NABOTH
Man who was killed so that Ahab could
seize the vineyard he coveted. Ahab's
wife, Jezebel, persuaded religious elders to
convict Naboth of blasphemy. He was
stoned to death, and Elijah warned Ahab
that he and his family would be punished.
*1 Kings 21*

NADAB
• Eldest son of Aaron, who became
a priest but later died for dishonoring
God.
*Exodus 6:23; Leviticus 10:1–2*
• Successor to his father, Jeroboam I,
as king of Israel (903–02BCE). He was
assassinated by Baasha.
*1 Kings 14:20; 15:25–28*

NAHASH
Ammonite king who became the first
victim of the union of the Israelites
under Saul and his army.
*1 Samuel 11; 12:12; 1 Chronicles 19:1–2*

NAHOR
Abraham's brother, and son of Terah.
He settled at Haran with his wife,
Milcah. He became the ancestor of
several Aramaean tribes.
*Genesis 11:27*

NAHUM
Prophet who prophesied against Nineveh.
*See pp.238–39*

NAOMI
Mother-in-law of Ruth, from Bethlehem.
She returned to Bethlehem with Ruth
after the death of her two sons.
*See pp.110–11*
*Ruth 1–4*

NAPTHALI
One of Jacob's 12 sons, ancestor of
one of the tribes of Israel.
*Genesis 30:8; 49:21*

NATHAN
Prophet who delivered God's judgment to
David after he and Bathsheba committed
adultery. He helped make Solomon king.
*2 Samuel 7:1–17; 12:1–15; 1 Kings 1;*
*1 Chronicles 17:1–15*

NATHANAEL OF CANA
One of the 12 Apostles named in John's
Gospel. He is probably the Bartholemew
mentioned by the other evangelists.
*John 1:45; 21:2*

NEBUCHADNEZZAR /
NEBUCHADREZZAR
King of Babylon who captured
Jerusalem and took the Judeans into exile
after extensive campaigns in Palestine

and Egypt. Daniel interpreted his dreams and was made one of the king's courtiers. He was a great builder of temples, canals, and palaces. According to Daniel, God humbled him with a temporary madness after which he honored God.

*2 Kings 24–25; 2 Chronicles 36:5–13; Jeremiah 21:2–52:30; Ezekiel 26:7; 29:18–20; 30:10; Daniel 1–4*

### NEBUZARADAN
Nebuchadnezzar's head guard, who had the responsibility of sending the Judeans into exile in Babylon after Jerusalem had been captured. He burned down the Temple, and the city was reduced to ruins. He treated Jeremiah kindly, allowing him to stay in Judah.

*2 Kings 25:8–20; Jeremiah 39:9–40:5*

### NECO / NECHO II
Egyptian pharaoh c.610–595BCE, who killed Josiah in battle at Megiddo, deposed Jehoahaz, and put Jehoiachim on Judah's throne. He was defeated by Nebuchadnezzar in 605BCE, after which Judah came under Babylonian power.

*2 Kings 23:29; 24:7; 2 Chronicles 35:20–36:4*

### NEHEMIAH
Cup-bearer to the Persian king, who returned to Jerusalem and organized the rebuilding of the city walls.

*See pp.162–63*

### NICODEMUS
Pharisee who came secretly to Jesus, who told him that a person could only enter the kingdom of God if he or she is reborn. Nicodemus later defended Jesus when the Pharisees called for his arrest. He helped Joseph of Arimathea bury Jesus' body and brought spices and oils to embalm the body.

*John 3:1–21; 7:50–51; 19:39–40*

### NIMROD
Grandson of Ham and a great hunter.

*Genesis 10:8–9*

### NOAH
Godly man in a time of great evil who was saved from the Flood that destroyed the rest of humanity.

*See pp.32–33*

## O

### OBADIAH
• Steward from Ahab's household who hid 100 prophets of God in an attempt to save them from the Jezebel.

*1 Kings 18:1–16*

• Prophet whose message against Edom is recorded in the book of Obadiah.

*See pp.228–29*

### OBED
Son of Ruth and Boaz, grandfather of David.

*Ruth 4:17*

### OBED–EDOM
Philistine in whose house the Ark of the Covenant remained after Uzzah's death.

*2 Samuel 6:10–12; 1 Chronicles 13:13–14*

### OG
Amorite king of Bashan, east of the Jordan. He was conquered by the Israelites and his land given to the tribe of Manasseh.

*Numbers 21:33; Deuteronomy 3:1–13; Nehemiah 9:22*

### OMRI
Powerful king of Israel who made Samaria his capital. He reigned for 12 years, c.885–73BCE. He made an alliance with the king of Sidon, whose daughter Jezebel he brought to Israel as a wife for his son Ahab. Omri tolerated worship of Baal.

*1 Kings 16:15–28*

### ONAN
Judah's son, who refused to follow his father's instructions to give children to his dead brother's wife, Tamar.

*Genesis 38:4–9*

### ONESIMUS
Runaway slave, owned by Philemon, who became a Christian and helped Paul in prison. Paul sent Onesimus back to his owner with a letter asking him to be pardoned, set free, and sent back to Paul.

*See pp.438–39*

*Colossians 4:9; Philemon vv.10–18*

### ORPAH
Moabite daughter-in-law of Naomi, who remained in Moab.

*Ruth 1:4–15*

### OTHNIEL
One of the first judges in Israel. He stopped the Israelites from worship of Baal and defeated the Mespotamian king, Cushan–Rishathaim.

*See pp.104–05*

*Joshua 15:16–17; Judges 3:7–11*

## P

### PASHUR
Priest who put Jeremiah in the stocks for saying that Jerusalem would be destroyed.

*Jeremiah 20:1–6*

### PAUL / SAUL
Apostle to the Gentiles.

*See pp.390–91, 396–97, 400–01, 408–09*

### PEKAH
Captain in Pekahiah's army who seized the throne of Israel from Pekahiah c.735BCE, and worshiped idols. He was murdered by Hoshea three years later.

*2 Kings 15:25–16:5; 2 Chronicles 28*

### PEKAHIAH
King of Israel c.736–35BCE, assassinated by Pekah.

*2 Kings 15:22–26*

### PENINNAH
Elkanah's second wife, who taunted the childless Hannah.

*1 Samuel 1:2–4*

### PETER
Apostle and leader of the early Church.

*See pp.386–87*

### PHILEMON
Christian owner of the slave Onesimus, to whom Paul wrote his letter.

*See pp.438–39*

*Philemon*

### PHILIP
• One of the 12 Apostles, he came from Bethsaida in Galilee.

*Matthew 10:3; John 1:43–48; 6:5–7; 12:21–22; 14:8–9; Acts 1:13*

• Son of Herod the Great and first husband of Herodias.

*Mark 6:17*

• Second son of Herod, tetrarch of Iturea.
*Luke 3:1*
• Deacon and evangelist of the early
Church. Paul stayed with him in Caesarea.
*See pp.388–89*
*Acts 6:5; 8:4–40; 21:8–9*

## PHINEHAS
• Priest and grandson of Aaron, who
killed some Israelites when they began
worshiping idols instead of God.
*Exodus 6:25; Numbers 25:7–13; 31:6;*
*Joshua 22:13; Judges 20:28*
• Son of Eli, killed by the Philistines
when they captured the Ark of the
Covenant.
*1 Samuel 4:11*

## PHOEBE
Christian woman known by Paul who
worked in a church in Cenchreae, near
Corinth. Benefactor of the early Church.
*See pp.428–29*
*Romans 16:1–2*

## PILATE
Roman procurator of Judea from 26–36CE.
Pontius Pilate presided over the trial
of Jesus.
*Matthew 27:11–26; Mark 15:1–15; Luke 3:1;*
*13:1; 23:1–25; John 18:28–19:16*

## POTIPHAR
Officer in the pharaoh's guard who
bought Joseph as a slave. Potiphar's
wife wanted Joseph to sleep with
her. He refused and was imprisoned,
charged with rape.
*Genesis 37:36; 39*

## PRISCILLA SEE AQUILA & PRISCILLA

## PUBLIUS
Elder on the island of Malta whose father
Paul healed after being shipwrecked on
the island.
*Acts 28:7*

## PUL I SEE TIGLATH–PILESER III

# Q

## QUIRINIUS
Governor of the province of Syria at the
time of the census when Jesus was born.
*Luke 2:2*

# R

## RABSHAKEH
Leader of delegation sent by Sennacherib
to negotiate with Hezekiah, king of
Judah, and to intimidate the people
when Jerusalem was under siege.

## RACHEL
Laban's daughter. She married Jacob,
who, in order to marry her, had worked
for seven years without pay. The mother
of Joseph and Benjamin, she died giving
birth to Benjamin.
*Genesis 29:9–31:35; 35:16–20*

## RAHAB
Prostitute from Jericho who hid Joshua's
two spies. In return, the spies promised
that no harm would come to her and
her family when Jericho was captured.
*Joshua 2:1–21; 6:22–23*

## REBEKAH / REBECCA
Wife of Isaac, brought to him by
Abraham's servant, Eliezer, and mother
of twin boys, Esau and Jacob. Jacob
(the younger) was her favorite, and she
tricked Isaac into blessing him instead
of Esau.
*See pp.40–41*
*Genesis 24; 25:19–26:16; 27*

## REHOBOAM
Solomon's son under whom the
kingdom divided. The northern
kingdom became known as Israel and
the southern kingdom as Judah. He
was king c.924–07BCE.
*1 Kings 11:43–12:24; 14:21–31;*
*2 Chronicles 9:31–12:16*

## REUBEN
Eldest of Jacob's sons, who tried to
save Joseph when his brothers were
plotting to kill him. Ancestor of one
of the tribes of Israel.
*Genesis 29:32; 37:21–22; 42:22, 37; 49:3*

## REUEL SEE JETHRO

## REZIN
Syria's last king, who made a pact with
King Pekah of Israel. He was killed by
Tiglath–Pileser III of Assyria.
*2 Kings 15:37–16:6*

## RHODA
Girl who was so astounded to hear Peter's
voice at the door after he had escaped
from prison that she forgot to let him in.
*Acts 12:13–14*

## RIZPAH
Saul's concubine, whose sons David
gave to the Gibeonites to put to death.
*2 Samuel 3:7; 21:8–12*

## RUTH
Moabite woman whose love for her
mother-in-law, Naomi, led her to
emigrate to Bethlehem. She became
the wife of Boaz and had a son, Obed,
who was the grandfather of King David.
*See pp.110–11*
*Ruth 1–4*

# S

## SALOME
• Daughter of Herodias, not named in
the Bible. Salome's dance in front of
Herod Antipas so pleased him that he
promised her anything she desired.
Herodias, angered by John the Baptist's
public criticism of her marriage to
Antipas, suggested she demand the
head of John the Baptist.
*Matthew 14:1–12; Mark 6:14–29*
• Mother of James and John; she
accompanied Jesus and the disciples from
Galilee. She was present at the Crucifixion
and on the Resurrection morning. She
may possibly have been the sister of
Jesus' mother, Mary.
*Mark 15:40; 16:1*

## SAMSON
Champion of Israel against the
Philistines in the time of the Judges,
famous for his strength.
*See p.107*
*Judges 13–16*

## SAMUEL
Priest and leader who anointed Israel's
first two kings, Saul and David.
*See pp.118–19*
*1 Samuel 1–4; 7:3–16:13; 19:18–22; 25:1*

## SANBALLAT
Persistent Samaritan opponent of
Nehemiah's attempt to rebuild the

walls of Jerusalem.
*Nehemiah 2:10, 19; 4:1–9; 6:1–4; 13:28*

## SAPPHIRA
With her husband Ananias she was guilty of deceiving the Church.
*Acts 5:1–11*

## SARAH
• Wife of Abraham, who remained childless until old age, when she gave birth to Isaac. Sarah sent her maid Hagar, together with Abraham's son, Ishmael, away after Isaac's birth. When she died, Abraham bought a cave near Hebron as her burial chamber.
*See pp.38–39*
*Genesis 11:31–12:20; 16:1–18:15; 20:1–21:10; 23*
• Daughter of Raguel who married Tobias.
*Tobit 3, 7, 8, 10–12*

## SAUL
First king of the united Israel c.1050–1010BCE.
*See pp.120–121*

## SENNACHERIB
King of Assyria (705–681BCE) whose army shut Hezekiah up in Jerusalem. On Isaiah's advice, Hezekiah refused to surrender, and the Assyrian army came under attack from the Egyptians from the south. Sennacherib returned to Assyria, where he was assassinated by two of his sons.
*2 Kings 18:13–19:37; 2 Chronicles 32:1–23; Isaiah 36–37*

## SERGIUS PAULUS
Proconsul of Cyprus, who asked to hear Paul's message. He was influenced by a magician named Elymas.
*Acts 13:7*

## SETH
Third son of Adam and Eve, who was born after Cain had murdered Abel.
*Genesis 4:25*

## SHADRACH
One of Daniel's three companions in exile at Babylon who was thrown into the furnace, but remained unscathed.
*Daniel 1:7; 2:49; 3:13–30*

## SHALLUM
• Usurping king of Israel who reigned

for only one month c.745BCE before being assassinated by Menahem.
*2 Kings 15:10–15*
• One of King Josiah's sons; *see* JEHOAHAZ.

## SHALMANESER V
Successor to Tiglath-Pileser III of Assyria, who captured Samaria and took the Israelites into exile. Ruled c.727–22BCE.
*2 Kings 17:3–6*

## SHAMGAR
One of Israel's judges.
*Judges 3:31; 5:6*

## SHAPHAN
Official of Josiah who reported to him the discovery of the book of God's Law.
*2 Kings 22; 2 Chronicles 34:8–18*

## SHEBA
• The Queen of Sheba (part of ancient Ethiopia) is not named in the Bible but in Muslim legends is known as Balkis or Bilkis. She visited Solomon to verify his riches and wisdom and gave him gifts of gold and spices.
*See pp.130–31*
*1 Kings 10:1–13; 2 Chronicles 9:1–12*
• Benjaminite in the time of David, who rebelled against David and was subsequently besieged by David's army in the town of Abel of Beth-Maachah. To save their city, the inhabitants cut off Sheba's head and threw it to the attackers.
*2 Samuel 20*

## SHEBNA
State official under Hezekiah who talked with King Sennacherib's Assyrian delegation.
*2 Kings 18:18–19:7; Isaiah 22:15–25; 36:2–37:7*

## SHECHEM
Son of King Hamor, who raped Jacob's daughter, Dinah.
*Genesis 34:1–26*

## SHEM
Eldest of Noah's three sons.
*Genesis 6:10; 7:13; 9:18; 10:1, 21–31; 11:10–11*

## SHESHBAZZAR / SANABASSAR
Led the exiled Jews back to Jerusalem c.537BCE after the Persian king Cyrus allowed them to return. Sheshbazzar

laid the foundations for the Second Temple in Jerusalem.
*Ezra 1:8; 5:14; 1 Esdras 2:12*

## SHIMEI
Benjamite who cursed David at the time of Absalom's rebellion and accused David of murdering Saul.
*2 Samuel 16:5; 19:16–23; 1 Kings 2:8–9*

## SHISHAK / SHESHONK
Egyptian pharaoh c.945–924BCE.
*1 Kings 11:40; 2 Chronicles 12:2–9*

## SIHON
Amorite king east of the Jordan River in the 13th century BCE. His land was defeated by the Israelites after he refused to allow Moses and his people to pass through to reach Canaan.
*Numbers 21:21–35; 32:33; Deuteronomy 2:24–35; 1 Kings 4:19; Nehemiah 9:22*

## SILAS / SILVANUS
Leader of the Jerusalem church who accompanied Paul on his missionary travels and acted as his secretary for some of the letters to the churches.
*Acts 15:22–17:15; 18:5; 2 Corinthians 1:19; 1 Thessalonians 1:1; 2 Thessalonians 1:1; 1 Peter 5:12*

## SIMEON
• One of Jacob's 12 sons, ancestor of one of the tribes of Israel, who was left as a hostage with Joseph in Egypt. He and his brother Levi avenged the rape of their sister, Dinah, by the Shechemites. Jacob rebuked them on his deathbed.
*Genesis 29:33; 34:25; 42:24; 49:5; Joshua 19:1–9*
• Devout old man in the New Testament who gave two prophesies about Jesus. In the Temple he held the infant Jesus in his arms and gave praise to God.
*Luke 2:25–35*

## SIMON
• Simon Peter; *see* PETER.
• Simon the Zeal, one of the 12 Apostles.
*Matthew 10:4; Acts 1:13*
• One of Jesus' brothers or half-brothers.
*Matthew 13:55*
• Simon the leper, to whose house at Bethany Jesus was invited. While

Jesus was there, a woman anointed
his head with oils.
*Matthew 26:6; Mark 14:3*
• Pharisee who invited Jesus to his house
where a woman wept at Jesus' feet,
then dried them with her hair.
*Luke 7:40–44*
• Simon of Cyrene, who helped Jesus
carry his cross.
*Matthew 27:32; Mark 15:21–22; Luke 23:26*
• Simon Magus. He tried to buy the
gift of the Spirit from the Apostles
but was told that God's power could
not be bought.
*See pp.378–79*
*Acts 8:9–24*
• Tanner in whose house at Joppa Peter
had his vision.
*Acts 9:43*

### SISERA
Canaanite army commander who
made life miserable for the Israelites
for many years. He was killed by Jael,
who drove a tent peg through his
head after he took refuge in her tent,
having been defeated by Deborah
and Barak.
*Judges 4; 5:20, 26*

### SOLOMON
Son of David and Bathsheba who became
king of Israel (c.970–30BCE).
*See pp.130–33*

### SOSTHENES
Ruler of the synagogue at Corinth,
who was attacked after failing to
persuade the Roman governor Gallio
to imprison Paul.
*Acts 18:17*

### STEPHANAS
He was among the few Corinthians
to be baptized by Paul personally.
*1 Corinthians 1:16; 16:15*

### STEPHEN
One of seven deacons chosen to take
care of practical matters in the church at
Jerusalem. He became the first Christian
martyr, stoned to death for speaking
against the Temple and against the Law
and customs of Moses. Saul (Paul),
persecuting Christians at this time, was
a witness to Stephen's death.
*Acts 6, 7*

### SUSANNA
Wife of the wealthy Joakim, who was
tricked by two elders wishing to have
intercourse with her. They said she had
been with a younger man, and for this
she was condemned to death. But Daniel
saved her by questioning the elders,
and finding out they were liars when
each gave a different answer.
*See pp.254–55*
*Susanna*

# T

### TABITHA
Woman from Joppa noted for her good
works. She was raised from the dead
by Peter. Her Greek name was Dorcas.
*Acts 9:36–41*

### TAMAR
• Daughter-in-law of Judah, who bore
him twin sons, Perez and Zerah.
*Genesis 38:6–30; Ruth 4:12*
• David's daughter, who was raped
by Amnon, her half-brother. She
was avenged by her brother Absalom,
who planned Amnon's death two
years later.
*2 Samuel 13*

### TERAH
Father of Abraham. He led the
migration from Ur with Abraham,
but instead of continuing to Canaan,
he settled in Haran.
*Genesis 11:27–32*

### TERTULLUS
Orator hired by the High Priest Ananias
to lay accusations against Paul.
*Acts 24:1–8*

### THADDEUS
Named as one of the 12 Apostles in
Matthew and Mark's gospel. Perhap
the same as Judas. *See also* JUDAS.
*Matthew 10; Mark 3; Luke 6; Acts 1*

### THEOPHILUS
Roman to whom Luke's Gospel and
Acts were addressed. He may have been
high ranking. The name means "lover
[or friend] of God".
*Luke 1:3; Acts 1:1*

### THOMAS
One of the 12 Apostles, known as
Didymus, the twin. Absent when the
others first saw the risen Christ, he
would not believe them, saying he had
to touch the wounds before he could
believe that Jesus had risen. Jesus then
appeared to him and Thomas believed.
According to tradition, he became a
missionary to India.
*John 11:16; 14:5–7; 20:24; 21:1–2; Acts 1:13*

### TIBERIUS
Roman emperor in Jesus' lifetime. He
ruled from 14 to 37CE. In the Gospels
he is simply referred to as Caesar.
*Luke 3:1*

### TIGLATH-PILESER III
Powerful king of Assyria to whom Ahaz
turned for help against Syria and Israel.
Also known as Pul (745–27BCE).
*2 Kings 15:19; 16:7–10; 2 Chronicles 28:20*

### TIMOTHY
Paul's companion and fellow missionary.
*See pp.446–447*

### TITUS
Paul's companion and fellow missionary.
*See pp.446–447*

### TOBIAH
He opposed Nehemiah's attempt to
rebuild the walls of Jerusalem.
*Nehemiah 2:10; 4:3, 7; 6:1, 12–14; 13:4*

### TOBIAS
Tobit's son.
*Tobit 1:9–14:15*

### TOBIT
Blinded accidentally for eight years after
assisting Jews exiled by the Assyrians,
he was healed by a slave brought by his
son, Tobias.
*See pp.254–55*
*Tobit 1–14*

### TROPHIMUS
Ephesian Christian who went with Paul
to Jerusalem.
*Acts 20:4; 21:29; 2 Timothy 4:20*

### TUBAL-CAIN
Lamech's son by his second wife, Zilpah.
*Genesis 4:22*

## TYCHICHUS

Christian who went with Paul on his last visit to Jerusalem. He was a messenger for Paul when the Apostle was imprisoned in Rome, taking letters to Colossae and Ephesus.
*Acts 20:4; Ephesians 6:21–22; Colossians 4:7–9:2; Timothy 4:12; Titus 3:12*

# U

## URIAH

• Hittite warrior in David's army and Bathsheba's husband. He was sent to his death by David.
*2 Samuel 11*
• Priest in Jerusalem who built an altar for the Temple in Jerusalem.
*2 Kings 16:10–11*
• Prophet from Kiriath-jearim in the time of Jeremiah who was put to death by Jehoiachim for speaking out against the people of Judah.
*Jeremiah 26:20*

## UZZAH

Man in the time of King David who touched the Ark of the Covenant and was struck dead by God as a consequence.
*2 Samuel 6:3–8*

## UZZIAH

Godly king of Judah (eighth century BCE) who brought peace and prosperity. He was later punished with a skin disease after offering incense in the temple, something that only a priest was allowed to do. He was also called Azariah.
*2 Kings 14:21; 15:1–7; 2 Chronicles 26; Isaiah 6*

# V

## VASHTI

Queen whom the Persian king Ahasuerus divorced after she had disobeyed him.
*Esther 1:9–2:17*

# X

XERXES I SEE AHASUERUS

# Z

## ZACCHAEUS

Tax collector who climbed a tree at Jericho to get a glimpse of Jesus among the crowds. Jesus asked to come to his house, despite the disapproving crowds who maintained that Zacchaeus was a sinner. Zacchaeus was a changed man as a result and gave half of his property to the poor.
*Luke 19:1–10*

## ZADOK

Priest at David's court with Abiathar. After David's death he anointed Solomon king and was rewarded with the position of High Priest.
*2 Samuel 15:24–36; 17:15; 19:11; 1 Kings 1:7, 32; 2:35*

## ZEBEDEE

Father of the Apostles James and John and husband of Salome.
*Matthew 4:21–22*

## ZEBULUN

One of Jacob's 12 sons, who became ancestor of one of the Twelve Tribes of Israel.
*Genesis 30:19–20; 49:13*

## ZECHARIAH / ZACHARIAS

• Prophet after the Exile.
*See pp.242–43*
• King of Israel who reigned for six months c.745BCE before he was murdered by Shallum.
*2 Kings 14:29; 15:8–12*
• Prophet who spoke against the people.
*2 Chronicles 24:20*
• Father of John the Baptist, struck dumb when he refused to believe the angel telling him that his wife, Elizabeth, was going to give birth to a baby boy.
*Luke 1*

## ZEDEKIAH

Last king of Judah c.597–87/86BCE, whose rebellion brought Nebuchadnezzar's Babylonian army and destruction on Jerusalem. He was captured and taken as a prisoner to Babylon.
*2 Kings 24:17–25:7; 2 Chronicles 36:10; Jeremiah 21; 32:1–5, 34; 37:1–39:1*

## ZEPHANIAH

Prophet of the seventh century BCE.
*See pp.240–41*

## ZERAH

• Son of Judah and Tamar and twin of Perez. Forefather of the Judean clan of Zerahites.
*Numbers 26:20*
• Ethiopian who with a large Ethiopian and Libyan force invaded Judah.
*2 Chronicles 14:9–15*

## ZERUBBABEL

Leader of the exiles, who returned to Judah in 537BCE. He worked with Joshua as governor of Judea, and under their leadership the foundations for the new Temple in Jerusalem were laid.
*Ezra 2:2; 3:2–4:3; 5:2; Haggai 1–2; Zechariah 4*

## ZIBA

Saul's servant, who told David that his adopted son Mephi-bosheth was still alive.
*2 Samuel 9; 16:1–4; 19:17, 26–29*

## ZILPAH

Leah's servant, who bore Jacob two of his 12 sons, Gad and Asher.
*Genesis 19:24, 30:9–13*

## ZIMRI

Ruler of Israel for one week c.885BCE before being overthrown by Omri.
*1 Kings 16:15–20*

## ZIPPORAH

Jethro's daughter, who became the wife of Moses after he had escaped from Egypt. She bore him two sons.
*Exodus 2:21–22; 4:24–26; 18:2*

## ZOPHAR

One of Job's three friends.
*Job 2:11; 11; 20; 42:9*

# A-Z OF
# PLACES
## IN THE BIBLE

# A

### ABANA
One of the two rivers running through Damascus in Syria. Elisha's servant told the Syrian general Naaman to bathe in the Jordan River and be healed, but he despised the muddy Jordan when compared with the clear, flowing waters of Abana and Pharpar.
*2 Kings 5:12*

### ABEL OF BETH-MAACHAH
Town in the north of Israel, near Lake Huleh, to where Joab pursued Sheba. It was captured by Arameans of Damascus, and recaptured more than once.
*2 Samuel 20:14; 1 Kings 15:20*

### ABEL-MEHOLAH
Town where the Midianites fled after Gideon's attack. Hometown of Elisha.
*Judges 7:22; 1 Kings 19:16*

### ABILENE
Region northwest of Damascus, governed by Lysanias.
*Luke 3:1*

### ACHAIA
Roman province of southern Greece, governed from Corinth.
*Acts 18:12; 2 Corinthians 9:2*

### ACHOR
Valley near Jericho. Achan was killed here for disobeying God's command.
*Joshua 7:24–26; Isaiah 65:10; Hosea 2:15*

### ADAM
Place where the Jordan River was blocked, thus allowing the Israelites to cross into the Promised Land.
*Joshua 3:16*

### ADMAH
One of a group of five cities that included Sodom and Gomorrah. The kings of these cities formed an alliance and rebelled against four northern kings in the time of Abraham, whose nephew Lot was captured in the ensuing battle.
*Genesis 10:19; 14:2*

### ADRAMYTTIUM
Port near Troy and Troas on the west coast of modern-day Turkey. A ship from here took Paul and his fellow prisoners on the first stage of their journey to Rome.
*Acts 27:2*

### ADULLAM
Where David took refuge in a "cave" (or a fort) while evading King Saul. His family and 400 outlaws joined him, and three soldiers risked their lives to bring him water from the well at Bethlehem held by the Philistines.
*1 Samuel 22:1; 2 Samuel 23:13*

### AHAVA
Name of a canal and a region in Babylonia where Ezra assembled the second party of returning Jewish exiles. Before setting off on the 900 mile (1,448km) trip to Jerusalem, they prayed for protection.
*Ezra 8:15, 21, 31*

### AI
Site of one of Joshua's battles in the Promised Land. Its name means "the ruin."
*Joshua 7, 8*

### AIJALON
Amorite town of the tribe of Dan but given to the Levites. Joshua fought a battle against the Amorites in a nearby valley.
*Joshua 10, 19:42; 21:24; Judges 1:35; 2 Chronicles 11:10*

### AKKAD
City on the Euphrates in ancient Babylonia, center of a major empire and civilization 2360–2180BCE.
*Genesis 10:10*

### ALEXANDRIA
Important Egyptian seaport situated on the Nile Delta, founded by Alexander the Great. Under the Ptolemies it was the capital of Egypt and was a great center of culture, learning, and trade. This continued into Roman times, when a museum of arts and sciences, and a great library was located here. The city contained a large Jewish community, and this was where Apollos, an important teacher in the early Church, came from. It was here that the Hebrew Bible was first translated into Greek (the Septuagint).
*Acts 6:9; 18:24; 27:6; 28:11*

### AMMON
East Jordanian state whose capital was Rabbah (modern Amman).
*See also RABBAH*

### AMPHIPOLIS
Town in northern Greece through which Paul passed on his missionary travels.
*Acts 17:1*

### ANATHOTH
Town north of Jerusalem belonging to the Levites. Jeremiah's birthplace.
*Joshua 21:18; Jeremiah 1:1*

### ANTIOCH IN PISIDIA
City in Asia Minor (modern Turkey) that Paul and Barnabas visited on their first missionary journey. They were thrown out of the city by angry Jews who realized that non-Jews were responding to their message. Paul revisited the city a few years later as part of his mission to encourage the new Christians in their faith.
*Acts 13:14*

### ANTIOCH IN SYRIA
Modern Antakya, on the border of Turkey and Syria. Named after Antiochus, the father of one of Alexander's generals. Under the Romans, this city became the capital of the province of Syria, the third

largest city of the empire. Well-known for its culture, it was one of the earliest great centers of Gentile Christianity, where the followers of Jesus were first called Christians.
*See pp.392–93; Acts 11:19–27; 13:1; 15:35*

## ANTIPATRIS
Town named in honor of King Herod's father, Antipater. Paul spent the night here when taken from Jerusalem to Caesarea while his life was under threat.
*Acts 23:31*

## APHEK
Town where the Philistines camped and concentrated their forces before the battle in which they captured the Ark of the Covenant from the Israelites. Much later this town became Antipatris.
*1 Samuel 4:1*

## AR
Moabite city on the Arnon River. During their time in the desert the Israelites were told to leave this city in peace. God had given it to the Moabites, Lot's descendants.
*Numbers 21:15; Deuteronomy 2:9; Isaiah 15:1*

## ARABAH
The rift valley of the Jordan River, stretching from the Sea of Galilee in the north to the Dead Sea in the south. The "Sea of Arabah" is the Dead Sea.
*Deuteronomy 1:1; 3:17*

## ARAD
Canaanite city in the Negev (or Negeb), captured and occupied by the Israelites.
*Joshua 12:14*

## ARARAT
Place where Noah's ark came to rest after the waters of the Flood had subsided. The area, called Urartu in Assyrian inscriptions, is in Armenia, on the borders of Turkey and Russia. Mount Ararat itself is an extinct volcano.
*Genesis 8:4; Jeremiah 51:27*

## AREOPAGUS
Hill northwest of the Acropolis in Athens from which the Council of the Areopagus took its name.
*Acts 17*

## ARGOB
Part of the kingdom of Og in Bashan, located east of the Jordan. A strong, fertile region with many significant towns, it was given to the half-tribe of Manasseh.
*Deuteronomy 3:4, 13; 1 Kings 4:13*

## ARIMATHEA
Home of Joseph, secret disciple of Jesus. After the Crucifixion, Joseph had Jesus' body placed in his rock tomb.
*Matthew 27:57; Mark 15:43*

## ARMAGEDDON SEE MEGIDDO

## ARNON
River that runs into the Dead Sea from the east (now Wadi Mujib). It formed the southern border between the Amorites and the Moabites.
*Numbers 21:13ff.; Isaiah 16:2*

## AROER
City lying on the north bank of the Arnon River, east of Jordan. Part of the Amorite kingdom and later of the tribe of Reuben. Aroer is also the name of a town in the Negev, south of Beersheba.
*Deuteronomy 2:36; 2 Kings 10:33*

## ASHDOD
One of the five major Philistine cities. The captured Ark of the Covenant was taken to Ashdod by the Philistines. In Isaiah's time the city fell to King Uzziah of Judah. It was later called Azotus and was restored by King Herod in New Testament times.
*1 Samuel 5; 2 Chronicles 26:6; Isaiah 20:1; Acts 8:40*

## ASHKELON
One of the five Philistine cities, situated on the coast of Israel between modern Jaffa and Gaza. Samson killed 30 men in Ashkelon to pay what he owed in a debt. Over the years the city was ruled by Assyria, Babylonia, and Tyre. It was the birthplace of Herod the Great.
*Judges 1:18; 14:19; 1 Samuel 6:17; Jeremiah 47:5–7*

## ASHTAROTH / ASHTEROTH-KARNAIM
City on the east of the Jordan, named after the Canaanite mother-goddess, Ashtar. Captured by Chedorlaomer in Abraham's time, it later became a capital of King Og of Bashan. It was one of the cities given to the Levites.
*Genesis 14:5; Deuteronomy 1:4; 1 Chronicles 6:71*

## ASIA
In Roman times, the western part of Asia Minor (modern Turkey) including a number of important Greek city-states. The Roman province of Asia included all the west coast, with its important city of Ephesus. Paul carried out much of his missionary work in this region.
*Acts 2:9; 19:10; Revelation 1:4, 11*

## ASSOS
Port of Mysia in the Roman province of Asia (Turkey) from which Paul sailed on his last journey to Jerusalem.
*Acts 20:13*

## ASSYRIA
Area in north Mesopotamia, home of a dominant empire. *See pp.142–43*

## ATAROTH
Town situated east of the Jordan, given to the tribe of Reuben.
*Numbers 32:3, 34*

## ATHENS
Capital of Greece. A model democracy and cultural center from the fifth century when the Parthenon was built. It was stripped in 86BCE by the Romans. In c.50CE, when Athens was still a great city of learning, Paul arrived here on his missionary travels and spoke before the Athenian council.
*Acts 17:15–34*

## ATTALIA
Port used by Paul on his first missionary journey. Modern-day Antalya on the south coast of Turkey.
*Acts 14:25*

## AZEKAH
Town to which Joshua pursued the Amorites. It later became a fortified city bordering Judah.
*Joshua 10:10; Jeremiah 34:7*

# B

## BABEL
City, probably Babylon. In the time after

the Flood, when everyone spoke only one language, the people built a great tower, which would reach to heaven. God confused their language so that they could not understand one another.
*Genesis 10:10; 11:1–9*

## BABYLON

City situated on the Euphrates River 50 miles (80km) south of modern-day Baghdad. Founded in the third millennium BCE, it became the capital of Babylonia and the Babylonian empire, which grew after the defeat of the Assyrians in 612BCE. In 597 and 586BCE, King Nebuchadnezzar of Babylon conquered Jerusalem, and the people of Judah were carried into exile, among them the prophets Ezekiel and Daniel. Persians took the city in 539BCE and from then it went into decline.
*See pp.146–49*
*Genesis 10:10, 2 Kings 24:1; 25:7–13; Isaiah 14:1–23; Daniel 1–6*

## BASHAN

Region east of the Sea of Galilee. The Israelites, on route from Egypt to Canaan, defeated King Og of Bashan, and his land was given to the tribe of Manasseh.
*Deuteronomy 3; Psalm 22:12; Isaiah 2:13*

## BEERSHEBA

Town on the edge of the Negev desert, named after the well dug by Abraham. Hagar came close to death in the desert of Beersheba. It is also mentioned in connection with Elijah and Amos. The phrase "from Dan to Beersheba" became a common way of referring to the whole land, from north to south.
*Genesis 21:14, 30–32; 26:23–33; 1 Kings 19:3; Amos 5:5*

## BEROEA

Greek city 50 miles (80km) north of Thessalonica where Paul preached as part of his mission. He was welcomed by the Bereans because they studied the Scriptures, but he was forced to leave after the Jews stirred up trouble against him.
*Acts 17:10–15; 20:4*

## BETHANY

Village near Jerusalem, on the road to Jericho, where Mary, Martha, and Lazarus lived. Jesus visited them often, and here he raised Lazarus from the grave.
*Matthew 26:6–13; 24:50; John 11; 12:1–9*

## BETHEL

Place situated 12 miles (19km) north of Jerusalem, where Jacob dreamed of a staircase leading up to heaven. God promised to give the land to Jacob's descendants, and Jacob called the place "Bethel" (house of God). When the kingdoms of Israel and Judah divided, King Jeroboam of Israel set up an altar and Golden Calf at Bethel so that people could worship there instead of Jerusalem.
*Genesis 28:10–22; Judges 1:22–26; 20:18; 1 Kings 12:25–33; 2 Kings 2; 17:28; Nehemiah 11:31*

## BETHESDA / BETHZATHA

Pool in Jerusalem where many sick came to be healed. Fed by a bubbling spring, it was believed to have healing powers. Here, Jesus healed a man who had been ill for 38 years.
*John 5:1–15*

## BETH-HORON (UPPER AND LOWER)

Two towns that controlled the Valley of Aijalon and the ancient trade-route passing through it. Here, Joshua pursued the Amorite kings who had attacked the town of Gibeon.
*Joshua 10:10; 16:3–5*

## BETHLEHEM

City in the Judean hills 5 miles (8km) south of Jerusalem. Jacob's wife, Rachel, was buried here, and it was where Ruth and Naomi settled. The birthplace of David, it was also here that the prophet Samuel chose David as the king to succeed Saul. The prophet Micah foretold the birth of the Messiah at Bethlehem.
*See pp.320–21; Genesis 35:19; Ruth 1; 1 Samuel 16; Micah 5:2; Matthew 2; Luke 2*

## BETHPHAGE

Small village near Bethany, where Jesus came on his last journey to Jerusalem. From here he sent two disciples to fetch the colt upon which he was to make his triumphant entry into Jerusalem.
*Matthew 21:1; Mark 11:1; Luke 19:29*

## BETHSAIDA

Fishing town on the north shore of Lake Galilee. Philip, Andrew, and Peter, the disciples of Jesus, came from here. In Bethsaida, Jesus cured a blind man and warned the people of God's judgment. Despite witnessing this miracle, the people would not change their ways.
*Matthew 11:21; Mark 8:22; John 1:44*

## BETH-SHAN

Ancient city in northern Palestine. The Israelites tried to drive the Canaanites out of this area, but failed. After Saul and Jonathan were killed by the Philistines on Mount Gilboa, their bodies were put on Beth-shan's walls, but they were later retrieved by men from Jabesh-gilead. The city, known by the Greek name of Scythopolis in New Testament times, became one of the cities of the Decapolis.
*Joshua 17:11, 16; Judges 1:27; 1 Samuel 31:10–13; 2 Samuel 21:12; 1 Kings 4:12*

## BETH-SHEMESH

Fortified town 12 miles (19km) west of Jerusalem. The Philistines returned the Ark of the Covenant to Beth-shemesh. Amaziah of Judah was captured in a battle near here by Jehoash, king of the Northern Kingdom of Israel.
*Joshua 21:16; 1 Samuel 6:9–21; 1 Kings 4:9; 2 Kings 14:11–13*

## BETH-ZUR

City of Judah, 4 miles (6km) north of Hebron, settled by the family of Caleb. One of the 15 cities fortified by King Rehoboam. Men from Beth-zur helped rebuild Jerusalem under Nehemiah's leadership. Situated on a hill top, it was the site of a great Jewish victory in the Maccabean revolt.
*Joshua 15:58; 1 Chronicles 2:45; 2 Chronicles 11:7; Nehemiah 3:16*

## BITHYNIA

Roman province in Asia Minor (modern Turkey), where Paul was forbidden to preach by the Holy Spirit. Peter sent his first letter to Christian believers living in Bithynia. Important center of Christianity.
*Acts 16:7; 1 Peter 1:1*

## BOZRAH

Ancient city in northern Edom, south-east of the Dead Sea. The Prophets foretold the city would be destroyed.

*Genesis 36:33; 1 Chronicles 1:44; Isaiah 34:6; 63:1; Jeremiah 49:13, 22; Amos 1:12*

# C

## CAESAREA
Mediterranean port on the coast of Palestine, built by Herod the Great and named after the Roman emperor Augustus Caesar. Home of Philip the evangelist and Cornelius, the Roman centurion who sent for Peter, asking him to explain God's message. Paul used this port many times on his missionary travels, and it was here that he was taken for trial before Felix since the Roman governors lived here rather than in Jerusalem. Paul spent two years in prison in this town, and from here he sailed for Rome after his appeal to Caesar.
*Acts 8:40; 9:30; 10; 11; 18:22; 21:8; 23:33–26:32*

## CAESAREA PHILIPPI
Town at the foot of Mount Hermon. A large temple was built here by Herod the Great in honor of Augustus Caesar. One of his sons, Philip, changed the town's name from Paneas to Caesarea, and it was known as Philip's Caesarea to distinguish it from the port (*see above*). It was here that Jesus asked his disciples, "Who do they say I am?"
*Matthew 16:13–16*

## CALAH
Ancient Mesopotamian city (modern Nimrud in Iraq) that became an important city of the Assyrian empire.
*Genesis 10:11–12*

## CANA
Village in Galilee where Jesus turned water into wine at a wedding. One of Jesus' 12 disciples, Nathanael, came from Cana.
*See p.375; John 2:1–11; 4:46–53; 21:2*

## CANAAN
Land promised to the Israelites by God.
*See p.95*

## CAPERNAUM
Important town from Roman times, on Lake Galilee. It was Jesus' base while he was teaching in Galilee and was also the home of Levi (Matthew) the tax collector. Jesus performed many miracles in Capernaum. In spite of Jesus' preaching to the people many would not heed his words, and he had to warn them of coming judgment.   *See p.341*
*Mark 1:21–34; 2:1–17; Luke 7:1–10; 10:15*

## CAPPADOCIA
Area of eastern Turkey, once a Roman province. Jews from Cappadocia heard Peter in Jerusalem on the Day of Pentecost. Later, Peter sent his first letter to the Christians in Cappadocia.
*Acts 2:9; 1 Peter 1:1*

## CARCHEMISH
Hittite city on the Euphrates River on the border between Turkey and Syria. Nebuchadnezzar, the Babylonian king, defeated the Egyptians here in 605BCE.
*2 Chronicles 35:20; Isaiah 10:9; Jeremiah 46:2*

## CARMEL
Mountain range near the Mediterranean port of Haifa. God's prophet Elijah challenged the prophets of Baal to a contest on Mount Carmel.
*1 Kings 18:19–46; 2 Kings 2:25; 4:25*

## CHALDEA
Ancient region of Babylonia; Abraham's family home.
*Genesis 11:28; Isaiah 48:20*

## CHEBAR
Possibly a river in Babylonia, or a canal, leading from the Euphrates River. Here, in exile with the Jews in Babylonia, Ezekiel saw visions of God.
*Ezekiel 1, 3, 10, 43*

## CHERITH
Desert stream east of the Jordan beside which Elijah lived during the years of drought and famine.
*1 Kings 17:3–7*

## CHINNERETH
Name for Lake Galilee in Hebrew Bible.
*Numbers 34:11; Deuteronomy 3:17; Joshua 11:2; 1 Kings 15:20*

## CHORAZIN
Hill-top town near Capernaum where Jesus taught. He denounced it because the people did not show a change of heart after hearing his words.
*Matthew 11:21; Luke 10:13*

## CILICIA
Region in southern Asia Minor (modern-day Turkey) that became a Roman province. The capital, Tarsus, was Paul's birthplace.
*Acts 21:39; 22:3; 23:34*

## COLOSSAE
City on the main road to Ephesus (south-west Turkey). Paul wrote a letter to the church at Colossae.
*Colossians 1:2*

## CORINTH
Ancient Greek city situated on the narrow piece of land connecting mainland Greece with the southern peninsula, between the Aegean and Adriatic seas. It was destroyed and rebuilt by the Romans. Paul stayed in Corinth as part of his mission. He also founded a church here.
*Acts 18; 1 Corinthians 1:2; 2 Corinthians 1:1*

## CRETE
Island in the eastern Mediterranean. King David's bodyguards, the "Cherethites," probably came from Crete, and it was a home of the Philistines. Paul stopped off at Crete on his way to Rome, and he also left Titus there to help the newly formed church.
*Genesis 10:14; Deuteronomy 2:23; Jeremiah 47:4; Amos 9:7; Acts 2:11; Titus 1:5, 12*

## CUSH
Country in ancient Ethiopia of the supposed descendants of Cush, Noah's grandson. Comprises an area of north-east Africa covering approximately Nubia, Sudan, and southern (upper) Egypt.
*Genesis 10:6–8; Isaiah 11:11; 18*

## CYPRUS
Large eastern-Mediterranean island. In the New Testament it was the home of Barnabas. It was the first place visited by Paul and Barnabas, where they spread the good news to the non-Jewish world. They met the governor, Sergius Paulus, and his magician friend. Barnabas later paid another visit to Cyprus with Mark.
*Acts 4:36; 13:4–12; 15:39; 27:4*

## CYRENE
Greek city on the north coast of Africa, in modern-day Libya. Simon from Cyrene helped Jesus carry the cross

for part of the way to the Crucifixion.
*Matthew 27:32; Mark 15:21;*
*Acts 2:10; 6:9; 11:20*

# D

## DALMATIA
Roman province on the east coast of the
Adriatic Sea where Titus preached.
*2 Timothy 4:10*

## DAMASCUS
Syrian capital. Already well known
in Abraham's day, it is frequently
mentioned in the Hebrew Bible. The
city was captured by King David but
soon regained its independence. Isaiah
predicted the destruction of Damascus
and, after many attacks, it fell to the
Assyrians in 732BCE. From 64BCE to
33CE, it was a Roman city. It was on
the road to Damascus to persecute
Christians that Saul (Paul) met Jesus
himself, and his whole life changed.
He later had to escape from the city
when the Jews persecuted him.
*Genesis 14:15; 15:2; 2 Samuel 8:5; 1 Kings 20:34;*
*2 Kings 5:12; 8:7–15; Isaiah 17; Acts 9*

## DAN
City in the northern territory of
Canaan, named after the tribe
descended from Dan, fourth son
of Jacob. When the kingdom was
divided, Jeroboam I tried to keep
the loyalty of the northern tribes
by giving them two golden calves to
worship, one of which was at Dan.
*Joshua 19:40–48; 1 Kings 12:25–30*

## DEAD SEA SEE SALT SEA, ARABAH

## DECAPOLIS ("THE TEN TOWNS")
Area south of Lake Galilee named after
a league of ten Greek towns, including
Damascus, and mainly inhabited by non-
Jews. These people joined the crowds
that followed Jesus. Jewish Christians
fled to Pella, one of the towns in this
region, before the war with the
Romans in 70CE.
*Matthew 4:25; Mark 5:20*

## DERBE
City in Lycaonia, in southern Asia Minor
(modern Turkey), where Paul preached.
*Acts 14:20; 16:1*

## DOR
Canaanite town that joined the
northern alliance of kings who fought
unsuccessfully against Joshua. The tribe
of Manasseh was given the town but
failed to drive out the inhabitants.
*Joshua 11:1–15; Judges 1:27; 1 Kings 4:11*

## DOTHAN
Town on the route from Beth-shan
and Gilead to Egypt. Joseph was sold
by his brothers to the Ishmaelite traders
in Dothan, and it was here that Elisha
was rescued from the Syrian army.
*Genesis 37:17–28; 2 Kings 6:13*

# E

## EBAL
Rocky mountain close to ancient
Shechem and modern Nablus. Here
Moses commanded Joshua to build
an altar and to give the people a
choice: to obey God and enjoy the
divine blessing, or to disobey and be
punished.
*Deuteronomy 11:29; 27; Joshua 8:30*

## EDEN
Garden made by God for humankind,
from which Adam and Eve were banished
when they disobeyed God's command.
Two of the rivers in the Garden were
the Tigris and the Euphrates.
*Genesis 2:8–15*

## EDOM
Mountainous region south of the Dead
Sea where Esau's descendants settled.
*Genesis 32:3; Numbers 20:14ff.; 1 Samuel 14:47;*
*Isaiah 34:5ff.*

## EDREI
Place where the Israelites defeated
the army of Og, King of Bashan,
before entering the Promised Land.
Edrei is the modern-day Der'a, on
the border between Syria and Jordan.
*Numbers 21:33; Deuteronomy 1:4; 3:1, 10;*
*Joshua 12:4; 13:12, 31*

## EGLON
Amorite city conquered by Joshua.
*Joshua 10:34*

## EGYPT
Along with Babylonia, one of the
most important empires mentioned in the
Hebrew Bible. From the third millennium
BCE Egypt was a major center of culture,
religion, and civilization. It is the setting
of many biblical events, among them the
stories of Joseph, Moses, and the Exodus.
*See pp.46–47; Genesis 46; Exodus 1–14*

## EKRON
One of the five important Philistine cities
given to the tribe of Judah in the early
years of the Conquest, but it was soon
lost again to the Philistines. When the
Philistines defeated Israel and captured
the Ark of the Covenant, a plague broke
out in each of the cities. When the plague
reached Ekron, the Philistines decided
to return the Ark to the Israelites.
*Joshua 15:11, 45–46; Judges 1:18; 1 Samuel*
*5:10–6:17; 7:14; 17:52; 2 Kings 1:3–6; Amos 1:8*

## ELAH
Valley lying southwest of Jerusalem,
through which the Philistines marched
to invade Israel. David fought Goliath
in the valley of Elah.
*1 Samuel 17:2*

## ELAM
Country east of Babylonia with Susa
as its capital.
*Genesis 14:1; Isaiah 21:2; Daniel 8:2; Acts 2:9*

## EMMAUS
Village near Jerusalem, probably
modern-day El-Qubeibeh. Jesus appeared
to two of his followers on the day of
his Resurrection while they were on
the road to Emmaus.
*Luke 24:13–32*

## ENDOR
Place in northern Israel, near Mount
Tabor, where Saul consulted a medium.
*1 Samuel 28*

## ENGEDI
Spring to the west of the Dead Sea,
where David sought refuge from Saul.
*Joshua 15:62; 1 Samuel 23:29;*
*Song of Songs 1:14*

## EN-ROGEL
Spring in the Kidron valley southeast
of Jerusalem. One of King David's sons,

Adonijah, had himself anointed king before his father's death in an attempt to stop the kingdom from going to Solomon.
*1 Kings 1:9*

### EPHESUS
Capital of the Roman province of Asia (western Turkey). An important port and trade center between Europe and Asia, it was a magnificent city in Paul's day. By New Testament times it had a population of almost 250,000 and gradually grew as an important Christian center.
*See pp.398–99; Acts 18:19; 19; 20:17; 1 Corinthians 15:32; 16:8–9; Ephesians 1:1; 1 Timothy 1:3; Revelation 2:1–7*

### EPHRAIM
Land belonging to the tribe of Ephraim.
*Joshua 16:4–10*

### EPHRATHAH
Another name for Bethlehem.

### ESHCOL
Valley near Hebron. "Eshcol" translates as "cluster of grapes." When Moses sent spies into the Promised Land, they brought back bunches of grapes from this valley.
*Numbers 13:23–24; 32:9; Deuteronomy 1:24*

### ESHTAOL
A city to the west of Jerusalem where Samson grew up. It was here that the spirit of God first moved him to go out against the Philistines. Samson was buried near here.
*Joshua 15:33; 19:41; Judges 13:24–25; 16:31; 18:2ff.*

### ETHIOPIA
Called Cush in many translations of the Hebrew Bible, this is Sudan and not the Ethiopia of today.
*2 Kings 19:9; Isaiah 18:1; Jeremiah 38:7ff.; Acts 8:27ff.*

### EUPHRATES
River that rises in the east of Turkey and flows southeast to the Persian Gulf. Simply referred to in the Hebrew Bible as "the river." It is mentioned as one of the four rivers of Eden.
*Genesis 2:14; 15:18; Revelation 9:14; 16:12*

### EZION–GEBER
Settlement, later town, on the shores of the Red Sea where the Israelites camped on their way from Egypt to Canaan. King Solomon based a Red Sea trading fleet there, which King Jehoshaphat later attempted to revive, but his ships were wrecked. The town eventually came under the control of the Edomites.
*Numbers 33:35–36; Deuteronomy 2:8; 1 Kings 9:26–27; 22:48*

# F

### FAIR HAVENS
Port in Crete where Paul's ship docked on his voyage to Rome. Here Paul advised the owner and captain of the ship not to go to sea. However, they did set sail and the boat was caught in a storm, which drove them to shipwreck on Malta.
*Acts 27:8–12*

# G

### GAD
Land belonging to the tribe of Gad, which was formerly part of the Amorite kingdom and lay east of the Jordan River.
*Joshua 13:8–13*

### GADARA / GADARENES
One of the cities of the Decapolis, the inhabitants of which were known as Gadarenes. It was in this area that the miracle of Legion and the swine took place
*Matthew 8:28–34; Mark 5:1–17; Luke 8:26–37*

### GALATIA
Roman province in central Asia Minor whose capital was Ancyra (now Ankara). Many of the cities Paul visited were here: Pisidian Antioch, Iconium, and Lystra. Paul's letter to the Galatians was probably addressed to the people of these towns.
*Acts 16:6; 18:23; Galatians 1:2; 1 Peter 1:1*

### GALILEE
Lake and region in north Israel that was the homeland of Jesus and the majority of his disciples. Mentioned occasionally in the Hebrew Bible, this hilly area was greatly influenced by other nations. In New Testament times it was a fishing area, and many of the towns mentioned in the Gospels were found here, including Nazareth, Capernaum, Cana, and Bethsaida. The Sea of Galilee (the lake) is a focal point of many of the Gospel stories.    *See pp.340–41*
*1 Kings 9:11; 2 Kings 15:29; Isaiah 9:1; Luke 4:14; 5:1; John 21; Acts 9:31*

### GATH
In Hebrew Bible times, Gath was one of five Philistine strongholds. When the Ark of the Covenant was stolen it was taken here, and a plague followed. Goliath came from Gath, which was also home to other "giants." Soldiers from here helped King David when his son Absalom led a rebellion against him.
*Joshua 11:22; 1 Samuel 5; 17:4; 21:10–22:1; 27; 2 Samuel 15:18; 2 Kings 12:17; 2 Chronicles 11:8; 26:6*

### GATH–HEPHER
Town on the border of Zebulun and Naphtali. Birthplace of the prophet Jonah.
*Joshua 19:13; 2 Kings 14:25*

### GAZA
One of five Philistine strongholds in the Hebrew Bible. The city was conquered and then lost by Joshua, and where Samson was imprisoned and later died. In the New Testament, Philip was on the road to Gaza when he met the Ethiopian official and told him the good news about Jesus.
*Joshua 10:41; Judges 16; 1 Samuel 6:17; 2 Kings 18:8; Jeremiah 47; Acts 8:26*

### GEBA
Town (modern-day Jeba) 6 miles (10km) north of Jerusalem. Geba became the northern limit of the southern kingdom of Judah and was fortified by King Asa.
*Joshua 18:24; 21:17; 1 Samuel 13:16; 1 Kings 15:22; 2 Kings 23:8; 1 Chronicles 6:60; Ezra 2:26; Nehemiah 7:30; Isaiah 10:29; Zechariah 14:10*

### GEBAL
Ancient Phoenician city, more often known by its Greek name of Byblos, that stood on the coast of modern Lebanon, north of Berytus (Beirut). Men from Gebal helped build Solomon's Temple.
*Joshua 13:5; 1 Kings 5:18; Psalm 83:7; Ezekiel 27:9*

### GENNESARET
Town on the western shore of Lake

Galilee. The name, which means "garden of the prince," is also used of the lake itself.
*Mark 6:53; Luke 5:1*

## GERAR
Place in the Negev between Beersheba and Gaza where both Abraham and Isaac stayed. Abraham said that his wife, Sarah, was his sister, for her own safety. Abimelech, king of Gerar, wanted to take Sarah as his wife but God intervened.
*Genesis 20, 26*

## GERIZIM
Mountain of God's blessing, opposite Mt. Ebal in Samaria. It later became the Samaritans' sacred mountain, where they built their temple.
*Deuteronomy 11:29; 27:11–12; Joshua 8:33; John 4:20*

## GESHUR
Region and town in southern Syria. King David married the daughter of the king of Geshur. Absalom, their son, fled to Geshur after he had killed his half-brother, Amnon, in revenge for the rape of his sister, Tamar.
*Joshua 12:5; 2 Samuel 3:3; 13:38*

## GETHSEMANE
Garden situated across from Jerusalem and close to the Mount of Olives.
*See p.360–61; Matthew 26:36–56; Mark 14:32–51*

## GEZER
Town on the road to Jerusalem from Joppa – one of the Canaanite towns campaigned against by Joshua. It belonged to Egypt until one of the pharaohs gave it to his daughter, who was King Solomon's wife.
*Joshua 10:33; 1 Kings 9:15–17*

## GIBEAH
Home and capital city of King Saul, 4km (3 miles) north of Jerusalem. During the time of the Judges, the town was destroyed as a result of a crime committed by its people. The site is at Tell el-Ful, which overlooks the suburbs of Jerusalem.
*Judges 19:12–20:48; 1 Samuel 10:26*

## GIBEON
Town 6 miles (10km) north of Jerusalem. Joshua was tricked into a peace treaty

by the Gibeonites, after the fall of Jericho and Ai. Saul later broke the treaty. David's men fought the supporters of Saul's son, Ishbosheth, at the pool of Gibeon, to decide who would be king. The Tabernacle was kept at Gibeon, and King Solomon worshiped here. The people of Gibeon helped rebuild the walls of Jerusalem.
*Joshua 9; 2 Samuel 2:12–29; 20:8; 21; 1 Kings 3:4–5; 1 Chronicles 21:29*

## GIHON
One of the four rivers that flowed out of the Garden of Eden. Also the name of a spring at the foot of the hill on which the first city of Jerusalem stood. The Gihon spring water was essential to the city and, later, King Hezekiah cut a tunnel through the hills and inside the walls. The tunnel still exists today.
*Genesis 2:13; 1 Kings 1:38; 2 Chronicles 32:30; 33:14*

## GILBOA
Range of mountains in the north of Palestine. On Mount Gilboa, King Saul and his army took their last stand against the Philistines. Saul, Jonathan, and his other two sons were all killed here.
*1 Samuel 28:4; 31:1, 8; 2 Samuel 1; 21:12; 1 Chronicles 10:1, 8*

## GILEAD
Large area east of the Jordan River, extending north from the Dead Sea. The tribes of Reuben, Gad, and Manasseh each occupied part of Gilead. Jair, Jephthah, and the prophet Elijah all came from Gilead.
*Genesis 37:25; Joshua 17:1; Judges 10:3–4, 11; 1 Kings 17:1; Song of Songs 4:1*

## GILGAL
Place between Jericho and the Jordan River. The Israelites camped here after crossing the river, and set up stones to mark the event. They set out to conquer Canaan from Gilgal. It became the site of an important shrine and is mentioned in the stories of Elijah and also of Elisha, who dealt with a pot of "poisoned" stew here. Worship at Gilgal was condemned as empty ritual by the prophets Hosea and Amos.
*Joshua 4:20; Judges 3:19; 1 Samuel 7:16; 10:8; 2 Samuel 19:15; 2 Kings 2:1; 4:38–41; Hosea 4:15; Amos 4:4*

## GOLGOTHA
Place of the Crucifixion.
*See p.360–61*

## GOMORRAH
One of the five cities probably now beneath the southern end of the Dead Sea. It was destroyed along with Sodom because of the persistent sin here. The two towns are used throughout the Bible as warnings of God's judgment.
*Genesis 14; 19; Isaiah 1:9–10; Matthew 10:15*

## GOSHEN
Fertile area in the Nile Delta in Egypt. When Jacob and his family went to join Joseph they settled here. Goshen escaped the plagues suffered by the rest of Egypt, in the time just before the Exodus.
*Genesis 45:10; Exodus 8:22*

## GOZAN
Town on the River Khabbur in north-east Syria (modern-day Tell Halaf.) The Assyrians captured the Israelites from Samaria and took them to Gozan.
*2 Kings 17:6; 19:12*

## GREAT SEA
Name often used in the Hebrew Bible for the Mediterranean.

## GREECE
Alexander the Great brought Israel and the eastern Mediterranean lands under Greek control. The influence of Greek civilization and culture was strong in the last centuries before Christ and in New Testament times.
*See pp.246–47; Daniel 11:2; John 12:20; Acts 6, 17, 18*

# H

## HABOR
Tributary of the Euphrates River. The town of Gozan stood on its banks.
*2 Kings 17:6*

## HAMATH
Modern-day Hama, on the Orontes River in Syria; capital of a small kingdom in ancient times. During the reigns of David and Solomon, Israel had a peace treaty with King Toi of Hamath. Pharaoh Neco and then King Nebuchadnezzar

once made Hamath their headquarters.
*Joshua 13:5; 2 Samuel 8:9–11; 1 Kings 8:65;*
*2 Kings 17:24; 18:34; 2 Chronicles 8:4*

## HARAN / HARRAN

Town in present-day southeast Turkey.
The place where Abraham's father, Terah,
settled after leaving Ur, and also where
Jacob worked for Laban. Haran was
fortified by the Assyrians as a provincial
capital. After the fall of Nineveh, it was
the Assyrian capital for three years.
In 609BCE it fell to the Babylonians.
*Genesis 11:31; 12:4–5; 29:4; 2 Kings 19:12;*
*Ezekiel 27:23*

## HAROD

Spring, probably in northern Palestine, by
a stream that runs through the valley of
Jezreel. Gideon chose his army by looking
at the way they drank from this spring.
*Judges 7:1–8*

## HAZOR

Canaanite city in the north of Israel. It was
the king of Hazor, Jabin, who organized
an alliance against Joshua, but he was
defeated, and the city was burned. Along
with Megiddo and Gezer, Hazor was
rebuilt by King Solomon. It was destroyed
by the Assyrians in the eigth century BCE.
*Joshua 11; Judges 4; 1 Kings 9:15;*
*2 Kings 15:29*

## HEBRON

Town lying high in the Judean hills.
The old name for Hebron was Kiriath-
arba. Abraham and his family often
camped near Hebron; it was later
given to Caleb. Hebron was David's
capital before he captured Jerusalem.
Absalom staged his rebellion from
Hebron. Many Jews returned to live
there, much later after the Exile.
Traditional burial place of the
Ancestors at the Tomb of Machpelah.
*Genesis 13:18; 23; 35:27; 37:14; Numbers 13:22;*
*Joshua 14:6–15; 2 Samuel 2:1–4; 15:9–10;*
*Nehemiah 11:25*

## HELIOPOLIS SEE ON

## HERMON

Mountain on the Lebanon/Syria
border, sometimes called Sirion in the
Bible. Very close to Caesarea Philippi,
it may be the "high mountain" where

Jesus' disciples saw him in his glory.
*Joshua 12:1; Psalms 42:6; 133:3; Matthew 17:1*

## HESHBON

Prosperous town at the time of Isaiah and
Jeremiah, east of the Jordan River. It first
belonged to Moab, then to the Amorites,
and later to the tribes of Reuben and Gad.
*Numbers 21:25ff.*

## HIERAPOLIS

City in Roman province of Asia
(western Turkey). In his letter to
Colossae, Paul mentions the Christians
at Laodicea and Hierapolis. The hot-
water springs have since become the
waterfalls of stone in Pamukkale.
*Colossians 4:13*

## HINNOM

Valley south of Jerusalem. The kings Ahaz
and Manasseh set up a shrine here for the
god Molech, and children were offered to
him in sacrifice. This was destroyed by
Josiah, and Jeremiah denounced the evil
of the place. "Gehenna," meaning "Valley
of Hinnom," became a word for "hell."
*Joshua 15:8; 18:16; 2 Kings 23:10; 2 Chronicles*
*28:3; 33:6; Jeremiah 7:31; 19:2; 32:35*

## HOREB

Another name for Mount Sinai.

## HORMAH

Town in southern Canaan; the exact site
is uncertain. After the Conquest, it was
given to the tribe of Judah.
*Numbers 14:41–45; 21:3; Judges 1:17*

# I

## IBLEAM / IBLE-AM

Canaanite town north of Israel, where
Jehu killed King Ahaziah of Judah.
*Joshua 17:11–12; 2 Kings 9:27; 15:10*

## ICONIUM

Present-day Konya in central Turkey.
During New Testament times it was in the
Roman province of Galatia. Paul visited
Iconium on his first missionary journey
and was met with violent opposition.
*Acts 13:51; 14:1–6, 19–22; 2 Timothy 3:11*

## IDUMAEA

Greek name for the region known in

the Hebrew Bible as Edom. By New
Testament times, many Idumaeans had
settled west of the Jordan, in the dry
country in the south of Palestine. The
region was then called Idumaea. King
Herod was an Idumaean.
*Mark 3:8*

## ILLYRICUM

Region stretching along the eastern shore
of the Adriatic Sea. The southern part
was also called Dalmatia. When Paul
wrote to the Romans, he said he had
preached the Gospel from Jerusalem as
far west as Illyricum; this is the only
mention in Paul's work of this region.
*Romans 15:19*

## ISRAEL

Land occupied by the 12 tribes. After the
death of Solomon it was divided, and the
name *Israel* referred only to the northern
part of the kingdom.
*See pp.134–35*

## ISSACHAR

Land belonging to the tribe of Issachar,
situated south of Lake Galilee and west
of the Jordan River.
*Joshua 19:17–23*

## ITURAEA

Area north of the Jordan River. The
Ituraeans were probably the descendants
of the Hebrew Bible people callled Jetur.
In John the Baptist's time, Herod Philip
was ruler of Ituraea and Trachonitis.
*Luke 3:1*

# J

## JABBOK

River flowing into the Jordan from the
east, now known as the Zerqa. Jacob
wrestled with the angel beside the
Jabbok, which is also mentioned
in the Bible as a boundary.
*Genesis 32:22–30; Numbers 21:24;*
*Deuteronomy 3:16; Judges 11:13*

## JABESH-GILEAD

Town on the east of the Jordan. At
the time of the Judges, the wives of the
Benjaminites were killed in a civil war,
and the town of Jabesh-gilead provided
replacements. When Jabesh was besieged

by the Ammonites, Saul answered an appeal for help. Men from this town later risked their lives to remove his body from the walls of Beth-shan.
*Judges 21; 1 Samuel 11; 31:11–13*

## JAVAN
Name of one of the sons of Japheth. Javan is named as the father of a group of peoples, probably including those who lived in Greece and Asia Minor in early times. The name may also be connected with the Greek "Ionia" in western Turkey, and it is used in later parts of the Hebrew Bible to refer to Greece or the Greeks.
*Genesis 10:2; 1 Chronicles 1:5; Isaiah 66:19; Ezekiel 27:13, 19*

## JAZER
Amorite town east of the Jordan River that was captured by the Israelites and given to the tribe of Gad. Jazer was famous for its grapes.
*Numbers 21:32; Joshua 13:25; 1 Chronicles 26:31; Isaiah 16:8–9*

## JEBUS
Early name for Jerusalem.
*Joshua 18:28*

## JERICHO
Town west of the Jordan River, sometimes referred to as the "city of palms." In the Hebrew Bible it was a well-fortified town, and Joshua gained his first victory in the land at Jericho.
*See pp.96–97Joshua 2, 6; Judges 3:13; 2 Kings 2; Nehemiah 3:2; Mark 10:46–52; Luke 10:30–35; 19:1–10*

## JERUSALEM
The capital of Israel's early kings and later, of the Southern Kingdom of Judah. It was probably the "Salem" of which Melchizedek was king in Abraham's day. Before King David captured it and made it his capital, it was called Jebus. King David brought the Ark of the Covenant to Jerusalem, and his son, Solomon, built the Temple. From that time on, Jerusalem was the "holy city" for the Jews, and later for Christians and Muslims. Jerusalem was a political and religious center to which the people came for the great annual festivals.    *See pp.126–27, 276–77 Genesis 14:18; Joshua 15:63; 2 Samuel 5:4–10; 14:25–26; 2 Kings 12:17–18; 18:13–19:36;*

20:20, 25; Ezra 5; Nehemiah 3–6; Psalms 48, 122, 125; Luke 2:22–52; 19:28–24:49; John 2:23–3:21; 5; 7:10–10:42; Acts 2, 15

## JEZREEL
Town and plain in the north of Israel, close to Mount Gilboa. Before the Battle of Gilboa, Saul camped at the spring in the valley of Jezreel. King Ahab of Israel had a palace at Jezreel. The story of Naboth's vineyard took place in Jezreel. King Joram of Israel went to Jezreel to recover from his wounds, and Queen Jezebel was thrown from the palace window and died here.
*1 Samuel 29:1; 1 Kings 18:45–46; 21; 2 Kings 8:29; 9:30–37*

## JOPPA
Present-day Jaffa, close to Tel-Aviv. Joppa was the port for Jerusalem, 35 miles (56km) away. Jonah set sail for Tarshish (Spain) from Joppa. Dorcas (Tabitha), the woman Peter restored to life, came from Joppa. Peter was in Joppa when he had his dream about the "clean" and "unclean" animals.
*2 Chronicles 2:16; Jonah 1:3; Acts 9:36–43, 10*

## JORDAN
Israel's main river, repeatedly referred to in the Bible. It flows from Mount Hermon in the far north, through Lake Huleh and Lake Galilee, to the Dead Sea. Its name means "the descender," and it flows through the deepest rift valley on earth. Joshua led the people of Israel across the Jordan from the east into the Promised Land near to Jericho. David escaped across the Jordan at the time of Absalom's rebellion, and Elijah and Elisha crossed the Jordan just before Elijah was taken up to heaven. Elisha told the Syrian general, Naaman, to wash himself in the Jordan, and he would be healed. John the Baptist baptized people, including Jesus, in this river.
*Joshua 3; 2 Samuel 17:20–22;2 Kings 2:6–8, 13–14; 5; Jeremiah 12:5; 49:19; Mark 1:5, 9*

## JUDAH
The land belonging to the tribe of Judah. It later became the name of the Southern Kingdom, with Jerusalem as its capital.
*See pp.134–35; Joshua 15*

## JUDEA
Greek and Roman name for Judah, usually referring to the southern part of the country, with Jerusalem as its capital. The "Wilderness of Judea," associated with John the Baptist, is the desert west of the Dead Sea.
*Luke 3:1; 4:44*

# K

## KADESH-BARNEA
Settlement and oasis in the desert south of Beersheba. It is mentioned in the campaign of Chedorlaomer and his allies at the time of Abraham. It was near here that Hagar saw an angel. After the escape from Egypt, most of Israel's years of desert wanderings were spent in this region. Miriam died here, and Moses brought water out of the rock. It is later mentioned as a point on Israel's southern border.
*Genesis 14:7; 16:14; Numbers 13:26; 20:1; 33:36–37; Deuteronomy 1:19–25, 46; Joshua 10:41*

## KEDESH
Canaanite town in Galilee, given to the tribe of Naphtali after it was conquered by Joshua. It was the home of Barak and one of the first towns to fall to the Assyrians when Tiglath-Pileser III invaded Israel from the north (734–732BCE).
*Joshua 12:22; 15:23; 19:37; Judges 4; 2 Kings 15:29*

## KEILAH
Town north of Hebron where David stayed while evading Saul. David saved it from a Philistine attack.
*Joshua 15:44; 1 Samuel 23; Nehemiah 3:17–18*

## KIDRON
Valley separating Jerusalem and the Temple from the Mount of Olives. In the time of Absalom's rebellion, David crossed the Kidron on leaving Jerusalem. The reforming kings Asa, Hezekiah, and Josiah, destroyed idols in the Kidron valley. Jesus and his disciples would have crossed it on their way to the Garden of Gethsemane.
*2 Samuel 15:23; 1 Kings 15:13;2 Kings 23:4–6; 2 Chronicles 29:16; John 18:1*

## KING'S HIGHWAY
Road by which Moses promised to travel

peacefully through the land of Edom and the land of Sihon. Both kings refused his request, forcing the Israelites to avoid Edom and to fight and defeat Sihon. Probably the main north-south route along the heights east of the Jordan, between Damascus and the Gulf of Aqaba.
*Numbers 20:17, 21:22*

KINNERETH see CHINNERETH

### KIRIATHAIM
Town given to the tribe of Reuben, east of the Dead Sea. It was later taken over by the Moabites.
*Joshua 13:19, Jeremiah 48:1–25, Ezekiel 25:9*

### KIRIATH-ARBA
Early name for Hebron.

### KIRIATH-JEARIM
Town lying in the hills a few miles west of Jerusalem. One of the towns of the Gibeonites, who tricked Joshua into a peace treaty. The Ark of the Covenant was kept here for 20 years before King David took it to Jerusalem.
*Joshua 9:17, 1 Samuel 6:19–7:2,*
*Nehemiah 7:29, Jeremiah 26:20*

### KISHON
Small stream that flows across the plain of Megiddo (Esdraelon) and into the Mediterranean Sea. In the tale of Barak, the heavy rain raised the stream's water level so high that the surrounding ground turned to mud and bogged down Sisera's chariots, allowing Israel to be the victors. It was at the Wadi Kishon that Elijah killed the prophets of Baal.
*Judges 4, 5:21, 1 Kings 18:40*

### KITTIM
One of the sons of Javan, whose descendants settled on Cyprus and gave their name to the town of Kition (modern Larnaca).
*Genesis 10:4, Numbers 24:24, 1 Chronicles 1:7,*
*Isaiah 23:1, 12, Jeremiah 2:10, Ezekiel 27:6*

### KUE/COA
Region in the eastern part of Cilicia (the south of modern Turkey), where Solomon obtained his horses.
*1 Kings 10:28*

# L

### LACHISH
Important fortified town about 30 miles (48km) south of Jerusalem. Here, Joshua defeated the king of Lachish and four other Amorite kings. He attacked and captured Lachish and put its inhabitants to death. The town was rebuilt as a defense against the Philistines and Egyptians by King Rehoboam, son of Solomon. King Amaziah of Judah fled to Lachish for safety, but his enemies followed him and he was killed here. Sennacherib, the Assyrian king, besieged Lachish when he attacked Judah, cutting Jerusalem off from possible help from Egypt. Lachish fell, and Sennacherib had the siege pictured on the walls of his palace at Nineveh. At the time of the final siege of Jerusalem (589–586BCE), the Babylonian army attacked the town. Lachish again fell and the Babylonians burned it. After the Exile, Lachish was resettled but was never again a powerful city.
*See pp.143, 153, Joshua 10, 2 Kings 14:19,*
*18:14–17, 2 Chronicles 11:5–12,*
*Isaiah 36:1–3, Nehemiah 11:30, Jeremiah 34:7*

### LAODICEA
City in the west of present-day Turkey, in the Lycus valley. It became wealthy through trade and banking. Paul's letter to the Colossians was also intended for Laodicea, although he had not been here. The early Christian group in Laodicea may have been started when Paul was staying in Ephesus.
*Colossians 2:1, 4:13–16,*
*Revelation 1:11, 3:14–22*

### LEBANON
Area north of Israel famous for its forests of cedar trees; Lebanese cedars were used to build the Temple and royal palace at Jerusalem. The Bible also mentions the fertile soils of the land, which grew many fruits and vegetables. The Phoenician ports of Tyre, Sidon, and Byblos were all on the coast of Lebanon.
*1 Kings 5:1–11, Ezra 3:7, Psalm 72:16,*
*Isaiah 2:13, 14:8, Ezekiel 31*

### LIBNAH
Fortified town near to Lachish. It was

taken by Joshua and later rebelled in the reign of King Jehoram of Judah. The town survived a siege by the Assyrian king Sennacherib when plague hit his army.
*Joshua 10:29–30, 2 Kings 8:22, 19:8, 35*

### LO-DEBAR
Place in Gilead where Mephibosheth, Jonathan's son, lived in exile until David brought him to his court.
*2 Samuel 9, 17:27*

### LYCIA
Small, mountainous country in Asia Minor (modern Turkey). The ports of Patara and Myra where Paul landed were in Lycia.
*Acts 27:5*

### LYDDA
Town inland from Joppa where Peter healed a lame man, Aeneas, when visiting the first Christians here. Known today as Lod.
*Acts 9:32–35, 38*

### LYSTRA
Remote city in the Roman province of Galatia (near Konya in Turkey). On their first missionary journey, Paul and Barnabas went to Lystra, where Paul healed a crippled man. The people believed him to be Hermes (messenger of the Greek gods) and Barnabas to be Zeus. Paul was stoned and left for dead after the Jews from Iconium stirred up trouble. Some of the people became Christians, and Paul returned to see them on his later missionary travels.
*Acts 14:6–20, 16:1–5*

# M

### MAACAH
Small Aramaean state southeast of Mount Hermon, mentioned in David's campaigns.
*Joshua 12:15, 2 Samuel 10, 23:34*

### MACEDONIA
Region in northern Greece with its capital at Thessalonica. Other towns in this Roman province included Philippi and Beroea. Paul had a vision of a Macedonian man asking him to come and help them, so he crossed the Aegean to see them. It was the first stage in bringing the good news to Europe.

Three of Paul's letters are addressed to Macedonian Christians (Philippians, and 1 and 2 Thessalonians), many of whom gave generously to his relief fund for Christians in Judea and became his regular helpers.
*Acts 16:6–17:15; 20:1–6;2 Corinthians 8:1–5; 9:1–5*

## MACHPELAH
Plot of land at Hebron including the cave of Machpelah, which Abraham bought from Ephron the Hittite after Sarah died. Abraham himself was later buried here, as were Isaac, Rebekah, and Jacob. Herod the Great built a shrine around the place believed to contain the cave and the tombs, still an important pilgrimage site for Jews, Christians, and Muslims.
*Genesis 23; 25:9; 49:30; 50:13*

MAGOG see GOG AND MAGOG, p.484

## MAHANAIM
Place in Gilead, east of the Jordan River and near the Jabbok River. Before the reunion with his brother Esau, Jacob saw God's angels at Mahanaim. It was King David's headquarters during Absalom's rebellion. One of Solomon's district officers was based at Mahanaim.
*Genesis 32:2; 2 Samuel 2:8–10; 17:24–29; 1 Kings 4:14*

## MAKKEDAH
Canaanite town in the south, captured by Joshua. The five Amorite kings who had fought against him were found dead by Joshua in a nearby cave. The town was given to the tribe of Judah.
*Joshua 10:10, 16; 15:41*

## MALTA
Mediterranean island south of Sicily. Its ancient name was Melita. Paul's was shipwrecked here during his voyage as a prisoner to Rome.
*Acts 28:1–10*

## MAMRE
Place near Hebron where Abraham, and later Isaac, often camped. Here Abraham heard that Lot had been captured. It was here that God promised him a son and where Abraham pleaded with God to spare Sodom.
*Genesis 13:18; 14:13; 18; 23:17; 35:27*

## MANASSEH
Land belonging to the tribe of Manasseh. West Manasseh was the hill country of Samaria as far west as the Mediterranean Sea. East Manasseh was the land east of central Jordan.
*Joshua 13:6–31; 17:1–13*

## MAON
Town in the Judean hills where Nabal, Abigail's husband, lived. When David was an outlaw from King Saul he stayed in Maon twice.
*Joshua 15:55; 1 Samuel 23:14–25; 25*

## MARESHAH
Town in the low hills 20 miles (32km) south of Jerusalem. Fortified by King Rehoboam; King Asa later destroyed a great army from Sudan here. Micah prophesied disaster for this town.
*Joshua 15:44; 2 Chronicles 11:8; 14:9–10; 20:37; Micah 1:15*

## MASSAH
Place in the wilderness, so-named by Moses because the people put God to the test by demanding water. The name means "to test," "to try out."
*Exodus 17:7; Deuteronomy 6:16; 9:22; Psalms 95:8*

## MEDIA
Northwest Iran. The region came under Assyrian control but later helped the Babylonians to overthrow the Assyrians. Cyrus the Persian brought Media under his control. Later, the Medes rebelled under Darius I and II.

## MEGIDDO
Ancient city located on the edge of the plain of Jezreel, important in the Hebrew Bible. So many battles occurred here that the New Testament (Rev. 16:16) uses the name symbolically as the site of the great last battle: "Armageddon," or "the hill of Megiddo." The Canaanite king of Megiddo was defeated by Joshua when the Israelites conquered Canaan. It was given to the tribe of Manasseh, who made the Canaanites work for them but did not drive them out. It was chosen as one of Solomon's fortified towns. King Ahaziah of Judah died here after being wounded by Jehu's men. So too did King Josiah in his attempt to stop the advancing Egyptian soldiers, led by Pharaoh Neco.
*Joshua 12:21; Judges 1:27–28; 5:19; 1 Kings 9:15; 2 Kings 9:27; 23:29*

## MEMPHIS
Egypt's ancient capital, on the Nile River south of modern Cairo. The pyramids at Giza are near Memphis. Up until the time of Alexander the Great the city remained very important. Many of the Hebrew Bible Prophets referred to Memphis when they condemned Israel's trust in Egypt.
*Isaiah 19:13; Jeremiah 2:16; 46:14; Ezekiel 30:13*

## MERIBAH
Place in the wilderness, combined with Massah. It means "to strive with," "to contend against."
*Exodus 17:7; Deuteronomy 33:8; Psalms 95:8*

## MESOPOTAMIA
Land between the Tigris and Euphrates rivers, the center of one of the earliest civilizations that included such famous cities as Babylon, Ur, and Nineveh. Harran and Paddan-aram, the towns where some of Abraham's family settled, lay here. It was the home of Balaam, the prophet who was sent to curse the Israelites, and in the time of the Judges it was ruled by Cushanrishathaim. In the New Testament, people from Mesopotamia were in Jerusalem on the Day of Pentecost and heard Peter and the Apostles speak to them in their own languages.
*Genesis 24:10; Deuteronomy 23:4; Judges 3:8, 10; Acts 2:9*

## MICHMASH
Village today known as Mukhmas, 7 miles (11km) northeast of Jerusalem. The Philistines invaded Israel and camped in force at Michmash, threatening King Saul's capital at Gibeah. Michmash was on the route by which the Assyrians approached Jerusalem from the north. It was reoccupied after the Exile.
*1 Samuel 13–14; Ezra 2:27; Nehemiah 7:31; 11:31; Isaiah 10:28*

## MIDIAN
Region in Arabia, east of the Gulf of Aqaba. Moses went to Midian after killing an Egyptian overseer. He married

a Midianite wife and stayed there until God sent him back to Egypt to help free the Israelites. At the time of the Judges, Gideon defeated a large force of camel-riding invaders from Midian.
*Genesis 25:1–6; Exodus 2:15–21; Judges 6–7*

## MILETUS
Port on the west coast of present-day Turkey, where Paul stayed on his way back from his missionary travels. The elders from the church at Ephesus came to meet him here and heard his farewell message.
*Acts 20:15–38; 2 Timothy 4:20*

## MITYLENE
Important port and city on the Greek island of Lesbos. Paul stopped here over-night on his last voyage to Jerusalem.
*Acts 20:14*

## MIZPAH / MIZPEH
Name of a number of different places. Jacob and Laban called the place where they made a peace agreement Mizpah. A Mizpah in Gilead features in the story of Jephthah, at the time of the Judges. Israel's forces assembled here in preparation for war against Ammon. The most important Mizpah, where the Israelites met together, lay a few miles north of Jerusalem. This particular town was where Samuel presented Saul to the people as their king. After Jerusalem fell to the Babylonians the governor, Gedaliah, lived at Mizpah.
*Genesis 31:44–49; Judges 10:17; 11; 20:1; 1 Samuel 7:5–16; 10:17; 1 Kings 15:22; 2 Kings 25:23*

## MOAB
High plateau of land, east of the Dead Sea – the home of Ruth. Often at war with Israel, the country was repeatedly denounced by the Prophets. The Plains of Moab lay east of the Jordan River opposite Jericho, where the Israelites crossed into Canaan.
*Numbers 22:1; 35:1; Joshua 13:32; Judges 3:12–30; Ruth 1; 2 Samuel 8:2; 2 Kings 3; Isaiah 15*

## MOREH
Hill a few miles northwest of Mount Gilboa, where the Midianites camped before Gideon's attack.
*Judges 7:1*

## MORESHETH / MORESHETHGATH
Town thought to be near Mareshah, in the low country southwest of Jerusalem. Hometown of the prophet Micah.
*Jeremiah 26:18; Micah 1:1, 14*

## MORIAH
Mountains to which Abraham was told to go to sacrifice his son Isaac. (The Samaritans claimed that the place for the sacrifice was actually Mount Gerizim.) The author of 2 Chronicles wrote that Solomon's temple was "in Jerusalem, on Mount Moriah."
*Genesis 22:2; 2 Chronicles 3:1*

## MOUNT OF OLIVES / OLIVET
Hill that overlooked Jerusalem and its Temple area from the east; in Jesus' day it was planted with olive trees. When King David fled from Jerusalem at the time of Absalom's rebellion, he passed through this way. King Solomon built an altar here. During the Exile, the prophet Ezekiel saw the dazzling light of God's glory leave Jerusalem and move to the Mount of Olives. Zechariah foresaw God on the Day of Judgment, standing on the Mount, which would split in two. Jesus rode in triumph into Jerusalem from here. On its lower slopes lay the Garden of Gethsemane, where Jesus prayed on the night of his arrest.
*See p.349 2 Samuel 15:30; Zechariah 14:4; Luke 19:29, 37; 21:37; 22:39; Acts 1:12*

## MYRA
Port in Lycia (southwest Turkey). On his voyage to Rome, Paul and his party changed ships here.
*Acts 27:5*

## MYSIA
Land forming part of the Roman province of Asia (Turkey). Paul came here as part of his mission, but God prevented him from crossing the border from Asia into Bithynia.
*Acts 16:7–8*

# N

## NAHOR
City in Mesopotamia where Abraham's servant found a wife for Isaac.
*Genesis 24:10*

## NAIN
Town near Nazareth in Galilee, where Jesus brought a widow's son back to life.
*Luke 7:11–17*

## NAPHTALI
Land in Galilee belonging to the tribe of Naphtali.
*Joshua 19:32–39*

## NAZARETH
Town in Galilee, home of Jesus' parents, Mary and Joseph. Jesus grew up here but made his base in Capernaum when he began his public work. *See pp.320–21*
*Matthew 2:22–23; 4:13; Mark 1:9; Luke 1:26; 2:39, 51; 4:16–30; John 1:45–46*

## NEAPOLIS
Modern-day Kavalla but once the port in Macedonia (northern Greece) for Philippi. Here, Paul first set foot in Europe in answer to a call for help from Macedonia. On his last voyage to Jerusalem he also sailed from here.
*Acts 16:11*

## NEBO
City in Transjordan conquered by the Israelites. Also a mountain east of the north end of the Dead Sea, in Moab. Moses climbed Mount Nebo before he died and saw the whole of the Promised Land spread out before him.
*Deuteronomy 32:48–52; 34:1–4*

## NEGEV
Area of dry scrubland and desert in far south of Israel. It merges with the Sinai Desert on the way to Egypt. Abraham and Isaac camped here, as did the Israelites before they settled in Canaan.
*Genesis 20:1; 24:62; Numbers 13:17; 21:1; Isaiah 30:6*

## NILE
Egypt's great river, on which its whole economy depended. It flows from Lake Victoria in the heart of Africa to the Mediterranean Sea, totaling 3,500 miles (5,632km ) in length. It featured in the dreams of Joseph's pharaoh; at the time of Moses' birth the pharaoh ordered his people to drown all Hebrew baby boys in the Nile. Moses was hidden in a basket in the reeds at the river's edge. The Nile also features in the sequence of

plagues sent by God when the pharaoh refused to free the Israelites. It is often mentioned by the Prophets.
*Genesis 41:1–36; Exodus 1:22; 2:3–10; 7:17–8:15; Isaiah 18:2*

### NINEVEH
Important city in Assyria, especially in Sennacherib's reign. According to the Bible, it was founded by Nimrod the hunter. The site goes back to about 4500BCE. In 2300BCE the city had a temple to the goddess Ishtar. Nineveh became more important as Assyria's power increased, and several Assyrian kings had palaces here. Sennacherib undertook a great deal of rebuilding work. The relief carved on the walls of his palace shows his victories, including the siege of Lachish in Judah. Nineveh fell to the Babylonians in 612BCE. In the Bible, Jonah was sent to save Nineveh, and Nahum prophesied against it.
*Genesis 10:11; 2 Kings 19:36; Jonah 1:2, 3; Nahum 1–3; Luke 11:30*

### NOB
Thought to be at Mount Scopus, north of the Mount of Olives. When David escaped from King Saul's attempts to kill him, he received help from the priest Ahimelech at Nob. One of the king's men told Saul, and he had the priests at Nob killed. There was still a settlement at Nob when Nehemiah was rebuilding Jerusalem.
*1 Samuel 21–22; Nehemiah 11:32; Isaiah 10:32*

### OLIVES, MOUNT OF  SEE MOUNT OF OLIVES

### ON
Ancient city in Egypt, famous for its worship of the sun god Ra. Joseph married the daughter of the priest of On, and they had two sons, Ephraim and Manasseh. This city is mentioned later in the Prophets, once by its Greek name "Heliopolis" (city of the sun).
*Genesis 41:45, 50; 46:20; Ezekiel 30:17*

### OPHIR
Possibly a country famous for its gold that may have been in South Arabia, East Africa (Somalia), or India. But, *ophir* may

be Arabic for "abundance," meaning gold in abundance and may not be a place.
*1 Kings 9:28*

### PADDAN–ARAM
Area around Harran, north Mesopotamia. Abraham sent his servant to Paddan-aram to choose a wife for Isaac from the branch of the family that had settled there. Jacob later fled from Esau to his uncle, Laban, who was living at Paddan-aram at the time.
*Genesis 25:20; 28:2*

### PAMPHYLIA
Narrow coastal region on the south-west coast of modern Turkey. Paul visited the town of Perga, which was situated in Pamphylia. Jews from this area made the pilgrimage to Jerusalem for the Feast of Pentecost.
*Acts 2:10; 13:13*

### PAPHOS
Town in southwest Cyprus. Paul visited Paphos on his first missionary journey. He met the magician Elymas here. The governor of the island, Sergius Paulus, believed God's message.
*Acts 13:3–13*

### PARAN
Desert area near Kadesh-barnea, often refered to as the "wilderness of Paran." This is where Hagar's son, Ishmael, grew up. The Israelites passed through it after the Exodus, and from here spies were sent into Canaan.
*Genesis 21:20–21; Numbers 10:12; 12:16; 13:1–16*

### PATMOS
Island off the west coast of Turkey where John had the visions written in the book of Revelation.
*Revelation 1:9*

### PENUEL / PENIEL
Place near the Jabbok River, east of Jordan, where Jacob wrestled with the angel.
*Genesis 32:22–32*

### PERGA
City inland from Antalya in modern-day

Turkey. Paul visited here on his arrival from Cyprus on his first missionary journey, and again when he returned to the coast.
*Acts 13:13; 14:25*

### PERGAMUM
First administrative capital of the Roman province of Asia. The first temple to be dedicated to Rome and the Emperor Augustus was built at Pergamum in 29BCE. Pergamum was the center of the pagan cults of Zeus, Athena, and Dionysus. There was also a center of healing here connected with the temple of Asclepius (a fourth great pagan cult). The city was one of the seven churches to which the letters in the book of Revelation are addressed. The phrase "where Satan has his throne" may refer to emperor worship.
*Revelation 1:11; 2:12–16*

### PERSIA
Country that conquered Media and overthrew Babylon in the seventh century BCE to establish an empire that continued until Alexander the Great and his conquests in the fourth. Daniel was in Babylon when the city was taken by the army of the Medes and Persians. It was the Persian king, Cyrus, who allowed the Jews and other exiles to return to their homeland. Esther, a Jewish heroine, became queen to the Persian king, Xerxes I (Ahasuerus).
*See pp.156–57*
*Ezra 1; Esther 1; Daniel 5:24–28; 6; 8:20; 10:1*

### PHARPAR  SEE ABANA

### PHILADELPHIA
City in the Roman province of Asia (modern Alashehir, in western Turkey). One of the seven churches of Asia to which the letters in the book of Revelation were addressed.
*Revelation 1:11; 3:7–13*

### PHILIPPI
City 8 miles (12km ) inland from Neapolis on the coast of Macedonia (northern Greece). It was named after Philip of Macedon. Paul visited the city as part of his mission, after seeing a vision of a Macedonian man calling for help. The first Christian church in Europe was established at Philippi. Paul

and Silas were imprisoned here illegally but were later released after they revealed that they were Roman citizens.
*Acts 16:6–40; 20:6; Philippians 1:1; 1 Thessalonians 2:2*

PHILISTIA
Land of the Philistines on the coast of Israel.

PHOENICIA
Small but important trading state on the coast of Syria, north of Israel. Its main towns were Tyre, Sidon, and Byblos.
*Obadiah 20; Mark 7:24ff.; Acts 11:19; 15:3*

PHOENIX
Modern Finika on the south coast of Crete. Paul advised those at a conference at Fair Havens not to sail to Phoenix for the winter, but they set sail and were shipwrecked in a storm.
*Acts 27:12*

PHRYGIA
Land in the center of Asia Minor, whose main cities included "Pisidian" Antioch and Iconium. Three other Phrygian cities are mentioned in the New Testament: Laodicea, Colossae, and Hierapolis.
*Acts 16:6; 18:23*

PISGAH
One of the peaks of Mount Nebo.

PISIDIA
Remote and dangerous mountainous area in the south of modern-day Turkey. Paul passed through here on his missionary travels, on his way from Perga to Antioch.
*Acts 13:14; 14:24*

PITHOM
Egyptian city lying east of the Nile Delta. One of Pharaoh's two supply-cities, built by Israelite slave labor.
*Exodus 1:11*

PLAIN, CITIES OF THE
Group of five cities – Sodom, Gomorrah, Admah, Zebliim, and Bela (or Zoar) – now probably buried under the shallow southern tip of the Dead Sea.
*Genesis 13:12; 19:24–29*

PONTUS
Ancient name for the Black Sea and also

for the land along its south coast. It became a Roman province, stretching along most of the northern coast of Asia Minor (Turkey). It was one of the lands to which Peter sent his first letter. The Christian message may have reached Pontus very early, because Jews from here were in Jerusalem on the Day of Pentecost.
*Acts 2:9; 18:2; 1 Peter 1:1*

PTOLEMAIS
Greek name for an ancient city in northern Israel, known in the Hebrew Bible as Acco. On his last visit to Jerusalem, Paul sailed here from Tyre and spent a day with the Christians. It is now known by its early name of Akko (Acre).
*Judges 1:31; Acts 21:7*

PUT
African country, probably part of Libya.
*Genesis 10:6; Jeremiah 46:9; Ezekiel 27:10*

PUTEOLI
Port in Italy near Naples now known as Pozzuoli. Paul landed here on his way to Rome as a prisoner.
*Acts 28:13*

# R

RAAMSES / RAMESSES
Egyptian city on the east side of the Nile Delta. Pharaoh Ramesses II's palace was here. Raamses and another city, Pithom, were built by the Israelites as supply centers for the king. The Israelites set out from Raamses on their escape from Egypt.
*Exodus 1:11; 12:37*

RABBAH / RABBATH–AMMON
The capital city of the Ammonites, an ancient people whose name is preserved in the modern name Amman (now the capital of Jordan). This territory was given to the tribe of Gad but was still occupied by the Ammonites until David's general, Joab, captured Rabbah. David was helped at Rabbah when he fled from his rebellious son Absalom. The city's wickedness was denounced by the Prophets and its destruction prophesied. Later the Greek name of Philadelphia was given to the city, and it became one of the ten cities of the Decapolis.

*Deuteronomy 3:11; Joshua 13:25; 2 Samuel 11:1; 12:26–31; 17:27; 1 Chronicles 20:1–3; Jeremiah 49:2; Ezekiel 21:20; 25:5; Amos 1:14*

RAMAH / RAMATHAIM–ZOPHIM
Name, meaning "height," used for many hill towns, two of which are very important in the Hebrew Bible. One was at er-Râm, 5 miles (8km) north of Jerusalem. The prophetess Deborah lived near here. It was captured and fortified by Baasha, King of Israel, and recaptured by Asa of Judah. According to Isaiah, the Assyrians approached Jerusalem by way of Ramah. When Jerusalem later fell to the Babylonians, Jeremiah was set free at Ramah. Rachel's tomb was said to be near here. The second Ramah* was farther north and was probably the birthplace and home of the prophet Samuel. It may have been the same place as the New Testament Arimathea.
*Judges 4:5; 19:13; 1 Kings 15:17, 22; 2 Chronicles 16:1, 6; Isaiah 10:29; Ezra 2:26; Nehemiah 11:33; Jeremiah 31:15; 40:1; *1 Samuel 1:1; 2:11*

RAMOTH–GILEAD
City east of the Jordan River that changed hands several times in the wars between Israel and Syria. Thought to be the same place as Mizpah in Gilead and therefore the home of Jephthah in the time of the Judges. One of Solomon's 12 district governors was stationed at Ramoth. King Ahab of Israel was killed in battle here, and Jehu was anointed king.
*Joshua 20:8; 1 Kings 4:13; 22; 2 Kings 9:1–10*

RED SEA
The Hebrew words *yam suph* translated mean "Sea of Reeds." The account of the Exodus refers to the area of lakes and marshes between the head of the Gulf of Suez and the Mediterranean Sea (the Suez Canal area).
*Exodus 13:7–14:31; Numbers 33:10; Deuteronomy 1:40*

REPHAIM
Valley southwest of Jerusalem where King David fought and defeated the Philistines. Also the name of one of the peoples who lived in Canaan before the Israelite Conquest.
*2 Samuel 5:18*

## REUBEN

Land east of the Dead Sea belonging to the tribe of Reuben.
*Joshua 13:15–23*

## RHEGIUM

Port in Italy (modern Reggio di Calabria) on the Strait of Messina, opposite Sicily. Paul's ship called here on his way to Rome.
*Acts 28:13*

## RIBLAH

Town on the Orontes River in Syria, where King Jehoahaz of Judah was taken prisoner by Pharaoh Neco of Egypt. Nebuchadnezzar had his headquarters here. King Zedekiah, the last king of Judah, was taken to Nebuchadnezzar at Riblah for sentence following rebellion.
*2 Kings 23:33; 25:6–7*

## ROME

City on the Tiber River in Italy, capital of the Roman empire. It was probably founded in 753BCE. Jews from Rome were in Jerusalem on the Day of Pentecost and heard Peter's message. There appears to have been an early Christian group in the city. Aquila and Priscilla, the Christian couple whom Paul met at Corinth, had come from Rome. They had probably been forced to leave when the emperor Claudius expelled all the Jews from his capital. Paul's letter to the Romans names a number of Christians in Rome already known to him. For two years Paul was under guard in Rome, during which time he may have written a few of his letters to Christians in other places. According to tradition, Peter also worked in Rome and was martyred with Paul. Rome's evil and corruption are referred to in Revelation, where the city ("great Babylon") is pictured as a prostitute drunk with the blood of God's people.
See pp.402–03
*Acts 2:10; 18:2; 19:21; 28:14–30; Romans 1:7, 15; 2 Timothy 1:16–17; Revelation 17:5–18:24*

# S

## SALAMIS

Commercial center on the east coast of Cyprus. Home to many Jews, and where Paul preached in the synagogues.
*Acts 13:5*

## SALEM SEE JERUSALEM

## SALT SEA

Hebrew Bible name for the Dead Sea.

## SAMARIA

Capital of the Northern Kingdom of Israel. King Omri began work on building the city in c.875BCE, and Ahab, his son, added a new palace. This was built using so many pieces of ivory that it became known as the "ivory house." The people of Samaria worshiped pagan gods and were thus condemned by many of the Prophets of the Hebrew Bible, who warned them that their city would be destroyed. Samaria fell to the Assyrians in c.722BCE, and the people were exiled to Syria, Assyria, and Babylonia. With the fall of Samaria, the kingdom of Israel ceased to exist and the whole area, not just the city, became known as Samaria. The city was rebuilt by Herod the Great and renamed Sebaste (Greek for Augustus). The Samaritans, a group of mixed-race Jews who also worshiped the God of Israel, lived here during this period and were despised by the Jews in Judea. But Jesus showed a great concern for them by traveling through their land and staying with them. Philip went to Samaria to preach the gospel, and Peter and John also preached in the area.
*1 Kings 16:24, 32; 2 Kings 6:8–7:20; Isaiah 8:4; Luke 17:11; John 4:1–43; Acts 8:5–25*

## SARDIS

City in the Roman province of Asia (Turkey) that was a great trade center in Roman times. In the book of Revelation, one of the seven letters to the churches in Asia was addressed to the Christians at Sardis. At this time, the Church and the people had become apathetic, relying too much on their past instead of concentrating on the present. The city had once been the capital of the kingdom of Lydia under the rule of the wealthy Croesus.
*Revelation 1:11; 3:1–6*

## SEA OF GALILEE SEE GALILEE

## SEIR

Another name for Edom.

## SELA

Built on a rocky plateau high in the mountains of Edom, the name means "rock" or "cliff." About 300BCE, the Nabateans took Sela and carved the city of Petra (Greek for "rock") out of the rocky valley at the foot of the original settlement.
*2 Kings 14:7; Isaiah 16:1; 42:11*

## SELEUCIA (SELEUCIA PIERIA)

Port of Antioch in Syria, from where Paul and Barnabas set sail for Cyprus on their first missionary journey.
*Acts 13:4*

## SENIR

Another name for Mount Hermon, used also to describe a nearby peak, and sometimes for the whole range of mountains.

## SEPHARVAIM

Town captured by the Assyrians. The people were brought to Samaria after the Jews had been sent into exile.
*2 Kings 17:24, 31*

## SHARON

Israel's coastal plain, extending 50 miles (80km) from Joppa to Caesarea. Today, it is a rich agricultural area, but in biblical times few people lived there. It was land used as pasture for sheep.
*1 Chronicles 27:29*

## SHEBA

Present-day Yemen in southwest Arabia. A wealthy country, it traded in spices, gold, and jewels. In the tenth century BCE the Queen of Sheba traveled over 1,000 miles (1,600km ) by camel caravan to visit King Solomon and test his wisdom. It is possible that she also wanted to arrange a trade agreement.
*1 Kings 10:1–10, 13; Psalm 72:15; Isaiah 60:6*

## SHECHEM

Ancient Canaanite town in the hill country of Ephraim, near Mount Gerizim. Here, Abraham was told by God that this was the country that would be given to him for his descendants. Jacob also visited Shechem, setting up camp outside the town. After the Israelites had conquered Canaan, Joshua gathered all the tribes at Shechem to renew their promise to worship God and to reject all others. In the time of the Judges, Canaanite worship was practiced in Shechem. Gideon's

son Abimelech was given money by the inhabitants so that he could pay to have his 70 brothers killed. Abimelech made himself king of Shechem, but when the people turned against him, he destroyed the town in revenge. Solomon's son Rehoboam was rejected at Shechem. Jeroboam, the first king of the new Northern Kingdom, started to rebuild the city. Shechem survived the fall of Israel, becoming the Samaritans' most important city and the site of a great temple.
*Genesis 12:6–7; 33:18–35:5; 37:12–18; Joshua 24; Judges 9; 1 Kings 12*

## SHILOH
Town where the Tabernacle was set up; it thus became the center of Israel's worship. The tent was replaced by a more permanent building and an annual special festival was held here. Hannah and Elkanah traveled to Shiloh to worship God. When Hannah prayed for a son, she promised to give him back to serve God. When Samuel was born, Hannah kept her promise and brought him back to Shiloh, where he grew up in the temple under the care of Eli the priest. The town was destroyed about 1050BCE, probably by the Philistines. The prophet Jeremiah warned that the Temple in Jerusalem would be destroyed, just as the place of worship at Shiloh had been.
*Joshua 18:1; Judges 21:19; 1 Samuel 1–4; Jeremiah 7:12–16*

## SHINAR
Another name for Babylonia.

## SHITTIM / ABEL–SHITTIM
Place on the plains of Moab, also known as Abel-shittim ("field of acacias"). Just before crossing the Jordan into Canaan, the Israelites camped here. It was likely that they were at Shittim when the king of Moab tried to persuade Balaam to curse them. Here, Joshua was appointed as Moses' successor.
*Numbers 25:1; Joshua 2:1; 3:1*

## SHUNEM
Town (modern-day Sôlem) in northern Israel. The Philistines set up camp here before the battle on Mount Gilboa when Saul and Jonathan were killed. While staying here Elisha restored a child to life.
*Joshua 19:18; 1 Samuel 28:4; 1 Kings 1:3; 2 Kings 4:8–37*

## SHUR
Desert area in the northwest region of the Sinai peninsula. Hagar fled here after Sarah had treated her unkindly. The Israelites had to travel through this region after escaping from Egypt, and they complained bitterly about the lack of water.
*Genesis 16; Exodus 15:22–25*

## SIDDIM
Valley where Chedorlaomer, king of Elam, fought against the kings of the plain. Lot was taken prisoner during the fighting but was later rescued by Abraham.
*Genesis 14*

## SIDON
Phoenician port on the coast of modern Lebanon, famed for its skilled craftsmen exporting carved ivory, gold and silver jewelry, and glassware. Sidon was not taken when the Israelites conquered Canaan, and in the time of the Judges the people of Sidon attacked and harassed the Israelites. Gradually the cultures began to merge, and the Israelites were accused of worshiping the gods of Sidon – Baal and Ashtoreth. Jezebel was the daughter of a king of Sidon, and she promoted the worship of Baal in Israel. The town was opposed to Israel and the worship of God and so became a place destined to be destroyed, according to the Prophets. By New Testament times most of the people of Sidon were Greek. Many of them went to hear Jesus preach in Galilee. Jesus himself visited Sidon and the neighboring city of Tyre. Paul stopped at Sidon on his way to Rome.
*Judges 1:31; 10:12; 1 Kings 16:31; 17:9; Isaiah 23:1–12; Ezekiel 28:20–24; Matthew 15:20–28; Luke 6:17; Acts 27:3*

## SILOAM
Underground pool that was one of Jerusalem's main sources of water. When the Assyrians threatened to besiege Jerusalem, Hezekiah realized the city needed its own water supply in order to survive and had a tunnel cut through the rock to tap the Gihon Spring outside Jerusalem. Jesus cured a blind man by telling him to wash his eyes in this pool. The tower of Siloam, which collapsed killing 18 people, probably stood on the slope of Mount Zion, above the pool.
*2 Kings 20:20; Luke 13:4; John 9:1–12*

## SIMEON
Land in the Negev, southern Israel, given to the tribe of Simeon.
*Joshua 19:1–9*

## SINAI
Mountain in the Sinai peninsula and the area of desert around it. The Israelites set up camp here three months after leaving Egypt. God gave Moses the Ten Commandments on the mountain. The exact location of the mountain is not known.
*See p.95; Exodus 19–32, 34*

## SMYRNA
Port town, present-day Izmir in Turkey. In New Testament times it had many splendid public buildings, one of which was the temple built in honor of the emperor Tiberius (emperor worship was practied here). One of the letters to the seven churches in the book of Revelation is addressed to the Christians at Smyrna.
*Revelation 1:11; 2:8–11*

## SODOM
Lot settled in this town, famous for its immorality, which was destroyed along with Gomorrah because of this sinfulness. He escaped after being warned of the impending disaster. The town now probably lies submerged at the southern end of the Dead Sea.
*Genesis 13:8–13; 14; 19*

## SUCCOTH
• Egyptian town where the Israelites made their first camp on their journey out of the country.
*Exodus 12:37; 13:20; Numbers 33:5–6*
• Town in the Jordan valley, part of the territory of Gad. After Jacob and his brother Esau agreed to go their separate ways, Jacob stayed in Succoth for a while. In the time of the Judges the people of Succoth refused to provide Gideon and his army with food while he was fighting the Midianites. After Gideon's victory he returned and punished the town officials.
*Genesis 33:12–17; Judges 8:4–16*

## SUSA
Ancient city north of the Persian Gulf, capital city of the Elamite empire until it was destroyed in 645BCE by the king of Assyria, Ashurbanipal, exiling inhabitants to Samaria. It regained importance under the Medes and Persians, being one of the three royal cities of the Achaemenid (Persian) kings. Darius I built a palace here, the ruins of which can still be seen today. The story of Esther, the Jewish girl who became queen of Persia, took place at the royal court in Susa. The city was later captured by Alexander the Great.
*Ezra 4:9–10; Nehemiah 1:1; Esther 1:2*

## SYCHAR
Samaritan town (its exact site is unknown) where Jesus met and talked to a Samaritan woman who had come to draw water. When the inhabitants heard what the woman said about Jesus, many believed that he was the Messiah.
*John 4:1–42*

## SYENE
Place on the southern border of Egypt, modern-day Aswan. Isaiah pictures dispersed Jews returning to Jerusalem from as far away as Syene.
*Isaiah 49:12; Ezekiel 29:10*

## SYRACUSE
Ancient Sicilian city. Paul spent three days here on the last stage of his voyage to Rome after a shipwreck on Malta.
*Acts 28:12*

## SYRIA
In the Hebrew Bible, Syria is the land occupied by the Aramaeans to the north and northeast of Israel, with Damascus as its capital. In the New Testament, Syria was a Roman province whose capital was Antioch on the Orontes.

# T

## TAANACH
Canaanite city on the edge of the valley of Jezreel. Barak fought Sisera near Taanach. It became one of the cities of the Levites.
*Joshua 21:25; Judges 5:19*

## TABOR
Mountain in the Plain of Jezreel. Barak gathered his army here in the time of the Judges.
*Judges 4*

## TAHPANHES
Egyptian town in the east of the Nile Delta where the prophet Jeremiah was taken after the fall of Jerusalem. He probably died here.
*Jeremiah 43:5–10; Ezekiel 30:18*

## TARSHISH
Distant place to which Jonah set sail when he disobeyed God's command to go to Nineveh. It may have been Tartessus in Spain (in some modern versions of the Bible Tarshish is translated as Spain).
*Isaiah 23:6; Jeremiah 10:9; Ezekiel 27:12; Jonah 1:3*

## TARSUS
Town in southern Turkey, on the Cilician plain, an important university city in New Testament times, with a large population. Paul was born here and returned here shortly after becoming a Christian.
*Acts 9:11, 30; 21:39; 22:3*

## TEKOA
Town 6 miles (10km) south of Bethlehem in the Judean hills. A wise woman from Tekoa pleaded with King David to allow his son Absalom to come back to Jerusalem. The town was also the home of the prophet Amos.
*2 Samuel 14:2; Amos 1:1*

## TEMAN
Part of Edom where the people were famous for their wisdom.
*Jeremiah 49:7*

## THEBES
Ancient capital of upper Egypt on the River Nile, 330 miles (531km ) south of Cairo. The site is marked by two great temples of the God Amun (Karnak and Luxor). It was a wealthy city from 1500–1000BCE, when Amun was the official god of the Egyptian empire, with great riches and many treasures. The city fell to the Assyrians in 663BCE. Jeremiah and Ezekiel, the prophets, pronounced judgment on Thebes along with other Egyptian cities.
*Jeremiah 46:25; Ezekiel 30:14–15; Nahum 3:8–10*

## THESSALONICA
Macedonia's (northern Greece) principal city on the Egnatian Way, the main Roman road to the East. Paul visited the city as part of his mission, but angry Jews forced him to move on to Beroea. Soon after, Paul wrote two letters to the Thessalonian Christians.
*Acts 17:1–15; Philippians 4:16; 1 Thessalonians 1:1; 2 Thessalonians 1:1*

## THYATIRA
City in the Roman province of Asia (present-day Akhisar in western Turkey). The town was a manufacturing center for dyeing, fabrics, clothes, pottery, and brasswork. Lydia, the businesswoman from Thyatira who became a Christian when she met Paul at Philippi, was a "dealer in purple cloth." One of the seven letters in the book of Revelation was addressed to the church at Thyatira.
*Acts 16:14–15; Revelation 1:11; 2:18–29*

## TIBERIAS
Town on the west shore of the Sea of Galilee, founded by King Herod Antipas and named after the Roman emperor Tiberius.
*John 6:23*

## TIGRIS
Mesopotamia's second greatest river. The great Assyrian cities of Nineveh, Calah, and Assur were all built on the banks of the Tigris. It is mentioned as one of the four great rivers of Eden.
*Genesis 2:14; Daniel 10:4*

## TIMNAH
Town situated on the northern border of Judah that fell to the Philistines. It was the home of Samson's first wife.
*Judges 14:1–7*

## TIMNATH–SERAH / TIMNATH–HERES
Town situated in the hill country of Ephraim, northwest of Jerusalem. Joshua was given this town as his own and was buried here after his death.
*Joshua 19:50; 24:30; Judges 2:9*

## TIRZAH
Town in the north of Israel, captured

by Joshua. It was later the home of Jeroboam I and became the first capital of the Northern Kingdom of Israel. King Omri later moved the center of government to his new city of Samaria.
*Joshua 12:24; 1 Kings 14:17; 2 Kings 15:14–16; Song of Songs 6:4*

## TISHBE
Place in Gilead, east of the Jordan River (the actual site is not known). Elijah, the "Tishbite," probably came from here.
*1 Kings 17:1*

## TOB
Region south of Damascus where Jephthah lived as an outlaw in the time of the Judges. The people of Tob helped the Ammonites against David.
*Judges 11:3*

## TOPHETH
Place in the valley of Hinnom where children were sacrificed. The shrine was destroyed by King Josiah.
*2 Kings 23:10; Jeremiah 7:31, 19:6, 10–14*

## TRACHONITIS
Rocky volcanic area, east of Galilee and south of Damascus, linked with Ituraea. Together they made up the territory ruled by Herod Philip in the time when John the Baptist began his preaching.
*Luke 3:1*

## TROAS
Port near Troy in northwest Turkey used by Paul on his travels. Here Paul had his vision of a Macedonian man calling for help, and he sailed from here on his missionary travels to Europe.
*Acts 16:8–12; 20:5–12; 2 Corinthians 2:12–13*

## TYRE
Large port and city-state on the coast of Lebanon. It had two harbors, one on the mainland and one on an offshore island. After the Philistines plundered Sidon, the other important Phoenician port nearby, in 1200BCE, Tyre became the leading city. Tyre flourished in the time of David and Solomon. King Hiram of Tyre provided the wood and labor to build the Temple in Jerusalem. The city is often mentioned in the Psalms and by the Prophets, who condemned

its pride and luxury. Tyre was captured in succession by the Assyrians, Babylonians, and finally Alexander the Great and his Greek army. In the New Testament period, Tyre was visited many times by Jesus, who preached to its people.
*2 Samuel 5:11; 1 Kings 5; 9:10–14;Psalm 45:12; Isaiah 23; Ezekiel 26, 27;Matthew 15:21; Luke 6:17; Acts 21:3*

# U

## UR
From the third millennium BCE, a city on the Euphrates River in south Babylonia (modern Iraq); Abraham's home before he and his family moved to Harran. The city was abandoned in 300BCE after being occupied for several thousand years. The royal graves here (c.600BCE) contained many examples of beautiful craftsmanship.
*See p.35*
*Genesis 11:28–31*

## UZ
Job's home country, probably in the region of Edom.
*Job 1:1*

# Z

## ZAREPHATH / SAREPTA
Small town belonging to Sidon and later to Tyre. The prophet Elijah stayed here with a widow during the time of the drought. Later he restored the widow's dead son to life.
*1 Kings 17:8–24; Luke 4:26*

## ZEBOIIM
One of a group of five cities that included Sodom and Gomorrah. Zeboiim was also the name of a valley near Michmash, in the desert east of Jerusalem. It was the site of a Philistine raid in the days of Saul.
*Genesis 14:2, 8; Deuteronomy 29:23; 1 Samuel 13:18*

## ZEBULUN
Land belonging to the tribe of Zebulun, in Galilee.
*Joshua 19:10–16*

## ZIKLAG
Town in the south of Judah. It was given

to David by the king of Gath when he was an outlaw from King Saul. When Amalekites raided the town, David rescued the captives taken by them.
*1 Samuel 27:6; 30*

## ZIN
Desert region near Kadesh-barnea, where the Israelites camped after the Exodus.
*Numbers 13:21; 20:1; 27:14*

## ZION
Fortified hill that David captured from the Jebusites. The name became synonymous with Jerusalem .

## ZIPH
Hill town belonging to the tribe of Judah, southeast of Hebron. David hid from Saul in the desert near Ziph, and Jonathan came to encourage him there. The people of the town betrayed him to Saul, and he moved to Maon and Engedi. Later, Ziph was one of the places fortified by King Rehoboam. Today the site is still called Tell Zif.
*Joshua 15:55; 1 Samuel 23:14–29; 2 Chronicles 11:8*

## ZOAN / TANIS
Ancient Egyptian town in northeast of the Nile Delta. From about 1100 to 660BCE, Zoan was used as the capital of Egypt.
*Numbers 13:22; Isaiah 19:11*

## ZOAR
One of five cities, probably at the southern end of the Dead Sea. When Sodom and the other cities were destroyed, Lot fled to Zoar.
*Genesis 13:10; 14:2, 8; 19:18–30*

## ZOBAH
Aramaean kingdom between Damascus and Hamath defeated by David.
*2 Samuel 8:3; 10:6*

## ZORAH
Birthplace of Samson.
*Judges 13:2*

# GLOSSARY

**ABBA** An Anamaic word of affectionate respect, meaning "father"– not an abbreviation. It was used by Jesus of God.

**ALPHA AND OMEGA** "The first and the last": Alpha and Omega are the first and last letters of the Greek alphabet. In the book of Revelation, they refer to God at the beginning and the end, the all-encompassing.

**ALTAR** A raised table or cairn of stones in a holy place, where SACRIFICES and offerings are made to God.

**AMEN** From a Hebrew verb meaning "to be fixed, firm," hence "trustworthy." It is used to end prayers or religious statements to express strong assent to them (so be it).

**ANCESTORS** Forebears. The term is now commonly used in place of Patriarchs in recognition of the equally important part played by the Matriarchs.
See pp.34–35

**ANNUNCIATION** The announcement by the Archangel Gabriel to Mary that she would bear the Messiah.
See pp.318–19

**ANOINT** To apply oil or ointment to a person or object as a sign of its being dedicated to God. In the Hebrew Bible, priests, prophets, and kings are anointed as a sign of consecration. In the New Testament, the sick are anointed and prayed over.
See pp.114–15

**ANTICHRIST** An enemy of Christ. In the New Testament, the word is sometimes used as if there is one Antichrist behind all antichrists.
See p.445

**APOCALYPSE** from Greek for revelation. Hence Apocalyptic, writings claiming to reveal truths about things otherwise unknown – for example, future events and the end of the world.
See pp.260–61, 468–71

**APOCRYPHA, APOCRYPHAL WRITINGS** Hidden things. Protestants refer to the 14 books of the Greek version of the Hebrew Bible, found in the SEPTUAGINT but not included in the Hebrew Bible, as the Apocrypha. Some are included in Orthodox and Roman Catholic Bibles, where they are known as Deuterocanonical books.
See pp.253–61

**APOSTASY** from Greek for desertion. Losing one's religious faith and leaving one's religion.

**APOSTLE** from Greek for one sent out. Early Christian missionaries and leaders, especially the 12 disciples.
See pp.330–31

**ARK OF THE COVENANT** A rectangular wooden box, overlaid with gold both inside and out. Believed to represent the presence of God, this was the most sacred religious symbol of the Hebrew people, thought to have contained the stone tablets on which the Ten Commandments were written.
See p.61

**ASCENSION** Jesus' return to Heaven at the end of his life on earth.
See pp.382–83

**ATONEMENT** An English coinage, "At-one-ment," to translate the Hebrew kaphar, "to cover over." In the Hebrew Bible, human misbehavior leads to estrangement from God. Through personal repentance, symbolized by ritual sacrifice, the individual is reconciled to God. This applies to the entire people of Israel on the Day of Atonement (YOM KIPPUR). In the New Testament, Jesus' suffering and death on the cross make it possible for anyone to be reconciled to God.
See pp.422–23

**BAAL** Important Canaanite god, opposed by Hebrew Bible prophets such as Elijah. Worship may have involved cultic prostitution and sacrifice.

**BAPTISM** A ritual ceremony using water for the washing away of sins and for admission into the Kingdom or Church.
See pp.324–25, 409, 418–19

**BEATITUDES, THE** The sequence of blessings pronounced by Jesus in the Sermon on the Mount.
See pp.335

**BENE ISRAEL/JACOB** Lit. the sons/children of Israel/Jacob, the term used to describe the sons of the Ancestor Jacob, and subsequently the Twelve Tribes and the Israelite nation that descended from them.

**BODY OF CHRIST** The Church as a unit, mystically linked to Christ. Also a description of the bread at the EUCHARIST.

**CANAAN** The land between the Jordan River/Dead Sea and the Mediterranean Sea. The Israelites believed that it was promised to them by God after their flight from Egypt, so it is sometimes referred to as the Promised Land.
See pp.98–99

**CANON** from Greek for rule. The list of books accepted as belonging to the Bible. Hence canonical, a part of the Canon.
See pp.189, 474–75

**CHOSEN PEOPLE** A term applied to the people of Israel because they were elected to be God's witnesses in the world. With "chosenness" come particular responsibilities.
See pp.54–55

**CHRIST** from Greek translation of Hebrew MESSIAH, anointed one (anointed suggesting chosen and commissioned). Originally one of the titles of Jesus, later it became part of his name.

**CIRCUMCISION** Removal of the foreskin of an Israelite, later Jewish, male child when eight days old (occasionally an adult) as a sign of membership of the Covenant with God.
See pp.281, 394–95

**CLAN** A group of people related by ancestry or marriage. There were a number of clans within each of the tribes of Israel.

**CLEAN/UNCLEAN** The state of ritual purity or impurity.

**CODEX** Manuscripts in pages with writing on both sides, thus able to be made into books.
See p.474

**COMMUNION** Another name for the EUCHARIST. Also, the spiritual union between Christ, individual Christians, their churches, and their fellow Christians.

**COVENANT** A legally binding agreement, based on faithful loyalty (Hebrew chesed) between those involved. The Hebrew Bible knows a series of covenants between God and human beings: e.g., with Noah after the Flood; with Abraham; with the people of Israel at Mount Sinai; and with King David. By Christians, the Covenant with Israel is known as the Old Covenant, renewed and fulfilled in the New Covenant, or Testament, of Christ.
See pp.60–61

CULT  A system of religious worship. In the Hebrew Bible, the Temple cult was the system of sacrifices and rituals at the TEMPLE.
*See pp.376–77*

DAY OF ATONEMENT, THE
SEE YOM KIPPUR

DAY OF THE LORD, THE  A time at which God acts decisively. The phrase is often used to describe a future time when God will act in judgment, either on Israel or on all nations at the end of history.
*See pp.240–41, 263*

DECALOGUE  The Ten Commandments.

DEDICATION  SEE HANUKKAH

DETERMINISM  The belief that everything that happens is completely determined and necessarily caused by what came before so that there is no human freedom, and choice, therefore, is an illusion.

DEUTEROCANONICAL BOOKS
SEE APOCRYPHA

DEUTERONOMISTIC  Relating to the book of Deuteronomy. The word is used in particular when seeking to extrapolate from the characteristics of that book to a hypothetical school of historians or particular writers who wrote or edited other biblical books, or parts of them.
*See pp. 80–81, 105*

DEVIL  The most powerful evil being, seen as the primary enemy of God.
*See p.473*

DIASPORA  The dispersal of the Jews into lands other than Israel. It thus refers to Jews living outside Israel.
*See pp.159, 280–81*

DOCTRINE  *from Latin for* teaching. Beliefs.

DOXOLOGY  A verse or hymn in praise of God, especially one used in LITURGY.

DUALISM  The belief that reality is based on equally strong but opposing forces of good and evil.

ELDER  Traditional local leaders throughout the biblical period. Senior member of a church, with some responsibility for service and church discipline. Elders were a part of the structure of New Testament churches, although they are not always so in modern churches.

ELECTION  The doctrine that God chooses certain people for relationship with God and for Heaven.

ELOHIM  (Also EL.) Early Hebrew and Canaanite term for God. The form of the word in Hebrew is plural, hence in the Hebrew Bible it is used as a general term for "the gods" of the nations. When understood as a singular form, it is used of Israel's God who is also the Creator of the whole world.
*See pp.58–59*

EMMANUEL  SEE IMMANUEL.

END-TIME  The time leading up to the end of the world.

EPISCOPACY  Church government by bishops.

EPISTLE  Letter, in particular one of the letters adopted as a book in the New Testament.
*See p.405*

ESCHATOLOGY  *from Greek for* discourse of or study of last things. Doctrine concerning the end of the world, the return of the Messiah, and the final destiny of humankind.
*See pp.262–63*

ESSENES  An ascetic Jewish sect, flourishing at the time of Jesus, that followed strict purity laws.
*See p.289*

ETERNAL LIFE  According to the New Testament, the new, unending, and unlimited life that God bestows on those who are "in Christ" and "know God," in which they are united with Christ and thus reconciled to God, initially on earth and finally in Heaven.

ETHICS  Morals, considered systematically. The rules, principles, and values that should govern human conduct and the study thereof.
*See pp.466–67*

EUCHARIST  *from Greek for* thanksgiving. The Christian ceremony commemorating the Last Supper and Christ's PASSION.
*See pp.418–19*

EVANGELIST  *from Greek for* good news. One who preaches the GOSPEL of Christ. Also, the authors of the four Gospels are known as the four evangelists. Hence evangelical, concerned with the evangel, the good news of Christ and his work of salvation.

EXILE, THE  The period between 587/6 and 538/7BCE, when many of the inhabitants of Jerusalem and Judaea were deported to Babylon.
*See pp.146–47, 152–53*

EXODUS, THE  *from Greek for* the way out. The Israelites' departure from Egypt, led by Moses.
*See pp.48–49, 52–53*

EXPIATION  Making amends for sin, so that it no longer causes a breach with God.
*See p.422*

EXTREME UNCTION  The anointing with oil of those close to death.

FALL, THE  In Christian understanding, the disobedience of Adam and Eve and their fall from God's presence. Through the Fall, sin entered the world and human nature, which it has affected ever since.
*See pp.30–31*

FALSE PROPHET  One who falsely claims to speak for God. False prophecy is very strongly condemned throughout Scripture. In Revelation, a powerful figure of evil is called "the false prophet."
*See pp.196–98*

GENTILE  A translation of the Hebrew word *goy*, which simply means "nation" (including Israel) in the Hebrew Bible. Only in the Second Temple Period is it used to distinguish non-Jewish people from Jews.

GLOSSOLALIA  *from Greek for* tongues or languages; "speaking in tongues."
*See p.417*

GNOSTICISM  *from Greek for* knowledge. Umbrella term for second-century sects, which sought to escape the body to purely spiritual life-via secret knowledge (gnosis), known only to them. They included parts of the Christian story in their beliefs and claimed to have the true understanding of it. Hence gnostic.

GODHEAD  God, or the nature and state of being God. The word is often used when referring to the TRINITY, to stress that the persons of the Trinity are united in the Godhead.

GOSPEL  *from the Old English* "godspel" – good news. The teaching that God has redeemed humankind through Jesus Christ. Also refers to the first four books of the New Testament, the four Gospels, which deal with Jesus' life, death, and Resurrection.
*See pp.300–13*

GRACE  Abundant and unmerited love, freely given by God to humanity, especially, in the Christian view, in Christ.
*See pp.426–27*

HADES  Greek term, used in the New Testament, for a place of "departed spirits." Linked to the Hebrew Bible idea of SHEOL.

HALLELUJAH / ALLELUIA  *Hebrew for* "Praise the Lord." Commonly found in Psalms and used in Jewish and Christian worship as an exclamation of praise to, and adoration for, God.

**HANUKKAH** Means "dedication" and refers to a Jewish religious festival, lasting eight days, celebrating the victory of the Maccabees and the rededication of the Jerusalem TEMPLE.
See pp.68–69

**HELLENISM** In general, the spirit and characteristics of classical Greek civilization. Also, a movement and approach by the Seleucid Greek rulers, whose empire included Palestine, to "Hellenize" every country in their empire – i.e., to make them Greek in language, culture, and religion. It was broadly welcomed in most of their domain, but most Jews in Palestine were resistant on religious grounds.
See pp.246–47

**HERESY** from Greek for choice. Rejecting parts of the orthodox form of a religion and instead following beliefs that differ from it.

**HIGH PLACE** A raised place used for religious worship, hence a sanctuary. Especially used with reference to the holy sites of Canaanite religions.

**HOLINESS** Translation of the Hebrew word qadosh, "set apart," or "other." In the Hebrew Bible it refers to the quality that sets God apart from, and beyond, limited human qualities. People are called upon to aspire to holiness through obedience to God's will and in imitation of God's actions in the world.
See p.63

**HOLY OF HOLIES** The most sacred part of the TEMPLE in Jerusalem, containing initially the ARK OF THE COVENANT. It was curtained off and was entered only once a year on the Day of Atonement by the High Priest.

**HOLY SPIRIT** God present to people in the world, the agent of inspiration. In Christianity, the third person of the TRINITY, which consists of the Father, the Son, and the Holy Spirit.
See pp.409, 416–17

**HOSANNA** Greek form of Hebrew for "save now, we pray." An exclamation of praise of God found in Psalm 118 and subsequent Jewish liturgies. It was also used at the triumphal entry of Jesus into Jerusalem.

**HYMN** A song of praise, in particular a song of praise to God.

**IDOL** An image, often carved, which is worshiped as a god. Hence idolatry, worship of a false god.

**IMMANUEL/EMMANUEL** Hebrew for God with us. One of the names given to Jesus, because Christians identify him with the

child prophesied in Isaiah 7:14, who was to be called Immanuel.

**IMMORTALITY** Perpetual, unending life, not subject to death or decay. Greek and many Eastern philosophers believed that immortality belonged only to the SOUL. It does not occur in the Hebrew Bible. Christians believe that if the soul is reborn in Christ, the body will also be raised to new life, as Christ's was.

**INCARNATION** from Latin for in the flesh. The belief that God is present in a human life. Christians believe this of Jesus, believing also that the Son who took the initiative to be incarnate in Jesus is the pre-existing second Person of the TRINITY.

**JEHOVAH** A nonexistent name for God derived from an error. Since no vowels were written in the letters YHWH, this name of God cannot be pronounced. The vowels from Adonai, "my Lord," were inserted as a signal to pronounce that word instead. Trying to read this mixed word as written produces the impossible "Yahowah" or Jehovah.
See also YHWH.
See pp.58–59

**JERUSALEM COUNCIL** An early meeting of Church leaders at which the Apostles and elders decided that Gentile converts need not be circumcised and forced to obey the LAW.
See pp.394–95

**JUBILEE** In the TORAH, the fiftieth year was named the year of Jubilee, and decreed to be a time when slaves were liberated, debts were cancelled, and land returned to its original owners. Hence the word "Jubilee" is used of times, seasons, or anniversaries for rejoicing.

**JUDAISM** The religion of the Jewish people based on the TORAH, the "written law," and the traditional commentary, "oral law," that accompanied it according to rabbinic thought.
See pp.280–83, 288–89

**JUDGES** Leaders who ruled among the tribes of Israel from the death of Joshua to the time of Samuel; and the name of the book dealing with that period of Israelite history.
See pp.104–07

**JUSTIFICATION** The initial gift of God's GRACE by which a sinner is absolved by God.
See pp.422, 426–27

**KABBALAH** Jewish mystical teachings. In their earliest form they were derived from the Creation story in Genesis 1 and the first chapter of Ezekiel but, since the 12th century CE, based on the study of the Zohar, a mystical commentary on the TORAH.

**KINGDOM OF GOD, THE** Prophetic teaching that in time the entire world would come to accept the universal rule of Israel's God. The Kingdom of God or of Heaven is fundamental in the teaching of Jesus.
See pp.332–33

**KINGSHIP** SEE SACRAL KINGSHIP

**KINSHIP GROUP** An alliance of families, clans, and tribes in which the relationship is recognized but not always actively expressed. Hence the BENE ISRAEL are referred to as a kinship group.
See pp.102–03

**LAW, THE** An inadequate translation of the Hebrew word TORAH, which contains elements of law, teaching, and guidance. It refers to the set of laws and teachings given to the Israelites by God, aimed at creating an ideal society based on their obligations to each other, to the land, and to God under the COVENANT.
See pp.24–25

**LEVIATHAN** Huge marine animal representing a threat of chaos, defeated by God.

**LITURGY** The fixed forms of public services practiced by a community. In Judaism this may center on the reading from the TORAH; in Christianity on the EUCHARIST.

**LOGOS** from Greek for word or reason. A name by which the second person of the TRINITY, the Son, Jesus, is referred to, particularly in the Gospel of John.

**LORD'S SUPPER** Name in 1 Corinthians 11:20 for COMMUNION or the EUCHARIST. The first such meal was the final meal that Jesus shared with his disciples, known as the Last Supper.
See pp.350–51, 418–19

**LXX** A symbol for SEPTUAGINT.

**MAGI** Zoroastrian ritual experts, or priests, of ancient Persia (Iran), later a term used more generally for wise or learned men of various kinds, in particular those who traveled to bring gifts to the infant Jesus.

**MANNA** Food miraculously provided for the Israelites on their way through the wilderness from Egypt to the PROMISED LAND.
See p.72

**MARTYR** from Greek for witness. Initially used to refer to any who witnessed to Christ. Later used to refer only to those who died for their faith. Hence martyrdom.
See pp.459

**MASORETIC** from Hebrew for tradition. Relating to the Massora, or Massorah, the authoritative text with notes and commentaries of the Hebrew Bible as established by the Masoretic school of rabbis between the sixth and tenth centuries.

MATRIARCH See ANCESTORS
*See pp.112–13*

MENORAH Seven-branched candelabrum used in the TEMPLE, subsequently an emblem of Israel, and later of Judaism.

MESSIAH *from Hebrew for* anointed one. In the Hebrew Bible, a Messiah is a person chosen and commissioned by anointing for a special role, for example a king or High Priest. Visions of the future included the restoration of an anointed king on the throne of David, a "Messiah," for whom the Jewish people still wait, but who Christians believe was and is Jesus of Nazareth, the Christ.
*See pp.123, 346–47*

MIDRASH *from Hebrew for* to search. A Jewish commentary on the Hebrew Bible.

MILLENNIUM *from Latin for* a thousand years. In Revelation 20, a thousand-year reign of Christ is described but so vaguely that there have been unending speculations about its timing and nature.

MINISTRY *from Latin for* service. Spiritual work of all Christians, but the word now is increasingly used of those ordained.
*See pp.448–49*

MIRACLE The translation of a Hebrew term meaning "sign," it can refer to any event that signifies God's action or intervention in the world. More commonly it refers to a spectacularly supernatural event.
*See pp.342–45*

MISHNAH *from Hebrew for* instruction. A compilation of Jewish teachings collected together in the late second century CE. It forms the earlier part of the TALMUD.

MONOTHEISM The belief that there is only one God.

MONTANISM A Christian heresy founded by the prophet Montanus in Asia Minor in the second century CE. It focused on strict holy living and direct guidance by God through certain new prophets, especially Montanus.

MOSAIC Of Moses. Linked with Moses, as for example the Mosaic Law, or the Law of Moses, another name for the TORAH.

NAZIRITES / NAZARITES Individuals within ancient Israel who vowed to abstain from drinking alcohol, from cutting their hair, and from contact with a dead body

for a fixed period as evidence of special dedication to God.

ORACLE A prophecy, or a shrine at which prophecies are made. Also, the word used to refer to the Scriptures, which have been called the Oracles of God. In the Hebrew Bible it refers to the HOLY OF HOLIES.

ORDINATION A ceremony in which someone is commissioned into church ministry and leadership.

ORIGINAL SIN A Christian doctrine, it is a state of human nature involving inner corruption, bias toward sin, and being cut off from God, inherited by all people since sin originally entered the world at the FALL.

ORTHODOXY *from Greek for* right belief. A term applied to the central core of Jewish or Christian beliefs and practices. Also, a name sometimes applied to the Orthodox Churches as a whole.

ORTHOPRAXY *from Greek for* right behavior. The way of love and obedience that should accompany orthodox belief.

PAGAN *from Latin for* a country dweller, or a civilian, i.e., someone not in the ranks of Christ's army. Hence the word has come to mean someone who follows a local or unsophisticated religion.
*See pp.376–77*

PARABLE *from Greek for* placing beside, hence analogy. A short story that uses ordinary life to illustrate moral and spiritual truths.
*See pp.336–39*

PARACLETE *from Greek for* advocate or helper. A name for the HOLY SPIRIT in his role as comforter and helper: and for Jesus in 1 John 2:1.
*See p.313*

PARADISE Hebrew *pardes*, a Persian loan-word meaning "orchard." In later tradition a blessed place where the righteous live. Can refer to Heaven, or to Eden before the expulsion of Adam and Eve.

PAROUSIA *from Greek for* presence. A word for the presence of God in the final completion of the Kingdom, especially in association with Jesus.
*See p.444*

PARTICULARISM In theology, the doctrine that divine grace or salvation is restricted to a certain group (called "the elect") and not offered to all.
*See pp.232–33*

PASSION *from Latin for* suffering. Christ's suffering leading up to the Crucifixion.

Hence, the suffering and death of a MARTYR may be referred to as that martyr's passion.
*See pp.360–61*

PASSOVER Annual Jewish festival commemorating the EXODUS.
*See pp.68–69*

PASTORALS The three New Testament letters advising church leaders on the way to care for the churches in their charge.
*See pp.446–47*

PATRIARCH The male head of a tribe or family. Used of the Hebrew leaders before the time of Moses, in particular Abraham, Isaac, and Jacob, and also of the 12 sons of Jacob.
*See pp.34–35*

PAULINE Relating to Paul.

PENTATEUCH *from Greek for* five scrolls The first five books of the Bible: Genesis, Exodus, Leviticus, Numbers, and Deuteronomy. These books contain, and are also called, the TORAH.
*See pp.20–23*

PENTECOST *from Greek for* fiftieth. The Jewish Feast of Weeks (*Shavuot*) on the 50th day after Passover. On this day, the first fruits of the harvest were presented at the Temple. In the New Testament, the HOLY SPIRIT descended on the Apostles at Pentecost.
*See pp.384–85*

PEOPLE OF THE BOOK Muslim name for Jews and Christians. The book referred to is the Bible.

PERSECUTION Oppression or harassment, especially because of race or religion.

PHARISEES *from Hebrew for* interpreters, *also for* separated. One of the main Jewish groupings of the New Testament period.
*See pp.288–89*

POLYTHEISM The belief in, and worship of, more than one God.

PROMISED LAND SEE CANAAN

PROPHET Someone through whom God speaks, hence prophecy.
*See pp.195–99, 417*

PROSELYTE Someone newly converted to a religious faith, especially a Gentile newly converted to Judaism.

PROVIDENCE God's purposeful government of the world, in particular by way of care and protection of all creatures.

PSALM *from Greek for* a song accompanied on the harp. The 150 sacred songs, poems,

and prayers collected as one of the books of the Hebrew Bible. Often used in worship.
*See pp.176–77*

PSALTER  Another name for the book of Psalms, or for a book containing all the psalms, often with a musical setting.
*See pp.176–77*

PSEUDEPIGRAPHA  Writings that are attributed to someone other than the author, usually in order to give them more authority. This term is frequently used of pseudonymous Jewish and Christian works from the first century BCE onward.
*See pp.462–63*

PURIM  A Jewish festival commemorating the events recorded in the book of Esther, and God's protection of the COVENANT people at that time.
*See p.167*

RABBI  *from Hebrew for* master. A title of honor given to a qualified Jewish religious teacher. Hence rabbinic, relating to a rabbi, their teachings, or writings.

RECONCILIATION  In the New Testament, reconciliation particularly refers to the barrier between God and sinful humanity being removed by Christ's sacrificial death.

REDEMPTION  Bringing freedom to those who have been in bondage of some kind. In the Hebrew Bible, God's rescue of the Israelites from Egypt. In the New Testament, Christ's death on the cross, which brought freedom from slavery to sin and death.
*See p.422*

REFORMATION  A 16-century Christian movement in northern Europe that sought to purify the Church and put it under the authority of the Bible alone.

REMNANT  A righteous group that holds to the truth when all others fall away. At the time of Elijah, an archetypal such group remained faithful when BAAL worship was dominant for most of Israel. Also, a "remnant" of Jews returned to Israel from the Exile.

REPENTANCE  Sincere regret for sin, strong enough to cause the person repenting to turn away from sin.

RESURRECTION OF CHRIST  His passage through death to life. More than just a return to his previous life: his body no longer felt its previous limits. Christ's Resurrection gives Christians hope for a general resurrection at the end of time.
*See pp.364–65*

REVELATION  The disclosure of God's nature, purpose, and will through the Scriptures, the created order, and history; also through Christ.

SABBATH  The seventh day of the week, the Sabbath was set aside for the worship of God and for rest. It originally began on Friday evening for both Jews and Christians, but because the Resurrection took place on Sunday, it displaced the previous sabbath for Christians.
*See p.281*

SACRAL KINGSHIP  More loosely, sacred kingship; a view of kingship in which kings have a role as, in some measure, mediators between God and their people. In Hebrew Bible times the kings of Israel were seen as being chosen and anointed by God and having such a role.
*See pp.122–23*

SACRAMENT  One of the central Christian religious ceremonies, such as BAPTISM or COMMUNION, an enacted sign through which truth is expressed in nonverbal form.
*See pp.418–19*

SACRIFICE  An offering made to God, particularly a living animal. In the Hebrew Bible, the people of Israel made sacrifices to obtain forgiveness, or seal a COVENANT with God. By the seventh century BCE, sacrifice was confined to the TEMPLE in Jerusalem. For Christians, the Crucifixion of Christ is the one sacrifice that makes forgiveness by God possible.
*See pp.66–67, 376–77, 422–23*

SADDUCEES  In New Testament Israel, a conservative aristocracy of Jewish priests who dominated TEMPLE worship and the SANHEDRIN. They opposed both the PHARISEES and Jesus. Unlike the Pharisees, they rejected oral tradition, the resurrection of the dead, and the existence of angels.
*See p.288*

SALVATION  Rescue. In the New Testament, Christ is seen as having rescued sinner from sin and separation from God, through his death and Resurrection, for reconciliation with God on earth and final unity with God in heaven.

SANCTUARY  In the TEMPLE, it was the most holy area, the Holy of Holies. The section of a church containing the altar.
*See pp.132–33*

SANHEDRIN  A Jewish council, either local or, in the case of Jerusalem, supreme.
*See p.355*

SATAN  *from Hebrew for* adversary. An agent of God, he was a member of the divine court who, for example, challenged the righteousness of Job. Satan became the equivalent of the DEVIL, with a role of chief tempter and deceiver of humans, especially in the New Testament.
*See p.175, 473*

SCAPEGOAT  In the Hebrew Bible, a goat that was sent into the desert at the conclusion of New Year ceremonies of repentance and ATONEMENT. Today's transferred meaning of a person bearing the *unacknowledged* blame due to others, is a misunderstanding of the biblical concept.

SCHISM  *from Greek for* to split. A division in the Church, in which the disagreements are serious enough to break COMMUNION, but not so essential that one side is accused of HERESY.

SCRIPTURE / THE SCRIPTURES  The Hebrew Bible and/or the New Testament. Also, any book of writings considered to be sacred.

SECOND COMING  SEE PAROUSIA

SEER  Another name for a PROPHET.

SEPTUAGINT  Greek translation of the Hebrew Bible made in Alexandria, c.270BCE. It was the Bible of the early Church, to which the books of the New Testament were added as they became generally accepted. It contains the books known as the APOCRYPHA.
*See pp.253, 520*

SHADDAI  *Hebrew for* mighty one, an ancient Jewish name for God.

SHALOM  Common Hebrew greeting. It indicates security, contentment, good health, prosperity, friendship, and tranquillity of heart and mind.

SHEMA  *from the Hebrew* "Hear (O Israel)!" The opening of the central affirmation of the unity of God (Deut. 6:4). It commands Israel to love God with "all your heart, all your soul and all your might."
*See pp.82–83*

SHEOL  In the Hebrew Bible, the abode of the dead.
*See pp.178–79*

SIN  A general term that translates a number of Hebrew and Greek words for actions ranging from failure to live up to one's responsibilities to outright rebellion against God. In the Hebrew Bible such "sins" are regarded as individual acts consequent upon human free will, not a state of being. In Christian thought, the natural inclination of humans towards sin is referred to as ORIGINAL SIN, inherited from Adam and Eve after the FALL.
*See pp.30–31*

**SON OF MAN, THE** Phrase (not a title) used by Jesus to speak of himself and possibly of another who would come to inaugurate the final Kingdom of God. The meaning of the phrase is much debated. Jesus probably combined two major meanings of the phrase in the Bible, "humanity that has to die," and (Dan. 7) "those who are faithful to God, even in persecution, and who are vindicated by God beyond death." Thus Jesus saw himself as one who, like all humans, must die, but who will be vindicated beyond death.

**SOUL** The SPIRIT or noncorporeal part of a person. Body and soul combine to make up a human being. They may be separated by death.
*See pp.182–83*

**SPEAKING IN TONGUES** A phenomenon, described in the New Testament, in which people inspired by the Holy Spirit speak in languages not known to them, or in sounds that do not correspond to any language.

**SPIRIT** A noncorporeal being, not confined to a body. God is spirit in a unique sense, unconfined by body, space, or time. Also, the third person of the Trinity, the Holy Spirit. Also, another way of referring to the human soul.
*See pp.182–83*

**SUFFERING SERVANT** One who bears pain and punishment on behalf of others.
*See p.203*

**SUKKOT** A Jewish autumn harvest festival, remembering the time when the Hebrews lived in the wilderness after the EXODUS. Also called the Feast of Tabernacles.
*See pp.68–69, 73*

**SYNAGOGUE** *from Greek for* a gathering. A Jewish place of worship or congregation that meets for worship and religious study.
*See pp.280-81*

**SYNCRETISM** The amalgamation of the beliefs and/or practices of two or more religions or philosophies.

**SYNOPTIC** *from Greek for* seeing things together. The Gospels of Matthew, Mark, and Luke are known as the Synoptic Gospels, because they share much material and have the same basic framework.
*See pp.300–03*

**TABERNACLE** The large portable tent that formed the sanctuary in which the Israelites carried the ARK OF THE COVENANT during their journey from Egypt to Canaan.
*See pp.53, 116–17*

**TALMUD** An extensive Jewish religious work containing interpretation of, and

commentary on, the TORAH, the primary source from which the rest of Jewish religious law has developed. Made up of the MISHNAH and the Gemara, which records debates on the interpretation of the Mishnah.

**TANAKH** An acronym based on the initial letters for the three sections of the Hebrew Bible in the form used by Jews: the (T)orah (the Teaching/Law), (N)ebi'im (the Prophets), and (K)ethubim (the Writings).

**TEMPLE, THE** In Jerusalem, the Temple was the only place where sacrifices could be made, and the centre of Jewish worship. The first Temple was built by Solomon (c.970–933BCE), and was destroyed by the Babylonians (586BCE). The second was built after the EXILE (c.520BCE). The third Temple was built by Herod the Great, and was the one that Jesus knew.
*See pp.116–17, 132–33, 286–87*

**TEMPTATION** The desire to do something wrong. Not in itself a sin, it is the moment of choice when doing right is difficult.
*See pp.326–27*

**TERAPHIM** Household gods or images venerated by ancient Semitic peoples.

**THEODICY** The branch of theology that tries to explain the problem of evil and to defend God against blame for it.

**THEOLOGY** Reflections on God and the implications of belief in God.

**TORAH** A term meaning "teaching" or "direction" that includes the idea of "law." Originally it applied to the PENTATEUCH, the five books of Moses, but in Jewish tradition it came to mean the whole of the Hebrew Bible and teaching derived from it through interpretation.
*See pp.24–25*

**TRANSFIGURATION** The unveiling of Christ's glory, which happened once during his life on earth, witnessed by his three closest disciples Peter, James, and John.

**TRIBE** A group of people who share a common ancestry and some degree of social unity. The 12 sons of Jacob founded the 12 tribes that made up the people of Israel.
*See pp.102-03*

**TRINITY** God in three persons, the Father, the Son, and the Holy Spirit. A central doctrine of the Christian faith.
*See p.413*

**UNIVERSALISM** The belief that God's purposes embrace those beyond the Jewish community. In Christian theology, the belief

that all will be saved.
*See pp.232–33*

**VULGATE** The fourth-century translation of the Bible into Latin by Jerome.
*See p.520*

**WAY, THE** One of the names Jesus gave to himself. Also, early Christians were sometimes described as "followers of the Way."

**WEEKS** SEE PENTECOST

**WILDERNESS, THE** The wilderness of Sinai, between Israel and Egypt.
*See pp.72–73*

**WISDOM / WISDOM LITERATURE** An important element of the Hebrew Bible, including the Psalms, Proverbs, Ecclesiastes, the Song of Songs, and the Book of Job.
*See pp.168–71, 256–57*

**YHWH** The most sacred Hebrew name for God, given by God to Moses. The form Yahweh has become common, but the original vowels and pronunciation are unknown.
*See pp.58–59*

**YOM KIPPUR** The Day of Atonement. The most solemn day in the Jewish calendar. An annual festival, it is a day of fasting and repentance.
*See pp.68–69*

**ZEALOTS** Groups of Jewish rebels against Rome at the time of Jesus.
*See p.289*

**ZION** The hill adjacent to Jerusalem that became a synonym for Jerusalem. The word is also used to refer to Israel or to Heaven. Symbolically, it could be said to represent the place of God.

# BIBLIOGRAPHY

## TRANSLATIONS OF THE BIBLE

From the earliest days (even before the canons of the Jewish and Christian Bibles had been agreed), the biblical books were translated into other languages. Of major importance are the Septuagint (LXX), from Hebrew into Greek (c. third–first centuries BCE), the Peshitta (Hebrew into Syriac, c. first century CE onward), and the Vulgate (Hebrew, based on LXX, into Latin, late fourth century CE). The Targums (*see below*, 543) are translations of the Hebrew into Aramaic, often incorporating the interpretation of difficult passages made in synagogues, made over a long period of time from c. first century CE onward. The New Testament was translated into many languages, most of which are helpful in questions concerning the text.

Translations into English (*see below*, 36) owe much to William Tyndale (c.1494–1536). To resolve competition between the Bishops' Bible and the Geneva Bible, King James I ordered the version that appeared in 1611 (the Authorized Version, or King James Bible). The Revised Version brought the Authorized Version up to date in terms of scholarship but is little used now. The Revised Standard Version took that process even farther, eliminating archaisms. For Roman Catholics, the Rheims-Douai version appeared (1582, 1610), based on the Vulgate. Many new translations have subsequently appeared. Of enduring importance have been The New English Bible (1961, 1970; revised as The Revised English Bible, 1989), a departure from the tradition of the Authorized Version supported by most non-Catholic British churches and aiming at a timeless literary style; The Jerusalem Bible (1966; revised as The New Jerusalem Bible, 1985), the English version of an originally French Catholic translation, notably modern in its translation of the

tetragrammaton as "Yahweh" rather than "the Lord"; The Good News Bible (1966, 1967), a version in simple, nonecclesiastical language published by the Bible Societies; The New American Bible, a translation (1952–70, revised 1978) undertaken by Roman Catholics; The New Revised Standard Version (1989, 1995), a translation remarkable for its attention to gender-inclusive language (and the version used throughout this *Handbook*); The New American Standard Bible (1960–63, but with subsequent editions containing corrections, etc); and The New International Version (1965–75, revised 1985), a widely used version aiming at natural English style and conformity to conservative evangelical understanding. The New Living Translation (1996) is a revision of an existing paraphrase, *The Living Bible Paraphrased*. The original was guided by "a rigid evangelical position." The revision is intended to bring it closer to a translation. Among Jewish translations, particularly important is *Tanakh: The Holy Scriptures*, The Jewish Publication Society, 1985.

All translation is interpretation. There is no single "original meaning of the text" to which the translators are attempting to get back. The text in its original languages often allows several different, but equally legitimate, possibilities of meaning. Scholarship continues to uncover new possibilities. Thus, any translation has to make unending judgments about text and meaning. For that reason, there are, in addition to translations, paraphrases that try to convey the underlying intention of the original text. Among the earliest and best of these was J.B. Phillips, *The New Testament in Modern English* (rev. ed. 1972). *The Precise Parallel New Testament*, ed. J.R. Kohlenberger, OUP, 1995, gives the Greek and seven of the above translations.

1 **Aberbach, M.** *The Roman-Jewish War* (66–70 AD), Golub, 1966

2 **Ackroyd, P.R.** *Exile and Restoration: A Study of Hebrew Thought of the Sixth Century BC*, SCM Press, 1972

3 **Ackroyd, P.R.** *Israel under Babylon and Persia*, OUP, 1970

4 **Ahlström, G.W.** *Royal Administration and National Religion in Ancient Palestine*, Brill, 1982

5 **Aland, D. Gutherie et. al.** *The Authorship and Integrity of the New Testament*, SPCK, 1965

5a **Aland, K.** *Synopsis of the Four Gospels*, Stuttgart, 1984

6 **Albertz, R.** *A History of Israelite Religion in the Old Testament Period*, 2 vols, SCM Press, 1994

7 **Albrektson, B.** *History and the Gods*, Lund, 1967

8 **Albrektson, B.** *Studies in the Text and Theology of the Book of Lamentations*, Lund, 1963

9 **Allen, L.C.** *The Books of Joel, Obadiah, Jonah and Micah*, Eerdmans, 1976

10 **Alsup, J.E.** *The Post-Resurrection Stories of the Gospel Tradition*, SPCK, 1975

11 **Alter, R.** *The Art of Biblical Narrative*, Allen and Unwin, 1981

12 **Anderson, A.A.** *The Book of Psalms*, 2 vols., New Century Bible Commentary, 1972

13 **Anderson, A.A.** "Sacrifice and Sacrificial Offerings," in *Anchor Bible Dictionary*

14 **Anderson, B.W.** (ed.) *Creation in the Old Testament*, SPCK, 1984

15 **Anderson, B.W.** *The Living World of the Old Testament*, Longman, 1988

16 **Anderson, F.I. & Freeman, D.N.** 'Amos', in *Anchor Bible Commentary*, Doubleday, 1989

17 **Anderson, F.I. & Freeman, D.N.** "Hosea," *Anchor Bible*, Doubleday, 1980

18 **Archer L.** *Her Price is Beyond Rubies: The Jewish Woman in Graeco-Roman Palestine*, JSOT, 1990

19 **Arnold, C.E.** *Ephesians: Power and Magic*, CUP, 1989

20 **Arnold, C.E.** *Powers of Darkness*, InterVarsity Press, 1992

21 **Asali, A.J.** (ed.) *Jerusalem in History*, Buckhurst Hill Scorpion, 1989

22 **Ashton, J.** *Understanding the Fourth Gospel*, Clarendon Press, 1991

23 **Auerbach, E.** *Moses*, Lehman, 1975

24 **Auld, A.G.** *Joshua, Judges, and Ruth*, St. Andrew, 1984

25 **Auld, A.G.** *Kings without Privilege*, T&T Clark, 1994

26 **Aune, D.E.** *Greco-Roman Literature and the New Testament*, Scholars Press, 1988

27 **Aune, D.E.** *The New Testament in Its Literary Environment*, Westminster, 1987

28 **Avigad, N.** *Discovering Jerusalem*, Blackwell, 1984

29 **Bach, A.** (ed.) *The Pleasure of her Text: Feminist Readings of Biblical and Historical Texts*, Trinity Press, 1990

30 **Badia, L.F.** *The Qumran Baptism and John the Baptist's Baptism*, University Press of America, 1980

31 **Bailey, K.E.** *The Manger and the Inn*, *Theological Review*, II, 1979

32 **Bailey, K.E.** *Poet and Peasant: A Literary Cultural Approach to the Parables in Luke*, Eerdmans, 1976

33 **Bailey, K.E.** *Through Peasant Eyes: More Lucan Parables, Their Culture and Style*, Eerdmans, 1980

34 **Bailey, L.R.** *Noah: The Person and the Story in History and Tradition*, University of South Carolina Press, 1989

35 **Bailey, L.R.** *Where is Noah's Ark: Mystery on Mt. Ararat*, Abingdon, 1978

36 **Bailey, L.R.** *The Word of God: A Guide to English Versions of the Bible*, 1982

37 Baines, J. & Malek, J. *Atlas of Ancient Egypt*, Phaidon, 1980

39 Bal, M. *Lethal Love: Feminist Literary Readings of Biblical Love Stories*, Indiana University Press, 1987

40 Bal, M. *The Politics of Coherence in the Book of Judges*, Chicago University Press, 1988

41 Baldwin, J.G. *1 & 2 Samuel*, InterVarsity Press, 1988

42 Baldwin, J.G. *The Message of Samuel*, InterVarsity Press 1990

43 Baltzer, K. *The Covenant Formulary*, Fortress, 1971

44 Bammel, E. (ed.) *The Trial of Jesus*, SCM Press, 1970

45 Bammel, E. & Moule, C.F.D. *Jesus and the Politics of His Day*, CUP, 1984

46 Banks, R. *Paul's Idea of Community: The Early House Churches in their Historical Setting*, Paternoster, 1980

47 Banstra, A. *In the Company of Angels: What the Bible Teaches and What You Need to Know*, CRC Publications, 1995

48 Barclay, W. *Educational Ideals in the Ancient World*, Baker, 1974

49 Barker, M. *The Gate of Heaven: The History and Symbolism of the Temple in Jerusalem*, SPCK, 1991

50 Barnett, P. *The Message of 2 Corinthians*, InterVarsity Press, 1988

51 Barr, J. *Biblical Words for Time*, SCM Press, 1962

52 Barr, J. *Escaping from Fundamentalism*, SCM Press, 1984

53 Barr, J. *The Garden of Eden and the Hope of Immortality*, SCM Press, 1992

54 Barrett, C.K. *Church, Ministry and Sacraments in the New Testament*, Paternoster, 1985

55 Barrett, C.K. *Jesus and the Gospel Tradition*, 1967

56 Barrett, C.K. *Paul: An Introduction to his Thought*, Chapman, 1994

57 Barrett, C.K. *2 Corinthians*, A&C Black, 1973

58 Barrois, G. *Jesus Christ and the Temple*, St. Vladimir Press, 1980

59 Barrow, R.H. *The Romans*, Penguin, 1990

60 Bartchy, S.C. "Greco-Roman Slavery," in *Anchor Bible Dictionary*

61 Bartlett, D.L. *Ministry in the New Testament*, Fortress, 1993

62 Barton, J. *Amos's Oracles against the Nations*, CUP, 1980

63 Barton, J. *Ethics and the Old Testament*, London, 1998

64 Barton, J. *Isaiah 1–39*, Sheffield Academic Press, 1995

65 Barton, J. *Oracles of God: Perceptions of Ancient Prophecy in Israel after the Exile*, Darton, Longman and Todd, 1986

66 Barton, S.C. (ed.) *The Family in Theological Perspective*, T&T Clark, 1996

67 Barton, S.C. *People of the Passion*, Triangle, 1994

68 Barton, S. & Stanton, G.N. (eds.) *Resurrection. Essays in Honour of Leslie Houlden*, SPCK, 1994

69 Bauckham, R. *Jude and the Relatives of Jesus*, T&T Clark, 1990

70 Bauckham, R. *The Relatives of Jesus in the Early Church*, T&T Clark, 1990

71 Bauckham, R. *Jude, II Peter*, World Books, 1983

72 Bausinger, H. *Folk Culture in a World of Technology*, Indiana University Press, 1990

73 Beard, M. & Crawford, M. *Rome in the Late Republic*, Duckworth, 1985

74 Beasley-Murray, G.R. *Baptism in the New Testament*, Eerdmans/Paternoster, 1997

75 Beasley-Murray, G.R. *Jesus and the Kingdom of God*, Eerdmans/Paternoster, 1986

76 Beattie, D.R.G. *Jewish Exegesis of the Book of Ruth*, JSOT, 1977

77 Becker, J.C. *Paul the Apostle: The Triumph of God in Life and Thought*, T&T Clark, 1980

78 Behe, M.J. *Darwin's Black Box*, Free Press, 1996

79 Ben-Amos, D. "Folklore in the Ancient Near East," in *Anchor Bible Dictionary*

80 Berg, S.B. *The Book of Esther*, Scholars Press, 1979

81 Bernheim, P.-A. J. *James, Brother of Jesus*, SCM Press, 1997

82 Bernstein, A. *The Formation of Hell*, UCL Press, 1993

83 Best, E. *Following Jesus: Discipleship in the Gospel of Mark*, JSOT, 1981

84 Best, E. *Disciples and Discipleship*, T&T Clark, 1986

85 Best, E. *Temptation and Passion: The Markan Soteriology*, CUP, 1990

86 Best, M.E. *The Gospel as Story*, T&T Clark, 1983

87 Betlyon, J.W. "Coinage," in *Anchor Bible Dictionary*

88 Betz, H.D. *Essays on the Sermon on the Mount*, Fortress Press, 1985

89 Beyerlin, W. *Origins and History of the Oldest Sinaitic Traditions*, Blackwell, 1963

90 Biale, R. *Women and Jewish Law*, Schocken, 1984

91 Bickerman, E. *Four Strange Books of the Bible*, Schocken, 1967

92 Bickerman, E. 'The Babylon Captivity', in *The Cambridge History of Judaism vol. 1*, (eds.) W.D. Davies & I. Finkelstein, CUP, 1984

93 Bienkowsky, P. *Jericho in the Late Bronze Age*, Ars & Phillips, 1986

94 Bigger, S. *Creating the Old Testament*, Blackwell, 1989

95 Biran, A. (ed.) *Temples and High Places in Biblical Times*, Jewish Institute of Religion, 1981

96 Birch, B.C. *Let Justice Roll Down: The Old Testament, Ethics and Christian Life*, Westminster/John Knox, 1991

97 Birch, B.C. *The Rise of the Israelite Monarchy*, Missoula MT, 1976

98 Blakely, J.A. & Bennett, W.J. *The Pottery of Palestine: Neolithic to Modern*, Eisenbrauns, 1994

99 Blenkinsopp, J. *Ezekiel, Interpretation*, John Knox, 1990

99a Blenkinsopp, J. *Ezra-Nehemiah*, Westminster, 1988

100 Blenkinsopp, J. *A History of Prophecy in Israel*, SPCK, 1984

101 Blenkinsopp, J. *The Pentateuch: An Introduction to the First Five Books of the Bible*, SCM Press, 1992

102 Blenkinsopp, J. "The Quest for the Historical Saul," in *No Famine in the Land*, (eds.) J.W. Flanagan & A.W. Robinson, Missoula MT, 1975

103 Blenkinsopp, J. *Sage, Priest, Prophet*, Westminster, 1995

104 Blenkinsopp, J. *Wisdom and Law in the Old Testament*, OUP, 1983

105 Blocher, H. *In the Beginning: The Opening Chapters of Genesis*, InterVarsity Press, 1984

106 Blomberg, C.L. *Interpreting the Parables*, InterVarsity Press, 1990

107 Boardman, J., Griffin, J. & Murray, O. (eds.) "Greece and the Hellenistic World," in *The Oxford History of the Classical World*, OUP, 1991

108 Boardman, J., Griffin, J. & Murray, O. (eds.) *The Roman World*, OUP, 1991

109 Bockmuehl, M. *This Jesus: Martyr, Lord, Messiah*, T&T Clark, 1994

110 Boecker, H.J. *Law and the Administration of Justice in the Old Testament and Ancient East*, SPCK, 1980

111 de Boer, M.C. *The Defeat of Death: Apocalyptic Eschatology in 1 Corinthians and Romans*, JSOT, 1988

112 Borg, M.J. *Jesus. A New Vision: Spirit, Culture and the Life of Discipleship*, SPCK, 1993

113 Bornkamm, G. *Paul*, Hodder & Stoughton, 1971

113a Borowitz, E.B. *Ehad: The Many Meanings of God is one*, 1988

114 Borowski, O. *Agriculture in Ancient Israel*, Eisenbrauns, 1987

115 Bottéro, J. *Mesopotamia*, University of Chicago Press, 1992

116 Bourdillon, M.F.C. & Fortes, M. *Sacrifice*, Academic Press for the Royal Anthropological Institute, 1980

117 Bovon, F.C. *Luke the Theologian: Thirty-three Years of Research*, Delachaux & Niestle, 1978

117a Bowker, J.W. *Is God a Virus?*, SPCK, 1995

118 Bowker, J.W. *The Meanings of Death*, CUP, 1991

119 Bowker, J.W. "Mystery and Parable: Mark 4.1–20," in *Journal of Theological Studies, XXV*, 1974

120 Bowker, J.W. *The Oxford Dictionary of World Religions*, OUP, 1997

121 Bowker, J.W. *Problems of Suffering in Religions of the World*, CUP, 1990

122 Bowker, J.W. *The Religious Imagination and the Sense of God*, Clarendon Press, 1978

123 Bowers, R.H. *The Legend of Jonah*, Martinus Nijhoff, 1971

124 Boyce, G.E. *The Egyptian Contribution to the Wisdom of Israel*, Bucknell University Press, 1979

125 Boyce, M. *Zoroastrianism: Its Antiquity and Constant Vigour*, Routledge, 1979

126 Bradley, K. *Slaves and Masters in the Roman Empire*, OUP, 1987

127 Brandon, S.G.F. *The Trial of Jesus of Nazareth*, Batsford, 1968

128 Brenner, A. *Naomi and Ruth, Vetus Testamentum 33*, Brill, 1983

129 Brenner, A. *The Israelite Woman, Social Role and Literary Type in Biblical Narrative*, JSOT, 1985

130 Brichto, C.C. *Toward a Grammar of Biblical Poetics: Tales of the Prophets*, OUP, 1992

131 Bright, J. *A History of Israel*, SCM Press, 1981

132 Brooten, B.J. *Women Leaders in the Ancient Synagogues*, Scholars Press, 1982

133 Brower, K.E. & Elliott, M.W. (eds.) *The Reader Must Understand: Eschatology in Bible and Theology*, Apollos/InterVarsity Press, 1997

134 Brown, C. *Miracles and the Critical Mind*, Eerdmans, 1984

135 Brown, J.C. & Bohn, C.R. (eds.) *Christianity, Patriarchy and Abuse: A Feminist Critique*, Pilgrim Press, 1989

136 Brown, R.E. *The Birth of the Messiah*, Chapman, 1993

137 Brown, R.E. *The Community of the Beloved Disciple*, Paulist Press, 1979

138 Brown, R.E. "The Epistles of John," in *Anchor Bible Dictionary*

138a Brown, R.E. *An Introduction to New Testament Christology*, Chapman, 1994

139 Brown, R.E. *The Virginal Conception and Bodily Resurrection of Jesus*, Chapman, 1973

**140** Brown, R.E. & Meier, J.P. "Antioch and Rome," in *New Testament Cradles of Catholic Christianity*, Paulist Press, 1983

**140a** Brown, R.E. et al. *Mary in the New Testament*, Paulist Press, 1978

**140b** Brown, R.E. et al. *Peter in the New Testament*

**141** Bruce, F.F. *The Epistle to the Galatians, A Commentry on the Greek Text*, Paternoster, 1982

**142** Bruce, F.F. *The Epistle to the Hebrews*, Marshall, Morgan & Scott, 1964

**143** Bruce, F.F. *The Spreading Flame: The Rise and Progress of Christianity from its First Beginnings to the Conversion of the English*, Paternoster, 1982

**144** Brueggemann, W. *Genesis*, John Knox, 1982

**145** Brueggemann, W. *Hopeful Imagination: Prophetic Voices in Exile*, Fortress, 1986

**146** Brueggemann, W. *The Message of the Psalms*, Augsburg Publishing, 1984

**147** Brueggemann, W. *Tradition for Crisis: A Study in Hosea*, John Knox, 1968

**148** Budd, P.J. 'Holiness and Cult," in *The World of Ancient Israel*, (ed.) R.E. Clements, CUP, 1989

**149** Burge, G.M. *The Anointed Community: The Holy Spirit in the Johannine Tradition*, Eerdmans, 1987

**150** Burns, R. *Has the Lord Indeed Only Spoken Through Moses? A Study of the Biblical Portrait of Miriam*, Scholars Press, 1987

**151** Burridge, R.A. *Four Gospels, One Jesus?*, SPCK, 1994

**152** Caird, G.B. *The Gospel of Saint Luke*, Penguin, 1963

**153** Caird, G.B. *The Language and Imagery of the Bible*, Duckworth, 1980

**154** Caird, G.B. *Paul's Letters from Prison*, OUP, 1976

**155** Caird, G.B. *Principalities and Powers: A Study in Pauline Theology*, Clarendon Press, 1956

**156** Caird, G.B. *The Revelation of St. John the Divine*, A&C Black, 1966

**157** Camp, C.V. *Wisdom and the Feminine in the Book of Proverbs*, Almond, 1985

**158** von Campenhausen, H. *The Formation of the Christian Bible*, A&C Black, 1972

**159** Carcopino, J. *Daily Life in Ancient Rome*, Penguin, 1956

**160** Carlson, R.A. *David, the Chosen King*, Amqvist & Wiksell, 1964

**161** Carmichael, C.M. *Law and Narrative in the Bible*, Cornell University Press, 1985

**162** Carroll, R.P. *From Chaos to Covenant*, SCM Press, 1981

**163** Carroll, R.P. *Jeremiah*, JSOT Press, 1989

**164** Carroll, R.P. *Jeremiah: A Commentary*, SCM Press, 1986

**165** Carson, D.A. *How Long, O Lord?*, InterVarsity Press, 1990

**166** Carson, D.A. *Showing the Spirit: A Theological Exposition of 1 Corinthians*, Paternoster, 1995

**167** Cassidy, R.J. *Society and Politics in the Acts of the Apostles*, Orbis, 1987

**168** Cassuto, U. *A Commentary on the Book Of Exodus*, Magnes Press, 1967

**169** Catchpole, D.R. *The Trial of Jesus*, Brill, 1971

**170** Cerny, J. *Ancient Egyptian Religion*, London, 1952

**171** Cerny, J. *Paper and Books in Ancient Egypt*, Chicago, 1977

**172** Chadwick, H. *The Early Church*, Penguin, 1967

**172a** Charlesworth, J.H. (ed.) *The Messiah: Developments in Earliest Judaism and Christianity*, T&T Clarke, 1995

**172b** Chester, A. & Martin, R.P. *The Message of 1 Peter*, CUP, 1994

**173** Chester, A. & Martin, R.P. *The Theology of the Letters of James, Peter, and Jude*, CUP, 1994

**174** Childs, B.S. *Exodus, A Commentary*, SCM Press, 1974

**175** Childs, B.S. *Introduction to the Old Testament as Scripture*, Fortress, 1979

**176** Childs, B.S. *Isaiah and the Assyrian Crisis*, SCM Press, 1967

**177** Childs, B.S. *Isaiah and the Deliverance of Jerusalem*, Sheffield, 1980

**178** Chilton, B.D. *A Feast of Meanings*, Brill, 1994

**179** Clark, E.A. *Women in the Early Church*, Michael Glazier, 1983

**180** Clarke, E.G. "Wisdom of Solomon," in *Anchor Bible Dictionary*

**181** Clements, R.E. *Beyond Traditional History: Deutero-Isaianic Development of First Isaiah's Themes*, JSOT 31, 1985

**182** Clements, R.E. *Deuteronomy*, Sheffield Academic Press, 1989

**183** Clements, R.E. *God and Temple*, Blackwell, 1965

**184** Clements, R.E. *Isaiah 1–39*, Eerdmans, 1980

**185** Clements, R.E. *Jeremiah: Interpretation*, John Knox Press, 1988

**186** Clements, R.E. (ed.) *World of Ancient Israel*, CUP 1989

**187** Clifford, R. *Fair Spoken and Persuading: An Interpretation of Second Isaiah*, Paulist Press, 1984

**188** Clines, D.J.A. *The Esther Scroll: The Story of the Story*, JSOT, 1984

**188a** Clines, D.J.A. "Ezra, Nehemiah, Esther" in *New Century Bible Commentary*, Marshall, Morgan and Scott, 1984

**189** Clines, D.J.A. *The Theme of the Pentateuch*, JSOT, 1978

**190** Clines, D.J.A. *What Does Eve Do to Help?*, JSOT, 1990

**191** Clowney, E.P. *The Message of 1 Peter*, InterVarsity Press, 1988

**192** Coats, G.W. *Moses*, Lehman, 1975

**193** Coats, G.W. *Rebellion in the Wilderness*, Abingdon, 1968

**194** Cody, A. *A History of the Old Testament Priesthood*, Pontifical Biblical Institute, 1969

**195** Coggins, R.J. *First & Second Books of Chronicles*, CUP, 1976

**196** Coggins, R.J. *Haggai, Zechariah, Malachi*, JSOT Press, 1987

**197** Coggins, R.J. & Reemi, S.P. (eds.) *Israel among the Nations: A Commentary on the Books of Nahum and Obadiah*, Handsel Press, 1985

**198** Cohen, A. (transl.) *Leviticus Rabbah*, Soncino Press, 1939

**199** Cohen, Shaye J.D. "Masada: Literary Tradition, Archeological Remains and the Credibility of Josephus," in *Journal of Jewish Studies*, 1982

**200** Collins, A.Y. (ed.) *Feminist Perspectives in Biblical Scholarship*, Scholars Press, 1985

**201** Collins, J.J. *Daniel, with an Introduction to Apocalyptic Literature*, Eerdmans, 1984

**202** Collins, J.N. *Diakonia: Reinterpreting the Ancient Resources*, OUP, 1990

**203** Collins, R.F. *Introduction to the New Testament*, SCM Press, 1992

**204** Contenau, G. *Everyday Life in Babylonia and Assyria*, Norton, 1966

**205** Conzelmann, H. *An Outline of Theology of the New Testament*, SCM Press, 1969

**206** Coogan, Michael, D. "Life in the Diaspora; Jews at Nippur in the Fifth Century BC," in The Biblical Archaeologist 37, 1974

**207** Cook, J. M. *The Persian Empire*, Dent, 1983

**208** Coote, R.B. *Amos Among the Prophets*, Fortress, 1981

**209** Coote, R.B. (ed.), *Elijah and Elisha in Socioliterary Perspective*, Ga. Scholars, 1992

**210** Coote, R.B. & Whitelam, K.W. *The Emergence of Early Israel in Historical Perspective*, Almond, 1987

**211** Cosby, M.R. *Sex in the Bible*, Englewood Cliffs, 1985

**212** Cousar, C.B.A. *Theology of the Cross*, Fortress, 1990

**213** Crenshaw, J.L. *Ecclesiastes, A Commentary*, SCM Press, 1987

**214** Crenshaw, J.L. *Joel*, Doubleday, 1995

**215** Crenshaw, J.L. *Old Testament Wisdom*, SCM Press, 1981

**216** Crenshaw, J.L. *Prophetic Conflict: Its Effect Upon Israelite Religion*, BZWA, de Gruyter, 1971

**217** Crenshaw, J.L. *Samson: A Secret Betrayed, a Vow Ignored*, SPCK, 1979

**218** Crenshaw, J.L. (ed.) *Theodicy in the Old Testament*, Fortress, 1983

**219** Crenshaw, J.L. *A Whirlpool of Torment: Israelite Traditions of God as an Oppressive Presence*, Fortress, 1984

**220** Croatto, J.S. *Exodus: A Hermeneutics of Freedom*, Orbis Books, 1981

**221** Cross, F.M. *Canaanite Myth and Hebrew Epic*, Harvard, 1973

**222** Cullmann, O. *Prayer in the New Testament*, SCM Press, 1995

**223** Dalley, S. *Myths from Mesopotamia*, OUP, 1989

**224** Dancy, J.C. *The Shorter Books of the Apocrypha*, CUP, 1972

**225** Daniel-Rops, H. *Daily Life in the Time of Jesus*, Hawthorn Books, 1962

**226** Daniels, D.R. *Hosea and Salvation History*, de Gruyter, 1990

**227** Davidson, R. *The Courage to Doubt: Exploring an Old Testament Theme*, SCM Press, 1983

**228** Davies, E.W. *Hosea*, Waco.

**229** Davies, E.W. *Prophecy and Ethics*, 1981

**229a** Davies, G.I. *Hosea*, JSOT, 1993

**230** Davies, G.I. *The Way of the Wilderness*, CUP, 1979

**231** Davies, P.R. *In Search of 'Ancient Israel'*, JSOT, 1992

**232** Davis, J.G. *He Ascended into Heaven: A Study in the History of a Doctrine*, Lutterworth, 1958

**232a** Davis, J.J. *Biblical Numerology*

**233** Davis, M. *Matthew*, JSOT Press, 1993

**234** Davies, M. *The Pastoral Epistles*, Sheffield Academic Press, 1996

**235** Day, J. "Canaan, Religion of", in *Anchor Bible Dictionary*

**236** Day, J. "The Development of Belief in Life after Death in Ancient Israel," in *After the Exile*, (eds.) J. Barton & D.J. Reimer, Mercer University Press, 1996

**237** Day, J. *God's Conflict with the Dragon and the Sea*, CUP, 1985

**238** Day, J. *Psalms*, Sheffield Academic Press, 1990

**239** Day, P.L. *An Adversary in Heaven: Satan in the Hebrew Bible*, Scholars Press, 1988

**240** Diamond, A.R. *The Confessions of Jeremiah in Context*, JSOT Press, 1987

241 Dibelius, M. James, Fortress, 1976

242 Dodd, C.H. The Interpretation of the Fourth Gospel, CUP, 1953

243 Dodd, C.H. Historical Tradition in the Fourth Gospel, CUP, 1963

244 Dodd, C.H. The Parables of the Kingdom, Scribners, 1961

245 Donfried, K.P & Marshall, I.H. The Theology of the Shorter Pauline Letters, CUP, 1993

245a Doorly, W.J. Prophet of Justice, Paulist Press, 1989

246 Doty, W.G. Letters in Primitive Christianity, Fortress, 1973

247 Douglas, M. Purity and Danger, Routledge, 1966

248 Dozeman, T.B. God on the Mountain, Scholars Press, 1989

249 Drane, J.W. Introducing the Old Testament, Lion, 1987

250 Drane, J. W. Paul: Libertine or Legalist? SPCK, 1995

251 Driver, G.R. Canaanite Myths and Legends, T&T Clark, 1956

252 Dudley, D. Roman Society, Penguin, 1991

253 Duke, P.D. Irony in the Fourth Gospel, John Knox, 1985

254 Duncan, R. Judas, Anthony Blond, 1960

255 Dundes, A. Folklore Matters, University of Tennessee Press, 1989

256 Dunn, J.D.G. The Acts of the Apostles, Epworth Press, 1996

256a Dunn, J.D.G. The Epistle to the Galatians, A&C Black, 1993

257 Dunn, J.D.G. Jesus and the Spirit: A Story of the Religious and Charismatic Experience of Jesus and the First Christians, SCM Press, 1975

258 Dunn, J.D.G. Jesus' Call to Discipleship, CUP, 1992

259 Dunn, J.D.G., 1 Corinthians, Sheffield Academic Press, 1995

260 Dunn, J.D.G. "Pseudepigraphy," in Dictionary of the Later New Testament and its Developments, InterVarsity Press, 1997

261 Dunn, J.D.G. The Theology of Paul the Apostle, T&T Clark, 1998

262 Dunn, J.D.G. Unity and Diversity in the New Testament, SCM Press, 1977

263 Eaton, J.H. Job, JSOT, 1985

264 Eaton, J.H. Kingship and the Psalms, SCM Press, 1976

265 Eaton, J.H. "Music's Place in Worship: A Contribution from the Psalms," in Prophets, Worship and Theodicy, Oudtestamentische Studiën 23, 1984

266 Edelman, D. King Saul and the Historiography of Judah, Sheffield Academic Press, 1991

267 Edelman, D.V. "Saul," in Anchor Bible Dictionary

268 Ehrman, B.D. The Orthodox Corruption of Scripture, OUP, 1993

269 Eichrodt, W. Ezekiel, SCM Press, 1970

270 Eichrodt, W. Theology of the Old Testament, SCM Press, 1961

271 Emmerson, G.I. Hosea: An Israelite Prophet in Judean Perspective, JSOT, 1984

272 Emmerson, G.I. Isaiah 56–66, JSOT, 1992

273 Emmerson, G.I. Prophets and Poets: A Companion to the Prophetic Books of the Old Testament, Bible Reading Fellowship, 1994

274 Emmerson, G.I. "Women in Ancient Israel," in The World of Ancient Israel: Sociological, Anthropological and Political Perspectives, (ed.) R.E. Clements, CUP, 1989

275 Epp, E.J. The Theological Tendency of Codex Bezae Cantabrigiensis in Acts, CUP, 1966

276 Epsztein, L. Social Justice in the Ancient Near East and the People of the Bible, SCM Press, 1986

277 Erman, A. The Ancient Egyptians: A Sourcebook of Their Writings, Harper & Row, 1966

278 Eskenazi, T.C. In an Age of Prose: A Literary Approach to Ezra Nehemiah, Society of Biblical Literature, 1988

279 Esler, P.F. Community and Gospel in Luke-Acts, CUP, 1987

280 Esler, P.F. (ed.) Modelling Early Christianity, Routledge, 1995

281 Eusebius Ecclesiastical History, (trans.) R.J. Deferrari, Catholic University of America Press, 1965

282 Evans, C.F. Saint Luke, SCM Press, 1990

283 Fackenheim, E.L. God's Presence in History, Harper & Row, 1970

284 Fackenheim E.L. The Jewish Bible After the Holocaust: A Re-reading, Manchester University Press, 1990

285 Falk, M. Love Lyrics from the Bible: A Translation and Literary Study of the Song of Songs, HarperCollins, 1990

286 Falk, W. Hebrew Law in Biblical Times, Wahrmann Books, 1964

287 Fee, G.D. The First Epistle to the Corinthians, Eerdmans, 1987

287a Fee, G.D. God's Empowering Presence, Hendrickson, 1994

288 Fee G.D. 1 & 2 Timothy, Titus, Hendrickson, 1988

288a Fensham, F.C. The Books of Ezra and Nehemiah, Eerdmans, 1982

289 Fenton, J.C. The Gospel According to John, Clarendon Press, 1970

290 Ferguson, E. Backgrounds of Early Christianity, Eerdmans, 1993

291 Fiorenza, E.S. Bread Not Stone: The Challenge of Feminist Biblical Interpretation, Beacon, 1984

292 Fiorenza, E.S. In Memory of Her: A Feminist Theological Reconstruction of Christian Origins, SCM Press, 1983

293 Fiorenza, E.S. "Missionaries, Apostles, Coworker: Romans 16 and the Reconstruction of Women's History," in Feminist Theology: A Reader, (ed.) Ann Loader, SPCK, 1990

294 Firmage, E. "Zoology," in Anchor Bible Dictionary

295 Fisch, H. Poetry with a purpose: Biblical Poetics and Interpretation, Indiana University Press, 1990

296 Fish, H. "Ruth and the Structure of Covenant History," Vetus Testamentum 32, 1982

297 Fishbane, M. Biblical Interpretation in Ancient Israel, Clarendon Press, 1985

298 Fitzmyer, J.A. Responses to 101 Questions on the Dead Sea Scrolls, Paulist Press, 1992

299 Flanagan, J.W. David's Social Drama, A Hologaram of Israel's Early Iron Age, Almond, 1988

300 Flower, M. Centred on Love: The Poems of Saint John of the Cross, The Carmelite Nuns, 1983

301 Fohrer, G. History of Israelite Religion, SPCK, 1973

302 Fokkelman, J.P. Narrative Art and Poetry in the Books of Samuel, Van Gorcum, 1981

303 Fokkelman, J.P. Narrative Art in Genesis, JSOT, 1991

304 Fox, M.V. Character and Ideology in the Book of Esther, University of South Carolina Press, 1991

305 Fox, M.V. Qohelet and his Contradictions, Almond, 1989

306 Francis, J. "Children and Childhood Imagery in the New Testament," in The Family in Theological Perspective, (ed.) S. Barton, T&T Clark 1996

306a Frank, D.H. (ed.) A People Apart: Choseness and Ritual in Jewish Philosophical Thought, Albany, 1993

307 Frankfort, S.H. Kingship and the Gods: A Study of Near Eastern Religion as the Integration of Society and Nature, University of Chicago Press, 1948

308 Freedman, K.N. (ed.) "Zoology: Animal Profiles: Birds," in Anchor Bible Dictionary

309 Fretheim T.E., Deuteronomic History, Abingdon, 1983

310 Freyne, S. Galilee, Jesus and the Gospels, Fortress, 1988

311 Friberg, J. "Numbers and Counting," in Anchor Bible Dictionary

312 Frick, F.S. The Formation of the State in Israel, Almond, 1985

313 Frick, F.S. The Social World of Biblical Antiquity, 1985

314 Friedman, R.E. Who Wrote the Bible?, Prentice Hall, 1987

315 Frymer-Kensky, R. "Tit for Tat," in Biblical Archaeologist, 43, 1980

316 Furnish, V.P. Theology and Ethics In Paul, Abingdon,1968

317 Gager, J. Curse Tablets and Binding Spells from the Ancient World, OUP, 1992

318 Gamble, H.Y. The New Testament Canon: Its Making and Meaning, Fortress, 1985

319 Garcia Martinez, F. "The Dead Sea Scrolls Translated," in The Qumran Texts in English, (trans.) W.G.E. Watson, Eerdmans, 1996

320 Garnsy, P. & Saller, R. The Roman Empire: Economy, Society and Culture, University of California Press, 1987

321 Garrett, S.R. The Demise of the Devil: Magic and the Demonic in Luke's Writings, Fortress, 1989

322 Garstang, J. & J.B.E. The Story of Jericho, Marshall, Morgan & Scott, 1948

323 Gartner, B. Iscariot, Fortress Press, 1971

324 Gaster, T.H. Myth, Legend and Custom in the Old Testament, Duckworth, 1969

325 Gaston, L. "No Stone on Another: Studies in the Significance of the Fall of Jerusalem," in The Synoptic Gospels, Brill, 1970

326 Geus, C.H.J. The Tribes of Israel, Van Gorcum, 1976

327 Gibson, J.C.L. Canaanite Myths and Legends, T&T Clark, 1976

328 Gillingham, S.E. The Poems and Psalms of the Hebrew Bible, OUP, 1994

329 Gledhill, T. "The Message of the Song of Songs," in The Bible Speaks Today, InterVarsity Press, 1994

330 Godwin, M. Angels: An Endangered Species, Boxtree, 1990

331 Goldingay, J. After Eating the Apricot, Solway, 1996

332 Goldingay J. Daniel, Word Books, 1989

333 Goldingay, J. Models For Scripture, Eerdmans, 1994

334 Goldstein, J.A. 1 Maccabees, Doubleday, 1976

335 Goldstein, J.A. 2 Maccabees, Doubleday, 1983

336 Golka, F.W. The Leopard's Spots: Biblical and African Wisdom in Proverbs, T&T Clark, 1993

337 Good, E.M. Irony in the Old Testament, Almond, 1981

338 Goodman, M. The Roman World 44 BC–AD 180, Routledge, 1997

339 Gordis, R. The Book of Job, Jewish Theological Seminary, 1978

**340 Gordis, R.** *Koheleth: The Man and his World*, New York, 1968

**341 Gordis, R.** *Poets, Prophecy, and Sagas*, Bloomington, 1971

**342 Gordon, R.P.** *1 & 2 Samuel: A Commentary*, Paternoster, 1986

**343 Gottwald, N.K.** *The Tribes of Yahweh*, SCM Press, 1980

**343a Gowan, D.** *Eschatology in the Old Testament*, T&T Clark, 1987

**344 Grabbe, L.L.** *Judaism from Cyrus to Hadrian*, SCM Press, 1994

**345 Grabbe, L.L.** *Priests, Prophets, Diviners and Sages*, Trinity Press, 1995

**346 Gray, J.** *The Canaanites*, Thames & Hudson, 1964

**347 Gray, J.** *1 & 2 Kings*, SCM Press, 1977

**348 Grayson, A.K.** "Mesopotamia, History of Assyria," in *Anchor Bible Dictionary*

**349 Grayson, A.K.** "Mesopotamia, History of: History and Culture of Babylonia," in *Anchor Bible Dictionary*

**350 Grayston, K.** *Dying We Live*, Darton, Longman & Todd, 1990

**351 Green, J.B.** *The Death of Jesus*, JCB Mohr, 1988

**352 Green, M.,** *Freed to Serve*, Hodder & Stoughton, 1996

**353 Green, T.A.** *Folklore: An Encyclopedia of Beliefs, Customs, Tales, Music and Art*, Santa Barbara (ABC-CLIO), 1997

**354 Greenberg, M.** "Ezekiel 1–20," in *Anchor Bible Dictionary*

**355 Greenspoon, L.** "The Warrior God, or God, the Divine Warrior," in *Religion and Politics in the Modern World* (eds.) P. Mirkl and N. Smart, 1983

**356 Guelich, R.A.** *The Sermon on the Mount*, Word, 1982

**357 Gunkel, H.** *The Legends of Genesis*, Schocken, 1964

**358 Gunn, D.** *The Fate of King Saul*, JSOT, 1980

**359 Gunn, D.M.** *The Story of King David*, JSOT, 1982

**360 Gunther, J.J.** *Paul: Messenger and Exile: A Study in the Chronology of his Life and Letters*, Judson, 1972

**361 Gustafson, J.M.** *Christ and the Moral Life*, Chicago University Press, 1968

**362 Gutman, S.** *Ancient Synagogues: The State of Research*, Michigan University Press, 1981

**363 Gutiérrez, G.** *On Job: God-Talk and the Suffering of the Innocent*, Orbis, 1987

**364 Habel, N.C.** *The Book of Job*, Westminster, 1985

**365 Haenchen, E.** *The Acts of the Apostles*, Westminster, 1971

**366 Halas, R.B.** *Judas Iscariot:* *A Scriptural and Theological Study*, Catholic University of America, 1946

**367 Hall, S.** *Doctrine and Practice in the Early Church*, SPCK, 1991

**368 Hamilton, V.P. & Collins, R.F.** "Marriage," in *Anchor Bible Dictionary*

**369 Hamlin, E.J.** *At Risk in the Promised Land: A Commentary on the Book Of Judges*, Eerdmans, 1990

**370 Hanson, P.D.** *The Dawn of Apocalyptic: The Historical and Sociological Roots of Jewish Apocalyptic Eschatology*, Fortress, 1979

**371 Haran, M.** *Temples and Temple Service in Ancient Israel*, Clarendon Press, 1978

**372 Harden, D.** *The Phoenicians*, Penguin, 1980

**373 Harris, M.J.** *Raised Immortal: Resurrection and Immortality in the New Testament*, Marshall Morgan & Scott, 1983

**374 Harrison, R.K.** *Old Testament Times*, Eerdmans, 1974

**375 Hartman, L.F. & di Lella, Alexander A.** *The Book of Daniel*, Doubleday, 1978

**376 Harvey, A.E.** *Strenuous Commands: The Ethic of Jesus*, SCM Press, 1990

**377 Hay, D.M.** *Glory at the Right Hand: Psalm 110 in Early Christianity*, Abingdon, 1973

**378 Hayes, J.H.** *Amos the Eighth Century Prophet: His Times and His Preaching*, Abingdon, 1988

**379 Hays, R.B.** *First Corinthians*, John Knox Press, 1997

**380 Hays, R.B.** *The Moral Vision of the New Testament*, HarperCollins, 1996

**381 Hayward, C.T.R.** *The Jewish Temple*, Routledge, 1996

**382 Heaton, E.W.** *A Short Introduction to the Old Testament Prophets*, Oneworld, 1996

**383 Heaton, E.W.** *Solomon's New Men: The Emergence of Ancient Israel as a Nation State*, Thames & Hudson, 1974

**384 Heidel, A.** *The Gilgamesh Epic and Old Testament Parallels*, Phoenix Books, 1949

**385 Hendrickx, H.** *The Miracle Stories of The Synoptic Gospels*, Chapman, 1987

**386 Hendrickx, H.** *The Parables of Jesus*, Chapman, 1986

**387 Hendrickx, H.** *The Sermon on the Mount*, Chapman, 1984

**388 Hengel, M.** *The Atonement*, SCM Press, 1981

**388a Hengel, M.** *Between Jesus and Paul*, SCM Press, 1983

**389 Hengel, M.** *The Charismatic Leader and His Followers*, Crossroad, 1981

**390 Hengel, M.** *Crucifixion in the Ancient World and the Folly of the Message of the Cross*, SCM Press, 1977

**391 Hengel, M.** *The Hellenization of Judaea in the First Century after Christ*, SCM Press, 1989

**392 Hengel, M.** *Jews, Greeks and Barbarians*, SCM Press, 1980

**393 Hengel, M.** *The Johannine Question*, Trinity Press, 1989

**394 Hengel, M.** *Judaism and Hellenism,*, SCM Press, 1974

**395 Hengel, M.** *The Pre-Christian Paul*, SCM Press, 1991

**395a Hengel, M.** *Studies in Early Christology*, T&T Clarke, 1995

**396 Hengel, M.** *Studies in the Gospel of Mark*, Fortress, 1985

**397 Hengel, M.** *Was Jesus a Revolutionist?* Fortress, 1971

**398 Hengel, M.** *The Zealots*, T&T Clark, 1988

**399 Hengel, M. & Schwemer, A.M.** *Paul between Damascus and Antioch*, SCM Press, 1997

**400 Hennecke, E.** *New Testament Aprocrypha*, 2 vols, Lutterworth, 1963-5

**401 Hepper, F.N.** *Planting a Bible Garden*, HMSO, 1987

**402 Hermann, S.** *A History of Israel in Old Testament Times*, SCM Press, 1980

**403 Heron, A.** *Table and Tradition*, Handsel Press, 1983

**404 Hertzberg, H.W.** *1 & 2 Samuel*, SCM Press, 1960

**404a Heschel, A.J.** *The Prophets*, Jewish Publication Society, 1962

**405 Higgins, A.J.B.** *The Lord's Supper in the New Testament*, SCM Press, 1952

**406 Hill, C.C.** *Hellenists and Hebrews: Reappraising Division within the Earliest Church*, Fortress, 1992

**407 Hill, E.** *Being Human*, Chapman, 1984

**408 Hillers, D.B.** "Lamentations," in *Anchor Bible*, Doubleday, 1973

**409 Hillers, D.R.** *Micah*, Fortress, 1984

**410 Hobbs, T.R.** *A Time for War: A Study of Warfare in the Old Testament*, Michael Glazier, 1989

**411 Hoehner, H.W.** "Herodian Dynasty," in *Dictionary of Jesus and the Gospels* (eds.) J.B Green, S. McKnight & I.H. Marshall, InterVarsity Press, 1992

**412 Hoehner, H.W.** "Pontius Pilate," in *Dictionary of Jesus and the Gospels*, (eds.) J.B Green, S. McKnight & I.H. Marshall, InterVarsity Press, 1992

**413 Hoerth, A.J. Mattingly, G.L. & Yamauchi, E.M.** (eds.) *People of the Old Testament World*, Lutterworth, 1996

**414 Holladay, J.S.** "House (Israelite)," in *Anchor Bible Dictionary*

**415 Holladay, W.L.** *Isaiah: Scroll of a Prophetic Heritage Commentary*, Eerdmans, 1978

**416 Holtz, B.W.** (ed.) *Back to the Sources: Reading the Classic Jewish Texts*, Summit Books, 1984

**417 Hooker, M.D.** *The Message of Mark*, Epworth, 1983

**418 Horsely, R.A. & Hanson, J.S.** *Bandits, Prophets and Messiahs*, Winston, 1985

**419 Houlden, J.L.** *The Pastoral Epistles* SCM Press, 1989

**420 House, P.R.** *Zephaniah: A Prophetic Drama*, Almond, 1988

**422 Humphreys, W.L.** *Joseph and his Family*, University of South Carolina Press, 1988

**423 Hurtado, L.W.** *One God One Lord. Early Christian Devotion and Ancient Jewish Monotheism*, SCM Press, 1988

**424 Ishida, T.** *The Royal Dynasties in Ancient Israel*, BZAW, 1977

**424a Jacob M.M.** *Ezra, Nehemiah*, Doubleday, 1965

**425 Jacob I. & Jacob W.** 'Flora,' in *Anchor Bible Dictionary*

**426 Jagersma, H.** *A History of Israel from Alexander the Great to Bar Kochba*, SCM Press, 1985

**427 Jeansonne, S.P.** *The Women of Genesis: From Sarah to Potiphar's Wife*, Fortress, 1990

**428 Jeremias, J.** *The Eucharistic Words of Jesus*, SCM Press, 1966

**429 Jeremias, J.** *Jerusalem in the Time of Jesus*, SCM Press, 1967

**430 Jeremias, J.** *The Parables of Jesus*, SCM Press, 1963

**430a Jeremias, J.** *The Prayers of Jesus*, Allenson, 1967

**431 Jewett, R.** *A Chronology of Paul's Life*, Fortress, 1972

**432 Jewett, R.** *The Thessalonian Correspondence*, Fortress, 1986

**433 Johnson, A.R.** *The Vitality of the Individual in the Thought of Ancient Israel*, University of Wales Press, 1964

**434 Johnson, L.T.** *The Acts of the Apostles* Collegeville: Liturgical, 1992

**435 Johnson, L.T.** *The Writings of the New Testament*, SCM Press, 1986

**436 Johnson, M.D.** *The Purpose of the Biblical Genealogies*, CUP, 1969

**437 Jones, G.H.** *1 & 2 Chronicles*, Sheffield Academic Press, 1993

**438 Jones, G.H.** *1 & 2 Kings*, Eerdmans, 1984

**439 Jones, I.H.** *The Gospel of Matthew*, Epworth Commentaries, 1994

**440 Jones, I.H.** "Music and Musical Instruments," in *Anchor Bible Dictionary*

**441 Josephus, F.** *Jewish Antiquities*, Heinemann, 1981

**442 Josephus, F.** *The Jewish War*, Penguin, 1981

**443** Juel, D. *Luke-Acts*, SCM Press, 1983

**444** Kaiser, O. *Isaiah 1–12*, SCM Press, 1980

**445** Kaiser, O. *Isaiah 13–39*, SCM Press, 1980

**446** Kapelrud, A.S. *Central Ideas in Amos*, Oslo University Press, 1961

**447** Kapelrud, A. S. *The Message of the Prophet Zephaniah: Morphology and Ideas*, Oslo University Press, 1975

**448** Kee, H.C. (ed.) *Cambridge Annotated Study Apocrypha*, CUP, 1994

**449** Kee, H.C. *Community of the New Age*, SCM Press, 1977

**450** Kee, H.C. *Good News to the Ends of the Earth*, SCM Press, 1990

**451** Kee, H.C. *Medicine, Miracle and Magic in New Testament Times*, CUP, 1986

**452** Kee, H.C. *Miracle in the Early Christian World*, Yale University Press 1983

**453** Kendon, F. *A Life and Death of Judas Iscariot*, Bodley Head, 1926

**454** Kenyon, K.M. *Digging up Jericho*, Ernest Benn, 1979

**454A** Kenyon, K.M. *Digging Up Jerusalem*, Ernest Benn, 1974

**455** Kidner, D. *Proverbs*, Tyndale Press, 1964

**456** Kiene, P. *The Tabernacle of God in the Wilderness of Sinai*, Zondervan, 1977

**457** King, P.J. *Jeremiah: An Archeological Companion*, Westminster/John Knox, 1993

**458** King, P.J. "Jerusalem," in *Anchor Bible Dictionary*

**459** Kingsbury, J.D. *The Christology of Mark's Gospel*, Fortress, 1989

**460** Kingsbury, J.D. *Conflict in Mark*, Fortress, 1989

**461** Kirkpatrick, P.G. *The Old Testament and Folklore Study*, JSOT, 1988

**462** Klein, R.P. "Books of Ezra-Nehemiah," *Anchor Bible Dictionary*

**463** Klein, R.W. *Ezekiel: The Prophet and his Message*, University of South Carolina Press, 1988

**464** Klein, R.W. *Israel in Exile: A Theological Interpretation*, Fortress, 1979

**465** Knight, D.A. "Cosmology and Order in the Hebrew Tradition," in *Cosmology and Ethical Order*, (eds.) R.W. Lowin & F.E. Reynolds, University of Chicago Press, 1985

**466** Koo, H.C. *Medicines, Miracles and Magic*, CUP, 1983

**467** Koo, H.C. *Miracles in the Early Christian World*, Yale University Press, 1983

**468** Kopp, C. *The Holy Places of the Gospels*, Nelson, 1963

**469** Kraeling, C.H. *John the Baptist*, Scribners, 1951

**470** Kraus, H. J. *Worship in Israel*, Blackwell, 1966

**471** Kugel, J.L. *The Idea of Biblical Poetry: Parallelism and its History*, Yale University Press, 1981

**472** Kümmel, W.G. *Man in the New Testament*, Epworth Press, 1963

**473** Laato, A. *Josiah and David redivivus*, Almqvist & Wiksell Int.,1992

**474** Lacoque, A. *The Book of Daniel*, SPCK, 1979

**475** Lacoque, A. *The Feminine Unconventional: Four Subversive Figures in Israel's Tradition*, Fortress, 1990

**476** Lambert, W.G. & Millard, A. *Atra-hasis: The Babylonian Story of the Flood*, Clarendon Press, 1969

**477** Landy, F. *Paradoxes of Paradise: Identity and Difference in the Song of Songs*, Almond, 1983

**478** Lang, B. *History of Heaven*, Yale University Press, 1988

**479** Lang, B. (ed.) *Anthropological Approaches to the Old Testament*, SPCK/Fortress, 1985

**480** Lang, B. *Wisdom and the Book of Proverbs: An Israelite Goddess Redefined*, Pilgrim, 1986.

**481** de Lange. N. *Apocrypha: Jewish Literature of the Hellenistic Age*, Viking Press, 1978

**482** de Lange, N. *Judaism*, OUP, 1986

**482a** Larkin, K. *Ruth and Esther*, Old Testament Guides, Sheffield Academic Press, 1995

**483** Larue, G. *Sex and the Bible*, Buffalo, 1983

**484** Laurentin, R. *The Truth of Christmas Beyond the Myths: The Gospels of the Infancy of Christ*, St. Bede's Publications, 1986

**485** Laws, S. *A Commentary on the Epistle of James*, A&C Black, 1980

**486** Lehrman, S.M. *The Song of Songs*, in A. Cohen (ed.) *The Five Megilloth*, Soncino, 1952

**487** Leibowitz, N. *Studies in the Pentateuch*, 5 vols, World Zionist Organization, 1980

**488** di Lella, A, "Wisdom of Ben-Sira," in *Anchor Bible Dictionary*

**489** Lemaire, A. "Education (Israel)," in *Anchor Bible Dictionary*

**490** Lemche, N.P. *Early Israel*, Brill, 1985

**491** Leon, H.J. *The Jews of Ancient Rome*, Jewish Publication Society, 1960

**492** Levenson, J. *Sinai and Zion*, New York, 1985

**493** Levine, A.J. *The Social and Ethnic Dimensions of Matthaen Salvation History*, Edwin Mellen Press, 1988

**494** Levine, B. *Numbers 1–20, A Translation with Introduction and Commentary*, Doubleday, 1993

**495** Levine, L.I. *The Synagogue in Late Antiquity*, American School of Oriental Research, 1987

**496** Lieu, J., North, J. & Rajak, T. (eds.) *The Jews among Pagans and Christians in the Roman Empire*, Routledge, 1994

**497** Lincoln, A.T. & Wedderburn, A.J.M. *The Theology of the Later Pauline Epistles*, CUP, 1993

**498** Lincoln, A. *Ephesians*, Word Books, 1990

**499** Lincoln, A. *Paradise Now and Not Yet*, CUP, 1981

**500** Lindars, B. *John*, Sheffield Academic Press 1990

**501** Lindblom, J. *Prophecy in Ancient Israel*, Fortress, 1962

**501a** Lohmeyer, E. *The Lord's Prayer*, Collins, 1965

**502** Long, A.A. & Sedley, D.N. *The Hellenistic Philosophers, vol. 1*, CUP, 1987

**503** Longenecker, R.N. *Galatians*, Waco, 1990

**504** van der Loos, H. *The Miracles of Jesus*, Brill, 1968

**505** Lüdemann, G. *Paul, Apostle to the Gentiles: Studies in Chronology*, Fortress, 1984

**506** Lundquist, J. *The Temple: Meeting Place of Heaven and Earth*, Thames & Hudson, 1993

**507** Mack, B.L. *Rhetoric and the New Testament*, Fortress, 1990

**508** Macquarrie, J. *A Guide to the Sacraments*, SCM Press, 1997

**509** Magonet, J. "Book of Jonah," in *Anchor Bible Dictionary*

**510** Magonet, J. *Form and Meaning: Studies in Literary Techniques in the Book of Jonah*, Almond, 1983

**511** Magonet, J. *A Rabbi Reads the Psalms*, SCM Press, 1994

**512** Magonet, J. *The Subversive Bible*, SCM Press, 1997

**513** Malandra, W.W. *An Introduction to Ancient Iranian Religion*, University of Minnesota Press, 1983

**514** Malherbe, A.J. *Social Aspects of Early Christianity*, Fortress, 1983

**515** Malina, B. *The New Testament World*, Westminster, 1993

**516** Mann, T. *Joseph and his Brothers*, Secker & Warburg, 1981

**517** Marrou, H.I. *A History of Education in Antiquity*, Sheed & Ward, 1956

**517a** Marshall, I.H. *The Epworth Preachers Commentary*, 1992

**518** Marshall, I.H. *The Gospel of Luke*, Eerdmans,1978

**518a** Marshall, H.I. *Last Supper and Lord's Supper*, Paternoster, 1980

**519** Marshall, I.H. *Luke: Historian & Theologian*, Zondervan, 1970

**520** Martin, D.B. *Slavery as Salvation*, Yale University Press, 1990

**520a** Martin, J.D. *Proverbs*, Old Testament Guides, Sheffield Academic Press, 1995

**520b** Martin, J.D. *Galatians*, Doubleday, 1997

**520c** Martin, R.P. *Philippians*, Tyndale New Testament Commentaries, InterVarsity Press, 1987

**520d** Martin, R.P. *The Spirit and the Congregation*, Eerdmans, 1984

**521** Martin-Achard, R. *From Death to Life*, Oliver & Boyd, 1960

**522** Martin-Achard, R. *A Light to the Nations: A Study of the Old Testament Conception of Israel's Mission to the World*, Oliver & Boyd, 1962

**523** Mason, R.A. *The Books of Haggai, Zechariah, and Malachi*, CUP, 1977

**524** Mason, R.A. *Micah, Nahum, Obadiah*, Sheffield Academic Press, 1991

**525** Mason, R.A. *Zephaniah, Habakkuk, Joel*, JSOT, 1994

**526** Matera, F.J. *Passion Narratives and Gospel Theologies*, Paulist Press, 1986

**527** Matter, E.A. *The Voice of My Beloved: The Song of Songs in Medieval Christianity*, 1990

**528** Matthew, I. *The Impact of God: Soundings from St. John of the Cross*, Hodder & Stoughton, 1995

**529** Mauser, U.W. *Christ in the Wilderness*, SCM Press, 1963

**530** Mayes, A.D.H. *Israel in the Period of the Judges*, SCM Press, 1974

**531** Mayes, A.D.H. *Judges*, JSOT, 1989

**532** Mayes, A.D.H. *The Story of Israel Between Settlement and Exile: A Redactional Study of the Deuteronomistic History*, SCM Press, 1983

**533** Mays, J.L. *Amos*, SCM Press, 1970

**534** Mays, J.L. *Micah*, SCM Press, 1974

**535** Mazar, B. *The Mountain of the Lord*, Doubleday, 1975

**536** McCann, J.C. *The Shape and Shaping of the Psalter*, Sheffield Academic Press, 1993

**537** McConville, J.G. *Judgement and Promise: An Interpretation of the Book of Jeremiah*, Apollos, 1993

**538** McGrath, A. *Christian Theology: An Introduction*, Blackwell, 1994

**538a** McGrath, A. *Iustitia Dei: A History of the Christian Doctrine of Justification*, CUP, 1986

**539** McKane, W. *Prophets and Wise Men*, SCM Press, 1983

**540** McKane, W. *Proverbs: A New Approach*, SCM Press, 1970

**541** McKane, W. *Studies in the Patriarchal Narratives*, Handsel Press, 1979

**542 McKeating, H.** *Ezekiel*, Sheffield Academic Press, 1993

**542a McKinnon, J.W.** *Music in the Ancient World*

**543 McNamara, M.** *The Aramaic Bible*, Michael Glazier (series)

**543a Meade, D.G.** *Pseudonymity*

**544 Meeks, W.A.** *The First Urban Christians: The Social World of the Apostle Paul*, Yale University Press, 1983

**545 Meeks, W.A.** *The Moral World of the First Christians*, SPCK, 1987

**546 Meeks, W.A.** *The Origins of Christian Morality*, Yale University Press, 1993

**547 Meier, J.P.** *A Marginal Jew: Rethinking the Historical Jesus. vol. 1*, Doubleday, 1991

**548 Meier, J.P.** *A Marginal Jew: Mentor, Message and Miracles, vol. 2*, Doubleday, 1994

**548a Mettinger, T.N.D.** *The Civil and Sacral Legitimisation of the Israelite Kings*, 1976

**549 Mettinger, T.N.D.** *In Search of God*, Philadelphia, 1988

**550 Mettinger, T.N.D.** *King and Messiah*, CWK Gleerup, 1976

**551 Mettinger, T.N.D.** *Solomonic State Officials*, Lund, 1971

**552 Metzger, B.M.** *An Introduction to the Apocrypha*, OUP, 1957

**553 Meyer, B.** *The Aims of Jesus*, SCM Press, 1979

**554 Meyer, B.F.** *One Loaf, One Cup*, Mercer University Press, 1993

**555 Meyers, C.** *Discovering Eve: Ancient Israelite Women in Context*, OUP, 1988

**556 Meyers, E.M.** *Jewish Ossuaries: Reburial and Rebirth*, Biblical Institute Press, 1971

**557 Meyers, E.M. & Strange, J.F.** *Archaeology, the Rabbis and Early Christianity*, SCM Press, 1981

**558 Milgrom, J.** *Cult and Conscience*, Brill, 1976

**558a Milgrom, J.** *Numbers*, Jewish Publication Society, 1990

**558b Millard, A.R. & Wiseman, D.J.** *Essays on the Patriarchal Narratives*, InterVarsity Press, 1980

**559 Miller, J.M. & Hayes, J.H.** *A History of Ancient Israel and Judah*, SCM Press, 1986

**560 Miller, P.D.** *Sin and Judgement in the Prophets*, Scholars Press, 1982

**561 Miller, P.D. et al.** *Ancient Israelite Religion*, Fortress, 1987

**562 Miller, R.J.** *The Complete Gospels*, HarperCollins, 1994

**562a Moberly, R.W.L.** *Genesis 12–50*, Sheffield Academic Press, 1992

**562b Moberly, R.W.L.** *The Old Testament of the Old Testament*, Fortress Press, 1992

**563 Mollenkort, V.R.** *The Divine Feminine: The Biblical Imagery of God as Female*, Crossroad, 1983

**564 Montenat, C.** *How to Read the World: Creation in Evolution*, SCM Press, 1985

**565 Montet, P.** *Everyday Life in Egypt in the Days of Ramesses the Great*, Arnold, 1958

**566 Moore, C.A.** *Tobit, Judith and the Additions*, Doubleday

**567 Moore, W.H.** "Book of Esther," in *Anchor Bible Dictionary*

**568 Moore, W.H.** "Galilee," in *New International Dictionary of Biblical Archaeology*, (eds.) E.M. Blacklock and R.K.Harrison, Zondervan, 1986

**569 Morenz, S.** *Egyptian Religion*, Cornell University, 1978

**570 Morgan, R.** *Romans*, Sheffield Academic Press, 1992

**571 Morris, L.L** *The Cross in the New Testament*, Eerdmans, 1965

**572 Moscati, S.** *The Face of the Ancient Orient*, Routledge, 1960

**573 Moscati, S.** (ed.) *The Phoenicians*, Harmondsworth, 1971

**574 Moule, C.F.D.** *Essays in New Testament Interpretation*, CUP, 1982

**575 Moule, C.F.D.** *The Holy Spirit*, Mowbray, 1978

**576 Moule, C.F.D.** *The Origin of Christology*, CUP, 1977

**577 Moxnes, H.** (ed.) *Constructing Early Christian Families*, Routledge, 1997

**578 Murphy, R.E.** *The Song of Songs*, Fortress, 1990

**579 Murphy-O'Connor, J.** *The Holy Land: An Archaeological Guide from Earliest Times to 1700*, OUP, 1932

**580 Murphy-O'Connor, J.** *Paul: A Critical Life*, Clarendon Press, 1996

**581 Murphy-O'Connor, J.** *The Theology of 2 Corinthians*, CUP, 1991

**582 Myers, C.** *Discovering Eve: Ancient Israelite Women in Context*, OUP, 1988

**583 Myers J.M.** *1 & 2 Chronicles*, Doubleday, 1983

**584 Naveh, G. & Shaked, G.S.** *Amulets and Magic Bowls: Aramaic Incantations of Late Antiquity*, Brill, 1985

**585 Naveh, J.** *Early History of the Alphabet*, Brill, 1982

**585a Nelson, R.D.** *Raising up a Faithful Priest: Community and Priesthood in Biblical Theology*, Westminster/ John Knox Press, 1993

**585b Neher, A.** *The Prophetic Existence*, Yoseloff, 1969

**586 Newsome, J.D.** *By the Waters of Babylon: An Introduction to the History and Theology of the Exile*, John Knox, 1979

**587 Nicholson, E.W.** *Deuteronomy and Tradition*, Blackwell, 1967

**588 Nicholson, E.W.** *Exodus and Sinai in History and Tradition*, John Knox, 1973

**589 Nicholson, E.W.** *God and his People: Covenant and Theology in the Old Testament*, Clarendon Press, 1986

**590 Nicholson, E.W.** *The Pentateuch in the Twentieth Century*, Clarendon Press, 1998

**591 Nickelsburg, G.W.E.** *Jewish Literature Between the Bible and the Mishnah*, SCM Press, 1981

**592 Nickle, K.F.** *The Collection: A Study in Paul's Strategy*, SCM Press, 1966

**593 Niditch, S.** *Chaos to Cosmos: Studies in Biblical Patterns of Creation*, Scholars Press, 1985

**594 Niditch, S.** *War in the Hebrew Bible*, OUP, 1993

**595 Nineham, D.E.** *St. Mark*, Penguin, 1963

**596 Nock, A.D.** *Cremation and Burial in the Roman Empire*, Harvard Theological Review, 1932

**597 Noll, S.** *Thinking Biblically About Angels*, InterVarsity Press/Apollos, 1998

**597a North, C.R.** *Isaiah 40–55*, SCM Press, 1952

**598 Noth, M.** *The Deuteronomistic History*, JSOT, 1981

**599 Noth, M.** *Exodus*, Old Testament Library, SCM Press, 1962

**600 Noth, M.** *The Laws in the Pentateuch and Other Essays*, SCM Press, 1984

**601 Noth, M.** *Leviticus*, SCM Press, 1977

**602 Noth, M.** *Numbers*, SCM Press, 1968

**603 O'Connor, K.M.** *The Confessions of Jeremiah*, Scholars Press, 1988

**604 Ogletree, T.W.** *The Use of the Bible in Christian Ethics*, Fortress, 1983

**605 Olsen, D.T.** *The Death of the Old and the Birth of the New*, Scholars Press, 1985

**605a Orchard, J.B.** *A Synopsis of the Four Gospels in a New Translation*, Macon, 1982

**606 Osborne, G.R.** *The Resurrection Narratives: A Redactional Study*, Baker, 1984

**607 Ottoson, M.** *Temples and Cult Places in Palestine*, Uppsala, 1980

**608 Palmer, B.** *Medicine and the Bible*, Paternoster, 1986

**609 Parr, J.** *Sowers and Reapers: A Companion to the Four Gospels and Acts*, Bible Reading Fellowship, 1994

**610 Parsons, M.C.** *The Departure of Jesus in Luke-Acts*, Academic Press, 1987

**611 Patrick, D.** *Old Testament Law*, SCM Press, 1985

**612 Perkins, P.** *Jesus as Teacher*, CUP, 1990

**613 Perkins, P.** *Ministering in the Pauline Churches*, Paulist Press, 1982

**614 Perkins, P.** *Resurrection: New Testament Witness and Contemporary Reflection*, Doubleday, 1984

**614a Peters, P.E.** *Jerusalem*, Princeton, University Press, 1985

**615 Petersen, D.L.** *Haggai and Zechariah 1–8*, SCM Press, 1984

**616 Petersen, N.R.** *Rediscovering Paul: Philemon and the Sociology of Paul's Narrative World*, Fortress, 1985

**616a Petuchowski, J.J. and Brocke, M.** (eds.) *The Lord's Prayer and Jewish Liturgy*, Burns & Oats, 1978

**617 Phillips, A.** *Ancient Israel's Criminal Law, A New Approach to the Decalogue*, Blackwell, 1970

**618 Phillips, A.C.J.** *Deuteronomy*, CUP

**619 Phipps, W.E.** *Genesis and Gender: Biblical Myths of Sexuality and Their Cultural Impact*, Praeger, 1989

**620 Pitman, M.** *Adam and Evolution*, Rider, 1984

**621 Polzin, R.** *Moses and the Deuteronomist: A Literary Study of the Deuteronomic History*, Seabury, 1980

**622 Polzin, R.** *Samuel and the Deuteronomist*, Harper & Row, 1989

**623 Pope, M.** "The Song of Songs," in *Anchor Bible Dictionary*

**624 Porten, B.** *Archives from Elephantine: The Life of an Ancient Jewish Military Colony*, University of California Press, 1968

**625 Powell, M.A.** "Weights and Measures," in *Anchor Bible Dictionary*

**626 Prevost, J.P.** *How to Read the Apocalypse*, SCM Press, 1993

**627 Prinsloo, W.S.** *The Theology of the Book of Joel*, de Gruyter, 1985

**627a Prior, M.** *The Bible and Colonialism: A Major Critique*, Sheffield Academic Press, 1997

**628 Pritchard, J.B.** (ed.) *Ancient Near Eastern Texts Relating to the Old Testament*, (3rd ed. with supplement), Princeton University Press, 1969

**629 Pritchard, J.B.** (ed.) *Solomon and Sheba*, 1974

**630 Provan, I.** *Lamentations: The New Century Bible*, Marshall Pickering, 1991

**631 Provan, I.** *1 & 2 Kings*, Sheffield Academic Press, 1997

**632 Purvis, J.D.** *Jerusalem, the Holy City: A Bibliography*, 2 vols., Scarecrow, 1991

**633 Quirke, S.** *Ancient Egyptian Religion*, British Museum Press, 1992

**634 Quirke, S. & Spencer, J.** (eds.) *The British Museum Book of Ancient Egypt*, British Museum Press, 1992

**635 von Rad, G.** *Deuteronomy, A Commentary*, SCM Press, 1966

**636 von Rad, G.** *Genesis*, SCM Press, 1972

**637 von Rad, G.** 'The Joseph Narrative and Ancient Wisdoms,' in *The Problem of the Hexateuch and Other Essays*, Oliver & Boyd, 1966

**638** von Rad, G. *Wisdom in Israel*, SCM Press, 1975

**639** Ramsey, G. W. *The Quest of the Historical Israel*, SCM Press, 1982

**640** Ramsey, G.W. "Samuel," in *Anchor Bible Dictionary*

**641** Rappaport, U. 'The Maccabean Revolt,' in *Anchor Bible Dictionary*

**642** Rawson, B. (ed.) *The Family in Ancient Rome: New Perspectives*, Croom Helm, 1986

**643** Redford, D.B. *Akhenaton, the Heretic Pharaoh*, Princeton University Press, 1984

**644** Reisner, R. "Galilee," in *Dictionary of Jesus and the Gospels*, (eds.) J.B. Green, S.McKight, & H. Marshall, InterVarsity Press, 1992

**645** Rhoads, D.M. *Israel in Revolution 6–74 CE*, Fortress, 1976

**646** Richards, K.H. & Gulley, N.R. "Death," in *Anchor Bible Dictionary*

**647** Richardson, A. & Bowden, J. (eds.) "Christology" and "Trinity," in *A New Dictionary of Christian Theology*, SCM Press, 1983

**648** Riches, J. *Jesus and the Transformation of Judaism*, Darton, Longman & Todd, 1980

**649** Riches, J. *Matthew*, Sheffield Academic Press, 1996

**649a** Ringgren, H. *Israelite Religion*, SPCK, 1966

**650** Ringgren, H. *The Messiah in the Old Testament*, SCM Press, 1956

**651** Ringgren, H. *Religions of the Ancient Near East*, SPCK, 1976

**652** Roberts, J.J.M. *Nahum, Habakkuk and Zephaniah*, Westminster/John Knox, 1991

**653** Robertson, O.P. *The Books of Nahum, Habakkuk and Zephaniah*, Eerdmans, 1990

**654** Robinson J.A.T. *In the End, God...*, *A Study of the Christian Doctrine of the Last Things*, James Clarke & Co., 1950

**655** Robinson, J.A.T. *Jesus and His Coming: The Emergence of a Doctrine*, SCM Press, 1957

**656** Robinson, J.A.T. *The Priority of John*, SCM Press, 1985

**657** Robinson, J.A.T. *Wrestling with Romans*, SCM Press, 1979

**658** Rogers, G.M. *The Sacred Identity of Ephesus: Foundations Myths of a Roman City*, Routledge, 1991

**659** Rogerson, J.W. *Anthropology and the Old Testament*, Blackwell, 1978

**660** Rogerson, J.W. *The Supernatural in the Old Testament*, Lutterworth, 1976

**661** Rogerson, J. & Davies, P. *The Old Testament World*, CUP, 1989

**662** Rousseau, J.J. & Arav, A. *Jesus and His World*, Fortress, 1995

**663** Roux, G. *Ancient Iraq*, Harmondsworth, 1980

**664** Rowland, C. *The Open Heaven*, SPCK, 1982

**665** Ruether, R.R. (ed.) *Religion and Sexism*, Simon & Schuster, 1974

**666** Rush, A.C. *Death and Burial in Christian Antiquity*, Catholic University Press of America, 1941

**667** Russell, D.S. *Divine Disclosure*, SCM Press, 1992

**668** Russell, D.S. *The Jews from Alexander to Herod*, CUP, 1967

**669** Russell, D.S. *The Method and Message of Jewish Apocalyptic*, SCM Press, 1964

**670** Russell, L.M. (ed.) *Feminist Interpretation of the Bible*, Westminster, 1985

**671** Russell, L.M. *The Liberating Word: A Guide to Non-Sexist Interpretation of the Bible*, Westminster, 1976

**672** Safrai, S. "The Jewish Cultural Nature of Galilee in the First Century," in *The New Testament and Christian-Jewish Dialogue, Immanuel*, nos. 24/25 (ed.) M. Lowe.

**673** Safrai, S. & Stern, M. *The Jewish People in the First Century*, Fortress, 1976

**674** Saggs, H.W.F. *Everyday Life in Babylonia and Assyria*, Batsford, 1965

**675** Saggs, H.W.F. *The Might That Was Assyria*, Sidgwick & Jackson, 1984

**676** Salters, R.B. *Jonah & Lamentations*, JSOT, 1994

**677** Sanders, E.P. *The Historical Figure of Jesus*, Penguin, 1993

**678** Sanders, E.P. *Jesus and Judaism, Part 1*, SCM Press, 1985

**679** Sanders, E.P. *Judaism: Practise and Belief 63 BCE – 66 CE* SCM Press, 1992

**680** Sanders, E.P. *Paul*, 1991

**681** Sanders, E.P. *Paul and the Law and the Jewish People*, Fortress, 1983

**682** Sanders, E.P. *Paul and Palestinian Judaism*, Fortress, 1977

**683** Sanders, E.P. (ed.) *Twentieth-Century Interpretations of the Book of Job*, Englewood, Cliffs, 1986

**684** Sanders, E.P. & Davis, M. *Studying the Synoptic Gospels*, SCM Press, 1989

**685** Sarna, N.M. "The Book of Exodus," in *Anchor Bible Dictionary*

**686** Sarna, N.M. "Exodus," in *The Jewish Publication Society Torah Commentary*, 1991

**687** Sarna, N.M. *Exploring Exodus: The Heritage of Biblical Israel*, Schocken, 1987

**687a** Sarna, N.M. *Understanding Genesis*, 1966

**688** Sass, B. *The Genesis of the Alphabet and Its Development in the Second Millennium BC*, Wiesbaden, Harrassowitz, 1988

**689** Sasson, J.M. "Jonah," in *Anchor Bible Dictionary*

**690** Sasson, J.M. *Ruth: A New Translation*, John Hopkins University Press, 1979

**691** Sawyer, J.F.A. *Isaiah*, Westminster, 1986

**692** Sawyer, J.F.A. *Prophecy and the Prophets of the Old Testament*, OUP, 1987

**693** Sawyer, J.F.A. *Reading Leviticus: A Conversation with Mary Douglas*, Sheffield Academic Press, 1996

**694** Schmidt, B. "Canaan (Place)," in *Anchor Bible Dictionary*

**695** Schmidt, B. *Israel's Beneficent Dead*, Tübingen, 1994

**696** Scholem, G. *Major Trends in Jewish Mysticism*, Schocken, 1946

**697** Schottroff, L. *Lydia's Impatient Sisters*, SCM Press, 1995

**698** Scobie, C.H.H. *John the Baptist*, Fortress, 1964

**699** Segal, A. F. *Paul the Convert, A Jewish Viewpoint*, Yale University Press, 1990

**669a** Seifred, M.A. *Justification by Faith*, Brill, 1992

**699b** Sendrey, A. *Music in Ancient Israel*

**700** Sheriffs, D. *The Friendship of the Lord*, Paternoster, 1996

**701** Sherwood, Y. *The Prostitute and the Prophet: Hosea's Marriage in Literary-Theoretical Perspective*, Sheffield Academic Press, 1996

**702** Sigal, P. *The Emergence of Contemporary Judaism, 1.1: From the Origins to the Separation of Christianity*, Pickwick Press, 1980

**703** Skehan, P.W. & di Lella, A, *The Wisdom of Ben Sira*, 1987

**704** Skinner, J. *Prophecy and Religion*, CUP, 1961

**705** Smalley, S.S. *1,2,3 John*, Waco, 1984

**706** Smallwood, E.M. *The Jews Under Roman Rule: From Pompey to Diocletian*, Brill, 1981

**707** Smith, D.L. *The Religion of the Landless: The Social Context of the Babylonian Exile*, Meyer-Stone Books, 1989

**708** Smith, D.M. *First, Second & Third John*, John Knox, 1991

**709** Smith, J.Z. *Drudgery Divine: on the Comparison of Early Christianity and the Religions of the Late Antiquity*, University of Chicago Press, 1990

**710** Smith, M. *The Word Is Very Near You*, Darton, Longman & Todd, 1990

**711** Smith, M.S. *The Early History of God*, Harper & Row, 1990

**712** Smith, M.S. *The Laments of Jeremiah and Their Contexts*, Scholars Press, 1990

**713** Snaith, J.G. *Ecclesiasticus*, CUP, 1973

**714** Snodgrass, K. *The Parable of the Wicked Tenants*, Mohr, 1983

**715** Soggin, J. A. *Judges*, SCM Press, 1987

**716** Soggin, J. A., *The Prophet Amos*, SCM Press, 1987

**717** Souter, A. (rev. C.S.C. Williams) *The Text and Canon of the New Testament*, Duckworth, 1954

**718** Sparks, H.F.D. (ed.) *The Apocryphal Old Testament*, Clarendon Press, 1984

**719** Spencer, A.J. *Death in Ancient Egypt*, Harmondsworth, 1982

**720** Spencer, A.J. "Levites and Priests," in *Anchor Bible Dictionary*

**721** Spronk, K. *Beatific Afterlife in Ancient Israel and in the Ancient Near East*, Neukirchen-Vluyn & Kevelaer, 1986

**722** Stambough, J. & Balch, D. *The Social World of the First Christians*, SPCK, 1986

**723** Stamm, J.J. & Andrew, M.E. *The Ten Commandments in Recent Research*, SCM Press, 1967

**724** Stanton, G. *A Gospel for a New People*, T&T Clark, 1992

**725** Stanton, G. *The Gospels and Jesus*, OUP, 1989

**726** Stanton, G. *Gospel Truth? New Light on the Gospels*, HarperCollins, 1995

**727** Stein, R.H. *The Synoptic Problem*, Baker, 1987

**728** Stern, E. (ed.) *The New Encyclopedia of Archaeological Excavation in the Holy Land*, Simon & Schuster, 1993

**729** Stern, M. "The Province of Judaea," in *The Jewish People in the First Century*, (eds.) S. Safrai & M. Stern, Fortress, 1974

**730** Stern, M. "The Reign of Herod and the Herodian Dynasty," in *The Jewish People in the First Century*, (eds.) S. Safrai & M. Stern, Fortress, 1974

**731** Sternberg, M. *The Poetics of Biblical Narrative*, Indiana University Press, 1987

**732** Stevenson, J. *A New Eusebius: Documents Illustrative of the History of the Church to AD 337*, SPCK, 1957

**733** Stone, M.E. *Jewish Writings of the Second Temple Period*, Philadelphia, 1984

**734** Stone, M.E. *Scriptures, Sects, and Visions*, Blackwell, 1982

**735** Stott, J.R.W. *The Letters of John*, InterVarsity Press/Eerdmans, 1988

**736** Strange, J.F. "Nazareth," in *Anchor Bible Dictionary*

**737** Strange, W.A. *Children in the Early Church*, Paternoster, 1996

**738** Strecker, G. *The Sermon on the Mount, An Exegetical Commentary*, Abingdon, 1988

739 Stuart, D. K. *Hosea-Jonah*, Waco, 1987

740 Sweet, J. *Revelation*, SCM Press, 1979

741 Tamez, E. *The Scandalous Message of James: Faith without Works is Dead*, Crossroad, 1990

742 Tannehill, R.C. *The Narrative Unity of Luke-Acts*, Fortress, 1986

743 Taylor, J. *Ezekiel, Tyndale Old Testament Commentaries*, InterVarsity Press, 1969

744 Terrien, S. *Till the Heart Sings*, Fortress, 1985

745 Theissen, G. *The Miracle Stories of the Early Christian Tradition*, T&T Clark, 1983

746 Theron, D.J. *Evidence of Tradition*, Bowes & Bowes, 1957

747 Thompson, M.M. *The Humanity of Jesus in the Fourth Gospel*, Fortress, 1988

748 Thompson, M.M. *1-3 John*, InterVarsity Press, 1992

748a Throckmorton, B.H. *Gospel Parallels*, Nash, 1979

749 Thurston, B.B. *The Widows: A Women's Ministry in the Early Church*, Fortress, 1989

749a Tiede, C.P. *Simon Peter: From Galilee to Rome*, Paternoster, 1986

750 van de Toorn, K. *Sin and Sanction in Israel and Mesopotamia*, Van Gorcum, 1985

751 Torczyner, H. *Lachish 1: The Lachish Letters*, OUP, 1938

752 Tov, E. *Textual Criticism of the Hebrew Bible*, Fortress, 1992

753 Travis, S.H. *I Believe in the Second Coming of Jesus*, Hodder & Stoughton, 1982

754 Trebilco, P. *Jewish Communities in Asia Minor*, CUP, 1991

755 Tribble, P. *God and the Rhetoric of Sexuality*, Fortress, 1978

756 Tribble, P. *Texts of Terror: Literary-Feminist Readings of Biblical Narratives*, Fortress, 1984

757 Tubb, J.N. & Chapman, R.L. *Archaeology and the Bible*, British Museum Press, 1990

758 Tuckett, C.M. *Luke*, Sheffield Academic Press, 1996

759 Turner, M.M.B. *The Holy Spirit and Spiritual Gifts, Then and Now*, Paternoster, 1996

760 Turner, M.M.B. *Power from on High: The Spirit in Israel's Restoration and Witness in Luke-Acts*, Academic Press, 1996

761 Twelftree, G.H. 'Temptations of Jesus', in *Dictionary of Jesus and the Gospels*, (eds.) J.B. Green, S. McKnight & I.H. Marshall, InterVarsity Press, 1992

762 Vanderkam, J.C. *The Dead Sea Scrolls Today*, Eerdmans, 1994

763 Van Seters, J. *Abraham in History and Tradition*, Yale University Press, 1975

764 Van Seters, J. *In Search of History*, Yale University Press, 1983

765 Van Seters, J. *The Life of Moses*, Westminster/John Knox Press, 1994

766 de Vaux, R. *Ancient Israel*, McGraw-Hill, 1965

767 de Vaux, R. *Ancient Israel: Its Life and Institutions*, Darton, Longman & Todd, 1994

768 Vawter, B. *Job and Jonah: Questioning the Hidden God*, Paulist Press, 1983

769 Verhey, A. *The Great Reversal: Ethics and the New Testament*, Eerdmans, 1984

770 Vermes, G. *The Complete Dead Sea Scrolls in English*, Allen Lane, 1997

771 de Vries, S.J. *Prophet Against Prophet*, Eerdmans, 1978

772 de Vries, S.J. *Yesterday, Today and Tomorrow: Time and History in the Old Testament*, SPCK, 1975

773 Walsh, J.P.M. *The Mighty from their Thrones: Power in the Biblical Tradition*, Fortress, 1987

774 Walton, J.H. "The Mesopotamian Background of the Tower of Babel Account and its Implications,"Bulletin for Biblical Research 5, 1995

775 Walzer, M. *Exodus and Revolution*, Basic Books, 1985

776 Wanamaker, C.A. *The Epistles to the Thessalonians*, Exeter Paternoster, 1990

777 Waskow, A. *Seasons of Our Joy: A Modern Guide to the Jewish Holidays*, Beacon Press, 1982

778 Watson, D.F. "Angels," in *Anchor Bible Dictionary*

778a Watson, F.B. *Paul, Judaism and the Gentiles*, CUP, 1986

779 Watts, J.D.W. *The Books of Joel, Obadiah, Jonah, Nahum, Habakkuk and Zephaniah*, Word Books, 1975

780 Watts, J.D.W. *Isaiah 1-33*, Word Books, 1985

781 Watts, J.D.W. *Isaiah 34-66*, Word Books, 1987

782 Webb, B.G. *The Book of Judges: An Integrated Reading*, JSOT, 1987

783 Weber, H.R. *Jesus and the Children*, World Council of Churches, 1979

784 Wedderburn, A.J.M. *Baptism and Resurrection*, JCB Mohr, 1987

785 Weeks, S. *Early Israelite Wisdom*, Clarendon Press, 1994

786 Weems, R. *Just a Sister Away: A Womanist Vision of Women's Relationships in the Bible*, LuraMedia, 1988

787 Weinfeld, M. *Deuteronomy and the Deuteronomic School*, Clarenden Press, 1967

788 Weippert, M. *The Settlement of the Israelite Tribes in Palestine*, SCM Press, 1971

789 Wenham, G.J. *The Book of Leviticus*, Eerdmans, 1979

790 Wenham, J. *Easter Enigma: Do the Resurrection Stories Contradict One Another?* Paternoster, 1984

791 Westbrook, R. "Punishments and Crimes," in *Anchor Bible Dictionary*

792 Westermann, C. *Creation*, SPCK, 1974

793 Westermann, C. *Genesis 1-11; Genesis 12-36; Genesis 37-50*, Ausburg, 1984-86

795 Westermann, C. *Isaiah 40-66*, SCM Press, 1969

796 Westermann, C. *Lamentations: Issues and Interpretation*, T&T Clark, 1994

797 Westermann, C. *Praise and Lament in the Psalms*, John Knox Press, 1981

798 White, J.L. *The Body of the Greek Letter*, Society of Biblical Literature, 1972

799 Whitelam, K.W. *The Invention of Ancient Israel*, Routledge, 1996

800 Whybray, R.N. *Isaiah 40-66*, Eerdmans, 1975

801 Whybray, R.N. *The Making of the Pentateuch*, JSOT, 1987

801a Whybray, R.N. "Proverbs" in *New Century Bible Commentary*, Marshall Pickering, 1994

802 Whybray, R.N. *The Second Isaiah*, JSOT, 1983

803 Whybray, R.N. *The Succession Narrative*, SCM Press, 1968

804 Wiener, A. *The Prophet Elijah in the Development of Judaism*

805 Wildberger, H. *Isaiah 1-12*, Minneapolis, 1991

806 Wilkinson, N. *Jerusalem as Jesus Knew It*, Thames & Hudson, 1982

807 Williams, C.S.C. *Alterations to the Text of the Synoptic Gospels and Acts*, Blackwell, 1951

808 Williams, D.J. *Acts*, Paternoster, 1990

809 Williams, J.G. *Those Who Ponder Proverbs: Aphoristic Thinking and Biblical Literature*, Almond, 1981

810 Williamson, H.G.M. "The Composition of Ezra i-vi," in *Journal of Theological Studies*, 1983

811 Williamson, H.G.M. *Ezra and Nehemiah*, JSOT, 1987

812 Williamson, H.G.M. *Israel in the Books of Chronicles*, CUP, 1977

813 Williamson, H.G.M. *1 & 2 Chronicles*, Marshall, Morgan & Scott, 1982

814 Wills, L.M. *The Jewish Novel in the Ancient World*, Cornell University Press, 1995

814a Wilson, S.G. *The Gentiles and the Gentile Mission in Luke-Acts*, CUP, 1973

815 Wilson, S.G. *Luke and the Law*, CUP, 1983

816 Wink, W. *John the Baptist in the Gospel Tradition*, CUP, 1968

817 Winston, D. "Wisdom of Solomon," in *Anchor Bible Dictionary*

818 Winter, P. *On the Trial of Jesus* (rev. ed.), de Gruyter, 1974

819 Wire, A.C. *The Corinthian Women Prophets*, Fortress, 1990

820 Wiseman, D.J. (ed.) *Peoples of Old Testament Times*, OUP, 1973

821 Wison, R.R. *Genealogy and History in the Biblical World*, Yale University Press, 1979

822 Witherington, B. *The Acts of the Apostles: A Socio-Rhetorical Commentary* Paternoster, 1988

823 Witherington, B. *Conflict and Community in Corinth*, Eerdmans, 1995

824 Witherington, B. *Friendship and Finances in Philippi*, TPI, 1994

825 Witherington, B. *Women and the Genesis of Christianity*, CUP, 1990

826 Wolff, H.W. *Anthropology of the Old Testament*, SCM Press, 1974

827 Wolff, H.W. *Joel and Amos*, Fortress, 1977

828 Wolff, H.W. *Micah*, Neukurchener Verlag, 1982

829 Wolff, H.W. *Obadiah and Jonah: A Commentary*, Ausburg, 1986

830 Wright, C.J.H. *Living as the People of God: The Relevance of Old Testament Ethics*, InterVarsity Press, 1983

831 Wright, D.F. (ed.) *Chosen by God*, Marshall Pickering, 1989

832 Wright, N.T. *The Climax of the Covenant: Christ and the Law in Pauline Theology*, T&T Clark, 1991

833 Wright, N.T. *Jesus and the Victory of God*, SPCK, 1996

834 Wright, N.T. *What St. Paul Really Said*, Lion, 1997

835 Yadin, Y. *The Art of Warfare in Biblical Lands*, Jerusalem, 1983

836 Yadin, Y. *Jerusalem Revealed*, Jerusalem, 1975

837 Yadin, Y. *Masada: Herod's Fortress and the Zealot's Last Stand*, Weidenfield & Nicolson, 1966

838 Yarborough, O.L. *Not Like the Gentiles: Marriage Rules in the Letters of Paul*, Scholars Press, 1985

839 Yee, G.A. *Jewish Feasts and the Gospel of John*, Michael Glazier, 1989

840 Young, B.H. *Jesus and his Jewish Parables*, Paulist Press, 1989

841 Young, F. *The Theology of the Pastoral Epistles*, CUP, 1994

842 Ziesler, J. *Pauline Christianity*, OUP, 1990

843 Ziesler, J. *Paul's Letter to the Romans*, SCM Press, 1989

844 Zohary, M. *Plants of the Bible*, CUP, 1982

# GENERAL REFERENCE

845 Aichele, G. et al .The Postmodern Bible, Yale University Press, 1995

846 Alter, R. The Art of Biblical Poetry, T&T Clark, 1990

847 Alter, R. The World of Biblical Literature, Basic Books, 1992

848 Bar-Efrat, S. Narrative Art in the Bible, Almond, 1989

848a Barrett, C.K. The New Testament Background: Selected Documents, SPCK, 1956

849 Barton, J. Reading the Old Testament, Darton, Longman & Todd, 1984

850 Boadt, L. Reading the Old Testament, an Introduction, Paulist Press/Fowler Wright Books, 1984

851 Brown, R.E. An Introduction to the New Testament, Doubleday, 1997

852 Brueggeman, W. The Theology of the Old Testament, Fortress, 1997

853 Campbell, A.F. The Study Companion to Old Testament Literature, Michael Glazier, 1989

853a Casson, L. Travel in the Ancient World, Allen & Unwin, 1874

854 Charlesworth, J.H. The Old Testament Pseudepigrapha, Darton, Longman & Todd, 1985

855 Davies, W.D. & Finkelstein, I. The Cambridge History of Judaism, CUP, 1984

856 Dillard, R.B. and Longman, T. An Introduction to the Old Testament, Apollos, 1995

856a Dunn, J.D.G. (general ed.) New Testament Theology, CUP

856b Dunn, J.D.G. & Mackey J. (eds.) New Testament Theology in Dialogue, SPCK, 1987

857 Fisch, H. Poetry with a Purpose: Biblical Poetics and Interpretation, Indiana University Press, 1990

858 Freed, E.D. The New Testament: A Critical Introduction, SCM Press, 1994

859 Gardner, P. Who's Who in the Bible, Marshall Pickering, 1995

860 Goldingay, J. The Bible As a Whole, Bible Reading Fellowship, 1994

861 Green, J.B. et al. Dictionary of Jesus and the Gospels, InterVarsity Press, 1992

862 Hawthorne, G.F. & Martin, R.P. Dictionary of Paul and his Letters, InterVarsity Press, 1993

863 Holtz, B.W. (ed.) Back to the Sources: Reading the Classic Jewish Texts, Summit Books, 1984

864 Josipovici, G. The Book of God: A Response to the Bible, Yale University Press, 1988

865 Kee, H.C. et al. The Cambridge Companion to the Bible, CUP, 1997

866 Kee, H.C. et al. The Origins of Christianity: Sources and Documents, Prentice-Hall, 1973

867 Leon-Dufour, X. Dictionary of Biblical Theology, Geoffrey Chapman, 1967

868 Magonet, J. A Rabbi's Bible, SCM Press, 1991

869 Mills, W.E. (ed.) Lutterworth Dictionary of the Bible, Lutterworth, 1994

870 Moule, C.F.D. The Birth of the New Testament, A&C Black, 1981

871 Newsom, C.A. The Women's Bible Commentary, SPCK, 1992

872 Nickelsburg, G.W.E. Jewish Literature Between the Bible and the Mishnah, SCM Press, 1981

873 Rendtorff, R. The Old Testament: An Introduction, SCM Press, 1985

873a Roaf, M. Cultural Atlas of Mespotamia and the Ancient Near East, OUP, 1990

874 Shanks, H. (ed.) Ancient Israel, SPCK, 1989

875 Stern, E. (ed.) The New Encyclopedia of Archaeological Excavation in the Holy Land, Simon & Schuster, 1993

876 Theissen, G. & Merz, A. The Historical Jesus: A Comprehensive Guide, SCM Press, 1998

877 Vermes, G. et al. The History of the Jewish People in the Age of Jesus Christ (rev. Emil Schurer), 3 vols. T&T Clark, 1973–79

## DICTIONARIES AND COMPANIONS

879 Achtemeier, P.J. HarperCollins Bible Dictionary

880 Bromiley, G.W. International Standard Bible Encyclopedia

881 Browning, W.R.F. (general ed.) A Dictionary of the Bible, OUP, 1997

882 Buttrick, G.A. The Interpreter's Dictionary of the Bible 4 vols (& Supplement by K. Crim), 1976

883 Coggins, R.J. & Houlden, J.L. A Dictionary of Bible Interpretation

884 Davids, P.H. & Martin, R.P. Dictionary of the Later NT and its Developments

884a Freedman, D.N. (editor-in-chief) Anchor Bible Dictionary, Doubleday

885 Green, J.B. et al. Dictionary of Jesus and the Gospels

886 Hawthorne G.F. et al. Dictionary of Paul and his Letters

887 McKenzie, J.L. Dictionary of the Bible, Geoffrey Chapman, 1965

888 Metzger, B.M. & Coogan, M.D. (eds.) The Oxford Companion to the Bible, OUP, 1994

889 Mills, W.E. Lutterworth Dictionary of the Bible (also published as The Mercer Dictionary)

890 Myers, A.C. Bible Dictionary, Eerdmans

891 Rogerson, J.W. et al. The Cambridge Companion to the Bible

• On Jewish interpretations, general points and introductions can be found in:

892 Roth, C. (ed.) The Encyclopedia Judaica, Keter Publishing/MacMillan, 1972

893 Wigoder, G. (ed.) The Encyclopedia Judaica

894 Jacobs, L. The Jewish Religion: A Companion

## COMMENTARIES

There are many commentaries on each book in the Bible, many more than can be listed here. There are also many series of commentaries, either complete or in progress. They vary from the technical (often commenting on the Hebrew or Greek text) to the accessible. Among the important series (in English) are:

*Anchor Bible*
*Augsburg Commentary on the New Testament*
*Cambridge Bible Commentary*
*Expositors Bible Commentary*
*Harpers Bible Commentaries*
*Interpreters Bible*
*InterVarsity Press New Testament Commentary*
*The Jewish Publication Society Torah Commentary*
*New American Commentary*
*Old Testament Library Commentary Series*
*Oxford Bible Commentary*
*Torch Bible Commentary*
*Tyndale Commentaries*
*Trinity Press International New Testament Commentaries*
*World Biblical Commentary*

• There are also one- or two-volume commentaries, including:

Anderson, B. W. *The Book of the Bible*

Brown, R.E., Fitzmyer, J.A. & Murphy, R.E. (eds.) *New Jerome Biblical Commentary*, Geoffrey Chapman, 1989

Dunn, J.D.G. & Rogerson, J. (eds.) *Commentary 2000*, Eerdmans, 1999

Laymon, C.M. *The Interpreter's One Volume Commentary*

Mayes, J.L. *Harper's Bible Commentary*

Newsom, C.A. & Ringe, S.H. *The Women's Bible Commentary*

• Note also the study guides to both Testaments published by the Sheffield Academic Press (general eds. R.N. Whybray, Old Testament & A.T. Lincoln, New Testament). Also:

*Guides to Biblical Scholarship* series, Fortress Press

Mays, J.L., Newson, C.A. & Petersen, D.L. (series eds.) The Old Testament Library Series, SCM Press

## ATLASES

Grollenberg, L. The Penguin Shorter Atlas of the Bible, Penguin, 1978

May, H.G. The Oxford Bible Atlas, OUP, 1984

Pritchard, J.B. The Harper Atlas of the Bible, Harper & Row, 1987

Rogerson, J.W. Atlas of the Bible, Phaidon, 1989

## CONCORDANCES

Concordances list in alphabetical order the words that occur in the Bible. There are concordances to all the major translations. Useful is R. Youngs' *Analytical Concordance to the Holy Bible*, to the AV, because it divides the English words under the differing Hebrew, Aramaic, or Greek words of the original.

## BIBLIOGRAPHIES

Books and articles on the Bible appear at an undiminished rate, so that bibliographies rapidly become dated. However, a useful starting point may be:

Fitzmyer, J.A. An Introductory Bibliography for the Study of Scripture, Pontifical Biblical Institute, 1990

Harrington, D.J. The New Testament: A Bibliography, Michael Glazier, 1985

Zannoni, A.E. The Old Testament: A Bibliography, Liturgical Press, 1992

## CD ROMS

There are now many CDs containing one or (usually) more translations with concordances and other programmes for Bible search and reading.

## DAILY READING

Guides to daily and devotional reading are numerous. Noteworthy are:

*Daily Bread* (The Scripture Union)
*Daily Study Bible*
*The People's Bible Commentary* (D. Winter)
*New Daylight* (Bible Reading Fellowship)
See also 331, 609, 710, 860

# INDEX

*Headings and page numbers in bold type refer to main entries. For minor biblical people and places not mentioned in the main text see the A–Z of People (pp.478–495) and the A–Z of Places (pp.496–513).*

Aaron 49, 50, 51, 52, 63, 65, 71, 112, 118, 160, 265, 266, 347, 379, 478
Aaronides 65
Abba 333, 416, 522
Abdon 104, 105
Abednego 217, 478
Abel 26, 30, 31, 55, 60, 66, 478
Abiathar 124
Abigail 112, 113, 125, 478
Abihu 63, 478
Abijah, King 135, 151
Abimelech 36, 105, 107, 478
Abiram 71, 478
Abishag 125, 478
Abner 115, 478
**Abraham** 21, 26, 27, 28, 31, 34, 35, 36, 37, **38-39**, 40, 41, 45, 61, 87, 92, 93, 103, 112, 136, 141, 153, 174, 179, 186, 191, 200, 208, 209, 232, 239, 268, 306, 411, 424, 425, 427, 430, 451, 454, 472, 473, 498
Abram *see* Abraham
Absalom 115, 125, 130, 478
Academy 452, 453
Achaicus 373
Achan 93, 478
Achior the Ammonite 254
Achsah 107
**actions of God 222-23**
Actions, prophetic *see* prophetic actions
**Acts, book of** 60, 221, 260, 279, 293, 310, 311, 314, 315, 330, 331, 345, 347, 367, 370, 374, 376, 378, 379, **380-81**, 382, 383, 384, 385, 386, 387, 388, 389, 390, 391, 392, 393, 394, 395, 396, 397, 399, 403, 410, 417, 418, 421, 432, 434, 436, 442, 446, 449, 452, 467
acts of God *see* God, activity of
*Acts of Paul and Thecla* 391
**Adam** 6, 26, 27, **30-31**, 32, 150, 182, 183, 192, 231, 240, 261, 310, 347, 408, 411, 432, 461, 478
first and second 31, 33, 408, 411, 423
Adonai 59
Adonijah 130, 479
Adonis 365
Adullam 124, 498
adulterer, adulteress 151, 187
adultery 33, 56, 57, 86, 87, 115, 187, 193, 213, 218, 219, 254, 255, 335, 525
Aegean Sea 274, 397, 433
Aelia Capitolina 276
aetiological 109
Africa 368
afterlife (*see also* life after death) 46, 141, 182, 377
after the Hijrah (AH) 237
*agape* 409, 414
agora 452, 453
agricultural seasons 69, 237
agriculture, agricultural 32, 46, 68, 69, 97, 98, 283, 285
Agrippa I *see* Herod Agrippa I, King
Agrippa II *see* Herod Agrippa II, King
Ahab, King 113, 129, 135, 138, 139, 198, 479
Ahasuerus *see* Xerxes I, King
Ahaz, King 133, 135, 200, 235, 479
Ahaziah, King 135, 479
Ahijah 128, 197, 226, 479
Ahimelech 64, 479
Ahura Mazda 141
Ai 93, 94, 498
Akhenaten, King 141
Akiba, Rabbi 190, 191, 347, 362
Akkad 122, 148, 498
Akkadian 98, 148
Alexander Jannaeus 251, 259, 294
Alexander the Great 137, 156, 157, 246, 248, 249, 250, 452
Alexandria 189, 246, 247, 275, 377, 451, 474, 498
**after Alexander 248-49**
aliens 395, 456
allegories 191, 425
almonds, almond tree 31, 265
almsgiving (*see also* collection) 255
alphabet 77, 99, 165
North Semitic 165
altars 32, 37, 38, 41, 65, 66, 67, 105, 108, 109, 116, 117, 125, 134, 138, 155, 214, 225, 249, 250, 286, 376, 522
'am ha'arez 289
Amalekites 49, 89, 119, 121, 125, 166
Amarna 18, 98
Amaziah, King 135, 225, 479
Amen 260, 417, 522
Amenemope 171, 185
Amenhotep III, King 78
Amidah 282
Ammon 18, 99, 100, 123, 141, 213, 225, 498
religion of 100
Ammonites 100, 101, 103, 104, 105, 107, 119, 120, 121, 232
Amnon 125, 479
Amon, King 135, 479
Amorites 98, 99
Amos 54, 55, 137, 212, 221, 224, 225, 227, 235, 238, 241, 242, 263, 479
**Amos, book of** 117, 143, 175, 195, **224-25**, 228
Amoz 200
amphictyonies 109
amulets 37, 82, 282, 379
Amun 141
An 140
Ananias 362, 381, 385, 391, 479
Anat 99
Anathoth 64, 199, 206, 208, 498
Anatolia 18, 47, 396
**Ancestors** 21, 22, 26, 31, **34-37**, 41, 42, 44, 48, 70, 88, 94, 100, 112, 153, 207, 209, 232, 257, 319, 408, 522, 525
Patriarchal Age, Period 35, 96
patriarchal customs 35
patriarchal names 35
Patriarchal Narratives 34, 35
Patriarchal society 112, 164, 322
**religion of the 36-37**
ancestors 100, 110, 178, 207, 363
Andrew 328, 329, 330, 331, 386, 479
Andronicus 410
angelic executioners 214, 473
Angel of the Lord 42
**angels** (*see also* archangels) 21, 41,

42-43, 75, 109, 139, 149, 157, 175, 215, 255, 260, 288, 309, 318, 319, 326, 327, 364, 387, 391, 410, 442, 445, 450, 451, 460, 461, 469, 470, 471, 472, 473
fallen 43, 472
Uriel 43
worship of 438
anger 125, 208, 219, 279, 338
**animals** 31, 32, 33, 40, 62, 66, 79, 140, 191, 193, 196, 205, 233, **268-69**, 282, 423, 458
blood 451
clean 32
husbandry 283
sacrifice 66, 67, 283
skins 40
unclean 62
Anna 318, 319, 480
Annals of the Kings of Israel 129
Annals of the Kings of Judah 129
Annas 275, 354, 480
Annius Rufus 279
**Annunciation 318-19**, 522
anointed 145
king 243
Lord's anointed 115
one 215
anointing 114, 119, 120, 121, 264, 346, 353, 418, 419, 454, 455, 522
anthropology 74, 182, 183, 409
Antichrist 443, 445, 465, 522
Antigones 246
Antigonus 251
**Antioch** 246, 248, 307, 380, 381, 387, 388, 389, **392-93**, 394, 396, 397, 417
Antioch in Pisidia 449, 498
Antioch in Syria 275, 389, 392, 397, 424, 498
Antiochus I, King 249
Antiochus II, King 249
Antiochus III, King 247, 249, 250
Antiochus IV Epiphanes, King 216, 217, 247, 249, 250, 251, 261, 281, 461
Antiochus V, King 249, 269
Antipas *see* Herod Antipas
Antipater 298, 499
anti-Semitism 381
Antonia Fortress 276, 353, 357, 361, 400
Anu 140
Anubis 140
Aphrodite 246
**Apocalypse** 43, 242, 260, 261, 445, 468, **470-71**, 522
four beasts of 260, 261
Markan 309
of Isaiah 201
of John 216
**Apocalyptic** 236, 243, **260-61**, 443, 445, 471, 473, 522
literature, writings 77, 153, 159, 160, 214, 216, 365, 468, 469, 470, 471
**Apocrypha** 12, 25, 76, 91, 97, 131, 160, 166, 169, 170, 179, 189, 250, **253**, 254, 255, 256, 257, 258, 259, 300, 470, 522
**apocalyptic 260-61**
**fiction 254-55**
**history 258-59**
Jewish apocryphal works 252, 461
Protestant 253
**wisdom 256-57**
apocryphal gospels *see* gospels, apocryphal
*apokalupsis* 243
Apollo 376, 433
Apollonia 274
Apollonius of Tyana 343, 365
Apollos 399, 451, 480
apologist 475

apostasy 37, 71, 105, 134, 250, 475, 522
apostles 241, 274, 316, 329, 331, 345, 367, 379, 381, 385, 389, 394, 395, 396, 410, 414, 421, 425, 431, 436, 437, 448, 449, 522
apostolic tradition 463, 475
Appian Way 370, 401
Apuleius 377
*Aqedah* 38, 39
aqueducts 279, 368, 402
Aquila 285, 399, 403, 435, 436, 437, 480
Arabah 101, 499
Arabia 19, 131, 275, 369, 391
Arabic 98
Arad 66, 71, 499
Aram 123
Aramaic 98, 216, 246, 360, 388
Aramaean 142
archangels 42
Raphael 43, 255
Gabriel 42, 43, 316, 384
Michael 42, 43, 167, 473, 491
Archelaus *see* Herod Archelaus, King
Areopagus 452, 499
Aristobulus I 251
Aristobulus II 251
Aristotle 440, 452
ark 32, 33, 265, 266, 267, 268
Ark of the Covenant 25, 53, 60, 61, 63, 64, 84, 108, 114, 115, 116, 117, 118, 125, 126, 127, 132, 145, 155, 180, 282, 522
Armageddon *see* Megiddo
Armenia 142, 369
armies 18, 40, 41, 94, 104, 107, 145, 263, 368, 372, 373, 402, 433
armor of God 429
Arnon, River 299, 499
arrogance 229, 240
art 99, 107, 165, 222
Artaxerxes I, King 137, 157, 160, 161, 162, 480
Artaxerxes II, King 157, 161, 480
Artaxerxes III, King 157
Artemis 370, 377, 398, 399
Asa, King 129, 134, 135, 151, 480
Asaph 177, 480
**Ascension** 179, 263, 272, 310, 311, 317, 349, 367, 381, **382-83**, 385, 418, 458, 522
ascetic, asceticism 453, 459
Asclepius 377
Ash Wednesday 221
Asher 102, 480
Asherah 99
Ashkelon 141, 499
Ashtar 100
Ashtart 99
Ashur 140, 143
Ashurbanipal, King 122, 145, 480
library of 33
Asia Minor 246, 248, 275, 369, 370, 374, 376, 393, 394, 398, 399, 446, 456, 461, 468, 499
Asmodeus 255
asphyxiation 359
assassinated, assassination, 250, 456, 457
Asshur 19, 142, 143, 156
associations 283
assumption 317
assurance 464
**Assyria** 18, 19, 29, 55, 100, 101, 123, 128, 137, **142-43**, 144, 145, 149, 156, 201, 218, 219, 225, 234, 238, 239, 275, 369, 499
destruction of 201
exile in 134
fall of 149
Assyrians 60, 122, 127, 128, 134, 135, 137, 140, 142, 143, 148,

233, 238, 254, 255
Astarte 192, 246
astrology 149, 377, 378, 429
astronomical data 148
astronomy 452, 470
Aswan 159
Atalus III, King 398
Aten 141
Athaliah, King 113, 135, 480
Athanasius of Alexandria 474
atheism, atheist 453, 458
Athens 272, 374, 443, 452, 453, 499
Athirath 99
**atonement** (*see also* Day of Atonement) 67, 359, 408, **422-23**, 450, 522
Attis 365
augur 149
Augustine, St. 335, 384, 410
Augustus Caesar 78, 274, 318, 368, 369, 372, 373, 374, 379, 458, 480
authority 8-10, 98, 115, 119, 121, 122, 189, 245, 256, 257, 260, 279, 307, 329, 332, 339, 354, 356, 361, 373, 382, 389, 413, 419, 425, 428, 449, 460, 461, 463, 464, 465, 469, 473
apostolic 331, 421, 439
Jewish 354
Avesta 157
*'avodah* 25
Azariah *see* Uzziah, King
Azazel 86
Azekah 153, 499

Baal 36, 59, 99, 105, 135, 138, 139, 149, 198, 199, 218, 480, 522
prophets of 138, 141, 199, 223, 333, 461
worship 218
Baasha 135, 480
Babel, Tower of 26, 31, 33, 34, 75, 149, 385, 499
**Babylon** 19, 29, 96, 101, 123, 128, 140, 143, 144, 145, 148, 149, 153, 154, 155, 156, 159, 161, 162, 170, 176, 199, 203, 207, 214, 216, 229, 238, 241, 245, 246, 281, 469, 500
**Exile to** 35, 43, 63, 68, 126, **146-47**, 152, 153, 154, 159, 192, 202, 204, 206, 212, 216, 217, 229, 237, 242, 243, 276
Hanging Gardens of 122
king of 473
return from 204
**Babylonia**, Babylonians 18, 19, 41, 61, 122, 126, 127, 133, 135, 137, 140, 143, 144, 145, 148, **148-49**, 153, 156, 202, 206, 211, 214, 224, 233, 238, 239, 255
conquest 158, 162
invasion of Judah 148, 228
Bacchides, fortress of 97
Bacchus 453
Bagoas 247, 480
Balaam 71, 74, 217, 268, 461, 480
Balak, King 480
bandits 94, 104, 107, 276, 396
baptism 299, 324, 325, 326, 327, 365, 367, 391, 399, 409, 418, 419, 438, 522
**John's 324-25**, 399
of the dead 419
baptize 364, 378, 384, 387, 389, 417

*bara* 29, 204
Barabbas, Jesus 355, 356, 480
Barak 106, 107, 480
Bar-Jesus 379, 480
barley 78, 110, 265
bar mitzvah 24, 286
Barnabas 309, 376, 381, 389, 392, 393, 394, 395, 396, 449, 481
*Barnabas, Epistle of* 284, 474
barrenness 113
Bartholomew 330, 331, 481
Bartimaeus 77, 348, 481
Baruch 206, 207, 481
**Baruch, book of** 195, 253, **256-57**
*basar* 182
Bashan 333, 500
bathing 113, 193
baths 284, 398, 402
Bathsheba, wife of Uriah 115, 125, 130, 131, 187, 193, 306, 481
Battle of Ipsus 248
battles 88, 93, 105, 106, 125, 145, 215, 263, 372, 445, 471, 473
beast, horned 77
beasts 77, 216, 468, 469, 473
Beatitudes 334, 335, 455, 522
beauty 28, 76, 167, 191
bedouin 52, 72
Beersheba 18, 500
**behavior** 62, 170, 204, 224, 225, **226-27**, 409, 414, 443, 447, 452, 461, 466
Christian 415, 423
beheaded 459
Bel 149, 254, 255, 480
temple of 255
**Bel and the Dragon** 254-55
beliefs 29, 74, 108, 126, 131, 145, 149, 178, 188, 201, 214, 222, 233, 282, 335, 363, 414, 450, 454
folk **74-75**, 284
Jewish 458
religious 248
believers 215, 284, 384, 387, 388, 391, 392, 393, 409, 411, 415, 416, 417, 417, 428, 429, 434, 438, 443, 448, 456, 457, 458, 464, 467
Greek 395
Christian 414, 432, 438, 443, 465
Gentile 392, 393, 394, 397
Jewish 387, 392, 394
Roman 410
Belshazzar, King 149, 217, 379, 481
Ben-Ammi 100, 481
*Bene Israel, Bene Jacob,* 102, 103, 522
benedictions, eighteen 282, 458, 522
benefactors 283, 449
Benjamin 44, 64, 102, 104, 481
tribe of 103, 390
Benjaminites 314
*berith* 80
bestiality 193
Bet Din 355
Bethany 277, 299, 348, 353, 382, 500
Bethel 18, 34, 41, 108, 117, 128, 224, 500
Hiel of 96, 97
**Bethlehem** 111, 234, 298, 299, 315, 318, 319, **320-21**, 500
Bethphage 298, 348, 500
Bethsaida 299, 500
Bethulia 255
betray, betrayal 219, 331, 471
**betrayal of Jesus** (*see also* Jesus, betrayal of) **352-53**
betrothal 187, 418
Bibles 21
Christian 21, 91, 169, 190, 195, 253, 468
Jewish 21, 195, 211, 253, 256, 257, 290
Orthodox 91, 257
Protestant 253, 256
Roman Catholic 91, 169, 195, 253, 256, 257
translations of 520
bier 362

bigotry 55
Bildad 172, 173, 481
Bilhah 102, 103, 481
biography 300, 305
*bioi* 305
**birds** 32, 33, 79, 233, **266-67**, 282
birth 43, 48, 102, 107, 109, 122, 123, 139, 165, 179, 201, 209, 284, 409, 430, 445
new 456
second 223
birthright 34, 40, 409
bishops 373, 437, 447, 448
Bithynia 369, 500
Bitter Lakes 52
Black Sea 18, 369
blasphemy 33, 86, 139, 255, 355
blessings (*see also* Beatitudes) 26, 33, 34, 35, 37, 40, 41, 64, 70, 71, 73, 80, 81, 113, 123, 127, 158, 187, 201, 219, 220, 221, 224, 241, 284, 310, 342, 351, 382, 407, 416, 421, 424, 443, 449, 458
spiritual 410, 427
universal 430
blind 41, 105, 202
blindness 145, 342, 379
of Saul 390
blood 32, 66, 67, 178, 193, 350, 351, 376, 408, 422, 423, 468, 471, 473
of Christ 415
boats 33, 46, 344, 345
Boaz 110, 111, 132, 133, 321, 481
body, flesh 63, 99, 178, 179, 182, 183, 192, 214, 343, 350, 351, 362, 363, 365, 383, 384, 409, 411, 415, 421, 425, 427, 430, 439, 445, 448, 451, 458, 465, 473
dead 62
immortal 415
of Christ 351, 373, 409, 411, 415, 419, 428, 429, 448, 467, 522
one 414
Boethius 185
bones 125, 179, 214, 363, 376
Bonhoeffer, Dietrich 456
Book of Consolation 207
Book of Life 179
Book of the Covenant *see* Covenant, Book of the
Book of the Law 113
Booths *see* Tabernacles, festival or feast of
boys 164, 165, 196, 323, 362
bread 67, 199, 265, 333, 343, 350, 351, 364, 419, 443
breaking of 350, 351, 419, 434, 435
bread of life 313
bread of the Presence 117
breastfeeding 192, 284
bride 112, 190, 191, 284, 375
dream of 191
father of 187
bridegroom 187, 190, 191, 284, 375
brothers 31, 35, 40, 41, 190, 223, 251, 311, 314, 315, 338, 384, 454, 467
Jesus' 455
buildings 76, 278, 280-81, 373
**burial** 112, 134, 143, 178, 179, 284, 321, **362-63**
place 360
ritual 255
burning bush 50, 51, 59, 63
Byblos 18

# C

Caesar 285, 357, 400, 401, 403, 481
Caesarea 275, 276, 278, 283, 298, 321, 357, 369, 381, 388, 432, 434, 501
Caesarea Philippi 297, 308, 332, 386, 501

Caiaphas 275, 353, 354, 355, 481
Cain 26, 30, 31, 55, 66, 471, 481
Caleb 92, 93, 103, 481
calendars 68, 69, 237
Caligula, Emperor 279, 372, 373
call 28, 31, 51, 107, 118, 207, 212, 220, 223, 241, 244, 245, 313, 375, 386
Calvary 361
Cambyses II, King 157, 161
camels 268, 269
Cana 299, 317, 344, 375, 501
Canaan (the Promised Land) 18, 21, 34, 35, 36, 37, 38, 44, 48, 51, 52, 53, 64, 70, 71, 72, 81, 88, 92, 93, 94, 95, 96, 98, 99, 100, 104, 105, 106, 111, 176, 232, 264, 280, 311, 327, 451, 481, 501, 522
conquest of 81, 92, 94, 95, 96
religion of 141, 143
**Canaanites** 32, 36, 37, 40, 58, 89, 93, 95, 97, **98-99**, 104, 105, 106, 117, 165, 219, 232
beliefs 99
culture 99
gods 73, 105
influence 237
language 99
tribes 104
women 37
cannibalism 458
**canon**
**Christian** 25, 166, 188, 245, 253, 256, 407, 462, 463, 470, **474-75**, 522
83, 189, 191
Jewish 83, 189, 192, 253, 258, 462, 475
Capernaum 299, 321, 332, 333, 342, 345, 501
Cappadocia 369, 501
capital punishment 356
captives 143, 149, 205
captivity 34, 77, 146-47, 199, 206, 397
captivity letters *see* prison letters
Carchemish 18, 143, 145, 501
Carmel, village of 193
Carmel, Mount 138, 139, 223, 333, 501
carpenter 315, 413
Carthage 459
catacombs
Jewish 402
Roman 231, 391
catastrophe, cosmic 471
Catholic letters 404, 454, 460
Cedar of Lebanon 265
celebration 68, 283, 284, 351
celibacy 291, 375
Cenchreae 274, 410
census 70, 71, 115, 125, 151, 285, 319, 320
centurion 387, 431, 434
Cephas (*see also* Peter) 457
ceremonies 157
religious 372
Chaldeans 148, 149, 156, 202
chaos 27, 28, 122, 123, 141, 263, 378, 471
chariot mysticism 215, 391, 468
chariots 89, 106, 214, 369, 468
of fire 138
*charismata,* charisms 417
charitable giving (*see also* alms giving, collection) 421
chastity 167, 193
Cherith 198, 501
cherubim 42, 132
child-bearing 31
childbirth 192
child, children 24, 35, 39, 40, 41, 48, 50, 51, 55, 57, 63, 109, 123, 125, 130, 164, 165, 171, 187, 193, 198, 210, 218, 281, 282, 284, 307, 311, 318, 319, 322, 323, 374, 375, 425, 440, 445, 446
of light 429
of the devil 473
slaughter of 295
tombs of 294
childless, childlessness 39, 86, 111
child-rearing 284, 374

choices 26, 54, 55, 184, 473, 523
moral 472
*chokmah* 170
Chosen People (*see also* **Covenant People**) 54, 55, 470
chosen race 456
*chozeh* 196, 469
*Chrestus* 403, 410
Christ (*see also* Jesus) 27, 29, 43, 67, 191, 236, 267, 312, 313, 317, 347, 382, 384, 390, 392, 393, 395, 396, 408, 412, 415, 424, 426, 430, 450, 458, 465, 522
birth of 43
Body of *see* body of Christ
brother in 439
death of 421, 424, 439, 473
incarnation of 473
Jesus our Lord 410
love of 190
ministry of 451
return of, coming of 43, 311, 415, 443, 445, 461
risen 414, 443
rule of 439
victory of 429, 472
**Christian Ethics** (*see also* ethics) **466**
Christianity, Christian religion 66, 67, 81, 82, 139, 175, 183, 248, 262, 281, 284, 293, 364, 372, 373, 374, 377, 380, 381, 390, 393, 394, 395, 397, 398, 399, 402-03, 406, 411, 413, 424, 426, 428, 437, 439, 452, 454, 455, 458, 475
**beginnings of 367**
Eastern 418
**in Rome 402-03**
spread of 402, 403, 406, 434
Western 418
Christians 29, 39, 51, 57, 76, 82, 95, 127, 179, 197, 247, 254, 263, 277, 287, 301, 311, 317, 319, 346, 347, 351, 357, 360, 370, 380, 382, 388, 390, 391, 393, 401, 402, 405, 406, 409, 412, 414, 417, 418, 419, 421, 422, 423, 424, 428, 432, 435, 436, 440, 441, 442, 446, 447, 449, 450, 454, 456, 458, 459, 468, 469, 470, 471, 474
poor, needy 410, 421
early 416, 434
Gentile 247, 306, 307, 392, 403, 427, 430, 456
Hebrew 389
Hellenist 367, 389
Jewish 307, 331, 347, 392, 400, 403, 410, 413, 427, 429, 430, 433, 450, 456, 461
name 380, 393
Orthodox 91
Roman 403
**Chronicles, books of** 129, 134, 143, **150-51**
**First** 91, **150-51**, 163, 169, 175
**Second** 88, 91, 130, 131, 134, 143, 144, 145, **150-51**, 160, 163, 169, 258
*chronos* 237
compensation 87
Church, churches 190, 191, 305, 307, 310, 330, 356, 360, 367, 373, 375, 381, 383, 384, 385, 386, 387, 390, 391, 393, 396, 397, 401, 406, 409, 410, 412, 414, 416, 417, 418, 423, 424, 428, 430, 432, 433, 434, 435, 438, 441, 446, 447, 448, 459, 461, 466, 467, 469, 472, 474
Antioch, first Gentile 392, 393
buildings 459
Christian 221, 247, 285, 306, 310, 316, 317, 323, 351, 365, 375, 380, 412, 413, 430, 431, 433, 435, 442, 448
Corinth 282, 420, 421, 435, 441
denominations 447
early 181, 272, 274, 314, 316, 323, 330, 331, 361, 385, 392, 394, 395, 405, 416, 417, 419, 436, 445, 447, 448, 453, 458

Ephesus 399
Ethiopic 462
Gentile 410, 421, 423
**house 434-35**
household 403, 436
Jerusalem 315, 386, 389, 394, 395, 419, 425, 449, 455
leaders 446, 447
life 446, 447
members 388
of Jews and Gentiles 428
Orthodox 256
Philippi 433
Rome 410, 475
seven in Asia 468
Church of the Holy Sepulchre 361
Cicero 406, 440, 453
Cilicia 369, 396, 501
circumcised 276, 318, 387, 395, 425, 427, 457
circumcision 34, 38, 61, 92, 109, 139, 152, 165, 281, 317, 394, 397, 409, 424, 427, 522
cities 283, 467, 468
of refuge 70, 71, 86
citizens
Roman 359, 368, 373, 390, 400
free-born 373
city 351, 369, 469
bride- 468
harlot- 468
City of Palms 97
city-states 98, 99, 109, 122, 123, 136, 148, 453
clans 95, 103, 186, 522
class system, Roman 372
Claudius, Emperor 372, 373, 403, 410, 482
clean, cleanliness 62, 63, 71, 268, 522
ritual 283
cleansing 418
cleansing of the Temple *see* Temple, cleansing of
*Clement, Letters of* 474
Cleopatra 246
client kings 278, 279, 325
Codes, Domestic or Household *see* domestic codes
Codex, codex 407, 474, 522
coffin 362
coins 78, 79, 293
coitus interruptus 192
collection for the poor 385, 401, 410, 421
Colossae 275, 397, 399, 435, 438, 501
Colosseum 402
**Colossians, letter to the** 28, 291, 397, 401, 405, 408, 409, 412, **438-39**, 441, 446, 453
colt 348
Comforter 313
**Coming Kingdom 444-45**
commandments (*see also* Ten Commandments) 71, 196, 213, 282, 339, 431
great 333
second, great 282
commission, commissioning 107, 331, 346, 351, 364, 387, 396
communication 196, 406, 407, 468
communion 67, 351, 419, 522
communities 283, 342
Christian 367, 385, 405, 416, 428, 431, 438, 442, 443, 445, 446, 447, 451, 460
Gentile 284
Hurrian 35
Jewish 284
Qumran 73, 217, 324
compassion, compassionate 204, 220, 221, 230, 231, 310, 332, 344
compensation 87
complaints, complaining 173, 174, 211, 245, 342
**composition of the Pentateuch 22-23**
conception
virginal 315, 316, 317, 319
conciliation 87
concubines 39, 82, 103, 130, 186, 374, 440

condemnation 225, 229, 239, 339, 409, 422, 427, 460, 461
confessions 163, 208, 407, 412, 418
  of Jeremiah 208-09
confirmation 418, 419
conflicts 27, 28, 31, 38, 39, 43, 98, 99, 124, 125, 208, 209, 336, 368, 372, 387, 388, 414, 420, 424, 432, 439, 456
confrontation 172, 174, 210
congregation 25, 417, 464
conquests 88, 92, 93, 108, 125, 248
  Assyrian 142, 281, 333
conscience 451, 467
consecration 116
consolation 205, 213
conspiracy 125, 254
Constantine, Emperor 246
consuls 372
consummation 190
contest 31, 98, 99, 138
context commands 466, 467
contraception 192
contract 187
  legal 284
conversions 225, 323, 367, 387, 389, 392, 403, 409, 416, 418, 419, 431, 446, 467
  of Cornelius 387
  of Saul 381, 390-91
converts 33, 283, 367, 394, 399, 401, 417, 420, 424, 429, 433, 442
  Gentile 424, 427, 430
Corinth 247, 274, 373, 376, 387, 391, 397, 403, 410, 414, 415, 435, 443, 446, 501
Corinthians 397, 415, 420, 421, 471
Corinthians, letters to the 390, 399
  First 351, 375, 383, 385, 387, 397, 405, 408, 409, 412, 414-15, 417, 419, 420, 425, 428, 436, 441, 448, 453
  Second 391, 397, 405, 409, 413, 420-21, 445, 446
Cornelius 283, 367, 387, 392, 434, 482
coronations 123, 177, 180, 383
corpses 179, 415
corruptions 175, 201, 205, 234, 240
cosmetics 47
cosmic renewal 29, 471
Cosmic Tree 31
cosmos 412, 453
Council
  divine 199
  Jerusalem 381, 387, 393, 394-95, 396, 430, 524
  Jewish 386
  of elders 353, 355
  of Jamnia 189
counselor 313
coups 113, 128
courage 162, 231, 257
court, courts of law 369, 414
Covenant, Book of the 66, 80
covenant, Covenant 21, 22, 23, 24, 26, 31, 32, 33, 34, 36, 38, 39, 48, 49, 55, 60-61, 63, 72, 80, 81, 82, 85, 86, 89, 92, 93, 94, 95, 108, 115, 129, 135, 179, 187, 201, 205, 212, 218, 219, 226, 227, 232, 233, 235, 244, 256, 258, 262, 277, 280, 281, 282, 351, 359, 384, 408, 409, 423, 425, 431, 450, 451, 522
  blessings 218
  book of Leviticus 48
  Code 48, 224
  Davidic 125, 155
  law 35, 145, 243
  Mosaic 61, 135
  new 291, 350, 416, 419, 450, 451
  Noachide 33
  old 450
People 52, 54-55, 92, 102, 110, 111, 127, 150, 223, 232, 248, 280, 287, 332

promise 239, 245
relationship 86, 234, 350
Renewal Festival 80
  with God 33
coveting, covetousness 56, 57
craftsmanship, craftsmen 35, 407
Creation 21, 25, 26, 27, 28-29, 30, 31, 32, 42, 49, 57, 67, 81, 148, 151, 172, 176, 185, 203, 217, 222, 233, 239, 240, 241, 256, 261, 281, 312, 410, 413, 428, 430, 432, 438, 440, 467, 471, 472
  Babylonian creation stories 29
  created order 188
  new 27, 28, 29, 204, 257, 312, 409, 425
  science 29
  stories 22, 27, 85, 148, 327
  theology 233
  traditions 232, 233
Creationists 29
creator 42, 57, 109, 182, 184, 203, 207, 222, 224, 233, 236, 239, 345, 411, 439, 469
credal fragments 407
creed 233, 432
cremation 284, 362
Crete 18, 274, 446, 447, 501
crime, criminal 40, 86-87, 359
crisis 106, 261, 451
criticism
  feminist and womanist 305
  form 304
  historical 304
  ideological 23, 305
  narrative 23, 305
  reader-response 23, 305
  redaction 304
  rhetorical 23, 305
  source 304
  structuralist 305
crops 69, 219, 283, 445, 467
cross 31, 263, 265, 317, 331, 358, 359, 360, 364, 365, 383, 395, 414, 415, 419, 420, 421, 422, 423, 424, 432, 444, 467
crown, crowned 25, 107, 199, 355
crucifixion, crucified 31, 231, 277, 289, 297, 301, 307, 309, 310, 311, 313, 329, 347, 352, 354, 355, 356, 357, 358-59, 360, 361, 383, 389, 418, 436, 445, 457
  Peter's 459
cruelty 229, 278
cubit 79, 371
cults 84, 115, 141, 149, 157, 177, 196, 226, 229, 243, 333, 366, 376-77, 379, 435, 523
  Artemis 399
  cultic prostitute 218
  fertility 190, 198
  imperial, Emperor 369, 399, 403, 468
  Isis 377
  Mithra, Mithras 377
  Roman imperial 398
  Temple 366, 377, 470
culture, Greek 248, 251
cuneiform script, writing 142, 148, 165, 170
cup 302, 303, 350, 351
cup-bearer 162
curriculum 323
curses, cursing 32, 37, 80, 81, 96, 172, 173, 208, 219, 363, 423, 471
customs 14, 278, 279, 284
Cyaxares the Mede 156
Cynic 453
Cyprus 18, 246, 275, 369, 379, 381, 388, 389, 391, 393, 394, 396, 501
Cyrene 369, 501
Cyrus the Great, King 51, 103, 137, 149, 151, 153, 154, 155, 156, 157, 160, 161, 200, 202, 203, 216, 255, 258, 482
  decree of 137, 161

D 22
D (Western text) 9, 395
Dacia 369
Dagon 61, 99
Dalmatia 368, 502
Damascus 18, 123, 143, 145, 225, 275, 277, 381, 390, 391, 502
Damascus Gate 361
Dan 22, 102, 104, 117, 482, 502
dance, dancing 112, 181
danger 396, 403, 432
Daniel 216, 217, 254, 255, 309, 379, 445, 482
Daniel, Additions to 217, 253, 254, 255
Daniel, book of 43, 45, 169, 178, 179, 181, 195, 216-17, 243, 249, 254, 255, 261, 309, 347, 412, 445, 468, 470, 471
Darius I, King 137, 155, 156, 157, 161, 258, 482
Darius II, King 157
Darius III, King 157
Darius the Mede 216, 217, 482
Darwin, Charles 29
Dathan 71, 482
daughters 100, 107, 130, 173, 193, 207, 279, 345, 389
  inheritance 71
  Pharaoh's 51
daughters-in-law 111
David, King 23, 31, 44, 61, 64, 89, 95, 103, 108, 110, 111, 113, 114, 119, 120, 121, 123, 124-25, 126, 127, 128, 129, 130, 131, 132, 133, 134, 135, 145, 150, 151, 155, 155, 160, 177, 187, 193, 199, 201, 230, 233, 235, 242, 243, 267, 287, 288, 319, 321, 327, 346, 347, 447, 462, 482
  city of 276, 277
  house of 134, 153
  Jesus' descent from 306, 310, 314, 315, 347, 447
  kingdom of 126
  reign of 77, 114, 136, 269
  son of Jesse 129
Day of Atonement 48, 63, 68, 69, 73, 155, 180, 205, 221, 230, 275, 282, 286, 287, 450, 523
Day of Judgment 174, 333
Day of the Lord 89, 220, 221, 224, 225, 229, 236, 237, 240, 241, 243, 245, 262, 263, 443, 445, 451, 461, 523
Day of the Son of Man 241
deacons 281, 410, 436, 437, 447, 448, 449
dead 62, 119, 122, 141, 149, 358, 378, 393, 400, 428, 444, 447, 448, 473
Dead Sea 101, 215, 228, 294, 299, 370, 502
Dead Sea Scrolls 166, 206, 289, 290-91, 346, 347, 359, 431
  sectarian 290, 291
deaf, deafness 202, 342
death 29, 31, 86, 99, 109, 111, 112, 119, 122, 125, 140, 170, 175, 178, 179, 182, 187, 188, 189, 190, 193, 199, 208, 211, 230, 249, 255, 256, 262, 278, 279, 284, 298, 312, 335, 347, 348, 351, 355, 356, 358, 359, 362, 363, 365, 377, 380, 386, 390, 401, 409, 410, 411, 412, 413, 420, 423, 426, 427, 430, 431, 432, 438, 443, 445, 446, 451, 453, 459, 464, 469
  fear of 453
  of Egyptian firstborn 257
  penalty 87
  power of 409
Deborah 104, 105, 106, 107, 112, 113, 165, 482
Deborah, Song of 102, 103, 105, 106, 112
debts 63, 111, 224, 440
Decalogue see Ten Commandments

deceit, deception 35, 203, 223, 471
deceivers 421, 465
Decius, Emperor 459
deeds 457
  good 110, 165, 231, 447, 451
  heroic 107
defeat 121, 176, 199, 202
defilement 193, 212, 333
deities 66, 98, 99, 141, 196, 202, 369, 378
Delian League 246
Delilah 107, 482
deliverance 68, 127, 166, 167, 178, 196, 220, 235, 239, 241, 257, 261, 439
deliverers 104
Delphi 376
Demetrius, King 285, 482
Demetrius II, King 251
demons 175, 255, 288, 330, 467
  demon-possessed man 75
  desert 69
  host of 473
denarius 371
denial, Peter's 267, 386
deportation 142, 149, 199
Derbe 375, 381, 393, 502
descendants 34, 41, 115, 186, 411, 424, 425
descent 186, 306, 314, 346
deserts 51, 53, 70, 95, 138, 193, 266, 298, 311, 319
destitute 211, 227
destruction 88, 121, 128, 131, 143, 178, 199, 201, 210, 211, 212, 214, 220, 229, 333, 459, 461, 470, 472, 473
determinism, determinist 288, 452, 453, 523
Deuterocanonical books see Apocrypha
Deuteronomistic 226, 257, 523
Deuteronomistic history 80, 105, 108, 128, 129, 135, 226
Deuteronomy, book of 21, 22, 24, 37, 50, 56, 60, 64, 66, 69, 70, 80-81, 82, 84, 85, 87, 92, 101, 105, 108, 109, 111, 119, 128, 131, 135, 149, 159, 193, 195, 196, 197, 207, 218, 219, 226, 232, 235, 263, 356, 357, 359, 362, 466
devil see Satan
devotion, devoted 66, 67, 88, 110, 145, 259, 326, 360
diakonos 437
dialect 107
  Hebrew 98
  Phoenician 98
Dialogue Between the World Weary and his Soul 185
Diana see Artemis
Diaspora 147, 153, 159, 167, 245, 247, 248, 280, 281, 286, 322, 388, 523
  synagogues 396
Diatessaron 475
diatribe 407
Didymus see Thomas
diet 67, 152, 438
  dietary laws, regulations 37, 282
Diocletian, Emperor 459
Dion 299
Dionysius of Alexandria 469, 482
Diotrephes 449, 465, 482
disasters 105, 207, 222, 224, 225, 260, 263, 469
discernment 467
disciples 77, 202, 297, 307, 311, 319, 331, 351, 386, 391, 393, 436, 463
  beloved 313, 317, 330
  of Jesus 243, 302, 303, 310, 311, 313, 317, 323, 328-29, 331, 333, 337, 338, 344, 345, 346, 347, 349, 350, 352, 353, 358, 364, 365, 375, 380, 382, 383, 384, 385, 387, 412, 418, 419, 436, 440, 444, 449, 471
  of John 325
  the twelve 285, 330-31; 352, 469
discipleship 309, 311, 323, 329, 331, 337, 467

discipline 69, 164, 259, 439, 451
discrimination, racial 456
diseases 165, 342
disobedience 81, 105, 115, 119, 121, 130, 135, 192, 212, 223, 226, 230, 327, 411, 430, 432
disorder 31, 472
dissension 455
divided kingdom see kingdom, divided
divination, divining 149, 170, 377, 378
divine see God
divine right of kings 119
divorces 131, 160, 187, 206, 218, 245, 278, 284, 335, 374, 375, 467
Documentary hypothesis see Pentateuch 21-23
Dome of the Rock 276
domestic crafts 164
Domestic or Household Codes 323, 375, 434
Dominical sacraments 418
Domitian, Emperor 369, 373, 398, 456, 459, 468
donkeys 119, 120, 217, 268, 269, 349, 371
  talking 74
doom 206, 207
door of the sheep 313
Dorcas see Tabitha
doubt 176
doves 32, 231, 265, 267, 413, 416
dowry 375
doxology 407, 523
dragon 148, 255, 469
  of chaos 472
dreams 44, 106, 178, 190, 217, 260, 318, 319, 355, 379, 470
dress 65, 67
  codes 67
drought 95, 138, 139, 220, 221
drunk, drunkenness 32, 254, 255, 453
dry bones 214, 215
dualism 141, 157, 523
dunamis 413
Dura-Europas 73
dynasties 107, 115, 128, 133, 134, 250, 346

E 22
Ea 140
eagle 261, 266
early religion of the Israelites 108-09
earth 28, 30, 31, 32, 41, 42, 73, 122, 139, 178, 179, 189, 205, 233, 235, 312, 333, 383, 412, 438, 461, 469, 472
  new 29, 205, 262, 469, 471, 472, 473
earthquakes 53, 73, 139, 225, 364, 471
Ecce Homo arch 361
Ecclesiastes, book of 131, 169, 170, 171, 174, 182, 185, 188-89, 190, 191
Ecclesiasticus, book of (see also Wisdom of Jesus ben Sira, or Sirach) 163, 169, 171, 256, 257
economy, rural 283
ecstatic prophets, prophecy 196, 198, 212, 475
ecstatic states 120
Eden 27, 203, 262, 263, 327, 471, 502
  Garden of 30, 31, 467, 472, 473
edim 223
Edom 18, 41, 57, 71, 99, 101, 141, 213, 225, 228, 229, 244, 502
Edomites 101, 228, 232
  shrine of 100, 101
education, educated 29, 74, 374, 440

in ancient Israel 164-65
in New Testament times 322-33
  moral 113
  religious 113
Egerton Gospel 463
Egnatian Way 442
Egypt 18, 24, 33, 34, 44, 46-47, 48, 49, 50, 51, 52, 53, 68, 69, 72, 76, 86, 95, 98, 100, 106, 122, 123, 137, 142, 143, 144, 145, 149, 152, 153, 156, 157, 159, 165, 171, 201, 203, 206, 207, 209, 213, 219, 223, 232, 246, 247, 248, 249, 251, 256, 259, 274, 301, 318, 319, 320, 321, 345, 350, 369, 376, 379, 451, 452, 502
  18th Dynasty 96
  famine in 27
  luxury goods of 47
  power of 145
  river economy of 46
Egyptians 27, 37, 50, 68, 89, 127, 145, 165, 232, 233, 257
  princess 51
  rule 95
Ehud 104, 105, 483
ekklesia 188, 307
El 36, 58, 59, 99, 108, 109
El Salvador 457
Elah, King 135
elders 65, 87, 114, 119, 164, 254, 255, 339, 356, 381, 392, 394, 446, 447, 449, 469, 523
Eleazar, son of Aaron 259, 483
Eleazar, son of Jairus 295
election see choice
election traditions 232, 233
Elephantine 152, 159, 184, 247
Elhanan 150
Eli 64, 115, 117, 118, 119, 483
Eliakim, Jehoiakim 145, 483
Elias 189
Eliezer 112, 483
Elihu 172, 173, 483
Elijah 96, 97, 128, 129, 134, 136, 138-39, 141, 179, 196, 197, 198, 199, 223, 226, 230, 245, 266, 302, 303, 311, 325, 333, 346, 365, 383, 454, 461, 483
  ministry of 139
Elimelech 110, 111, 483
Eliot, T. S. 163
Eliphaz 172, 173, 483
Elisha 96, 97, 128, 129, 134, 136, 139, 198, 223, 269, 343, 365, 483
elite, elitism 285, 372, 420
Elizabeth 316, 317, 320, 324, 483
Elizabeth, Grand Duchess of Russia 456
Elkanah 118, 483
Elkosh 239
Elohim 22, 58, 61, 141, 523
Elon 104, 105
Elymas see Bar-Jesus
embalment 362
Emmanuel see Immanuel
Emmaus 298, 311, 364, 365, 382, 502
emotions 208, 210, 409
emperors 369, 400, 458, 459, 468
  Roman 433, 445
empires 136-37
  Achaemenid 156
  Assyrian 143, 200, 206
  Babylonian 148
  Second, Neo-Babylonian 149
  Greek 217, 246, 359
  Lydian 154, 156
  Medo-Persian 154
  Mitannian 142
  Persian 156, 157, 246, 248
  Roman 278, 368-69, 371, 372, 376, 379, 380, 392, 402, 433, 434, 440, 447, 453, 458, 467
encouragement 345, 432, 451, 455, 471
Endor 119, 121, 378, 502
end-time, end of time, end of days 24, 217, 261, 291, 333, 365, 383, 445, 451, 468, 523

endurance 223, 455
enemies 60, 81, 104, 106, 107, 127, 175, 183, 205, 208, 209, 211, 224, 230, 241, 260, 261, 312, 332, 339, 353, 363, 422, 423, 440, 473
  of God 261, 473
  of Israel 232, 233, 261, 263
Enki 140
Enlightenment 185
Enlil 140
Enoch 77, 179, 365, 460, 462, 470, 483
Enoch, First book of 179, 290, 461, 462
entry into Promised Land (see also Promised Land) 94-95
entry into Jerusalem 348
Enuma Elish see creation
Epaphras 438, 483
Ephesians, letter to 291, 397, 401, 405, 408, 409, 428-29, 430, 431, 448, 449, 462, 473
Ephesus 274, 285, 317, 325, 369, 370, 379, 381, 397, 398-99, 428, 429, 446, 447, 449, 456, 465, 469, 503
ephod 65, 117
Ephraim 45, 102, 103, 483, 503
Ephraimites 107
Ephrathah 503
Epic of Atrahasis 33
Epictetus 453
Epicureans, Epicureanism, Epicurus 452, 453
episcopacy 448, 523
epistles 314
epistles or letters 405, 406-07, 454, 460, 464, 523
  Pastoral 401, 405, 406, 446, 462, 463, 464, 523
  Prison or Captivity 397, 399, 401, 405
Eresh-kigal 140
eretz Israel 289
Eridu 19
Eriduu 19
Esau 27, 35, 40, 41, 55, 98, 101, 113, 228, 244, 483
escape 52, 68, 69
eschatology, eschatological 220, 221, 241, 260, 262-63, 307, 357, 365, 523
  future 263
  realized 263
eschaton 262
Esdras 160, 258, 484
Esdras, books of
  First 160, 253, 258, 259
  Second 160, 189, 253, 260, 261, 470
  Third 160
Essenes 288, 289, 290, 324, 331, 385, 523
Esther 112, 166, 167, 189, 223, 483
Esther, Additions to 253, 258, 259
Esther, book of 45, 68, 69, 91, 166-67, 169, 189
eternal life 33, 182, 312, 313, 333, 338, 339, 350, 375, 464, 466, 523
ethical dualism 157
ethics (see also morality) 197, 226-27, 235, 407, 409, 414, 453, 457, 523
  Christian 466-67
  prophets 226-27
Ethiopia 46, 131, 503
ethnicity 282
Eucharist (see also Last Supper) 67, 343, 350, 418, 523
Euergetes 257
Eunice 484
eunuchs 389
  Ethiopian 367, 389
Euphrates River 18, 19, 36, 141, 142, 148, 503
Eusebius 399, 401
evangelism 345, 380, 389
evangelists 301, 302, 307, 324, 325, 329, 331, 333, 336, 342, 357, 389, 436, 448, 449, 523
Eve 26, 30-31, 182, 183, 192, 484

everyday life 46-47, 282-85
evil 31, 32, 175, 183, 226, 229, 230, 239, 240, 241, 333, 342, 356, 379, 403, 413, 439, 445, 470, 472, 473
  forces 260, 345
  powers of 166, 408
  spirits 342, 344
evolution, Darwinian theories of 29
exclusion 87
executed 362, 458
executions 187, 354, 355, 356, 357, 358, 359, 361, 401, 459
exhortation 451
Exile, exile 27, 28, 31, 61, 65, 68, 84, 96, 111, 115, 126, 127, 129, 131, 144, 145, 146-47, 148, 149, 150, 151, 154, 155, 158, 159, 160, 165, 167, 176, 178, 186, 193, 198, 200, 202, 203, 206, 207, 208, 212, 213, 218, 219, 220, 231, 238, 241, 242, 243, 244, 245, 250, 255, 257, 258, 260, 281, 287, 333, 399, 468, 470, 523
  return from 154-55, 204
  religion of the 152-53
exiles 152, 153, 161, 162, 163, 175, 199, 207, 212, 214, 216, 217, 259
Exodus, book of 21, 22, 23, 47, 48-49, 50, 51, 52, 56, 59, 60, 64, 66, 68, 69, 72, 80, 84, 98, 116, 132, 149, 150, 179, 231, 232, 422, 468
Exodus, the 21, 28, 49, 52-53, 54, 72, 77, 96, 112, 131, 136, 137, 153, 180, 203, 219, 225, 232, 267, 311, 350, 523
exorcisms 337, 342, 345, 378
expiation 66, 422, 523
exposure of children 284
extermination 93
extinction 473
extreme unction 418, 523
eye for eye 87
Ezekias see Hezekiah
Ezekiel 61, 153, 155, 196, 198, 199, 212, 213, 215, 242, 468, 484
Ezekiel, book of 127, 147, 153, 175, 179, 189, 195, 199, 212-13, 214, 216, 228, 239, 260, 309, 391
  visions of 214-15
Ezion-Geber 152, 503
Ezra 31, 84, 111, 155, 156, 159, 160, 161, 163, 189, 200, 248, 258, 260, 261, 484
Ezra, book of 91, 150, 155, 160-61, 162, 163, 169, 258

**F**

failure 92, 421
faith 39, 49, 50, 53, 59, 70, 71, 92, 95, 110, 127, 139, 140, 152, 153, 158, 159, 173, 176, 176, 179, 188, 202, 203, 217, 222, 223, 239, 257, 259, 282, 317, 330, 331, 332, 342, 345, 348, 365, 378, 382, 386, 397, 401, 408, 409, 411, 414, 417, 418, 419, 420, 421, 422, 424, 425, 426, 427, 430, 431, 432, 433, 438, 439, 442, 443, 447, 450, 451, 454, 455, 456, 458, 460, 461, 464, 467, 469, 475
  Christian 323, 379, 387, 420, 422, 450, 451
  hero, heroes of 119, 461
  Jewish 247, 259, 394, 471
  people of 261
faithfulness 92, 223, 245, 315, 327, 399, 416, 467
faithful, the 178, 215, 241, 261, 385
faithlessness 245
fall (see also Adam, first and second) 31, 183, 262, 523

false accuser 473
false prophets see prophets, false
falsehood 453
family, families 32, 33, 40, 48, 63, 64, 74, 80, 81, 103, 107, 108, 109, 112, 113, 119, 120, 121, 139, 151, 152, 164, 178, 184, 186-87, 189, 193, 200, 228, 255, 282, 283, 284, 285, 305, 333, 338, 374-75, 406, 448
  group, groups 23, 118, 192
  Hellenistic Jewish 390
  life 80, 81, 257, 284
  meal 68
  relations 284
  royal 113, 149
  tomb 363
famine 27, 61, 111, 139, 210, 266, 338, 385, 469
  relief 392
farming, farms 54, 164, 283, 285, 333, 372, 440
fasting 69, 205, 227, 231, 327, 335, 351, 449
fasts 62, 68-69, 205, 230, 326, 383
  of Jesus 77
  of petition 69
fate 170, 452
father 25, 35, 98, 107, 171, 193, 310, 311, 339
  the Father 76, 333, 413
  faults 31, 40, 41, 128, 231
favoritism 41
fear 456
  of the Lord 184
feasting 351, 445
feasts 62, 68-69, 217, 338
  idolatrous 414
Felicitas 459
Felix, Marcus Antonius 279, 373, 400, 484
female and male 30, 285
Fertile Crescent 18, 137
fertility 140, 192, 246, 399
  cult 64, 198
  goddess 113
  rites 218
festivals 67, 68-69, 149, 164, 177, 236, 237, 263, 282, 283, 313, 349, 355, 376, 439
  days 176, 237
  harvest 69
  sacrifices 70
Festival Scrolls see Megilloth
Festus, Porcius 279, 400, 484
fetus 192
fidelity 187
fiery furnace 217, 255
fig 31, 264, 471
fig tree, barren 309
fires 43, 50, 53, 59, 73, 107, 138, 139, 149, 162, 262, 324, 337, 385, 403, 442, 451, 458, 461, 473
  unholy 63
firmament 29
First Jewish war 292-93
firstborn 40, 55, 68
  death of 49
fish 76, 230, 231, 233, 282
  hook 231
fishermen 329, 331, 332, 340, 386
fishing 23, 298, 329, 331, 332, 333, 340
Five Scrolls 166
Flavius Silva 294
flax 54, 265
fleece 107
flock, flocks 31, 41, 69, 124, 268, 460
Flood, floods 26, 27, 32-33, 77, 92, 106, 148, 265, 267, 268, 471
  stories 33
folklore 51, 74-75, 107, 111, 130, 230
followers 285, 423
folly 131, 185, 187, 188, 189, 335
foods 31, 40, 62, 69, 92, 145, 189,

210, 255, 264, 266, 267, 268, 282, 283, 338, 344, 350, 388, 389, 395, 402, 414, 434, 435, 447, 454, 468
  laws 62, 282, 395, 409
  sacrificed 415
forces 258
  evil 260, 445
foreigners 110, 193, 204, 205, 330
forgiveness 48, 68, 219, 230, 235, 286, 297, 324, 332, 342, 345, 348, 351, 409, 413, 422, 423, 429, 439, 467
Former Prophets 91, 194
fornication 395, 468
Fortunatus 473
forty 77
forum, Forum 369, 372, 402
four species 73
four last things 262
frankincense 65, 265, 318
Frazer, Sir James 74
free birth 372
free-born citizens 373
free man 338, 414
free woman 425
freedom 48, 72, 229, 279, 284, 335, 373, 396, 415, 425, 440, 441, 467
  religious 250
freedmen 373
free will 288, 473
French Revolution 119
friends 171, 172, 191, 210, 257, 285, 422, 433, 440
  of God 454
friendship 432, 453
Frost, Robert 231
fruitfulness 29
fruits, first 384
fulfillment 92, 93, 197, 236, 242, 384
fullness 438, 439, 444
funerals 180, 234, 362, 363
  customs 284
  gifts 99
future 197, 199, 202, 203, 216, 236, 243, 260, 263, 444, 469

**G**

Gabbatha 353, 360, 361
Gabriel see archangels
Gad 102, 103, 115, 484, 503
  tribe of 93
Gadara 299, 503
Gaius, Emperor 373, 435
Galatia 369, 381, 503
Galatians 424, 425
Galatians, letter to 322, 359, 387, 390, 391, 394, 395, 397, 405, 409, 424-25, 430, 433, 446
Galba 373
Galilee 117, 274, 275, 277, 278, 281, 288, 293, 297, 298, 299, 309, 310, 311, 313, 320, 321, 325, 328, 329, 331, 332, 333, 334, 340-41, 347, 355, 364, 375, 386, 503
Galilee, Lake or Sea of 236, 298, 299, 333, 335, 340, 344, 512
Gallia 368
gallows 167
Gamaliel, Rabbi 390, 484
games 284
  board 261
  sacred 283
Garden community 453
Garden Tomb 361
Gathas 157
Gaugamela 157
Gaulanitis 293, 299
Gaza 18, 99, 107, 142, 277, 503
Gedaliah, fast of 69
gemilut hasadim 25
genealogies 150, 236, 306, 310, 314, 347
Genesis, book of 21, 22, 26-27, 28, 29, 30, 31, 32, 34, 35, 36, 39, 40, 41, 44, 45, 47, 48, 54,

55, 61, 75, 98, 102, 109, 112,
117, 126, 150, 159, 175, 179,
180, 182, 183, 192, 193, 214,
226, 233, 240, 262, 312, 461,
462, 468
Gennesaret 299, 332, 503
genocide 74
Gentiles 33, 36, 67, 100, 101,
110, 111, 140, 141, 160, 221,
231, 245, 247, 261, 280, 283,
284, 310, 311, 331, 332, 342,
357, 362, 367, 381, 387, 388,
391, 393, 394, 395, 396, 403,
410, 411, 423, 425, 428, 430,
431, 435, 441, 457, 470, 523
congregations 400
Court of 431
mission 282, 381, 388
Gerar 34, 504
king of 36
people of 36
Gethsemane 302, 303, 311, 352,
360, 361, 504
Garden of 302, 330
Ghiberti 107
ghosts 149, 345, 363
Gibeon 108, 504
Gideon 104, 105, 106, 107, 484
gifts 409, 412, 415, 416, 417, 420,
421, 448, 449
Gilboa, Mount 121, 125, 504
Gileadites 107
Gilgal 94, 108, 343, 504
*Gilgamesh, Epic of* 33, 148
girls 164, 190, 284, 322, 323, 345
Giza 136
gleaning 111
glorification 383
glory, Glory 25, 51, 204, 205,
214, 243, 313, 383, 426, 433,
440, 443, 445, 461
*glossolalia* 385, 417, 523
Gnostic, Gnosticism 300, 301,
325, 465, 523
gospel 474
Naasene Gnostics 301
pre-Gnosticism 465
goats 69, 86, 267, 268, 338
**God** 22, 24, 26, 36, 37, 51, 55,
57, 59, 71, 75, 80, 82, 88, 93,
105, 106, 109, 118, 122, 133,
139, 151, 163, 172, 173, 191,
199, 202, 203, 206, 207, 219,
222, 233, 342, 350, 351, 353,
384, 408, 409, 412, 440, 441,
468, 469
**actions**, activity of 76, **222-
23**, 308, 310, 319, 332, 342,
351, 408
agents of 42
appearance of 205, 384
as Father (Abba) 333, 522
as judge 225, 342
as King 202
as love 467
authority of 49, 307, 425
blessing of 93, 199, 310, 335,
425, 429
call of 200, 325, 333, 411
children of 312, 456, 457, 465
choice 54, 55, 187
commands of 466
compassionate 29, 134, 203,
219, 221, 339
consciousness of 23
deliverance of 50
derivation of all life 26
endurance of 188
faithfulness, fidelity of 54, 61,
71, 92, 153, 187, 201, 207, 218,
259, 411, 451
favor of 170, 409, 427
fear of 36, 39
forgiveness of 282, 411
freedom of 212
fullness of 439
gifts of 282
glory of 25, 201, 213, 214,
257, 312, 422, 467, 469, 471,
472
goodness of 110, 111
grace of 411, 423, 424, 426,
428, 430, 456, 460
guidance of 25, 33, 48, 50, 73,
223

holiness of 42, 201, 212, 213
honor of 48
house of 450, 451, 472
household of 429, 430
justice of 71, 84, 87, 179, 185,
239, 261
law of 50, 115, 236, 240, 297,
306
love of 191, 218, 219, 228,
238, 244, 245, 267, 410, 422,
461, 465, 473
majesty of 312, 408
mercy of 105, 176, 230, 231,
233
messages of 42, 43, 196, 207,
337
mind of 319
mission of 231
mystery of 439
**names** 50, **58-59**, 80, 108,
109, 153, 166
**nature**, character of **58-59**,
93, 99, 173, 226, 408, 465, 474
one 56, 225, 229, 245, 263
pain of 208
patience of 461
people of 42, 70, 107, 150,
159, 176, 206, 212, 224, 238,
240, 241, 282, 345, 387, 391,
394, 395, 396, 409, 413, 425,
427, 430, 448, 449, 456
plan of 34, 44, 243, 310, 428
power of 48, 49, 52, 63, 118,
178, 203, 213, 239, 297, 342,
345, 411, 416, 420, 421, 428,
429
presence of 23, 42, 49, 61, 71,
73, 116, 127, 133, 158, 159,
201, 212, 215, 232, 286, 342,
351, 383, 385, 416, 421, 450,
470
promises of 26, 27, 36, 39, 92,
95, 128, 133, 134, 152, 219,
262, 280, 306, 307, 342, 394,
425, 429, 451, 461
protective care of 73, 170, 258
providence of 49, 111, 150,
166, 167, 223, 233, 255, 327,
381
punishment of 205, 223, 243
purposes of 23, 26, 27, 41, 42,
43, 49, 71, 111, 150, 197, 202,
225, 226, 228, 229, 232, 236,
238, 239, 240, 243, 256, 258,
263, 307, 309, 319, 342, 345,
381, 385, 408, 409, 411, 416,
428, 430, 455
rejection of 211
relationship with Israel 35, 60,
80
response of 172, 173
retribution of 240
revelation of 466
righteousness of 411
rule of 216, 233, 470
salvation of 176, 203, 232, 411
saving design 315
sons of 472
sovereignty of 197, 201, 212,
229, 231, 444, 451, 467
Spirit of 45, 411, 427, 467
sustenance of 222, 351
the Father 416
threats of 262
transcendence of 23, 408
truth of 256, 258
victory of 28, 345, 468, 469,
471
ways of 24, 171
will of 34, 56, 119, 159, 173,
196, 197, 229, 239, 309, 317,
319, 353, 467
Word of 67, 119, 197, 198,
199, 203, 209, 226, 233, 243,
260, 411, 449
works of 21, 29, 33, 310
wrath, anger of 51, 88, 89,
105, 176, 207, 219, 263, 422,
426
God-fearers 283, 392
Godhead 413, 523
godliness 447
**gods, goddesses** 77, 85, 134,
135, **140-41**, 145, 149, 154,
157, 175, 184, 187, 197, 199,

230, 232, 246, 247, 369, 376,
398, 453, 458, 468
Canaanite 36, 98-99
Egyptian 141
fertility 113
household 141, 143
of Babylon 149, 152
other 27, 28, 36, 81, 101, 193
gold 35, 78, 79, 98, 131, 170,
199, 217, 318
*Golden Bough, The* 74
Golden Calf 48, 49, 51, 59, 72
Golgotha 358, 360, 361, 504
Goliath 89, 121, 124, 150, 484
Gomer 198, 218, 219, 484
Gomorrah 36, 38, 209, 461, 504
good, goodness 31, 183, 188,
240, 262, 427, 457
Gordon, General 361
Goshen 47, 52, 504
gospel, the 300, 379, 380, 381,
387, 388, 389, 392, 393, 394,
395, 397, 409, 410, 411, 412,
420, 425, 429, 433, 434, 441,
442, 447, 464, 523
**Gospels, the** 109, 216, 223, 242,
278, 297, **300-05**, 313, 314,
315, 317, 322, 324, 329, 336,
340, 343, 344, 346, 347, 348,
349, 351, 352, 354, 357, 357,
358, 359, 363, 365, 407, 413,
436, 437, 463, 467, 475, 524
Apocryphal 252, 300, 301
canonical 300
*Egerton Gospel* 301
**Synoptic** 300, 301, **302-03**,
304, 312, 313, 326, 327, 329,
336, 349, 350, 353, 358, 463,
527
tetramorphs 308
Goths 399
government 119, 164, 165
Roman 456
governors 320, 331, 372
provincial 372
grace 59, 213, 332, 409, 411, 418,
449, 451, 523
graves 119, 178, 179, 182, 190,
203, 363
Great Commission 418
Greco-Roman society 283
Greece 18, 76, 123, 136, 156,
157, 216, 246-47, 248, 272,
381, 393, 414, 432, 442, 461,
467, 504
greed 182, 353, 378, 460
**Greek Empire**, Greeks 77, 148,
**246-47**, 285, 310, 365, 392,
400, 467
translation 24
Greek 18, 76, 123, 136, 156,
grief, grieving 68, 207, 210, 211,
365
groom *see* bridegroom
ground 30, 32
guidance 42, 64, 83, 84, 197, 222,
446, 467
guilt, guilty 33, 113, 175, 210,
211, 359, 422, 423, 426
Gunkel, H 75
*gymnasium, gymnasia* 246, 284, 323,
398

H

Habakkuk 239, 255, 484
**Habakkuk, book of** 174, 195,
**238-39**
Habiru 94
Hadad 99, 484
Hadrian, Emperor 276, 369, 398
Temple of 369
Hagar 38, 39, 41, 42, 186, 425,
485
Haggadah, The 49
Haggai 155, 158, 242, 243, 485
**Haggai, book of** 195, **242-43**
Haifa 333
Halitzah 111
Hall of Hewn Stones 355

Hallel collections 177
Ham 32, 33, 98, 485
Haman 68, 166, 167, 485
Hamath 145, 504
Hammurabi, Code of 85, 87, 148,
149
Hammurabi, King 123, 136, 148,
149
Hananiah 199, 206, 485
Handel, George Frederic 107, 173
*Messiah* 173
*Samson* 107
hanged, hanging 353, 359
Hanina ben Dosa 343
Hannah 112, 113, 115, 118, 316,
319, 485
song of praise 113
Hanukkah 68, 250, 282, 524
Hapiru 94
happiness 184, 190, 445, 453
Haran, Harran 18, 34, 40, 485,
505
harbors 369, 373, 398
harlots 130, 198
harmonies, Gospel 304, 475
harmony 28, 31, 183, 205, 467,
471, 475
harvests 69, 73, 110, 224, 339,
384, 455
Hasmonai 250
**Hasmonean period**, dynasty
137, **250-56**, 287, 294
Hasmonean rulers, kings 97, 251,
259
Hasmoneans 155, 250, 258, 259
stronghold of 361
Hazor, King of 106
healings 309, 329, 334, 342, 343
Bartimaeus and another blind
man 343
blind man at Bethsaida 343
blind men 343
boy with epilepsy 343
Canaanite woman's daughter
343
centurion's servant 343
deaf and mute man 343
leper 343
Malchus' ear 343
man blind, mute, and possessed
343
man born blind 312, 343
man mute and possessed 343
man possessed 343
man with a withered hand 343
official's son 312, 343
paralyzed man 343, 345
Peter's mother-in-law 343, 434
sick man 312
sick man at pool of Bethesda
343
ten lepers 343
two Gadarenes 343
woman bent double 343
woman with a hemorrhage 343
woman with dropsy 343
health 342, 406
healing, to heal 26, 33, 74, 97,
297, 330, 331, 342, 343, 344,
345, 367, 378, 401, 417, 448
heart 82, 182, 190, 409, 466
heathen defilement 243
**Heaven**, heavens 42, 43, 73, 95,
109, 122, 138, 139, 179, 233,
235, 245, 262, 312, 333, 344,
382, 383, 384, 385, 412, 419,
428, 438, 439, 442, 443, 444,
445, 450, 451, 461, 462, 468,
469, 470, 475, 524, **472-73**
Babylonian 31
gates of 472
host of 472
new 29, 205, 262, 469, 471,
472, 473
third 391
heavenly bodies 472
*hebel* 188
**Hebrews** 37, 94, 95, **388-89**,
472
**Hebrews, letter to** 67, 327, 346,
383, 405, 406, 412, **450-51**,
452
Hebron 18, 34, 38, 103, 298, 320,
505
hegemony 122, 123

heirs 111, 187, 339
**hell** 185, 231, 262, **472-73**
Hellenism, **Hellenists** 247, 248,
249, 277, 282, **388-89**, 524
Hellenization 246, 248, 251
help, helper 30, 219, 339, 422,
448
Hercules 51
*herem* 93
heresy 465, 524
heretics 458, 473
Hermes 376
Hermon, Mount 333, 505
Herod Agrippa I, King 278, 279,
485
Herod Agrippa II, King 279, 400,
485
Herod Antipas, King 275, 278,
279, 321, 325, 333, 355, 357,
381, 485
Herod Archelaus, King 275, 278,
485
Herodians 353
Herodias 278, 485
Herodium 278, 292, 294, 295,
299
Herod Philip, King 278, 279, 493
Herod the Great, King 97, 101,
127, 181, 274, 275, 276, 277,
278, 279, 282, 286, 287, 294,
295, 318, 319, 353, 361, 369, 485
death of 97
Herodium 295
Herodotus 6
Hezekiah, King 126, 127, 133,
134, 135, 143, 200, 203, 234,
235, 241, 347, 485
tunnel of 126
hieroglyphic script 165
high priesthood 251
high priests 65, 122, 155, 158,
160, 243, 248, 249, 251, 257,
279, 286, 287, 352, 354, 355,
356, 357, 445, 450, 451
Hiram, King 130, 132, 486
*Hishonim* 253
history 6, 74, 75, 164, 170, 260,
261, 262, 310, 452
Historical books 91
Hittites 47, 60, 98, 122
Hivites 98
holiness 23, 37, 55, 62, 63, 64,
89, 117, 133, 155, 163, 200,
226, 286, 332, 333, 429, 431,
457, 472, 524
Holiness Code 70, 84
Holocaust 167
holocaust 66
Holofernes 254, 255, 486
holy, Holy 54, 62, 63, 67, 202,
205, 457
days 438
Family 275, 277
Land 281
living, lives 423, 442, 443
place, places 250, 450
War 232
Holy of Holies 66, 132, 155, 190,
215, 259, 277, 286, 287, 524
Holy One, of Israel 63, 202
**Holy Spirit, the** 25, 76, 104,
221, 231, 237, 262, 308, 310,
311, 316, 318, 319, 324,
325, 326, 327, 364, 367, 378,
379, 380, 381, 384, 385, 387,
389, 399, 409, 412, 413, **416-
17**, 418, 424, 425, 428, 429,
430, 431, 442, 444, 447, 448,
449, 467, 470, 475, 524, 527
fruits of the Spirit 416, 425,
467
gifts of the Spirit 383, 384,
385, 391, 409, 416, 428, 448
power of 411, 428
presence of 418
homes 113, 164, 282, 374, 434,
435
homily 400, 464
homosexuality 193
honor 322, 333, 338, 372, 375, 408
hope 152, 199, 201, 202, 207,
211, 217, 219, 224, 229, 234,
234, 235, 243, 263, 310, 346,
413, 416, 433, 439, 445, 456
living 456

Hophni 64, 486
Horeb *see* Sinai
horn of oil 114
Horus 141
Hosanna 349
Hosea 61, 76, 137, 198, 218, 219, 221, 234, 238, 242, 486
**Hosea, book of** 143, 179, 195, 207, **218-19**, 226
Hoshea, King 135, 486
hospitality 331, 437
house arrest 401
**house churches 434-35**
house group 435
Household Codes *see* Domestic Codes
households 113, 164, 186, 373, 434, 439, 447, 453
  managers 113
  of God 434
house of prayer 67
houses 97, 345, 434
Huldah 112, 113, 165, 486
**human** 31, 49, 51, 86, 196, 378, 471
  beings 63, 178, 182, 183, 230, 231, 409
  condition, predicament 26, 27, 54, 422
  creations 25
  flesh 411
  life 184, 188, 189, 223
  **nature 182-83**, 408, **409**, 426
  race 30
humanity 240, 310, 311, 383, 411
humankind 27, 28, 30, 32, 33, 184, 232, 233, 351
humble, the 240, 241, 310, 455, 472
humility 121, 257, 323, 332, 339, 432, 433
hunger, hungry 210, 466
hunting 47, 97
husbands 110, 113, 186, 187, 193, 255, 323, 373, 374, 375, 457
Hyksos kings 52
hymns 25, 125, 176, 177, 201, 224, 233, 255, 346, 352, 407, 412, 432, 435, 470, 524
  Zion 232
hypocrisy 335
Hyracanus II 251
Hyrcanus, John 251, 258
hyssop 265

# I

I am 50, 203, 313
Iamblichus 462
Ibzan 104, 105
Iconium 275, 381, 393, 449, 505
identity 126
idolatry, idolaters, idolatrous 33, 36, 57, 59, 65, 83, 86, 87, 93, 138, 140, 141, 204, 205, 212, 218, 219, 222, 239, 240, 254, 257, 263, 282, 414, 469
idols 82, 134, 202, 203, 206, 217, 255, 415, 442, 467, 468, 524
Idumea 101, 278, 298, 505
Ignatius 399, 459
illness *see* healing
images, imagery (*see also* idolatry, idols) 109, 171
  graven 56
  pagan 279
  sexual 192
Immanuel 198, 201, 524
immorality (*see also* life after death) 414, 467
  sexual 415, 443
immortality 33, 179, 256, 524
imprisonment 87
  Peter's 367
impurity 110, 193
  ritual 67
incarnation 315, 345, 413, 465, 524
incense 64, 65, 100
  burner 65, 180

incest 33, 192, 458
independence 103, 114, 115, 145, 155, 158, 250, 251
  Jewish 251
  political 250
India 248
inerrancy 7
infancy narratives 302
infection 62
infertile 192
infidelity 57, 59, 61, 92, 94, 119, 198, 206, 218, 219, 468
inheritance 34, 64, 102, 120, 129, 186, 247, 338, 339, 429, 430, 456
  female 70, 71
  Jewish 455
initiation 418
injustice 175, 189, 201, 204, 205, 225, 234, 239, 263, 298, 335, 471
inner courts 431
innocence, innocent 172, 173, 174, 175, 209, 267, 357, 426
inspiration 8-9, 417, 475
instruct, instruction 24, 25, 63, 84, 164, 165, 322, 323, 452, 467
instruments, musical 180
intercession 37, 196, 383
intermediary 51
internal organs 66
interpretation, interpreters 288, 417
  Jewish 77
  Kabbalistic 77
investigation 355, 356
Irenaeus 399, 468
**Isaac** 27, 34, 36, 37, 38, **40-41**, 112, 113, 136, 186, 411, 486
Isaiah 24, 29, 79, 128, 137, 155, 179, 195, 198, 200, 201, 202, 212, 226, 234, 235, 238, 241, 263, 269, 313, 319, 321, 324, 337, 389, 462, 470, 471, 486
**Isaiah, book of** 195, 229, 232, 243, 337, 347, 463
  **Chapters 1-39** 129, 143, 178, **200-01**, 202, 205, 239, 260, 277, 327, 341
  **Chapters 40-55** 27, 28, 52, 147, 153, 175, 179, 182, 200, **202-03**, 204, 233, 238, 300, 347, 430
  **Chapters 56-66** 29, 67, 127, 200, **204-05**, 297, 385
Ish-Bosheth, Ishbaal 115, 125, 486
Ishmael 39, 41, 87, 186, 486
Ishmaelites 22, 57
Ishtar 140, 246
  Gate 148
Isis 141, 256, 367
Islam 39, 82, 237
**Israel** 24, 25, 26, 27, 35, 35, 37, 40, 41, 46, 47, 50, 55, 60, 61, 63, 66, 71, 76, 79, 84, 86, 87, 88, 89, 96, 98, 99, 100, 102, 103, 104, 107, 108, 109, 114, 115, 119, 120, 121, 122, 123, 125, 128, 131, 134, 134, 135, 136, 137, 142, 143, 151, 155, 161, 176, 190, 191, 196, 198, 199, 203, 204, 211, 215, 219, 222, 224, 225, 228, 229, 232, 234, 235, 236, 237, 238, 241, 263, 265, 268, 289, 305, 310, 311, 312, 313, 314, 318, 319, 329, 331, 332, 333, 345, 346, 356, 381, 411, 427, 430, 431, 454, 466, 468, 470, 486, 505
  children of 48, 139
  defeat of 225
  founding of 34
  God of 101, 229, 475
  history of 114, 124, 129
  Holy One of 200
  journey of 70, 71
  King of 88, 120, 130
  **kings of** 115, **134-35**, 158, 257
  leaders of 339
  **neighbors of 100-01**
  origins of 81, 95
  people of 21, 24, 31, 48, 50,

54, 70, 77, 86, 92, 102, 118, 119, 140, 153, 158, 212, 215, 220, 408
  rebellion of 219
  religion of 36, 66, 140, 143, 149, 158
  renewed 384
  restoration of 149
  State of 191
  **Twelve Tribes of** 41, 65, 77, 93, **102-03**, 104, 113, 120, 215, 236, 329, 330
Israelites 33, 35, 36, 45, 49, 50, 51, 52, 54, 55, 59, 65, 67, 68, 73, 88, 94, 95, 96, 99, 101, 104, 105, 131, 132, 137, 149, 151, 152, 175, 187, 193, 203, 230, 237, 241, 245, 254, 255, 269, 329, 343, 345, 346, 395, 411, 451
Issachar 102, 104, 486, 505
*I Will Praise the Lord of Wisdom* 148, 185

# J

J 22, 27, 49
Jabbok River 299, 505
Jabesh-Gilead 120, 505
Jabin, King 106, 487
Jachin 132, 133
**Jacob** 21, 22, 26, 27, 34, 35, 36, 37, 40-41, 44, 45, 55, 75, 102, 103, 113, 136, 203, 268, 329, 486
Jael 106, 107, 487
*Jahwe* 22
Jair 104, 105
Jairus 330, 345, 487
James, brother of Jesus 314, 315, 395, 461, 487
  martyrdom 315
James, brother of John 302, 303, 329, 331, 332, 352, 386, 457, 487
  death of 279
**James, letter of** 173, 285, 315, 405, **454-55**
James, son of Alphaeus 330, 331, 487
Jamnia/Yavneh 189
Japha 321
Japheth 32, 33, 487
*Jashar, Book of* 114, 125
Jason 249, 487
jawbone 107
Jebel Musa 53
Jebus 126, 506
Jebusites 95, 115, 121, 123, 125, 126, 127
Jedidiah 130
Jehoahaz II, King 135, 145, 487
Jehoahaz, King 135, 487
Jehoash 133
Jehoiachim, King 133, 135, 487
Jehoiachin, King 135, 145, 149, 487
  release of 128
Jehonadab ben Rechab 129
Jehoram, King 135, 487
Jehoshaphat, King 88, 135, 487
Jehovah 59, 524
Jehu, King 128, 135, 487
Jephthah 104, 105, 107, 487
Jephunneh 103
jeremiad 207
Jeremiah 37, 61, 64, 127, 129, 146, 153, 155, 197, 198, 199, 203, 206, 207, 208, 209, 210, 211, 212, 227, 242, 243, 257, 324, 349, 450, 487
  **Confessions of** 206, **208-09**
  ministry of 207
  pain of 209
**Jeremiah, book of** 146, 147, 153, 174, 195, **206-07**, 208, 211, 226, 228, 291, 349
Jeremiah, letter of 233, 257
**Jericho** 18, 93, 94, **96-97**, 145, 180, 223, 290, 299, 339, 348, 363, 371, 506

Jeroboam I, King 103, 117, 128, 134, 135, 487
Jeroboam II, King 123, 135, 218, 224, 225, 487
Jerome 166, 242, 253, 259
  Latin Bible of 475
**Jerusalem** 18, 34, 37, 41, 60, 61, 64, 69, 81, 83, 84, 95, 96, 97, 99, 108, 115, 116, 121, 123, 125, **126-27**, 133, 134, 135, 137, 145, 148, 151, 153, 155, 156, 157, 158, 159, 160, 161, 162, 163, 179, 192, 200, 201, 202, 203, 204, 207, 212, 213, 214, 220, 228, 232, 233, 234, 240, 241, 242, 243, 245, 248, 249, 251, 258, 259, 265, 267, 275, **276-77**, 278, 281, 283, 286, 287, 288, 291, 292, 293, 295, 297, 298, 307, 309, 310, 311, 314, 315, 316, 318, 320, 321, 326, 327, 328, 329, 331, 332, 333, 339, 348, 349, 353, 354, 356, 357, 358, 360, 361, 363, 367, 370, 371, 372, 381, 382, 384, 385, 386, 388, 389, 390, 391, 392, 394, 395, 397, 400, 403, 410, 415, 417, 421, 431, 434, 446, 471, 472, 506
  conquest, capture of 125, 127
  destruction of 101, 126, 127, 145, 159, 210, 211, 228, 241, 293, 306, 458, 471
  fall of 103, 127, 145, 152, 189, 207, 213, 261, 288, 293, 294
  heavenly 277, 475
  new 469
  rebuilding, restoration of 205, 255
  siege of 69, 199, 275
  walls of 249
Jesse 103, 124, 487
**Jesus** (*see also* Christ) 27, 31, 76, 77, 82, 95, 97, 171, 179, 189, 197, 199, 201, 203, 205, 207, 216, 223, 231, 236, 241, 243, 264, 265, 267, 275, 276, 277, 279, 282, 287, 288, 289, 292, 293, 299, 300, 301, 302, 303, 304, 305, 306, 308, 309, 310, 313, 316, 321, 323, 324, 329, 330, 332, 333, 334, 335, 339, 342, 346, 347, 348, 350, 351, 353, 354, 355, 356, 358, 362, 367, 377, 380, 382, 383, 385, 386, 390, 391, 393, 397, 403, 408, 409, 412, 416, 418, 424, 430, 431, 432, 434, 440, 444, 448, 449, 450, 451, 454, 455, 458, 459, 463, 464, 475, 487
  actions of 336, 419
  **arrest of** 297, 307, 311, 313, **352-53**, 360, 380
  authority of 297, 336, 339, 345, 348, 412
  baptism of 267, 297, 307, 308, 309, 325, 413, 419
  **betrayal of** 297, 307, **352-53**
  birth narratives 302
  birth of 297, 306, 307, 311, 318, 319, 413
  body of 361
  burial of 313, 364
  call of 329, 386
  character of 305
  childhood of 297, 299
  conception of 318
  **death of** 67, 263, 277, 297, 300, 307, 308, 310, 312, 345, 347, 350, 353, 354, 356, 357, **358-59**, 360, 364, 380, 382, 383, 384, 389, 408, 409, 411, 419, 422, 423, 426, 431, 444, 450, 458, 466
  divinity of 343
  **entry into Jerusalem** 199, 242, 268, 312, 347, **348-49**
  **family of 314-15**, 339
  finality of 450
  final promise of 384
  great commission 307, 364
  healings of 309, 329, 334
  historical 300, 304, 308
  humanity of 413
  importance of 305

interrogation of 352, 353, 354
  is the judge 412
  journey of 310, 311, 401
  King of Israel 312, 349
  King of the Jews 355, 357, 358
  **life of** 242, 263, **297**, 304, 306, 310, 312, 319, 336, 345, 408, 422, 431, 444, 466
  **lordship of 412-13**
  **Messiah** 306, 307, 310, 314, 317, 319, 320, 325, 327, 330, 343, 344, **346-47**, 349, 383, 391
  message of 297, 304, 306, 330
  ministry of 73, 223, 241, 297, 298, 299, 300, 306, 308, 310, 311, 312, 315, 320, 321, 322, 324, 327, 328, 329, 332, 336, 347, 351, 375, 402, 431, 436, 466
  mission of 297, 336, 357, 431
  post-Resurrection appearances 364, 365
  presentation of 277, 311
  purpose of 312, 336, 359
  Resurrection appearances 381, 383
  return of 419, 442, 469
  risen 416, 418
  Son of God 308
  sufficiency of 387
  **teachings of** 205, 263, 282, 285, 297, 306, 307, 309, 314, 319, 330, 331, **332-33**, 348, 354, 355, 375, 385, 388, 407, 415, 444, 454, 455, 460, 466, 467
  **temptations of** 77, 307, 309, 311, **326-27**
  times of 304
  tomb 331, 363
  **trials of** 279, 297, 307, 311, 313, 353, **354-57**, 372
  victory of 327
  vindication of 445
  wisdom of 314
  words of 109, 419
  work of 263, 331, 450
Jesus son of Sirach 256, 488
Jethro 49, 51, 488
Jew, Jews 29, 33, 39, 49, 51, 57, 58, 67, 68, 82, 84, 112, 126, 139, 149, 153, 154, 155, 156, 157, 158, 159, 165, 166, 167, 242, 244, 246, 247, 248, 251, 254, 256, 258, 259, 261, 276, 277, 279, 280, 281, 282, 283, 285, 286, 287, 288, 289, 292, 293, 298, 306, 307, 313, 332, 333, 339, 342, 346, 347, 351, 355, 356, 358, 359, 362, 363, 370, 378, 380, 381, 384, 388, 391, 392, 393, 395, 399, 400, 402, 403, 409, 410, 411, 424, 425, 427, 430, 431, 434, 435, 451, 452, 458, 467, 470, 471, 473, 474
  Diaspora *see* Diaspora
  Orthodox 62, 85
  persecution of 216
  Roman 403
jewels, jewelry 47, 78, 99, 170, 472
Jewish life 351, 471
Jewish New Year 221, 383
**Jewish War, First** 279, 285, 290, 291, **292-93**, 391, 467
Jewish wars 471
Jewish year 282
Jezebel 113, 131, 139, 198, 488
Jezreel 198, 506
  plain of 106
Joab 125, 488
Joanna 436, 488
Joash, King 135, 488
Job 75, 171, 172, 173, 175, 208, 209, 326, 327, 454, 455, 460, 488
**Job, book of** 27, 28, 75, 169, 170, 171, **172-73**, 174, 175, 182, 185, 188, 233, 235
*Job, Testament of* 173
Joel 220, 221, 263, 471, 488
**Joel, book of** 195, **220-21**, 228, 231, 243, 260, 384, 385

Johanan 247, 488
Johanan ben Zakkai, Rabbi 391
John 302, 303, 313, 329, 331, 332, 350, 352, 353, 367, 381, 386, 395
son of Zebedee 469
**John, Gospel of** 28, 277, 291, 300, 301, 304, 305, **312-13**, 315, 317, 319, 320, 321, 325, 329, 341, 343, 345, 347, 349, 350, 353, 354, 355, 356, 357, 358, 359, 360, 361, 362, 364, 365, 375, 383, 385, 386, 413, 418, 458, 463, 465, 475
**John, letters of** 445, 454, **464-65**
**First** 405, 406, **464-65**, 467, 469
**Second** 405, **464-65**, 469
**Third** 405, 449, **464-65**, 469
John Mark 309
John of Gischala 293
John of the Cross 191
John the Apostle 469, 488
**John the Baptist** 139, 267, 278, 289, 299, 301, 310, 316, 319, **324-25**, 326, 327, 328, 329, 347, 365, 384, 399, 407, 417, 488
birth of 311
ministry of 324, 325
John the Elder 465, 469
John the Seer, of Patmos 468, 469, 470, 473
Jonah 75, 217, 230, 231, 233, 264, 488
**Jonah, book of** 178, 195, 221, 228, **230-31**, 233
Jonathan 115, 124, 125, 488
Jonathan Maccabeus 251, 259, 294, 489
Joppa 275/298, 381, 387, 506
Jordan River 72, 81, 92, 93, 94, 100, 102, 120, 141, 145, 299, 325, 506
Jordan Valley 267, 269, 324
Joseph, husband of Mary 315, 316, 318, 320, 321, 488
Joseph of Arimathea 329, 488
family of 361
**Joseph, son of Jacob** 26, 27, 41, **44-45**, 46, 52, 102, 170, 223, 259, 319, 379, 489
Joseph the Tobiad 249
Josephus 163, 207, 279, 281, 288, 289, 290, 292, 293, 294, 295, 325, 332, 333, 347, 357, 361, 385, 452, 453
Joses, brother of Jesus 314, 315, 489
Joshua 36, 70, 71, 80, 81, 83, 89, 92, 93, 95, 96, 104, 141, 175, 180, 243, 489
death of 93, 105
sermon of 93
the High Priest 155
**Joshua, book of** 70, 80, 91, **92-93**, 94, 95, 103, 104, 105, 108, 109, 128, 182, 195, 341
**Josiah, King** 69, 81, 82, 113, 117, 133, 134, 135, 137, 143, **144-45**, 151, 152, 153, 206, 207, 241, 258, 259, 489
Jotham, King 135, 200, 235, 489
journeys 21, 35, 43, 68, 70, 71, 132, 161, 381, 391, 396, 400, 410, 446
Jubal 180, 489
Jubilee 63, 524
*Jubilees, Book of* 179
**Judah** 45, 46, 81, 96, 100, 103, 111, 113, 115, 122, 125, 126, 128, 129, 132, 134, 135, 136, 137, 142, 143, 145, 148, 149, 150, 152, 153, 154, 158, 161, 162, 167, 190, 198, 199, 200, 201, 202, 207, 212, 216, 220, 221, 224, 225, 228, 229, 234, 235, 238, 240, 245, 263, 290, 489, 506
desert of 215
**kings of** 115, **134-35**, 144, 219, 227
Lion of 469
monarchy 290

rebellion of 207
tribe of 25, 102, 103, 125
**Judaism** 31, 33, 57, 66, 67, 77, 82, 110, 129, 133, 153, 158, 163, 175, 245, 247, 248, 250, 253, 255, 259, **280-81**, 282, 283, 284, 286, 288, 293, 306, 319, 324, 329, 355, 374, 391, 392, 394, 396, 413, 424, 433, 438, 450, 454, 458, 460, 461, 524
rabbinic 248
Judas Barsabas 489
Judas Iscariot 330, 331, 352, 353, 355, 357, 361, 489
Judas Maccabeus 189, 250, 259, 294, 489
Judas, son of James 330, 489
**Jude, letter of** 315, 454, **460-61**, 470
Jude or Judas, brother of Jesus 314, 315, 461
Judea 162, 254, 274, 275, 276, 278, 279, 281, 292, 293, 294, 298, 313, 320, 339, 348, 357, 369, 386, 388, 389, 392, 506
hills of 251
Judean Desert 298, 299, 324
Judean dynasty 258
judgments 24, 37, 42, 54, 55, 64, 88, 92, 104, 105, 121, 127, 134, 159, 167, 183, 197, 201, 202, 205, 207, 213, 218, 220, 221, 224, 225, 225, 228, 229, 235, 236, 238, 239, 240, 241, 261, 324, 325, 331, 333, 335, 338, 339, 356, 417, 422, 445, 451, 461, 469, 473
divine, God's 128, 134, 175, 176, 197, 206, 207, 219, 227, 234, 235, 238, 239, 263, 293, 324, 349, 379, 422, 430, 461
final 175, 257, 262, 288, 469
moral 43
seat 353
judges 70, 81, 86, 87, 88, 104, 105, 106, 107, 110, 113, 114, 119, 121, 443
minor 104, 105
righteous 220
**Judges, book of** 88, 91, 92, 94, 103, 104-07, 108, 109, 110, 111, 117, 128, 193, 195, 321
Judith 264, 489
**Judith, book of** 91, 253, **254-55**
Julian-Claudian dynasty 372
Junia 410, 437
Jupiter 276
just, the 239, 256
justice 27, 29, 33, 85, 87, 88, 89, 123, 171, 173, 174, 197, 201, 203, 205, 208, 209, 224, 226, 227, 229, 234, 250, 263, 333, 346, 422, 439, 441, 453
social 224, 225
**justification** 291, 411, 422, 425, **426-27**, 455, 524
Justinian, Emperor 53

# K

Kabbalah 77, 215, 524
Kadesh-Barnea 52, 53, 506
*kairos* 237
Keats, John 111
*kashrut* 282
*katholikos* 404
Kemosh 101
Kenites 51
tribe 106
Kenyon, K. M. 96
*Kethubim see* Writings
Khirbet *see* Qumran
Khorsabad 132
Kidron Valley 134, 179, 360, 506
kindness 223, 226, 227, 335, 375, 416
loving 25
**kingdom** 25, 236, 261, 417, 455, 473

**coming 444-45**
new 342
kingdom, divided 125, 128, 129, 134, 135, 137
kingdom of God 83, 89, 306, 307, 308, 310, 312, 319, 327, 329, 330, 331, 332, 333, 335, 336, 337, 344, 345, 346, 350, 351, 355, 357, 365, 375, 387, 433, 444, 445, 455, 461, 470, 524
kingdom of Heaven *see* kingdom of God
King, Martin Luther, Jr. 456
**kings** 24, 28, 81, 85, 98, 99, 105, 107, 113, 114, 115, 118, 119, 120, 121, 122, 123, 125, 129, **134-35**, **136-37**, 138, 144, 176, 184, 197, 198, 200, 202, 206, 218, 225, 226, 233, 237, 242, 243, 256, 263, **278-79**, 282, 319, 331, 346, 379, 383, 472
divine right of 119
**Kings, books of** 91, 114, **128-29**, 134, 135, 143, 150, 151, 176, 207, 232, 259
**First** 52, 76, 80, 91, 114, 124, **128-29**, 130, 131, 132, 134, 138, 151, 195, 341
**Second** 69, 84, 91, 101, 105, 114, 117, **128-29**, 134, 138, 143, 144, 145, 150, 151, 179, 195, 223, 225, 230
**kingship** 88, 115, 119, 121, **122-23**, 125, 246, 318
kingship, sacred 122, 123, 383, 526
kinship group 36, 37, 53, 72, 95, 102, 103, 109, 114, 115, 126, 186, 524
kinship laws 113
kinsman 110, 111
Kish 120, 166, 489
kiss 352, 361
of peace 458
knowledge 25, 26, 31, 75, 170, 184, 192, 197, 207, 217, 220, 232, 390, 439, 449, 451, 470
of heaven 453
of reality 453
of the world 453
spiritual, religious 407, 465
Koine 246
*koinonia* 417
Korah 70, 71, 177, 489, 490
*kurios* 412
Kübler-Ross, Elisabeth 211

# L

Laban 40, 41, 490
labor, laborers 29, 31, 65, 68, 283, 285, 373, 445
Lachish 98, 99, 142, 143, 146, 153, 507
Letters 153
siege of 137
ladder 41, 42, 43
lake of fire 263, 473
Lamb, lambs 203, 205, 350, 469, 473
of God 313, 325
sacrificial 469
spring 69
Lamech 32, 490
**Lamentations, book of** 127, 169, 195, 207, **210-11**
*Lamentations Rabbah* 211
lamenting, laments 176, 177, 204, 208, 210, 234, 362, 470
David's 114, 125
land, Land 37, 41, 48, 63, 64, 69, 70, 79, 86, 92, 93, 94, 95, 101, 102, 110, 111, 113, 144, 145, 153, 154, 158, 159, 176, 186, 191, 193, 198, 204, 218, 220, 224, 232, 233, 263, 282, 283, 298, 345, 395
foreign 111, 214
of milk and honey 50
landlords 283

landowner 339, 372
languages 31, 148, 171, 203, 223, 461
Aramaic 98, 216, 246, 360, 388
Greek 388
Semitic 98
Laodicea, Laodiceans 274, 399, 401, 438, 507
last days 383, 384
**Last Supper** 181, 199, 297, 309, 311, 313, **350-51**, 352, 353, 361, 365, 415, 419
last things *see* eschatology
Late Monarchy 96
Law, **law** 22, 23, 24, 25, 31, 53, 62-63, 64, 69, 84, 86, 105, 113, 128, 155, 161, 164, 165, 197, 207, 224, 243, 244, 263, 307, 322, 333, 335, 339, 339, 367, 411, 416, 423, 424, 425, 426, 427, 430, 450, 454, 455, 467, 475, 524
apodeictic 84
**biblical 84-85**
book of the law 144
casuistic 84
Code, codes 80, 81, 84, 85, 87, 123, 148
Jewish or Israelite 83, 85, 135, 159, 186, 249, 259, 277, 279, 281, 288, 289, 290, 306, 324, 355, 395, 400, 424, 431, 450, 455
levirate 111
of Moses, Mosaic law 37, 145, 245, 284, 387, 394, 401, 431, 451, 467, 525
royal 455
tablets of 21, 50, 51
laws 21, 22, 48, 49, 56, 57, 69, 70, 71, 80, 81, 85, 86, 108, 149, 189, 193, 204, 226
code of 368
cultic 62
Hittite 85
Roman 372, 402, 433, 439
scientific 28
lawcourt of God 235
lawsuits 415
lawyers 332, 333, 339, 402
laying on of hands 367, 419, 449
Lazarus 277, 311, 362, 363, 365, 437, 490
leaders 65, 70, 81, 92, 103, 104, 106, 129, 218, 225, 386, 391, 393, 395, 406, 420, 447, 448, 461
church 373, 446, 447
Jewish 345, 473
military 81, 105
religious 339
leadership 36, 71, 72, 92, 113, 118, 119, 121, 160, 232, 242, 251, 420, 437, 447, 449
pastoral 331
Leah 27, 41, 102, 103, 112, 490
learning 28, 148, 149, 164, 165
*leb* 182
Lebanon 132, 265, 507
legal rights 112, 373
legends 74, 75, 109
legendary themes 99
legislation 62, 83
leper, leprosy 67, 112, 201
lesbianism 193
*Letter of Aristeas* 259
**letters** 77, 284, 390, 391, 401, **405-07**, 410, 414, 420, 424, 428, 442, 443, 446, 450, 461, 463, 464, 468, 474
Catholic 405
Hellenistic 406, 407
paranesis, paranetic 407, 447
Levi 64, 102, 118, 150, 346, 490
tribe of 65, 103
*Levi, Testament of* 290
Leviathan 132, 265, 507
levirate law 111
Levita 189
Levites 62, 65, 67, 70, 71, 73, 93, 102, 150, 151, 163, 314, 336, 339
**Leviticus, book of** 21, 22, 37, 50, **62-63**, 64, 66, 67, 70, 72,

81, 83, 84, 111, 192, 193, 200, 205, 218, 278, 395, 455, 466
liberation 52, 166, 225, 350
liberation theology 49
liberty 205, 454
life 29, 165, 170, 171, 173, 178, 179, 182, 188, 189, 210, 211, 262, 333, 335, 377, 382, 390, 410, 412, 416, 417, 464, 467
agricultural 32
Christian 466
church 446, 447
daily (*see also* everyday life) 336
in the Spirit 416
moral 229, 466
new 29, 206, 207, 409, 413, 423
nomadic 32
religious 36, 282
risen 408
**life after death** (*see also* immortality) 173, **178-79**, 188, 189, 214, 257, 261, 288, 365
future life 417
life before death 178
life everlasting *see* eternal life
lifestyle 465
Christian 454
cosmopolitan 282
light of the world 313
lights 69, 204, 313, 396, 464, 465, 469, 471
Lilith 30
linen cloths 362
lions' den 217, 255
Lipit-Ishtar 123
literacy 165, 322
literature 99, 107
liturgical assembly 447
liturgical life 67, 80
liturgies 48, 57, 123, 177, 210, 221, 235, 306, 524
Babylonian 177
Egyptian 177
Jewish 67, 71, 112
living, Christian 464
living, the 444
Lo-Ammi 198
Lo-Ruhamah 198
locusts 220, 221, 223
Logos *see* Word
Lord of Creation 28, 412
LORD, Lord *see* God
Lord's Prayer 312, 333, 334
Lord's Supper 350, 409, 414, 415, 418, 419, 435, 524
Lord's table 419
Lot 27, 34, 38, 39, 100, 490
lots 68, 167, 230, 358
divine 64, 65
love 23, 48, 59, 71, 80, 82, 110, 129, 182, 190, 191, 219, 223, 234, 246, 267, 305, 313, 333, 339, 409, 411, 414, 415, 416, 417, 420, 425, 427, 428, 432, 437, 439, 441, 448, 451, 457, 464, 465, 466, 467, 473
Christian 414, 415
God and your neighbor 466
love-matches 186
lover 190, 193, 206
love song 25, 190-91
loyalty 245, 248, 331, 458, 473
Lucius 373
Luke 306, 310, 380, 381, 385, 386, 387, 392, 490
**Luke, Gospel of** 52, 277, 293, 297, 298, 300, 301, 302, 303, 304, 308, 309, **310-11**, 314, 315, 316, 317, 318, 319, 320, 321, 322, 324, 325, 327, 329, 330, 331, 332, 333, 334, 335, 337, 340, 343, 347, 349, 351, 353, 355, 356, 357, 358, 360, 363, 364, 365, 381, 382, 383, 413, 445, 466, 473
lust 125, 187
Luther, Martin 217, 445, 455
LXX (Greek) version *see* Septuagint
Lydda 298, 381, 507
Lydia 283, 370, 374, 433, 490
Lystra 275, 376, 381, 393, 446, 449, 507

# M

Maat 141, 185
Maccabean period 250-51, 423
Maccabean revolt 137, 175, 189, 215, 249, 250, 259, 281, 289, 292
**Maccabees** 68, 217, 247, **250-51**, 257, 258, 349
**Maccabees, books of 258-59**
  **First** 91, 250, 253, **258-59**
  **Fourth 258-59**
  **Second** 91, 163, 189, 253, **258-59**
  **Third** 253, **258-59**
Macedonia 246, 248, 369, 374, 381, 420, 433, 442, 446, 507
Machaerus 292, 294, 299
Machir 103
Machpelah, cave of 38, 103, 508
Madonna and child 315
Magdalene *see* Mary
magi *see* wise men
**magic** 148, 282, 347, 363, 376, **378-79,** 381, 429
  spells 148, 149, 379
magicians 49, 378, 379, 389
Magnificat 113, 118, 316, 317, 319
Mahershalal-hash-baz 198
Mahlon 111
Maimonides 57, 167
majesty 201, 461, 472
Malachi 155, 245, 490
**Malachi, book of** 139, 179, 195, **244-45**
Malchus 353, 490
males 30, 63, 92, 193, 285, 424
Malta 61, 508
Mamre 38, 508
Manasseh 45, 102, 103, 200, 490, 508
  half-tribe of 93
Manasseh, King 133, 134, 135, 150, 151, 490
Manasseh, Prayer of 253, 255
Mandaeans 325
manger 318, 319
Mann, Thomas 45
manna 51, 72, 92, 95, 257, 524
mantle 121, 139, 165, 319
  of prophet 119
  Torah 25
manumission 440, 441
Mara *see* Naomi
*maranatha* 445
Mara bar Serapion 357
Marathon 157
Marcion 475
Marcionite practice 419
Marcus Aurelius, Emperor 459
Marduk 122, 123, 140, 149, 156
  dragon of 148
Mari 18, 19, 105, 196
Mark 306, 331, 457, 490
**Mark, Gospel of** 300, 301, 302, 303, 304, 307, **308-09,** 310, 311, 316, 317, 325, 327, 329, 330, 331, 333, 337, 340, 343, 347, 349, 351, 353, 355, 356, 357, 358, 360, 361, 364, 365, 380, 385, 413, 455, 463, 467
**marriage** 30, 57, 81, 109, 111, 130, 160, 161, 162, 165, 178, 190, 193, 206, 218, 219, 244, 245, 282, 284, 395, 415, 418, 447, 453, 467
  arranged 373
  breakdown 218
  **in ancient Israel 186-87**
  **in New Testament times 374-75**
  mixed, intermarriage 37, 93, 111, 192, 248, 431
  remarriage 467
married couples 193
Martha 277, 436, 437, 490
martyrdom 217, 259, 359, 386, 389, 432, 459
  of Eleazar 259
martyred 200, 259, 331, 403, 459
martyrs 175, 206, 423, 456, 459, 467, 525

Mary Magdalene 359, 364, 383, 436, 490
**Mary, mother of Jesus** 67, 191, 113, 311, 314, 315, **316-17,** 318, 320, 321, 359, 375, 384, 399, 413, 436, 437, 490
Mary, sister of Jesus 315
Mary, sister of Martha 277, 436, 437, 490
**Masada** 278, 290, 291, 292, 293, **294-95,** 298, 299
*mashal* 336
*mashiach* 114, 346
Masoretes 58, 59
mass 457
Masoretic text, Hebrew 166, 221, 525
Matriarchs 34, 36, 112, 525
Mattaniah 145
Matthias 250, 258, 259, 490
Matthew, also called Levi 285, 306, 307, 329, 330, 331, 491
**Matthew, Gospel of** 52, 111, 269, 284, 298, 300, 301, 302, 304, **306-07,** 308, 309, 310, 314, 315, 316, 318, 319, 320, 321, 325, 327, 329, 330, 331, 333, 334, 335, 337, 340, 343, 349, 351, 353, 355, 356, 357, 358, 360, 361, 364, 365, 387, 413, 431, 455, 463
Matthias 331, 491
meals 283, 351, 419, 435
**measurement,** measures **78-79,** 84, 157, 371
meat 32, 268, 269, 282, 283, 376, 467
Medes 149, 156, 157, 238, 255
Media 216, 255, 508
mediator 55, 61, 64, 312, 313, 450
medicine 74, 165, 264, 452
meditation 214, 468
Mediterranean 136, 165, 274, 333, 367, 370, 377, 387, 388, 391, 398, 405, 410, 428, 440
  Sea 18, 99, 274, 298, 368, 369
  world 280, 281, 390, 402, 452
mediums 113, 121, 378, 379
Megiddo 66, 117, 123, 141, 143, 145, 508
  Battle of 106
*Megilloth* 110, 191
Melchizedek 37, 123, 451, 491
Melqart 132
Memphis 18, 247, 508
men 30, 31, 32, 41, 46, 57, 86, 87, 107, 114, 164, 182, 185, 187, 191, 192, 206, 268, 295, 342, 412, 415, 423, 436, 437
Menahem, King 135, 491
Menelaus 249
menopause 192
*menorah* 31, 64, 76, 155, 292, 525
menstruation 62, 192, 193
Merab 124, 491
merchants 79, 219, 285, 433
  life 285
mercy 48, 59, 61, 219, 221, 227, 231, 286, 307, 312, 333, 411, 422, 451, 466
mercy seat 116, 422
merkabah (Chariot) 139, 215, 391
Merneptah 47
Meshach 217, 491
Mesha, King 101
Mesopotamia 33, 34, 35, 75, 76, 106, 122, 123, 142, 148, 149, 156, 165, 171, 246, 248, 250, 275, 369, 508
  cities of 122
  religion of 140
messages 198, 199, 205, 206, 208, 209, 212, 214, 219, 224, 226, 351, 383, 464, 468
  carrying 226
  prophetic 226
messengers 24, 42, 43, 51, 109, 139, 143, 201, 217, 244, 245, 319, 371, 417, 472
**Messiah** 74, 89, 111, 114, 115, 122, 123, 125, 139, 153, 155, 201, 215, 256, 261, 263, 280, 291, 298, 305, 306, 307, 308, 310, 312, 314, 317, 318, 319, 325, 327, 328, 329, 330,

332, 342, 345, **346-47,** 349, 355, 383, 390, 391, 410, 424, 434, 458, 525
Messianic age 205, 261, 461
Messianic claims 347, 355
Messianic hope 115, 123, 155, 346
Messianic implications 357
Messianic oracles 89, 123, 177
secret Messiah 309
two messiahs 346
meteorology 470
*mezuzot* 83
Micah 24, 117, 212, 234, 235, 298, 491
**Micah, book of** 143, 195, 200, 226, **234-35,** 320
Micaiah ben Imlah 128, 196, 491
Michal 124, 491
Midian 50, 71, 508
Midianites 122, 104, 105, 106, 263
Midrash 82, 525
  Great Midrash 110
Midrashim 221, 254, 255
Miletus 274, 381, 509
milk, milk products 268, 269, 282
Milkom 101
millennium 217, 469, 525
ministers 419
**ministry** 319, 415, 421, 423, 429, 431, **448-49,** 525
  Apostle John's 399
  Christian 421
  Ezekiel's 214
  healing 332
  heavenly 383
  Paul and Barnabas' 393
  Paul's 397, 399, 403, 420, 423, 430
**miracles** 223, 297, 304, 307, 309, 312, 317, 326, 333, **342-45,** 379, 381, 385, 393, 417, 434, 525
  calming of the storm 344
  catch of fish 343
  coin in a fish's mouth 343
  feeding of the 4,000 343
  feeding of the 5,000 312, 332, 343, 344, 347, 350
  fig tree withered 343
  healings (*see also* healings) 343
  natural 343, 344
  **of Jesus** 285, **344-45**
  other catch of fish 343
  raising a widow's son at Nain 343
  raising of Jairus' daughter 343, 345
  raising of Lazarus 312
  walking on water 312, 343, 344, 345
  water into wine 312, 332, 343, 344, 375
Miriam 71, 112, 165, 491
Mishnah 109, 159, 189, 286, 322, 355, 525
mission 274, 310, 367, 371, 381, 383, 385, 386, 387, 389, 391, 403, 410, 412, 416
  Aegean 396
missionaries 389, 397, 424, 461
missionary or apostolic journeys 387, 388, 391, 397, 424
missionary work 367, 386, 387, 393, 396, 397, 410, 423, 431, 432
*Mithraeum* 377
Mithra, Mithras 377
Mizpah, Mizpeh 108, 509
*mizvot* 375
Moab 18, 57, 99, 100, 101, 110, 123, 141, 213, 225, 491, 509
  conquest by Babylon 101
  plains of 51, 81, 92
Moabites 71, 101, 104, 232
Moabitess 110
monarchy 35, 65, 81, 94, 104, 105, 108, 114, 117, 128, 133, 135, 154, 155, 158, 186, 198, 224
money 78-79, 82, 121, 133, 249, 251, 255, 279, 338, 353, 371, 421, 432, 433, 440, 441
money-changers 370
monogamy 187, 193
monotheism, monotheistic 36, 81, 82, 93, 157, 206, 225, 280, 413, 525

Montanus, Montanism 475, 525
moon god 140
  Sin 149
moons 237, 439, 469, 471
moral 192, 222
  code 225
  instruction 322
  tradition 467
morality (*see also* Ethics) 37, 56, 57, 69, 86, 93, 192, 193, 224, 226, 227, 395, 409, 414, 465, 466, 467
Mordecai 166, 167, 491
Morphology of the Folktale, The 75
**Moses** 21, 22, 24, 25, 27, 31, 34, 36, 37, 48, 49, **50-51,** 52, 53, 54, 55, 58, 59, 61, 63, 64, 65, 67, 69, 71, 72, 77, 80, 82, 83, 92, 93, 95, 107, 112, 116, 139, 141, 159, 161, 163, 177, 179, 203, 220, 223, 231, 232, 233, 259, 264, 266, 280, 302, 303, 307, 311, 319, 329, 332, 333, 343, 346, 359, 379, 383, 408, 450, 451, 460, 462, 491
  birth of 51
  blessing of 81
  death of 21, 81
  Song of 51, 81
Mot 99
mother-in-law 110
mothers 30, 35, 102, 103, 112, 113, 164, 190, 210, 251, 316, 317, 318, 360
  of Israel 113
Mount of Olives *see* Olives, Mount of
Mount, Sermon on the *see* Sermon on the mount
mountains 33, 298
mourners 284, 362, 363
mourning 29, 167, 180, 181, 210, 211
movement, Christian 386, 390
movements 391, 393, 397, 417, 435
Murabba'at 290
murder, murderers 33, 57, 86, 87, 115, 151, 193, 355, 464, 471
*mysterion* 418
mystery 28, 192, 418, 423, 428, 429
mysticism, ascetic 438
mystics 215
myths 74, 99, 108, 109, 376, 377
  mythological themes 99

# N

Nabal 103, 113, 491
Nabatean princess 278
*nabi* 196
Nabonidus 149, 154
Nabopolassar 148, 149
Naboth 113, 139, 491
Nadab 63, 491
Nadab, King 135, 491
Nahash 120, 492
Nahor 36, 40, 141, 492, 509
Nahum 238, 492
  prophecy of 239
**Nahum, book of** 143, 195, 231, **238-39,** 359
Nain 363, 509
naked, nakedness 31, 32, 192
names 30, 39, 41, 51, 126, 198, 218, 238
**names of God 58-59**
Naomi 58, 110, 111, 113, 321, 492
Naphtali 102, 104, 509
Nathan 80, 114, 115, 125, 128, 197, 226, 492
Nathanael 321, 328, 330, 492
nationalism 233
  Jewish 69, 359
nationality 233
nations 34, 35, 39, 80, 101, 119,

124, 131, 154, 164, 170, 200, 202, 225, 229, 233, 238, 262, 338, 409
  foreign 468
  holy 63, 456
  leader of 119
  states 131
**Nativity 318-19**
nature 149, 191
  forces of 344
  human *see* human nature
  laws of 342, 345
nature, human *see* human nature
Navjote 157
Nazarenes 380, 424
**Nazareth** 205, 299, 310, 314, 315, 318, **320-21,** 332, 333, 413, 509
Nazirites 24, 71, 104, 107, 321, 525
Nazis 45
Neapolis 274, 509
Nebat 134
Nebi'im *see* **Prophets**
Nebuchadnezzar I, King 149
Nebuchadnezzar II, King 137, 143, 145, 148, 149, 153, 207, 212, 216, 217, 254, 255, 379, 492
Neco, Necho II 137, 145, 492
necromancy 378
needy, the 204, 227, 385
Negev Desert 18, 99, 100, 101, 509
Nehemiah 137, 155, 156, 160, 161, 162, 163, 245, 248, 258, 492
**Nehemiah, book of** 91, 150, 160, 161, **162-63,** 169, 231, 258, 260
neighbors 57, 80, 89, 100, 224, 228, 282, 333, 339, 455, 466
neo-Darwinism 29
Nergal 140
*nephesh* 182
Nero, Emperor 78, 293, 365, 372, 373, 401, 403, 456, 459
  massacre of Christians by 468
*neshamah* 182
new age 261, 310, 346
New Year Festival 149
New Year for Trees, festival of 69
New Year's Day 180
news, good 239, 274, 300, 309, 311, 318, 343, 347, 364
Nicodemus 301, 333, 492
Nicolaitans 399
Nicolaitans 399
Nile 18, 44, 46, 159, 247, 407, 509
  delta 46, 265
  Valley 18
Nimrod 492
Nineveh 19, 33, 122, 142, 143, 156, 230, 231, 238, 255, 264, 510
  defeat of 239
  destruction of 255
Ninevites 231, 233
Nippur 19, 33
Noachide covenant 33
**Noah** 21, **32-33,** 61, 73, 98, 266, 267, 268, 461, 469, 492
Nob 64, 117, 124, 510
Nod 31
nomadic people, nomads 18, 32, 35, 69, 100, 104, 268
Northern Kingdom 22, 81, 102, 103, 128, 134, 135, 142, 145, 151, 200, 218, 219, 224, 225, 237, 333
Notre Dame de Sion, convent of 361
**Numbers, book of** 21, 22, 23, 50, 64, **70-71,** 72, 74, 81, 150, 175
**numbers** 73, **76-77,** 133
numeracy 165
Nuzi 35
Nympha 435

# O

oasis 53, 96, 97
Obadiah 128, 228, 229, 492
**Obadiah, book of** 41, 195, **228-29,** 230
obedience 32, 39, 51, 92, 93, 105,

115, 121, 153, 197, 230, 235, 243, 244, 245, 307, 316, 401, 419, 432, 443, 467
occupations 164, 283, 284, 285
Oded 150
Oedipus 51
offerings 31, 63, 64, 66, 69, 71, 83, 108, 141, 155, 163, 243, 255, 267, 423
offspring 192, 430
oil, oil-press 360, 362
old age 187
olive leaf, oil, tree, 32, 264, 265, 370, 427, 428, 431
Olives, Mount of 127, 303, 347, 348, 349, 350, 352, 360, 382, 471, 509, 510
omens 197, 377
Omri, King 129, 135, 492
*On Death and Dying* 211
Onan 192, 492
Onesimus 438, 439, 441, 493
Onesiphoros 391
Oniads 249
Onias II 249
Onias III 249
Ophrah 108
opposition 432, 442
oppressed 166, 205, 225, 229, 310, 311, 347, 466, 471
oppression 89, 179, 189, 239, 240, 298, 346
Egyptian 49
oppressors, Roman 346
oracles 64, 149, 180, 196, 198, 200, 201, 202, 204, 206, 207, 209, 212, 213, 214, 224, 225, 226, 227, 228, 229, 230, 234, 238, 239, 240, 242, 243, 470, 525
oral tradition (*see also* tradition) 109, 322
order 28, 141, 327
created 345
new heavenly 470
ordination 418, 525
orgies 458
Origen 160, 191, 459
original sin *see* sin, original
Orpah 111, 493
orphans 227
Orthodox Church 253
orthodoxy 465, 525
orthopraxy 465, 525
Osiris 141, 365, 377
ossuary 284, 359, 363
Ostia 377, 401, 402
Othniel 104, 105, 493
outcasts 311, 351, 466
outreach 386, 387, 396
overseers 49, 448
ox, oxen 205, 269

**P**

P 23, 27, 49
pagan, paganism 218, 393, 424, 442, 458, 459, 467, 525
pain 29, 31, 209, 305
palaces 97, 127, 132, 278, 294, 295, 369, 402
**Palestine** 18, 34, 35, 94, 96, 98, 99, 109, 137, 141, 142, 145, 248, 249, 250, 264, 265, 266, 267, 268, 269, 274, 278, 279, 282, 283, 285, 293, **298-99**, 304, 305, 331, 332, 336, 357, 359, 370, 371, 428, 461
palm branches, leaves 264, 265, 348, 349
Palm Sunday 242, 268
Pamphylia 393, 510
Panaetius of Rhodes 453
Pannonia 368
pantheon, Babylonian 149
deities 255
Papias 309, 469
papyrus 46, 165, 171, 265, 395, 407
**parables** 115, 301, 304, 309, 311, 312, 332, 334, **336-39**, 467, 525

alert servants 337
counting the costs 337
banquet 337
burglar 444
creditors and debtors 337
dishonest steward 337
faithful steward 337
fig tree as herald of summer 337
fig tree without figs 337
friend in need 337
Good Samaritan 97, 150, 277, 333, 336, 337, 339, 371, 467
great net 337
ground 336
hidden treasure 337
invitation to a wedding feast 337
lamp under a bushel 337
leaven 337
lost coin 337
lost sheep 332, 337
master and his servants 337
mustard seed 337
new cloth on old garment 337
new wine in old wineskins 337
of Jesus 283, 284, 298, 336, **336-39**, 444, 473
pearl of great value 337
persistent widow and unrighteous judge 337
Pharisee and the tax collector 277, 337, 339
places of honor at the feast 337
pounds 337, 444
prodigal son 338, 339, 467
rich fool 337
rich man and Lazarus 337
seedtime to harvest 337
sheep and the goats 337, 338, 339
sower 332, 336, 337
talents 337, 444
ten bridesmaids 337, 444
tenant farmers 283, 337, 339
two debtors, unforgiving servant 337
two sons 337
wheat and tares 337
wise and foolish builders 335, 337
workers in the vineyard 337
*parabole* 336
Paraclete 313, 525
paradigms 467
Paradise 358, 473, 525
*parakletos*, Paraclete 313
parallels 27, 28, 33, 35, 54, 61, 80, 82, 106, 148, 150, 171, 185, 218, 231, 263, 307, 310, 325, 327, 332, 335, 419, 431, 432, 449, 465
parallelism 177
paralysis 342
paralyzed man 345
*paranesis* 407
parchment 155, 407
parents 30, 41, 48, 50, 56, 57, 81, 164, 165, 178, 219, 257, 284, 310, 317, 322, 323, 333, 375
Parousia 444, 525
**particularism 232-33**, 525
**Passion** 275, 297, 300, 308, 312, 325, 327, 331, 349, 357, 525
historical sites of the 360-61
narratives 300, 305
Passover, festival or feast of 49, 53, 66, 68, 69, 71, 85, 92, 145, 152, 164, 176, 191, 247, 258, 259, 276, 277, 282, 283, 287, 297, 312, 313, 333, 348, 352, 353, 355, 357, 384, 408, 525
meal 350
new 311
sacrifice 351
Seder 139
past 256, 345, 444
pastoral
care 448
concern 420
Pastoral letters 405, 406, 446, 463
pastors 397, 448, 449
patience, patient 48, 172, 173, 220, 223, 259, 416, 455

Patmos 399, 468, 469, 510
Patriarchs *see* Ancestors
patronage 283, 285, 372
patrons 373, 410
**Paul** 29, 39, 181, 199, 216, 221, 247, 263, 276, 277, 279, 282, 285, 289, 309, 311, 314, 315, 323, 347, 351, 359, 363, 365, 367, 370, 373, 376, 379, 380, 381, 385, 387, 388, 389, **390-91**, 392, 393, 394, 395, 397, 398, 399, **400-01**, 403, 405, 406, 407, **408-09**, 410, 411, 412, 416, 420, 421, 423, 424, 425, 427, 428, 430, 431, 432, 435, 436, 437, 438, 439, 441, 442, 443, 445, 446, 447, 448, 449, 452, 453, 455, 457, 459, 463, 466, 467, 471, 475, 493
arrest of 381
**conversion** of 381, **390-91**, 396, 425
death of 381, 396, 446, 459, 463
**final years 400-01**
imprisonment of 367, 400
letters of 300, 314, 367, 383, 391, 395, 405, 408, 422, 424, 428, 440, 441, 445, 446, 453, 455, 463, 466, 467
message of 426, 427
ministry of 420, 425
**missionary journeys of** 371, 393, **396-97**, 446
preaching of 424
**teaching of** 375, **408-09**, 422, 423, 426
thorn in the flesh 421
visions of 391
visits to Jerusalem 395
work of 438
**Paul's Mission 396-97**
Pavement *see* **Gabbatha**
pax Deorum 458
Pax Romana 402, 403
peace 89, 105, 120, 201, 202, 205, 223, 225, 235, 248, 263, 265, 267, 278, 282, 320, 342, 345, 346, 416, 426, 430, 431, 433, 439, 454, 468
Pekah, King 135, 493
Pekahiah, King 135, 493
penance 418
penitence 69, 125
**Pentateuch** 20, **21-23**, 24, 25, 26, 34, 67, 70, 71, 83, 84, 109, 148, 159, 161, 219, 289, 462, 525
**Pentecost, festival or feast of** 68, 69, 110, 176, 221, 277, 316, 331, 367, 383, 384, **384-85**, 417, 419, 525
people of the Book 159, 474, 525
people of the land 289
peoples 37, 94, 114, 152, 155, 158, 203, 226, 228, 232, 234
dealings of God with 105
of faith 261
settled 81
sinful 207
perfection 24
Pergamum 274, 398, 510
Perpetua 459
**persecutions** 53, 177, 179, 217, 259, 279, 331, 381, 388, 392, 401, 402, 403, 421, 432, 456, **458-59**, 468, 475, 525
Persepolis 19, 156, 246
**Persia** 19, 123, **156-57**, 216, 510
king of 84
Persians 81, 156, 157, 242, 243, 248
*Pesiqta Rabbati* 207
Peter, Gospel of 301, 462
**Peter, letters of** 454
**First** 322, 323, 387, 393, 405, 431, 448, 449, **456-57**, 461, 473
**Second** 262, 405, 445, **460-61**, 462, 471
**Peter** 77, 301, 302, 303, 308, 309, 313, 328, 329, 330, 331, 332, 352, 353, 354, 364, 367, 380, 381, 384, 385, **386-87**, 389, 392, 393, 395, 396, 403, 410, 418, 434, 448, 457, 459, 460, 473, 493
death of 461
Pharaohs 24, 27, 38, 39, 47, 48, 49, 50, 52, 65, 122, 140, 145, 156, 263, 269, 379

army of 112
Pharisees 248, 251, 279, 288, 289, 311, 313, 322, 324, 329, 330, 331, 333, 335, 336, 339, 345, 353, 365, 390, 401, 452, 471, 525
pharmacology 470
Philadelphia 274, 299, 468, 473, 510
Philemon 435, 441, 493
**Philemon, letter to** 397, 401, 405, 406, **438-39**, 441
Philip 328, 330, 331, 378, 381, 386, 389, 493
mission of 367
Philip II of Macedon 157, 246
Philippi 274, 397, 432, 442, 448, 510
Philippians 432, 433
**Philippians, letter to the** 397, 401, 405, 408, 412, **432-33**, 446
Philistia 18, 123, 213, 225, 511
Philistines 52, 60, 61, 100, 102, 103, 104, 105, 107, 115, 118, 119, 121, 124, 125, 136, 141, 247, 321
temple 104, 107
women 107
Philo 247, 279, 289, 290, 357, 451, 452, 453
philosophers 452, 467
**philosophies 452-53**
Philostratus 300
Phinehas 49, 64, 289, 493
Phoebe 410, 437, 449, 493
Phoenicia 18, 123, 246, 511
Phoenicians 98, 100, 247, 370
Phrygia 381, 511
phylactery 83
physician 381
physics 452, 453
piety 113, 173, 175, 176, 279, 339, 363, 447
false 339
pigs 75, 338
pilgrimages 68, 69, 81, 116, 180, 233, 433
pilgrims 277, 349, 360, 370
Galilean 279
Jewish 400
Samaritan 279
pillar of cloud 53, 71, 73
pillar of fire 73
pillars 37, 76, 107, 108, 132
pistis 39, 409, 427
pit, the 178, 473
place, high and holy 472, 524
plagues 49, 51, 62, 71, 73, 115, 117, 125, 220, 223, 232, 265, 379
Plain, Cities of the 511
Plain, Sermon on the *see* Sermon on the Plain
**plants 264-65**
Plato, Platonic tradition 452
pleasure 453
God's 224
Pliny the Elder 289, 290, 333, 402
Pliny the Younger 458
plot 381, 391
Plutarch 377
*pneuma* 409
poems 99, 106, 190, 205, 210, 211, 239, 257, 305, 432
epic 28
poet, poetry 29, 70, 80, 172, 176, 177, 190, 198, 210, 222
love 192
poets, Greek 323
polygamy 112, 186, 193
polytheism 141, 525
Pompey 287
Pontius Pilate 275, 276, 279, 347, 353, 354, 355, 356, 357, 358, 360, 361, 372, 400
poor, the poor 69, 139, 201, 224, 225, 227, 234, 240, 257, 282, 310, 311, 317, 342, 343, 373, 385, 388, 400, 401, 417, 455
ports 274, 298, 414
Posidonius of Apamea 453
possessions 48, 63, 337, 385
Potiphar 44, 493
Potiphar's wife 44, 45
pottery 106, 283
poverty 185, 284, 373
powers 26, 49, 113, 114, 118, 119,

121, 122, 132, 137, 139, 142, 143, 144, 145, 148, 157, 172, 182, 217, 225, 238, 239, 241, 250, 256, 258, 260, 266, 269, 279, 327, 332, 342, 344, 345, 348, 357, 372, 378, 380, 382, 389, 409, 410, 411, 413, 423, 438, 444, 445, 461, 470, 473, 473
abuse of 227
divine 330, 414, 453
evil 149, 180, 429, 430
temporal 438
praise 51, 73, 92, 171, 180, 190, 191, 202, 255, 256, 311, 417, 429, 432
Prayer of Azariah 255
prayers 11, 42, 59, 67, 70, 83, 118, 161, 162, 176, 179, 208, 209, 211, 217, 222, 231, 254, 255, 277, 280, 282, 311, 332, 333, 335, 337, 352, 353, 376, 406, 407, 408, 412, 417, 429, 434, 439, 444, 445, 447, 448, 449, 455, 470
of dedication 152
prayer shawls 64
pre-rabbis 248
preachers 392
preach, preaching 233, 244, 331, 381, 389, 391, 392, 393, 395, 398, 399, 449, 475
pregnancy 192
prejudice 339, 466
present 236, 345, 410, 444, 470
pride 229, 240, 257, 420, 450
priesthood 37, 49, 62, 64, 65, 67, 73, 79, 126, 163, 165, 176, 244, 349, 448, 457
high 249
holy and royal 448, 456
Jewish 250, 293
**priests** 24, 25, 37, 42, 55, 57, 62, 63, **64-65**, 66, 67, 70, 81, 112, 114, 115, 117, 118, 119, 122, 123, 124, 132, 150, 151, 155, 159, 165, 177, 180, 193, 196, 196, 201, 218, 219, 225, 234, 240, 243, 245, 248, 255, 260, 265, 282, 314, 324, 336, 339, 346, 369, 437, 448
chief priests 339, 353, 355, 356
of Bel 255
of Isis 377
of Zeus 376
robes 264
Priscilla 285, 399, 403, 435, 436, 437, 480
prison 107, 399, 428, 432, 438, 446
prison letters 397, 401, 404, 428, 432, 446
prisoners 89, 101, 292, 355, 357, 401, 423
privilege 54, 55, 118
procreation 192, 374, 375
**procurators 278-79**, 292, 293, 372, 400
**Promised Land, entry into** 70, 72, 92, 93, **94-95**, 96, 97
Promised Land *see* Canaan
promises 34, 93, 128, 204, 205, 216, 219, 224, 225, 232, 408, 411, 425
property 57, 63, 81, 86, 87, 186, 192, 385, 457
family 110
prophecies 64, 70, 74, 128, 139, 159, 180, 197, 198, 199, 200, 201, 204, 207, 212, 214, 218, 220, 226, 230, 236, 241, 260, 297, 307, 319, 320, 321, 357, 381, 384, 415, 417, 436, 461, 468, 470
gift of 384
Messianic 74, 321
ministry of 389
spirit of 243
prophetesses 104, 107, 112, 113, 165, 167, 318, 319
**prophetic actions 198-99**, 348, 349, 351, 418
**Prophets**, Nebi'im 12, 61, 83, 91, 105, 152, 169, 179, 189, 194, **195-99**, 214, 219, 226-27, 229, 230, 232, 236, 257, 260, 262, 263, 417, 468
Former 91, 92, 104, 129, 195

Latter 195
Minor 218, 220, 230
post-exilic 155
prophets 25, 37, 42, 55, 67, 74, 80, 81, 82, 88, 95, 96, 114, 118, 119, 120, 121, 128, 134, 138, 139, 149, 153, 155, 159, 177, 180, 196, 197, 198, 200, 201, 205, 206, 209, 212, 214, 218, 220, 221, 223, 224, 225, 226, 228, 234, 238, 239, 240, 242, 243, 245, 260, 313, 319, 324, 329, 333, 335, 343, 346, 347, 349, 351, 355, 356, 383, 411, 417, 431, 448, 449, 468, 469, 470, 471, 472, 525
court 165
cultic 176, 197, 225, 226, 229
false 81, 196, 197, 473, 523
ministry of prophets 417
of God 113
school of 96, 97
suffering 207
the four hundred 128
the hundred 128, 343
prosecution 202
proselytes 283, 322, 387, 394, 424, 525
prostitutes 113, 193, 218, 414
profane 113
prostitution 198
prostitution, cultic 64, 113
Protestants 12, 256, 455
proud 240, 241, 339, 455
proverbs 74, 109, 184, 185, 188
**Proverbs, book of** 45, 110, 113, 131, 164, 169, 170, 171, **184-85**, 190, 233, 256, 455
providence 222, 327, 453, 526
psalmists 24, 176, 177
psalms 73, 124, 125, 170, 176, 177, 202, 208, 211, 230, 239, 245, 283, 435, 468, 526
Coronation Psalms 383
royal Psalms 232
**Psalms, book of** 24, 27, 28, 52, 61, 83, 88, 99, 124, 125, 126, 127, 149, 169, 170, 171, **176-77**, 178, 179, 180, 182, 183, 196, 208, 209, 231, 232, 233, 327, 341, 347, 349, 383, 412
Psalms of Lament 173, 174
Psalms of Solomon 346
Psalter 176, 177, 233, 234, 526
Psammeticus II 145
**pseudepigrapha** 462-63, 526
*psyche* 409
Ptolemais 275, 298, 511
Ptolemies 216, 248, 250
Ptolemy 137, 246, 248, 249, 259
Ptolemy III, King 249
Pul I *see* Tiglath-Pileser III
**punishment** 33, 42, 48, 55, 70, 71, **86-87**, 94, 105, 112, 115, 121, 125, 130, 139, 153, 175, 208, 209, 211, 212, 213, 219, 225, 226, 230, 235, 261, 262, 263, 342, 358, 443, 451, 453, 472
capital 356
corporal 87
eternal 339
Jerusalem's 214
Uzziah's 150
purification 66
Purim, festival or feast of 68, 166, 167, 287, 526
purity 62, 63, 64, 84, 110, 121, 133, 162, 212, 267, 335
regulations, laws 62, 152, 291, 342
ritual 212, 289
purple 370, 374
pyramids 122, 136, 368
Pythagoras 462

Q 301, 302, 307, 310
*Qaddish* 333
Qadesh 47
Qiriath Sepher 164

Qohelet 171, 188
Qos, Qaus 101
Qu'ran 45, 131
quails 51, 71, 72, 267
Quirinius 320, 493
**Qumran** 109, 255, **290-91**, 298, 346, 362

R

rabbis 25, 57, 63, 139, 163, 173, 185, 190, 191, 205, 257, 280, 281, 284, 287, 288, 289, 303, 322, 333, 336, 362, 471, 526
Rachel 27, 41, 44, 102, 103, 112, 321, 494
Rahab 306, 454, 494
rainbow 32, 33, 214, 469
rains, rainstorm 106, 445
raising the dead (*see also* miracles) 344
Ramah, Ramathaim-Zophim 119, 511
Ramesses II 47, 52, 89, 136, 406
Ramesses III 101
ransom 179, 423
rape 86, 125, 193
Ras Shamra 99
Re 141
realized eschatology 263
reason 222, 453
Rebekah 40, 41, 112, 113, 494
rebellion 43, 70, 71, 72, 95, 133, 145, 149, 207
rebirth 205, 377
Rechabites 129
reconciliation 174, 351, 359, 394, 422, 431, 439, 526
Red Sea, Reed Sea 18, 49, 51, 52, 112, 232, 267, 269, 511
crossing of 223
redeemer 111, 173, 184, 203, 469
redemption 31, 111, 121, 174, 203, 222, 332, 408, 411, 413, 422, 426, 469, 526
law of 111
Reformation 166, 253, 418, 526
Reformers 231
refuges 40, 125
cities of 70, 71, 86
Rehoboam, King 103, 127, 128, 129, 134, 135, 321, 494
relationships 21, 26, 27, 34, 35, 54, 55, 57, 60, 62, 103, 131, 149, 161, 163, 172, 190, 198, 210, 211, 219, 230, 233, 257, 333, 351, 441, 466, 467
pastoral 433
with God 263, 421, 425, 444, 450
**religion** 29, 36, 37, 72, 74, 93, 129, 134, 140, 141, 144, 154, 199, 212, 247, 261, **376-77**, 378, 408, 452, 458, 470
after the Exile 158-59
ancient 31
Babylonian 31, 149
Canaanite 99, 108, 109
Egyptian 141
Greek 251, 376
Indian 141
Jewish or **Israelite** 24, 64, 69, 81, **108-09**, 214, 232, 283, 402, 452
Mosaic 36
of the Ancestors 36-37
of the Exile 152-53
Persian 141
Phoenician 141
Roman 376
Samaritan 67
state 37
Temple-based 199
Ugaritic 99
religious practice 36, 84, 248
remnant 101, 203, 225, 526
renewal 241, 319, 384
movements 336
repair 26, 31, 33, 262, 319, 408
repent, repented 105, 324, 325, 332
repentance 25, 68, 105, 139, 150,

161, 173, 205, 207, 219, 220, 221, 223, 224, 230, 231, 233, 241, 243, 244, 245, 287, 324, 326, 329, 336, 353, 409, 467, 526
Rephaim 100, 511
rescue 88, 149, 178, 204, 343, 408, 422, 423, 426
Reshef 135, 141
resistance, nonviolent 456
respect 48, 80, 164, 187, 439, 457
response 55, 223, 238, 339
responsibilities 31, 262
rest, resting 68, 77, 81, 95
restoration 153, 161, 173, 179, 180, 201, 202, 204, 207, 213, 225, 235, 342
**Resurrection** 43, 141, 157, 173, 179, 215, 217, 231, 263, 288, 297, 300, 306, 307, 309, 310, 311, 312, 313, 330, 331, 338, 346, 349, 358, 360, 363, **364-65**, 375, 380, 381, 382, 383, 385, 386, 401, 408, 409, 411, 418, 419, 420, 422, 423, 426, 428, 429, 433, 436, 439, 455, 458, 466, 473, 526
and life 313
body 415
of the dead 400, 415
resuscitations 342
retribution 87, 189
return 154, 155, 160, 161, 213, 219
**return from Exile 154-55**
Reuben 45, 102, 494, 512
tribe of 93
Reuel *see* Jethro
reunification 199
revelation 24, 55, 51, 139, 216, 255, 260, 291, 310, 395, 417, 460, 462, 470, 473, 526
**Revelation, book of** 31, 77, 175, 261, 285, 308, 317, 399, 445, 459, **468-69**, 470, 471, 472, 473, 475
revenge 87, 113
reward 110, 179, 208, 226, 256, 257, 261, 262
rib 235
rich (*see also* wealthy) 203, 248, 257, 268, 282, 342, 414, 447
Riders of the Chariot 215
righteous 45, 178, 189, 239, 240, 254, 257, 339, 455
righteousness 32, 85, 197, 204, 226, 250, 262, 335, 411, 426, 427
Rilke, R.M. 121
**ritual** 23, 48, 62, 63, **66-67**, 70, 71, 73, 81, 83, 99, 115, 121, 164, 176, 177, 190, 197, 201, 212, 236, 285, 333, 379, 433
impurity 67
law 424
purity 64
religious, sacred 125, 429
washing 62
roads 157, 274, 298, 339, 361, 368, 371, 402, 440
robbers, robbery 83, 339, 466
rock, Rock 51, 71, 163, 386, 387, 457
rod, Aaron's 65
*roeh* 196
Roman Palestine 280, 281
Roman period 97
**Roman society 372-73**
Romans 79, 127, 211, 250, 251, 276, 278, 287, 288, 290, 291, 293, 294, 295, 298, 310, 330, 333, 339, 353, 355, 356, 365, 368, 369, 370, 371, 431, 444
authorities 357, 381, 435, 458
power 381
standards of 279
world of 284, 384, 468
**Romans, letter to** 221, 383, 397, 405, 407, 408, 409, **410-11**, 412, 413, 421, 422, 431, 437, 440, 448
**Rome** 123, 136, 229, 261, 266, 274, 279, 281, 283, 285, 289, 292, 347, 355, 363, 367, 368, 369, 372, 377, 381, 386, 387, 391, 397, 398, 400, 401, **402-03**, 410, 432, 438, 440, 446,

449, 458, 459, 467, 468, 471, 512
bishop of 403
**Christianity in 402-03**
Roman sources 359
Romero, Oscar 457
Rosh Hashanah *see* Jewish New Year
royal law 455
rule, Roman 274, 282, 284, 359
rulers 109, 112, 113, 219, 339, 410
Russian Orthodox Church 418, 456
Ruth 58, 110, 111, 113, 233, 306, 321, 494
**Ruth, book of** 91, **110-11**, 169, 230, 233

S

Sabbath 25, 56, 57, 68, 70, 72, 85, 152, 163, 217, 221, 224, 237, 247, 259, 281, 282, 333, 362, 364, 409, 439, 526
observance 37
**sacraments** 418-19, 526
**sacrifice** 31, 32, 33, 38, 39, 42, 63, 64, **66-67**, 70, 71, 89, 104, 108, 116, 119, 121, 138, 158, 159, 160, 162, 196, 197, 201, 205, 215, 218, 224, 226, 244, 245, 250, 266, 267, 268, 277, 281, 287, 291, 324, 333, 349, 351, 369, 376, 383, 422, 423, 433, 450, 451, 526
blood 60, 62, 66
human 107
illegitimate 249
sacrificial blood 265, 366
Samaritan 67
Temple 268
sacrificial duties 65
sacrificial system 67, 423
Sadducees 257, 288, 289, 322, 357, 365, 401, 524
saints 415, 429, 431, 448, 449, 456, 468
Salem *see* Jerusalem
Salome 278, 494
Salome Alexandra 251
death of 251
Salome, sister of Jesus 315
salvation 37, 93, 178, 202, 204, 205, 206, 219, 221, 229, 232, 233, 234, 235, 241, 310, 311, 313, 325, 351, 377, 381, 395, 408, 411, 412, 425, 427, 444, 445, 460, 464, 474, 526
human 416
universal 311
Samaria 18, 103, 142, 218, 235, 275, 277, 278, 279, 298, 313, 333, 367, 381, 382, 386, 388, 389, 512
Samaritans 67, 161, 311, 336, 339, 378, 431
Samaritan, good *see* Parables, good Samaritan
villages 386
Samson 24, 75, 104, 105, 107, 269, 494
*Samson Agonistes* 107
**Samuel** 80, 104, 113, 114, 115, 117, 118-19, 120, 121, 124, 136, 197, 268, 319, 321, 378, 494
**Samuel, books of 114-15**, 128, 150, 151, 176, 232, 259
**First** 61, 80, 88, 89, 91, 108, 110, 120, 121, 124, 180, 195, 317, 378
**Second** 61, 80, 91, 129, 130, 133, 151, 175, 195
Sanballat the Horonite 162, 247, 494
sanctuaries 53, 62, 64, 65, 66, 67, 70, 81, 98, 108, 109, 118, 214, 215, 218, 224, 225, 286, 383, 431, 450, 451, 526
heavenly 383
sandals 63, 65, 265, 298, 338, 407
Sanhedrin 355, 356, 357, 381, 400, 526
Sapphira 381, 385, 494

Sarah 34, 38-39, 41, 87, 112, 186, 425, 494
of Media 255
Sarai (*see also* Sarah) 38, 39
Sargon II, King 77, 132, 137, 142, 143
Sargon, legend of 51
*sarx* 408, 409
Satan 77, 151, 157, 172, 173, 174, 175, 299, 308, 326, 327, 353, 386, 429, 442, 461, 468, 469, 472, 473, 523, 526
satraps 156, 249
**Saul, King** 103, 114, 115, 117, 118, 119, **120-21**, 123, 124, 125, 129, 135, 136, 166, 197, 267, 268, 378, 494
Saul *see* Paul
Savior 201, 317, 318, 342, 346, 414, 443, 461
*Sayings of Ahiqar, The* 171
scapegoat 69, 86, 423, 458, 526
schism 129, 526
schools 29, 161, 165, 202, 322, 406, 407, 453, 462
science 29, 222, 470
scientific positivism 222
scribes 155, 159, 160, 165, 171, 177, 207, 329, 333, 335, 339, 406
Mesopotamian 77
Scriptures 8-9, 280, 288, 289, 290, 306, 308, 322, 327, 335, 341, 383, 390, 427, 468, 526
scrolls 24, 25, 129, 144, 161, 191, 379, 469, 471, 474
Festival 110
of parchment 84
sealed 473
sea 99, 230, 231, 233, 344, 345, 363, 393, 396, 400, 471, 473
heavenly 472
seafarers 377, 398
seals 98, 469
seasons 69, 99, 261, 472
seat of life 66
Second Coming 412, 443, 444, 445, 460, 526
sects 397, 435, 458
Seelim 290
seers *see* prophets
Seleucia 246, 512
Seleucid rule 137, 247, 249
Seleucids 216, 247, 250, 251, 258
Seleucus I, King 246, 249, 250
Seleucus II, King 249
Seleucus III, King 249
Seleucus IV, King 249, 250
self-control 223, 257, 375, 416
semen 62, 192
Senate, senators 372, 373
Seneca 406, 440, 453
Sennacherib, King 137, 143, 234, 494
separatism, separatists 248, 288
Sepphoris 283, 299, 321, 332, 333
**Septuagint** 12, 24, 109, 114, 115, 166, 189, 206, 247, 253, 254, 255, 256, 257, 259, 385, 412, 451, 524, 526
seraphim 42, 43, 200, 201
Serapion 462, 463
Serapis 377
Sergius Paulus 283, 379, 495
**Sermon on the Mount** 301, 307, 333, **334-35**, 454, 455, 466, 467
Sermon on the Plain 335
sermons 81, 206, 310, 450
of Joshua 93
serpent 30, 31, 71, 175
Servant of God 203
servant, servants 40, 41, 112, 113, 193, 284, 316, 339, 350, 449, 450
ministry 449
of Christ 421
Servant Songs 203
Servant, Suffering 203, 347, 527
service 54, 55, 319, 335, 401, 423, 431, 448, 468
of God 257
Seth 32, 141, 495
settlement 69, 93, 104, 105, 106, 152, 153
seven 76, 77
Seven Last Words 359
Seven, the 389

seventy, the 310, 329
**sex 192-93**, 453
sexual beings 43
sexual ethics, Christian 414, 415
sexual partners 190, 191, 192, 193
sexual relations, relationships 57, 87, 187, 192, 375, 415
sexual rites 64
**sexuality** 131, 190, 191, **192-93**
Shadrach 217, 495
Shalkim, King 135
Shallum, King 495
Shalmaneser III, King 135
Shalmaneser V, King 137, 142, 495
Shamash 149
shame 165, 210, 322, 372
Shamgar 104, 105, 495
sharing 385, 388, 414, 421, 434, 435
Shavu'ot, festival of 73
Shear-Jashub 198
Sheba 115, 125, 495, 512
Sheba, Queen of 123, 131, 495
Shechem 18, 23, 34, 81, 107, 108, 495, 512
sheep 268, 269
shekel 78, 84, 371
shelters 69, 73, 338
Shem 32, 33, 495
**Shema** 71, 81, **82-83**, 123, 280, 282, 526
Sheol 178, 179, 182, 473, 526
Shepherd, Good 313
*Shepherd of Hermas* 474
shepherd-king, shepherds 31, 225, 242, 268, 318, 319, 343
Sheshbazzar, Sanabassar 154, 495
*shibboleth* 107
Shiloh 61, 64, 81, 108, 117, 118, 513
ships 230, 371, 401, 402, 440
shipwrecks 363, 371, 391, 401
shrines 23, 61, 66, 69, 81, 109, 116, 117, 120, 132, 159, 181, 226, 243, 376
Edomite 100, 101
shroud, linen 284
*Sicarii* 289, 292, 294, 295, 353
Sicily 274
sick 342, 344, 454, 455, 466
Sidon 213, 246, 513
siege 89, 143, 199
signs 107, 120, 121, 224, 225, 305, 312, 313, 342, 345, 365, 379, 384, 418
Silas, Silvanus 433, 442, 443, 457, 495
silver 78, 79, 141, 199, 217
trumpet 181
silver, thirty pieces 243, 353
silversmiths 285, 399
Simeon 311, 317, 318, 319, 495, 513
tribe of 102
Simeon II 257
Simon, a tanner 285, 387, 495
Simon Bar-Giora 293
Simon Bar Kokhba 347
Simon, brother of Jesus 314, 315, 495
Simon Maccabeus 97, 251, 259
Simon Magus 378, 389, 495
Simon of Cyrene 358, 360, 495
Simon Peter see Peter
Simon the Zealot 289, 330, 331, 495
sin 31, 38, 48, 66, 69, 71, 86, 89, 92, 125, 134, 160, 161, 172, 174, 175, 182, 183, 212, 213, 219, 224, 234, 240, 254, 261, 329, 333, 339, 342, 345, 351, 408, 409, 411, 415, 418, 419, 422, 423, 424, 426, 427, 429, 439, 450, 451, 461, 473, 526
conviction of 413
of the people 67, 69, 450
original 31, 183, 262, 525
Sinai 18, 21, 22, 24, 34, 37, 39, 48, 49, 59, 60, 61, 69, 70, 72, 80, 95, 264
desert 52, 53
Mount 25, 34, 48, 49, 51, 52, 53, 62, 65, 70, 73, 76, 77, 231, 513
sinners 77, 289, 339, 425, 431, 455

**Sirach, book of** 160, 165, 170, 253, **256-57**, 290
Sisera 106, 495
sisters 314, 315, 454, 467
'666' 77
skills 164, 170, 368
military 164, 165
skin disease 151
skulls 96, 97, 361
slaves 39, 46, 53, 63, 72, 84, 87, 94, 203, 227, 283, 285, 322, 338, 352, 358, 359, 373, 374, 375, 402, 408, 414, 422, 423, 425, 432, 439, 440, 441, 447, 457
girl 433, 458
Jewish 441
slave-traders 370
**slavery** 48, 49, 52, 63, 68, 72, 111, 219, 232, 345, 350, 425, 439, **440-41**
sling 89
Smyrna 274, 468, 473, 513
snake 401
bronze 71
stoning 86
**society** 74, 85, 112, 285
Hellenistic 181, 281, 323, 452
**Roman 372-73**
Socrates 452
Sodom 27, 36, 37, 38, 39, 174, 193, 209, 461, 471, 513
destruction of 472
soldiers 89, 355, 358, 371, 374, 475
Roman 361, 400
*Solomon, Acts of* 129, 130
**Solomon, King** 37, 80, 103, 108, 115, 116, 123, 125, 126, 127, 128, 129, **130-31**, 132, 133, 134, 135, 151, 160, 171, 184, 185, 188, 189, 190, 191, 286, 287, 288, 462, 463, 470, 495
accession of 129
city of 277
empire of 134
prayer of 67
reign of 77, 129, 136
*soma* 409
son of David 349
Son of God 42, 76, 305, 308, 309, 312, 327, 330, 391, 413, 445, 451
Son of Man, the 182, 216, 302, 303, 308, 309, 312, 347, 348, 444, 445, 468, 469, 527
**Song of Songs, book of** 82, 131, 169, 189, **190-91**, 192, 264
Song of the Three Young Men 255
songs 22, 70, 109, 181, 198
of praise 112, 461
spiritual 435
thanksgiving 202
sons 25, 31, 32, 33, 34, 40, 41, 102, 103, 107, 110, 111, 113, 118, 121, 145, 171, 173, 207, 251, 278, 279, 311, 316, 317, 318, 338, 339, 446, 450
of Aaron 64
of Zebedee 302
older 339
younger 339
sorcerer, sorcery 149, 379
soul 30, 82, 178, 179, 182, 191, 215, 365, 377, 408, 409, 466, 527
Southern Kingdom 103, 128, 134, 135, 142, 200, 219, 225, 237
Spain 401, 410
Sparta 374
speeches 80, 171, 254, 381, 383, 385, 390, 400
impediments 342
spies 71, 92
Spirit of Christ 361
Spirit of God see Holy Spirit
Spirit of the Lord 198, 221
spirits 63, 149, 182, 365, 408, 409, 433, 465, 527
spiritual
beings 43
development 71
experience 325
forces 417, 429, 473
fruits 416
insight 414
journey 72
light 237
powers 423, 438, 473

spirituality 83, 176, 414, 438, 439
St. Catherine, Monastery of 53
St. John of the Cross 191
St. Peter's 387
stars 282, 318, 319, 377, 471, 472
state, Jewish, destruction of 206
Stations of the Cross 360
Stephen 45, 287, 356, 357, 389, 390, 496
martyrdom 381, 389, 392
stewardship, good 85
Stoicism, Stoics 407, 452, 453, 456
stoning 86, 87, 187, 355, 357, 390, 393
storm god 99
**studying the Gospels 304-05**
Succession Narrative 111
Suetonius 403, 410
Suez, Gulf of 52
**suffering** 70, 148, 171, 172, 173, **174-75**, 178, 179, 188, 189, 203, 207, 208, 209, 212, 223, 261, 297, 305, 309, 347, 420, 421, 423, 432, 433, 447, 455, 456, 457, 459, 469
of Christ 420, 421
Suffering Servant see Servant, Suffering
suicide 121
Sukkot see Tabernacles, festival or feast of
Sumer, Sumerians 122, 123, 148
culture 148
epics 148
sun god 140
Shamash 149
supernatural beings 75
supernatural events 223
superstition 458
supremacy 450
of Christ 438
Susa 19, 246, 514
Susanna 436
**Susanna, Story of 254-55**, 496
symbols 76, 133, 165, 395
symbolism 57, 67, 73, 131, 212, 348
Christian 395
pagan 395
symbolic dreams 44
symbolic language 183
symbolic significance 56
synagogue 25, 73, 133, 159, 165, 167, 189, 205, 281, 283, 288, 314, 321, 322, 323, 331, 333, 334, 345, 391, 393, 396, 399, 402, 403, 413, 434, 435, 458, 527
Jewish 442
Roman 410
Synoptic Gospels see Gospels, Synoptic
Syria 18, 35, 98, 99, 109, 141, 142, 143, 149, 153, 171, 248, 250, 275, 293, 320, 347, 359, 369, 372, 396, 465, 514
Palestine 145, 171
Syrians 198, 233

# T

**Tabernacle** 48, 49, 51, 53, 61, 65, 69, 70, 71, 73, 103, **116-17**, 132, 128, 450, 450, 527
Tabernacles, festival or feast of 68, 69, 73, 163, 176, 189, 263, 277, 283, 384, 527
Tabitha 448, 496
Table of Nations 98
Tablet of Destinies 140
tablets 35, 53, 196
clay 33, 142, 170
of stone 80
writing 323, 407
Tabor, Mount 106, 320, 333, 335, 514
Tacitus 279, 357, 362, 403
talent (see also parables) 371
Talmud 109, 115, 159, 167, 322, 527
Babylonian 57
Palestinian 333

Tamar 125, 192, 306, 496
Tarshish 230, 514
Tarsus 275, 388, 390, 392, 514
Tatian 475
tax-collectors 97, 285, 307, 311, 330, 339
taxes 134, 248, 250, 251, 283, 284, 285, 368, 403
tax, Temple 79, 277, 281, 283, 293, 370, 371
teacher, authorized 277, 348, 354, 356
teachers 24, 87, 297, 306, 313, 323, 329, 338, 348, 412, 436, 439, 448, 449
false 447, 461
Jewish 466
of the Law 355
teachings 24, 25, 81, 159, 165, 171, 225, 244, 307, 319, 350, 356, 405, 406, 417, 434, 435, 447, 449, 453, 467, 475
false 447, 461, 464, 465
**of Jesus 332-33**
Pauline 408, 467
Christian 455
Tekoa 225, 514
Tel el-Amarna 18
Temple Mount 126, 132, 179
**Temple**, temples 34, 49, 61, 64, 77, 79, 84, 105, 108, 113, **116-17**, 125, 126, 127, 131, 132, 133, 135, 137, 144, 145, 150, 151, 152, 153, 154, 156, 157, 158, 159, 160, 161, 162, 165, 176, 200, 201, 202, 204, 205, 206, 212, 213, 214, 217, 226, 232, 241, 242, 243, 245, 247, 248, 250, 259, 276, 277, 281, 282, 285, **286-87**, 288, 292, 293, 307, 309, 313, 317, 318, 319, 322, 324, 326, 327, 333, 333, 339, 348, 354, 355, 356, 357, 358, 368, 369, 376, 383, 389, 391, 398, 399, 400, 423, 431, 434, 441, 445, 458, 467, 469, 527
building of 128, 129
cleansing, purification 259, 348, 349
clearing of, by Jesus 199, 348, 349
curtain 308, 358
dedicated to gods 149, 366
dedication of 52, 67
destruction of 65, 67, 69, 127, 133, 158, 228, 445, 471
First 69, 130, 132, 133, 215, 287
guard 353
in Ephesus 398
in Rome 402
Jerusalem 61, 64, 65, 76, 250, 279, 298, 369, 445, 470
living 291
new 215
**of Solomon** 76, 115, 117, 127, **132-33**, 215, 265
offerings 221
Phoenician 132
rebuilding, (restoration) 81, 137, 144, 145, 154, 159, 204, 242, 243, 258, 259
rebuilt 260
rededication 68, 69
Scroll 359
Second 23, 63, 69, 73, 127, 153, 155, 244, 286, 287
tradition 163
treasury 279
worship 25, 150, 181, 202, 206, 229, 264, 265
Temple Vision 200-01, 214
temptation 175, 326, 327, 429, 451, 473, 527
**temptations of Jesus 326-27**
**Ten Commandments** 21, 48, 49, 51, 53, **56-57**, 60, 76, 80, 81, 82, 84, 85, 138, 139, 332
tent of meeting 53, 108, 116, 286
ten plagues 49
Terah 36, 141, 496
teraphim 127, 527
Tertullian 401
test 38, 39, 121, 326

testing 28, 77, 175, 297, 333, 386
texts 9
Mari 105
Ugaritic 99
Thaddeus 330, 331, 496
thankfulness, thanksgiving 66, 69, 73, 115, 174, 230, 286, 311, 342, 350, 406, 409, 433, 439
Thebes 239, 514
theodicy 172, 174-75, 527
Babylonian 185
Theodotion 254
theology 71, 80, 202, 222, 257, 389, 410, 468, 527
Pauline 408, 463
theophany 48, 49, 53
Theophilus 310, 311, 381, 496
Thessalonians 443, 471
**Thessalonians, letters to the 442-43**
**First** 405, 409, **442-43**, 446
**Second** 405, **442-43**, 445, 446
Thessalonica 274, 442, 443, 514
Theudas 347
Thomas 301, 331, 364, 496
*Thomas, Gospel of* 300, 301
thorn in the flesh 421
thorns, crown of 355, 358
Thucydides 385
thummim 64, 65
Thyatira 274, 370, 514
Tiberias 277, 283, 299, 332, 333, 340, 364, 514
Tiberius Alexander 279, 372, 373, 496
Tiglath-Pileser III, King 103, 137, 142, 218, 496
Tigris River 18, 19, 142, 148, 514
**time** 77, **236-37**, 262
Timnah 101, 514
Timothy 323, 438, 443, 446, 496
**Timothy, letters to 446-47**
**First** 383, 405, 406, 436, 446-47
**Second** 405, 406, **446-47**
Tishri 237
tithe, second 277
tithes, tithing 64, 245, 289
Titus 395, 446, 496
Titus, Emperor 276, 292, 293, 373
Arch 292
**Titus, letter to** 405, 406, **446-47**
Tobiads 249
Tobiah the Ammonite 162, 496
Tobias 42, 255, 496
Tobit 254, 255, 496
**Tobit, book of** 91, 253, **254-55**, 290
Tola 104, 105
*Toledoth Jeshu* 357
tombs 35, 46, 78, 101, 134, 203, 284, 291, 295, 361, 363, 364, 386, 469
empty 309, 329, 365
of Zechariah 179
tongues 384, 385, 415, 417, 455, 527
speaking in 197, 387, 417, 435, 436, 527
**Torah** 21, 22, 23, **24-25**, 31, 33, 39, 51, 57, 62, 64, 72, 83, 84, 86, 109, 133, 155, 159, 161, 163, 164, 165, 167, 170, 183, 185, 189, 196, 197, 200, 226, 227, 245, 246, 248, 251, 256, 258, 259, 260, 261, 280, 281, 282, 288, 289, 292, 293, 332, 333, 354, 356, 367, 394, 395, 401, 424, 426, 430, 527
'613 commandments of' 33, 62, 235
Oral Torah 25, 109, 159, 288
prohibitions of 33
scrolls 83, 282
*she be'al peh* 109, 288
*Torat Kohanim* 63
torture 441, 459, 473
**trade** 18, 78, 247, 284, 285, 298, **370-71**
routes 34, 267, 398
tradition
Christian 176, 231, 320, 330
Jewish 23, 25, 39, 43, 57, 67, 73, 99, 109, 131, 139, 163, 164, 167, 176, 200, 205, 232, 462

Trajan, Emperor 368, 369, 398, 458
transcendent, transcendence 202, 333
Transfiguration 119, 302, 309, 311, 330, 383, 386, 527
trans-Jordanian tribes 93
**travel 370-71**, 411, 415, 446
travel narrative 310, 311
treason, high treason 224, 359
Tree of Life 25, 31
tree of the knowledge of good and evil 30, 31
Tree of Truth 31
**trial of Jesus 354-55**
trials 255, 337, 361, 400, 401, 455, 456
tribe 23, 34, 41, 45, 48, 70, 77, 93, 95, 102, 103, 104, 113, 118, 119, 120, 121, 124, 125, 126, 129, 131, 134, 138, 184, 236, 390, 527
northern 125, 129
tribute 104, 133, 142, 143, 149, 200, 248, 249
Trinity 76, 413, 527
Troas 274, 419, 515
Trumpets, festival or feast of 68
trust 49, 60, 127, 164, 202, 219, 223, 257, 327, 378, 409, 467
in God 331
truth(s) 29, 36, 141, 222, 258, 312, 313, 345, 418, 448, 449, 452, 453, 457, 464, 465, 468, 473
Trypho 251
Turkey 122, 142, 387, 389, 424, 438
Twelve *see* disciples, the twelve
Twelve Tribes *see* tribes
Tychicus 438, 496
Tyre 18, 130, 132, 213, 225, 246, 275, 332, 515
*tzedaqah* 204
*tzitzit* 71

## U

Ugarit 18, 99
unclean 63, 201, 268, 333, 522
food 387
people 387
underworld 99, 183, 472, 473
unfaithfulness *see* infidelity
**unity** 103, 417, 429, **430-31**, 432, 467
**universalism** 230, **232-33**, 239, 244, 311, 527
conditional 233
universality 381
universe 28, 29, 233, 262, 345
unleavened bread 107, 283
Unleavened Bread, festival or feast of 68, 69
upper room 350
Ur 19, 34, 35, 38, 153, 515
Urartu 142
Uriah 125, 153, 187, 193, 496
Uriel 261
urim 64, 65
Uruk, Erech 19, 33
Utnapishtim 33
Uzzah 63, 497
Uzziah, King 135, 151, 200, 225, 255, 497

## V

Valerius Gratus 279
Valley of Bones 214
vanity of vanities 188
Varus 321
Vashti, Queen 167, 497
vengeance 41, 221, 238
Vespasian, Emperor 293, 373, 402
Via Dolorosa 360, 401
victories 27, 92, 112, 120, 176, 180, 201, 224, 228, 238, 263, 265, 291, 332, 408, 423, 429, 439, 464, 473

divine 263
vindication 173, 220, 263
vines 129, 264, 265, 351, 471
vineyard 79, 139, 339
violence 71, 107, 203, 212, 230, 333, 335
virgin 87, 125, 193, 315, 316, 319, 413
birth 314, 316, 319, 413
virginity 107
Virgin Mary *see* Mary
virtues 40, 41, 55, 212, 375, 407, 453, 455
visionary state, experiences 212, 327, 391, 438
**visions** 24, 29, 105, 127, 138, 153, 159, 200, 201, 205, 212, 213, 214, 215, 216, 217, 220, 224, 225, 226, 235, 242, 243, 245, 260, 302, 332, 347, 367, 381, 387, 390, 391, 401, 468, 469, 470, 471
Daniel's 260, 468
**of Ezekiel** 155, **214-15**
Jacob's 42, 43
vows 70, 107
baptismal 419
Vulgate 166, 253, 256, 257, 527

## W

**war** 81, **88-89**, 104, 164, 201, 232, 241, 250, 263, 269, 469
civil 125, 143, 468
washing of feet 350, 432,, 449
watchman 239
water, waters 32, 33, 40, 49, 51, 95, 106, 112, 126, 127, 319, 338, 368, 375, 451, 461, 471, 472
holy 418
Way of the Sea 145
Way, the 279, 380, 527
followers of 393
way, truth, and life 313
weaknesses, human 413, 420, 450
weak, the 204, 227, 240
wealth 78, 120, 123, 131, 185, 188, 227, 241, 269, 285, 311, 333, 372, 373, 385
wealthy 205, 282, 284, 373
weapons 35, 88, 89
weddings 180, 187, 255, 283, 285, 344, 374, 418
Weeks, festival or feast of *see* Pentecost
weights 78, 84, 157
wells 40, 112, 180
West Bank 96
Western Wall 64, 83, 127, 158, 276, 277, 286
whore 185, 206
wicked 88, 174, 175, 178, 189, 203, 205, 208, 209, 229, 239, 260, 261, 262, 473
wickedness 32, 119, 175
widows 110, 111, 113, 138, 139, 187, 227, 251, 255, 385, 388, 389, 447
wife, wives 32, 33, 37, 40, 41, 55, 57, 71, 87, 98, 103, 112, 113, 130, 160, 161, 163, 172, 186, 193, 206, 207, 213, 218, 251, 278, 284, 318, 323, 375, 386, 387, 414, 457
barren 35, 107
good 188
Pilate's 355, 357
Uriah's *see* Bathsheba
**wilderness** 21, 25, 42, 48, 51, 53, 62, 63, 65, 69, 70, 71, **72-73**, 77, 80, 81, 86, 95, 129, 132, 133, 139, 202, 203, 227, 250, 257, 297, 311, 324, 326, 327, 343, 383, 396, 527
wine 47, 67, 78, 129, 199, 264, 283, 350, 351, 375, 419, 453
harvest 69
making 32
**Wisdom**, wisdom 24, 27, 28, 31, 74, 76, 85, 97, 123, 130, 131, 165, 166, **170-71**, 172, 184,

185, 187, 188, 189, 224, **256-57**, 259, 333, 335, 379, 413, 414, 417, 439, 449, 452, 455, 463, 467, 470, 527
**book of** 169, 170, 179, 253, **256-57**
**literature**, books 12, 25, 27, 84, 148, 168, **169-93**, 184, 233, **256-57**, 527
of Amenemope 171
of Ben Sira 25, 256
of Solomon 131, 256, 452
tradition 188, 455
wise men 264, 265, 306, 318, 319, 524
wise women 119, 121, 378, 379
witchcraft, witches 378, 473
witnesses, witnessing 311, 319, 330, 365, 381, 382, 449, 454, 462, 467
wizards 378
woes 239, 335
**women** 29, 30, 31, 32, 40, 46, 57, 86, 107, 111, **112-13**, 124, 162, 165, 170, 186, 187, 190, 191, 192, 193, 255, 257, 295, 306, 311, 317, 328, 329, 331, 342, 353, 359, 364, 373, 374, 378, 379, 388, 415, 433, 436, 437, 445, 447, 466
Jewish 375
**ministry of** 431, **436-37**
of Jerusalem 190
pregnant 113
role of 431, **436-37**, 447
tombs 291
Word, the 312, 313, 413, 454, 525
Word of God 6, 7-8
words of institution 351
works 46, 81, 188, 189, 203, 281, 282, 285, 383, 397, 427, 443, 454, 475
good 110, 455
manual 285
world 26, 28, 31, 55, 74, 75, 88, 109, 116, 122, 156, 171, 178, 183, 184, 189, 200, 222, 228, 231, 232, 239, 240, 241, 256, 310, 312, 313, 332, 333, 355, 364, 380, 381, 408, 413, 423, 443, 444, 451, 464, 470, 471
seven wonders of 399
symbolic 467
to come 416
worship 27, 36, 42, 48, 49, 51, 57, 65, 81, 86, 105, 106, 108, 109, 115, 116, 123, 131, 134, 138, 141, 149, 150, 151, 152, 156, 158, 159, 161, 163, 176, 180, 181, 182, 199, 202, 206, 207, 209, 212, 215, 224, 225, 227, 233, 245, 255, 263, 286, 287, 333, 388, 389, 403, 407, 408, 415, 416, 417, 431, 432, 433, 434, 445, 447, 451, 457, 458, 467, 472, 475
ancestor 96
Christian 414, 415
dishonest 263
false 267, 219
heavenly 291
idolatrous 206, 415
of angels 438
pagan 376
public 342
sacrificial 450
writing on the wall 217
Writings, *Kethubim* 25, 83, 166, 169, 189, 190, 194, 195, 211, 216
wrongdoing, wrongdoers 32, 48, 172, 178, 422

## X

*xenolalia* 385
xenophobia 228, 239
Xenophon 301
Xerxes I, King 137, 157, 161, 479

## Y

Yahweh *see* YHWH
Yam 99
Yasna 157
*yezer* 183
YHW 247
YHWH 22, 36, 37, 51, 57, 58, 59, 61, 71, 80, 82, 93, 105, 106, 107, 109, 116, 138, 141, 145, 149, 151, 163, 176, 199, 201, 202, 203, 206, 219, 229, 233, 239, 383, 527
yoke 83, 199, 424
Yom Kippur *see* Day of Atonement

## Z

Zacchaeus 97, 264, 497, 497
Zadok 64, 65, 114, 160, 251, 288, 497
Zadokites 64, 65
Zealots 288, 289, 292, 293, 527
Zebedee 279, 313, 497
Zebulun 102, 103, 497, 515
Zechariah 155, 158, 179, 199, 242, 243, 311, 316, 324, 407, 497
**Zechariah, book of** 55, 175, 195, 227, 232, 233, **242-43**, 260, 349, 470, 471
Zechariah, King 135, 497
Zedekiah, King 133, 135, 145, 149, 198, 207, 497
Zeira, Rabbi 110
Zelophehad, daughters of 70, 71
Zeno of Citium 453
Zephaniah 240, 241, 497
**Zephaniah, book of** 143, 195, **240-41**, 263
Zerubbabel 137, 154, 161, 162, 242, 243, 258, 259, 287, 497
Zeus 250, 376
ziggurats 34, 75, 149
Zilpah 102, 103
Zion 126, 127, 202, 232, 261, 316, 527
Zion, Mount 152, 249, 277, 515, 527
Zophar 172, 173
Zoroaster, Zoroastrianism 141, 157

## INDEX OF FEATURED ARTISTS

*in page order:*
Albert Herbert 1
Tamas Galambos 2l
Kathy Baxter 2r
Fra Angelico 3c
Dina Bellotti 5 bc
Henry Moore 8 tr
Antonio Ciseri 9
Albrecht Dürer 11
Mathias Grünewald 28
Lucas Cranach 30
Tamas Galambos 32
Jacopo Bassano, school of 35
William Blake 40
Bartolome Esteban Murillo 41
Hans Memling 42
Francesco di Giovanni Botticini 43-43
Gustave Moreau 43
Tamas Galambos 56
John Martin (after) 58
Sébastien Bourdon 60
Tamas Galambos 74-75
Briton Riviere 77
Rembrandt 80
Salomon Alexander Hart 84
Dora Holzhandler 85
William Holman Hunt 86
H. Melville (after; engraved by R. Staines) 87

Nicolas Poussin 88-89
Jean Fouquet 93
Michael Rothenstein 94
Gustave Doré 106
Simeon Solomon 110
Bartolomé Esteban Murillo 112
John Singleton Copley 118
Otto Dix 120
Francken (Frans the Elder) 123
Francisco Goya 152
Georges de la Tour 173
Simone Martini 181
Edward A. Armitage 180-81
Albrecht Dürer 182
Leonardo da Vinci 183
Brueghel (Pieter the Younger) 184
Rembrandt 186bl
Horace Vernet 186cr
Nicola Pellipario 187
Steenwyck 188
Marc Chagall 190
Wolfgang Krodel 193
Mathias Grünewald 200
Julius Schnorr von Carolsfeld 208
J.B. Pratt 216
Michelangelo 220
Juan de Borgoña 224
Albert Herbert 230
R.T. Bayne 233
André Beauveveu 234
John Martin 238
John Martin 240
David Algranati 242
Gustave Doré 250
Domenichino 252-53
Artemisia Gentileschi 254
Gustave Doré 258
Duccio di Buoninsegna 272
Lucas Cranach 278
Priechenfried Alois 280
Marc Chagall 281
Dora Holzhandler 283
Mané-Katz 287
Domenico Morelli 296-97
Albrecht Dürer 304
Sir John Everett Millais 314
Georges de la Tour 315
Henry Moore 317
Kathy Baxter 318
J. Wolff 319
William Holman Hunt 322cr
Dora Holzhandler 322bl
J.A. Lecomte de Nouy 323tr
Duccio di Buoninsegna 328
Consadori 330
Albrecht Dürer 333
Fra Angelico 334
S. Labo 342
Giorgio de Chirico 344
Dina Bellotti 348
Leonardo da Vinci 350
Giotto di Bondone 352
Gerrit van Honthorst 354
Antonio Ciseri 356
N. Nikolai 357
Alberto Viani 358
Tsuguharu (Léonard) Foujita 359
Maurice Denis 362
Caravaggio 365
James Tissot 372
Dora Holzhandler 374
J.M.W. Turner 378
Liberale da Verona 378
F. Cayley Robinson 379
Raphael 396
Graham Sutherland 412
Cretan 412
Theodor Werner 420
Georgia O'Keeffe 422
Norman Rockwell 430
Ford Madox Brown 432
William Blake 437
Georges Rouault 438
Marco Comirato 440
Fra Angelico 442
Tommaso Masolino 448
Caravaggio 453
Michelangelo 459
Pablo Picasso 460
Sister Theresa Margaret 468
Hieronymus Bosch 472
Luca Signorelli 473

# ACKNOWLEDGMENTS

## A GUIDE TO THE BIBLE

When you arrive on vacation in an unfamiliar city, it is useful to have a guidebook to tell you how to get around and what you can expect to see. *The Complete Bible Handbook* is a guide of that kind. The Bible is not a single book but a collection of many books of very different kinds and dates. This *Handbook* will give you initial guidance to help you to find your way around and to know what you can expect to find. But it can only take you to the door. You then have to go inside and look at things for yourself.

The *Handbook* was written to include different points of view and different understandings of the books of the Bible and of what is in them. Jews as well as Christians are divided on these matters. Original drafts were prepared by a team of contributors and were then reviewed by me and at least three different consultants, who represented not only the highest levels of scholarship but also the differences that exist among Jewish and Christian communities about the status and interpretation of the Bible. As far as possible, the different points of view were incorporated, even though I have sometimes had to put them side by side as alternatives. The final text was written by myself, and no one else should be held responsible for it. It proved to be an immensely complicated task, and I am grateful to the contributors for their work, to the Consultant Editors and Consultants for their willingness to give so much time and knowledge to this work, and to the staff at Dorling Kindersley for their skill.

Above all, the thanks of all of us go to Peter Jones and Susannah Steel who, with the assistance of Caroline Hunt and Julie Oughton, did the unbelievably difficult work of editing this book, to the designers, to Luci Collings and Claire Legemah, the team managers, and to Sean Moore, from whom the initiative for this book came.

The thanks of all of us, but especially of myself, go to Margaret Bowker. In my uncertain state of health, I could not take on a work of this kind, but she made it possible by undertaking much of the work involved – especially by coping with the mountains of paper that revisions of revisions of drafts involved. She is the true author of this book. Finally, this book is in itself a thanksgiving to the One whose words these are: "The grass withers, the flower fades; but the word of our God will stand for ever" (Isaiah 40:8).

**John Bowker**

**Dorling Kindersley would like to thank:**
all their Consultant Editors and Consultants for their time and patience The Reverend Professor John Barton, Professor James D. G. Dunn, Rabbi Professor Jonathan Magonet, The Reverend Professor C.F.D. Moule, The Reverend Father Henry Wansbrough, Dr. Claude-Bernard Costecalde, and Donald C. Kraus (Executive Editor Bibles, Oxford University Press).

**Additional Editorial Assistance:**
AD Publishing Services Ltd (Index and Reference Section; with special thanks to Annette Reynolds), Janice Anderson, Jo Bicknell, Penny Boshoff, Nicola Bull, Gwen Edmonds, Elrose Hunter, Janice Lacock (proof-reading), David Pickering, Jane Sarluis, Laura Strevens, Derek Williams.

**Additional Design Assistance:**
Ngaio Ballard, Helen Cruse, Janice English, Sasha Howard.

# PICTURE CREDITS

*Abbreviations: t=top; b=bottom; c=center; l=left; r=right; ph.=photographer*

**Dorling Kindersley would like to thank the following for their kind permission to reproduce their photographs:**

Graphische Sammlung Albertina: 11 b.

AKG, London: 106, 122 cr, 127 t, 170 r, 172, 174, 175, 180 c, 181 cl, 186 bl, 198, 208, 228, 256, 293 t, 453 tc, 473; Birmingham City Museum and Art Gallery – 322 tr;

Erich Lessing – 44, 67 tl, 136 tc, 137 bl, 149 tl, 149 cr, 154 bl, 157 tl, 186 cr, 277 tl, 284 bl, 290 c, 292 b, 293 c, 315, 379 cr, 380, 440 cr, 462 bl; Erich Lessing / Kunsthistorisches Museum – 193 br; Erich Lessing / New York Jewish Museum – 104; Hilbich – 402 bl.

Ancient Art & Architecture Collection: 38, 53 tr, 53 tl, 64 bl, 141 br, 168–169, 197, 250 bl, 258, 267 br, 285 tl, 290 cl, 408; Ronald Sheridan – 31, 33 br, 143 tl, 272 c, 373 tl.

Andes Press Agency: Carlos Reyes-Manzo – 316, 387, 464.

Ardea, London: 16 bl, 52 cr.

Artothek / Blauel Gnamm, München, Arte Pinakothek: 304 bl, 304 br.

A.S.A.P.: 16 br, 113 tl; Aliza Auerbach – 72 bl; Bouky Boaz – 95 tr; Eitan Simanor – 145, 167; Eyal Bartov – 67 br; Garo Nalbandian – 97 cl, 320 bl; Israel Talby – 68 c; Joel Fisham – 68 cr; Lev Barodulin – 476–477; Shai Ginott – 273 tr, 341 tc.

shmolean Museum, Oxford: 164 cr.

ildarchiv Preussischer Kulturbesitz / Klaus Goken: 148.

Daniel Blatt: 66 l, 68 bl, 69 tl, 9 br, 100 cr, 108, 117 cl, 117 br, 251 tl, 69 tl, 423.

The Bodleian Library / Oxford Ms. Douce: 13; fol.187 v – 102 br.

ridgeman Art Library: 312 bl, 368 b, 77 bl, 377 tr, 399 t; Akademie der Bildenden unste, Vienna – 472; Architectural Museum, stanbul – 248 tl; Bible Society, London – 74 br, 474 bl; Biblioteca Medicea aurenziana, Florence / A.S.A.P. – 160; ibliotheque Nationale, Paris / Giraudon – 3, 234, 390; Bonham's, London – 216, 80 bl; Brancacci Chapel, Santa Maria del armine, Florence – 448; British Library, ondon – 7, 40, 50, 130, 150, 193 tl, 260, 75; British Museum, London – 137 tr, 06 cr; Cappella Paolina, Vatican – 459 tl; hristie's Images, London – 84 c, 184, 359; ourtauld Institute Galleries, University London – 30; Dahlem Staatliche emäldegalerie, Berlin – 80; Ephesus useum, Turkey – 399 br; Fitzwilliam useum, University of Cambridge – 378 bc, 59 bl; Galleria degli Uffizi, Florence – 2–43, 254; Galleria dell'Accademia, enice – 183; Giraudon, Paris 136 cr; uildhall Art Gallery, Corporation of ondon – 77 tc, 180–181 b, 323 t; ermitage, St Petersburg – 41, 88–89 c; ouvre, Paris – 85 tl, 144 br, 377 tl; utherhalle, Wittenberg – 56; Maguar emzett Galeria, Budapest – 74–75; anchester City Art Galleries – 432; usée Condé, Chantilly / Giraudon – 444; usée Départemental des Vosges, France – 73; Musée Gustave Moreau, Paris – 43 br; useo Archeologico Nazionale, Naples – 58 cr; Museo Archeologico Nazionale, aples – 373 tr; Museo Catedralicio, uenca – 224; Museo Correr, Venice – 87 br; Museo e Gallerie Nazionali di apodimonte, Naples – 323 bl; Noortman ondon) Ltd. – 123 br; O'Shea Gallery, ondon – 249 tl; Palazzo Ducale, Mantua 379 tc; Partridge Fine Arts, London – 41 bl; Petit Palais, Geneva – 287 tc; ado, Madrid – 112 bl; Private Collection – bl, 2 br, 23, 32, 48, 62, 77 br, 85 tr, 10, 120, 132 tl, 318, 440 bl; Santa Maria elle Grazie, Milan – 350–351; Sculthorpe hurch, Norfolk – 233; Sheffield City Art alleries – 94 l; Siena Cathedral – 272 bl, 28; Tretyakov Gallery, Moscow – 357; niversity of Liverpool Art Gallery and ollections – 413; Unterlinden Museum, olmar, France – 28, 200; Valley of the ueens, Thebes, Egypt – 140 c; Vatican useums and Galleries, Rome – 220, 452 tc;

by courtesy of the Board of Trustees of the Victoria & Albert Museum, London – 196, 238, 396, 437 tl; Villa dei Misteri, Pompeii – 374 tl; Wadsworth Atheneum, Hartford, Conneticut – 278 tr; Wallace Collection, London – 42 c; Marc Chagall *The Synagogue* 1917 oil on cardboard Private Collection / ADAGP, Paris and DACS, London 1998 – 281 tr; Maurice Denis *The Raising of Lazarus* (detail) 1919 Private Collection / ADAGP, Paris and DACS, London 1998 – 362 cl; Dora Holzhandler *Passover Feast* Rona Gallery, London – 283 b; Dora Holzhandler *The Rabbi Teaching* 322 bl; Dora Holzhandler *Wedding Couple with Flowery Canopy* Rona Gallery, London – 374 b; Henry Moore *Madonna and Child* reproduced by permission of the Henry Moore Foundation – 8 tr, 317; Georgia O'Keeffe *Black Cross, New Mexico* Art Institute of Chicago / ARS, New York and DACS, London 1998 – 422; Picasso *Guernica* Museo National Centro de Arte Reina Sofia, Madrid / Succession Picasso, Paris and DACS 1998 – 460; George Roualt *The Holy Face* Galerie Daniel Malingue / ADAGP, Paris and DACS, London 1998 – 438; Graham Sutherland *Christ in Glory* Coventry Cathedral, Warwickshire / PRO LITTERIS, Zurich and DACS, London 1998 – 412.

British Library, London: 267 cl, 300, 463 l.

British Museum, London: 47 tr, 47 br, 79 br, 88 l, 89 tl, 135 tl, 137 tl; 143 tr, 153, 157 cr, 171 tl, 192 bl, 246, 290 cr, 293 br, 331 b, 403 tr, 407 tl, bl.

By permission of the Syndics of Cambridge University Library, U.L.MS.L1.10 ff.2v, 12v, 21v and 31v: 306, 308, 310, 312.

Circa Photo Library: 273 c, 346, 436–437; William Holtby – 446.

Bruce Coleman Ltd.: Wayne Lankinen – 266–267 b; Antonio Manzanales – 266 cr; Kim Taylor – 272 br, 416.

Convent of the Holy Name / Sister Theresa Margaret, ph. Jake Matchett: 468.

Corbis: 457 bl; Bettman – 456 bc; Dave Bartruff – 11 t, 305.

John and Kathleen Court: 382.

C.M. Dixon: 321 br, 371 c.

Dover Publications Inc.: *The Complete Engravings, Etchings and Drypoints of Albrecht Dürer* ed. Walter L. Strauss, fig. 42 – 182 b; *The New Testament – A Pictorial Archive from 19th Century Sources* ed. Don Rice, figs. 272, 135, 115, 283, 297 – 394 bl, 407 tr, 434 cr, 436 c, 459 tr.

Private Collection, courtesy of England &

Co. Gallery, London: Albert Herbert *St George and the Dragon, Jonah in the Whale and The House of God* 1990–1991 oil on wood 26 x 8 ½ inches: 1, 230 (detail).

E.T. Archive: 20–21, 138, 264–265 b, 268 br; Biblioteca dell'Escorial, Spain – 192 c; Biblioteca Marciana, Venice – 43 tc; Bibliothèque Nationale, Paris – 22; British Library – 176; Egyptian Museum, Cairo – 86–87 b; Palatine Library, Parma – 301; Galleria degli Uffizi, Florence – 453 bc.

Mary Evans Picture Library: 33 l, 58, 86 tr, 103 tr, 314, 338–339, 379 bl, 441 br.

Werner Forman Archive: 244.

Germanisches Nationalmuseum, Nurnberg, Echternacher Evangeliar, fol. 20 r: 326.

Glasgow Museums: 69 bl.

The Granger Collection, New York / Marc Chagall *Song of Songs* / ADAGP, Paris and DACS, London 1998: 190 c.

Grand Lodge Library and Museum Charitable Trust, Freemasons' Hall, London WC2: 76 cr.

Graphische Sammlung Albertina, Wien: 333.

Sonia Halliday Photographs: 3 bl, 10, 54, 178, 199, 206, 212, 236, 250 br, 267 tr, 279, 282 bl, 282 tc, 283 cr, 291 br, 298 cl, 298 bc, 299 tr, 340 bl, 349, 360 c, 363 cr, 369 t, 369 b, 372, 376 c, 389 b, 391, 392, 398 br, 398 bl, 402 br, 496–513 478–495; Barry Searle – 147 cr, 180 bl, 295 bc; FHC Birch – 292 cl, 370 cr; Laura Lushington – 17 br, 43 tl, 87 br, 166, 266 bl, 268 cl, 276, 291 cl, 294, 299 cr, 327, 336, 364.

Robert Harding Picture Library: 86 c, 122 bl, 126 tl, 127 b, 156, 159, 165 bl, 389 tl; A.S.A.P. / Talby – 340 cr; Christina Gasgoigne – 341 tl; E. Simanor – 14–15, 70, 95 b, 277 b; Fred Friberg – 320 cr; Gene Stein – 59; Richard Ashworth – 34 bl.

Ursula Held: 463 br.

Michael Holford Photographs: 388; Canterbury Cathedral – 401 tl.

Hulton Getty Images: 456 bl.

Hutchison Library: 52 tl, 53 br, 97 tr, 418–419; Andrey Zvoznikov – 418 bl; J Davey – 458 bl.

IKONA: Alberto Viani *Cristo*, ph. Antonio Masatti, Raccolta Lercaro, Bologna – 358; Dina Bellotti *Li'Ingresso di Gesu in Gerusalemme* Galleria d'Arte Sacra dei Contemporanei, Milano – 5 bc, 348; Domenico Morelli

*Cristo che cammina sulle acque* Galleria Nazionale d'Arte Moderna, Roma – 296–297; J. Wolf *Re Magi* Collezione d'Arte Religiosa Moderna, Vaticano, ph. A. Bracchetti – 319; Consadori *Il Discorso della Montagna* Collezione d'Arte Religiosa Moderna, Vaticano, ph. A. Bracchetti – 330 c; S. Labo *Guarigione del Paralitico* Collezione Arte Religiosa Moderna, Vaticano, ph. A. Bracchetti – 342; T. Werner *Crocifissione* Collezione d'Arte Religiosa Moderna, Vaticano, ph. A. Bracchetti – 420.

Images Colour Library: 395 br.

Image Select: Ann Ronan Collection – 452 bl.

The Israel Museum, Jerusalem: 8 bl, 98–99 b, 124, 242, 298 tr; David Harris – 290 bl, 375 tr.

Jewish Museum, London: 25; Andy Crawford – 165 t.

Jewish National and University Library, Jerusalem: 45.

Kobal Collection: 332, 470; Arco / Lux 345.

Frank Lane Picture Agency: 214; D. Hall – 202 bc; E. & D. Hosking – 265 tr; J.F. Hosking – 202 c.

Magnum: Bruno Barbey 157 tr.

By courtesy of the Trustees of The National Gallery, London: Bassano *Departure of Abraham* – 35; Bourdon *The Return of the Ark* (detail) – 60; Steenwyck *Still Life* – 188; Domenichino *Landscape with Tobias Laying Hold of the Fish* (detail) – 252–253; Gerrit van Honthorst *Christ Before the High Priest* – 354; Fra Angelico *Christ Glorified in the Court of Heaven* – 442.

Board of Trustees National Museums & Galleries on Merseyside, Lady Lever Art Gallery, Holman Hunt *The Scapegoat*: 86 bl.

N.H.P.A.: Vicente Garcia Canseco 264 tr.

*The Golden Rule*, Norman Rockwell printed by permission of the Norman Rockwell Family Trust copyright ©1961 The Norman Rockwell Family Trust: 430.

Panos Pictures: Jean Leo Dugast – 209; Crispin Hughes – 227; David Reed – 232; Sami Sallinen – 418 tc; J.C. Torday – 222, 226; Tiny Tweedie – 3 br; Jasper Young – 147 tr, 204.

Zev Radovan, Jerusalem: 5 cl, 6, 16 c, 26, 34 br, 36, 37, 39, 46 tr, 46–47, 47 cl, 47 tl, 55, 61, 64–65 b, 65 tc, 65 tl, 65 cr, 65 br, 66 r, 66 c inset, 72 tl, 73 cr, 73 bc, 73 tl, 74 bl, 75 tc, 75 cr, 76 cl, 77 cl, 78 b, 78 c,
79 cl, 82, 83 b, 83 t, 84 bl, 89 tr, 90–91, 92, 97 bl, 97 br, 100 bl, 100 bc, 101 tl, 101 tr, 101 br, 103 cr, 109, 112 br, 113 br, 113 tr, 113 bl, 114, 116, 117 tr, 123 tl, 126 cr, 128, 131, 132 cl, 133 t, 133 br, 134 br, 135 tr, 140 bl, 140–141 b, 141 tl, 144 cl, 144 cr, 144 bl, 146, 154 br, 155 tr, 158 b, 162, 170 bl, 171 bl, 179, 181 br, 187 tr, 187 cl, 187 cr, 194–195, 210, 249 tr, 251 tr, 264 cl, 278 bl, 281 br, 284 cr, 286 bl, 287 br, 288 l, 288 br, 289 br, 289 tc, 295 tr, 321 t, 330 tr, 335, 341 tr, 341 br, 360 tr, 360 bc, 361 tc, 361 bl, 362–363, 369 cr, 371 t, 375 b, 376 bl, 394 cr, 403 tl, 426, 434 bl, 449, 462 c; BLMJ Borowski Collection – 181 tr.

Red Cross: 2 bc, 466.

Réunion des Musées Nationaux: Chuzeville – 165 c, 406 bl; Louvre–Chuzeville – 375 cl.

Rex Features: 419 bc, 428, 454; George Carey – 437 cr; SIPA Press – 450.

Rheinisches Landesmuseum, Trier, ph. Thomas Zuhmer: 273 b, 285 b, 371 bl.

Scala: 325, 435 b; Battistero degli Ariani, Ravenna – 324; Cappella Scrovegni, Padova – 352; Giorgio de Chirico *Christ and the Tempest* DACS 1998 / Collezione d'Arte Religiosa Moderna, Vaticano – 344; Antonio Ciseri *Ecce Homo* Galleria d'Arte Moderna, Firenze – 9, 356; Museo di San Marco, Firenze – 3 bc, 334; Pinacoteca di Brera, Milano – 365.

Science Photo Library: Chris Butler – 29.

The Stock Market: 289 cl, 395 c.

Tony Stone Images: 237, 404–405; Bill Aron – 24; Oliver Benn – 419 tl; Tim Brown – 410; Paul Chesley – 270–271; Claire Hayden – 384; Andy Sacks – 164 bl; Manoj Shah – 471; Paul Sisut – 263; Robert Slant – 262; Kaluzny Thatcher – 424; David C. Tomlinson – 366–367.

Tate Gallery, London: John Martin *Great Day of His Wrath* – 240 b; J.M.W. Turner *Sunrise with Sea Monsters* – 378 c.

Topham Picturepoint: 17 c, 218, 400 b.

Wadsworth Atheneum, Hartford: the Ella Gallup Sumner and Mary Catlin Sumner Collection Fund, John Singleton Copley *Samuel Relating to Eli the Judgements of God upon Eli's House*: 118.

WaterAid: Caroline Penn – 414.

Werner Braun: 299 b.

World Council of Churches: Photo Oikoumene – 456 br.

Jacket: Andes Press Agency / Carlos Reyes-Manzo – inside front; A.S.A.P. – back tr, cbl; Bridgeman Art Library – back ctl; Siena Cathedral – front; Sonia Halliday Photographs – back tl, bl, br; Zev Radovan – spine; Red Cross – back cr.

DK special photography: Calcografia Nacional, Madrid – 152; Centro Mostre di Firenze, Soprintendenza per i beni artistici e storici / Brancacci Chapel / Alison Harris – 385, 386; Andy Crawford – 389 tr; Archaeological Receipts Fund – 247 t, 247 cr; Churches Ministry among the Jews – 283 tc; Alan Hills – 269 br; Dave King – 269 cr; John Heseltine – 331; Jerry Young – 269 c.

Additional Photographers:
Max Alexander, Peter Anderson, Geoff Brightling, Jane Burton, Peter Chadwick, John Chase, Andy Crawford, Geoff Dann, Philip Dowell, Mike Dunning, Neil Fletcher, Alan Gilliam, Nick Goodall, Steve Gorton, Frank Greenaway, Paul Halliday, Mark Harwood, Peter Hayman, Steven Head, John Heseltine, Alan Hills, Ellen Howden, Paul Kenward, Barnabas and Annabel Kindersley, Dave King, Andrew McRobb, Ray Moller, David Murray, Nick Nichols, Martin Norris, Stephen Oliver, Gary Ombler, Janet Peckham, Laurence Pordes, Susanna Price, Tim Ridley, Kim Sayer, Jules Selmes, Karl Shone, Steve Tanner, Kim Taylor, Matthew Ward, John Williams, Barbara Winter, Jerry Young.

Illustrators:
Stephen Conlin, Peter Dennis, Eugene Fleury, John Hutchinson, Kenneth Lilly, Jamie Oliver.

## DATE DUE

| | |
|---|---|
| | |
| | |
| | |
| | |
| | |
| | |
| | |
| | |
| | |
| | |
| | |
| | |
| | |
| | |
| | |
| | |
| | |
| | |
| | |
| | PRINTED IN U.S.A. |